ENCYCLOPEDIA
YEAR BOOK
1983

GROLIER

This annual has been prepared as a yearbook for general
encyclopedias. It is also published as *The Americana Annual.*

Contents

Feature Articles of the Year

The Alphabetical Section

Separate entries on the continents, major nations of the world, U.S. states, Canadian provinces, and chief cities will be found under their own alphabetically arranged headings.

American Broadcasting Companies, Inc.

The Year in Review

By Peter Jennings ABC News

In 1982 wars were again in rich supply, optimism a rare commodity.

Great Britain and Argentina fought in the remote reaches of the South Atlantic. For both countries, the Falkland Islands (Islas Malvinas) became a focal point of national pride. The two nations sacrificed hundreds of lives for the right to fly a national flag. At great financial as well as human cost, Britain prevailed.

Despite a highly publicized national election, El Salvador remained engaged in a seemingly endless struggle. For the Reagan administration, whose support the right-wing National Alliance Party deemed essential, the Salvador conflict has been a study in frustration and discouragement. Washington's own ambassador and the international human-rights organization, Amnesty International, pointed accusing fingers at the San Salvador government's record in human rights.

For the Soviet Union, the quagmire of Afghanistan provided few bright spots. Antigovernment forces, which have not been in a position to prevail since the Soviet invasion in late 1979, nevertheless remained potent enough to deny the Soviets and the Afghan government freedom to rule at will.

Again in 1982, the most explosive corner of the globe remained the Middle East. Iran and Iraq were still deadlocked in conflict. By the time the winter rains had settled in, Iran had scored some significant military gains, within Iranian territory. Analysts of this little-reported war believed Iran was in a stronger position by year's end. The lack of a settlement kept the more conservative Arab states to the west of Iraq in a year-long state of apprehension.

The region's bloodiest and most complex conflict was played out on the shores of the Mediterranean. The Israeli invasion of Lebanon, ostensibly to secure Israel's northern border, became a full-scale onslaught against the Palestine Liberation Organization. The PLO was forced to leave its Lebanese haven, but the Israeli siege of West Beirut forced the government of Prime Minister Menahem Begin to face widespread anger in Israel and internationally. The military defeat of the PLO in Lebanon led to its dispersal throughout the Arab world, the resurgence of militant Christian authority in Lebanon, and the deepest involvement of the United States in Lebanese affairs since Lebanon became a modern state. The postwar massacre of Palestinian civilians in their West Beirut refugee

About the Author: Peter Jennings is the London anchorman of ABC's *World News Tonight* and the network's chief foreign correspondent. His 1982 travels took him to the Middle East at the height of the Lebanon crisis for talks with the various leaders, including Yasir Arafat of the PLO, and to Poland at the time of Solidarity's demise. A Canadian by birth, Mr. Jennings earlier served as a parliamentary correspondent and network anchorman in Ottawa and Montreal.

camps, widely believed to have been conducted by right-wing Christian gunmen—but while Israel was ostensibly in control—set off the most profound debate on Israeli morality in the 36-year history of the Jewish state.

In the Soviet Union, the death of President Leonid Brezhnev came as no surprise. The transition to a new leadership was both swift and definitive. Brezhnev's successor, Yuri Andropov, had been head of the KGB for 15 years. His appointment as leader of the Soviet Communist party touched off considerable soul-searching about the frail state of East-West relations. By year's end there was nothing concrete to suggest any diminution of tension between Moscow and Washington. There was no significant progress to report from any of the groups negotiating bilateral arms reductions.

The new Soviet leader inherited a foreign policy which, in the last years of Mr. Brezhnev's life, had reaped more failure than success. In Poland, however, yearlong martial law had removed much of the threat to Socialist stability that had stemmed from the creation of the Warsaw Pact's first independent union, Solidarity. Without having to send in Soviet troops, Moscow was able to emasculate the once-powerful union. When Lech Walesa, the charismatic leader of the now-outlawed union, was released from internment, it seemed clear that Moscow and the military leadership in Warsaw no longer regarded him as a threat to the authority of the Polish Communist party.

If Soviet-American relations remained extremely uncertain at the end of the year, and they did, relations between the United States and its Alliance partners were also troubled. Disputes over technology for the Soviet gas pipeline to Western Europe, the steel trade, the political value of sanctions against the Soviet bloc, and economic policy were some of the divisive issues. Tension eased somewhat with short-term compromises on European steel imports to the United States and with President Reagan's decision to remove sanctions on companies that supply parts for the pipeline. Once again, however, it was a year during which the nature of the European-American relationship was the subject of consider-

The Israeli invasion of Lebanon was a full-scale onslaught against the PLO. After months of fighting, however, hundreds of thousands of Palestinian and Lebanese civilians were left homeless.

© James Nachtwey/Black Star

East-West relations were the coldest in decades, as both sides continued to build military strength. At a parade in Red Square marking the 65th anniversary of the Bolshevik Revolution, a new Soviet personnel carrier went on display. President Brezhnev called for détente but warned that any aggression would be met with a "crushing strike." Brezhnev's death later that month did not seem to ease tensions. Meanwhile, in the West, the Versailles summit conference in June resolved few differences among the industrialized powers. Nuclear arms, sanctions against the Soviet bloc, and economic and trade policy were some of the issues that shook the U.S.-Western European alliance.

able debate and perhaps unusually intense scrutiny. The French foreign minister touched a nerve when he spoke of progressive divorce. There was little doubt that on each continent the relationship was being seriously reevaluated.

In the United States during the year, a dangerous lunatic stabbed at the nation's nerve ends by lacing headache tablets with cyanide. Many Americans asked themselves whether the country had more than its share of crazies. The answer was probably not. John Hinckley was found not guilty, by reason of insanity, of trying to assassinate the president and was committed to a mental hospital.

The year 1982 marked the requiem for Reaganomics. The influential *New York Times* suggested it was only a slogan at best. Lower taxes and smaller government remained elusive. Though by the end of the year the stock market had signaled a recovery with a record-breaking surge, no one had predicted it and few could explain it. Most other economic indicators remained gloomy. Unemployment was the highest since the Great Depression. In October the Department of Labor announced that the jobless rate stood at 10.4%. Not only in the United States, but elsewhere in the industrialized world and particularly in the developing world—where 300 million people were unemployed—there were nagging doubts about long-term social stability.

Baldev/Sygma

In the Third World, where conflict and economic malaise also clouded the year, one bright spot was the beginning of reconciliation between two previously hostile nations—India and Pakistan. Their leaders met and agreed to establish a permanent joint commission to work out differences. Indira Gandhi went to Delhi airport to meet Zia ul-Haq.

There was, and is, acute concern about the international banking system. Western banks, having accumulated vast deposits from the oil-producing countries and then lending it aggressively to developing countries, now see international debt at a perilous level. In Mexico, for example, an $80,000,000,000 debt and impending default led to sudden panic and a swift emergency loan. The continuing crisis has brought home to bankers and governments the extent of their interdependence with Third World economies.

Back in the United States, the antinuclear movement burgeoned, but the political effectiveness of the women's movement waned. The antinuclear movement leaped across the Atlantic from Western Europe. More and more Americans demanded progress toward arms control. Americans were not only thinking more actively about the unthinkable, but they began a national debate on how to reduce the awesome nuclear arsenals held by the superpowers. The message, in its simplest form, was that nuclear arms control was too important to be left only to politicians. There was unexpected and welcome support for the movement when the Nobel Peace Prize was awarded to two longtime advocates and campaigners for nuclear disarmament, Alva Myrdal of Sweden and Alfonso Garcia Robles of Mexico. The campaign to win ratification of the Equal Rights Amendment did not thrive in similar fashion. By the deadline for its passage, pro-ERA forces were three states short of the 38 needed for ratification. Its supporters declared every intention of trying again.

So that future generations won't think the nation was in a totally parlous state during 1982, they should know that during the summer Americans were completely captivated by a space romance called *E.T.* Everyone seemed to cry during this record money-making film. One young American said, *"E.T.* is our generation's *Wizard of Oz."* At least three icons of international film and theater died in 1982—Ingrid Bergman, Henry Fonda, and Jacques Tati. Princess Grace of Monaco, the former film actress, died. The comic actor John Belushi was the best-known person to die from an overdose of drugs. Drug use, especially among the affluent, increased.

Some things were taken for granted—in the United States, democracy, perhaps. Less than 50% of eligible voters turned out to exercise their franchise in the midterm elections. In Spain, by contrast, where democracy is a mere seven years old, almost 80% of those eligible elected the first Socialist government since the end of the Spanish Civil War. In America football was also taken for granted, at least until the National Football League went on strike for the first time in 63 years. When the dispute was resolved, much of the nation seemed in better humor on weekends.

On Veterans Day 1982, the United States inaugurated a memorial to the men who had died during the war in Vietnam. The president characterized U.S. intervention in Vietnam as a "noble cause." Others continued to characterize America's war in Talleyrand's words: "It was worse than a crime—it was an error." In a year of wars, the sentiment was likely felt in many other parts of the globe as well.

January

3 President Chun Doo Hwan of South Korea dismisses Prime Minister Nam Duck Woo and five other cabinet members, four of whom were in charge of the economy. Yoo Chang Soon is named as Nam's successor.

4 President Hosni Mubarak of Egypt swears in a new cabinet. Two days earlier, Mubarak relinquished the premiership to Ahmed Fuad Mohieddin and ordered him to form a new government.

U.S. National Security Adviser Richard V. Allen resigns his post because of controversy over his acceptance of $1,000 from a Japanese magazine to help arrange an interview with First Lady Nancy Reagan in 1981. William P. Clark, Jr., is named as his replacement.

5 A federal district judge in Arkansas declares unconstitutional a state law requiring that "creation science" be given equal time in any school in which the theory of evolution is taught.

7 U.S. President Ronald Reagan announces the resumption of military draft registration for 18-year-olds.

8 The U.S. Justice Department announces the settlement of its eight-year-old antitrust suit against American Telephone & Telegraph Co. (AT&T) and the dropping of its 13-year-old antitrust case against International Business Machines Corp. (IBM).

A member of the National Transportation Safety Board inspects the wreckage of a Boeing 737 that crashed into a bridge in Washington, DC, January 13. The board conducted an extensive investigation to determine the cause of the accident, which took the lives of 78 persons.

UPI

11 In Brussels, at the first emergency meeting ever held by the North Atlantic Treaty Organization (NATO), foreign ministers of 14 member countries issue a communiqué denouncing the Soviet Union for its active support of "repression" by the martial law regime in Poland.

12 The United States and the Soviet Union resume negotiations in Geneva on the limitation of medium-range nuclear missiles in Europe.

In a policy reversal from the week before, President Reagan calls on Congress to pass legislation banning tax exemptions for schools that discriminate on the basis of race.

13 Flight Lt. Jerry Rawlings, who assumed power in Ghana in a December 31 coup, names a seven-member council to act as the nation's central authority.

An Air Florida jetliner crashes into a bridge over the Potomac River shortly after take-off from Washington's National Airport, killing 78 persons.

14 Adil Carcani is named prime minister of Albania, replacing the late Mehmet Shehu.

16 At a two-day meeting in Key Biscayne, FL, representatives of the world's major trading nations agree to fight protectionism and to refrain from curbing imports.

19 A one-day general strike, called by eight national trade unions to protest the labor policies of Prime Minister Indira Gandhi, halts industry and public services throughout India.

20 The United States vetoes a UN Security Council resolution calling for punitive measures against Israel for its annexation of the Golan Heights in December 1981.

24 The San Francisco 49ers win the championship of the National Football League by defeating the Cincinnati Bengals, 26–21, in Super Bowl XVI.

26 In his first State of the Union Message, President Reagan calls for a "new federalism," whereby $47,000,000,000 in social programs would be turned over to state and local governments.

U.S. Secretary of State Alexander Haig, Jr., and Soviet Foreign Minister Andrei Gromyko hold eight hours of talks in Geneva. The Polish situation is the focus of these first high-level discussions between the two countries in four months.

27 Roberto Suazo Córdova, a civilian, is inaugurated as the president of Honduras, ending nine years of military rule.

28 U.S. Brig. Gen. James L. Dozier, who had been kidnapped by Red Brigade terrorists Dec. 17, 1981, is rescued from an apartment in Padua by Italian special police.

29 The U.S. government announces that it will pay $70 million in debts owed by Poland to ten American commercial banks.

U.S. Brig. Gen. James L. Dozier presents his wife, Judith, with a belated Christmas gift, a gold necklace with the insignia of the North Atlantic Treaty Organization. In Padua, Italian special police had rescued the high-ranking NATO official from captivity by Red Brigade terrorists January 28.

UPI

February

1 The neighboring West African nations of Senegal and Gambia formally unite, creating the confederation of Senegambia.

2 Egyptian President Hosni Mubarak arrives in Washington for two days of talks with President Reagan.

5 Great Britain becomes the first European member of NATO to join the United States in imposing economic and diplomatic sanctions against Poland and the Soviet Union for the imposition of martial law in Poland in December 1981.

Laker Airways, the pioneer of reduced-fare transatlantic flights, declares bankruptcy.

6 The Reagan administration unveils its budget for fiscal 1983, calling for $757,600,000,000 in expenditures, a deficit of $91,500,-000,000, an 18% increase in defense spending, and reductions in social programs and tax revenues.

7 Luis Alberto Monge of the National Liberation Party is elected president of Costa Rica.

Before an Organization of American States meeting in Washington, DC, February 24, U.S. President Ronald Reagan unveils his program to improve conditions in the Caribbean basin and Central America.

10 Chan Sy is named chairman of the Cambodian Council of Ministers, replacing Pen Sovan who was removed in December 1981.

13 A U.S. military adviser in El Salvador is ordered home after being seen on film carrying an M-16 rifle in violation of regulations.

14 The leaders of 11 member nations of the Organization of African Unity (OAU) conclude four days of talks in Nairobi. The conflicts in Western Sahara and Chad were the main topics of discussion.

16 In a letter to Israeli Prime Minister Menahem Begin, President Reagan denies charges that the United States is drifting from its policy of full support for Israel. Begin had sent Reagan a letter of protest over statements made in Jordan by U.S. Secretary of Defense Caspar Weinberger suggesting that the United States would sell advanced antiaircraft missiles and fighter planes to that country.

17 Prime Minister Robert Mugabe of Zimbabwe dismisses political rival Joshua Nkomo from his cabinet, accusing him of plotting to overthrow the government.

18 The government of Iran announces that the Ayatollah Ruhollah Khomeini, 81, will eventually be replaced by a three- to five-man ruling council.

19 Pope John Paul II concludes an eight-day, four-nation tour of West Africa. It is his first trip abroad since the attack on his life in May 1981.

22 Finance ministers of the European Community (EC) nations agree to a realignment of the European Monetary System. The Belgian franc is devalued by 8.5%, the Danish krona by 3%.

Representatives of 44 Third World nations begin a three-day conference in New Delhi to develop strategies for restructuring global economic relations.

24 In an address to the Organization of American States (OAS), President Reagan announces a far-reaching trade and economic assistance program for the Caribbean basin and Central America.

27 Wayne B. Williams, a 23-year-old photographer, is found guilty of murdering two black youths during the period in which 28 such killings were discovered in Atlanta, GA. He is sentenced to two consecutive life terms in prison.

In Atlanta, GA, Wayne B. Williams is convicted of the murder of two black youths. During a nine-week, closely followed trial, the prosecution depicted Williams as a "Dr. Jekyll and Mr. Hyde" personality.

March

1   Greek Prime Minister Andreas Papandreou concludes a three-day visit to Cyprus, the first ever by a Greek premier. During his stay, Papandreou called for an international conference on the island's problems.

Rank and file of the International Brotherhood of Teamsters ratify a new, 37-month labor agreement with the U.S. trucking industry. The union makes major concessions.

2   At the conclusion of a two-day visit to Moscow, Polish Prime Minister Wojciech Jaruzelski pledges closer ties with the Soviet Union and a continuation of efforts to stop "in the most resolute manner" uprisings against Communist rule in Poland.

3   French President François Mitterrand arrives in Israel on the first visit to that country by a European head of state.

4   Bertha Wilson becomes the first woman appointed to the Canadian Supreme Court.

President Reagan names Gen. John W. Vessey, Jr., chairman of the Joint Chiefs of Staff.

5   Comic actor John Belushi, 33, is found dead of a drug overdose in Hollywood, CA.

9   Charles Haughey of the Fianna Fail Party is elected prime minister by the Irish parliament, defeating incumbent Garret FitzGerald by 86 to 79.

11   Sen. Harrison A. Williams, Jr. (D-NJ) resigns his seat in the face of imminent expulsion for misdeeds in the FBI's Abscam probe.

13   Col. Muammar el-Qaddafi of Libya concludes three days of talks with high government officials in Austria. It is his first formal visit to Western Europe since 1973.

15   The Sandinist government of Nicaragua suspends all constitutional rights for 30 days and declares a state of siege to combat anti-Sandinist "counterrevolutionary" attacks.

16   In a highly publicized trial at Newport, RI, socialite Claus von Bülow is found guilty on two counts of attempting to murder his wealthy wife, Martha (Sunny) von Bülow.

20   At a two-day meeting in Vienna, the Organization of Petroleum Exporting Countries (OPEC) agrees to cut crude oil production by 700,000 barrels per day to reduce the world's oversupply.

23   Dissident army officers overthrow the Guatemalan government in a bloodless coup and install a three-man military junta. The rebels charge that March 7 presidential balloting had been rigged to ensure the victory of government-backed candidate Gen. Angel Anibal Guevara.

After tie votes on three no-confidence motions, Israeli Prime Minister Menahem Begin proposes the resignation of his government. The cabinet refuses by a vote of 12 to 6, and Begin agrees to remain in power. The parliamentary no-confidence resolutions had been made in response to Begin's handling of unrest on the West Bank.

24   In Bangladesh, army chief of staff Gen. Hossein Mohammed Ershad overthrows President Abdus Sattar, ending three years of civilian rule.

Roy Jenkins, a founder of Great Britain's year-old Social Democratic Party, wins a parliamentary by-election in Glasgow, Scotland.

UPI

Sen. Harrison A. Williams (D-NJ), who had been convicted in connection with the FBI's Abscam investigation, speaks to reporters after resigning from the Senate March 11. Mrs. Williams is at the senator's side.

In El Salvador's countryside, a large crowd attends a government-sponsored campaign rally. The immediate results of the March 28 elections were indecisive.

28 In closely-monitored elections for the El Salvador constituent assembly, moderate Christian Democrats make a strong showing, but five rightwing parties together gain a majority of votes. Negotiations for a coalition begin immediately. The unexpectedly large voter turnout is seen as a rejection of leftist rebel groups, who had called for an election boycott.

29 The University of North Carolina Tar Heels win the NCAA men's basketball championship by defeating the Georgetown Hoyas, 63–62.

30 The U.S. space shuttle Columbia completes its third and longest test flight. Col. Jack Lousma and Col. C. Gordon Fullerton land the craft at White Sands Missile Range, NM, after eight days in space.

Leaders of the ten European Community (EC) nations conclude a two-day summit meeting in Brussels.

April

3 An Israeli diplomat, Yacov Barsimantov, is shot to death in the lobby of his Paris apartment by an unknown woman assailant.

5 Great Britain launches its largest naval assault force in 25 years on an 8,000-mi (13,000-km) voyage to the Falkland Islands off the coast of Argentina. Three days earlier, Argentina seized control of the British-held islands, claiming that they "form part of our national patrimony."

6 The Polish government and its major foreign commercial creditors sign an agreement to reschedule payment of $2,400,000,000 owed by Poland in 1982.

11 A U.S.-born Israeli soldier goes on a shooting spree in the Temple Mount, a Muslim shrine in Old Jerusalem, killing two Arabs and setting off widespread, angry protests.

12 President Reagan ends a five-day "working holiday" in Jamaica and Barbados, during which he met with the leaders of five Caribbean nations.

14 China issues a strong protest against a U.S. decision to proceed with a $60 million sale of military equipment to Taiwan.

15 Five Muslim extremists are executed for the October 1981 assassination of Egyptian President Anwar el-Sadat. Seventeen others received prison sentences and two others were acquitted in the March 6 ruling of a military tribunal.

16 Keeping a campaign promise, President Reagan announces a proposal for tuition tax credits for families who send their children to private elementary or secondary schools.

17 Amid pomp and ceremony in the Canadian capital of Ottawa, Queen Elizabeth II of Great Britain signs a formal proclamation—the Constitution Act, 1982—giving Canada complete legal and statutory independence from the United Kingdom. The provincial government of Quebec boycotts the ceremony.

19 Former Iranian Foreign Minister Sadegh Ghotbzadeh admits that he participated in a plot to assassinate the Ayatollah Ruhollah Khomeini.

Portuguese President Antonio Ramalho Eanes concludes a triumphant four-day visit to the former colony of Angola.

20 American poet Archibald MacLeish dies in Boston at age 90.

21 Israeli fighter planes attack Palestinian-controlled villages in southern and coastal Lebanon, breaking a nine-month-old cease-fire between Israel and the Palestine Liberation Organization (PLO).

22 Ending rumors of a serious illness, Soviet President Leonid Brezhnev appears at a rally in Moscow marking the 112th anniversary of the birth of Vladimir Lenin.

During the first national congress of the Social Democratic Party since 1979, West German Chancellor Helmut Schmidt wins a major political battle when his party votes down a nuclear freeze motion.

Amid mounting criticism of his economic policies, Chilean President Augusto Pinochet Ugarte replaces all 16 of his cabinet ministers.

In Ottawa, April 17, Queen Elizabeth II signs the Constitution Act, 1982, granting Canada complete independence from Great Britain.

© John DeVisser/Black Star

25 The Egyptian flag is raised over the northern and eastern Sinai, as Israel returns the last portions of the peninsula in accordance with the peace treaty of 1979. The Israeli withdrawal follows days of turmoil in the northern settlement of Yamit, the stronghold of militant nationalistic and religious opposition to the pullout. Army troops had to be called in to remove town residents.

27 The National Front coalition of Malaysian President Mahathir bin Mohamad wins an overwhelming majority in parliamentary elections.

The West German government announces a number of changes in its cabinet; Manfred Lahnstein is named to succeed Hans Matthoefer as finance minister.

29 The constituent assembly of El Salvador elects Alvaro Alfredo Magaña, a moderate conservative banker, as the nation's interim president.

30 Ending eight years of diplomatic bargaining, delegates to the UN Law of the Sea Conference overwhelmingly approve a comprehensive treaty on the use and exploitation of the world's seas. However, U.S. opposition raises questions about the treaty's effectiveness.

May

1 Serious fighting breaks out between British and Argentine troops on the Falkland Islands and surrounding waters. One day earlier the United States abandoned efforts to mediate the dispute and announced its support for the British position.

The 1982 World's Fair officially opens in Knoxville, TN.

4 In the wake of violent protests in several cities on the May Day holiday, the Polish government reimposes tough martial law restrictions, which it had lifted less than one week before.

The Chinese government announces that 11 vice-premierships have been eliminated and that the overall number of ministers and vice-ministers has been reduced by two thirds, completing the second phase of a major bureaucratic reorganization.

The ruling Golkar coalition sweeps national legislative elections in Indonesia.

5 President Dawda Jawara of Gambia is overwhelmingly reelected.

6 President Reagan formally endorses a constitutional amendment authorizing organized prayer in public schools.

9 In a commencement address at Eureka (IL) College, his alma mater, President Reagan proposes that the United States and the Soviet Union reduce their arsenals of nuclear missile warheads by at least one third. The cutback would be part of a "practical, phased reduction plan" for strategic nuclear forces.

U.S. Vice-President George Bush completes a two-week tour of Japan, South Korea, Singapore, Australia, New Zealand, and China.

12 U.S. evangelist Billy Graham returns home from a five-day visit to the Soviet Union amid controversy over a statement that the thousands of churches "seem to have liberty to have worship services."

At the shrine of Fatima in Portugal, Pope John Paul II emerges unscathed from an assassination attempt by a 32-year-old Spanish priest who ran toward him carrying a bayonet.

U.S. evangelist Billy Graham is one of more than 400 persons to attend a five-day conference on disarmament, sponsored by the Russian Orthodox Church and held in Moscow in May.

Wide World

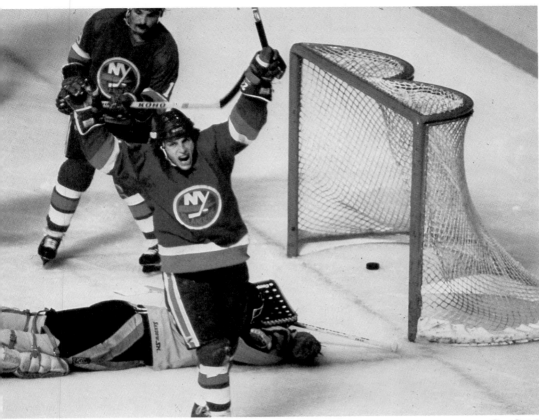

13   Braniff International, the eighth largest U.S. airline, files for bankruptcy in a surprise move.

16   The New York Islanders capture their third consecutive National Hockey League (NHL) championship.

18   Wall Street is shaken by an announcement that Drysdale Government Securities Inc., a brokerage house specializing in federal securities, has defaulted on payment of $160 million in interest.

       The Rev. Sun Myung Moon, founder and leader of the Unification Church, is found guilty by a federal court in New York on four separate counts of income tax evasion.

21   In response to Rumania's economic problems, Premier Ilye Verdet and at least 12 other officials are dismissed.

24   The Iranian government announces that its troops have recaptured the key port city of Khorramshahr, which Iraq had taken at the outbreak of the Persian Gulf war in October 1980.

       A bomb explosion at the French embassy in Beirut, Lebanon, leaves at least 12 persons dead and 27 wounded.

29   Highlighting a six-day visit to Britain, the first ever by a pontiff, Pope John Paul II joins with Archbishop of Canterbury, the Most Rev. Robert Runcie, in an emotional religious service that ends 450 years of division between the Church of Rome and the Church of England.

30   Spain officially becomes the 16th member of the North Atlantic Treaty Organization (NATO).

31   Belisario Betancur Cuartas of the Conservative Party is elected president of Colombia.

Mike Bossy of the Islanders is jubilant after scoring a Stanley Cup goal. The high-scoring winger, who led the New Yorkers to their third consecutive championship, was voted the play-offs' most valuable player.

Alon Reininger/Contact

*Israeli troops sweep to the out-
skirts of Beirut as they continue
their invasion of Lebanon to
crush PLO strongholds.*

3 Beginning a nine-day visit to Europe, President Reagan confers with France's President François Mitterrand in Paris.

Shlomo Argov, Israel's ambassador to Great Britain, is shot and seriously wounded outside a London hotel.

Lina Wichser, a 28-year-old American who had been teaching in Peking, is released from government detention and given 48 hours to leave China. She is charged with violating China's law by stealing "secret information."

6 In Versailles, France, the leaders of the seven major industrialized democracies conclude their annual conference with limited agreement on the subjects of East-West trade and currency fluctuations.

7 Ground and air fighting intensify between Israeli and Syrian forces as hostilities widen during the second day of Israel's drive into Lebanon to destroy the main military bases of the Palestine Liberation Organization (PLO).

In the civil war in Chad, the rebel forces of former Prime Minister Hissène Habré capture the capital of Ndjamena and overthrow the government of President Goukouni Oueddei.

8 The Los Angeles Lakers capture the National Basketball Association championship series, defeating the Philadelphia '76ers four games to two.

9 Brig. Gen. Efrain Rios Montt dissolves Guatemala's three-man junta and declares himself president.

10 By a 219–206 vote, the U.S. House of Representatives approves a budget for fiscal year 1983. The measure, which is considered a victory for President Reagan, awaits approval by a Senate-House conference.

In the Bahamas, the ruling Progressive Liberal Party of Prime Minister Lynden O. Pindling wins a new five-year mandate in parliamentary elections.

11 Pope John Paul II meets with President Leopoldo Galtieri at the beginning of a two-day visit to Argentina.

12 In New York City, more than 500,000 demonstrators stage an antinuclear weapons rally.

Meeting in Brussels, the finance ministers of the European Monetary System nations announce agreement on a realignment of their currencies.

In parliamentary elections in Mauritius, the opposition—the Militant Mauritian Movement and its ally, the Mauritian Social Democratic Party—is overwhelmingly victorious.

13 Saudi Arabia's King Khalid dies of a heart attack and is succeeded by Crown Prince Fahd.

17 Following public protests by Agentines over their nation's defeat in the war with Great Britain over the Falkland Islands, Leopoldo Galtieri resigns as president, commander in chief of the Army, and member of the ruling junta. Ten weeks of fighting had come to an end with a June 14 surrender by Argentina and a cease-fire.

President Reagan addresses the UN Second Special Session on Disarmament.

20 Iraq's President Saddam Hussein announces that Iraqi troops have begun withdrawing from Iran.

21 A jury finds John W. Hinckley, Jr., not guilty by reason of insanity of the shooting of President Reagan and three others in March 1981.

President Reagan and Israel's Prime Minister Menahem Begin meet at the White House to discuss the Lebanon crisis.

The Princess of Wales gives birth to a boy, who becomes second in line to the British throne, behind his father, Prince Charles.

22 Maj. Gen. Reynaldo Benito Antonio Bignone is named president of Argentina.

The U.S. Department of Justice announces that 18 Japanese businessmen have been charged with conspiring to steal computer information from the International Business Machines Corp.

24 Soyuz T-6 is launched from the Soviet space center. Jean-Loup Chrétien, 43-year-old French Air Force colonel, joins Soviet cosmonauts Col. Vladimir A. Dzhanibekov and Aleksandr S. Ivanchenkov aboard the spacecraft.

25 President Reagan announces the resignation of Alexander M. Haig, Jr., as secretary of state and the appointment of George P. Shultz to the post.

28 Special Prosecutor Leon Silverman declares that "there was insufficient credible evidence to warrant prosecution" of Raymond J. Donovan for any alleged crimes the secretary of labor may have committed while he was an executive of a New Jersey construction company.

29 In Geneva, representatives of the United States and the Soviet Union open strategic arms reduction talks (START).

President Reagan signs into law a bill extending for 25 years the enforcement provisions of the 1965 Voting Rights Act.

30 The proposed Equal Rights Amendment to the U.S. Constitution is officially defeated as the deadline for ratification passes with only 35 of the required 38 state legislatures having approved.

Key members of the Reagan administration—James Baker (far left), William Clark, and Edwin Meese (far right)—gather with the president at Camp David to confer with secretary of state-designate George P. Shultz (second left).

Michael Evans/The White House

July

© William Karel/Sygma

Philip C. Habib, U.S. special emissary to the Middle East, spends much of the summer shuttling between the capitals of the Middle East and meeting with the area's leaders. His mission: a peaceful solution to the conflict in Lebanon.

4 Miguel de la Madrid Hurtado is elected president of Mexico.

After seven days orbiting the earth, the Columbia space shuttle, with Capt. Thomas K. Mattingly 2d and Henry W. Hartsfield, Jr., aboard, lands safely at California's Edwards Air Force Base.

In the annual tennis championships at Wimbledon, England, Jimmy Connors defeats John McEnroe to win the men's singles title. Martina Navratilova took the women's crown on July 3.

9 The Reagan administration transmits to Congress a call for a reduced federal role in urban policy.

A Pan American World Airways jet crashes in a residential area of New Orleans, LA, killing at least 154 persons.

10 Members of the Organization of Petroleum Exporting Countries (OPEC) conclude a two-day meeting in Vienna, Austria, without agreement on production and price guidelines.

11 Italy wins the World Cup soccer championship, defeating West Germany, 3-1, in the tournament final.

12 The Reagan administration lifts the economic sanctions it imposed against Argentina during the Falklands war.

13 The U.S. Environmental Protection Agency issues new regulations for the dumping of hazardous wastes in land sites.

14 Iran launches a major military drive into Iraq, toward the oil refining city of Basra.

16 Following unanimous confirmation by the U.S. Senate, George P. Shultz is sworn in as the 60th U.S. secretary of state.

18 A strike by British railway workers comes to an end as rail engineers accept a management plan for a flexible workday.

20 Nine British soldiers are killed and some 50 persons are injured as two bombs explode in two London parks. The Irish Republican Army (IRA) claims responsibility for the attacks.

21 In Poland, Gen. Wojciech Jaruzelski announces the release of more than 1,200 persons detained under martial law and the easing of travel and communications curbs.

The British government announces that "serious errors and omissions" by the police permitted an intruder to enter the Buckingham Palace bedroom of Queen Elizabeth II on July 9.

In Bolivia, Army Chief of Staff Gen. Guido Vildoso Calderon is sworn in as president, succeeding Gen. Celso Torrelio Villa, who resigned July 15.

23 The International Whaling Commission votes to ban all commercial whaling, effective in 1986.

25 Zail Singh is installed as president of India, a largely ceremonial post.

29 Meeting at the White House, President Reagan and India's Prime Minister Indira Gandhi agree to improve scientific, cultural, and economic ties between the United States and India. It is also agreed that a third nation, France, will provide low-enriched uranium for a U.S.-built atomic power plant near Bombay.

30 Arístides Royo Sanches resigns as president of Panama. He is to be succeeded by Vice-President Ricardo de la Espriella.

August

1 President Daniel arap Moi announces that Kenya's police and army units have crushed an attempt by members of the air force to overthrow the government.

4 Israeli planes, gunboats, and artillery stage a major attack across West Beirut, Lebanon. Casualties are said to be "in the hundreds."

6 Harvard's Martin Feldstein is named to succeed Murray L. Weidenbaum as chairman of the U. S. Council of Economic Advisers.

7 Armenian gunmen attack the airport at Ankara, Turkey. At least 9 persons are killed and 72 are reported injured in the terrorist incident, which the Armenians called a protest against the "Turkish fascist occupation of our land."

9 A federal judge finds that there is "clear and convincing evidence" that presidential assailant John W. Hinckley, Jr., is mentally ill and dangerous, and orders him to a mental hospital for an indefinite period.

In Paris, France, unidentified gunmen attack a kosher restaurant in a Jewish neighborhood, killing 6 persons and wounding 22.

12 Israeli jets bomb West Beirut for 11 hours, and Lebanon responds by suspending negotiations on the withdrawal of Palestinian guerrillas from Lebanon.

Actor Henry Fonda, 77, dies in Los Angeles.

16 Salvador Jorge Blanco is inaugurated as president of the Dominican Republic.

17 The United States and China issue a joint communiqué, the result of ten months of negotiations, in which the United States pledges gradually to reduce military sales to Taiwan and China promises to continue to seek "a peaceful solution to the Taiwan question."

At the New York Stock Exchange, the Dow Jones Industrial Average registers its best one-day gain in history.

Lines are long and the questions are numerous at banks and local financial exchange centers in Mexico. The peso was devalued for the second time in six months on August 5.

© Rosales/Gamma-Liaison

Polish troops held a tight grip on daily life in Warsaw and other cities. In late August, riot police quelled pro-Solidarity uprisings with a strong hand.

19 The Israeli cabinet approves a plan for the withdrawal of Palestinian and Syrian fighters from west Beirut in exchange for the release of two captured Israeli soldiers. U.S., French, and Italian troops are to supervise the withdrawal.

20 U.S. Secretary of Agriculture John R. Block announces that the Soviet Union has accepted President Reagan's offer of a one-year extension of the grain sales agreement.

23 Giovanni Spadolini forms Italy's 42nd post-World War II government; it has the same makeup as the one that fell August 7.

25 U.S. Rep. Frederick W. Richmond (D-NY) pleads guilty to tax evasion and two other charges and agrees to resign.

26 The Reagan administration orders trade sanctions against a company owned by the French government and the French subsidiary of a U.S. company for violating a U.S. embargo against the delivery of equipment to the Soviet Union for the construction of a natural gas pipeline to Western Europe.

27 Leroy Williams, a former congressional page, admits that he lied when he asserted in March that he had had homosexual liaisons with members of Congress.

The Soviet Soyuz T-5 spacecraft returns to earth after an eight-day mission. Crew member Svetlana Savitskaya is the second woman to have traveled in space.

31 Polish riot police break up demonstrations in Warsaw and several other cities marking the second anniversary of the establishment of the trade union Solidarity.

September

1 In a televised address, President Reagan endorses "full autonomy" under Jordanian supervision for Palestinians living in the West Bank and Gaza Strip; demands a freeze on Israeli settlements; and calls for negotiations leading to an undivided Jerusalem. The speech comes on the same day that the last Palestinian and Syrian fighters leave west Beirut.

Mexico's President José López Portillo delivers his final State of the Union address, in which he calls for the nationalization of private banks and full currency-exchange controls. In a recent financial crisis the value of the peso fell some 75%.

3 President Reagan signs into law a bill providing $98,300,000,000 in tax increases and $17,500,000,000 in spending reductions for the fiscal years 1983–85.

9 William S. Paley, the founder and chairman of CBS, announces his retirement effective April 20, 1983.

A rescue mission by Swiss police secures the freedom of five diplomats held hostage inside the Polish Embassy in Bern, Switzerland. Four gunmen demanding the lifting of martial law in Poland had seized the building three days earlier.

10 Israel rejects a Mideast peace plan announced the previous day at the Arab League summit in Fez, Morocco. The plan called for an independent Palestinian state but gave implicit recognition to the existence of Israel. A week earlier Israel rejected the plan put forward by President Reagan.

12 The Chinese Communist Party concludes its 12th national congress, during which it adopted a new constitution that restructures the party to eliminate vestiges of Maoism.

13 A special U.S. prosecutor again reports that he could find no evidence of illegal activity by Labor Secretary Raymond Donovan.

14 President-elect Bashir Gemayel of Lebanon is killed in a bomb blast at Phalangist Party headquarters in east Beirut; he was elected August 23 and was to take office September 23.

Princess Grace of Monaco, the former actress Grace Kelly, dies of injuries sustained in a car crash the day before.

15 PLO leader Yasir Arafat meets at the Vatican with Pope John Paul II and in Rome with Italian government leaders.

Sadegh Ghotbzadeh, Iran's foreign minister during the U.S. hostage crisis, is executed by firing squad for having plotted to assassinate Ayatollah Ruhollah Khomeini.

President Ferdinand Marcos of the Philippines arrives in the United States for his first visit in 16 years.

18 First details emerge of the massacre of more than 600 Palestinians by Christian militiamen at the Sabra and Shatila refugee camps in west Beirut. Israel denies any responsibility.

19 Former Prime Minister Olof Palme and his Social Democratic Party are returned to power in Sweden.

The New York Cosmos defeat the Seattle Sounders, 1–0, in Soccer Bowl-82.

20 India's Prime Minister Indira Gandhi arrives in Moscow.

21 The National Football League Players Association (NFLPA) goes on strike after negotiations with the league management council for a new basic agreement break down. The players are demanding a fixed percentage of owners' revenues, including TV.

22 President Reagan signs legislation ending a four-day strike which had shut down much of the nation's railroad system.

24 British Prime Minister Margaret Thatcher agrees with leaders in Peking to hold formal talks on the future of Hong Kong.

Ending a lengthy takeover battle, Allied Corp. announces that it has acquired Bendix Corp. for some $1,900,000,000.

29 Israeli Prime Minister Menahem Begin, succumbing to mounting international and domestic pressure, requests an independent judicial inquiry into the mid-month Palestinian massacre.

UPI

NFL ON STRIKE

His coalition dissolved, West Germany's Chancellor Helmut Schmidt (right) lost a "constructive no-confidence motion" October 1. The parliamentary measure simultaneously elected conservative Christian Democrat Helmut Kohl (third from left) as his successor.

1 The West German Bundestag (lower house) votes to oust Chancellor Helmut Schmidt, electing Christian Democrat Helmut Kohl to succeed him. Schmidt's coalition had broken up September 17.

The maker of Extra-Strength Tylenol orders a recall of some 264,000 bottles after seven persons in the Chicago area died from capsules that had been laced with cyanide.

The United States signs a "compact of free association" giving limited independence to the Federated States of Micronesia.

4 In a conciliatory move, President Amin Gemayel of Lebanon, a Christian Phalangist who was elected September 21 after the assassination of his brother, President-elect Bashir Gemayel, asks Chafiq al-Wazan, a Muslim, to stay on as prime minister.

6 The second round of strategic arms reduction talks (START) between the United States and Soviet Union opens in Geneva.

7 Former Prime Minister Olof Palme of Sweden, leader of the Social Democratic Party (SDP), is sworn in as premier. Palme and the SDP won a solid victory in September 19 general elections.

8 The Polish parliament votes overwhelmingly to outlaw the independent trade union Solidarity.

10 Hernan Siles Zuazo is sworn in as president of Bolivia, ending 17 years of military rule. The national congress, reconvened after more than two years, elected him October 5.

12 Prime Minister Zenko Suzuki of Japan announces his resignation as president of the Liberal Democratic Party and as premier.

The leaders of Egypt and Sudan sign a "charter of integration" providing for unification of political and economic policies.

Alva Myrdal of Sweden and Alfonso García Robles of Mexico, activists for international nuclear disarmament, are named corecipients of the 1982 Nobel Peace Prize.

19 Automobile executive John De Lorean is arrested in Los Angeles for possession of, and conspiracy to distribute, cocaine.

20 The St. Louis Cardinals defeat the Milwaukee Brewers, 6-3, in Game 7 of baseball's World Series.

21 The United States and the European Community reach an accord limiting European steel exports to the United States.

22 A delegation of the Arab League headed by Morocco's King Hassan meets at the White House with President Reagan to discuss recent U.S. and Arab peace proposals for the Middle East.

27 A Chinese census reports a population of 1,008,175,288, nearly one fourth that of the entire world.

28 Felipe González Márquez becomes Spain's first socialist prime minister since the Civil War, as his Socialist Workers' Party wins a strong majority in parliamentary elections.

November

1 Ending the first talks between leaders of the two countries in 10 years, Prime Minister Indira Gandhi of India and President Zia ul-Haq of Pakistan agree to set up a permanent joint commission to resolve future disagreements.

2 In U.S. midterm elections, the Democratic Party increases its majority in the House of Representatives by 26 seats and wins 27 of 36 state gubernatorial races. The Republican majority of 54 to 46 in the Senate, however, remains unchanged.

4 Queen Beatrix of the Netherlands swears in a new center-right coalition headed by Christian Democrat Ruud Lubbers, ending a government crisis that began October 13 with the resignation of Andreas van Agt as party leader.

5 Some 10,000 Canadian members of the United Auto Workers go on strike for higher wages at six Chrysler plants in Ontario.

6 President Ahmadou Ahidjo of Cameroon resigns after 22 years in power, naming Prime Minister Paul Biya as his successor.

7 Voters in Turkey approve by more than 90% a new constitution proposed by the military junta of Gen. Kenan Evren, who automatically becomes president for a seven-year term.

In Upper Volta, a predawn coup led by Maj. Jean-Baptiste Ouedraogo ousts Col. Saye Zerbo. A military junta takes control.

9 Pope John Paul II ends a 10-day visit to Spain.

Rank and file of the United Mine Workers elect 33-year-old Richard L. Trumka as union president, replacing Samuel Church.

10 Soviet President Leonid Ilyich Brezhnev, 75, dies in Moscow.

Australia and New Zealand announce agreement on a Close Economic Relations (CER) accord, by which tariff and duty restrictions between the two nations will be phased out.

Geoffrey Arthur Prime, a longtime Russian translator at the British electronic intelligence center in Cheltenham, England, pleads guilty to seven charges of espionage.

12 Former KGB chief Yuri Andropov, 68, is chosen secretary-general of the Soviet Communist Party, succeeding Leonid Brezhnev.

13 President Reagan lifts U.S. sanctions against companies selling equipment to the USSR for the natural gas pipeline from Siberia to Western Europe. U.S. allies welcome the decision.

Spanish Socialist Felipe González ran successfully for the premiership in parliamentary elections October 28. His campaign slogan—"For A Change"—obviously struck a note with voters, as the nation got its first left-wing government since the pre-Franco era.

Gamma-Liaison

Lech Walesa addresses a crowd at his Gdansk apartment November 14 after being released from detention.

15 As a major step in the government's policy of *abertura* (opening up), Brazilians vote in the country's first free municipal, legislative, and gubernatorial elections in 17 years.

16 The U.S. space shuttle *Columbia* returns to earth after a successful five-day mission. *Columbia*'s first operational flight was highlighted by delivery into orbit of two commercial satellites. Two days earlier, Soviet cosmonauts aboard the Salyut 7 space station broke the record of 185 days in space.

Representatives of the National Football League Players Association (NFLPA) and the NFL Management Council reach a tentative accord in the 57th day of the players' strike.

19 China's Foreign Minister Huang Ha and Defense Minister Geng Biao are removed from office and replaced by Wu Xueqian, 60, and Zhang Aiping, 72, respectively.

22 In a nationally televised address, U.S. President Reagan calls for the deployment of 100 MX missiles in the controversial "dense pack" basing mode. The missiles would be based in a cluster of silos near Cheyenne, WY, at an initial cost of $26,400,000,000.

25 Police in Rome, Italy, arrest an employee of the Bulgarian national airline, charging him with complicity in the May 1981 assassination attempt against Pope John Paul II.

27 New Japanese Prime Minister Yasuhiro Nakasone, 64, and his 21-member cabinet are installed in office. Nakasone was elected in a special session of the Diet the day before.

29 Representatives of 88 nations end a six-day meeting of the General Agreement on Tariffs and Trade (GATT), held in Geneva. Though the conference was extended by three days, fundamental trade issues remained unresolved.

December

1 On the first leg of a five-day, four-nation goodwill tour of Latin America, U.S. President Reagan extends $1,230,000,000 in short-term credit to Brazil.

Miguel de la Madrid Hurtado is sworn in for a six-year term as president of Mexico. De la Madrid was elected July 4.

Prime Minister-designate Amintore Fanfani announces a new four-party coalition cabinet, ending a government crisis that began with the resignation of Prime Minister Giovanni Spadolini on November 13.

U.S. Sen. Edward M. Kennedy (D-MA) announces that he will not run for president in 1984.

2 Medical history is made at the University of Utah Medical Center in Salt Lake City, as doctors implant a permanent artificial heart in 61-year-old retired dentist Barney Clark.

3 U.S. Department of Labor statistics for November report a national, seasonally adjusted unemployment rate of 10.8%, a post-World War II high.

4 Leaders of the 10 European Community (EC) nations conclude two days of discussions in Copenhagen on trade policy, economic cooperation, and East-West relations.

6 During its 15-day annual session, the Chinese National People's Congress ratifies a new, 138-article constitution. Earlier in the congress Prime Minister Zhao Ziyang unveiled the country's sixth economic five-year plan, covering 1981 through 1985.

8 Pakistan's President Zia ul-Haq concludes his first official visit to Washington, during which he held talks with President Reagan and other officials on a proposed U.S. economic package and Zia's intentions regarding nuclear weapons.

Norman Mayer, a 66-year-old advocate of nuclear disarmament, is shot to death by police at the Washington Monument in Washington, D.C., after taking over the structure for 10 hours and threatening to blow it up.

The U.S. Senate confirms Donald Hodel as energy secretary.

9 Meeting near Frankfurt, West Germany, finance officials of the United States, Great Britain, West Germany, and France agree to increase the lending power of the International Monetary Fund (IMF) by 50%.

12 Employees of Chrysler Canada Ltd. vote to ratify a new contract, ending their 38-day strike.

13 An earthquake in Yemen leaves more than 2,800 dead.

14 Garret FitzGerald is elected prime minister of Ireland, after the Labor Party agreed to accept a coalition with his Fine Gael.

Spain opens its border to the British colony of Gibraltar, ending a 13-year blockade.

15 The International Monetary Fund agrees to a $4,500,000,000 loan for Brazil to help it keep up its foreign debt payments.

Teamster President Roy L. Williams is found guilty by a federal jury of conspiring to bribe a U.S. senator and of defrauding the union's pension fund.

16 Anne Gorsuch, head of the U.S. Environmental Protection Agency (EPA), is held in contempt of Congress for refusing to submit documents requested by a House committee.

20 The U.S. Environmental Protection Agency issues its "national priority list" of the 418 most hazardous toxic waste sites to be cleaned up under a federal law.

21 Soviet Communist Party leader Yuri Andropov offers a proposal for the reduction of medium-range missiles in Europe. The United States, Great Britain, and France reject the plan.

23 The U.S. Senate passes, 54–33, a bill providing for a 5¢-per-gallon increase in the gasoline tax to finance highway repairs and mass transit. After the vote, the 97th Congress adjourns, ending its 25-day lame duck session.

The leading political opposition figure in South Korea, Kim Dae Jung, is freed from prison after serving two-and-a-half years of a 20-year sentence and leaves Seoul for the United States.

27 The Dow Jones industrial average closes at a record 1,070.55.

28 Talks between Israel and Lebanon on the withdrawal of foreign troops from Lebanese territory open in the coastal town of Khalde. The second session is to be held in Kiryat Shemona, Israel.

Violence breaks out in downtown Miami following the shooting of a young black man by a city police officer.

30 Martial law in Poland is partially lifted.

In Finland, Prime Minister Kalevi Sorsa reconstitutes his coalition government. The prime minister names members of his Social Democratic Party to the ministries of education, labor, and traffic.

President Reagan announces that the United States will not pay a United Nations assessment "destined to finance the very aspects of the Law of the Sea Treaty which are unacceptable to the United States." The treaty was signed by 117 nations December 10.

Anne Gorsuch, administrator of the U.S. Environmental Protection Agency, became the first cabinet-level officer ever to be held in contempt of Congress. She was cited for refusing to turn over documents.

UPI

The Falklands— An Unlikely War

By Richard C. Hottelet

Patriotic zeal in Great Britain was evidenced by an emotional farewell for 3,000 reinforcement troops leaving Southampton aboard the re-outfitted luxury liner Queen Elizabeth II on May 12. According to the Defense Ministry, the speed, size, and facilities of QE II made her "uniquely suited" for carrying troops to the Falklands.

On April 2, 1982, the Falkland Islands, located in the far South Atlantic, emerged out of the mists of time and years of tortuous diplomacy to bring Great Britain and Argentina to war. Since World War II, the world has seen many international conflicts bigger and bloodier than this. But, for the first time since 1945, two Western powers fought over territory. The Falklands were a most unlikely speck on the map to stir up such a storm, and underlying the sounds of war were frequently posed questions about the reasons for and necessity of such a confrontation.

East and West Falkland are twin islands, separated by a narrow sound, some 250 mi (400 km) off the coast of Argentina and 300 mi (480 km) due east of the Straits of Magellan. They cover an area about the size of Connecticut. The climate is terrible: rainy, foggy, and cold. A sharp west wind makes tree growth just about impossible, but grass thrives and feeds the 650,000 sheep that are the livelihood of the 1,800 inhabitants. The Falkland Islands Company, chartered by the British Crown in the middle of the 19th century, owns half the land and all the sheep. It markets the islands' main exports, wool and mutton. The Falklands are, in effect, company islands, but offer the quiet, remote, rural British life-style that appeals to the people, who are almost entirely of British origin.

Villalobos/Gamma-Liaison

Nationalistic fervor was also at a high pitch in Argentina. Mass demonstrations filled the streets of Buenos Aires.

None of the obvious reasons explains why anyone should covet this territory or its administrative dependencies, South Georgia Island and the South Sandwich Islands, practically uninhabited pinpoints scattered about 1,000 mi (1 600 km) eastward. No one has discovered oil or gas in any quantity on the islands; and if it were there, the cost of drilling and transporting it would be prohibitive. The Falklands have no mineral wealth, only grass, sheep, and 10 million penguins plus seals and birds and kelp, the seaweed that grows thickly around the island and gives the population its nickname, kelpers.

History. The Falklands had a certain strategic value when London colonized them in 1833. Prior to the building of the Panama Canal, the islands dominated the only passage between the Atlantic and Pacific oceans. Great Britain, as a global empire, wanted no other power—Spain and France at the time—in position to pose a challenge there. Today the islands have little or no military meaning. Of some theoretical interest, however, possession of all the islands might be used to bolster British or Argentine territorial claims in Antarctica, now suspended by the Antarctic Treaty of 1959, an international agreement that has prevented possible trouble in the area.

About the Author: Richard C. Hottelet has served as United Nations correspondent for the Columbia Broadcasting System since 1960. In this capacity, he reported regularly during the spring of 1982 on the Falklands crisis. Associated with CBS for more than 35 years, Mr. Hottelet previously was a correspondent for United Press and worked for the Office of War Information during World War II. He is a member of the Association of Radio News Analysts and the Council on Foreign Relations.

Spooner/Gamma-Liaison

UPI

Vital to the British war effort was the neutralization of Argentine air superiority. Sea Harrier jump jets from the British aircraft carriers Hermes, above, and Invincible made strategic attacks on island airfields. Below: Argentine weapons lay idle in the snow near the airstrip at Goose Green, a major stronghold captured by British ground troops only days after they landed on East Falkland.

Outweighing every other consideration has been the political dynamic of nationalism, infusing the issue with patriotic fervor. Britain and Argentina each claim title to the islands and deny each other's facts. France was the first to build a settlement on what mariners from St. Malo had named Les Isles Malouines, whence the Spanish name Las Malvinas. But France withdrew its colonists when Spain asserted its original sovereignty. Britain, founding a colony in 1765 on West Falkland (named by a British captain after the first lord of the admiralty, Viscount Falkland), saw it overwhelmed by a Spanish force sent in from Buenos Aires in 1770. Patriots in Britain demanded war, and a powerful fleet was assembled to throw the Spaniards off the islands. But the prime minister, Lord North, troubled by the gathering storm in the North American colonies, looked for a compromise. The great Dr. Samuel Johnson wrote a pamphlet which observed, among other things, that "patriotism is the last refuge of the scoundrel." The crisis passed. Spain affirmed its sovereignty, which Britain did not dispute. The British colony remained in place until it was abandoned in 1774 as "uneconomic." Essential for the future was the fact that Spain never ceded its sovereign rights to Great Britain. It never signed a treaty, as it had done for Gibraltar.

When Britain returned in 1833, Spain was gone from the Western Hemisphere. Its colonies had become independent states which insisted, under international law, on inheriting the rights and boundaries drawn by the mother country. Britain today argues that Spain had already abandoned the Falklands, that Argentina had never effectively colonized them, and that Britain reoccupied practically uninhabited islands without firing a shot. Argentina asserts that Spanish and then Argentine governors administered the Malvinas in an unbroken line and that Britain took the islands by force in 1833, expelling Argentine authorities and citizens. Argentina has never acknowledged British rights on the islands.

For 125 years this legal argument did not disturb British control of the Falklands. Then, in the late 1950s, the United Nations launched a decolonization movement which turned scores of imperial possessions into independent nations. Argentina seized the opportunity to gain, or regain, the Falklands. Negotiations with Britain began in 1966. Argentina's goal was sovereignty. Britain, while willing to discuss ways to reduce tension, refused to discuss what it called its valid, legal title; at one point, however, it did seem to bend that resolve by considering a formula under which Argentina would have the islands but lease them back to Britain for long-term autonomous administration. Representatives of the islanders, almost certainly encouraged by the Falklands company and a formidable Falklands lobby in London, turned it down.

By June 7 British ground forces had swept across East Falkland and launched an artillery attack on the capital of Port Stanley. The Argentine command called it an "indiscriminate bombardment" of the civilian population. The International Red Cross called for the establishment of a neutral zone in the city, and both sides agreed.

Sygma

Argentina's 12,500-man occupation garrison had the advantage of being dug in on rugged Falklands terrain. Every military setback, therefore, came as a major psychological blow.

The 1982 Crisis. In February 1982, Argentina concluded that negotiations were going nowhere. It broke them off and prepared to seize the islands. In Buenos Aires, Gen. Leopoldo Galtieri, who had maneuvered his way to the top of the ruling military junta in December 1981, faced a bleak national prospect. Argentina's economy was in serious trouble with high inflation and unemployment. Social friction and political frustration ignited a demand for constitutional democracy as well as a wave of strikes and protest demonstrations. The Roman Catholic Church condemned what it called the moral crisis of the thousands who had been assassinated or had disappeared in the six years since the military regime seized power. Workers took to the streets in the largest numbers since the time of Juan Perón, clashed with police, and were arrested by the thousands. Galtieri and his generals may well have regarded the capture of the Falklands as an act of patriotism that would co-opt the mounting opposition.

On April 2, Argentine forces landed on the Falklands, quickly overcoming the handful of British marines stationed there. On the next day, they seized South Georgia and the South Sandwich group, ignoring an appeal by the president of the United Nations Security Council that both parties not use or threaten force, as well as a Security Council resolution demanding immediate cessation of hostilities, withdrawal of all Argentine troops, and negotiation of a settlement.

On April 1, U.S. President Ronald Reagan had tried personally to avert war. In a long telephone conversation with General Galtieri he sought, according to Argentine sources, to persuade Galtieri that force would not solve the problem, warning that Britain would respond furiously and with enormous military power. Further, Reagan is said to have underscored the intimacy of Anglo-American relations and made it clear that he would not only join in no action against Britain but would also help America's closest ally if need be. The sources described the general as visibly shaken, but it was too late. The force was on its way; there was no turning back. Galtieri had counted on a quick victory over a tired, uncertain, distant Britain.

Britain was, indeed, some 8,000 mi (13 000 km) from the scene, but it responded at once to what it felt as humiliation by a second class power. Merchant ships were swiftly requisitioned, at their head the luxury liner *Queen Elizabeth II* (*QE 2*), and a fleet was sent to sea as the British people set aside political and other divisions in a burst of patriotic resolution. The spirit was much the same in Argentina, where the crowds that had cursed the junta only the day before turned out tenfold to cheer and wave flags.

At the United Nations, Britain accused Argentina of violating the UN Charter, plunging into aggression instead of settling differences peaceably. London invoked the inherent right of self-defense. Argentina replied that Britain had taken the Falklands illegally in the first place and now wanted to perpetuate an intolerable colonial presence in the Western Hemisphere. As for self-defense, Argentina snorted that the Falklands were "8,000 miles from British territory," making the argument absurd. Britain accused Argentina of trying to colonize the islands, trampling the Falklanders' right of self-determination. Argentina retorted that, in the liquidation of colonialism, restoration of territorial integrity took precedence over self-determination.

UPI

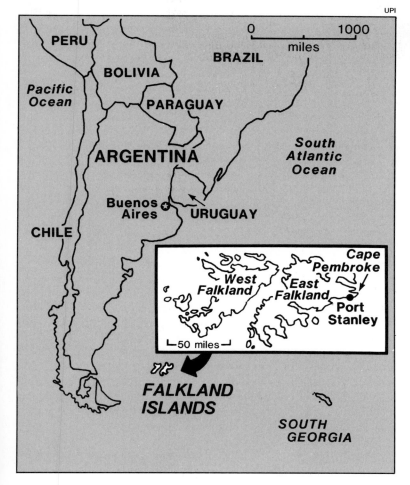

Samuel Johnson on the Falklands, 1771: "islands thrown aside from human use, stormy in winter, barren in summer."

For 12 days in April, U.S. Secretary of State Alexander M. Haig, Jr. (below, left) acted as a go-between in an effort to avert war. In Buenos Aires, President Leopoldo Galtieri (below, right) and his advisers developed "specific ideas for discussion." The U.S. diplomat then transmitted them to Britain for their views. Right, Sir Anthony Parsons and Jeane Kirkpatrick, British and U.S. envoys to the UN, smiled only briefly during the UN Security Council's emergency session on the Falklands in late May. Some three weeks earlier, the United States had announced that it was siding with the British.

UPI

UPI

President Reagan, distressed by a collision between two friends of the United States, ordered Secretary of State Alexander Haig to use his good offices. For 12 days, Haig shuttled between London and Buenos Aires but could not break the vicious circle. His first goal was to avert full-scale war by an agreement to a cease-fire. However, Britain would not accept a truce unless Argentina withdrew its troops. And Argentina would not pull out its forces without the assurance that whatever negotiations ensued would affirm its sovereignty over the Falklands. Britain dismissed that as a mockery of negotiation which ignored the islanders' rights, to boot.

Meanwhile, preparations for war went forward. Argentina moved more than 10,000 men to the Falklands. Britain threw a war zone of 200 mi (320 km) around them and on April 25 reoccupied South Georgia. The task force steamed south, touching base halfway at Ascension Island. It was a hellishly difficult job for a navy that, with no thought of having to defend the Falklands, was being transformed to play its NATO role of antisubmarine defense in the North Atlantic. The aircraft carrier *Invincible,* which became part of the British assault force, already had been sold to Australia. Several destroyers had been ordered mothballed. Had Argentina's rulers waited until the following winter, Britain could not have mustered the fleet and the short-range air support now on their way.

On April 30, with the climax clearly approaching, President Reagan changed diplomatic course from impartiality to open support for Britain. He ruled out direct U.S. military involvement but promised such logistical support as fuel, spare parts, and ammunition. Argentina later accused the United States of making its intelligence resources available to Britain, as well as providing satellite coverage of the war zone, monitoring Argentine military communications, and even analyzing Argentine radar frequencies for British planes to home in on.

Soon there were major naval and air encounters. On May 2 a British submarine sank Argentina's only cruiser, the *General Belgrano,* as it approached the war zone. Casualties were several hundred dead and missing. On May 4, Argentine planes using French Exocet long-range cruise missiles sank the destroyer *Sheffield,* on picket duty beyond air cover, with the loss of 30 lives.

Against this background of rising danger and increasing casualties, and with the United States no longer impartial, Secretary-General Javier Pérez de Cuellar of the United Nations took up the diplomatic effort. His immediate purpose, like Haig's, was to obtain a cease-fire and the departure of Argentine forces. They were to be replaced on the Falklands not by the British, who would keep their distance, but by a UN-peacekeeping contingent; and the United Nations would administer the islands for an indefinite period, with a possible role for both Britain and Argentina. The two parties would then negotiate the islands' future status, resolving the issues of sovereignty, economic interests, and inhabitants' rights. There would be no prior conditions. Face would be saved on both sides, making settlement easier.

Fighting at full stretch in that harsh and dismal region, a third of the way around the world, with increasing losses of ships and men, in the face of a desperate Argentine air attack, Britain was ready to go along with Pérez de Cuellar. But the Argentine junta would not see what this meant. They did not recognize that with the UN on the Falklands, British sovereignty was effectively ended and that negotiations under UN auspices precluded future delay of the sort Argentina had found unbearable. Buenos Aires gave no clear answer and missed the chance. On May 20 the secretary-general abandoned his effort. On May 21, British troops landed in strength on East Falkland Island.

Establishing a beachhead near Port San Carlos under persistent air attack, British troops moved south over the sodden, boggy ground to take the settlements of Darwin and Goose Green and then turned southeastward against the Falklands' capital, Port Stanley, effectively encircling it on May 31. In the cold of the sub-Antarctic winter, the British pressed forward despite bombs and shells and mines. On June 14 the Argentine force surrendered.

Prime Minister Margaret Thatcher frequently maintained that "negotiations do not close [Britain's] military options." On May 20 the House of Commons held its first vote on the Falklands crisis and strongly endorsed the Thatcher government's handling of the situation.

UPI

Argentine prisoners of war relaxed on Ascension Island before going home. The Galtieri government was held responsible for Argentina's defeat, and Reynaldo Benito Bignone, below, became president.

Consequences-Aftermath. Britain sent the nearly 12,000 prisoners of war home without delay, cheered its own returning men and ships, and celebrated a great victory—a welcome taste of the power that had been slipping from the nation's hands since World War II. Prime Minister Margaret Thatcher won universal praise for her courage and dogged defense of what most of her countrymen saw as British rights and British soil. The more than 250 fallen were heroes; there was no trace of any Vietnam-like doubt. The $1,300,000,000 the campaign had cost (approximately $750,000 per Falkland Islander) and the additional $1,700,000,000 projected to replace equipment and to garrison the islands over the next three years were not contested. The bitter complications of victory were not apparent.

One was that the Falklanders' peaceful, archaic way of life, which Britain had come to defend, was gone forever. The unexploded bombs and shells scattered over the islands and the plastic Argentine land mines that defy detection will be removed in time, although it may be years before the people walk carefree across the land. The Falklands are now a fortified outpost, with a garrison that far outnumbers the population. Fighter planes and artillery will guard them. Because Latin America sided with Argentina in denouncing British policy, the islands now must be supplied directly from the United Kingdom, at enormous expense. A bigger harbor and an intercontinental airstrip are needed.

Argentina refused to accept the outcome as final and continued to claim the Falklands as a matter of right. Psychologically exhausted by the incompetence and vainglory that had ensured defeat, economically burdened by the terrible cost pushing the country literally toward bankruptcy, depressed by the hundreds of dead—many of them ill-trained conscripts, confused by their leaders, the people seemed to move blindly from day to day without absorbing the lesson of the tragedy. Galtieri and his junta colleagues were swept away, but the system survived. Other military men took their place and soon raised doubts about the promised

transition to constitutional democracy. As the year ended, the junta was asking for guarantees that would protect it from an investigation of its mismanagement of the war, its corruption, and its violation of human rights in the preceding six years. It spoke also of retaining residual power after the transition.

The United States had as little reason to be happy with the political aftermath as with the war itself. Having begun, in grave concern about Latin American relations, by being impartial in its good offices, then giving Britain full materiel support in its war effort, the United States moved away from Britain's political position. On November 4, over Britain's most urgent protest, the United States voted for a UN General Assembly resolution calling upon London and Buenos Aires to resume negotiations for a peaceful solution of the sovereignty dispute concerning the Falklands. Britain saw that as a tilt toward Argentina. Washington, for its part, feared that this festering problem could endanger the inter-American system by forcing it again to choose sides. It wanted passions to cool, making a peaceful solution possible at last.

Although the war left the islands a fortified garrison, Falklanders resumed their routines. The return of the Union Jack and the naval ensign to South Georgia, a Falklands dependency, presaged Britain's victory.

Territorial Jurisdiction Disputes

Although wars have been fought strictly over territory for centuries, such conflicts are now rare. In addition to the Falklands, however, numerous territories remain areas of dispute. For example, Belize, independent since 1981, is not recognized as such by Guatemala; Gibraltar, the "Rock" in the Mediterranean, is officially a British crown colony but in 1982 Spain reaffirmed its desire to integrate it under Spanish sovereignty; three islands in the Beagle Channel near the tip of South America are a cause of near-war between Chile and Argentina; the Western Sahara, from which Spain withdrew in 1975, is disputed by Moroccan and Algerian-backed Polisario Front forces; mineral-rich regions of Guyana are claimed by Venezuela; and Navissa, a 2-mi- (3.2-km-) long, uninhabited Caribbean rock, is contested by Haiti and the United States.

Personal Investing in the 1980s

Andrew Popper/Business Week

By Ray Brady

Sears Roebuck has come a long way since the days when it was simply a mail-order company. Now, in eight of its stores, in cities from Atlanta to Los Angeles, the company is operating a new kind of financial center. The customer, who may have come to Sears to buy tires or kitchenware, has only to stroll into a center to be able to handle virtually all of his or her financial needs. If the customer wants to invest in stocks, bonds, or mutual funds, Sears has a salesman ready to serve. If it is a matter of opening an individual retirement account (IRA), that, too, can be handled, and if the customer wants to put money into a money market fund, Sears has its own, operated by a brokerage house owned by the huge merchandising company.

While the Sears centers are still an experiment for the company, the idea of a one-stop financial shopping points up the massive change that is occurring in how—and where—Americans invest their money. The change is expected to accelerate as the United States moves farther into the 1980s. Only a few years ago, the overwhelming majority of Americans were content to keep their money in passbook savings accounts, where they could depend on a steady 5.25% to 5.5% return on their money. But inflation—and the era of high interest rates—changed all that. As the rising cost of living ate into their savings, they acquired a new degree of financial sophistication: they began to look for investments offering a rate of return that would keep up with inflation, and perhaps make them a little money, as well.

Sears Financial Network, available at eight branch stores on an experimental basis in 1982, offers a complete line of one-stop financial services, including stock and real estate brokerages, as well as insurance coverage.

New Attitudes and Government Policies. People who used to talk at cocktail parties and other social gatherings about how their homes were rising in value, shifted to new topics as terms like CD (certificate of deposit), "yield," and IRA entered the general vocabulary, and everyone began comparing notes on where the highest return was to be found. Even as they were beginning to talk about rates of interest, a tidal wave of mergers was sweeping away the lines that used to separate the various financial institutions. American Express, the credit card company, acquired a giant brokerage house, Shearson Loeb Rhoades, and began to offer a whole host of financial services. Merrill Lynch Pierce Fenner & Smith, the nation's biggest brokerage house, proffered services, devised to keep a customer's money working at all times, that remarkably resemble bank checking accounts. And banks started to shake off their old ways, realizing that they, too, had to change if they were to keep up with the competition for investment dollars.

This scramble in the financial marketplace is partly the result of saving incentives adopted by the federal government. American industry has entered a period of reindustrialization in which many of the nation's obsolete factories must be rebuilt if the United States is to hold its own against foreign competition. Modernizing the automobile industry, to manufacture smaller, more fuel-efficient cars, for instance, requires the expenditure of billions of dollars, part of the billions of dollars in capital that must be raised

About the Author: Ray Brady, a business-financial correspondent for the CBS network, appears regularly on its morning and evening news programs. Mr. Brady has served as associate editor and assistant managing editor of *Forbes,* associate editor of *Barron's,* and editor of *Dun's Review.* He has lectured on financial topics at several universities, and is a member of the board of governors of the New York Financial Writers Association.

CBS News

Courtesy, Pandolfi Properties
Danbury, CT

Unusually high interest rates have adversely affected real estate investments. In the early 1980s, many for-sale homes were on the market for a considerable period of time.

during the remainder of the 1980s to pay for the reindustrialization. Raising that money, however, requires changes in the way people think about saving money. During the high inflation period of the 1970s, the rate of saving in the United States dropped sharply. People reasoned: "Why save money, if every year what we've saved is losing more of its value?"

In an effort to alter that psychology, the Reagan administration introduced a series of measures designed to make saving more attractive, and thus to accumulate the dollars that industry needs if it is to modernize and expand. The cornerstone of the Reagan policy is the Economic Recovery Tax Act of 1981, which cut the tax rate sharply over a three-year period. While the measure was criticized by some economists as cutting government revenues too much, its basic aim was to stimulate people to work harder, and to put at least some of their after-tax income into savings.

If there was one predominant form of investment to encourage Americans to save and invest—and one which brought about a lot of changes in government regulations—it was the ingenious idea called money market funds. In 1975, a year after the Reserve Fund of New York launched the first one, 32 funds, handling $3,600,000,000 in assets, were functioning. The funds' popularity has since generated an explosive rise in assets. By mid-1982 a total of $233,500,000,000 was being managed by 245 funds. The concept is simple. Traditional securities that offer high yields require a minimum investment of $10,000, which puts them out of the reach of most small investors. By accepting minimum investments as low as $1,000 and offering high yields and full liquidity money market funds opened the door to tens of thousands of small investors. The money funds place the investor's money in short-term debt instruments, such as Treasury bills, bankers' acceptances, and Eurodollar deposits. An investor made apprehensive by banks with financial problems, or worried about the general condition of the economy, can opt for a more secure investment by going into an offshoot of the money funds, one that invests only in securities that are backed by the U.S. government. The trade-off is that the rate of return tends to be slightly less than the rate for money market funds. Whatever the type of fund, its rate of return ran well ahead of anything being paid out by thrift institutions and commercial banks. At one point in 1982, as interest rates declined, the money fund rate of return was just below 12%. That was still well ahead of the return on a passbook account at the bank.

But if the money market funds showed the way, it remained for the federal government to develop what may be the biggest single influence in the investing trends of the future. The government act that cut taxes also liberalized the rules under which Americans could save money—the individual retirement account (IRA)—and it also gave the banks a chance to survive the battle against the money funds and other competitors by letting them offer a brand new kind of investment.

Few financial observers will ever forget the days when savings banks introduced the government-approved "All Savers" Certificates. "Why wait?" demanded one ad. "Earn up to $2,000 tax-exempt interest without leaving your living room." In and around banks decked out in red, white, and blue bunting, long lines formed of people waiting to buy the new certificates. The purpose of "All Savers" was to stop the drain of savers' money away from the hard-pressed banks. In return for the money they left in the banks' management the savers were promised a heady return: generally speaking, each could get up to $1,000 in tax-free interest—a married couple would be eligible for $2,000 tax-free. At the time of offering that worked out to 12.6%. Since the certificates were designed to help the ailing banks of the United States, they would run for just one year. Still, it was an offer that few American savers could resist, and some $42,500,000,000 was raised through them.

Other parts of the 1981 recovery act are expected to have even greater ramifications in the way Americans handle their money henceforth. Until recently, only a limited number of persons could take advantage of Keogh and individual retirement account plans. Under those plans, which were mainly for those not covered by other pension programs, the individual could put aside certain specified sums of money before taxes, in order to finance retirement. The tax would be paid when the money was withdrawn during retirement, when it was presumed that the retiree would be taxed at a lower rate. In the meantime, the money had been earning compound interest. As another means of enabling industry to raise additional capital, such plans have been liberalized. Now, for example, nearly every worker, whether covered by a pension plan or not, can subtract up to $2,000 a year from his or her taxable income by depositing that amount of money in a special retirement fund (IRA). Just as no tax is paid on the $2,000 of income deposited, none is exacted on the amount it earns, until the funds are withdrawn. The Keogh plan for the self-employed also has been liberalized.

While IRAs are still new, they are particularly attractive to those whose incomes have been pushed into higher tax brackets because of inflation, and a variety of investment devices are available for IRAs. With the 1981 legislation, moreover, the total num-

© Roir/Rothco

"TELL ME MORE ABOUT YOUR I.R.A."

ROTHCO
ORIGINAL

ber of people permitted to open IRAs doubled. In the past, those who had been eligible for IRAs often were in lower-paying jobs, the kind in which the worker did not get a pension. Now, those in higher paying positions can take out IRAs. It is expected that many professionals will put their wives on the payroll, so that they too may share in the benefits of an IRA. By the end of 1982 it was too early to know how many million Americans were joining new IRA plans, but many financial institutions made no secret of the fact they expect millions of investment dollars to come from the plans.

Money Management Accounts and Other Plans. As new investment incentives pushed up the stakes, the dividing lines between financial institutions blurred. The Wall Street firm of Merrill Lynch pioneered in offering the Cash Management Account (CMA), which is banking and brokerage services all rolled into one. As it works, the investor keeps his securities at the brokerage firm and deposits spare cash in the firm's money market fund. But even as the money is drawing a higher rate of interest in the fund, checks can be written and charged against a Visa or American Express debit card. If one should happen to write a check for more than the account contains—which caused a check to "bounce" in the old days—the account automatically gets a loan against the value of securities kept with the brokerage house. Initially, an account of this type required about $20,000 in cash and securities to get started, but as Merrill Lynch's business boomed—some people are believed to have pulled their stocks out of safe deposit boxes in order to open CMAs—a number of brokerages began lowering the initial requirements.

To remain competitive, banks offer a competing service, with money market funds and checking account privileges. At Citibank, the nation's second biggest bank, the service is called the Asset Network Account, but it is basically patterned on Merrill Lynch's CMA. California's BankAmerica moved to buy Charles Schwab and Company, a discount stock brokerage, and other banks were known to be looking at discount brokerages, which would enable the banks to buy and sell stocks at rates that are generally lower than those charged by the major Wall Street brokerage houses. As if all that were not enough, banks were offering a variety of other investment programs, including the popular CDs. With a CD, the saver gets a rate of return that is pegged to the rate being paid on 26-week Treasury bills. While the minimum amount that can be invested in CDs is $10,000, some banks and thrift institutions have been selling the so-called loophole certificates, lending the buyer enough money to invest the full $10,000. Banks also have been marketing "repos," banker's shorthand for retail repurchase agreements. While the name sounds technical, it actually means an investment that pays a fairly high rate of return, and may run for a term of from 8 to 90 days. Then there are the small savers certificates, which are exactly what the names implies. The minimum investment in these certificates can be as low as $100. While the funds are tied up for at least 2 to 2½ years, the rate of return is a competitive one.

The high rate of taxation has made Americans aware of the benefits of tax-free municipal bonds, a form of investment that used to be pretty much the province of insurance companies. In 1971, for example, individuals bought only 1% of municipal bond

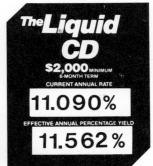

The Cash Management Account (CMA), left, which combines a brokerage fund with a regular bank checking account, a money fund, a charge or debt card, and automatic borrowing privileges, was introduced by Merrill Lynch during 1977. The plan, called a "financial department store," became so successful that a dozen companies were offering similar ones throughout 1982. Recent deregulation of interest rates and changes in the tax law have led to the introduction of a variety of CDs (certificates of deposit) which are available at fixed as well as at varied rates of interest.

issues coming to market. Ten years later, the percentage stood at 64%. Many bond customers buy through investment trusts, where the individual may purchase a trust unit for about $1,000, and the trust itself uses professionals to buy a variety of tax-free bonds.

The Stock Market. While these new investment programs were getting under way, there was a sleeping giant at the corner of Broad and Wall streets in New York City, the heart of the nation's financial center. Simply put, a lot of money was available for money funds, CD, and other programs because the stock market had been an unattractive place for investment. As one broker put it: "Who would put money in stocks, when you can get 14% on a certificate of deposit and sleep soundly at night?"

It was a compelling argument, but in late summer of 1982 the giant gave signs of stirring. Slowly, the U.S. inflation rate was coming down, meaning interest rates would be falling as well. And once business started picking up, the stock market could be an attractive place again.

And then it came. In two rapid-fire days in mid-August that left even veteran brokers breathless, the most widely watched of all stock market indicators, the Dow Jones Industrial Average, shot up by 39 points, the biggest one-day move in its history. Two months later, the sleeping giant flexed still another muscle. Powered mostly by big institutional buying, the volume of shares traded on the New York Stock Exchange (147 million) broke every record in the book. Some market analysts were predicting that this could be the start of the hoped for bull market of the 1980s. (*See also* STOCKS AND BONDS, pages 491–92.)

There is no denying that the stock market remains the hub of the U.S. investment world. More than 32 million Americans own shares in U.S. corporations. Still others—133 million by most estimates—have indirect ties to the stock market. They have corporate pensions which have been invested in stocks, or they are the beneficiaries of money that has been invested by bank trust departments and life insurance companies. One way or another, the constituency of the stock market is huge, and when stock prices make headlines, or prices rise in a meaningful way, the stock market acts as its own publicity agent and entices even the most reluctant buyer. As Michael Metz, vice-president of the investment firm of Oppenheimer and Company, puts it: "One person says to another, 'Hey, I bought a stock for $10 last week, and I sold it yesterday for $12'—and once you get a few people with stories like that, the news spreads quickly and the investors come flocking in."

In an age when everyone is tax conscious, the stock market has a new advantage going for it. If a stock or other capital asset is held for a year or longer, the gain on it is taxed at a new low rate of 20%. Wall Street analysts believe that most investors are still not aware of that change, but they feel that once investors earn some profit from stocks and experience the satisfaction of having to give only a comparatively small percentage of it to Uncle Sam, they will send still more money flooding into the stock market. If that happens, the investment outlook for the 1980s will grow even more glittering, and it is to be hoped investors will have the funds to cash in on all the new ideas that will be designed to catch their attention.

Reprinted by permission of Tribune Company Syndicate Inc.

STRESS

By Dr. Herbert Pardes

In a recent national survey of American family health, fully 82% of respondents indicated a need for less stress in their daily lives. Those surveyed agreed that stress is a major obstacle to health. National leaders share the public's concern. In late 1981, the Institute of Medicine, a component of the U.S. National Academy of Sciences, issued a major review of research on stress and health. In a preface to the report, Institute President David Hamburg noted that during the late 1970s "no aspect of health and disease elicited more interest among leaders of the United States government . . . (than) the possible effects of very difficult life experiences on health."

Scientific attempts to understand stress have gone hand in hand with the increasing concern of government leaders and the general public. Over the past several decades, the concept of stress has emerged as a dominant unifying concept in the health and social sciences. It links such diverse fields as basic biology, medicine, psychology, and the study of social and organizational behavior. Important new insights have been gained into the meaning, measurement, positive and negative effects, control, and treatment of stress.

About the Author: Dr. Herbert Pardes has served since 1978 as director of the National Institute of Mental Health in Rockville, MD. Prior to that he was chairman of the departments of psychiatry at the University of Colorado Medical Center (1975–78) and the State University of NY Downstate Medical Center (1972–75). He is a regular contributor of this publication's Mental Health review (*see* page 337).

Meanings and Models. Though many persons view the present as an era of stress, the phenomenon is certainly not new to the 20th century. Stress is an essential ingredient of life. As Dr. Hans Selye, one of the world's foremost authorities on stress, points out, the complete absence of stress is death. Stress forces adaptation to change, and adaptation allows survival. It was Selye who some 40 years ago formulated the "stress syndrome," or "general adaptation syndrome" (GAS). The GAS, according to Selye, is a three-phase physiological response that occurs when an organism is confronted by a threatening stressor. In the first stage of *alarm,* the organism recognizes the stressor and prepares to fight or flee. The chain of command in this arousal process begins in the brain, which first notifies the pituitary gland; from there, a hormonal message is sent to the adrenal gland which, in turn, activates a variety of systems essential to physical response. Heart rate and blood pressure increase, pupils dilate, perspiration begins, and digestive processes slow to allow blood to be sent to the muscles. In the second stage of *resistance,* the organism, fully prepared to meet the threat, begins to repair bodily damage resulting from the arousal. Because the organism cannot indefinitely maintain the physiologic state of full readiness, however, the third stage, *exhaustion,* follows if the stress does not abate. Without a return to a steady state, prolonged exhaustion places health and even survival in jeopardy.

The general adaptation syndrome extends the doctrine of homeostasis that was proposed early in the 1900s by Harvard University physiologist Walter B. Cannon. He described homeostasis as the means by which the body, using hormonal feedback devices, maintains a state of equilibrium despite environmental stressors. Emotional arousal, he suggested, evokes the "fight or flight" response to prepare an organism for a defensive struggle.

Though Selye defined biologic stress as "the nonspecific response of the body to any demand," his initial interest was in physiological responses to such physical stressors as infection, extremes of temperature, and traumatic injury. As social and psychological research on stress evolved from his original work, investigators attempted to develop refined models of stress that would avoid simple cause-and-effect explanations of stress and its consequences. A representative current model, developed by the Institute of Medicine task force, specifies four factors common to an interaction between an individual and the environment: an *activator* (or stressor) in the environment that produces a *reaction* (condition of stress) that leads to a *consequence.* Both steps in this sequence—from activator to reaction and from reaction to consequence—can be influenced by *mediators* that exist either in the environment or in the individual's biological or psychological makeup. By virtue of these mediators, an experience that one person views as extremely stressful might be seen by another as the spice of life.

Even with more flexible conceptualizations of stress, some researchers question the fitness of the term, given the diverse contexts in which it is used. Writing in the *International Encyclopedia of the Social Sciences,* University of California stress expert Richard Lazarus noted that the concept of stress has been applied to post-operative metabolic imbalances, failure to succeed in experimental tasks, bereavement, psychopathology associated with extreme hardships, and social disruptions stemming from natural di-

MASSACHUSETTS STATE EMPLOYMENT SERVICE

Wide World

UPI

Viewed as an adaptive response to some threatening circumstance, stress actually helps the individual survive a catastrophic event. The greater the stress, however, the greater the threat to physical and mental health. Loss of home and livelihood are among the most serious "stressors" one can face.

sasters. The varying needs and interests of scientists representing diverse disciplinary perspectives encourage further refinement of definitions and process models. Psychologist Lazarus, for example, views stress in terms of "cognitive appraisal" of a situation. He suggests that an individual appraises the demands of a given stressor in light of available personal adaptation resources. If the perceived demands exceed the assessed resources, the individual will view and react to the stressor as a threat; if the resources exceed the demands, the individual will more likely view the stressor as a positive challenge.

Despite all the ambiguity and controversy, the concept of stress is likely to continue to be used in science. In a review article published in the *Journal of Human Stress,* Dr. John Mason observed that "perhaps the notion of a generic term which somehow ties together the threatening or taxing demands of the environment on living organisms strikes some deep, responsive chord within us which keeps alive the use of stress terminology in spite of all the confusion it creates."

Stress and Health in Everyday Life. Since life is a series of interactions between an individual and his or her biological, social, and psychological environments, all life events can be said to be stressful. But not all stress is bad. Lazarus refers to "threats" and "challenges," terms that parallel Selye's designation of "distress," which is harmful or unpleasant, and "eustress," which is associated with good or pleasant events. Challenges, and even mild stress, have been shown in research to enhance learning, improve job performance, and generally add an invigorating edge to life. Excessive stress, on the other hand, has long been associated anecdotally—and increasingly by research—with poor health and performance. But here lies another quirk of stress. Even apparently positive events—for example, reunion with a long-lost

While minimal compared with severe emotional trauma, excessive tension in daily family life can have negative long-term health consequences.

© Laimute Druskis/Taurus Photos

loved one or winning a competition—can affect health adversely. While identifying "distressful" experiences is important both for the prediction and prevention of health risks, it is also a complex problem.

Much of the direct evidence for the effects of stress on health results from studies of victims of unique or catastrophic events. Early in the history of stress research, combat veterans and concentration camp survivors were frequent research participants and did, in fact, show a high rate of adverse physical, emotional, and psychosomatic consequences. More recent studies of such victims support those findings. In 1977, Dr. Lenore Terr of the University of California studied a group of 26 children who, after being kidnapped from their school bus and buried alive, managed to escape to safety more than a day later. Each of the children showed signs of emotional trauma, ranging from major personality change to declining school performance. So well documented are the post-traumatic effects of severe stress that survivors—such as former prisoners of war in Vietnam and U.S. embassy personnel held hostage in Tehran—are routinely offered psychological therapy to minimize negative aftereffects. In 1980, the American Psychiatric Association added "Post-traumatic Stress Disorder" to its official manual of diagnostic categories.

Because most people never experience such severe stressors as captivity or catastrophic disaster, a more pressing task confronting stress researchers is to identify routine life events that may turn out to be health-threatening stressors. One approach to this problem that has gained prominence over the past decade was introduced by University of Washington researchers Thomas Holmes and Richard Rahe in the late 1960s. While working with tuberculosis patients, the two researchers noted that the onset of TB often followed a major or difficult event in the patient's life. Using information they had collected from thousands of patients over two decades, Holmes and Rahe compiled a list of life events that had preceded health problems encountered by the subjects. These events—both positive and negative—were organized into categories: health, work, family, finances, and community/social relations. The researchers then asked a smaller group of subjects to rank 43 representative events in terms of intensity and the amount of time necessary to accommodate their impact on the "steady state" of day-to-day life. When numerical values, or "life change units," were assigned to the events, the resulting list ranged from "death of a spouse" (100 points), to "outstanding personal achievement" (28 points), to "minor violation of the law" (11 points). Holmes and Rahe posited that a rapid succession of major life events occurring within a specified period could indicate an increased risk of illness. Over the past decade, Holmes' and Rahe's original Social Readjustment Rating Scale has been critiqued and refined on technical grounds. More importantly, however, the original hypothesis was borne out statistically, and the study of life events offers a potentially rigorous research strategy for future understanding of stress.

Research on life events has underscored the complexity of stress and considerably weakened simplistic cause-and-effect explanations of stress and its effects. The duration and frequency of stressors and the degree to which they are predictable and controllable (or unpredictable and uncontrollable) can greatly influence an individual's reaction, as well as the physical and mental

All too frequently, Americans cope with routine stress by going to the medicine cabinet. Sedatives and tranquilizers represent a multibillion-dollar industry.

© Sybil Shelton/Peter Arnold

"THAT'S WHERE WE DIFFER. I FIND DRIVING RELAXING."

Sidney Harris

While individuals may react differently to the same situation, all work is potentially stressful. And though a certain level of stress may increase efficiency, a variety of factors can cause a dangerous excess.

health consequences. The stress associated with elective surgery, for example, may differ significantly from the stress imposed by chronic, debilitating illness. Similarly, the death of a spouse in late life, while being a serious stressor, is more predictable and thus more readily subject to accommodation than might be the death of a spouse at age 30. Institute of Medicine panel members compiled a partial list of mediators in the relationship between stress and illness. The list includes *personal* factors, such as personality traits, coping resources, genetic variables that might predispose one to illness, and such sociodemographic variables as age, sex, race, and economic status. Among *environmental* modifiers of stress are the availability of social supports, the physical setting or climate in which a stressor is encountered, and such social or cultural factors as prejudice or institutionalized means of dealing with change.

Stress and Work. Testifying before Congress in 1981, the Washington Business Group on Health, a national organization representing 500 major corporations, estimated that industry loses more than $1,000,000,000 each year on stress-related problems through loss of time and productivity, accidents, and medical costs. The organization attributed an additional $42,000,000,000 annually to costs stemming from alcohol and chemical dependency. Dr. Michael Lerner, director of the Institute for Labor and Mental Health in Oakland, CA, sees the problem from the viewpoint of employees. "The impact of occupational stress on health, mental health, crime, lowered industrial productivity, and family breakdown can no longer be ignored," contends Lerner.

While research has documented the exceptional stress-related consequences of certain occupations—most notably, perhaps, that of air traffic controllers, who must maintain a high state of preparedness while remaining outwardly calm and physically inactive—all work is potentially stressful. Sources of job stress are varied. Stressors can be physical, such as excessive noise or poor lighting and ventilation, or psychosocial, such as conflicting job demands, lack of control over work, inadequate recognition for performance, or lack of job security. Any of these stressors can trigger physiological responses, but many employees see little opportunity to vent their tension. The employee under continuing stress can succumb to the physiologic stage of exhaustion and greatly increase his or her susceptibility to physical or mental illness.

In recent years, strategies aimed at occupational stress and its consequences have been as varied as the causes. Employee assistance programs, now common in large companies, offer services extending from case finding to referral and treatment, either through company health care providers or contracted community health and mental health agencies. A greater emphasis on prevention is seen in company-sponsored programs to assist employees to avoid excessive stress or to enhance their coping capacities. Approaches run the gamut from providing athletic facilities as a healthy outlet for stress-generated tension, to training in various relaxation response procedures, techniques through which such physiologic functions as blood pressure, once considered involuntary, can be controlled through mental effort. Harvard scientist Dr. Herbert Benson notes that transcendental meditation, exercise, and periods of quiet can be as effective in increasing stress tolerance as the clinically developed "relaxation response."

Many occupational stress experts, however, advise that the most effective solutions to job stress must ultimately be found within the work setting. Lerner and his colleagues recommend many beneficial ways to restructure the work environment. If

The physiological components of stress can be monitored, and sometimes even controlled, with the help of biomedical technology. The stress test is increasingly offered by private companies and other institutions.

K. Sherman/Bruce Coleman

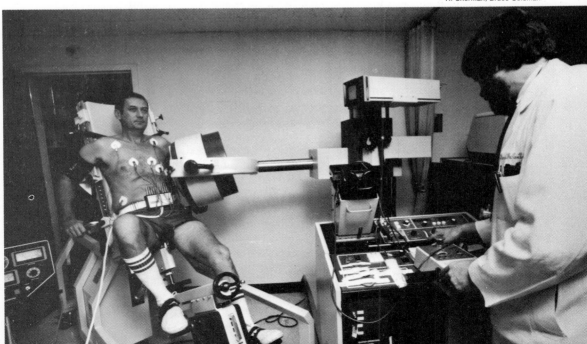

physical stressors—high sound levels and poor light, air, and climate—cannot be eliminated, workshifts should be shortened to avoid excessive stress, they suggest. To reduce the impact of psychosocial stressors, the researchers call for management's increased sensitivity to the personal and family needs of workers; for greater opportunity for employees to form social support groups; and for the restructuring of tasks to allow workers a decision-making role in the way work is done. A well-publicized series of innovations in Swedish automobile plants, in which mass production workers were allowed to work on a team basis rather than an assembly line basis, have offered a successful model for job restructuring. Workers in the experimental plants were found to suffer lower rates of absenteeism and health problems and to have more personal concern for the quality of the product.

Directions in Research. Publication of Selye's first article on stress in 1936, "A Syndrome Produced by Diverse Nocuous Agents" in the British journal *Nature,* marked the beginning of modern stress research. Today, the literature on stress includes hundreds of thousands of articles. Yet, in the opinion of stress authority Dr. John Mason, a shortcoming of the field historically has been a lack of communication between the two major lines—physiological and psychosocial—of research.

The 1981 Institute of Medicine report suggests that contemporary research is redressing this failing. Advances in both the neurosciences and the behavioral sciences have elucidated the role of the brain in controlling the endocrine and autonomic nervous systems. Because the former is involved primarily in regulating internal biochemical processes and the latter in mediating an organism's relation to the environment through behavior, demonstration of interaction between the two has underscored the role of stress as a unifying concept in health research. In recent decades, discovery and identification of the roles of neuroregulators—biochemical substances that are involved in interneuronal communication throughout the body—have contributed to an improved understanding of stress reactions. Also, hormones in addition to those identified by early stress researchers have been shown to be responsive to stress. Studies of genetic factors also will further elaborate individual differences in response to stressful experiences and may suggest sharply focused preventive interventions.

Repeated studies have shown that people show a great diversity of responses under a given set of environmental circumstances, however difficult. Thus, psychosocial studies of stress, which are placing an increasing emphasis on how people cope, also offer a potentially useful approach to preventing or intervening in maladaptive responses to stressors before they produce an increased risk of illness. The Institute of Medicine report notes that "The promise of such interventions is clearest with respect to mental health, but is directly relevant to general health. Failure of coping to reduce stress can contribute to physical illness, and coping patterns that harm health, including smoking, alcohol use, and risky driving, weigh heavily in the burden of illness."

Modern science has made significant inroads in the understanding of stress. Continuing progress in the neurosciences, in genetics, and in the behavioral study of adaptation and coping offer promise that the immense health risk stemming from stress-related disorders will lessen in the future.

The corporate gymnasium provides employees a healthful outlet for venting tension.

J. Fortuny/Texaco

SPORTS on TELEVISION
The Game Changes...

Hand-held cameras and on-field microphones bring TV viewers closer to the game, and its stars, than stadium spectators ever get. Demanding a fixed share of the league's growing television revenue, NFL players went on strike in 1982.

By William Oscar Johnson

It had its beginnings more than four decades ago on a glistening spring afternoon—May 17, 1939—at Columbia University's Baker Field in Manhattan. The occasion was an Ivy League baseball game between Columbia and Princeton—the first real sporting event ever to be televised. It was carried on W2XBS, an experimental station owned by the NBC network, and the man who barked the first greeting to the world's first television sports fans—*"Good afternoon, ladies and gentlemen!"*—was none other than the late Bill Stern, then America's most renowned radio sportscaster. The telecast was not an unmitigated success. Years later, Stern recalled: "God, we were dunces. In that one game we learned a complete lesson in how not to televise a sports event."

A single camera, a bulky old Iconoscope, was on hand to follow the action, and it simply could not do the job. Whenever a ball was hit, fair or foul, the camera would sweep clumsily, blindly about, trying to keep the streaking sphere in its lens. "We got so

About the author: William Oscar Johnson is a Senior Writer for *Sports Illustrated* magazine and has written extensively on the subject of television and sports. Among his several books are *Super Spectator and the Electric Lilliputians* (1970, Little, Brown) and a recent novel, *Hammered Gold* (1982, Pocket Books), about TV sports and a plot to fix the 1984 Olympics.

THE VIEW THE RADIO 'EYE' SAW

Scene from the Columbia-Princeton game on Wednesday were covered by the iconoscope shown here on an elevated platform. The actual pictures reached televisors in homes and hotels via portable sets and the NBC station on the Empire State Building.

How Ball Game Was Televised

Iconoscope Follows Plays in First Sports Event to Be Shown in Local Homes.

By SAMUEL KAUFMAN.

Television came to the baseball diamond for the first time last Wednesday and stole the show. The ten-inning second game of the double header between the Columbia and Princeton nines at Baker Field was presented visually and audibly over W2XBS via N. B. C.'s relay station on wheels.

It was a literal field day for the television crew and the video lads conceded that they learned a lot about sports pickups through the experiments. The overtime game—originally intended for seven innings—covered two hours seventeen and a half minutes.

Folks in the vicinity of Marble Hill—even those some distance from the athletic field—knew that there were some strange goings-on at the Columbia sports grounds. The giveaway was the appearance of an odd-shaped antenna strung up the tall flagpole. Even a distance it may have seemed like the weathervanish frame of a river box kite, but an close inspection carefully proved lead-in wires used to stay leading down to the transmitter van of the famous television relay station which feeds the Empire State transmitter. The relay antenna point, near Broadway and 230th street, was about 500 feet from the playing diamond. Feeding the receivers was an easy task for the video station who merely followed a long stretch of coaxial cable—made practical by a new set of receivers with thin red flags on the second van covering the way....

Columbia University Athletic Club

The first televised sporting event was a Columbia-Princeton baseball game in 1939. "It was a literal field day for the television crew," read the above newspaper account, "and the video lads conceded that they learned a lot about sports pick-ups through the experience. The overtime game—originally intended for seven innings—covered two hours seventeen and a half minutes."

we were actually praying for all the batters to strike out," said Stern. "That was one thing we knew the camera could follow." Mercifully, only a few thousand people—most of them spectators idling through the exhibits at the RCA Pavilion at the New York World's Fair in Flushing, NY—saw that historic telecast. *The New York Times* radio critic wrote of the event: "To sit for two hours in a darkened room on a beautiful sunny day in May to watch a baseball game on a miniature screen stirs thoughts on the future of television in sports. The imprisoned baseball fan becomes restless. His eyes tire. He knows that he is missing so much." But *Life* magazine reviewed the W2XBS telecast from a far more positive—and accurate—perspective: "No fuzziness could hide what television will mean for American sports. Within ten years an audience of 10 million, sitting at home or in movie theaters, will see the World Series or the Rose Bowl Game. Thousands of men and women who have never seen a big-time sports event will watch the moving shadows on the television screen and become excited fans. . . ."

And so it has come to pass—except that "thousands" is never the term used to count TV crowds anymore. Now it's "millions." These days, even a total of 10 million people watching major league sports on network television is considered just average—or below. And 10 million is a mere fraction for such blockbuster events as the World Series, the Olympic Games, and the Super Bowl—that latter-day invention which did not come into existence until 28 years after that historic first telecast in 1939 and which now makes the Rose Bowl and all other sporting events look puny by comparison. The first game of the 1980 World Series between the Philadelphia Phillies and the Kansas City Royals broke all records for a TV baseball audience by pulling no fewer than 79,070,000 viewers. The January 1982 Super Bowl between the San Francisco '49ers and Cincinnati Bengals attracted an astonishing 110,230,000—the largest multitude of Americans to watch a telecast of anything. Indeed, five of the six highest-rated shows in TV history are Super Bowls. Only *Roots,* with an audience of 98,700,000, ranked with Super Bowls, and it finished third.

Big Business. TV sport is a massive industry. The three major networks—CBS, NBC, and ABC—have a combined sports department budget of about $1,000,000,000 per year. With the addition of all the local television sports operations around the country, plus cable and pay-TV, the overall budget for TV sport in America is probably approaching $2,000,000,000 per year. Advertisers flock to buy commercial time on sports programs, and they pay and pay and pay. A one-minute spot on an ABC Monday Night football game goes for at least $225,000. The 1982 Super Bowl on CBS produced the single highest per-minute commercial price in the history of television—*$690,000!* Clearly, the million-dollar-minute is not far off.

The money that the three networks generate through advertising has been the bulwark, the foundation, the single most essential source of support for nearly all big-time sports in America. As Roone Arledge, the innovative and highly motivated president of ABC News and Sports, once said: "So many sports organizations have built their entire budget around television that if we ever withdrew the money, the whole structure would just collapse."

Courtesy, American Broadcasting Companies, Inc.

The pioneer of television sports programming, Roone Arledge of ABC created such longtime favorites as Wide World of Sports *and* NFL Monday Night Football. *As executive producer of virtually all the network's sports broadcasts—including the 1964, 1968, and 1972 Olympics—he introduced such techniques as slow motion, stop action, and instant replay. Today Arledge is president of both ABC Sports and ABC News.*

While that is basically true, it is more true for some sports than for others. For example, the National Football League (NFL) depends on network television revenue more than any other major league sport. And today it is more dependent than ever before. In 1970, the NFL's television package was worth $40 million per year, split equally among the 26 teams—about $1.5 million per team. In those days, revenues from TV made up about 40% of a team's total income, with 60% derived from tickets, concessions, parking, and other stadium revenue. In early 1982, NFL Commissioner Alvin "Pete" Rozelle produced the coup of the century by getting the three networks to agree to a $2,000,000,000, five-year contract guaranteeing each team an average of $14.2 million per season—an increase of more than 900% from 1970. Thus, the ratio of TV-to-stadium income in the NFL will now be almost exactly reversed—60% from television and 40% from the stadium.

With coverage of several events on a given afternoon, cameras at every vantage point, videotape and split screen capabilities, audio controls, and commercial interruptions, producing a typical sports show requires precise timing and technical expertise in the control room.

Courtesy, ESPN

The NFL is by far the healthiest sports organization in the country, not only because of the enormous sums it attracts from TV but also because it has long lived by a strict and unswerving law that television revenue must be shared equally among all 28 teams. That insistence on parity ensures the well-being of every franchise, whether it is located in a major media market, such as New York, or an utter tank town, such as Green Bay. In major league baseball, by contrast, there are potential competitive inequities among the franchises because of huge differences in TV revenue from one club to another. The major leagues do pool their network revenue (which comes to about $1.5 million per team per year), but local television income, which usually exceeds network fees by a great deal, is kept by the individual teams. Thus, the Montreal Expos club, which taps almost all of Canada for television outlets, has a monumental income of about $10 million per year, while such small-town teams as Kansas City, Seattle, and Milwaukee get barely $3 million apiece.

However it is distributed, money for televised sporting events continues to pour in. Every year, sports on TV are fetching increasingly higher, boom-town prices. In 1970, broadcast rights for the Rose Bowl cost NBC $1.5 million; in 1984, 1985, and 1986, NBC will be paying $11 million per contest. TV rights for the 1980 Olympic Games in Moscow were awarded to NBC for $85 million, while ABC paid a whopping $225 million for the 1984 Games in Los Angeles. In 1981, ABC and CBS signed a four-year, $132 million contract with the National Collegiate Athletic Association (NCAA) for college football games—a 110% increase over the previous agreement.

The clout of network television shows itself in ways other than large sums of money. In the spring of 1982 a brand new professional football organization, the 12-team United States Football League (USFL), landed a $22 million-a-year contract with ABC. While that is not an enormous amount of money, ABC made the deal even though the USFL would not play its first game until March 1983. *March?* Yes, March. The USFL is going to play a "reverse season" schedule, from March to July. While, this is a wildly risky experiment, to say the least, the very presence of ABC's money—regardless of the amount—gave the USFL an immediate credibility that it could have achieved in no other way. Many people had been predicting an early demise for the league, but the prevailing opinion switched completely after the deal with ABC was made public.

The Future. Until now, the three broadcast networks have been the single most influential force in TV sport. It was their money and their mass exposure that produced the spectator sports boom of the 1960s and 1970s. It was the networks' money and exposure that boosted salaries, prize money, and endorsement fees, making dozens—perhaps hundreds—of athletes multi-millionaires. It was also network TV that dictated truly bizarre starting times for games, such as Sunday morning; insisted on extra timeouts for commercials; and caused the World Series to be played late in October and at night, when subfreezing temperatures are a very real possibility. Indeed, it was network TV that held the power—economically, politically, and esthetically—over the way the games were played and the way they developed over the last 25 years.

Television has aided the expansion of professional sports, created whole new events, and had far-reaching effects on existing games. The proposed U.S. Football League was given a boost by landing a network contract; officers of the New York franchise, above, and 11 other teams could look to the future with optimism. The Superstars, pitting well-known athletes from different sports in head-to-head competition is a popular made-for-TV event. The commercial time-out is just one of the changes that affects play itself.

"SLOW DOWN. TWO QUICK HITS, A PICKOFF, A STEAL—WE HAVE TO PAUSE AND LET THE STATION GET IN A COUPLE OF COMMERCIALS."

But now that era seems to be over. TV sport is facing an incipient revolution which could make some mighty differences. Don Ohlmeyer, the former long-time executive producer of NBC Sports, said: "The structure of sports on TV will change so radically it will be hardly recognizable. The networks have been enormously successful as monopolies, but that's all over. Cable television and pay television are here. They are real." These non-network systems for transmitting TV signals are by no means new. They have existed for many years. Yet it is only now, at the beginning of the 1980s, that cable, satellite, and pay-per-view TV systems have begun to proliferate enough to make them a potential force in American TV sport. For example, thanks to satellite transmission, it is now possible for a single major event to be sent out—for pay—over its own national network. Gustave Hauser, co-chairman of Warner Amex Cable, said: "You can create a network for any one-of-a-kind event—the Masters, the NCAA basketball final, the Super Bowl. Instead of three big networks, we can have 40 or 50 satellite networks. They can serve every freaky appetite in the country."

One such satellite network that some think serves a fairly freaky public is the Entertainment and Sports Programming Network (ESPN), which broadcasts sports programs 24 hours a day, seven days a week, 365 days a year. A subsidiary of Getty Oil, ESPN currently reaches 16.5 million homes. It signed a separate contract with the new USFL but that, so far, is about as major league as most of its programming gets. ESPN serves its viewers—jokingly called "sports junkies"—a widely diverse menu of odd and mainly minor sports, ranging from polo to rodeos to amateur boxing to full-contact karate. ESPN gets a small fee for each viewer from the various cable systems that carry it, but most of its revenue comes from advertising. ESPN is growing, but it is far from being a profitable operation—yet.

Many experts wonder if advertising money is television's best source of revenue to underwrite the increasingly huge rights costs for major sports events, or even for day-to-day sports programming. Many experts feel that some form of pay TV—through subscriptions or on a pay-per-view basis—in the only way that *any* kind of network will be able to afford to transmit big-time sports.

Mobile units equipped with audio and visual relay systems provide golf coverage—from tee to green on all 18 holes—to millions of homes.

ESPN, a cable network headquartered in Bristol, CT, offers sports junkies 24 hours of programming every day. Coverage ranges from rodeo, lacrosse, soccer, and full-contact karate to in-depth news and interview shows.

The eye of the camera takes in the drama of sport in all its aspects. From a post-game locker room celebration to the tension-filled corner of the champ, it affords vivid images otherwise inaccessible to the public.

"Prism," for example, is a very successful pay-cable network in Philadelphia which began in 1976. Prism transmits a lot of movies and a good, nourishing menu of major league baseball, basketball, and hockey, as well as some college games. Jim Barniak, sports director of Prism, sees that operation, or an extension of it, as the true wave of the future: "I think you'll see everything go pay-per-view. You watch something and they'll send you a bill for it. If Prism were to switch from $10-a-month subscription to, say, $2 a game, we could take in $460,000 a night." This version of more frequent superpaydays is what dazzles sports entrepreneurs today. They all recall the night of Nov. 25, 1980, when "ON TV," a movie-and-sports subscription channel in Los Angeles, put on the second Sugar Ray Leonard-Roberto Duran boxing match. ON TV charged its subscribers an extra $15 for the fight, and 165,000 homes anted up an impressive $2.5 million to receive that event alone.

> *The structure of sports on TV will change so radically it will be hardly recognizable. . . . Cable television and pay television are here. They are real.''*
>
> Don Ohlmeyer

If one were to charge the same $15 fee to the immense viewing audiences generated by some of our more celebrated events, the revenue would be absolutely mind boggling: a single Super Bowl would draw more than $1,000,000,000 and a seven-game World Series, $2,100,000,000.

Is this, then, the future of TV sport? Will we be paying directly for our sports on television—$15 for a Super Bowl, $100 for a full Olympics? Will the major networks become powers of the past? Gerald Levin, vice-president of the Time Inc. video group, says, "The networks will continue to deliver the single largest mass audience and, thus, they will continue to have the showcase events. The networks are still the best way to merchandise a sport, because you can reach the largest number of people with a single exposure."

That is true—for now. But many people believe that the day will inevitably come when American sports entrepreneurs will not be able to resist the temptation to go to the source of the greatest amount of money—no matter how big (or small) the audience. There is certainly no possibility that a single network—or even all *three* networks as we know them today—could afford to spend $1,000,000,000 to televise a single Super Bowl. Yet, can we really expect the owners of NFL franchises to forego such a guaranteed gold rush once the technology exists to produce it? Some people believe firmly that Congress would prohibit any action that would limit the number of American TV homes which could receive such "American institutions" as the Super Bowl or the World Series. But one must wonder if Congress would really force NFL owners—or any other businessmen—to sacrifice enormous amounts of money that they have, in effect, earned and thus have a right to receive.

Whatever the answer, one thing is certain. TV sport is in the process of radical, perhaps even violent, fluctuation. Even the experts cannot predict what the future—even the immediate five-year future—will hold. When we look back on that first flawed, fuzzy telecast over W2XBS, we can see that there was no certain way to predict what future was contained in the clumsy Iconoscope camera, big as an icebox, and the few hundred tiny TV tubes, small as auto headlamps, that received its blurry images. Oddly enough, despite all the progress in the intervening decades, or perhaps *because* of it, it is even more difficult today to guess with any certainty what lies ahead.

Dick Clark Remembers...
25+ Years of Rock 'n' Roll

David Redfern/Retna Ltd.

Bill Haley and His Comets recorded "Rock Around the Clock," and a new era in music was under way.

By Dick Clark

Rock 'n' roll can no longer be described as a phenomenon. It has become an institution. After more than 25 years, the music form has gained total acceptance.

Generally, 1955 is designated as the year of the birth of this rhythmic music to which kids can dance. Dance was what the youngsters of the mid-1950s wanted to do most. Rock 'n' roll is a combination of various kinds of music. The music form combined the "race" music of the late 1940s and early 1950s, "rhythm and blues" or "soul," and the roots of country music, then known as "rockabilly."

The foremost rock names of 1955 were Fats Domino, Chuck Berry, Lavern Baker, and Bo Diddley. However, if one single performer or group introduced the music form, it probably was Bill Haley and His Comets with "Rock Around the Clock." The song was recorded in 1954 and became the theme of the 1955 movie *The Blackboard Jungle.*

Editor's Note: Dick Clark of *American Bandstand,* a television show geared to teenagers and featuring recorded music, dancing by members of the audience, and singing by new and established performers, has been a center figure on the rock 'n' roll stage from the beginning. The show originated in Philadelphia in 1952 and moved to the ABC network in 1957.

The Early Days. Rock had begun to emerge even before 1955. As early as April 1950, "The Fat Man" by Fats Domino was in the Top Ten charts for black artists, and in 1951, Johnny Otis and Mel Walker had a song called "Rockin' Blues." That same year, Piano Red hit the charts with "Rockin' with Red," and a couple of months later came Amos Milburn's "Let's Rock Awhile."

In 1950 a novelty tune, "Rag Mop," that even today has the "feel" of rock, enjoyed enormous success. "Rag Mop" is indicative of the influences that combined to become rock 'n' roll. The song was a Top Ten number for both the Ames Brothers and Ralph Flanagan's Orchestra. At the same time it was a rhythm and blues hit for Lionel Hampton at one end of the spectrum and for Doc Sausage and Joe Liggins at the other. To top it off, "Rag Mop" was a country hit for Johnnie Lee Wills.

It was this melding of country music, black music, and a little bit more that gave birth to rock 'n' roll. The step which Bill Haley took with "Rock Around the Clock," and which Elvis Presley later enhanced, grew out of a feel for the black music of the day. Chuck Berry, who was black, had a feel for country music that provided the same sort of meld to his songs.

Someone suggested recently that we could establish an official birthday for rock 'n' roll by choosing the date when the first record with the words rock and roll in its title reached the top ten in the pop charts. That would have been January 1956, and the record was Kay Starr's "Rock and Roll Waltz," hardly a true rock 'n' roll roots recording.

It is interesting that the growth of rock 'n' roll changed the music audience and took the Big Band vocalists off the top of the charts. The Big Band vocalists, including Patti Page, Teresa Brewer, Joni James, Jo Stafford, Georgia Gibbs, Rosemary Clooney, and Kay Starr dominated the charts in the early 1950s.

UPI   UPI

Early favorites Fats Domino (left) and Chuck Berry were instrumental in the development of rock 'n' roll.

Debbie Reynolds was one of two female vocalists to be represented in the top charts in 1957. Her "Tammy," a movie theme, was Number 12.

Wide World

In 1954 ten of the top 30 singles were recorded by these big band vocalists. In 1955 that number dropped to seven, then to four in 1956. In 1957, Debbie Reynolds' "Tammy" and Gale Storm's "Dark Moon" were the only two records by female vocalists in the Top 30. In 1958, "Sugar Time," an almost rock number by the McGuire Sisters, was the only hit in the charts by a female or female group.

Connie Francis, Elvis, Disc Jockeys, and The Rock Explosion. Way down the charts in position number 39 in 1958 was a recording by the first female vocalist from the rock 'n' roll generation. Connie Francis had her first hit, "Who's Sorry Now?" This was the first step on a path that would make Connie the "First Lady of Rock 'n' Roll." But, with few exceptions, rock 'n' roll was an all male world. Elvis Presley was its king.

Wide World
UPI

By the late 1950s, rock 'n' roll fans had crowned their royalty. Elvis Presley was king; Connie Francis was queen.

Chubby Checker introduced ''The Twist,'' the dance craze of the early 1960s, on American Bandstand, which has been hosted by Dick Clark (below) since July 1956. To mark the show's 30th anniversary on television, the original lectern was presented to the Smithsonian Institution in Washington, D.C, in a special 1982 ceremony.

Rock 'n' roll was having an impact on America, and the impact of *American Bandstand* was as massive as it had been unpredictable. We knew we had a large following in Philadelphia, but some people were not certain that teenagers dancing to records in an Eastern city would attract all of America's teens. It did. Rock 'n' roll had gone national and the "rock explosion" had begun.

Alan Freed, a disc jockey who started in Cleveland and later moved to New York City, was already calling the new music rock 'n' roll. Todd Storz at WTIX in New Orleans and Gordon McLendon at KLIF in Dallas had come up with a new radio format. It was *all* top 40 music plus some news and sports. This innovative form of radio was a natural partner for rock 'n' roll.

Many things could be said about Elvis Presley's contribution to rock 'n' roll. A significant fact was that his early hits opened a two-way street between black and white music. Presley was on the rhythm and blues charts, as well as the pop charts. That made it legitimate to feature black artists as "rockers."

Bandstand was the showcase. Little Richard, The Platters, Frankie Lymon and the Teenagers, and, most of all, Chuck Berry, became rock stars. Pat Boone and Paul Anka added a softer sound to the hard-driving rock of Jerry Lee Lewis and Buddy Holly.

The Platters were one of the most popular early rock 'n' roll groups. In 1956 alone, they had three hits—"My Prayer," "Great Pretender," and "The Magic Touch."

UPI

Over the years *Bandstand* introduced thousands of artists and, in the early days, it was the main source of exposure for new artists. There were still such black artists as The Coasters, Jackie Wilson, and Lloyd Price, but there were also such teen idols as Frankie Avalon, Fabian, and Bobby Rydell. The mixture continued through most of the early rock years. There also was the building of legends. Bobby Darin was one.

The 1960s. The biggest innovation of 1960 was a dance. Chubby Checker, who took his name from being a "little Fats Domino," popularized "The Twist." While there had been a long list of dances introduced on *Bandstand,* there had been nothing like the Twist. What made it so important to rock 'n' roll was that it was not just a dance for kids. It became the "in" dance for an older generation and expanded the audience for rock 'n' roll.

Rock rolled along for a couple of years until California was heard from. Surf, sand, and cars became the symbols of the young generation in the form of The Beach Boys. And then came the "Invasion from England."

Even more importantly, then came the Beatles. They were adopted by America from the moment they arrived in February 1964. Adults shook their heads in dismay at the spectacle of screaming teenage girls and insisted that their sons not let their hair grow long, to no avail. No group had a more profound effect on rock music than these four youngsters from Liverpool. John Lennon, Paul McCartney, George Harrison, and Ringo Starr did many very special things for rock 'n' roll. They silenced many of its critics. America's youth could respond to their parents' criticism. "Listen to the words, listen to the music." An ever growing number did listen, and the generation gap narrowed. The record business began to grow into a multibillion dollar industry. In radio, the airwaves were filled with the sounds of rock 'n' roll.

Top Popular Record of the Year

Year	Artist / Song	Year	Artist / Song	Year	Artist / Song
1952	Leroy Anderson *Blue Tango*	1962	Mr. Acker Bilk *Stranger on the Shore*	1972	Roberta Flack *First Time Ever I Saw Your Face*
1953	Percy Faith *Song from Moulin Rouge*	1963	Jimmy Gilmer & The Fireballs *Sugar Shack*	1973	Tony Orlando & Dawn *Tie A Yellow Ribbon 'Round The Ole Oak Tree*
1954	Kitty Kallen *Little Things Mean A Lot*	1964	Beatles *I Want to Hold Your Hand*	1974	Barbra Streisand *The Way We Were*
1955	Prez Prado *Cherry Pink and Apple Blossom White*	1965	Sam the Sham & The Pharoahs *Wooly Bully*	1975	Captain & Tennille *Love Will Keep Us Together*
1956	Elvis Presley *Heartbreak Hotel*	1966	S/Sgt/Barry Sadler *The Ballad of the Green Berets*	1976	Wings *Silly Love Songs*
1957	Elvis Presley *All Shook Up*	1967	Lulu *To Sir With Love*	1977	Rod Stewart *Tonight's the Night*
1958	Domenico Modugno *Volare*	1968	Beatles *Hey Jude*	1978	Andy Gibb *Shadow Dancing*
1959	Johnny Horton *Battle of New Orleans*	1969	Archies *Sugar Sugar*	1979	The Knack *My Sharona*
1960	Percy Faith *Theme from a Summer Place*	1970	Simon & Garfunkel *Bridge Over Troubled Waters*	1980	Blondie *Call Me*
1961	Bobby Lewis *Tossin' and Turnin'*	1971	Three Dog Night *Joy to the World*	1981	Kim Carnes *Bette Davis Eyes*

Later Developments. There were innovations, not only in the music but also in the instrumentation. Electronics began to play as much of a role in rock music as it did in the space program. Rock instrumentals took their own special place. Even a rock opera, *Jesus Christ Superstar,* opened on Broadway in October 1971.

Beginning with the late 1960s, there were new giants in the business—The Rolling Stones, Simon and Garfunkel, The Doors, Otis Redding, Blood, Sweat and Tears, Chicago, Carole King, Stevie Wonder, Alice Cooper, Elton John, Fleetwood Mac, The Bee Gees, Bob Dylan, Rod Stewart, Donna Summer, Peter Frampton, Led Zeppelin, Bruce Springsteen, John Denver, and Billy Joel. Each of them fairly well dominated at least one year of rock music. In addition, hundreds of other performers made an impact on a growing audience.

The Beach Boys again had a hit in 1976.

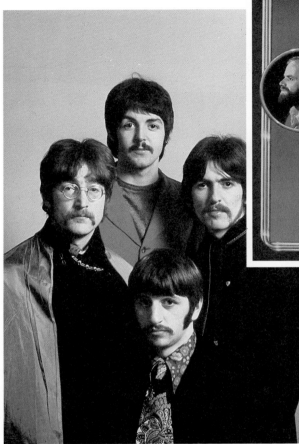

The Beatles (clockwise from left): John, Paul, George, Ringo.

Billy Joel won several Grammys in 1979–1980.

"Children of the World" was a 1977 success for the Bee Gees, the Gibb Brothers who became popular in Australia in the 1960s.

Bob Dylan, a master of the protest song in the 1960s, became a rock superstar.

What is the future of rock 'n' roll? I do not see superstars of the magnitude of Elvis or the Beatles. Today's rock 'n' roll is diverse. There is Power Pop, just as there has been New Wave and Punk Rock, the Big Band sound and the Ballads, Disco and the Twist. What is interesting is that each of these forms has built its own following and that each following remains. Rock is a lot of things to a lot of people, and I expect it to stay that way.

Etty/Retna

The Image Bank

"Rock 'n' roll is here to stay." New artists, including Deborah Harry (left), the lead singer of Blondie, and Bruce Springsteen (page 69), constantly come to the fore. In fact, Springsteen "burst just like a supernova" onto the scene in 1975 with the album "Born to Run," and "Call Me," by Blondie was the Number 1 single of 1980. Elvis Presley (above) remained king until his death at the age of 42 in 1977, and Dionne Warwick (page 69) believes

Adam Scull/Black Star

Someone said that the only constant in rock music since the mid-1950s has been *American Bandstand*. I guess that is true, and I hope that it remains so for another generation or two. I look back with a lot of satisfaction at having been a part of the evolution of this now broad spectrum of music, but I am still looking ahead.

Rock 'n' roll is not just memories. It lives and grows, reflects the mood of today, and indicates the music of tomorrow.

Mary Alfieri

that "her different kind of sound was accepted by both the rhythm and blues audience and the pop audience." Discomania, whereby enthusiasts danced the night away at New York City's Studio 54 (page 68 bottom) and other discotheques, peaked in the late 1970s. Rock concerts, including the Rolling Stones 1981 tour of 25 American cities (below), continue to draw record crowds to music halls, ball parks, and country fields.

Mike Prior/Retna

Gary Gershoff © Retna Ltd.

People, Places and Things

The 1982 World's Fair in Knoxville, TN—formally named the Knoxville International Energy Exposition—attracted some 11 million visitors in the six months it was open. The theme of the fair was "Energy Turns the World," and its symbol was the 266-ft (81-m) Sunsphere (top, center). Some 23 nations, 30 corporations, and 7 states had pavilions.

Snowdon/Camera Press London

People in the news: *France's Col. Jean-Loup Chrétien was launched June 24 aboard a Soyuz T-6 spacecraft with two Soviet cosmonauts, making him the first person in space not from the United States or a Communist country. On July 29, six-week-old Prince William of Wales—William Arthur Philip Louis—posed with his parents on the occasion of their first wedding anniversary. In New York City, the proposed demolition of the venerable Morosco and Helen Hayes theaters led to an impassioned but unsuccessful protest by such notables as (left to right) Celeste Holme, Liza Minnelli, Christopher Reeve, and Joseph Papp (looking down).*

Gamma-Liaison

UPI

Elissa Spiro/Wallace Berrie & Co., Inc.

Tiny blue creatures called Smurfs, above, won the hearts of American children—and merchandisers—in 1982. First created in Belgium more than 20 years ago, smurfs began appearing on lunch boxes, bed sheets, and clothes, not to mention their own hit TV show. When they weren't playing with smurfs, kids flocked to video game arcades to steer through the monster-infested maze of Pac-Man. Video games grew into a $5,000,-000,000 industry.

Yvonne Hemsey/Gamma-Liaison

FDR Centennial Commission

"Floriade," a floral extrava-
ganza held every ten years in
Holland, blossomed at a 135-
acre (55-ha) site in Keukenhof,
near Amsterdam, from April 8
through October 10.

Centenaries: The 100th birthday of Franklin Delano Roosevelt was marked by a ceremony
at his Hyde Park, NY, estate
(opposite page, bottom), on
January 30. The mansion was
damaged by fire only one week
before. Below: The 100th birthday of Irish author James Joyce
was February 2, but the celebration was not held until June
16, designated by Joyce as
"Bloomsday," after Leopold
Bloom, the hero of his novel
Ulysses. To mark the occasion,
100 actors in Dublin dressed up
in Edwardian costume and performed scenes from Joyce's
work.

© Homer Sykes/Woodfin Camp

Malak

In cities throughout the United States, artist Richard Haas covers barren walls with deceptive trompe l'oeil murals. His façade in New York City's Soho district, right, creates a quaint and fanciful baroque atmosphere. In central Florida, Walt Disney Productions opened a vast, futuristic exhibition and amusement park called the EPCOT Center. EPCOT—which stands for ''environmental prototype community of tomorrow''—showcases the latest advances in science and technology. A massive geosphere called ''Spaceship Earth'' forms the entrance to the $800 million, permanent facility.

Ira Berger

© Ray Fairall/Photoreporters

The Alphabetical Section

The Vietnam Veterans Memorial, inscribed with the names of the 57,939 Americans killed or missing in the Vietnam War, was dedicated officially on the Washington Mall in November.

ADVERTISING

In all probability, the year 1982 will go down in U.S. economic and advertising history as "The Recovery that Wasn't." Though the national economy passed through a watershed in the battle against inflation, hammering down the rate to a respectable 6%, the much-heralded midyear turnaround came instead in the muted tone of a whisper. Despite the Reagan administration tax cut in July, consumers kept a tight lid on their money; in August, retail sales actually declined. Although interest rates fell, they were still well above the levels of past economic recoveries; interest rates on consumer loans were especially high. And in the book of big business, Chapter 11 was well thumbed, as bankruptcy felled corporations in numbers exceeded only by the Great Depression.

The nation's 125 leading advertisers reported a total 6.7% decline in earnings by the middle of the year, with little hope for improvement. As for the advertising agencies themselves, 1982 was yet another year of low profitability due to high interest rates, major increases in overhead costs, and slower payments.

On the bright side, advertisers for the most part bucked the trend of previous recessions by holding the line on advertising budgets and in some cases increasing them. The total outlay for advertising in the United States in 1982 was an estimated $68,300,000,000, an 11.4% gain over the year before. The rate of increase easily outdistanced that of inflation (at 6%) and the gross national product (about 3%).

Laws and Regulations. In the course of the year, advertisers saw the first major reorganization of the laws governing their industry since 1938, when the government began regulating the then-fledgling broadcast industry. Seriously affected by the Reagan administration effort to reduce bureaucratic regulatory power was the Federal Trade Commission (FTC), whose slashed budget resulted in a reduction of staff lawyers and a curtailment of the agency's rule-making powers. In various stages of approval were congressional bills that would strip the FTC of its powers to 1) ban advertisements that it considers to be "unfair"; 2) police the business practices of doctors, lawyers, and other professionals; 3) force manufacturers to prove "natural" food claims on product labels; and 4) restrict the marketing practices of beer, wine, and liquor manufacturers. Still at issue was the FTC's power to define and regulate so-called "deceptive" advertisements.

Under pressure from the Justice Department, the National Association of Broadcasters (NAB)—a self-regulating trade association for the television networks and some 660 stations nationwide—agreed to end its regulation of the quantity, length, and placement of television advertisements and other nonprogram material by member stations. It also agreed to stop limiting the number of products or services that can be promoted in a single commercial. At that point the NAB ceased its advertising clearance activity altogether. The Federal Communication Commission's (FCC's) guidelines restricting the amount of advertising that can be broadcast in any given hour were also under review. This, together with the dismantling of the NAB, left unclear what television advertising regulations, if any, will exist in years to come.

Volume. U.S. advertisers were expected to increase total outlays to some $68,300,000,000 in 1982, an increase of 11.4% over the previous year. On a year-to-year basis, however, the increase was 1.2% less than the 1981 gain. As in recent years, nearly one third of the overall outlays came in newspaper buys, which totaled $19,200,-000,000, for a 10.3% increase. Surprisingly, the year's largest gains were in the smallest category—outdoor advertising—up 14.3% to $800 million; television was up 14.2% to $14,500,-000,000; and miscellaneous (a catchall category for anything from bus-shelter advertising to skywriting) was up 12.2% to $13,800,000,000. The increases in the outdoor and miscellaneous categories suggested that recession-weary advertisers were looking for cheaper buys. The overall increase in television advertising outlays reflected the dramatic jump in spot buying (up 16.2% to $4,300,000,000), the increase in network buying (up 14.2% to $6,400,000,000), and the not-so-dramatic local gain (up 11.8% to $3,800,000,000). The year's weakest increases were recorded in magazine advertising, up 8.6% to $3,800,000,000, and radio advertising, up 9.5% to $4,600,000,000. Also below the year's total advertising growth rate were the previously strong direct mail category, up only 10.3% to $9,600,000,000, and business publications, up 11.1% to $2,000,-000,000.

Canada. Total advertising outlays in Canada for 1982 were expected to be $4,473,000,000, an increase of only 6% over the previous year, reflecting the continued adverse effects of a recessionary economy. Daily newspapers still accounted for the largest share of media expenditures (at $1,095,000,000), but this figure represented an increase of only 1% over 1981; weekend supplements were up 9% to $38 million, and weekly newspapers gained 5% to $230.7 million. The outlay for radio advertising was an estimated $455 million (up 4%); outdoor advertising, $290 million (up 9%); and direct mail, $884.8 million (up 5%). In the periodical category, advertising expenditures in farm publications were $17 million (up 6%); directory advertising, $290 million (up 5%); religious, $12.5 million (up 4%); and business publications, $145 million (down 1%). Canadian advertising's brightest stars in 1982 were television, up 16% to $800 million, and general-interest magazines, up 13% to $215 million.

EDWARD H. MEYER
Grey Advertising Inc.

AFGHANISTAN

© William Campbell/Sygma

Afghanistan, an economically troubled nation heavily dependent on agriculture, remains a battleground as well.

The situation in Afghanistan during 1982 can be briefly summarized: no peace; no Soviet withdrawal; no diplomatic solution.

The Military Situation. In 1982 the USSR recognized its inability to pacify the country short of a major military escalation, a move it was not yet prepared to undertake. Soviet tactics changed accordingly. The destruction of villages, the burning of crops, and the slaughter of people and livestock diminished as the Soviets recognized that these terror tactics only consolidated countrywide resistance. Soviet forces adopted defensive postures, venturing from their fortified areas only when the *mujahidin* (freedom fighters) threatened major strategic positions.

In one such area, the Panjshir Valley, the Soviets attacked at three separate times during the year. This valley adjoins the main supply route from the Soviet border to Kabul, and from it insurgents threatened Soviet supply columns and the principal military airbase at Bagram. The Soviets committed major elite units to clear the valley. The guerrillas, led by a brilliant young commander and former engineering student, Ahmad Shah Massoud, simply melted into the high mountains and ambushed the supply columns. The mujahidin severely defeated the Soviets, causing high personnel and materiel losses and capturing large amounts of arms.

A similar fiasco occurred in Paktia province in July, when Soviet reinforcements were sent to the besieged forts of Kopkia and Debgai, which control access to the strategic town of Khost. Three large columns of armor and mechanized infantry were ambushed by mujahidin. The columns suffered heavy casualties and finally retreated. The garrisons at Kopkia and Debgai then killed the Russian advisers and surrendered, joining the guerrillas. Large amounts of arms and supplies were captured by the mujahidin. In November an explosion, caused by the collision of a fuel truck and the lead vehicle of a Soviet convoy, temporarily closed the Salang pass tunnel on the main supply route between Kabul and the Soviet border. Soviet forces sealed off the entrances causing many deaths.

© William Campbell/Sygma

Afghani street merchants offer fresh bakery products as well as weapons and ammunition. Below, members of the Hizb-i-Islami group of freedom fighters take position south of the city of Kandahar. Although the freedom fighters were more united in 1982, political disorganization continued to prevent them from taking full advantage of their tactical edge over the Soviet occupiers.

Roland Neveu/Gamma-Liaison

Although militarily the Soviets were on the defensive in 1982, the freedom fighters were unable to capitalize fully on their advantage because of lack of weapons and poor logistic and political organization. Their efforts to control large urban centers such as Herat and Kandahar failed when the Soviets mounted determined, well-armed counteroffensives. Urban terrorist attacks were more successful in keeping the Soviets off balance. In the countryside, on the other hand, the freedom fighters had almost total control. Several foreign observers noted that the insurgents moved openly in daylight throughout most of the country.

A new and important trend in military leadership emerged among the guerrillas during 1982. Previously, insurgent leaders came mostly from tribal or other rural elites and tended to be uneducated and inexperienced in battle. In 1982, intellectuals and former military men began to assume leadership, adding a new dimension of strength and skill to the resistance. It became more common for neighboring resistance groups to participate in joint military operations. Former army officers and NCOs provided new capabilities for training and repairing equipment.

The year, then, brought a shift in military balance in favor of the mujahidin. They were not organized enough to expel the invaders, but they drove the Soviets into defensive positions.

The Political Situation. Reduction in Soviet military action was accompanied in 1982 by a much stronger political effort. The Soviets applied pressure on the Afghan government to reconcile the Parcham and the Khalq factions of the communist Peoples' Democratic Party of Afghanistan (PDPA). The feud had turned to deadly hostility in 1979 when the Soviets replaced Hafizullah Amin (Khalq) with Babrak Karmal (Parcham) as Afghan president. The underground war between Parchamis and Khalqis frustrated Soviet efforts to organize a responsive government in Kabul and to broaden its support.

In May, Karmal was called to Moscow, ostensibly for a few days of medical consultation. Instead he stayed for two months. On his return to Kabul he launched an unsuccessful program to reconcile the Khalqis in the party, the government, and the army. In one widely reported case, Parchamis arranged to send young Khalqi party activists to the Panjshir valley to back up the Soviet military offensive. The young Khalqis were slaughtered, and bitterness between the two factions greatly increased. Mujahidin asserted that Khalqi adherents in the government and army secretly informed them of forthcoming military operations, enabling the guerrillas to ambush or evade the attackers.

The Soviets also attempted to balkanize Afghanistan into linguistic and ethnic regions to prevent a unified resistance. This tactic worked in the 1920s against the rebellious Muslim Basmachis in Soviet Central Asia. In 1982 the reorganized Ministry of Tribes and Nationalities offered the various ethnolinguistic groups in Afghanistan autonomy and the freedom to retain their traditional customs and religion if they would lay down their arms. For the Pushtun tribes, with their penchant for anarchy, the offer of an autonomous Pushtun Republic undercut the center of greatest tribal resistance to the Soviet presence.

In longer-range political actions, the Soviets courted the allegiance of women and youth. To women they promised total liberation from rigid Muslim traditional restraints. To youth the Soviets offered extensive educational opportunities. Russian became the second language of instruction. Hundreds of young children were sent to school in the USSR and thousands participated in summer vacation programs in Soviet Central Asia.

Politically, the mujahidin inside Afghanistan became more independent from the exiled leaders in Pakistan. The political groups in Pakistan, despite feeble attempts to unite, continued to bicker. Meanwhile, the freedom fighters in actual combat began to call themselves "free mujahidin," and many independent groups developed close liaisons, cooperating despite different political convictions. Non-Pushtun elements of the Afghan population joined the freedom struggle. The Hazaras of the central highlands formed their own government headed by an elected *Shura* (parliament) and organized village militias to defend their areas.

In terms of political independence, self-reliance, and cooperative organization, the mujahidin made important strides during 1982.

The International Situation. Diplomatically, there was little progress toward a political solution. The Soviets showed no inclination to withdraw. On the contrary, the construction of permanent barracks, a new road and railroad bridge across the Amu Darya river, plans to extend the Soviet railroad to Kabul, the expansion and modernization of the military airfields at Bagram and Shindand, extensive Russianization of the educational system, and total control of the

---

AFGHANISTAN • Information Highlights

Official Name: Democratic Republic of Afghanistan.
Location: Central Asia.
Area: 251,773 sq mi (652 090 km^2).
Population (1982 est.): 15,100,000.
Chief Cities (1979 census): Kabul, the capital, 913,-164; Kandahar, 178,409; Herat, 140,323.
Government: Head of state, Babrak Karmal, president (took power Dec. 1979). Head of government, Soltan Ali Keshtmand, prime minister (named June 1981). Policymaking body—57-member Revolutionary Council.
Monetary Unit: Afghani (50.6 afghanis equal U.S.$1, Jan. 1982).
Gross National Product (1981 U.S.$): $3,230,000,-000.
Economic Index (1980): Consumer Prices (1978–79=100), all items, 112.6; food, 104.
Foreign Trade (1980 U.S.$): Imports, $924,000,000; exports, $729,000,000.

Afghan government machinery all pointed to a Soviet resolve to dig in.

In June, Pakistani and Afghan officials met in Geneva and discussed a political settlement through a UN intermediary. In July the United States conducted special talks with the USSR in Moscow on the same subject. U.S. Secretary of State Alexander Haig and his successor, George Shultz, in talks with Soviet Foreign Minister Andrei Gromyko, insisted that U.S.-USSR relations could not be normalized so long as Soviet troops remained in Afghanistan. The Soviets remained obdurate in their position that they would not withdraw unless there was an international guarantee ensuring the survival of the communist government in Kabul.

Pakistan grew increasingly concerned as the flood of Afghan refugees into Pakistan continued unchecked. The 2.8 million refugees began to settle more permanently in Pakistan, converting the huge tent camps into villages with *kacha* (adobe) huts. The addition of this populace into the oversensitive North West Frontier Province had alarming implications for Pakistan.

During 1982 the international community maintained a high level of rhetorical pressure on the USSR, but the Soviets remained oblivious to world opinion.

For the fourth time in three years, the UN General Assembly passed a resolution calling for the "immediate withdrawal of foreign troops from Afghanistan" and insisted on the right of the Afghans to "determine their own form of government." The United States accused the USSR of causing 3,000 deaths in Afghanistan through the use of poison gas. The U.S. Congress, the Council of Europe, and the European Parliament declared March 21, the first day of the Afghan new year (Nauroz), to be Afghanistan Day. U.S. President Ronald Reagan issued the proclamation in a highly publicized White House ceremony, praising the Afghan freedom fighters and dedicating the forthcoming space shuttle flight to Afghan freedom. However, the Europeans financed the Soviet gas pipeline and President Reagan lifted the Soviet grain embargo. The nonaligned movement, at its meeting in Havana in June, called for the withdrawal of foreign troops from Afghanistan. But none of the Western countries, the Arabs, or the nonaligned nations made any serious effort to supply the mujahidin with the weapons, medicines, communications equipment, or money they so desperately needed. As for U.S. sympathy for the Afghan cause, groups of Afghan political refugees arriving in New York and San Francisco were promptly thrown into jail by U.S. immigration authorities.

The Economic Situation. With the countryside devastated, the Afghan government could not feed its urban population. The USSR was forced to make up the deficit, despite its own severe grain shortage. In return, the Soviets tightened their stranglehold on the Afghan economy. Prime Minister Soltan Ali Keshtmand announced that Afghan-Soviet trade had more than doubled in 1981 and that nearly all Afghan foreign commerce was with the Soviet bloc. To help balance this trade monopoly, new agreements were signed to expand natural gas pipelines and production from Afghan fields to supply the growing industrial sector of the Soviet Central Asian republics. The integration of the Afghan power grid with the Soviet system and the new transportation links between the two countries would enable the Soviets to absorb the Afghan economy into the Soviet bloc.

The Soviet economic commitment in Afghanistan was high and rising, providing further evidence that the USSR was paying a high price for its Afghan venture.

LEON B. POULLADA
Northern Arizona University

Well-equipped military men guard the People's House, the official Kabul residence of President Babrak Karmal.

David Lomax / Camera Press

AFRICA

For Africa, 1982 was a time of turmoil, despair, and uncertainty about the future. Never before in the 20th century had the continent experienced so many threats to its survival. It was a year of accelerating economic decline and mounting debt. African countries reeled under heavy debt service commitments, escalating balance of payments deficits, crippling fuel costs, and severe food shortages. Mineral exporting countries, particularly Zambia, Zaire, Zimbabwe, Botswana, and South Africa, were hard hit by the drop in world prices for copper, cobalt, diamonds, gold, and other basic metals. Other countries groaned under the calamitous fall in prices for such agricultural commodities as cocoa, coffee, and peanuts. With falling world demand, African exports weakened in value and could buy fewer imports. An acute foreign exchange crisis developed everywhere, and many countries fell into arrears on payments of loans. Factories shut down for lack of essential imported machinery and spare parts. Agricultural output declined almost everywhere as farmers found it difficult or impossible to obtain import licenses for fertilizer, seed, pesticides, and equipment. As debts mounted, growing numbers of countries called upon hard-pressed creditors for postponement or rescheduling of loan payments. In 1978, only two African members of the International Monetary Fund (IMF) had credit arrangements. By mid-1982 the number had exploded to 21. This came at a time when multinational public and private lending institutions were struggling to maintain liquidity in the face of a global recession, inflation, tight money, and historically high interest rates. In February, the World Bank proposed severe cutbacks in noninterest loans to sub-Saharan Africa by its affiliate, the International Development Association (IDA). And the IMF cut off funds or withdrew portions of loan commitments to countries missing repayment targets or failing to fully institute mandated austerity programs. Many countries were indeed failing to meet so-called performance criteria.

Economic austerity programs generated tension, popular demonstrations, and general political instability. Most governments responded to the unrest with greater repression of civil liberties, human rights, and free speech. Government leaders resorted to extralegal measures to prevent the formation of opposition parties. President Daniel arap Moi of Kenya, fearful of losing the forthcoming national elections, declared his country officially a one-party state and detained those leaders calling for a multiparty democracy. In Zaire and Sudan, Presidents Mobutu Sese Seko and Jaafar al-Nemery, respectively, imprisoned dissident parliamentarians who tried to form an opposition party. And Gabon's President Omar Bongo used his secret police to arrest members of MORENA, a political protest group seeking representation in government. Moreover, numerous black African countries followed South Africa's lead in requiring its citizens to carry identity cards. In 1982, Amnesty International reported a "pattern of severe violations of basic human rights in Uganda" after collecting data on hundreds of cases of detention without trial, as well as systematic torture and murder committed by the national army. In Ghana, the bar association expressed outrage over the abduction and murder of three Supreme Court justices and the creation of "People's Tribunals."

Significant assaults were also made on the right to be kept informed, as the independent press came under heavy attack for its criticism of government policies. In Kenya, the government sacked the editor-in-chief of *The Standard,* the nation's second-largest daily, after he editorialized against the current practice of detentions without trial. Zaire and Gabon arrested several highly respected editors; and Uganda and South Africa, among several countries, threatened greater restrictions on press freedom. Government police and military battled dissidents from within and without their countries. Antigovernment guerrilla movements were creating chaos in Zimbabwe, Uganda, Ethiopia, Sudan, Somalia, Angola, Mozambique, and South Africa.

The fabric of African unity was also under severe strain at the international and Pan-African levels. For lack of a quorum, the annual summit of the Organization of African Unity (OAU) was postponed for the first time in history. Members were deeply divided over several fundamental issues, including the seating of the Polisario representative of the Saharan Arab Democratic Republic as the group's 51st member. Morocco and its allies refused to recognize the republic, which claims territory taken by Morocco after Spain's withdrawal from the Western Sahara. A late November attempt to convene an OAU summit also was abandoned. This time the issue was the seating of the Habré government in Chad. Such African nations as Nigeria and Cameroon, Ethiopia and Somalia, Zaire and Zambia clashed in border disputes. South Africa continued to violate Angolan territorial sovereignty by staging several invasions aimed at weakening guerrilla (SWAPO) operations against Namibia (South-West Africa).

Things went a bit better in the search for economic unity. Nine African countries signed in Zambia a treaty establishing a preferential trade area for east and southern Africa. Defensive in nature, it seeks to create a regional trade zone free from South African interference.

Africa's political troubles were exacerbated by soaring population growth rates and deepening problems of food availability and distribution. Many countries, but most acutely Ghana and Tanzania, were suffering from food shortages in 1982. The United Nations estimates that one in five Africans are malnourished. The World Bank adds that people in only 7 of 45

Military men carefully guard Ghana's new leader, Flight Lt. Jerry Rawlings (seated center), at a student rally.

sub-Saharan countries are getting enough to eat. And nearly every country in Africa is a net food importer. A host of them received emergency food assistance from the West and imported costly staples from Zimbabwe, South Africa, and Cameroon.

Africa's political and economic torment was momentarily forgotten with the return of Pope John Paul II. On a visit to Nigeria, Gabon, Equatorial Guinea, and Marxist-led Benin, he defended the traditional social, ethical, and religious values of Africa. The pontiff called for peace and for a renewed reverence for the family and the brotherhood of all mankind.

West Africa

In Ghana, the year opened with the return to power of Flight Lt. Jerry J. Rawlings. His overthrow of the elected Hilla Limann regime on Dec. 31, 1981, was the fifth military coup in Ghana's 25 years of independence. Rawlings had previously ruled in 1979 but returned power to civilian status after four months. The 1981 coup occurred amid the worst foreign exchange crisis in the nation's history and perhaps the deepest economic depression in a century. Rawlings quickly established a Provisional National Defense Council (PNDC) as an interim government and launched a virulent campaign against the "reactionary" middle class which consisted mainly of local merchants, independent journalists, large landowners, and many professionals. By year's end he had failed to win broad support, to restore public confidence, or to substantially

improve the economy. The nation's infrastructure continued to deteriorate and many of the country's most talented citizens had fled.

The year also commenced on a note of hope with the establishment of a confederation between Senegal and Gambia, two of Africa's most democratic countries. The unification began with an integration of the armed forces, the development of a common monetary and economic system, and political coordination on foreign policy. The Senegambia confederation is the culmination of nearly a century of attempts to unify French-speaking Senegal with tiny English-speaking Gambia, which is geographically surrounded by its big brother.

Nigeria came a step closer toward national unity with the political pardon and tumultuous return of the former Biafran leader, Odumegwu Ojukwu, from exile in Ivory Coast. His pardon and the pardoning of Yakubu Gowon, respective leaders of secessionist Biafra and of Nigeria during the civil war (1967–70), closed a bloody and bitter chapter in that nation's history. Nigeria could now devote its full energies to preparations for the 1983 national elections. Nigeria continued to be a major cultural leader, especially in pop music, poetry, and drama. Wole Soyinka, widely recognized as one of black Africa's most versatile and creative writers, received international acclaim for his autobiography. Moreover, African soul music, called "Afrobeat," was fast being replaced by Sunny Ade's "Juju Music," which commands a wide following.

Many West African governments were locked in a bitter power struggle with trade unions. Once a power in most African countries, the unions have suffered from maladministration, weak leadership, and corruption. Nevertheless, organized labor has recently grown more vocal, and governments are attempting to bridle them. In 1982, the military government in Upper Volta dissolved the powerful Voltaic Trade Union Confederation; and in Ghana, the Trade Union Congress was attacked by its own rank and file for corruption and mismanagement.

North East Africa

In the territorially vast republic of Sudan, long-simmering discontent erupted into sporadic violence. Even though the protracted civil war between the Muslim north and the Christian-animist south ended in 1972, the coexistence of the two regions has been fragile and tense. Sudan's army consists mainly of southerners, but the central government is northern-controlled. Before 1982, President Nemery allowed considerable autonomy to the southerners, who are culturally, religiously, and racially distinct. But the south now clamors for semi-independence, a demand that the government has refused.

Sudan and its neighbor, Egypt, have drawn closer together since the 1976 defense treaty. They moved a step nearer in 1982 with an agreement to coordinate their respective economic and political policies. The Nemery government is dependent on Egyptian economic and military aid for its political survival. The country has been threatened by Libya and Ethiopia on its western and eastern borders, and internally by dissident southerners and hungry urbanites. Recurrent street disturbances in the country's urban centers have been caused by severe shortages of food staples and discontent over the economic austerity program imposed by the IMF.

In the Horn of Africa, fighting intensified between the Ethiopian-funded Somali Democratic Salvation Front and the West Somali Liberation Front. The latter, supported by the Somali government, seeks the Ogaden region's independence from Ethiopia. Marxist Ethiopia was also fighting secessionist movements in its northern provinces of Tigre and Eritrea. Even though Ethiopia's President Mengistu Haile Mariam continued to rely heavily on the Soviet Union for military support, his army had failed to contain these potentially disastrous centrifugal tendencies that threaten the country's existence.

In Somalia, escalating border clashes with Ethiopia placed an enormous economic and political strain on the government of President Mohammed Siad Barre. The United States, Egypt, and Italy rushed in needed military supplies.

East Africa

Africa and the West were deeply shaken by the abortive coup in Kenya on August 1. Since independence in 1963, Kenya had enjoyed a global reputation for political stability and economic growth within the framework of relative democracy and free speech. But 1982 opened with massive deficits, inflation, shortages of imported goods, and growing dissatisfaction with the performance of President Daniel arap Moi. Uncharacteristically, the Moi government responded with repression. Prominent dissident intellectuals and newspaper editors were threatened or arrested. On August 1 junior cadres in the air force staged a poorly coordinated coup which fizzled within hours. But it triggered massive civilian rioting and looting in downtown Nairobi, the capital, and left many shops in ruin, particularly those under Asian ownership. Popular outrage over economic conditions has been directed toward Kenya's 100,000 or so Asians as well as at the Moi government. While Asians comprise less than .5% of the country's population, they control more than 25% of Kenya's gross domestic product and three quarters of its retail business. The aborted coup weakened the Moi government and thrust the army for the first time into a position of enormous influence. The entire air force was disbanded and more than 3,000 persons were arrested, including high-ranking officers in the police. Clearly, Kenya's image of peaceful stability had been tarnished by 1982 events.

Uganda, which until the early 1970s enjoyed a reputation for tranquility, continued to be jolted by violence. Its political and economic conditions were a bit less precarious, though extremely tense. The economy showed faint signs of recovery from the devastations of the former dictator, Idi Amin. Exports increased, modest amounts of foreign aid flowed in, and the country, with its resilient subsistence agricultural sector, was able to feed itself. President Milton Obote secured the return of a few wealthy Asian businessmen to assist in national reconstruction. Although Obote had consolidated his political power at the center, he still faced severe opposition from the powerful Baganda people and from antigovernment guerrillas in the Muslim north. Tanzania's withdrawal of its last troops from Uganda only increased Obote's vulnerability. Moreover, Uganda's image was again tarnished by reports of atrocities committed by the national army.

Tanzania's economic situation was the most acute of the three East African countries. Food shortages had become endemic; and with an almost bankrupt treasury, even essential exports dwindled. President Julius Nyerere's great Ujamaa socialist experiment in economic and social self-reliance faltered in the face of deep depression. Indeed, in most respects Tanzania was less self-reliant in 1982 than it was at the time of independence nearly two decades earlier. Though popular discontent grew, the sheer force of President Nyerere's personality kept the body politic of Tanzania on a rather steady if uneasy course.

Central Africa

Peace was restored in Chad, after another round in the long off-again, on-again civil war. Hissène Habré emerged as new head of state after a sanguinary two-year struggle with Libyan-backed Goukouni Oueddei. Habré's victory was due in part to substantial military support from Egypt and the Sudan. In late 1981, Libya's Qaddafi withdrew its army from Chad, leaving Oueddei without military support. A 1,500-man OAU peacekeeping force filled the vacuum but refused to involve itself in the war. In mid-June, Habré, with backing from his allies, defeated Oueddei and installed himself in the capital. The OAU force then withdrew. By September, Habré's army had secured the vital southern region and thus claimed control over nearly the entire country. Though Oueddei had fled in exile to neighboring Cameroon, he left behind many supporters poised to renew the struggle. In Chad, it was a fragile stability.

Zaire and Zambia, both major mineral exporters, slid deeper into debt and were unable to meet the IMF's performance criteria or to fulfill their debt service commitments. The calamitous fall of the price of copper on international markets prevented the two nations from covering even production costs. Zaire's relations deteriorated with the United States, its major creditor and military supplier. President Mobutu became the first African leader to resume ties with Israel, allegedly out of concern over growing American criticism of continuing repression and corruption. For that decision, he won almost universal condemnation in Africa. Relations between Zaire and Zambia, cool since the 1977 Shaba invasion, went into deep freeze after a new series of violent border skirmishes. Both governments steadily lost popular support.

Neighboring Marxist Angola also experienced severe internal problems. The fragile economy was weakened further by the high cost of fighting the União Nacional para Independência Total de Angola (UNITA) antigovernment guerrillas in the country's central and southern regions. UNITA continued to sabotage the vital Benguela Railway and to deny Lobito-port access to goods from Zaire, Zambia, and Angola's potentially rich interior. The Angolan civil war provoked a bitter cabinet shake-up.

A glimmer of hope came to Equatorial Guinea in 1982 when voters approved a new constitution that guarantees human rights, a free judiciary, and universal suffrage. It is one of the most liberal constitutions in Africa and comes after more than a decade of political repression under the regime of the late dictator, Francisco Macías Nguema. Equatorial Guinea, like its neighbors Gabon and Cameroon, is experiencing a measure of economic prosperity. In November, Ahmadou Ahidjo, Cameroon's leader for nearly 25 years, turned over power to Prime Minister Paul Biya.

Southern Africa

White South Africa staggered under an unprecedented degree of political disunity, economic recession, and black labor militancy. Di-

The Queen Mother (left) leads mourners at the September funeral of Sobhuza II, king of Swaziland for 61 years.

Louise Gubb/Liaison

visions within the white Afrikaner community were deeper and more profound than they have been in more than four decades. In March, a group of Nationalists under the powerful Transvaal leader, Dr. Andries Treurnicht, broke away and formed the more right-wing Conservative Party. Though unable to win seats in the National Assembly, the Conservatives gained electoral power at the local polls. Not since the National Party came to power in 1948 has it been so seriously challenged from within its own ranks. But growing numbers of Afrikaners oppose Prime Minister P. W. Botha's constitutional plan to share government with Asians and people of mixed racial ancestry, or Coloreds. They also criticize his easing of segregation of public amenities and his abolition of job reservation for whites. Seemingly overlooked is Botha's tightening of enforcement of the fundamental tenets of grand apartheid, namely the pass laws, residential segregation, and the laws against African participation in the political process.

Africans, on the other hand, demonstrated a renewed sense of unity and purpose. The power of the banned African National Congress (ANC) has grown with the demise of the Pan-African Congress (PAC) and the black power movement. The Zulu mass organization, Inkatha, and the more militant black labor unions have drawn closer to the ANC. Black factory workers have begun to use the new labor relations system as a vehicle for political mobilization. The Botha government can take credit for initiating sweeping labor reforms. But fear of the growing power of organized black labor has led to repressive measures to discipline it. Militant labor leaders, journalists, and attorneys have been banned or harassed. And Dr. Neil Aggett, a physician and trade union organizer, died in a Johannesburg jail in February. He was the first white ever to die in security police custody. His passing signalled a new wave of mass work stoppages. And during the year, the AMC bombed key rail and utility installations. In response, the government decreed that all white men under age 60 must register for military duty.

Tumbling world prices for gold and other minerals, combined with rising imports, provoked a serious balance of payments crisis in South Africa and forced the government to borrow heavily. Its application for a $1,100,000,000 loan from the IMF in late October stirred objections in the UN and the U.S. Congress. But as South Africa slipped into recession, many workers, especially blacks, lost their jobs. Especially hard hit was agriculture, a sector that supplies essential staples not only to South Africa but to food-deficit countries to the north.

South Africa came under greater global censure at a meeting of the World Council of Reformed Churches in Ottawa, Canada. The organization, representing 70 million members, declared apartheid a heresy and expelled South Africa's major Reformed Church body.

High-level talks on the independence of Namibia reached an impasse in October. South Africa and the United States insisted that the transition to majority rule be conditional upon Cuban troop withdrawal from Angola. Angola, the OAU, and other members of the Western Contact Group insisted on a separation of the two issues. The Angolans argued that a Cuban military presence is essential to protect the country from South African raids and the UNITA insurrectionists.

In Zimbabwe, Prime Minister Robert Mugabe struggled to consolidate his power and to achieve national unity. But the essential fabric of cooperation was torn by the dismissal of cabinet member and Patriotic Front leader, Joshua Nkomo, on unproven charges of attempting to overthrow the government. Even though Nkomo's party holds 20 parliamentary seats to Mugabe's 57, its influence in governance has steadily declined. Government opposition is centered in the southwestern region of Matabeleland, a Nkomo stronghold and home of the Ndebele, who represent 17% of the nation's population. Many Ndebele members of the armed forces defected in 1982, returned to the bush, and disrupted law and order. In July, unidentified guerrillas destroyed a major air base and a large number of recently purchased aircraft. Moreover, six foreign tourists were kidnapped and others were killed. Curfews went into effect in many western areas as government forces clashed with armed dissidents. Prime Minister Mugabe blamed Nkomo and South Africa for attempting to destabilize the regime. By October, Zimbabwe was sliding toward open civil war.

A long chapter in southern African history closed with the death in August of Sobhuza II, king of Swaziland, at age 83. Since 1921, he had provided stable, paternalistic, though dictatorial rule in the New Jersey-sized realm. The Queen Mother will govern until a successor is chosen. The selection process is likely to be prolonged and divisive. King Sobhuza's passing leaves the kingdom's future in considerable doubt. Swaziland has supported South Africa's offer of the territories of Kangwane and Ingwavuma (Kwazulu) because it will give them access to the sea. However, black South Africans are vehemently opposed, arguing that 800,000 Swazi-speakers would lose their South African citizenship in the deal.

South Africa's relations with Marxist Mozambique turned increasingly sour over the issue of destabilization. By late 1982, the South African-supported black guerrilla movement held nearly half the country and was dislocating the already anemic economy. In desperation, President Samora Machel took a more pragmatic foreign policy stand and sought more aid and trade from his former colonial master, Portugal, and other Western powers.

RICHARD W. HULL
New York University

Urban Surprises

When one daydreams of Africa, thoughts of architecturally modern cities are generally few. Since Africa is one third desert and next to the least urbanized of the seven continents, this reflects a preconception that is understandable. In fact, only an estimated 28% of the continent's mid-1982 population of 498 million lived in urban areas. Nevertheless, as is evident from the accompanying photographs, Africa does have some large, beautiful metropolises. Such cities are usually national capitals, are growing at extremely rapid rates, and account for a high percentage of the urban population. As much as the desire to escape eternal burdens—poverty, soil exhaustion, drought, famine, disease—the magic of these cities steadily draws Africans from their countryside. Although many of Africa's cities have undergone extensive redevelopment of late—the East African nation of Malawi moved its capital from Zomba to Lilongwe in the mid-1970s—the urban centers are by no means free of such problems as housing shortages, unemployment, inadequate food and transport, and political instability.

© Guido Rossi/The Image Bank

© Robert Caputo

Many of Africa's major cities, including Tunis, Tunisia, above, are located in the north. A statue in honor of Habib Bourguiba, the president-for-life, was built in the mid-1970s. The Hotel du Lac (left, rear) was a response to Tunisia's growing tourism industry. Inadequate housing, not only in Lagos, Nigeria, left, but throughout the continent is a prime concern. Active open-air markets and new construction are features of Abidjan, page 87, top left, the financial center of the prospering Ivory Coast. Uhuru Park enhances the beauty of downtown Nairobi, Kenya. The Parliament Building (clock) and the new Kenyatta International Conference Center with a revolving, rooftop restaurant, are nearby. The Carlton Centre in Johannesburg, South Africa, was constructed in the 1970s. It includes office buildings, a hotel, and a shopping area with some underground stores, page 87, bottom.

Shostal Associates

James Church/Alpha

© Terry Madison/The Image Bank

AGRICULTURE

The 1982 crop year started with unfavorably wet weather in major agricultural regions of the United States. However, conditions improved as the growing season progressed, and the nation had a very large grain crop. Production of corn and other feed grains and soybeans set new records. The cotton crop also was very large. Corn production was 1% greater than in the record year 1981. Soybean production was 14% greater than the 1981 record. Wheat production was 1% lower than in 1981, but the yield per acre was greater. Consequently prices, which were low throughout the beginning of the year, receded even further as the large 1982 crops became apparent.

Prices. The large crops of corn and wheat, along with large stocks of both crops, caused the year-end carryover of both to be at record levels. By mid-August the central market prices per bushel were $2.12 for corn, $3.04 for wheat, and $5.25 for soybeans. The price per pound of cotton was 62 cents. Mid-August 1981 prices for these four major crops were $2.80, $4.16, $6.76, and 68 cents, respectively. Prices eased even more as harvest began.

Prices for poultry products were down about 12% from 1981 on the same date. Vegetable and beef prices were about even or down modestly, while pork prices were up about 22%. Hog prices reached an all-time high in August.

With prices low in 1981 and even lower in 1982, a large number of farmers were caught in a financial pinch. In real terms, total net farm income was lower than at any time since the depression of the 1930s. Of course, net income in current dollars per farm family was much higher because there now are many fewer farms and the majority of families have income from off-farm sources. The financial pinch was caused by low farm commodity prices and high interest rates. Farmers who had purchased land at high prices in recent years were especially pressed, and a considerable number went bankrupt during the year. The price of farmland, which skyrocketed in the 1970s, declined throughout the year. Depressed farm income reduced the demand for durable equipment, and farm machinery firms had to lay off many workers and retract production. Farms continued to grow larger; by 1982, two thirds of net farm income was earned by 1% of U.S. farms.

U.S. Farm Bill. Congress was expected to pass a new farm bill in 1981 but did not do so until far into 1982. Both President Ronald Reagan and Secretary of Agriculture John Block initially talked of freeing U.S. agriculture from government programs and making it more market oriented. However, they did support the $11,-000,000,000 farm bill passed by Congress. President Reagan opposed the program initially proposed, which would have cost a third more. The new bill raised price supports or loan rates on major agricultural and dairy commodities. Dairy support prices were separated from the previous 80%-of-parity requirement. Large surpluses of dairy products had accumulated under the parity concept and were given away to low-income families in 1982. Support prices for feed grains, wheat, and rice are to be adjusted annually, based on production costs. Those for soybeans, cotton, and peanuts are based on a formula specified by Congress.

A grain shipment leaves New Orleans for the USSR. The U.S.-Soviet grain agreement was extended in 1982.

Set-Aside Program. While it had opposed production-control programs earlier, the administration approved a paid cropland set-aside or supply-control program for grains in 1983 as low farm income and large production prospects continued into the year. The program rewards farmers for keeping land idle by granting eligibility for price supports or commodity loans and by making direct cash payments. Few farmers participated in the 1982 program, which did not include cash payments for idling land.

The 1982 set-aside program initially was suggested by Office of Management and Budget Director David Stockman to lessen the cost of farm programs. The purpose of the set-aside is to reduce production and increase market prices for feed grains and wheat.

U.S. Exports. The value of U.S. farm exports in 1982 declined for the first time in 12 years. However, the actual tonnage increased. The largest increases in sales in recent years have been to the Middle East, especially Egypt and Saudi Arabia, and to Nigeria. Growth of sales also has been rapid in Eastern Europe, Mexico, Venezuela, and developing countries. The United States exported more than 50 million t* of wheat, nearly a fourth more than in 1981, and captured nearly all the growth in the world wheat trade. U.S. feed grain exports also were at a record level.

President Reagan lifted the partial embargo that President Carter had invoked on USSR grain purchases following the Soviet invasion of Afghanistan. The legislation spelling out the details of these exports was to have expired in 1982. The president suggested that he might not renew the agreement for grain exports, to protest continued Soviet pressure on Poland. However, in early August he announced that he would extend the current U.S.–Soviet grain agreement for one year. In October, he increased the offer to 23 million t.

USSR. The USSR suffered its fourth consecutive poor crop in 1982. Total grain production was estimated at only 170 million t. The crop shortfall over the four years amounted to more than an annual crop. After the partial embargo on grain shipments was lifted, the USSR was willing to negotiate each time the opportunity arose but initially showed little hurry to buy more than the contracted amount of grain. In September, at the end of the sixth year of the U.S.–USSR grain agreement, the Russians had purchased 18 million t over the previous 12 months. It was expected, because of their poor harvest, that they would enter the market on a fairly large scale in early 1983. Under the extended contract, they are required to buy 6 million t of grain and may buy up to 23 million t without informing U.S. officials.

The USSR strove to increase meat production but was restrained by the succession of poor crops and by the complexities of buying feed

*1 metric ton (t) equals 1.102 short tons.

grain on the world market. With shortages in feed supplies, livestock inventories were maintained at light weights and low productivity. Marketing weights of both hogs and cattle declined in 1982. Production for the year was less than in 1981.

With considerable failure in its farm programs, the USSR held a top-level meeting of agricultural experts and government officials in 1982 to assess future strategies. Little word seeped to the outside world on the decisions at this meeting.

Soviet agricultural grain purchases now total about $20,000,000,000 annually, represent a quarter of all imports, and place a heavy drain on foreign exchange reserves.

Eastern Europe. In the rest of Eastern Europe, the area sown to grains increased slightly in 1982. Supplies of fertilizer were inadequate, especially in Poland and Rumania. Grain imports in the region were about 12 million t. Rising per-capita meat consumption halted over the last two years and fell in Poland. Most countries raised food prices. Poland raised prices 260% for meat, 250% for dairy products, and 350% for sugar.

Western Europe. Weather and production over most of the region was nearly normal in 1982. Political and economic differences slowed agreement among European Community (EC) countries on price increases for agricultural commodities. A record-high increase of 11% for 1982–83 was finally accepted. Imports of Western European countries from the United States increased about 7% to $12,000,000,000.

The Falkland Islands War had no lasting effect on grain imports by the EC countries despite the embargo on grain purchases from Argentina. The EC nations used special incentives to encourage use of more feeds from these countries for livestock. The United States opposed these efforts because of the impact on grain exports. Wine supplies and prices remained a source of conflict in the EC countries.

Other Grain Exporters. Canada's 1982 crop was about the same size as the previous year's record. The area planted was up slightly and weather was favorable. After declining in 1981, livestock production recovered in 1982. Beef and poultry production increased somewhat, while pork production declined. Under a more favorable exchange rate, the value of agricultural exports increased by about 12%.

Australian production increased by about 13% from July 1981 to June 1982, following a 1981 drought. Crop output increased 25%, while livestock production declined slightly. With higher cost and lower commodity prices, net farm income declined. The 1981–82 winter wheat crop was 50% larger than the 1980–81 crop, and wheat exports increased by 20%.

Argentina's 1982 export supplies were 14.5 million t of grains and 0.5 million t of beef. Exports quickened in the first quarter but slowed

UPI

In Iowa, President Reagan promised farmers that he would seek more foreign trade for their products.

rains caused preharvest losses in India and Pakistan, and India returned to rather large grain imports. The grain situation remained critical in Bangladesh.

Africa and Middle East. Reduced oil earnings in 1982 caused Nigeria to place restrictions on imports, including grains, except rice. Zimbabwe's corn production was down nearly 50% from 1981, but it had a record carryover and was able to export some of its corn. Botswana declared a drought emergency and imported more grain from Zimbabwe and South Africa. Morocco, Algeria, and Tunisia imported more feed grains than in 1981 in order to increase meat production.

The late 1981 drought caused reduced crops in the eastern Mediterranean area. Israel's grain harvest was less than half that of 1981. Australian and Argentine competition reduced U.S. sales to Iran. Thailand supplied the major part of Iran's rice imports. Iraq became a major importer of U.S. farm products.

Latin America. Good growing weather caused Latin American agricultural production to increase. However, weak commodity prices, inflation, and high interest rates caused farmers to reduce the planted area. Brazil's growth in farm output, while still strong, was lower than in 1981 due to dry conditions. Central America's growth was about 2%, while Cuban growth slowed from its previous 6%.

Latin American exports (the United States provided half the market) increased along with crop production in 1982. With larger crops, Latin American imports declined, the impact falling mainly on the United States.

World Policy and Trade. The ICCO agreed to double the 1-cent-a-pound levy on cocoa to establish a buffer stock plan and obtain a Brazilian loan. Members extended the International Sugar Agreement for two years and set a global goal of 18.3 million t for exports. The United States imposed an emergency import quota on sugar to stem a price decline. The International Coffee Organization set quotas at 14 million bags (60 kg each) for the January-March period because the price was above the $1.20-per-pound threshold level. Later the price fell below this level.

The United States signed a policy agreement with Jamaica for the exchange of dairy products for bauxite. The Canadian Wheat Board signed a new three-year agreement with Communist China to deliver from 10.5 to 12.6 million t. India signed an agreement to provide the USSR with rice, and Argentina concluded a five-year trade agreement to supply Algeria with grain.

The U.S. Wool Growers Association withdrew its petition to the International Trade Commission for an investigation of the harm being brought to the U.S. sheep industry because of imports of New Zealand lambs.

See also FOOD.

with the Falklands crisis. Brazil's soybean exports declined, due to lower output. Following a small 1981 crop, South Africa reduced exports in 1982. However, exports of coffee, sugar, cocoa, meat, and orange juice were high.

World cocoa production in 1981–82 set a third consecutive record, largely from increases in the Ivory Coast, Malaysia, and Nigeria. After a year of operation, the International Cocoa Organization (ICCO) agreement was not able to keep the price at the floor level of $1.10 per pound, and prices reached a five-year low of 70 cents per pound. World cotton trade was up somewhat.

Asia. Following gains in 1981, grain production in Communist China was up slightly in 1982. Total imports declined somewhat, but cotton imports declined by 19%. Although U.S. farm exports to China in 1982 were about 13% lower than in 1981, China was the sixth largest importer of U.S. farm commodities.

Japan reduced its surplus rice stocks after two bad harvests. The United States pressed Japan for greater access to its farm commodity markets, and Japan announced 67 nontariff actions to remove trade barriers.

Imports of wheat by medium-high-income East Asian countries grew only slightly in 1982 because of slow economic growth and concern over trade deficits. Burma and Thailand had reduced rice exports to South Korea and Indonesia. The latter country had a record main-season rice harvest. Poor weather in several South Asian countries limited 1982 crop production. Heavy

EARL O. HEADY
Iowa State University

ALABAMA

Politics and the economy dominated Alabama news during 1982.

Election Results. Maverick Democratic Gov. Fob James announced on July 9 that he would not be a candidate for a second term. In the September primaries, former Gov. George C. Wallace defeated Lt. Gov. George D. H. McMillan, Jr., to become the Democratic gubernatorial nominee for the fourth time: Wallace received an estimated 30–40% of the black vote. Wallace also was the overwhelming favorite of blacks and of working class and rural whites in the November 2 general election, in which he won a fourth term as governor with 60% of the vote over Montgomery's Republican Mayor Emory Folmar. Wallace received approximately 80% of the black vote.

State legislative elections were conducted under terms of a temporary federal court order of June 23 that required districts to be revised in the near future to ensure greater opportunities for the election of blacks. In 1982, 17 blacks were elected to the state House of Representatives, and three were elected to the Senate. Oscar Adams, in winning a seat on the state supreme court (to which he had been appointed to fill an unexpired term), became the first black to be elected to statewide office in recent times.

In the congressional elections, Democrats took the Birmingham seat, which had been filled by a Republican since the 1964 election. Jefferson County Commissioner Ben Erdreich (D) defeated first-term Rep. Albert Lee Smith (R). After the elections, Alabama's U.S. House delegation comprised five Democrats and only two Republicans.

Legislative Sessions. The Alabama legislature met in one regular session and three special sessions during 1982. In its regular session the legislature approved 15% annual pay raises for teachers and 11% salary boosts for other state employees. The total education budget was $1,462,000,000; the general fund budget was $433.7 million. However, on September 27, be-

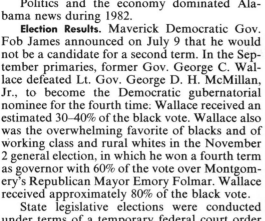

Diego Goldberg/Sygma

Capturing some 80% of the black vote, former Gov. George Wallace was returned to office for a fourth term.

cause of revenue shortfalls, Governor James ordered a 15% reduction in general fund appropriations and a 10% reduction in educational funds. Proration was necessary because Alabama law requires a balanced budget. In the special sessions Governor James secured approval of proposals to encourage voluntary school prayer and to give public agencies more weapons for combating crime. The governor's crime package was put in jeopardy, however, because his office failed to deliver the bills to the secretary of state within the required ten days after they were passed by the legislature.

The prayer bill adopted by the legislature included a suggested prayer written by the governor's son. The law was challenged in federal court by a Mobile parent who contended that it represented a violation of the constitutional principle of church-state separation.

Unemployment. Alabama's unemployment rate was among the highest in the nation throughout 1982, second only to Michigan's. In September, when the national unemployment rate of 10.1% was cited as the worst since 1940, Alabama's rate was 14.3%. Within the state, the highest unemployment figure was registered for Gadsden, where 20.7% of the labor force was reported to be out of work. It was estimated that Alabama had lost 33,900 production jobs in the past year.

WILLIAM H. STEWART
The University of Alabama

ALABAMA · Information Highlights

Area: 51,705 sq mi (133 916 km²).

Population: (1980 census): 3,893,888.

Chief Cities (1980 census): Montgomery, the capital, 178,157; Birmingham, 284,413; Mobile, 200,452.

Government (1982): *Chief Officers*—governor, Forrest H. James, Jr. (D); lt. gov., George McMillan, Jr. (D). *Legislature*—Senate, 35 members; House of Representatives, 105 members.

State Finances (fiscal year 1981): Revenues, $5,105,-000,000; expenditures, $4,374,000,000.

Personal Income (1981): $32,198,000,000; per capita, $8,219.

Labor Force (Aug. 1982): *Nonagricultural wage and salary earners,* 1,319,300; *unemployed,* 239,800 (14.2% of total force).

Education (Fall 1981): *Enrollment*—public elementary schools, 518,534; public secondary, 224,914; colleges and universities (1981–1982), 166,375 students. *Public school expenditures* (1980–81), $1,-086,372,000 ($1,384 per pupil).

ALASKA

On November 2, Alaskans went to the polls in record numbers to elect a governor, lieutenant governor, congressman, and most of their state legislators. The electorate also voted on several constitutional amendments and ballot propositions.

Election. Alaskans overwhelmingly chose Anchorage hotelier and businessman William Sheffield (D) as governor. Defeated gubernatorial candidates were Tom Fink (R) of Anchorage, Richard L. Randolph of Fairbanks (Libertarian), and Joe Vogler, a Fairbanksan and founder of the Alaskan Independence Party. Sheffield and his running mate, Steve McAlpine, the mayor of Valdez, succeeded Republican incumbents Jay Hammond and Terry Miller.

It seemed clear that the candidacy of Libertarian Dick Randolph pulled significant support from Fink, while only slightly diminishing Sheffield's edge. The implications of so large a percentage of Libertarian votes (14%) would be a matter for further study, but it appeared that a significant number of Alaskan voters found the traditional parties inadequate for their needs.

Rep. Don Young (R) easily won reelection, and the Republican Party scored gains in both branches of the state legislature.

Several important questions were on the ballot. Alaskans voted against the expenditure of $2,840,000,000 to move the state capital from Juneau to a new site in Willow. The decision not to authorize the expenditure was a setback in a lengthy series of efforts to move the state capital to a more central location. Voters approved the move in 1974 and selected Willow as the site in 1976. However in 1979, opponents of the move succeeded in passing the so-called "Frank Initiative," which required voter approval of "all bondable costs" of the move. The November initiative was on those costs.

In a second initiative, Alaskans voted to retain a 1978 state law that gives priority to subsistence hunters of fish and game. Alaskan law recognizes three major categories of wildlife use: sport; commercial; and subsistence, or traditional and customary uses. When game or fish are in seriously short supply and access is restricted, subsistence hunters—largely native Alaskans—take precedence over other users of the resources. Some sports hunters—mainly whites—felt this preference was a denial of equal treatment and sought to have the law abolished through the initiative. The issue had been of particular concern because of its divisive nature—pitting whites against nonwhites and urbanites against rural dwellers.

The voters did choose to assert state claims to all lands within the borders of Alaska by approving the "Tundra Rebellion" initiative. The initiative is merely advisory, authorizing the state to pursue a variety of actions to gain control over Alaska lands held by the federal government. The ultimate purpose is to accomplish the transfer of publicly held lands to private ownership.

Economy. During the first several crucial weeks of the salmon fishing season, most commercial fishermen were on strike for higher pay from the canneries. A considerable part of the runs had passed by the time a settlement had been reached. Still, it was a record year for the salmon fishery.

On the other hand, the crab fishermen, especially on Kodiak, found the harvest both disappointing and frightening. Barren females comprised much of the small take, indicating a severe drop in the reproduction rate and promising a long downturn in future crab harvests. The forecast presented a depressing prospect for the crabbers.

Gas Line. The likelihood grew even dimmer that a natural gas pipeline would be constructed to carry gas from Prudhoe Bay to the "lower 48" along the Alaska Highway. The companies proposing the project failed to obtain funding either in the private or the public sector, and as a consequence the major contractor pulled out of the project. Proponents of a natural gas pipeline continued to urge that the state enter the project at least to the extent of guaranteeing loans from private banks. Opponents argued that the project must stand on its own merits.

Permanent Fund Dividend. During the year the U.S. Supreme Court handed down its decision that the legislative scheme for distributing Permanent Fund benefits on the basis of length of residency was not constitutional. The state, in a backup plan, immediately moved to distribute dividend checks of $1,000 each to all residents of at least six months. Under the plan, residents would receive less than $500 in 1983. There were those who objected to the dividend plan, urging instead that the Permanent Fund money be used to provide roads and airports and other collective benefits.

ANDREA R. C. HELMS
University of Alaska, Fairbanks

ALASKA · Information Highlights

Area: 591,004 sq mi (1 530 700 km²).
Population (1980 census): 401,851.
Chief Cities (1980 census): Juneau, the capital, 19,-528; Anchorage, 173,017; Fairbanks, 22,645; Sitka, 7,803.
Government (December 1982): *Chief Officers*—governor, William Sheffield (D); lt. gov., Steve McAlpine. *Legislature*—Senate, 20 members; House of Representatives, 40 members.
State Finances (fiscal year 1981): *Revenues*, $5,134,-000,000; *expenditures*, $2,543,000,000.
Personal Income (1981): $5,667,000,000; per capita, $13,763.
Labor Force (July 1982): *Nonagricultural wage and salary earners*, 199,400; *unemployed* (Aug. 1982), 17,600 (8.4% of total force).
Education: *Enrollment* (fall 1981)—public elementary schools, 63,756; public secondary, 27,102; colleges and universities (1981–82), 24,754 students. *Public school expenditures* (1980–81), $476,904,-000 ($5,010 per pupil).

ALBANIA

The People's Socialist Republic of Albania celebrated the 70th anniversary of its independence in 1982. There were numerous top-level changes in the government and in the ruling Albanian Party of Labor (APL) following the reported suicide in December 1981 of Prime Minister Mehmet Shehu, the second-ranking member of the Albanian leadership.

Domestic Developments. It appeared that Shehu's death stemmed from differences over foreign and domestic policies that had developed between him and APL First Secretary Enver Hoxha. Hoxha regarded the suicide of his longtime colleague as an act of disloyalty and accused Shehu of having plotted "with internal and foreign enemies" to seize power.

At the January 1982 session of the People's Assembly, Adil Carcani, who had served as first deputy prime minister since 1974, was elected prime minister. In his inaugural address, Carcani enthusiastically endorsed Hoxha's policies, which had been approved by the eighth APL congress in November 1981. Two additional cabinet changes were announced in January 1982. Deputy Prime Minister Qirjako Mihali was named minister of finance, and a veteran party functionary, Hekuran Isaj, was appointed minister of the interior. At the June session of the People's Assembly, Reis Malile became minister of foreign affairs, Deputy Prime Minister Pali Miska was appointed minister of energy, and Ajil Alushani was named minister of health. In November, APL Politburo member Ramiz Alia, apparently being groomed as Hoxha's successor, became head of state.

In June, with much fanfare, the government announced price reductions for consumer goods and services. It contrasted this development with the erosion of the purchasing power of workers in Western Europe and the United States.

In late September the Albanian press reported that the nation's armed forces had crushed an attempted invasion of the country by anti-Communist political exiles. This episode resulted in renewed appeals for vigilance against the country's internal and external enemies.

Foreign Relations. Albanian-Yugoslav relations remained tense as Tiranë continued to support the demands of the ethnic Albanians of Kosovo that their province be granted republic status in the Yugoslav federation.

Albania enthusiastically supported Argentina in the Falkland Islands crisis. Tiranë harshly criticized Israel's "invasion" of Lebanon and continued to demand the establishment of an independent Palestinian state.

Albania seemed willing to expand its commercial and cultural ties with Western Europe. In this connection, Tiranë hinted that it would be interested in entering into discussions with Great Britain and West Germany to establish diplomatic relations.

However, Albania showed no signs of changing its attitude toward the Soviet Union and the United States. Moscow was taken to task for its "aggression" in Afghanistan and its "oppression" of Poland. Tiranë castigated the Reagan administration for its support of "reactionary regimes" in Latin America and "Zionist imperialism" in the Middle East.

NICHOLAS C. PANO, *Western Illinois University*

ALBERTA

Only in 1982 did Albertans really begin to suffer from abnormally high unemployment, inflation, and interest rates. Unemployment rose from 4.6% in January 1982 to above 8% by fall, and bankruptcies increased sharply. Many recent newcomers from Eastern Canada returned home.

Economy. Worsening economic conditions, restrictions of National Energy Policy, and a slump in oil prices forced cancellation or postponement of the third oil-sands plant at Fort McMurray, the heavy oil project at Cold Lake, and the Alaska gas pipeline. These developments and the prolonged shutdown of the coal mine at Grande Cache adversely affected the provincial economy. However, completion of Alberta legs of the Alaska pipeline provided new, if limited, markets for Alberta's gas, and work began on a new coal mine near Hinton.

Except for apartment developments, housing construction was slow. Commercial building continued apace in Edmonton and Calgary, although in both it was decelerating by fall. Apartment vacancy rates climbed from .1% to about 5%, but rents remained high. Some large real-estate firms merged or ceased operations.

All aspects of the province's tourist-related business suffered declines. Particularly hard hit was the town of Jasper because of the discontinuance of transcontinental VIA rail service. The closing of a major uranium mine in northern Saskatchewan dealt a severe blow to Athabasca River transportation. The provincial government announced the forthcoming sale of its Pacific Western Airline.

ALBANIA · Information Highlights

Official Name: People's Socialist Republic of Albania.
Location: Southern Europe, Balkan peninsula.
Area: 11,100 sq mi (28 749 km²).
Population (1982 est.): 2,800,000.
Chief Cities (1975): Tiranë, the capital, 192,000; Shkodër, 62,400; Dürres, 60,000.
Government: *Head of state,* Ramiz Alia, president of the Presidium (took office November 1982). *First secretary of the Albanian Party of Labor,* Enver Hoxha (took office 1941). *Head of government,* Adil Carcani (took office January 1982). *Legislature* (unicameral)—People's Assembly, 250 members.
Monetary Unit: Lek (7 lekë equal U.S.$1, March 1982—noncommercial rate).
Gross National Product (1978 U.S.$): $1,850,000,-000.

Alberta's Premier Peter Lougheed (above) led the Conservatives to victory over Gordon Kesler, a former rodeo rider and new Western Canada Concept Party leader.

For the first time in many years, the Lougheed government budgeted for a deficit, nominal rather than actual, as it still earmarked part of resource revenue for its Heritage Fund, a trust fund that approximates C$11,000,000,000. Part of its revenue would now be used for subsidizing home mortgages and assisting small business and farming operations.

As a result of the 1981 census, Alberta gained six seats in the House of Commons. The province's population grew by 37% during the decade 1971–81. In January boundaries of Edmonton were extended, doubling its area and making it in size the largest major city in Canada but adding only about 35,000 to its population.

Education. In 1982, all postsecondary educational institutions reached new enrollment highs. Elementary school registrations remained sta-

UPC

Government and Politics. With the 1981 resignation of Opposition leader Bob Clarke from the Legislature, the once-powerful Social Credit (SC) Party appeared to collapse. The remaining three SC legislators indicated they would not again be Social Credit candidates for election. To wide astonishment, Gordon Kesler captured Clarke's vacated seat. He was later chosen as leader of Western Canada Concept Party, a reactionary separatist movement.

Proclaiming that "the sun is shining and we [the Progressive Conservatives] are in the mood," Premier Peter Lougheed called a provincial election for November 2. To Kesler's disappointment, the PCs won a near sweep.

ALBERTA • Information Highlights

Area: 255,285 sq mi (661 189 km²).
Population (1981 census): 2,237,724.
Chief Cities (1981 census): Edmonton, the capital, 532,246; Calgary, 592,743; Lethbridge, 54,072; Red Deer, 46,393; St. Albert, 31,996.
Government (1982): *Chief Officers*—lt. gov., Frank Lynch-Staunton; premier, Peter Lougheed (Progressive-Conservative); atty. gen., Neil S. Crawford. *Legislature*—Legislative Assembly, 79 members.
Education (1982–83): *Enrollment*—elementary and secondary schools, 455,700 pupils; postsecondary, 50,240 students.
Public Finance (1982 fiscal year, est.): *Revenues,* $10,184,600,000; *expenditures,* $8,037,400,000.
Personal Income (average weekly salary, June 1982): $434.86.
Unemployment Rate (August 1982, seasonally adjusted): 8.3%.
(All monetary figures are in Canadian dollars.)

tionary or continued to decline, and government austerity continued to cause financial difficulty to school administrations.

Agriculture. For the first time in three years, adequate snowfall averted danger of spring drought, but dry weather in May and June caused anxiety. Precipitation thereafter resulted in abundant harvests, except in Peace River country, which suffered virtual crop failure. However, rising costs and declining meat and grain prices put severe pressure on farmers and ranchers.

JOHN W. CHALMERS
Concordia College, Edmonton

ALGERIA

Algeria celebrated its 20th year of independence from France in July 1982 under the pragmatic leadership of President Chadli Benjedid. Completing his third year in office in 1982, Chadli continued to follow a nonaligned path while seeking closer political and economic ties with the West. On the economic front, traditional socialist policies were being liberalized and prolonged negotiations with foreign buyers of Algeria's liquefied natural gas were successfully concluded.

Political Developments. President Chadli's continued efforts to distance himself from the rigid socialist line of his predecessor, the late President Houari Boumedienne, were manifested in late 1981 by the removal from the ruling National Liberation Front (FLN) Central Committee (politburo) of three leading figures of the previous government: Abdelaziz Bouteflika, foreign minister for 15 years; Belaid Abdesselam, minister of industry and energy (1965–77); and Ahmad Ghozali, former head of Sonatrach, the state oil and gas corporation, who had led the program of heavy industrialization under Boumedienne—a program under fire in 1982 for causing excessive foreign borrowing and waste.

Foreign Minister Mohamed Benyahia, who mediated the release of American hostages from Iran, died in May when his plane was shot down by unidentified fighters just inside Iran's borders. He was traveling to Iran to discuss efforts to end the Iran-Iraq war. Dr. Ahmed Taleb Ibrahimi was appointed to replace him.

Algeria's second general elections since independence in 1962 were held in March, and with a 72.6% voter turnout, representatives to the National People's Assembly were elected. All candidates were selected by the FLN, and only 68 of the 261 deputies were reelected.

Economy. Chadli's reappraisal of the economic policies of his predecessor, involving a shift in emphasis from heavy industry toward lighter industries and basic development needs, resulted in an encouragement of Algeria's small private sector and efforts to attract Western investment. Huge state organizations controlling production and distribution of most goods were decentralized; the investment code dating back to 1966 was revised and simplified; and greater emphasis was placed on meeting the needs of an expanding population via ambitious housing programs and incentives to farmers to reduce the high level of food imports.

Algeria's 19th international trade fair in September attracted a record attendance with 1,300 companies from 50 countries represented. The United States was represented for the first time at the fair, and American exports to Algeria increased by 20% to $504 million during the first half of 1982.

Negotiations with foreign buyers over the export price of liquefied natural gas (LNG) met with success in 1982 as France and Italy concluded new long-term contracts and two American companies, Panhandle Eastern and Distrigas, were awaiting U.S. government approval of renegotiated agreements at above-market prices.

Sonatrach had been seeking to rewrite the contracts pegging the gas price to that of its oil. After two years of negotiation, Gaz de France agreed to a higher price. In return, Algeria pledged to place orders for $2,000,000,000 worth of French technology and industrial goods.

Algeria's income from oil and gas declined by one third to about $9,500,000,000 in 1982, because of conditions on international markets and the ongoing LNG negotiations, but revenues from gas exports were expected to triple.

Foreign Relations. Relations with Algeria's former colonial power, France, continued to improve, particularly in the wake of the December 1981 official visit to Algiers by French Socialist President François Mitterrand and the LNG agreement with Gaz de France.

The Reagan administration was warned against increasing military assistance to Morocco and Tunisia as harmful to peace, as Algeria continued to support the Polisario front in its war against Morocco over the Western Sahara. Economic cooperation appeared to be improving.

MARGARET A. NOVICKI, *"Africa Report"*

ALGERIA · Information Highlights

Official Name: Democratic and Popular Republic of Algeria.
Location: North Africa.
Area: 919,595 sq mi (2 381 751 km^2).
Population (1982 est.): 20,100,000.
Chief Cities (1980 est.): Algiers, the capital, 2,200,-000; Oran, 633,000; Constantine, 384,000.
Government: *Head of state,* Chadli Benjedid, president (took office Feb. 1979). *Head of government,* Mohammed Ben Ahmed Abdelghani, prime minister (took office March 1979).
Monetary Unit: Dinar (4.54 dinars equal U.S.$1, March 1982).
Gross National Product (1981 U.S.$): $36,800,000,-000.
Economic Index (1980): *Consumer Prices* (1970= 100), *all items,* 225.0; *food,* 281.4.
Foreign Trade (1980 U.S.$): *Imports,* $10,811,000,-000; *exports,* $13,656,000,000.

ANGOLA

Declining oil and diamond prices and worsening security problems in the south plagued the People's Republic of Angola in 1982.

Domestic Affairs. Angola's smoldering guerrilla conflict, an outgrowth of the 1976 civil war, continued as the opposition movement, União Nacional para Independência Total de Angola (UNITA), expanded its operations in the southern part of the country. In Cabinda, after a period of quiet, the Front for Liberation of the Cabinda Enclave (FLEC) mounted sabotage raids against the ruling Movimento Popular de Libertação de Angola (MPLA). Many prominent MPLA members were purged from the party and the government in what appeared to be a strengthening of Soviet and Cuban control. In August, President José Eduardo dos Santos found it necessary to shake up his cabinet and to dismiss his foreign trade minister.

Economy. The decline in world oil prices contributed to a weakened economy in Angola. The diamond market also remained depressed. These developments, together with a poor coffee harvest, seriously eroded the previous trade surplus. Food lines were frequent, and black market and barter circulated more goods than did the official market where prices were low but goods were scarce. Whereas Angola was formerly an exporter of food, the loss of agricultural production in the central highlands because of guerrilla activity necessitated the importing of foodstuffs.

Foreign Affairs. Angola's foreign policy continued to be dominated by South African raids into the southern region to attack bases of the South West African People's Organization (SWAPO), which seeks independence for Namibia. It was reported during the year that South African forces had established two bases in Angola near the Namibian border.

Soviet bloc support remained strong as the USSR agreed to provide $2,000,000,000 in aid by the end of the decade, and East Germany and Bulgaria signed economic pacts. Cuba continued to have troops and advisers in Angola.

Three Americans who had been held prisoner in Angola were freed in an exchange for three Soviet prisoners.

THOMAS H. HENRIKSEN

ANGOLA • Information Highlights

Official Name: People's Republic of Angola.
Location: Southwestern Africa.
Area: 481,351 sq mi (1 246 700 km²).
Population (1982 est.): 6,800,000.
Chief Cities (1970 census): Luanda, the capital, 480,-613; Huambo, 61,885; Lobito, 59,258.
Government: *Head of state and government,* José Eduardo dos Santos, president (took office 1979).
Monetary Unit: Kwanza (63.75 kwanza equal U.S.$1, October 1981).
Gross National Product Per Capita (1980 U.S.$): $470.
Foreign Trade (1979 U.S.$): *Imports,* $440,780,000; *exports,* $620,241,000.

ANTHROPOLOGY

The year 1982 was a momentous one, not just for anthropology, but for science in general. It saw the results of the "creation science trial" in Little Rock, AR, the reporting of several fossil finds of major significance to the understanding of human evolution, the publication of major research results in linguistics, and the death of the well-known anthropologist Alexander Lesser.

Creationism. In January, a federal district judge threw out an Arkansas law requiring "balanced" classroom treatment for the theories of evolution and "creation science." His opinion declared that "creation science" is not science at all but an attempt to introduce the biblical account of creation into public schools. Arkansas was permanently enjoined from enforcing that law.

Fossils. Fossil hunter R. T. Bakker, a paleontologist at Johns Hopkins University in Baltimore, announced the discovery of foot bones from what he believes is the oldest known true primate. These fossils, found in 50-million-year-old rocks in Wyoming, provide evidence of the earliest known animal with a grasping big toe. Such a trait is a definitive element in the evolution of primates. It allowed greater freedom of movement in trees and thus ensured survival over less agile forms. The fossil animal *Cantius trigonodus* has been known since 1878, but not enough of the skeleton had been collected to reconstruct the whole form.

Anthropologists J. Desmond Clark and Tim White of the University of California at Berkeley, announced the discovery of fossil bones in Ethiopia which they believe are the oldest human ancestors yet found. These fossils are 400,000 years older than "Lucy," *Australopithecus afarensis,* found by Donald C. Johanson in 1974 and a source of contention ever since. This new fossil belongs to the same species as Lucy but is apparently a male. Dr. White maintained that the absence of any significant physical differences indicate that the species was stable over a long period of time.

Hidemi Ishida of Osaka University in Japan and Richard E. Leakey announced the discovery of a jaw bone of a humanlike form estimated to be eight million years old. Professor Ishida described the fossil jaw as having five teeth and "some humanoid characteristics and some apelike characteristics." If the dating is confirmed, this form will fill the gap in the fossil primate record between *Ramapithecus,* at about 12 million years old, and *Australopithecus,* at about 4 million years old.

The position of the Ramapithecines as possible human ancestors has also been affected by recent fossil finds. Davis Pilbeam, a Harvard University anthropologist, announced the discovery of a fossil skull clearly of the Ramapithecine line but having many orangutan-like features. While Pilbeam is cautious about

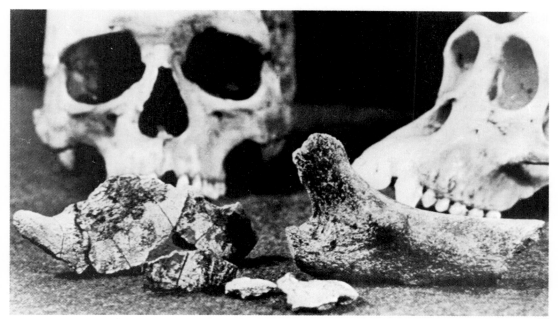

UPI

University of California scientists reported the discovery in Ethiopia of a 4-million-year-old human ancestor.

"constructing evolutionary stories," others conclude that Ramapithecus can no longer be considered a direct ancestor of humans. These finds support biochemical and African fossil evidence that hominid evolution began five to six million years ago.

Language. Derek Bickerton, a linguist at the University of Hawaii, has suggested that creole languages, which are descendants of pidgin languages, may provide a clue to the understanding of the origin of human language in general. Creole, as used by linguists, refers to a type of language which develops in an area where several languages come into contact. The way creoles develop, says Bickerton, is most insightful. He finds an unusual degree of uniformity in first-generation, native-born speakers and believes that this is due to a "bioprogram," a genetically determined process of language acquisition and development. This suggests that human language is genetically programmed more than previously believed.

Death. The noted anthropologist Alexander Lesser, a student of Franz Boas, died Aug. 7, 1982. A native–New Yorker, Lesser wrote and lectured extensively on the Plains Indians. He edited Boas' collected papers, published in 1940 under the title *Race, Language, and Culture.* Lesser had a lifelong concern for the subject of race, believing that it was an improper, arbitrarily used, and unscientific concept. His major work was the *Pawnee Ghost Dance Hand Game* (1933).

HERMAN J. JAFFE
Brooklyn College
City University of New York

ARCHAEOLOGY

An unusually large number of significant archaeological finds were made in the field and laboratory during 1982. And while the practical application of archaeological information continued to accelerate, the chief value still lay in the intrinsic interest of the finds themselves. Unfortunately, the ruination of sites by well-organized looters and profiteers also attained an all-time high, with armed "artifact rustlers" operating in the American West.

Eastern Hemisphere

Palaeolithic Practices. An apparent chopping tool found in Miocene deposits in the Siwalik hills of India again raised the possibility that *Ramapithecus,* a small primate with human-like teeth, was a sometime tool user. Additional perspective on this issue came from a report by Pat Shipman on the excavations at Fort Ternan, an east African locality which earlier produced a possible Ramapithecine tool.

A rare human fossil of the Steinheim level, which falls between the older *Homo erectus* and later Neanderthal, shows evidence of the cultural practice of scalping. The 300,000-year-old Bodo cranium was found by University of California researchers in Ethiopia.

Spanish and U.S. archaeologists discovered a Middle Magdalenian sanctuary at El Juyo cave on Spain's northern coast. Some 14,000 years ago, a band of hunters set up a cylindrical shrine made of different colored earths. A rough, free-standing stone sculpture shows half its face as a mustachioed human male and the other half as that of a large feline, such as a cave lion.

Stone Age Farmers. Chinese archaeologists probing the virtually unknown prehistory of Tibet found a stratified neolithic site at Karuo with habitation going back 5,000 years. The early dwellings of clay and wood were semi-subterranean, containing thousands of stone tools but very few made of bone. Painted and cloth-impressed pottery amplify the evidence for weaving already provided by ceramic spindle whorls. The ancient people hunted such wild animals as buffalo but kept domestic pigs and raised crops. Agriculture was feasible because the plateau was 213 ft (65 m) lower than it is today.

The Corded Ware culture of Europe (3,000–2,500 B.C.) is famous for its individualized but egalitarian graves, with special rites for men, women, and children. At Esbjerg, Denmark, a dog was buried with the stone battle axe normally reserved for a human warrior. A warrior with a battle axe, mace, and amber bead was in a nearby grave. The dog was about the same size and appearance as a Norwegian elkhound.

Ancient Civilizations. Three royal mummies were found in King Aminhat's long-known pyramid at Saqqara, Egypt, by a Vienna University project. In the Queen's Hall were found King Aminhat himself along with the sarcophagi of his queen and a princess.

Israeli investigations at ancient Lachish, 31 mi (50 km) southwest of Jerusalem, confirmed the biblical account of the slaying of most of the city's population at the time of the Israelite invasion in the 14th century B.C. Level XI of the unfortified city had been destroyed by fire, and on the floors of houses lay the skeletons of men, women, and children. In the temple, an embossed gold plate depicts a nude goddess brandishing a cup while standing on the back of a horse.

Some insight finally emerged on the origins of Chinese bronze metallurgy, which flourished dramatically ca. 1500 B.C., during the Shang dynasty. Copper and bronze artifacts were unearthed in late neolithic contexts (2,000 B.C.) in Kansu in northwest China. Two rod fragments of the same age from Shangtung in the east turned out to be copper and zinc, making them the oldest known brasses in the world.

Anthropologists at Herculaneum, an ancient Roman town buried by the same volcanic eruption that destroyed nearby Pompeii in A.D. 79, reported the discovery of 80 complete human skeletons, the largest group yet unearthed from Roman times. The find was expected to provide a wealth of information about the life of the average citizen.

The glass of ancient Egypt, Greece, and Rome survives well in the soil, with the original surface still intact after 3,000 years. Glasses made according to ancient recipes, as reconstructed by laboratory analysis, could be used as containers for radioactive wastes until natural decay has rendered the wastes harmless. Silica and sodium-lime glasses buried in a dry environment show the greatest promise.

Iron Age Europe. A crannog island settlement submerged in Loch Tay, Scotland, is being excavated by University of Edinburgh divers. The excavation is being done under water instead of by draining, in order to keep intact the perfectly preserved materials of the habitation. Numerous flaxen artifacts include rope, clothing, baskets, and oil wicks for lamps fueled by animal fat.

Medieval Cities. An Anglo-Saxon helmet was recovered in October 1981 by archaeologists at the Coppergate, York, England. The iron helmet from ca. A.D. 700 is the latest of three known Anglo-Saxon helmets. It features cheek pieces, a nose-guard, and a chain mail neck protection.

A deeply stratified tell near Jenne, Mali, explored by a Rice University husband-and-wife team has yielded remains of the city of Jenne-jeno, which flourished from 250 B.C. until its abandonment ca. A.D. 1400. In a fertile region of the Niger floodplain, Jenno-jeno sent foodstuffs and gold to the north in exchange for Mediterranean salt and glass beads. Gold earrings show local consumption of metal, with other ornaments being of copper and iron, which was also used for such items as spears, knives, and fishhooks.

Western Hemisphere

Palaeo-Indians. At Mesa Verde, Chile, Tom Delahaye of the University of Kentucky found more evidence of Palaeo-Indian use of wood 13,000 years ago. A wishbone-shaped house structure had foundations of wooden stubs; inside the structure, bone and wood digging sticks

A stone face half human and half feline was found in a 14,000-year-old sanctuary in the El Juyo cave, Spain.

L.G. Friedmann

Donald S. Whitcomb and Janet H. Johnson

Excavations at Quseir, on the Red Sea in Egypt, have told much about trade during the Roman and Mamluk empires.

were also discovered. Mastodon bones found at the site are the southernmost remains of that animal yet unearthed in the Western Hemisphere.

At the American Chemical Society meetings in September 1982, confirmation of the Soviet thermoluminescence (TL) dating of loess was announced. The tests on dated Missouri loesses verified that the Shriver industry of northwestern Missouri is 4,000 years older than the well-dated Clovis complex of ca. 9,000–10,000 B.C.

At Pigeon's Roost Creek in eastern Missouri, Michael O'Brien and associates found a sealed-in Dalton site ca. 9,500 years old. There was evidence that these hunters also collected hazel nuts, walnuts, hickories, and possibly ragweed seeds.

Settled Communities. Pipeline construction workers came upon an unusual village on federal land near Denver, CO. At an elevation of 8,200 ft (2 500 m), houses of wattle and daub construction burned ca. 3,000 B.C. The high elevation suggests that it was a semi-sedentary summer village set up for quarrying the nearby outcrops of jasper to make hunting and gathering tools.

The interior of a 30-ft- (9-m-) high pyramid discovered at Cuello, Belize, by Rutgers University archaeologists provided evidence for the lowland origin of the Maya Culture. Although the final level of the pyramid was constructed as late as A.D. 300, the site began as a village with a low, plaster ceremonial platform built ca. 2,200 B.C. A higher temple platform contained a mass burial of more than 20 humans sacrificed by means of ceremonial flint daggers recovered in the dig. The more normal grave of a child contained a ceramic bird whistle, which 3,000 years later can still be played.

Archaeological investigations of the El Cumbre canal, constructed 50 mi (80 km) from the Chimu Culture city of Chan Chan (Peru) to the Chicama River, provide some practical in-

formation for modern times. In about A.D. 1300, the canal and water-starved capital city had to be abandoned because tectonic movements in the Andes were raising up parts of the canal bed. Today, the Peruvian government uses archaeological data on the rate of uplift in its plans to build a similar but more viable canal for modern irrigation.

It was long thought that the Spanish Conquistadores had completely torn down the main temple of the Aztecs at their capital of Tenochitlan, now Mexico City. However, after subway construction hit the bases of earlier temples over which the main one had been built, complete earlier pyramids were found nested underneath. The oldest, innermost, and smallest one had at its summit virtually intact shrines to the rain god Tlaloc and the war god Huitzilopochtli.

More than 650 years ago, the Crow Creek Plains Village site in South Dakota was burned and suddenly abandoned, with a few body parts left in fortification ditches and near houses. Below the village on the Missouri River, archeologists found the mass grave of nearly 500 people who had been killed, scalped, and mutilated after a great battle ca. A.D. 1325. The population was malnourished, suggesting that there had been wars over declining croplands.

Eskimo Bonanza. A joint Dutch-American expedition at Barrow, AK, accidentally found the remains of two winter houses which had been crushed by an icefall early in the 19th century. Furnishings found in the houses included bows and arrows, harpoons, bowls, cups, ladles, and two parkas left on a rack to dry. Some of the people trapped inside had become skeletonized, but permafrost had kept two of them frozen in a near perfect state of preservation.

RALPH M. ROWLETT
Department of Anthropology
University of Missouri-Columbia

ARCHITECTURE

The year 1982 marked the 50th anniversary of the term International Style, first used in an exhibition in New York City, and subsequently used as the description of the stark and functional aesthetic ("modern") that would prevail among many leading architects almost to this anniversary. While some architects were continuing on this route, many more were pursuing different, more decorative directions—labeled historic recall, post-Modernism, or regionalism.

Design. The Renaissance-style AT&T headquarters in New York City, designed by Philip Johnson, was nearing completion. Johnson had been among the inventors of the term International Style and among its foremost promoters. Yet his new building may have done more to break the style's grip than any other. There was a strong interest in such architects as Mario Botta, who used modern forms in very novel and imaginative ways. Post-Modernism co-founder Robert Venturi delivered a lecture at Harvard entitled the "Relevance in Historicism."

The art of drawing for aesthetic effect was seeing a rebirth, as witnessed by gallery shows; by the conservation of drawings from the previous great period, the Beaux Arts; and by high prices paid by collectors for drawings from current and historic periods. The interest in a more decorative architecture carried over into a continued growing interest in the preservation or reuse of older buildings.

Romaldo Giurgola (*left*) won AIA's annual Gold Medal.
Courtesy, The American Institute of Architects (AIA)

The Pritzker Architecture Prize, conceived in 1979 by the family of that name to fill a gap in the categories of the Nobel Prizes, went to Kevin Roche. The jury said that Roche's formidable body of work, in a time of overnight fashion swings, "sometimes intersects fashion, sometimes lags it, and more often makes it."

Once again, the winners of American Institute of Architects (AIA) national awards competitions reflected a concern with small-scale design in the belief that the prevailing large-scale construction might not be consistent with prevailing architectural thought. Despite the completion of many large-scale buildings that displayed the desired qualities of increased awareness of their environment, historic context, and human scale, the twelve winners of the national competition were as follows:

(1) A library for the blind and physically handicapped in Chicago by Joseph W. Casserly, an architect working for the city, and Stanley Tigerman Associates. The jury remarked: "The building is joyful, while solving pressing needs."

(2) The Garfield Elementary School in San Francisco by Esherick Honsey Dodge and Davis. The building was segmented to fit into a residential neighborhood.

(3) The LeJeune residence in Orino, MN, by Frederick Bentz/Milo Thompson/Robert Rietow, Inc. The jury made the award on the basis of the successful screening of a nearby road, while opening views to the lakefront location.

(4) Lath House at Heritage Square in Phoenix, AZ, by Robert R. Frankeberger. The open structure for public gatherings makes stylistic references to a Victorian-house neighbor.

(5) A residence in East Hampton, NY, by Eisenman Robertson. The house makes strong references to the historic shingle-style of the area.

(6) The Talbot House in Nevis, West Indies, by Taft Architects. The structure makes use of the stone from an earlier plantation to create a native sensitivity to climate conditions.

(7) Macondray Terrace, San Francisco, by Hood Miller Associates. The apartment complex successfully copies the initimate scale of its Victorian residential neighbors.

(8) Schulman house addition in Princeton, NJ, by Michael Graves. The jury described this project as "a knitting together of fragments."

(9) The Curtis Park Face Block Project in Denver, by Long Hoeft Architects and McCrystal Design and coordinated by Historic Denver, Inc. The architects restored the exteriors of 43 Victorian houses for low-income tenants.

(10) Scoville Square Building in Oak Park, IL, by John Vinci Inc. A Prairie School-style building was restored as the headquarters of the Industrial Fire and Casualty Company.

(11) The Valley National Bank in Des Moines, IA, by Charles Herbert & Associates. This was a thorough restoration of a 1931 building with some minimal intrusion for improved lighting.

(12) The American Academy of Arts by Kallman, McKinnel & Wood. It is a design from Europe, California, and the Midwest.

The Profession. Progress was made in setting new standards by which architects are licensed. The National Council of Architectural Registration Boards (NCARB) announced the findings of a two-year study of the basic skills required by new architects and the council's intention of seeing these newly defined skills become the basis of a standardized national qualifying examination. Previously, each state had administered its own examination. Included in the list of necessary skills were many new qualifications—such as legal, ecological, and economic analysis training.

The AIA made two major changes in its 125th anniversary year. First was a management reorganization which consolidated five branches into three. A second proposal, ratified by members at the annual convention, transferred many of the former national services, including ongoing professional education, to the state chapters. The purpose was to free the national AIA to set policy and to publicize the values of architecture.

The volume of construction, which normally determines the amount of architectural activity, remained at a very low level, despite the easing somewhat of high interest rates. Part of the problem was said to be the reluctance of lenders to make mortgage commitments while interest rates remained unstable. Nonetheless, many architects reported a negligible slump in work. This was due to efforts to broaden the base of types of projects in which architects were involved and to continued high levels of construction activity outside the United States.

The U.S. federal government acted in ways that were both cheered and decried by architects. Prominent in the latter category were continued attacks on the Brooks Law, which made the quality of services and not the architect's fee the basis for initial selection of architects on federal projects. The Office of Procurement found the law to be contrary to uniform practice. More popular among architects was a Reagan administration proposal for Urban Enterprise Zones that would give tax credits for business investment in mid-city areas, where architects' services are most often used. Mixed reviews were given to the relaxation of design guidelines on federal work that would have provided for easier access for the handicapped. The design changes would involve considerable cost increases on new and remodeling construction. The right of architects to control the use of their plans for subsequent construction after a commissioned building had been built from them was upheld by the Nebraska Federal District Court, and the ruling promised to be a precedent for future decisions. Similarly, the Supreme Court refused to hear appeals by manufacturers that the specification of a particular product by architects was a breach of antitrust statutes.

Courtesy, Kevin Roche John Dinkeloo and Associates

Kevin Roche received the 1982 Pritzker Prize.

Techniques. Energy-conscious design did not seem to be the visible issue that it had been in previous years. Nonetheless, architects were practicing such conservation in their designs. A survey of cost-effectiveness in buildings winning the Owens-Corning Fiberglas awards for energy conservation during the previous ten years showed impressive improvements. It also revealed that the state of the art had moved from exotic conservation techniques, such as active solar systems, to better orientation, increased insulation, and natural ventilation and lighting.

The National Institute of Building Sciences and the Office of Technology Assessment recommended greater energy efficiency in existing buildings. Energy conservation was responsible for a large number of buildings built either underground or surrounded by earth berms. Notable was the University of Michigan Law Library underground addition by Gunnar Birkerts, which had the added advantage of preserving open space in the downtown Ann Arbor location. Structural breakthroughs included the use of stretched fabric roofs on such buildings as department stores and schools.

Personalities. Romaldo Giurgola was the recipient of the American Institute of Architects annual Gold Medal for an outstanding contribution to architecture. Among his cited designs were the addition to the Missouri State Office Complex and his winning entry in the international competition to design the Parliament House in Canberra, Australia.

George M. White, controversial Architect of the Capitol, was again criticized—this time by the General Accounting Office—for cost overruns.

CHARLES HOYT
Associate Editor, "Architectural Record"

ARGENTINA

Argentina's unsuccessful attempt in the South Atlantic to wrest the Falkland (Malvinas) Islands from Great Britain dominated the country's foreign and domestic affairs in 1982. (*See* feature article, page 28.) This military fiasco was followed by a series of political upheavals as the ruling junta tried to restore some measure of public confidence. At the same time, Argentina's economic problems reached crisis proportions.

Government and Politics. Maj. Gen. (ret.) Reynaldo Benito Bignone was sworn into the presidency on July 1, replacing Lt. Gen. Leopoldo Galtieri, whose brief term ended with his resignation on June 17, three days after the Falklands surrender. Galtieri, in turn, had ousted Lt. Gen. Roberto Viola from the executive office in December 1981, after Viola had served only eight months of a three-year term.

Ignoring cries for an immediate return to civilian rule, the incoming army commander in chief, Lt. Gen. Cristino Nicolaides, a noted "hard-liner," chose General Bignone for the vital executive position. Before his military retirement, Bignone had served as liaison between the military government and the country's leading politicians. His program of government had featured a dialogue with civilian political forces on the economic, social, and political aspects of an eventual return to democratic rule. While civilian leaders pressured Bignone for an early return to civilian government, the chief executive was inflexible: national elections would be held late in 1983, with the installation of newly elected leaders to come on March 29, 1984.

Bignone became president in the absence of the customary military junta of ranking officers of the three branches within the armed forces. The navy and air force had insisted on their domination of the executive power, but that solution to the midyear power struggle was rejected by the predominant army, even though the army bore the brunt of defeat in the South Atlantic. Both the naval and air forces favored a civilian alternative over continued army dominance. After that solution also was vetoed by the army, the navy and air force pulled out of the junta and the administration, leaving the army to govern alone while coping with the consequences of a public display of disunity in the armed forces.

By September 21, the junta had been reestablished, with the navy and air force endorsing army decisions made since July. Representing the navy and air force on the junta were, respectively, Adm. Oscar Rubén Franco and Brig. Gen. Augusto Hughes. Bignone named a civilian to repair an economy that had virtually collapsed from unparalleled mismanagement, corruption, and personal greed. However, José María Dagnino Pastore soon lost the confidence of the president and was replaced by Jorge Wehbe.

Bignone favored civil liberties for all except the Communists. Human-rights activist José Westerkamp was charged in July with attacking the judicial system in Chubut province and was held for trial. In October, when some 10,000 human-rights activists marched in Buenos Aires, insisting that the military rulers account for their actions, the regime resurrected legislation laying down minimum prison sentences of three to eight years for newspaper reporters who wrote stories detrimental to "social peace" and "institutional order."

Speaking for the junta, Admiral Franco indicated that the armed forces would not allow themselves, under any pretext, to stand accused on human rights, which they had always defended. But among the embarrassments to the regime was the discovery in September of perhaps a thousand bodies in unmarked graves in a pauper's cemetery near Buenos Aires.

Peronism. Pushing the Bignone government into concessions beyond the lifting in July of the six-year-old ban on political party activity, the militant Brazil Street faction of the Peronist-dominated General Confederation of Workers (CGT) held illegal but well-attended demonstrations and strikes. None of the protests was suppressed. After one such event, on September 23, in which 20,000 workers and political activists participated, the government announced that the 42 unions under military control since 1976 would be placed under transitional commissions and that leaders would be elected from among union members. The curbs on strikes by labor unions would be revoked and labor leaders would be consulted on wage matters.

Former President Isabel Martínez de Perón would not be a presidential candidate in 1983. The supreme court ruled on August 24 that she would be prevented from holding public office in Argentina because, as president, she fraudulently used funds from a state-run charity.

Economic Policy. During his abbreviated presidency, General Galtieri had attempted to mend the economy, and to that end he had named the

---

ARGENTINA · Information Highlights

Official Name: Republic of Argentina.
Location: Southern South America.
Area: 1,068,302 sq mi (2 766 902 km^2).
Population (1980 census): 27,862,771.
Chief Cities (1980 census): Buenos Aires, the capital, 2,908,001; Córdoba, 990,007; Rosario, 935,471.
Government: Head of state and government, Maj. Gen. Reynaldo Bignone, president (took office July 1, 1982). *Legislature*—Congress (dissolved March 24, 1976).
Monetary Unit: New Peso (41,640 new pesos equal U.S.$1, Dec. 13, 1982).
Gross National Product (1981 U.S.$): $124,600,000,-000.
Economic Indexes: *Consumer Prices, all items* (1970=100), 529,776; *food* (1974=100), 123,-800. *Industrial production* (March 1982, 1975=100), 77.
Foreign Trade (1981 U.S.$): *Imports,* $10,544,000,-000; *exports,* $8,016,000,000.

Villalobos/Gamma-Liaison

Officially prohibited, the "March for Life" human rights rally October 5 in Buenos Aires still drew 5,000 people.

experienced Roberto T. Alemann as his economics minister. Alemann maintained that by "privatizing" the economy—that is, selling off government-owned industrial enterprises and financial entities, as well as reducing the military's share of the budget by 10%—the economy would be on its way to recovery.

Before Alemann's program had had a chance to demonstrate its effectiveness, Galtieri and his junta had gone to war over the Falklands. Soon the folly of pursuing the war had become evident to most of the military leadership, but Galtieri held out for continued belligerence, even after the British had recaptured Stanley. Galtieri resigned on June 17.

The task of strengthening the war-weakened economy fell upon veteran financier Jorge Wehbe in September. Wehbe found that U.S. $2,310,000,000 was overdue from unmet obligations in the first half of 1982, and that $12,600,-000,000 in principal and interest would fall due in the second half of the year. Even with available reserves and a favorable trade balance, Argentina would be unable to pay such amounts. Hoping to find contingency funding for payments falling due in the latter half of the year, Wehbe attended a meeting of the International Monetary Fund (IMF) in Toronto in September. By then, the total Argentine public and private foreign debt had reached almost $40,000,000,000.

An impediment to a refinancing of the foreign debt was removed later in September when British and Argentine officials ended financial sanctions that had been in place since April, freeing $1,000,000,000 of Argentine assets in British banks and $3,000,000,000 of British assets in Argentina. In November the IMF announced a $2,100,000,000 emergency loan for Argentina.

The government in Buenos Aires unveiled other economic policies in September, confirming a move away from the free-market policies pursued after the military coup in 1976. In order to reactivate consumer demand, price controls were placed on the products of leading companies, and to protect living standards, price ceilings were placed on bread and milk. The "commercial peso" was devalued to 28,000 to the dollar, an effective drop of 12%, aimed at narrowing the gap between the commercial and the "financial peso," officially exchanged at about 40,000 to the dollar in September. The value-added tax was reduced from 12% to 8%.

By October, inflation had reached the 200% level, and unemployment, while conservatively estimated at 18% overall, had surpassed 55% in construction and some other industries. The biggest strike of the year—indeed, the first nationwide strike under the military regime—occurred on December 6 when an estimated 9 million workers remained away from work for 24 hours in protest against both inflation and abuses of human rights and liberties. No effort was made to disrupt the strike.

Foreign Affairs. Relations with the United States plummeted as a result of the U.S. decision in May to side with Great Britain in the Falklands crisis. In September, after Argentina's defeat, the United States resumed deliveries of military spare parts, but Argentine foreign policy continued to move away from the United States and toward Third World countries and the Communist bloc. In the 1981–1982 international marketing year, Argentina had exported a record 13 million metric tons of grain to the Soviet Union. Relations with the USSR became even more friendly after the Falklands war.

Prior to the ill-fated South Atlantic operation, Argentina had become closely identified with U.S. policies and practices in Central America. Once the United States decided to back its European ally rather than Argentina in the Falklands, Argentina withdrew its anti-guerrilla trainers from Central America and its military personnel from the U.S.-operated School of the Americas in the Canal Zone.

LARRY L. PIPPIN, *Elbert Covell College*

ARIZONA

In unusually high numbers for a nonpresidential election year (more than 60% turnout), Arizonans went to the polls on November 2 to vote for a governor, a senator, five congressmen, and other state officials. In addition, 10 referenda issues were on the ballot.

Although known as a conservative state, Arizona voters follow no consistent partisan pattern. Since 1952 the state has gone Republican in every presidential election and "Mr. Conservative," Barry Goldwater, has been a U.S. senator since January 1953. But this year incumbent Democrats Bruce Babbitt (governor), Dennis DeConcini (U.S. senator), and Morris Udall (congressman) easily trounced their Republican opponents for reelection. Moreover, in a vigorously contested race for Arizona's newly created fifth-district congressional seat, Democrat James McNulty defeated his Republican opponent by a margin of 49% to 48%. This occurred in spite of the fact that the district had been drawn, most observers agreed, to favor a Republican candidate.

Republicans, however, reelected Congressmen Eldon Rudd and Bob Stump and elected a newcomer, John McCain, to retain their edge in the Arizona congressional delegation (3 Republicans and 2 Democrats). Similarly, Republicans retained their control in both houses of the state legislature.

On referenda issues, voters rejected 7 of the 10 propositions considered. Among those rejected were the proposed "nuclear-weapons freeze," a "bottle bill" that would have required deposits on beer and soft drink containers, and pay raises for state legislators and other selected state officials.

Voters also kept the so-called Sage Brush Rebellion alive in Arizona by voting down a proposed repeal of the state law that permits the state to pursue its claims on federally owned land. Voters showed a get-tough attitude toward criminals by voting overwhelmingly for a bill that will prohibit bail for persons charged with a felony and who pose a danger to society. Another bill—enabling Arizonans to register to vote when they apply for their driver's licenses—was approved by a slim margin.

The Economy. Following the national trend, economic gloom in the form of unemployment has penetrated Arizona's sun-belt economy. The layoff of some 12,000 copper miners and more than 30,000 construction workers pushed the state's unemployment rate above 10%. The devaluation of the Mexican peso also contributed to a decline in the state's economy, especially in towns along the international border.

Other Matters. The U.S. Department of Interior finally approved construction of the Tucson portion of the Central Arizona Project, but federal funding will provide only half the construction money needed. Thus, the water problems of southern Arizona remain unresolved until the state can generate the needed revenue.

The Arizona legislature passed a stringent drunken-driving law that will impose stiff fines, eliminate plea-bargaining in such cases, and require mandatory jail terms for offenders.

JAMES W. CLARKE
University of Arizona

During a national protest against acid rain pollution in February, Claire O'Brien and Davis Stewart of the Greenpeace environmental group perched themselves atop the left smokestack at the Magma Copper Co. smelter in San Manuel, AZ, and unfurled a 60-ft (18-m) banner.

Wide World

ARIZONA · Information Highlights

Area: 114,000 sq mi (295 260 km^2).
Population (1980 census): 2,718,425.
Chief Cities (1980 census): Phoenix, the capital, 764,-911: Tucson; 330,537; Mesa, 152,453; Tempe, 106,743.
Government (1982): *Chief Officers*—governor, Bruce E. Babbitt (D). *Legislature*—Senate, 30 members; House of Representatives, 60 members.
State Finances (fiscal year 1981): *Revenues*, $3,405,-000,000; *expenditures*, $3,076,000,000.
Personal Income (1981): $27,256,000,000; per capita, $9,754.
Labor Force (Aug. 1982): *Nonagricultural wage and salary earners*, 1,003,400; *unemployed*, 149,500 (11.3% of total force).
Education: *Enrollment* (fall 1981)—public elementary schools, 355,275; public secondary, 151,924; colleges and universities (1981–82), 205,169. *Public school expenditures* (1980–81), $1,103,550,000 ($1,914 per pupil).

ARKANSAS

An exciting gubernatorial campaign, the most expensive in the state's history; antics of a Pulaski county sheriff raiding a Little Rock toga party; and the crowning of Terri Lee Utley of Cabot as Miss USA provided relief from the depressing economic reports about record unemployment, factory cutbacks, and business failures in Arkansas during 1982. A tornado killed two persons in the Little Rock area in early December.

Elections. A determined Republican challenge to the Democratic control of public office was checked. Liberal Democrat Bill Clinton made a remarkable comeback from his disastrous defeat in the 1980 election for governor by conservative Republican Frank White. In 1982, Clinton decisively beat Governor White by winning 55% of the total vote cast in the general election. While most Republican candidates lost, the two Republican incumbent U.S. representatives were reelected, and Republicans made small gains in the Arkansas General Assembly by maintaining their seven state House seats and increasing their number to three in the state Senate. A successful campaign to repeal the constitutional 10% maximum limit on interest rates was almost as flamboyant as the gubernatorial race.

State Government. Governor White held the line on state expenditures. When revenue collections did not meet expectations, agency budgets were reduced. Funding for the state highway department became critical. New state prison facilities were not constructed fast enough to house the increasing prison population and some prisoners began to stack up in local jails. A nine-day special legislative session in November 1981 failed to resolve pressing problems, and some became outstanding campaign issues in 1982. Among them were the reform of utility regulations and the setting of a maximum 80,000 lb (36,287 kg) limit on truck weights. The federal appeals court rejected the state law redrawing congressional districts to conform to 1980 popu-

UPI

Rice is unloaded at a Stuttgart cooperative. U.S. rice production was down, but carry-over stocks were abundant.

lation changes, and the court selected an alternate plan after the governor refused to call a special legislative session to redo the task.

The Judiciary. In a year of judicial activism, state and federal courts struck down a number of state laws: a 1981 statute requiring the teaching of creation science in public schools; at-large city council elections in West Helena for discriminating against black voters; a 1981 act requiring popular election of the mayor in Little Rock, a city-manager city in which the city council appoints the mayor from its membership; and the financial aid law distributing state funds to school districts on the basis of property wealth. Pulaski County Sheriff Tommy Robinson was jailed for two days because of his conflict with federal District Judge George Howard over control of the county jail.

Education. In Little Rock, where massive state resistance to integration began 25 years ago when nine black students attempted to attend Central High School, white student enrollment dwindled to 34% because of white flight from the city.

Utilities. Popular resentment against utility rate increases led to two unsuccessful attempts to initiate constitutional amendments requiring the election, instead of the appointment, of the three Public Service commissioners. One attempt failed when sponsors did not obtain enough signatures on the petition; another was rejected because the state supreme court found its title defective. Bill Clinton then promised to support legislation requiring their election.

WILLIAM C. NOLAN
Southern Arkansas University

ARKANSAS · Information Highlights

Area: 53,187 sq mi (137 754 km²).

Population (1980 census): 2,286,435.

Chief Cities (1980 census): Little Rock, the capital, 158,461; Fort Smith, 71,384; North Little Rock, 64,419.

Government (1982): *Chief Officers*—governor, Frank White (R); lt. gov., Winston Bryant (D). *General Assembly*—Senate, 35 members; House of Representatives, 100 members.

State Finances (fiscal year 1981): *Revenues,* $2,529,-000,000; *expenditures,* $2,356,000,000.

Personal Income (1981): $18,467,000,000; per capita, $8,044.

Labor Force (Aug. 1982): *Nonagricultural wage and salary earners,* 719,300; *unemployed,* 100,400 (9.7% of total force).

Education: *Enrollment* (fall 1981)—public elementary schools, 305,030; public secondary, 132,091; colleges and universities (1981–82), 76,032. *Public school expenditures* (1980–81), $768,672,000 ($1,571 per pupil).

ARMS CONTROL

Little was accomplished in the area of arms control in 1982. Regarding both theater nuclear weapons in Europe, and strategic intercontinental nuclear weapons, the United States position was generally that the Soviet Union enjoyed quantitative advantages that would have to be reduced before Washington could enter into serious negotiations for arms control and disarmament. In other words, the Reagan administration wanted the Soviet Union to make reductions in the numbers of certain weapons deployed as a necessary first step in the negotiations process. The Soviets countered that the United States had postulated a false Soviet superiority in order to justify a buildup in American weapons.

From time to time in Washington there was official talk of proposing "confidence-building" measures to the Soviet Union as a means of setting the stage for substantive arms-control agreements later. Such measures were described as being activities in which the two superpowers could engage that would minimize the chances of either nation's launching nuclear weapons in response to a false alarm. In June, President Reagan announced that the United States would shortly ". . . approach the Soviet Union with proposals in such areas as notification of strategic exercises, of missile launches, and expanded exchange of strategic data."

Arms Control and Politics. Several prominent political figures, seeking to challenge the Reagan administration, voiced suggestions for future American arms-control initiatives. Sen. Edward Kennedy (D-MA), for example, supported the proposed nuclear freeze at current levels of U.S. and Soviet nuclear arsenals (*see* special report, page 108). Sen. Gary Hart (D) of Colorado offered a different proposal. His suggestion was a variant on the nuclear-freeze proposal: that both superpowers freeze the number of strategic nuclear warheads on missiles at current levels. Then, Hart suggested, both sides should substitute single warheads for multiple warheads now carried on many strategic missiles. Finally, any new missiles built in the future should be small ones, capable of carrying only one warhead each.

Throughout the year various individuals and groups, generally Democratic, voiced support for reviving the SALT II (Strategic Arms Limitation Talks) treaty negotiated by President Jimmy Carter with Soviet President Leonid Brezhnev in 1979. That agreement was criticized as "fatally flawed" by President Reagan when he successfully campaigned for the presidency in 1980. After his election the president continued his opposition to SALT II on the grounds that the agreement as written would provide certain advantages to the Soviet Union.

Arms Control and Space. Some arms controllers expressed concern in 1982 that if action was not taken soon, the availability of new weapons for space would generate pressures for their deployment that would undermine hopes for arms control in space. A major concern was that after some 25 years of generally peaceful exploration of space and the ratification of the Outer Space Treaty of 1967, the United States and the Soviet Union might be on the verge of embarking on an immense military effort in space. Persons fearful of such a possibility pointed to a number of disturbing developments.

First, there was the successful flight-testing of the American space shuttle *Columbia*. It was noted that the space shuttle is capable of carrying military payloads into space, including components from which manned space battle stations could be built. These fears about an altered role for the space-shuttle program were borne out to some degree when the Air Force announced it would be using some future space shuttle flights for classified military operations. According to Robert Cooper, director of the Defense Advanced Research Projects Agency, the Department of Defense plans to spend nearly $11,000,000,000 for various space-shuttle operations of a military nature, including 20 military flights, in the next five years. The first such use of the space shuttle will be in 1983. After that flight, approximately one third of the planned 300 shuttle flights to 1994 will be military in character.

Another reason arms controllers worry about an arms race in space is the proportion of money proposed for military-space programs as compared with funding for civilian-space activities. According to Department of Defense budget records, the amount of funding for military-space activity ($6,400,000,000) exceeded that spent on civilian-space programs ($5,500,000,000) for the first time in 1982. For the fiscal year beginning in October 1982, the Reagan administration requested $8,500,000,000 for military-space operations and $6,800,000,000 for civilian activities. According to Edward Aldridge, undersecretary of the Air Force, military spending for space will reach $14,000,000,000 annually within five years.

Another clue to the expanding emphasis placed by the military on space is the plan to construct a Consolidated Space Operations Center for the Air Force. It will be located near the Air Force Academy, outside of Colorado Springs, CO.

Arms controllers were also worried by news reports in 1982 that Dr. Edward Teller, the eminent nuclear-weapons scientist, had suggested a radical new weapons possibility for space deployment. The core of the proposed weapon would be a nuclear bomb. The explosion of the bomb would release energy to power laser beams that could be used to destroy Soviet warheads launched by missiles, or to destroy Soviet bombers. There was no consensus among space scientists that Dr. Teller's concept could be developed into an operative weapons system. However, as-

© Pressens Bild/Photoreporters   UPI

For their "patient and meticulous" efforts to promote international nuclear disarmament, 80-year-old Alva Myrdal of Sweden (left) and 71-year-old Alfonso García Robles of Mexico were named corecipients of the 1982 Nobel Peace Prize.

suming that it could, there would be created substantial pressure to deploy the new system before the Soviets could follow suit. Such activity has been characteristic of the arms race between the United States and the Soviet Union— a rush to be the first to deploy a new weapons system.

Somewhat sensitive to charges that it is gearing up for an arms race in space, the Reagan administration claimed in 1982 that it had no specific plan to place weapons in orbit. Nevertheless a five-year strategic plan titled *Defense Guidance* carries the statement that "The United States space program will contribute to the deterrence of an attack on the United States or, if deterrence fails, to the prosecution of war by developing, deploying, operating, and supporting space systems."

Endangered Treaties. Contemporary arms developments could create pressures for changing—or possibly even abrogating—two major arms-control treaties: the ABM (Antiballistic Missile) Treaty of 1972 and the Outer Space Treaty of 1967.

Regarding the ABM Treaty, one of the proposals for protecting the "dense-pack" MX missile deployment system (*see* MILITARY AFFAIRS) calls for the installation of ABM's around the initial MX complex. The protection of one MX complex would appear to be in accord with the 1974 protocol to the ABM Treaty, which permits one intercontinental ballistic missile (ICBM) complex to be so protected. However, should the United States seek to protect more than one MX complex with ABM's, it probably would be necessary to abrogate the treaty or to negotiate substantial changes in it with the Soviet Union.

Two provisions of the Outer Space Treaty relate directly to arms control. One prohibits the treaty signatories from placing in orbit around the earth, installing on the moon or any other celestial body, or otherwise stationing in outer space nuclear weapons or other weapons of mass destruction. The second prohibition limits the use of the moon and other celestial bodies exclusively to peaceful purposes.

The placement in earth orbit of satellites for surveillance, weather observation, communication, and navigation assistance—all possibly for military purposes—does not violate the terms of the Outer Space Treaty. Such satellites have been launched by both the United States and the Soviet Union. However, satellites propagating laser beams derived from the energy released by nuclear explosions could be interpreted as being in violation of the treaty.

In November, President Reagan reiterated his call for the Soviets to join in making "deep cuts" in strategic nuclear weapons in accord with the spirit of what the president terms START (Strategic Arms Reduction Talks). He reaffirmed the invitation for Moscow to cooperate in confidence-building measures such as exchanging advance warning of pending missile tests and military maneuvers.

In December, Soviet party chairman Yuri Andropov announced that the Soviets would limit their SS-20's in Eastern Europe to the number of French and British missiles in Western Europe, about 162, if the United States would agree not to deploy the Pershing 2 and cruise missiles to Europe in December 1983.

ROBERT M. LAWRENCE
Colorado State University

The Nuclear Freeze Movement

As the UN special session on disarmament opens in June, some 500,000 persons stage a peace rally.

Since the detonation of the two American atomic bombs on the Japanese cities of Hiroshima and Nagasaki in 1945, there have been a variety of protests in the United States and elsewhere against nuclear weapons. For example, in the 1950s and early 1960s there was the Ban the Bomb movement. This was never a mass activity, and it faded away following the adoption by the United States and the Soviet Union in 1963 of the treaty that prohibits nuclear weapons tests that contaminate the earth's atmosphere and space. The Ban the Bomb movement and periodic protests since then have typically not been grass-roots actions involving large numbers of citizens. However, the character of the antinuclear activity in the United States changed dramatically in 1982. For the first time, substantial numbers of Americans, including many clergymen, rallied behind a proposal for the United States and the Soviet Union to adopt an immediate, mutual, and verifiable freeze on the testing, manufacture, and deployment of nuclear weapons, to be followed by systematic reductions in the number of nuclear weapons possessed by the superpowers.

In addition, an unusual number of books discussing the threat of nuclear war were published. Jonathan Schell's *The Fate of the Earth*, which was excerpted in *The New Yorker*, made the best-sellers list.

Several explanations exist for what is generally referred to as "the nuclear freeze." One explanation is that the contemporary American movement was sparked by the antinuclear rallies and demonstrations in Western Europe, particularly West Germany, during the past several years. Much of the focus of the European antinuclear activism has been to prevent the proposed deployment in 1983–84 of new cruise missiles and Pershing II missiles to its

NATO allies by the United States. By late 1982, the European antinuclear protests had failed to persuade West European governments and the United States to drop the proposed action.

A second explanation of the nuclear freeze movement is more complex. It initially credits a young woman living near Boston with doing much to spread the idea to traditional peace groups and the small antinuclear organizations existing in 1980. According to this perspective, Randall Forsberg, with support from Quaker groups, traveled throughout the United States advocating the nuclear freeze as a modification of a proposal for a nuclear weapons moratorium made several years before by the American Friends Service Committee. It is ironic to note that the election in 1980 of Ronald Reagan as president may have given Forsberg and the relatively small group of nuclear freeze supporters at that time a boost. Analysts point out that Reagan's efforts to rally citizens in support of his call for substantially increased levels of nuclear weapons, and his occasional remarks that nuclear war was not impossible, frightened many into believing the nuclear arms race was becoming too dangerous, involved too many nuclear weapons, and thus should be halted with a nuclear freeze.

Still another explanation for the nuclear freeze movement is that those Americans supporting the freeze have been duped into accepting a perspective which is congruent with, and orchestrated by, the Soviet Union. A widely read example of this explanation appeared as the major article in the October 1982 issue of the *Reader's Digest*. The article, titled "The KGB's Magical War for Peace," was written by the magazine's senior editor, John Barron. The thesis of the article, and the belief of many who oppose the nuclear freeze, is that the Soviets are cleverly manipulating the sincere desire to avoid nuclear war by many Americans in a way to advance the interest of the Soviet Union. That interest is said to be the tricking of the United States into accepting a freeze which would prevent Washington from deploying new nuclear weapons that would offset the current superiority in weapons it is claimed Moscow enjoys. Persons accepting this explanation of the origins of the nuclear freeze movement oppose the freeze on the grounds that it would freeze Soviet superiority to the detriment of the United States.

President Reagan's Perspective. President Reagan opposes a nuclear freeze unless certain critical preconditions are met. He is joined by the Secretary of Defense Caspar Weinberger, Secretary of State George Shultz, and numerous others in and out of the government. The president and his supporters state that there exists a "window of vulnerability" between the United States and the Soviet Union which would be maintained to the disadvantage of the United States should a nuclear freeze be instigated without substantial changes being made. What the president means is that in his view the USSR has achieved nuclear weapons superiority and that this condition places America in a vulnerable position, and that is unacceptable.

As a counter to the nuclear freeze proposal, the president has suggested an alternative arms control plan. It is that before a halt is called in the nuclear arms competition one of two developments must occur. Either the Soviets must substantially reduce their arsenal of nuclear weapons, or the United States must substantially increase its supply of nuclear weapons. The anticipated consequence of either action would be, according to the president, establishment of equality between the nuclear arsenals of both nations. This would be the administration's necessary precondition for negotiating a halt in the nuclear arms race.

The Rationale of the Nuclear Freeze Movement. The premise upon which those who support the nuclear freeze rest their case is quite different from the foundation of the president's thinking. It is that rough nuclear equality currently exists between the United States and the USSR. Rough nuclear equality is defined as Soviet numerical superiority regarding some nuclear weapons and American numerical superiority regarding other nuclear weapons. Further, nuclear freeze supporters contend that in general U.S. nuclear weapons are qualitatively superior to those of the USSR. Given this view, nuclear freeze advocates believe that now is an opportune time to halt the nuclear weapons competition because both sides would be more likely to agree to restraint when both are equal in a nuclear weapons context. Nuclear freeze proponents also suggest that for the United States to increase its nuclear arsenal, as the Reagan administration desires, would worsen U.S.–Soviet relations and possibly create instabilities that might increase the dangers of nuclear war by either accident or design.

The Nuclear Freeze Compared with the Anti-Vietnam War Movement. The 1982 nuclear freeze movement has both similarities and differences to the anti-Vietnam War movement of the late 1960s and early 1970s. A major difference is that to date (late 1982) the nuclear freeze movement has been nonviolent in character. This was not always the case with the anti-Vietnam War effort. Antiwar demonstrators and protesters frequently clashed with police in ways that led to injuries to both sides, property damage, and numerous arrests. There has been no incident associated with the nuclear freeze movement even remotely resembling the most violent of the anti-Vietnam War confrontations, the killing of four young persons by the Ohio National Guard on the campus of Kent State University in May 1970. Another major difference is that many voters in 1982 had the opportunity directly to register their feelings regarding the nuclear freeze proposal in local and statewide balloting, which was not the case in the earlier period. As part of the general elections in November, one out of four Americans had the nuclear freeze proposal on their ballots. This was true in nine states—Arizona, California, Massachusetts, Michigan, Montana, New Jersey, North Dakota, Oregon, and Rhode Island. Of the nine states, only Arizona recorded a no vote on the freeze issue. The District of Columbia voted in favor of the freeze, as did such major cities as Chicago, Denver, Miami, and Philadelphia. Previously Wisconsin voters had supported the freeze.

The results of the November balloting on the nuclear freeze question did not legally bind the federal government. The voting did, however, constitute substantial political pressure on the Reagan administration to modify its position regarding arms control negotiations with the Soviet Union. The basic similarity between 1982 and the anti-Vietnam War era is that in each case the opposing sides tried to assist politicians who were favorable to their point of view, while they worked to defeat politicians who differed with them.

Among the groups supporting the nuclear freeze are Common Cause, Federation of American Scientists, Physicians for Social Responsibility, Union of Concerned Scientists, Lawyers Alliance for Nuclear Arms Control, National Council of Churches, and the Council for a Livable World. Sen. Mark Hatfield (R-OR) and Sen. Edward Kennedy (D-MA) were active in supporting the nuclear freeze.

ROBERT M. LAWRENCE

ART

After reaching a high point in 1978–79, the 20-year art boom is over, and the auction business is suffering a decline. Although the volume of art sales continues to be high, profits are falling. The two leading art auction houses, Sotheby Parke-Bernet and Christie's, experienced drops of about 30% and 15%, respectively, during the 1981–82 art season. Since Sotheby in recent years had been expanding around the world and into diverse markets, including real estate, the news that it was retrenching came as a shock. Its worldwide staff was cut by 500; in London, the Belgravia branch, specializing in Victoriana, was transferred to the Bond Street headquarters; the showrooms and an office in Los Angeles ceased; and the small galleries on New York City's East 84th Street were closed. But it was the announcement in June that the principal New York galleries, on Madison Avenue at 76th Street, were to be vacated in September that really startled the art world. When Parke-Bernet moved from 57th Street to the elegant Madison Avenue building in the early 1950s, the uptown trend started. It was the center of a neighborhood toward which the art life of New York naturally gravitated. Museums, libraries, art galleries, bookstores, and the Institute of Fine Arts Foundation are nearby. Now Sotheby's only New York headquarters will be at York Avenue at 76th Street.

The reasons for the decline are varied. Economic recession has been blamed for a shortage of cash flow. Lower rates of inflation coupled with continuing high interest rates caused speculators to invest in money markets instead of buying art works. At the same time there were no major collections for sale, and a general decline in the volume of objects occurred. Moreover, the institution of a buyer's premium (charging the buyer 10% of the hammer price) in addition to the usual 10% commission caused some consumer resistance.

When the annual figures were released in July, the decline was particularly noticeable in certain areas: jewelry sales were off 43% at Sotheby's, and 19% at Christie's from the previous year; modern and Impressionist paintings were off 31% at Sotheby's and 47% at Christie's; Art Nouveau and Art Deco were off 46% at Sotheby's and 60% at Christie's. But other areas did better. For example, post-World War II art rose 113% at Christie's; American furniture 137%; and silver 25%. Records continued to be made in individual cases: Wassily Kandinsky's 1910 *Sketch for Composition II* sold at Christie's for $1.1 million, a record for the artist; Paul Gauguin's *Man with the Axe* was sold privately for $6 million; Henry Moore's *Reclining Figure* sold for $1,150,000 at Sotheby's, the highest price ever paid for a sculpture by a living artist. A 1912 Piet Mondrian *Composition in Gray-Blue* sold for $1,080,000 at Sotheby's in

Scofield Thayer bequeathed his collection, including the above Matisse, to New York's Metropolitan Museum of Art.

London, at an auction in which 70% of the lots remained unsold, because bidding—though high—did not reach the reserve price set by the owner. These examples show that works of quality will continue to command high prices but that the idea that anything is salable and at unrealistically high prices no longer holds true.

Morse Painting. Samuel F. B. Morse's "The Gallery of the Louvre" was privately sold by the University of Syracuse to Daniel J. Terra, founder of the Terra Museum of American Art in Evanston, IL. Morse, better known as the inventor of the telegraph, had a distinguished career as a painter and as an educator, having been the first professor of Fine Arts at New York University. In 1832 he painted *The Gallery of the Louvre,* showing the Salon Carré filled with famous Old Masters carefully copied in miniature scale. In the foreground he put himself correcting the work of a copyist, while in the doorway his friend, James Fenimore Cooper, with his wife and daughter, appear. The writer had commissioned Morse to do this painting, which was to be sent on tour in order to acquaint Americans with the cultural heritage of Europe. For nearly

U.S. cultural affairs ambassador Daniel J. Terra purchased Morse's "The Gallery of the Louvre" for $3.25 million.

a century it had belonged to Syracuse University and was virtually never exhibited. Now the proceeds from the sale would be used for the purchase of books and other items for the research libraries, while the painting itself will be on permanent view. It will be one of the main showpieces of the Terra Museum, founded in 1980 and specializing in American art of the 18th, 19th, and 20th centuries. The price of the painting, $3.25 million, topped the previous record for an American painting. Frederic Edwin Church's *Icebergs* sold for $2.5 million in 1977.

Museum News. Salvador Dali, the popular 76-year-old Spanish surrealist painter, is the sole artist featured in the museum bearing his name, which opened in March 1982 in St. Petersburg, FL. The donors of the new museum's works, Mr. and Mrs. A. Reynolds Morse of Cleveland, OH, started collecting Dali in 1943. The collection, valued at $35 million, consists of 93 oil paintings, 200 watercolors and drawings, 1,000 prints, as well as films, sculptures, designs for furniture and clothing, and a 2,500-volume library on Dali and surrealism. It was presented to St. Petersburg because the city promised to keep it intact and persuaded the Florida state legislature to appropriate $2 million to renovate a former marine warehouse for the museum.

The new addition to the Fogg Museum in Cambridge, MA, announced in 1981 as a $7.8 million project to be designed by a noted British architect to add badly needed gallery, storage, and classroom space, was endangered when Harvard University announced early in 1982 that the plans had to be abandoned for financial reasons. Previously, an attempt to raise money for the expensive project by deaccessioning $3 million worth of the Fogg's art works had also been abandoned following severe criticism by the art world. After the announcement, a last minute money-raising effort to provide funds for operating costs succeeded in persuading Harvard's administration to continue with the building of the new wing.

The Museum of Modern Art reached the halfway mark of its $85.6 million building program. The original structure is being renovated, and new wings are being added to provide more office, gallery, theater, and restaurant space. In addition, the air rights are being used to build a 44-story condominium tower, of which the first six floors will be occupied by the museum. When the program is completed, there will be space to exhibit the museum's large collection adequately. It has been estimated that no more than 15% of its paintings and sculpture have been displayed at any one time; and other media, such as prints, photographs, and drawings, also need space commensurate with their importance among the museum's holdings.

In spite of the confusion engendered by the construction, the museum has remained open. A selection from its permanent collection is on view in the new West Wing, the first floor of which was given to a loan exhibition featuring the works done by Giorgio de Chirico between

1911 and 1917. This Italian painter, who was born in Greece in 1888 and died in Rome in 1978, is considered to have done his most significant work during this early period of his long career. The museum showed 75 paintings and 20 drawings of his surrealist period, a few earlier ones revealing his links with German painting of the turn of the century, and some later works which are considered by many critics to be merely repetitions and less imaginative. He had a great influence on painting in the 20th century and continues to fascinate viewers with his haunting empty cities and mannequin figures.

Another pioneer of 20th century art is Wassily Kandinsky. He was the favorite painter of the Solomon Guggenheim Museum when it was known as the Museum of Non-Objective Painting. In 1982 he was featured in a series of shows spanning his entire career. The first, "Kandinsky in Munich: 1896–1914," opened in February at the Guggenheim. The Russian-born painter studied in Paris for a time, but it was in Munich—an important art center in those years—that he began to free himself from the dominant style (Jugendstil, parallel to Art Nouveau) and to move toward the abstraction that became the most important manifestation of modern art. The exhibition included the work of his contemporaries and also documents and objects relating to the theatrical, musical, and architectural life of Munich in the early part of the century. A curiosity was the production at a local theater, in conjunction with the exhibition, of a multimedia stage work, *The Yellow Sound,* created by Kandinsky between 1909 and 1912, and never before performed.

The Metropolitan Museum of Art became the beneficiary of three large donations. A col-

lection of 60 works of Chinese painting and calligraphy was donated to it in December 1981 by John M. Crawford, Jr. Worth at least $18 million and ranging from the 11th to the 18th century, the collection represented the last great concentration of paintings and calligraphies still available outside China.

The second gift was presented by Belle Linsky, founder and partner with her late husband, Jack, of the stationery company, Swingline Inc. During 40 years of collecting, the Linskys amassed Old Masters, French furniture, porcelains, bronzes, and Renaissance jewelry, all of consistently high quality and thought to be worth at least $60 million. Mrs. Linsky chose the Met in preference to other American museums eager to acquire her collection, in part at least, because she is a lifelong New Yorker. She stipulated that the collection would go elsewhere were the museum to deaccession or place in storage any part of it. It is to be exhibited in specially designed small rooms to simulate a private collection.

An unexpected gift came to the Met from the estate of the late Scofield Thayer (1890–1982), editor from 1919 to 1925 of the avant-garde New York literary magazine *The Dial.* In the 1920s he started collecting Picasso, Matisse, Braque, and other French painters as well as the Norwegian Edvard Munch and the Austrians Gustav Klimt and Egon Schiele, the latter three unknown in the United States at that time. The collection consists of 450 works, bulk drawings, lithographs, and watercolors. It had been exhibited for years at the art museum in Worcester, MA, Thayer's native city.

New York's Metropolitan Museum presented remarkable and little-known treasures of the art

The $18 million Michael C. Rockefeller Wing at the Metropolitan Museum of Art, which opened in February 1982, is devoted to the display of some 2,000 objects of primitive art from Africa, the Pacific Islands, and the Americas.

of Central Asia, dating from the 6th to the 10th centuries. The show, "Along the Ancient Silk Routes: Central Asian Art from the West Berlin State Museums," was on loan to the museum. The Museum für Indische Kunst in West Berlin acquired these relics of a lost culture from two German archeologists who discovered them in the early years of the 20th century. The desert area enclosed by high mountains, now Chinese Turkestan, was once the scene of lively traffic between Asia Minor and China and also between India and China. The exchange that took place in the area involved not only silk and other commodities but also religion and culture. During the first century missionaries from India brought Buddhism to the area; it remained the dominant religion until Islam was introduced in the region about 1000 and the flourishing cities and temples were destroyed. The treasures were buried by sand and, except for the local inhabitants who despoiled them of what could be reached, remained unknown until Europeans discovered them about the turn of the 20th century. The installation at the Met was admired for its success in displaying the beautiful objects, mainly pieces of sculpture and frescos, in settings painted and lighted to simulate the caves in which many of them were originally.

London was the site of an eight-month Festival of India, probably the largest such manifestation in honor of a country by another country. The program consisted of some 20 exhibitions of Indian culture. At the Hayward Gallery a most extraordinary show, "In the Image of Man," brought together 480 objects, mostly sculpture and painting from 53 Indian collections, including provincial and site museums rarely accessible to the average tourist, and from English museums. At the same time, the Tate showed modern paintings; the Victoria and Albert Museum displayed "The Indian Heritage: Court Life and the Arts under Mughal Rule, 1500–1850"; and the British Library featured "The Art of the Book in India." Private galleries and stores also joined in showing Indian products.

A Forgery? A painting at the Metropolitan Museum was publicly called a fake, giving rise to the cause célèbre of the year. The authenticity of *The Fortune Teller* had already been questioned by some art scholars. It had been acquired by the Metropolitan in 1960 for $675,000 and was attributed to the 17th century French painter Georges de la Tour, whose paintings are relatively rare and highly valued. The painting was considered a fake on the basis of such details as the clumsy drawing of some figures and the anachronistic parts of some costumes. In the spring these objections reached a wider public when the CBS broadcast *60 Minutes* aired them without, according to the museum, giving the opposite view sufficient consideration. The uproar was given much press publicity, and it seemed that the Metropolitan would take the case to court. However, in the end, the publicity

National Gallery of Art, Washington, DC

"Saint Martin and the Beggar" was featured at the "El Greco of Toledo" show in Washington, Toledo, and Dallas.

was used to advertise an exhibition at the Met, "France in the Golden Age: 17th Century French Paintings in American Collections," in which this painting was one of the central pieces.

Exhibits. There were several important exhibitions during the year which were shown in cities across the United States but, for one reason or another, not in New York. For the first time a major exhibition of Spanish masterpieces was arranged. "El Greco of Toledo" was hailed as a "once-in-a-lifetime" experience. In return for the loan to Spain in 1981 of about 30 paintings from U.S. museums, many of El Greco's paintings, never before exhibited outside Spain, were permitted to form part of the show. It opened at the National Gallery in Washington and continued to the Toledo (OH) Museum of Art and the Dallas Museum of Fine Arts. Also opening in Washington was "Dutch Paintings from the Mauritshuis." The exhibit of 40 paintings was a part of the celebration of 200 years of diplomatic relations between the United States and the Netherlands. It included such masterpieces as the *Head of a Girl* by Jan Vermeer. The exhibition was to continue to the Kimball Art Museum in Fort Worth, the Chicago Art Institute, and the Los Angeles County Art Museum.

Another exhibition planned with the cooperation of the Dutch was "De Stijl: 1917–1931, Visions of Utopia." A definitive survey of the Dutch avant-garde movement, it was organized by the Walker Art Center in Minneapolis and shown there and at the Hirshhorn Museum in Washington, as well as at two museums in the Netherlands from which many of the works exhibited had been loaned. The movement known as "De Stijl" embraced architecture, furniture, photography, typography, and industrial design, as well as painting and sculpture, and it profoundly influenced the art and culture of the 20th century. Its most famous exponents were Piet Mondrian and Theo van Doesburg.

American Artists. The centenary of the birth of George Bellows was observed by a display of 65 prints and 12 paintings at the Met. Although he was only 43 when he died, he founded the "Ashcan School" and was an influential force in American painting. His subjects come from everyday life and are portrayed with great realism.

A four-wall panorama of American life by Thomas Benton was sold by the New School for Social Research in New York, for which it had been painted in 1931. Called "among the pioneering mural paintings in America," the panels were in need of attention and were sold as much to preserve them as for the sake of endowment funds. They were sold to a dealer who promised to keep them as a group.

The Whitney Museum was in danger of losing the popular Calder composition *The Cir-cus,* lent to it by the artist in 1970. It is a collection of 50 wire and cloth sculptures begun in the 1920s, constituting a troupe of performers and animals and housed in a large Plexiglas cage in the lobby of the museum. After Calder's death in 1976, the complicated tax situation of his estate caused the executors to order the sale of the work for $1.25 million. In a 15-day campaign to help the Whitney buy the collection, donors rallied to make it possible for the group to stay in the place the artist himself had chosen for it.

Isamu Noguchi's spectacular 17-ft- (5.2-m-) long, 1,600-lb (725.8-kg) aluminum rhomboid, commissioned in 1975 to hang point down in the lobby of the New York headquarters of the Bank of Tokyo, had to be removed on the grounds that it frightened both employees and public. Since 1980 it has been lying in pieces in storage. The city of Jacksonville, FL, expressed interest in having it set up as part of its new convention center. Noguchi refused because moving it would violate his intentions. He strongly supports a bill introduced in the New York State Assembly to protect works of art from alteration, defacement, mutilation, or other modification after they are sold. Noguchi's life-long contribution to the arts was recognized with the award of the Edward MacDowell Medal for 1982.

Finally, the American painter Jackson Pollock was given a comprehensive showing at the Beaubourg in Paris. The show ranged from a self-portrait done when the artist was in his twenties to his drippings in the 1950s. This was the first large Pollock show in Paris since one in 1951, which was not well received.

See also CANADA—The Arts; GREAT BRITAIN—The Arts.

ISA RAGUSA
Princeton University

"De Stijl: 1917–1931, Visions of Utopia" was presented in Minneapolis and Washington as well as in the Netherlands.

Courtesy, Walker Art Center

ASIA

The year 1982 was one of relative respite from Asia's all too frequent violence. Only one coup d'etat took place—that of army chief Gen. Hossein Mohammed Ershad in Bangladesh—while largely political maneuvering to influence future change occurred elsewhere on the continent. Japan's government underwent a peaceful change late in the year.

Internationally abetted warfare continued in Afghanistan, Cambodia, and Burma, however, and a Muslim separatist uprising persisted in the southern Philippines. But the scope of the violence was on a more modest scale than it had been in most years of the second half of the 20th century in Asia.

Spotlight on China. No country in Asia faced more difficult choices in 1982 than did China. Deng Xiaoping, top man in the Politburo and chairman of a new "advisory commission," sought continued reversal of policies of the last years of the late Mao Zedong.

The September session of the 12th congress of the Communist Party was expected to result in the retirement of several major aging political figures. This did not occur to the extent anticipated, partly because of persisting opposition to Deng within the People's Liberation Army. Mao's intended successor, Hua Guofeng, was dropped from the Politburo, however, and the power of Deng allies Hu Yaobang (party chairman) and Zhao Ziyang (premier) was strengthened.

Externally, China faced several choices involving the United States, the USSR, Vietnam, North Korea, and Hong Kong. Critical of American arms sales to Taiwan, China nonetheless joined the United States on August 17 in a vague communiqué stating that Peking would seek only peaceful reunification with Taiwan and that Washington would eventually end its weapons supply to Taipei.

Soviet leader Leonid Brezhnev, seeking to capitalize on Sino-U.S. differences, called for renewed Moscow-Peking talks. The talks took place for the first time in three years, on a low level, in October. Defense Minister Geng Biao stated, however, that improved relations were not possible as long as Soviet troops remained in Afghanistan and Vietnamese forces were in Cambodia. China's Foreign Minister Huang Hua, who was subsequently replaced, held talks with the new Soviet leader, Yuri Andropov, and Foreign Minister Andrei Gromyko following Brezhnev's funeral in November.

Tension increased along the Sino-Vietnamese border during the year, while China lavishly hosted North Korean leader Kim Il-Sung, who publicly endorsed Chinese support of anti-Vietnamese (and anti-Soviet) rebels in Cambodia. British Prime Minister Thatcher and Deng Xiaoping agreed to start talks on Hong Kong, Britain's lease of which will expire in 1997.

The Cambodian Coalition. The key to China's Southeast Asia policy was the Vietnamese alliance with the USSR. The Vietnamese occupation of Cambodia very much concerned China, which was most disturbed by the weak military showing of the Peking-aided anti-Vietnamese Khmer Rouge forces in early 1982. The insurgents' weakness also troubled Vietnam's anti-Communist Southeast Asian neighbors, the five member states of the Association of Southeast Asian Nations (ASEAN), as well as Burma.

China and the ASEAN governments combined diplomatic efforts to induce previously opposed anti-Vietnamese (Communist and anti-Communist) Cambodian elements to form a new political coalition against the Hanoi-sponsored Phnom Penh regime. Prince Norodom Sihanouk became president of the Coalition Government of Democratic Cambodia, set up in July. Communist Khieu Samphan of the Khmer Rouge became vice-president, and anti-Communist Son Sann became premier. The military arm of the coalition government—the Khmer People's National Liberation Front, estimated to number 9,000 troops—took the initiative against Vietnamese forces in the second half of the year (as contrasted with the Khmer Rouge's largely defensive activity of early 1982).

The Vietnamese Response. Vietnam's reaction to Chinese-ASEAN-rebel Cambodian cooperation lacked the finesse of past Hanoi diplomacy. The Vietnamese midyear claim to have withdrawn some of their troops from Cambodia was disputed by the United States and other countries. Vietnam's foreign minister, Nguyen Co Thach, visiting ASEAN countries and India, made a number of diplomatic mistakes. In Southeast Asia, he threatened to grant bases to the USSR in Vietnam and to support insurgent movements in ASEAN lands. And in India he openly attacked China.

Internally, relations with the USSR also appeared to be an issue, as three key officials associated with a pro-Soviet posture were dropped from the Politburo.

With its northern defense along the Chinese border strengthened, however, the Vietnamese government prepared at year's end to step up its military activity in Cambodia.

Soviets on the Defensive. The USSR was very much on the defensive in Asia in 1982. The Soviet military effort to strengthen the position of puppet President Babrak Karmal in Afghanistan registered some successes, particularly the pacification of the Panjsher valley in midyear. But the cost was high: fresh troops had to be dispatched to Afghanistan; there were reports of Soviet military defections; desertions of Afghan government soldiers to the anti-Communist resistance increased; and ailing Babrak Karmal was rumored to be increasingly at odds with Moscow. The diplomatic efforts of UN Secretary-General Javier Pérez de Cuellar to encourage Soviet leader Brezhnev to reduce the USSR's military

China's Premier Zhao Ziyang (left) confers with Japan's Prime Minister Zenko Suzuki in Tokyo in June.

presence in Afghanistan hardly enhanced Moscow's prestige in Asia.

Even though the USSR expanded its military presence at the former U.S. base at Cam Ranh Bay in Vietnam, supporters of Moscow in the Soviet-allied Southeast Asian government lost influence during the year. And friendly India was visibly offended when the Soviet defense minister, Dmitri Ustinov, in response to an invitation extended before Prime Minister Gandhi's return to power, traveled to New Delhi with an excessively visible 40-man delegation, including the heads of the Soviet Air Force and Navy.

The Anti-Communists Cooperate. The strongest regional group in all Asia, ASEAN, observed its 15th anniversary in 1982, and its political importance was never more evident. Each of the ASEAN members—Indonesia, Thailand, Singapore, Malaysia, and the Philippines—played a part in the negotiation and material support of the new anti-Vietnamese coalition front in Cambodia.

Anti-Communist South Korean President Chun Doo Hwan, hosting Australian Premier Malcolm Fraser, called for a "Pacific community" meeting of the leaders of the lands on both sides of the world's largest ocean. And talk of greater cooperation among the seven South Asian countries also continued but made little progress, primarily because of fear that India's size would result in domination of its partners, but also because of persisting Indo-Pakistani differences.

America Seeks Friends. President Ronald Reagan sought to widen the circle of U.S. friends in

Asia as Vice-President Bush traveled to that continent and several of the continent's foremost figures visited Washington.

Prime Minister Indira Gandhi, who also visited Moscow and London, had her own purposes in traveling to Washington, not least of all to demonstrate the Indian government's intention to be viewed as genuinely neutral (and not as an excessive partisan of the USSR). Mrs. Gandhi, who discussed Afghanistan with both U.S. and Soviet leaders, also sought to mend fences with neighbors China and Pakistan. The Indian and Pakistani leaders met in November. In April the Indian leader also visited Saudi Arabia.

Another visitor to both the United States and Saudi Arabia was Philippine President Ferdinand Marcos. Aging and ailing, Marcos sought Saudi counsel in ending the Muslim uprising in the southern Philippines, as well as a display of American friendship to bolster his sagging popularity at home.

Other ASEAN leaders hosted by Washington were Singapore's Premier Lee Kuan Yew and Indonesia's President Suharto, whose world tour took him also to Japan, South Korea, and Spain— all strong anti-Communist lands. Suharto's government party (called Golkar) scored a strong, if government-aided, electoral victory in May.

U.S.-Japanese ties continued to be close, although not without serious problems. Japan agreed to increase its air and naval capabilities, but trade differences and private Japanese computer espionage hurt relations.

RICHARD BUTWELL
The University of South Dakota

ASTRONOMY

The astronomical event that most captured the public's attention in 1982 was the grand "alignment" of all nine planets. Enormous press coverage was sparked by the predictions of John R. Gribbin and Stephen H. Plagemann that this situation would result in a rash of earthquakes and other natural disasters. Astrologers, other pseudoscientists, and doomsayers dominated the electronic media, at the expense of astronomers who tried to assure the public that nothing unusual would happen. As it turned out, March 10th passed without worldwide calamity; in doing so it swept away the bogus idea outlined in the 1974 Gribbin-Plagemann book *The Jupiter Effect*.

Venus. A truly significant event was the arrival on Venus of two Soviet space probes, Venera 13 and 14. They landed on March 1 and 5, respectively, and returned a cornucopia of data. Their on-board cameras recorded mainly rocky plains, sometimes marked by outcrops, and soil-like patches. There was also evidence for chemical erosion, which would be expected from Venus' hot and corrosive atmosphere.

The historic portion of these missions, however, involved the first detailed sampling of the planet's crustal chemistry. It seems that the surface of Venus consists of basalts, rocks formed by heat and extruded from the interior. (The earth's ocean floor is covered with similar material.) This finding suggests that volcanic activity may be a major molding force on our sister planet.

Comets. In August 1979, a military satellite recorded the first instance of a comet crashing into the sun. In 1982 we learned of two more comets that probably met similar fates, in January and July of 1981. Again, satellite observations were needed. According to Herbert Gursky of the U.S. Naval Research Laboratory, it now appears that several comets a year may strike the sun. These are probably small bodies whose presence cannot be readily detected by ground-based observers.

Stars. Since the 17th century the sun has been known to rotate in about 25 days. And since the 19th century the number of spots on the sun has been known to change in an 11-year cycle. Now astronomers have proved, not surprisingly, that stars akin to the sun exhibit properties similar to it.

By measuring the amount of light emitted by calcium atoms in these stars' atmospheres, a team of American astronomers has determined that these luminaries rotate in 12 to 48 days. Arthur Vaughan of Mount Wilson and Las Campanas Observatories and his colleagues conclude that rotation periods are slower among relatively older stars as well as those that are relatively less massive. Starspot cycles were found to span 5 to 12 years.

X-ray Bursters. Among the numerous X-ray sources in our galaxy, a few repeatedly undergo outbursts in which their luminosity increases tenfold within a second or so. Most astronomers have long believed these bursters to be binary systems containing a collapsed object, such as a neutron star, and a rather ordinary stellar companion. The hitch was that no binary X-ray burster had even been discovered.

This situation changed in January 1982, when a team, headed by Stewart Boyer of the University of California, announced the binary nature of 4U 1915−05, an X-ray burster in the constellation of Aquila. Dimmings in the system's X-ray emission at 50-minute intervals could be readily interpreted as eclipses of the neutron star by a bulge of matter on a disk surrounding it. This bulge is produced by matter drawn from the companion; its impact on the disk causes the X-ray emission.

Star Death. Recent spectroscopic observations of Eta Carinae, a star in the southern constellation of the Ship's Keel, indicate that it is old. And because of the star's huge mass, perhaps more than 100 suns, it will continue to age rap-

The longest lunar eclipse since 1736 was visible in the Western Hemisphere on July 6, 1982. Astronomers expressed the belief that a cloud of volcanic dust surrounding the earth caused the eclipse's rich red and orange color. In the photographs, below, the approximate Eastern daylight times are shown as the moon passes into the earth's shadow.

UPI

1:41 A.M.   2:00 A.M.   2:15 A.M.   2:35 A.M.

idly. Furthermore, this bulk will not allow Eta Carinae to die peacefully. Nolan Walborn of the NASA-Goddard Space Flight Center and his co-workers predict that within the next several thousand years this star will explode as a supernova. At that time it will temporarily outshine everything in the sky except the sun and moon.

Milky Way. Stunning increases in our ability to "see" through the dense clouds of dust and gas that lie between the earth and the center of our galaxy have yielded a pretty consistent picture of the object that resides there. Radio, infrared, X-ray, and gamma-ray observations all suggest the presence of a black hole with a mass of several million suns. Of course, we can never see the black hole itself, for no radiation can escape its intense gravitational pull. But we can observe the hole's effects on gas in its vicinity, as well as the high-energy radiation emitted by the matter it consumes.

How big is this "pivot" around which our galaxy spins? According to Robert Brown of the U.S. National Radio Astronomy Observatory, it is less than a light-day in diameter. Thus, the core of the Milky Way spans at most only about a hundred millionth the diameter of the galaxy—the width of a period at the end of a 10-mile-long sentence.

Quasars. These apparently starlike and enormously energetic objects have been an astronomical bugaboo since their discovery in 1963. Fundamental questions concern whether the quasars lie at enormous distances and, if so, how their power is generated. During recent years, evidence has been accumulating that quasars are nothing more than the highly luminous and compact cores of distant "active" galaxies.

In 1981 some quasars were shown to be surrounded by a fuzzy envelope, as a typical galaxy would be. And in 1982 T. Boroson and J. Oke at Palomar Observatory found that the envelope of at least one object (called "3C 48") is composed of stars, just like our Milky Way. Furthermore, these stars are young—they must have formed within the last billion years. What kind of galaxy is 3C 48? It appears to be a superbright spiral, some 100 times more luminous than our galaxy.

Clusters of Galaxies. It has long been known that galaxies prefer to occur in clusters. More recently, it has been proved that these huge assemblages themselves tend to congregate in superclusters.

Our Milky Way is part of a cluster (albeit a mini one with only 30-odd members). In 1982 R. Tully of the University of Hawaii determined that this so-called Local Group is situated on the outskirts of a supercluster, whose center lies some 50 million light-years away in the constellation of Virgo. At least a half dozen clusters of galaxies make up this huge array.

Cosmology. One major problem confronting cosmologists today is to explain the clumpy structure of the universe. A basic tenet, the so-called cosmological principle, says that the universe should be homogeneous on the largest scale. Thus, galaxies and clusters of galaxies must be irrelevant eddies.

But what to make of a hole in the heavens some third of a billion light-years across? Although this void, discovered by Robert Kirschner of the University of Michigan and his colleagues, is the largest yet known, its volume still encompasses only a hundred thousandth of the universe today. This is sufficiently large to have resulted from local variations in the density of the early universe, but it is still too small to cause trouble for the cosmological principle.

LEIF J. ROBINSON, *"Sky and Telescope"*

ATLANTA

On Jan. 4, 1982, Andrew Young, former U.S. congressman and ambassador to the United Nations, was sworn in as Atlanta's 55th mayor. A week later the city came to a standstill when 5 inches (12.7 cm) of snow and ice fell during the afternoon rush hour. National Guard troops were mobilized to unsnarl 10,000 vehicles stranded in the "snow jam 82."

Williams Trial. Wayne B. Williams, a 23-year-old aspiring talent scout, was found guilty of and sentenced to two consecutive life prison terms for the murders of Nathaniel Cater and Jimmy Lee Payne, the last of 28 young blacks slain in a two-year period in Atlanta. Prosecutors were allowed to introduce evidence from ten of these cases to establish a pattern that linked Williams to the victims by bloodstains, witnesses, and especially carpet fibers found on the bodies. Since investigators believed that Williams was responsible for 24 of the murders, these cases were closed and a special task force was disbanded. After black leaders protested the decision, the police commissioner established a new task force to investigate all homicides.

Gun Law. Kennesaw, a small suburb of Atlanta, made national headlines when its city council passed an ordinance requiring every head of a household to own and "maintain a firearm and ammunition."

Reapportionment. A three-judge federal court ruled that Georgia's new legislative remap plan split the city's black community and violated the 1965 Voting Rights Act. In a special assembly session, state legislators provided for a revised 65% black majority 5th district, including Atlanta, which was approved by the federal court. State officials then appealed the case to the U.S. Supreme Court. (*See also* GEORGIA.)

Baseball. Atlanta baseball fans were treated to an exciting season. Under new manager Joe Torre, the Braves got off to an excellent start and finished first in the Western Division. They lost in the play-offs, however, to St. Louis.

KAY BECK, *Georgia State University*

AUSTRALIA

The Australian National Gallery, designed by Colin Madigan and costing A$62,000,000,000, officially opened October 12.

In Malcolm Fraser's seventh year as prime minister, Australia faced its most severe and intractable economic problems since the 1930s. The sharp setback reflected both world recession and "loss of competitiveness" associated with wage increases stemming from premature hopes of boom in minerals and energy resources. Inflation (above 10%), widespread drought, and record interest rates (easing toward year-end) went with higher unemployment (6–8% range), indifferent industrial output, and an adverse balance of trade. The government responded to official inquiries that revealed widespread tax dodging with legislation to enable retroactive tax collection.

A mood of concern and irritation was seen in heightened criticism of the ruling Liberal-National Party (L-NP) coalition. The Australian Labor Party (ALP) and its leader, Bill Hayden, directed barbs against Fraser's leadership style and economic policies as well as the government's administrative competence and fairness in the handling of such overall issues as taxation. Hayden's attacks—the most frequent, wide-ranging, bitter, and intense seen in years—gained generous media coverage. Innuendo, invective, and accusation in parliamentary attacks on individuals led both to flaring headlines and to some media reaction cautioning against politically motivated smearing.

Meanwhile, official investigations revealed instances of union-linked crime and resulted in some indictments.

Politics. Although possessing a sound majority in the House of Representatives, Fraser faced a Senate in which ALP and minor elements could combine to thwart his measures. In fact the government secured passage of the bulk of its legislation program, with nongovernment senators moving cautiously in order to avoid precipitating a general election.

In April differences between Fraser and former Cabinet minister Andrew Peacock resulted in a Liberal Party leadership challenge that Fraser turned back comfortably. With the issue defused, the Liberals closed ranks. Peacock rejoined the ministry in October following the resignation of Sir Philip Lynch. Fraser overcame some policy divergence within the party, and the Liberals remained united behind Fraser in spite of continued media attacks against him. Opinion polls suggested that popular support for the government had not fallen seriously.

The ALP also underwent a leadership battle when Bob Hawke's supporters pressed a party vote. Hayden retained the leadership on July 16, after which personal differences appeared to subside; but most observers believed the highly publicized clash revived serious factionalism within the ALP involving Hawke's right-wing supporters and the "socialist left" group whose votes Hayden held. Earlier the ALP had gained electoral victory in Victoria, the second most populous state, after 27 years in which the Liberals held uninterrupted power.

While economic issues held the spotlight, nuclear concerns were kept alive by demonstrators and unionists. The future of uranium mining, the proposed establishment of an enrichment facility (endorsed by the government in October), and the dangers of nuclear war were key issues. While groups within the ALP promoted an antinuclear stand, the national party, fearful of providing Fraser with a ready-made electoral issue, opted for a cautious approach and at a national conference in June adopted ambivalent policies. Similarly, ALP support of the U.S.-Australian alliance was qualified. In November, Fraser underwent surgery to relieve a painful back ailment. This put an end to speculation about an early election.

Environmental concerns—especially related to dam building and wilderness preservation—also remained at the fore.

The Economy. By midyear the recession was widely felt, with the effects of a widespread drought adding to a slack economy and lower prices of export commodities. Drift of the Australian dollar (A$) to a record low point (A$1=U.S.$0.95) failed to correct an adverse balance of trade; only an unprecedented capital inflow maintained the overall balance of payments and overseas reserves. Housing construction was variable, but business fixed-investment showed good growth. Depressed prices for minerals, combined with higher labor costs, resulted in reversals for mining companies; the corporate sector generally suffered a reduction in profitability. Wage increases and the spread of reduced hours of work led to markedly higher production costs. Demand for labor continued to wane. In the 12 months to June 30, average earnings rose sharply: a 17.4% rise in total male earnings to an average of A$325 per week and a 5% rise in female weekly earnings to A$262.50.

The budget presented in August represented a retreat from the government's aim of a reduced public sector and lessened tax burden. Features included personal income tax cuts by way of changes in the tax scales and rebates and some tax easing for industry, matched by increased consumer taxes; social welfare assistances (including family allowances and other benefits) rose; and capital works expenditure was increased. Total outlays showed a 14% rise (3% in real terms), with 11.3% higher receipts, resulting in a lift in the overall deficit to A$1,674,000,000.

Official estimates pointed to a considerable decline in the volume of rural output. Farm spokesmen foretold of a precipitate fall in returns to farmers. At Australian wool auctions, weakness in demand resulted in heavy purchases by the price-support authority, the Australian Wool Corporation, while trade buyers were reported to be virtually out of the market at some sales. Important resource finds included a vast new copper deposit in South Australia and extended reserves of oil and natural gas.

Defense and Foreign Affairs. The government signaled an increased defense presence in the eastern sector of the Indian Ocean with naval exercises involving warships and aircraft from Australia, New Zealand, and the United States, and with the strengthening of Australian air units in Western Australia. A new air force base was opened in Darwin. Reports indicated that the U.S. Air Force was now seeking greater operational involvement with Australian units in the aim of protecting sea lanes and strengthening security resources in the area.

In August, Prime Minister Fraser visited Peking for discussions with China's leaders. An agreement provided for the two countries to work jointly on relations between rich and poor nations.

National Policy and Milestones. In October the government announced increased expenditure on its Antarctic division, with provision for the purchase of an Antarctic supply and science ship and construction of three runways (to take Hercules aircraft) in the Australian Antarctic Territory.

A national crime commission with sweeping powers to crack down on organized crime was announced following revelations by a temporary commission of widespread criminal conduct. A new Omega communications base completed the worldwide satellite network.

After 14 years of construction, the Australian National Gallery in Canberra was opened by Queen Elizabeth II in October. Described as showing "the total visual art history of the nation in painting, drawing, sculpture, furniture, ceramics, silver, and folk art in comprehensive displays," the gallery also "exhibits the art heritage of many other cultures, including those of the Australian Aborigines, the pre-Columbian Americas, and Australia's neighbors in Asia and the Pacific."

Research scientists in Adelaide announced that they are now able to design Very Large-Scale Integrated (VLSI) computer microchips for special purposes.

The 12th Commonwealth Games were held in Brisbane in October. Some 2,000 athletes from 45 nations took part. Australia, with fine performances from its women swimmers, collected 39 gold medals.

R. M. YOUNGER, *Australian Author*

AUSTRALIA • Information Highlights

Official Name: Commonwealth of Australia.
Location: Southwestern Pacific Ocean.
Area: 2,967,900 sq mi (7 686 861 km^2).
Population (1982 est.): 15,000,000.
Chief Cities (June 1980): Canberra, the capital, 245,-500; Sydney, 3,231,700; Melbourne, 2,759,700.
Government: *Head of state,* Elizabeth II, queen; represented by Sir Ninian Martin Stephens, governor-general (took office July 1982). *Head of government,* Malcolm Fraser, prime minister (took office Dec. 1975). *Legislature*—Parliament: Senate and House of Representatives.
Monetary Unit: Australian dollar (1.0688 A. dollars equals U.S.$1, Nov. 1, 1982).
Gross Domestic Product (1981 A.$): $148,235,000,-000.
Economic Indexes (1981): *Consumer Prices* (1970= 100), all items, 295.3; food, 296.4. Industrial production (1980, 1975=100), 111.
Foreign Trade (1981 U.S.$): Imports, $23,656,000,-000; exports, $21,664,000,000.

AUSTRIA

The year 1982 was characterized by political stability, as Austria faced the general elections to be held in the spring of 1983. At the same time the economy remained sluggish.

Foreign Affairs. On January 6, the Jewish Agency, the official Israeli agency overseeing the immigration of Soviet Jews to Israel, announced it would curtail its activity in Vienna because the Austrian government permitted other agencies to contact Soviet Jewish émigrés and persuade them to settle in countries other than Israel. In response, Chancellor Bruno Kreisky asserted the right of every person stepping on Austrian soil to emigrate to wherever he wished. As for the Polish refugees in Austria, it was announced on April 23 that the United States had promised to take 1,000 each month and that Canada would accept 1,500 by year's end.

Col. Muammar el-Qaddafi of Libya made an official visit to Austria on March 1–13. An Austrian-Libyan statement issued at the conclusion of the visit stressed agreement on the need for détente. A five-day official visit of President Rudolf Kirchschläger to the Soviet Union late in May led to a joint communiqué calling for increased efforts in the direction of détente, disarmament, and economic cooperation. On June 16–17, President François Mitterrand of France made an official visit to Vienna. In a joint declaration the two countries demanded that Israel respect UN resolutions calling for an immediate cease-fire and the withdrawal of Israeli troops from Lebanon.

On April 7 Austria banned military sales to Argentina at the time of the Falkland Islands crisis. A new law sponsored by both leading political parties provided that weapons could not be exported to "a country where repeated violations of human rights may lead to the risk that the exported arms could be used to oppress human rights." The government was required to issue an annual report showing to which countries weapons had been sold.

UPI

Austria's Foreign Minister Willibald Pahr gave a key speech at the UN special session on disarmament.

Economy. The gross domestic product (GDP) increased by only 0.7% in the first quarter of 1982, with an increase of 1.5% forecast for the year. It was estimated that unemployment would reach 3.6% in 1982. The inflation rate rose slightly but remained around 6%. Austria had a trade deficit of $5,200,000,000 in 1981, and the indications were that 1982 would bring only slight improvement. In February, Austrian banks announced a loan to the Soviet Union of $596.6 million over the next two years, at a low interest rate of 7.8%. The loans were intended to further exports to Russia but were not connected with the controversial pipeline being built from Siberia to Western Europe. Austria signed a 25-year agreement to buy 53,000,000,000 ft^3 (1,500,800,000 m^3) of gas annually from the Soviet Union.

Internal Events. The peace and antinuclear movement accelerated during the year, and an estimated 70,000 turned out for a rally in Vienna in May. A new Jewish Museum at Eisenstadt in Burgenland was opened, financed by the federal government and the nine provinces. On September 1, Lorin Maazel, until then conductor of the Cleveland orchestra, took over the post of manager and artistic director of the Vienna State Opera.

ERNEST C. HELMREICH, *Professor of History, emeritus, Bowdoin College*

AUSTRIA • Information Highlights

Official Name: Republic of Austria.
Location: Central Europe.
Area: 32,376 sq mi (83 653 km^2).
Population (1981 census): 7,559,440.
Chief Cities (1981 census): Vienna, the capital, 1,515,666; Graz 243,405; Linz, 197,962; Salzburg, 138,213.
Government: *Head of state,* Rudolf Kirchschläger, president (took office July 1974). *Head of government,* Bruno Kreisky, chancellor (took office April 1970). *Legislature*—Federal Assembly: Federal Council and National Council.
Monetary Unit: Schilling (17.63 schillings equal U.S.$1, Oct. 1982).
Gross National Product (1981 U.S.$): $65,500,000,000.
Economic Indexes (1981): *Consumer Prices* (1970=100), *all items,* 196.4; *food,* 180.2. *Industrial production* (1975=100), 112.
Foreign Trade (1981 U.S.$): *Imports,* $21,049,000,000; *exports,* $15,846,000,000.

AUTOMOBILES

The U.S. auto industry remained in the grip of a gnawing recession in 1982. Production of 1982 passenger car models plunged 22.4% from the 1981-model total as consumer resistance to high prices and interest rates, called "sticker shock," doomed forecasts of an upturn for the fourth consecutive year.

All five domestic automakers sustained deep production curtailments, raising the number of indefinitely laid-off auto workers above the 200,-000 mark. The squeeze on cash flow and profits caused by the drop in new-car sales induced the United Auto Workers (UAW) for the first time to renegotiate collective bargaining contracts with the Big Three and American Motors so that concessions in future wage and fringe benefits could ease producer labor costs.

By the end of September, the U.S. auto industry had built 5,177,833 cars bearing 1982 model designations. This fell sharply from the 1981-model count of 6,673,324 cars and was the lowest total since the 1950s, trailing even the 1961 volume of 5,407,256. By contrast, 9,526,024 cars were built as recently as the 1979 model run, second only to the record of 9,915,802 in 1973.

General Motors (GM) was hardest hit of the U.S. automakers during the 1982 run, producing nearly one million fewer cars than it did during 1981. The GM decline of 23.9% to 3,172,183 cars underscored continued sales weakness in the corporation's lowest priced models, although GM's full-size and intermediate series fared relatively well, as did the restyled Chevrolet Camaro and Pontiac Firebird sports coupes.

Although the Ford Escort subcompact was the No. 1 domestic nameplate in production and sales, Ford Motor Company as a whole suffered an 11.6% decline in 1982-model output, to 1,233,-864 cars. Ford's weaknesses were centered in the midsize and compact segments, which had not been redesigned in many years and lacked the front-wheel-drive feature of competitors.

Chrysler Corporation, still operating under federally guaranteed loans, incurred a 25.1% slide to 592,605 cars in the 1982 run. Higher-priced models, such as the New Yorker and new LeBaron convertible, scored modest sales upturns for Chrysler, but the financially plagued No. 3 automaker experienced setbacks in its volume of compacts and subcompacts and sold its tank plant for $450 million to raise operating cash.

The recession was felt severely at American Motors (AMC) and Volkswagen of America (VW). AMC, whose principal owner is the French automaker Renault, fell 45.2% in 1982, to 75,201 cars. The company counted on a revival in 1983 with the introduction of the Renault Alliance. VW production of Rabbit subcompacts at its New Stanton, PA, plant tumbled 42.1% to 103,980 units and the subsidiary of Volkswagenwerk in West Germany postponed plans to add a

second U.S. assembly facility at Sterling Heights, MI.

Truck sales, often a harbinger of a turnaround in cars, provided a bright spot for the U.S. industry. The Big Three unveiled domestic mini-compact pickup trucks early in 1982, challenging Japanese imports for the first time, and truck production rose 18.7% to 1,521,365 units in the first nine months of 1982. The domestic junior-edition pickups were the Chevrolet S-10, GMC S-15, Ford Ranger, and Dodge Rampage.

GM's Chevrolet division barely exceeded the one million mark in 1982-model production, finishing with 1,054,481 cars. Ford division assembled 765,429 cars of 1982 vintage, of which 334,-850 were Escorts. Chevrolet's Chevette was second to Escort with 232,957 completions. Buick outproduced Oldsmobile for third place among domestic automakers, 725,207 to 694,229. Pontiac's top-volume marque was the Firebird at 116,219, while the Camaro finished second to the Chevrolet Chevette with 189,211. Four GM divisions introduced front-wheel-drive intermediate "A-cars" in 1982—the Chevrolet Celebrity, Pontiac 6000, Buick Century, and Oldsmobile Ciera—but sales fell far short of expectations.

The 1983 Models. With gasoline prices stabilized, performance replaced fuel efficiency as a primary 1983-model feature. Full-size body styles held up well in sales throughout the recession-plagued 1982-model year, prompting several domestic manufacturers to add "upscale" series or body styles for 1983. Each U.S. automaker was required to meet a federal Corporate Average Fuel Economy (CAFE) of 26 miles per gallon on its 1983-model fleet.

WORLD MOTOR VEHICLE DATA, 1981

Country	Passenger Car Production	Truck and Bus Production	Motor Vehicle Registrations
Argentina	139,428	32,922	4,176,131
Australia	351,570	40,044	7,441,600
Austria	6,987	7,923	2,455,144
Belgium	216,055	41,401	3,513,239
Brazil	406,004	373,832	10,159,942
Canada	803,117	519,663	13,210,810
Czechoslovakia	181,785	46,268	2,644,333
France	2,611,864	407,506	21,720,500
East Germany	178,000	40,000	3,146,129
West Germany	3,577,807*	319,200	24,791,850
Hungary	—	13,788	1,158,800
India	42,106	106,781	1,194,533
Italy	1,257,340	176,403	19,120,890
Japan	6,974,131	4,205,831	37,856,174
Korea, S.	68,760	64,324	527,729
Mexico	355,497	241,621	4,847,383
Netherlands	76,125	11,878	4,647,000
Poland	244,600	48,200	3,067,167
Portugal	—	98	1,205,000
Rumania	76,000	51,000	368,000
Spain	855,325	132,149	8,937,400
Sweden	258,261	55,286	3,077,323
Switzerland	—	1,178	2,564,926
United Kingdom	954,650	229,555	17,357,746
United States	6,253,138	1,682,893	155,889,692†
USSR	1,324,000	868,600	15,508,600
Yugoslavia	257,000	31,000	2,654,436
Total	27,469,550	9,749,344	411,112,525‡

* Includes 296,572 micro-buses. † U.S. total includes 121,723,-650 cars and 34,166,042 trucks and buses. ‡ World total includes 320,539,030 cars and 90,573,495 trucks and buses, of which 27,-870,138 vehicles are from nonproducing countries not shown above. Source: Motor Vehicle Manufacturers Association of the United States, Inc.

UPI

UPI

Although 1982 was a poor year for auto production, it did mark the return of the convertible. For the first time in nine years, the streamlined Mustang line included such a model. In September, Paul Tippett, chairman of the American Motors Corp., presented the Renault Alliance, the result of the AMC-Renault partnership.

The most dramatic departures in styling appeared on the 1983 Ford Thunderbird, Mercury Cougar, and Chevrolet Corvette. Rounded "aerodynamic" lines marked a turnaway from the boxy U.S. styling of the 1970s and early 1980s. Ford Motor Company also planned to draw on its new styling posture for Ford Tempo and Mercury Topaz compacts, due for introduction in the spring of 1983. New "upscale" entries included the Pontiac 6000 STE four-door sedan, Buick T-Types in five series, Dodge 600, and Chrysler E-Class and Town & Country convertible. The Chevrolet Cavalier, Ford Mustang, and Buick Riviera series also added convertibles.

Two foreign-headquartered automakers joined VW in production of U.S. cars. Renault teamed up with AMC for assembly at Kenosha, WI, of the Renault Alliance subcompact, a car derived from the Renault 9. The Honda Accord four-door sedan, previously imported from Japan, was put into production by American Honda at a new plant in Marysville, OH. Toyota, Japan's No. 1 auto builder, was nego-

tiating with GM on joint-venture production of a new Toyota subcompact in California. Nissan of Japan scheduled a late-1983 launch of pickup truck output at a new plant in Smyrna, TN.

The Imports. The second year of voluntary export restraints imposed by the Japanese government effectively reduced imported car sales in the United States by 9.1% in the first nine months of 1982, to 1,682,441 cars. However, while sales of the five highest-volume Japanese car imports fell, U.S. demand for most European sedans and sports coupes rose to record or near-record levels.

Toyota retained top position among U.S. imports, with 400,775 car sales in the period January-September 1982. Nissan/Datsun was second at 355,351; Honda third at 279,511; Mazda fourth at 121,480, and Subaru fifth at 111,459. A new entrant in the American market from Japan in late 1982 was Mitsubishi, which set up its own importing organization in addition to supplying "captive" cars for Chrysler marketing activities. MAYNARD M. GORDON, *"Motor News Analysis"*

BANGLADESH

Consistent with its history of political instability, Bangladesh suffered yet another military coup on March 24, 1982. Army Chief Lt.-Gen. Hossein Mohammed Ershad seized power, established martial law, appointed former Supreme Court judge Abul Fazal Mohammad Ahsanuddin Choudhury as figurehead president, and assumed the roles of chief martial law administrator and chief executive.

The bloodless coup ended the weak and ineffective civilian regime headed by septuagenarian President Abdus Sattar. Sattar, who had succeeded to power when Ziaur Rahman was assassinated in May 1981, was elected president in November 1981, but proved unable to stem public and military criticism of governmental corruption and inefficiency. Early in 1982, Sattar shuffled cabinets and created a National Security Council in response to army demands. Nevertheless, Ershad proceeded with his coup.

Following the military takeover, Ershad had several hundred former public officials arrested, most of them connected with Sattar's Bangladesh National Party, and charged them with corruption. He promised to hold general elections and to return Bangladesh to democratic rule "within two years." In July, Ershad extended by one year the terms of office of the country's 4,472 union parishads, or village-level committees, which are intended to play an important role in development activities.

Economic Developments. Economic growth in Bangladesh declined during the year. The gross domestic product in fiscal 1982 was estimated to have grown by a mere 0.1%, compared with 6.1% during the previous year. During the same period, the cost of living increased by nearly 20%. Externally, increased costs for imports, particularly for petroleum, were a major factor. Another problem was the declining price of jute.

Internally, drought resulted in a 5% shortfall in the production of food grains. Per capita income declined by 2.2% in fiscal 1982 after having risen 3.5% the previous year.

Wide World

Lt. Gen. Hossein Mohammed Ershad.

Among the new military regime's stated economic goals were a 7% growth rate in fiscal year 1983, the prevention of waste in the public sector, encouragement of private investment, self-sufficiency in food, and effective control of population growth. In presenting the fiscal 1983 budget in July, Finance Minister A.M.A. Muhith called for a "bold effort toward an increase in domestic savings and resources."

This approach is clearly one which an elected government would have found difficult to implement. Development spending was cut, as were energy and food subsidies. At the same time, taxes were increased. As in neighboring India, there was a shift from import substitution to export promotion as a strategy for improving the adverse balance of payments. The economic policies of the new government appeared generally in agreement with advice from the World Bank and other major donors of foreign aid, which continued to provide much of Bangladesh's development funds.

Foreign Relations. Relations between India and Bangladesh improved. The major issue continued to be the equitable distribution of river waters flowing from India into Bangladesh. The agreement that governed the allocation of Ganges water between the two countries from 1977 until Nov. 4, 1982, was replaced with an interim agreement as negotiators from both sides attempted to formulate a longer-term solution. A series of high-level diplomatic exchanges, including a summit meeting in New Delhi between General Ershad and Indian Prime Minister Indira Gandhi, helped to reduce tensions.

Under General Ershad, Bangladesh attempted to strengthen ties with Saudi Arabia and China. It also continued to play an active role in the United Nations, in the Nonaligned Movement, and in the South Asia Regional Forum.

WILLIAM L. RICHTER, *Kansas State University*

BANGLADESH · Information Highlights

Official Name: People's Republic of Bangladesh.
Location: South Asia.
Area: 55,126 sq mi (142 776 km²).
Population (1981 census): 87,052,024.
Chief Cities (1974 census): Dacca, the capital, 1,679,-572; Chittagong, 889,760; Khulna, 437,304.
Government: *Head of state,* Abul Fazal Mohammad Ahsanuddin Choudhury, president (sworn in March 27, 1982). *Head of government,* Hossein Mohammed Ershad, chief executive (assumed power March 24, 1982).
Monetary Unit: Taka (21.549 taka equal U.S.$1, March 1982).
Gross National Product (1980 U.S.$): $10,400,000,-000.
Economic Index (1980): *Consumer Prices* (1972= 100), *all items,* 401.6; *food,* 383.4.
Foreign Trade (1980 U.S.$): *Imports,* $2,616,000,-000; *exports,* $789,000,000.

BANKING

The year 1982 brought many changes to the U.S. banking industry.

On the legislative side, the key development was a new federal banking law which provides aid for the troubled savings and loans industry through governmental infusions of capital when needed and through new powers to diversify into business lending. The new law was necessitated by the heavy losses that many thrift institutions (thrifts) experienced during the year and the need to rescue many thrifts through merger, in many instances with aid from the federal insurance agencies. Adding to the problems of thrifts and the banks was the continued growth of money market funds, which grew to more than $225,000,000,000 during the year, thus continuing to drain money from both banks and specialized savings institutions.

In response, banks and thrifts introduced ingenious accounts by which customers funds above a certain minimum amount could be swept from savings deposits into higher-yielding bank repurchase agreements. And under the 1982 banking law, banks and thrifts soon would be able to offer their own money market funds, thus stemming the trend of movement of money away from banks and into brokerage industry funds.

The higher interest rates being paid on savings and the efforts to attract savings back from money market funds were part of a general trend of both banks and thrift institutions to cater more to the saver, even though it means higher charges for borrowers.

The days have passed when savers would take extremely low interest returns on their funds, and in return borrowers would pay interest rates that were below the rate of inflation. The fact that savers now want an attractive return and will move money out of banks and thrifts if they do not get it is one reason why interest rates on borrowings remained high in 1982. And general economic activity was extremely slack in large part because of an inability of potential borrowers to pay these high borrowing costs.

This slack in economic activity as well as high unemployment rates made banking a more difficult business, too. For the record levels of bankruptcies caused many bank loans to turn bad, and many banks suffered heavy losses due to business failures, mortgage defaults, and personal bankruptcies. On top of this, several notorious defaults in the brokerage industry, a major bank failure in Oklahoma, and serious difficulties in gaining repayment of some giant international loans, notably to Mexico, made U.S. banks more cautious in their credit policies. This was also true of Canadian banks, whose loans to an individual borrower can be larger than in the United States, leading to greater liability in the case of defaults.

Thus, in both the United States and Canada a more conservative banking posture is probable, as banks respond to the credit problems that resulted from their generous lending approaches of the past. Along with the slackened economic activity, greater loan problems, and higher interest returns for savers—accompanied by higher credit costs to borrowers—came a lessening of inflation. The maintenance of tight credit had as a major goal the reduction of inflation. This was achieved, even though the United States was experiencing the highest unemployment rate in more than 40 years. But the lower inflation rate was also affecting banking and investments in a significant way by lessening the attractiveness of such tangible assets as land, jewelry, and collectibles, and raising the worth of financial assets, notably stocks and bonds. Tangibles are used as inflation hedges, while financial assets flourish when inflation has lessened, and this was the situation in the United States in 1982.

The Outlook. The switch back to tangible assets should make banks more attractive as deposit vehicles. But, ironically, many banks are becoming more selective as to which customers they want because of the high cost of providing bank services. The result has been an "upscaling" of banking, with many banks charging small accounts to such a degree that people are switching their accounts from banks to thrifts and credit unions. Other banks, however, are responding by intensifying the development of automated banking through the use of teller machines, point of sale terminals, banking in the home, telephone transfer of funds, and other approaches that lessen the need for personal contact with the customer.

The result should be, in time, a banking industry that provides such routine banking services as deposits and withdrawals of funds automatically and that uses its employees to handle more complicated problems, to offer more sophisticated banking service, and to give the public a greater variety of service. This approach should include brokerage service, financial advice, automatic movement of funds for home and securities purchases and sales, and other activities that will make banks more like brokerage firms just as brokerage firms are trying to become more like banks. This diversification by both banks and brokerage firms, coupled with the new lending powers for thrifts under the 1982 banking act, should provide greater competition and better, cheaper service to the public.

The slow development of interstate banking, both through legal changes and the indirect advancement of banks from one state into others through loan production offices and traveling representatives, should also intensify the competition in the provision of banking service.

See also pages 38–44.

PAUL S. NADLER
Professor of Finance
Rutgers—The State University of New Jersey

BELGIUM

Belgian Foreign Minister Leo Tindemans served as president of the European Community Council of Ministers.

A new ministry with far-reaching legislative measures tried to rectify Belgium's many economic ills in 1982, but any improvement was difficult to see.

Domestic Affairs. The economic picture steadily worsened throughout the year, even though there were slight gains in the fight against inflation. The new coalition government of Prime Minister Wilfried Martens that assumed power in December 1981 announced a bold austerity program in February 1982. Having gained approval for special emergency powers that put aside any parliamentary obstacles for a year, the right-center government devalued the Belgian franc by 8.5% in order to stimulate exports, reverse the sharp fall in foreign buying, and cut down unemployment. Belgium's level of unemployment constituted the highest percentage in the European Community trading bloc, reaching an all-time high of 14.8% by year's end.

With the public debt above 15% of the gross national product and unemployment in February exceeding 500,000, Martens called for severe government retrenchment by trimming some $2,000,000,000 from the budget. The major spending cutbacks were reduced unemployment benefits and human services, mostly in education and medical areas. A substantial rise in the gasoline tax, lowered corporate taxes, and a general wage freeze emerged in the winter. The indexation system, which links wages to cost of living via periodic salary augmentation, was modified so that real wages went down 3% immediately.

By November, the business tax cuts seemed to work only minimally as investment incentives. The expected surge in exports from devaluation (the first since 1949) was not clearly fulfilled. Industrial productivity, which doubled in the 1970s, mostly out of huge foreign investments, continued to be unimpressive. A projected halt in joblessness due to government action did not come about, and unemployment increased from 11% in February to 14.8% in November.

The chronic economic headaches and the 1982 political program aimed at resolving these problems fanned regional and ethnic flames once again. The French-speaking Walloons of the south, already unhappy that Martens had excluded the Socialist party from the coalition of December 1981, felt that the extreme malaise of their region—particularly in steel, gas, and engineering—was not being addressed by a government representing the more prosperous Flemish north with its Dutch-speaking majority. The escalation of union unrest and numerous strikes in the industrial regions continued as the year drew to a close.

Foreign Affairs. The first six months of the year brought Belgium the rotating presidency of the European Community (EC) under Foreign Minister Leo Tindemans. A long-planned attempt to address major EC issues in this period failed, not only because economic recovery in the ten member nations was retarded, but also because the dispute concerning dumping of European steel in the United States preoccupied the Common Market powers. Furthermore, real political cooperation and progress, not only within Europe but also in Atlantic relations, were diminished by the controversy over U.S. sanctions against providing equipment for the Soviet natural gas pipeline and by the war in the Middle East. The October agreement between the United States and the EC, regulating and restricting European steel exports, did little to aid the most depressed industry in Belgium.

PIERRE-HENRI LAURENT, *Tufts University*

BELGIUM · Information Highlights

Official Name: Kingdom of Belgium.
Location: Northwestern Europe.
Area: 11,781 sq mi (30 513 km^2).
Population (1982 est.): 9,900,000.
Chief Cities (1980 est.): Brussels, the capital, 1,000,-221; Ghent, 239,959; Liège, 216,604; Antwerp, 190,652.
Government: *Head of state,* Baudouin I, king (acceded 1951). *Head of government,* Wilfried Martens, prime minister (formed new government Dec. 1981). *Legislature*—Parliament: Senate and Chamber of Representatives.
Monetary Unit: Franc (50.13 francs equal U.S.$1, Nov. 15, 1982).
Gross Domestic Product (1981 U.S.$1): $100,840,-000,000.
Economic Indexes (1981): *Consumer Prices* (1970= 100), *all items,* 219.0; *food,* 189.5. *Industrial production* (1980, 1975=100), 100.
Foreign Trade (1981 with Luxembourg U.S.$): *Imports,* $62,133,000,000; *exports,* $55,646,000,-000.

BIOCHEMISTRY

The year 1982 was a remarkable one for new discoveries and practical applications in the field of biochemistry.

Lesch-Nyhan Gene. Abnormalities in a single gene can have devastating effects, and this is most evident in Lesch-Nyhan syndrome. The syndrome occurs approximately once in 100,000 male births. The affected children have high uric acid levels in the blood (leading to kidney stones at a very young age) and suffer from compulsive self-mutilation and severe mental retardation. The apparent cause is absence of the enzyme hypoxanthine-guanine phosphoribosyl transferase (HPRT), an enzyme involved in nucleotide metabolism. (Nucleotides are chemical components of nucleic acids). How an absence of this enzyme leads to neurologic changes has remained a mystery. Theodore Friedmann and his co-workers at the University of California in San Diego have now succeeded in isolating the human gene for HPRT from the X-chromosome and cloning it in bacteria. This has resulted in the reproduction of the gene in sufficient amounts so that it should now be possible to determine what is wrong with the Lesch-Nyhan gene. The goal is to transplant copies of the HPRT gene into patients with Lesch-Nyhan syndrome to provide them with the enzyme they lack.

Bone Growth. In humans, bone is constantly being dissolved (resorbed) and new bone synthesized to replace it. In the healthy adult, the two processes occur at a constant rate so that bone volume remains constant. However, in certain diseases, such as osteoporosis and periodontal disease, the rate of bone destruction exceeds that of bone replacement so that bone becomes less dense and consequently more fragile. Many researchers believe that there is a chemical, the so-called coupling factor, that ensures a balance in bone destruction and rebuilding processes. John R. Farley, David J. Baylink, and their co-workers at Loma Linda University in California have succeeded in isolating from human bone a protein called skeletal growth factor (SGF). SGF stimulates the growth rate of bone cells by more than 1,000% but has no effect on other types of cells. These scientists believe that SGF is the coupling factor and speculate that it is released during bone destruction, which could then stimulate the formation of new bone. If this is true, several bone diseases might be due to abnormally high or low amounts of SGF. Indeed, abnormally high levels of SGF are reported in patients with Paget's disease, a disorder characterized by higher-than-normal bone destruction.

This research has important implications, since SGF might ultimately help physicians diagnose and treat certain bone diseases before the damage is visible on X-ray film.

Chemical Basis of Nonmotile Sperm. Reduced or absent sperm motility is one of the major causes of male infertility. (The other major cause is low sperm count). In some patients, lack of motility is due to structural flaws in the sperm tail, but in most cases no such defects are detectable. Richard J. Sherins and his colleagues at the National Institute of Child Health and Human Development in Bethesda, MD, have discovered that patients with nonmotile sperms have a deficiency of an enzyme called protein-carboxyl methylase (PCM). The researchers found that the amount of PCM in the semen of these patients was the same as that in vasectomized males but was only one fourth of that in fertile males. PCM apparently is required for sperm motility. Although this enzyme is found in various parts of the body, the largest amount is in spermatids, the precursor cells of sperms in testis. Interesting, PCM also is involved in controlling the movement of bacteria and certain white blood cells. It is expected that a complete understanding of the biochemistry of sperm motility may not only lead to treatment of certain cases of male infertility, but also to the development of chemical male contraceptives.

Biochemical Defect and Suicide. Scientists have long suspected that a biochemical defect may be the underlying cause of emotional illnesses. Now, two teams of scientists—one at Wayne State University and the other at the National Institute of Mental Health—have independently found that suicidal tendencies may indeed be due to a biochemical abnormality in the brain. The two teams compared the brain samples obtained at autopsies of suicide victims with nonsuicides killed violently. The researchers measured the ability of imipramine, an antidepressant drug, to bind to certain chemical sites—called "binding sites"—located in the cortex, or outer layer, of the brain. Imipramine binding, in turn, is believed to reflect the brain's ability to utilize serotonin, a naturally occurring chemical carrier of nerve impulses between brain cells. The results revealed that the suicides' brains had one-half to one-third fewer imipramine binding sites than did the control group brains. Recent studies have linked low serotonin levels to depression, aggression, and impulsiveness. The present research suggests that, regardless of personality disorder, abnormally low serotonin levels (as revealed by imipramine binding) may be the common biochemical factor in determining whether or not an individual attempts suicide.

Other recent studies have shown that the blood platelets of patients diagnosed as depressive also have fewer imipramine binding sites. In view of this, it is likely that a simple procedure utilizing the blood platelets will be developed to screen potential suicides at a very young age.

See also MEDICINE AND HEALTH—Mental Health.

PREM P. BATRA
Wright State University

BIOGRAPHY

A selection of profiles of persons prominent in the news during 1982 appears on pages 128–141. The affiliation of the contributor is listed on pages 589–92; biographies that do not include a contributor's name were prepared by the staff. Included are sketches of:

ANDROPOV, Yuri Vladimirovich

Succeeding the late Leonid Brezhnev as secretary-general of the Soviet Communist Party on Nov. 12, 1982, Yuri Andropov rose to the leadership of the USSR with a speed that surprised many Western observers and a high-level, behind-the-scenes support that gave testimony to his political skill. As former head of the State Security Committee (KGB)—1967 to 1982, longer than any security chief in Soviet history—Andropov is the first top leader of the USSR to have been a police minister. He is also the first to have been an ambassador, serving in Budapest from 1954 to 1956, when Soviet forces were sent in to put down the Hungarian revolution. Though experienced in diplomacy, police intelligence, and internal security, he has never been an economic manager or policymaker.

Background. Born on June 15, 1914, in the town of Nagutskoye in the north Caucasus, Andropov is the son of a Russian railwayman. He attended a trade school and, without graduating, went on to Petrozavodsk University. After working as a telegraph operator and Volga boatman, he became a recruiter for the Young Communist League (YCL) and was rapidly promoted to YCL first secretary for the Yaroslavl region. In 1940 he was transferred to the same post in the Karelo-Finnish soviet republic. In 1944 he was appointed second Communist Party secretary in Pe-

trozavodsk, the Karelo-Finnish capital, and in 1947 second party secretary for the entire republic.

Transferred to Moscow in 1951, Andropov worked in the party secretariat as an inspector and then a department chief. In 1953 he became an officer of the Soviet Embassy in Budapest, and in 1954 the ambassador. Recalled again to Moscow in 1957, he was made head of the secretariat section negotiating with other Communist parties in the Soviet bloc. Five years later he was made a party secretary.

Andropov's rise continued under Leonid Brezhnev. He was made a nonvoting Politburo member and head of the KGB in 1967, and a full Politburo member in 1973. Six months before Brezhnev's death, in May 1982, he returned to the secretariat as a party secretary. His bid for power is said to have begun at that time.

At 68, Yuri Andropov is the oldest person in Soviet history to take over the top leadership. He is considered a mild Communist and has promised publicly to continue Brezhnev's internal and foreign policies. At the same time, he is regarded as flexible and open-minded. He speaks English and has a taste for Western music, scotch whiskey, and tennis.

ELLSWORTH RAYMOND

ARAFAT, Yasir

In his checkered *kaffiyeh* (cloth headdress), dark sun glasses, and khaki military fatigues, Yasir Arafat is one of the most familiar figures on the world scene. As chairman of the Palestine Liberation Organization (PLO), he leads a fervent nationalist movement whose aspirations and guerrilla tactics have been the major points of contention in the most volatile region of the globe. Since taking over as head of the PLO in 1969, Arafat has developed its constituent commando groups into a more cohesive, well-trained fighting force and established a variety of political and social institutions. In recent years Arafat has focused his efforts on winning international recognition of the rights of Palestinians and of the PLO as the official diplomatic representative of the Palestinian people.

The year 1982 represented a major turning point for Arafat and the PLO. The Israeli military offensive into Lebanon and 10-week siege of Beirut finally forced the guerrillas and their leader out of the country in which they had based their operations since 1971. The PLO was dispersed throughout the Arab world, and Arafat sailed August 30 for Greece. With a vow to "continue the struggle," he resumed his international diplomatic crusade. Now operating out of Tunisia, he traveled to Rome in mid-September, where he met with Pope John Paul II and Italian government leaders.

Background. Said to be a descendant of Palestinian nobility, Yasir Arafat was born in Jerusalem in August 1929. Though accounts differ, he apparently was reared in Gaza, where his father was a businessman. After the Arab-Israeli war of 1948, in which he was a gun runner, Arafat

Andropov, Yuri Vladimirovich

Tass from Sovfoto

Yasir Arafat

Photoreporters, Inc.

studied civil engineering at Fuad I (now Cairo) University and headed the Palestinian Student Federation. At the same time he began learning guerrilla tactics and after graduation attended the Egyptian military academy. In 1956 he served as a demolitions expert in the Suez campaign.

Arafat worked as an engineer in Kuwait in the late 1950s, but his activities in the Palestinian movement continued to grow. He helped establish al-Fatah, a clandestine organization which began carrying out commando raids into Israel in the early 1960s. After the Six-Day War of June 1967, al-Fatah emerged as the best organized of many Palestinian liberation groups, and Arafat was idolized as its leader. By February 1969 he was named executive chairman of the PLO. The PLO was given a major boost in October 1974, when it was named the legitimate representative of the Palestinian people at an Arab summit in Rabat, Morocco. A month later—on Nov. 13, 1974—Arafat scored his greatest diplomatic success with an appearance before the United Nations General Assembly. In familiar garb and with a side arm on his hip, he delivered a plea for the creation of a Palestinian state that would include Muslims, Christians, and Jews. He was accorded the status of chief of state and won new support for his cause.

CLARK, William Patrick

A year after he was criticized as an undistinguished choice for the number-two job at the U.S. State Department, William P. Clark was elevated to assistant to the president for national security affairs (national security adviser), replacing the hapless Richard Allen, who resigned under pressure. Despite his lack of foreign-policy expertise, Clark's promotion was applauded as likely to bring needed order to President Reagan's fractious foreign-policy establishment.

A former California judge, Clark played a key role in forcing Secretary of State Alexander Haig's resignation, ostensibly over U.S. policy toward Israel and the extent of trade sanctions affecting America's European allies. In both cases, Haig was in the minority with Clark urging a tougher approach. But White House aides let it be known that Haig's tempestuous personality was at the heart of his premature departure. Although Clark had originally served as a buffer between Haig and Reagan's ruling "troika" of advisers, after he moved to the White House, he came to the conclusion that Haig had to go.

Clark shares Reagan's conservative instincts and, as a long-time associate, has unlimited access to the oval office. He instituted daily morning briefings with the president, a practice that had lapsed during Allen's tenure. When President Reagan vacations at his California ranch, Clark helicopters over from his own nearby spread to keep the president up-to-date, a sharp contrast to Aug. 19, 1981, when Reagan was allowed to sleep through a U.S. air battle with Libya.

Clark is heralded for his personal qualities, chiefly a winning modesty and an ability to mediate successfully both policy and personality disputes. He describes himself as "an honest broker of ideas" interested only in putting Reagan's mark on foreign policy. To that end, "the judge," as he likes to be called, shies away from media appearances.

Background. A fifth-generation Californian, William Patrick Clark was born on Oct. 23, 1931, in Oxnard, CA. After a lackluster academic performance that included dropping out of both Stanford University and Loyola Law School, Clark studied privately and passed the bar on his second try. A small-town lawyer, he signed on as a county chairman of Reagan's first gubernatorial campaign in 1966. As Governor Reagan's chief of staff, he created the famous "mini-memos" that are still the president's hallmark. Beginning in 1969, Reagan appointed Clark to a series of judgeships that culminated in a 1973 seat on the State Supreme Court.

Clark and his wife, Joan, have five children.

ELEANOR CLIFT

DE LA MADRID HURTADO, Miguel

Miguel de la Madrid Hurtado was sworn in as president of Mexico on Dec. 1, 1982, to serve a single six-year term, his first elective public office. The candidate of the government's Institutional Revolutionary Party (PRI), de la Madrid was the chosen successor of outgoing President José López Portillo. His victory over six other candidates in the July 1982 balloting was a foregone conclusion, since no opposition candidate had ever won a Mexican presidential election. Nevertheless, de la Madrid campaigned vigorously to make himself known to the public and to gather information on citizen problems and demands.

The 47-year-old candidate made the traditional promises to continue the Mexican Revolution by promoting social justice for the masses, maintaining an independent foreign policy, and developing the economy in a balanced

Miguel de la Madrid Hurtado

Randy Taylor/Sygma

fashion. He also promised a "moral renewal" for the nation. The new president was expected to revive the Global Development Plan, bring government spending and inflation under control, and increase economic planning. Considered a political moderate, he also was expected to give more concessions to private business and be friendly toward the United States.

De la Madrid entered the presidency after a career as a financial expert and bureaucrat. As minister of planning and budget under López Portillo, he was the architect of Mexico's economic development plan, which gave greater control to the government. Facing the consequences of a 40% currency devaluation in 1982, a staggering foreign debt, a high inflation rate, and decline in oil revenues, the new president sought to use his technical expertise to increase the solvency and economic competitiveness of Mexico.

Background. Miguel de la Madrid Hurtado was born in the western city of Colima on Dec. 12, 1934, the son of a middle class family. He is the first Mexican president from the State of Colima. In 1957 he earned a law degree from the National Autonomous University in Mexico City, where he studied under López Portillo. De la Madrid, who speaks fluent English, is also the first Mexican president to hold an academic degree from a U.S. university. With the aid of a scholarship, he earned a master's degree in public administration from Harvard University in 1965. He entered public service as an advisor to the Bank of Mexico in 1960, becoming subdirector general of public credit in 1965. In 1970 he moved to Petróleos Mexicanos (PEMEX), the government petroleum monopoly, as subdirector of finances. In 1972 he returned to the finance ministry as director general of credit. President López Portillo promoted him to deputy finance minister in 1975 and minister of planning and budget in 1979. He resigned that post when the ruling PRI made him its official presidential candidate in September 1981.

See also MEXICO.

DONALD J. MABRY

DOMINGO, Placido

In opera, this is the era of the lyric tenor, and Placido Domingo is a primary reason why. The Domingo voice is exceptional. Besides its variety of color, flexibility, and strength, its very tone makes his performances convincing in roles from the lightest of Donizetti to the heroic demands of *Otello*. With his ringing tenor voice, musicianship, acting ability, and strong physical presence, Placido Domingo is the picture of the hero.

Placido Domingo

Wide World

Reportedly receiving up to $15,000 a performance from major companies, Domingo meets a jet star's whirl-wind schedule—predominantly opera, but also concerts, television, opera films, and recordings. His discography exceeds 70 records, which include many of his 82 operatic roles as well as discs for the popular market. *Perhaps Love*, an album joining him with the pop singer John Denver, has sold almost one million copies internationally. Domingo continually emphasizes his great enthusiasm for opera. He believes strongly that by appearing in films and on television, as well as by recording popular songs, he helps to promote interest in the operatic form in the United States.

Background. Placido Domingo was born in Madrid in 1941 to parents who were noted singers in *zarzuela*, the Spanish operetta form. The family moved to Mexico when Domingo was eight. His piano studies began then, and a few years later he discovered his voice and stage talent. His precocity in his early teens extended to other fields as well—to soccer, baseball, bullfighting, marriage at 16 to a fellow pianist, and then to work in nightclubs. He made his operatic debut in 1961 with the Mexican National Opera in Monterrey. That same year, he sang opposite Joan Sutherland in *Lucia di Lammermoor*.

In 1962 he and his new second wife, Marta Ornelas, joined the Hebrew (now Israel) National Opera in Tel Aviv as that company's leading tenor and soprano. Over the next two and half years, he sang 280 performances of 12 roles. By 1965 he was singing with the New York City Opera. His debut in Vienna came in 1967 and at the Metropolitan Opera in New York in 1968.

By March of 1982, Domingo had given 1,582 performances. During the year, besides performing in several of the world's opera houses, he conducted *Die Fledermaus* in Vienna, filmed *La Traviata*, recorded a new pop album in London, sang concerts, and began recording the soundtrack for a film of *Carmen*.

His life in recent years has been a constant commute with his wife Marta from homes in New York, London, Monte Carlo, and Barcelona. Their two sons, Placido, Jr., and Alvaro, are in a boarding school in Switzerland. His oldest son José, from his first marriage, is studying in London. The opera star is devoted to his family and believes that it is "awful when you realize that you see more of people in cities where you sing than your own children." Time permitting, he still enjoys participating in an occasional game of soccer.

At just 41, Placido Domingo is universally placed among the great tenors of history.

See also MUSIC.

ROBERT COMMANDAY

FAHD, King

On June 13, 1982, upon the death of his half-brother, King Khalid, Prince Fahd ibn Abdul al-Aziz al-Saud, 60, became king of Saudi Arabia. As crown prince since 1975, Fahd played a leading role in maintaining close ties with the United States, establishing Saudi Arabia's leadership in the Organization of Petroleum Exporting Countries (OPEC), and in modernizing the Saudi economy. In 1981, Fahd initiated a peace plan which implicitly recognized the existence of Israel and was intended to end the Arab-Israeli dispute. Domestically, Fahd presided over the drafting and implementation of five-year development plans and supervised the construction by Bechtel, a U.S. corporation, of two new industrial cities designed to add petrochemical manufacturing and a natural gas collecting system to Saudi economic strength.

Background. Born in 1922, Fahd is the eldest of the highly influential "Sudeiri Seven," the sons of King Abdul al-Aziz (Ibn Saud), the founder of Saudi Arabia, and one of his wives, Hassa bint Ahmad al-Sudeiri. Fahd, who was educated at court and speaks English fluently, was the first minister of education of Saudi Arabia from 1953 to 1960. While in that position he established a number of new public and elementary schools, including a separate new system for girls. From 1962 to 1975, Fahd was minister of the

King Fahd

Regis Bossu/Sygma

interior, in charge of the police and internal security. In 1968 he was also named second deputy prime minister and subsequently chaired the supreme council for oil affairs and the U.S.-Saudi joint commission on economic and security cooperation.

After the assassination of King Faisal in 1975, Fahd was named crown prince by the new ruler, Khalid, who also entrusted Fahd with the day-to-day supervision of the government. Fahd overcame his earlier notoriety for extended vacations by shaping the $150,000,000,000 five-year plan (1975–80) to develop the Saudi infrastructure of ports, highways, water systems, and education. The takeover of the Great Mosque in Mecca by religious rebels in November 1979 led Fahd the following year to propose a constitutional system and consultative council, neither of which has yet been implemented. Instead, Saudi Arabia under Khalid and Fahd continued to function as an absolute monarchy, with no elections, political parties, or constitution.

Fahd and Oil Minister Ahmed Zaki Yamani sought to unify OPEC oil prices by changing the amount of oil that Saudi Arabia sells, but the Iran-Iraq war and declining world demand for petroleum have weakened OPEC's willingness to cooperate.

By appointing Prince Abdullah ibn Abdul al-Aziz, head of the national guard, to be his crown prince and successor, Fahd signaled upon his becoming king that he would continue prior government policies and practices with relatively few initial changes. He is considered a strong ally of the West and a moderate in the Arab bloc.

See also SAUDI ARABIA.

WILLIAM OCHSENWALD

GONZÁLEZ MÁRQUEZ, Felipe

Overwhelming support for the Socialist Workers Party in the Spanish parliamentary elections of October 1982 marked a sharp break with the Francoist past as Felipe González Márquez became the nation's first leftist prime minister since before the civil war that ended during March 1939.

An unprecedented 78% of the 27 million eligible voters cast ballots in contests that gave the Socialists an absolute majority in the 350-member national parliament (Cortés). Although King Juan Carlos immediately recognized the results, extremists on the left and right began conspiring against the boyishly handsome González and his new government.

The former labor lawyer was formally elected prime minister in parliament on December 2. At that time the new leader reaffirmed that his government would work to halt

Spain's integration into the North Atlantic Treaty Organization. He also said that "the process of putting obstacles to Spain's entry to the European Community cannot be permanent."

Background. Born on March 5, 1942, in Seville, Gonzáles grew up in humble circumstances. His father was a Socialist and owner of a small dairy. Felipe, the only one of four children to receive a university education, studied under Roman Catholic priests at universities in Seville and Louvain, Belgium. Upon completing his studies, he returned to Seville to practice law. However, politics soon claimed an increasing amount of his time.

He became active in the outlawed Socialist youth movement, assumed the underground name of Isidoro, and worked hard to revitalize the Socialist organization. In 1974 he emerged as the party's secretary general when he and other activists gained acceptance of the idea that the Socialists, who had operated from exile in Paris, should return to Spain to fight against the repressive dictatorship of Gen. Francisco Franco.

As the party came into the open after Franco's death in 1975, González reshaped its image from one of militancy to moderation. An especially bitter struggle focused on the inclusion of "Marxist" in the party's name. The pragmatic young leader, who refused to identify himself as a Marxist, resigned until he was recalled six months later with permission to drop the unacceptable label.

He demonstrated the same political acumen during the 1982 campaign. To allay conservative fears over his plea for a "historic change," González backed the monarchy, rejected massive nationalizations of private firms, emphasized job creation, and avoided inflaming class antagonisms. When asked whether he would use his authority to dispossess the wealthy, he responded: "No, we want to get rid of the poor."

Once viewed by journalists as a playboy, González discarded casual attire for tweed suits when electioneering. In line with his informal style, he is known throughout Spain as simply "Felipe."

He is married to Carmen Romero, a secondary schoolteacher. They have three young children and live in a modest apartment in Madrid.

See also SPAIN.

GEORGE W. GRAYSON

HABIB, Philip Charles

For nearly 11 weeks between June and August 1982, U.S. special envoy Philip Habib conducted a grueling seven-nation diplomatic mission to end the hostilities between Israeli forces and Palestine Liberation Organization guerrillas in Lebanon. The 62-year-old former foreign service officer, who had been summoned out of retirement by President Ronald Reagan in May 1981, represented the only real hope for a negotiated solution to the conflict. Working 18-hour days and shuttling among capitals throughout the Mideast and Europe, Habib convinced the principal parties that peace was in their best interest. Final agreement on his 14-point peace plan—calling for the departure of PLO forces from Beirut to other Arab countries—was called a "diplomatic miracle."

In recognition of his latest diplomatic efforts, Philip Habib was awarded the Presidential Medal of Freedom on September 7. And though the ending of the Beirut crisis was perhaps the most notable achievement of his long diplomatic career, he had played several key roles in U.S. foreign policy. He was a major figure in the U.S. negotiating team at the Vietnam peace talks in Paris, served as ambassador to South Korea, helped arrange meetings between President Jimmy Carter and Egyptian President Anwar el-Sadat that eventually led to the historic Camp David talks, and arranged a cease-fire in the Lebanese war of 1981. Habib's success as a diplomat has been attributed to his persistence, persuasiveness, amiable sense of humor, and ability to keep talks with foreign leaders private.

Background. The family background of Philip Charles Habib seems a good preparation for a Mideast diplomat. The son of a grocer who emigrated from Lebanon, Habib grew up in a section of Brooklyn, NY, that was heavily Jewish. He earned a B.S. degree from the University of Idaho in 1942 and served in the U.S. Army until 1946, having attained the rank of captain. By the time he was awarded his Ph.D. in economics by the University of California at Berkeley in 1952, he had already served three years in the foreign service.

From 1949 to 1962, Habib held posts in Canada, New Zealand, Trinidad, and the State Department in Washington. In 1962 he was sent to South Korea as counselor for political affairs. Three years later, with the war in Vietnam escalating, he joined the U.S. diplomatic team in Saigon. He became chief political adviser to Ambassador Henry Cabot Lodge, and his growing reputation as an expert in Southeast Asian affairs ultimately led him to the negotiating tables in Paris. Relieved from that mission in July 1970, he was nominated as ambassador to South Korea one year later and served until 1974. Named undersecretary of state for East Asian and Pacific affairs, he then concentrated his efforts on U.S. policy in Cambodia.

Habib's attention was turned to the Middle East in May 1976, when President Gerald Ford appointed him undersecretary of state for political affairs. President Jimmy Carter retained him in that post, but in early 1978 Habib, always a workaholic, suffered his second major heart attack and was forced to retire to golf and poker at his home in California. Three years later, circumstances in Lebanon prompted President Reagan to seek him out. Of his efforts, the president said: "What he accomplished was the vital first step . . . for launching a fresh start in the quest for peace" in Lebanon, Israel, and the area.

HENDERSON, Rickey

When, on August 27 at Milwaukee's County Stadium, Rickey Henderson of the Oakland A's stole his 119th base of the 1982 season, he broke one of major league baseball's most cherished records and kept a bold preseason promise. After predicting that he would eclipse Lou Brock's 1974 standard, the 23-year-old center fielder proceeded to steal bases at an unprecedented clip. "The Rickey Watch" was a highlight of the 1982 season. While it had taken Brock 153 games to rob his 118 bases, Henderson reached that mark in only the 128th game of the campaign. The record came the next evening and, characteristically, Henderson did it in explosive fashion. With his patented head-first slide, he stole *four* bases before calling it a night. By season's end he had amassed a total of 130.

By no account is base stealing the only talent of Rickey Henderson. In less than four full seasons in the major leagues, the 5'10" (1.78 m), 180 lb (82 kg) Oaklander has established himself as one of baseball's all-around stars. His instincts and sheer foot speed have made him a Gold Glove-caliber outfielder, and in the strike-shortened 1981 season he led the American League with 135 hits, batting .319. Though his batting average dropped to .267 in 1982, the walk-conscious lead-off man still managed to get on base more than 40% of the time. In an otherwise disappointing season for the A's, Henderson brought confidence, a boyish spirit, and—most of all—excitement to every game.

Background. Rickey Henderson was born on Christmas Day, 1958, in Chicago. When he was two his father left home, and his mother, Bobbie, moved the seven children to Pine Bluff, AR. Five years later they settled in North Oakland, CA. Bobbie worked as a nurse to support the family and reared her children with a firm hand. Rickey went to Oakland Tech, where he was an all-city running back on the football team. His heart was set on being a gridiron star, and he was offered at least a dozen college scholarships. Bobbie, however, felt he was too small for football and would have a longer career on the baseball diamond.

Signed to a contract by the A's right out of high school in 1976, Henderson honed his skills—including the head-first slide—in the minor leagues before being called up to the parent club in 1979. He gave notice of a bright future by batting .274 and stealing 33 bases in half a season. The following year, at age 21, he batted a healthy .303 and be-

came the first American Leaguer ever to steal 100 bases in a season. His total for 1982 not only shattered the major league mark, but it also made him the first player to steal triple figures twice in a career. He was still only 23.

JACOB, John Edward

When National Urban League President Vernon E. Jordan, Jr., announced his resignation in September 1981, the venerable civil-rights organization launched a three-month search for a successor. The winner among 30 candidates, including several high-profile public figures, however, turned out to be a quiet little man who had been at the league all along, the executive vice-president, John E. Jacob.

Though he is less adept at attracting publicity than the charismatic Jordan, Jacob proceeded to make headlines by assailing President Reagan's controversial budget cuts as an assault on America's poor. In the summer of 1982, Jacob called for a massive, $100,000,000,000-a-year job training program. Likened to a domestic version of the Marshall Plan that helped rebuild war-torn Europe, the program would unite the public and private sectors in an attempt to cure high unemployment, which is chronic among black Americans, and repair the decaying infrastructure of the country.

Background. John Edward Jacob was born Dec. 16, 1934, in Trout, LA, and reared in Houston, TX. He earned bachelor and master of social work degrees at Howard University, and worked with the Department of Public Welfare in Baltimore, MD, before joining the league as director of education for its Washington, DC, branch in 1965. Jacob moved up to acting executive director there, went on to head the San Diego, CA, branch, and returned as executive director of the Washington office in 1975. In 1978 he was named executive vice-president of the national office in New York with expanded responsibilities for day-to-day operation of the league's affairs.

Throughout his career, Jacob has earned high marks as a low-keyed but effective administrator and a skillful lobbyist and fund raiser. His talents were highlighted for several months in 1980 when he took control of the league after Jordan was critically wounded by a would-be assassin. Often asked to compare himself to his former boss, Jacob once answered that Jordan is 6'4" (1.93 m) and he is 5'7" (1.7 m). "I am not Vernon. I will not try to be Vernon," he said upon his promotion. In addition to unemployment, Jacob has targeted voter registration, black teenage pregnancy, and crime as key issues for the league. And at a time of fiscal retrenchment (which affected the league itself in the form of lost federal contracts), Jacob emphasized the need for self-reliance among black organizations.

Jacob lives in Hartsdale, NY, with his wife, Barbara. They have one daughter, Sheryl.

DENNIS A. WILLIAMS

JARUZELSKI, Wojciech

On Dec. 13, 1981, Eastern Europe's latest experiment in political liberty came to an end with the imposition of martial law in Poland. Over the previous 16 months, Polish workers had united behind Lech Walesa's independent trade union Solidarity, which challenged the Communist Party's economic and political leadership of the nation. The man who brought Poland its martial law regime, imprisoned Walesa, and drove Solidarity underground, was Gen. Wojciech Jaruzelski, chairman of the Council of Ministers and first secretary of the Communist Polish United Workers' Party (PZPR). A career soldier who in 1976 said that "Polish troops will never be used to fire upon Polish workers," Jaruzelski has subjected the Polish people to the harshest repression since World War II. Scores of workers were killed and many more imprisoned in the imposition of martial law. In the face of popular resentment, General Jaruzelski has tried to suppress the remnants of Solidarity and revive a badly lagging economy. Although Walesa was released from detention in mid-November and martial law was eased somewhat by year's end, he continued to maintain tight control over virtually every aspect of Polish national life.

Background. Wojciech Jaruzelski was born on July 6, 1923, in the village of Kurów in east-central Poland. Anomalously for a future Communist leader, he was the son of land-owning gentry. Sometime after the Soviet Union annexed Poland's eastern territories in September 1939, Jaruzelski and his family likely were deported to the USSR. In 1943, at age 20, he joined the Soviet-sponsored First Polish Army as a junior infantry officer and fought alongside Red Army forces in the advance on Poland and Germany. After the war, Jaruzelski fought Polish anti-Communist guerrillas until 1947. The following year he became a member of the Communist Party and entered the General Staff War College in Warsaw. Completing advanced officer training in 1951, Jaruzelski was promoted to brigadier general in 1956 and commanding officer of the 12th Motorized Division in 1957. He reached the peak of the military hierarchy in 1973, when he became a four-star general of the Army.

At the same time, Jaruzelski was advancing in the state and party hierarchies. Between 1960 and 1962 he served as chief political commissar of the Polish armed forces. From 1962 until 1968 he was deputy minister of defense, and from 1965 to 1968 he was also chief of the general staff. In 1968 he was named minister of national defense.

Jaruzelski joined the party Central Committee in 1964 and by 1970 was a member of the Politburo, the top policy-making organ. In 1981, Jaruzelski became the principal beneficiary of the growing labor crisis and the demands by Moscow for suppression of the unrest. On Feb. 9, 1981, he succeeded Jozef Pinkowski as premier, and on October 18 he was named first secretary of the PZPR, replacing Stanislaw Kania. Thus, during 1982, this slight, balding, notably reticent man had more power than any Polish leader since the mid 1930s.

Although little is known about the general's personal life, it has been reported that his wife was born in the Soviet Union.

ALEXANDER J. GROTH

JENKINS, Roy Harris

In July 1982 Roy Harris Jenkins became the first elected leader of Britain's new Social Democratic Party (SDP), having been chosen in a balloting of the party's membership. He won by a convincing majority over his only opponent, the former Foreign Secretary David Owen. His campaign for the SDP leadership was downbeat, stressing his experience, proven ministerial record, and essential conservatism.

Background. Jenkins was born Nov. 11, 1920, the son of a Welsh mining family with aspirations to middle-class gentility. When he was a small child his father was sent to prison for three months for alleged incitement to riot. To many working-class socialists, a prison sentence for a political cause would be seen as a badge of honor. The young Jenkins was told, however, that his father was on business abroad and he did not learn the true story until he was 16.

He was educated at the local grammar school, which in Britain meant a public school for bright children, and later went to Oxford. He lost his Welsh accent, or nearly all of it, being left only with an inability to pronounce the letter "r." He developed a taste for good living, fine wines, and elegant houses, none of which prevented him from entering Labour Party politics. He was also formidably intelligent.

In 1948 Jenkins was elected a member of Parliament (MP) and was distinguished more for his intellectual ability than for his devotion to his constituents. He had no great love for the city of Birmingham, part of which he represented following reelection in 1950.

When Labour came to power in 1964, Jenkins held a succession of ministerial posts and made a number of remarkable achievements. Unlike many ministers then and since, he appeared to be fully in command of his departments and made it clear that the important decisions would be taken by him and not by his civil servants. He is generally agreed to have been the most successful chancellor of the exchequer (treasury secretary) since World War II, and as home secretary (minister for the interior) he brought about a number of important liberal reforms, including ones on abortion and homosexuality.

Through the 1970s Jenkins displayed growing mistrust of the Labour Party's move toward the left, and shortly after losing the ballot for the party leadership in 1976 he resigned to become president of the European Commission—in effect leader of the Common Market. He was not a great success in a difficult job, and in 1980 he returned to British politics with a call for a realignment of the old parties. He was, therefore, the first moving spirit in the formation of the Social Democrats. In 1981 he caused a sensation by almost winning a safe Labour constituency in a by-election, and in March 1982 he was returned to Parliament as MP for a middle-class seat in the Scottish industrial city of Glasgow.

SIMON HOGGART

JOHNSON, Earvin ("Magic"), Jr.

At age 22, when many other players are just being graduated from college, Earvin ("Magic") Johnson was leading the Los Angeles Lakers to their second National Basketball Association (NBA) championship in three years. His strong rebounding, steady scoring, and sleight-of-hand passing earned him Most Valuable Player (MVP) honors in the 1982 play-offs, as the Lakers defeated the Philadelphia '76ers, four games to two, in the final series. For the 6'9" (2.06 m) guard, it was a repeat performance of the 1980 play-offs, when he became the first rookie ever to be voted tournament MVP. One of the most colorful and charismatic figures in sports, Magic Johnson carries an infectious enthusiasm onto the court whenever he plays. His exciting style, love of the game, and irrepressible smile have made him a media favorite and team leader.

Earvin Johnson
Courtesy, Los Angeles Lakers

Background. Earvin Johnson, Jr., was born in Lansing, MI, on Aug. 14, 1959. He was the sixth of ten children born to Christine Johnson, a school cafeteria supervisor, and Earvin Johnson, Sr., who worked at a General Motors auto body plant. Young Earvin learned the game of basketball at a local playground and practiced daily with his older brother Larry. At Everett High School in Lansing, he was a three-time All-State selection and led his team to a Class-A state championship in his senior year. As a college freshman in 1978, Johnson sparked Michigan State to its first Big Ten basketball title in 19 years. The following season Magic brought the Spartans to the NCAA tournament finals against undefeated Indiana State and Player of the Year Larry Bird. The Spartans came away with the national collegiate crown, and Johnson was voted tournament MVP.

After his sophomore year, Magic agreed to a four-year contract with the L.A. Lakers, estimated at $600,000 per year. As an NBA rookie he averaged 18.0 points, 7.7 rebounds, and 7.3 assists per game. His all-star season was capped by the NBA championship and play-off MVP award. Larry Bird, now of the Boston Celtics, edged him out in Rookie-of-the-Year voting.

The 1980–81 campaign was a disappointment for Johnson and the Lakers. Magic's statistics—21.6 points, 8.6 rebounds, and 8.6 assists—were much improved, but he missed 45 games in midseason with a serious knee injury. In the play-offs, the Lakers lost in an early round and were dethroned as champions by the Celtics.

As a vote of confidence, Lakers' owner Jerry Buss gave his floor leader a new contract in June 1981. It was one of the most lucrative in sports history—$25 million over 25 years. Johnson responded with his best season ever. His 2.67 steals per game led the NBA, and his 9.5 assists was second highest. His 9.6 rebounds and 18.6 points further attested to his all-around skills. Most importantly, his leadership and enthusiasm were the keys to another NBA title.

KEMP, Jack French

A self-proclaimed "neoconservative," U.S. Rep. Jack Kemp (R-NY) has emerged as one of the most influential figures on the American political scene. First elected to Congress in 1970, he gained national prominence in 1978 by submitting to that body the controversial Kemp-Roth bill, a comprehensive federal tax-cut package. His strong advocacy of supply-side economics and outspoken support for presidential candidate Ronald Reagan thrust the former professional football star into Washington's power elite in the 1980s. As an architect of President Reagan's economic policy, he was a staunch and articulate defender of the tax and budget cuts proposed by the new administration. By 1982, however, it had become clear that Kemp stood even farther to the right, economically, than Reagan. When, during the summer, the president submitted to Congress a $98,000,000,000 tax-increase bill, Kemp stuck to his supply-side guns and announced his opposition. The bill passed, but the ranks of disaffected conservatives were swelling fast. Prominent among them was the 47-year-old representative from New York State's 38th Congressional District. Perhaps inevitably, the tax bill fight fueled speculation about Kemp's aspiration to higher political office.

Background. Jack French Kemp was born in Los Angeles on July 13, 1935. He attended Fairfax High School in L.A., where he devoted most of his time and energy to football. As a quarterback at local Occidental College he impressed professional scouts, and upon graduation in 1957 he was drafted by the Detroit Lions of the National Football League (NFL). Cut from the Lions, he played for the Pittsburgh Steelers, New York Giants, and Calgary Stampeders of the Canadian Football League—and served one year in the Army—before finding gridiron success with the Los Angeles Chargers of the new American Football League (AFL) in 1960. He stayed with the team when it moved to San Diego the next year but was picked up by the Buffalo Bills in 1962. His outstanding play led the Bills to league championships in 1964 and 1965, and in the latter season he was named AFL Player of the Year. After 13 years in professional football, a series of injuries forced

Wide World

Jack Kemp

him to retire at the conclusion of the 1969 season. He took a job as public relations officer to the Marine Midland Bank of Buffalo.

Kemp's political career was launched in 1970, when local Republican leaders convinced him to run for Congress. In addition to his celebrity status, attractiveness, and speaking ability, Kemp had had some political experience working on several Republican campaigns. He took graduate courses in political science and began reading economic history. With the added endorsement of the Conservative Party, he won the 1970 election by a narrow margin. He has been reelected to each succeeding Congress by ever-increasing majorities. On Capitol Hill, Kemp quickly established himself as a conservative, especially on economic matters. His tax-cutting proposals, which reached full formulation in the Kemp-Roth bill, called for a one-third reduction in personal income tax and smaller cuts in corporate taxes. Though the measure was voted down, its ideology was brought into fashion by the election of Ronald Reagan.

KOHL, Helmut

Helmut Kohl, leader of the Christian Democratic Union (CDU), succeeded the Social Democrat Helmut Schmidt on October 1, 1982, as the first West German chancellor elected by a "constructive" vote of no-confidence against his predecessor. The Bundestag (lower house) voted in the 52-year-old conservative after the Social Democratic-Free Democratic coalition government of Chancellor Schmidt broke up over budgetary and other disagreements, and after a sufficient number of Free Democrats turned to the CDU for a majority. In his first major policy statements, Kohl said he would pursue Schmidt's foreign policy course of close cooperation with the West and avoidance of confrontation with the East. In domestic matters, however, his economic and social programs would be considerably more conservative than those of his predecessor. His goal, he said, was "to make freedom, dynamism, and self-reliance blossom again."

Background. Helmut Kohl was born on April 3, 1930, in Ludwigshafen, the son of a finance official. He has been involved in politics since his youth. In 1947 Kohl was one of the cofounders of the Young Union, the CDU youth organization. Two years later, at age 19, he was already making speeches on behalf of Bundestag candidates. Beginning in 1955 he held various positions in the CDU itself. In 1958 he received his doctorate in political science from the University of Heidelberg with a dissertation titled "The Reemergence of the Parties after the Collapse." After employment by the Chemical Industry Association for several years, he devoted himself completely to politics. Kohl rose quickly through the party ranks, though he owed his success more to his conciliatory way and administrative abilities than to any noteworthy political positions.

In 1969 Kohl was elected minister-president of the Rhineland-Palatinate state; the same year he became national deputy chairman of the CDU and head of the party's platform committee. Four years later he was elected chairman of the CDU. In 1976 Kohl lost narrowly to Schmidt in Bundestag elections for the chancellorship. He resigned as minister-president of the Rhineland-Palatinate to concentrate on the CDU chairmanship and his future candidacy for chancellor, but party losses in 1978 local elections led to charges that he was a weak leader. In 1980 the aggressive Franz Josef Strauss, head of the CDU's Bavarian affiliate, was selected as the chief opposition candidate for the chancellorship. Strauss lost decisively to the incumbent Schmidt, and Kohl's position as party leader was thereby strengthened.

Helmut Kohl was married to Hannelore Renner in 1960; they have two teenage sons.

ANDREAS DORPALEN

NELSON, Willie

Long known as a country music "outlaw," Willie Nelson has done more to popularize the form than perhaps any other country musician currently on the scene. A composer, singer, and instrumentalist, Nelson combines country, blues, and rock elements into a distinctive sound that took years to catch on but that finally brought vast new audiences into the fold. Nelson's full baritone voice, shoulder-length auburn hair—usually worn in a ponytail or braids, under a cowboy hat—baggy jeans and tee shirt, and warm stage presence have made him an international celebrity. He has won numerous music awards, including Country Music Association Entertainer of the Year for 1979 and four Grammys, for *Blue Eyes Cryin' in the Rain* (1975); *Georgia on My Mind* (1978); *Mama Don't Let Your Babies Grow Up to Be Cowboys*, with Waylon Jennings (1978); and *On the Road Again* (1980). The soft-spoken Texan, seen frequently on television, appeared in the mo-

Willie Nelson

Michael Putland/Retna Ltd.

tion pictures *Electric Horseman* (1979), *Honeysuckle Rose* (1980), and *Thief* (1981). In 1982 he played the title role in Fred Schepisi's Western fable, *Barbarosa*.

Background. Willie Nelson was born on April 30, 1933, in the small farming community of Abbott, TX. Willie and his sister, Bobbie, were reared by their grandparents and earned money picking cotton after school. Willie's grandfather, a blacksmith and amateur musician, gave Willie his first guitar and music lessons. By age 10 he was playing local dances, and by 13 he had his own band. In 1950 Willie dropped out of high school to join the Air Force but was discharged, for medical reasons, eight months later. He studied briefly at Baylor University, only to leave and take a variety of door-to-door salesman jobs. He did devote more and more time to his music, and in the late 1950s he worked as a radio disc jockey. By this time several of his songs—performed by others—began to gain notice, and Nelson went to Nashville in search of stardom.

He began recording his own songs in 1962, and a few of them reached the top ten charts. Nelson also played bass in the band of Ray Price, a well-known Nashville performer, and in 1964 became a regular member of the Grand Ole Opry. Still, the Nashville experience was a disappointment. Nelson's style was out of the country music mainstream and found little commercial success. Nelson returned to Texas disillusioned. He made his way to the Armadillo World Headquarters in Austin, where other prominent country western "outlaws" had gathered. The counterculture rock revolution of the late 1960s and 1970s began making room for a progressive country sound, and in 1973 Nelson finally made it big with the album *Shotgun Willie*. It wasn't long before he was a national phenomenon. July 4, 1975, was declared "Willie Nelson Day" in Texas. In May 1979 he visited the White House to present a special Country Music Association award to President Jimmy Carter, a longtime fan.

PÉREZ DE CUELLAR, Javier

The fifth secretary-general of the United Nations, Javier Pérez de Cuellar, began his five-year term on Jan. 1, 1982. The career diplomat from Peru—the first UN chief from Latin America—took office with a reputation as a man of honor but also of extreme caution, with no record of the innovative problem-solving that is needed to tackle the disputes before the UN.

Pérez de Cuellar's initial objective was to improve staff morale by deflecting governmental pressure in hiring and promotion. His first political test came in April, when Argentina invaded and occupied the Falkland Islands. Pérez de Cuellar mediated between the British and Argentines for three weeks, but both sides ultimately rejected his last proposal. Despite the failure of his diplomacy, the effort won praise for the 62-year-old secretary-general and enhanced his reputation as an "honest broker." His stands on disarmament and the Middle East demonstrated his eloquence, frankness, and compassion.

Background. Javier Pérez de Cuellar was born in Lima, Peru, on Jan. 19, 1920, and was graduated from the Catholic University law faculty there in 1943. The following year he joined the Peruvian foreign service, serving in France, Britain, Bolivia, and Brazil. After holding various senior posts in Lima, he became ambassador to Switzerland in 1964. He was Peru's first ambassador to the Soviet Union from 1969 to 1971, when he became Peru's UN representative.

In 1975 Pérez de Cuellar joined the Secretariat as the UN mediator in Cyprus, and in 1976 he persuaded leaders of the island's Greek and Turkish communities to open talks. After a stint as his country's ambassador to Venezuela, he returned to the UN in 1979 as an undersecretary in charge of UN peace forces. In that post he learned a great deal about UN personnel issues while serving on the board that supervises staff appointments and promotions. After the Soviet invasion of Afghanistan in 1980, he took on the difficult task of trying to negotiate an arrangement under which the occupation could be ended.

On Dec. 11, 1981, while still on the latter assignment, Pérez de Cuellar was recommended by the Security Coun-

Javier Pérez de Cuellar

Wide World

cil as a compromise choice to succeed Kurt Waldheim of Austria as secretary-general. The General Assembly approved him by acclamation three days later.

Pérez de Cuellar is married to the former Marcela Temple and has two grown children by a previous marriage. He is the author of two books on international law and likes to relax in the evenings by reading Spanish literature or listening to classical music. He has described himself as a man of diplomacy and peace, but "that doesn't mean I am mild. One has to impress people with your firmness."

MICHAEL J. BERLIN

SAWYER, Diane

In the competitive and pressurized world of television broadcasting, 37-year-old Diane Sawyer has made a household name for herself with a cool and sophisticated reporting style. As co-anchor with Bill Kurtis on *CBS Morning News*, a weekday broadcast which premiered in March 1982, she fills one of the most visible and demanding jobs on the air. A former aide to President Richard Nixon, Sawyer began building her reputation as a reporter and State Department correspondent in Washington. Among her reportorial assignments were the Three Mile Island nuclear accident and subsequent proceedings; the diplomatic efforts to free the American hostages in Iran; various aspects of the 1980 presidential election; the Reagan administration policy in El Salvador; and the role of former Secretary of State Alexander Haig. One of a handful of women to break the sex barrier of national broadcast journalism, the pretty blonde has earned a reputation among her colleagues as a hard worker. Her schedule, which she describes as "unmerciful," has her going to bed at 5:30 P.M. and rising at 1 A.M.

Background. The daughter of a judge and an elementary school teacher, Diane Sawyer was born in Glasgow, KY, on Dec. 22, 1945. Reared in Louisville, she was elected America's Junior Miss at age 17 and traveled around the country making several appearances a day. In 1967 she received her B.A. degree from Wellesley (MA) College and entered the University of Louisville Law School. After one semester she withdrew to begin her career in television.

From 1967 to 1970, Sawyer worked as a reporter for the CBS affiliate in Louisville, WLKY-TV. She was hired by the Nixon administration in October 1970 as an aide to the deputy press secretary. She subsequently moved up to administrative assistant to Press Secretary Ron Ziegler and then staff assistant to Nixon himself. From July 1975 to April 1978, she assisted the former president in the writing of his memoirs.

Returning to CBS in August 1978, Sawyer was made a reporter in the Washington Bureau, and she was named a correspondent in February 1980. Four months later she was assigned to the State Department, which she covered for one year. In September 1981 she was named co-anchor with Charles Kuralt on the 90-minute weekday news program *Morning*, the predecessor of *CBS Morning News*. The latter show's format is more information oriented than the competing broadcasts of other networks. Detailed reports, in-depth interviews, and a sober style suit the anchorwoman just fine. "We have a stubborn integrity about what we're doing," says Sawyer.

SCHLAFLY, Phyllis

For ardent antifeminist Phyllis Schlafly, 1982 was a banner year. After a decade of fighting the Equal Rights Amendment (ERA), she saw the proposed constitutional change go down in defeat. Schlafly and her Eagle Forum, a conservative group which she founded and heads, celebrated with a giant "Over the Rainbow" party on June 30, the day the amendment officially ran out of time, three states short of ratification. If enacted, it would have prohibited legal discrimination on the basis of sex.

The Alton, IL, self-described "housewife" launched her crusade against the amendment in 1972, the year it was passed by Congress. At the time, it was almost unopposed. Impeccably clad and usually unflappable in debate, she took her message coast to coast, charging that the ERA would destroy the American family. She regularly infuriated her opponents by labeling them "women's libbers" who care nothing about families but want to draft women and legalize homosexual marriage.

Feminists point to the irony of a woman as independent as Schlafly, a longtime political activist, author of several books, television-radio commentator, and public speaker, opposing the ERA. "I can do it all without the ERA," she replies. "Home, husband, family, and children have come first in my life," says Schlafly. "Everything else came afterward."

After ERA's defeat, she announced that her Eagle Forum would work for political candidates "who are pro-family," as well as institute campaigns against sex education and a nuclear freeze.

Phyllis Schlafly

Wide World

Background. Born in St. Louis on Aug. 15, 1924, Phyllis Schlafly was the first child of John and Odile Stewart. Her inventor-father lost his job during the Depression, but her mother found work to earn enough money to send her daughter to an elite Catholic school. Later, Schlafly test-fired ammunition in a St. Louis factory at night so that she could attend Washington University where she was graduated Phi Beta Kappa. She then completed a master's degree in government at Radcliffe before she was 21.

After marrying corporation lawyer Fred Schlafly, she ostensibly settled down to be a homemaker in Alton, IL, raising six children. However, she never strayed far from politics. She ran for Congress in 1952 and 1970, losing both times. In 1964 she wrote and published *A Choice, Not an Echo*, a book that helped catapult Barry Goldwater to the presidential nomination.

In 1967 she began to speak out on a variety of conservative issues, sending her monthly "Phyllis Schlafly Report" to a network of like-minded women. She later went to Washington University Law School to gain constitutional law credentials, and was admitted to the Illinois bar in 1979.

Schlafly and her husband, whose children are grown, live at their spacious Alton home where a staff handles her considerable correspondence.

JULIA MALONE

SHARON, Ariel

Revered for his military leadership, assailed for his combat excesses, Israeli Defense Minister Ariel ("Arik") Sharon is one of his nation's most controversial public figures. Israel's invasion of Lebanon in June 1982 further split domestic opinion and thrust the 54-year-old career soldier into the international spotlight. The portly, gray-haired Sabra (native Israeli) was highly visible throughout the conflict, observing the army's progress and inspiring his troops. "This is Arik's war," said one government official. The success of the campaign enhanced Sharon's already formidable reputation as a military strategist, but heavy civilian casualties, the lengthy siege of Beirut, and alleged foreknowledge of the Christian Lebanese massacre of Palestinian refugees in September aroused severe criticism at home and abroad.

A founder of the governing Likud alliance, Sharon was appointed defense minister in August 1981. He is a trusted adviser to Prime Minister Begin and, at least before the massacre, was considered Begin's most likely successor as leader of the Likud. Opponents of his hard-line Zionism, however, were joined by many other Israelis in expressing outrage at the events south of Beirut and in calling for Sharon's dismissal.

Background. Ariel Sharon was born in 1928 at Kfar Maalal, one of the first Jewish agricultural cooperatives in Palestine. His parents were Russian Jews who emigrated after World War I and joined with other Zionist settlers in defending their land from attacks by neighboring Arabs. As a teenager, Ariel joined Haganah, the clandestine Jewish defense force, and completed a training course for platoon leaders at age 17. In the 1948 war of independence he was seriously wounded in the stomach but eventually returned to combat as a company commander. After a leave of absence to study Middle Eastern history, he was recruited to organize an elite antiterrorist corps for retaliatory raids into Jordan. During the Suez War of 1956, Sharon commanded the Israeli paratroop corps and led his troops to an important victory at the strategic Mitla Pass in the Sinai. By the Six-Day War of 1967, Sharon had earned a law degree and advanced to the rank of major general. As commander of the Egyptian front he directed Israeli ground forces to a major victory at the Suez Canal. Sharon retired from active service in July 1973 but was recalled three months later upon the outbreak of the Yom Kippur War. The outstanding achievement of his military career was the crossing of the Suez Canal and the establishment of an Israeli bridgehead on Egyptian territory. He emerged from the war a hero.

In 1973 Sharon was elected to parliament, where he was a vital member of the new Likud coalition. The follow-

Ariel Sharon

Milner/Sygma

ing year Prime Minister Yitzhak Rabin chose him to be his military adviser, but in 1976 Sharon resigned to form a new political party. It was not powerful, winning only two seats, but it did help elect Begin in 1977. As minister of agriculture in the new administration, Sharon initiated programs to establish Jewish settlements in occupied Arab territories.

Ariel Sharon lives on a 1,000-acre (400-ha) farm in the Negev Desert with his wife, Lili, and two sons.

See also ISRAEL; MIDDLE EAST.

SHULTZ, George Pratt

At the swearing-in ceremony of his new secretary of state, President Reagan applauded him with an old saying, "Let George do it." After a tumultuous 18 months with Alexander Haig in the top diplomatic post, the president and his aides were relieved to usher in the coolly competent George Pratt Shultz, a direct opposite of the explosive Haig and a Washington-wise veteran of the Nixon years. The plaudit had been voiced by the Senate, which voted unanimously on July 15, 1982, to confirm Shultz as the nation's 60th secretary of state.

The holder of a doctoral degree in industrial economics, Shultz's experience has been chiefly in the domestic arena. Under President Nixon, he headed the Office of Management and Budget (July 1970–May 1972) and served as secretary of both labor (January 1969–June 1970) and treasury (June 1972–May 1974). He resigned to join the Bechtel Corporation, a construction conglomerate with extensive commitments in the Middle East.

As president of Bechtel, he traveled widely, acting in effect as a secretary of state for the huge firm. Because Bechtel has major projects in several Arab countries, particularly Saudi Arabia, Shultz was thought to be less apt to take Israel's side in Middle Eastern disputes than Haig.

During his confirmation hearings on Capitol Hill, Shultz declared that "the legitimate needs and problems of the Palestinian people must be addressed and resolved"—a statement that signaled his apparent determination to put the thorny subject of a Palestinian homeland at the top of the administration's priority list.

The arrival of Shultz at the State Department completed the takeover of Reagan's foreign policy apparatus by three of his longtime California associates. Together with Defense Secretary Caspar Weinberger and National Security Adviser William P. Clark, Shultz has been a confidant of Reagan's for some time, advising him on economic policy during the 1980 presidential campaign.

Shultz once wrote that the United States under Jimmy Carter was the "Prince Hamlet of world affairs, a superpower, but indecisive, with results that are dangerous for everyone." An advocate of U.S.–Soviet trade, he criticized Carter for placing restrictions on the sale of American technology to the Soviet Union. Reagan has since expanded that policy to include foreign companies licensed to sell U.S. technology. Although Shultz has endorsed Reagan's approach, he is thought to be less eager than his colleagues to wage economic warfare against the Soviets at the expense of the NATO alliance.

Shultz has a reputation for being a "good soldier." As Nixon's OMB director, he argued vehemently against wage and price controls. But when Nixon ignored his advice and imposed controls in August 1971, Shultz volunteered to run the program.

Nevertheless, Shultz knows how to stick to his principles. On the Watergate tapes, Nixon can be heard calling him a "candy ass" for refusing to order the Internal Revenue Service (IRS) to investigate Nixon's enemies. In *Economic Policy Beyond the Headlines*, a 1978 book he coauthored with academician Kenneth W. Dam (who in July 1982 was named deputy secretary of state), Shultz recalls that perhaps the two most important words he spoke during his five-plus years of government service were "do nothing" when confronted with Nixon's request regarding the IRS.

Background. George Pratt Shultz was born Dec. 13, 1920, in New York City. He took his B.A. at Princeton in 1942, then served as a Marine Corps captain in Hawaii where he met and married Army nurse Helena O'Brien, known as "Obie." He received a doctorate from the Massachusetts Institute of Technology (MIT) in 1949, and spent a total of 22 years on the faculties of MIT and the University of Chicago. In 1962, he became dean of the University of Chicago Business School.

While at Bechtel, he taught part-time at the Stanford University Graduate School of Business. He and his wife maintained a home on the campus. The Shultzes have five children. A pipe smoker, Secretary Shultz enjoys tennis and golf.

ELEANOR CLIFT

SMEAL, Eleanor Marie

Eleanor Smeal, the woman who spearheaded the drive to ratify the Equal Rights Amendment (ERA), stood grim-faced and determined before a crowd of supporters in Tallahassee, FL. "We will never give up," said the president of the National Organization for Women (NOW), minutes after the state legislature had refused to ratify the ERA, setting the seal on its final defeat.

A no-nonsense leader who has a reputation for working 20-hour days, Smeal had crisscrossed the United States since 1977. Her number one goal was winning the 38 states needed to ratify the constitutional amendment that would bar sex discrimination. But when the official clock ran out June 30, Smeal vowed to continue the fight for equality for women. NOW would move into politics to elect a new type of lawmaker dedicated to human rights, she said.

A former housewife with an impressive education, Smeal is the first homemaker to head NOW, which with some 216,000 members is the nation's biggest feminist organization. During her tenure as president (1977–82), NOW shifted toward the mainstream of women's interests and away from its earlier more radical image.

Despite the change, Smeal fought an uphill battle as she argued that the ERA meant justice, not unisex toilets, and that the amendment would add to, not subtract from, the rights of homemakers. As the ratification drive wound down, she concluded that a "silent lobby" of insurance

Eleanor Smeal   UPI

companies, which offer different rates to men and women, and other corporations had killed the ERA.

Background. Born on July 30, 1939, in Ashtabula, OH, Eleanor Marie Smeal was the youngest of four children of Peter and Josephine Cutri, Italian immigrants who believed firmly in education despite their own lack of schooling. Her father established an insurance business in Erie, PA, where Smeal grew up.

Smeal attended Duke University in North Carolina, graduating Phi Beta Kappa. A professor dissuaded her from choosing law school, arguing that as a woman she would not be allowed to practice law. Instead, she earned a master's degree in political science from the University of Florida in 1963.

She married Charles Smeal, a metallurgist with a Ph.D., and they settled outside Pittsburgh. The turning point in her life came after the birth of their second child, when a back ailment confined Eleanor to bed for a year and she made a close study of feminist literature. She and her husband joined NOW in 1971, and she advanced quickly up the ranks. When she was elected president in April 1977, it was her first paying job.

Eleanor and Charles Smeal, who moved to the outskirts of Washington, DC, to be near her work, live with their teenaged children, Tod and Lori.

JULIA MALONE

SMITH, Dean Edwards

Finally, Dean Smith has it all. He had entered the 1981–82 season as the seventh winningest coach of all time in major college basketball, he had gained the respect of his peers as one of the game's greatest innovators, and he had brought home countless trophies to the University of North Carolina—but he had never won "The Big One." Now he has. In his seventh trip to the National Collegiate Athletic Association (NCAA) tournament Final Four, Smith coached the Tar Heels to a 63–62 victory over Georgetown for college basketball's biggest prize. (*See* SPORTS—Basketball.)

Smith's team had been ranked at or near the top of the national preseason polls, and it occupied the Number 1 spot for several weeks during the season. The 1982 Tar Heels might not have been his greatest squad individually, Smith conceded, but it did have all the ingredients of a championship team—experience, a potent offense, and a stingy defense. Showing the poise and discipline that have become the trademark of Dean Smith teams, Carolina played its best basketball in the NCAA tournament and finally won one for "Coach."

Background. Dean Edwards Smith was born in Emporia, KS, on Feb. 28, 1931. The son of a high school basketball coach, Smith went to the University of Kansas on an academic scholarship. In addition to playing freshman football and varsity baseball, he was a guard on the Jayhawk basketball teams—coached by the legendary Dr. F. C. "Phog" Allen—that won the national championship in 1952 and finished second a year later.

Smith caught the coaching bug after graduation, while stationed in Germany as a member of the U.S. Air Force. His first team, made up of air policemen, was undefeated (11–0). While in Germany he met Bob Spear, who took him on as an assistant coach for the U.S. Air Force Academy's first basketball team. Smith held the job for three years before going to North Carolina as an assistant to Frank McGuire, later elected to the Basketball Hall of Fame. When McGuire left North Carolina three years later, he recommended Smith as his replacement. Although the young assistant was still relatively unknown, McGuire knew he would succeed. "Dean Smith will be one of the finest coaches in the nation in a very few years," McGuire predicted.

Smith's technical contributions to the game are many. Among them are the controversial "four corners offense," the "run and jump defense," and team huddles to set up defenses before free throws. In addition to the 1982 national championship, Smith's teams have won nine Atlantic Coast Conference (ACC) postseason tournaments and finished first in the regular season ten times. He has had ten 25-win seasons and led his team to seven NCAA Regional Championships. In 1976, Smith coached the U.S. Olympic team to the gold medal.

MARK ENGEL

Dean Smith

© Dan Helms/Duomo

Steven Spielberg   Philippe Ledru/Sygma

SPIELBERG, Steven

With two new hit movies in 1982—*E.T. The Extra-Terrestrial* and *Poltergeist*—35-year-old filmmaker Steven Spielberg seemed finally to shuck the label of motion picture "wunderkind." Released in early summer, *E.T.* and *Poltergeist* continued Spielberg's streak of movie blockbusters and established him as one of the most popular directors of his time. To his credit the maker of *Jaws* (1975), *Close Encounters of the Third Kind* (1977), and *Raiders of the Lost Ark* (1981), had two fantasy-adventures in 1982 that were a double box-office smash unprecedented in the history of the screen. *Poltergeist*—of which he was co-producer, co-screenwriter, and editing supervisor—is a modern-day ghost story, and *E.T.*—which he directed and co-produced—is a kind of science fiction fairy tale. (*See* MOTION PICTURES.) Both are stamped with Spielberg's unique combination of wit, enchantment, and suspense which develops before the backdrop of everyday life in America. More escapist than artistic, Spielberg's films aim to pique the imagination and, above all, to entertain the audience. Says one colleague, "Steven makes his movies sitting front-row center with popcorn. He *is* the audience."

Background. Steven Spielberg was born in Cincinnati, OH, on Dec. 18, 1947. He was the eldest of four children of Leah Posner Spielberg, a concert pianist, and Arnold Spielberg, an electrical engineer. The family moved from Ohio to New Jersey to Arizona, and when Steven was a teenager his parents divorced. A "weird, skinny kid with acne," young Spielberg found expression in an 8-mm movie camera. At age 12 he made his first short film, a collision between two Lionel trains. Dreaming up ever more elaborate scenes and stories, he made a two-and-a-half-hour science-fiction movie, *Firelight*, at age 16. Not accepted by any college with a film program, Steven attended California State College at Long Beach, where he received a B.A. in English.

In 1969, while still in school, Spielberg made a 16-mm short called *Amblin'*, which won awards at the Venice and Atlanta film festivals. After a series of routine but successful television jobs, Spielberg was offered his first contract for a major motion picture. *The Sugarland Express* (1974), a comedy-drama starring Goldie Hawn, was well received by the critics but unsuccessful at the box offfice. One year later *Jaws* was setting records, and Spielberg was being hailed as a great young talent. *Close Encounters*, a dazzling science-fiction fantasy, brought audiences back for multiple viewings. And *Raiders*—a collaboration with George Lucas, creator of *Star Wars*—was the summer hit of 1981, as well as an Oscar nominee for "Best Picture." Spielberg's only real miss was *1941* (1979), a World War II comedy.

Spielberg is tall and slim, with thick brown hair. He dresses casually, often in jeans and a sweater. He spends his spare time at home in California but admits, "The only time I feel totally happy is when I'm watching films or making them."

STAPLETON, Maureen

An actress long renowned for dedication to her craft, Maureen Stapleton received new accolades in 1982 for her masterful portrayal of American anarchist Emma Goldman in the film spectacular *Reds.* Film critics, heaping praise, referred to her performance as "hearty, funny. . . ," "marvelous and earthy," and showing "purity in her acting." The Academy of Motion Picture Arts and Sciences' voters, apparently in agreement, awarded her the Academy Award for "Best Performance in a Supporting Role."

Background. Of Irish descent, Maureen Stapleton was born in Troy, NY, on June 21, 1925. Soon after high school she headed for New York to become an actress. Her first job there—as a billing machine operator on a night shift—enabled her to take daytime acting classes. She described the classes as opening a "whole new world" where she learned "integrity in acting." A charter member of the famed Actors Studio, she studied there first with Robert Lewis and later with Lee Strasberg.

Her Broadway debut came in *The Playboy of the Western World* (1946) and was soon followed by a tour with Katharine Cornell in *The Barretts of Wimpole Street* and a Broadway stint, again with Miss Cornell, in *Antony and Cleopatra.*

In 1951 Stapleton achieved major prominence on the stage with the role of Serafina delle Rose in Tennessee Williams' *The Rose Tattoo,* for which she won a Tony award. Thereafter she often was associated with Williams' plays, appearing in his *Twenty-Seven Wagons Full of Cotton, Orpheus Descending* (and its film version, *The Fugitive Kind*), revivals of *The Glass Menagerie,* and the 1976 TV dramatization of *Cat on a Hot Tin Roof.*

Other important Broadway runs included *Toys in the Attic; Plaza Suite; The Gingerbread Lady,* for which she again received a Tony award; *The Country Girl;* and *The Little Foxes,* the 1981 production with Elizabeth Taylor.

Venturing into motion pictures, she debuted in *Lonelyhearts* (1958), with Montgomery Clift. Other major screen credits include *A View from the Bridge, Bye Bye Birdie, Trilogy, Plaza Suite,* and *Interiors.*

Stapleton's early appearances on television coincided with its so-called "golden age." Especially memorable were her performances in *All the King's Men* and *For Whom the Bell Tolls.* Recently she has starred in *Tell Me Where It Hurts, Queen of the Stardust Ballroom,* and *The Gathering,* receiving Emmy nominations for the latter two.

Twice married and divorced, she has two children. She especially fears flying.

UPDIKE, John

Despite criticism that his subject matter is too narrow, John Updike has emerged as one of America's most important contemporary writers. He has established himself as a brilliant prose stylist whose use of language is so evocative that he is paradoxically accused of writing "too well." But Updike has used his talents with admirable self-awareness; no one else has so clinically and so tenderly examined the crises of middle-class life in America. In 1982 he won the Pulitzer Prize and the American Book Award for *Rabbit is Rich,* his tenth novel and the third in the "Rabbit" trilogy. The fall publishing season then saw the release of a new short-story collection, *Bech is Back.*

Background. John Updike was born on March 18, 1932, in Shillington, PA. He attended Harvard University (B.A., 1954) in part because of the opportunity to draw and write for the *Harvard Lampoon.* In 1953 he married Mary

Pennington, with whom he had four children. After graduation Updike traveled to England to study at the Ruskin School of Drawing and Fine Art, but he decided to devote himself to writing. His first literary sale, a short story to the *New Yorker,* began a lasting association with that magazine. Updike was divorced in 1977 and currently lives in Georgetown, MA, with his second wife, Martha Bernhard.

Updike signaled his remarkable talent and productivity in 1959 with his first collection of stories, *The Same Door,* and his first novel, *The Poorhouse Fair,* an amazingly mature study of life in an old-age home. *Rabbit, Run* (1960), the first of three novels about Harry Angstrom, a sort of American Everyman who is trying to puzzle out his life, established Updike as an important young writer. *Rabbit Redux* (1971) deals with the turbulent 1960s, and *Rabbit is Rich* (1981) shows Harry as a middle-aged man in the summer of 1979.

Updike's novels are often controversial. *The Centaur* (1963) attempted to give cosmic scale to a Pennsylvania family by the daring use of classical mythology. Graphic sexual description and constant introspection mark *Couples* (1968), *A Month of Sundays* (1975), and *Marry Me* (1976). *The Coup* (1978) imagines the thoughts and feelings of a contemporary African dictator.

Perhaps Updike's most thoroughly successful works are his stories, which perfectly balance style, scale, and subject. His collections are *Pigeon Feathers* (1962), *Olinger Stories* (1964), *The Music School* (1966), *Bech: A Book* (1970), *Museums and Women* (1972), *Too Far to Go* (1979), and *Problems* (1979). A long story, *Of the Farm* (1965) is occasionally regarded as Updike's masterpiece.

Updike is more than a chronicler of the surfaces of American life. He uses language not for ostentatious effect but to create unforgettable sensations which lead to shocks of recognition. Influenced by theologians Karl Barth and Paul Tillich, he addresses the search for love, the quest for understanding, and the yearning for a spiritual meaning of life. He writes that "by taking pains, word by word, to be accurate, we put ourselves on the way toward making something useful and beautiful, and, in a word, good."

JEROME STERN

VESSEY, John William, Jr.

In a surprise appointment, announced by the White House on March 4, 1982, President Ronald Reagan named Gen. John W. Vessey, Jr., chairman of the Joint

John W. Vessey, Jr.

Russell F. Reederer/U.S. Army Audiovisual Center

Chiefs of Staff, succeeding Gen. David C. Jones. Following confirmation by the Senate, the 60-year-old general, who had served as vice chief of staff of the Army since July 1979, took over as chairman on July 1.

A general who had worked with Vessey pointed out that the president's new senior military adviser "is a very cool and calm man . . . very meticulous about detail." Gen. Edward C. Meyer, the Army chief of staff, said that Vessey would "do the kinds of things that the chairman ought to be doing, which are looking at broad policies and being able to articulate the issues so that we make the right decisions in the very critical period ahead."

A battlefield commander, General Vessey is the recipient of many military decorations, including the Defense Distinguished Service Medal, the Distinguished Service Cross, the Army Distinguished Service Medal, and a Purple Heart for being wounded in Vietnam.

Background. Born in Minneapolis, MN, on June 29, 1922, the future military leader enlisted in the Minnesota National Guard in May 1939 and was called to active duty 21 months later. He received a battlefield commission as a second lieutenant of field artillery at the Anzio Beachhead in Italy on May 6, 1944. Before World War II ended, he also saw action in North Africa.

General Vessey later was executive officer of the 25th Infantry Division Artillery in Vietnam, served two tours with the 3d Armored Division in Germany, and was deputy chief of the U.S. Military Advisory Group in Thailand. Vessey spent March 1973 through September 1974 in Washington, DC, as director of operations of the office of the deputy chief of staff for operations and plans of the U.S. Army, and October 1974 through August 1975 at Fort Carson, CO, as commanding general of the 4th Infantry Division (Mechanized). He was promoted to lieutenant general in 1975, and was deputy chief of staff for operations of the U.S. Army and senior Army representative at the UN from September 1975 through October 1976. A full general since November 1976, he served in Korea from October 1976 to July 1979.

The general did not obtain his bachelor's degree (a B.S. from the University of Maryland) until he was 41 years old and a lieutenant colonel. He attended several military schools and was awarded a master's degree in business administration by George Washington University in 1965. A member of Phi Kappa Phi, General Vessey is married to the former Avis C. Funk. They are the parents of three children.

WEINBERGER, Caspar Willard

Caspar Weinberger made his reputation as a budget-cutter, describing himself as almost "heretical" when it came to practicing fiscal restraint. As secretary of Health, Education, and Welfare (HEW) during the Nixon administration, he sliced so many programs he became known as "Cap the Knife." When President-elect Reagan named him secretary of defense, the military establishment feared he was miscast to preside over what promised to be the biggest peacetime build-up in history.

They need not have worried. The diminutive Weinberger fights so hard for his department's full budget share that White House aides complain he is "a captive of the generals" and that he is undermining their efforts to bring the federal budget under control.

Weinberger maintains that "without a strong defense, a strong economy has no meaning," and he vows to stick with his mission "to rearm America." Among the programs he has pushed to assure that the United States is not second militarily to the Soviet Union is a controversial mobile missile system, the MX; a new bomber, the B-1; two additional nuclear-powered aircraft carriers; and the expansion of the current 400-ship Navy to 600 vessels by 1990.

Despite an ongoing recession and drastic reductions in domestic spending, President Reagan has backed Weinberger every step of the way, counting his fellow Californian among his most trusted advisers. The two first worked together in 1968 when Weinberger, serving as Governor Reagan's finance director, turned a state budget deficit into a surplus and won an inscribed picture of himself with

Caspar W. Weinberger

Sygma

a joyous Reagan. The notation read, "The smile is for real, thanks to you." In recent years, Weinberger's influence has prevailed to the extent that Reagan calls him, "my Disraeli."

Weinberger frequently clashed with former Secretary of State Alexander Haig over the role of America's NATO allies in any modern-day cold war. Where Haig tended to sympathize with the European desire to keep détente alive, Weinberger usually carried the day with a tougher approach, including unpopular trade sanctions. An ardent Anglophile, Weinberger has said that he sees "some rather deadly parallels" between Sir Winston Churchill's often lonely efforts to persuade a reluctant Europe to rearm against the Germans and President Reagan's ongoing battle for the necessary dollars to ward off the Soviet threat.

Though he is soft-spoken and deferential in manner, Weinberger is a relentless taskmaster, at one point ordering lie-detector tests for officials suspected of unauthorized leaks to reporters.

Background. Caspar Willard Weinberger was born on Aug. 18, 1917, in San Francisco, CA. His Ivy League credentials include both Harvard and Harvard Law School. He made his Washington debut during the Nixon administration in a series of high-profile jobs: chairman of the Federal Trade Commission (1970); deputy director and director of the Office of Management and Budget (1970–72, 1972–73); counsellor to the president (1973); and HEW secretary (1973–75). A year after Nixon resigned the presidency, Weinberger returned to California to become chief legal counsel for the Bechtel Group, a construction conglomerate.

He and his wife, the former Jane Dalton, have two children.

Eleanor Clift

BOLIVIA

Peter McFarrety/New York Times Pictures

Miners stage a rally for candidate Hernán Siles Zuazo.

The most important event in Bolivia in 1982 was the inauguration on October 10 of Hernán Siles Zuazo as the first democratically elected constitutional president in two decades. He had first been chosen as the result of the election of 1980, but a coup in August of that year had prevented his taking office.

Siles was the third Bolivian president in 1982. During the early months of the year, Gen. Celso Torrelio Villa sought unsuccessfully to combat the economic crisis. In February, he devalued the peso from 24.51 to the U.S. dollar to 44 to the dollar, increased gasoline prices by 20%, froze prices of some foods, and decreed a 130% wage increase for low-paid workers. On April 21 he announced that new elections would be held in April 1983, and soon after he lifted the ban on political parties and labor unions that had been in effect since August 1980.

However, on July 15, Torrelio was forced to resign as president, giving way to a three-man military junta, which on July 21 installed still another general as president, Guido Vildoso Calderón. He promised to "rebuild the economy, bring back full democracy, defeat defeatism, and restore faith in the fatherland." He also promised to crack down on the $2,000,000,000-per-year cocaine trade. Nevertheless, civilian opposition to the military regime continued.

Hernán Siles, who had headed a symbolic "government in exile" from Peru since August 1980, demanded new elections. Late in September, President Vildoso announced that the Congress elected in 1980 would be allowed to convene and elect a new president. The Congress met during the first week of October and overwhelmingly chose Hernán Siles. He returned triumphantly to Bolivia on October 8 and was inaugurated two days later.

President Siles appointed a 14-person cabinet, including six from his Nationalist Revolutionary Movement of the Left, six from the Leftist Revolutionary Movement of Vice-President Jaime Paz Zamora, and two from the pro-Soviet Communist Party of Bolivia.

The day after his inauguration, Siles replaced all of the top military command with officers reputed to be supporters of constitutional rule. He also began negotiations to reschedule the $2,500,000,000 foreign debt, on which Bolivia had defaulted. He promised to move against the cocaine trade, take steps to curtail the inflation rate of more than 125% a year, and help poorly paid workers.

In June, Bolivia was one of the five producing countries to sign the Sixth International Tin Agreement. At the same time, it got a loan of $26.7 million from the International Monetary Fund to help finance its contribution.

During the crisis over Argentina's invasion of the Falkland (Malvinas) Islands, Bolivia supported Argentina. It joined other Andean Pact countries in promising to increase trade with Argentina.

In April, Guido Salinas, Central Bank president, resigned when accused of selling foreign exchange reserves held in the United States to government insiders just before February's devaluation. In May a paramilitary group called "Sovereignty" threatened to murder U.S. Ambassador Edwin Corr for allegedly accusing Lt. Col. Luis Arce Gomez of being engaged in the cocaine trade. About the same time, Bolivia's cultural attaché in Mexico, Victor Vargas, was arrested at Kennedy Airport in New York, charged with carrying 11 lbs (5 kg) of cocaine in his luggage.

ROBERT J. ALEXANDER, *Rutgers University*

BOLIVIA · Information Highlights

Official Name: Republic of Bolivia.
Location: West-central South America.
Area: 424,164 sq mi (1 098 585 km²).
Population (1982 est.): 5,600,000.
Chief Cities (1980 est.): Sucre, the legal capital, 68,426; La Paz, the actual capital, 719,780; Santa Cruz de la Sierra, 330,635; Cochabamba, 236,564.
Government: *Head of state and government,* Gen. Hernán Siles Zuazo, president, inaugurated Oct. 10, 1982. *Legislature*—Congress: Senate and Chamber of Deputies.
Monetary Unit: Peso (44 pesos equal U.S. $1, Oct. 20, 1982).
Gross National Product (1981 U.S.$): $7,400,000,000.
Economic Index (1981): *Consumer Prices* (1970= 100), *all items,* 741.4; *food,* 824.4.
Foreign Trade (1980 U.S.$): *Imports,* $833,000,000; *exports,* $1,033,000,000.

BRAZIL

Brazil in 1982 inched forward toward a restoration of democracy after 18 years of military rule. As the economy showed signs of slowing down, the government sought to improve relations with the United States, most particularly in the area of trade.

Elections. National elections were held on November 15 for all 479 seats in the House of Representatives, 25 of the 69 Senate seats, legislatures in all 23 states, and governorships in 22 states. The government's Social Democratic Party (PDS) maintained control of the House and Senate and won an ample majority of the state legislatures and governorships, but the opposition, especially the Brazilian Democratic Movement (PMDB), made significant gains in such populous states as São Paulo, Minas Gerais, and Rio de Janeiro. The elections were peaceful, with an estimated 50 million people voting out of a potential electorate of 58.5 million.

The composition of the national Senate and House is important because the Congress, together with six representatives from each state, make up the electoral college, which will choose a successor to President Gen. João Figueiredo, whose term ends in March 1985. On the basis of the election results, it seems likely that a military man will rule the country for another six years, but the gains registered by the civilian opposition are evidence of the continuing commitment of the country's generals to the process of *abertura* ("opening") to democracy.

U.S. Relations. Presidents Reagan of the United States and Figueiredo of Brazil exchanged state visits in 1982. Reagan was in Brazil for two days, December 1–2, as part of a tour of four Latin American countries. Figueiredo went to Washington in May. Both visits were cordial, and in Brasília, Reagan announced a $1,230,000,000 emergency loan to Brazil, but a number of troublesome issues remained between the two countries.

Brazil, increasingly export-minded, has seen U.S. markets steadily closing to a variety of its products under the impact of increasing protectionism. The United States has "graduated" a number of Brazilian products from the U.S. Generalized System of Preferences (GSP), which provides duty-free access to the U.S. markets for nearly 3,000 products from developing countries. The "graduation" principle is applied to products in which the U.S. government judges a country to have become relatively competitive in world markets. Brazil argues that, particularly in these difficult economic times, it should not be penalized for what it considers modest success in some export areas.

Another critical issue centers on Brazil's practice of offering subsidies to a broad range of exported goods to enable them to compete in the markets of the industrialized countries. The United States, under terms of the General Agreement on Tariffs and Trade (GATT), imposes additional (countervailing) import duties on such subsidized products. Brazil, along with most other Third World countries, believes that the developing nations should receive special treatment from the developed countries and should not be forced to offer reciprocal privileges for exports of the industrialized world. Subsidized Brazilian products in contention in 1982 ranged from frozen concentrated orange juice to steel and twin-engine turboprop airplanes.

A third problem between the two countries involves trade in services, a broad category that includes engineering and construction, banking, accounting, shipping, insurance, commercial aviation, communications, and franchising. The United States has proposed a new round of GATT negotiations to regulate trade in services. Brazil, which is moving into such areas as overseas construction, shipbuilding, and export of alternative fuel technologies, opposes moves to regulate the services trade.

Economy. Until the beginning of this decade, Brazil had one of the fastest-growing economies in the developing world. The current worldwide recession, along with Brazil's mounting foreign debt problem, have taken some of the steam out of the economy over the past two years. Although Mexico passed Brazil as the Third World's leading debtor nation in 1982, Brazil still finished the year with a foreign debt load of more than $80,000,000,000. Part of the debt has been amassed in financing ambitious development projects and borrowing to expand exploitation of the country's rich natural resource base. But a substantial part of the increasing foreign debt burden results from a weakening of demand for such traditional commodity exports as sugar and coffee. High interest rates and the long-term rise in the cost of imported petroleum also are factors. Oil imports and interest payments absorbed 86% of Brazil's export revenues in 1981.

At the beginning of 1982, the government had projected a balance of trade surplus of

---

BRAZIL · Information Highlights

Official Name: Federative Republic of Brazil.
Location: Eastern South America.
Area: 3,286,478 sq mi (8 511 965 km²).
Population (1980 census): 121,075,669.
Chief Cities (1980 census): Brasília, the capital, 1,202,683; São Paulo, 8,584,896; Rio de Janeiro, 5,184,292; Belo Horizonte, 1,814,990.
Government: *Head of state and government,* João Baptista Figueiredo, president (took office March 1979). *Legislature*—National Congress: Federal Senate and Chamber of Deputies.
Monetary Unit: New Cruzeiro (236.66 n. cruzeiros equal U.S.$1, Dec. 13, 1982).
Gross National Product (1980 U.S.$): $240,980,000,-000.
Economic Indexes: *Consumer Prices* (Nov. 1981, 1972=100), *all items,* 3,223.2; *food,* 3,580.1. *Industrial production* (1981, 1975=100), 115.
Foreign Trade (1981 U.S.$): *Imports,* $24,007,000,-000; *exports,* $23,172,000,000.

Morel/Gamma-Liaison

A carnival atmosphere attended party campaigning before Brazil's first free national elections since 1964.

$3,000,000,000. By year's end it seemed certain that the surplus would fall below $500 million. By contrast, interest payments on the foreign debt amounted to $10,000,000,000 during the year. Nonetheless, international bankers showed considerable confidence in Brazil's potential, and during much of the year Brazil refinanced its debt without recourse to the International Monetary Fund (IMF). By November, however, it became apparent that IMF help would be needed. In December the IMF approved a $546 million loan to cover a shortfall in export earnings and gave tentative approval to a $4,900,000,-000 financing package over the next three years.

Internally, the economic panorama was far from favorable. In 1981 the industrial output declined for the first time in 40 years. The gross domestic product slipped by 1.9%. Inflation hovered around 100% through 1982, and nominal interest rates were between 140 and 150%. In September the government announced an austerity plan, including restrictions on imports. Immediately after the November elections, it imposed a series of price increases for basic commodities and public services. On the other hand, the government stepped up its drive to expand Brazilian exports, and for the first time opened a lobbying office in Washington to secure more favorable treatment for Brazilian products in the U.S. market.

Energy. Work on the giant Itaipú hydroelectric project on the Paraná River neared completion in 1982. The sluice gates on the Itaipú dam were closed, and the Paraná began backing up behind it to form one of the largest lakes in Latin America. Itaipú's first turbine was scheduled to go into operation in February 1983. When the $17,000,000,000 project is operating at full capacity, it will generate 12,870 megawatts of electricity, three times the capacity of the Grand Coulee Dam in the United States, and the equivalent of 500,000 barrels of oil a day in a thermal generating plant. Although Itaipú is a joint project of Paraguay and Brazil, most of the power will go to Brazil. Itaipú eventually will produce as much electricity as all of New York State, including New York City, consumes.

The nation's austerity program has set back plans for development of a nuclear energy network. The budget of Nuclebrás, the government energy corporation, will be cut by 50% in 1983, to a level of $50 million. Brazil's first nuclear energy generating plant, Angra I, dedicated in 1981, was shut down early in 1982 because of design problems in a steam generation unit. When Angra I was restarted a few months later, it was authorized to operate at only 50% of total capacity, pending a solution of its problems.

Jari Project. In January, a consortium of 22 Brazilian companies assumed control of Jari, a huge agro-industrial Amazon project. The size of Belgium, Jari had been the property of Daniel K. Ludwig, an American businessman, who reportedly lost $1,000,000,000 on the venture.

RICHARD C. SCHROEDER
Washington Bureau Chief, "Vision"

BRITISH COLUMBIA

Low prices and weak world markets resulted in employee layoffs and production shutdowns throughout the forestry and mining industries. In the first half of 1982, sawn lumber production declined by 24% and pulp and paper by more than 7%. Only three metal mines, each with a precious metal component, remained profitable. Despite earlier production and price increases for coal, a cutback in demand from the Japanese steel industry threatened coal mining. Meanwhile, construction of the $2,500,000,000 northeast coal development project continued. In the first six months of 1982, 66,000 jobs were lost in British Columbia. In August unemployment reached a record high of 13.9%. British Columbia Hydro's proposed Site C power project on the Peace River was the subject of public hearings. Sabotage of a power substation on Vancouver Island caused an explosion that destroyed equipment valued at $6 million.

Government and Politics. In February, Premier William Bennett announced a plan to limit increases in government spending and imposed wage guidelines for all provincial public sector employees in a two-year Compensation Stabilization Program. Maximum basic income increases were initially set at 10% for 1982–83, with up to an additional 2% adjustment for compensation experience and a further 2% for special circumstances. In July the maximum basic increases were reduced to 6% in the first year and 5% for the second.

In 1981–82, provincial government revenue was $173.6 million below operating expenditures of $7,042,000,000. The budget for 1982–83 estimated total consolidated revenue fund expenditures at $7,689,000,000 and revenues of $7,331,-000,000. By the fall, a deficit as high as $1,000,000,000 seemed a possibility. Medicare premiums were increased and the corporation capital tax on banks was raised to 2%. At the spring sitting of the legislature, new waste management and wildlife acts were also approved. Other legislation removed the restrictions on the holdings of British Columbia Resource Investment Corporation shares and required cabinet approval of changes in the controlling interests of public utilities. A Housing and Employment Development Financing Authority was established with provision for a bond issue to finance capital projects.

A 15-month contract was concluded with the 40,000-member provincial Government Employees' Union after four and a half months of negotiations. During the dispute, the union had organized two province-wide strikes and selective regional and occupational strikes.

Questions concerning the expense accounts of Corporate and Consumer Affairs Minister Peter Hyndman were referred to the auditor general. In an August cabinet shuffle, Hyndman and two other ministers resigned. Provincial Progressive Conservative leader Brian Westwood resigned to join the separatist Western Canada Concept Party.

A fall sitting of the legislature was held. The government adopted a recommendation to increase the number of legislative seats from 57 to 64 but subsequently allowed the proposal to die when faced with accusations of gerrymandering. Additional restraint measures provided for a one-year, 6% limit on rate increases for Crown corporations and the Worker's Compensation Board, and suspension of the denticare program. Homeowner interest-free loans to reduce mortgage payments to a 12% level and small business development loans were offered as part of a plan for economic recovery. A commitment to a balanced budget was ended in new financial authority for treasury bill borrowing.

NORMAN RUFF, *University of Victoria*

BRITISH COLUMBIA · Information Highlights

Area: 366,255 sq mi (948 600 km²).

Population (1981 census): 2,744,467.

Chief Cities (1981 census): Victoria, the capital, 64,-379; Vancouver, 414,281; Prince George, 67,559; Kamloops, 64,048; Kelowna, 59,196; Nanaimo, 47,069.

Government (1982): *Chief Officers*—lt. gov., Henry Bell-Irving; premier, William R. Bennett (Social Credit party); atty. gen., L. Allan Williams. *Legislature*—Legislative Assembly, 57 members.

Education (1982–83): Enrollment—elementary and secondary schools, 537,100 pupils; postsecondary, 50,620 students.

Personal Income (average weekly salary, April 1982): $440.21.

Employment Rate (August 1982, seasonally adjusted): 13.9%.

(All monetary figures are in Canadian dollars.)

BULGARIA

In domestic affairs the government directed its efforts toward strengthening the economy, revising the penal code, and encouraging the "Socialist way of life." In foreign affairs it continued to toe the Soviet line.

Domestic Affairs. The year 1981 had ended with the publication of Bulgaria's 8th Five-Year Plan. Its targets were significantly more modest than those of the preceding plan. Soon after, the government established the New Economic Mechanism to reduce waste and provide some degree of autonomy to industrial units, which were to participate in national planning.

In April, the 9th Congress of the Trade Unions was held in Sofia. More than 2,900 delegates representing some 4,000,000 members discussed achievements of their organization, friendship with the Soviet Union, solidarity with the Polish Communist Party, and further expansion of international labor cooperation. President and First Secretary Todor Zhivkov called for the strengthening of the workers' collectives.

Bad weather reduced the yields for various crops. The areas sown with wheat and barley

BULGARIA · Information Highlights

Official Name: People's Republic of Bulgaria.
Location: Southeastern Europe.
Area: 42,823 sq mi (110 912 km^2).
Population (1982 est.): 8,900,000.
Chief Cities (1979 est.): Sofia, the capital, 1,047,920; Plovdiv, 342,000; Varna, 286,382.
Government: *Head of state,* Todor Zhivkov, president of the State Council and general secretary of the Communist party (took office July 1971). *Head of government,* Grisha Filipov, chairman of the Council of Ministers (took office June 1981).
Monetary Unit: Lev (0.85 lev equals U.S.$1, March 1982).
Gross National Product (1981 U.S.$): est. $30,200,-000,000 to $39,100,000,000.
Foreign Trade (1980 U.S.$): *Imports,* $9,650,000,-000; *exports,* $10,372,000,000.

were increased from 3.46 million acres (1.38 million ha) to 3.83 million acres (1.53 million ha).

The National Assembly revised the penal code. Some minor offenses were decriminalized, while penalties for economic crimes were increased.

In May, Zhivkov addressed 2,750 delegates to the 14th Congress of Bulgaria's Komsomol (Communist Youth League). He spoke of Bulgaria's "Golden Age of Socialist Culture" under the past leadership of his recently deceased daughter, Lyudmila. The First Secretary of the Komsomol, Stank Shopova, called upon Bulgarian youth to follow the "Socialist way of life," avoiding consumerism, idleness, criminality, as well as the misuse of tobacco and alcohol.

Foreign Affairs. As in the past, there was unqualified support of Soviet domestic and foreign policies. This was accompanied by increased criticism of U.S. policies and initiatives. In May, Poland's Communist Party secretary, Gen. Wojciech Jaruzelski, visited Sofia. In a public statement Zhivkov expressed "full understanding and support" for Jaruzelski's measures against "counterrevolution and anarchy" in Poland.

Also in May, an international symposium on industrial cooperation between the East and the West was held in Varna. Some 100 prominent business representatives from 26 countries, including the United States, West Germany, and Japan, discussed how most effectively to increase Bulgaria's foreign trade. But the poor quality of Bulgarian goods as well as a shortage of hard currencies proved to be the main obstacles.

JAN KARSKI, *Georgetown University*

BURMA

Burma enjoyed political stability and economic growth in 1982 despite continued insurgency at home and unsettled conditions in nearby Indochina.

Politics. President San Yu, successor to longtime military strongman Ne Win, experienced no challenges to his governmental leadership in his first year of office. But ailing Ne Win, who retained the chairmanship of the single Burma Socialist Program party when he relin-

quished the presidency in 1981, continued as the real power. Gen. Aye Ko, holding both party and cabinet posts, and Brig. Tin Oo, regaining favor with Ne Win, were potential replacements for San Yu as Ne Win's long-term successor.

The Economy. Burma anticipated a 7% increase in real gross domestic product (GDP) for the year. Indications were that the country would have the highest GDP growth in Southeast Asia. Aiding Burma economically were Japan, which extended a $112 million energy-transportation loan; the World Bank's International Development Association, which granted an $80 million hydroelectric and thermal power loan; and West Germany, which provided $55 million for power, agriculture, and railroads.

Insurgencies. Burma received increased support from two major non-Communist governments in its continuing struggle with multisided insurgencies. Eight insurrections controlled half the country and a third of its people.

U.S. Assistant Secretary of State John Holdridge visited Rangoon to promise continued American help in combating narcotics smuggling—a chief source of income for Burma's 12,000-man Communist insurrection. Through 1982, 27 helicopters and seven fixed-wing aircraft had been supplied. Ne Win visited West Germany in pursuit of new arms. The first German assault rifles arrived late in the year.

Foreign Relations. Burma was wooed by Communist and anti-Communist governments alike. The foreign ministers of Thailand and Singapore separately visited Rangoon on behalf of the anti-Communist Association of Southeast Asian Nations (ASEAN). Burma approved ASEAN's call for withdrawal of Vietnamese forces from Cambodia, but Foreign Minister Chit Hlaing indicated that his government would again abstain on United Nations recognition of the pro-Vietnamese Cambodian government. The Vietnamese foreign minister's midyear visit to Rangoon did little to temper Burma's fears of Vietnam's intentions. The Burmese government endeavored to retain its neutral foreign policy.

RICHARD BUTWELL, *University of South Dakota*

BURMA · Information Highlights

Official Name: Socialist Republic of the Union of Burma.
Location: Southeast Asia.
Area: 261,218 sq mi (676 555 km^2).
Population (1982 est.): 37,100,000.
Chief Cities (1973 census): Rangoon, the capital, 2,-056,118; Mandalay, 417,000; Moulmein 171, 767.
Government: *Head of state,* U San Yu, president (took office Nov. 1981). *Head of government,* U Maung Maung Kha, prime minister (took office March 1977). *Legislature* (unicameral)—People's Assembly.
Monetary Unit: Kyat (7.7182 kyats equal U.S.$1, March 1982).
Gross National Product (1981 U.S.$): $4,800,000,-000.
Economic Index (1980): *Consumer Prices* (1970= 100), *all items,* 274.2; *food,* 289.5.
Foreign Trade (1980 U.S.$): *Imports,* $353,000,000; *exports,* $471,000,000.

BUSINESS AND CORPORATE AFFAIRS

Larry Lambert/Picture Group

More U.S. businesses went bankrupt than in any year since the Great Depression. Countless others just closed up.

U.S. businessmen faced a difficult economic environment throughout most of 1982. The recession deepened, forcing many companies into bankruptcy, and interest rates remained high until the later months of the year. The only bright spot for businessmen was the reduction in the inflation rate from the double-digit levels of 1981 to less than 5% by the end of October 1982.

Corporate mergers were being negotiated at a faster pace than in 1981, though the number of "blockbuster" deals decreased by several. (*See* special report, page 149.)

Profits and Losses. U.S. corporate profits dropped sharply in the first quarter of 1982. According to Standard & Poor's they fell 11% compared with the first quarter of 1981. The worst-hit industries included airlines, savings and loans, trucking, paper, tire and rubber, construction, and mining. By the second quarter the profit slide was even worse, off 16% from the same period the previous year. The recession continued to hurt the basic "smoke stack" industries, including steel and machinery. However, it also spread to retailers, who reported sharply falling sales as unemployment spread. Automobile manufacturers reported profits in the first and second quarters as they reduced production runs to match sales and gained contract concessions from the United Auto Workers.

In the third quarter, earnings continued to wane. Economists estimated that profits would

be down by 15–20% from the same quarter in 1981. Although companies benefited from lower interest rates and from spending cuts enacted earlier in the year, demand remained weak. Nevertheless, corporate earnings did show some improvement compared with the second quarter, and many economists were hoping to see even more improvement by year's end.

The nation's steel manufacturers took some major losses in the third quarter, as factories operated at only about 40% of capacity. After reaching a settlement with European steel makers, who agreed to limit their exports to the United States, the American companies vowed to force other foreign steel makers to cut down on their exports as well.

The housing industry remained mired in a slump through much of the year. There was some improvement during the summer, however, and by September housing starts picked up by about 30% compared with the depressed levels of September 1981.

Bankruptcies. The continuing recession pushed many U.S. corporations into bankruptcy. According to Dun & Bradstreet, 20,365 companies had declared bankruptcy by October 21, the most since 1932.

The first major bankruptcy of the year came in May, when San Diego-based retailer Wickes Cos., burdened by a $2,200,000,000 debt and deteriorating relations with its suppliers, filed under Chapter 11 of the bankruptcy code. Analysts blamed Wickes' failure on the recession, years of bad management, and an ill-timed acquisition. Later in the year another major retailer, F.W. Woolworth, announced that it would close all of its 336 Woolco stores and try to sell its 52% interest in more than 1,000 Woolworth stores in Britain.

Braniff International Corp., the parent of Braniff Airlines, also closed its doors in May. The Dallas-based airline, widely known for its multicolored jets, had expanded its operations too rapidly during the deregulation of the airline industry and found itself financially overextended when the recession set in. An attempt by the company to shift from a jet-set image to a low-fare, economy image came too late. When the company shut down operations, it owed its creditors some $1,100,000,000, or about $100 million more than its assets.

There were rumors throughout the year that International Harvester, a major employer in the Midwest, would also be declaring bankruptcy. The farm equipment manufacturer did manage to restructure its massive debt, however, and by the end of October had still avoided going into bankruptcy. In the effort to stay alive, the company had to pare down its work force and close many of its factories.

New York employees demonstrate against the collapse of Britain's Laker Airways, a leader in cut-rate fares.

UPI

Another major bankruptcy came as a result not of the recession, but of lawsuits. Manville Corp., a Denver-based manufacturer of asbestos insulation, filed for bankruptcy because of thousands of lawsuits instituted against it seeking damages for asbestos-related deaths and other injuries. According to a study compiled by the company, Manville could expect some 32,000 lawsuits with a potential liability of $2,000,000,000; the company's total assets at the end of 1981 were $2,200,000,000. Many critics believed the bankruptcy was designed to force the government to provide aid to the industry, while lawyers representing the aggrieved parties claimed the bankruptcy was a dodge. Congress began hearings on the situation.

The declaration of bankruptcy by a small brokerage firm, Drysdale Government Securities Corp., shook Wall Street in the spring. The firm announced in May that it would not be able to meet payments due to several major banks, including Chase Manhattan. The new brokerage house had become involved in some highly complex transactions involving government securities, and when the highly volatile markets moved against it, the result was default. Chase Manhattan and the other banks agreed to pay the interest due on the securities and to absorb Drysdale's losses in their own earnings.

In another financial fiasco, the Penn Square Bank, located in Oklahoma City, closed its doors after many of its loans to oil drillers turned bad. In addition the bank had "packaged" $2,000,000,000 in loans and then sold them to some large money-center banks, including Continental Illinois National Bank and Trust Co.; Seafirst Corp., a Seattle bank; and Chase Manhattan. Continental had to write off $120 million in bad debts from the Penn Square loans, while the other banks wrote off lesser amounts.

Among the other companies moving into Chapter 11 of the bankruptcy code was Revere Copper & Brass, which traced its roots to the patriot Paul Revere. Analysts cited depressed aluminum markets and poor management as the reasons for its failure.

De Lorean. One of the year's most shocking corporate developments was the arrest on October 19 of John De Lorean, the chairman of De Lorean Motor Co. and a former executive of General Motors Corp., for alleged trafficking in cocaine. De Lorean was picked up near Los Angeles International Airport and charged with conspiring to distribute cocaine for the purpose, authorities maintained, to raise capital for his ailing car company. De Lorean Motors was in receivership in Belfast, Northern Ireland, and the British government had announced plans to close the plant permanently. At the same time, a U.S. company, Consolidated International, Inc., said it would try to buy the Belfast factory. De Lorean pleaded innocent to the charges.

RON SCHERER
"The Christian Science Monitor"

Mergers and Antitrust

Neither a tepid economy nor high interest rates could keep down merger activity in U.S. business during 1982. Though the number of "blockbuster" mergers which had characterized 1981 actually declined, there were several major acquisitions and the overall trend toward corporate mergers was growing. Settlement early in the year of two longstanding antitrust cases promised to have far-reaching consequences for the business community and the public.

Mergers. According to W. T. Grimm, a Chicago-based firm which specializes in mergers, there were 1,198 mergers in the first half of 1982, compared with 1,184 in the first half of 1981. There were 58 mergers with a value of more than $100 million in the first half of 1982, compared with 55 in the first six months of 1981. However, there were only 6 mergers with a value of $500 million in the period January–June 1982, compared with 12 during the same period of 1981.

The slowdown in billion dollar bidding was caused in large part by the recession. Corporations, watching earnings fall, were hesitant to commit their cash to buying other companies even though stock prices were depressed. They reasoned that it was not worth buying another company and getting stuck with it if the economy continued to falter. Later in the year, sharply rising stock prices again inhibited takeovers, as bargains disappeared. Still, U.S. companies remained confident that the Reagan administration would review antitrust cases more loosely than its predecessors, and merger activity continued at an unprecedented rate.

The biggest merger of the year involved Cities Service Company, a Tulsa-based oil producer. In early June, Mesa Petroleum of Amarillo, TX, made an offer to buy 15% of Cities, the nation's 18th largest oil company, for $45 per share. Once it had the 15%, said Mesa, it would buy up to 45% of the company for $50 per share and then purchase the rest of the company for some form of stock or debt. Cities Service immediately rejected the offer and itself offered to buy Mesa for either $17 per share if Mesa contested the bid, or $21 per share if it did not.

While these two companies locked horns, Cities hunted for a "white knight" to rescue it. The Tulsa company corralled Gulf Oil, the nation's sixth largest oil company, which offered to pay $63 per share for Cities stock. The transaction, valued at $5,000,000,000, would have been the third largest merger in corporate history, following that of DuPont De Nemours and Conoco, valued at $7,200,000,000, in 1981,

and that of U.S. Steel and Marathon Oil, valued at $6,000,000,000, in early January 1982. The new company would be the seventh largest industrial corporation in the United States.

The proposed Gulf-Cities Service merger was a test of the Justice Department's new antitrust guidelines, as drawn up by Assistant Attorney General William Baxter. The new rules, Baxter said, were designed to "indicate regions of safe harbors where management can plan corporate affairs without significant worry that the antitrust division will pop out of the closet." The gist of it was that neither the antitrust division nor the Federal Trade Commission (FTC), the two antitrust enforcers, would interfere with a merger in an uncontested market.

In this first test of the new guidelines, however, the FTC said it would fight the merger unless Gulf agreed to divest itself of certain assets. Gulf than shocked both Cities Service and Wall Street by announcing in August that it was withdrawing its offer because of the antitrust objections. Analysts, however, believed that Gulf got cold feet because it felt it was paying too high a price. Cities announced that it would sue Gulf for breach of contract and immediately set out to find a new merger partner. Within a week it was entertaining Occidental Petroleum, a Los Angeles-based oil company, from whom it ultimately accepted an offer of $55 per share, or $4,000,000,000. Although many traders made money on the deal, the ones who did not instituted lawsuits against Gulf.

In another hotly contested merger, NLT Corporation, a Nashville-based insurance company, announced during the summer that it would acquire American General Corporation, an insurance company based in Houston. Both companies subsequently made offers to buy each other, an example of the "Pac Man" strategy—attempting to gobble up the other company before being gobbled up by it. In mid-August the two companies finally agreed to merge in a complicated financial deal.

The Pac Man strategy was adopted again in early September, when Bendix Corporation, a Michigan-based company made an offer to buy Martin Marietta, an aerospace company in Bethesda, MD, for $1,500,000,000. Marietta, in turn, recruited United Technologies, a Hartford, CT, defense contractor, to make a joint bid for Bendix, for $1,500,000,000. In return for the bid, United would get certain of Bendix's assets, while Marietta, in return for $600 million in cash, would get the aerospace part of Bendix. Bendix, in the meantime, led by Chairman William Agee, purchased 50% of Marietta's shares and subsequently bought another 20% on the open market. Marietta, after fighting off Bendix lawsuits, then purchased more than 50% of Bendix's stock. The final winner, it appeared, would be determined by the courts. Negotiations, which had begun at the 11th hour, broke down. Then, Allied Corporation, an oil and chemical company in Morristown, NJ, offered to join Bendix in its bid to buy Marietta. But Allied failed to file the necessary documents on time and could not prevent Marietta from buying a controlling interest in Bendix. In subsequent negotiations, Allied agreed to buy all of Bendix and a 39% interest in Marietta for $1,900,000,000. The 39% was part of the 70% held by Bendix. Allied would then swap the remaining Marietta shares held by Bendix for Marietta's 50% interest in Bendix. Later, Allied said it would buy the rest of the Bendix stock and bonds.

In other major mergers during the year, the Interstate Commerce Commission approved the merger of the Union Pacific Railroad with the Missouri Pacific and Western Pacific railroads, creating the third largest rail system in the country. Coca-Cola acquired Columbia Pictures for $629.7 million; Allied Corp. and Continental Group jointly acquired Supron Energy for $711 million; Aetna Life & Casualty purchased the 71% of Geosource it did not already own, for $609 million; and Pittsburgh National Bank and Provident National Bank merged in a deal worth $599 million.

Antitrust Cases Dropped. Early in the year, on January 8, the U.S. Justice Department made history when it rendered two important antitrust decisions in one day. First, Assistant Attorney General Baxter announced that the Justice Department had reached a settlement with American Telephone & Telegraph (AT&T), resolving a seven-year lawsuit. Then Baxter announced that the department had also reached a settlement with International Business Machines (IBM) after 13 years of litigation.

In the IBM settlement, the Justice Department basically decided to drop its case against the giant computer company because Baxter simply decided that the government did not have one. He argued that under Section 2 of the Sherman Antitrust Act, IBM could not be sued simply because it held a monopoly. Rather, he reasoned, to have broken the law it would have had to obtain that monopoly illegally. The Justice Department also noted that IBM's dominance in the computer field had eroded in recent years, mitigating the need for the case. Dropping the action, lawyers said, would save both the government and IBM several million dollars a year in legal fees.

The AT&T settlement was even more far-reaching. In return for allowing Ma Bell to enter the unregulated telecommunications business,

George Tames/New York Times Pictures

Asst. Attorney General William Baxter (left) and AT&T Chairman Charles L. Brown announce a settlement in the longstanding antitrust suit against that company.

AT&T agreed to divest itself of the 22 operating companies that provide most of the nation's telephone service. These subsidiaries, with assets of $83,000,000,000—two thirds of the company's assets—would be spun off to the shareholders in a complicated formula to be worked out later by AT&T and its investment bankers. However, Bell was allowed to keep its long-distance network, its manufacturing arm—Western Electric, and Bell Labs.

The implications of the Bell agreement were enormous. First, the telephone company said it expected its 141 million customers to see their phone rates rise more quickly than normal over the next five years. Profits from the long-distance subsidiary, pointed out AT&T President William Ellinghaus, would no longer subsidize local operations. AT&T did admit later that inflation would have increased rates anyway.

The settlement of the lawsuit, which had already cost Bell $360 million in legal fees, was viewed as a coup for the company. It was allowed to keep the most profitable part of the system while spinning off the part that was most heavily regulated. Judge Harold Greene later made some modifications, permitting the operating companies to produce the "yellow pages," which had been relegated to the parent company, but not to manufacture telephone equipment. He also ruled that AT&T could not use its transmission facilities for electronic publishing.

RON SCHERER

CALIFORNIA

The economic recession affected California in many ways during 1982, including high unemployment, a sharp increase in mortgage foreclosures and unpaid property taxes, and a great drop in tax revenues. The elections set records for campaign spending and allowed voters to decide many controversial issues.

Recession. The unemployment rate in the state was the worst in 42 years, running at or above the national average throughout the year. Foreclosures more than doubled the rate of the previous year, and the statewide average percentage of delinquent property taxes exceeded that of the 1938–39 Depression year. Although the state's large high-technology electronics industry continued to expand, the important aerospace industry suffered major cutbacks.

Elections. With no incumbents taking part in the races for governor and U.S. senator, the primary elections were crowded and costly. A record of more than $40 million was spent; the general election, involving more than $60 million, also set a new high. There were 18 candidates for governor and 24 for senator, but only the Republican contests were close.

In November, Attorney General George Deukmejian (R) upset the favored Mayor Tom Bradley by 52,000 votes out of 7.6 million cast in the governor's race. In the Senate contest, controversial Gov. Edmund G. Brown, Jr. (D) fought an uphill battle but lost by six percentage points to Mayor Pete Wilson of San Diego.

As usual, voters paid little attention to party affiliations. All new state elective officers except the governor were Democrats, and the legislature remained firmly in Democratic hands. The state sent 28 Democrats and 17 Republicans to the U.S. House of Representatives, a gain of six seats for the former. The delegation, with three more members than in the 97th Congress, includes three blacks, three Chicanos, two women, and an Asian-American.

UPI

Governor-elect George Deukmejian (left) meets with outgoing Gov. Edmund G. Brown, who lost a U.S. Senate bid.

Redistricting. Population increases in the state relative to the nation and in southern California relative to northern California made for a difficult and highly controversial problem of redistricting. The Democrats drew up a legislative plan, but the Republicans cried "Foul!" and voters rejected the plan in June, though it was allowed to be used for one election. A proposal to turn redistricting over to a permanent commission was voted down in November, and the matter was returned to the legislature.

Propositions. Many political issues were again left to the voters. In June they adopted a "Crime Victims' Bill of Rights," which modified many existing rights of the accused and thereby assured future court tests. Another proposal virtually eliminated state inheritance and gift taxes.

In the fall voters rejected by two-to-one a proposal to adopt the most restrictive handgun law in the nation; San Francisco did adopt a similar proposal in June, but it was overturned by the state Court of Appeal. To the surprise of many observers, voters approved all five bond issues on the ballot. A proposal to require deposits on all beer and soft-drink bottles and cans was soundly defeated. An advisory referendum for a bilateral nuclear arms freeze was adopted, though not overwhelmingly.

Water. Important issues of water distribution again came up in 1982. In the June primary election, voters rejected by a large margin a proposal to build a multibillion-dollar canal around

---

CALIFORNIA • Information Highlights

Area: 158,706 sq mi (411 049 km²).

Population (1980 census): 23,667,565.

Chief Cities (1980 census): Sacramento, the capital, 275,741; Los Angeles, 2,966,763; San Diego, 875,504; San Francisco, 678,974; San Jose, 629,-546.

Government (1982): *Chief Officers*—governor, Edmund G. Brown, Jr. (D); lt. gov., Mike Curb (R). *Legislature*—Senate, 40 members; Assembly, 80 members.

State Finances (fiscal year 1981): *Revenues,* $39,-552,000,000; *expenditures,* $38,846,000,000.

Personal Income (1981): $288,481,000,000; per capita, $11,923.

Labor Force (Aug. 1982): *Nonagricultural wage and salary earners,* 9,901,500; *unemployed,* 1,249,-500 (10.2% of total force).

Education: *Enrollment* (fall 1981)—public elementary schools, 2,769,788; public secondary, 1,276,368; colleges and universities (1981–82), 1,885,757. *Public school expenditures* (1980–81), $11,242,-472,000 ($2,594 per pupil).

the delta of the state's two largest rivers; this would have made a permanent allocation of Sacramento River water to southern California. In the November election, voters rejected another costly proposal, this one to require state-approved local water conservation plans, with allocations and new sources to be controlled by a state agency.

Legislative Session. The legislature's principal theme for the year was the rewriting of welfare laws and rules of eligibility for medical care for the poor; both were restricted.

Dissatisfaction with the state's educational system led to the election defeat of Superintendent of Public Instruction Wilson Riles, by Bill Honig, who urged a return to "basics" without promising additional funds.

The legislature was expected to concentrate on educational issues in 1983, though it was also faced with a deficit likely to exceed $1,000,000,-000 in the 1982–83 fiscal year and even more in the following year unless the recession ends quickly or taxes are raised. The manner in which the shortfall may be dealt with was complicated by the announced opposition of Governor-elect Deukmejian to any tax increases.

CHARLES R. ADRIAN
University of California, Riverside

CAMBODIA

In 1982, as for many years past, Cambodia's fate was controlled by forces outside the country. A 200,000-man Vietnamese army had occupied Cambodia since 1979, and thousands of Vietnamese and Soviet advisers continued to dominate a client government in the capital, Phnom Penh.

Politics. In June 1982, a coalition of Communist and non-Communist resistance groups was formed after many months of prodding by the governments of China, Malaysia, Singapore, and Thailand. The purpose of the coalition was mainly political. A majority of UN members could be more easily persuaded to support the coalition than the Communist resistance alone, because the Communists had murdered thousands of their own people while they were in power from 1975 to 1979.

Prince Norodom Sihanouk, the former leader of Cambodia, was named president of the coalition. Son Sann, prime minister under Sihanouk, was named prime minister. Khieu Samphan, a former member of Pol Pot's Communist regime, was named vice-president in charge of foreign affairs. The aim of the coalition was to revive the spirit of Cambodian nationalism, which had taken a severe beating during more than a decade of war and oppressive rule. If a sense of nationalism could be revived, Vietnam might be persuaded to withdraw some of its forces and civilian advisers from Cambodia and broaden the regime in Phnom Penh to include Prince Sihanouk.

Economics. According to reports by visiting journalists, the food situation in Cambodia was gradually improving in 1982. However, some food aid was still being provided by foreign governments to Cambodian refugees clustered along the Thai-Cambodian border and to the government in Phnom Penh for distribution inside the country. But the 1982–83 rice harvest would probably come closer to feeding the population than any harvest for the past 10 or 12 years. (Before the wars of the 1970s, Cambodia exported a substantial amount of rice and other food products.)

Small amounts of rubber, once a major export, also were being produced. This probably helped to pay for machinery and other imports from the USSR. However, production in Cambodia's small industrial sector continued to be hampered by a shortage of skilled workers—many of whom were killed in the 1970s—and by a shortage of spare parts for machinery. The government tolerated a brisk trade in black-market consumer goods smuggled in from Thailand.

According to press reports, one of the two railroads—from Phnom Penh to Sihanoukville on the Gulf of Thailand—was running normally. But the other railroad line, from Phnom Penh to the Thai border, was sometimes disrupted by resistance forces. The same was true of some of the major highways.

Foreign Relations. The Association of Southeast Asian Nations (ASEAN) backed the coalition of Cambodian resistance groups and called on Vietnam to withdraw its forces from Cambodia. (ASEAN includes Indonesia, Malaysia, the Philippines, Singapore, and Thailand.) In a series of UN debates and resolutions over the previous three years, the ASEAN position had gained the support of about 95 UN members. (Most other countries outside the Soviet bloc abstained.) The ASEAN countries and their supporters hoped to persuade Vietnam to accept a neutral, non-Communist Cambodia.

In July, Prince Sihanouk visited a Cambodian refugee camp in Thailand; thousands of refugees flocked around him and asked him to lead them home. Following the visit, Sihanouk traveled extensively through Africa, Eastern and Western Europe, and Asia seeking support for the newly formed coalition. He received a standing ovation when he addressed the UN General Assembly in September.

PETER A. POOLE

CAMBODIA · Information Highlights

Official Name: The People's Republic of Kampuchea.
Location: Southeast Asia.
Area: 69,898 sq mi (181 036 km^2).
Population (1982 est.): 6,100,000.
Chief City (1979 est.): Phnom Penh, the capital, 200,-000.
Government: *Head of state and government,* Heng Samrin (took office 1981).
Monetary Unit: Riel (4 riels equal U.S.$1, Dec. 1981).

CANADA

For Canadians, 1982 should have been a year of proud achievements. After two years of debate and compromise, Canada finally had a homemade charter of rights and freedoms. In Toronto, a glittering new concert hall opened to resounding praise. Two young Canadians achieved the ascent of Mount Everest.

Such accomplishments were overshadowed by deepening economic recession. The sharp decline which had begun in mid-1981 gained momentum throughout 1982 until the toll of unemployment and business failure could only be compared to the Great Depression of the 1930s. As the economy slumped, opinion leaders embraced stringent measures to cut wages, purchasing power, and welfare programs. The conservatism of the Reagan administration south of the border became increasingly the conventional wisdom of provincial governments and editorial commentators.

The Constitution. Balked by resistance from the provinces and the opposition parties, Pierre Elliott Trudeau's Liberal government had failed to patriate Canada's constitution from Great Britain by July 1, 1981, Canada's national day. Only a dramatic predawn compromise on November 5, 1981, had produced a constitutional package acceptable to the central government and nine of the provinces. Quebec, the province for which constitutional reform had been initiated in 1980, was the ultimate dissenter. Its separatist government under Premier René Lévesque sought in vain to derail the final stages of patriation through court challenges. Canada's native people and feminists, dissatisfied by final compromises, took their protests to Britain.

Despite predictions of a lively debate, the British Parliament showed no sign of wishing to meddle with Canadian concerns. After a short and often ill-informed debate, the Canada Bill passed a crucial second reading by 334 votes to 44 in the House of Commons. By March 27, it had passed both houses and received Royal Assent. In Ottawa on April 17, Queen Elizabeth II, in her continuing role as Canada's queen, proclaimed the new Constitution Act. The law included the former British North America Act (Canada's constitution from 1867 to 1982), a complex amending formula, and a 34-part Charter of Rights and Freedoms. (*See also* pages 584–88.)

For the prime minister and many Canadians, the charter was the main achievement in the long constitutional debate. Many of its newly entrenched guarantees—freedom of belief and expression; equality on the basis of religion, nationality, sex, and age; and the right to counsel on arrest—would be familiar in any democracy. Others reflected Canadian circumstances or substantial lobbying. Physical and mental handicap, for example, could no longer be a basis for dis-

Springtime in Canada

Langley in The Christian Science Monitor © 1982

crimination. Canadians would have the right to live and work anywhere in the country but provinces could still discriminate in favor of their own residents in such matters as land ownership. Canadians would have the right to education, in French or English, but only "where numbers warrant." A "notwithstanding" clause allowed provinces to annul certain rights in special circumstances. All the rights in the charter were subject to "such reasonable limits prescribed by law as can be demonstrably justified in a free and democratic society."

While many Canadians welcomed their newly patriated constitution, others believed that the process had done more to divide then unite the country. Opinion polls suggested that 27% of Canadians felt that confederation was doomed, compared with only 18% in 1981. Only long and costly litigation would demonstrate the significance of the new charter. One major decision by Quebec's chief justice, Jules Deschênes, used the new charter to overthrow a section of the province's language law that limited English language education to children whose parents had been educated in Quebec. Deschênes's ruling extended the right to all English-speaking Canadian children in Quebec.

Nor did constitutional reform satisfy the very different grievances of western Canadian separatists. Gordon Kesler, victor in an Alberta provincial by-election and new leader of the Western Canada Concept Party, could campaign on Western resentment of bilingualism and alleged Quebec domination in Ottawa. He and other provincial leaders in and out of power could also capitalize on a widespread belief that Ottawa policies had contributed to hard times. (Kesler's party did, however, lose to Peter Lougheed's Progressive Conservatives in a November election in Alberta.)

The Recession. If Trudeau's government reaped little political credit for its constitutional exertions, it was because most Canadians were more preoccupied with the economy. During the previous decade, Canadians had worried about inflation at 10–12% and unemployment rates of 6–8% but they believed that they were doing as well as their American neighbors. That meager comfort vanished in 1982. In mid-1981, Canada had begun to follow the United States into the deepest recession since World War II, and its plunge exceeded the U.S. experience. Manufacturing and construction had been early casualties of an inflation-fighting policy of high interest rates. Now Canada's resource industries—its major source of export income—began to dry up with the loss of markets in the United States and Japan. Even remaining markets were threatened by reviving American protectionism.

As a symptom of economic difficulties, the Canadian dollar, once above par with its U.S. counterpart, tumbled to U.S. $.77 by June and recovered only to hover at U.S. $.80–.82. Canadian interest rates, firmly controlled by the

Unemployed workers begin lining up the night before the opening of a temporary employment office in Vancouver.

UPC

state-run Bank of Canada, fell more slowly than American rates in an attempt to prevent a flight of capital. In any event, hard-pressed head offices of foreign-owned corporations in Canada pulled all the money they could out of Canada, a record capital exodus that underlined the country's dangerous dependence on the whims of foreign investors. While inflation persisted at an annual rate of 10–11%, unemployment almost doubled, from 790,000 in August 1981 to 1,480,-000 a year later. Not since the Great Depression had a greater proportion of the Canadian work force been vainly hunting for jobs. Influential voices in the business community protested that Canada's unemployment insurance system, launched in 1940, had become so costly that it might well prevent economic recovery.

Unemployment insurance was only one policy devised by Canada's federal government to guarantee that the misery of the 1930s would never return. Postwar governments in Ottawa had been committed to Keynesian strategies for damping the peaks and troughs of the business cycle; they also held impressive powers and fiscal reserves to make such policies work. In the long era of prosperity following 1945, Ottawa's strength had waned. Massive transfers to provinces, individuals and corporations, guaranteed by law, left the central government little fiscal leverage. Going into debt only fed inflation and sent interest rates soaring. While farms and businesses went bankrupt at record rates, and as unemployment climbed, the Trudeau government continued to insist that inflation was Canada's main economic problem.

During 1982 many of the government's critics and even its own ministers argued that the nationalistic policies adopted by the Liberals after their 1980 election victory were hurting the economy. The National Energy Policy, aimed at majority Canadian ownership of the oil and gas industry by 1990, was blamed for the collapse of activity in Alberta's once-thriving Oil Patch. Ottawa's claim to control development of offshore resources led to a compromise with Nova Scotia but not with Newfoundland. The glowing promise of wealth from the Hibernia field off the Newfoundland coast remained a mirage, rendered more tragic by the sinking of a huge oil rig, the *Ocean Ranger*. All aboard were lost.

Under sharp domestic and foreign criticism, the Trudeau government began to reverse its policies. Its retreat was punctuated by the crumbling of the so-called megaprojects with which it had hoped to achieve energy self-sufficiency for Canada by 1990 and economic stimulation in between. At the end of April, the proposed Alsands synthetic oil plant near Fort McMurray, Alberta, was finally abandoned after projected costs had soared to $14,000,000,000. Manitoba's massive northern hydroelectric development plan, designed to feed a prairie power grid, was cancelled. In Washington, the Reagan administration reversed a pledge of former Presi-

The sinking of the oil rig "Ocean Ranger" during a winter storm was a major blow to those who invested in the Hibernia oil field, off Newfoundland.

dent Carter and cut off the Alaska natural gas pipeline. Canadian nationalists, opposed to a Canadian-financed prebuild of the line to tap cheaper Canadian gas, had their fears confirmed.

Economics and Politics. While Prime Minister Trudeau hoped that his constitutional success would allow him an honorable retirement, his party's standing was battered by economic troubles. Provincial governments, all of them politically opposed to Trudeau's Liberals, demanded a role in charting a national economic recovery. When Trudeau met the premiers for three days in February, there was no meeting of minds. Ottawa refused to moderate its anti-inflation policies; the provinces rejected temporary wage controls. To regain a little fiscal leverage, the federal government unilaterally decided to trim its transfer payments to the provinces. On March 29, Parliament approved a five-year formula that promised the provinces $5,860,000,000 less than they would have received under previous agreements. The days when provinces could "kick us in the teeth and ask for more" were over, claimed the prime minister.

In November 1981, Finance Minister Allan MacEachen had devised a budget designed to tighten belts, plug tax loopholes, and fight inflation. After six months of humiliating retreats and the admission of forecasting errors, MacEachen and his officials felt compelled to present a new federal budget on June 28. It was a dismaying demonstration of how frail Ottawa's fiscal influence had become after decades of decentralizing federalism. In six months, a projected federal deficit of $10,500,000,000 had climbed to $19,600,000,000, and estimates would climb far higher by the end of the year. Instead of stimulation, MacEachen was obliged to raise taxes by eliminating indexing features. Govern-

ment desperation was apparent as the finance minister proclaimed "a two-year national effort to break inflation." As a first step, collective bargaining rights for federal employees were cancelled and pay increases would be limited to 6% for the twelve months beginning July 1, 1982, and 5% for the following year.

While experts argued the effectiveness and justice of the new restraint program, most Canadians welcomed the drastic curbs on public-sector incomes. Some provinces, notably British Columbia and Quebec, had already led the way with public-sector restraint programs. While provincial premiers, at their annual meeting, refused to join the Trudeau government's "6 & 5" crusade, suspecting that it was a partisan gimmick, their own financial difficulties and readings of voter opinion led all but Manitoba's New Democratic Party government into comparable restraint programs before the end of 1982.

Though provincial governments could legislate arbitrary restraint programs for employees of government departments and such crown corporations as Air Canada and the Canadian Broadcasting Corporation, they only urged private sector employees to follow suit. Government ministers and members of Parliament preached the message of restraint. In November the new finance minister, Marc Lalonde, urged Canadians simultaneously to tighten their belts and spend more. Meanwhile, he reopened most of the tax loopholes his predecessor had plugged a year earlier. Business leaders, increasingly suspicious and hostile to the Trudeau policies, responded with satisfaction.

Labor's Response. In 1980 Trudeau's party had sought an election comeback by displaying its radical side; by 1982 the Liberals were taking on the coloration of Ronald Reagan's Republican administration. It was reasonable to expect

Prime Minister Trudeau listens intently as Finance Minister Allan MacEachen presents a new federal budget June 28.

that Canada's labor movement, mustering 40% of Canada's work force, would respond powerfully. It did not.

In May, when the Canadian Labor Congress (CLC) met in Winnipeg for its biennial convention, its president, Dennis McDermott, announced that he and fellow leaders had "signed in blood" their commitment to resist wage concessions; however, McDermott could not speak for 250,000 members of the Canadian Federation of Labor (CFL) formed in March by locals of American-based construction unions. The new CFL had no sympathy with public-sector workers and every desire to speak with the voice of moderation. Almost 1 million other Canadian unionists had refused to join any central labor body. Restraint programs and massive unemployment found Canada's labor movement far more powerful but almost as divided as it had been in the 1930s.

Far from leading protests, the CLC's leaders confessed at the end of August that their first task would be to educate their own members.

CANADA • Information Highlights

Official Name: Canada.
Location: Northern North America.
Area: 3,851,809 sq mi (9 976 185 km²).
Population (Jan. 1982): 24,347,400.
Chief Cities (1981 census): Ottawa, the capital, 295,163; Montreal, 980,354; Toronto, 599,217.
Government: *Head of state,* Elizabeth II, queen; represented by Edward Schreyer, governor-general (took office Jan. 22, 1979). *Head of government,* Pierre Elliott Trudeau, prime minister (took office March 1980). *Legislature*—Parliament: Senate and House of Commons.
Monetary Unit: Canadian dollar (1.24 dollars equal U.S.$1, Dec. 2, 1982).
Gross National Product (second quarter 1982 C$): $342,504,000,000.
Economic Indexes (1981): *Consumer Prices* (1970= 100), all items, 243.7; food, 293.6. *Industrial production* (1975=100), 117.
Foreign Trade (1981 C$): *Imports,* $79,129,400,000; *exports,* $83,678,000,000.

Almost two thirds of union households backed the "6 & 5" formula. Unions could point to statistics showing a steady fall in the purchasing power of Canadian industrial workers since 1976 and their fall from second to fourteenth place among workers of industrialized nations since 1971. While some militant unions organized strikes, most followed the example of the United Auto Workers, which publicly refused to imitate the "giveback" policy of its American majority but shrewdly purchased peace from Ford and General Motors at the expense of a few days of paid leave. Chrysler's workers struck in November.

Politics and Conservatism. If most unions retreated because of the nervous conservatism of their members, politicians struggled to adjust to the mood. Progressive Conservatives won every provincial election they contested in 1982, defeating even the successful and widely respected New Democratic (NDP) government of Allan Blakeney in Saskatchewan by a wide margin. In Ontario, where the Liberals had won in the 1980 federal election, three by-elections went to the opposition. The Conservatives gained their first federal seat in northern Ontario in decades. Only a bitter split in Tory ranks allowed the New Democrats to retain a Toronto constituency.

Trudeau's Liberal Party saw its former lead in the polls dwindle to the lowest level in history and wondered whether its leader would carry out his promise to retire before the next federal election in 1983 or 1984. Despite his own apparent unpopularity, Pierre Elliott Trudeau remained the man more Canadians wanted as their prime minister than Joe Clark of the Progressive Conservatives or Ed Broadbent of the New Democrats. As head of a government, Trudeau could at least take the initiative. In a three-stage shuffle of cabinet ministers, Trudeau returned Allan MacEachen to the external affairs department and appointed Marc Lalonde as minister of finance. Jean Chretien, one of the few Liberal ministers to make friends in Western Canada, took over the controversial energy portfolio, while Herb Gray, advocate of economic nationalism, was banished to the obscurity of the treasury board. If businessmen really had the answers to Canada's acute economic difficulties, Trudeau's made-over government presented a far friendlier face at the end of 1982 than it had at the beginning of the year.

External Relations. If Canadians still admired their prime minister, often it was because they believed that his experience and influence carried weight in the world. When seven national leaders met in Versailles for the 1982 economic summit, it was conspicuous that Trudeau had by far the longest tenure in office. At the same time, domestic difficulties eclipsed Trudeau's earlier enthusiasm for the North-South dialogue between rich and poor nations. His forthcoming retirement encouraged him to lecture a North Atlantic Treaty Organization (NATO) summit meeting on the risks of nuclear annihilation and the silliness of the organization's prearranged communiqués.

Such views did not improve Canada's relations with its neighbor, the United States. The Reagan White House found plenty to complain about in Ottawa, from Canada's Foreign Investment Review Agency to major Canadian timber exports to the American market. Canadian concerns about acid rain, the flooding of British Columbia's Skagit Valley, and the bellicose American attitude toward the Soviet bloc found little sympathy in Washington. However, as the year progressed, conservatism and pragmatism gradually prevailed in Ottawa. The Trudeau government held firm on its promise to allow testing of the Cruise missile in Canada, despite public protests and the bombing of a Toronto building. Having spent much of the winter pushing the National Energy Policy through Parliament, a reshuffled cabinet did its best to reassure foreign investors that neither it nor the Foreign Investment Review Agency would be allowed to impede the flow of foreign capital into Canada.

Native People. A consequence of the constitutional debate was a growth in the visibility of Canadian Indians and Inuit as a political force and a social concern. While native leaders had failed to win more from the constitution-drafters than a guarantee of "existing aboriginal and treaty rights," they forced Ottawa and the provinces to promise an early conference to determine what those rights really meant. In Regina in July, Canadian Indians celebrated their new self-confidence by playing host to the World Assembly of First Nations. The conference drew 2,000 delegates from 24 nations.

Another demonstration of the determination of native people to control what remained to them was a referendum in the Northwest Territories on April 14. By a significant majority, inhabitants voted to divide the huge region into a

THE CANADIAN MINISTRY

Pierre Elliott Trudeau, prime minister
Allan Joseph MacEachen, minister of external affairs
Jean-Luc Pepin, minister of transport
Jean Chrétien, minister of energy
John Munro, minister of Indian affairs and northern development
H. A. (Bud) Olson, government leader in the Senate
Herb Gray, president of the treasury board
Eugene Whelan, minister of agriculture
André Ouellet, minister of consumer and corporate affairs
Marc Lalonde, minister of finance
Ray Perrault, minister responsible for fitness and amateur sport
Roméo LeBlanc, minister of public works
John Roberts, minister of the environment
Monique Bégin, minister of national health and welfare
Jean-Jacques Blais, minister of supply and services
Francis Fox, minister of communications
Gilles Lamontagne, minister of national defence
Pierre De Bane, minister of fisheries and oceans
Hazen Argue, minister of state for the wheat board
Gerald Regan, minister of state for international trade
Mark MacGuigan, minister of justice
Robert Kaplan, solicitor general
James Fleming, minister of state for multiculturalism
William Rompkey, minister of state for small business
Pierre Bussières, minister of national revenue
Charles Lapointe, minister of external relations (francophone nations)
Yvon Pinard, president of the Privy Council
Ed Lumley, minister of industry and regional expansion
Donald Johnston, minister of state for economic and regional development
Lloyd Axworthy, minister of employment and immigration
Paul Cosgrove, minister of state (finance)
Judy Erola, minister of state for mines and minister responsible for the status of women
Jack Austin, minister of state for social development
Charles Caccia, minister of labor
Serge Joyal, secretary of state
Bennett Campbell, minister of veterans affairs

predominantly Inuit-inhabited Nunavut and a more southerly territory of Denendeh in which Indians would be a majority. Against the will of the white minority, the decision was promptly endorsed by the territorial assembly.

Other News. Results of the 1981 decennial census were released in 1982. A total of 24,343,-181 Canadians had been found, a 12.9% increase since 1971. It was the smallest ten-year growth since the 1930s. Among Canadians in the news was Bertha Wilson, the Scottish-born clergyman's wife who had put herself through law school, established her brilliance at the bar to become, on March 4, the first woman to be named a justice of the Supreme Court of Canada.

In November the report of the federal task force on cultural policy, appointed by the Clark government in 1979, proposed removal of the CBC's television-production role and abolition of the award-winning National Film Board. The government appeared unconvinced.

In a year of discouragement and self-doubt, Canadians could take pride in skier Steve Podborski, who took the World Cup men's downhill title for 1982; Angela Taylor and Alex Baumann, who won honors for Canada at the Commonwealth Games in Brisbane, Australia; and in the team of Canadians who endured hardship and tragedy to reach the summit of Mount Everest.

DESMOND MORTON
Erindale College, University of Toronto

The Economy

The Canadian economy continued in a downward spiral in 1982, impelled by punishingly high interest rates and tight monetary policies in unhappy coincidence with shrinking world trade. By December, with the end of the 17-month-long global recession nowhere in sight, a growing sense of desperation had arisen in the country. Soaring levels of unemployment and business bankruptcies combined with slashed corporate profits and housing starts to provide dismal confirmation of the particularly severe effects of the downturn on Canada. During the year the gross national product (GNP) fell by an estimated 4.9%, the worst contraction among industrialized nations.

As 1982 began there were hopes that the recession which began in mid-1981 would end in the coming months. Instead, the economy suffered a series of setbacks outstripping any since the Great Depression. First came the currency crisis in early summer when rising U.S. interest rates prompted a rush of capital to the U.S. dollar. That, in turn, sent the Canadian unit plummeting to an all-time low of $.7686 to the U.S. dollar on June 21. Worried by the inflationary effects of the Canadian dollar's fall—the rising cost of imports drives up domestic prices—the Bank of Canada intervened heavily in the foreign exchange markets, spending more than C$3,000,000,000 in May and June to prop up the dollar. More significantly, the central bank also drove up domestic interest rates in an attempt to maintain a margin above U.S. rates that would make the Canadian dollar more attractive. By August, the currency was again above the $.80 (U.S.) level, but only after the prime interest rate—charged to corporate customers—soared to 18.25% in July.

The central bank's fixation on propping up the currency, and the resultant stratospheric level of interest rates, took a heavy toll on an already foundering economy. Business bankruptcies soared 30% above 1981 levels as undercapitalized and debt-burdened firms defaulted on loans. A flurry of bank-financed acquisitions by oil companies in 1981, prompted by the Canadianization goals of the National Energy Program, came back to haunt the companies as their debt crises worsened. Dome Petroleum Ltd., one of the nation's largest oil companies, averted collapse by signing a C$1,000,000,000 bailout plan with its bankers and the federal government. Slumping demand conspired with high interest charges to slash corporate profits by more than 30% from 1981. Worst hit was the country's large primary resource sector. The mining and forestry industries, in particular, were devastated by falling world demand and prices for their products.

For consumers, the situation was equally bleak. Unemployment rose to a post-Depression high of 12.8% in December, and personal dis-

UNEMPLOYMENT RATE

Seasonally Adjusted

1980 1981 | J F M A M J J A S O | 1982

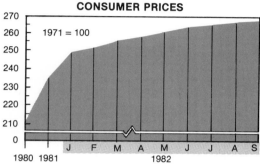

CONSUMER PRICES

1971 = 100

1980 1981 | J F M A M J J A S | 1982

Source of Information: Statistics Canada

posable income fell by 2%, prompting a deepening mood of pessimism that was reflected in drastically high rates of saving. Canadians were hoarding 13 cents of every dollar, a situation that aggravated the sorry condition of businesses. The housing industry, in particular, felt the effects as real estate prices plummeted and housing starts fell 30% from 1981.

Amid the onslaught, the federal government implemented modest make-work programs worth C$1,100,000,000. But it was unable to apply more stimulative balm because of a ballooning budget deficit predicted to reach at least C$23,600,000,000.

The current account balance was one of the few bright spots. It was forecast to register a C$500 million surplus after a C$5,300,000,000 deficit in 1981. The reason was a predicted C$15,000,000,000 surplus in the merchandise trade balance which was more than enough to offset a deficit in services and transfers. But the positive balance in merchandise trade was due more to weak demand for imports of industrial and consumer products than to an increase in exports.

There were some tenuous harbingers of recovery late in the year. In August interest rates began a decline that sparked a rally on the stock and bond markets. Inflation moderated from 12.5% in 1981 to about 10%. But progress on these fronts proved insufficient to spark a turnaround. Moreover, serious long-term structural problems meant that a 1983 upturn would be more a period of convalescence than recovery.

JAMES FLEMING
Business Editor, "Maclean's" Magazine

The Arts

As traditionalists among Canadian folk-singers revived hard-times songs of the 1930s and annual arts festivals slashed their budgets, artists lost their last illusions about attainable security, and museum directors abandoned extension programs that had taken years to build up. From coast to coast desperate efforts were made to maintain established organizations while waiting for the coming revision of the government's cultural policy. In 1982 the resilience and resourcefulness of the cultural sector were tested almost everywhere in the Western world. Canada was no exception.

The Canada Council's 25th anniversary was celebrated appropriately. By the end of its 1982–83 fiscal year, it had distributed more than $53.5 million throughout Canada in grants to arts organizations and individual artists.

Visual Arts. The year marked the 10th anniversary of The Canada Council Art Bank and its two ongoing programs: the purchase of contemporary Canadian art and the rental of these acquisitions to government departments, eligible agencies, and institutions at home and abroad. Art Bank, valued at $10 million, in 1982 listed 10,384 items by 1,286 artists; 75% of the collection was rented at a yearly rate of 12% of the purchase price. Alberta, British Columbia, Nova Scotia, Quebec, and Saskatchewan have developed their own Art Banks.

Many museum exhibitions began or continued nationwide and international shows. Among them were retrospective shows of Canadian painters Jean-Paul Riopelle (b. 1923), at the Musée du Québec and the Musée National d'Art Moderne, Paris; Greg Curnoe (b. 1936), at the National Gallery of Canada; Gershon Iskowitz (b. 1921), at the Art Gallery of Ontario; and Frederick H. Varley (1881–1969), at the Edmonton Art Gallery. Canadian cultural centers in Brussels, London, Paris, and New York organized their own exhibitions. In February, Elizabeth the Queen Mother opened the expanded and updated Art Gallery at Canada House in London. A major display of contemporary Canadian tapestries was featured during the inaugural season at London's Barbican Centre for Arts and Conferences. At the Venice Biennale, Montreal-born painter Paterson Ewen represented Canada. West Berlin's Akademie der Kunste hosted "OKanada." This event was the most ambitious exposition of contemporary Canadian culture ever mounted in Europe.

In Toronto, a major exhibition (with daily demonstrations by 40 Chinese craftsmen) produced by the Ontario Science Centre and the China Science and Technology Palace, Peking, offered a display of Chinese cultural and scientific history on a scale never seen before in the Western world. "China—7,000 Years of Discovery" was sent to Canada with the arrangement that half of the proceeds from admission fees would go toward the purchase of the Ontario Science Centre's traveling "Science Circus" and its modern mobile exhibits, chosen by the Chinese government as a model for popular scientific education.

Performing Arts. The 30th anniversary season of the Stratford Festival coincided with the 150th birthday of the community where Tyrone Guthrie launched his brave Ontario venture. Artistic director John Hirsch offered 10 major productions. "Stratford Summer Music" staged 70 concerts, and the Gallery/Stratford mounted an exhibition, "Leslie Hurry: A Painter for the Stage." (Hurry designed 10 Stratford productions between 1956 and 1974.) Michael Langham, Guthrie's successor, returned to direct

The Shaw Festival at Niagara-on-the-Lake, Ontario, staged Shaw's "Too Good to Be True" in a desert setting.

Courtesy, Shaw Festival Theatre

an operatic version of George Bernard Shaw's *Arms and the Man.* Douglas Campbell, a guest actor in the festival's first year, played Falstaff again in Shakespeare's *The Merry Wives of Windsor.* Tanya Moiseiwitsch, designer of the festival theater's famed thrust stage, did the costumes for Hirsch's handsome revival of Friedrich Schiller's *Mary Stuart.* Guy Sprung staged Brian Friel's *Translations,* while Brian Bedford directed and played Charles in Noel Coward's *Blithe Spirit.* Brian MacDonald took a new look at the Gilbert and Sullivan favorite, *The Mikado,* which gave Stratford its biggest 1982 success. Hirsch directed *The Tempest,* with Len Cariou playing a very executive Prospero. At the Shaw Festival at Niagara-on-the-Lake, a joyful revival of the 1926 musical *The Desert Song* was presented. Shaw plays included *Pygmalion; The Music Cure;* and an entrancing *Too Good to Be True,* set in a science-fiction desert.

Festival Ottawa Opera Plus '82 at the National Arts Centre opened with the spectacular premiere of Handel's *Rinaldo,* with Marilyn Horne in the title role. The style of 1711 (the year of *Rinaldo*'s first performance) was followed. This rarely performed work was Canada's gift to the Metropolitan Opera's 1983–84 Centennial.

The Canadian Opera Company introduced four firsts in the 1982–83 season: Verdi's *Falstaff,* Puccini's *La Fanciulla del West* (Girl of the Golden West), Monteverdi's *L'Incoronazione di Poppea* (The Coronation of Poppaea), and Strauss's *Elektra.* The Opéra de Montréal, the only opera company in Canada showing a profit during inflationary times, drew capacity audiences with Puccini's *Madama Butterfly,* Donizetti's *L'Elisir d'Amore,* and Verdi's *Il Trovatore.* Charles Dutoit, musical director of the Orchestre Symphonique de Montréal, received the 1982 Canadian Artist of the Year award, presented by the Canadian Music Council.

A new theater in Montreal, Espace Libre (Free Space), under the direction of playwright Jean-Pierre Ronfard, provided a base for the Nouveau Théâtre Expérimental and two mime troupes, Les Enfants du Paradis and Mime Omnibus. In Edmonton, Alberta, The Citadel Theatre entered its 18th season. At the Manitoba Theatre Centre, Winnipeg, artistic director Richard Ouzounian's high camp contemporary 1982 production of *The Taming of the Shrew* was both loved and hated. The second-ever Indigenous People's Theatre Association's Celebration, held at the Curve Lake Reserve near Peterborough, Ontario, brought 25 international companies together.

At L'Aquila, Italy, "Musikarchitettura," the annual International Festival of Music and Architecture, was devoted entirely to Canada.

Les Grands Ballets Canadiens, at New York's City Center (April 7–11), presented Ronald Hynd's *Les Valses;* Brian MacDonald's *Etapes,* set to *Concerto for Two Pianos and Orchestra* by Canadian composer Roger Matton; John Butler's *Othello* pas de trois; and Linda Rabin's *Tellurian.* The Royal Winnipeg Ballet (artistic director, Arnold Spohr) toured with a new *Firebird* production by Vicente Nebrada, the Peter Wright version of *Giselle,* and George Balanchine's *Allegro Brillante.*

Motion Pictures. Canadian film festivals continued. Between August and October the International Animation Festival, Ottawa; the Banff International Television Film Festival, Alberta; the World Film Festival of Montreal; and the Festival of Festivals, Toronto, were followed by the International Festival of Films on Art, Montreal. Important feature films of 1982 were Jean-Pierre Lefebvre's *Les Fleurs Sauvages,* winner of the International Critic's Prize for best film not in competition at the Cannes Film Festival; *The Grey Fox,* directed by Vancouver's Phillip Borsos; and *Quest for Fire,* by French director Jean-Jacques Annaud. Frédéric Back (CBC/Radio Canada) won, among other awards, the Oscar for *Crac,* a 15-minute animated film about Québec history. The National Film Board of Canada released 112 movies during its 1981–82 fiscal year, earning 89 international awards. Most successful were *Getting Started, Premiers Jours, The Sweater,* and *The Tender Tale of Cinderella Penguin.*

Broadcasting. CBC/Radio Canada introduced two series: *Heart of Gold* and *Canadian Portraits.* On FM radio, there were Sunday concerts from Toronto's Roy Thomson Hall.

HELEN DUFFY, *Art Critic, Toronto*

Marilyn Horne sings the title role in Handel's "Rinaldo" during the National Arts Centre's 1982 opera festival.

Courtesy, National Arts Centre

CARIBBEAN

The major developments throughout the Caribbean in 1982—political contests, strikes and unrest, financial belt-tightening, the Caribbean Basin Initiative, and a growing Soviet influence—all reflected worsening economic conditions.

The bleak economic picture did have one bright spot, however. For the second consecutive year, the Caribbean was spared destruction by the powerful hurricanes that normally swirl through the region. Only four storms were registered during the 1982 hurricane season, and all of these either rapidly dissipated or traveled in a northwesterly direction away from the Caribbean Islands. Temperatures remained one or two degrees above normal, and rainfall in most of the islands was slightly below expected levels.

Political Activity. Concern for civil rights prompted a U.S. federal judge in Miami to order the speedy release of hundreds of illegal Haitian immigrants being held in detention centers in the United States and Puerto Rico. In Haiti itself, President for Life Jean-Claude Duvalier released a prominent opposition leader, who immediately left the country with his family, in exchange for the renewal of financial assistance from West Germany.

In the British Associated State of St. Kitts-Nevis, the announcement by Premier Kennedy Simmonds of the government's plan for independence in 1983 brought on violent protests and public demonstrations. Although the immediate cause of protest was the rivalry between St. Kitts and the smaller associated island of Nevis, the deeper reason was concern over independence at a time of economic uncertainty.

In 1982, elections were held in the Dominican Republic, Virgin Islands (*see* page 557), the Netherlands Antilles, St. Lucia, and the Bahamas. In the Bahamas, Prime Minister Lynden Pindling and his Progressive Liberal Party won another five-year term in office, thus extending his 15-year hold on the nation's politics.

In St. Lucia, a five-day strike called by both business and labor leaders at the beginning of the year forced the government of Prime Minister Winston Cenac to schedule elections in May. At the polls, the conservative United Workers Party, led by John Compton, won 14 of the 17 seats in the island's parliament. Compton began his second term as prime minister, having led the island to independence from Great Britain in 1979.

In the five-island government of the Netherlands Antilles, a split between the political leaders of Aruba and Curaçao forced the ruling coalition to call for general elections. The balloting resolved nothing, as it produced the same leadership as before the crisis. Former Prime Minister Don Martina was asked to form a new coalition government from the 22 members of the nation's parliament.

On May 16, almost three million voters in the Dominican Republic went to the polls to elect a new president. The candidate of the party in power, Salvador Jorge Blanco, easily turned back the challenge of former President Joaquin Balaguer. Before Jorge Blanco could take his post, however, the nation was shocked by the suicide on July 4 of the incumbent president, Antonio Guzmán, who had honored his pledge not to run for a second term. The constitutional process was adhered to precisely, as Vice-President Jacobo Majluta Azar, whom Jorge Blanco

During an April visit, President Reagan met in Barbados with the leaders of five eastern Caribbean nations. He used the occasion to promote his Caribbean Basin Initiative and to warn against communist influence in the region.

Bill Fitz-Patrick/White House

© J.L. Atlan/Sygma

President-elect Salvador Jorge Blanco of the Dominican Republic visited Washington with his wife in July.

had earlier defeated in a struggle for the nomination of the Partido Revolucionario Dominicano, assumed the presidency for six weeks before giving way to Jorge Blanco.

Economic Activity. The Dominican Republic, with a foreign debt estimated at $1,500,000,000, an unemployment rate conservatively estimated at more than 40%, a trade deficit of some $600 million, and an annual inflation rate of 30%, reflected the economic woes of the nations of the Caribbean. The region's major export products—sugar, coffee, cocoa, and bauxite—were getting the lowest prices in recent memory. After the world price of sugar dropped to a new low of less than 7¢ per pound, President Jorge Blanco in October banned the exportation of sugar until the situation improved. Other new economic measures were equally drastic: salary cuts for government workers, sharp restrictions on imports, and increased taxes.

Caribbean Basin Initiative. Regional leaders, such as Prime Minister Edward Seaga of Jamaica, looked with hope to U.S. President Ronald Reagan's economic development plan for the region, known as the Caribbean Basin Initiative. (*See* LATIN AMERICA, pages 302–303.) This measure, built around a $350 million aid package, had actually been vetoed by its creator and saved only when Congress passed over the veto of a 1982 budget bill. Much of the aid will go to Central America, where $150 million alone is assigned to El Salvador and Costa Rica. The remaining $200 million averages out to a mere $6.00 per person for the rest of the Caribbean. As

President Reagan pointed out, any further aid would have to come from private initiative stimulated by the promise of reduced tariff barriers on some Caribbean products for a 12-year period, a relief measure which had been proposed but not yet received congressional approval.

In Miami at the end of October, some 500 to 600 business executives participated in a U.S. government-sponsored conference designed to promote trade and investment in the Caribbean region. The United States also established import quotas for Caribbean sugar at protected prices set about 10¢ per pound above the current world price.

In the case of Jamaican bauxite, which supplies 75% of that island's foreign exchange earnings, production in 1982 was cut back some 30% from the already declining figure of the previous year. One of the two major producers on the island operated at a mere 8% of capacity during the year. Even this reduced level was possible only because the United States was committed to stockpiling a specific amount of the ore in the face of a drastically declining market.

From November 15 to 18, the heads of government from English-speaking Caribbean nations that are members of the Caribbean Economic Community—commonly known as CARICOM—met on the north coast of Jamaica. The last regular meeting of that group was held in December 1975 on the island of St. Kitts. The failure to meet in more recent years has been attributed to the less than harmonious relationship between the recently deceased Prime Minister Eric Williams of Trinidad and Tobago and the leaders of the other Caribbean nations. Participants in the Jamaica meeting faced long-delayed decisions regarding international organizations, as well as the economic consequences on the Caribbean Common Market of trade restrictions by member states trying to cope with their rapidly growing balance of payments deficits. The change in attitude of the leaders of Trinidad and Tobago reflected the worsening economic conditions in that tiny, oil-producing nation.

Soviet Influence. In the spring of 1982, after a visit to the Soviet Union, Prime Minister Maurice Bishop of Grenada announced a multi-million-dollar agreement between his small nation of about 100,000 people and the USSR. The bilateral agreement would cover trade, science, and culture. The Soviets loaned Grenada $7.5 million over a 13-year period at 3% interest for the construction of a satellite ground station and a water and sewage system. Another $1.5 million was provided for clothing, flour, and steel purchases. In exchange, Moscow agreed to buy the island's principle product, nutmeg, at an unspecified price for a five-year period.

THOMAS MATHEWS
Institute of Caribbean Studies
University of Puerto Rico

CENTRAL AMERICA

© M. Philippot/Sygma

Orlando José Tardencillas Espinoza (with bullhorn) was to testify in Washington that he had been trained as a Marxist guerrilla and sent to fight in El Salvador. However, the Nicaraguan, 19, recanted and returned home a hero.

On Feb. 24, 1982, President Ronald Reagan addressed the delegates to the Organization of American States convened in Washington to discuss the state of affairs in Central America and the Caribbean region. He talked of common history and common goals, the sick economies, and the very dangerous polarization taking place in the last few years. He declared his intention to do something about the "economic siege," as he called it, which forced small nations to produce five times as much coffee or twice as much sugar to buy one barrel of oil in 1982 as in 1977. As a partial solution to some of these problems, he proposed six broad points that came to be called the Caribbean Basin Initiative:

1. Free trade into the United States of Caribbean exports—current and future for 12 years—that period being designed to encourage the development of new products. Only textiles and clothing would be exempted, since they are already under preferential quotas.

2. To encourage investment in the basin he would ask Congress for significant tax-incentive legislation.

3. He would seek a supplemental appropriation for direct economic assistance for the Caribbean nations hardest hit by the recession.

4. Technical assistance would be offered to the private sector of all basin states in investment promotion, marketing, production, and many forms of training.

5. He would ask more developed nations to assist in the initiative.

6. Additional aid would be provided Puerto Rico and the U.S. Virgin Islands because of their special relationship with the United States.

Except for point three, little of this program was accomplished in 1982. The president seemed to have concentrated on Jamaica as a sort of experimental grounds for the rest of the area. In spite of severe White House pressure, the lame duck Congress adjourned December 23 without acting on other parts of the plan. In the words of Secretary of State George P. Shultz, America had already waited too long, and its credibility "was at stake." Meanwhile, however, overall economic assistance to Central America for 1982 doubled that provided by the United States in 1981.

The administration often expressed its aim in Central America as being one of seeking political solutions in El Salvador and Nicaragua, but it appeared that major efforts were being made to lure Costa Rica, Honduras, and Panama away from their preferred neutrality to a position of more direct support of the United States against the Communist influence in Nicaragua.

As a further indication of the president's interest in the area, Reagan concluded an early December trip to Latin America with stops in Costa Rica and Honduras. He conferred with the leaders of Costa Rica and El Salvador in San

Luis Alberto Monge campaigned successfully for the presidency as democracy continued to prevail in Costa Rica.

José, Costa Rica, and with the leaders of Honduras and Guatemala in San Pedro Sula, Honduras. In Costa Rica, the president again called on the U.S. Congress to enact his program for the region. He also said that "foreign support for terrorists and subversive elements" in Central America must end.

Belize. When the tiny republic of Belize celebrated its first anniversary of independence from Great Britain in September 1982, Prime Minister George Price acknowledged his nation's thanks to the British for their continued protection against Guatemala's frequent threats of invasion. Even though trade between the two Central American states grew throughout the year, Guatemala withdrew its promise of diplomatic recognition to Belize. The protection kept some 7,000 British troops tied down in Belize, guarding the borders and the Guatemalan trade routes at a cost of $50 million per year for the army and several jet aircraft.

Belize has a population of about 200,000, mostly English-speaking blacks, with substantial minorities of Indians, whites, and various mixtures of all three colors. The nation is quite literate, largely Protestant, working class. The Anglo blacks (Creoles) have become increasingly concerned about the number of Indian and mestizo refugees entering Belize from portions of Central America tormented by civil war and death squads.

The nation is not well off and needs the petroleum resources for which it seeks within its borders without success so far. Pemex, the Mexican national oil agency, suddenly demanded payment of an overdue oil bill of nearly $4 million under threat of cutting off fuel supplies to the nation's power system. Prime Minister Price held talks with Washington and the International Monetary Fund (IMF) seeking to borrow enough to meet this emergency. Belize also hoped for $10 million in aid from President Reagan's Caribbean Basin Initiative.

Costa Rica. Amid signs that Costa Rica's policy of neutrality and near-isolationism in Central America was being threatened by political instability and civil war, the nation conducted a peaceful presidential election in 1982. Luis Alberto Monge was chosen to succeed Rodrigo Carazo Odio. Monge, 56, a social democrat, former union organizer, diplomat, and congressman, immediately announced steps to try to cope with the nation's economic problems.

Monge proposed a "one-hundred day" plan to cope with the most pressing of the nation's problems—the degree of austerity needed to save the nation from bankruptcy. In 1981, President Carazo Odio had failed to reach an agreement with the IMF about the requirements for additional financing to meet the foreign debt; in the face of high fuel costs, high interest rates, and low coffee prices, the nation's credit and foreign exchange supply were being strangled. Inflation remained very high, while unemployment occasionally reached 15%. The foreign debt approached $3,000,000,000. President Monge told the Costa Ricans that they must be prepared to make new sacrifices, and he urged a "Back to the Land" movement, which seemed to imply increased self-sufficiency on the part of both families and nation. To get the help Monge sought, the IMF apparently would insist upon devaluation of the colón, an end to export subsidies, tax cuts, and reductions in the budget, while holding the line on wages. Whether Monge's long political experience and his reputation as a friend of labor would help ease the pains of severe austerity could not be seen in 1982.

In international affairs, Costa Rica faced an old nuisance in a new guise. Always a haven for the political exile from elsewhere in Central America, the nation increasingly encountered the problem of refugees planning the overthrow of a neighboring government or staging attacks from within Costa Rican boundaries. Severe tensions with Nicaragua and Guatemala resulted, and the Costa Rican government found it necessary to deport many refugees for this kind of activity. Their presence in large numbers also aggravated the unemployment and relief programs in Costa Rica.

President Monge did not want to worsen relations with Nicaragua, but subversive actions of the Sandinistas and many border incidents prevailed upon him to ask the Reagan administration for $2 million to strengthen the Guardia Civil, Costa Rica's only military establishment. In October the nation hosted a regional meeting promoting peace in the Caribbean. Apparently aimed at Nicaragua, discussions centered on how the nations of the region could reduce the flow of arms and political propaganda and support the democratic yearnings of the majority.

For the past decade Costa Rica has been engaged in construction of vast hydroelectric projects, largely financed by the Inter-American Development Bank, at costs of at least $140 million. Much of this work has been completed, and by early 1983 it was hoped that the power capacity of the nation would be doubled, perhaps even making possible the sale of some electricity to Panama and Nicaragua.

El Salvador. In 1982, Salvadoreans suffered from their third-consecutive year of civil war, kidnappings, and assassinations with no sign of cessation or even moderation. Yet in March more than 1.4 million citizens, nearly 90% of those eligible, turned out to cast their ballots for a constituent assembly. Many guerrillas had vowed to boycott the election and some of that feeling may have been reflected in the large number of blank ballots cast. Nevertheless, the election, which was witnessed by hundreds of foreign observers and reporters, made an impressive display of faith in the democratic process. More difficult was the correct interpretation of the vote. Supported by the United States, the Christian Democrats won a plurality of seats with about 35% of the votes. But a coalition of right-wing parties led by Roberto d'Aubuisson won a majority of the 60 seats in the assembly and probably could control affairs in that body. The vote meant an end to the junta leadership of José Napoleón Duarte.

The new interim president of El Salvador is Alvaro Magaña, heading a completely civilian government. Magaña, 56, is a wealthy banker and political moderate. Educated in economics at the University of Chicago, he was initially favored by Washington. Within a few months, however, visiting American congressmen reported that Magaña lacked political power, and that it rested in the hands of d'Aubuisson or the defense minister. Magaña's administration

Amid civil war and strife in El Salvador, some 90% of those eligible believed that their vote was the solution.

© M. Philippot/Sygma

caused significant differences of opinion in the United States. Although the State Department certified to Congress in July that El Salvador had made improvements in its human-rights record and was entitled to continued U.S. military aid, some congressmen, led by Sen. Christopher Dodd, called the report a "sham" and declared that they had found little improvement at all.

The war, which seemed even more intense late in the year than during the early months, cost an estimated 32,000 lives by late 1982. The guerrillas pressed the government hard in about one half of the provinces and twice in two weeks succeeded in blacking out much of the countryside by sabotage. The Farabundo Martí National Liberation Front (FMLN) appeared to be willing to achieve a stalemate and seek a political settlement, but the army continued to drive for a military solution. At least 500 officers and one entire battalion of troops have been trained in the United States, and President Reagan sought funds to include more men in that program. El Salvador reportedly has 20 U.S. helicopters and six new jet fighters. Since early 1981 the nation has received $125 million in U.S. military aid. Approximately 2,000 soldiers have been killed in the past two years in civil fighting often reported as "fierce."

The unity of the military was threatened late in the year by a power struggle between d'Aubuisson, who is president of the constituent assembly charged with drawing up a new constitution, and Defense Minister Gen. José Guillermo García. If the split widens it could seriously damage the army, just as similar divisions resulted in the assembly's lack of progress on a new constitution.

In November it appeared that U.S. policy toward El Salvador might be reaching a crossroads. Ambassador Deane Hinton, apparently disturbed by the failure of Salvadorean courts to punish anyone for the murder of the American land-reform specialists, publicly castigated the justices concerned and threatened the Salvadorean government with the cessation of American military and economic aid if right-wing death squads were not brought under control. The Reagan administration seemed surprised and upset by the speech, but it probably reflected more recent Washington attitudes toward the failure of the Magaña government to control either right- or left-wing extremism. The United States could still hope for the rise of some new centrist coalition in El Salvador, but that possibility seemed remote at the end of the year. Meanwhile, Magaña named a government's Commission on Human Rights.

The major economic issue remained the vast agrarian-reform project, three of whose planners were murdered in January 1981, for which crime no one was punished in 1981–82. Both Salvadorean officials and American observers have found it hard to agree on the progress of the program. According to the Reagan government

Etienne Montes/Gamma-Liaison

In Guatemala, violence and the human rights issue dominated the initial months of the Efraín Ríos Montt rule.

about 11,000 land titles had been given to landless peasants at the time that the law was suspended by the assembly to "perfect" the measure; but Salvadoreans claimed that the law was dead. Given its uncertain status, judgment is premature, but by year-end the land redistribution did not seem likely to solve the Communist threat as originally hoped.

As if the land had not been plagued enough, El Salvador suffered from a seven-point earthquake in June, killing several persons and completely destroying a number of villages. October produced five days of rain and a torrential flood; 700 were known dead, hundreds more were missing, more villages were carried off by the waters, and hundreds of millions of dollars worth of crops ruined. And once again smugglers bringing Salvadoreans into the United States were responsible for their deaths. This time four persons suffocated in a van in Texas.

Guatemala. A presidential election also was held in Guatemala in 1982. The outgoing president, Romeo Lucas García, supported a general who won, but the opposition claimed that the election had been "rigged" and performed a bloodless coup overturning the results and installing another general, Efraín Ríos Montt. A career officer who ran for president in 1974 after retiring from the army, Ríos Montt soon removed the other members of the ruling junta and by June was ruling alone. Again there was no violence.

For five years the government of Guatemala had been unable to receive military assistance from the United States because the Carter administration had judged the degree of human-rights violations to be excessive. By May of 1982, the Reagan government was reported considering restoring military aid; many American congressmen declared that the Ríos Montt government did not qualify; he retorted that he did not need it. The State Department insisted that the rights record was improving and that Guatemala needed help against Cuban-backed guerrillas.

Early in the Ríos Montt administration domestic violence did decline, as did censorship and control over the schools, church, and the press. The president announced, under pressure, that political prisoners in the future would get public trials instead of secret military tribunals. But by July, Ríos Montt had installed a state of siege and said that he would use the death penalty against captured terrorists. The army was accused of an expanded program of war on Indians, who until 1981 had been more or less safe from both sides in this strife; the conservative Council of Bishops charged that Ríos Montt had instituted a program of genocide. The government replied that the deaths were caused by the guerrillas and that the army had been providing much food to the Indian villages. Amnesty International continued its claims that the army was guilty of torture and mass executions, once again denied by the government.

A new element expanded the civil war and more and more Guatemalans fled their lands to exile. Guatemalan peasants entered Mexico and had to be fed by the Mexican government. Occasionally the Guatemalan army raided across the border seeking certain guerrillas to bring back to Guatemalan jurisdiction. The border, more than 500 mi (800 km), was impossible to police, and incidents were numerous, adding to the tensions between the two nations.

Guatemala's unfavorable trade balance with most of Central America provoked the imposition of restrictions in July against all of the region except Honduras. Guatemala's demand for dollars or quetzales in payment could well destroy the small amounts of trade still functioning among those states. Such developments made the prospect of U.S. aid more palatable to Ríos Montt.

Honduras. In an honest election in November 1981, the Hondurans chose their first civilian president since December 1972. In a land where the military has usually controlled elections, the victory came as a pleasant surprise and made it possible for the Reagan administration to support Roberto Suazo Córdova, who was inaugurated as president in January.

Since the election the role of Honduras in Central American affairs has changed drastically from the years when its neighbors promised to keep the land neutral and free of all military activity. For now Honduras is the center of the region's border troubles. On the Salvadorean front, in land still jointly claimed from the days of the 1969 Soccer War, both Honduran and

Honduran troops patrol near a Miskito refugee camp. The Indians were a source of Honduran-Nicaraguan conflict.

© Randy Taylor/Sygma

© Susan Meiselas/Magnum Photos, Inc.

A poster (top) helps Nicaraguans recall the events surrounding the 1979 overthrow of President Somoza.

Salvadorean troops attempt to control the activities of thousands of persons fleeing from the latter government and settling in refugee camps in Honduras. They pose significant economic problems in addition to the strain they place on the relationship between the two states whose war settlement has not yet been totally accepted. In July, Suazo Córdova complained that Salvadorean guerrillas were participating with their Honduran counterparts in staging kidnappings and bombings to weaken his government.

On a much longer frontier, Honduras faced serious difficulties with Nicaragua, especially in the Miskito Indian area along the Caribbean coast. This region has long been in dispute between the two nations, but the situation has been aggravated by the attempts of the Sandinista government to incorporate the Indians more tightly into Nicaraguan society. Honduras charged that the Sandinistas terrorized the Indians, and thousands have fled to Honduras; Nicaragua complained that Honduras deliberately sowed the seeds of separatism among the Indians to weaken the Nicaraguan government. There also are many former Somoza guardsmen along the frontier, frightening the Sandinistas into the belief that Honduras is acting as a base for a U.S.-supported overthrow of the Nicaraguan government. In November, President Reagan admitted that the U.S. Central Intelligence Agency (CIA) was sponsoring covert action of Nicaraguan exiles to weaken that nation's aid to leftists in El Salvador. This program had been started by Argentines, who pulled out at the time of the Falkland Islands war. As the United States relies more and more on Honduras as an ally and base, military aid to that nation has increased sharply. Reagan promised an increase from about $8 million in 1980–82 to $60 million for 1982–84. This support could weaken the relative position of Honduras' military and civilian strength in the government, however.

Honduras, which is the poorest of the Central American states, also faces a heavy foreign debt and the necessity of an austerity program. The Venezuela Trust Fund has given $1 million and the Caribbean Basin program promises more. However, unemployment is rising and the economy shows little sign of growth.

Nicaragua. Some of the unity of the first few revolutionary years seemed to be cracking as the Nicaraguan economy slowed down considerably in 1982. The growth for 1980 and 1981 had averaged about 9% per year, but in 1982 preliminary estimates saw less than 1% growth. Like all of Central America, Nicaragua suffered from declines in trade triggered in part by continued strife in the region and in part by worldwide slumps that affected even the smaller states. The World Bank promised to help meet the outstanding foreign debt, some of it carrying over from Somoza days. Gas rationing was implemented in August, and government expenditures and capital investment had to be sharply reduced. Disillusioned with the revolution, many so-called moderates went into exile, including the famous military hero Captain Zero, Edén Pastora Gómez, and Alfonso Robelo Callejas, once a member of the ruling junta. In exile, these men refused to work with former Somoza guardsmen, but raised their objections to the Sandinista regime separately. Relations between church and state were better than early in the revolutionary days; religious freedom seemed assured, and frequent talks between the government and Archbishop Miguel Obando y Bravo served to ease some of the tensions of 1981.

Ill-will between Nicaragua and Honduras, however, clearly escalated in 1982. The latter nation, backed by the United States, complained of the substantial military buildup by Managua whose armed forces probably approached 30,000 plus 150,000 questionably prepared militia. Managua pilots trained in Bulgaria, and large numbers of Cuban, and to a lesser degree, Soviet military advisers, were evident in Nicaragua. In a July meeting, representatives of Costa Rica, Honduras, El Salvador, and Guatemala declared that they would not tolerate further buildup, nor Nicaraguan meddling in their affairs. The United States added that aerial photographs proved that Nicaragua was receiving USSR and Cuban support, well beyond Nicaragua's needs for defense.

The war of words continued while the United States supported a retaliatory assistance program for Honduras. It was along the Honduras-Nicaragua border that the struggle began to center. The long-ignored Miskito Indians were wooed by both governments, and when many of the Indians fled into Honduran territory, that government charged that Nicaraguan forces pursued them into Honduras and killed 200 fugitives. The Miskitos, who are of mixed blood and often speak English but not Spanish, have lived in isolation for centuries, and their relations with the Nicaraguan governments have usually been poor. It is believed that they number more than 100,000 and occupy nearly one third of Nicaragua, much of it land long disputed by Honduras. This sudden interest on the part of two governments has frightened them and led many to express hope for independence.

Although U.S. military support for Honduras implies no lessening of the cold war with Nicaragua, and even an escalation in military terms, the U.S. State Department did forward proposals to ease the strife. Assistant Secretary of State for Latin America, Thomas Enders, suggested in August that all Central America should begin to limit arms and remove foreign military advisers. The Central American reaction was both modest and mixed, but the Nicaraguan coordinator of the junta, Daniel Ortega Saavedra, thought that the message was at least worthy of discussion.

Panama. Like so much of the region, Panama found itself with a new president in 1982, the chief difference being that to Panamanians the change came as a sharp surprise. In July, President Aristides Royo Sanchez resigned in favor of the vice-president, Ricardo de la Espriella. The reasons for the resignation were variously assigned to a bad throat and to pressure from the always powerful National Guard which had been objecting to corruption in the government, inflation, and the declining economy. Royo had been president since 1978, named by the late strong man Gen. Omar Torrijos Herrera. The new president, Espriella, 47, had been an economics student at Louisiana State University and Stanford and for 10 years served as manager of the Bank of Panama. Still to be clarified was the new role of the national guard; its leader, Brig. Gen. Rubén Dario Paredes del Rio, who may have engineered the resignation, was reconfirmed as commanding general of the guard in September. It is assumed that General Paredes would like to be president in his own name, but for the moment will play the Torrijos role of collecting support from both the left and the right and maintaining the true power of the state.

Some of the conditions which prompted the change in administration included an unemployment figure of 130,000 out of a population of less than 2 million, a freeze on government wages, poor housing, strikes, and a foreign debt of more than $3,000,000,000. However, in the wake of the 1978 U.S.-Panama treaty which is changing the ownership of the Panama canal to Panama in the year 2000, traffic reached its all-time peak, and Panama might earn $100 million in 1982 from the charges made upon shipping. The canal needs modernizing. It is often full to capacity, and a 24-hour wait to begin the 9-hour trip through the canal is fairly common. Panama is benefiting in that a large number of American-citizen employees have retired or left the Canal Zone turning their jobs over to Panamanians.

Panama contains a variety of wealth. Surrounded by the thousands of very poor people are fashionable shops and many great banks, symptoms of the size and value of the international trade that the nation enjoys. New pipelines were ready to carry Alaskan oil "across the continent" in 1982, and this also should enhance the economy in time. The nation has probably relied too heavily upon its location to provide easy international banking and tax-free foreign trade to the detriment of internal development. Signs are still few that such change has begun.

In Panama City in September, the government of Panama warned both Cuba and Nicaragua about the need for reducing Central American arms races and the amount of tensions created by them, and declared that an attack on Costa Rica would be viewed with great concern.

THOMAS L. KARNES, *Arizona State University*

CENTRAL AMERICA · Information Highlights

Nation	Population (in millions)	Area in sq mi	(km²)	Capital	Head of State and Government
Belize	0.2	9,000	(23 310)	Belmopan	Elmira Minita Gordon, governor-general George Price, prime minister
Costa Rica	2.3	19,575	(50 700)	San José	Luis Alberto Monge, president
El Salvador	5.0	8,260	(21 392)	San Salvador	Alvaro Magaña, interim president
Guatemala	7.7	42,042	(108 890)	Guatemala City	Efraín Ríos Montt, president
Honduras	4.0	43,277	(112 087)	Tegucigalpa	Roberto Suazo Córdova, president
Nicaragua	2.6	50,193	(130 000)	Managua	Daniel Ortega Saavedra, junta coordinator
Panama	1.9	29,209	(75 650)	Panama City	Ricardo de la Espriella, president

CHAD

Civil war continued to wrack Chad despite the efforts of individual states and the Organization of African Unity (OAU) to compromise on differences between contending parties.

Bowing to world pressure, Libyan President Muammar el-Qaddafi in November 1981 removed Libyan army units that had supported Chadian President Goukouni Oueddei's faction. Their place was taken by an OAU multinational force. A government of National Unity was formed with Oueddei as president, Wadal Abdelkader Kamougue as vice-president, and Ahmat Acyl as foreign minister. Hissène Habré, the major dissident leader whose strength was in the north, retired to Sudan. His party, *Forces Armées du Nord* (FAN) was soon strong enough to begin attacking the government stations in eastern Chad. The weak coalition government soon fell apart. Kamougue retired with his army, the *Forces Armées Tchadienne* (FAT), into the most populous area of southern Chad. Ahmat's private army also remained intact.

In January, President Oueddei held a three-day meeting with the Sudanese leader Jaafar al-Nemery, but their announced agreement did not stop Sudan's support of Habré. Oueddei's position was worsened in February when the OAU called for a cease-fire and a new constitution that would bring Habré's faction into the government. France also cut its arms supply to Oueddei, and pressure from neighboring African states for a new settlement increased. A visit to Libya by Oueddei failed to secure Qaddafi's intervention.

By early June, Habré's forces had advanced to Massaguet, 50 mi (80 km) north of Ndjamena, the capital. After a major battle there, the FAN army defeated the government's forces. The way was thus cleared for Habré to occupy Ndjamena, which was taken without fighting on June 7. President Oueddei fled to Cameroon, and Ahmat and Kamougue immediately declared their willingness to negotiate. Habré soon announced his desire to normalize relations with France and the United States. The OAU withdrew its peacekeeping forces. The accidental death of Ahmat in July and the departure of southern strongman Kamougue to Cameroon in September eliminated the last of Habré's rivals.

HARRY A. GAILEY, *San Jose State University*

CHAD · Information Highlights

Official Name: Republic of Chad.
Location: North-central Africa.
Area: 495,800 sq mi (1 284 122 km²).
Population (1982 est.): 4,600,000.
Chief Cities (1979 est.): Ndjamena, the capital, 303,000.
Government: *Head of state and government,* Hissène Habré, president (seized control June 7, 1982).
Monetary Unit: CFA franc (283.65 CFA francs equal U.S. $1, December 1981).
Gross National Product Per Capita (1980): $120.

CHEMISTRY

Controversy over the hazards of chemicals continued to hold public attention in 1982, and research advances were scored in organic synthesis, splitting of water, and the creation of a new element.

Chemical Hazards. Several events during the year marked the potential dangers posed by chemicals. Since the late 1970s, the Love Canal area of New York State has stood as a symbol of chemical waste contamination. In 1980 President Jimmy Carter declared a federal emergency, allowing members of the community to relocate. President Carter sought to protect them from toxic residues seeping from an abandoned chemical dump site. On July 14, 1982, the U.S. Environmental Protection Agency (EPA) released a report concluding that migration of chemicals from the dump site was less than many had feared, and that most of the Love Canal area was again "habitable." The report drew strong criticism from some environmental scientists, who claimed it was based on inadequate controls and contained data of unknown accuracy. One day earlier, the EPA announced its long-awaited final rules for disposal of hazardous wastes in land sites.

Also in July a study of Virginia's Shenandoah River basin showed severe mercury contamination left over from an acetate fiber plant that ceased using the metal in 1950. The report concluded that any attempt to clean up mercury locked in sediments near the plant would do more harm than good.

In September the EPA announced a settlement with more than 100 chemical companies to share costs for cleaning up a chemical waste site in Hamilton, OH. The cost to the companies was $2.4 million, and the EPA said it would sue companies that refused to settle. Later that month a dramatic example of chemical hazards occurred when a train of chemical tank cars derailed in Livingston, LA, igniting a string of explosions. Resulting fires and the release of toxic fumes led to the evacuation of 2,700 persons from the area.

Controversy followed a report by the International Agency for Research on Cancer which failed to conclude that benzene exposure increases the risk of getting leukemia; critics charged industry pressures. A jury awarded $58 million to 47 railway workers who were exposed to the toxic chemical dioxin three years earlier when cleaning up a tank car spill. The Manville Corporation filed for protection under Chapter 11 of the bankruptcy laws, claiming it could not cope with an expected flood of lawsuits dealing with asbestos health hazards. And the United States and Canada continued to argue over acid rain, with the United States calling for more research and Canada urging regulations.

Synthesis. The "Möbius strip" has held the fancy of generations of mathematicians and schoolchildren. Named after a 19th-century mathematician, it can be formed by taking a strip of paper, twisting one end by 180°, and joining the two ends. The resulting figure has just a single continuous side. David Walba and co-workers at the University of Colorado announced that they had synthesized a molecular equivalent of the Möbius strip using double polyether strands composed of carbon and oxygen atoms. Joining the two ends of the strips without a twist gave "cylinders," and with a twist, the Möbius molecules. Next the Coloradoans hope to separate the strands lengthwise, possibly yielding a compound with joined rings.

Splitting Water. Gabor Somorjai and other research workers at the University of California at Berkeley described a technique which they said could break down water into hydrogen and oxygen using only visible light and inexpensive materials. Previous attempts in this direction have generally employed both expensive materials, such as platinum, and high-energy ultraviolet light. The Berkeley scheme employed two pressed iron oxide electrodes, one doped with silicon dioxide and the other with magnesium oxide. Although the efficiency of the original system was quite low, future improvements were predicted. Some scientists praised the development; others remained skeptical.

New Element. In late September scientists from Darmstadt, West Germany, announced that they had succeeded in creating a new element. Element 109 was formed by bombarding bismuth with fast-moving iron atoms. The feat was hailed as "an incredible technological feat," especially the subsequent detection of a single atom of the element. Uranium, with atomic number 92, is the heaviest element occurring in nature; heavier elements have been created, but they tend to be unstable. Element 109 lasted only a tiny fraction of a second.

Supersonic Jets. During the last few years, Donald Levy at the University of Chicago has pioneered the use of supersonic jet expansions in spectroscopy. These streams of molecules allow one to obtain exceedingly sharp molecular spectra, partly because the molecules are isolated, but more importantly because they are drastically cooled by the expansion. In 1982 Levy described a further use of his technique in studying how two molecules of the same type stick together. Tetrazine is a flat molecule with a ring containing four nitrogen and two carbon atoms. Using laser-induced fluorescence, Levy showed that tetrazine forms two types of weakly bound dimers (double molecules), one with the rings side-by-side and the other with a T-shaped arrangement. Separately, an Israeli research group demonstrated some of the analytical potentials of the technique. The Israelis were able to identify several large organic molecules from the sharp spectra, and they also used the method to determine minor impurities and isotopic composition.

PAUL G. SEYBOLD, *Wright State University*

CHICAGO

With a mayoral election coming up in 1983, the often controversial Mayor Jane M. Byrne was frequently in the news headlines in 1982. An expected challenge from Cook County State's Attorney Richard M. Daley, son of the longtime Chicago mayor, made Byrne's course difficult. Almost all polls showed Daley a favorite to win.

Byrne launched a campaign to remind voters that a man named Daley was no longer the "boss" in Chicago. The Byrne name appeared everywhere—for example, three city-sponsored events were advertised as Mayor Byrne's Chicagofest, Mayor Byrne's Taste of Chicago, and Mayor Byrne's Farmer's Market.

The year also saw the removal of George Dunne, president of the Cook County Board and a Daley man, as chairman of the powerful Democratic Party of Cook County. Byrne's handpicked choice for the new party chairman was Chicago Alderman Edward Vrdolyak, whom the mayor once described as part of "an evil cabal" of aldermen on the City Council.

The mayor was less successful in ousting black Alderman Allan Streeter. During the height of an aldermanic election she charged that Streeter was under federal investigation for accepting bribes. The United States attorney found no basis for the charges. Streeter handily defeated Byrne's choice for alderman, and thus gave support to a move to run a black against Byrne in the 1982 mayoral race.

A black mayor in 1983 seemed unlikely. Although blacks comprise 40% of the city's population, their turnout at the polls is much smaller. State's Attorney Daley, meanwhile, went through all the motions of running for mayor. By late November, Byrne, Daley, and Rep. Harold D. Washington, a black, had entered the race.

The death in April of John Cardinal Cody brought both sorrow and relief to the city's large Catholic community. Cody's autocratic stewardship of the archdiocese had been under attack, and a federal grand jury was looking into charges that he diverted church funds to an old friend, Helen Dolan Wilson of St. Louis. Cody's death ended that inquiry.

The arrival in August of Chicago's new archbishop, Archbishop Joseph L. Bernardin of Cincinnati, brought a week of celebration and a new sense of direction for the 2.4 million Catholics in the archdiocese. (*See also* RELIGION—Roman Catholicism.)

A fire in Chicago's Conrad Hilton Hotel killed four persons and injured 23 in May. The Hilton Hotel chain also scrapped plans for a new hotel in the North Loop area after it was denied a tax break.

Meanwhile, the long-awaited redevelopment of the North Loop moved slowly. Revival of that decaying area has been one of the goals of the Byrne administration.

ROBERT ENSTAD, *"Chicago Tribune"*

CHILE

The most important events of 1982 in Chile included the third reshuffling of the cabinet in less than a year, a surprise 18% devaluation of the peso on June 15, and a statement by President Augusto Pinochet Ugarte on September 11 that a return to democracy would not be speeded up.

Government and Political Events. The most important appointment in President Pinochet's new cabinet of eight civilians and nine military men in the shuffle of August 30 was Rolf Lüders, who was to head a newly combined Ministry of Economics and Finance in an effort to implement an economic recovery program and to restore support of the government by business and labor.

On two separate occasions in July, Pinochet claimed that "an aristocratic clique" wanted to rule the country. He also reaffirmed his "opposition to the reestablishment of political parties and a pluralist democracy." On July 27, Pinochet refused to meet with representatives of the four most important national confederations of workers, including the Confederation of Copper Workers, who had petitioned him to discuss unemployment and other economic problems with them. Pinochet said that he might "talk with unions individually" if their leaders "are not Communists." He also refused to meet with Leon Vilarin, leader of the Confederation of Truck Owners, whose August 1973 strike precipitated the downfall of President Salvador Allende Gossens.

In August, Felice D. Gaer, executive director of the International League for Human Rights, reported that 837 people had been arrested and charged with political offenses between January and June 1982, as compared with 614 in the same period of 1981. Not a single conviction had resulted from more than 400 cases of torture presented to the courts since the constitution of 1980 went into effect.

Andrés Zaldivar, president of the Christian Democratic Party, and three other exiled party members were not allowed to enter Chile for the funeral of former President Eduardo Frei Montalva, who died in Santiago on January 22.

The Economic Crisis. The government's devaluation of the peso in June came after earlier measures failed to increase foreign investments or to strengthen the peso enough to slow down an alarming increase in bankruptcies (362 between January and June 1982, as compared with an average of 117 a year between 1970 and 1975). Unpaid domestic loans had increased to $1,400,000,-000 in April 1982 from $513 million in 1981.

In other economic measures, salaries of senior government officials, including the military and 38 government-owned companies, were cut by 6-24%; cost-of-living adjustments were ended; a new 75% tax was levied on all automobiles costing more than $15,200; and the Central Bank bought the bad-debt portfolios of 15 private banks, totaling some $1,500,000,000. On September 1, the president of the Central Bank, Miguel Kast, resigned his office.

As a consequence of a 30.2% increase in exports of agricultural and seafood products and an 8.9% increase in copper exports between January and May 1982, along with a 32.5% drop in imports—principally consumer and semimanufactured goods—the annual trade deficit projected for 1982 dropped to $202 million from $1,030,000,000 in 1981. But the demand for dollars for imports and trips abroad—especially to inflation-ridden Argentina—left only $2,900,-000,000 in reserves, enough to finance 45 days of imports. On September 17, therefore, the Central Bank announced that it would try to renegotiate the payment of $1,800,000,000 in principal on the foreign debt due in 1982—an amount equal to $1,500 per capita, the world's third highest.

The government announced two measures in August and September to improve purchasing power and slow increasing unemployment, which reached 24% in September. On August 5 the government announced that it would expand the money supply in an effort to reactivate "national productive capacity." In September it announced that it would increase monthly wages for some 210,000 workers in a Government Minimum Employment Program from 1,300 to 2,000 pesos (from $22.03 to $33.90), while employers would receive a monthly subsidy of 1,200 pesos ($20.34) for each worker hired after March 31.

Foreign Relations. In the wake of the Falkland Islands War, Chile and Argentina sought to improve relations, which had deteriorated since late 1977 over sovereignty in the Southern Beagle Channel. The two countries agreed on September 15 to a papal proposal extending for six months a provisional agreement over the channel.

The Pinochet regime continued to resist extradition of three Chilean military officers indicted by a U.S. grand jury in the 1976 murder of Chilean diplomat Orlando Letelier in Washington, DC.

NEALE J. PEARSON, *Texas Tech University*

CHILE • Information Highlights

Official Name: Republic of Chile.
Location: Southwestern coast of South America.
Area: 292,132 sq mi (756 622 km^2).
Population (1982 est.): 11,500,000.
Chief Cities (June 1981 met. est.): Santiago, the capital, 3,946,281; Viña del Mar, 281,389.
Government: *Head of state and government,* Gen. Augusto Pinochet Ugarte, president (took power Sept. 1973). *Legislature*—Congress (dissolved Sept. 1973).
Monetary Unit: Peso (66 pesos equal U.S.$1, Oct. 26, 1982, floating rate).
Gross Domestic Product (1980 U.S.$): $28,080,000,-000.
Economic Index (1981): *Consumer Prices* (1970=100), *all items,* 502,215; *food,* 572,281.
Foreign Trade (1980 U.S.$): *Imports,* $5,821,000,-000; *exports,* $4,818,000,000.

CHINA (People's Republic of)

Deng Xiaoping (right) offers a toast to visiting U.S. Vice-President George Bush in early May.

The year 1982 saw China taking far-reaching measures to reorganize the party leadership and overhaul the administrative structure. The 12th party congress affirmed Deng Xiaoping's supremacy and his program of modernization.

China adopted an economic plan to quadruple its industrial and agricultural output in two decades. Collective and individual enterprise would be expanded to supplement state operations, while foreign technology would continue to be imported to advance the nation's industrial development. (*See* special report, page 177.) The huge and rapidly growing population remained a burden on the economy.

Taiwan became a critical issue in relations between China and the United States. A new Sino-American accord in August relieved the tension but left all parties dissatisfied. China resumed talks with the Soviet Union in October, but improved relations were not immediately expected. The death of Moscow party chief Leonid Brezhnev and replacement by Yuri Andropov left basic issues in abeyance at year's end.

Domestic Affairs

Congresses. The 12th national congress of the Chinese Communist Party was held September 1–11 in Peking. Hu Yaobang, chairman of the party, delivered the political report, in which he proposed sweeping structural changes. The congress accepted the report and adopted a new party constitution, which eliminated the posts of chairman and deputy chairman, created a special advisory commission, and expanded the power of the secretariat. The constitutional

changes represented a breaking away from a structure that was closely identified with Mao Zedong. The new constitution also called for reexamination of the qualifications of 39 million party members; the plan was aimed at weeding out leftists and incompetents and ensuring the loyalty of the party's rank and file.

The 12th congress affirmed the paramount position of Deng Xiaoping in the party. It elected him chairman of the new Central Advisory Committee and reelected him chairman of the party's Military Commission. It endorsed his constitutional proposals, elected his protégés to the top leadership, and dropped Hua Guofeng, Mao Zedong's chosen successor, from the Politburo. Denouncing Mao's dogmatism and personality cult, the congress endorsed Deng's pragmatic line and modernization programs.

To the surprise of many, the new advisory commission, which had been set up to encourage semiretirement by aging leaders, took in only two Politburo members besides Deng Xiaoping.

In late November and early December, the annual meeting of the National People's Congress (parliament) brought other important changes. A new, 138-article national constitution, the fourth of the Communist regime, was ratified. A variety of political, economic, and bureaucratic changes contained in the document further eliminated vestiges of Maoism. Also during the session, Prime Minister Zhao Ziyang unveiled a new five-year economic plan (1981–85).

Administrative Overhaul. Earlier, in March, Peking launched an extensive administrative overhaul to streamline its unwieldy and inefficient bureaucracy. The number of deputy prime

François Guenet/Gamma-Liaison

The two-lane Karakorram Highway was extended through the Khunjerab Pass in the Himalayas to Pakistan.

ministers was reduced from 13 to 2, while 98 ministries and commissions were consolidated into 52. Each ministry was allowed a minister and only two to four deputy ministers, whereas previously there could have been eight or more. The plan would trim the 600,000 administrative staff of the central government by 200,000, replacing aged, incompetent workers with younger ones trained in modern technology.

The Military. Because of limited funding for the defense establishment, China had a long way to go before its armed forces could be fully modernized. Peking did not entirely abandon the old concept of the peoples' war. The army believed that massive manpower and guerrilla tactics could still be used to supplement modern strategies and equipment. On the other hand, China's explosion of a simulated tactical nuclear weapon during a July military exercise against a staged Soviet invasion, showed Peking's readiness to stop the enemy at the border and its moving away from the peoples' war concept. The successful test-firing of its first submarine-launched missile in October further testified to China's emphasis on sophisticated weapons.

Economic Development. An ambitious economic plan was announced by Chairman Hu Yaobang at the 12th party congress. China was to quadruple its industrial and agricultural out-

put by the year 2000, from $366,000,000,000 in 1981 to $1,400,000,000,000. Collective and individual enterprises were to supplement state undertakings, and individual incentive was encouraged to achieve higher productivity. Economic relations with foreign countries would be expanded to create more markets for Chinese products and to bring in advanced technology for China's industrial development. By the time the program is completed, said Hu, China will have advanced to the front ranks of the world's industrial nations.

Import of foreign technology developed rapidly under the program of industrial modernization. The machine-building industry was one of the largest importers of new technology to update existing facilities. In March 1982 Peking listed 130 projects, both in heavy and light industry, which might seek Western capital and technology. The projects would have a reliable supply of raw materials and a matching contribution of capital from the Chinese government. Peking's offer signified a vigorous resumption of economic modernization, which had been cut back three years earlier because of insufficient financial resources.

In foreign trade, China was shifting from a decentralized system—which had resulted in excessive competition between regions, price fluctuation, and supply shortages—to more central control. Peking maintained that the move was not a total reversal of the decentralization policy and that local corporations could still sign contracts directly with foreign firms. In 1982 China lowered import duties on 149 categories of industrial equipment and raw materials needed for its modernization program. On the other hand, Peking introduced export duties as high as 60% on many raw materials, including coal, pig iron, rice, soybeans, and sugar, in an effort to reserve supplies for internal use.

The new five-year plan announced by Zhao in November—China's sixth—called for a continuation of these general "economic readjustments." Emphasis would be given to increased productivity, higher profitability, and "real growth"—projected at a moderate 4–5% annually. Increased exports and foreign capital would help spur overall economic growth.

Commune Reorganization. China began to phase out the commune system, which had been established by Mao Zedong in the 1950s as the shortcut to "pure" communism. Communes were giving way to "xiang" (rural townships), and production brigades to villages, as units of local government. The economic functions of such units were assigned to agricultural-industrial-commercial companies expressly responsible for rural output. The Chinese rural economy was no longer limited to agriculture, as industrial enterprises rose rapidly on farms that had too little land and too many people. Rural factories manufactured a great variety of products, including bricks, glue, glass, and clothes. These sideline industries increased earnings by as much as 40% in some areas and offered work to peasants who would otherwise drift off to overcrowded cities.

Population. The official 1982 Chinese census—the largest in history—revealed a population of 1,008,175,288. Despite strong family-planning incentives, the annual growth rate was a high 1.4%, a serious burden on China's economic development. A shortage of arable land simply makes it impossible to grow enough grains to feed the vast and growing population. In 1981 China imported 15 million tons of grain, thus losing enormous foreign exchange that otherwise could be used for modernization purposes. Peking also paid out huge subsidies, estimated at $18,000,000,000 in 1981, to stabilize prices of food and other necessities.

Culture and Communism. While China's modernization program requires economic and technical exchanges with capitalist countries, these may bring foreign influences that threaten the Communist way of life. It is therefore necessary, said Hu Yaobang, "to guard against, and firmly resist, the corrosion of capitalist ideas and to combat any worship of things foreign or fawning on foreigners." The official press launched a concerted attack on the "poisoning" of capitalist ideology and the "pollution" it produces. The government forbade unauthorized contacts with foreigners and banned social dancing, Western rock music, and racier videotapes and books. Hardening its attitude toward what it castigated as "bourgeois liberalism," Peking insisted that the main task of literature is to heighten people's enthusiasm for socialism.

Foreign Affairs

United States. Peking made the Taiwan question a test of its relations with the United States. In April 1982, when the Reagan administration was ready to proceed with a $60-million sale of military parts to Taiwan, China protested loudly, contending that in the Shanghai Communiqué of 1972, the United States acknowledged only one China and that Taiwan was an integral part of it. Consequently, said Peking, arms sales to Taiwan constituted an interference in China's internal affairs and an infringement of its sovereignty over Taiwan. Deng Xiaoping warned that his country was "well prepared" to downgrade diplomatic relations with the United States if no agreement could be reached over the Taiwan problem.

Recognizing the sensitivity of the issue, President Reagan wrote three letters to the leaders of China in April and May, in which he acknowledged as "significant" Peking's plan of Sept. 30, 1981, for peaceful reunification with Taiwan. (The plan, which offered to let Taiwan retain its socioeconomic system as well as its armed forces, had been rejected by Taipei as a trick.) President Reagan expressed the view that "in the context of progress toward a peaceful solution, there would naturally be a decrease in the need for arms by Taiwan." On August 17, after much delicate negotiation, the countries issued a joint communiqué in which China stated that its message to Taiwan on Jan. 1, 1979, "promulgated a fundamental policy of striving for peaceful reunification of the motherland" and that the plan put forward on Sept. 30, 1981, "represented a further major effort under this fundamental policy to strive for a peaceful solution to the Taiwan question." On its part, the United States stated that the arms sales to Taiwan "will not exceed, either in qualitative or in quantitative terms, the level of those supplied in recent years," and that it "intends to reduce gradually its sales of arms to Taiwan, leading over a period of time to a final resolution."

The communiqué contained enough ambiguities to patch up differences, but it immediately gave rise to conflicting interpretations. The U.S. pledge to reduce arms sales to Taiwan, said President Reagan, was based on "the full expectation" that China would seek reunification with Taiwan by peaceful means. But the Chinese leadership took exception to any linkage between the U.S. pledge to reduce arms sales to Taiwan and Peking's policy to seek peaceful reunification. "They were two separate questions of an entirely different nature," said the official New China News Agency.

Beyond the Taiwan question, China and the United States made good progress in the expansion of economic and technical cooperation. Peking recognized the importance of its friendship with the United States in the face of the Soviet challenge, as well as the value of U.S. technology in its modernization program. As Washington liberalized its export policy toward Peking, trade between the two countries rose sharply, with China becoming the 14th largest trading partner of the United States.

Western Europe. The future of Hong Kong was the major subject of discussion when Prime Minister Margaret Thatcher of Great Britain visited Peking, September 22–26. Hong Kong was ceded to Britain in 1842, but the New Territories on the Kowloon side were acquired by the British under a 99-year lease, which expires in 1997. Without the New Territories, which make up 88% of Hong Kong's area, the colony would not survive as an independent entity.

China made it clear that it planned to regain sovereignty over Hong Kong, though it assured island residents that they had no cause for concern. Chinese sales to the colony brought $5,000,000,000 in revenue, about 40% of Peking's foreign exchange earnings. Apparently interested in an orderly transition, Peking had hinted that the island might become a "special administrative region" to ensure continued trade development. On September 24, after a lengthy conference with Deng Xiaoping, Prime Minister Thatcher read a joint statement announcing that

China and Great Britain had agreed to enter talks through diplomatic channels "with the common aim of maintaining the stability and prosperity of Hong Kong." No details were given as to their respective positions, but on September 30 Peking declared that China was not bound by the 19th-century treaties that ceded Hong Kong to Britain. The statement was intended to contradict Thatcher, who said in Hong Kong that the treaties were valid under international law and that their abrogation would be "very serious indeed."

Peking received a French delegation in August to discuss the purchase of Mirage 2000 jet fighters, which had proved effective in Argentine attacks on the British navy in the Falklands war. In June, Chinese Foreign Minister Huang Hua visited West Germany, holding talks with Chancellor Helmut Schmidt and Foreign Minister Hans-Dietrich Genscher. The German leaders expressed support for a coalition of Cambodian resistance groups fighting against Vietnam and urged China to use its influence in that effort.

Soviet Union. Exploiting China's tension with the United States over Taiwan, Soviet President Leonid Brezhnev proposed on March 24 that Moscow and Peking resume border talks, which had been suspended in 1978, and discuss measures to improve relations. China's response was cautious. The Soviet threat to its security remained significant, and Peking had long recognized that the best way to deter the Soviets was strategic cooperation with the United States. When Brezhnev on September 26 appealed for "a normalization, a gradual improvement of relations," Peking finally agreed to increase contacts. On October 5 talks were resumed in Peking, with Deputy Foreign Minister Qian Qichin leading the Chinese team and Deputy Foreign Minister Leonid Ilyichev the Soviet.

Foreign Minister Huang Hua led the Chinese delegation to Brezhnev's funeral on November 15. The next day Huang met with his Soviet counterpart, Andrei Gromyko, in the first high-level talks between the two superpowers in 13 years. One week later, in his first major policy speech, new Soviet party chief Yuri Andropov promised to seek improved relations with China.

Japan. Peking expressed anger at the revision of material in Japanese high school textbooks regarding Japan's invasion of China in the 1930s and 1940s. The Chinese protested strongly against the use of such words as "advance" and "expansion" to whitewash its aggression in China and the glossing over of Japanese wartime atrocities, particularly the 1937 massacre at Nanjing. In August, Japan said that it would make "necessary amendments" in 1985.

On September 26 Japanese Prime Minister Zenko Suzuki arrived in Peking on an official visit to commemorate the 10th anniversary of the normalization of relations between the two countries. In his talks with Chinese leaders, Suzuki agreed to increase Japanese investment in offshore oil exploration by $400 million, to a total of $600 million.

Southeast Asia. China played an instrumental role in the formation of a Cambodian guerrilla coalition on June 22, when that country's three major resistance leaders signed a declaration to join forces in the struggle against Vietnamese occupation. The three men—Prince Norodom Sihanouk, a former head of state; Son Sann, a former prime minister; and Khieu Samphan, a leader of the Communist Pol Pot forces—had been so bitterly divided that only strong pressure from Peking, which provided arms to all three factions, could bring them together. The coalition was necessary to strengthen the anti-Vietnamese forces and to win support from non-Communist Southeast Asian countries. Considering Vietnamese occupation of Cambodia a direct menace to East Asian stability, China was determined to fight Vietnam on all fronts.

Numerous conflicts occurred along the Chinese-Vietnamese border during 1982, with many Chinese peasants reported killed or wounded. On March 3 two Vietnamese gunboats shelled a number of Chinese fishing boats in the South China Sea, setting three of them on fire. Eighteen Chinese fishermen were missing and six wounded. The next day, apparently in retaliation, China seized a Vietnamese reconnaissance boat near the Paracel Islands.

Others. China and India held talks in May on the 20-year-old border dispute that had been the obstacle to normal relations between the two countries. Peking proposed that the discussions be extended to include economic relations, technological cooperation, and cultural exchanges. No accord was reported, but the two sides agreed to meet again.

Over protests from New Delhi, China and Pakistan opened the Khunjerab Pass on August 27. Situated at the end of a highway from Xinjiang into Pakistan, the pass links the two countries along the ancient Silk Road.

On December 20, Prime Minister Zhao set out on a month-long, 10-nation tour of Africa to strengthen ties with the Third World.

See also TAIWAN.

CHESTER C. TAN, *New York University*

CHINA · Information Highlights

Official Name: People's Republic of China.
Location: Central part of eastern Asia.
Area: 3,691,500 sq mi (9 560 985 km²).
Population (1982 census): 1,008,175,288.
Chief Cities (1980 est.): Peking, the capital, 9,335,-000; Shanghai, 12,382,000; Tianjin, 4,657,000.
Government: *General secretary of the Chinese Communist Party,* Hu Yaobang (took office June 1981). *Head of government,* Zhao Ziyang, premier (took office Sept. 1980); Deng Xiaoping, chairman, Central Advisory Commission. *Legislature* (unicameral)—National People's Congress.
Monetary Unit: Yuan (1.73 yuan equal U.S.$1, December 1981—noncommercial rate).
Foreign Trade (1980 U.S.$): *Imports,* $19,530,000,-000; *exports,* $18,255,000,000.

Foreign Investment

© Greenhill/Black Star

A variety of Western goods have been available in China for several years. Of late the Communist government has encouraged foreign companies to expand their investment in consumer goods, as well as in major industrial projects.

Investment by foreign companies in the People's Republic of China slowly has grown in the early 1980s, taking on increasing importance to Western business and the Chinese economy. The rate of future growth is uncertain, but the outlook remains promising.

Opening Up. Accurate data on foreign investment in China are difficult to obtain, and available statistics are complicated by inconsistent definitions, but by any measure the amount is becoming sizable. For the period between China's enactment of a joint-venture code in 1979 to the end of 1981, estimates range from $700 million to $2,000,000,000; Chinese claims tend toward the higher figure. Between late 1979 and early 1982, China discussed or arranged more than 400 joint and cooperative projects with companies from more than 30 nations. By the end of the first quarter of 1982, 40 joint ventures had been approved, of which 27 were in operation. Of the initial ventures, 19—calling for about $20 million in foreign investment—were established in 1981; 20 others—for about $177 million of foreign investment—were set up in 1980. Nearly $90 million in foreign investment has been made.

Among the goods and services for which China has accepted foreign investment are beer brewing, soft drinks, food products, photocopiers, movies and other entertainment, vehicle manufacturing, natural resource marketing, and production and distribution of electronic products. The arrangements with foreign companies represent a variety of investment concepts, including licensing, leasing, developing, outright joint equity, cooperative enterprises, and compensation pacts.

Many of the projects are being established in special economic zones (SEZs), set up to attract foreign capital by offering inexpensive land and labor, as well as tax advantages. The four zones, located in the southern provinces of Guangdong and Fujian, are Shenzhen, Zhuhai, Shantou, and Xiamen. Since 1979, potential contracts in excess of $2,600,000,000 allegedly have been brought to Guangdong alone. Other areas also have been given greater leeway in making deals with foreigners, and reports in early 1982 suggested that other special areas, akin to SEZs, might be formed.

In March 1982, China broadened its approach to foreigners, inviting overseas firms to invest $1,000,000,000 to $1,500,000,000 for 130 industrial projects. Those projects, ranging in cost from less than $1 million to $150 million, would be for consumer goods, machinery, com-

Courtesy, R.J. Reynolds Tobacco International, Inc.

In a joint project with the Chinese, R.J. Reynolds Tobacco International makes filter cigarettes in Xiamen. The first full year of production was completed in 1982.

munications equipment, textiles, and building materials.

That offering followed by about one month Peking's invitation to 46 foreign oil firms in 12 nations—including 23 companies in the United States—to prepare bids for offshore drilling leases in Chinese waters. The entire project was expected to require an investment of $10,-000,000,000 to $20,000,000,000 over a period of 10 to 15 years. In September, Peking awarded a contract, the first ever to a U.S. oil concern, to Atlantic Richfield.

At about the same time, China began renegotiating canceled contracts and making various other arrangements .with foreign businesses. Among the most important was one with Occidental Petroleum Corp. for a feasibility study which could lead to a major joint coal venture and, eventually, an investment by Occidental of about $230 million.

Loans, Credit, and Banking. Underscoring these developments, China, between 1977 and the end of 1981, arranged or began negotiating for $35,000,000,000 to $40,000,000,000 in loans and credits from Western banks and government and international institutions. Through 1981, China apparently used only a fraction of the available funds. These loans also represent a variety of approaches—conventional bank-

customer arrangements; government loans; syndicated loans; credits from export banks; and buyers' credits, involving long-term deposits in the Bank of China.

Significantly, too, more than a dozen foreign banks had representative offices in China by mid-1982, and reports indicated that nearly 60 others were anxious to establish themselves. Similarly, China has established a number of joint banking and finance ventures in other countries; made progress on plans to sell Chinese bonds to foreigners to raise development capital; and expanded the Bank of China's operations in Japan and the United States. In late 1981, the Chinese formed an investment bank to obtain medium- and long-term funds from international and other organizations, as well as to provide loans for joint ventures.

China has also continued to establish correspondent relationships with foreign banks. Since 1978 it has established ties with nearly 65 U.S. banks and, according to one estimate, up to 1,000 worldwide. To facilitate trade and business, Chinese national and provincial units from 1979 through 1981 made agreements with such U.S. institutions as First National Bank of Chicago, Chase Manhattan Bank, Allied Bank International, and Chemical Bank.

Uncertainties. However promising the trend of recent years, the pace of investment growth in China hinges on imponderables. Among the questions that remain to be answered are whether China's pragmatic modernization plans will be interrupted by political upheaval, and how far and fast the country plans, with foreign help, to develop its natural resources, particularly coal and oil, and perhaps nuclear power.

Clarification and enactment of additional regulations governing investment, as well as the effectiveness of their administration, also will weigh heavily in investment decisions. Many new rules have been introduced since China adopted its joint-venture law, and complementary action must be taken by Western nations. Likewise, the success of China's efforts to streamline the government bureaucracy and facilitate the conduct of business will be an important consideration to potential investors.

Finally, diplomatic affairs may play a crucial role. Investment by U.S. companies (of which about 80 had offices in China by mid-1982) could be influenced by Washington-Peking relations. Some American executives have expressed concern for future opportunities if relations sour, especially over the Taiwan issue. In 1981, however, the Netherlands sold two submarines to Taiwan and diplomatic relations between Peking and Amsterdam were downgraded, but business arrangements with private Dutch firms were not canceled.

ARTHUR W. SAMANSKY

CITIES AND URBAN AFFAIRS

Although many urbanists remained convinced that U.S. cities are poised on the edge of a "golden era," 1982 was marked by deep dents in the urban revitalization movement in the older cities of the Northeast and Midwest, and by drastically curtailed growth in the Sun Belt communities. The major forces shaping urban affairs during the year were 1) the depressed economy, which resulted in urban disinvestment by both the public and private sectors; 2) conflict over the Reagan administration's New Federalism policy; 3) a new focus on "public-private partnerships"; and 4) the increased use of pension funds for economic development.

The Economy. The fiscal stress experienced by U.S. cities in 1981 worsened during 1982, even though interest rates and inflation began to decline toward year's end. The national unemployment rate, which edged over 10% in September, was exacerbated in the cities, where many firms in the automotive, steel, and farm implement industries either closed down or drastically cut back production. Not even high-tech industries were immune to the ravages of the economy, as firms in California's "silicon valley" instituted layoffs for the first time.

Home loan foreclosure proceedings threatened a record number of American families (150,000) in 1982. The beleaguered housing industry showed brief signs of recovery in the spring, but it lapsed quickly when mortgage rates remained high. Unemployment in the construction industry hovered near 20% in 1982, and construction firms continued to fail at an alarming rate.

Although most of the major cuts in federal urban programs were effected in 1981, it was only in 1982 that the consequences really began to be felt. The Comprehensive Education Training Act (CETA), for example, was terminated on Sept. 30, 1982, with future vocational training left to the discretion of cities and private industry with little or no federal assistance. Other categorical aid programs were being terminated, merged, or rearranged within the framework of the president's New Federalism.

The New Federalism. President Reagan's plan to significantly restructure the lines of authority and responsibility among federal, state, and local levels of government was unveiled in January 1982. While the major thrust of the plan—full federal responsibility for Medicaid in exchange for state assumption of Aid to Families and Dependent Children (AFDC), food stamps, and 61 smaller federal grant programs—dealt primarily with federal-state relationships, its implications for cities—dependence upon state governments to provide funds to maintain essential services—caused grave concern among U.S. mayors. (*See* special report, page 539.)

The cities were also dissatisfied with the provisions of the proposed "turnback" mechanisms, whereby a federal trust fund would provide states with revenue to help meet new obligations for the programs turned back to them under New Federalism. Cities feared that the states would not "pass through" sufficient federal trust fund payments to compensate for the loss of categorical federal grants.

The release of the president's draft urban policy statement in June pledged continued support for a program favored by mayors—Urban Development Action Grants (UDAGs)—but the overall tone of the report was "survival of the fittest," and it concluded that "cities are not guaranteed eternal life." The most controversial points in the statement were that 1) federal programs to aid cities have been largely counterproductive and have transformed mayors from "bold leaders of self-reliant cities to wily stalkers of federal funds," 2) cities could expect the federal government to play a passive role in urban policy, and 3) the economic recovery program *is* the administration's urban policy, and cities must learn to rely on themselves, their states, and the private sector.

Public-Private Partnerships. While public-private partnerships represent one of the cornerstones of the Reagan urban policy, it is not a new concept. What is new is that the federal government's partnership role will be passive and limited. UDAG grants requiring a minimal 5:1 ratio of private-to-public investment dollars will remain a federal tool, and the administration supported legislation to establish Urban Enterprise Zones, a proposal to induce entrepreneurial investment in depressed areas of cities by reducing taxes and regulations. Critics have pointed out that the zones will have limited effect, since only 75 would be authorized over a three-year period and since most of the financial burden (new public facilities, for example) would fall on cities and states.

Other forms of urban public-private partnerships which do not necessarily rely on federal involvement include the loan of corporate management experts to city government, city contracts with private firms to provide services, and collaboration on downtown development projects.

Pension Funds. One bright spot in an otherwise bleak year for cities was the acceleration of public pension fund investments in urban economic development. Federal program cutbacks, coupled with the shift of responsibility to the states and cities, heightened interest in pension funds as an alternative source of financing for urban programs. Of an estimated $800 billion in pension funds, 25% is in more than 6,500 public funds. Development investing of pension funds focuses on "capital gaps" in the housing market, primarily the buying of federally guaranteed mortgages in the secondary market. Such investments can assist neighborhood development in an era of declining resources.

LOUIS H. MASOTTI, *Northwestern University*

COINS AND COIN COLLECTING

The 250th anniversary of the birth of the first president of the United States occurred in 1982 and was commemorated by a number of special coin and medal issues. For the first time in more than 30 years, a legal tender U.S. commemorative coin was authorized and issued. The 90% silver half-dollar was designed by Elizabeth Jones, chief sculptor-engraver of the U.S. Mint. The obverse of the coin depicts George Washington on horseback, and the reverse features a view of Washington's Mount Vernon home.

Much controversy surrounded the proposed 1982 legislation for the minting of 29 special U.S. commemorative coins to be issued in conjunction with the 1984 Olympic Games. Many numismatic experts felt that 29 coins were too many, and that few people other than the very serious collector would be able to acquire the entire set. Successful legislation introduced by Rep. Frank Annunzio (D-IL) in August, and supported by testimony from many of the hobby's most active members, assured that not more than six coins would be minted, and that the marketing and distribution would be done by the Treasury Department rather than by an outside agency, as called for in the original legislation. Representative Annunzio also successfully presented a resolution stating that the third full week in April shall perpetually be known as National Coin Week.

The American Numismatic Association, the largest and most active numismatic organization in the world, completed a $1 million addition to its Colorado Springs, CO, headquarters building. Early in the year a time capsule containing full sets of current coinage and other memorabilia was placed in the foundation of the building. The completed addition was dedicated in June and included the inauguration of an expanded museum and library, which are open to the public free of charge. Dignitaries at the dedication

U.S. Mint

A 90% silver half-dollar was issued by the U.S. Mint in honor of the 250th birthday of George Washington.

included Astronaut James B. Irwin, who opened the museum's exhibit of moon rocks obtained by Irwin's Apollo 15 mission of July 1971.

The familiar one-cent piece underwent a significant change during the year when most of the cent's copper content was replaced with zinc. Although they remain the same in appearance, the new cent pieces comprise 99.2% zinc and are barrel plated with 0.8% copper. The switch to zinc was made because of the rising costs of copper.

One of the most exciting events in the numismatic world during 1982 was the identification and recovery of the 1804 Linderman silver dollar. The coin, one of only 15 1804 silver dollars known to exist throughout the world, was stolen from its owner in 1967. In 1981 it was brought to the American Numismatic Association Certification Service for authentication and grading. A thorough investigation soon led to its identification as the long-missing piece. Valued at $750,000, the coin went on permanent display at the association's museum in June.

In late October a $3 gold piece struck at the San Francisco Mint in 1870 sold for a record $687,500 in New York City.

MARY JANE JOYAL
Associate Editor, "The Numismatist"

Numismatists welcomed the return of a rare 1804 Linderman silver dollar, which was stolen from its owner in 1967.

American Numismatic Association

COLOMBIA

The election of Conservative Belisario Betancur as president dominated Colombian events in 1982. Betancur won a four-man race in which the normal Liberal party majority was split between "official" candidate (and former president) Alfonso Lopez Michelsen and "New Liberal" candidate Luis Carlos Galán. The Liberals did gain a narrow, if divided, victory in the March congressional elections.

Politics. The midyear presidential elections that brought Belisario Betancur to power were marked by increased participation; voter abstention has long plagued Colombian politics. Some 7 million people, or about 55% of the electorate, voted, an increase of 15% over the previous presidential contest. Betancur received 47% of the vote, with Lopez garnering about 40%. Carlos Galán, backed by former President Carlos Lleras Restrepo, received 12%; leftist candidate Gerardo Molina, backed by the Communist and Socialist parties, received slightly more than 1%. The Liberal split virtually assured Betancur's win, as the March congressional elections showed a clear and continuing liberal majority among the voters. The March elections presaged the presidential result, as congressional slates pledged to Lopez and Galán fought for available Liberal votes. The final Liberal total was split, with 2.3 million for slates pledged to Lopez and more than 500,000 for candidates pledged to Galán. Congress was split into five factions—three Liberal and two Conservative.

Betancur's first days in office promised a renewed presidential initiative. He filled six of 13 available cabinet posts with Liberals and appointed 10 women to deputy cabinet posts. In his inaugural address on August 7, Betancur promised that his administration would be "close to the poor" and that he would "lift the white flag of peace" to the antigovernment guerrillas. The president also stated that Colombia would consider joining the movement of nonaligned nations, but would not renew diplomatic relations with Cuba so long as that nation continued to train Colombian guerrillas. In a subsequent speech, President Betancur promised that the government would allocate more money for low-income housing.

Guerrillas. For the first time in recent years, guerrilla activity in Colombia seemed to wane. Betancur's prospects of dealing successfully with the guerrilla problem were improved by outgoing President Gabriel Turbay Ayala's announcement on July 20 of an end to a six-year state of siege. Despite the failure of the Turbay government to back the unconditional amnesty proposed by an independent peace commission, the lifting of the state of siege and the election of the populist Betancur contributed more toward a solution of the guerrilla problem than any event since 1948. Betancur's alliance with the remnants of ANAPO, the populist political organization of former dictator Gustavo Rojas Pinilla, also held promise. ANAPO is the organizational and ideological source of the M-19 guerrilla group.

Economy. Real growth in the Colombian economy rose to 3.9%, up from 2.5% in 1981. Inflation for the year stood at 21.3%, down from 1981 and substantially lower than other Latin American countries. Unemployment at midyear was estimated at 8.1%, with underemployment at 16%. The rates in the larger cities were considerably higher. The controlled devaluation of the peso continued, with the U.S. dollar worth 63.6 pesos at year-end. Colombia incurred a balance of payments deficit of $550 million during the first half of 1982. Coffee still accounted for a major share of the nation's official foreign exchange earnings. Illegal exports of marijuana and cocaine to the United States earned more than all the official exports together. The creation of a new "Mafia" as a result of the trade in illicit drugs was a national problem.

Foreign Affairs. Colombia was one of four members of the Organization of American States (OAS) to abstain on an OAS resolution backing Argentine claims to the Falkland Islands. (The others were Chile, Trinidad and Tobago, and the United States.) But Colombia, along with other Andean Pact nations, stepped up trade with Argentina during the Falkland crisis. Colombia opened talks with Venezuela in an effort to solve border problems between the two countries.

Relations with the United States remained good. Colombia was an early supporter of President Reagan's Caribbean Basin Initiative plan, and in March the United States and Colombia opened talks concerning U.S. air bases in Colombia. The Colombian government continued to cooperate with U.S. drug enforcement efforts, and in February officials of the two nations announced the seizure of 6.4 million lbs (2.9 million kg) of marijuana.

In his first months in office, President Betancur took steps to distance his country from a strict U.S. alignment, prompting President Reagan to make a stop in Bogotá during his late-year Latin American tour.

ERNEST A. DUFF
Randolph-Macon Women's College

COLOMBIA • Information Highlights

Official Name: Republic of Colombia.
Location: Northwest South America.
Area: 440,831 sq mi (1 141 752 km^2).
Population (1982 est.): 25,600,000.
Chief Cities (1979 est.): Bogotá, the capital, 4,055,-909; Medelín, 1,506,661; Cali, 1,316,137.
Government: *Head of state and government,* Belisario Betancur Cuartas, president (took office Aug. 1982). *Legislature*—Congress: Senate and Chamber of Representatives.
Monetary Unit: Peso (44 pesos equal U.S.$1, Oct. 1982).
Gross National Product (1980 U.S.$): $32,740,000,-000.
Economic Index (1981): *Consumer Prices* (1970= 100), *all items,* 882.6; *food,* 1,071.8.
Foreign Trade (1980 U.S.$): *Imports,* $4,333,000,-000; *exports,* $3,852,000,000.

COLORADO

UPI

Denverites welcome the opening of the 16th Street Mall.

Colorado faced increasing economic problems in 1982 as its voters elected a governor, U.S. representatives, and other officials.

Election. Incumbent Gov. Richard D. Lamm (D) won a record-breaking election victory margin of 67.5% on November 2, but Republicans easily retained control of both chambers of the state legislature. Republicans also wrested the attorney general's office from the Democrats when Duane Woodard defeated Gail Klapper in the race to succeed retiring Attorney General J. D. MacFarlane (D). Klapper's bid to be the first woman elected to that office in the nation failed narrowly in the only close statewide race.

Incumbent Republican Representatives Ken Kramer and Hank Brown won reelection, as did incumbent Democrats Patricia Schroeder, Timothy Wirth, and Ray Kogovsek. Republican Jack Swigert captured the new sixth district seat. The former astronaut died of cancer at year-end, and a special election would be held in 1983 to fill the vacancy.

Economy. Governor Lamm had little time to savor his victory because of a worsening fiscal picture. Even before the election, he had to order $30 million cut from state spending. Actually, however, many states would have envied Colorado's economic position. When the budget cuts were made in August, the state's unemployment rate was only 4.9%—exactly half the national average. However, a year earlier it was 3.6%.

As the recession hit the state, a number of highly publicized events seemed to send consumers into hiding, leveling off retail sales and sales tax collections. The most dramatic event was Exxon Corporation's decision to mothball its huge oil shale project in western Colorado. However, Union Oil, which enjoys a $400 million federal purchase guarantee, said it would continue with its project and expected to produce diesel and jet fuel from oil shale.

Meanwhile the sagging automobile and steel markets caused layoffs at CF&I Steel Corp. in Pueblo and the AMAX Inc. molybdenum mines in the state. The continuing international oil slump and relatively depressed crude oil prices began to slow the building boom by natural-resource companies in the Denver area.

The recession caused state sales tax revenues, expected to rise by 7% in 1982, to remain even with 1981 receipts in the July–September period. Pointing to needs ranging from new jails to a highway maintenance program to help Colorado cope with its growing population, Governor Lamm said that gasoline taxes, truck ton-mile taxes, cigarette taxes, and other levies might be raised.

Meanwhile private charities and local governments dealt with the worsening economic problems as best they could. A church-sponsored shelter for 300 homeless residents was opened in Denver at a former high school.

Other Events. Regional Environmental Protection Agency Director Steve Durham warned that Colorado's clean-air plan was inadequate and might force federal sanctions on the state.

The United Methodist Church's Judicial Council upheld Denver-area Bishop Melvin Wheatley's ruling that homosexuals are not prohibited from serving in the ministry of that church.

A four-week strike by bus drivers in the Regional Transportation District caused little disruption for most of the 80,000 residents who normally ride the system.

BOB EWEGEN, *"The Denver Post"*

COLORADO • Information Highlights

Area: 104,091 sq mi (269 596 km²).

Population (1980 census): 2,889,735.

Chief Cities (1980 census): Denver, the capital, 491,-396; Colorado Springs, 214,821; Aurora, 158,588.

Government (1982): *Chief Officers*—governor, Richard D. Lamm (D); lt. gov., Nancy Dick (D). *General Assembly*—Senate, 35 members; House of Representatives, 65 members.

State Finances (fiscal year 1981): *Revenues,* $3,501,-000,000; *expenditures,* $3,311,000,000.

Personal Income (1981): $33,256,000,000; per capita, $11,215.

Labor Force (Aug. 1982): *Nonagricultural wage and salary earners,* 1,281,200; *unemployed,* 114,100 (7.2% of total force).

Education: *Enrollment* (fall 1981)—public elementary schools, 376,043; public secondary, 168,131; colleges and universities (1981–82), 167,977. *Public school expenditures* (1980–81), $1,532,345,000 ($2,656 per pupil).

COMMUNICATION TECHNOLOGY

In 1982, advances were made in all of the technologies basic to modern communication: digital transmission and switching systems, lightwave systems, communication satellites, direct satellite-to-home TV broadcasting, and high-capacity mobile radio telephone systems. New technology for the local telephone exchange and for broad-band links to the user's terminal began to appear. Experimental trials of data and pictures via two-way information systems for the home and office were indications that a new era might be announcing itself.

Transmission and Switching Systems. Lightwave transmission systems became increasingly important during the year. The Bell System was installing more than 60 such systems in areas all across the United States. Bell Canada moved forward with the installation of thousands of kilometers of optical-fiber cables.

Successful experiments were conducted on lower-loss, longer-wavelength systems and on multiplexed systems using three different wavelengths of light simultaneously. With multiplexing, a 144-fiber cable could handle 300,000 two-way telephone conversations at once.

In a Bell Labs experiment, a 274 mb/sec lightwave signal was transmitted a distance of 63 mi (101 km) without amplification along the way. At such high pulse rates, 150 pages of text can be sent in about one second. Such a system might someday be used for high-capacity transoceanic undersea telecommunications.

COMSAT announced plans for deployment in 1984 of six new INTELSAT *V*-A satellites, each with a capacity of approximately 30,000 simultaneous telephone calls.

The U.S. communication system moved steadily toward the goal of an all-electronic-switched network. By mid-1982, more than 50% of the almost 90 million subscriber lines were served by electronic switching offices, with new ones being cut into service at the rate of one every two days. The latest of these, No. 5 ESS, is a new digital switching system already in commercial service in Seneca, IL. It marks an important step in the progress toward an integrated national digital network which will provide voice data and video services on an end-to-end basis.

Communication Services. Direct satellite-to-home TV transmission, supplying 30 channels and receivable by a small rooftop antenna, approached broader public use. More than a dozen companies responded to a midyear announcement by the FCC that applications would be accepted for the Direct Broadcast Service (DBS). Operation was expected to begin in 1986.

Nationwide mobile radio telephone service, using a new high-capacity cellular system, moved ahead with FCC acceptance of applications. The technology is based on electronically-switched, lower-power transmitters in a number of small contiguous cells. The available frequencies are used many times over, thus increasing the number of customers who can be served.

Technology for bringing all kinds of information into and out of homes and offices continued to be developed. "Videotex," a two-way information service utilizing the home TV screen and telephone or cable TV lines, and "teletext," a one-way service conveyed in a coded format over standard broadcast or cable TV channels, are representative of the multiplicity of new systems being tested by more than 20 companies. They provide news, weather reports, stock quotations, transportation schedules, and myriad other information. Some systems have a keyboard that enables the user to do at-home shopping and banking.

Microelectronics. A number of U.S. and other companies began production of 256-kilobit random access memory (256 K RAM) chips used in processors for electronic switching systems and general-purpose computers. Also, significant reductions in size and cost were made in 32-bit microprocessors, logic devices now containing the equivalent of 150,000 transistors on a single chip about 0.4 inch (1 cm) square.

In 1982, a high-speed ultra-miniature data processor, consisting of 548 Josephson junction switches operating at the temperature of liquid helium, was demonstrated by Bell Labs. The processor, on a chip the size of a small button, carried out complex logic operations in a time of 30 nanoseconds (30 billionths of a second) with a power consumption of less than one milliwatt. It is predicted that, using the Josephson junction technology, microelectronic circuitry contained within a few cubic inches, could process the same amount of information that is now handled by a roomful of computers, in less time.

M. D. FAGEN, *Formerly, Bell Laboratories*

COMPUTERS

Computers were clearly a major part of the American economy and society in 1982. Ironically, the proof of the industry's importance was the fact that it could not escape the economic recession. Just as sales of such staples as automobiles and homes sagged, sales of computers slowed and the manufacturers' profits lagged those of previous years.

The good news for consumers was that the prices of home computers plummeted during 1982. These computers typically attach to a television and can perform a variety of tasks, ranging from playing games and tutoring children to helping to balance household finances. In July, Timex Corp. staged a computer first by selling its personal computer for $99.95 through the 100,-000 retail outlets that carry its watches. Then, Texas Instruments Inc. introduced a home computer that sold for $199—just one fifth the price that same model sold for in 1980. Commodore International Ltd. cut the price of its VIC 20 to

As prices fell and more versatile, convenient systems hit the market, home computers became the latest appliance craze. The growing software industry has provided a wide range of home uses, from tutoring to cataloguing recipes.

under $200 and Tandy Corp.'s Radio Shack stores shaved $100 off the Color Computer to bring its price to $299. Similarly, Atari, the video game leader, reduced the price of its popular Model 400 by 25% to under $300. As a result of these price drops, consumers bought an estimated 1.5 million home computers during 1982—five times the number purchased in 1980.

More sophisticated personal computers were also gaining in popularity among such professionals as doctors, stock brokers, and small business owners. For example, the International Business Machines (IBM) Corp., which only entered the personal computer business in 1981, was expected to sell 200,000 computers by the time the year was out. Computers also became more portable during 1982. Osborne Computer Corp. set off the portability craze by introducing the Osborne 1, a 24-lb (10.8-kg) computer built into a briefcase that sold for $1,795—less than many desk-bound models. Quasar Co. and Panasonic Co. introduced a hand-held computer that weighs less than 1 lb (.45 kg) and sells for about $600. Perhaps the most sophisticated portable unit was the Compass, introduced by Grid Systems Inc. Priced at a steep $8,150, the unit was quickly recognized as the Porsche of the computer industry.

Computers were already widely used in business. But the combination of lower prices and new features found more and more executives using the machines in 1982. For example, the Supreme Court went electronic, as the justices and their staffs began using a network of 65 computer terminals to keep track of the approximately 5,000 cases they consider each session. A Philadelphia congressman began using an electronic mail system to receive and reply to messages from his constituents.

To prepare them for the computerized world, many universities began equipping their students with personal computers. For example, a test at Rensselaer Polytechnic Institute showed that the 20 freshmen to whom the school gave computers used them much more in their studies than a similar group of students who did not have their own machines and had to go to the computer center. So to encourage students to seek out computers, Rensselaer, Carnegie-Mellon, Dartmouth, and other institutions are now equipping all their students with the machines.

To make computers available to those who can not or do not want to buy them, many libraries are beginning to install computers. Some 200 libraries put in coin-operated computers in 1982. Time on personal computers, such as those made by Apple Computer or Radio Shack, can be bought by inserting coins or dollar bills into the vending machine hardware attached to the computer. The price was $2 to $6 per hour.

While home computers were getting smaller and less expensive, business computers were getting more powerful than ever. IBM, Sperry Univac, and Honeywell introduced new top-of-the-line mainframe computers that could perform as many as 20 million instructions per second. These new machines—the biggest ever built by these companies—are intended for businesses, such as banks, which perform more and more transactions on computer-controlled automatic teller machines, and other corporations that increasingly utilize computerized files.

Although slowed by the recession, demand for computers grew between 15% and 20% during the year. This encouraged more new companies to enter the business than ever before. These young firms intend to use microprocessors—those miniaturized computers that fit on a semiconductor chip just .5 square inches (1.27 cm^2)—to build computers that are easier to use, more reliable, smaller, and less expensive.

ANTHONY DURNIAK, *"Business Week"*

CONNECTICUT

William A. O'Neill, who became governor on Dec. 31, 1980, when the cancer-stricken Ella T. Grasso resigned, won a four-year term on his own. In November he defeated Republican Lewis B. Rome, a former state senator. The O'Neill-Rome contest was a face-off between candidates who each promised he would cut spending and veto any personal income tax bill.

Although the Democrats retained control of the state government, they were unable to unseat U.S. Sen. Lowell P. Weicker, Jr., a moderate Republican who had alienated conservative Republicans by his failure to support fully the Reagan administration. Weicker had to fight off a challenge for the Republican senatorial nomination by Prescott Bush, Jr., brother of the vice-president, but was reelected to a third term. He defeated Democratic U.S. Rep. Toby Moffett, who had represented the sprawling sixth congressional district for four terms and had a reputation as a liberal who supported consumer-oriented legislation.

Moffett's vacated sixth-district seat was captured by Republican Nancy L. Johnson, who defeated state Sen. William E. Curry, Jr. The Johnson victory added a second woman to the state's six-member congressional delegation. The other woman is U.S. Rep. Barbara B. Kennelly, a first-district Democrat who was first elected in January 1982 to fill the unexpired term of the late William R. Cotter. She was easily reelected.

Although the Republicans won Moffett's old seat, the partisan makeup of the congressional delegation remained four Democrats and two Republicans because Democrat Bruce A. Morrison narrowly defeated incumbent Republican Lawrence J. DeNardis in the third congressional district. Other winners include Democrat Sam Gejdenson in the second congressional district, Republican Stewart B. McKinney in the fourth district, and Democrat William R. Ratchford in the fifth district.

Business. When the politicians were offstage in 1982, the spotlight turned toward the business

UPI

A 3-lb (1.4-kg) meteorite (inset) startled a Wethersfield household when it plunged into the family's living room.

community. Two Connecticut companies were involved in mergers that attracted national attention. In March two insurance giants, Connecticut General Corporation of Bloomfield and INA Corporation of Philadelphia, merged to become CIGNA Corporation. Heublein Inc., the Farmington-based producer of alcoholic beverages and food, was acquired in October by R. J. Reynolds Industries Inc., a tobacco, energy, food, and ocean-transport concern.

In other business-related news, the 1982 state legislature set a national precedent when it enacted a "lemon law." The law requires that the manufacturer of a new car or truck must either reimburse a purchaser or replace a vehicle that fails to function properly after four repair attempts or remains nonfunctioning for 30 consecutive days.

Highly toxic compounds were discovered at a sludge pile of Environmental Waste Removal, Inc., a Waterbury hazardous-waste treatment plant. The company was ordered to clean up.

Other News. An April 6 blizzard buried springtime Connecticut under 12 inches (30 cm) of snow but caused nowhere near the havoc of a June 6 flood. Twelve persons died in the flooding.

In July the drinking age for alcoholic beverages was raised to 19 by the state legislature.

In November a meteorite about the size of a grapefruit crashed through the roof of a home in Wethersfield, surprisingly the second to strike Wethersfield in 11 years.

ROBERT F. MURPHY, *"The Hartford Courant"*

CONNECTICUT • Information Highlights

Area: 5,018 sq mi (12 997 km²).

Population: (1980 census): 3,107,576.

Chief Cities (1980 census): Hartford, the capital, 136,-392; Bridgeport, 142,546; New Haven, 126,109.

Government (1982): *Chief Officers*—governor, William A. O'Neill (D); lt. gov., Joseph J. Fauliso (D). *General Assembly*—Senate, 36 members; House of Representatives, 151 members.

State Finances (fiscal year 1981): *Revenues,* $3,873,-000,000; *expenditures,* $3,740,000,000.

Personal Income (1981): $40,164,000,000; per capita, $12,816.

Labor Force (Aug.1982): *Nonagricultural wage and salary earners,* 1,395,800; *unemployed,* 105,200 (6.6% of total force).

Education: *Enrollment* (fall 1981)—public elementary schools, 347,490; public secondary, 157,896; colleges and universities (1981–82), 162,367. *Public school expenditures* (1980–81), $1,374,460,000 ($2,697 per pupil).

CRIME

Presidential assailant John Hinckley suffered "process schizophrenia," according to testimony at his trial.
© Marty Katz/Woodfin Camp & Associates

Fear of crime continued in 1982 to unnerve large numbers of Americans, despite statistical reports that indicated a leveling off in the rate for some serious offenses and a decline in the rate for others. These public fears of crime were captured in a magazine cartoon in which a man says to his wife: "Cover me, I'm going out to get the paper."

U.S. Crime Statistics. In New York City, 46% of the population rated crime as the area's most pressing problem—the highest response on any particular issue. *The New York Times,* commenting on the poll, could offer little solace. Crime results from "enormously complex, often capricious social events," the paper observed editorially. It felt that criminal justice agencies could hardly be held responsible for such crime-producing matters as the sudden influxes of Cubans and Haitians, or for the creation of new centers of international drug trafficking in Latin America. The *Times* thought that the performance of agencies such as the police ought better be measured in terms of fairness and justice than in regard to crime rates. It was not an argument that the public found persuasive.

What has captured the public mind are reports such as that by the federal Bureau of Justice Statistics indicating that members of U.S. households are more likely to be raped, robbed, or assaulted than to experience a household fire or to be injured in an automobile accident. Also, more American households will be victimized by a robber than will experience cancer or heart disease. Despite such vulnerability, the bureau at the same time reported a decrease in the number of households victimized by crimes of violence.

The figure for 1982 was just below 25 million, about 30% of the nation's households, and contrasted with the 32% rate for 1975. The most vulnerable households were those of blacks, those with residents in the higher income brackets (for thefts), and households in the central areas of the large cities.

The reported decline in the percentage of households experiencing crime was mirrored in the Uniform Crime Reports (UCR), the annual tabulation prepared by the Federal Bureau of Investigation, based on reports from the nation's law enforcement agencies. There was a decrease of 1.7% in the Index Crimes (murder, forcible rape, robbery, aggravated assault, burglary, larceny-theft, and arson). Of the group, the sharpest declines were in arson, down 5.2%, and murder, which dropped 3.9%. The only increase was in robbery, up 2.9%.

Arson, recently added to the Index Crime list by congressional mandate, is defined in the UCR as "any willful or malicious burning or attempt to burn, with or without attempt to defraud, a dwelling house, public building, motor vehicle, or aircraft, personal property of another, etc." Fires of suspicious or unknown origin are not included in the figures; only those determined through investigation to have been willfully or maliciously set.

There were 97,202 arson offenses reported in 1981. The largest percentage of cases (23.4%) was directed at single-occupancy residences. Twenty percent involved automobiles, the next highest target category. There were more than 20,000 arrests for arson (about one arrest for each five incidents). Of all persons arrested for the offense,

42% were under 18 years of age, and 67% were under 25. Males made up 89% of all arson arrestees, and whites, 78%. The 78% was 10 percentage points higher than the white arrest rate for any other index crime. Those rates ranged from 39% for robbery to 69% for burglary.

The Reagan Crime Plan. Responding to the public's concern about crime, the Reagan administration in September proposed to Congress a series of controversial measures. The core proposal was to allow courts to consider illegally obtained evidence, if such evidence was secured in a "reasonable and good-faith belief" that it was lawfully acquired. Under current law, all such evidence is barred in court, and convictions at times are lost because of the rule. The Reagan proposals also would limit federal courts' consideration of petitions that seek to overturn state convictions on constitutional grounds to only issues that had been raised in the state proceedings. The administration plan also would limit appeals to federal courts to a period of one year following conviction. A restriction in the use of the defense of "irresistible impulse," under which a defendant can claim that he or she lacked the ability to control the behavior involved in the criminal act, also was proposed. The president further recommended that judges be allowed to hold without bail defendants deemed likely to flee or to be dangerous to others, that drug penalties be raised, and that policies be inaugurated to allow easier confiscation of the proceeds of illegal activities, such as drug smuggling.

The Reagan plan would alter federal sentencing by eliminating parole and limiting time off for good behavior to about one tenth the sentence. At present, inmates generally receive a one-third reduction in their sentence for good behavior. The bill also would require a minimum sentence of two years in prison for anyone committing a federal felony with a gun, and at least five years for repeat gun offenders. Congress adjourned without final action on the program.

Crime in Canada. Americans' fear of crime is duplicated among Canadians, though crime rates in Canada are only about a fifth of those in the United States. Anthony N. Doob and Julian V. Roberts of the University of Toronto's Center of Criminology believe that Canadians develop their fears of crime from watching American television news and entertainment programs. They absorb American information and apply it, incorrectly, to conditions in their own country. Doob and Roberts also believe that the Canadian mass media sensationalize unusual crime cases, leading people to believe that such cases occur more often than they actually do. In Toronto, they point out, newspapers devoted large amounts of space to the murders of three young women and the brutal rape of a woman sunbathing in a public park. This resulted, the criminologists suggest, in "a moral panic—a false

sense that Toronto was caught in a terrible crime wave."

Doob and Roberts point out that the total number of homicides in Canada declined to 647 in 1981, as compared with 668 in 1976, the year when the country abolished capital punishment. Yet two thirds of Canadian citizens responding to a poll thought that the number of homicides in the country had risen. New York City, with about half the population of Canada, has about three times as many homicides.

Crime in the News. Sensational cases dominated the mass media in the United States, as well as in Canada, during the year. In June, John W. Hinckley, Jr., was found not guilty by reason of insanity on 13 counts of shooting President Reagan and three other men on March 30, 1981. The jury verdict, coming after 25 hours of deliberation over four days, meant that Hinckley, 27, would be confined to a mental hospital until authorities declare him competent. The test for this will be whether "by a preponderance of evidence he is not likely to injure himself or other persons due to mental disease."

Hinckley became the first person to avoid conviction on charges of attempting to assassinate a sitting president since 1835, when a jury took five minutes to find Richard Lawrence not guilty by reason of insanity, after Lawrence tried to shoot President Andrew Jackson at close range with two pistols that misfired. The acquittal of Hinckley on grounds of insanity led to a barrage of criticism, much of it focused on the legal concept of criminal responsibility. (*See* page 307.)

In March, Wayne B. Williams, 23, was convicted of the murders of two Atlanta men, and subsequently sentenced to a pair of consecutive life terms. Williams was suspected of having perpetrated an additional 27 killings that terrorized Atlanta for 22 months and prompted the wearing of green ribbons throughout the United States as a symbol of concern. The trial jury, which heard 197 witnesses, was convinced of Williams' guilt by a web of circumstantial evidence. Most damaging was the fact that police reported seeing Williams drive across a bridge not far from where a victim's body was found, and shortly after a splash had been heard in the water. Green fibers and dog hairs found on the victims' bodies were said to be similar to the carpet in Williams' bedroom and the hair of his German shepherd. That no further slayings occurred after Williams was taken into custody is regarded by some persons as strong inferential evidence of his guilt.

In Rhode Island, Claus von Bülow, a 55-year-old, Danish-born man, was found guilty in March of twice having tried to murder his wife through the use of insulin injections. Von Bülow's motive was said to be a desire to inherit $14 million, earmarked for him in her will, and then to be free to marry his lover. Von Bülow was given a 30-year prison sentence. Outside the

Ira Wyman/Sygma

In a dramatic televised trial, Claus von Bülow (left) was found guilty of trying to murder his wealthy wife.

court, when the verdict was announced, crowds cheered von Bülow and chanted, "Free Claus!" "Many people are starving for heroes," the prosecutor said, in attempting to explain this public reaction.

The vulnerability of the consumer to sudden, impersonal demise was brought home in the fall by the death of seven persons living in the Chicago area who took Extra-Strength Tylenol. The capsules had been laced with cyanide, a deadly poison. Only a few capsules in each bottle had been contaminated, apparently while the Tylenol was on the shelves in drug stores and groceries. Late in the year, James W. Lewis, considered a key figure in the case, was arrested in New York City and extradited to Chicago. Although not charged with the murders, he was accused of trying to extort $1 million from the Tylenol manufacturers to "stop the killing." Prior to the arrest, new packaging regulations for such drug products were introduced.

In other crime news of the year, Jack Henry Abbott, author of the widely acclaimed book, *In the Belly of the Beast,* was convicted of first-degree manslaughter for the slaying of a waiter in the East Village district of New York City. Abbott had been free from prison for only six weeks when he stabbed the waiter because he believed that he was being threatened by him. Abbott called the killing "a tragic misunderstanding" caused by the paranoia he had acquired from 24 years spent in prison.

In Los Angeles, William Bonin, a 34-year-old truck driver, was convicted in January of murdering 10 boys and young men and abandoning their bodies near freeways in 1979 and 1980.

The Penalty of Death. Frank J. Coppolla, a convicted murderer who declared that he wished to die, was executed at the Virginia State Penitentiary in Richmond in the electric chair on August 10, shortly before midnight. Coppolla, a former seminary student, basketball player, and policeman, was convicted of the brutal slaying of a woman during a 1978 robbery. He asked to be executed in the summer, to minimize the taunts by classmates of his two school-age sons. In Texas, December 7, Charlie Brooks, a convicted murderer, became the first person to be executed by a lethal injection.

New Jersey became the 37th state during the year to adopt the death penalty. More than 1,000 prisoners are now on U.S. death rows, 13 of them women. It is believed that there will be a huge surge in the number of executions by late 1984, when avenues of court appeal will have been exhausted. Florida has the largest number of inmates under sentence of death, followed by Texas, Georgia, and California. Meanwhile voters in Massachusetts approved a measure to reimpose the death penalty.

Gun Control. In June, the San Francisco Board of Supervisors banned the ownership of pistols by most residents, making the city the first large jurisdiction in the nation to take such action. Possession of a pistol became punishable by up to 30 days in jail and a $500 fine. Rifles and shotguns were not included in the prohibition. Exemptions were provided for police, military and security personnel, gun collectors, private investigators, licensed target shooters, and private store owners who obtain permission from the police. The ordinance was invalidated by the state Court of Appeal in October, pending an appeal to the state Supreme Court. Also in California, voters defeated a measure seeking to freeze the number of handguns in the state.

Crime and the Media. A report by the National Institute of Mental Health declared that an analysis of a decade's research on the effects of television viewing had concluded that there now exists "overwhelming" scientific evidence that "excessive" violence on television leads directly to aggression and violent behavior among children and teenagers. (*See* page 337.)

Crime shows and crime fiction, notwithstanding this finding, enjoyed a bumper year. Analysts tied the outpouring of crime materials to the economic recession. Anthony M. Hoffman, a media commentator, noted that in hard times a considerable amount of day-dreaming takes place. "People wish they could pull a bank job and get away with it, and that affects their choice of literature, their television watching, and their moviegoing."

Crime-related television programs making their debut in the fall included *Matt Houston* (ABC), *The Good Witch of Laurel Canyon* (ABC), and *The Devlin Connection* (NBC), all featuring detective heroes.

GILBERT GEIS, *University of California, Irvine*

CUBA

Cuba's economy suffered a telling setback in 1982, principally because of a sharp drop in the price of sugar and the worldwide recession. However, the country was able to avoid disaster thanks to the continued support of the USSR.

The Economy. Ironically, Cuba found itself in a serious economic predicament despite having produced 8,207,178 metric tons or t (9,044,310 tons, T) of sugar, one of the largest harvests of its main export. The price of sugar on the world market, which in 1974 had soared to 60 cents per pound, plummeted in 1982 to 6 cents, well under the island's production cost and diminishing Cuba's already meager foreign exchange reserves. As a result, Cuba had less money to buy Western raw materials, badly needed for its vital industries, and to pay its foreign debt, estimated at $3,500,000,000, principally to Canada, France, West Germany, Spain, and Japan.

Another irony was that in 1981 the Cuban government, counting on higher sugar prices, had borrowed heavily in the West. The necessity to service its old and new loans, with payments of close to $1,000,000,000 on interest and principal due by mid-1983, forced the government of President Fidel Castro to drastically reduce public spending and imports. While pledging to continue interest payments, Cuba asked commercial banks in the West and Japan to postpone for three years loan payments due in 1982, 1983, and 1985.

The future appeared bleak, President Castro conceded in a July speech. "We are going to have difficulties in the coming years, and the difficulties could be major.... Simply stated, we shall have to do more with less.... It may be necessary in some cases to reduce hours or days of work, affecting as little as possible the income of workers." Castro disclosed that Cuba also had "serious difficulties" in selling nickel, its second-ranking cash export, and other products for which demand had fallen. All this would result in little if any economic growth in 1982, the president said, indicating that production plans for 1983 and beyond were also scaled down.

Foreign Relations. Soviet assistance to Cuba in 1982 was estimated at $3,000,000,000, essentially

At the Havana convention center, with President Castro attending, Foreign Minister Isidoro Malmierca opens a meeting of the foreign ministers of the Nonaligned Nations.

CUBA · Information Highlights

Official Name: Republic of Cuba.
Location: Caribbean Sea.
Area: 42,823 sq mi (110 912 km²).
Population (1981 census): 9,706,369.
Chief Cities (1981 census): Havana, the capital, 1,924,886; Santiago de Cuba, 345,289; Camagüey, 245,235.
Government: *Head of state and government,* Fidel Castro Ruz, president (took office under a new constitution, Dec. 1976). *Legislature* (unicameral)—National Assembly of People's Power.
Monetary Unit: Peso (0.81 peso equals U.S.$1, March 1982—noncommercial rate).
Gross National Product (1980 U.S.$): $18,400,000,-000.

---

the same as in 1981. Moscow pays four times the world price for Cuban sugar and supplies the island with cheap oil and other products, including grain. Cuban ruble debt is equivalent to some $10,000,000,000, which Russia does not expect to collect.

The Soviet Union also provides, free of charge, large quantities of weapons for the Cuban armed forces. According to a U.S. report, Cuban military strength increased dramatically with the delivery in 1981 of 66,000 t (72,732 T) of military equipment, the largest annual shipment of materiel since 1962, including advanced supersonic MiG-23B fighters. Cuba had an army of 100,000 plus reservists, a navy of about 11,000, and an air force of 16,000, as well as a large paramilitary force and militia units. About 35,-000 troops were stationed abroad.

The deployment of 18,000 Cuban soldiers in Angola became an issue affecting independence for neighboring Namibia (South-West Africa). South Africa, which administers Namibia, conditioned its military withdrawal on the Cubans' leaving Angola. The Reagan administration made it clear that the presence of Cuban troops, whom Washington views as essentially protecting a leftist government without popular mandate, was for it a major irritant. On Feb. 4, 1982, Cuba and Angola signed a joint declaration in which Havana agreed to remove its military forces once real and potential aggression against Angola had ceased and when asked to do so by the Luanda regime.

A few weeks after that accord, although in an apparently unrelated move, the U.S. government announced new regulations that in effect banned tourist and business travel to Cuba after May 15. Only official travel, trips by media personnel or academic researchers, and travel for family reunification (the last applicable mainly to Cuban exiles) were allowed. The regulation, described by the Treasury Department as "designed to reduce Cuba's hard-currency earnings from travel," indicated the continuation of a hard line against Cuba despite possible signals by Havana that it was interested in improving relations with Washington. But almost all senior officials in the administration were unimpressed by Cuban hints and promises of better behavior. These officials contended that Cuba's apparent desire to talk basically reflected the weakness of a regime beset by internal and external problems. Another view on Cuban-U.S. relations was expressed by Wayne S. Smith, chief of the U.S. diplomatic mission in Havana from 1979 to 1982. He stated publicly that it was desirable to deal with Castro, who then conceivably could moderate his policy in a diplomatic quid pro quo. Smith's opinions were rejected by administration officials. They continued to accuse Cuba of using Nicaragua as a platform for supporting guerrilla movements in Central America.

While strains remained unabated between Washington and Havana, Cuba's ties with Latin America became friendlier in 1982. Chiefly as a result of Cuba's resolute support for Argentina during the Falklands crisis, there was a thaw in Cuba's relations with Argentina, Venezuela, and Colombia. To underline their new friendship, Argentina and Cuba signed in June a $100 million trade agreement. Venezuelan diplomats, who had stayed away from Havana for two years, returned to their posts, and the Colombians were to follow suit. Brazilian businessmen who visited Havana pressed for a restoration of Cuban-Brazilian trade, with Havana promising to buy a yearly minimum of $200 million in Brazilian goods.

Fidel Castro's term of office as chairman of the Nonaligned Movement ended in 1982 with the group more divided than ever. His efforts to mediate the war between two members, Iran and Iraq, came to nought.

President Castro went to Moscow for President Brezhnev's funeral and held discussions with the new Soviet leadership.

GEORGE VOLSKY
Florida International University

CYPRUS

During 1982, for the eighth year, almost 40% of Cyprus remained occupied by Turkey.

Government. In the occupied territories, all situated in the north, Rauf Denktaş ruled as president of the "Turkish Federated State of Cyprus." This political entity had never gained international recognition by any country other than Turkey. The Turkish government contended that its military presence on the island was necessary to protect the Turkish Cypriot minority that had concentrated in the occupied territories after the 1974 Turkish invasion.

The rest of the island was governed in 1982 by the internationally recognized Republic of Cyprus with its Greek Cypriot president, Spyros Kyprianou. The United Nations maintained a peacekeeping force on Cyprus and sponsored the continuation of intercommunal talks between the Greek Cypriots and the Turkish Cypriots. These proved fruitless.

International Relations. During the year President Kyprianou attempted to find some solution to the problem brought about by the *de facto* division of the island. He met with many world leaders, including former West German Chancellor Willy Brandt and UN Secretary-General Javier Pérez de Cuellar, who had once served as a special UN representative to Cyprus. Kyprianou was one of the last foreign visitors to be received by the late Soviet President Leonid Brezhnev, and he was present at Brezhnev's funeral in Moscow in November.

Kyprianou's closest contacts outside Cyprus were with the Greek government and Greek Premier Andreas Papandreou. Papandreou made a spectacular visit to Cyprus on the weekend of February 27. He was the first Greek premier to go to the island since its independence in 1960. Papandreou was greeted by cheering throngs of Greek Cypriots, who seemed to feel that he could help bring about a solution to the partition, something no other Greek leader had been able to accomplish. While on Cyprus, Papandreou met with Archbishop Chrysostomos, head of the Greek Orthodox Church there, and received the Cypriot church's highest decoration.

CYPRUS · Information Highlights

Official Name: Republic of Cyprus.
Location: Eastern Mediterranean.
Area: 3,572 sq mi (9 251 km^2).
Population (1982 est.): 600,000.
Chief Cities (1978 est.): Nicosia, the capital, 121,500; Limassol, 102,400.
Government: *Head of state and government,* Spyros Kyprianou, president (took office Aug. 1977). *Legislature*—House of Representatives.
Monetary Unit: Pound (4.5861 pound equals U.S.$1, February 1982).
Gross National Product (1980 U.S.$): $2,176,000,-000.
Economic Index (1981): *Consumer Prices* (1977= 100), *all items,* 147.8; *food,* 144.0.
Foreign Trade (1981 U.S.$): *Imports,* $1,166,000,-000; *exports,* $562,000,000.

Papandreou called for the "internationalization" of the Cyprus problem and stressed his government's solidarity with the Greek Cypriots. Both Kyprianou and Papandreou emphasized repeatedly that the Turkish occupation had to be brought to an end for a lasting solution, and both agreed that Cyprus should remain an independent state.

In May, Turkish Premier Bülent Ulusu visited the Turkish-occupied north, sparking protests from Greek Cypriots.

Recourse to the UN. In October, Kyprianou addressed the UN General Assembly and called for a special Assembly debate on Cyprus. His preference, voiced to the press, was that such a discussion come after the Cypriot presidential elections, scheduled for early 1983. He had announced in April that he was a candidate for reelection and that he had the additional support of the Cypriot Communist party, AKEL.

The Economy. Despite the occupation of the north, the part of Cyprus controlled by Greek Cypriots continued to thrive economically. More and more foreign businesses were attracted to the republic's sector, and tourism there rose markedly in 1982. The north, by contrast, was far less prosperous.

GEORGE J. MARCOPOULOS
Tufts University

CZECHOSLOVAKIA

In 1982 events in Czechoslovakia followed much the same pattern as in 1981. The performance of the nation's economy was mediocre; the regime's campaign against dissidents and the churches continued unabated; and Soviet-style conformism pervaded the sessions of the Communist Party's Central Committee and the congresses of the Czechoslovak Writers' Union and the Trade Unions.

Economy. In January prices of a number of goods were again increased. For example, the prices of meat and poultry rose 27%, rice 100%, cigarettes 30%, and fish and venison 14%. The difficulties plaguing Czechoslovakia's economy were also apparent in the government's semiannual report on the performance of the economy. In the first half of 1982, industrial production rose by a mere 1.4% over the corresponding period in 1981, and production costs were lowered by only 0.5%. Better results were attained in the output of engineering goods, which rose by 4.4% and of light industry, up by 2.4%. But the planned targets were not met in mining and construction. Overall food output fell by 2.7% and meat by 8.2%. The volume of foreign trade with the Soviet Union rose by 20% while trade with nonsocialist countries fell by 5.6%. Preliminary reports on the 1982 grain harvest indicated that it would be better than the bad harvest of 1981 but that the planned target of 11 million metric tons (12.1 million T) would not be achieved.

Anti-religious Campaign. Repression of dissidents and the anti-religious campaign remained as harsh as ever. Anxious to restrict contacts by Czechoslovak Roman Catholics with their Western co-believers, the regime denied visas to a group of West German prelates led by Joseph Cardinal Hoeffner, who had been invited by František Cardinal Tomášek of Prague to take part in a religious commemoration in June. Visas requested for the same purpose were also refused to four French priests. The regime attacked even the pope for his alleged attempts to "integrate anti-communist forces."

Foreign Relations. The main event in Czechoslovak-U.S. relations was the conclusion of an agreement by which Czechoslovakia was to pay $81.5 million in compensation for the property of U.S. citizens that had been nationalized after World War II. In return, the United States released the gold that had been looted from Czechoslovakia by Nazi Germany and subsequently held by the United States, Britain, and France pending the settlement of their respective financial claims.

Czechoslovakia's foreign minister traveled to Vienna in April to pave the way for President Husák's visit to Austria later in the year.

A visit by the Polish Communist leader Gen. Wojciech Jaruzelski in April led to an agreement on long-term economic cooperation of the two countries. In June a Czechoslovak government delegation headed by President Husák agreed in Moscow to strengthen Czechoslovak-Soviet economic cooperation by establishing eight joint associations for research, development, and production in a number of fields. An agreement calling for greater economic and scientific-technical cooperation between Czechoslovakia and Rumania was signed in Prague in September; and a Czechoslovak-Libyan agreement on friendship and cooperation was concluded during a visit to Prague by Libyan leader Muammar el-Qaddafi in the same month.

EDWARD TABORSKY
University of Texas at Austin

CZECHOSLOVAKIA · Information Highlights

Official Name: Czechoslovak Socialist Republic.
Location: East-central Europe.
Area: 49,374 sq mi (127 879 km²).
Population (1982 est.): 15,400,000.
Chief Cities (1979 est.): Prague, the capital, 1,182,-294; Bratislava, 381,165; Brno, 371,376.
Government: *Head of state,* Gustav Husák, president (took office 1975). *Head of government,* Lubomir Strougal, premier (took office 1970). *Communist party secretary-general,* Gustav Husák (took office 1969). *Legislature*—Federal Assembly: Chamber of House of Nations and Chamber of House of the People.
Monetary Unit: Koruna (11.64 koruny equal U.S.$1, March 1982—noncommercial rate).
Gross National Product (1981 U.S.$): est. $73,100,-000,000 to $121,000,000,000.
Economic Index (1981): *Industrial production* (1975= 100) 121.
Foreign Trade (1981 U.S.$): *Imports,* $15,148,000,-000; *exports,* $14,891,000,000.

DANCE

Martha Swope

In a departure from its often abstract ballets, the New York City Ballet premiered "The Magic Flute."

Events and concerns that extended beyond artistic matters affected the dance world in 1982, but the year also produced new faces and new works of distinction.

Economic News. Amid worries of cutbacks in government funding, both managements and members of dance companies sought a more secure future. After an approximate two-month lockout in a prolonged labor dispute, American Ballet Theatre's dancers won a four-year contract with unprecedented gains such as vacation pay, severance pay, and significant wage increases. The dispute, however, led to the cancellation of a season in Paris and postponement of two new productions.

Seeking wider financial support, the Joffrey Ballet became the first major American dance company to establish a dual residence as it announced that it would become the resident ballet company of the Los Angeles Music Center and also keep its regular New York season. Observers predicted that more companies would need to find two "homes" to support them in the face of increasing economic needs.

In Transition. An internal dispute at the Pennsylvania Ballet, which faced a large deficit, led to the resignation of its founder, Barbara Weisberger, as director, and later, of Benjamin Harkarvy, as artistic director. Robert Weiss, until then a principal dancer in the New York City Ballet, became the Philadelphia company's artistic director, with Peter Martins, another New York City Ballet principal, agreeing to serve as "artistic adviser."

Other changes included the departure from Ballet Theatre of Alexander Godunov, who had defected from the Bolshoi in 1979. Godunov said he had been dismissed by Mikhail Baryshnikov, a childhood classmate in the Soviet Union and now Ballet Theatre's artistic director. The company said that Godunov had been asked to take a leave of absence because the coming season had no roles for him.

In the fall, Dame Margot Fonteyn, one of the foremost international ballerinas, took on a new role as hostess of a six-part PBS television series, *The Magic of Dance.* The series focused on the world of dance, past and present, and on the great choreographers and dancers from Louis XIV of France, who is credited as a founder of classical ballet, to modern dance groups, such as the Dance Theater of Harlem.

Stravinsky Celebrations. The centennial of Igor Stravinsky's birth led many companies to create ballets to his music. The major celebration came from the New York City Ballet, which had held a Stravinsky Festival in 1972, a year after the composer's death. The 1982 nine-day event was organized by George Balanchine, the company's artistic director, and presented acknowledged Balanchine-Stravinsky masterpieces from the past. The "Stravinsky Centennial Celebration" also included new works. Some were brief, such as Balanchine's *Tango* and *Elégie,* Peter Martins' *Piano-Rag-Music,* Jacques d'Amboise's *Pastorale,* and Lew Christensen's *Norwegian Moods.*

The longer new ballets were John Taras' *Concerto for Piano and Wind Instruments,* Martins' *Concerto for Two Solo Pianos,* and d'Amboise's *Serenade en La.* The most successful was Jerome Robbins' *Four Chamber Works.* Balanchine also staged two choral works with dancing—*Noah and the Flood* and *Persephone,* with Vera Zorina as the narrator.

The Ballet Season. The season indicated that, artistically, choreographers remained pluralistic. An influx of European companies showed a greater interest in dramatic works than that shown in the United States.

Prior to the Stravinsky tribute, Jerome Robbins' *Gershwin Concerto* gave the City Ballet a popular success. Martins' *The Magic Flute* and Joseph Duell's *La Creation du Monde* entered the company's repertory.

At American Ballet Theatre, *Great Galloping Gottschalk,* a breezy new work by Lynne Taylor-Corbett, was enthusiastically received by the public. Merce Cunningham's modern-dance work *Duets* was a more substantive success for the company. Its production of Roland Petit's *Carmen* proved a failure, and Peter Anastos' *Clair de Lune* was a minor premiere. Baryshnikov was sidelined as a dancer for part of 1982 following microsurgery on his knee but resumed dancing during the summer. Young dancers who were noticed were Susan Jaffe, who made an acclaimed debut in *Swan Lake,* and Peter Fonseca.

Dance Theater of Harlem surprised its public by emphasizing dramatic works over its usual plotless ballets in the revivals of Valerie Bettis' *A Streetcar Named Desire* and *Frankie and Johnny* by Ruth Page and Bentley Stone, as well as the new *Firebird* by John Taras and *Equus: the Ballet* by Domy Reiter-Soffer. Geoffrey Holder contributed *Banda* and *Songs of the Auvergne.*

Other ballet events of importance included the first American production, by the Oakland Ballet, of Bronislava Nijinska's 1923 Stravinsky ballet, *Les Noces.* The Feld Ballet found a permanent home in New York when Eliot Feld opened the Joyce Theater, a former movie house remodeled for the dance company. The Feld Ballet presented the premieres of *Over the Pavement, Play Bach,* and *Straw Hearts.*

The San Francisco Ballet, nearing its 50th anniversary, was given some needed East-Coast exposure when it performed in the Washington area at Wolf Trap. The primary traits of the company suggest a strong ensemble spirit and a certain emphasis on the works of resident choreographers.

A new choreographic talent was seen in William Forsythe, an American living in Germany. His *Say Bye Bye,* a critique of pop culture, proved a sensation of the Netherlands Dance Theater season in New York. The company's director, Jiri Kylian, offered his version of *Les Noces* and the new *Nomads* and *Songs of a Wayfarer.*

The most popular visiting company was the Royal Danish Ballet, which delighted audiences with works by August Bournonville and *Coppélia.* Lis Jeppesen and Arne Villumsen stood out among the dancers, who also performed Glen Tetley's modern-dress version of *The Firebird.*

Tetley's *The Tempest,* given by the Norwegian National Ballet, launched the Brooklyn Academy of Music's "Ballet International" series, which included Sweden's Cullberg Ballet Company and the Dutch National Ballet. Britain's Ballet Rambert made a New York debut.

The Joffrey Ballet, facing financial difficulties, scheduled a late New York season with a premiere by the modern-dance experimentalist Laura Dean and the architect Michael Graves. Ron Reagan, President Reagan's son, was promoted from the Joffrey II Dancers to the Joffrey Ballet.

Modern Dance. Miss Dean created *Skylight* for her own company. Modern dance's established companies were active. Paul Taylor's new *Mercuric Tidings* and *Lost, Found and Lost* were highly acclaimed. Merce Cunningham had one of his best attended seasons in New York with *Trails* and *Gallopade.* Martha Graham's season revived great works such as *Primitive Mysteries, Dark Meadow,* and *Herodiade,* as well as *Acts of Light,* and presented the new *Andromache's Lament* and *The Golden Hall.* Alvin Ailey scheduled a new piece to Ravel after his troupe performed Elisa Monte's *Pigs and Fishes,* Talley Beatty's *The Stack Up,* and Rodney Griffin's *Sonnets.* Alwin Nikolais offered *The Mechanical Organ II* and the *Pond.* Murray Louis' quirky style was evident again in his premieres—*A Stravinsky Montage* and *Many Seasons.*

Other News. The dance world was saddened by the deaths of dance critic Walter Terry and choreographers Valerie Bettis, Eugene Loring, Igor Schwezoff, and in Britain, Marie Rambert.

On the happier side, recognition was given to Martha Graham in the form of the $25,000 Algur Meadows award from Southern Methodist University. The second annual Samuel H. Scripps-American Dance Festival award, also $25,000, went to Merce Cunningham.

ANNA KISSELGOFF, *"The New York Times"*

DELAWARE

UPI

It is time for a family celebration as William V. Roth, Jr. (R-DE) captures another six years in the U.S. Senate.

In 1982 attention in Delaware, as in the rest of the nation, was focused largely on the economy and the elections.

Elections. In the first election since legislative districts were reapportioned because of population shifts, Democrats maintained control of the Senate (13–8) and took control of the House (25–16). The General Assembly was to begin a new two-year session in January.

In the five statewide elections, Thomas R. Carper (D) defeated Rep. Thomas B. Evans, Jr., the Republican incumbent; William V. Roth, Jr. (R) maintained his seat in the U.S. Senate; Dennis E. Greenhouse (D) won over the incumbent state auditor; Janet Rzewnicki (R) was elected state treasurer; and Charles M. Oberly III (D) was chosen over the incumbent as state attorney general. With good weather prevailing, about 67% of Delaware's registered voters went to the polls on November 2.

Legislative Session. The 131st General Assembly's second session came to a close at midnight, June 30, 1982. Legislation approved in 1982 included: the "Bottle Bill," a law banning no deposit–no return bottles at the wholesale level in November and in retail stores in January, a new law raising the governor's salary from $35,000 to $70,000, a tougher "Drunk-Driving Law," and a bill giving the General Assembly control over all appropriations, including special grants, which in some instances had been under the control of individual agencies.

Economy. Delaware's economy showed signs of vitality. As a result of the 1981 Financial Cen-

ter Development Act, 12 bank holding companies, including some of the nation's largest banks, were setting up operations in Delaware. It is expected that these 12 banks will create at least 2,000 new jobs in the state by the end of 1983.

While efforts to stimulate the Delaware economy continued through several state and local programs in 1982, Delaware experienced an increase in unemployment (seasonally adjusted), from 7.3% in July 1981 to 10% in August 1982. Even so, in 1982 the unemployment rate in Delaware had dropped below the national rate for the first time since the 1974–75 recession.

Schools. Enrollment in public schools continued to decline. Public school enrollment in grades K-12 decreased from 99,403 in the 1980–81 school year to 95,072 in the 1981–82 school year. Private school enrollment (including parochial schools) again showed an increase, from approximately 23,000 in the 1980–81 session to 24,096 in the 1981–82 session. The decline in public school enrollment prompted the closing and sale of several public schools. The Department of Public Instruction developed new rules for certification to ensure basic competence of new teachers and to provide for continued training and better supervision of experienced staff.

Health Care. After much controversy, ground was broken in New Castle County for the new 780-bed Southwest Division of the Wilmington Medical Center. At the completion of the hospital, two of the Wilmington Medical Center's three hospitals, located in the city of Wilmington, will close. Total cost of the new project will be approximately $140 million.

Budget. In fiscal year 1982 the state held a no-growth stance in government spending, resulting in a balanced budget for the fifth consecutive year. The bond rating for the state was upgraded for the fourth time since 1977, and the state's debt held constant.

JEROME R. LEWIS
University of Delaware

DELAWARE · Information Highlights

Area: 2,044 sq mi (5 294 km²).
Population (1980 census): 594,317.
Chief Cities (1980 census): Dover, the capital, 23,512; Wilmington, 70,195; Newark, 25,247; Elsmere, 6,493.
Government (1982): *Chief Officers*—governor, Pierre S. duPont IV (R); lt. gov., Michael N. Castle (R). *General Assembly*—Senate, 21 members; House of Representatives, 41 members.
State Finances (fiscal year 1981): Revenues, $1,123,-000,000; expenditures, $1,029,000,000.
Personal Income (1981): $6,640,000,000; per capita, $11,095.
Labor Force (Aug. 1982): *Nonagricultural wage and salary earners,* 259,100; *unemployed,* 30,500 (10.0% of total force).
Education: *Enrollment* (fall 1981)—public elementary schools, 60,287; public secondary, 34,785; colleges and universities (1981–82), 32,061 students. *Public school expenditures* (1980–81), $270,240,-000 ($2,781 per pupil).

DENMARK

In the autumn of 1982, Poul Schlüter became Denmark's first Conservative prime minister in 81 years. Schlüter's rise to power came after several months of struggle on the part of Prime Minister Anker Jørgensen, who on Dec. 30, 1981, had presented his fifth Social Democratic cabinet, having managed to ride out the storm brought on by a number of intractable economic problems. The main change in Jørgensen's cabinet, based on a Social Democratic minority in the Folketing (parliament), was the dropping of Ritt Bjerregaard, the somewhat controversial minister of social affairs.

The spring and summer of 1982 brought very little improvement in the economy, and the leaders of the nonsocialist parties deemed the time ripe for a transfer of power. An adverse vote in parliament on the issue of the state budget and the use of pension funds led to the resignation of the Anker Jørgensen cabinet in early September.

Following negotiations among party leaders, Queen Margrethe asked Conservative Party leader Poul Schlüter to form a government to include representatives of Conservative, Center Democrat, Liberal, and Christian People's parties. Liberal Party leader Henning Christophersen was appointed finance minister and deputy premier, and Uffe Ellemann-Jensen succeeded Kjeld Olesen as foreign minister.

Economy. The deficit in the Danish state budget in 1982 set a per-capita world record and in 1983 was slated to amount to 9.2% of the gross national product. The state budget also revealed that outlays amounted to 50% more than income. A step to aid the economy, especially Denmark's export industries, was taken on February 21, when a 3% devaluation of the krone was announced.

Denmark joined other Western European nations in making known its opposition to the U.S. sanctions imposed on firms supplying equipment to the Soviet gas pipeline project. In Washington on August 12, Danish Ambassador Otto Borch handed a protest note to the U.S. secretaries of state and commerce. A few days later, then Foreign Minister Olesen (also the chairman of the European Community [EC] Council of Ministers) discussed the matter with U.S. government officials.

Greenland. A dispute with West Germany regarding the size of its codfish haul off the coasts of Greenland was settled, but strong feelings about EC fishing quotas in Greenlandic waters led to a referendum on February 23 as to whether Greenland should leave the EC. (Greenland had joined the EC with Denmark, of which it is a part, in 1973.) The solely advisory referendum gave a 1,400 majority against Greenland's membership. Final withdrawal, however, would be decided by the Danish Folketing. Even if carried out, the Greenlanders may favor a future loose relationship with the

UPI

Prince Henrik (left) inspects some Royal Copenhagen porcelain during a New York City exhibit of Danish art.

EC, which has granted Greenland more than $150 million in grants since 1975.

The 1,000th anniversary of the discovery of Greenland by Erik the Red was celebrated at the Julianehåb House of Culture in Greenland on August 3. Queen Margrethe and Prince Henrik, President Vigdís Finnbogadóttir of Iceland, and Governor-General Edward Schreyer of Canada attended.

Cultural News. The "Scandinavia Today" program in the United States commenced in early September. Denmark was represented by Prince Henrik. Included in the various exhibitions (to be on view into 1983) were Danish furniture and paintings by Asger Jorn.

ERIK J. FRIIS
"The Scandinavian-American Bulletin"

DENMARK • Information Highlights

Official Name: Kingdom of Denmark.
Location: Northwest Europe.
Area: 16,631 sq mi (43 074 km²).
Population (1982 est.): 5,100,000.
Chief Cities (1981 est.): Copenhagen, the capital, 1,206,622; Aarhus, 245,565; Odense, 169,183.
Government: *Head of state,* Margrethe II, queen (acceded Jan. 1972). *Head of government,* Poul Schlüter, prime minister (took office Sept. 1982). *Legislature* (unicameral)—Folketing.
Monetary Unit: Krone (8.93 kroner equal U.S.$1, Oct. 8, 1982).
Gross Domestic Product (1981 U.S.$): $57,800,000,000.
Economic Index (1981): *Consumer Prices* (1970=100), *all items,* 285.5; *food,* 182.
Foreign Trade (1981 U.S.$): *Imports,* $17,530,000,000; *exports,* $15,735,000,000.

DISASTERS AND ACCIDENTS

AVIATION

Jan. 13—In Washington, DC, an Air Florida jetliner crashes into a traffic-crowded bridge and falls into the Potomac River, killing 78 persons.

Jan. 23—A Soviet jetliner reportedly crashes in Siberia, killing about 150 people.

Feb. 3—A plane carrying French Foreign Legion paratroopers crashes in Djibouti, killing 36 persons.

Feb. 9—A Japanese jetliner crashes into Tokyo Bay, killing 24 of 174 persons aboard.

Mar. 19—In northern Illinois, a U.S. National Guard jet tanker crashes, killing 27 persons.

April 2—Eleven persons are killed when a U.S. Navy plane crashes near the coast of Crete.

April 26—Near Guilin, China, a Chinese jetliner crashes, killing all 112 persons aboard.

June 8—Near Fortaleza, Brazil, a Brazilian airliner crashes into a mountaintop, killing 137.

June 22—An Air India jet crash-lands in a rainstorm at Bombay International Airport, killing 19.

July 6—A Soviet jetliner crashes just after takeoff from Moscow; the 90 persons thought to be aboard are reportedly killed.

July 9—A jetliner crashes in a residential area just after takeoff from New Orleans, killing all 146 persons on board and eight on the ground.

Sept. 11—Near Mannheim, West Germany, a U.S. Army helicopter carrying an international parachuting team crashes, killing 46 persons.

Sept. 13—A DC-10 jetliner crashes on takeoff from Málaga, Spain; 56 persons are dead.

Nov. 29—Near Quetame, Colombia, a twin-engine domestic airliner crashes, killing 22 persons.

Dec. 24—A Chinese airliner bursts into flames in an emergency landing in Canton, killing 23.

EARTHQUAKES AND VOLCANOES

Mar. 29—In southern Mexico eruptions of the Chichón volcano kill as many as 100 people.

Dec. 13—An earthquake strikes North Yemen, killing some 2,800 people and destroying 21 villages.

FIRES AND EXPLOSIONS

Jan. 19—An explosion in an elementary school in Spencer, OK, kills six persons.

Jan. 20—In Floyd County, KY, a coal-mining explosion kills seven men.

Feb. 8—Fire in a Tokyo hotel kills at least 23.

Mar. 6—In a Houston hotel, 10 persons die in a fire.

April 25—An explosion and fire at a building housing an antiques exhibition northeast of Rome kill at least 33 people.

April 30—A fire in a residential hotel in Hoboken, NJ, kills 12 persons.

May 25—In Aire, France, fire in a home for mentally handicapped teenagers kills at least 18.

July 5—In Waterbury, CT, fire in two tenement buildings kills six; 10 others are missing.

Sept. 4—In Los Angeles a fire in an apartment building kills 24 persons.

Nov. 2, 3?—In Afghanistan a fuel truck explodes in a mountain tunnel, killing hundreds of Soviet soldiers and Afghan civilians trapped inside.

Nov. 8—A fire in the county jail in Biloxi, MS, kills 29 prisoners and injures 61 others.

Dec. 19–21—A fuel-tank fire rages out of control near Caracas, Venezuela, killing at least 129 people.

LAND AND SEA TRANSPORTATION

Jan. 26—In Algiers a passenger train derails, killing at least 120 people and injuring 150 others.

Jan. 26—Near Tuxpan, Mexico, a bus falls from a bridge into a river, killing 19 persons.

Feb. 15—An oil-drilling rig off the coast of Newfoundland sinks during a storm, killing 84 men.

Feb. 16—In heavy seas of the North Atlantic, a Soviet freighter, the *Mekhanik Tarasov*, sinks, killing at least 18 people; several others are missing.

Mar. 6–7—In the mid-Atlantic an explosion sinks the supertanker *Golden Dolphin;* nine are missing.

Mar. 20—Near Warangal, India, an express train crashes into a bus, killing 40 persons.

Mar. 28—Near Rangoon, Burma, a ferry capsizes in a canal, killing nearly 130 people.

April 7—A tanker truck and a bus collide in the Caldecott Tunnel of California, killing seven.

April 11—Near Henzada, Burma, a ferry capsizes; more than 160 people are presumed drowned.

April 20—In the Sinai near El Arish, a bus accident kills 14 Greek tourists; 34 others are injured.

July 11—A train traveling in Mexico from Nogales to Guadalajara derails, killing 120 persons.

July 25—The tourist ship *Coral Island* catches fire in Manila Bay; 21 crewmen are missing.

July 31—Near Beaune, France, 53 persons, including 44 children on their way to an Alpine vacation camp, are killed in a multiple bus-car collision.

Sept. 12—Near Zurich, Switzerland, a locomotive strikes a bus, killing 39 persons.

Nov. 8 (reported)—In Saraburi Province, Thailand, 26 persons are killed when a bus, attempting to pass another bus, crashes into a truck.

STORMS AND FLOODS

Jan. 3–6—In the San Francisco Bay area, mudslides and floods leave more than 30 dead.

Jan. 4—Across the United States from Oregon to Massachusetts and into the South, storms have led to 34 deaths since New Year's Eve.

Jan. 8–9—In Great Britain snowdrifts cause 11 deaths; in Sweden two die from the cold.

Jan. 9–13—Record-breaking cold, snowstorms, and winds grip the Middle West, East, and South, contributing to the deaths of 143 persons.

Jan. 23–24—Torrential rains in the Peruvian jungle cause the flooding of the Chontayacu River; at least 600 people are dead or missing.

Mar. 13–20—Flooding in the Midwest—particularly Fort Wayne, IN, and sections of Michigan and Ohio—kills seven.

Mar. 15—In Santa Cruz, Bolivia, rains and flooding leave 50 families missing and thousands homeless.

April 1–10—A spring storm system, moving from California to the Southwest, Midwest, and the Northeast and producing tornadoes, snow, high winds, and flooding, kills at least 64 people.

May 12—In the province of Guangdong, China, severe floods have killed at least 430 people.

May 28 (reported)—Floods in Nicaragua and Honduras cause the deaths of 226 persons.

May 29 (reported)—In Hong Kong flooding and landslides cause the deaths of at least 20 people.

June 3—In Cuba, Hurricane *Alberto* kills 24.

June 3—On Indonesia's Sumatra island, heavy floods kill 225 persons and leave about 3,000 homeless.

June 4—A hurricane hits the Indian state of Orissa, killing 200 persons and leaving 200,000 homeless.

June 5–6—Flooding in Connecticut kills 12.

June 25–26—In the state of Paraná, Brazil, windstorms kill 43 persons.

July 23—Flooding in and near the city of Nagasaki, Japan, kills at least 307; 43 others are missing.

Aug. 2—Typhoon *Bess* hits Japan, causing 80 deaths.

Sept. 17–25—Flooding in El Salvador, Guatemala, and Mexico causes the deaths of 600 in El Salvador and 560 in Guatemala. Missing are 1,200 in Guatemala and 10 in Mexico.

Oct. 20–22—Flooding in northern Spain kills 113.

Nov. 10 (reported)—In the western Indian state of Gujarat, a hurricane kills 275 persons.

Dec. 1–3—A major storm system of wind, rain, and snow moves from California eastward and southward, and contributes to the deaths of 38 persons.

MISCELLANEOUS

Mar. 14—Near Grenoble, France, nine avalanches in five ski areas of the Alps cause 11 deaths.

Mar. 21—In Japan, avalanches in the Yatsugatake and Hokendake mountains kills 13; two are missing.

April 15—In East Chicago, IN, an unfinished highway bridge collapses, killing 12 workers.

DRUG AND ALCOHOL ABUSE

Recent surveys show that such stimulants as cocaine and amphetamine are increasing in popularity, and that methaqualone (Quaalude) use is also on the increase. Meanwhile, the number of users of marijuana and phencyclidine (PCP) has been decreasing. Other drugs show no significant change in use patterns. Because of the poor quality of the heroin on the street, regional outbreaks of prescription narcotics abuse have occurred. In the Midwest, a combination of "Ts and blues," pentazocine (Talwin) and pyribenzamine, an antihistamine, is favored. In Southern California, "loads," codeine-Doriden mixtures, are preferred.

Cocaine. A century ago, after the successful extraction of cocaine from coca leaves, an epidemic of excessive cocaine use was seen in Europe and the United States. Sigmund Freud, among many, extolled the virtues of cocaine for a long list of ailments, including depression, alcoholism, and neurasthenia. A few years later he had to retract his glowing endorsement as instances of overdose, insatiable craving, and psychosis emerged.

What we are observing now appears to be a repetition of the events of the 1880s. We have repeated the errors of those days, and our delivery systems have become more malignant than they were a hundred years ago.

It is not cocaine's physical effects that are of public health consequence, although occasional hypertension, nasal perforations, and overdose deaths do occur. Rather, it is the psychological impact that concerns mental health workers who are seeing increasing numbers of people locked into compulsive cocaine usage. This is especially true of those who use the rapid delivery systems—intravenous use or freebase smoking—but it also can happen to the snorter of the substance.

Smoking freebase is relatively new. Street cocaine is cocaine hydrochloride mixed with adulterants. It is treated with an alkali and a solvent to form cocaine base. The base has a low vaporizing point, and when heated in special pipes can be inhaled. This provides an instantaneous euphoria which lasts for a few minutes. The intravenous route also gives an immediate brief "high." These mood elevations are so intense that the desire to continue the use as long as possible is the rule. Another factor that compels the user to continue use as long as any cocaine remains is a post-cocaine depression at the end of a "run" that can be "cured" by another "hit" of cocaine. A final effect of sustained cocaine use is a paranoid psychosis that resembles paranoid schizophrenia and is usually associated with delusions of persecution and full-blown hallucinations.

Cocaine is the most reinforcing (rewarding) of all drugs. A monkey will continue working for a cocaine reward until it collapses or dies, not stopping for food or water. Such behavior mimics humans who have unlimited access to cocaine. Fortunately, even cocaine adulterated with sugar, amphetamine, or local anesthetics like procaine is expensive, and this acts as a deterrent against use.

Marijuana. Reports by the World Health Organization (1981), the Institute of Medicine of the National Academy of Sciences (1982), and the National Institute on Drug Abuse (1982) emphasized the adverse consequences of prolonged marijuana use. The three reports agreed that marijuana is many times more potent than it was a few years ago, that younger age groups are becoming involved in its use, and that users are indulging daily. A 1982 National Research Council report recommended the abolition of all criminal penalties for the personal use of marijuana, however.

Marijuana contains all the irritants and cancer-causing chemicals that are found in tobacco, some in higher concentrations. Bronchitis is a well-known effect of chronic use, and in times chronic obstructive lung disease is a possibility. Like tobacco, the cannabis tars in marijuana induce tumors and cancers when painted on mouse skins, and the tars react in a manner similar to tobacco in tests to discern carcinogenicity.

Driving a car or piloting a plane under the influence of marijuana results in impaired performance. Decreased reaction time, peripheral vision, and impaired memory are present. Up to 80% of users state that they drive an auto while "stoned." Increasing numbers of accidents are being recorded that involve motorists who have THC, marijuana's main psychoactive component, in their blood.

Perhaps the most serious result of chronic marijuana use is the loss of motivation, ambition, and drive that develops over months or years. This is particularly noted in young people whose adaptive or coping skills have not matured completely. If the marijuana smoking behavior persists, the person remains at a psychologically immature level of development.

Alcohol. Alcohol excess continues to be the most damaging of substance abuse, with 10% of the drinking population affected by serious health, vocational, or family consequences. Focus on the death and destruction caused by intoxicated drivers of automobiles, particularly among the young, has resulted in a number of social and political moves. Some of the states that lowered the legal drinking age during the 1970s have reversed that decision, and many states have enacted or are considering new legislation increasing the penalties for those convicted of drunk driving. In addition, President Reagan established a Presidential Commission on Drunk Driving "to act as a catalyst for grassroots action" against the problem.

SIDNEY COHEN, M.D.
UCLA School of Medicine

ECUADOR

In spite of serious economic difficulties, the democratic regime installed in August 1979 remained in power in Ecuador during 1982.

Government and Politics. The coalition behind President Osvaldo Hurtado Larrea was modified in March, when the Izquierda Democrática (ID) party declared that it would offer "firm, objective and belligerent opposition" to "errors of the regime," although it would continue to back the positive moves of the government.

This change in the pro-government coalition was reflected in the new officials of the Chamber of Representatives (Congress) when it began its regular sessions in August. Raul Baca Carbo of the ID was replaced as president of the body by Rodolfo Daquerizo Nazur of the Concentracion de Fuerzas Populares (CFP). The vice-president and secretaries also were drawn from the pro-administration Roldósista, CFP, and Democratic parties. The ID was given only one representative on the presiding body of the Congress.

Another important political event of the year was the acceptance by Congress in August of the report of a multiparty commission it had appointed to investigate the causes of the airplane crash on May 24, 1981, in which President Jaime Roldós Aguilera and his wife had been killed. The commission had obtained the help of the scientific service of the Zurich, Switzerland, police force in the investigation, and the Swiss authorities had reported that there was no evidence of sabotage, concluding that the accident was due either to unexplained mechanical failure or to human error in the maintenance or operation of the doomed vehicle.

Economy. The country's economic difficulties were due largely to the slump in the oil industry, which in 1981 had provided 9.9% of the gross domestic product and 67.2% of the country's total exports. It was estimated that the cut in oil prices would reduce foreign exchange earnings in 1982 by $140 million. The oil minister, Eduardo Ortega Gomez, was censured by Congress and resigned on September 8. With the government's expected revenues drastically reduced, the economic situation was complicated by the country's large foreign debt, amounting early in the year to some $5,500,000,000.

In April, the Hurtado government took steps to try to deal with the economic crisis. Among these was postponement of programs to build a large steel mill and to expand the highway system. The government also sought new financing abroad, including a three-year $900-million loan from European banks to finance firms in the private sector, and $1,200,000,000 for the public sector.

In his annual report to Congress in August, however, President Osvaldo Hurtado noted that important sectors of the Ecuadorean economy were still showing progress. Although he reported inflation running at an annual average rate of 14.5%, he said that the agriculture and fishing sector had grown by 4.3% in 1981, and was expected to surpass that increase in 1982. He also noted progress in the fields of hydroelectricity, highways, and construction. A total of 12,145 housing units had been built in 1981, equal to half the number constructed in the entire previous decade. The president claimed that illiteracy had decreased from 22% in 1979 to 12% in 1982.

The Ministry of Industries, Commerce, and Integration reported in September that there had been a substantial increase in the rate of foreign investment in Ecuador—an increase of 67.2% between August 1981 and July 1982.

Early in August 1982 a new hydrocarbons law was passed, designed to increase the participation of foreign firms in exploration for oil. However, principal responsibility for control of the national oil industry remained in the hands of the government's firm, the Corporacion Estatal Petrolera Ecuatoriana.

Foreign Affairs. President Osvaldo Hurtado traveled extensively during the year, reinforcing Ecuador's relations with neighboring countries. In February, on a four-day trip to Brazil, he signed a treaty of amity and cooperation with President João Baptista Figueiredo. In the following month he visited Venezuela and Colombia, speaking before the Congress of Venezuela and being decorated with the "Order of Democracy" by that of Colombia. Then in August he attended the inauguration of President Belisario Betancur of Colombia, and in October he was present at the installation of President Hernán Siles Zuazo of Bolivia.

During the Falkland Islands dispute, Ecuador joined with other Andean bloc countries in support of Argentina but also condemned the use of force to resolve international disputes.

In May the government ordered cessation of operations of the Summer School of Linguistics, a Protestant missionary group from the United States which for 30 years had been active in the country, particularly in translating the Bible into local Indian languages.

ROBERT J. ALEXANDER, *Rutgers University*

ECUADOR • Information Highlights

Official Name: Republic of Ecuador.
Location: Northwest South America.
Area: 109,484 sq mi (283 564 km²).
Population (1982 est.): 8,500,000.
Chief Cities (1974): Quito, the capital, 635,713; Guayaquil, 941,009.
Government: *Head of state and government,* Osvaldo Hurtado Larrea, president (took office May 1981). *Legislature* (unicameral)—Congress.
Monetary Unit: Sucre (58.10 sucres equal U.S.$1, Sept. 23, 1982).
Gross National Product (1980 U.S.$): $10,840,000,000.
Economic Indexes (1980): *Consumer Prices* (1970= 100), *all items,* 327.3; *food,* 380.9.
Foreign Trade (1979 U.S.$): *Imports,* $1,986,000,000; *exports,* $2,013,000,000.

EDUCATION

School prayer and busing were two major issues faced by government leaders and educators in 1982.

In his second year in office, President Reagan accelerated his efforts to reduce the federal role in education in favor of state and local initiative and to reduce the federal role as stimulator of social experiments.

In 1982 the Reagan administration merged 29 federal categorical programs (for specific educational needs) into block grants for the states to use as they see fit for educational purposes. The administration and its allies attempted to bar federal courts from jurisdiction over busing for integration and over school prayer cases. To stimulate the private sector, the president urged tax rebates to parents with children in private elementary and secondary schools. So sudden a reversal of the educational policies prevalent for decades inevitably brought massive resistance from liberals in and out of Congress.

In Japan, revision of school textbooks that glossed over its World War II and earlier military atrocities raised international objections, especially from mainland China and from North and South Korea.

Busing-Desegregation. On March 2, after an eight-month fight, the Senate passed, 57-37, the most stringent anti-busing, anti-school desegregation bill in history. Foes in the House hoped to defeat the bill, which consisted of three riders to a Justice Department authorization bill: one by Sen. Jesse Helms (R-NC) barring the Justice Department from ruling on busing cases; the second by Sen. J. D. Johnston (D-LA) limiting lower federal court-ordered busing to no more than 5 mi (8 km) or 15 minutes from home to a neighborhood school; and the third by Sen. Howell Heflin (D-AL) allowing removal or reduction of existing court-ordered busing plans. Opponents of the bill, calling it unconstitutional and dangerous, saw it as an attempt by conservatives to have Congress rather than the federal courts interpret the Constitution. Others saw it as a ravaging of the Constitution in order to return the Supreme Court's 1954 desegregation decision to the 1896 separate-but-equal doctrine. Black leader Jesse Jackson said that opposition to busing was a coverup for racism; that demagogues used schoolchildren politically to discredit busing; and that, where competent white leaders supervised busing for integration, it worked well. In a letter released May 6, U.S. Attorney General William French Smith said that in the opinion of the Justice Department, the Senate-passed anti-busing bill was constitutional.

On June 30 the U.S. Supreme Court gave conflicting decisions on busing cases in California and Washington state. California state courts had imposed busing in Los Angeles, whose schools were segregated but not intentionally so. California voters then approved a state amendment (Proposition 1) stating that busing may only be ordered to correct intentional segregation. Under this amendment, Los Angeles would have to dismantle its busing plan. Los Angeles then appealed to the Supreme Court. The court upheld by an 8-1 vote the state constitutional amendment requiring the Los Angeles busing plan to be dismantled, indicating that state voters could countermand state court action. Washington state had passed Initiative 350 barring local school districts from undertaking mandatory busing. The Supreme Court voted (5-4) to strike down the law, making the fine distinction that a state may not arbitrarily block its local districts from making busing plans.

In other desegregation news, the Justice Department, trying since 1981 to substitute voluntary for court-ordered desegregation, on February 12 endorsed a voluntary plan for Chicago schools. Civil rights lawyers, however, said such voluntary plans were ineffective in Chicago and elsewhere and had been found unconstitutional by the Supreme Court.

Similarly, on August 9 in East Baton Rouge, LA, the Reagan administration, determined to enlist federal courts in rolling back mandatory busing, asked the federal appeals court to try a voluntary rather than a mandatory desegregation plan. In both the Chicago and the East Baton Rouge cases, Assistant Attorney General for Civil Rights William B. Reynolds defended the administration's voluntary desegregation plans. He stated that mandatory desegregation leads to white flight and thus to tax losses for city schools. An opposite view was advanced by a study, released on March 3 by Vanderbilt University, that stated that mandatory desegregation is more effective in reducing racial isolation than voluntary plans. Another study in Cleveland, released on September 9, challenged the white flight theory. The study found that fewer students than previously thought left Cleveland schools after 1978 because of forced desegregation.

Tax Relief for Racially Biased Schools. Since 1970, the Internal Revenue Service (IRS) has denied tax exempt status to private schools and colleges that discriminate racially. In October 1981, the Supreme Court agreed to consider a suit challenging the IRS stand against tax relief for Bob Jones University in Greenville, SC, and the Goldsboro (NC) Christian schools. On Jan. 8, 1982, the Reagan administration announced that it would lift the 12-year IRS ban on racially biased schools and asked that the Bob Jones and Goldsboro School cases be held moot. An immediate storm of protest forced President Reagan four days later to reverse his stand, restoring IRS policy. Accepting the onus for the reversal flap, the president insisted that the IRS had, by bureaucratic fiat and not by congressional authority, imposed its 1970 ban. Incensed civil rights groups pointed out that IRS action was government policy, long backed by the federal courts, and that President Reagan's January 8 reversal was intended to placate southern conservative leaders in South Carolina and Mississippi where most of the discriminatory private schools, including Bob Jones University, are located and are demanding tax relief because they are hard-pressed financially. The furor declined after the Supreme Court on April 19 appointed William T. Coleman, Jr., a black Republican and secretary of transportation in the Ford administration, as a special counsel to argue in favor of the IRS stand. The Supreme Court was expected to rule on the case during its 1982-83 session.

Tuition Tax Credit Bill. President Reagan's tuition tax credit bill, unveiled before a Chicago meeting of the National Catholic Education Conference on April 15, would allow parents with children in private elementary and secondary schools to qualify for a tax credit of up to 50% of their annual cost for tuition. A maximum deduction of $100 per child would be available for the first year, $300 the second year, and $500 thereafter. The amount of the deduction would be reduced for families with $50,000 to $75,000 incomes, and no credit would be available for families with incomes beyond that level. Opponents of the proposal, including the National Education Association and the American Federation of Teachers, charged that the bill's estimated cost matches President Reagan's federal education cuts and is part of the administration's design to subsidize private education and supplant public schools. They charge the president with trying to recapture middle class urban Catholic voters, the main users of parochial schools. Polls showed that the group's support of the president had slipped following budget cuts and high unemployment.

Advocates, who believe it only fair to reimburse parents paying both public school taxes and their children's private school fees, also see private schools as forcing public schools to improve. Opponents say that the measure strips children, money, and middle class support from already weakened public schools; that it unconstitutionally aids religious schools, some of which discriminate against blacks and other minorities; that it benefits only the 10% of U.S. children in private schools while hurting the 90% in hard-pressed public schools; that it is a payoff to Moral Majority conservatives and affluent Reagan supporters; and that it divisively encourages educational, racial, and religious segregation. Most press opinion agreed with Republican Robert Dole, chairman of the Senate Finance Committee that is responsible for studying the bill, that Congress, worried about the huge federal deficit, would not act on this controversial measure.

Public School Prayer. On January 25 the Supreme Court struck down as unconstitutional a Louisiana voluntary school prayer. In March an appeals court similarly ruled on school prayer in Lubbock, TX. A federal court later halted Alabama's school prayer. On May 6, which President Reagan had proclaimed as a National Day of Prayer, he endorsed a constitutional amendment to permit but not force public school prayer. The amendment was later sent to Congress. In a letter to Sen. Strom Thurmond, chairman of the Senate Judiciary Committee, U.S. Attorney General Smith expressed doubt on the constitutionality of bills that would strip federal courts and the Supreme Court of jurisdiction over school prayer cases. His opinion was aimed at Sen. Jesse Helms's pro-prayer and anti-abortion amendments to a national debt ceiling bill. Helms's pro-prayer amendment was defeated by a liberal filibuster and a vote in the Senate on September 23.

Aliens. On June 15 the Supreme Court voted, 5-4, that Texas must provide children of illegal aliens a free public education, thus striking down a 1975 Texas law barring state funds from educating children of illegal Mexican aliens. Federal court opposition had kept that law from implementation. The Supreme Court said that withholding education "imposes a lifetime hardship on a discrete class of children not accountable for their disabling status." Texas' fear of being swamped by 100,000 or more alien children at a cost of $124 million per year had been exaggerated. Since 1980 when a lower federal court first struck down the Texas law, some 25,000 such children had enrolled in Texas schools. No significant increase was expected following the June 15 ruling, the first time in U.S. history that equal protection has been extended to persons not legally admitted to the United States.

Censorship. A survey published by the *Los Angeles Times* reported that book censorship in both schools and libraries was increasing. The American Library Association (ALA) recorded up to 1,000 cases of censorship in 1981 and estimated that only about 25% of actual censorship incidents come to its attention.

A leading case in 1982 was a student-initiated lawsuit charging violation of First Amendment freedom of speech when in 1975 the Island Trees Union Free School District (NY) school board banned nine high school library books as being "anti-American, anti-Christian, anti-Semitic, and just plain filthy." On June 25 the Supreme Court rejected the board's assertion of having absolute authority over school library books. In a 5-4 decision the court returned the case to federal district court for trial. In September the school board returned the banned books to the library, requiring that parents be notified when their children borrow the books.

On February 2 at a Girard, PA, high school assembly, author Studs Terkel defended his 1974 bestseller, *Working.* A group of parents and students had attacked the book for its profanity. It was assigned reading for 14 vocational students. Terkel defended the book's graphic quotations of working people talking about their lives and jobs. Terkel later said that his literature was "really about . . . the good hard working people who live in places like Girard."

Aspects of the complex censorship problem can be seen in Texas, one of some 22 states where one textbook committee approves up to five titles per subject each year. Local school systems must then choose from the approved list. Because Texas spends so much on a few textbooks ($51.5 million in 1981), its choices influence which textbooks publishers will promote nationally.

Other censorship cases in 1982 centered on Mark Twain's *The Adventures of Huckleberry Finn,* called a racist book in a Fairfax, VA, school, and *Newsweek,* replaced as too liberal by *U.S. News & World Report* in a Minot, ND, school.

Handicapped. On June 28 the Supreme Court said that under the 1975 Education for All Handicapped Children Act (P.L. 94-142), school boards need only provide services "sufficient to maximize each child's potential commensurate with the opportunity provided other children." The court's 6-3 vote overturned two earlier federal court rulings requiring a Westchester County school district to provide deaf student Amy Rowley (she was then in the fourth grade) with an interpreter in class. The court held that she had passed from grade to grade and was thus receiving a meaningful and appropriate education. Educators of the handicapped, glad that the basic provisions of P.L. 94-142 were being upheld, feared that the decision might lead some school districts to reduce services to some handicapped children. Most school officials were relieved by the decision, having feared possible escalating demands for high-cost services needed by some handicapped children.

President Reagan in 1981 had sought a 25% cut in education aid for the handicapped. Congress, which resisted these cuts and others, set off a storm of protest when the Department of Education on August 3 announced a seemingly more restrictive interpretation of the 1975 legislation. For example, a proposed revised rule would allow schools to discipline handicapped children who disrupt classes. In response to protests and after public hearings, Education Secretary T. H. Bell on September 29 withdrew the proposed regulations.

S.A.T. Scores. For the first time in 19 years, the average verbal and mathematical Scholastic Aptitude Test (S.A.T.) scores increased. Although the exact reasons for the rise were unknown, it was suggested that the high school seniors of 1982 may have benefited from courses in English, mathematics, science, and foreign languages, which have been reinstated in the curriculums.

Enrollment Down, Costs Up. Elementary and secondary school enrollment declined for the seventh consecutive year, while higher education enrollments reached an all-time high. School statistics for 1982-83 (1981-82 in parentheses) were: Enrollments, kindergarten through grade 8—30,945,000, decline is expected to reverse in mid-1980s (31,145,000); high school—13,875,-000, with decline projected through the 1980s (14,325,000); higher—12,500,000, with decrease projected 1982-90 (12,372,000); total, 57,320,000, or −1.0% (57,842,000). The record total enrollment of 61,300,000 was in 1975.

Education directly involved 61,000,000 persons, or 26% of the total U.S. population of 232,-000,000. Expenditures were: public elementary and secondary schools, $120,300,000,000 ($112,-800,000,000); nonpublic elementary and secondary, $15,300,000,000 ($14,000,000,000); public higher education, $53,200,000,000 ($48,300,000,-000); nonpublic higher education, $26,500,000,-000 ($23,200,000,000), a total of $215,300,000,-000 ($200,000,000,000). Of this amount, 9% would come from the federal government, 39% would come from state governments, and 25%

would come from local governments; 27% would come from other sources, including tuition, fees, endowment earnings, and private gifts and grants.

Number of teachers, elementary and secondary, 2,450,000 (2,470,000); higher, 870,000 (860,000); total, 3,320,000 (plus 300,000 administrators and other staff).

Graduates, high school, 3,000,000 (3,050,- 000), with more than 2,800,000 expected in 1983; (high school graduate peak in 1977 was 3,161,- 000); bachelor's degrees, 965,000 (945,000); first professional degrees, 74,000 (72,000); master's, 307,000 (300,000); and doctorates, 33,000 (same).

See also LAW—U.S. Supreme Court.

FRANKLIN PARKER
Benedum Professor of Education
West Virginia University

EDUCATION/SPECIAL REPORT

The College Cost Factor

The cost of higher education in the United States has been rising at a rate well above inflation, fluctuating between 12 and 16% annually in the past decade. The trend will continue in the 1982–83 academic year, with increases in tuition at state-financed public institutions averaging 20% and at privately-financed independent colleges and universities 13%, according to the College Scholarship Service.

Tuition and fees charged by public four-year institutions would average $979, up from $815 in the previous year. At private institutions, average tuition has risen from $3,552 in 1981–82 to $4,021 in the current year. At public two-year community colleges, tuitions are up to almost $600 from just above $500 in 1981–82, an increase of almost 18%. The rise at private two-year institutions was 11%, from $2,238 to $2,486.

Actually, of course, the cost of going to college is considerably higher than these figures suggest. When room and board as well as other incidental expenses are included, the total annual bill at public institutions may range from $3,500 to $6,000 and from $6,000 to $12,000 on private campuses. The latter amount is the approximate cost at Ivy League and equivalent institutions.

The result of rapidly escalating costs has shifted the enrollment balance even further toward public institutions. In 1981–82, undergraduate enrollment dropped 2.7% at the nation's private colleges, and the National Association of Independent Colleges and Universities predicted an even sharper downward curve for 1982–83. At the same time, enrollments rose sharply at community colleges and at those four-year public institutions to which students are able to commute, thus saving dormitory fees. But even commuting students are experiencing a 12.5% increase in college costs at public four-year institutions.

One serious consequence of these trends has been a dramatic reduction in the number of students from low-income families on prestigious high-cost private college campuses. In the period from 1979 to 1982, these institutions have experienced a drop of 39% in enrollment of students from families with incomes between $6,000 and $24,000. During the same period, as financial pressures on all families increased, the number of students from higher-income families receiving financial aid showed a substantial rise. Among those with family incomes of more than $36,000, the aid increase was 156%.

Student Aid. The problem of escalating costs has been aggravated by uncertainties and contradictions concerning student aid. Although the White House has denied that student aid has been reduced, academic observers point out that the administration's budget request for fiscal 1983 proposed cutting the $6,000,000,000 student aid package by almost one third. The administration forecast, however, that even though there would be a reduction of nearly $1,000,000,000 in federal funds for guaranteed student loans, private banks would increase loans to students to a record level of more than $10 million in fiscal 1983. But critics of such forecasts point out that interest rates on such loans would be costly to students, and that many banks might not be willing to extend loans to students from low-income families.

The Congressional Budget Office estimated that total loan volume will drop from $7,200,- 000,000 in 1982 to $4,800,000,000 in 1983, rather than rise to the $10,000,000,000 level predicted by the administration. Direct aid to students, known as Pell Grants, under the administration's budget request, would have declined from $2,300,000,000 to $1,400,000,- 000 in the new academic year. But ultimately, Congress defied President Reagan, overrode his veto, and added $217 million in grant money for needy students. Congressional adjustments were expected to bring the Pell Grants to $2,280,000,000, only about $10 million below the 1982 total.

Despite such last-minute adjustments, college financial aid officers said that many needy students have been frightened away by the er-

Timothy A. Murphy/U.S. News & World Report

With tuition costs rising and federal aid declining, students now must seek new avenues of financial assistance.

roneous belief that they would be ineligible for scholarship or loan support. Yet, no matter how cuts are interpreted by the administration and its critics in academia, direct federal aid to needy students in fiscal 1983 was being reduced 17%, not counting the additional reduction in funds available for the Guaranteed Student Loans. Until October 1982, such low-interest loans were available to all students, regardless of family income; now, students whose families earn more than $30,000 are barred from such loans unless they can show extraordinary need.

Looking at the total picture, the College Board estimated that student aid from all sources in the 1981–82 academic year amounted to about $20,000,000,000. This estimate included at least $3,000,000,000 provided by the colleges themselves, and $1,000,-000,000 each from the states and from employer tuition plans.

A study of financial aid at public colleges, conducted at the University of Wisconsin, shows that students who get subsidies also tend to work to meet their educational expenses. Approximately one third of those receiving aid are completely self-supporting. About 2.2 million students, or 23% of all students attending public colleges, depend on federal aid to meet their expenses. More than half of such aid goes to families or individuals earning less than $9,200 a year, the figure defined by the 1981 census as the poverty line for a family of four.

Expenses for the Institutions. Financial pressures on colleges themselves have been aggravated by high energy costs and aging faculties, with an increasing number of professors at the top levels of the salary scale and little room for advancement to the tenured ranks of less costly junior faculty members. Declining enrollments on some private campuses raise the total cost of operations. Further pressure on budgets stems from the mounting expense of scientific and technological equipment and the escalating costs of library acquisitions and maintenance.

Perhaps the most serious concern, however, among representatives of higher education's independent sector, which before World War II enrolled approximately 60% of all students, is the accelerated shift to state-financed campuses. In 1982 some of the public institutions reported increases of 10% or more in the number of freshmen applications, at a time when the private institutions, with the exception of a relatively few top-prestige campuses, reported a decline. Enrollment at independent colleges stood at 2.6 million, compared with 9.6 million at the public ones.

This situation tends to hide the fact that many public institutions also face serious financial difficulties as state legislatures cut budgets. This constitutes an added threat as scholarship aid is reduced and admissions standards at the relatively low-cost public institutions are tightened. Many observers fear that if less affluent youths are shut out, the racial minorities will be most seriously affected, and higher education's role in keeping the society open and upwardly mobile may be diminished.

FRED M. HECHINGER

EGYPT

Hosni Mubarak, who succeeded the assassinated Anwar el-Sadat as president of Egypt, completed his first year in office on Oct. 14, 1982. The year had a curiously humdrum air, marked by neither spectacular success nor manifest failure. Egypt's greatest problems remained economic.

Basic Problems. The unchanging dilemma for any ruler of Egypt is posed by people and poverty, problems compounded by the dead hand of a vast, slow-moving, and poorly paid bureaucracy. The population, some 45 million in 1982, increases by about 100,000 per month, or 3% per year. Almost half the food consumed in Egypt is imported. The cost of subsidizing low prices for such staples as rice, cooking oil, and gasoline rose to some $3,000,000,000 in 1982. Inflation in 1982 continued at an annual rate of about 25%. Wages remained extremely low, even for those with special job qualifications or academic degrees. As a result, some three million Egyptians—1 in 15—work abroad, mostly in other Arab countries where wages and salaries are much higher.

Economic Policy. Since taking office, Mubarak has given priority to economic questions. Two major cabinet shuffles, as well as many official pronouncements, testified to this in 1982. On January 2, Mubarak gave up the premiership, which he had also held since October 1981, and named Ahmed Fuad Mohieddin as the new prime minister. Mohieddin, 55, has been prominent in Egyptian public life since the time of Nasser; before his elevation he was first deputy prime minister. Mohieddin's new cabinet was announced January 3 and sworn in the next day. All economic posts were reallocated. The new economics minister was Abdel Fattah Ibrahim, governor of the central bank. Two of the nine dismissed ministers had recently been touched by financial scandal.

In announcing his cabinet, Mohieddin said the new government would "seek the solution of urgent economic problems as soon as possible." He undertook to continue, but also to revise, the "open door" (*infitah*) economic policy—encouraging foreign investment and free enterprise—upon which Sadat had embarked in 1974. Mohieddin said that steps would be taken to make the policy more productive and to orient it more toward serving the poor. The same moral was preached on January 26, when Mubarak assumed the chairmanship of the National Democratic Party. Describing the national economy as "our primary interest," he called for a broad-based conference of economic experts to advise the government and draw up a five-year plan. The conference met February 13–15, but there was apparently more consensus on the problems than on desirable remedies. When Prime Minister Mohieddin outlined the government's economic policy in a parliamentary speech on Feb-

ruary 20, the most specific change was the imposition of new regulations restricting imports. Expansion of vocational training, the negative effects of large subsidies, and the need for greater efficiency in the public sector were also discussed.

The second cabinet shuffle of the year took place on September 1, when seven ministers were replaced, including the two chiefly responsible for economic policy. Informed opinion held that the seven ousted ministers had been in favor of reducing the budget deficit by means of cuts in subsidies.

Though Egyptian oil sales lagged in the face of a worldwide glut, thus reducing foreign-exchange earnings, not all the economic news was bad. Suez Canal revenues were steadily rising. A subsidiary of Royal Dutch Shell discovered a huge oil pool in the Western Desert, estimated to contain as much as 30 million barrels. And General Motors announced in August that it would invest $10 million in a truck factory in Egypt; this was exactly the kind of solid, employment-creating foreign investment that the late President Sadat had hoped his "open-door" policy would attract.

Security. The government continued to be concerned with security problems, but the tight measures instituted in the aftermath of the Sadat assassination were soon eased. By the end of March 1982, half of the 1,500 political and religious opponents of the government who had been jailed on Sadat's orders in September 1981 had been released. Among them were the prominent journalist Dr. Heikal, now supportive of the government, and Fuad Serageddin, former leader of the banned Wafd party. A number of Coptic clergy were also freed, and though Shenouda III, the Coptic leader, remained in prison, he too adopted a friendly attitude toward Mubarak. In August about 600 more of the 1981 detainees were released.

Where reconciliation was not possible, however, as with Muslim fundamentalists, Mubarak showed a determination to be ruthless. Several score young men of this group were arrested in

---

EGYPT · Information Highlights

Official Name: Arab Republic of Egypt.
Location: Northeastern Africa.
Area: 385,229 sq mi (997 743 km^2).
Population (1982 est.): 44,800,000.
Chief Cities (1976 census): Cairo, the capital, 5,074,-016; Alexandria, 2,317,705; El Giza, 1,230,446.
Government: *Head of state,* Hosni Mubarak, president (took office Oct. 1981). *Head of government,* Ahmed Fuad Mohieddin, prime minister (took office Jan. 1982). *Legislature* (unicameral)—People's Assembly.
Monetary Unit: Pound (0.70 pound equals U.S.$1, Nov. 15, 1982).
Gross National Product (1980 U.S.$): $20,600,000,-000.
Economic Index (1981): *Consumer Prices* (1970= 100), *all items,* 271.1; *food,* 338.7.
Foreign Trade (1981 U.S.$): *Imports,* $8,839,000,-000; *exports,* $3,233,000,000.

After a 3½-month trial, 22 Muslim extremists were convicted of taking part in the 1981 assassination of Anwar Sadat.

the spring and summer. In early October the government said that the fanatic Muslim threat was still strong enough to justify a one-year extension of the emergency law curbing constitutional rights.

Trial of Assassins. The trial of the 24 men accused in the assassination of President Sadat, begun on Nov. 21, 1981, was concluded on March 6, 1982, when 22 of the defendants were found guilty. Five were sentenced to death, and 17 others were given sentences of between five years and life in prison, with hard labor. The five executions were carried out April 15.

Foreign Affairs. Mubarak's pledge to continue the policies of his predecessor was substantially carried out in the field of foreign affairs, though he seemed to be striving to distance Egypt a little from the United States and to demonstrate that it was no client state. Mubarak made his first U.S. trip as president, February 2–4, and his foreign minister, Kamal Hassan Ali, visited Washington in November. On the other hand, in a partial healing of Sadat's breach with the USSR, the government announced on January 24 that it had invited 66 Soviet industrial experts to come to Egypt as advisers.

The great fruit of continuity, of course, was the regaining of the Sinai, the last third of which Israel returned on April 25 in accordance with the 1979 Egyptian-Israeli peace treaty. Thereafter the Egyptian attitude toward Israel remained

correct though cool, growing even cooler after the Israeli incursion into Lebanon in early June. Nevertheless, Egypt continued to fulfill its agreement to sell Israel 40,000 barrels of oil per day, though freely criticizing Israeli policy.

Because new preoccupations had arisen—especially Iraq's failure in the war with Iran and the events in Lebanon—Egypt in 1982, though still faced with the unremitting hostility of Libya and Syria, became less of a pariah in the Arab world. Though formal diplomatic links were, in most cases, not restored, friendly overtures were received from Jordan, Oman, Saudi Arabia, and Iraq. Egypt made substantial arms sales to help Iraq in its war effort. In July, Egypt accepted an invitation to attend the meeting of nonaligned states scheduled for September in Baghdad, though the conference was postponed to 1983 and the site changed to India.

Union with Sudan? On October 12 in Khartoum, President Mubarak and President Jaafar al-Nemery of Sudan signed a "charter for integration," envisaging a future unity of defense, economic, and social policies. The agreement established a joint council chaired by the two presidents and supported by a parliament comprising 30 members from each country. A variety of other steps toward unification were foreseen for the next 10 years.

ARTHUR CAMPBELL TURNER
University of California, Riverside

ENERGY

The world energy situation in 1982 was characterized by contradictions and instability.

As world demand continued to decline, the oil surplus of 1981 grew into a glut. Although there was no major break in the price of oil as a result of the glut, prices did soften. Declining demand resulted from three factors. First, the world economy experienced one of the most severe recessions since World War II. Second, consumers throughout the world implemented major oil conservation measures. Third, with softening oil prices, the major international oil companies met demand by drawing down the quantities of oil they had in storage rather than buying new production.

The 13 members of the Organization of Petroleum Exporting Countries (OPEC) saw their share of the world market continue to decline. OPEC production, which had peaked at 31 million barrels per day in 1977, was down to 17 million barrels per day during some months of 1982. The drop in OPEC production was precipitous, declining by nearly 5 million barrels per day.

Benefits and Costs. Abundant, lower-priced oil delivered a mixed set of benefits and costs. On the benefits side, the oil surplus allowed the world to experience two Middle Eastern conflicts, invasions of Iraq by Iran and of Lebanon by Israel, without a serious threat of oil disruption. In a number of industrial countries, particularly the United States, consumers enjoyed an absolute reduction in the prices they paid for petroleum products. Those price reductions, in turn, contributed significantly to a decline in the rate of inflation. Finally, the U.S. government took advantage of the changed circumstances and accelerated the rate at which it was filling its Strategic Petroleum Reserve.

The beneficial effects of the oil glut, however, were counterbalanced by a number of negative impacts. The most threatening development was a pervasive pattern of instability in the world's financial system. In the years of scarce oil and rising prices following the 1973 oil embargo, three developments had occurred in the world's financial system. First, a number of the largest oil exporters had enjoyed financial returns on their sales far in excess of what they were able to spend. Most world oil is sold for dollars and the surplus dollars were deposited primarily in U.S. and Western European banks. These surplus dollars triggered a vigorous search by Western banks for places to lend the petrodollars. The primary recipients of the petrodollar loans were less-developed countries (LDCs). Loans to LDCs between 1973 and 1981 grew at a truly awesome rate, from $100,000,000,000 to $540,000,000,000.

In 1982, one of the curious contradictions of the energy crisis decade came to the fore. Non-oil producing, less-developed countries found themselves heavily in debt as a result of their need to borrow to pay for the increased costs of imported oil. As the oil-price-driven worldwide recession reduced demand for the products sold

Photo: Thomas Leighton/Texaco Inc.

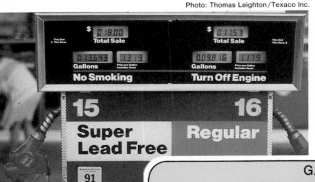

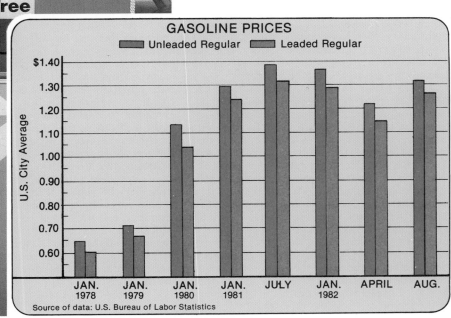

Source of data: U.S. Bureau of Labor Statistics

by LDCs, growing numbers of these countries were hard pressed to meet their debt obligations.

On the other hand, many of the oil-exporting LDCs have committed themselves to vigorous economic development programs based on the belief that the demand for oil would remain high and that prices would continue to increase. To underwrite this rapid development, many of the oil-exporting LDCs also borrowed heavily. With declining demand, even many of the largest oil exporters were faced with cutting back on their development programs. The oil exporters with the largest debts found themselves threatened with economic collapse.

The most severe and graphic case of disruption caused by the oil glut was Mexico. In 1982, Mexico's debt reached an estimated level of $80,000,000,000. In August, Mexico announced that it was incapable of meeting its debt obligations. To stave off bankruptcy, the Mexican government took an extreme set of actions, including a massive cutback in its development program, a devaluation of the peso, and nationalization of all privately owned banks. To help Mexico overcome an imminent financial collapse, the United States led a major effort by Western creditors to put together an emergency short-term loan. In addition, the United States made an advance payment of $1,000,000,000 to Mexico for oil that was to be delivered later to the U.S. Strategic Petroleum Reserve.

At the annual joint meeting of the International Monetary Fund and the World Bank, held in Toronto, Canada, in September, the world's central bankers expressed fear that what had occurred in Mexico was only the first of what was likely to be a number of similar situations. Triggered first by oil shortages and rising prices and then by an oil glut and softening prices, the world's financial system was experiencing instability and disorder.

On another level, the world oil glut triggered conflict and instability within OPEC and significantly weakened the capacity of Saudia Arabia to enforce oil price stability. In an effort to maintain the OPEC-established benchmark price of $34 a barrel in the face of declining demand, Saudia Arabia led an effort to establish a maximum OPEC production level. A part of this effort involved establishing production quotas for the various members. OPEC initially set its overall production ceiling at 17.5 million barrels per day. When world demand dropped below that level, a number of OPEC members cut prices in an effort to increase sales.

Meeting in July, OPEC sought to reestablish production quotas that would keep a floor under the OPEC-established price. Conflicts among the cartel members, however, were so serious that the meeting adjourned without agreement on either production levels or price.

To maintain price stability, the Saudis have, in the past, increased or reduced production as necessary to maintain a world supply-demand balance. The Saudi capacity to do this resulted from two factors. First, the Saudis have the capability to produce more than 11 million barrels of oil per day. Second, their financial needs can be met by production that many observers believe is only half to two thirds of that maximum production capability. However, during 1982, Saudi production fell below the level believed needed to meet its revenue needs. Declining demand for oil reduced their flexibility and therefore, the Saudis' capacity to maintain a world supply-demand balance. One late-in-the-year report indicated that the Saudis were concerned about their declining sales. Most observers saw the Saudi sales problem resulting from their insistence on the $34 a barrel price. It is a reflection of what occurred during the year that the Saudi commitment to the maintenance of price stability had converted their oil from the cheapest in OPEC throughout most of the decade to the highest priced oil in 1982.

Energy was the trigger for a major political conflict of another kind during 1982. This occurred when the European nations, motivated by a desire to reduce their energy dependence on Mideastern oil, went ahead with an agreement, signed in 1981, to buy major quantities of Siberian natural gas. Under the terms of the agreement, the Soviets will build a 3,500-mi (5 633-km) natural gas pipeline from their Siberian gas fields to a connection with Western European pipelines.

The Reagan administration opposed the pipeline for two reasons: first, a fear that at some future date the Soviets would use either the threat of or the actual cutoff of gas to Western Europe as a political instrument, and second, a concern that the Soviets would use the hard currency gained from the sale of gas to enhance their military capability.

Over vigorous European objections, the Reagan administration sought to block the construction of the pipeline by denying the Soviets access to U.S. pipeline technology either directly or through European subsidiaries and licensees of American companies. Although both the United States and its European allies sought to play down the split, it was viewed by many observers as the most serious policy conflict between the United States and its European allies since the end of World War II.

Domestic Consequences. During 1982, overall energy consumption in the United States remained relatively steady, with petroleum consumption declining slightly, averaging approximately 15.5 million barrels per day. Domestic petroleum production remained on a par with the level of 1981, about 10 million barrels per day.

In striking contrast, oil imports into the United States dropped by more than half, to as low as 2.5 million barrels per day during some months of the year. Throughout most of the year, oil imports were below the level needed to

Solar One, the world's largest solar power plant at 10,000 kw, was opened in the Mojave Desert near Daggett, CA. Some 300 heliostats, or giant movable mirrors, reflect the sun on a 300-ft (91-m) "power tower" to make steam.

fill the gap between domestic production and consumption. The difference was made up by drawing down the levels of oil industry had in storage.

Again, a curious contradiction resulted from the oil glut. At the same time that the federal government's Strategic Petroleum Reserve was being added to on an accelerated basis, private storage was declining. It appeared likely that when the figures were in for the year, the combination of government and private storage would be lower than it had been early in the year.

The high cost of much of the privately held oil, plus high interest rates, made drawing down storage a wise business decision. One effect of that decision, however, was to reduce the amount of cushion the nation would have available should a sudden and unpredictable disruption of supply occur, and it was still widely believed that the nation would face such a disruption at some point in the future. Those who expressed concern about the lack of adequate emergency preparedness noted that the nation's need for 5 to 5.5 million barrels of imports per day was only 1 million barrels per day less than at the time of the embargo.

The oil glut had a range of other negative domestic energy impacts. Perhaps most striking was what occurred with regard to oil drilling. U.S. industry, stimulated by the deregulation of domestic oil and the partial deregulation of natural gas, had accelerated drilling to the highest rate in history during 1981. In December 1981, 4,530 rigs were working in the United States. Late in 1982, the number of working rigs had declined to less than 2,700.

Rising oil and gas prices had attracted vast quantities of capital into the oil and gas industry in the previous two years. New oil operators entered the business. Many of these operators were not adequately financed to face a softening in oil and gas prices and, when that occurred, the bottom dropped out of the drilling boom.

During 1982, oil industry profits experienced significant declines. Even Exxon, the world's largest corporation, undertook a program to reduce the number of its employees in an effort to respond to its declining profits. By the end of the year, some oil and gas industry trade journals were referring to a recession in the industry.

The nation's decision to move massively and systematically toward the development of a commercial synthetic fuels industry, represented by the establishment of the Synthetic Fuels Corporation in 1980, suffered a serious blow during the year. The $5,000,000,000 Colony Oil Shale Project of the Exxon Corporation and the Tosco Corporation was canceled in May. This project, located in western Colorado, involved not only opening a huge mine and constructing a plant, but the building of a new city. At the time the decision was made, nearly $1,000,000,000 had been invested in the project. Exxon indicated that a combination of rising construction costs and soft world oil prices was behind the decision.

The role of nuclear power in the United States continued to decline in 1982. A growing number of utilities canceled plants. In a report issued in March, the Nuclear Regulatory Commission estimated that as many as 19 already committed nuclear plants might be canceled during the year. In addition, the nation was no

208

more successful in formulating a policy for nuclear waste management than it had been in previous years. Some electric utilities indicated that the failure to establish storage sites for spent fuel would lead to the early shutdown of a number of operating nuclear plants. At present, utilities store used nuclear fuel in water tanks located at the plant sites. A number of these on-site storage facilities are within two or three years of capacity. With no place to dispose of the presently stored fuel, plant shutdown is the only option.

Finally, many energy experts worried that the most severe consequence of the oil glut would be a significant weakening in the commitment of Americans to energy conservation. Between 1973 and 1981, energy conservation had resulted in savings that were the equivalent of more than 7 million barrels of oil a day. With lower prices, however, it appeared that many Americans were moving back to a pattern of more inefficient energy usage. One illustration of this was the renewed popularity of large fuel-inefficient autos. Late in the year, both General Motors and the Ford Motor Company issued reports that indicated significant growth in the sales of their Cadillac and Lincoln cars.

Government Policy. During its first year in office, the Reagan administration had developed an energy approach with four components: 1) a reduction in federal regulations impeding energy development by the private sector, 2) more rapid leasing of federal land, 3) vigorous support for the nuclear fast-breeder reactor, and 4) withdrawal of direct federal financial support for nonnuclear energy sources. During 1982 the Reagan administration continued its efforts to reduce regulation by cutting the budgets and reducing the personnel levels of the regulatory agencies as well as modifying their regulations. Both the administration's supporters and critics agreed that real changes were occurring in the way the federal government enforced its environmental and health and safety regulations.

The most striking change with regard to leasing federal lands was represented by a new five-year schedule for Outer Continental Shelf (offshore) oil and gas leases. The new schedule called for offering approximately 1,000,000,000 acres (404 million ha) for lease during 1982–87. Under this new program, the industry would have much greater freedom in selecting the areas it wished to lease. Further, the new program put greater reliance on competitive bidding to set lease prices than had previously been the case. A number of states and environmental interest groups vigorously objected to this new leasing program and announced that they would challenge it in court. By the end of the year, it appeared that a number of the lease areas might be blocked until the courts were able to decide the issues.

Finally, the Reagan administration continued its efforts to reduce federal funding for the development of new energy resources. The most striking changes in that connection were in the Department of Energy's research and development (R&D) budget. The Reagan administration's budget proposals called for an absolute reduction of 44% from the last budget submitted by the Carter administration. Three sources—fossil fuels (primarily coal), energy conservation, and solar energy—suffered 80% of the total cut. In the case of fossil fuels, the R&D budget dropped from $991 million to $106 million. The energy conservation budget dropped from $201 million to $19 million, and the solar budget was lowered from $549 million to $73 million. The administration argued that these funding cuts would allow the economic marketplace to more effectively determine the appropriate energy sources which should be developed for the future.

During 1982, President Reagan sought to implement his campaign promise to eliminate the Department of Energy (DOE), calling for the majority of the department's functions to be transferred to the Department of Commerce. The administration argued that eliminating the Department of Energy would save anywhere from $250 million to more than $1,000,000,000 a year. Late in the year, however, the General Accounting Office issued a report that concluded that the administration had not demonstrated that those savings would occur. At the time, it was generally thought that the president would not be successful in eliminating the department.

Late in 1982, Energy Secretary James B. Edwards resigned to become president of the Medical College of South Carolina. President Reagan named Donald P. Hodel, 47-year-old undersecretary of the interior and administrator of the Bonneville Power Administration (1972-77), to the energy post. Hodel had been a member of the Oregon Alternate Energy Development Commission. Although Hodel supports the president's efforts to merge major portions of the DOE into the Commerce Department, he said that he would not launch a "major effort" to dismantle existing federal energy programs.

In another organizational change, the administration consolidated the management of energy on public lands by establishing a new Minerals Management Service in the Department of the Interior from portions of the U.S. Geological Survey and the Bureau of Land Management. The administration argued that this organizational change would make it possible to more effectively accelerate the development of mineral and energy resources on public lands.

Finally, although a majority in Congress felt that the president should have a standby rationing program in case of another oil disruption, the administration argued that the marketplace would more effectively manage energy resources than would the federal government.

DON E. KASH
University of Oklahoma

ENGINEERING, CIVIL

Many high-priority construction projects with favorable benefit-cost ratios were being built by the public and private sectors in the United States and other countries during 1982.

Bridges

United States. More than two years after a freighter knocked part of Florida's Sunshine Skyway Bridge into Tampa Bay, work began on its replacement. When the bulk carrier smashed into a concrete pier during a rain squall in May 1980, it ripped away more than 1,300 ft (396 m) of truss span. Completed in 1971 with a 160-ft (49-m) vertical clearance, the two-lane crossing was the twin to an 11-mi (18-km) causeway-bridge built in 1954. Each structure carried two lanes of one-way traffic, and the undamaged older bridge presently carries two-way traffic. The first bridge cost $12.5 million and the second $20.5 million; the new four-lane structure is expected to cost some $215 million. It will have a 1,200-ft (366-m) horizontal and 175-ft (53-m) vertical clearance. It is scheduled for completion in 1985, and it will carry both I-275 and U.S. 19. The superstructure will be cable-stayed, either precast-concrete segmental box-girder or steel box-girder. The new 4.2-mi (6.8-km) bridge will replace the deep-water portion of the twin two-lane structures. Work was begun on the piers in 1982. Understandably, protection against damage in the future by heavy river traffic is an important aspect of the design of the new piers.

At Lulig, LA, about 15 mi (24 km) upstream from New Orleans, the state has built a new $121 million steel stayed-girder bridge across the Mississippi River. Construction started in 1975 and was finished in 1982. Its main span, 1,222 ft (372 m) between the A-shaped twin towers, sets a U.S. record for its kind. Its 82-ft- (25-m-) wide orthotropic deck, 14-ft- (4-m-) deep trapezoidal box girders, and tower sections—all of weathering steel—were fabricated in segments in Japan and shipped from Kure. All field connections are bolted. The steel bridge deck has a 2.25-inch (5.7-cm) epoxy asphalt wearing surface. Routes I-10 and U.S. 61 are north of the bridge, with U.S. 90 to the south.

The state of Iowa also built a new bridge across the Mississippi. The four-lane vehicular structure, easing traffic conditions between Dubuque and the left-bank boundary of Wisconsin and Illinois, has a 670-ft (204-m) tied steel arch span, flanked by 1,200 ft (366 m) of steel approach girders on one side and 840 ft (256 m) on the other. The top of the arch is 207 ft (63 m) above the river. Bolted connections are used throughout. The $14.7 million structure was completed in 1982.

The new Mississippi River Bridge at Luling, LA, is the longest (1,222 ft; 372 m) steel stayed-girder span in the United States. Red weathering steel for the $121 million project was brought in from Japan.

State of Louisiana Department of Highways

Canals

United States. A 4,300 ft- (1 311-m) canal is being dug from the right bank of the Columbia River in the State of Washington to the west shore of Vancouver Lake. Its purpose is to clean up the lake and improve the aquatic environment. The unlined flushing channel is 200 ft (61 m) wide and 43 ft (13 m) deep. Water will be returned to the river via an outlet at the north end of the lake. Hydraulic dredges handle the excavating. At the lake end, two culverts 84 inches (213 cm) in diameter, equipped with sluice and flap gates, control the flow of water. Sponsored by the Port of Vancouver, the dredging will cost $12 million. Completion of the canal and lake restoration was scheduled for 1983.

Egypt. With financial assistance from Japan, Egypt plans to enlarge its 101-mi (163-km) Suez Canal so as to accommodate 260,000-T (235 868 t) tankers. Present passage is limited to 150,000-T (136 078-t) ships. Dredging will widen the canal from 525 to 755 ft (160 to 230 m) and deepen it from 65 to 80 ft (20 to 24 m). Some 524 million yd^3 (401 million m^3) will be dredged, with another 16 million yd^3 (12 million m^3) excavated by earthmoving equipment. Japanese contractors will assist in the construction. The Canal Authority anticipates an increase in revenue when larger ships use the passage.

Dams

United States. Time and money were saved by the use of roller-compacted concrete in the construction of Willow Creek Dam near Heppner, OR. For the first time in the United States, lean concrete was placed in continuous horizontal lifts with earthmoving equipment rather than conventional cranes or cableways. The flood-control gravity dam, with a central overflow spillway, is 160 ft (49 m) high, 1,700 ft (518 m) long, and 16 ft (5 m) wide at the top, with a sloping downstream face and vertical upstream face of concrete panels to support the rolled concrete lifts. The dam contains 410,000 yd^3 (313 467 m^3) of concrete, spread by crawler dozers. Dual-drum, self-propelled vibratory rollers compacted the concrete into 12-inch (30-cm) layers. Scheduled for completion in 1983, the project will cost $14 million.

Ketchikan, at the southeastern tip of Alaska, is building Swan Lake Dam 22 mi (35 km) to the northeast on Revillagigedo Island. The hydro-electric project has the first elliptical, double-curved arch dam in the United States. It will be 174 ft (53 m) high, 17 ft (5 m) thick at the base, 6 ft (2 m) at the crest, and 430 ft (131 m) long; it will contain 25,000 yd^3 (19 114m^3) of concrete. Its 22-Mw powerhouse will replace diesel-driven generators now servicing the city, which gets an average annual rainfall of 150 inches (381 cm).

A 670-ft (204-m) tied arch span over the Mississippi River at Dubuque, IA, was opened in 1982. Four vehicular lanes over the bridge were expected to reduce traffic at the Iowa-Wisconsin-Illinois border.

William Crawford

The Swan Lake Project at Revillagigedo Island, AK, includes the first elliptical double-curved arch dam in the United States. The hydroelectric complex is expected to be completed in 1984 at a total cost of $100 million.

The $100 million project, which is both city- and state-financed, is expected to be completed in 1984.

Canada. British Columbia is building the $1,600,000,000 Revelstoke power project on the Columbia River in the eastern part of the province. The main structure, a concrete gravity dam 1,500 ft (457 m) long and 600 ft (183 m) high, has a spillway and powerhouse at its base. Concrete totals 2.9 million yd³ (2.2 million m³). The project includes an earthfill wing dam 3,800 ft (1 158 m) long and 415 ft (126 m) high, containing 16 million yd³ (12 million m³). The concrete and earthfill barriers will form a reservoir 80 mi (129 km) long with a storage capacity of 4.3 million acre-ft. The 2,700-Mw powerhouse and dams were completed in 1982.

Peru. Condoroma Dam on the Colca River in southern Peru is taking shape as the first of the six-dam Majes river-control, irrigation, and hydroelectric project. The 320-ft (98-m) high and 1,650-ft (503-m) long rockfill dam contains 6.5 million yd³ (5 million m³) of fill. At elevation 13,-450 ft (4 100 m), the dam taps glacier-fed rivers flowing from the Andes Mountains, to irrigate the coastal desert plains and impound water for electrical power. The first stage of the work is scheduled for completion in 1985. A five-nation consortium—Canada, Great Britain, South Africa, Spain, and Sweden—is engaged on the Majes project.

Tunnels

United States. The Massachusetts Bay Transportation Authority (MBTA) is extending its Red Line subway 3.2 mi (5 km) through Cambridge in open-cut tunneling. The complicated extension begins under the Harvard Square station across the Charles River from Boston. The tunnel follows north, along Massachusetts Avenue at an average depth of 35 ft (11 m), to Porter Square, where it drops to 120 ft (37 m) below grade for the new station. From there it continues to Davis Square in Somerville. The $600-million extension is scheduled for completion in 1984.

The city of Pittsburgh is building a new 1.1-mi (1.8-km) subway connecting the upper and lower parts of the Golden Triangle, its downtown business section. The light rail transit line, constructed by the open-cut method, will cross the Monongahela River on a bridge and tie into existing trolley lines and bus connections. Sponsored by the Port Authority of Allegheny County, the subway will cost about $70 million and is expected to be completed in 1984.

The State of Washington's Department of Transportation is boring a 1,500-ft (457-m) vehicular tunnel through Mt. Baker Ridge between downtown Seattle and Lake Washington. The 63-ft (19-m) inside-diameter bore will make it the largest soft earth tunnel in the country. The middle of three inside levels will carry a three-lane westbound roadway for I-90; the lower level will carry two reversible traffic lanes; and the upper will be a pathway for pedestrians and bicycles. Two existing tunnels will be rebuilt to carry three eastbound lanes. The bore is scheduled for completion in 1986 and will cost about $70 million.

Canada. The Canadian Pacific Railway is boring a 9-mi (14-km) one-track rock tunnel through Selkirk Mountain in eastern British Columbia near Rogers. It is part of a 21-mi (34-km) relocation at Glacier National Park. A 1,200-ft (366-m) deep ventilation shaft is at the midpoint of the line. Work started in 1982 and is scheduled for completion in 1986 at a cost of $550 million.

WILLIAM H. QUIRK
Construction Consultant

ENVIRONMENT

The year 1982 marked the 10th anniversary of the Stockholm United Nations Conference on the Human Environment. International environmental groups used the occasion to examine the progress they have made since then, especially as concerns Third World nations, and view the problems that lie ahead. A cause for hope was that Third World countries, despite immense social and economic problems are demonstrating increased awareness that environmental conservation deserves attention and action. Environmental affairs in the United States were dominated by an assault on Reagan administration environmental policies by conservation organizations. Seldom if ever have various conservation groups put up such a unified front.

World Developments

Clean-up of the oceans was hailed as a major achievement of international conservation by the present and former executive directors of the United Nations Environment Program (UNEP). Maurice Strong of Canada, UNEP's first director and now head of the International Energy Development Corporation, was secretary-general of the Stockholm conference. During an interview in the spring of 1982, he cited the Regional Seas Program of UNEP as an important "positive effect" of the conference.

The delegates to the 1972 conference, representing 113 nations, committed themselves to an "action program" and formed UNEP to promote its goal of safeguarding the world environment. Assessing UNEP's progress during the decade, present director Mostafa Tolba noted that "the previous 10 years have seen environmental degradation gather pace on every front" but added that the Regional Seas Program is a "notable exception."

Regional Seas. On April 3, 1982, as part of the Regional Seas Program, 16 Mediterranean nations and the European Community approved a treaty commiting them to a network of protected areas around their common sea. The treaty calls for establishing 100 protected zones for endangered species, migratory birds, public beaches, and sites of architectural or historic importance.

Third World Progress. In the decade since the Stockholm Conference, the number of countries with environmental agencies increased from less than one dozen to more than 100, most of them in the Third World. "The importance these countries now attach to the environment is a source of great encouragement," declared Tolba. He added that UNEP, headquartered in the developing nation of Kenya, has completed a "teething" process and is looking for more international support in the decade ahead.

Tropical Forests and Primates. Early in 1982 the International Union for the Conservation of Nature and Natural Resources and the World Wildlife Fund began planning a campaign to conserve tropical forests and the primates living in them. Several meetings were held during the year to pinpoint regions where action is needed and to develop projects for them. Among the projects scheduled for nations with tropical forests are the development of two or three national parks in Cameroon, improving the protection and management of the important Tai National Park in the Ivory Coast, and preservation of coastal forests in Brazil.

Whaling Ban. The 39-nation International Whaling Commission voted on July 23 to phase out commercial whaling in the next three years,

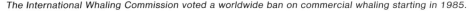

The International Whaling Commission voted a worldwide ban on commercial whaling starting in 1985.

G. Williamson/Bruce Coleman

although the prohibition may not be totally effective. Under the ban, the handful of nations that is engaged in commercial whaling—Japan and the Soviet Union prominent among them—can continue to take several species, such as minke and fin whales, until 1985. Even after that, complains the Whale Protection Fund of Washington, DC, the whaling nations may still harvest whales if they decide to leave the commission. Moreover, the commission action allowed countries that oppose the ban to file "objections."

World Parks Conference. Government officials, conservationists, scientists, business people, and others from all over the globe met in Bali, Indonesia, October 11–22, for the Third World Conference on National Parks. The first conference was held in Seattle 20 years earlier, the second in Grand Teton National Park a decade after that. Participants in the 1982 conference considered the management and future of the more than 1,000,000,000 acres (400 million ha) of wild land and water areas held in protected status by 120 countries, especially as these areas relate to development in the Third World.

The major part of the conference examined case histories of parks and their management in all parts of the world. Workshop sessions focused on both terrestrial and marine parks, as well as on the training of people to manage them. Manuals were produced to help countries in each of these areas of concern.

Experts from several countries pinpointed what they viewed as major issues affecting parks. These included the use of parks for monitoring ecological ups and downs, as storehouses for genetic resources, and as land that can be developed. The challenge, they said, is to use protected natural areas without sacrificing their conservation.

U.S. Developments

Major environmental organizations such as the National Wildlife Federation, National Audubon Society, and dozens of others waged what amounted to open warfare with the Reagan administration over what conservationists saw as attempts to roll back regulations and laws protecting the environment. In mid-October, Reagan did sign the first major piece of conservation legislation of his presidency, barring federal subsidies for the development of about 700 mi (1 127 km) of the nation's barrier islands. By year's end, however, the outcome of the conservationists' struggle was still uncertain.

Endangered Species Act. Environmentalists won a big battle—or rather, the fight never materialized—when in June the Congress voted to extend the Endangered Species Act by reauthorizing its funding for three years. Conservation groups had expected attempts to weaken provisions of the act that protected habitats critical to imperiled species. Reauthorization was accomplished, however, with little controversy.

Public Land Sales. The Reagan administration's budget for fiscal 1983 projected $17,000,000,000 in income from the sale of federal lands to private interests over a five-year period. The plan drew the wrath of environmental groups and also of some of the "Sagebrush Rebels," westerners who had backed the administration's promises to reduce the federal role in administering land in the western states. One of their worries was that big business interests would take advantage of the land sale at the expense of small farmers and ranchers.

According to the Reagan plan, which was challenged by conservation organizations in the courts, 35 million acres (14 million ha)—5% of land owned by the federal government—would be placed on the block. Federal agencies such as the Forest Service and Bureau of Land Management were asked to pinpoint land that could be considered excess. Conservationists noted that although federal lands have been sold in the past the administration was considering the disposal of acreage on a scale never before attempted. By fall, however, the agencies that had been asked to list their surplus lands had identified only a fraction of the total envisioned by the administration.

Backers of the plan pointed out that profits from the sale would lower the national debt and claimed that private interests would manage the land better than the federal government. Typical of the reaction by conservationists was that of National Wildlife Federation President Jay Hair. He urged "public outcry . . . to make the administration realize the folly of its yard sale."

DDT Ban Anniversary. The year 1982 also marked the 10th anniversary of the banning of

Topsoil erosion, caused primarily by moldboard plowing, threatens more than one third of working U.S. farmland.

Tim McCabe/Soil Conservation Service

Short of food, hundreds of deer in Florida's Everglades had to be slain in July to ensure the survival of the herd.

the pesticide DDT in the United States. It was banned because of its harmful environmental impact, including damaging effects on the reproductive system of birds. DDT poisoning was blamed for the alarming decrease in the population of several species, including the bald eagle, peregrine falcon, and brown pelican. Since the ban went into effect, all of these species have shown signs of recovery, in some cases rather dramatically.

Eagles are appearing in places from which they have been absent for many years. Several states—New Hampshire and Rhode Island, for instance—have initiated "eagle watch" programs to chart the progress of the birds within their borders.

Peregrines are also returning to many areas. The natural increase has been helped considerably by scientists who have reared birds in captivity from eggs obtained in the wild; the captive birds are released upon fledging. Peregrines have been reintroduced in both rural and urban areas. Several have been released in eastern cities such as New York and Baltimore. A female loosed in the latter community reared three young during the year.

Perhaps the most impressive comeback is by the brown pelican, whose population has increased by many thousand along the southeastern and Gulf coasts.

Poaching for Asia. Oriental folk medicine has long used various animal parts and products, ranging from snake venom to rhinoceros horn, for the treatment of ailments and as tonics. The demand for some of these materials has inspired poaching of wildlife in many parts of the world.

During 1982, conservationists expressed mounting fear that the poaching of animals for the Asian folk medicine market had spread to the western United States. The targets were bear and elk. The gall bladder of bears and the antlers of elk taken in the United States bring high prices in medicine shops in Far Eastern cities because both are considered aphrodisiacs.

White-Eye Invasion. California was alarmed during the summer by the realization that exotic birds called white-eyes, which may have escaped from the San Diego Zoo in the mid-1970s, had established themselves and were multiplying rapidly. White-eyes can be serious agricultural pests. They eat berries, buds, and fruit, as well as insects. One of the items on their diet has special significance in California: grapes. While there has been no significant damage yet, California authorities estimated that if the white-eyes become numerous they could cause as much as $2 million annually in agricultural losses. For this reason, state officials are attempting to eliminate the birds. White-eyes are great colonizers and once settled in a new area can become exceedingly numerous.

Wetlands Task Force. Co-chaired by Secretary of the Interior James Watt and outgoing Alabama Gov. Forrest James, a private-sector organization to save wetlands was established during the year. A major object of the group, Protect Our Wetlands and Duck Resources, is to encourage owners of wetlands to donate them to state agencies, conservation groups, or the U.S. Fish and Wildlife Service.

EDWARD R. RICCIUTI
Free-lance Environment Writer

The U.S. National Park System

America's cherished national parks—those repositories of the best and most inspiring of the nation's natural and cultural heritage—are in dire straits. The problems are complex; and they affect the most remote, isolated national parklands as well as those near large metropolitan centers. The fact is that Congress has been unable to draw a boundary around a tract of land, declare it a national park, and ensure that the area inside the boundary will remain unchanged and undamaged forever. National parks are not immune to the quest for new sources of energy, to the effects of widespread pollution, to political pressure, and to poor management decisions.

State of the Parks Report. "It is clear that events are taking place that are causing demonstrable and severe damage to the natural and the cultural resources of the nation's national parks, monuments, historic sites and other units," the National Park Service reported to Congress in May 1980 in a document entitled "The State of the Parks—1980." Examples of these damaging events abound:

—Off-road vehicles damage vegetation and wildlife habitat at many national seashores.

—Sewage disposal pollutes the water at Fire Island National Seashore, NY, and Chattahoochee River National Recreation Area, GA.

—Feral goats, burros, and pigs damage vegetation and compete for food and water with native species of animals in Hawaii Volcanoes National Park, Death Valley National Monument, and Great Smoky Mountains National Park.

—Massive energy developments threaten archaeological treasures in and surrounding Chaco Culture National Historical Park, NM.

—Remote Glacier National Park on the Canadian border in Montana is surrounded by threats to its resources, including the threatened grizzly bear and the endangered bald eagle. Threats include livestock trespass, poaching, housing development, logging, road building, oil and gas exploration, air pollution from a nearby aluminum plant, and air and water pollution from a proposed open-pit coal mine and power plant in Canada.

—Geothermal drilling threatens the world's largest hot water lake at Lassen Volcanic National Park, CA, and even the famous geysers and hot springs at Yellowstone National Park.

The water at Fire Island National Seashore, off the south shore of Long Island, NY, is being polluted by sewage. Off-road vehicles also ravage vegetation and wildlife habitats at many otherwise scenic national seashores.

Sam Falk

H. Thompson/Death Valley National Monument

The burro is one of several animals that damage vegetation and compete with native species at Death Valley National Monument, left, and other parklands. Gas exploration is one of a variety of development projects that threaten Glacier National Park in Montana, below.

Dewitt Jones

—Acid rain is damaging resources in at least 83 national parks and monuments.

—A huge open-pit strip mine operates within the borders of Death Valley National Monument, and more are proposed.

—Uprating the generators at Glen Canyon Dam to increase peak electrical power will further alter the natural regime of the Colorado River in Grand Canyon National Park.

—Coal strip mines, power plants, tar sands drilling, and a proposed nuclear waste dump threaten to bring air pollution and road and railroad construction to the remote slickrock national parks and monuments of southern Utah and could contaminate the Colorado River with radioactive wastes for thousands of years.

In fact, the threat to national parks may be even greater than known, because the National

Park Service lacks adequate baseline data regarding park resources, as well as the staff and funding to adequately monitor, research, and document the damage that is occurring.

Cultural Report. The 1980 "State of the Parks" report focused mainly on natural resources. In April 1982 the National Park Service released another report, "Threats to Cultural Resources." It, too, cited a long list of problems. As urbanization spreads, the report said, historical parks are becoming "islands of green in a sea of development." Consequent problems include overcrowding; use of park roads in some cases as traffic corridors; degradation of historical ambience; and increasing vandalism, including graffiti, damaged artifacts, and even arson. Although the National Park Service is responsible for more than 10 million historical artifacts—a collection second only to that of the Smithsonian Institution—only 10% of them have been cataloged. Buildings and collections are deteriorating because of insufficient professional staffing and funding to provide the necessary care.

Expansion. The tremendous popularity and growth of the National Park System have contributed to these problems. Recreational visits to the system increased from 165,700,000 in 1972 to 238,600,000 in 1981. The 95th Congress (1977–78) added 20 new units to the National Park System, and in 1980 Congress doubled its total area by adding 43.6 million acres (17.7 million ha) in Alaska. The staff and budget of the National Park Service, however, have not kept pace with the expansion of the system, the growth in visitation, or inflation. As the number of park units and visitors increases and buying power decreases, funds and staff have been spread ever thinner.

The Watt Controversy. Many of these problems are not new, but some of them have intensified since the Reagan administration took office. Secretary of the Interior James Watt advocates commercial and industrial development on public lands, and his policies affecting the national parks emphasize recreation rather than protection of park resources. His policies include proposals to promote hunting, trapping, and commercial fishing in the National Park System. Despite the findings of the "State of the Parks" report, conservationists point out that little action has been taken to mitigate the problems cited, or even to document those that are known but not scientifically proven. Watts' proposed operating budgets have drawn fire as not adequate to fund the interpretation and protection of the resources that the parks were established to preserve.

As a budget-cutting measure, Secretary Watt recommended early in 1981 that drastic cuts be made in land acquisition appropriations for the National Park Service from the Land and Water Conservation Fund. Congress had set up this fund in 1964 partly to purchase land for national parklands. This money is needed to acquire the backlog of lands already authorized by Congress for the National Park System but not yet acquired. The secretary further recommended that the fund be used for maintenance and construction of national park roads and facilities instead of for land acquisition. He also considered de-authorizing five National Park System units. Citizen and congressional opposition largely defeated the secretary's budget recommendations. Congress provided substantially more money for land acquisition than recommended, but less than needed.

Air Quality. According to the "State of the Parks" report, air quality is threatened in nearly half the units of the National Park System. The reauthorization of the Clean Air Act of 1977 was due to be completed by the 97th Congress (1982–83). Industry and the Reagan administration advocated significantly weakening the protection given national parks by this law. The outcome of congressional debate will have far-reaching effects on future air quality in national parks, especially in the West, where pristine air will be threatened by expanding coal mining and more coal-fired power plants.

Conclusion. The enabling legislation of the National Park System in 1916 clearly defined its mandate "to conserve the scenery and the natural and historic objects and the wild life therein and to provide for the enjoyment of the same in such manner and by such means as will leave them unimpaired for the enjoyment of future generations." It is becoming more difficult to carry out that mandate in the face of misplaced priorities, insufficient funds, political pressure, and increasing levels of global pollution. In order to meet its mandate, the National Park Service needs more support from the administration and from Congress. And, as the "State of the Parks" report admits, it also needs to reorder its own priorities and to reallocate staff and funds toward more research and resource protection.

Millions of American and foreign tourists will visit U.S. national parks each year and will find their visits immensely rewarding. Nevertheless, as the "State of the Parks" report concluded, "no parks of the System are immune to external and internal threats. . . . There is no question but that these threats will continue to degrade and destroy irreplaceable park resources until such time as mitigation measures are implemented. Often this degradation or loss of resources is irreversible. It represents a sacrifice by a public that, for the most part, is unaware that such a price is being paid."

EUGENIA HORSTMAN CONNALLY

ETHIOPIA

In 1982, Ethiopia intensified its military attacks against neighboring Somalia, initiated another offensive against Eritrean rebels, increased repression against religious minorities, and began stabilizing its foreign affairs.

War with Somalia and Eritrea. In early July, about 7,000 Ethiopian troops, in support of the Somali Democratic Salvation Front, invaded and occupied two Somali villages along the border east of the Ethiopian-controlled Ogaden desert. The Ethiopian air force bombed Somali troop positions in the frontier villages.

The Ethiopian attack was in response to continued Somali support for the Western Somali Liberation Front's attempt to wrest the Ogaden from Ethiopia. Sporadic fighting in the Ogaden had taken place throughout the early part of 1982, during which time 250 Ethiopian soldiers were reported killed. Somali President Siad Barre appealed to the United States to help "stop the naked aggression of Ethiopia's invading forces." In late July the United States announced that it was airlifting $5.5 million in military equipment to Somalia. One month later, Somalia declared a state of emergency along the Ethiopian border, and the intensity of the fighting diminished.

Beginning in February, Ethiopia opened its seventh full-scale offensive in an attempt to eradicate the Eritrean secessionist movement. The secessionists have continued to fare badly against Ethiopia, and their struggle for independence has been curtailed by military losses.

Domestic Repression. In August the United Nations Human Rights Commission cited Ethiopia as a major violator of human rights, claiming that "political disappearances," "terror," "abductions," and "body mutilations" were sanctioned by the government. Sweden and Norway maintained in early 1982 that the Ethiopian Evangelical Church had been seized by the government and that 600 Lutheran churches had been closed. At the same time the Canadian Association for Ethiopian Jews and the Los Angeles-based Simon Wiesenthal Center accused Ethiopia of arresting and torturing Ethiopian

UPI

Fighting between Ethiopia and Somalia over the disputed Ogaden territory continues. Above, Somalia forces position themselves near the Ethiopian border.

Jews (Falashas) and of engaging in a general campaign of anti-Semitism.

International Affairs. In late 1981, Ethiopia became a member of the East and Southern Africa Preferential Trade Area. In January 1982, Cuba announced plans to finance and construct a major cement factory in Ethiopia; and in February, Egypt and Ethiopia signed a $25 million trade agreement.

Early in 1982 the U.S. government announced that because of the stabilization of political conditions in Ethiopia, it was preparing to return to Ethiopia many of the Ethiopian refugees living in exile in the United States, estimated to number up to 30,000. Although the exiles reacted unfavorably, Ethiopia said that they would be welcome to return since they were needed to help in developing the country.

The New York Times reported in August that Ethiopia was considering offering land to the Palestine Liberation Organization, whose forces had been evacuated from Beirut, Lebanon, and maintained that the PLO might use the land as a base for reorganizing part of its army.

PETER SCHWAB
State University of New York at Purchase

ETHIOPIA · Information Highlights

Official Name: Ethiopia.
Location: Eastern Africa.
Area: 472,435 sq mi (1 223 607 km²).
Population (1982 est.): 30,500,000.
Chief Cities (1978 est.): Addis Ababa, the capital, 1,-125,340; Asmara 373,827; Dire Dawa, 72,202.
Government: *Head of state and government,* Mengistu Haile Mariam, chairman of the Provisional Military Administrative Committee (took office Feb. 1977).
Monetary Unit: Birr (2.07 birr equal U.S. $1, March 1982).
Gross National Product Per Capita (1980 U.S.$): $140.
Economic Index (1980): *Consumer Prices* (1970=100), *all items,* 247.3; *food,* 271.0.
Foreign Trade (1979 U.S.$): *Imports,* $567,000,000; *exports,* $418,000,000.

ETHNIC GROUPS

National Urban League's John Jacob (left) presented his views to many legislators, including Sen. D'Amato (R-NY).

Wide World

Perhaps the best news for ethnic and racial minority groups in the United States in 1982 was that their numbers were growing. Statistics released from the 1980 census, for example, showed that the United States was the seventh-largest Spanish-speaking country in the world. Continued immigration, legal and otherwise, from Latin America was certain to continue the trend. At the same time, newcomers from Southeast Asia established themselves as the fastest-growing ethnic group in the country, and a large group of refugees from Haiti created a legal snarl that severely tested U.S. immigration policy.

The Administration and Civil Rights. Off and on throughout the year, the Reagan administration was plagued by criticism that it was insensitive to the needs and concerns of minorities—criticism that the administration firmly rejected. The first incident occurred on January 8 when the administration announced the reversal of an 11-year-old policy withholding tax-exempt status from schools that discriminate on the basis of race. When the policy change provoked an outcry from those who said it would amount to a federal subsidy of discrimination, the administration relented. Instead, the president tried to persuade Congress to pass a law affirming the existing policy of denying tax exemptions to schools that discriminate.

Congress declined, but the issue was already headed for the U.S. Supreme Court. Bob Jones University in Greenville, SC, which did not admit blacks until 1975 and still prohibits interracial dating, and the Goldsboro Christian Schools of Goldsboro, NC, had sued the govern-

ment. The Christian fundamentalist schools held that their discriminatory policies were religiously ordained, and that the government's denial of tax-exempt status was a breach of freedom of religion. The court heard arguments in the case in the fall, but the sting of the administration's reversal remained. One White House aide at the time described it as "our biggest public-relations and political disaster yet." It was not the last.

In February, the administration suffered two more civil-rights embarrassments. First, Detroit businessman William Bell asked President Reagan to withdraw his name as a candidate to head the Equal Employment Opportunity Commission (EEOC). Bell was the owner of a small minority-recruiting firm that had failed to place any employees in a year. Since Bell did not seem to have the expertise or experience required to run a large federal agency charged with monitoring fair-hiring rules, critics saw his nomination as an attempt to undercut the effectiveness of the EEOC. (The post was later filled by Clarence Thomas.)

Soon afterward the president had to reconsider his nomination of the Rev. B. Sam Hart, a black Philadelphia evangelist and broadcaster, for a seat on the U.S. Civil Rights Commission. Hart drew criticism by saying that he opposed the Equal Rights Amendment and busing for racial integration, and that homosexuality was not a civil rights issue. Republican Sen. John Heinz of Pennsylvania summarized the concern over Hart when he said the nominee was not "an advocate for civil rights as most people understand the term." Hart's name was withdrawn.

In September, 33 state advisers to the U.S. Civil Rights Commission accused the president of presiding over a "dangerous deterioration in federal enforcement of civil rights." And the Washington Council of Lawyers issued a report that found the Justice Department wanting in its pursuit of open-housing cases. A regular target of such complaints was William Bradford Reynolds, chief of the civil rights division of the Justice Department. Reynolds opposed court-ordered busing, affirmative-action hiring quotas, and a tougher extension of the Voting Rights Act of 1965. (The Voting Rights Act extension was eventually approved, with the endorsement of President Reagan.)

The president responded to his critics on September 15 in a speech before the National Black Republican Council in Washington. He declared that President Lyndon Johnson's Great Society program had been "tragic" for blacks and said that any suggestion that his administration did not vigorously support civil rights was "just plain baloney."

The 1982 Elections. By November, the Republican Party was justifiably concerned about the minority vote. The unemployment rate had topped 10% for the first time in 40 years (black unemployment had passed 17% nine months earlier), helping to reunite President Franklin Roosevelt's Democratic coalition of blue-collar workers and ethnic minorities. The voter turnout was the highest in an off-year election in 20 years, largely because of an energetic black vote. The biggest increase was in the South, where black voters ironically swept onetime segregationist George Wallace to his fourth term as governor of Alabama. They were also credited with helping Mark White win an upset victory in the Texas gubernatorial race. The black vote also cushioned Mario Cuomo's narrow gubernatorial victory in New York and nearly carried Adlai Stevenson III to an upset in Illinois.

Black voters could not carry Los Angeles Mayor Tom Bradley in his unsuccessful California bid to become the nation's first elected black governor, or send Robert Clark to Washington as Mississippi's first black congressman in 100 years. Still, the Congressional Black Caucus reaped a net gain of three seats as representatives from Brooklyn, NY, Kansas City, MO, and Gary, IN, raised black membership in Congress to a modern high of 21.

Immigration. Of the nearly 6,000 Haitian refugees who had fled poverty and political repression at home to seek asylum in the United States, 1,800 were interned in 14 detention camps in seven states and Puerto Rico. They were there because of a tough new policy (begun under the Reagan administration) of incarcerating the Haitians, whose legal status as refugees was questioned, until their cases could be decided individually. Previously they had been released on parole until their immigration hearings were held.

In June a federal judge ordered their release because, he said, the government had violated its own immigration procedures by detaining the Haitians without prior public notice. Angry government officials unsuccessfully sought a stay of the release order, then issued new regulations spelling out the government's intent to jail any illegal immigrant except pregnant women, children, those with medical problems, or those who had relatives in the country who could vouch for them.

In July the first 17 Haitians were released from Miami's Krome Avenue detention camp, an abandoned military base. Others followed slowly, mostly from the Miami camp. In the meantime, 50 Haitians in a Brooklyn, NY, detention center had been detached from the Miami groups because of overcrowding and then pursued a separate lawsuit to gain their release. They lost, and were not included in the ruling that freed the others. The released Haitians were scheduled to show up for immigration hearings 30 days later. About one third of them failed to appear. Of those who returned, only one was granted asylum in the first round of hearings. Others appealed, indicating that a final resolution of the situation would be a long time coming.

In June the U.S. Supreme Court declared unconstitutional a 1975 Texas law that allowed school districts to bar illegal-alien children from public schools or charge them tuition. A group of parents, with the help of the Mexican American Legal Defense and Educational Fund, challenged the law in Tyler, TX, in 1977. The Carter administration had supported the parents, and the Reagan administration took an officially neutral posture. Nevertheless the Supreme Court ruled that the state could not deprive the children of free public education, even though they were in the country illegally. The ruling, it was felt, would probably not become a basis for extending other privileges, such as food stamps, to illegal-alien adults.

The Census. Numbers compiled from the demographic snapshot of the United States taken on April 1, 1980, showed a continuation of recent trends in the population. The percentage of Hispanic Americans increased from 4.5 in 1970 to 6.4 (14.6 million) in 1980. The number of U.S. Mexicans almost doubled. More than 6% of the national population was foreign-born (the first increase since 1920), and one person in ten spoke a language other than English at home.

One California study projected that by the year 2000, non-Hispanic white Americans (86% of the population in 1970, and 80% in 1980) would decline to 75%. At the same time, Hispanics would increase by 58% to 23 million, and Asians would increase by 90% to 10.6 million. Clearly, the melting pot was continuing to bubble.

See also BIOGRAPHY—Jacob, John.

DENNIS A. WILLIAMS, *"Newsweek"*

EUROPE

In the year that marked the 25th anniversary of the European Community (EC), deepening economic recession had far-reaching political consequences across the continent. It foiled the efforts of recently elected governments, like that of President François Mitterrand in France, to engage in fundamental reform; it caused the defeat of long-standing governments, like that of Chancellor Helmut Schmidt in West Germany; and it brought into power governments promising radical change, like that of Olof Palme in Sweden and Felipe González in Spain. Repression in Poland dispelled the hope that Communist regimes in Eastern Europe might be willing to liberalize from within, made relations between the Western alliance and the Soviet bloc more tense, and provoked dissension among the Western powers over what steps should be taken to influence events in Poland. And finally, terrorism throughout Western Europe remained a scourge.

Economic Problems. The cost of oil imports continued to hold back economic recovery, especially in the poorer countries of southern Europe. Although prices declined, the European powers were compelled to pay in U.S. dollars when their own currencies had slumped in relation to the dollar. When European governments attempted to compete with high U.S. interest rates, which were stimulating European investment in the United States, they dampened industrial spending and created unemployment, which reached almost 10% for Western Europe as a whole. Even West Germany, whose purchases had often acted as a stimulant to other EC economies, saw its gross national product decline and its unemployment reach 7.5%. Italy, which showed a small increase in real growth, suffered 16% inflation.

Government policies prolonged the recession. Nationalization of private banks and several large industrial companies frightened French business, provoking a 10% devaluation of the franc in relation to the German mark. The cost to Britain of fighting the Falklands war was high. Not only did it lose 255 lives and several warships, but the financial cost disrupted an already flagging economy. In the aftermath of victory, Britain faced expenses of more than $4,000,000,000 annually to garrison the islands. The international monetary situation did stabilize somewhat after the leaders of seven major non-Communist powers (Britain, Canada, France, Italy, Japan, United States, and West Germany) decided at their June summit conference in Versailles, France, to intervene more often to prevent disparities in their currency values. The leaders also considered the dangers to their own economies of the large loans made to the Communist bloc, including $15,000,000,000 to Poland alone, but decided only to increase interest rates charged to the USSR and more prosperous Communist states.

Political Instability. Victory in the Falklands restored the popularity of the Conservative government of British Prime Minister Margaret Thatcher and defused the challenge of the new Social Democratic Party. Elsewhere, however, there was a revulsion against governments in power. In France, President Mitterrand had enjoyed public support for his reform programs in the months following his election in May 1981. But support for the Socialists waned throughout 1982, as the economy slumped, unemployment rose, and Mitterrand was forced to cut back on his proposals for greater government spending.

U.S. efforts to halt construction of a gas pipeline from Siberia to Western Europe troubled European leaders.

Leaders and ministers from the 10 EC nations met for two days in Brussels in late March. The summit produced several foreign policy agreements but avoided major economic issues, such as farm prices and budget restructuring.

In Italy, radical Prime Minister Giovanni Spadolini fell from power in August, when his Socialist allies refused to support a new austerity program; he was reappointed 17 days later, only to resign again in November. Perhaps the most dramatic repudiation of an entrenched leader occurred in West Germany in October. After eight years as chancellor, Socialist Helmut Schmidt was voted out of office upon the defection of his coalition partners, the Free Democrats. Schmidt has been under attack from the Left—young members of his own party and the increasingly popular antinuclear and environmental groups. The Free Democrats objected to his plan to increase social security payments and raise taxes to pay for job programs. The Christian Democrats, in alliance with the Free Democrats, named Helmut Kohl as chancellor.

Elsewhere, however, discontent was a boon to Socialists. Andreas Papandreou, leader of the Panhellenic Socialist Movement in Greece, increased his popularity by threatening to withdraw Greece from NATO and by forcing the EC to make greater concessions to Greek farmers. In Sweden in September, fears of unemployment and a reduction in welfare benefits triggered the victory of Socialist Olof Palme over incumbent Prime Minister Thorbjörn Fälldin. And in Spain, voters elected the first leftist government since the pre-Franco era. Still, there was little sign that the West Europeans were turning to the Communist parties, and the French and Italian Communist leaders found it necessary to disassociate themselves from the repression in Poland.

In no European country was political disillusionment more evident than in Poland. After a heady 18 months in which the Poles had come to believe that they could democratize their society on the foundation of free trade unions, Gen. Wojciech Jaruzelski, premier and Communist Party secretary, imposed martial law in December 1981. Hundreds of members of Solidarity, the principal trade union, were interned, but resistance to the regime continued in 1982 in the form of demonstrations, underground newspapers, and unwillingness to work.

U.S.-West European Disagreements. Attempts by the U.S. government to pressure the Soviet regime into a more conciliatory attitude toward Poland backfired. President Reagan attempted to prevent the construction of a natural gas pipeline from Siberia to Western Europe by forbidding European subsidiaries of American companies to provide equipment. West European governments reacted angrily, continuing to allow the supply of equipment and credits to the USSR, and Reagan lifted the sanctions in mid-November. However, at the Conference on Security and Cooperation in Europe, held in Madrid in February, West European governments did condemn the imposition of martial law in Poland; they also strongly endorsed the opening in July of new U.S.-Soviet talks in Geneva on reduction of strategic nuclear weapons.

Terrorism. Paris remained the city in which terrorists seemed most brazen. Assassination attempts were carried out there against U.S. and Iraqi diplomats, and a vicious series of attacks were made against the Jewish community during the summer. In Italy, considerable progress was made in uncovering the organization of the Red Brigade after the freeing of kidnapped U.S. Gen. James L. Dozier in January. But the Sicilian Mafia killed the general responsible for much of that progress when he was sent to Palermo to launch a new investigation of organized crime. London was shocked in July at two bomb attacks by the Irish Republican Army (IRA) against the royal cavalry and a military band.

F. ROY WILLIS
University of California, Davis

FASHION

The word that best described fashion in 1982 was lean. The shape was linear, elongated, and narrow; the look was clean, uncomplicated, and uncluttered. All of this was in sharp contrast to the billowing fullness, the layers, ruffles, and garish ornamentation that characterized the ethnic and costume approach to fashion in the previous year. The trend toward simplification was named "Minimalism" and was hailed as pure design that was truly aristocratic and elegant.

Part of the inspiration for this return to understatement was the impact of the television adaptation of *Brideshead Revisited,* a novel by Evelyn Waugh that charted the life of an aristocratic English family in the years between World Wars I and II. The costumes of the women in the production were typical of the period—languid and unadorned, unconfining yet sensual, the epitome of the emerging emancipated woman. For today's emancipated women, staging their own rebellion against impractical and expensive fashion, the look was appealing, and for designers, already bored with their excesses, this simplicity was a refreshing inspiration.

The Minimalists. Just as in the 1920s when such breakthrough designers as Chanel and Patou were instrumental in changing the direction of fashion, in the 1980s there were the champions of minimalism—Norma Kamali, Zoran, and Rolandus Shamask. Working in basic colors, their designs were equally spare and functional, yet each had a distinct personality and approach.

Norma Kamali's inspiration was the locker room with its fabrics and styles calculated for ease of movement and comfort. Actionwear such as jogging outfits, baseball jerseys and jackets, and dancer's practice clothes were the launching pad for her youthful pants, tops, and short, flippy skirts of jersey or sweatshirting fabric.

Zoran, on the other hand, created a wardrobe of buttonless, zipperless, sometimes seamless basics in cashmere or cotton knit that mixed, matched, or layered to become as individual as the wearer. His spare, stripped-down tank tops, T-shirt dresses, slim skirts, lanky cardigans, and easy pants were effortless chic at its best.

Rolandus Shamask was the fashion architect. His intricate and ingenious cut and seaming created sharply geometric shapes that were works of art as well as very functional clothes.

The Apparel. The year's shape was streamlined—slim and straight as a column. Suits, favored for day and evening, were prime examples of the long, lean look, with tunic-length jackets topping narrow skirts. Coat styles were slim reefers, coachman types cut with military precision, or tapered wrap coats. The body-skimming chemise in challis, crepe, or jersey dominated the dress market, but the sweater dress was a close second.

© P. Vauthey/Sygma

In fashion, it was the year of the streamlined dress.

For evening, it was black tie, and the tuxedo was the ensemble for women as well as for men. Black wool and velvet suits with blazers or cutaway jackets featured satin lapels; others were styled as smoking jackets to be worn with trousers. To complete the look, there were white blouses with wing collars and the pleated fronts or tucked bibs typical of men's dress shirts.

Attempts to revive the dying jeans business included the promotion of black as the "new" jeans color and the introduction of stone-washed and overdyed jeans. The denim was stone washed to fade and soften, then overdyed in vivid colors.

Fabric and Color. Fabrics in natural fibers were still preferred by most designers, and tweeds, flannels, gabardines, and linen were prominent in daytime suits. Jersey, challis, crepe, and sweater knits were the popular choices in the dress market; while traditional poplin, chino, seersucker, and madras were reserved for classic sportswear. For formal evening attire, designers relied on velvet, moiré, satin, faille, and matte jersey for their tuxedo interpretations or their sheath dresses, draped in the Greek manner.

Color palettes were specific by market. Black, gray, beige, and taupe tones dominated the coat and suit scene, while grayed or heathered pastels saturated the dress market. Black was the only significant color for evening.

Courtesy, Ralph Lauren

The blazer ''Tuxedo Look'' was a must for evening.

The long slim coat was cut with military precision.

Courtesy, Ralph Lauren

Bright colors such as scarlet, chrome yellow, turquoise, and jade were featured only as accents. There were, however, vivid colors used in sportswear and active wear, and these often were combined to form vibrant color blocks on sweaters and casual tops.

Prints, which had been such an important and colorful part of fashion in past years, were virtually nonexistent. Patterns were mainly stripes or traditional plaids, and the few prints that were to be seen were geometrics or abstract motifs. Another notable absence was the metallic look. Except in jewelry, the gold rush was over.

Accessories. In accessories, gloves were the number one design accent and the most colorful. Leather or knit gauntlets in red, yellow, blue, or green set off the sedately colored fashions on European designers' runways. Some were fancifully feathered, beaded, studded, or embroidered.

While the boldest and wittiest accessory was the glove, the finishing touch was the hat. A cloche, tricorn, or fedora was the necessary topping for the long, lean line.

The most popular accessories at all price levels were those that were part of the "Tuxedo Look." Cummerbunds, pocket handkerchiefs, bow ties in black or brightly colored silk, and vests of brocade or moiré transformed any sensible black suit into proper evening attire. Studs, stickpins, and cuff links perfected the look.

Crystal and jet were the jewelry materials in vogue, and the important shapes were geometric or Art Deco inspired. Ropes of pearls, long gold chains mixed with gemstones, or dramatic pins set off the simpler styles.

Shoes remained flat or low-heeled, often with shaped or molded wedge bottoms. T-straps, ghillies, and kilted oxfords provided the daytime looks, as did classic pumps done in lush suede and highly polished nappa leather. For evening, there was the tuxedo flat in moiré or satin or the basic pump, ornamented with a cockade or clip. Casual shoes were styled as ballet slippers, jazz oxfords, or athletic footwear but were done in brightly colored leathers and brushed pigskin, and in poplin, chintz, and corduroy.

The classic wafer-heeled riding boot in polished calf was still a favorite, but perhaps due to 1981's hard winter, consumers looked for something more practical. Best sellers were the rain- and snow-repellant footwear made of "Gore-tex," treated nylon fabric.

Menswear. Menswear in 1982 strongly reflected the "Brideshead" influence. The polished elegance and sophisticated coordination of the fashions had the subtle touches of Savile Row. Whether done in gentry tweeds, flannels, or corduroy, the fashions were a blend of fine tailoring, quality fabrics, and ease of fit that made for maximum masculine enhancement. Navy blue and gray flannel were suitable for the boardroom, while glen plaids and pinstripes were flattering to the confident executive. District checks, tweedy herringbones, corduroys, and flannels in brown, rust, and olive tones served as well for the office as for country weekends.

The four- or six-button double-breasted look was strong in business suits, casual sports jackets, and vests. Lapels were high and peaked, shoulders were natural, and the fit was easy. Trousers had single or double pleats at the waist but were lightly tapered to the ankle, and vests were often an integral part of the suit or the important accessory.

Dress shirts had button-down, tab, or contrasting colored collars in plain oxford cloth or finely striped cotton broadcloth. The tie was understated in classic pencil stripes, club motifs, or foulard prints on dark silk or challis. Casual shirts were bolder in colorful checks, plaids, or wide stripes and were worn with solid-colored knit ties or under classic Shetland pullover sweaters.

For evening, it was traditional black and white. The tuxedo took over after dark, complete with starched shirt with wing collar and tucked bib, a satin cummerbund, studs, and cuff links.

Shoes had the same polish as the clothes. For business, wingtips and slip-ons in smooth calfskin properly complemented the impeccably tailored suit. For the country, there were grainy leather brogues, rubber-soled suede or leather oxfords, or the traditional riding boot. Jewelry was kept to the minimum—watch, tie bar or collar pin, and cuff links. The hat, for those who could wear it, was the bowler.

The business of fashion was as lean as the silhouette. Even the so-called recession-proof affluent minority that had heavily supported fashion seemed to have rearranged its priorities and was not buying. Retailers and manufacturers were forced to cut back, close unprofitable divisions or stores, edit lines, and generally trim operations. With selective buying becoming a way of life, they wooed their customers with special sales, catalogs, private label merchandise, and other promotions.

ANN ELKINS, *"Good Housekeeping Magazine"*

The double-breasted sports jacket and double-pleated slacks were part of the "in" look in 1982 menswear.

Courtesy, Calvin Klein

FINLAND

A number of candidates, representing the entire spectrum of Finnish politics, campaigned in late 1981 and early January 1982 for the post relinquished by ailing 81-year-old President Urho K. Kekkonen on Oct. 27, 1981. Mauno Koivisto, who as prime minister had succeeded to the office of acting president, was nominated for the presidency by his Social Democratic Party, but he faced strong opposition from the nonsocialist parties and more specifically from Johannes Virolainen of the Center Party. According to the constitution, the election of an electoral college is the first step in the selection of a president, and the nationwide election of January 18 gave 145 votes, a sizable plurality, to Mauno Koivisto. The closest contenders, Harri Holkeri and Johannes Virolainen, had 58 and 53 backers, respectively, in the 301-seat electoral college. On January 26, the electors gave the former prime minister a total of 167 votes, with only 151 needed for election.

In his inaugural speech of January 27, Koivisto, Finland's first left-wing president, said that he would remain aloof from all parties and act in the interest of the entire nation. He also stated that he would continue the foreign policy line laid out by former presidents Juho Kusti Paasikivi and Kekkonen. The cabinet, according to custom, resigned at the time of the president's accession.

On February 17, a new cabinet, with Social Democratic leader Kalevi Sorsa as prime minister, took office. The coalition cabinet was made up of members of the Social Democratic Party, the Center Party, the Swedish People's Party, and the Finnish People's Democratic League, in addition to one no-party minister. Pär Stenbäck of the Swedish People's Party headed the foreign ministry. Earlier, Johannes Virolainen had been reelected as speaker of parliament.

President Koivisto in March traveled to the Soviet Union and conferred with President Leonid Brezhnev. In September the president made an unofficial visit to Hungary.

The Economy. As one step in the fight against inflation, unemployment, and trade deficits, interest rates were reduced by 0.75% in May. However, the highest lending rate of the banks was to remain at 12.5%. In October, the government devalued its currency by 4%, imposed a price freeze until mid-December 1982, and altered some tax schedules.

Anniversaries. On May 25 the Finnish parliament (Eduskunta) marked its 75th anniversary. Important dignitaries from the other Scandinavian countries, as well as the Soviet Union, took part in various festivities. In their speeches, both President Koivisto and the speaker of parliament broached the subjects of parliamentarism and a possible revision of the constitution. The Finnish Trade Union Confederation also marked its 75th anniversary.

UPI

Kalevi Sorsa, 51-year-old chairman of Finland's Social Democrats, returned as prime minister in February.

Nordic Council. The Nordic Council met for its 30th annual session in Helsinki in March. Among the achievements of the session were the renewal of an agreement on Nordic labor markets and the continued cooperation on a prospective Nordic television satellite. The Nordic Council of Ministers also decided that a new Nordic Institute for further education in public health would be established in Helsinki.

Culture. Finnish representation in "Scandinavia Today," an American celebration of Scandinavian culture, included performances by the Tapiola Choir and an exhibition of the paintings of Akseli Gallen-Kallela.

ERIK J. FRIIS
Editor
"The Scandinavian-American Bulletin"

FINLAND · Information Highlights

Official Name: Republic of Finland.
Location: Northern Europe.
Area: 130,129 sq mi (337 034 km²).
Population (1982 est.): 4,800,000.
Chief City (1980 est.): Helsinki, the capital, 484,014.
Government: *Head of state,* Mauno Koivisto, president (took office Jan. 27, 1982). *Head of government,* Kalevi Sorsa, prime minister (took office Feb. 17, 1982). *Legislature* (unicameral)—Eduskunta.
Monetary Unit: Markka (5.10 markkaa equal U.S.$1, Oct. 8, 1982).
Gross National Product (1981 U.S.$): $712 million.
Economic Indexes (1981): *Consumer Prices* (1970=100), *all items,* 327.6; *food,* 339.4. *Industrial production* (1975=100), 129.
Foreign Trade (1981 U.S.$): *Imports,* $14,201,000,-000; *exports,* $14,015,000,000.

FLORIDA

© Karen Borchers/Picture Group

A federal judge ordered the release of 1,900 Haitians from a detention camp near Miami.

The major events of 1982 in Florida were concerned with the elections, congressional reapportionment, economic difficulties, and continuing problems with crime and the environment. Year-end rioting broke out in Miami's Overtown neighborhood following the shooting of two youths by policemen.

Elections. The Democratic Party continued its domination of the Florida political scene as U.S. Sen. Lawton Chiles and Gov. Bob Graham, both Democrats, defeated their Republican opponents by almost a 2-to-1 margin. Despite the endorsements of such top national Republicans as President Ronald Reagan and Sen. Jack Kemp, State Sen. Van Poole, who challenged Chiles, and gubernatorial candidate Congressman L.A. "Skip" Bafalis failed to win voter support. Unlike the national trend, however, Republicans retained all the congressional seats they formerly held, including the one vacated by Bafalis. In addition, Republicans won two of the four new seats Florida gained as a result of population growth in the 1980 census.

The congressional victories proved to be the GOP's only cause for celebration, however, because Republicans lost many seats in the Florida legislature. The number of Republican senators dropped from 13 to 8, and the number of GOP House members was reduced from 40 to 36. Although the Republicans now hold only 20% of the seats in the Senate, they have formed a coalition with conservative Democrats and, as a result, they chair several committees.

Reapportionment. The always controversial process of reapportionment, necessitated by the 1980 census, was undertaken by the Democrat-controlled legislature amid threats of court challenges from various groups if the results appeared unfair to minorities and the Republican Party. The results were acceptable to the courts.

The most controversial change was the surprising decision to go from multimember districts for the legislature to single-member districts. Supporters who advocated the change in order to increase representation by blacks were apparently vindicated by the 1982 elections, which increased black legislators from 5 to 12.

Legislature. Florida's legislature rejected the Equal Rights Amendment and was bitterly divided over issues of taxation, reapportionment, and crime-fighting strategy. It enacted Florida's first major tax increase in more than a decade by increasing the sales tax from 4% to 5%. One half of the anticipated annual revenue of $770 million will be distributed to cities and counties according to a complex formula, to compensate them for revenue lost when the homestead exemption was increased from $5,000 to $25,000 in 1980. The remaining new revenue was used to increase significantly teachers' salaries; to employ new highway patrolmen, prosecutors, and judges to aid in the war on crime; and to expand overcrowded prisons.

Economy. Florida's unemployment rate in October was 8.7% when the national rate was 10.4%, indicating that the state's economy remained relatively strong, even though people were moving into the state faster than the job market could absorb them.

The phosphate industry, hit hard by high interest rates and declining fertilizer sales, made massive layoffs, resulting in double-digit unemployment in Polk County and other areas.

The overall strength of the economy is due to new industry moving to Florida and a relatively strong tourism rate, due in large measure to the opening in October of the spectacular Epcot Center at Disney World (*see* page 74).

J. LARRY DURRENCE, *Florida Southern College*

FLORIDA • Information Highlights

Area: 58,664 sq mi (151 940 km²).
Population (1980 census): 9,746,342.
Chief Cities (1980 census): Tallahassee, the capital, 81,548; Jacksonville, 540,898; Miami, 346,931; Tampa, 271,523; St. Petersburg, 236,893.
Government (1982): *Chief Officers*—governor, Bob Graham (D); lt. gov., Wayne Mixson (D). *Legislature*—Senate, 40 members; House of Representatives, 120 members.
State Finances (Fiscal year 1981): *Revenues,* $9,029,-000,000; *expenditures,* $8,274,000,000.
Personal Income (1981): $103,502,000,000; per capita, $10,165.
Labor Force (Aug. 1982): *Nonagricultural wage and salary earners,* 3,698,500; *unemployed,* 378,700 (7.8% of total force).
Education: *Enrollment* (fall 1981)—public elementary schools, 1,035,323; public secondary, 452,398; colleges and universities (1981–82), 426,570. *Public school expenditures* (1980–81), $3,460,-021,000 ($2,262 per pupil).

FOOD

In 1982, the key word in describing the world's food supply was uncertainty—uncertainty in the role of inflation, in the effects of slow or lowered economic growth on purchasing power, in overall harvest yields, and in the ability of countries to ensure an adequate diet for their citizens.

Food and energy remained two of the most important needs of the world's population. International turmoil in the Middle East, Poland, and other areas intensified the problem of providing these commodities to many dislocated or deprived people. While the supply of petroleum remained relatively stable throughout the world, inflation decreased its availability to those who depend upon it for the transportation and preparation of food.

World Food Supply. While natural factors such as droughts and floods affected crop yields, total food supply in 1982 was expected to be greater than in the past several years. However, problems of distribution, politics, and weather created isolated shortages of food. Out of a world population of approximately 4,585,000,000, some 400–500 million people were classified by the UN Food and Agriculture Organization (FAO) as malnourished or severely malnourished.

While parts of Africa reportedly were low in nutrients or food supplies, growing conditions in all but the southern part seemed to have improved. The FAO reported a drop in countries reporting abnormal food shortages, from 22 in 1981 to 15 in 1982. Further, unfavorable crop conditions were reported by only five countries, lending hope for a better 1982 crop year. In Australia, drought conditions in the eastern wheat area delayed or reduced plantings, decreasing overall crop estimates.

In the Far East, excessive monsoon rains—or lack of them—created varying problems. In areas of China and India, paddy and summer cereal crops were heavily affected by flooding, while growing areas in Bangladesh, Burma, the Philippines, and Vietnam benefited from normal precipitation. In Latin America, coarse grain harvesting proceeded in Argentina, Brazil, and Mexico, while other countries in the region suffered from the effects of natural disasters.

In both Eastern and Western Europe, crop prospects appeared to be good with the exception of Poland, Italy, and Czechoslovakia, where dry conditions lowered crop estimates. In the USSR, dry weather in May affected the outlook for winter and spring grain crops in the key grain areas of the southern Ukraine and northern Caucasus. In July, rain aided spring grains but delayed harvesting of the winter grain crops. Drought affected oilseed crops in the eastern USSR. Overall, 1982 production was expected to be some 50 million metric tons or t (55 million short tons or T) below the projected target of 238 million t (262 million T).

Because of its reduced grain production, the USSR continued to make outside purchases from the United States and Canada. During the summer, the Soviet Union agreed to a year's extension of the grain purchase agreement with the United States. It also agreed to a five-year, 25 million-t (27.5 million-T) grain deal with Canada, further indicating grain shortages in the USSR. In other foods, reports indicated shortages in potatoes and meat, leading experts to speculate that the USSR would continue to import needed supplies to offset lowered crop yields.

Worldwide, it appeared that supplies of wheat, coarse-grass, and rice would be close to 1981 production levels. It was expected that this level would be sufficient to meet world import demands.

U.S. Food Production and Supply. In the United States, food and feed production forecasts for corn, wheat, soybeans, and meat indicated a bumper year. Only rice and eggs were forecast to be less than 1981 production levels. The 1982 corn crop was expected to produce a record 211 million t (233 million T), or 1% more than 1981.

With the economy lagging and world food supplies uncertain, three U.S. Congressmen decry waste. The goods before them were recovered from supermarket dumpsters.

UPI

Further, per-acre yield was up by 4 bushels over 1981's records. In all, a record U.S. feed grain crop of some 252 million t (278 million T) was expected. These record crops also meant a possible record carry-over of feed grain stocks in the amount of 88 million t (97 million T), despite hopes for expanded domestic use and improved exports.

In wheat, harvest figures indicated a 1% drop below 1981's record production, but with a record yield of 35.1 bushels per acre. With the expected 1982 harvest of 75.4 million t (83 million T), carry-over stocks were expected to rise 15% to 35.8 million t (39 million T). The U.S. crop, when combined with other world wheat production, was expected to stabilize prices into 1983. While rice production was predicted to be some 16% below 1981 levels, carry-over stocks remained high. In soybeans, the record U.S. crop was forecast at some 62 million t (68 million T), marking the second consecutive year in which the crop increased by 6 million t (6.6 million T) or more. As a result, world stocks of soybeans were expected to be of record size.

Pork and turkey production declined in 1982, while beef remained even, and chicken rose slightly. While prices varied, there were indications that the public was changing its consumption habits. Some reports showed that beef had lost favor in the consumer's view, while chicken and pork had increased. Reasons for such changes are associated with cost, health awareness, and changing tastes.

The U.S. Food Industry. The U.S. food industry, like other industries, has been buffeted by inflation, weather, energy costs, and selective consumer buying. Additionally, the industry was changed in 1982 by mergers (Heublein was purchased by R.J. Reynolds and Libby by California Canners and Growers), and by the introduction of new products and lines. In 1982, consumer concern over excess salt consumption affected the food industry. Both the U.S. Food and Drug Administration (FDA) and the Food Safety and Inspection Service of the U.S. Department of Agriculture (USDA), while not ordering sodium labeling, have defined sodium terms. Under FDA guidelines food with nutrition labeling would be required to include sodium content. Chemically, salt or sodium chloride is 40% sodium; 2000 milligrams of sodium are contained in a teaspoon of salt. The regulatory definitions per serving are: sodium free (5 mg or less), low sodium (35 mg or less), moderately low sodium (140 mg or less), and reduced sodium (specially processed foods). In addition to salt, other common ingredients can increase sodium levels when added to food for flavor, curing, or preservation. The consumer interest in sodium has spawned such products as low-sodium soups and canned or frozen vegetables that have no salt added.

In another health-related area, aspartame, a low-calorie sweetener, will reenter the market-place. Now approved by the FDA, it will be marketed under controlled conditions by different companies to specified markets, and will compete with saccharin, the only other approved low-calorie sweetener. Within the same caloric field, "starch blockers" were banned by the FDA after reports of user reactions. Some 200 firms were ordered to stop selling the pills, which are made from kidney bean extract. The marketers of the pills claimed that a chemical in the beans slowed starch digestion, allowing consumers to lose weight while continuing to eat starchy foods. The FDA planned to continue its ban until more was known about the effects and mode of action of the pills. In a different approach to aid the calorie-conscious, "lite" or reduced-calorie foods and beverages appeared with greater frequency in the marketplace. The drop in calories was achieved through substitution (for example, saccharin or aspartame for sugar), reformulation (reduction of fat and starch levels), and reduction (for example, lower alcoholic content).

Food Safety. A suspected outbreak of botulism (an illness caused by toxin produced by the bacteria *Clostridium botulinum* and associated with low-acid foods) created havoc in the American canned salmon industry. A suspected illness in Connecticut and a death in Belgium resulted in the second-largest canned food recall in U.S. history. The recall uncovered only some 30 defective cans out of 55 million.

Nutrition. Rising food prices and increased living costs in 1982 forced many Americans to search for alternate food sources or monetary assistance. On Oct. 1, 1982, the start of fiscal 1983, U.S. food stamp recipients received an average 8% increase in benefits, the first adjustment since January 1981. However, an overall reduction in U.S. food programs was planned, leaving some low-income groups in precarious nutritional and financial positions. As always, misfortune engenders profits—profiteering in food stamps appeared to be growing. Some 22 million Americans received more than $11,000,000,000 in food stamps in 1982. While most are properly used, a black market has developed whereby food stamps can be exchanged for a variety of goods or services. Such acts, combined with regulatory actions, have a negative effect on the programs and on those who are dependent on them. Proponents of the cutbacks stated that the programs being reduced or closely monitored would have little or no effect on those who need them most.

Many consumers began to explore new ways of reducing food costs. Whether growing their own, picking their own, buying direct from the farmer or at farmer's markets, or forming cooperatives, Americans are attempting to reduce or eliminate the cost of the middleman in the food distribution process. For others, food coupons or bartering help save money.

See also AGRICULTURE.

KIRBY M. HAYES
University of Massachusetts

FOOD/SPECIAL REPORT

Light Foods

Catering to an increasingly weight-conscious consumer, the American food and beverage industry has served up a whole new menu of products which provide alternatives to the conventional diet fare of celery, carrots, and skim milk. "Light" or "lite" foods, as they are called, generally contain about one-third less calories than their full-bodied counterparts and, the industry claims, with no loss of taste. While a variety of low-cal foods have appeared in recent years, supermarket shelves in 1982 seemed to have new and surprising items almost every week. Light spaghetti, light pancake mix, light frozen dinners, and even light snack foods were among the choices. Following the success of diet soft drinks and light beer, wine makers also decided to get into the act. By one account, light foods and beverages accounted for nearly 10% of the nation's $300,000,000,-000 grocery bill in 1982.

Courtesy, K Graphic Design Co.

Courtesy, The Stouffer Corporation

For the weight conscious, pasta has been a "no-no." According to the manufacturers, properly cooked light spaghetti and elbows contain one-third fewer calories. The Lean Cuisine line includes a lasagna that substitutes zucchini for meat. To cure the thirst, there are diet sodas. For the social pause, there is even a "light" wine.

Courtesy, Paul Masson Vineyards

FRANCE

Habans/Sygma

Anti-Semitic terrorism reached a peak with the August attack on a Jewish restaurant in Paris, killing 6.

The Left, which had come to power in 1981, began to learn the harsh realities of French government in 1982. After the initial enthusiasm raised by political changes and social reforms, President François Mitterrand and his Socialist government had to face serious economic difficulties and severe criticism of their often-wavering policies. They were also confronted by an unprecedented wave of terrorism connected with the international situation and the Mideast in particular.

Domestic Affairs

In spite of a decree on January 13 giving all salaried workers a 39-hour workweek and a fifth week of paid vacation, the prevailing impression at the beginning of 1982 was that President Mitterrand's "state of grace" had definitely ended. The cabinet suffered two serious disappointments in a matter of days in mid-January. The first came on January 16, when the Constitutional Council rejected, on several counts, the draft bill on industrial nationalization; the cabinet was forced to revise its text and give more favorable compensation to company shareholders. The second disappointment came on January 17, when opposition candidates won four separate legislative by-elections.

Another test came two months later in district-level, or cantonal, elections. A restructuring of the districts by Interior Minister Gaston Defferre was expected to give an advantage to the government majority, but the opposition parties united for the fight, and the campaign was more political than is customary on such occasions. The two rounds of voting, on March 14 and 21, represented another blow to the Left. The right-wing opposition made modest gains in the first round and an even stronger showing in the second.

Some days later, as if to make up for the defeat, the cabinet announced new social measures, including the right to retirement at age 60, professional training for youths aged 16 to 18, and new rights for salaried workers. By the month of April, however, there were noises of dissension inside the cabinet. For example, Interior Minister Defferre wanted to retain the controls established by the previous government in response to spreading delinquency, while Justice Minister Robert Badinter wanted to drop them. President Mitterrand succeeded in appeasing both ministers but, once again, Prime Minister Pierre Mauroy was said to lack authority over the members of his cabinet.

On June 9, President Mitterrand held the second press conference of his presidency, in which he announced the beginning of "the second phase of action." At the time it was not quite understood what he meant. By the end of June, however, National Solidarity Minister Nicole Questiaux, who had been reproached for a tendency to spend lavishly in her department, was replaced by Pierre Bérégovoy, who became "social affairs minister." Bérégovoy, who was already the president's chief of staff, was known as a good manager. The change appeared to signal a slowdown in the program of expensive social reforms.

Shortly thereafter, on June 30, the government announced its plan to divide the administration of Paris among its 20 *arrondisements,* or neighborhood municipalities. This caused the anger of Jacques Chirac, the mayor of Paris and leader of the main opposition party, the Rassemblement pour la Republique (RPR). The project appeared to have been designed to undermine his authority. In view of the turmoil provoked by the whole affair, the cabinet drew back and in autumn presented a new, less revolutionary draft. The Socialists did continue their attacks against Jacques Chirac, but the center and right-of-center opposition remained united in their attacks against the government. On September 16, former President Valéry Giscard d'Estaing appeared on television for the first time since he lost the presidential elections and severely criticized the government economic policy: "Socialism does not work," he said. By October even the Communists, represented in the cabinet by four ministers, were disapproving some of the measures taken by the Socialists.

Economy. At the beginning of 1982 it was learned that prices had increased by 14% in 1981. And the rise continued to be strong during the first months of 1982. In March the French franc hit record lows against the U.S. dollar and the West German mark. On May 21, Prime Minister Mauroy announced that it was necessary to limit the increase in income and wages. On June 12 the European Monetary System (EMS) voted to devalue the franc 10% against the mark and Dutch florin. The dollar was at 6.70 francs after the devaluation and went up even further in the following months, reaching 7.30 in November.

Drastic measures were taken to stabilize the franc and slow up inflation. On June 13, one day after the EMS action, prices and wages were frozen until October 31. But this was not sufficient to solve France's economic problems. The nation's industries, which now had to pay huge sums for social programs, were, according to their managers, "on the edge of an abyss," and investment was low. The foreign trade deficit for the first seven months of 1982 had already reached 52,300,000,000 francs, compared with only 51,000,000,000 for all of 1981. Since unemployment had passed the two million mark, it was announced on July 28 that civil servants and non-wage earners would pay into a "solidarity fund for employment."

On September 1 the cabinet presented a draft of the 1983 budget which provided for a reduction in public spending and a restriction of the deficit. Representing a return to financial austerity, the budget was a departure from the expansionary policies of 1982 and even resembled the budgets of former Prime Minister Raymond Barre. It was not, therefore, universally applauded. Some labor unions quickly made it understood that its support for government action had its limits. And at the beginning of October, doctors, lawyers, and other professionals went into the streets to demonstrate their discontent.

Terrorism. On January 18, Lt. Col. Charles Ray, the assistant military attaché to the U.S. Embassy, was assassinated in Paris. Responsibility for the attack was claimed by the Revolutionary Factions of the Lebanese Army in Beirut. On February 11 and 12 a wave of bombings by Corsican nationalists swept the island, killing one soldier of the French Legion and badly injuring two others; throughout the year,

Corsica was a theater of terrorist activity, with several hundred incidents reported. On March 29 a bomb placed in a first class train bound from Paris to Toulouse killed five persons. On April 3 a member of the Israeli Embassy was assassinated in Paris; an inquiry proved that the weapon used was of the same make as that used against Charles Ray. On April 22 the explosion of a car bomb in the neighborhood of the Champs-Elysées in Paris killed one woman and wounded at least 60 other people; the attempt, aimed at the offices of a pro-Iraqi Arab newspaper, was attributed by the French to the Syrian secret police. On May 24 a car-bomb explosion at the French Embassy in Beirut killed 11.

Paris continued to be a prime target for international terrorism during the summer. On July 22 the explosion of a bomb hidden in a garbage can in the Latin Quarter wounded 15 customers of a café. The following day, the assistant director of the Palestine Liberation Organization (PLO) in Paris was assassinated. While the whole nation was still somewhat in shock over a July 31 highway bus crash that killed 53, nearly all of them children, the year's bloodiest terrorist action took place on August 9 in the rue des Rosiers, at the heart of Paris' Jewish district. Two men armed with automatic weapons opened fire inside a restaurant and then began shooting at pedestrians outside. Six persons were killed and 22 wounded. Two days later, five persons were slightly wounded after the explosion of a delivery truck outside the Iraqi Embassy.

In the face of the emotion raised by this wave of violence, President Mitterrand on August 17 announced a series of measures to combat terrorism. These could not prevent another attack on August 21, this time against U.S. Commercial Attaché Roderick Grant. The parcel-bomb placed near his car exploded in the hands of two detonations experts who were defusing it; one was killed instantly, the other died from injuries 15 days later. On September 17 a car belonging to a member of the Israeli Embassy exploded near a school in Paris; 51 people were wounded, most of them children. In October the police ap-

---

FRANCE · Information Highlights

Official Name: French Republic.
Location: Western Europe.
Area: 211,207 sq mi (547 026 km^2).
Population (1982 est.): 54,200,000.
Chief Cities (1975 census): Paris, the capital, 2,317,227; Marseille, 914,356; Lyon, 462,841; Toulouse, 353,176.
Government: *Head of state,* François Mitterrand, president (took office May 1981). *Chief minister,* Pierre Mauroy, prime minister (took office May 1981). *Legislature*—Parliament: Senate and National Assembly.
Monetary Unit: Franc (7.185 francs equal U.S.$1, Nov. 1, 1982).
Gross Domestic Product (1981 U.S.$): $570,510,-000,000.
Economic Indexes (1981): *Consumer prices* (1970= 100), *all items,* 285.0; *food,* 289.5. *Industrial production* (1975=100), 114.

During a March visit to Israel, the first ever by a French head of state, President Mitterrand addressed the Knesset (parliament). His call for a Palestinian state was coldly received.

Mingam/Gamma-Liaison

peared to be on the track of terrorists; two important members of l'Action Directe, an extreme left-wing organization linked with international anti-Zionist and pro-Palestinian groups, were arrested in Paris.

Foreign Affairs

On March 3–4, President Mitterrand made an official state visit to Israel. In a speech before the Knesset (Israeli parliament), Mitterrand evoked the right of Palestinians to have a homeland, which drew a rather acerbic reply from Prime Minister Begin. That position, said Begin, was the main obstacle to Franco-Israeli friendship. The French president also faced criticism from pro-Palestinian Arabs, who reproached him for being the first head of a European country to visit the Hebrew state.

A week later, on March 12, Mitterrand made the shortest of visits to the United States. In the morning he flew from Paris to Washington on the Concord and, after a three-hour discussion with President Reagan, returned home aboard the supersonic jet. In mid-April he visited Japan for four days, primarily to discuss trade policies. France resolutely aligned itself with Great Britain in the Falkland Islands dispute, respecting the embargo on Argentine goods voted by the European Community (EC) in April. At the same time, however, there were persistent differences between Paris and London regarding Britain's contribution to the EC budget.

In the Lebanon war beginning in early June, France again joined with its EC partners, this time to condemn the Israeli invasion. The close relationship that France has always maintained with Lebanon, as well as the existence in France of a very important Jewish community, made the government's position particularly delicate. President Mitterrand did his best to arrange a ceasefire and, once the final pullout plan was in effect, France participated in the Multinational Force of Intervention sent to Beirut in late September.

From June 4 to 6, leaders of the world's seven major industrial democracies met at the Château de Versailles, the royal palace near Paris. President Mitterrand had wanted this to be a special occasion with bright festivity. The setting was indeed splendid, but the results were disappointing to the French president. Mitterrand had hoped for a promise of more active U.S. cooperation in his fight to strengthen the franc. The devaluation of the French currency less than one week after Versailles showed that his efforts had failed. Another point of friction between Paris and Washington were the contracts concluded by French firms for the construction of the Euro-Siberian natural gas pipeline, as well as France's agreement on January 23 to buy from the Soviets billions of cubic feet of gas over a 25-year period. In June the Reagan administration prohibited licensees and foreign subsidiaries of U.S. companies to sell pipeline equipment to the Soviets. The following month France and other European nations ordered companies to honor their contracts in spite of the U.S. embargo.

This is not to say that Mitterrand's policy toward European Communist countries was especially cooperative. On several occasions he voiced his disapproval of the situation in Poland. In another connection, on July 27 he cancelled a visit to Rumania scheduled for September. The cancellation seemed to be connected with the mysterious disappearance in May of Virgil Tanase, a dissident Rumanian writer living in France. Tanase had published an article hostile to Rumanian President Nicolae Ceauşescu, and it was generally believed that he had been kidnapped by the Rumanian secret service. On August 31, however, Tanase reappeared in Paris and explained that his alleged kidnapping had in fact been organized by the French secret service to avoid his murder, ordered by President Ceauşescu. President Mitterrand's opponents blamed him for having been personally involved in this strange plot.

MONIQUE MADIER, *French Writer and Editor*

GARDENING AND HORTICULTURE

Two insect pests that made headlines in 1981 continued to be newsworthy in 1982. The Mediterranean fruitfly, which had caused serious crop damage in California, seemed to have been brought under control by quarantine and pesticide spraying. No new flies were trapped in the spring of 1982, and quarantines were lifted in three counties. In June, however, a fertile male fly was trapped for the first time in San Joaquin County. A quarantine was imposed and spraying was begun at once in an 81-sq mi (210-km^2) area. Several other states continued monitoring in 1982.

Another pest, the gypsy moth, defoliated trees in forests and urban areas in increasing numbers during 1980 and 1981—more than 5 million acres (2 million ha) in 1980 and nearly 13 million acres (5.3 million ha) in 1981. The spread continued into 1982. The moth and caterpillar, long confined to New England, have been found as far away as Florida and California. Gypsy moth larvae feed on more than 300 species of plants, many common to the eastern United States but others found elsewhere. The transport of egg masses on vehicles and camping equipment has contributed to the spread.

Production and Sales. Federal budget cuts resulted in the cancellation of "Floriculture Crops," published annually by the U.S. Department of Agriculture Reporting Service. The 1981 report indicated that the wholesale value of all sales for the 17 crops reported was $1,020,000,-000, a 7% increase over 1980. Decreases were reported for standard chrysanthemums, standard carnations, and sweetheart roses, while increases were noted for miniature carnations, roses, pompom chrysanthemums, gladioli, foliage, and bedding plants.

A recent study conducted by a major seed company showed that marigolds lead all other flower seed crops in volume of sales, testimony to the adaptability of the flower throughout the United States.

A 1979 Horticulture Speciality Census revealed that in the previous 20 years nurserymen grew an increasingly large percentage of plants in containers. In 1959, about 85% of plants were field-grown and 15% container-grown, whereas in 1979 about 72% were field-grown and 28% container-grown.

New Cultivars and Plants. All-America Selections, a nonprofit organization for evaluating and introducing new seed-grown plants, celebrated its 50th anniversary in 1982. All-America awards for annuals and vegetable plants for 1983 were the Acapulco Silver kochia, Red Picotee petunia, and Candlelight ornamental pepper. All-America Rose Selections awards were made to Sun Flare, a bright yellow floribunda, and Sweet Surrender, a clear pink hybrid tea.

New cultivars and breeding lines listed in *Hortscience* through June 1982 included 7 ornamentals, 21 fruits and nuts, and 11 vegetables. The National Arboretum released two viburnums, Eskimo and Chesapeake, and two crape myrtles, Muskogee and Natchez. A series of dwarf and weeping crape myrtles developed and patented by David Chopin of Baton Rouge, LA, was introduced by a commercial firm.

Meetings and Expositions. "Floriade/82," an international horticultural exhibition, was held near Amsterdam, the Netherlands, from April 8 to Oct. 19, 1982. The Floriade, held every ten years, spanned the spring, summer, and autumn flowering seasons. (*See page 73.*) "Grow Show '82," sponsored by The Society of American Florists, was held in Louisville, KY, and the 15th annual trade show and conference of Bedding Plants, Inc., was held in Orlando, FL. The American Society for Horticultural Science held its 79th annual meeting at Iowa State University in Ames, IA, in August; and the 21st International Horticultural Congress was held in Hamburg, West Germany, from August 9 to September 24.

Courtesy, All-America Rose Selections

Sun Flare, hybridized by Bill Warriner of Tustin, CA, became the first clear yellow floribunda to win an All-America Rose Selection award in 25 years.

E. N. O'ROURKE
Department of Horticulture
Louisiana State University

GENETICS

The year 1982 brought continuing advances in the understanding of genetic processes and the application of genetic research. One discovery, if confirmed, reveals a new pattern of gene-protein interaction. There was also important new information about cancer genes, and a novel approach to increasing the world's food production was explored.

Gene-Protein Interaction. For many years scientists have been studying a fatal degenerative disease of the brain in sheep called scrapie, which resembles the human brain disorders of Creutzfeldt-Jakob disease and kuru. All three are infectious diseases whose causative agents replicate very slowly in their hosts, producing symptoms months and sometimes even years after infection. A recent analysis of the scrapie agent by Dr. Stanley B. Prusiner of the School of Medicine of the University of California at San Francisco revealed that it is only one hundredth the size of the smallest known virus and that it consists only of protein.

Because the scrapie agent is composed of protein and is infectious, it has been called *prion* (pronounced pree-on). The question has been raised as to how the prion, a protein, can reproduce itself. One relatively simple explanation is that the prion turns on a particular host gene that is capable of specifying the synthesis of more prions. The presence of such a gene in the host cell would indicate that, in its origin, a prion was a normal cellular protein that has become transmissible from cell to cell.

A very different postulation of prion reproduction holds that the prion codes for its own replication. This might be accomplished by some process of protein-directed protein synthesis. Alternatively, it might involve the prion directing, in some fashion, the synthesis of DNA (deoxyribonucleic acid), followed by a normal pattern of protein synthesis—DNA to messenger RNA (ribonucleic acid) to protein. Both protein-directed protein synthesis and protein-directed DNA synthesis have up to now not been known to occur in any organism.

Which of the above mechanisms applies to prion replication will have to await the findings of further research. However, if it is found that the prion codes for its own replication, the overall picture of gene-protein interaction will have to be significantly expanded.

Cancer Genes. The genetic material of the Harvey sarcoma virus contains a segment that is able to produce tumors in rats and is also able to transform normal mouse cells, growing in tissue culture, into cancerous ones. The segment consists of two components. One is called *onc* (from the Greek *onkos*, meaning mass). Onc is a protein-producing gene that is responsible for the actual transformation of cells. The other component is the *control element*, which determines whether the onc gene is turned on or off. Neither component alone causes cancer. Of great importance to cancer researchers is the fact that normal rat cells contain the onc gene. However, the rat onc gene will not cause cancer in mouse cells unless it is first linked to the viral control element.

Dr. Robert Weinberg at the Massachusetts Institute of Technology recently discovered that human bladder cancer cells contained a small DNA sequence that could also cause cancer in mouse cells. This genetic material is virtually identical to DNA sequences found both in healthy human cells and in the onc component of the Harvey sarcoma virus. The control element of the human bladder cancer gene has not yet been isolated. Other researchers have discovered similar cancer-causing DNA sequences in human lung, colon, and nerve cell cancers.

The above findings support the theory that cancer results from a mutational-type change in the control element of an onc gene, caused variously by an infecting virus, exposure to radiation, or ingestion of a chemical. This change in the control element causes a previously suppressed onc gene to produce large amounts of the protein needed for cell division, resulting in a rapid and uncontrolled growth of the particular tissue—the cancer process.

Food Production. With the world's human population ever increasing, there is an ongoing search for ways to improve food production. One approach has been the hybridization of genetically diverse plant strains, followed by the selection of plants with desirable qualities from among the descendants of such hybrids. Another approach, more recently advanced by Dr. James F. Shepard of Kansas State University, has been the asexual propagation of somatic cells from leaf, stem, or root with the aim of finding desirable genetic variants. The desired types can be cloned to produce large numbers, which can later be regenerated into adult plants. This process has been quite effective in identifying disease-resistant plants. Another attraction of the asexual approach to plant improvement is the ability to fuse the cells from vastly different plants, as has been done successfully with the tomato and potato. This in effect hybridizes two species that are sexually incompatible. If this species-hybrid type of cell can be regenerated into an adult, plant breeders will have available a tremendous amount of genetic variability for selecting desirable traits. New and more abundant foods would result.

Creationism vs. Evolution. Arkansas' Balanced Treatment for Creation-Science and Evolution-Science Act of 1981, requiring schools to give the biblical account of creation whenever the scientific evidence for evolution is discussed, was declared a violation of the First Amendment by a federal district judge on Jan. 5, 1982.

LOUIS LEVINE
Department of Biology
City College of New York

GEOLOGY

Geological research continued in a healthy state in 1982 with progress reported in all branches of the science. Although there were no new explorations of other solid bodies of the solar system, the earth furnished more than enough data to keep geologists busy. Not all of the year's problems were academic. The problems of declining energy resources, shortages of raw materials, dangers from natural disasters, threats to the environment, and the exigencies of national defense all called for immediate action and practical solutions.

International Programs. What promises to become a most productive cooperative geologic venture—the International Lithosphere Program—has been proposed. Its main objective is the elucidation of the nature, dynamics, origin, and evolution of the outer brittle shell of the earth (the lithosphere or crust, plus the upper mantle). This layer is mobile upon the underlying hot plastic asthenosphere, and the interactions of the two layers produce the integrated worldwide geologic activity known as plate tectonics. Nine working groups and eight coordinating committees have been set up with members from 13 countries.

Long-range plans to continue scientific ocean drilling under the Advanced Ocean Drilling Program (AODP), to succeed the existing Deep Sea Drilling Project (DSDP), have been announced. International cooperation in this program is expected to continue and expand. A cooperative project involving various states, Canada, and Mexico will produce a number of geologic cross sections of the continental shelves and deep into the adjacent continent.

Mexican Volcano. Just as 1980 was the year of Mount St. Helens, so 1982 was the year of a little-known Mexican volcano, El Chichón, located on the Yucatan peninsula. In its first recorded eruption, the volcano became active late in March and exploded violently on April 4. The summit was destroyed, leaving a crater about 0.6 mi (1 km) wide and great flows of water-saturated debris and falls of ash in the immediate vicinity. Villages within a 4.5-mi (7-km) radius were destroyed or heavily damaged. A temporary dam burst, releasing a flood of hot water to create additional havoc. At least 187 persons were killed and thousands were forced from their homes.

The quantity of erupted material from El Chichón is thought to have been 20 times more than that of Mount St. Helens. Whereas the Mount St. Helens blast was directed mainly horizontally and produced relatively more solid particles, El Chichón expelled a great vertical cloud heavily charged with gaseous material. Originally expelled to a height of 13.5 to 16.1 mi (22-26 km), the cloud rose even higher to about 20 mi (32 km). From this elevation ultrafine particles tend to settle slowly to earth, leaving sulfur

UPI

Mexico's Chichón volcano erupted several times during March and April, spewing huge columns of steam and ash.

dioxide gas and sulfuric acid droplets. Estimates are that the cloud carries as much as 10 million T (9 million t) of sulfuric acid, and that 2.2 million T (2 million t) of sulfur have been deposited on the ground.

The sulfur-rich cloud, impelled by the trade winds, drifted westward in a broad belt between the equator and 30° North Latitude. It eventually covered more than one quarter of the earth's surface and, where thickest, blocked out as much as 10% of the sun's total radiation.

Confronted with their greatest natural experiment in atmospheric effects of volcanic eruption, specialists predicted varied climatic consequences. The sulfuric acid droplets will cause whatever surface cooling that may occur by scattering sunlight back into space. In general there should be a slightly warmer stratosphere and a cooler earth surface. Some observers forecast a cooling of an average of 1°F in the Northern Hemisphere and earlier frost in 1982 and 1983. The effects were not expected to influence human lifestyles significantly, but it may be five years before the atmosphere clears. Thorough study of the El Chichón eruption as an isolated event will be important in understanding the effects of clusters of eruptions that may have brought on ice ages in the geologic past.

California Tremors. Citizens of California were warned officially that an eruption may be brewing in the Mammoth Lakes area on the east front of the Sierra Nevada, just east of Yosemite National Park. Past geologic history includes major, widely spaced eruptions in that part of the country. The last, some 700,000 years ago, is calculated to have ejected 600 times more material than Mount St. Helens. Spasmodic earth tremors give evidence that magma is now moving upward, but for the time being the situation is being treated as justifying a mild alert but not as an immediate hazard.

Floods. The year 1982 was one of low earthquake activity, but floods were unusually widespread and destructive. In January, a flood on the Chontayacu River northeast of Lima, Peru, buried an estimated 600 persons under mud and debris, and left 2,500 homeless. In May, record floods in southern China killed at least 430 persons and left tens of thousands homeless.

In July the worst storms in 25 years struck Kyushu, Japan. Some 18 inches (46 cm) of rain fell in seven hours, leaving 350 people dead or missing and at least 50,000 homeless. In September, flooding that claimed an estimated 600 lives and left 30,000 homeless was the worst natural disaster to strike El Salvador in the 17 years since the great earthquake of 1965. In Guatemala, the same floods left an estimated 560 dead and 1,200 missing.

Rainfall records were broken in many sections of the United States in 1982. Although damage was high, the loss of life was relatively low.

Nuclear Waste Disposal. Large quantities of fissionable material for atomic power and weaponry have been mined and processed, producing dangerous waste that has been piling up for some 35 years. It is urgent that this waste be disposed of without delay. Suggestions for its disposal include shooting it into space, perhaps into the sun; burying it in Antarctic ice; throwing it into active volcanoes; and interring it in ocean deeps that are grinding downward beneath the continents. But these exotic schemes are too risky, and geologists are confronted with the task of finding safe disposal sites in the crust of the earth.

Possible disposal sites with relatively safe geologic conditions include basalt fields in Washington state, welded volcanic tuff in Nevada, and salt deposits in Texas, Louisiana, New Mexico, and Utah. Requirements for safe disposal are strict because repositories must remain intact for at least 10,000 years until the contents are no longer dangerous. They must not be too shallow or too deep; there can be no drill holes or mining; they must not interfere with present or projected resource development; they must not infringe on existing lands dedicated to other uses; and the contents must be accessible for inspection and retrieval at all times.

Buried material must not reach the outside environment by any conceivable means. The actual and potential movement of ground water is probably the most troublesome problem, since data can be obtained only by actual measurements, and these cannot be made without drilling—which itself might upset the repository.

Although geologists may specify satisfactory sites, numerous environmental, political, and sociological problems must also be faced. In Utah, for example, a prime site is very near Canyonlands National Park, and environmentalists are opposed to disposing of nuclear waste there.

Gold. A romantic find of the year was that of a 615-oz (17,435-g) gold nugget at Serra Talhada in the heart of the Amazon jungle. Brazilian sources credit the find to Clovis Tavaras, a former baker, and proclaim the nugget to be the largest found in Brazil and the second largest in the world. It is valued at about $400,000.

Creationism. Geologists are becoming unwilling participants in the creationist-evolutionist controversy. On such matters as the age of the earth, the origin of species, and the history of mankind, their methods and conclusions have been called into question by creationists. Creationists claim that much geologic evidence is so speculative that it is no better than that which can be brought forth to support traditional interpretations of Genesis.

In its annual meeting held in October in New Orleans, the Geological Society of America devoted a special technical session to the science-creationism controversy. The consensus, as expressed by one participant, was that "creation science" has "no credibility whatsoever in the domain of science." Creationists ask that equal emphasis be given their Bible-based interpretations in the public schools. One result of this controversy is that geologists are giving closer attention to establishing proof of their methods and conclusions.

See also DISASTERS and ACCIDENTS.

WILLIAM LEE STOKES
University of Utah

GEORGIA

Legislative activity and elections attracted the attention of Georgians during 1982.

Legislature. Law and order was the focus of General Assembly activity during the year as more than a dozen bills aimed at strengthening criminal laws were introduced. A bill that would permit the empaneling of a second jury for sentencing in death-penalty cases was passed but vetoed by Governor Busbee. Also vetoed by the governor was a controversial bill allowing juries to sentence convicted murderers to life imprisonment without parole. Both houses passed a bill providing for a plea of guilty but mentally ill, requiring a prison sentence at the conclusion of psychiatric treatment.

In other action the assembly defeated the Equal Rights Amendment by a vote of 116-57 in the House and rejected legislation designed to upgrade the status of women. Bills that would have required the equitable division of property in divorce proceedings, eliminate the "marriage tax," and base population requirements for militia districts on the number of adult persons rather than males were deemed "anti-family" and refused consideration.

A Reagan administration recommendation received some attention when legislators approved a work-force program to study the possibilities of employing welfare recipients.

Elections. For their new governor, Georgians chose a conservative businessman, Joe Frank Harris, from the northern part of the state. The original group of six gubernatorial candidates, which included former Jimmy Carter presidential aide Jack Watson, was reduced to two in a runoff between Harris and U.S. Representative Bo Ginn. Although Ginn finished first, leading by more than 10% and capturing endorsements of the four runners-up, Harris won a narrow victory and then went on to defeat soundly his Republican challenger, state Representative Bob Bell, in the general election. Harris based his campaign on a "common-sense" government with no tax increase.

Keza/Gamma-Liaison

The town council of Kennesaw, an Atlanta suburb, passed an ordinance requiring every household to possess a firearm and ammunition. Police held instruction classes.

In other political action, Max Cleland, former head of the Veterans Administration under President Carter, was elected secretary of state; and Carter's one-time Office of Management and Budget director, Bert Lance, became state Democratic Party chairman.

Of five congressional races, Democrats held four seats; and Georgia's single Republican in the House, Newt Gingrich, won by a narrow margin. Three Democratic candidates were unopposed. A delay in completing reapportionment forced postponement of congressional elections in the 4th and 5th districts until November 30. In both districts, Democrats were reelected.

Savannah River Plant. Governor Busbee actively opposed the federal government's plans to expand the Savannah River plutonium-production facility in South Carolina when a rare blood disease linked to radiation exposure was found to occur at a high rate near the plant. In his letter of protest, the governor also cited the fact that levels of radioactive tritium in Georgia's milk and water are 50 times higher than what is normally expected.

Unemployment. Georgia appeared to be surviving the recession better than some other states. Its single-digit unemployment rate (7.4% in August) was well below the national and southeastern rates.

Cumberland Island. The natural beauty of this island on the coast of Georgia was given federal protection when President Reagan signed legislation giving wilderness status to 8,440 acres (3,416 hectares) on the island.

KAY BECK, *Georgia State University*

GEORGIA · Information Highlights

Area: 58,910 sq mi (152 577 km^2).

Population (1980 census): 5,463,105.

Chief Cities (1980 census): Atlanta, the capital, 425,-022; Columbus, 169,441; Savannah, 141,634.

Government (1982): *Chief Officers*—governor, George D. Busbee (D); lt. gov., Zell Miller (D). *General Assembly*—Senate, 56 members; House of Representatives, 180 members.

State Finances (fiscal year 1981): *Revenues,* $5,848,-000,000; *expenditures,* $5,401,000,000.

Personal Income (1981): $49,797,000,000; per capita, $8,934.

Labor Force (Aug. 1982): *Nonagricultural wage and salary earners,* 2,149,800; *unemployed,* 200,100 (7.4% of total force).

Education: *Enrollment* (fall 1981)—public elementary schools, 736,565; public secondary, 319,552; colleges and universities (1981–82), 191,384. *Public school expenditures* (1980–81), $1,946,011,000 ($1,652 per pupil).

GERMANY

Helmut Kohl, Christian Democratic Union leader, is the new chancellor of West Germany.

Relations between the Federal Republic of Germany (West Germany) and the German Democratic Republic (East Germany or DDR) changed little during 1982. A meeting in December 1981 between West German Chancellor Helmut Schmidt and East German Chief of State Erich Honecker on East German soil yielded no concrete results. It did stress the fact, however, that good relations between the two states is a precondition for peace in Europe. Both Germanys recognized their special stake in peace and stability, since the two states would be the immediate battlefield of an East-West war. For this reason they were seen as bearing a special responsibility to work for an arms reduction within their respective blocs. There was some talk of increased cultural contact and additional tourist exchange opportunities for young people, but little came of these discussions. Overshadowing such efforts were the DDR's continued insistence on being treated as a completely separate state and West Germany's continued refusal to do so.

Federal Republic of Germany (West Germany)

The most significant event in the Federal Republic in 1982 was the changeover from a Social Democratic (SPD)-Free Democratic (FDP) coalition government headed by Helmut Schmidt (SPD) to a Christian Democratic (CDU)-Free Democratic coalition headed by Helmut Kohl. The change was not totally unexpected; tensions between the moderately leftist SPD and the

middle-of-the road FDP had haunted the social-liberal coalition for many months. The major source of these disputes was the budget. With the economy in recession, the problem of drafting a balanced budget acceptable to both parties proved unsolvable. The SPD wished to maintain the country's elaborate social security system and called for increased borrowing and higher taxes; the FDP wished to reduce some social programs, lower taxes, and encourage investments to stimulate the economy. Moreover, the FDP, which had been losing ground in a number of state elections, feared being driven completely from the political stage unless it dissociated itself from the SPD. It therefore joined forces with the more conservative CDU.

On September 17, the four FDP cabinet members withdrew from the 13-year-old coalition, leaving Schmidt with a minority government. On October 1, the Bundestag (lower house) passed (256–235) a vote of no-confidence, with 28 FDP deputies voting against Schmidt and only 25 continuing to support him. In Schmidt's place Helmut Kohl, CDU chairman, was elected as the new chancellor. Kohl formed a coalition cabinet of the CDU and FDP, as well as one member of the Christian Social Union (CSU), the right-wing Bavarian offshoot of the CDU. (See also BIOGRAPHY.)

Schmidt departed from office a highly respected figure who had steered the Federal Republic through difficult times and secured it a major position in the Western community of nations. He announced that for reasons of health he would not run as the SPD's candidate for the chancellorship in new Bundestag elections tentatively scheduled for March 6, 1983.

The New Government. Kohl promised to hold the March 1983 elections to give the nation an opportunity to pass judgment on his government. The move was not without risk, since such elections conceivably could wipe out the badly split FDP and pit Chancellor Kohl directly against an increasingly powerful antiestablishment ecology party, the Greens, possibly leaving him without a majority.

In the meantime, Kohl's new program emphasized the growth of private enterprise, to be implemented by tax relief and aid to continuously depressed areas. Special attention would be paid to high-technology industries, the aerospace industry, and the development of nuclear power. On the other hand, social expenditures would be cut, proposed pension increases postponed, and unemployment benefits reduced. Kohl called also for curbs on the immigration of foreign workers, thus hoping to reduce unemployment and assuage the anti-foreigner feelings of many of his countrymen.

In foreign affairs, Kohl stressed West Germany's commitment to the Western community and to NATO, but declared also that economic cooperation with the East was of great importance to the nation's economy and would be maintained.

The Greens. The change in government was not merely a consequence of economic conditions, budget disputes, and party politics. It also reflected a growing concern with the stability of a country whose social and political system was under attack from large circles of young people. German youth rebelled against what it saw as increasing materialism, ruthless exploitation of the environment, mounting armaments, and the use of nuclear power regardless of its dangers.

Although these anticapitalist, antiestablishment groups were part of no formal political party, they did elect delegates to various state parliaments under the name of "The Greens." In the case of one state, Hamburg, this caused considerable difficulty. The city's SPD minority government needed the Greens' votes to enact its policies, and a stalemate developed. The Greens refused to support the government's budget on the grounds that it called for increased use of nuclear energy and the expansion of Hamburg's harbor, which they felt was not needed and would merely add to air and water pollution. Hamburg's parliament, which had been elected only four months earlier, was dissolved in October, and new elections were called for in December.

The SPD struggled to neutralize the Greens by incorporating some of their demands into its own program. The CDU-CSU, on the other hand, remained rigidly opposed to them. The Kohl government sought to curb their influence; the new minister of the interior, Friedrich Zimmermann (CSU), is a staunch conservative.

UPI

President Reagan assures the West German parliament that the U.S. will not abandon the Western alliance.

Economy. The West German economy continued to decline throughout the year. Unemployment reached a new high; in September 1.82 million people, 7.5% of the work force, were without jobs. The number would have been even higher had management not retained as many of its skilled workers as it could, remembering earlier recessions when it proved very difficult to find skilled labor after a new economic upswing set in. Joblessness among young workers was therefore much more widespread than among older, more experienced workers.

Bankruptcies, too, rose to a new high, including among them AEG Telefunken, one of West Germany's leading electronics manufacturers. Inflation, however, receded from 5.8% in 1981 to 5.2% in 1982. To Germans, ever mindful of the ravages of inflation in 1922–23, this was still a frightening figure.

What shielded the economy from even harsher blows was the continued maintenance of a positive balance of trade. Exports, which constituted 25.6% of the Gross National Product in 1981 (compared with 8% in the United States), were estimated to have risen by 5% in 1982, while imports declined by 2%.

Social Conditions. An issue of growing importance was the antiforeigner feeling rife in the

WEST GERMANY · Information Highlights

Official Name: Federal Republic of Germany.

Location: North-central Europe.

Area: 96,011 sq mi (248 668 km^2). West Berlin, 186 sq mi (481 km^2).

Population (1982 est.): 61,700,000.

Chief Cities (1980 est.): Bonn, the capital, 287,100; West Berlin, 1,898,900; Hamburg, 1,648,800; Munich, 1,298,900.

Government: *Head of state,* Karl Carstens, president (took office July 1979). *Head of government,* Helmut Kohl, federal chancellor (took office Oct. 1982). *Legislature*—Parliament: Bundesrat and Bundestag.

Monetary Unit: Deutsche mark (2.55 d. marks equal U.S.$1, Nov. 1, 1982).

Gross Domestic Product (1981 U.S.$): $687,120,-000,000.

Economic Indexes (1981): *Consumer prices* (1970= 100), *all items,* 174.0; *food,* 160.8. *Industrial production* (1975=100), 118.

Foreign Trade (1981 U.S.$): *Imports,* $163,907,000,-000; *exports,* $176,085,000,000.

country. It was directed principally against the 4.6 million foreign workers and their families, mainly Turks, who were held responsible in large part for the unemployment of West German workers. In reality, foreigners tended to hold jobs which West Germans shunned—in mining, sanitation, and the hotel and restaurant business. But West Germans also seemed to fear that foreigners would undermine the social fabric of their society. The birthrate among Turks, Yugoslavs, Greeks, and Italians—the largest contingents of foreign labor—vastly exceeded that of the Germans, whose own birthrate was the lowest in the world (0.5 births per 1,000 inhabitants). The new Kohl government promised to deal with this problem by reducing immigration and calling on the foreigners to integrate themselves into German society, ignoring the widespread German resistance to any such efforts. As the Schmidt government already had pointed out, with the West German birthrate as low as it was, the foreign offspring would soon be needed to provide the necessary manpower for the economy.

The antiforeigner feelings also extended to troops from other countries stationed in West Germany. American soldiers, in particular, found themselves barred from taverns, restaurants, and other places of entertainment and were the victims of assaults by neo-Nazi groups. At the same time, however, the great majority of West Germans recognized the vital need for U.S. military protection.

Housing, too, remained an unresolved problem. An estimated 4 million people had inadequate housing, although some 700,000 apartments remained vacant. That situation was partly the result of tenant protection laws which made it possible for many to continue living in inexpensive subsidized housing even though their incomes no longer qualified them, while those who were entitled were not able to get in. Another cause of the housing shortage was the practice of many apartment house owners to keep their buildings vacant, let them deteriorate until they became uninhabitable, and then have them zoned for conversion into more profitable office buildings. Bitter protests, in the form of "squat-ins" in unoccupied buildings, led several times to severe clashes with police.

Foreign Policy. The foreign policy of the Federal Republic was based on the precarious West German location at the border between the Eastern and Western blocs. Chancellor Schmidt repeatedly stressed the need for accommodation rather than confrontation with the East. That stand caused serious disagreements with the United States, which assumed a much more militant attitude toward the Soviet Union and the other Eastern bloc countries. Bonn disapproved of Washington's imposition of economic sanctions against Poland and the USSR, thinking they were ineffective, added needlessly to East-West tensions, and hurt the people of Poland more than the Communist regime. Bonn also had an ongoing fear that heightened tensions between the Communist bloc and Western alliance would endanger East-West German relations.

The United States, in turn, objected to West Germany's intensified economic collaboration with the USSR. West Germany's participation in the construction of a natural gas pipeline from Siberia to Western Europe gave rise to a particularly heated controversy. The West Germans saw the transaction as a commercial deal which at the same time would make them less dependent on Middle Eastern oil. The United States, on the other hand, considered the projected sale of gas by the Soviets as a source of hard currency that could be used for military purposes and thereby strengthen the Kremlin's hand. It would also make Bonn dependent on Soviet gas, a contention denied by the former given the comparatively small portion of energy resources (5 to 6%) it would thus obtain. The Kohl government made it clear that it would maintain the pipeline agreement, but the issue was resolved when President Reagan announced the lifting of the U.S. boycott on November 13. Two days later, Kohl met with Reagan on his first official visit to the United States. Talks focused on Western relations with the Soviet Union.

Another source of controversy was the planned deployment of U.S. Pershing II and Cruise missiles on West German soil to counter the growing deployment of Soviet SS missiles directed against Western Europe. The Greens and other pacifist and antimilitarist groups were bitterly opposed to the U.S. plan and tried to block it by organizing massive demonstrations and circulating vast amounts of literature. Both Schmidt and Kohl supported the plan, however, provided that the Soviets did not agree to a withdrawal of their SS missiles at the disarmament talks under way at Geneva. Schmidt even threatened to resign if his own Social Democratic party rejected this strategy.

German Democratic Republic
(East Germany)

In the DDR, too, a peace movement tried to assert itself, there under the auspices of the Lutheran church. Many, especially among the young, took to wearing badges expressing their opposition to the East-West armament race and bearing the inscription: "Make peace without arms." In Dresden a gathering sponsored by the church in mid-February attracted some 4,000 people who called for a mutual reduction of armaments. The meeting also criticized the DDR government for applauding peace movements in the West while frowning on similar endeavors at home. The "Berlin Manifesto," signed by 200 East Germans of all social strata and circulated widely, demanded the conversion of Europe into a nuclear-free zone. It also asked for the withdrawal of all foreign troops from the two German states and the open discussion of peace and arms reduction.

The East German government, which does not recognize conscientious objectors and already trains schoolchildren in paramilitary activities, allowed these antiwar efforts to continue for a short time. When the movement really appeared to be gaining ground, however, it repressed them as anticonstitutional. The Free German Youth, the Communist youth organization, arranged a series of meetings in which the need for military preparedness as a prerequisite for peace was stressed. The Lutheran church maintained its pacifist position but, so as to avoid any confrontation with the government, did not encourage further protest activities.

Economy. Poorly endowed with mineral resources, the DDR was very much affected by rising world prices for raw materials. Efforts to increase exports to offset this trend were only partly successful. The economic collapse of Poland, the main source of relatively cheap coal and a major buyer of East German machines, also hurt the economy. New techniques were developed to save on energy and raw materials; the

Eastfoto

East German trucks are ready for export to Algeria. Adapting to foreign market demands is a national goal.

present five-year plan envisages annual reductions of 6.1% in the use of both. All in all, projected economic growth rates proved unattainable (3% in the first half of 1982, as against the goal of 4.8%), but the country still had the highest standard of living in the Eastern bloc.

Environmental protection was badly neglected for the sake of industrial growth. Air and water pollution were particularly noticeable in the industrial regions around Halle, Leipzig, and Karl-Marx-Stadt, with serious effects on public health. In the area around Halle, 10 to 15% more people suffered from heart and circulatory disease than in the country as a whole; life expectancy was 5% below the national average.

Social Conditions. The status of women continued to improve. Increasing numbers of women obtained managerial positions, and their pay for jobs on all levels was equal to that of men. Nine out of 10 women between the ages of

---

EAST GERMANY · Information Highlights

Official Name: German Democratic Republic.
Location: North-central Europe.
Area: 41,768 sq mi (108 179 km²).
Population (1982 est.): 16,700,000.
Chief Cities (1980): East Berlin, the capital, 1,145,-743; Leipzig, 563,388; Dresden, 516,284.
Government: *Head of state,* Erich Honecker, chairman of the Council of State. *Head of government,* Willi Stoph, chairman of the Council of Ministers Presidium. General secretary of the Socialist Unity (Communist) party, Erich Honecker (took office 1971). *Legislature* (unicameral)—Volkskammer (People's Chamber).
Monetary Unit: DDR mark (2.35 DDR marks equal U.S.$1, March 1982—noncommercial rate).
Gross National Product (1981 U.S.$): $96,800,000,-000—$142,130,000,000.
Economic Index (1980): *Industrial production* (1975= 100), 127.
Foreign Trade (1980 U.S.$): *Imports,* $19,082,000,-000; *exports,* $17,312,000,000.

243

16 and 60 were gainfully employed, largely because of the continued need for additional labor and the high price of everything but the basic necessities. As a result of their growing employment, women gained greater financial independence, contributing to the breakup of many marriages. With a rate of 2.7 per 1,000, the DDR had the world's highest divorce rate.

In the most crucial area—the affairs of the (Communist) Social Unity Party—however, women had not yet achieved anything like full equality with men. There were no women in the Politburo, except for two longstanding candidate members, and none of the party's district secretaries were women.

Among young people, the restlessness that had led to serious disturbances in 1980–81 was not as noticeable in 1982. Whatever uneasiness remained was largely channelled into the more disciplined peace movement. There seemed to be more emphasis on meeting the demands of school and thereby preparing for future jobs.

Foreign Policy. The DDR undertook no major foreign political initiatives during the year but continued to provide economic and military aid to a number of African and Asian states. The DDR had become one of the pillars of the Eastern bloc, with worldwide ties strengthened by Chief of State Honecker's trips to Mexico, Japan, and Austria. Relations with the USSR remained as close as ever.

East Berlin retained its detached attitude toward Poland, lest Poles striving for greater freedoms began to influence the East German population. Actually, the DDR regime need not have worried; the East German people strongly disapproved of the demands of the Polish Solidarity movement. Its calls for better working conditions were seen as a symbol of Polish laziness and disorderliness and an obstacle to economic growth.

West Berlin

This Western island within East Germany wrestled with its usual problems in 1982, as well as new financial setbacks. Despite large subsidies from the Federal Republic—which underwrote 53% of the city's $7,400,000,000 budget—West Berlin's economy was greatly affected by the worldwide recession. Some 20,000 jobs were lost since early 1981; the subsidies from West Germany were to be cut because of budgetary reductions in Bonn; and declining tourism would mean a drop in badly needed retail trade.

The severe housing shortage led to the continued occupation of vacant apartment buildings by youthful squatters, an almost routine occurrence in city life.

West Berlin was also hurt by the DDR's ecological abuses. There were recurrent "smog alarms," warning children and elderly people to stay off the streets and drivers not to use their cars until pollution levels had subsided.

ANDREAS DORPALEN, *The Ohio State University*

GHANA

Flight Lt. Jerry Rawlings returned to power as the result of another military takeover on Dec. 31, 1981. The democratic constitution was suspended and all political parties banned. Rawlings became the chairman of the Provisional National Defense Council (PNDC), which was designated to replace President Hilla Limann and his cabinet. Limann and other senior officials were arrested, many charged with "crimes against the people," and special revolutionary tribunals not governed by usual legal procedures were created to mete out "revolutionary justice."

The takeover was popular throughout Ghana, since the Limann government had been unable to deal with Ghana's economic problems. Long-and-short-term loan payments—combined with shortfalls in cocoa production, an extremely high inflation rate, and the need to import food and high-priced petroleum—had confronted a series of military and civilian governments with insoluble problems over the previous 20 years. As in 1979, Rawlings evoked a patriotic response from all segments of the community and promised that the revolution would restructure society in favor of the common people.

Operating with scant reserves, the PNDC reached an agreement with Nigeria on oil shipments, kept the Volta Aluminum Company smelter at Tema from closing, and received loans from Japan, the European Community, and the United Nations. The council supported Colonel Qaddafi of Libya at the aborted Organization of African Unity summit in August and received financial guarantees in return. Flight Lt. Rawlings announced a goal of agricultural self-sufficiency, hoping to cut back on food imports. The new regime was able to stand clear of complicity in the murders of three high court judges in June.

Rawlings' popularity withstood the persistent economic crisis. The inflation rate continued high, consumer goods were expensive and in short supply, and cocoa exports were unstable. Despite foreign loans, Ghana's cash inflow remained low. Western nations were hesitant to give immediate aid because of the increasingly radical stance of the regime.

HARRY A. GAILEY
San Jose State University

GHANA • Information Highlights

Official Name: Republic of Ghana.
Location: West Africa.
Area: 92,100 sq mi (238 539 km²).
Population (1982 est.): 12,400,000.
Chief Cities (1977 est.): Accra, the capital, 840,000; Kumasi, 353,000; Tema, 169,500.
Government: *Head of state and government,* Flight-Lt. Jerry Rawlings (assumed power Dec. 1981). *Legislature*—Constituent Assembly (dissolved, Dec. 1981).
Monetary Unit: New cedi (2.75 new cedis equal U.S.$1, December 1981).
Gross National Product Per Capita (1980): $420.

GREAT BRITAIN

The Barbican Centre for Arts and Conferences, near St. Paul's in London, opened in March after years of controversy about its cost. It includes three cinemas, two exhibition halls, an art gallery, a conservatory, and apartments.

In 1982 British public and political life was almost entirely dominated by the Falklands War (*see* feature article, page 28). In March the Conservative government headed by Margaret Thatcher appeared to be facing almost certain defeat at the next general election. The number of unemployed was heading rapidly to an unprecedented 3.5 million and there was no sign whatsoever of the long-promised revival in the economy. Indeed all the indications were that problems would worsen before they improved.

With the war, however, Mrs. Thatcher's standing in the polls suddenly rose. Her party held a clear and unchallenged lead in all the polls taken in the nine months following the war's outbreak—an achievement unmatched by a British government since polling began. At the end of the year it was widely assumed that a general election (these must be held in Britain every five years, but can be called earlier by the prime minister of the day) would provide Mrs. Thatcher with a further mandate for her policies. The reason for this became known, rightly or wrongly, as the "Falklands Factor." Whatever people thought of the war—and there were many doubting voices raised in Britain in the course of the fighting—it was clear that Mrs. Thatcher had set herself upon a course and had followed it resolutely to the end. Amid the doubters, she had been unwavering, and she, in the end, had proved successful.

Politics. The implication, openly stated by many Conservatives, was obvious. Just as she followed her convictions to ultimate victory in the South Atlantic, so she would with the British economy. The party lost few chances of reminding the voters of this; even the slogan adopted for the Conservatives' annual conference was "The Resolute Approach." Months after the fighting had ended, the news media were filled with Falklands stories—the return of ships from the battle zone, the award of military honors (two men won Britain's highest award, the Victoria Cross, for bravery, both posthumously), services, and parades—that continued to remind the public of the war. Books about the war poured from the presses; both big broadcasting networks produced videotapes so that ordinary citizens could relive the excitement in the comfort of their own homes.

Another swift effect of the fighting and the admiration won by Mrs. Thatcher was a serious setback in the prospects of the so-called SDP/Liberal Alliance. Two parties—the Liberals, who dated back to the 19th century and at times had seemed near extinction in this era, and the brand new Social Democratic Party—had come together to offer a moderate, centrist alternative to the increasingly right-wing Conservatives and the more stridently left-wing Labour Party. In 1981 the Alliance scored some remarkable electoral successes, and these appeared to be continuing in March 1982 when Roy Jenkins (*see* BIOGRAPHY) won the difficult Glasgow seat of Hillhead for the SDP. At this point the Falklands war intervened, and the Alliance's support began to drop rapidly. Its performance in the May local elections—even before the war was won—was exceedingly poor. Jenkins suffered personally too. He had been assumed to be front-runner for the leadership of the new party, but he found himself challenged by a much younger, brasher politician, David Owen. Owen had been foreign secretary (secretary of state) during a previous, hitherto unpublicized Falklands crisis, when he and the then Labour Prime Minister James Callaghan had privately made it clear to Argentina that any invasion of the islands would be met by British retaliation. Owen was able to claim that his prompt handling of the situation had averted the bloody crisis the country was now facing. In the subsequent SDP lead-

ership elections, Owen did much better than anyone had expected. Owen received 20,864 votes to 26,256 for the winning Jenkins. Paradoxically, Mrs. Thatcher's own popularity continued high even though there were many who suspected that she could, by more sensitive and flexible diplomatic action, have avoided the whole Falklands thing in the first place.

Meanwhile the hapless Labour Party, which has formed the government of Britain for just about half the years since World War II, was also slumping in the polls and looking less likely every day to be the next government. Led by grass-roots activists, encouraged by a sense of despair and disillusion with the old, failed economic remedies, the party had moved steadily to

Politically the year belonged to Margaret Thatcher. The prime minister's standing in the polls increased dramatically as a result of her handling of the war in the Falklands. Shortly after Argentina's defeat, Mrs. Thatcher personally thanked President Ronald Reagan for U.S. help. Roy Jenkins was also a political force. In July he overcame a challenge from David Owen and was elected leader of the new Social Democratic Party.

UPI

J. Sutton/Gamma-Liaison

the left. This drift became symbolized in the minds of many traditional, centrist Labour supporters with the success of "the Militant Tendency," an avowedly Trotskyist group of uncertain numbers but with a powerful influence in some local Labour parties. After years of indecision and inaction, the party leadership decided that members of the group should be expelled, or rather, that all groups within the Labour Party would have to be registered. Those groups that did not conform to the constitution would then be ejected. The decision was a sloppy compromise that immediately hit confusing legal difficulties as members of the Militant group fought to hold onto their position within the party. Other left-wingers made it clear that they regarded the attack on the strange and sectarian Militants as the precursor of an attack upon them, and they prepared to resist. In many constituencies local Labour parties chose ultra-left candidates, and it became clear that the Conservatives would have ample scope for alleging a Marxist menace at the next election, an opportunity they were unlikely to miss.

Michael Foot, Labour's leader, whose poll ratings were the lowest of any senior politician since World War II, won some comfort at the party's annual conference, where the right wing took over several important posts in Labour's governing committee. This newly constituted body set about purging the Left with great vigor but against considerable opposition. The party's electoral prospects seemed brighter, but at the end of 1982 few people were predicting that Foot would become the nation's leader.

The Thatcher Approach. It was supremely Mrs. Thatcher's year. The British prime minister was passionately admired by perhaps half of her people and disliked or even loathed by the rest. She proved, however, a number of unexpected truths that will change the course of British history, and to an extent that of the entire Western world.

First she showed that it was possible to govern a country in something near tranquility while living standards are falling and about 12% of the working population are unemployed. Politically she demonstrated that a consensus between various viewpoints from right to left is not necessary for practical government. She made it a habit to sack those who disagreed with her, largely ignored her opponents, and got away with it entirely. While in 1981 her own party had been wondering when it would be possible to ditch her, at the end of 1982 she was untouchable. Even the riots which had caused such fear and damage in the biggest British cities in 1981 were not repeated, except in tiny and isolated instances.

Mrs. Thatcher also tore up old notions of liberal coexistence with other countries. She was unashamedly and unabashedly nationalistic, whether in her dealings with Argentina, other countries in the European Community, or even with the United States. Apart from Prime Minister Pierre Elliott Trudeau of Canada, she was the longest-serving head of any major Western government, and while her own people might not love her they certainly respected her.

She had also developed a style of presidential government that had not been seen before in Britain. Traditionally the electorate votes for individual Members of Parliament (MPs) who then choose their own prime minister (almost invariably the leader of the largest party). The head of government therefore draws authority and power from MPs, to whom he or she feels most immediately responsible. Mrs. Thatcher, however, tries to appeal to the voters over the heads of Parliament, and even over the Cabinet she herself appoints. Often she gives the impression of "blaming the government" like a discontented housewife rather than the head of the government itself.

The Economy. Her consistent poll ratings were achieved in the face of a yet more disastrous economic situation. Apart from the appalling unemployment statistics, there was the number of bankruptcies and liquidations, totaling about 15,000 companies in 1982. The most notable was the famous cut-price Laker Airways. Unemployment pay reached the stunning figure of 28% of all public spending. For years, Conservative ministers have been predicting that the recession would end, and that British industry, "leaner and fitter," would be well placed to take quick and remunerative advantage. But as the year went by, their claims sounded more and more hollow as the closures and dismissals remorselessly increased.

The government could claim some successes. Inflation, which a few years earlier was in the high twenties, was at only 6.3% by the end of 1982. Interest on loans and mortgages was correspondingly decreased.

The declining interest rates also brought down the value of the pound sterling, helped on its way by the world glut of oil. Britain is an oil-exporting nation, and this fact is not always a blessing. However the lower pound was a help to exporters, especially through a sudden 10% fall against the German mark, one of Britain's chief rivals. Britain exports a higher proportion of its goods than any other large manufacturing nation, and the threat of a worldwide trade war caused much anxiety.

The reduced rate of inflation also helped the country's generally fraught and difficult labor relations. Several of the largest groups of workers, such as car makers at the British Leyland factories and the generally militant coal miners, decided not to go on strike for higher wages. The miners' decision was all the more remarkable because their president, a flamboyant left-winger named Arthur Scargill, had toured the country asking for a strike. He held packed meetings of near evangelical fervor and distributed videotapes of his speeches to union members who could not otherwise hear him. In spite of this, the union voted to stay at work, and the decision was hailed as a considerable success for Mrs. Thatcher's lowering of national expectations. Railroad engineers did strike, but their claim was virtually ignored until they returned to work. A walkout by hospital workers, demanding a 12% pay increase, disrupted several hospitals, but in the end the workers were obliged to accept a sum only triflingly more than they had originally been offered. Pay rises over the year averaged only 5.5%, much less than the rate of inflation. Grumblingly and unwillingly, the public appeared to be settling for less.

Mrs. Thatcher's determination to roll back the frontiers of socialism led her to sell off into private hands a number of industries that until 1982 had been publicly owned. Amersham International, a radio-isotope company, was offered to the market at too low a price, and fortunate investors made a financial killing. So the state oil company, Britoil, was offered at too high a price, and only 30% of the shares were subscribed, leaving the underwriters with a loss of some $65 million. Next in line for sale was British Airways, which returned a loss of $882 million in 1982, though cynics claimed that this was a bookkeeping swindle designed to make the 1983 results look remarkably good.

The most crippling and unexpected financial burden of the year was, of course, the Falklands War. Figures were unreliable, but it was estimated that the total cost of the lost shipping and aircraft and of maintaining a garrison on the islands that could resist an attack from Argentina would be at least £2,000,000,000 ($3,240,000,000)—more than $1.8 million for every man, woman, and child on the Falklands who are, in any case, greatly outnumbered by the troops who are guarding them. The cost was increased by the refusal of other South American countries to grant landing and refueling rights to Britain, largely because Britain refused to negotiate with

Argentina over future sovereignty of the territory. Mrs. Thatcher made it plain that she would never enter such negotiations.

Papal Visit. In spite of the Falklands War, Pope John Paul II paid his planned visit to Britain in May. The pope made plain his deep repugnance at any war as a means of settling disputes between nations, though the thousands of people who saw him during his six-day visit seemed happy enough to hear him and still hope for a British victory. The pope held a joint service at Canterbury Cathedral with Archbishop Robert Runcie, the head of the Church of England, thus marking a truce between the two churches after a schism that began some 400 years ago.

Royal Family. The most extraordinary distraction for the British people, during a year of unparalleled international and domestic problems, was its own Royal Family. It had been generally assumed that after the 1981 marriage of Queen Elizabeth's heir, Prince Charles, to Lady Diana Spencer, public interest would begin to lapse. Instead it increased to unprecedented, even obsessive, heights, helped by a number of bizarre incidents. Michael Fagan, an unemployed man, arrived in the queen's bedroom early one July morning, the culmination of a number of visits he had made to Buckingham Palace during which he was never once apprehended by the guards. Alarm bells were ignored, and the queen's "panic button" was disregarded until Fagan, by now in amiable conversation with his ruler, asked for a cigarette. The maid, summoned to bring it, arrived to remark: "Bloody hell, Ma'am, what's he doing here?" Thanks to a strange anomaly in British law, Fagan could not be charged with entering the bedroom and was even acquitted on the lesser count of stealing some wine. He was instead sent to a hospital for observation while security was tightened at the palace.

The queen's bodyguard, Cmdr. Michael Trestrail, was then revealed as an active and promiscuous homosexual by a young man who tried to sell the story of their affair to a newspaper. The hapless commander was dismissed.

Prince Andrew, the queen's second son, served as a helicopter pilot in the Falklands War and returned home to a considerable welcome. He promptly left for a vacation on the West Indian island of Mustique, taking with him a young and beautiful American actress named Koo Stark. This would have aroused less interest if her acting career had not been for the most part in soft-core porn movies. Prince Edward, the queen's fourth child and third son, went to teach at a high school in New Zealand, a country of which his mother is still the nominal ruler.

In the midst of all these peculiar events, Princess Diana, wife of Prince Charles, gave birth to a son who was christened William. The new prince is now second-in-line to the throne behind his father.

GREAT BRITAIN · Information Highlights

Official Name: United Kingdom of Great Britain and Northern Ireland.
Location: Island, western Europe.
Area: 94,250 sq mi (244 108 km²).
Population (1981 census): 55,945,000.
Chief Cities (1981 census): London, the capital, 6,696,008; Birmingham, 1,006,908; Glasgow, 763,162; Leeds, 704,974; Sheffield, 536,770; Liverpool, 510,306.
Government: Head of state, Elizabeth II, queen (acceded Feb. 1952). Head of government, Margaret Thatcher, prime minister (took office May 1979). Legislature—Parliament: House of Lords and House of Commons.
Monetary Unit: Pound (0.6225 pound equals U.S.$1, Dec. 27, 1982).
Gross Domestic Product (1981 U.S.$): $449,850,000,000.
Economic Indexes (1981): Consumer Prices (1970= 100), all items, 403.6; food, 429.2. Industrial production (1975=100), 103.
Foreign Trade (1980 U.S.$): Imports, $119,935,000,000; exports, $115,149,000,000.

The IRA claimed responsibility for two London bombings July 20, one directed against the Queen's Household Cavalry.

Espionage. It was not only the queen's security that led to anxiety. Geoffrey Prime, who had been highly placed in the British secrets communications center in the sleepy country town of Cheltenham, was revealed to be a Russian spy who had passed a horrifying list of secrets to the Soviets. There were two especially worrying aspects of the case. It made cooperation between Britain and its understandably jumpy allies, especially the United States, more difficult, and secondly, Prime was unmasked not by the authorities but by his wife, to whom he had confessed. He was also arrested for sexual offenses against small girls, and but for this predilection it is possible that the police would never have caught him.

Peace Movement. More worries mounted for the United States with the growth in the "peace movement" in Britain. The number of people who were opposed to the use of nuclear weapons continued to rise, and they became far more vocal than before. Tens of thousands of women surrounded a base at Greenham Common in southern England, a possible launch site for American cruise missiles. The revelation that the United States planned another European military base not far from London as a back-up for the headquarters in Western Germany caused more anger. The fear was growing that Europe, far from being protected by the United States, was merely regarded by the White House and Pentagon as a convenient and dispensable forward base to prevent missiles from hitting the United States. Whatever the rights and wrongs of this argument, the Americans showed no signs of successfully countering it, and the peace movement continued to expand—in spite of the increasingly aggressive stance of the USSR.

Northern Ireland. Again, and almost inevitably, the worst suffering in Britain came in Northern Ireland, where the warring sides showed less willingness than ever to reach an accommodation. The worst atrocity occurred in December, when Catholic extremists support-

ing a united Ireland blew up a crowded pub in the tiny town of Ballykelly. The bomb was meant to kill off-duty British soldiers, but also caught a number of local people, especially girls, who had been drinking with them. Some 18 persons died. In July, London had another taste of the horrors of the conflict. A bomb exploded as a troupe of the Queen's Household Cavalry was riding to take part in the changing of the guard ceremony at Whitehall, and another vast bomb exploded under soldiers who were playing music on a bandstand during the lunch hour in Hyde Park. Eleven persons died and 51 were injured; seven horses also died. Each such horror was followed by politicians claiming that the British people would be made even more resolute as a result; there was little clear evidence of this. While Londoners are certainly shocked at bombings near home, it should be remembered that the city's population is twice that of the whole of Ireland and that the police have been generally more successful in catching Irish Republican terrorists away from their home base. In Northern Ireland itself there were several other atrocities. The headmaster of a school was shot in front of his pupils, and several men were killed in full view of their wives and children.

In the hopes of getting some political movement, the minister in charge of Northern Ireland, James Prior, summoned a special Assembly, a democratically elected body which would at first merely talk, but which might later have power devolved to its members, provided they showed that Catholic and Protestant were willing and able to work together. The results were not what he and the London government hoped for. Catholics gave more votes than expected to the extremist Sinn Fein (Irish for "Ourselves Alone"), which supports the terrorist Irish Republican Army. In any event all Catholic parties refused to attend the Assembly which was, in consequence, merely a platform for the Protestants.

SIMON HOGGART, *"The Observer," London*

The Arts

Despite war, recession, value-added tax still on ticket prices, and an identity crisis at the Arts Council (which at one point left six key committee jobs unfilled), the arts still managed to flourish in Britain in 1982. An inspired choice for the new chairman of the Arts Council—Sir William Rees-Mogg, former editor of the *Times* newspaper—and a 9% increase in the Arts Council budget helped to keep gloom at bay. However, constant debate centered on the Arts Council policy of giving more than one quarter of its budget to the four "centers of excellence" in London—the Royal Opera House, the English National Opera, the National Theatre, and the Royal Shakespeare Company (RSC).

Theater. The RSC moved from its run-down London home of 21 years, the Aldwych, to a new auditorium in the Barbican Centre for Arts and Conferences in London, a complex opened by the Queen in March (*see also* London). The company opened in June in epic style with *Henry IV*—Parts I and II, played on alternate nights. The new theater auditorium proved dark and intimate despite its size (1,200 seats) and offered perfect sight lines and acoustics. Transfers from Stratford, including Trevor Nunn's Chekhov-style *All's Well That Ends Well,* made for a strong first Barbican season, while at Stratford-on-Avon, Derek Jacobi appeared first in *Much Ado About Nothing,* then in *Peer Gynt,* and finally in *The Tempest.* Jacobi drew critical acclaim with his portrayal of *The Tempest*'s Prospero.

Opening in December 1981 and continuing in 1982, Peter Hall's National Theatre production of *The Oresteia,* by Aeschylus, provided audiences with more than five hours of mask-clad declamation which transported them to ancient Greece. The award-winning production was later invited to Epidaurus to open the Athens Festival, the first non-Greek company ever to appear there. Some of the actors from *The Oresteia* changed nightly from their masks and hoofed their way through the National's revival of *Guys and Dolls.*

London saw new plays by Harold Pinter, Alan Ayckbourn, Peter Nichols, and Michael Frayn. Julian Mitchell's *Another Country* was well received. A huge performance was given by Alec McCowen as an aged Adolf Hitler in Christopher Hampton's dramatization of the George Steiner novel, *The Portage to San Cristobal of A.H.*

Dance. Ballet Rambert saw the opening of two major works by choreographer Christopher Bruce—*Ghost Dances* and *Berlin Requiem,* performed to the music of Kurt Weill. A major presentation was Peter Wright's production for the Sadler's Wells Royal Ballet of *Swan Lake.* Seen in Manchester and elsewhere, the production will visit London's Covent Garden in 1983. Another Sadler's Wells production which drew interest was the September London opening of David Bintley's ballet *The Swan of Tuonela.* Kenneth Macmillan's *Orpheus,* part of the Stravinsky centenary celebrations, and Rudolf Nureyev's exciting *The Tempest* were among works premiered.

Music. The London Symphony Orchestra moved to its new concert hall and permanent home in the Barbican Center. Through a much more flexible scheduling of concerts in the new hall, a new musical audience became apparent. Concert going in London has normally started at 8 P.M., but younger audiences were turning up at the Barbican not only for lunchtime performances but also at 6:30 P.M. A quiet breakthrough in the presentation of contemporary music on the South Bank was achieved with eight concerts entitled "Music of Eight Decades." Among new works performed for the first time was Peter Maxwell-Davies' *Black Pentecost.*

The overall operatic picture in 1982 was one of fewer new productions and less risk-taking. The 106-year-old D'Oyly Carte Opera Company closed in February, ending a longtime Gilbert and Sullivan tradition.

Visual Arts. The Victoria and Albert Museum along with the Hayward Gallery produced two of the most sumptuous exhibits in a nationwide Festival of India, the first comprehensive look at Indian culture ever in the West. At the Hayward show, "In the Image of Man," 500 works of art, including sculpture spanning some 2,000 years, were on loan from India. At the Victoria and Albert, "The Indian Heritage" focused on the extravagances of court life under the Mughal rule. Other events were a retrospective at the Tate of the work of Sir Edwin Landseer, Queen Victoria's favorite painter, and the launching of the first museum of industrial design, The Boilerhouse, financed by the Conran Foundation.

Films and Television. After the success of *Chariots of Fire,* the usual homilies over the grave of the British film industry have been suspended. Alan Parker's *The Wall,* based on the Pink Floyd record album, aroused interest as did Richard Attenborough's *Gandhi.*

Even those confined to their television sets did not need to feel totally cut off from the best of artistic endeavor. When *Brideshead Revisited* closed its final chapter, viewers were offered David Bowie in *Baal,* by Bertolt Brecht; Laurence Olivier in *A Voyage Round My Father,* by John Mortimer; Alec Guinness' return in *Smiley's People;* and a serialization of the Barchester novels of Anthony Trollope. In celebration of his 60th birthday, the poet Philip Larkin offered a reading from his harsh works. Britain boasts proportionately more owners of videotape recorders than any other Western nation, a fact which suggests that British viewers actually want to record and keep many of the current programs.

MAUREEN GREEN
Author and Journalist, London

GREECE

Anastesselis/Gamma-Liaison

Greece's Andreas Papandreou welcomed Yasir Arafat after the PLO leader left Lebanon.

Andreas Papandreou's Socialist government, which had come to power in October 1981, consolidated its political control of the government and strengthened its standing with the Greek electorate, winning substantial victories in municipal elections.

A More Moderate Stance in Victory. As a political candidate before becoming prime minister, Papandreou, leader of the Panhellenic Socialist Movement (PASOK), had called for sweeping changes in government, including the withdrawal of Greece from NATO, a possible withdrawal from the European Community (EC), and the elimination of U.S. bases from Greek soil. But as prime minister, Papandreou assumed a more moderate stance on these issues.

NATO Membership. Papandreou kept Greece in NATO in spite of Greece's continuing conflict with Turkey over Cyprus and over rights in the Aegean Sea. (As a NATO member, Turkey would be left with significant advantages if Greece were to withdraw from the alliance.) But in November the Papandreou government canceled NATO military exercises scheduled to be held in Greece when the Greek island of Lemnos, located close to Turkey in the Aegean, was not included in the operation.

Greece and the European Community. Greece also remained a member of the EC, receiving from it agricultural price supports and other help. But Papandreou's government refused to join other EC members in any plan to impose economic sanctions against Poland.

The U.S. Bases. Prime Minister Papandreou seemed to take an ambivalent position on the U.S. bases, of which there are four major ones and a number of smaller ones in Greece. He said that eventually they would have to be fully controlled by Greece, but he did not indicate when that would be. Before formal talks between the United States and Greece on the future of the bases began on Oct. 27, 1982, Papandreou warned that if a solution acceptable to Greece could not be reached, the status of the bases might be changed.

Foreign Affairs. Greece steered an independent course in foreign affairs. The government assisted in the removal of PLO fighters from Beirut during the Lebanon crisis, and Yasir Arafat, the PLO leader, made Athens his first stop on September 1 after he left Beirut. In November, Papandreou announced that Greece and Rumania had agreed to discuss making the Balkans a zone free of nuclear weapons. In the same month it was revealed that Gen. Wojciech Jaruzelski of Poland had asked the Greek government to oppose imposition by the West of economic sanctions against Poland. Papandreou agreed, on the condition that Polish martial law be eased.

Internal Changes. The voting age was lowered from 20 to 18, and for the first time in Greek history civil marriages were allowed. Additionally, Papandreou moved to decentralize administration and bring about the formation of voluntary farm cooperatives.

Municipal Elections. Municipal elections held on October 17 and 24 strengthened PASOK. The party won handily in about two thirds of the country's villages and more than 60% of the 276 cities and towns.

Greek Royalty in Exile. Deposed King Constantine II, cousin of Britain's Greek-born Prince Philip, served as a godfather at the christening of the Prince and Princess of Wales' son, William.

GEORGE J. MARCOPOULOS, *Tufts University*

GREECE • Information Highlights

Official Name: Hellenic Republic.
Location: Southwestern Europe.
Area: 50,961 sq mi (131 990 km²).
Population (1981 census): 9,740,151.
Chief Cities (1981 census): Athens, the capital, 885,-136; Salonika, 402,443; Piraeus, 187,458 (1971).
Government: *Head of state,* Constantine Caramanlis, president (took office May 1980). *Head of government,* Andreas Papandreou, prime minister (took office Oct. 1981). *Legislature*—Parliament.
Monetary Unit: Drachma (71.45 drachmas equal U.S.$1, Nov. 30, 1982).
Gross Domestic Product (1981 U.S.$): $40,200,000,-000.
Economic Indexes (1981): *Consumer Prices* (1970=100), *all items,* 472.4; *food,* 553.3. *Industrial production* (1975=100), 129.
Foreign Trade (1980 U.S.$): *Imports,* $10,531,000,-000; *exports,* $4,933,000,000.

GUYANA

During 1982, Guyana suffered its worst economic crisis in decades. In April, President Lynden Forbes Burnham announced that the country was bankrupt and could not pay its debts.

Economy. Prices of the country's principal exports—bauxite, sugar, and rice—had fallen drastically. Partly due to this, but also because of admittedly faulty management, the government-owned firms that dominate all of these fields were running large financial deficits. In October, Guyana's net international reserves were reported to be $250 million in the red.

The Burnham regime took many steps during the year to try to confront the economic crisis. It sought to cut expenditures; by October some 9,000 employees of government and of state-run firms had been dismissed. Substantial numbers of workers in the private sector also lost jobs.

The government also stopped importing a variety of consumer goods, including canned fish, fruit, split peas, cheese, cooking oil, and malted beverages. Other products, such as wheat flour, were unavailable in the regular markets. The government encouraged the consumption of domestically produced rice flour in place of the wheat flour.

At the same time, Guyana's foreign exchange crisis seriously damaged its limited manufacturing sector. Shortages of raw materials forced many industrial plants to work at reduced capacity or to close down.

Government and Foreign Relations. The regime of President Forbes Burnham had no difficulty remaining in power despite the national economic crisis, although the opposition called for his resignation. In April the Guyana Council of Churches organized a meeting of religious organizations, political parties, unions, and other groups, which issued a call for the installation of an all-party "government of national reconstruction."

Guyana was faced with a grave external problem in September when Venezuela refused to renew a 12-year "standstill agreement" on the question of Venezuela's territorial claims to five eighths of Guyana. In the face of this refusal, the Guyana government suggested that the issue be submitted to the World Court, but Venezuela insisted on bilateral negotiations.

On several occasions during the year, Guyana accused the Venezuelan air force of making illegal flights over Guyanese territory. In October, President Forbes Burnham announced that Guyana would purchase reconnaissance planes and armored personnel vehicles from Brazil for use in case of an armed conflict with Venezuela.

ROBERT J. ALEXANDER, *Rutgers University*

HAWAII

Hawaiians entered 1982 with trepidation, since the islands had not yet felt the full effect of the recession. Their fears were not unfounded.

In late November hurricane Iwa, the first to hit Hawaii in more than 20 years, caused extensive damage.

Economy. The sugar industry, which had enjoyed prosperity in 1980, was caught in a maelstrom of fluctuating world prices in 1981 and 1982. Only presidential action in imposing quotas on imported foreign sugar saved the industry from disaster in 1982. Hawaii's pineapple industry did not have similar administration support, and as a result faced competition from inexpensive foreign products. The sugar and pineapple industries both cut back their work forces, causing unrest within the ranks of the International Longshoremen's and Warehousemen's Union, which represents some 26,000 unionized workers throughout the islands.

Despite the recession, tourism, Hawaii's largest industry, had its biggest year ever. Nearly as gratifying was the growth in military spending, rising 20% above the 1981 amount of $1,470,000,-000. Construction took a tumble in 1982 and faced another year of crisis in 1983; the years-long conflict continued over construction of the proposed "H-3" trans-Oahu highway. Diversified agriculture ran into trouble in 1982 because of wet weather, but the state administration vowed to continue efforts to wean Hawaiians from their dependency on imported foodstuffs.

Gov. George Ariyoshi announced in September that he did not anticipate any increases in taxes or service cutbacks in fiscal 1982–83.

Politics. Democrats strengthened their control of the legislature in the 1982 elections, gaining three seats in the state Senate and three in the House to post their heaviest majorities since the historic landslide of 1954. The Democrats would go into the 1983 session outnumbering the Republicans 20–5 in the Senate and 43–8 in the House. The GOP had hoped that reapportionment, which they helped institute by a lawsuit, would work to their advantage.

Democratic Governor Ariyoshi, seeking his third four-year term, easily defeated Republican

---

GUYANA · Information Highlights

Official Name: Cooperative Republic of Guyana.
Location: Northeast coast of South America.
Area: 83,000 sq mi (214 970 km²).
Population (1982 est.): 900,000.
Chief City (1976 est.): Georgetown, the capital, 205,-000 (met. area).
Government: *Head of state,* Lynden Forbes Burnham, president (took office Jan. 1981). *Head of government,* Ptolemy Reid, prime minister (took office Oct. 1980). *Legislature* (unicameral)—National Assembly.
Monetary Unit: Guyana dollar (3.00 G. dollars equal U.S.$1, March 1982).
Gross National Product Per Capita (1980 U.S.$): $690.
Economic Index: *Consumer Prices* (May 1981, 1970=100), *all items,* 310.6; *food,* 309.6.
Foreign Trade (1980 U.S.$): *Imports,* $417,000,000; *exports,* $396,000,000.

D. G. Anderson and Independent Democrat Frank F. Fasi, a former mayor of Honolulu, in the first major three-way gubernatorial race since statehood was achieved in 1959.

U.S. Sen. Spark Matsunaga and U.S. Reps. Daniel K. Akaka and Cecil Heftel, all Democrats, had only token opposition.

Health Hazards. A state Senate investigation was launched after fresh milk was found to be contaminated with heptachlor, a pesticide known to cause cancer in animals. The director of the state health department resigned over the controversy, and his department came under fire.

Millions of cans of locally canned tuna were recalled in June after flaws were detected in the seals on some cans. There were, however, no reports of illness.

Well water from a rural Oahu area was tested over a period of several years and found to contain traces of the pesticide dibromochloro-propane (DBCP). The well was shut down as a precautionary measure.

CHARLES H. TURNER
"The Honolulu Advertiser"

HAWAII · Information Highlights

Area: 6,471 sq mi (16 760 km^2).
Population (1980 census): 964,691.
Chief Cities (1980 census): Honolulu, the capital, 365,-048; Pearl City, 42,575; Kailua, 35,812; Hilo, 35,269.
Government (Dec. 1982): *Chief Officers*—governor, George R. Ariyoshi (D); lt. gov., John Waihee (D). *Legislature*—Senate, 25 members; House of Representatives, 51 members.
State Finances (fiscal year 1981): *Revenues*, $2,085,-000,000; *expenditures*, $1,838,000,000.
Personal Income (1981): $10,823,000,000; per capita, $11,036.
Labor Force (Aug. 1982): *Nonagricultural wage and salary earners*, 403,300; *unemployed*, 34,700 (7.6% of total force).
Education: *Enrollment* (fall 1981)—public elementary schools, 109,272; public secondary, 53,533; colleges and universities (1981–82), 48,121. *Public school expenditures* (1980–81), $354,633,000 ($2,121 per pupil).

HONG KONG

Concern over Hong Kong's future colored events in 1982, a year in which Sir Edward Youde became the colony's 26th governor. He succeeded Sir Murray MacLehose.

Links With China. Britain's 99-year lease on the New Territories—which account for the bulk of the colony's land—will expire in 1997, and China will regain sovereignty. In September 1982, British Prime Minister Margaret Thatcher met with Chinese leaders to begin discussions on Hong Kong's transition to Chinese control.

In February, the Millie's Group of Hong Kong signed a joint venture with the authorities of Boji County, bordering the Shenzhen Special Economic Zone, to set up an industrial estate for medium- and small-scale factories from Hong Kong. In April, a new immigration and customs building was opened at Man Kam To near the China border to handle the increased coach traffic. An agreement was signed with Shenzhen municipality for the construction of four bridges over the Shenzhen River between China and Hong Kong.

Economy. In the first half of the year, Hong Kong's exports increased by 6%, imports by 5%, and reexports by 10%, compared with the same period in 1981.

In February, Sun Hung Kai Finance Ltd. became the first local firm to be granted a banking license since the 1960s. This brought the total number of banks in Hong Kong to 125. In August, a government sale of prime real estate to Peking's Bank of China at half the market price raised doubts about Hong Kong's fate and caused the Hang Seng index to plummet.

Between 1976 and 1982, $2,200,000,000 were spent on road and mass transit railway (MTR) projects. The tunnel connecting Happy Valley with Aberdeen was completed in April 1982 and the MTR's extension to Tsuen Wan in May.

To cope with the increasing demand for low-rental accommodations, the government established new housing estates at Ap Lei Chau and Tsing Yi Island. New towns were being developed or planned at Junk Bay, Ma On Shan, Three Fathoms Cove, and other locations.

A new pattern of district administration was introduced in 1982, consisting of 10 urban districts and 8 rural districts in the New Territories, each served by a district board and a district management committee.

Closed Camp Policy. In May, about 10,000 Vietnamese refugees were awaiting resettlement. In order to deter the influx of Vietnamese, a new policy took effect on July 2 that confined the refugees in closed camps and forbade them to work. The government hoped that the UN office of the High Commissioner for Refugees would pay half of the $8.3 million cost of the policy and resettle all the refugees.

CHUEN-YAN DAVID LAI, *University of Victoria*

Hong Kong Gov. Sir Edward Youde welcomes Britain's Margaret Thatcher for talks on the colony's future.

UPI

HOUSING

An ominous cloud of high prices and high interest rates in 1982 cast deep shadows over the housing landscape, where just a few years before a rainbow pointed to the American dream.

Most families were priced out of the housing market by mortgages that exceeded 17%, a rate which the National Association of Home Builders estimated left only 15.4% of families able to afford a $60,000, 30-year mortgage. Often, however, that mortgage was not available even to those who could afford it. Unable to compete for savings, U.S. thrift institutions—savings banks and savings and loan associations—had little money to lend. Like builders and sellers, they too were fighting to keep from going under. By any measure, the housing industry had fallen into the pit of depression.

New-home production plunged to between 1 million and 1.1 million units for the year, the lowest counted by the home builders association since World War II, and barely one half the rate many housing analysts believed was needed to meet the bulge of 42 million Americans reaching age 30 in the 1980s.

The National Association of Realtors (the Realtors), which counts existing home sales, reported an annual rate of only 1.82 million transactions in August and September, less than one half the 1978 rate of 3,863,000. And what deals were made often had to be accompanied by a mortgage from the seller.

Throughout the year, mortgage delinquencies rose and some people lost their homes. The Mortgage Bankers Association reported that of 8.3 million home loans surveyed, 5.56% were at least 30 days past due in the quarter ending in June, and that 0.2% were being foreclosed. Bankers expressed a reluctance to call in mortgages, however, and some praised the diligence with which homeowners were paying bills. Still, the foreclosure rate was said to be a record.

The housing collapse did not come all at once. By most criteria, it was first detected in October 1978, but by late 1982 it had become the longest in four decades. Time alone did not convey the intensity of the impact, because the onset coincided with perhaps the most bullish feeling toward housing that most Americans had ever witnessed. Housing, it was said, was the best investment anyone ever made. To own a home was a right, some claimed, and almost everyone agreed it made for better citizens. To own your own home, it was said repeatedly, was to share in the American dream.

The dream almost died, as was indicated by the titles the U.S. League of Savings Associations has given to its homebuyer reports. The league, which represents the largest category of home-mortgage lenders, titled its 1978 report "Realizing the American Dream." A year later the report was titled "Coping With Inflation." And early in 1982 it published "The American Dream Adrift." The latter called into question "the mix of policies that is denying the dream of homeownership to a new generation of American families."

In an April 29 report, President Reagan's Commission on Housing proposed a new direction for federal housing policy, emphasizing aid to poor families, the termination of such government regulations as rent control, and more participation by the private sector to finance housing. Although legislation was enacted in May authorizing the secretary of housing and urban development to provide mortgage assistance for lower income families, no legislation action was completed on the commission's recommendations in 1982.

Mortgages. As the housing problem grew deeper, separate elements of the industry were forced to probe deeply for solutions. The old fixed-rate, long-term mortgage was proclaimed dead (prematurely, as it turned out), and in its place came an assortment of variable and adjustable rates that confused both borrowers and lenders. At one point, Jack Carlson, chief economist of the Realtors, counted 84 varieties. Almost all the new loans and their many adaptations had one thing in common: Either the interest rates or the monthly payments fluctuated with economic or money-market conditions. No longer, said lenders, would they be caught with fixed-rate mortgages that might become overwhelmed by rising interest rates.

The most popular new lending plan appeared to be the adjustable rate mortgage, pegged to an index of money costs. The indexes used varied but generally were based on a formula related to short-term Treasury bills or longer-term Treasury securities. Also enjoying some success were graduated payment mortgages, under which a buyer could make relatively small monthly payments in the early years of the loan, when income theoretically is lower. While such arrangements helped qualify more buyers, especially young couples, they also threatened to burden them before their children were grown. For this reason, some couples preferred the shared equity mortgage, in which an investor provided part or all of the down payment, or a portion of the monthly payments, in return for a share in the equity of the property. The drawback to this format was clear: The dream of a home was to be shared with an outsider, and so the sense of ownership was to be diluted. Because of this, the future of the shared equity was in doubt as the year ended.

Nothing seemed to succeed in moving housing better than a bit of help from the seller. It became common for converters of apartment houses to cooperative or condominium status to "buy down" the mortgage rate by several points for the first three years, thus making the purchase more affordable for the buyers of individual units. Single-family homeowners also participated. In order to facilitate sale of their property, the sellers often offered the buyers a small mortgage at below-market rates. At times, the Realtors said, more than one half of existing-home sales involved such financing.

In spite of these market difficulties, housing prices seemed to hold up remarkably well. Late in the year, the Census Bureau estimated that new, single-family dwellings had a median sale price of $72,000, about the same as a year before. According to the Realtors, existing single-family homes were selling for $68,000, or 1.5% higher than a year earlier. Some analysts pointed out, however, that inflation during the year had reduced the purchasing power of dollars a lot more than that, and that seller financing at below-market rates had depressed prices in some instances by as much as 25%.

Regardless, averages did not tell the full story. If you had to sell your house, you may indeed have had to take a substantial loss. Where you lived had a good deal to do with that. The Realtors found that the average price of existing homes in San Francisco was $147,100 during the autumn, but that in Detroit the average was just $54,600. In Washington, DC, the average price was $104,200 and in New York City $100,900. But in between those two cities, the average price in Philadelphia was a mere $65,100.

Averages and prices hid other changes too. To hold prices down, more single-family houses were being built with shared walls and backyards. Multiple baths and fourth bedrooms were becoming less common, and the size of the typical house was shrinking. In 1978, a Realtor survey showed, the median living area was 1,655 sq ft (154 m^2). In 1981 it was only 1,550 sq ft (144 m^2). And a random survey of builders suggested that when the results for 1982 were analyzed, a further decline would be revealed.

Outlook. Every element of the housing industry—builders, sellers, lenders, and buyers—was adjusting to the new situation. But probably the most significant adjustment of all was the willingness of ordinary Americans to accept a diminished dream. Whether the dream would expand again could not be answered as the year came to an end, but it was obvious that the rainbow had regained some of its luster, and that once again there seemed to be a home at its end. The reason, of course, was that interest rates were falling.

From more than 17% early in the year, fixed-rate mortgages had dropped to a range of 14% by early December. A survey by the Realtors showed that adjustable rate mortgages were being offered for even less, some as low as 12.75%. A decline of that magnitude, statisticians said, could raise to more than 15 million from just 9 million the number of families who could qualify for a $60,000, 30-year mortgage. "More people have begun searching for homes to purchase as a result of declining mortgage interest rates," said the Realtors' Carlson. After four years, he said, September was the final month of

AMERICAN HOME BUYERS

	1981	1979	1977
WHO THEY WERE			
A Demographic Profile			
Median age	34 yrs.	33 yrs.	32 yrs.
Unmarried	29.6%	22.4%	17.0%
One- and two-person households	57.4%	51.9%	45.8%
An Economic Profile			
Median household income	$39,196	$28,110	$22,700
Importance of second income*	52.1%	53.9%	47.2%
Median household net worth	$70,519	$52,277	$31,800
First-time Buyers	13.5%	17.8%	36.3%
WHAT THEY PURCHASED			
Condominiums	21.5%	11.0%	NA
New homes	26.1%	30.8%	25.4%
Homes 25 or more years old	29.5%	27.5%	23.7%
Median size of home (sq. ft.)	1,450	NA	NA
THE COST			
Median purchase price	$72,000	$58,000	$44,000
Median down payment	$16,100	$12,282	$ 9,000
Median total monthly housing expense	$816	$550	$400
Mortgage payment	$624	$401	$273
Real estate taxes	$ 72	$ 58	$ 54
Utilities	$100	$ 75	$ 60
Hazard insurance	$ 20	$ 16	$ 13
HOW THEY AFFORDED THEIR PURCHASE			
Less than 20% down payment	30.9%	42.9%	32.1%
Housing expense exceeding 25% of household income	44.9%	45.7%	38.1%

* Percentage of households with two adults in which income contributed by a second earner accounted for 10% or more of total household income.

Source: U.S. League of Savings Associations

slow sales in the existing-home market. The association forecast a sustained recovery through 1983 and into 1984, a recovery that would bring resale activity to a 2.8 million annual rate by the end of 1983. "No boom," said Kenneth Kerin, an economist who worked on the forecast, but "a sustained recovery."

The National Association of Home Builders agreed. Late in the year Robert Sheehan, director of economic research, said builders were preparing to begin work on 1.35 million new single-family homes in 1983, and that the rate might rise to 1.7 million before peaking in 1986. "We're cautiously optimistic," he said. So too were the lenders. James Christian, chief economist of the U.S. League of Savings Associations, forecast a "modest improvement" in home sales, and said interest rates were likely to follow a jagged path lower, primarily because the outlook for less inflation was "very favorable."

After four years, the great housing depression appeared to be at an end. But in that time it had changed the very concept of what constitutes a house, as well as the building, financing, and selling of it.

See UNITED STATES: The Economy.

JOHN CUNNIFF
The Associated Press

Manufactured Homes

Factory-built housing, once the embarrassment of most beauty- and safety-conscious communities, is fast overcoming its former reputation for shoddy, uninspired, unsafe construction. Just as the mobile home helped fill the housing needs of the post-World War II years, today's manufactured housing, with multiple-type structures to choose from, has become an alternate means to home ownership for millions of people who otherwise could not afford to buy a home.

The manufactured home (a term mandated by Congress as a substitute for the historical term "mobile home") is a factory-built dwelling transported in one or more sections to the home site, where it is placed on concrete strips, slab, or foundation. Currently, about 4.6 million manufactured homes are used as primary dwellings, with roughly 50% of these located in manufactured-housing communities. Their average price per square foot, excluding land, is roughly half that of site-built housing, and they constitute about 80% of all single-family homes sold for under $40,000.

The most common type of manufactured housing is still the single-section home, typically 14 ft (4 m) wide and 60 to 75 ft (18–23 m) long, which offers up to 960 sq ft (90 m^2) of living space. A multisection house, which typically has 1,440 sq ft (134 m^2) of living space, is two single units built separately and joined horizontally at the site to form a single unit. Because of the additional living space provided, sales of multisection homes have risen from less than 10% of all manufactured-home sales in the 1960s to roughly 30% in 1982. The modular home, a third type, is essentially a multisection house designed to be permanently placed on a foundation. In fact, 97% of the manufactured homes are never moved once they reach their destination.

Restrictive zoning regulations in many areas still limit the location of manufactured homes, although these zoning barriers are coming down as the home designs improve. Rental space in a manufactured-housing development, typically with paved sidewalks and streets, underground utilities, off-street parking, and recreational facilities, is also available.

Historically the industry developed from the manufacture of trailer-coaches for leisure use in the 1930s. By the end of that decade, to the surprise of the manufacturers, about half of the output was being used as permanent housing. By 1952, the transition to the use of mobile homes as primary housing was complete. The trailer-coach industry split into two different entities—the mobile-home and recreational-vehicle industries.

Paralleling this history was the evolution of ever higher standards of construction quality. After World War II, the mobile-home industry initiated a long-term program of self regulation designed to develop uniform production standards. By the mid-1970s, this code served as the basis for the federal manufactured-home standards which were established in 1976. (Modular homes are built to codes other than the federal standards, and traditional builders are subject to many different codes within the local communities.)

The manufactured-housing industry now is comprised of four sectors: supply, production, distribution, and land development. About 1,500 suppliers serve the roughly 190 firms that produce the homes. There are approximately 10,000 dealerships. About 60% of them are involved in manufactured-housing community operations, of which there are now more than 24,000.

ARTHUR D. BERNHARDT

Today's mobile, or manufactured, home even comes in a contemporary design with two bedrooms and two bathrooms.

Courtesy, LCS

HUNGARY

Hungary's government concentrated on furthering economic reforms and modernization at home and on strengthening ties with the West.

Domestic Affairs. Hungary continued to loosen bureaucratic centralization of the economy by breaking up giant trusts (notably coal), closing inefficient state enterprises, and allowing some 330 private enterprises with up to 30 workers to compete with nationalized companies.

The value of agricultural production per capita rose to the highest in Europe, and the agricultural growth rate was exceeded only by that of the Netherlands. The combined harvest of wheat, rye, barley, oats, and corn for 1982 exceeded that of 1981 by some 1.5 million metric tons (1.65 million T), reaching a record 14.2 million metric tons (15.6 million T).

The 1981–1985 Five-Year Plan envisaged the construction of 270,000 privately financed dwellings, representing 70% of the total built. Government credits and various governmental facilities became widely available to prospective private entrepreneurs. A five-day work week was introduced in all manufacturing enterprises in January 1982. In September it was extended to all educational institutions.

Demonstrations in support of the Polish Solidarity trade union movement took place in Budapest in August. Security forces dispersed the demonstrators and arrested their leaders, including sociologist Gábor Demszky.

Some illegal *samizdat* publications, notably *Beszelo,* have been appearing since 1981. Privately printed and distributed, these uncensored publications offer its readers facts and critical comments unavailable elsewhere.

The Academy of Sciences founded the Political Science Society "to prove once and for all the Marxist character of political science."

Foreign Trade and Foreign Affairs. The traditionally negative trade balance showed a surplus in 1981 of 1,075,000,000 forints. Half of Hungary's foreign trade was now with the West. Exports of agricultural products brought in some $2,000,000,000 in hard currencies. Imports of oil were reduced as oil was replaced by cheaper Soviet natural gas. In May, Hungary was admitted to the International Monetary Fund. The allocated quota of 375 million Special Drawing Rights would allow Hungary to borrow up to $2,600,000,000 from the fund. In July, Hungary joined the World Bank.

Hungary's Communist party chief, János Kádár, visited Bonn in April. Soon after, Poland's prime minister, Wojciech Jaruzelski, made an official visit to Budapest. In the middle of the summer France's President François Mitterrand was received in Hungary's capital; a strengthening of cultural and economic ties was promised in a joint communiqué.

In September, Hungary's deputy foreign minister Imre Hollai was elected president of the 37th annual session of the UN General Assembly.

JAN KARSKI, *Georgetown University*

ICELAND

The government of Gunnar Thoroddsen effectively became nonviable after it resorted to drastic economic measures, announced in August during the parliamentary recess. The premier, formerly deputy chairman of the conservative Independence Party (IP), sought to buy time for the peculiarly constituted three-element coalition. As the year wore on, the government was backed by just three IP legislators, with growing unease in the camps that formed its parliamentary backbone—the centrist Progressive Party (PP) and the leftist People's Alliance (PA). Early national elections, perhaps in April 1983, seemed a foregone conclusion. While the IP scored big gains at the municipal polls in May 1982, speculation continued over the split in the party's ranks that had opened up when Thoroddsen defied the IP caucus to form the government in early 1980. Foreign Minister Ólafur Jóhannesson (PP) reaffirmed the traditional national security stance—membership in NATO and U.S. military presence, both anathema to the PA. The state visit of President Vigdís Finnbogadóttir to Great Britain was given ample publicity by foreign media, as was her role at the opening ceremonies of "Scandinavia Today," a cultural festival in the United States.

Economy. The emergency measures taken in August included a sharp currency devaluation and limits on wage indexation. The controversial package was met with notably docile reactions from key labor unions, which had settled for modest contracts. Central to the alarming economic outlook was a plunging output in the fisheries sector, compounded by some market difficulties, overinvestment in the trawler fleet, and soaring inflation (estimated at 50–60%). A 5–6% drop in national income was predicted, along

---

HUNGARY · Information Highlights

Official Name: Hungarian People's Republic.
Location: East-central Europe.
Area: 35,920 sq mi (93 033 km²).
Population (1982 est.): 10,700,000.
Chief Cities (1981 est.): Budapest, the capital, 2,060,-644; Miskolc, 209,287; Debrecen, 193,946.
Government: *Head of state,* Pál Losonczi, chairman of the presidential council (took office April 1967). *Head of government,* György Lázár, premier (took office 1975). First secretary of the Hungarian Socialist Workers' Party, János Kádár (took office 1956). *Legislature* (unicameral)—National Assembly.
Monetary Unit: Forint (35 forints equal U.S.$1, March 1982, noncommercial rate).
Gross Domestic Product (1981 U.S.$): $37,700,000,-000–$52,800,000,000.
Economic Indexes (1981): *Consumer Prices* (1970= 100), *all items,* 162.5; *food,* 170.7. *Industrial production* (1975=100), 121.
Foreign Trade (1981 U.S.$): *Imports,* $9,128,000,-000; *exports,* $8,712,000,000.

ICELAND · Information Highlights

Official Name: Republic of Iceland.
Location: North Atlantic Ocean.
Area: 39,709 sq mi (102 846 km²).
Population (Oct. 1982): 238,958.
Chief Cities (Oct. 1982): Reykjavik, the capital, 84,-593: Kópavogur, 13,996; Akureyri, 13,605.
Government: *Head of state,* Vigdís Finnbogadóttir, president (took office Aug. 1980). *Head of government,* Gunnar Thoroddsen, prime minister (took office Feb. 1980). *Legislature*—Althing: Upper House and Lower House.
Monetary Unit: Króna (15.63 krónur equal U.S.$1, October 1982).
Economic Index (1980): *Consumer Prices* (1970= 100), *all items,* 1,750.9; *food,* 1,921.4.
Foreign Trade (1981 U.S.$): *Imports,* $1,033,000,-000; *exports,* $888,000,000.

with a trade deficit equal to 8–9% of the GNP. Farm subsidies were a drain on the treasury.

Fisheries. Total catches at midyear stood at just 425,600 metric tons (468,200 T), down by 208,000 metric tons (228,800 T) from the June 1981 figure—primarily because of a ban on capelin fishing. Groundfish landings, mainly cod, were also down by a painful margin after growing steadily since 1979. A boosted take of herring was authorized for 1982.

Energy. High priority continued to be given to harnessing domestic sources, now accounting for more than 50% of total energy use. Two big geothermal heating systems were completed, and work started on a new hydro project. The gap in the national power grid narrowed.

HAUKUR BÖDVARSSON, *"News From Iceland"*

IDAHO

Dismal economic news pervaded Idaho in 1982. Income was down in agriculture, lumber, mining, and tourism, plunging the state deep into recession. By the fourth quarter, unemployment reached 11.1%, with rates of more than 35% reported by a few northern counties.

The largest single job loss (2,100) occurred on New Year's Day 1982, when Gulf Resources and Chemical Corporation permanently closed the Bunker Hill Mine in Kellogg. Depressed prices for silver, lead, and zinc frustrated Gulf Resources' attempt to sell the mine and smelter. Accusations flew when a group of prospective Idaho investors withdrew an offer in late January, citing intransigence on the part of the United Steel Workers Union. The union, in turn, charged that the purchase offer was insincere, a ploy to gain support for right-to-work legislation. In late October Gulf Resources finally sold Bunker Hill to the in-state investors. Still, there was no prospect of the mine or smelter reopening soon.

Legislature. The Bunker Hill furor galvanized both houses of the Republican-dominated legislature into passing a right-to-work bill. Democratic Gov. John Evans' veto of the bill was narrowly sustained in the Senate.

The most protracted legislative battle was over the future of the state's public television stations. Ultimately, the three stations were incorporated under a single manager. Though retaining their own call letters, the stations in Pocatello and Moscow became "satellites" of KAID in Boise. To persons outside Idaho the most notable legislative action was elimination of the insanity plea in criminal cases.

The General Fund budget approved for fiscal 1983 was $464,729,900, an increase of 9.8% over fiscal 1982. Education received 71.3% of this total, while health and welfare received 15.3%.

Budget. The ink was hardly dry on the fiscal 1983 budget when the state faced a deficit for fiscal 1982. In May, Governor Evans ordered a 3.85% cutback of state agencies for fiscal 1982. He also ordered a four-day workweek for state employees. Even so, the General Fund fell $13.8 million short for fiscal 1982, and that sum had to be paid out of fiscal 1983 revenues. In July, Evans ordered an 8.5% cutback for fiscal 1983. Tax revenues showing no sign of recovery, the governor followed in October with an additional 1.5% cutback.

Election Results. The gubernatorial campaign was dominated by the right-to-work issue and by charges from the Republican challenger, Lt. Gov. Phil Batt, that Governor Evans had violated the constitution by recording a deficit in fiscal 1982. Evans won reelection by a scant 3,500 votes.

First district Rep. Larry Craig and second district Rep. George Hansen, both Republicans, were returned to Congress. State Treasurer Marjorie Moon and state Auditor Joe Williams, both Democrats, likewise were reelected. Attorney General David Leroy (R) won the lieutenant governor's post, while Jim Jones (R) won election to replace Leroy as attorney general.

Democrats gained two seats in the Idaho Senate and five in the House. Republicans, however, retained their overall edge. A record 16 women were elected to the legislature.

M. C. HENBERG, *University of Idaho*

IDAHO · Information Highlights

Area: 83,564 sq mi (216 431 km²).
Population (1980 census): 944,038.
Chief Cities (1980 census): Boise, the capital, 102,-160; Pocatello, 46,340; Idaho Falls, 39,590.
Government (1982): *Chief Officers*—governor, John V. Evans (D); lt. gov., Philip E. Batt (R). *Legislature*—Senate, 35 members; House of Representatives, 70 members.
Senate Finances (fiscal year 1981): *Revenues,* $1,224,000,000; *expenditures,* $1,139,000,000.
Personal Income (1981): $8,574,000,000; per capita, $8,937.
Labor Force (Aug. 1982): *Nonagricultural wage and salary earners,* 311,800; *unemployed,* 39,700 (8.9% of total force).
Education: *Enrollment* (fall 1981)—public elementary schools, 145,547; public secondary, 58,977; colleges and universities (1981–82), 42,758 students. *Public school expenditures* (1980–81), $392,165,-000 ($1,780 per pupil).

ILLINOIS

The bizarre Tylenol poisonings, the recession, and a close gubernatorial election dominated Illinois news in 1982.

Poisonings. Seven Chicago-area persons died after taking Extra-Strength Tylenol capsules filled with deadly potassium cyanide. Three of the victims were from one family; the rest were from scattered parts of the Chicago area.

Investigators believed that the pain-killing capsules were pried open, filled with the poison, and then returned to their containers and randomly placed back on shelves of stores. There were no intended victims and the motive for the crime remained a mystery.

In the aftermath of the tragedy, millions of containers of Extra-Strength Tylenol were removed from stores across the nation. The city of Chicago banned the sale of the Tylenol capsules in Chicago, and in Washington the federal government drafted new rules for tamper-proof packages for drugs. Late in the year, James W. Lewis was arrested and charged with trying to extort $1 million from the Tylenol manufacturers to "stop the killing."

Economy. Illinois felt the impact of the national recession, with an unemployment rate that was one of the highest in the nation. In late fall the state's jobless rate stood at 12.5%, more than 2% above the national average. Hardest hit were the state's manufacturers of durable goods and heavy equipment. Cities such as Rockford, Peoria, and Rock Island, which are big producers of farm implements, had among the highest unemployment rates in the nation.

In October, employees of the Caterpillar Tractor Company in Peoria went on strike, along with Caterpillar employees in four other states. The company had sought wage and benefit concessions from the union, claiming that business had been damaged by the recession and by an increase in foreign competition.

Illinois farmers were hurt by near-record corn and soybean yields that brought record low prices. (*See* AGRICULTURE.)

Election. The recession became a big issue in the election race between James R. Thompson, the Republican incumbent governor, and Democrat Adlai E. Stevenson 3d, a former U.S. senator. Stevenson, whose father twice ran for president, was an early favorite, but the campaign took some unusual twists.

Thompson admitted, following newspaper disclosures, that as governor he had accepted oil paintings, antiques, china and crystal, $500 in cash from a Teamster union official, $2,500 worth of gold Krugerrands, and other lavish gifts from bankers, real estate developers, and other admirers. The governor denied that the gifts had influenced any decisions he made. However, he set a new policy for himself, under which he would no longer accept gifts worth more than $100.

That scandal quickly dimmed when Thompson's wife, an attorney, announced that she was seeking a federal judgeship in Chicago. Questions were raised about her qualifications to don a robe and the propriety of the governor's wife sitting on the bench. Jayne Thompson ultimately withdrew her application after the Illinois State Bar Association refused to recommend her for the judgeship.

Everything in the campaign seemed to be going Adlai Stevenson's way—until Stevenson accused Thompson of portraying him as "some sort of wimp." The governor, who tried to project a forceful image of himself in the campaign, denied that he ever called Stevenson a wimp. Stevenson publicly stated that he was not a wimp, complaining that he was hampered by a weak image just as his famous father was damaged by his reputation as an "egghead." To many voters, Stevenson's actions did more to perpetuate the image than abolish it. Editorial cartoons and jokes took up the controversy, and Stevenson's standing in the polls began to slide.

Stevenson's campaign was based on a call for new leadership in Springfield to revive the state's sagging economy. Thompson stressed that he had held the line on tax increases and brought balanced budgets to Illinois. He claimed that he, rather than Stevenson, could bring the necessary leadership to the office.

By election day every poll in the state indicated that Governor Thompson, who was looking for a wide margin of victory, would for the third time win the governorship by a landslide. It was not to be. For four days after the November election, the lead jumped back and forth. Final returns made Thompson the victor by only 5,000 votes out of nearly four million cast. Democrats won most other major offices in the state.

Illinois voters overwhelmingly approved a constitutional amendment to deny bail to accused felons who face a life sentence if convicted. That proposition won 85% of the vote.

ROBERT ENSTAD
Reporter, "Chicago Tribune"

ILLINOIS • Information Highlights

Area: 56,345 sq mi (145 934 km²).

Population (1980 census): 11,426,596.

Chief Cities (1980 census): Springfield, the capital, 99,637; Chicago, 3,005,072; Rockford, 139,712.

Government (1982): *Chief Officers*—governor, James R. Thompson (R). *General Assembly*—Senate, 59 members; House of Representatives, 177 members.

State Finances (fiscal year 1981): *Revenues,* $14,250,000,000; *expenditures,* $13,934,000,000.

Personal Income (1981): $132,675,000,000; per capita, $11,576.

Labor Force (Aug. 1982): *Nonagricultural wage and salary earners,* 4,615,900; *unemployed,* 651,100 (11.4% of total force).

Education: *Enrollment* (fall 1981)—public elementary schools, 1,304,192; public secondary, 619,892; colleges and universities (1981–82), 659,623 students. *Public school expenditures* (1980–81), $4,652,477,000 ($2,441 per pupil).

INDIA

© Shepard Sherbell/Picture Group

Indira Gandhi's U.S. visit signaled a new interest in free enterprise and ties to the West.

On Aug. 15, 1982, India celebrated the 35th anniversary of its independence, recognizing both progress and unresolved problems in political, social, and international affairs. Prime Minister Indira Gandhi remained in firm control of the country's politics, in spite of divisions in her own Congress (I) party, mounting criticism of her domestic policies, increasing signs of deterioration and corruption in public life, frequent outbreaks of violence and unrest, and a failure to deal effectively with growing economic and social problems. The economy registered some significant gains, mostly of a short-term nature. The year was a particularly active one in foreign policy, with Prime Minister Gandhi making official visits to the United States and the Soviet Union, and with preparations under way for hosting the nonaligned summit meeting in early 1983.

Politics and Public Affairs. The ruling Congress (I) party continued to be dominated by Prime Minister Gandhi, who chose new members for the party's Working Committee and Parliamentary Board (its two top agencies), appointed and ousted chief ministers of several states with little concern for their local standing, handpicked a candidate to succeed President N. Sanjiva Reddy, and in general applied the test of loyalty to important figures in the party and government. Opposition, both within the Congress (I) and in the other major parties, was weak and fragmented. Early in the year, an attempt to merge the three leading opposition parties—the Bharatiya Janata party, the Congress (U), and the Lok Dal—proved abortive. The Communist Party of India (CPI), which had supported Gandhi during the 1975–77 Emergency, withdrew its support and associated itself with the other major communist party—the Communist Party of India (Marxist-Leninist). While the close association was no serious challenge to

Gandhi on a nationwide scale, it was a significant factor in West Bengal, where the CPI(M) dominated the ministry, and in Kerala, where the two communist parties posed a major challenge to the Congress (I)-dominated government.

Elections in May for the legislatures of four states—Haryana, Himachal Pradesh, Kerala, and West Bengal—and for seven seats in the Lok Sabha (lower house of national parliament) indicated some decline in support for Gandhi as well as the divided state of the opposition. No party won a majority of seats in the legislatures of Haryana, Himachal Pradesh, or Kerala. In the first two, Congress (I) was able to continue in power, though with reduced majorities, and in Kerala the result was a virtual stalemate. In West Bengal, as expected, the ruling leftist government, dominated by the CPI(M), won more than three fourths of the seats. And in the Lok Sabha, Congress (I) gained all but two of the seven seats up for election.

The presidential election—by an electoral college comprising members of both houses of parliament and the state legislatures—was held on July 12. Gandhi's candidate, Zail Singh, home minister and former chief minister of the Punjab, received some 73% of the vote even though most of the opposition parties were united behind H.R. Khanna, a former justice of the supreme court. Singh became the seventh president of India and the first member of the Sikh sect to hold the office.

While the prime minister dominated the political scene, she was not so successful in dealing with grave social problems, including what then-President Reddy described in his address on the eve of Republic Day (January 25) as declining moral standards and corruption in public affairs. Serious unrest continued as a regular phenomenon in the troubled northeast and flared up sporadically in many other parts of the country. In the Punjab and New Delhi, militant Sikhs battled with police during demonstrations for greater autonomy for the Sikh-dominated Punjab; in August alone more than 10,000 demonstrators were arrested. On October 11 Sikh militants stormed the parliament house in New Delhi, leaving at least four persons killed and 65 injured. Bombay was paralyzed for several days in August, when 22,000 state police constables rioted over labor grievances. And in the Muslim-dominated state of Kashmir, Buddhists rioted in January over how they were being treated.

India's fledgling space program was seriously retarded when its first commercial satellite, INSAT 1A, failed. The $130-million spacecraft, with an expected life of seven years, was launched at Cape Canaveral on April 10 but ceased to be operational five months later because the fuel propellant was depleted.

Among prominent Indians who died in 1982 were Acharya Kripalani, a veteran of the freedom struggle, former president of the Indian National Congress, and later a leading opponent of the Congress; Sheikh Abdullah, "the lion of Kashmir" (see OBITUARIES); and C. D. Deshmukh, a former finance minister.

Economy. Relatively optimistic predictions for the economy early in the year were substantially modified as a result of increases and decreases in the 1982–83 budget and the problems being experienced in many sectors.

In a broadcast to the nation on January 14, Prime Minister Gandhi announced a production-oriented Twenty-Point Program to accelerate development in all sectors of the economy. On February 18, in his address opening the parliamentary budget session, President Reddy stressed the importance of the new program, stated that all major industries had made significant progress in the previous nine months, an-

nounced that there would be record food grain production, and called on all Indians to make 1982 a successful "Productivity Year."

A grimmer picture was presented in the Economic Survey, presented to parliament on February 24, and in the central budget for 1982–83, presented by the finance minister three days later. The Economic Survey reported that the government's finances were "coming under increasing pressure" because of larger defense expenditures, growth of nondevelopmental expenditures, and an increase in the cost of projects under the Sixth Five-Year Plan (1980–85). The new budget reflected these increases, including a rise in defense spending of 21.4% and in Five-Year Plan outlays of 27.6%. Total receipts for 1982–83 were estimated at $30,000,000,000 and total disbursements were expected to reach some $32,000,000,000.

In June the 13-nation Aid India Consortium, meeting in Paris, pledged some $3,700,000,000 for fiscal 1982–83, an increase of 5.7%.

Indian officials, including Prime Minister Gandhi herself, repeatedly expressed concern over the growing reluctance of the major donor countries, especially the United States, to fulfill their pledges of support to the International Monetary Fund (IMF) and International Development Association (IDA), the soft-loan affiliate of the World Bank. In the past India has been the main beneficiary of IDA loans, but the decline in contributions to that organization and the likelihood that China, a recent adherent to both the IMF and IDA, might draw heavily on both funds caused many Indians to express concern over the amount of assistance that could be expected from the two sources.

In 1982 the government expanded its efforts to make India more attractive to foreign investors and traders. It gave wide publicity to its liberalization of investment and import policies, which was described as a "major if somewhat

Zail Singh (center, front) became India's seventh president and first member of the Singh faith to hold the office.
© Dilip Mehta/Contact

UPI

Residents of Oriassa state battle flooding, a perennial problem in northern and eastern India, in September.

quiet change taking place in the economic policies of India."

Inflation, which the government claimed had been reduced virtually to zero by the spring, again became a problem later in the year, especially because of substantial price increases for food grains and other necessities. Unemployment and underemployment continued to be major problems.

Promoting trade was the main objective of the International Trade Fair, held in New Delhi from November 1 to 14. Nearly 50 countries, the European Community, and some 3,000 private companies participated; attendance was estimated at three million. Shortly after, from November 19 to December 4, the Asian Games were held in New Delhi. Hundreds of athletes from most nations in the continent participated in events observed by several million people. In preparation for the Games, the government of India spent vast amounts of money (estimated as high as $1,000,000,000) on new buildings, including sports facilities and many luxury hotels. The Games were certainly one of the year's highlights, but the exhorbitant cost was a serious drain on the budget.

INDIA • Information Highlights

Official Name: Republic of India.
Location: South Asia.
Area: 1,269,346 sq mi (3 287 606 km²).
Population (1982 est.): 713,800,000.
Chief Cities (1971 est.): New Delhi, the capital, 3,600,-000; Bombay, 6,000,000; Calcutta, 3,200,000.
Government: *Head of state,* Zail Singh, president (took office July 1982). *Head of government,* Indira Gandhi, prime minister (took office January 1980). *Legislature*—Parliament: Rajya Sabha (Council of States) and Lok Sabha (House of the People).
Monetary Unit: Rupee (9.74 rupees equal U.S.$1, Nov. 10, 1982).
Gross National Product (1981 U.S.$): $157,800,000,-000.
Economic Indexes: *Consumer prices* (1981), *all items,* 233.1; *food,* 232.9 (1970=100). *Industrial production* (1980), 126 (1975=100).
Foreign Trade (1980 U.S.$): *Imports,* $12,937,000,-000; *exports,* $6,328,000,000.

Foreign Affairs. There were many indications during the year that India was determined to play a more assertive role in foreign affairs. Its determination to be a more active leader of the developing nations was evidenced by several initiatives: its convening of a "South-South" conference in New Delhi in February—formally called the "New Delhi Consultations"—in which representatives of 44 developing countries sought, without much success, to evolve a unified strategy for dealing with the world's industrialized powers; its agreement in August to replace Iraq as the host for the seventh nonaligned summit conference in March 1983; and the special attention its leaders gave to heads of other developing countries through official visits, the extending of invitations, and other gestures.

Relations with the United States seemed to improve as a result of Prime Minister Gandhi's official visit in late July and early August. It was her first trip to the United States since the somewhat ill-fated visit in late 1971, when the United States was tilting toward Pakistan and away from India, just before the war between those two countries. Unlike the previous visit, her stay in the United States was relaxed and generally successful. Her long talks with President Reagan and other high-ranking U.S. officials seemed to go off well. A concrete evidence of the improvement in U.S.-Indian relations was the agreement, announced July 29, to end the impasse over the vexing issue of enriched uranium for the nuclear power plant at Tarapur, near Bombay. By that arrangement France, not the United States, would supply the uranium; the agreement seemed to be in jeopardy before year's end, however, because of a Franco-Indian dispute over the conditions of delivery.

Indo-Soviet relations continued to be extensive in spite of evidence that India was trying to develop a more balanced approach in its relations with the USSR, China, and the United States. In March a large Soviet military delegation came to India, led by Minister of Defense

Dmitri Ustinov and including the commanders of the Soviet navy and air force, the deputy commander of the army, and a number of senior generals. It was said to be the highest-ranking Soviet military delegation ever sent outside the Soviet bloc. On September 22 Prime Minister Gandhi made her first official visit to the Soviet Union since her return to power in January 1980. The two days in Moscow were more routine and subdued than her visit to the United States, but she was very warmly received. President Leonid Brezhnev greeted her on her arrival, hosted several meetings in her honor, spent many hours in conversation with her, and saw her off at the Moscow airport. Her visit, which also included Tallin and Kiev, was marked by repeated declarations of friendship and cooperation between the two countries, as well as a number of agreements for further cooperation on economic and cultural matters. Upon taking office in November, new Soviet party leader Yuri Andropov promised strong ties with India.

The prime minister's busy itinerary in 1982 also included official visits to England in March, where she joined Prime Minister Thatcher in inaugurating the "Festival of India" exhibition (*see* ART); to Saudi Arabia in April; to Japan in August; and to Mauritius and Mozambique in late August. Before leaving office, President Reddy made official visits to Sri Lanka in early February, where he was the guest of honor at celebrations commemorating the 34th anniversary of that country's independence, and to Ireland and Yugoslavia in May. The new president, Zail Singh, went to Houston, TX, in late September for medical treatment.

Little progress was made during the year in Sino-Indian relations, but the second round of official talks between the two nations was held in New Delhi in May. Though their 20-year-old border dispute was still unresolved, there was reported to be some narrowing of differences.

In Indo-Pakistani relations, several meetings were held at the foreign minister level in an effort to speed up the normalization process. Then, on November 1, Prime Minister Gandhi and Pakistani President Zia ul-Haq met in New Delhi, and a breakthrough was made. The two leaders agreed to set up a permanent joint commission to resolve any disputes that might arise, as well as to increase trade and other contacts.

Among the many heads of state or government to come to India during the year were the kings of Bhutan and Spain, the presidents of Algeria, Bangladesh, Greece, Mozambique, and Tanzania, and the prime ministers of Sweden and Great Britain.

NORMAN D. PALMER, *Emeritus Professor of Political Science and South Asian Affairs University of Pennsylvania*

Hindus gather yearly in the eastern town of Puri to celebrate the birth of Lord Jaggarnath, king of the universe.

Gamma-Liaison

INDIANA

No clear pattern emerged from the results of the 1982 elections in Indiana, enabling both major political parties to claim victory. The 30-day, alternate-year "short session" of the General Assembly was aimed at keeping the state treasury in the black. Devastating floods and growing unemployment also headlined events.

Election. As in the rest of the nation, Indiana Democrats gained in local and state elections but fell short of winning a mandate against conservative Republican policies. Republicans retained control of both houses of the state legislature, but by slimmer margins: 57–43 in the House instead of 63–37, and 32–18 in the Senate as opposed to 35–15. In a surprise victory Democrats won the state auditor's race, but Republican incumbents retained the other state offices. Voting for the first time in the recently redrawn congressional districts, Hoosiers split their congressional delegation 5–5; Republicans had hoped for a 6–4 margin. Elected in the first district was Democrat Katie Hall of Gary, the first black and third woman to represent Indiana in the national House of Representatives. As expected, Republican Sen. Richard Lugar easily defeated challenger Floyd Fithian to become Indiana's first GOP senator to be reelected in 26 years. Approximately 62% of Indiana's registered voters went to the polls, a surprisingly large turnout.

Legislature. Faced with severe economic problems, Indiana legislators concentrated on keeping the state solvent—and not much else. A one-time-only measure requiring retailers and employers to remit state sales-tax collections and income taxes withheld from employees by the 20th day of the following month rather than the 30th day removed the short-term fiscal pressure. Republicans expect positive long-term results from a bill increasing from 3% to 4% the supplemental net income tax on corporations making a profit, retroactive to Jan. 1, 1982. To offset this increase, Indiana businesses can more rapidly depreciate new equipment, machinery, and buildings on state income-tax returns. Split on this Republican-sponsored measure, Democrats conceded that the corporate-tax increase and accelerated depreciation would cancel each other out in the first few years but predicted a net loss for the state over the next eight years as the depreciation continues to accelerate. Despite these and other fiscal measures, Hoosiers fear a $450 million deficit, tax increases, and tax restructuring during 1983.

A last-day compromise reaffirmed a 1981 legislative decision to provide $1,000,000,000 in state tuition support to local schools in 1982–83 and authorized transfer of schools' Cumulative Building Funds to General Funds to pay for an extra $9.2 million in energy costs in 1983. Democrats condemned the "compromise" energy measure. Other significant legislative measures required physicians to notify parents before performing abortions on minors and permitted most motorists to renew drivers' licenses without taking a written test. A bill amending Indiana's Constitution to allow the state to operate a lottery was defeated.

Other. The worst flood in 50 years hit Fort Wayne, at the confluence of the St. Joseph, St. Marys, and Maumee rivers, in the early spring. An unemployment rate exceeding 11% ranked Indiana as one of the hardest-hit states in the nation economically. Particularly affected were the automotive towns of Anderson, Kokomo, Muncie, and Columbus.

LORNA LUTES SYLVESTER
Indiana University

Severe flooding struck Fort Wayne in the spring. Only heroic work by the public stopped complete inundation.

UPI

INDIANA • Information Highlights

Area: 36,185 sq mi (93 719 km^2).
Population (1980 census): 5,490,260.
Chief Cities (1980 census): Indianapolis, the capital, 700,807; Fort Wayne, 172,028; Gary, 151,953.
Government (1982): *Chief Officers*—governor, Robert D. Orr (R); lt. gov., John Mutz (R). *General Assembly*—Senate, 50 members; House of Representatives, 100 members.
State Finances (fiscal year 1981): *Revenues,* $5,488,-000,000; *expenditures,* $5,664,000,000.
Personal Income (1981): $53,147,000,000; per capita, $9,720.
Labor Force (Aug. 1982): *Nonagricultural wage and salary earners,* 2,005,300; *unemployed,* 283,200 (11.1% of total force).
Education: *Enrollment* (fall 1981)—public elementary schools, 690,810; public secondary, 334,362; colleges and universities (1981–82), 251,826 students. *Public school expenditures* (1980–81), $2,-062,572,000 ($1,793 per pupil).

INDONESIA

Elections for parliament and regional assemblies were held in May for the third time in the 16-year history of President Suharto's New Order regime. The government Golkar party won 64% of the vote, followed by the Islamic-oriented Development Unity Party with 28% and the nationalist-Christian Indonesian Democracy Party with 8%. Of particular importance was Golkar's victory in Jakarta, with 45% of the vote against 40% for Development Unity, reversing the results of the 1977 voting. The 1982 election was an important step in the reelection campaign of President Suharto; that vote is scheduled for March 1983.

Foreign Affairs. The relationship between the Soviet Union and Indonesia was further weakened by two incidents. First was the broadcast on Indonesian-language radio in Moscow of a message to President Brezhnev from the banned Indonesian Communist Party. All three political parties condemned the Soviets, and Foreign Minister Mochtar Kusumaatmadja issued a formal protest. In February, the government expelled a Soviet assistant military attaché and the local manager of the Soviet airline Aeroflot, accusing them of espionage.

Diplomatic relations between Indonesia and its eastern neighbor, Papua New Guinea, suffered in May when Indonesian troops made repeated incursions across the border in search of guerrillas of the separatist Free Papua Organization who were allegedly holding hostage employees of an Indonesian timber company. Both countries briefly recalled their ambassadors, but the issue was apparently resolved when the Indonesian army rescued the hostages.

President Suharto and several cabinet ministers visited Washington, Cape Canaveral, Houston, and Honolulu in October. Topics of discussion included the appointment of a new U.S. ambassador to Indonesia, U.S. rejection of the Law of the Sea Treaty strongly supported by Indonesia, Indonesian fears of Japanese rearmament, and a range of economic issues.

© P.J. Griffiths/Magnum

The Galunggung volcano in Java erupted twice in April.

Economy. World recession hurt the Indonesian economy. Gross domestic product grew by only 7.6% in 1981, down from the 9.9% recorded in 1980. Oil exports, which account for more than half of Indonesia's foreign exchange earnings and budget revenues, declined by about 30% in the first half of 1982. Other exports, such as rubber, timber, and coffee, fared little better. Foreign exchange reserves dropped from $6,100,-000,000 in December 1981 to $4,900,000,000 in July 1982. On the positive side, inflation was reduced from 16.0% in 1980 to 7.1% in 1981 and 7.0% for the first half of 1982.

The government sought new sources of revenue to maintain development programs. In January new policies designed to increase non-oil and non-gas exports were adopted, including a controversial provision requiring foreign suppliers to the government to export goods of equal value. Domestic oil and food subsidies were also cut substantially, releasing more than $1,000,-000,000 for other programs. Finally, the government began to borrow more heavily from foreign commercial banks, increasing its foreign indebtedness by nearly $1,000,000,000.

Volcano. The Galunggung volcano on the island of Java, east of the town of Garut, erupted twice in April, killing at least 11 persons and injuring at least 20 others. The eruptions forced several thousands of persons to flee their homes and destroyed several villages.

R. WILLIAM LIDDLE, *The Ohio State University*

INDONESIA · Information Highlights

Official Name: Republic of Indonesia.
Location: Southeast Asia.
Area: 735,432 sq mi (1 904 769 km^2).
Population (1982 est.): 151,300,000.
Chief Cities (1979 est.): Jakarta, the capital, 5,690,-000; (1974 est.): Surbaya, 2,000,000; Bandung 2,000,000; Medan, 1,000,000.
Government: *Head of state and government,* Suharto, president (took office for third five-year term March 1978). *Legislature* (unicameral)—People's Consultative Assembly.
Monetary Unit: Rupiah (675 rupiahs equal U.S.$1, Oct. 1982).
Gross National Product (1980 U.S.$): $67,660,000,-000.
Economic Index (1981): *Consumer Prices* (1970= 100), *all items,* 175.4; *food,* 175.7.
Foreign Trade (1980 U.S.$): *Imports,* $10,834,000,-000; *exports,* $21,909,000,000.

INDUSTRIAL PRODUCTION

Courtesy, Bethlehem Steel Corp.

INDUSTRIAL PRODUCTION		
1967 = 100	1981	mid-1982 (preliminary)
Canada	164.8	147.5
France	157.0	159.0
Great Britain	118.2	117.7
Italy	162.6	153.6
Japan	239.3	241.8
United States	151.0	138.5
W. Germany	160.0	157.0
Seasonally Adjusted		Source: Economic Indicators

Industrial production declined sharply in North America in 1982 while its performance in major European countries was sluggish at best. Growth slowed in the newly industrialized East Asian countries as well as in the Communist countries in Eastern Europe.

The United States. Industrial production in the United States dropped nearly 8% in 1982, the second steepest drop in the post-World-War-II period, according to preliminary estimates by the Federal Reserve Board of Governors (FRB). The sharp drop follows a feeble gain of 2.7% in 1981. The rate of capacity utilization declined from the 78.5% in 1981 to barely 70%.

The recession, combined with a decline in petroleum prices, hit mining output especially hard, pulling the index down 11%, following a 7% gain in 1981. Manufacturing production dropped 8%, after growing 2.4% in 1981. The

Editor's Note: The figures cited in the above table represent the industrial-production levels during June 1982. The author's estimates are for the year.

only sector to show an increase, although an anemic one, was utilities with a 0.3% gain—half the increase registered for 1981.

Manufacturing output losses were greatest in business equipment, down 13% after a gain of 4.5% in 1981. Production of consumer goods declined nearly 3%, following a 1.7% increase. Output of intermediate products decreased 7%, compared with an increase of 1.6%. Materials output shrank 11%, after rising 2.7%. The only area to show growth in 1982 was defense with production up nearly 6%, a gain better than the 4.5% registered for 1981.

As in every recession, production cuts were considerably sharper in durable-goods manufacturing—down almost 11%, after gaining 2.7% in 1981—than in nondurable-goods manufacturing—down a little less than 5%, compared with an increase of 2.2%. Primary-metals production plummeted almost 30%, after a recovery of 5.4%. Iron and steel output was down 37%, after increasing about 8%. Nonferrous-metals production dropped almost 18%, following a gain of 2.4%.

Losses were heavy in nonelectrical-machinery production. With the group down some 13% after gaining 5.1%, the brunt of the drop fell on farm equipment, which declined almost 29%, following a loss of 9%. Construction equipment decreased more than 20%, following a gain of 3.5%. Metal-working machinery lost more than 13%, after a 1.5% decline. Industrial machinery was down 18%, following a gain of 0.7%. Even the office-machinery group was down, losing nearly 6% after a brisk 12.7% increase. Production of instruments decreased almost 4%, after slipping 0.5%.

Electrical-machinery production decreased 4.5%, after growing 3.2%. Household appliances were down 12%, after gaining 0.1%. Major electrical equipment lost nearly 19%, following an increase of 2.8%. Output of television and radio sets declined more than 10%, after increasing 2.3%.

Increased defense spending was instrumental in boosting ordnance output nearly 7%, following a 3.4% gain in 1981. It also helped communications equipment gain almost 4%, nearly as strong an increase as in the preceding year. Electronic-components production grew only about 0.5%, compared with 2.2%.

Production of transportation equipment was down about 9.5%, following a decrease of 0.7%. Auto production dropped 14%, following a 0.2% decline. Truck, bus, and trailer output increased more than 10%, after a 0.4% gain. Motor-vehicle parts production fell almost 10% following a gain of 5.8%. Reflecting the dive in airline profits, output of aircraft and aircraft parts fell some 7%, after declining 1.1%. After rising 1.2% in 1981, production of ships and boats fell about 10%. Railroad equipment nearly repeated the 51.1% production loss recorded for 1981. Output of mobile homes was up marginally, after rising 8.4%. Fabricated-metal products registered a nearly 15% drop.

Even production of such staples as food slowed in 1982, down 0.3%, compared with an increase of 1.6%. Output of tobacco products was down about 0.5%, following a 1.8% gain. Apparel production declined more than 10% and textile-mill products were down 7%, following respective drops of 5.2% and 2.2%. Leather and leather-products output dropped some 13%, after eking out a gain of 0.1%. Drugs and medicines increased about 1.5%, following an increase of 8.6%. Output of soaps and toiletries dropped about 2.5%, after gaining 3.6%. Printing and publishing output grew nearly 1%, following an increase of 3.2%. Paper and paper products declined about 3%, following a 2.5% gain.

Industries whose fortunes are largely tied to construction activity suffered substantial production losses in 1982. Output of concrete and clay products was down almost 30%, following a 5.4% increase. Glass and glass products dropped about 16%, after declining 5.6%. Cement and structural clay products fell almost 15%, after squeezing out a 1% gain in 1981. Lumber and wood products dropped about 6%, following a decline of 0.3%. Paint production was down about 8%, after a loss of 2.9%. Hardware, plumbing, and other structural-materials production lost about 13%.

Reflecting the depression in residential construction, household-furniture output declined 7%. Output of fixtures and office furniture in-

creased close to 1%, partly due to the boom in office-building construction.

Production of chemicals dropped about 9%, after growing 4%. Basic chemicals were hit hardest, down about 16%, following a slide of 0.3%. Synthetic materials declined about 12%, after increasing 6.7%. Agricultural chemicals decreased 10%, after growing 4.7%. Production of petroleum products slipped about 5.5%, following a decline of 2.5%. Rubber and plastics products were down about 6%.

Investment in new plant and equipment by American industry in 1982 amounted to $320,-000,000,000, a drop of .5% following an increase of 8.7% in 1981. After taking price changes into account, the investment decline in 1982 is closer to 5%. On a constant dollar basis, capital spending by manufacturing industries dropped 9%: almost 12% in durable-goods manufacturing and about 7% in nondurables industries. Investment in the rest of the economy slipped about 3%. The biggest increase in new plant and equipment was by the steel industry, which increased its dollar outlays from $3,100,000,000 in 1981 to more than $3,900,000,000 in 1982. The largest cutback was by motor-vehicle manufacturers, who reduced their outlays from $10,000,000,000 in 1981 to $7,400,000,000.

American steel industry poured 74 million tons (67 million metric tons or t) of raw steel in 1982, 39% less than in 1981, a year that registered an increase of 8.1%. Steel shipments amounted to only 60 million tons (54 million t), a 31% drop. It was by far the worst year for the industry in the post–World-War-II period. With capacity utilization dropping close to 30% in some weeks—the lowest in 50 years—the industry closed obsolete mills while modernizing others in the hope of bringing operating rates closer to a profitable 70–75% range. As it was, the industry's capacity utilization was a meager 48%, compared with 78.3% in 1981. One third of the industry's workers were unemployed.

The steel industry in Western countries has been ailing for seven years. In addition to persistent overcapacity, the industry has been plagued by recessions three years in a row that have crippled the industry's major customers, the automobile and construction industries. Moreover, users have been switching to competing materials as well as thinner but stronger alloy steels. Aggravating the industry's woes in the West is output from new, efficient mills in South Korea, Brazil, Spain, and East Germany. Ironically, steel mills in these countries have the latest Western technology and steelmaking equipment.

American auto industry had its third disappointing year in a row with output dropping 20% to 5.1 million in 1982. It was the worst performance since 1958. About 30% of the industry's workers were unemployed. Truck production did perk up in 1982 by 13%.

Crude-oil production in the United States in 1982 increased 0.2% to a daily rate of 8.59 million barrels. Bituminous-coal production increased about 2.5% to 835 million tons (757 million t). Electricity generation was unchanged at 2,297,000,000,000 kilowatt-hours. Total energy use in the United States fell 3.2% in 1981 to about 73 quadrillion Btu as petroleum consumption declined 6.4%. Natural-gas consumption declined. In 1982 total energy consumption declined 1.8% as petroleum consumption dropped further by 3.5%. Total petroleum consumption in the United States has declined for four consecutive years. Petroleum production in the non-Communist world dropped 6% in 1982 to about 43 million barrels per day. OPEC accounted for most of the drop, cutting production from the 22.5 million barrels per day rate in 1981 to a rate of 18.45 million in 1982.

Given the worldwide oversupply of petroleum in 1982, drilling activity in the United States suffered its sharpest setback since World War II. Compared with the 4,530 oil rigs in operation in December 1981, the number was halved by year 1982. Oilmen claimed that the 1982 prices did not justify drilling at the record levels reached in 1981. But development still continues. A big payoff was the discovery of a new field off the southern California coast in 1982, the biggest find since Alaska's Prudhoe Bay field was discovered in 1968. The Point Arguello discovery is initially estimated to have reserves of about 1,000,000,000 barrels.

The hottest product in 1982 was the small computer. About 180,000 small business computers, price about $5,000, were sold in 1982, 75% more than in 1981. The personal computer market zoomed. (*See* COMPUTERS.)

Worldwide. Major European economies experienced further weakening in industrial production in 1982. Industrial activity was strongest in Belgium, with production up about 1.5% in 1982, following a nearly 6% drop in 1981. Italy's production was down 1.7% after falling 2.3% in 1981. The United Kingdom registered a gain of about 0.5%, following a 4% drop. France showed a 0.7% decrease, compared with a 1.7% drop. The Netherlands saw its production fall 2.1%, following a decline of 1.6%. West Germany's factory output dropped 2.5%, compared with a decline of 2.1%.

Industrial production in Canada increased 1.1% in 1981 but plunged about 10% in 1982. Especially hard hit was the furniture industry, with production down about 20%. Output of primary metals declined nearly 15%, and transportation-equipment production dropped at about the same rate. Wood production decreased about 18%. Overall, output of durable goods was down about 13% while nondurables output slowed by about 6%. Utilities increased their output by nearly 4%. Metals mining showed a slight increase while the production of mineral fuels dropped about 5%, and nonmetal mining plummeted some 16%. In 1982 Canadian industry was plagued by low labor productivity.

Industrial production in Japan slowed in 1981 but still registered a gain of 3.1%. Output gains slowed further in 1982, to about 1.5%. Manufacturing capacity utilization dropped below 80% for the first time since the 1974–75 recession. The country's performance was dampened by a declining export demand.

Doing their utmost to emulate Japan's success in industrial development are South Korea, Hong Kong, Taiwan, and Singapore. These areas are rapidly moving out of labor-intensive industries such as textiles, shoes, and simple electronic items, and into high-technology industries. Output in these countries is growing at a rate roughly double that of Japan's. These areas already excel in the production of such products as black-and-white television sets, offshore oil rigs, ships, and steel. In 1981, Singapore and South Korea increased their industrial output by 9% and 11% respectively, with gains at about half those rates indicated for 1982.

Industrial output in the Soviet Union slowed in 1982. Data published for the first nine months showed output growing at a rate of 2.7% compared with a 3.3% growth rate for the comparable period of 1981. Steel production was 1% lower. Coal production rose 2% and was heading close to the record 724 million tons (656 million t) reached in 1978. Oil production was up only 0.2%, but gas production increased 8%.

According to plan, Soviet industrial production was to average a growth rate of 4.7% in the 1981–85 period. Output rose 3.4% in 1981, while labor productivity rose 1.5%, about one third of what was planned. Much of the shortfall is attributed to inefficiencies in capital investment. It is estimated that about 330,000 investment projects were underway in 1981. Since it is impossible for central planners to make sure that all projects get the equipment they need on time, wasteful delays are commonplace. That means the machines are obsolete by the time they reach the farms.

Total output of factories and mines in Poland dropped some 14% in 1981, and despite martial law, it continued to plummet in 1982. Poland's industrial production in 1982 utilized about one third of its productive capacity. The country's foremost foreign exchange earner—coal—made a comeback, with production reaching 190 million tons (172.3 million t), a 16% increase from 1981.

Many of the East European countries' industrial problems can be traced to shortcomings in planning. In Poland, investments made in the late 1970s were three times as energy-intensive as those made in the West, thanks to the cheap oil provided by the Soviet Union and the underpricing of Poland's own coal. In retrospect, there was too much reliance on imported Western technology. In Rumania, the oil-refining and petrochemical industries were expanded just when its own oil resources were exhausted.

AGO AMBRE, *U.S. Department of Commerce*

INDUSTRIAL PRODUCTION/SPECIAL REPORT

Robots

Once a science fiction fantasy, robots today serve a variety of functions in major industries and businesses. Indeed, automated manufacturing equipment is seen as vital to the growth of industrial productivity, and the robotics industry is growing rapidly. Japan is the world leader in robot production and sales, producing 57% of the world's robots. U.S. sales were estimated at $200 million in 1982, and annual growth was expected to average 35% for the rest of the 1980s. While they do not resemble the human-like robots of science fiction, computerized machine tools can have advantages over human workers—speed, accuracy, and the willingness to perform tedious or dangerous jobs. George Brosseau of the National Science Foundation points out that "in the past, whenever a new technology has been introduced it has always generated more jobs than it displaced. But we don't know whether that's true of robot technology. There's no question but that new jobs will be created, but will there be enough to offset the loss?"

More akin to the robots of *Star Wars* are automatons that perform routine functions in the office or showroom, such as delivering mail, conducting tours, or giving a sales pitch. It is generally agreed, however, that maids and butlers are still a few years off.

Denby (right), a third-generation robot, has complete mobility, speaks, and distributes promotional material. The auto industry (below) utilizes industrial robots for two of their major functions, welding and paint spraying.

Courtesy, World of Robots

Chrysler Corporation

INTERIOR DESIGN

Toshi Yoshimi/Swimmer Cole Martinez Curtis

The trend toward romanticism is epitomized by the French Room in Dallas' Adolphus Hotel. Its arched ceiling, ornate chandeliers, murals, and elegantly crisp napery—all in muted pink and blue—create an Old World atmosphere.

Romanticism is fashionable again. The appeal of comfort, pretty colors, and enticing decor is regarded by many interior designers as a revolt against Bauhaus functionalism. As presently used, however, romanticism is less a singular style than an attitude, a way of putting emotion back into decorating. It is a turning back to the security of older traditions at a time when things are no longer as they used to be. The antecedents of the movement in decorating range from the 18th century to the Belle Epoque—a period sometimes referred to as the Age of Romanticism. The present trend also includes a touch of the Victorian.

In decoration the emphasis is on comfort—easy furniture upholstered in bright, large-scale floral patterns, with an abundance of plump cushions; quality silks or floral-patterned draperies, bed hangings, and wall coverings; and an assemblage of other carefully chosen objects. Popular colors are gray, lilac, pale pink, yellow, and soft blue.

Perhaps the most elaborate and lush interpretation of romantic decor is the dressing room of designer Françoise de la Renta. It is lavishly decorated, with ruffled silk draping the windows and dressing table, and ornate silver and crystal appointments set against a wall papered with lively, large-scale decadent cabbage roses and leaves. More restrained but equally romantic is designer John Saladino's use of classic forms and themes to evoke a nostalgic atmosphere at his home in Litchfield, CT.

Between the lavish and restrained is the conventional romanticism of the English country house. This look is exemplified in two residences—a Victorian home redesigned by William Diamond and the private home of the Fitzpatricks, innkeepers in New England's Berkshire Mountains—with floral-patterned chintzes and carpets, fresh flowers, and large cushions on oversized sofas and chairs. Indeed, every designer has his or her own variations for home decorating. "Soft edge romance" is how Mario Buatta describes his use of floral chintz, traditional furniture, and muted colors in a city apartment.

The romantic trend is also spilling over into hotels, restaurants, and other public places. Few designers have ventured so far as Jill Kurden Cole in Dallas' Adolphus Hotel. The arched ceiling over the French Room is adorned with murals of clouds, garlands, and putti in blues, pinks, and whites. Ornate chandeliers and floral carpeting in the Savonnerie style add to the Belle Epoque atmosphere. The Lalique restaurant in Bal Harbour, FL, is distinctly Art Deco in color, scale, and furniture design. Walls, flooring, upholstery and tablecloths are done in pink and beige-gray, with pink reiterated in large fresh floral arrangements. Glass murals are etched in the frosty style of the late French jeweler René Lalique.

JEANNE WEEKS

A New York City living room designed by Mario Buatta combines the traditional warmth of floral chintz, comfortable pillows, and furniture of several periods with modern paintings and clean white walls. At the Lalique restaurant in Bal Harbour, FL, subtle lighting focuses attention on the Art Deco etched glass.

INTERNATIONAL TRADE AND FINANCE

In many regards, 1982 was the worst year economically and financially since the 1930s. It was a year of widespread disinflation, and the consequences were multifold:

—The growth of world output, as estimated by Wharton Econometric Forecasting Associates, was a mere 0.3%. There was no growth in the real gross domestic product of the industrial nations, and the developing countries saw their output grew only slightly—by 0.5%.

—Reflecting this slowdown, foreign trade was shrinking. In the first nine months of 1982, the value of exports of industrial countries totaled $868,700,000,000, compared with $895,800,000,000 during the same period in 1981. The value of imports for that same period was $923,100,000,000 in 1982, as against $963,300,000,000 for the year-earlier period.

—Unemployment rose sharply. It was nearly 11% by fall in the United States, a rate not seen since 1932. In most West European nations, the jobless rate was also uncomfortably high. The Organization for Economic Cooperation and Development (OECD) predicted that the number of jobless in its industrial nation members could reach 32 million by 1983, or 9% of the labor force.

—Mexico's debt crisis in August precipitated world concern over the stability of the international financial system. The developing nations had more than $600,000,000,000 in external debts, and commercial bankers and others were wondering if some of those obligations might not be repaid.

—Interest rates in the United States and other industrial countries remained higher than at any time in the past two decades, though they were on a declining pattern as the year went on. In the United States, for example, the average level of both short-term and long-term interest rates from the third quarter of 1979 to the fall of 1982 was approximately 13%. For the seven major industrial countries as a group, the weighted average was about 12%. Real interest rates—those after the inflation rate is subtracted—were also extreme. They averaged at least 4% in the United States during 1982 and the previous two years. Moreover, interest rates generally have been three to four times as volatile as they had been in the 10 years prior to 1973.

For bankers and other financiers 1982 was an exciting year, with interest rates jumping up and down like a pianist's fingers on the keyboard, and with the risks of foreign loans seeming to change monthly as elections, coups, wars, policy changes, and other unforeseen events altered the scene in developing countries. Even loans to Communist countries, once regarded as relatively secure, suddenly became shaky. That was particularly so for Poland.

Despite the uncertainties and prevalent pessimism, the world quietly made a surprising amount of progress in dealing with its financial and economic problems. For instance:

—Inflation dropped relatively rapidly. By September, the average rise in consumer prices in the 24 OECD industrial nations was the lowest yearly rate since early 1973—7.4% for the previous 12 months. In the United States, consumer prices were rising at a less than 5% annual rate by autumn.

—Interest rates were at last plunging. In the United States the prime rate—the interest commercial banks claim to charge their most creditworthy customers—was 17% early in 1982 and widely expected to go higher with a recovery. Instead it slipped to 11.5% by mid-December. Three-month Treasury bills, which had returned more than 14% in the winter, paid about 8% by late autumn. West European politicians complained sharply during the winter about high American interest rates, which, they maintained, forced them to keep their own interest rates so high as to depress their economies. But as the year progressed, rates in Europe also followed a declining pattern.

—In the United States, the recession had bottomed out by autumn, and, although it took much longer than anticipated to move off that bottom, there were some signs of better times ahead as the year came to a close. Western Europe also was slow to recover. Nonetheless, some economists maintained that the industrial nations were building a solid base for some years of steady, less inflationary economic growth.

—Excited by the prospect of a more stable economic recovery and lower inflation, investors, particularly such institutions as mutual funds and pension funds, jumped into the U.S. stock markets with both feet. Starting August 12, prices exploded. The Dow Jones industrial average, which bottomed out earlier at 776.92, moved above 1,050 by the first week of November. On the New York Stock Exchange, the average price of shares was more than 35% above its mid-August price. That was the fastest 11-week rise in the six bull markets of the last two decades. Volume soared to new peaks, often topping 100 million and breaking all volume records November 4 with a historic 149.35 million.

Stock prices in several industrial nations—including Canada, Great Britain, France, Japan, West Germany, and, to a lesser degree, Switzerland—echoed the U.S. market with solid price gains.

—An oil glut prompted an approximate 15% drop in spot oil prices. Conservation and the world economic slowdown had reduced demand.

So, despite the prevalent deep gloom, not all was dark in 1982.

Trade. Beside the reduction in trade volume, there was a considerable increase in protectionism. As stated in an International Monetary Fund (IMF) paper released in November,

Canadian Prime Minister Trudeau opens the 37th annual joint IMF-World Bank meeting in Toronto, September 6.

"... the current economic difficulties have increased pressures on governments to adopt protective policies to maintain employment by supporting ailing industries or erecting trade barriers."

In the United States, for example, Congress considered, but did not pass, legislation which would have required foreign automobile manufacturers exporting to the American market also to assemble in the United States or to use parts made in the United States. The administration said it would veto this "domestic content" bill. Another unsuccessful bill would have limited Japan's share of the U.S. market to 14%. However, a three-year bilateral arrangement with Japan in May 1981 still limited Japanese automobile imports.

In the case of steel—another U.S. industry hard hit by both the domestic slump and imports—the International Trade Commission in February upheld 38 industry complaints of dumping and improper subsidies on imported steel. Later in the year, the Department of Commerce reached a preliminary decision to levy substantial penalties on steel imports from nine countries, including seven from the European Community (EC). Under this threat, the Community agreed in the fall to restrain its exports to the United States.

The EC extended an arrangement with 13 steel supplier countries, and concluded an additional arrangement with South Korea, permitting somewhat larger steel imports in 1982 than in 1981, but less than in 1980. Several European countries also limited auto imports from Japan. Italy permits only 2,200 Japanese cars in each year. France keeps Japanese auto imports to 3% of the domestic market. The United Kingdom has been more generous at 11%.

Textiles were another sensitive trade area. Here the EC moved to roll back imports by reducing quotas. The United States would let imports grow by 1.5% per annum for several years, less than the 6% rate previously allowed. As of late 1982, the United States received imports in manufactured goods from non-oil developing countries amounting to 1.04% of its gross national product. The equivalent figure for the United Kingdom was 1.16%; for France, 0.42%; for West Germany, 0.8%; for Japan, 0.55%; and for Canada, 0.81%.

Worried by the protectionist trend, U.S. Trade Representative William Brock in November proposed a seven-point program to seize the initiative on trade issues in Washington. Among other things, the program called for a speedup in procedures for processing complaints by U.S. industries about unfair trade practices by foreigners, and an expansion of government export-financing efforts.

A ministerial meeting of the General Agreement on Tariffs and Trade (GATT) was held

November 24–29 in Geneva. The Reagan administration, with its free-trade philosophy, pushed to limit new forms of trade restrictions and to ease barriers in the service industries (such as insurance, engineering, consulting, and accounting). But the negotiations, as expected, proved difficult, and not much was accomplished.

International Debt. Some nations' debt crises were resolved, at least temporarily.

For example, on November 10 Mexico's government announced that it had reached an agreement with the IMF on an austerity program designed to reduce its debt program. Under the deal, Mexico was to get $3,840,000,000 worth of credit over three years. The agreement also opened the door for other credits from private foreign institutions and provided access to $1,000,000,000 of a $1,850,000,000 emergency credit granted to Mexico in late August by the Bank of International Settlements in Basel, Switzerland, a sort of bank for central bankers. In turn, Mexico agreed to slash public spending, raise taxes, and curb imports. Government officials expected this program to bring an economic slowdown, further unemployment, and a reduced living standard. But, noted Finance Minister Jesus Silva Herzog, "This agreement enables us to avoid defaulting on our foreign debt of $78,000,000,000." That is the highest foreign debt of any nation.

On the same day, the IMF approved a $2,100,000,000 credit for Argentina to help that country meet payments on its nearly $40,000,-000,000 in foreign debt. Further, the United States and several European governments made more than $3,000,000,000 in emergency loans to Brazil to help it cover an expected shortfall in its international debt payments. Hungary and the IMF also tentatively agreed on a $580 million loan package that required the country to adopt a new austerity program that should help ease its debt problems. Still awaiting agreement in December was a $1,000,000,000 credit package for Yugoslavia.

One worrisome factor was the sudden slowdown in new loans to the developing countries, especially those in Latin America, and a tendency to make most short-term loans. Commented the Amex Bank Review: "Reliance on short-term credit lines . . . is probably inevitable while recession continues and banks remain cautious." This trend, though, makes it more difficult for the developing nations to service their loans.

International Monetary Affairs. At the joint annual meetings of the IMF and World Bank in Toronto, September 6–10, the governors decided to try to accelerate an agreement on enlarged Fund quotas to April 1983 from September 1983. The quotas determine how much money a nation can borrow to help it over an international payments crisis. But because ratification takes time, that might not occur until 1985. Moreover, the United States wanted quotas increased by far less than the $100,000,000,000 or so sought by the debt-ridden developing countries. The United States did propose a special emergency fund that would be available earlier to help in any debt crisis.

Also at the meeting, some 22 donor nations agreed to provide some $3,500,000,000 for the International Development Association in 1984. This World Bank affiliate makes easy-term loans to the world's poorest countries. The amount represented an increase of $800 million from that available the year before.

Foreign Exchange. Despite lower interest rates in the fall, the U.S. dollar remained extraordinarily strong. Foreigners apparently still regarded the United States as a relatively safe country for their investments. During the third quarter, the trade-weighted value of the dollar rose to a 13-year peak, more than 21% higher than the effective rate for March 1973, when the current period of managed floating exchange rates began. To U.S. businessmen faced with Japanese import competition, the weakness of the yen was especially annoying. A study by Citibank found that the strength of the dollar made the United States the least competitive of major industrial countries in hourly compensation in manufacturing.

Monetary Policy. American financial markets were buoyed greatly after the October meeting of the Federal Reserve System's policy-making Open Market Committee. Alarmed by the refusal of the U.S. economy to rise from the recession floor, the 12-person committee decided to temporarily ease credit conditions. The Fed signaled this by lowering to 9.5% the discount rate it charges on loans to commercial banks. And Federal Reserve Board Chairman Paul A. Volcker announced that for some months thereafter the Fed would attach much less weight to movements in M1, a measure of the nation's money supply that includes currency in circulation and checking accounts. M1, for technical reasons, would not be a suitable measure. Rather, the Fed would pay closer attention to larger money measures, M2 and M3. The action implied that the Fed's target for 1982 of 2.5 to 5.5% growth in M1 may have become too restrictive. Moreover, there was concern that the overly strong U.S. dollar was hurting American exports too much. It was depressing growth in the American economy and costing sizable numbers of jobs.

This more flexible approach to monetary policy increased market expectations that the powerful U.S. economy would recover shortly. Several European governments—West Germany, the Netherlands, Belgium, and Austria—responded by lowering their central bank discount rates. As the year closed, economic hopes were rising.

DAVID R. FRANCIS
"The Christian Science Monitor"

IOWA

The November elections, high unemployment, and legislative concern for increased taxes and crime prevention were among the topics of major concern in Iowa in 1982.

Elections. Former Democratic governor and U.S. senator Harold Hughes withdrew from the Iowa gubernatorial primary race when it was ruled that he did not meet the Iowa constitutional requirement of two years residency immediately prior to the election. The Democrats then nominated Roxanne Conlin as their candidate for governor as she defeated Jerry Fitzgerald and Ed Campbell. She was the first woman to be nominated for governor by a major party in Iowa.

Republican Gov. Robert Ray, who held the post of governor for 14 years (eight years longer than any other Iowan) announced that he would not be a candidate for a sixth term in 1982. Lt. Gov. Terry Branstad was unopposed in the Republican primary in his bid to succeed Ray.

On November 2, Iowans turned out in record numbers for a nonpresidential election and split their tickets. Lt. Gov. Terry Branstad defeated Roxanne Conlin in the gubernatorial race, while Democrat Robert Anderson won over Larry Pope in the contest for lieutenant governor. In other state elections, the Democrats won the attorney general and state treasurer posts, while the Republicans won the offices of secretary of state, state auditor, and secretary of agriculture. All six incumbent members of the U.S. House of Representatives (three Democrats and three Republicans) were reelected.

Further demonstration of the split-ticket voting was evident with the Democrats' taking over both houses of the General Assembly. The 1983 assembly will have 60 Democrats and 40 Republicans in the House, while the Senate will have 28 Democrats and 22 Republicans.

Unemployment. Unemployment in Iowa was higher in 1982 than in any year since the Great Depression. The statewide unemployment rate

UPI

Roxanne Conlin (right) is congratulated by her mother after becoming the first woman to be nominated for the governorship of Iowa. The Democrat lost on November 2.

was 8.3% in October. Dubuque was listed during one month as having more than 23% of the labor force unemployed. During the year the state was forced for the first time to borrow from the federal government to keep the unemployment compensation fund solvent.

Legislature. The 1982 legislative session lasted 104 days and enacted 268 bills into law. Both houses were controlled by the Republicans. According to Governor Ray's staff, 47 of the governor's 56 proposals to the General Assembly were approved. The governor's budget recommendations were accepted with few changes. A new law requires persons working in Iowa but living in another state to pay Iowa income taxes on the money earned in Iowa.

The diesel fuel tax was increased by 2 cents a gallon to 15½ cents, and the tax on gasohol also was raised by 2 cents to 8 cents. The legislature also toughened penalties for drunken driving. The maximum penalty for second-degree murder was increased from 25 to 50 years, and that for attempted murder was increased from 10 to 25 years. Convicted criminals will henceforth be required to pay restitution to their victims. Likewise, criminals convicted of felonies involving force may be denied bail.

Crops. The 1982 corn yield in Iowa totaled 1,610,000,000 bushels, or 124 bushels per acre. The soybean crop averaged 38 bushels per acre for a total yield of 325 million bushels.

University. James O. Freedman, former dean of the University of Pennsylvania Law School, became president of the University of Iowa.

RUSSELL M. ROSS, *University of Iowa*

IOWA · Information Highlights

Area: 56,275 sq mi (145 752 km²).

Population (1980 census): 2,913,808.

Chief Cities (1980 census): Des Moines, the capital, 191,003; Cedar Rapids, 110,243; Davenport, 103,-264.

Government (1982): *Chief Officers*—governor, Robert D. Ray (R); lt. gov., Terry E. Branstad (R). *General Assembly*—Senate, 50 members; House of Representatives, 100 members.

State Finances (fiscal year 1981): *Revenues,* $3,670,-000,000; *expenditures,* $3,617,000,000.

Personal Income (1981): $30,362,000,000; per capita, $10,474.

Labor Force (Aug. 1982): *Nonagricultural wage and salary earners,* 1,026,400; *unemployed,* 113,000 (8.3% of total force).

Education: *Enrollment* (fall 1981)—public elementary schools, 341,218; public secondary, 174,998; colleges and universities (1981–82), 143,105. *Public school expenditures* (1980–81), $1,396,925,000 ($2,560 per pupil).

IRAN

Sygma

The Iran-Iraq war continues. Above, Iranian troops march jubilantly after retaking their oil and port city of Khorramshahr in late May. Iran won a series of victories in the early months of the year.

Iran's Islamic regime was able to score a number of significant achievements during 1982, particularly in its war with Iraq and in suppressing domestic opposition. Nevertheless, there were serious negative developments in the clergy-run country. Perhaps the greatest threat to the regime's stability was the power struggle over who would succeed the ailing supreme ruler, the Ayatollah Ruhollah Khomeini. The economy was in dire straits, and foreign relations were deteriorating on several fronts.

War. Iran's armed forces staged a series of major offensives during the first half of the year which steadily drove back the Iraqi invaders. The Iranians used "human wave" tactics, which resulted in enormous casualties for their own forces but which overwhelmed their foes. Some of the Iranian volunteers in this bloodletting were youngsters in their early teens who believed it an honor to die for the Ayatollah Khomeini and his fanatical brand of Shiite Islam.

Originally, Khomeini and other Iranian leaders denied any intention to invade Iraq. But flushed with success, the Tehran government ordered its forces to drive into Iraq.

Between July and November the fighting was particularly bloody. Iran was able to muster as many as 150,000 troops for a single battle, and tens of thousands sacrificed their lives. The direction of the fighting, however, was changing in favor of Iraq. Iranian troops were not as effective as they had been in liberating their own territory, while at the same time the Iraqi resistance stiffened. By December the Iranians held only small parcels of Iraqi land, and the war had once more become one of attrition and stalemate for both sides.

Peace Efforts. During the time that Iranian troops were winning the war, the Tehran regime resisted efforts by the Nonaligned Movement, the Islamic Conference Organization, and individual countries seeking to mediate the conflict. Indeed, Iran actually increased its conditions for a peace settlement. In addition to demanding that all Iraqi forces leave Iranian soil, Tehran was now demanding the ouster of Iraqi President Saddam Hussein as well as reparations of $150,-000,000,000. The fact that Iraq wanted an armistice only made Iran more intransigent. By December, when the war was once again at a virtual stalemate, Tehran was not so shrill in vowing to continue the war. Nevertheless, 1982 came to an end without any real prospects for peace.

IRAN • Information Highlights

Official Name: Islamic Republic of Iran.
Location: Southwest Asia.
Area: 636,300 sq mi (1 648 017 km²).
Population (1982 est.): 41,200,000.
Chief Cities (1976 census): Tehran, the capital, 4,496,159 (met. area); Isfahan, 671,825; Meshed, 670,180.
Government: *Head of state,* Mohammed Ali Khamenei, president (took office Oct. 1981). *Head of government,* Mir Hussein Moussavi, premier (took office Oct. 1981). *Legislature* (unicameral)—Parliament.
Monetary Unit: Rial (86.70 rials equal U.S.$1, Dec. 23, 1982).
Gross National Product (1980 U.S.$): $112,100,000,-000.
Economic Index (1981): *Consumer Prices* (1970= 100), *all items,* 411.4; *food,* 495.9.
Foreign Trade (1980 U.S.$): *Imports,* $12,247,000,-000; *exports,* $14,251,000,000.

Terror. The Islamic regime successfully used terror against those seeking to overthrow Khomeini's government. In the process, many innocent people were imprisoned, tortured, and executed. Terror was also used against those openly objecting to or unwilling to comply with the stringent Islamic laws imposed by the Ayatollah Khomeini.

Khomeini's security forces could claim major successes against such leftist terrorists as the Islamic Marxist Mujahedeen-e-Khalq (People's Fighters or Holy Warriors). The leftists had been spectacularly successful in 1981, killing many leading members of the ruling Islamic Republican Party. But in 1982 the regime's security forces killed scores of leftist terrorists and broke up much of their organizational structure. Antigovernment terrorism declined but did not disappear. Prominent followers of Khomeini continued to be assassinated. In October a terrorist bomb exploded in central Tehran, killing at least 60 persons and wounding several hundred others.

In the Kurdish region of the northwest there was fierce fighting between government forces and Kurds seeking independence or autonomy. Other ethnic groups were restive, including the Azerbaijanis.

The rule of Iran's mullahs (clergy) through the Islamic courts was strengthened during 1982. Particularly affected were women, who were required to wear the *chador* (veil) and forbidden to use makeup or to dress in Western-style clothes. Strict male and female segregation was enforced in public life. The religious courts revived ancient Islamic punishments, such as flogging for adultery and the amputation of a hand for thievery. Vigilante justice was often the rule.

Plot. In April the government announced that it had smashed a plot to assassinate the Ayatollah Khomeini, involving former Foreign Minister Sadegh Ghotbzadeh, military officers, and "several others." Though a longtime supporter of Khomeini, Ghotbzadeh—who opposed the taking hostage of U.S. Embassy personnel in 1979—had been too moderate for the Islamic fundamentalists. On television April 19, Ghotbzadeh admitted his participation in the assassination plot, and on September 15 he was executed.

The Issue of Succession. The power struggle over who would succeed the 82-year-old Khomeini severely divided Khomeini's own fundamentalist followers. The two major factions were both Muslim fundamentalists, and the reasons for disagreement were often explained in abstruse Shiite Moslem theological terms. Underneath all the theological terminology, however, were differences over the future economic and political structure of the country. One faction wanted more radical nationalization of the economy and a stricter, more centralized state. This faction included the Ayatollah Hussein Ali Montazari, regarded by many to be Khomeini's

own choice as successor. The other major faction favored less radical nationalization of the economy and a less totalitarian system.

In December nationwide elections were held to choose an Assembly of Islamic Experts which would decide whether Khomeini would be succeeded by a single leader or by a council of ayatollahs. The less radical faction favored the council idea in order to prevent Montazari or any other individual from assuming Khomeini's dictatorial powers.

Economy. In 1982 Iran successfully boosted its oil production to more than 2 million barrels per day. While this earned needed foreign exchange to help finance the war, it also caused conflict with other OPEC (Organization of Petroleum Exporting Countries) members because Iran exceeded its OPEC quota and was selling oil below OPEC's established prices.

Despite the increased oil revenue, the domestic economy remained a shambles. There were food shortages, raging inflation, and a flour-

Shiite Islam remains at the center of Iranian life. Below, with photos of the Ayatollah Khomeini in view, children at an Islamic school in a small village pray to Allah.

© J. Guichard/Sygma

flourishing black market. The clergy proved to be bad managers of the country's industrial and agricultural structure.

Foreign Relations. Iran's relations with such Gulf states as Saudi Arabia and Kuwait remained poor. These states continued to provide military aid to Iraq because they feared that Khomeini would attempt to export his Islamic revolution throughout the region.

Relations with the Soviet Union deteriorated, particularly because of the continued Soviet occupation of Afghanistan and because of the innate anticommunism of the Iranian clergy. The Moscow-controlled Iranian Communist Party (the Tudeh) had its newspaper closed down, and a number of Communists were ousted from key government positions. Nevertheless, Soviet-made arms continued to flow to Iran through Libya and North Korea.

Mood. The year that began with fanaticism and military victories ended in an atmosphere of disillusionment. There was increasing popular resentment of the heavy war toll and economic sacrifices. The number of volunteers for the armed forces declined sharply, and fewer people turned out for government-staged demonstrations. Khomeini still held the allegiance of the masses, but it was questionable whether his successor or successors could count on such support.

AARON R. EINFRANK
Free-lance International Correspondent

IRAQ

Iraq under the leadership of President Saddam Hussein had a very bad year in 1982. A total disaster was avoided in the war with Iran, but little positive except survival could be claimed by the government.

Fighting. During the first half of the year, Iraq was pushed out of virtually all the Iranian territory it had occupied since President Hussein ordered his troops into Iran in September 1980. During the second half of the year, Iraqi forces fighting on their own territory did manage to stop advancing Iranian troops. The most the Iranians could capture were small border areas only a few miles inside Iraq. Baghdad said that Iranian casualties were much higher than its own, but in light of the smaller Iraqi population, losses were indeed severe. Conservative estimates put the Iraqi dead at more than 10,000, with many more wounded.

Peace Pleas. President Hussein was placed in the humiliating position of begging for a cease-fire. He made every effort to mobilize the support of the Nonaligned Movement, as well as friendly Muslim states, in trying to get peace talks started. Hussein even accused the United States and the Soviet Union of not doing enough to end the fighting—as if Moscow or Washington could dictate to the Islamic regime in Tehran. Iran caustically dismissed Hussein's peace overtures,

demanding that he be ousted from power and that Iraq pay reparations of $150,000,000,000. Only the stubborn defensive performance of the Iraqi army saved Hussein's regime from such an end.

Economy. The war with Iran, which entered its third year in September, forced Hussein to announce strict economic austerity measures. Major development projects were reduced or postponed. The Iraqi economy did not come to a complete halt, but a generalized slowdown was visible. In order to reduce popular discontent, the government continued to subsidize a variety of consumer goods.

Syria, which was supporting Iran, announced in April that Iraqi oil would no longer be allowed to flow through the Syrian pipeline system to the Mediterranean Sea. This left only the pipeline through Turkey to carry Iraqi oil exports to the outside world, since the Persian Gulf was controlled by the Iranian navy. Iraqi oil exports were estimated at a little more than one fourth of the 3.5 million barrels per day that the country had exported prior to the outbreak of war.

What saved Iraq from total financial collapse was the continuation of massive loans from Saudi Arabia and other Gulf states that feared the spread of Iran's Islamic revolution.

Politics and Government. Though during the year rumors circulated that President Hussein would be ousted, nothing materialized. In June personnel changes designed to strengthen Hussein's rule were made in the powerful Revolutionary Command Council and the government cabinet. The ruling Baath (Arab Socialist) Party still seemed to be solidly behind the president. One advantage that Hussein enjoyed was that once Iran began its invasion of Iraq, the war was no longer a foreign adventure but a life-and-death struggle involving both Hussein and the Iraqi people.

Anti-Hussein Iraqi dissidents operating out of Tehran and the Syrian capital of Damascus did not appear to have much influence on domestic events during the year.

President Hussein continued his policy of harsh reprisals against Iraqi Shiite-sect Muslims who showed any sympathy to Iran's Shiite

---

IRAQ · Information Highlights

Official Name: Republic of Iraq.
Location: Southwest Asia.
Area: 169,284 sq mi (438 446 km²).
Population (1982 est.): 14,000,000.
Chief Cities (1970 est.): Baghdad, the capital, 2,183,-800 (met. area); Basra, 370,900; Mosul, 293,100.
Government: *Head of state and government,* Saddam Hussein Takriti, president (took office July 1979).
Monetary Unit: Dinar (0.29532 dinar equals U.S.$1, July 1982).
Gross National Product (1980 U.S.$): $38,980,000,-000.
Economic Index (1978): *Consumer Prices* (1973=100), *items,* 151.9; *food,* 153.4.
Foreign Trade (1978 U.S.$): *Imports,* $4,213,000,-000; *exports,* $11,061,000,000.

Thousands of Iraqi troops were taken prisoner as Iranian forces pushed ahead in the early part of the year. At the Arab summit in Fez, Iraq's President Saddam Hussein (right) aired differences with King Hussein of Jordan.

leader, the Ayatollah Ruhollah Khomeini. The Hussein government, however, which is dominated by Sunni-sect Muslims like the president himself, made friendly overtures to Iraqi Shiites by renovating and beautifying their mosques and other religious sites. The Iraqi Shiites make up slightly more than half of the country's population. There were also reports during the year that Hussein was seeking a modus vivendi with Kurdish guerrillas fighting the government.

Foreign Relations. The war between Iraq and Iran caused the cancellation of the Baghdad summit of the Nonaligned Movement, scheduled for September 1982. This proved to be a major setback for Hussein's years-long effort to gain prestige within the movement, since Iraq was to have assumed the chairmanship. The summit was put off until 1983, when it would be held in New Delhi, India.

Moscow generally continued its policy of trying to ride both horses in the Iran-Iraq war. In 1982, however, the USSR did appear to be tilting slightly back toward Iraq, with which it has a friendship treaty. There were reports of increased Soviet arms shipments, particularly helicopter gunships, which played a major role in stopping the Iranian invasion.

At the end of the year, even Syria seemed somewhat less hostile to Baghdad than it had been, probably because Damascus, while disliking Hussein, does not want its neighboring country dominated by Khomeini-type religious fanatics.

Traditionally armed with Soviet equipment, Iraq during 1982 sought arms deals with the West. France reportedly signed a contract to sell artillery and ground-to-air missiles. Earlier in the year the French government promised to rebuild the Osirak nuclear reactor, destroyed in a 1981 Israeli air attack. The United States continued to bar military sales to Iraq, but it did open the way for civilian sales by removing Iraq from its official list of "terrorist" countries.

Future. Hussein's tightly controlled police state did not seem likely to collapse as the result of popular opposition. At the same time, however, the Iraqi president still faced two very real threats—a decisive defeat at the hands of the Iranian invaders and a coup. The former would appear to warrant the greater concern. A coup could come only from within the inner circle of the Baath political and military leadership, which President Hussein continued to dominate at year's end.

AARON R. EINFRANK
Free-lance International Correspondent

IRELAND

The ailing economy of the Irish republic left its mark on national politics when Prime Minister Garret FitzGerald resigned as leader of the Fine Gael-Labour coalition on Jan. 27, 1982. Faced with a growing national debt, high inflation, and weakened confidence in the Irish pound, the prime minister had introduced an austerity budget that raised the value-added tax (VAT) as well as excise and income taxes, while reducing government food subsidies. The Fianna Fail opposition party then combined with several Independents in the Dail (lower house) to defeat the budget by one vote. The president, Patrick Hillery, accepted FitzGerald's resignation and called for a general election on February 18. Although the voters gave no party a clear majority, Fianna Fail gained three seats for a total of 81, compared with Fine Gael's 63 and Labour's 15. The recently founded Sinn Fein, the Worker's Party (SFWP), won three seats, and Independents took four; the balance of power now belonged to these seven deputies (TDs).

After some tense negotiations, the SFWP members and two Independents agreed to support Fianna Fail, and on March 9 Charles J. Haughey was made prime minister (Taoiseach) for the second time, by a vote of 86 to 79 in the Dail. Elections for the Senate (upper house) were held in April and resulted in 28 seats for Fianna Fail, 19 for Fine Gael, 6 for Labour, and 7 for Independents. Two of Haughey's Senate appointments were Northern Irishmen.

Problems for the New Government. In August, Attorney General Patrick Connolly caused his party serious embarrassment when a man accused of two murders in late July was arrested in his private apartment in a Dublin suburb. Although the attorney general insisted that he knew nothing about his friend's alleged crimes, he was forced to resign amid a shrill outcry.

Mounting criticism of Haughey's leadership within his own party came to a head on October 7, when the Fianna Fail deputies met to consider a move to oust their leader. In an open ballot, Haughey won a vote of confidence by 58 to 22. The negative vote would have been considerably higher had members been allowed to vote in secrecy. To add to Haughey's troubles, two cabinet ministers resigned in the wake of the meeting.

Economy and Budget. During the elections, party leaders had stressed the importance of economic recovery and promised to ease the heavy burden of taxes and inflation. But with unemployment rising to more than 140,000 and a budget deficit in excess of 680 million Irish pounds (as of March), the new government faced a formidable task. Upon taking office, Haughey called "the tragic problem of Northern Ireland" the government's first priority, but he spent much of his time working on a budget that would relieve some of the economic malaise. The budget introduced on March 25 preserved the food subsidies and increased social welfare benefits by 25%. To pay for these and other concessions, new levies were imposed on banks and insurance companies, and increases were made in the capital gains tax and VAT on imports at the point of entry into the country. These proved to be only stopgap measures. By October economists estimated the budget deficit at close to 1,000,000,000 Irish pounds; unemployment had risen to 161,000; and the inflation rate had fallen only to 17%. Under pressure to effect strict economies, the cabinet announced that 300,000 public service employees would have to forego the pay raise they had been promised. This decision provoked an angry reaction from the unions.

FitzGerald Returns. On November 4, in a test of his economic policies, Prime Minister Haughey lost a confidence motion in the Dail, 82-80. New general elections were held November 24, and although no party was given an outright majority, it appeared likely that the Fine Gael and Labour parties would agree to join in a new coalition. The agreement was finally reached on December 12, with the result two days later that Garret FitzGerald was voted back into office. Upon his election, FitzGerald warned of "strenuous efforts and great sacrifices" to restore economic well-being.

Foreign Affairs. In foreign affairs, Prime Minister Haughey incurred unpopularity in Britain by refusing to support the EC's economic sanctions against Argentina during the Falkland Islands crisis. The explosion of two IRA bombs in central London on July 20, killing 11 persons and injuring at least 50 others, also damaged Anglo-Irish relations. Haughey did enhance the old Irish-American connection, however, by paying an official visit to Washington on St. Patrick's Day (March 17), where he lunched with President and Mrs. Reagan at the White House and met senior administration officials.

Back in office, Prime Minister FitzGerald promised an "open and positive" dialogue with Britain on the Northern Ireland problem.

L. PERRY CURTIS, JR., *Brown University*

IRELAND · Information Highlights

Official Name: Republic of Ireland.
Location: Island in the eastern North Atlantic Ocean.
Area: 27,136 sq mi (70 282 km²).
Population (1981 census): 3,440,427.
Chief Cities (1981 census): Dublin, the capital, 525,-360; Cork, 136,269; Limerick, 60,721.
Government: *Head of state,* Patrick J. Hillery, president (took office Dec. 1976). *Head of government,* Garret FitzGerald, prime minister (took office Dec. 1982). *Legislature*—Parliament: House of Representatives (Dail Eireann) and Senate (Seanad Eireann).
Monetary Unit: Pound (0.7270 pound equals U.S.$1, Dec. 17, 1982).
Gross National Product (1981 U.S.$): $17,490,000,-000.
Economic Indexes: *Consumer Prices* (1981, 1970= 100), *all items,* 433.6; *food,* 424.3. *Industrial Production* (1980, 1975=100), 136.
Foreign Trade (1981 U.S.$): *Imports,* $10,621,000,-000; *exports,* $7,763,000,000.

ISRAEL

A series of national crises had Menahem Begin (center) facing stiff opposition in the Knesset.

Traumatic developments shook Israel to its core in 1982. There was a vehement conflict over the transfer to Egypt of northern Sinai, controversy over the annexation of Golan, and the turbulent dissolution of the Israeli national airline. The major source of national trauma, however, was the war in Lebanon and its multifaceted repercussions.

Sinai. Turmoil racked the country as opposition mounted against the relinquishing, in accordance with the Camp David Agreement, of the third and final segment of the Sinai to Egypt. In this arid region, Israel had developed modern cities, agricultural settlements, cultivated fields, and paved highways. Yamit, a carefully planned and now flourishing model city, was the center of controversy in early 1982. Three months before the projected Egyptian takeover in April, thousands of protestors joined Yamit residents in barricading themselves in the city and vowing to resist evacuation. For the first time in the history of the state, one Israeli was pitted against another in direct confrontation, as army units were ordered to remove the resisters by force.

Golan Annexation. Tensions were also increased by the government's December 1981 vote to apply Israeli law to the Golan Heights, captured from Syria in the Six-Day War. The Golan's 7,000 Jewish settlers were jubilant, but the majority of Druze residents expressed opposition. They were joined by the U.S. State Department, which deplored the action, and by the UN Security Council, which voted sanctions against Israel. In late January 1982, however, the United States did veto the UN resolution.

El Al. Major labor disputes, leading to strikes and violent demonstrations, ravaged El Al, the Israeli national airline, and caused heavy damage to the economy. The airline's troubles were compounded by a cabinet decision to ban flights on the Sabbath and Jewish holidays. The ban was vigorously opposed by El Al employees. A decision by El Al management to sell the company to private interests was deferred to government deliberations, which resulted in a recommendation to liquidate the airline.

War in Lebanon. The June 3 assassination attempt by Palestinian hitmen of Israeli Ambassador Shlomo Argov in London triggered Israel's attack, called "Operation Peace for Galilee," on PLO bases in Lebanon. The initial objective—to destroy the network of Palestinian military strongholds and establish a 25-mi (40-km) buffer zone in southern Lebanon to protect the Galilee from repeated shelling and terrorist infiltration—was expanded to the encirclement of Beirut and expulsion of the PLO from that city.

Israelis rallied behind the government as the armed forces crossed into Lebanon on June 6. Shelling of the Galilee stopped the next day, as Israeli forces captured Tyre and Beaufort Castle, two major Palestinian artillery positions. On June 8 the Israel Defense Force (IDF) captured Sidon and Damur on the coast, and approached the Beirut-Damascus Highway in the east.

ISRAEL • Information Highlights

Official Name: State of Israel.
Location: Southwest Asia.
Area: 7,848 sq mi (20 326 km^2).
Population (1982 est.): 4,100,000.
Chief Cities (1979 est.): Jerusalem, the capital, 386,-600; Tel Aviv-Jaffa, 339,800; Haifa, 229,000.
Government: Head of state, Yitzhak Navon, president (took office May 1978). Head of government, Menahem Begin, premier (took office June 1977). Legislature (unicameral)—Knesset.
Monetary Unit: Shekel (30.94 shekels equal U.S.$1, Nov. 15, 1982).
Gross National Product (1981 U.S.$): $21,100,000,-000.
Economic Indexes: Consumer Prices (1981, 1970=100), all items, 7,015.1; food, 7,785.7. Industrial production (1980, 1975=100), 119.
Foreign Trade (1980 U.S.$): Imports, $7,875,000,-000; exports, $5,294,000,000.

As the year began, Defense Minister Ariel Sharon (above, second from left), held talks with Egypt clearing the way for Israel's final withdrawal from the Sinai in April. The major obstacle proved to be Israeli residents of the town of Yamit (left), who had to be removed by force.

Armed intervention by Syria prompted the cabinet to approve military operations to destroy Syrian missile batteries in the Bekaa Valley. Israeli fighter planes launched the attack on June 9, and the government claimed overwhelming success. Influenced by mounting domestic and world pressure, Israel declared a cease-fire, accepted by the Syrians on June 11 and the PLO on June 12. Renewed hostilities by the PLO, however, resulted in the destruction of their power base in Beirut and a siege of the city by Israeli forces. (*See* LEBANON.)

Despite the brilliant military victory, the mood in Israel was not jubilant. National grief over heavy Israeli losses (368 killed and 2,383 wounded) and moral anguish over Lebanese civilian casualties was deepened by distress over world condemnation, which many felt was based on biased media coverage.

The Massacre. The extension of the war beyond its initial objectives created domestic dissent, which reached a high point in September after the massacre by Christian militia of hundreds of Palestinians in west Beirut refugee camps. Mass demonstrations called for an official probe into the atrocity and the resignation of Defense Minister Ariel Sharon (*see* BIOGRAPHY). Prime Minister Menahem Begin bowed to pressure and instructed the Supreme Court to set up a commission of inquiry into the circumstances that permitted such an occurrence despite Israeli military presence in the area.

International bodies were nearly unanimous in condemning Israel and in failing to censure the actual perpetrators of the massacre. Egypt recalled its ambassador from Israel; the U.S. Congress launched an investigation into the use of American military aid to Israel; a UN General Assembly resolution called for the expulsion of Israel; Italian airport workers boycotted flights to and from Israel; and the International Telecommunications Union proposed to oust Israel from its ranks. Several Christian groups, however, expressed support for Israel, emphasizing the fact that the atrocity was in fact committed by Christian Phalangists. Groups of Christian theologians in the United States issued similar statements of solidarity with Israel, and 4,000 Evangelical Christians from around the world gathered in Jerusalem to reinforce their pledge of friendship.

World Jewry. Some of the harshest criticism of Israel's role in Lebanon and some of its most passionate defense came from world Jewry. Jewish communities around the globe found themselves targets of abuse because of antagonism toward Israel. Despite such abuse and sometimes despite their own agonizing indignation, world Jewry generally rallied in support of Israel.

Economy. The Israeli economy was greatly affected by the Lebanon war. The cost of the campaign was distributed among an already heavily taxed citizenry. Special levies, as on travel and the sale of securities, were imposed; import duties on luxury items and taxes on income, sales, and telephone use were raised. Because of adverse publicity abroad and the threat of PLO terror, tourism, one of the nation's major sources of income, dropped to an all-time low. The closing of El Al and the Italian boycott also added to the difficulties of the tourist trade.

The economic difficulties were evidenced by an average monthly increase in the Consumer Price Index of some 7.6%, indicating an annual inflation rate of 135%. The International Monetary Fund approved a loan of $140 million, and world Jewry was asked to contribute $300 million to an emergency fund.

The production of goods continued at a peacetime rate, and industrial exports, with the exception of diamonds, were also not affected by the war effort. This was because of a highly efficient and selective military call-up, with many key specialists exempted from mobilization. Agricultural production was facilitated by volunteers from abroad and by high school students who devoted part of their summer holidays to help in harvesting, fertilization, and irrigation.

Israel proceeded with the construction of a canal project linking the Mediterranean with the Dead Sea. The drop in elevation of nearly 1,300 ft (396 m) would provide the generating capacity for a 700-megawatt power station near the Dead Sea and save billions of dollars in energy production. It would also save the Dead Sea itself, which has been sinking at an alarming rate. Meanwhile, the Tzuk Tamrur I oil well began producing some 400 barrels per day.

Foreign Relations. Zaire, one of the African countries to break relations with Israel in 1973, resumed full diplomatic and military cooperation in August. Welcoming the new ambassador, President Yitzhak Navon expressed confidence that other African nations would follow the lead.

In a similar gesture, Costa Rica moved its embassy back to Jerusalem; it was one of the 13 nations which, following the 1980 Knesset declaration of "undivided" Jerusalem as Israel's capital, had moved their embassies to Tel Aviv. The participation of two Israeli scientists at the Third International Conference on the Theory of Relativity in Shanghai in October marked the first time in 20 years that Israeli passport holders were admitted into China.

Politics. The Telem party, founded by the late Moshe Dayan, voluntarily dissolved, and its two parliamentary representatives joined the government coalition. This was followed by the entry into the coalition of the ultra-nationalist Tehiya faction, giving the government a parliamentary majority of 64–56.

Late-Year Developments. The sudden death of Premier Begin's wife caused him to interrupt his visit to the United States in November and reschedule his meeting with President Reagan for early 1983.

The year ended on a hopeful note, as peace negotiations between Israel and Lebanon began on December 28.

LIVIA E. BITTON JACKSON
Herbert H. Lehman College, CUNY

Demonstrators criticized the government for not preventing the Lebanon massacre and demanded an investigation.

© S. Nackstrand/Sipa-Black Star

ITALY

UPI

The manhunt for kidnapped U.S. Gen. James Dozier finally met with success in late January.

Italy in 1982 suffered a serious economic downturn. Amid continued political instability, neither the Christian Democrats nor the Socialists was able to reverse the slide.

Politics and Domestic Affairs

Spadolini Governments. A major shift in Italy's political pattern occurred in June 1981, when the Christian Democrats were forced to relinquish the premiership, which they had controlled since 1945, to Giovanni Spadolini, leader of the small, secular Republican Party. Premier Spadolini's five-party government, made up of Republicans, Christian Democrats, Liberals, Social Democrats, and Socialists, remained in office longer than many observers expected. It drew up an austerity budget that called for reduction of public health spending and unemployment payments, and for an increase in the value-added tax (sales tax), in railway fares, and in gasoline and electricity charges.

Spadolini's government survived confidence votes in March and July 1982, but on August 7 it had to resign when the Socialist Party withdrew its support. The Socialists and Christian Democrats had split over proposals to make oil companies pay taxes early on refined products. Bettino Craxi, leader of the Socialist Party, favored new parliamentary elections rather than a reshuffling of the government, thinking that the Italian Socialists would be the beneficiaries of the same voting trends that had occurred recently in France, Greece, and Spain. President Alessandro Pertini, though himself a Socialist, resisted Craxi's strategy.

After several days of consultations with various party leaders, President Pertini persuaded Spadolini to form a new government—a carbon copy of the one that had resigned. On September 2 this second Spadolini government won a vote of confidence in the Chamber of Deputies. The opposition was led by the Communists, who had been shut out of the government. On October 27, the new government won another vote of confidence on tax measures decreed three months earlier as part of its austerity program. However the new government lasted only until mid-November. Prime Minister Spadolini's resignation, which was refused by the president on November 11, was accepted two days later.

On November 30, Amintore Fanfani, a Christian Democrat who had led four governments between 1954 and 1963, formed a four-party government with Socialists, Social Democrats, and Liberals. Fanfani's compromise economic proposals included a more flexible *scala mobile* (wage indexation), tax increases, and a $10,000,000,000 spending cut.

Christian Democrats. At their party congress in May, the Christian Democrats, Italy's largest party, elected a new leader as part of a strategy to regain the premiership. The new party secretary was a 54-year-old southerner, Ciriaco De Mita, a member of the party's center-left wing. While his ideological stance put him in a good position to deal with Italy's Socialists—the second major force in the country's coalition government—De Mita was expected to take a tough attitude toward his Socialist rivals. He succeeded Flaminio Piccoli, who supported De Mita over former Premier Arnaldo Forlani.

Communist Party. The Polish government's crackdown on Solidarity in December 1981 caused Enrico Berlinguer, secretary of the Italian Communist Party (PCI), to criticize openly the Soviet and Eastern European Communist leadership. "A period has ended," Berlinguer declared. "The propulsive forces which instigated the October Revolution have become exhausted just as the capacity to renew has become exhausted in Eastern European societies."

Berlinguer's denunciation elicited a 5,000-word editorial in Moscow's *Pravda* on January 24 that nearly excommunicated the Italian party. *Pravda* accused the PCI of "slandering" the USSR and of "giving direct aid to imperialism."

Berlinguer coolly rejected the Soviet charges and again expressed doubt about the relevance of the "Soviet model." He also accused Kremlin leaders of perpetuating the gross Stalinist errors that had been confessed by Khrushchev in 1956. Despite the bitter exchange, a complete breach between Moscow and the PCI seemed unlikely. But many of the 1.7 million rank and file in the PCI were confused, and many heaped blame on Berlinguer. Armando Cossutta remained the chief PCI supporter of the Soviet Union.

Many observers believed the PCI to be in serious trouble. Although the PCI won 30% of the vote in nationwide elections in 1979 and controlled the local governments in Italy's largest cities, it was consistently denied a place in the 20 regional governments.

Terrorism. On Dec. 17, 1981, U.S. Brig. Gen. James Lee Dozier, deputy chief of staff in NATO's southern European headquarters in Verona, was abducted from his apartment by the Red Brigade. The governments of Italy and the United States refused to negotiate for his release. An intensive manhunt was conducted by 6,000 Italian policemen. As a result of information disclosed by a captured terrorist, antiterrorist forces stormed an apartment in Padua on Jan. 28, 1982, freeing the general without firing a shot. Despite his prolonged isolation in a tent inside the apartment, Dozier was in good health. Officials in both Italy and the United States honored the general on his release and congratulated the police on the operation.

In the course of the manhunt, scores of terrorists in northeastern Italy were arrested. Some of General Dozier's captors were linked to the killing of former Premier Aldo Moro.

Mafia. With hundreds of Red Brigade terrorists behind bars, Italian authorities began to concentrate on the older, more deeply rooted Italian phenomenon—the Mafia. In recent years the Mafia has shifted from protection rackets to international trafficking in drugs. The upsurge of its activity, not only in Palermo and western Sicily but in Calabria and Naples, alarmed politicians, police, and civilians alike. Gen. Carlo Alberto Dalla Chiesa was named prefect of Palermo and charged with the crackdown.

On September 3, Dalla Chiesa and his wife were murdered by gunmen as they drove through downtown Palermo. Cries of outrage echoed throughout Italy. In Palermo, Salvatore Cardinal Pappalardo preached a hard-hitting funeral sermon in the presence of Italy's president and premier. Parliament quickly enacted a law that for the first time in Italian history made it a crime to associate with the Mafia. The government appointed the head of Italy's secret service, Emanuele De Francesco, to be the new prefect and special high commissioner in Palermo.

Anti-Jewish Violence. In Rome on October 9 unidentified terrorists threw hand grenades and fired submachine guns at Jewish worshipers who were leaving Rome's synagogue at the end of Sabbath services. The attack killed a two-year-old child and wounded 34 other Italian Jews. Italy's president, the premier, the pope, and all of Italy's political parties except the neo-Fascists immediately condemned the atrocity.

Banco Ambrosiano Scandal. A major financial crisis—the worst since the Michele Sindona banking scandal of 1974—rocked Italy throughout the summer. The nation's largest private bank, the Banco Ambrosiano of Milan, was found to be deeply involved in a murky web of irregular foreign and domestic dealings. Its president, Roberto Calvi, came under investigation for the loss of $1,400,000,000 in bank funds. In June, Calvi fled to London, where he was later found hanged under Blackfriars Bridge. An inquest ruled his death a suicide, but many Italians suspected foul play. Calvi had been a member of the secret "Propaganda-2" Masonic Lodge, whose conspiratorial, right-wing activities had

Italy's triumph in the World Cup soccer tournament was a source of national pride—and some wild celebrations.

Gamma-Liaison

brought down the Forlani government in 1981.

Investigation revealed that some of the missing funds had been obtained through unrepaid loans guaranteed by the Vatican bank. The Vatican appointed a team of three outside financial experts to look into the Vatican's relationship with the Banco Ambrosiano. In August, Italian banking authorities ordered the liquidation of Banco Ambrosiano.

In September, Licio Gelli, the fugitive Grand Master of the "Propaganda-2" Masonic Lodge, was arrested in Switzerland as he tried to withdraw millions of dollars from a blocked account. Italy immediately sought Gelli's extradition so that he could also be charged with banking fraud in connection with the Banco Ambrosiano. (*See* special report, page 551.)

Tax Evasion. In July 1980 the movie actress Sophia Loren was convicted *in absentia* of failing to report the equivalent of $180,000 on her 1963 income tax returns. On May 19, 1982, having been a fugitive for two years, she voluntarily returned to Italy, claiming that her tax consultant had made the error. She agreed to serve a 30-day sentence in a women's prison in Caserta, but was released after 17 days.

Economy

In June the government devalued the lira by 2.75% against the European Monetary System.

That same month the Confederation of Italian Industrialists declared that they would pull out of the agreement reached with the labor unions in 1975 on the *scala mobile* system of quarterly indexing of wages. Negotiations on this thorny problem got under way with labor leaders in the autumn.

In October parliament passed the new Spadolini government's austerity budget. By that time, most Italian economic indicators were gloomy. GNP was up only 1% above that of 1981. Unemployment, which already amounted to 9.2% of the work force, or 2.1 million persons, was expected to rise. It was especially high among young people. Paying for the government's deficit (which was expected to be at least $50,000,000,000, up from $38,700,000,000 in 1981) pushed interest rates to more than 20%; increased the money supply; and kept inflation at 17%, more than double the European Community (EC) average. The trade deficit was expected to reach $9,300,000,000.

Foreign Policy

Falkland Islands Invasion. When Argentine forces invaded Britain's Falkland (Malvinas) Islands in May, Italy at first went along with the EC's temporary economic measures designed to back up Britain. On May 17, however, Italy abstained from the continuation of these measures, arguing that Britain was overreacting. The fact that 40% of Argentina's population is of Italian origin was also significant.

United States. Italy's President Pertini visited the United States from March 24 to April 1. He received a warm welcome in Washington, New York, San Francisco, and elsewhere.

In June, U.S. President Ronald Reagan flew to Rome in the course of his trip to Versailles for a Big Seven economic conference and a NATO summit meeting. He met with President Pertini, Premier Spadolini, and Pope John Paul II.

In July, Italy sided with Britain, France, and West Germany in rejecting President Reagan's attempts to get them to rescind agreements they had made for construction of a pipeline that would bring Soviet natural gas into Western Europe. In September, the United States retaliated by blacklisting Italian firms fulfilling contracts for the pipeline construction. In November, Premier Spadolini flew to Washington to confer with the Reagan administration in an effort to resolve this dispute. Shortly thereafter, the U.S. president announced that he was lifting the pipeline sanctions. Otherwise, Italy was very supportive of U.S. policy in Europe. It moved forward with NATO plans to base Pershing II and cruise missiles in Sicily in 1984.

Algeria. In September, Italy and Algeria reached agreement on terms for shipment of natural gas to Italy through the new trans-Mediterranean pipeline, thus ending a deadlock that had delayed its opening by nearly one year.

Lebanon. In the wake of Israel's invasion of southern Lebanon and Beirut, Italy joined the United States and France in dispatching peacekeeping forces to Beirut. Italy expressed sharp criticism of Israel's military action.

When Yasir Arafat, leader of the Palestinian Liberation Organization, visited Rome in September, he was received by Italy's president, premier, and also by the pope—to the displeasure of Israel and of Italian Jews.

Bulgaria. Relations with Sofia worsened late in the year, when Italian police alleged that three Bulgarians had masterminded the 1981 assassination attempt against Pope John Paul II.

CHARLES F. DELZELL, *Vanderbilt University*

ITALY · Information Highlights

Official Name: Italian Republic.
Location: Southern Europe.
Area: 116,318 sq mi (301 264 km^2).
Population (1982 est.): 57,400,000.
Chief Cities (Dec. 1980): Rome, the capital, 2,916,-414; Milan, 1,655,599; Naples, 1,219,362; Turin, 1,143,263.
Government: *Head of state,* Alessandro Pertini, president (took office July 1978). *Head of government,* Amintore Fanfani, prime minister (took office Nov. 1982). *Legislature*—Parliament: Senate and Chamber of Deputies.
Monetary Unit: Lira (1,489.5 lire equal U.S.$1, Nov. 15, 1982).
Gross Domestic Product (1981 U.S.$): $350,154,-000,000.
Economic Indexes (1981): *Consumer Prices* (1970= 100), all items, 441.1; food, 420.0. *Industrial production* (1975=100), 127.
Foreign Trade (1981 U.S.$): *Imports,* $91,011,000,-000; *exports,* $75,214,000,000.

JAPAN

Domestic affairs in Japan were climaxed in late November by the election of the nation's 17th postwar prime minister, 64-year-old moderate Yasuhiro Nakasone. His Liberal-Democratic Party (LDP), which had emerged from the dual elections of 1980 with a comfortable majority, spent much of the year preparing for the party presidential election scheduled for that month. Prime Minister Zenko Suzuki, who had been the leading candidate for president of the LDP (and therefore likely to be reelected prime minister) unexpectedly announced in mid-October that he would resign the premiership and party presidency. That set the stage for Nakasone's ascendancy. Meanwhile, the LDP remained under a political cloud as the so-called Lockheed case moved steadily through court action toward some resolution. The Japanese press predicted that former Prime Minister Kakuei Tanaka, involved in the case since 1976, would eventually be convicted. Although Tanaka has remained in the Diet (parliament) as an independent member, he actually headed the largest faction of the LDP (109 Diet members).

In 1982, according to the Finance Ministry, Japan showed a modest overall surplus in world trade and, indeed, ran a deficit in the service category. But its merchandise surplus with both the United States and European Community (EC) were at such record heights as to cause severe friction with its closest allies. Pressure on Japan to reduce exports and increase imports was felt at the Versailles summit conference in June, and in bilateral contacts with the United States, Great Britain, France, Italy, and even members of the Association of Southeast Asian Nations (ASEAN).

Domestic Affairs

The LDP continued to enjoy a strong majority in both houses of the Diet. After Prime Minister Suzuki reshuffled his cabinet in 1981, the LDP held 287 of 511 seats in the (lower) House of Representatives and 136 of 252 seats in the (upper) House of Councillors. The Japan Socialist Party (JSP), with 104 seats in the lower and 47 seats in the upper house, made up the chief opposition, followed by representatives of the Clean Government (Komeito) Party, the Democratic Socialist Party (DSP), and the Japan Communist Party (JCP).

Party Politics. Although Suzuki was favored to win the fall LDP presidential election (and thus to remain prime minister), he continued to be hampered by a stubborn recession, falling revenues, and a towering budget deficit. In September, according to a poll by the Kyodo News Service, 37.5% of Japanese voters did not want him to win the party balloting. On October 12 in a surprise move, Suzuki resigned as LDP president and Japanese prime minister for the sake of

Wide World

Yasuhiro Nakasone, 64, a pro-Western conservative, was elected the new prime minister of Japan on November 26.

"harmony and unity in the party." His announcement sent LDP factional leaders jockeying for position to succeed him.

Despite moves by top party officials to choose a leader without a divisive showdown, four LDP leaders registered their candidacies on October 16. This forced a party primary on November 23, the second one since the system was introduced in 1978. Yasuhiro Nakasone, director general of the Administrative Management Agency, led the mainstream group, supported by the factions of Suzuki and Tanaka. The three non-mainstream candidates were Toshio Komoto, director general of the Economic Planning Agency; Shintaro Abe, minister of international trade and industry; and Ichiro Nakagawa, head of the Science and Technology Agency.

In the primary, involving about 1 million party members, Nakasone captured 58% of the vote, more than twice as much as his nearest opponent, Komoto. In the final voting November 25, in which only LDP Diet members cast ballots, Nakasone won a comfortable majority. The new prime minister was said to favor reductions in government spending, curbs on budget deficits, and better ties with the United States. His cabinet, announced immediately, reflected those policies, as well as the support of the controversial Tanaka.

Some redistribution of strength in the House of Councillors was expected in the election scheduled for 1983, because of the Diet's adoption in August 1982 of new procedures for the selection of upper house members from the national constituency. The new system provides

287

proportional representation, to be applied to half (or 50) of the nationwide seats elected for three-year terms. The reform was expected to benefit the LDP and JSP.

Economy. The Economic Planning Agency estimated a nominal growth rate of less than 5% for the year ending December 1981, with the gross national product (GNP) at about $1,200,-000,000,000 (U.S. trillion). Early in the year the government approved a fiscal 1982 budget, balanced with deficit bonds at $191,000,000,000. The total marked a 6% increase over 1981, the lowest rate of expansion in more than two decades. Defense appropriations totaled $11,800,-000,000 (about 0.9% of GNP), but increases in arms expenditures exceeded those for ordinary functions, including welfare. On July 9 the cabinet approved the policy goal of a zero-based budget for 1983; defense, foreign aid, and pensions were exempted from austerity planning.

Meanwhile, on June 16, the Ministry of Health and Welfare announced that during the previous fiscal year (April 1980–March 1981), $94,600,000,000 was paid into social welfare programs. Over one decade, total welfare payments had increased sevenfold.

Social Issues. On August 6, some 43,000 people gathered at the Peace Park in Hiroshima, site of the first atomic bomb explosion 37 years before. Mayor Takeshi Araki sent a telegram to U.S. Ambassador Mike Mansfield protesting underground nuclear tests conducted by the United States on the eve of the anniversary.

On September 21, in a rare display of unity among opposition forces, five minority political parties and four major labor unions demanded retraction of a government decision to freeze pay increases for public employees in 1982. They also agreed to press for a one trillion-yen tax cut, employment measures, and steps to support smaller enterprises. Agreement was reached among delegates from the JSP, Komeito, DSP, General Council of Trade Unions (Sohyo), Japan Confederation of Labor (Domei), and two smaller labor federations.

JAPAN • Information Highlights

Official Name: Japan.
Location: East Asia.
Area: 147,470 sq mi (381 947 km²).
Population (1982 est.): 118,600,000.
Chief Cities (1980 est.): Tokyo, the capital, 11,468,-516; Yokohama, 2,773,822; Osaka, 2,648,158; Nagoya, 2,087,884.
Government: *Head of state,* Hirohito, emperor (acceded Dec. 1926). *Head of government,* Yasuhiro Nakasone, prime minister (took office Nov. 1982). *Legislature*—Diet: House of Councillors and House of Representatives.
Monetary Unit: Yen (249.20 yen equal U.S.$1, Nov. 30, 1982).
Gross National Product (1981 U.S.$): $1,153,000,-000,000.
Economic Indexes (1981): *Consumer Prices* (1970=100), *all items,* 248.1; *food,* 246.7. *Industrial production* (1975=100), 146.
Foreign Trade (1981 U.S.$): *Imports,* $143,287,000,-000; *exports,* $152,027,000,000.

Japan's population continued to show change, not so much in quantity as in quality. A government survey reported an adjusted death rate in 1980 of 469.3 per 100,000 among men, and of 362.7 among women (down from 535.8 and 433.1, respectively, in 1975). Increases in the older population had profound effects on social policy.

Disasters. The Japanese suffered a series of disasters in 1982. Among the man-made was a hotel fire in the Akasaka district of Tokyo on February 8, which claimed 32 guests as victims and injured 30 others. The next day, a Japan Air Lines (JAL) DC-10 crashed in shallow waters off Haneda Airport, Tokyo, killing 24 and injuring 150 others. Pilot errors were also responsible for serious near-accidents at Osaka International Airport on July 19, involving another JAL DC-10; and at Chitose Airport in Hokkaido, August 19, involving a JAL Boeing 747.

Nature also dealt repeated blows. On March 29 a maximum-intensity earthquake centering on Urakawa in Hokkaido injured more than 100 persons and caused extensive property damage. On July 24–25, torrential rainfall and subsequent landslides left a death toll of 275 in Kyushu and southwestern Japan; flood damage was estimated at 315,000,000,000 yen. On August 1, Typhoon No. 10 cut a swath of destruction across central Japan, leaving 59 dead and 24 missing. Soon thereafter, on September 13, powerful Typhoon No. 18 went on a two-day rampage through the central, eastern, and northern parts of Honshu and Hokkaido. Maximum winds of 75 mph (125 km/h) flooded 80,000 homes, ruined more than 10,000 acres (4 000 ha) of rice paddies, washed out bridges and roads, paralyzed rail traffic, and left 30 persons dead or missing.

Foreign Affairs

In several settings during the year, Prime Minister Suzuki set forth the main themes in Japan's foreign policy. In his policy speech to the Diet in January, Suzuki promised to work on solutions to the problems of trade friction. He also vowed to continue a defense buildup so that Japan might meet its responsibilities as a leading member of the Free World. At the Versailles summit he responded to foreign criticism of Japan's towering trade surpluses, emphasizing that he was doing his utmost to open domestic markets.

While he focused on economic issues, Suzuki also appealed for world cooperation on global security. On June 9, as the first speaker at the UN Disarmament Conference in New York, the Japanese prime minister spelled out a three-stage proposal calling for disarmament, the transfer of resources from arms to economic development, and reinforcement of peace through the UN. On June 19, Prime Minister Suzuki underlined his position by delivering to the UN an antinuclear petition with more than 87 million Japanese signatures.

At the United Nations on June 9, then-Prime Minister Zenko Suzuki symbolized Japan's concern for global security by ringing the Peace Bell. Speaking at the UN Disarmament Conference that day, he warned that nations were being "trapped in a vicious circle . . . by building up their armaments."

United States. In 1981 the United States had a merchandise trade deficit with Japan of between $13,400,000,000 (Japanese customs estimate) and $15,800,000,000 (U.S. estimate). In January, in a personal message conveyed to U.S. President Ronald Reagan by Minister of International Trade and Industry Shintaro Abe, Prime Minister Suzuki promised to try to resolve bilateral trade friction. On February 20, Masumi Esaki, a key LDP official, led a delegation to Washington to work out a list of 67 sectors in which trade barriers could be reduced or eliminated.

On a visit to Tokyo, April 23–25, U.S. Vice-President George Bush expressed Washington's desire to obtain increased Japanese imports of American farm produce. Two Japanese business organizations supported the Bush request: Keidanren proposed that the government remove residual restrictions on some 27 items; Keizai Doyukai urged further liberalization of agricultural imports. Shizuma Iwamochi, president of an umbrella organization of agricultural cooperatives (Zenshu), however, rejected the proposal: "The six million farmers we represent will strenuously protest any move whatsoever toward appeasing U.S. demands on the agricultural issue."

During the year many Japanese came to think that the United States took trade issues into its own judicial system. On July 21 a federal grand jury in San Jose, CA, handed down indictments against the Mitsubishi Electric Corporation and four of its employees. Arrest warrants were also issued for employees of Hitachi Ltd., a Japanese electronics firm. It was charged that $648,000 had been paid to an undercover U.S. federal agent in order to obtain computer software belonging to International Business Machines (IBM). Hitachi claimed that it had paid a normal consulting fee; Mitsubishi denied all FBI allegations. The Japanese press alternated between criticism of the firms' methods of obtaining technological data and denunciation of what was called a "sting" operation.

On the heels of the so-called Silicon Valley case came yet another action. On July 20, a federal grand jury indicted the U.S. subsidiary of Mitsui & Company for allegedly conspiring to sell imported Japanese steel at unfair prices. Mitsui promptly announced that a mistake had been made in applying import procedures and that it would seek an out-of-court settlement.

There were other, more subtle differences between the allies. When he was in Tokyo in April, Vice-President Bush urged Japan to support the U.S. proposal to tighten regulations on new credit offers to the USSR. In Paris in June, however, Prime Minister Suzuki asked President Reagan to exclude from sanctions the Japan-Soviet natural gas and oil exploration project off Sakhalin. Suzuki contended that the project's bankruptcy would deal a heavier blow to Japan than to the USSR.

Although the Suzuki government had provided a marked increase (7.8%) in budget appropriations for defense in 1982–83, Washington officials persisted in pointing out that the outlay constituted less than 1% of Japan's GNP. This was what some Americans referred to as Japan's "free ride" in security arrangements. In Tokyo in late March, U.S. Defense Secretary Caspar Weinberger proposed that Japan's defense programs include the capability to protect sea lanes 1,000 nautical miles from its coasts. Tokyo agreed to discuss the plan in bilateral security meetings scheduled to be held in Honolulu later in the year. There was a serious question, however, as to whether Japanese constitutional restrictions (Article 9) would permit utilization of the nation's growing defense potential that far from the nation's shores.

Western Europe. Among the EC nations, too, Japan encountered stiff resistance to its growing merchandise trade surplus. In 1981, Japan earned its biggest trade surplus with the EC, estimated at $10,300,000,000, a sharp increase from the 1980 record of $8,800,000,000.

At the Versailles summit meeting of advanced industrial nations, Japan was on the defensive.

In his visit to Japan, March 9–14, President Sandro Pertini of Italy urged business leaders to engage in long-range discussions to lessen trade friction with Western Europe. Pertini also paid a formal call on Emperor Hirohito, exchanged views with Prime Minister Suzuki, addressed the Diet, and visited Hiroshima and Kyoto.

On April 14, President François Mitterand of France, his wife, and five ministers began a five-day stay in Japan. It was the first visit by a French head of state. Foreign Minister Claude Cheysson warned that Japan's trade imbalance with France ($1,000,000,000 in 1981) was fast becoming a political issue. Preparing an agenda for the June summit, in which he was to take up the question of transfers of technology, Mitterand also visited Japan's new Tsukuba Science City.

On a two-week tour of Asia, Prime Minister Margaret Thatcher of Great Britain arrived in Tokyo on September 17. In talks on economy and trade, she requested that Prime Minister Suzuki take steps to reduce Japan's $2,000,000,000 trade surplus with her country. Rather than simply ship goods from Japan, business should invest directly in the United Kingdom, she argued. The Japanese press, represented by *Yomiuri,* was skeptical in light of the 3.3 million unemployed in Britain.

Eastern Bloc. Both U.S.-Japanese and Soviet-Japanese relations were affected by events in Poland during the year. On February 23 the Suzuki government imposed limited sanctions on the military regime in Warsaw and what were called its Soviet supporters. Japan was the third U.S. ally (after Britain and West Germany) to withhold official credits and to refuse rescheduling of Poland's debts. Meanwhile, relations between Tokyo and Moscow continued to be exacerbated by the so-called northern territories issue, involving islands northeast of Hokkaido under occupation by Soviet forces since World War II. During the week of September 6, some 2,800 people from various parts of Japan attended an LDP-sponsored rally in Tokyo and demanded return of the islands in the southern Kuriles.

China and Korea. In 1981 trade between Japan and China reached a record total of $10,400,000,000. Japan suffered its first trade deficit with mainland China in 17 years, however, as steel exports went into a steep decline. In terms of customs-cleared trade, Japanese exports totaled $5,100,000,000; imports soared 22% over the 1980 total, reaching $5,300,000,000.

By July 1982, hopes were high in Tokyo that terms could be worked out for low-interest government loans to South Korea. The funds were designed to aid Seoul in its five-year (1982–86) development plan. At that point, however, relations with both South Korea and China were severely strained by the textbook revision case.

In Japan, school textbooks are reviewed by expert panels, and revisions are approved by the Education Ministry. In July 1982 it became apparent that most recent changes in high school history texts had altered treatment of Japanese activities on the continent prior to 1945. What Chinese regarded as "aggression" was described in the textbooks as Japan's "advance" into China. Similarly, uprisings in March 1919 against harsh Japanese rule in Korea were described as unlawful "riots." Reactions in Peking and Seoul were immediate and angry. On July 28 Japan's minister in Peking, Koji Watanabe, told the Chinese government that there had been no change in his country's attitude, made clear in the 1972 joint communiqué in which Japan accepted responsibility "for causing enormous damages in the past to the Chinese people through war and deeply reproaches itself." In late August, Japan assured South Korea that it was trying "in good faith" to settle the textbook issue and pledged that the material in question would be rewritten by 1985. China rejected the proposal.

ARDATH W. BURKS
Professor emeritus of Asian Studies
Rutgers University

"The Bridge to the Four Islands," a 42-ft (13-m) high monument, was built on the Cape of Noshappu to symbolize Japan's desire for the return from the USSR of the "northern territories."

JORDAN

Jordan's King Hussein, who celebrated his 30th year on the throne in August 1982, was able to revive his pivotal role in the search for a lasting Middle East peace. His support for Iraq in its bitter war with Iran increased his status among Arab moderates early in the year, and his July 26 decision to accept Palestinian Liberation Organization (PLO) troops evacuated from Beirut was a key to averting a potentially devastating Israeli ground assault on the Lebanese capital. More importantly, Hussein's reconciliation with PLO leader Yasir Arafat was a critical contribution toward defining the Arab response to a new American peace plan.

Iran-Iraq War. Jordan's support for Iraq was based on a fear shared by Saudi Arabia and the Gulf emirates that an Iranian victory would unleash radical Muslim fundamentalism on the Arab world.

On January 28, Hussein dramatically increased Jordan's commitment to Iraq by forming a volunteer force which he offered personally to lead into battle on the Iraqi side. In previous months, Jordan's support for the Iraqi war effort had been limited to ensuring that supplies reached Baghdad overland from the Jordanian port of Aqaba.

Hussein's attention was diverted, however, first by Israel's June 6 invasion of Lebanon, and then by a scarcely veiled Soviet warning during his June 24–28 visit to Moscow not to oppose Iran's summer offensive.

Lebanon and the U.S. Proposal. Hussein's offer of amnesty to PLO guerrillas—the same troops he had violently expelled from Jordan after they threatened his throne in 1970—not only paved the way for the lifting of Israel's siege of west Beirut but also may have served as a pretext for the role assigned to Jordan in U.S. President Reagan's peace initiative.

On September 1 Reagan unveiled a peace plan that went beyond the stalled Camp David negotiations. The proposal, calling for an Israeli withdrawal from the territories occupied since 1967 and the creation of a Palestinian entity on

Mattison/Gamma-Liaison

Jordan's King Hussein and PLO leader Yasir Arafat (left) held their first discussions in 12 years during 1982.

the West Bank and Gaza in association with Jordan, revived the so-called "Jordanian option" even though Hussein had been stripped of his role as spokesman since 1974.

Hussein, who had been secretly consulted by U.S. officials before the plan's announcement, carried out a pragmatic and careful program to reassert his role as a legitimate, if not primary, representative for the Palestinians while avoiding being denounced by the PLO and Arab radicals for dealing with the United States.

PLO Negotiations. To address the U.S. plan effectively, Hussein had first to consult with PLO spokesman Yasir Arafat. Hussein met with him initially at the September 6–9 Arab summit in Fez, Morocco, but delayed serious discussions until Arafat arrived in Amman on October 9. The four days of talks appeared to yield little, but private understandings allowed Hussein to represent Palestinian interests on the thorny problem of mutual PLO-Israeli recognition during trips to Washington late in the year.

Economy. Hussein's diplomatic success was paralleled by significant achievements in Jordan's ambitious five-year social and economic development plan. In the first two years, Jordan experienced a healthy 8.5% annual increase in gross domestic product by directing 40% of all investment to mining, manufacturing, and transportation. Though Jordan will need $3,500,000,-000 in foreign aid to reach the plan's goals, it seems likely, barring catastrophe or a diplomatic reversal, that the goals will be met.

F. NICHOLAS WILLARD

JORDAN • Information Highlights

Official Name: Hashemite Kingdom of Jordan.
Location: Southwest Asia.
Area: 37,738 sq mi (97 740 km²).
Population (1982 est.): 3,500,000.
Chief Cities (Nov. 1979): Amman, the capital, 648,-587; Zarqa, 215,687; Irbid, 112,954.
Government: *Head of state,* Hussein ibn Talal, king (acceded Aug. 1952). *Head of government,* Mudar Badran, prime minister (took office Aug. 1980). *Legislature*—National Consultative Assembly.
Monetary Unit: Dinar (0.36 dinar equals U.S.$1, Nov. 1982).
Gross National Product (1980 U.S.$): $3,600,000,-000.
Economic Index (1980): *Consumer prices* (1970=100), *all items,* 173.3; *food,* 159.2.
Foreign Trade (1981 U.S.$): *Imports,* $2,130,000,-000; *exports,* $541,000,000.

KANSAS

Bill Fitz-Patrick/The White House

Kansan Alf Landon's 95th birthday celebration was highlighted by a presidential visit.

Kansas' economy reflected the problems experienced in other states in 1982. The unemployment rate rose as layoffs occurred in major industries such as aviation. By the middle of the year, Beech Aircraft Corporation, headquartered in Wichita, had laid off more than 3,000 workers, while Cessna Aircraft, also of Wichita, had more than 4,000 idle workers. The high unemployment level and other economic factors led to a decline in state revenues, which, in turn, led to a 4% budget cut for state agencies.

Agriculture. Kansas regained its top spot in wheat production in 1982 with a record 462 million-bushel harvest. This figure represented an increase of approximately 42 million bushels over the previous record set in 1980 and a 51% increase over the 1981 harvest, which was hampered by poor weather, insects, and disease. Production averaged 35 bushels per acre for 13.2 million acres (5.4 million ha) harvested. Despite the record harvest, low wheat prices (40 to 50 cents below 1981 prices) dimmed farmers' hopes for a profitable year.

Legislation. Gov. John Carlin, reintroduced the issue of a severance tax on oil, natural gas, and coal as a means of providing additional revenue for the state's schools and highways. The proposal, which was defeated in 1981 legislative session, again passed the House of Representatives but was defeated in the Senate. This set the stage for the 1982 governor's race, in which the severance tax was a major issue. The state's fiscal problems were highlighted in June when state agencies were asked to cut their budgets by 4% because revenues were falling below estimates of income. Late in the year, another budget cut was implemented. A 4% cut in state aid to school districts and reductions in welfare aid were mandated to reduce projected deficits.

Another issue of the legislative session was the need to redraw congressional districts based on the 1980 census. The legislature adopted what was generally called the "Republican plan." It was vetoed by Governor Carlin. The issue was settled ultimately by the U.S. District Court, with the judges adopting boundaries that favored the Democrats.

Election. The major contest in the November 2 election was the race for governor. Sam Hardage, a real-estate developer from Wichita, won a crowded Republican primary. He faced the incumbent Democratic governor, John Carlin, in the general election. A major issue of the campaign was the severance tax, generally opposed by Republicans. Hardage opposed the tax until the last days of the campaign, when he indicated that additional sources of revenue were needed. He failed to receive an endorsement from Wendell Lady, the speaker of the Kansas House of Representatives, a supporter of the severance tax and one of Hardage's opponents in the primary. Carlin was reelected, carrying all of the urban areas of the state, while Hardage carried most of the oil-producing counties.

The second congressional district seat was left open when incumbent Jim Jeffries (R) decided not to run for reelection. Jim Slattery (D) won the general election, defeating former gubernatorial candidate Morris Kay. In the other congressional districts, incumbents—Republicans Pat Roberts, Larry Winn, and Robert Whittaker, and Democrat Dan Glickman—were reelected.

A number of cities approved increases in the sales tax, taking advantage of laws that allowed cities to levy taxes above the 3% collected by the state.

PATRICIA A. MICHAELIS
Kansas State Historical Society

KANSAS · Information Highlights

Area: 82,277 sq mi (213 097 km²).
Population (1980 census): 2,364,236.
Chief Cities (1980 census): Topeka, the capital, 115,-266; Wichita, 279,835; Kansas City, 161,148.
Government (1982): *Chief Officers*—governor, John Carlin (D); lt. gov., Paul V. Dugan (D). *Legislature*—Senate, 40 members; House of Representatives, 125 members.
State Finances (fiscal year 1981): *Revenues,* $2,715,-000,000; *expenditures,* $2,618,000,000.
Personal Income (1981): $25,762,000,000; per capita, $10,813.
Labor Force (Aug. 1982): *Nonagricultural wage and salary earners,* 910,200; *unemployed,* 83,100 (7.1% of total force).
Education: *Enrollment* (fall 1981)—public elementary schools, 282,014; public secondary, 127,895; colleges and universities (1981–82), 138,453. *Public school expenditures* (1980–81), $1,079,259,000 ($2,714 per pupil).

KENTUCKY

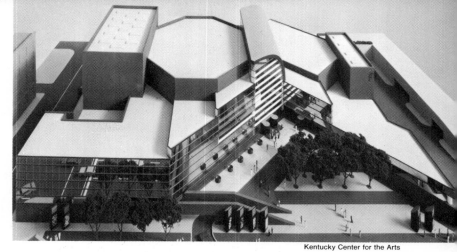

Kentucky Center for the Arts

A new $33-million, five-level arts center was under construction in Louisville.

Kentucky remained in the harsh grip of an economic recession throughout 1982. Unemployment remained high, particularly in Louisville, a center of heavy industry. The national economic slump led to continued low prices and limited production in the coal mines. The mining industry was plagued with a series of fatal accidents early in the year, most of them in small mines that used cheaper and more dangerous mining techniques. Farmers in the state were hurt by low prices for most crops, but tobacco farmers expected to benefit from a large crop.

Despite the general economic problems, major new hotel, office, and shopping complexes were opened in both Lexington and Louisville, and an arts center was under construction in Louisville. For many persons, the most encouraging development in Louisville was the return of minor-league baseball; in its first year the team set an attendance record for the minor leagues.

State Budget. The economic slump, which had led to a major state revenue shortfall during the 1980–82 biennium, confronted Gov. John Y. Brown, Jr., and the legislature with the necessity of raising taxes and curbing expenditures. The political leadership decided not to attempt any major overhaul of the tax structure. Negotiations between the governor and the legislature led to increased taxes on heavy trucks, alcoholic beverages, and insurance premiums, in addition to substantial increases in fees for a number of services.

The $5,000,000,000 biennial budget provided for increases in elementary and secondary education (much of it for teachers' salaries) and for a variety of human services. A proposal to shift higher education spending to help those universities with major graduate and professional programs encountered resistance from other universities and resulted in a compromise. Revenue shortfalls and concern over further cuts in federal aid led the legislature to establish a surplus of about $60 million. By the end of 1982 there were signs that lagging state receipts might require use of the surplus.

Other Legislative Action. Significant new laws were limited in number, but included a sweeping reform of the nursing home business and an automobile title law already found in the other 49 states. A fight among banks over a multi-county banking bill that dominated much of the session ended in a deadlock.

The legislature sought to assert its authority in relation to the executive branch. It passed laws giving its leaders and committees more power between legislative sessions in such areas as the budget, federal grants, appointments, and administrative regulations. The action led to a challenge in the courts to determine the scope of legislative authority. A lower-court ruling against the legislature was appealed to the state Supreme Court.

Electoral Politics. Politically, 1982 was a very quiet year. All incumbent congressmen were returned to office as a result of November elections. Voters in Louisville and Jefferson counties defeated a proposal to merge their two governments. The 1982 elections were overshadowed by preparations for the 1983 gubernatorial race. Three Democratic candidates had already raised a total of almost $1.5 million.

MALCOLM E. JEWELL, *University of Kentucky*

KENTUCKY • Information Highlights

Area: 40,409 sq mi (104 659 km^2).

Population (1980 census): 3,660,257.

Chief Cities (1980 census): Frankfort, the capital, 25,973; Louisville, 298,840; Lexington-Fayette, 204,165.

Government (1982): *Chief Officers*—governor, John Y. Brown, Jr. (D); lt. gov., Martha Layne Collins (D). *General Assembly*—Senate, 38 members; House of Representatives, 100 members.

State Finances (fiscal year 1981): *Revenues,* $4,618,000,000; *expenditures,* $4,821,000,000.

Personal Income (1981): $30,836,000,000; per capita, $8,420.

Labor Force (Aug. 1982): *Nonagricultural wage and salary earners,* 1,128,100; *unemployed,* 181,000 (10.8% of total force).

Education: *Enrollment* (fall 1981)—public elementary schools, 458,781; public secondary, 199,569; colleges and universities (1981–82), 144,154. *Public school expenditures* (1980–81), $1,050,372,000 ($1,569 per pupil).

KENYA

UPI

Nairobi saw much destruction following an abortive coup.

Kenya's reputation for domestic calm and political stability was shaken by a bloody attempt to overthrow the government, launched by junior air force officers on August 1. The rebels seized an air force base outside Nairobi and then took over the government radio station and the central post office, declaring that they wanted to end repression, corruption, and nepotism. The government's counterattack was swift and ruthless, and the coup collapsed after a day. However, at least 145 persons were killed in the upris-ing. A wave of looting and arson broke out in Nairobi, panic buying of food ensued, and radicalized students supporting the revolt ran wild in the streets before troops (who also committed excesses) restored order. More than 3,000 persons were arrested, including the entire air force, while the four coup leaders fled to Tanzania. Though the regime of President Daniel arap Moi seemed to be in full control, the coup attempt revealed deep and violent divisions in Kenyan society.

Economy. One cause of the revolt was Kenya's suddenly worsening economic situation. Due to a decline in coffee and tea sales, the country suffered a huge balance-of-payments problem, made worse by the higher cost of imported oil. As a result, the Kenya shilling was devalued by 40%, and the crucial state consumer grain subsidy of $1.00 per bag was in jeopardy. With an annual population growth of 4% and a GNP increasing at barely 2% each year, Kenya seemed certain to be heading for economic hard times.

Social Problems. The continued African resentment of Asian-descended Kenyans became acute in February, when President Moi accused the Asians of ruining the economy by smuggling currency and hoarding goods. Charging them with involvement in "all areas of social evil," he threatened to deport any or all of Kenya's 100,-000 Asians, even citizens, who were caught in such activities. Asians also were barred from the commodities and transportation businesses. Asian shops were a special target of looters during the coup. The government seemed willing to use Kenya's large and prosperous Asian community as a scapegoat for economic failures and social unrest. Many Asians planned to leave, taking with them capital and skills badly needed by Kenya.

Politics. Kenya officially became a one-party state in June, when the ruling Kenya African National Union (KANU) was made the sole legal party. President Moi moved to consolidate his control, pressuring newspapers who criticized the regime and transferring powerful cabinet ministers to prevent creation of alternative power centers inside KANU.

ROBERT GARFIELD, *DePaul University*

KENYA • Information Highlights

Official Name: Republic of Kenya.
Location: East Coast of Africa.
Area: 224,961 sq mi (582 649 km²).
Population (1982 est.): 17,900,000.
Chief Cities (1979 census): Nairobi, the capital, 827,-775; Mombasa, 341,148.
Government: *Head of state and government,* Daniel arap Moi, president (took office Oct. 1978). *Legislature* (unicameral)—National Assembly, 170 members.
Monetary Unit: Kenya shilling (10.580 schillings equal U.S.$1, February 1982).
Gross Domestic Product (1980 U.S.$): $6,400,000,-000.
Economic Index (1980): *Consumer Prices,* (1972= 100), *all items,* 234.5; *food,* 242.6.
Foreign Trade (1980 U.S.$): *Imports,* $2,305,000,-000; *exports,* $1,299,000,000.

KOREA

Relations between North and South Korea remained at a stalemate in 1982, with each government rejecting the other's reunification formulas. South Korean President Chun Doo Hwan proposed a Consultative Conference for National Reunification, through which delegates from the North and South could work out a joint constitution. He also suggested 20 pilot projects aimed at opening direct communications between the two halves of the country, as well as an inter-Korea presummit meeting. The North rejected these proposals, calling for a conference of

50 politicians from each side, but made it clear that withdrawal of U.S. troops from the South was still a prerequisite of negotiations and that it would not deal with Chun's government.

North Korea

For the Democratic People's Republic of Korea (DPRK—North Korea), the year was a demonstration of the durability of 70-year-old President Kim Il Sung and his elderly colleagues.

Politics. The February elections for the Supreme People's Assembly (SPA) reconfirmed President Kim's ability and intention to remain in power, as did the elaborate celebrations of his 70th birthday in April. His son and heir apparent, Kim Jong Il, gained a seat in the SPA—his first government post—and was awarded the rare title of Hero of the Democratic People's Republic of Korea.

To the surprise of most observers, the younger Kim was not made one of the DPRK's three vice-presidents in the election of top officials in April; nor was he made a member of the Central People's Committee, as also expected. Some interpreted this to mean that there was still resistance to the "Kim dynasty," especially from the military, and there were unconfirmed reports that 10 generals had been purged because of their opposition to Kim Jong Il. Others saw merely an indication that President Kim was not yet ready to hand over full power to his son. Kim Jong Il holds the second most important post after his father in the ruling Korea Workers' (Communist) party and therefore controls most of the day-to-day internal administration of the DPRK.

The Economy. President Kim's *juche,* or self-reliance, philosophy was a continuing feature of North Korea's economic policy, which remained essentially inward looking. The 1982 budget totaled $11,100,000,000, up 11% from 1981. Its emphasis was on economic development, with economic expenditures 11.5% higher than the previous year and with social and cultural expenditures only 5% higher. Defense expenditure was increased by 8.6% over 1981, representing 14.5% of the budget, the lowest percentage since 1972. However, sources outside North Korea said that a revision of budget classifications had disguised military spending, which in reality accounted for more than 30% of the total budget and about 24% of the current $16,200,000,000 gross national product (GNP).

Following a reorganization of the economic structure in 1981, which largely accounted for a drop in the growth rate that year, the GNP was expected to resume a 4–5% growth rate in 1982. Government-controlled consumer prices rose by an estimated 4–5% because of increased prices of imported raw materials, but government subsidies on basic necessities helped to compensate for reduced real wages.

Although the DPRK has not released its foreign trade figures for about 15 years, a South Korean expert on North Korean affairs put its total trade at about $3,000,000,000, with 43% in exports and 57% in imports. The outstanding debt to foreign creditors was estimated at $2,000,000,000 (or $3,200,000,000 including interest). Lack of foreign currency remained a problem.

Foreign Relations. Friendship between North Korea and China was reconfirmed by the exceptionally warm welcome given to Kim Il Sung when he visited China in September—his first trip there since the death of Mao Zedong in 1976. It was revealed that China's elder statesman, Deng Xiaoping, and party general secretary, Hu Yaobang, had paid a secret visit to Pyongyang earlier in 1982 for Kim's birthday celebrations.

South Korea

In the Republic of Korea (ROK—South Korea), a series of disasters in the early months of the year threatened the credibility of President Chun's government. Although Chun made numerous cabinet changes and twice replaced his prime minister, no serious opposition to his leadership emerged. Overall domestic stability was maintained, and the economy began to show signs of recovery after two years of recession.

Politics. President Chun began 1982 with a major cabinet reshuffle, officially to inject new vigor into the economy by bringing in more technocrats, but also to break any remaining ties with the former Park Chung Hee government. He replaced Prime Minister Nam Duck Woo, a key figure in the Park regime, with technocrat Yoo Chang Soon; appointed career banker Kim Joon Sung as deputy premier and economic planning minister; and changed four other ministers.

Then came the disasters that undermined public confidence in the government—a policeman running amok and killing dozens of people, an arson attack on the U.S. cultural center in Pusan, several fatal accidents on Seoul subway construction sites, and a gigantic scandal on the unofficial loan, or "curb," market. Mishandling of nearly $1,000,000,000 in promissory notes resulted in 15-year prison sentences for a husband and wife moneylending team and led to 29 other convictions, including an 18-month jail sentence

---

NORTH KOREA • Information Highlights

Official Name: Democratic People's Republic of Korea.
Location: Northeastern Asia.
Area: 46,540 sq mi (120 539 km^2).
Population (1982 est.): 18,700,000.
Chief Cities (July 1980 est.): Pyongyang, the capital, 1,445,000; Hamhung, 780,000.
Government: *Head of state,* Kim Il Sung, president (nominally since Dec. 1972; actually in power since May 1948). *Head of government,* Li Jong Ok, premier (took office Dec. 1977). *Legislature* (unicameral)—Supreme People's Assembly. The Korea Workers' (Communist) Party: General Secretary, Kim Il Sung.

for Lee Kyu Kwang, uncle of President Chun's wife, for accepting bribes.

Further cabinet reshuffles—including the appointment of former Korea University President Kim Sang Hyup as prime minister—together with a purge of the upper ranks of the ruling Democratic Justice Party (DJP) and a restructuring of the banking system, went some way to appease public opinion. But the scandal motivated the opposition parties to launch concerted criticism against Chun's government for the first time. In October the opposition Democratic Korea Party (DKP) and Korea National Party (KNP) called for greater political and press freedom. Then Chun's own party, the DJP, opposed a government bill prohibiting secret bank accounts.

Throughout the year, small groups of students staged sporadic antigovernment demonstrations, refusing to be mollified by liberal reforms such as the lifting of the 36-year-old curfew in January, amnesty for some 3,000 people, and the suspension of the prison sentence of leading dissident Kim Dae Jung. The authorities continued to deal harshly with some dissidents and with banned politicians. A publisher, Lee Tae Bok, was sentenced to life imprisonment in January for printing and distributing banned Marxist books; the leader of the former New Democratic opposition party, Kim Young Sam, was put back under house arrest in June after telling a foreign journalist that he thought President Chun could not continue in office beyond the autumn; and 567 former politicians remained barred from political activities.

The Economy. The early months of 1982 were marked by economic gloom as antirecession measures failed to have the desired effect. The financial scandal in May demonstrated the inadequacy of the highly controlled banking system to meet short-term capital needs. It forced the government to take drastic steps to rescue debt-ridden big business from resorting to the unregulated curb market.

At the end of June, bank interest rates were slashed almost across the board by four percentage points, thus ending the multicategory loans-interest system and bringing deposit and lending rates down to 8% and 10% respectively. Overdraft interest was reduced from 22% to 18%, and it was announced that corporate taxes would be reduced as much as 18% by early 1983. Three of the four remaining government-controlled commercial banks were denationalized, with the fourth scheduled to be turned over to the private sector early in 1983.

The government first revised the annual growth target for the broadly defined money supply (M2) from 20–22% to 22–25%, and later allowed it to increase to 25–30%. Fears about this relaxation of the former stabilization policy, which by keeping credit tight and prices down had reduced consumer price increases from 35% in 1980 to 12.5% in 1981, proved groundless. By September the consumer price index showed only a 4% increase rate, and government officials were confidently predicting a 1982 inflation rate of no more than 5–6%.

In the first nine months of 1982, the GNP grew by 5.3%, and with an excellent rice harvest, the year-end GNP growth rate was expected to reach 6%. Despite low exports, the curent account deficit was narrowed from $3,200,000,000 in August 1981 to $830 million a year later, primarily through a big reduction in oil imports and increased overall production. International Monetary Fund arguments for a sudden devaluation of the currency were rejected.

Disregarding improved economic indicators, foreign investors grumbled increasingly about the difficulties of operating in Korea, and the Dow Chemical Co., Korea's largest foreign investor, sold out in October. On the domestic front, a government official said "about one third of our businessmen are still on the verge of bankruptcy."

Foreign Relations. The Reagan administration continued its firm support of President Chun, and the annual South Korea-United States joint military exercise was scaled even larger than usual. Relations with Japan, always volatile, turned sour when Japan revised school textbooks to gloss over atrocities committed during its 1910–45 colonial rule in Korea. Negotiations, started the previous year, over Japanese economic aid to South Korea were abandoned indefinitely, though eventual agreement on a $4,000,000,000 Japanese loan was still expected.

President Chun proposed the creation of a 12-nation Pacific Community and suggested a summit meeting of Pacific leaders to Australian Prime Minister Malcolm Fraser and Indonesian President Suharto during their visits to Seoul, and to Canadian Prime Minister Pierre Trudeau in Ottawa. Chun also visited four African nations—Kenya, Nigeria, Gabon, and Senegal—with the twofold objective of enhancing economic relations and drumming up support for South Korea's position vis-à-vis the North.

JACQUELINE REDITT
Free-lance Correspondent, Seoul

SOUTH KOREA · Information Highlights

Official Name: Republic of Korea.
Location: Northeastern Asia.
Area: 38,022 sq mi (98 477 km^2).
Population (1982 est.): 39,331,147.
Chief City (1982 est.): Seoul, the capital, 9,074,127.
Government: *Head of state,* Chun Doo Hwan, president (formally inaugurated March 1981). *Head of government,* Kim Sang Hyup, prime minister (appointed June 24, 1982). *Legislature*—National Assembly.
Monetary Unit: Won (718.3 won equal U.S.$1, March 1982).
Gross National Product (1981 U.S.$): $63,100,000,-000.
Economic Indexes (1981): *Consumer Prices* (1970= 100), *all items,* 555.8; *food,* 663.7. *Industrial production* (1975=100), 232.
Foreign Trade (1981 U.S.$): *Imports,* $26,125,000,-000; *exports,* $21,254,000,000.

LABOR

In November, Richard L. Trumka (center), a 33-year-old lawyer with some mining experience, easily defeated incumbent Sam Church for the presidency of the United Mine Workers of America.

To labor in the United States, Canada, and most of the industrialized countries of Western Europe, the deepening recession of 1982 looked more and more like a dreaded depression.

United States

Bedeviled by unemployment, automation, and relentless international competition, American workers found few answers at the bargaining tables where employers sought concessions.

Unemployment. By November, unemployment had made more than 10.8% of the nation's work force idle. An estimated 11,987,000 workers were jobless, the most since 1940. Another 6.6 million had been cut back to part-time work, and 1.6 million more were so discouraged that they no longer actively hunted for work. A total of 99,032,000 were gainfully employed for one hour or more a week in November. Of these 18,484,000 worked only part time. The number working 35 hours or more a week declined 2,507,000 from November 1981. More then 2.5 million workers exhausted their unemployment compensation benefits in 1982, and their misery was compounded by cuts in food stamps and Medicaid.

The Elections. On November 2, workers turned out to vote in record numbers for a nonpresidential election. Two years earlier nearly half of them had voted against the advice of their unions to put Republican Ronald Reagan in the White House. This time, exit polls on election day indicated that 67% of union members voted for Democratic candidates.

The AFL-CIO, under President Lane Kirkland, was credited with mobilizing the union voters. For three years, Kirkland had worked to recreate a coalition of workers, blacks, Hispanics, women, senior citizens, environmentalists, and consumers who generally agree on economic issues. AFL-CIO computers addressed mailings to likely voters by name, and union volunteers registered 3.5 million new voters, while another 150,000 volunteers working phone banks in union halls placed a reported 10 million calls to voters.

AFL-CIO recommendations for dealing with the economic crisis, largely ignored before the election, took on a new importance. The organization has called for:

(1) A new Reconstruction Finance Corporation to aid ailing industries through loans, loan guarantees, and grants.

(2) A five-year program of grants to state and local governments to provide work for the long-term jobless.

(3) A National Industrialization Board with representatives of government, management, and labor, to oversee job-creating loans to private industry and to state and local governments.

(4) A comprehensive job-training program.

(5) A content law to require automobiles sold in the United States to be manufactured in large part with American labor and American-made parts.

In October, Congress adopted a modest program, the Job Training Partnership Act. It provides money for skills training, primarily for disadvantaged youths, dislocated workers, and older workers.

Collective Bargaining. Labor-management negotiations in 1982 were marked by continued efforts by management to reduce labor costs, either by freezing or cutting wages and benefits.

In turn, union negotiators sought more job security for workers.

Before the year ended, airline employees, steel workers, and auto workers rebelled against proposals for more concessions in the face of a steadily rising cost of living. Chrysler workers, for example, voted to strike if further negotiations failed to produce relief from the wage restraints accepted in 1979 to save that corporation from bankruptcy. Agreement on a one-year contract was reached in December.

The good news in bargaining was the settlement in electrical manufacturing. Three-year contracts between General Electric and Westinghouse and unions representing their 132,000 employees gave the average worker earning $9 an hour an immediate 7% raise and further increases of 3% in June 1983 and 1984. Cost-of-living adjustments were enriched, monthly pension benefits were increased, and job-security provisions were strengthened to include six-month advance notice of plant closings, along with provision of retraining funds.

Industrial wage settlements in the first half of 1982 provided for an average yearly increase of only 2.7% over the years of the contract, as compared with an average 7.7% increase a year earlier. Rising prices and reduced working hours offset this increase, forcing many families to lower their living standards. State and local government employees fared somewhat better. For the first half of 1982, their contract settlements averaged 8%, the same as in 1981. Teacher settlements averaged 6% to 8%.

Earnings. Weekly earnings of nonsupervisory employees averaged $270.05 in September, up from $259.74 in September 1981. Real average weekly earnings in September amounted to $167.63, compared with $168.88 a year earlier. In October the advance in consumer prices slowed to 5.1%, about one third what it had been a year earlier.

Organizing. While spreading layoffs thinned union ranks, organizing efforts were complicated by the fact that for the first time more Americans were working in the service industries than in the traditionally unionized manufacturing, mining, and construction industries. Employment has increased in banking, finance, insurance, and, most of all, in health care. Between April 1981 and April 1982, the number of health-care workers rose by 237,000 to 5.7 million.

Women make up another fast-growing segment of the work force. Their number has increased by more than 17% in five years, from 41,-810,000 in 1977 to 48,988,000 in 1982.

Efforts to strengthen unions through mergers continued. In July the Glass and Ceramic Workers merged with the Aluminum, Brick and Clay Workers, creating a joint union with 70,000 members. In August the Pottery Workers approved a merger with the Glass Bottle Blowers union. The new union has a combined membership of 90,000.

Strikes. Hard times and unemployment in 1982 reduced the number of strikes significantly from 1981. For most Americans, the year's most disruptive strike occurred when 1,500 organized football players struck for salaries comparable to those paid other professional athletes. Football players' salaries average considerably below those paid professional hockey, baseball, or basketball players. In football, the average career lasts only 4.2 years. With an eye on future revenue from cable television, the Players Association, an AFL-CIO affiliate, aimed at 55% of the National Football League's gross revenue. The owners offered a five-year package amounting to $1,600,000,000. After cancellation of 112 games and facing cancellation of the rest of the season, the association voted on November 16, after 57 days on strike, to accept terms of a negotiated settlement that permitted the fans to return to their normal viewing lives.

Court Cases. More than 5,000 employees of the Howard Johnson Co. are sharing a $5 million settlement for back pay, one of the largest awards ever made by a U.S. district court. Acting on a union complaint, the U.S. Department of Labor charged the company with violating the Fair Labor Standards Act. The dispute was settled on October 5.

In a wage settlement announced on October 21, the U.S. Postal Service agreed to pay $400 million for violating overtime pay requirements of the same act. The money will be shared by some 800,000 current and former postal workers.

In a landmark decision, the U.S. Supreme Court on July 2 unanimously reaffirmed the constitutional right of Americans to organize boycotts for political, economic, and social change. The decision settled a 16-year-old civil rights dispute and reversed a decision of a Mississippi court that had assessed $25 million damages plus interest against the National Association for the Advancement of Colored People for its economic boycott in Port Gibson, MS, in the 1960s.

International

In July the AFL-CIO reaffiliated with the International Confederation of Free Trade Unions (ICFTU), a worldwide organization of non-Communist trade unions that is headquartered in Brussels, Belgium. The AFL-CIO had left the organization in 1968 over disagreements on organizational policies.

Canada. Canada in 1982 suffered its worst economic crisis since the 1930s. Inflation and unemployment were at double-digit levels. An estimated 1.5 million workers (12.2% of the labor force) were jobless in September. By August, tens of thousands of workers were reaching the end of their 50-week unemployment benefits with no prospect of finding jobs.

More concerned over inflation, the government imposed ceilings of 6% and 5%, respectively, for the two years beginning July 1 on salary increases for 500,000 public servants and crown-corporation employees, and on such prices as are directly administered. Private employers and provincial governments were requested to observe the same ceilings on their wages and prices.

The Canadian Labor Congress (CLC) opposed this action with several affiliates staging brief protest strikes. The CLC advanced its own six-point program to deal with the crisis: reduce interest rates, control foreign exchange, invest in public works, use public sector pension funds for low-interest loans for housing, suspend home mortgage foreclosures, and protect the wages of those employed by firms in receivership or bankruptcy.

In the face of high unemployment, wage settlements were generally lower than those negotiated in 1981. They lagged behind the steadily increasing cost of living. However, a 15-month strike by farm workers ended with substantial wage increases, improved medical benefits, and union security. Auto workers were less fortunate, with management pressing for more concessions. Chrysler workers rebelled at a second round of concessions, and in November, Canadian UAW members struck Chrysler's Canadian plants. A new contract was approved during the following month.

A new national rival to the CLC was formed in March when 10 building trades unions—electricians, bricklayers, operating engineers, painters, plumbers, sheet-metal workers, insulators, plasterers, boilermakers, and elevator constructors—founded the Canadian Federation of Labor (CFL). The 10 unions are affiliates of international unions headquartered in the United States. They had been suspended by the CLC for withholding dues payments in a dispute over CLC policies. Politically, the new CFL is non-partisan, while the CLC is allied with the New Democratic Party.

To make up for the loss of revenue, the CLC convention at Winnipeg voted to raise payments of affiliates from 31 cents per member per month to 37 cents in 1982 and to 43 cents in 1983.

Great Britain. Over vigorous objections from unions and the Labour Party, the government adopted a new Employment Act restricting the closed shop (where employment is limited to those who already belong to the union) and secondary boycotts (where pressure is directed against a third party in the hope that that party will bring pressure on the employer directly involved).

Unemployment reached 3.34 million in September, nearly 14% of the work force. The rate of inflation, down from 20% in 1980, was still nearly 10%. Wage agreements in the first half of 1982 provided for increases averaging 7.3% in manufacturing, forcing workers to lower their living standards. Unemployment benefits were cut 5%, and reductions in other social programs were expected. The one bright spot was the improvement in productivity that reduced labor costs and increased exports.

The Labour Party, political arm of the trades unions, was beset by dissension, threatened on the Right by the new Social Democratic Party and on the Left by militant activists who want to abolish the monarchy, withdraw from NATO, and use extraparliamentary action, including a general strike, to bring down the Tory government.

Strikes were frequent but mostly of short duration. A strike by employees of the National Health Service was more serious, bringing on a one-day general sympathy strike on September 22 by affiliates of the Trades Union Congress (TUC). A strike by railroad engineers to preserve an eight-hour work shift collapsed after two

UPI

On December 9, Robert White (left), director of the Canadian United Automobile Workers, and Douglas A. Fraser, UAW president, announced a tentative agreement ending a five-week strike by Chrysler workers in Canada. Union members ratified the pact.

The British Trades Union Congress declared September 22 a Day of Action in support of the demands of health-care workers. Walkouts and a mass demonstration were held.

weeks when employees were threatened with dismissal by the state-owned railroad and the TUC refused to support the walkout.

France. Reversing its initial expansionist economic and social policies, the Social Democratic government cut federal expenditures for health care, social security, and other welfare programs. It devalued the French currency twice to stimulate lagging exports. Over the objections of France's three trade-union federations, the government in June froze prices and wages for four months. All 1982 wage increases were limited to 10%, and those increases of 1983 must be limited to 8%.

In spite of government efforts, unemployment stood at 8.25% in July, with 2.1 million people out of work. The government limited the entry of foreign workers, who now make up 8.5% of the active population.

Italy. The new Italian government of Amintore Fanfani pared expenditures in the hope of lowering the 16% inflation rate. Unemployment had risen to 11%, and cuts in pensions and higher taxes were being considered. Unions were struggling against an employer initiative to eliminate *scala mobile,* the automatic quarterly adjustment in wages to keep up with rising prices. The government decreed a 16% ceiling on labor cost increases.

Sweden. The September elections restored the Labor Party to power after a six-year absence. It immediately reversed some acts and plans of the previous government to cut social programs, notably those concerning health care. Instead, unemployment benefits and pensions were raised, and more was spent for job training and building roads, bridges, and housing. Higher taxes on sales and wealth are paying for these programs.

To increase exports, the new government in October devalued its currency by 16%, to the chagrin of its Nordic neighbors—Norway, Denmark, and Finland. The government also froze prices and took other austerity measures. Wage increases in 1981 lagged behind prices. Unemployment, at 3.5% in September, was high by Swedish standards. Immigration policies have been tightened. Aliens wishing to immigrate (except those from Nordic countries) must now show proof of employment.

The most critical issue in labor-management relations was the union's demand for a wage-earner fund. Management would be required to put 20% of its profits into a union-administered fund to buy shares in the business for the employees. Bitterly opposed by management, the plan was expected to face difficulties in parliament. The Labor Party is committed to the concept but not to any details of the union plan.

West Germany. The breakup of the coalition government of Social Democrats and the Free Democratic Party was caused largely by disagreement on how to deal with Germany's deepening economic crisis. By late 1982, unemployment, at 8.4% of the work force, involving 2.04 million workers, reached its highest level in 30 years. The national debt also was rising, and limits on social services were being considered.

The new government of Chancellor Helmut Kohl, a coalition of Christian Democrats and the Free Democrats, assumed power on October 1. It announced postponement of pension increases due in early 1983, cut other welfare programs, and considered freezing wages. Germany's strong 8-million-member labor federation, the DGD, protested these acts.

Two of the DGB's subsidiaries faced serious financial difficulties. A building society lost money because of questionable policies by its directors, and the Bank for Gemeinwirtschaft disclosed that it had made unguaranteed loans to Poland of $317 million.

Japan. Japan's unemployment rate was a little over 2%, the lowest of any industrialized nation. The annual spring labor offensive produced agreement on a 7% wage increase. The unions had sought increases of 9% and 10%.

Efforts to unify the trade unions continued to be hampered by divergent political views rather than by disagreement on economic or social issues. Of the two strongest federations, Sohyo favored disarmament and opposed nuclear weapons, while Domei stressed the importance of the Japan-United States security system and development of Japan's defense capabilities.

Poland. The attempts by Polish workers to establish a free trade-union organization in a Communist-controlled country appeared to have failed in 1982. The national union, Solidarity, was outlawed by the national legislature at the request of the military dictatorship in October. Polish workers are denied the right to strike and to form national labor organizations. Lech Walesa, Solidarity's leader, arrested without formal charges or hearing in December 1981, was released in November 1982, while other leaders remained in prison. Unrest and social tension continued. In December the government announced some easing of martial law restrictions, but not the prohibition against strikes and national labor organizations.

GORDON H. COLE and JOSEPH MIRE

LAOS

Laos underwent government changes in 1982, but the country's foreign policy mirrored that of neighboring Vietnam, much as in previous years.

Government. Prime Minister Kaysone Phomvihane was reelected leader of the Lao People's Revolutionary Party (LPRP) at the party's third congress. The congress also expanded the party's secretariat from 6 to 9 members and added three persons to its central committee. For the first time, party leaders revealed that the LPRP, the Communist country's only political party, had 40,000 members (1.1% of Laos' population).

Prime Minister Kaysone Phomvihane announced in April that a new constitution would be adopted in the near future. Changes in the cabinet in September appeared to reflect an enlargement of the number of ministries to be established under the new basic law.

Deputy Prime Minister Nouhak Phounsavanh, previously second in political command, relinquished his finance portfolio in the cabinet shuffle. Vice-Prime Minister Phoumi Vongvichit, a key politburo participant, gave up his responsibility for education, sports, and religion. Several new ministries were created, and various of the new ministers were recently trained returnees from Vietnam. They also were technically skilled individuals, suggesting new government reliance on experts, rather than on party ideologists.

Economy. The USSR and various Eastern European countries have been highly critical of the wasteful and inefficient use of economic aid supplied by them. In two meetings during the year with Prime Minister Kaysone Phomvihane, Soviet leader Leonid Brezhnev criticized poor economic planning by the Lao government, calling for the "more rational use of Lao resources" in the future. Moscow nevertheless pledged additional aid to the Vientiane government.

Because of Laos' limited linkages with the rest of the world economically, the worldwide recession did not have as great an impact on the country as it had on some of the more-developed lands of Southeast Asia. Shortages of goods persisted despite Soviet aid, increased imports of consumer products through Thailand, and a growing private market.

Guerrilla Warfare. Guerrilla activity was limited and posed no serious threat to the government, but, nonetheless, it increased during the year. Rebel units loyal to one-time neutralist military leader Kong Le were active in Luang Namtha province bordering China—Kong Le's chief supplier of weapons. Kong Le's forces also operated in central Laos, while right-wing troops of former anti-Communist leader Phoumi Nosavan were active in the south.

Foreign Relations. Vietnam maintained 50,000 of its troops in Laos. Two divisions of these troops were stationed in three of the northern provinces (Luang Namtha, Oudomsay, and Phong Saly) as a barrier to possible Chinese military action against either Laos or Vietnam.

At a meeting of Indochinese foreign ministers in Ho Chi Minh City in July, Laos joined in Vietnam's call for a 15-state conference on Cambodia (where Vietnamese and Chinese-aided Cambodian rebels continued to fight). In September, Foreign Minister Phoune Sipraseuth publicly appealed to Association of Southeast Asian Nations governments to endorse such a meeting, but the ASEAN countries called the Lao action a ploy in support of the attempt of the pro-Vietnamese Cambodian government to be seated in the UN General Assembly.

RICHARD BUTWELL
The University of South Dakota

LAOS · Information Highlights

Official Name: Lao People's Democratic Republic.
Location: Southeast Asia.
Area: 91,429 sq mi (236 800 km²).
Population (1982 est.): 3,700,000.
Chief Cities (1973 census): Vientiane, the capital, 176,637; Savannakhet, 50,690.
Government: *Head of state,* Prince Souphanouvong, president. *Head of government,* Kaysone Phomvihane, prime minister. *Legislature* (unicameral)—National Congress of People's Representatives.
Monetary Unit: New kip (10 new kips equal U.S.$1, March 1982).
Gross National Product (1980 U.S.$): $300,000,000.

LATIN AMERICA

Economic and political crises converged with devastating impact on the Western Hemisphere in 1982. It was the worst year, economically speaking, for Latin America since the end of World War II. Moreover, in 1982 for the first time in the 20th century, a major shooting war was fought in the hemisphere between a Latin American country and an extra-continental power. When the United States supported Britain in its brief but bloody conflict with Argentina over control of the Falkland Islands, inter-American unity was shaken to the core. (*See also* pages 28–37.)

Latin American Economies. Argentina tumbled into virtual economic chaos in the wake of the Falklands crisis, with the peso plunging to all-time lows, and inflation soaring out of control. But the conflict with Britain was not the underlying factor in the country's economic woes, nor was Argentina alone in its morass. Nearly all the Latin American countries experienced severe problems of mounting foreign debt and economic stagnation.

According to the 1982 annual report of the World Bank, 1981 marked the first time in the Bank's 36-year history that Latin America's gross domestic product (GDP) per capita experienced a significant decline. The overall rate of economic growth fell from 6% in 1980 to about 1% in 1981, not enough to keep up with an annual population increase of 2.4%.

Inflation averaged 60% throughout the region, exceeded 100% in Argentina, and remained at about that level in Brazil. The region's foreign debt spiral continued upward, approaching nearly $300,000,000,000 for Latin America as a whole. Three countries—Argentina, Brazil, and Mexico—accounted for $200,000,000,000 of the total. Mexico has become the largest debtor in the developing world, with obligations of more than $80,000,000,000; Brazil is not far behind at $70,000,000,000; Argentina owes more than $40,-000,000,000 to foreign creditors.

International bankers say the situation worsened in 1982. The Mexican peso went through a series of devaluations and lost 75% of its purchasing power in just six months. Inflation rose by more than 100% and unemployment and underemployment reached 40% of the work force. The Argentine peso plummeted even more precipitously, to an unofficial rate of more than 50,-000 to the U.S. dollar. In September, Bolivia defaulted on $60 million in foreign debt payments. Serious currency, debt, and other economic problems plagued other countries, such as Chile, Peru, Colombia, Venezuela, and Costa Rica. Brazil imposed a semi-austerity program, limiting imports and seeking new and expanded markets for its export sector.

The Latin American recession, and particularly the Mexican disaster, was felt in the United States. Throughout the border areas of the Southwest, retail and tourism businesses suffered heavy losses from the peso's decline. Mexican shoppers stopped making purchases in the United States, and U.S. customers deserted American stores for Mexican bargains. In September, the U.S. Small Business Administration announced an emergency $200 million bail-out program for border businesses in distress.

Inter-American System. The Organization of American States (OAS), which includes the United States and 30 countries of Latin America and the Caribbean, entered a period of intense stress during the Falklands conflict. Latin American government leaders and diplomats charged the United States with "betrayal" of its hemispheric commitments by supporting Britain against Argentina. Many Latin governments were unhappy with Argentina's invasion of the islands, but felt that a larger principle, that of hemispheric solidarity and collective security, was at stake in a clash with an extra-continental nation. The Latins said that the United States had breached the spirit of the Inter-American Treaty of Reciprocal Assistance (the Rio Treaty) and that fundamental changes were needed in the inter-American system. Some went so far as to suggest that the United States be expelled from the OAS, or that a new political organization, without U.S. participation, be created.

Tempers cooled somewhat toward the end of the year. The General Assembly of the OAS, meeting in November, voted to convoke a special meeting of foreign ministers which would, in turn, write an agenda for a summit meeting of hemispheric chiefs of state to seek reforms in the OAS charter and in the Rio Treaty. The chiefs of state were also expected to deal with a new and potentially unsettling issue: the imbalance in the organization caused by the entry over the past few years of ten small, relatively poor countries in the Caribbean. These countries, most of them English-speaking former British colonies, supported Britain in the Falklands crisis. The vote of a tiny state, such as Antigua-Barbuda, with scarcely 70,000 people and few resources, is equal in OAS councils to that of Brazil, for example, with a population of 125 million, or Mexico, with nearly 72 million.

The OAS was also challenged to action on Latin American economic problems. In October, the Inter-American Economic and Social Council called for a special Inter-American Conference on the region's rising debt and its lagging development effort. It seemed clear, at year's end, that the OAS would survive the present crisis, but that there would be fundamental changes in its structure and functioning.

Other Inter-American Institutions. The Inter-American Development Bank (IDB), in its annual report for 1981, issued in late March, showed a record level of lending to member states in the region. Loan totals in 1981 were nearly $2,500,000,000, 8% higher than in 1980.

Then U.S. Secretary of State Alexander Haig and Trade Representative William Brock (far right) met in New York on March 15 with foreign ministers from nations who supported the Caribbean Basin Initiative. That program strengthened ties with Latin America, but relations soured when the United States supported Britain in the Falklands dispute.

Borrowing by the bank in international capital markets also reached new highs. Bank officials said that, despite the region's dismal economic picture, the IDB's portfolio was in good shape and repayments were generally on schedule.

The Pan American Health Organization (PAHO), the Western Hemisphere branch of the World Health Organization (WHO), elected a new director at its annual meeting in September. PAHO chose Carlyle Guerra de Macedo, a 45-year-old Brazilian health planner, to succeed Dr. Hector R. Acuna of Mexico.

Caribbean Basin Initiative. In February, President Ronald Reagan unveiled his proposal for an innovative, multilateral development program for Central America and the Caribbean islands, which he called the "Caribbean Basin Initiative" (CBI). The focus of the president's plan was on strengthening the private sector in the area. The three main points of the CBI were (1) tax incentives to encourage U.S. manufacturers to locate new plants in the area; (2) a 12-year period of duty-free treatment for most Caribbean exports to the United States, except textiles and apparel products; and (3) an emergency aid appropriation of $350 million to help Caribbean basin countries overcome balance of payments. Reagan said he also expected Canada, Mexico, and Venezuela—which already had assistance programs in the area—as well as Colombia, to become donor countries to the CBI.

After months of political maneuvering, the aid portion of the CBI was approved as part of a supplementary appropriations bill for fiscal year 1982. Objecting to other parts of the bill, the president vetoed the legislation. Congress overrode the veto, thereby providing $355 million for the Caribbean. The tax and duty-free provisions, however, failed to clear Congress before it adjourned.

To shore up Latin American relations generally, President Reagan in early December went on a five-day good will tour of Brazil, Colombia, Costa Rica, and Honduras.

Arms. The Falklands conflict stimulated new interest on the part of Latin American military establishments in acquiring missiles, torpedoes, and other sophisticated weaponry that were used during the fighting. While U.S. officials cautioned against a new arms race in the region, Latin military men argued that more arms were necessary, since the United States had "abandoned" the Rio Treaty, and also that denial of weapons was based on an attitude in the United States that Latin American countries were "second-class powers." The United States, nonetheless, continued its ban on arms sales to Argentina and other Latin American countries.

Human Rights. The annual report of the Inter-American Commission on Human Rights, issued in October, showed little change in the panorama of human rights throughout Latin America. The commission said that respect for human rights remains "precarious" throughout the hemisphere, singling out the governments of Chile, El Salvador, Haiti, Nicaragua, and Uruguay for especially strong criticism. Cuba was not mentioned because of "the difficulty in gathering pertinent documentation." Guatemala was to be the subject of a separate report, to be released later. The commission called on the OAS to establish an inter-American authority to provide aid to the "millions" of refugees in the hemisphere, primarily from Central America.

RICHARD C. SCHROEDER
Washington Bureau Chief, "Vision"

The justices of the U.S. Supreme Court, photographed January 1982. Seated, from left: Marshall, Brennan, Chief Justice Burger, White, Blackmun. Standing: Stevens, Powell, Rehnquist, O'Connor.

The 1981–82 term of the U.S. Supreme Court was noteworthy for the debut of the first woman justice in the history of the court, Sandra Day O'Connor of Arizona. In the trial of John W. Hinckley, Jr., for the shooting of President Reagan and three others in March 1981, a federal jury in Washington, D.C. found the accused "not guilty by reason of insanity," creating new controversy over the insanity defense (*see* special report, page 307). And in the realm of international law, 1982 was marked by final passage, despite U.S. opposition, of the International Law of the Sea Treaty.

U.S. Supreme Court

Justice O'Connor quickly demonstrated an independent spirit and absence of awe for the male-dominated institution of the Supreme Court. She undertook a full load of decisions (12) and registered 27 dissents, sometimes speaking bluntly, as when she called one of Justice Brennan's opinions "incomprehensible." Her views were generally aligned with the court's two most conservative members, Chief Justice Burger and Justice Rehnquist, her former classmate at Stanford Law School. The first state judge to be named to the court in 25 years and a former state legislator, O'Connor was critical of federal restrictions on the states and advocated greater deference by Congress and the federal judiciary to state courts and legislatures. The financial disclosure required of all justices revealed O'Connor as one of the court's three millionaires.

The Supreme Court handed down 166 decisions, of which only 53 were unanimous, and an unprecedented total of 32 5-to-4 decisions, compared with 20 the previous term. The two liberals, Brennan and Marshall, had the most dissents, 48, and Rehnquist was next with 43, Burger 36, Stevens 32, Powell and Blackmun 28, and White 27. Rehnquist was ill for part of the term, and the chief justice seemed more concerned with administrative duties than cases, writing only one important decision. Two unprecedented events occurred during the year. A deaf lawyer argued a case before the court, and Justice White was physically attacked while making a speech in Salt Lake City.

Major Decisions. The court was less conservative and more assertive than might have been expected, striking down a number of state and federal statutes. It held unconstitutional (5-4) a Texas law denying free public education to children of illegal aliens (*Plyler v. Doe*). The NAACP was freed from heavy damages for a boycott of white businesses in Mississippi (*NAACP v. Claiborne*). A Washington state law forbidding cities to use school busing for racial integration was invalidated (*Washington v. Seattle School District*). And a Long Island, NY, school board was required (5-4) to explain why it removed certain books from the school library (*Island Trees Board of Education v. Pico*).

The court stayed the decision of an Idaho judge that an extension of the deadline for ratification of the Equal Rights Amendment (ERA) was unconstitutional, but failure of ERA backers to secure ratification made the issue moot (*NOW v. Idaho*). Former President Richard Nixon was held immune from any civil suits arising from his actions as chief executive, but presidential aides, it was determined, have only "qualified immunity" (*Nixon v. Fitzgerald; Harlan v. Fitzgerald*).

Criminal Prosecutions. The court ruled for the defense in two capital punishment cases. In *Enmund v. Florida* the court held (5-4) that a person cannot be sentenced to death for participation in a crime that resulted in death caused by someone else. In *Eddings v. Oklahoma,* a death sentence imposed on a defendant who was 16 at the time of the crime was reversed (5-4) for failure to consider mitigating circumstances, but the constitutional question of whether or not a juvenile can be executed was left unanswered.

The court extended police authority to search without a warrant in two cases. Reversing the previous term's ruling, *U.S. v. Ross* gave police sweeping authority to search automobiles stopped for probable cause. The search can include anything inside the car trunk, glove compartment, locked suitcases, or other closed containers. In *Washington v. Chrisman* an officer arrested a college student on campus and followed him into his dormitory room, where the officer saw evidence of drug use by the student's roommate and arrested him; the Supreme Court ruled that no search warrant was necessary.

The court continued to reduce the opportunity for persons convicted in state courts to secure habeas corpus review in federal court. A state prisoner can raise constitutional issues in federal court only if he or she can show cause for not bringing them up at the trial and that actual prejudice resulted from the errors (*U.S. v. Frady; Rose v. Lundy*).

The court held that a sentence of 40 years in prison for possession and distribution of 9 oz (255 g) of marijuana was not "cruel and unusual punishment" (*Hutto v. Davis*). It upheld an Illinois village ordinance regulating the sale of drug paraphernalia without actually prohibiting sale to adults (*Hoffman Estates v. Flipside*). The claim of a former Green Beret who had been convicted of murdering his wife and children nine years earlier that his constitutional right to speedy trial had been violated was rejected (*U.S. v. MacDonald*).

The court struck down a Massachusetts law requiring closed trials during the testimony of young rape victims but allowed judges to impose cloture on a case-to-case basis (*Globe v. Superior Court*).

First Amendment. States may ban the production, sale, or distribution of child pornography, whether or not it meets the legal definition of obscenity, the justices held in *New York v. Ferber.* The court let stand obscenity convictions, fines, and prison sentences imposed in Memphis, TN, on two distributors and the producer of the movie *Deep Throat,* rejecting contentions that it should determine whether the movie was legally obscene or should not have been judged by community standards (*Battista v. U.S.*).

Several efforts to invoke the Freedom of Information Act failed. The Defense Department was not required to make public the possible effects of storing nuclear weapons in particular locations, and the FBI was upheld (5-4) in refusing to disclose information originally compiled for law enforcement purposes but later used by the Nixon White House for political purposes (*Weinberger v. Catholic Action; FBI v. Abramson*).

Evenly divided, the court let stand a lower court decision upholding the right of political action committees and other independent groups to spend unlimited amounts of money in support of presidential candidates (*Common Cause v. Schmitt*). Nor may governments limit campaign contributions by individuals to organizations formed to support or oppose referendums and other ballot measures (*Citizens Against Rent Control v. Berkeley*).

Equal Protection. In an opinion by Justice O'Connor, the Mississippi University for Women (MUW), the last state-financed all-women's college in the country, was ordered to admit a male to its nursing school (*MUW v. Hogan*). But the court declined to accept a case in which a public school had refused to allow a girl to try out for the boys' athletic team (*O'Connor v. Board of Education*).

The court ruled that local school boards are not required to provide a sign-language interpreter for a deaf school child, but it did agree that handicapped children are entitled by federal law to instruction "with sufficient support services" to permit some educational benefit (*Board of Education v. Rowley*). The court also held that mentally retarded people in state institutions are entitled to safe conditions, freedom from unreasonable physical restraint, and "minimally adequate" training in caring for themselves (*Youngberg v. Romeo*).

In *American Tobacco Co. v. Patterson,* the court held that company seniority plans are constitutional regardless of their impact on women or minorities so long as they are not adopted for a discriminatory purpose. In *Sumitomo Shoji v. Avigliano,* the justices ruled that the 1964 Civil Rights Act applies to a Japanese firm doing business in the United States.

The court unanimously upheld awards for discrimination against air flight attendants who became mothers but not against those who became fathers (*Zipes v. TWA*).

The court let stand a California state court decision upholding the affirmative action program of the University of California Law School at Davis, developed after the *Bakke* decision. The plan takes account of "ethnic minority status" along with test scores, rigor of undergraduate studies, economic hardship, and other factors (*DeRonde v. Regents*).

Minority members denied jobs by labor union practices may sue the union but not the employer unless the company intentionally sets up a discriminatory system (*General Building Contractors Assn. v. Pennsylvania*). The fact that private institutions get government funding or are subject to government regulations does not mean that they can be subjected to civil rights suits (*Rendell-Baker v. Kohn*).

Federalism Issues. In several decisions, the Supreme Court rejected President Reagan's "New Federalism" and upheld federal controls over the states. *Santosky v. Kramer* gave federal courts increased power over a matter usually left to the states by ruling, 5-4, that parents may not be stripped of legal authority over their children unless there is "clear and convincing evidence" of parental abuse or neglect. Another 5-4 ruling upheld a 1978 federal act controlling state policies in public utility regulation (*Federal Energy Regulatory Cmsn. v. Mississippi*). *Zobel v. Williams* held that Alaska had denied equal protection by distributing $415 million in oil revenues to its citizens in shares based on length of residence in the state.

New Hampshire's attempt to prevent private utilities from selling energy to other states was held to obstruct interstate commerce, as was a Nebraska law barring the transfer of ground water to another state unless that state reciprocated (*New England Power Co. v. New Hampshire; Sporhase v. Nebraska*). But the court did reject an attack on the fairness of Missouri's tax system, saying that federal courts should apply the principle of comity and avoid interference in state affairs (*Fair Assessment v. McNary*).

Economic Issues. The states may not bar federally chartered savings and loan associations from enforcing due-on-sale clauses that require the seller of a house to pay the full balance of the mortgage when selling the property (*Fidelity Federal v. De La Cuesta*). The Bankruptcy Reform Act of 1978 conferred unconstitutional status on federal bankruptcy judges (*Northern Pipeline v. Marathon Pipeline*).

Having previously held that lawyers cannot be forbidden to advertise, the court ruled that states and bar associations can prohibit only advertising that is inherently misleading (*In re R.M.J.*). But the court did agree with New York court discipline of a lawyer who mailed flyers to local real estate brokers asking them to recommend him to their clients (*Greene v. Grievance Committee*).

The court upheld (4-4) a Federal Trade Commission order that the American Medical Association (AMA) permit doctors to advertise, compete for business, and enter into nontraditional financial arrangements for the practice of medicine (*AMA v. FTC*).

Labor Issues. Employees of a railroad owned by the state of New York have a right to strike under federal law in spite of a state law forbidding strikes by public employees (*United Transportation Union v. Long Island Railroad*). Federal courts may not enjoin politically motivated work stoppages under the Norris-LaGuardia Act (*Jacksonville Bulk Terminals v. I.L.A.*). But the refusal of longshoremen to load or unload Soviet ships after the USSR invaded Afghanistan was ruled an illegal secondary boycott, and the union was liable for damages (*I.L.A. v. Allied International*).

Minor management employees with access to confidential information are entitled to join unions and seek protection under federal labor laws (*NLRB v. Hendricks*). The court upheld (5-4) a labor union ban on financial contributions from nonmembers in elections for union office (*United Steelworkers v. Sadlowski*).

Religious Issues. The court invalidated a Minnesota law that imposed registration and reporting requirements on religions that secure more than half their contributions from nonmembers (*Larson v. Valente*). A lower court ruling that state laws providing for voluntary prayer sessions are unconstitutional was upheld unanimously (*Treen v. Karen B.*). But public universities that let secular organizations meet in their buildings must also make facilities available for use by campus religious groups (*Widmar v. Vincent*).

Amish businessmen must pay Social Security and unemployment taxes required of all employers, despite their belief that paying taxes is a sin (*U.S. v. Lee*). In a decision that will make it more difficult to litigate church-state issues, the court ruled that a citizen group had no standing to challenge government donation of surplus property to a church-run college (*Valley Forge Christian College v. Americans United*).

C. HERMAN PRITCHETT
*Department of Political Science
University of California, Santa Barbara*

International Law

Once again in 1982, nationalism, power politics, and economic selfishness were more conspicuous than the rule of law in international dealings.

Law of the Sea. After eight years of work on a treaty to regulate the economic and strategic uses of the world's ocean, the first comprehensive codification of international maritime law—the International Law of the Sea Treaty—was approved April 30 at the UN by a vote of 130 for, 4 against, and 17 abstained. The United States, Turkey, Venezuela, and Israel cast negative votes; Western Europe and the Soviet bloc abstained. The treaty was to be opened for signing in Kingston, Jamaica, in December and would take effect one year after ratification by 60 nations.

The United States opposed the treaty's formula for control of seabed production and sought a provision giving three industrial countries the power to veto any of the resolutions passed by the 36-member policymaking council. Though the developing nations would not agree to these 11th-hour amendments, the U.S. delegation did manage to win several protections for private companies already engaged in seabed mining.

The Insanity Defense

John W. Hinckley, Jr., did not deny that he planned to kill President Ronald Reagan, that he lay in wait until a propitious moment on March 30, 1981, and that he shot the president and several others, wounding them grievously. Nevertheless, at his trial in the spring of 1982, the federal jury returned a verdict of "not guilty by reason of insanity." A storm of controversy arose instantly.

Public outcry in reaction to a successful insanity plea was nothing new in Anglo-American legal history. Indeed the "M'Naghten test"—the classic definition of insanity—arose out of just such furor and the wrath of Queen Victoria when, in 1843, a former soldier named Daniel M'Naghten was acquitted on grounds of insanity after an attempt to murder the queen's prime minister, Sir Robert Peel.

Public outcry or no, such a defense has always been accepted in U.S. law, and most modern legal systems have a defense of this kind. The Hinckley case, however, served once again to raise the questions of whether it is justified and how it should be administered.

The Principle. The fundamental reason for allowing an insanity defense is that the seriousness of a criminal offense depends not only on the objective harm caused but also on the offender's state of mind. Can the law fairly punish as criminals those who have "lost their minds" to the point that they genuinely do not know they are doing wrong or cannot stop themselves from acting as they do? The law has consistently answered that although such persons may have to be treated for their illness or confined to prevent further harm, they cannot in fairness be morally blamed or punished as criminals. Few jurists or scholars have challenged this principle; the main reasons for controversy have had to do with its implementation.

Definition and Procedure. One commonly cited problem is the legal definition of insanity. In the United States, an insane offender is commonly defined as one who, because of a mental disorder, lacked awareness of the criminal nature of the act or lacked capacity for self-control in regard to the unlawful conduct. Whatever the technical variations, vague language has given inadequate guidance to juries.

Another problem is that expert witnesses often give contradictory opinions regarding the defendant's sanity, and the testimony is frequently esoteric and obscure. This has led to a widely held belief that criminal law and psychiatry cannot be mixed. But how could a fair insanity defense exclude psychiatric testimony?

The Hinckley case brought to the fore yet another major complication—the rules of procedure. In U.S. federal courts, when the defendant raises the insanity defense, the prosecution then has the burden of proving sanity (as it must all other elements of guilt) "beyond a reasonable doubt." Proving sanity is regarded by many as an unrealistic burden on the prosecution. As in the Hinckley trial, the defense usually brings in experts to testify in support of its claim of insanity. Logically, then, there can hardly fail to be at least a reasonable doubt as to the defendant's sanity. Even if the jury is on the whole persuaded that the defendant was sane, the existence of reasonable doubt obligates them to find the defendant not guilty. By contrast to the federal system, many state courts hold insanity to be a special, "affirmative" defense which puts the burden on the defense to show "by a preponderance of the evidence" that the defendant was insane. The Hinckley trial spurred Congressional interest in reforming the federal rule along those lines.

Once acquitted on grounds of being insane at the time of the offense, defendants may be sent to a mental hospital to determine if they are still insane and "dangerous." But the law is in ferment over this entire procedure. Since these persons have been acquitted of the crime and cannot be treated as criminals, basic civil liberties are at stake. Techniques for predicting "dangerousness" are notably unsatisfactory. Moreover, the medical and legal conceptions of "sanity" and "illness" are vague and can conflict. It would not be fair to keep every such person in confinement for life, since many of them do regain sanity and if freed remain law-abiding citizens. But if too many releases are authorized, errors will be made, and some truly dangerous persons will be released.

Future. By late 1982, eight states had adopted such compromise verdicts as "guilty but mentally ill," typically empowering criminal courts to imprison offenders under a criminal sentence if released too early from the hospital. In a more radical move, Idaho and Montana abolished the insanity defense altogether. The effectiveness and constitutionality of these steps remain to be seen.

Insanity cases represent a small proportion of criminal cases, but their symbolic-emotional impact is central. The plea evokes tensions among the main objectives of criminal law: the moral aim of punishing for guilt, the pragmatic aim of ensuring public safety, and the compassionate aim of rehabilitating offenders. The Hinckley trial was neither the first nor will it be the last to bring the tensions among these aims to the center of public attention.

HERBERT FINGARETTE

Langley/"The Christian Science Monitor"

The Law of the Sea Treaty does provide strategic and economic benefits to the United States. The Pentagon supported provisions dealing with navigation and overflights. By creating "exclusive economic zones" extending seaward for 200 mi (370 km) or to the edge of the continental shelves, the treaty assigns to coastal states control over offshore oil, fisheries, and other resources worth far more than is likely to be mined from the seabed. Despite these benefits, the treaty would likely have faced stiff opposition in the U.S. Senate because of its provisions for sharing technology with a multinational competitor, tapping profits for the benefit of developing nations, erecting obstacles to private exploitation of the seabed, and having a permanent Third World majority on the Seabed Authority. In 1980 Congress had passed the Deep Seabed Hard Mineral Resources Act, indicating its support for private exploitation of what the developing countries called "the common heritage of mankind." The Senate had also proven hostile to treaties with Canada and Mexico that set lines dividing the respective claims to territorial waters.

The next step for the United States was uncertain. One option was to persuade its industrial partners to enact national legislation with reciprocating provisions for seabed exploitation. Though Britain and possibly Germany and France might go along, Japan, Canada, and Belgium have kept aloof from such a mini-treaty. Ultimately the developing nations would ask the International Court of Justice to rule on these national laws.

If the United States does not eventually sign the treaty, it could lose its leadership position in undersea mining. Consortiums based in the United States would be ineligible for commercial mining permits. In the absence of a ratified treaty, meanwhile, countries continued to feud over maritime claims. For example, a dispute between Newfoundland and nearby French islands over cod fishing boundaries led in 1982 to a gunboat alert.

Whaling. In another oceanic matter, the International Whaling Commission (IWC) banned commercial hunting of whales worldwide for an indefinite period beginning in 1985. The moratorium, which required a three-fourths majority vote, was passed at Brighton, England, on July 23. Conservationists had fought for the ban for ten years, during which time annual quotas were reduced to less than one third of the total at the start of the campaign. In order to gain the three-fourths majority, the IWC was packed with small nonwhaling states, such as the Seychelles. Japan, which had not widely consumed whale meat until the days of scarcity following World War II, disputed the argument that whales are endangered. Japan and Norway invoked their sovereign rights to hunt whales within a 200-mi coastal economic zone.

Conflicts. Issues of international law were at the center of several major diplomatic disputes in 1982. In at least two notable instances, the result was war and new alleged abuses rather than peaceful arbitration.

A long-festering dispute between Argentina and the United Kingdom over the sovereignty of the Falkland (Malvinas) Islands erupted in war in April. Though the Argentine government had committed itself by treaty not to use force or the threat of force to settle territorial disputes, it argued that British intransigence left it no recourse. It opposed suggestions that the disputed issues be settled by arbitration in the UN, World Court, or other body. Britain, for its part, violated international law by declaring a 200-mi exclusion zone in the South Atlantic. (*See* feature article, page 28.)

In the Mideast, Israel was repeatedly censured by the UN for discrimination against the Arab population under its control. In turn, Israel's supporters stated that the West Bank administration was governed by the law of belligerent occupation. In its drive through Lebanon against the PLO, Israel indicated that it would not treat captured Palestinians as prisoners of war, lest that status be interpreted as a form of recognition of the PLO.

U.S. sanctions against the Soviet Union for its interventions in Poland and Afghanistan included a ban on the transfer of gas pipeline technology. Western European companies were to be part of the ban, but most of their governments considered the restriction contrary to international law and refused to comply.

MARTIN GRUBERG
Department of Political Science
University of Wisconsin-Oshkosh

LEBANON

UPI

An Israeli tank in a Beirut amusement park symbolizes the incongruity of Lebanon's tragedy.

The 1982 Israeli invasion of Lebanon, siege of Beirut, and occupation of the tiny, war-ravaged country demonstrated more clearly than ever before that Lebanon's sovereignty and its people remain hostages of the greater Arab-Israeli struggle.

Israeli Invasion. Since agreeing to a cease-fire with the Palestine Liberation Organization (PLO) in July 1981, Israel had been alarmed by what it alleged was an ongoing and potentially threatening PLO arms buildup in southern Lebanon. After nearly launching attacks in February and April, Israel finally did so upon the June 3 terrorist shooting of its ambassador to Great Britain.

On the morning of June 6, after two days of retaliatory air raids, three Israeli columns crossed the Lebanese frontier. Israel initially announced that its sole aim was to secure a 25-mi- (40-km-) wide buffer zone beyond the international border. However, Israeli forces made swift progress north along the coastal approaches to Beirut, through the Chouf Mountains in the center to threaten the vital Beirut-Damascus highway, and in the east toward the strategic Bekaa Valley.

In essence, Israel was attempting to secure its northern border by redrawing Lebanon's troubled political map. By destroying the PLO as a political and military force in Lebanon and by expelling the 30,000 Syrian peacekeeping troops that had occupied Lebanon since 1977, Israel intended to restore the authority of a strong, pro-Israeli central government dominated by its strongest ally against the PLO as well as the Syrians, Phalangist party militia leader Bashir Gemayel.

The military campaign's outcome was never seriously in doubt. In less than one week, Israel had achieved total air superiority and had at least 500 tanks and 60,000 men inside Lebanon. During the first three days, the PLO was forced to retreat from its strongholds at Tyre, Nabatiya, Beaufort Castle, Sidon, and Damour. By June 10 not only was the bulk of Syria's troops pinned down in the Bekaa Valley, but most PLO forces had withdrawn to the refugee camps south of the Lebanese capital or into Muslim west Beirut itself. Although cease-fires with the Syrians and the PLO were announced on June 11 and 12, respectively, Israel linked with Phalangist forces northeast of Beirut on June 17 to trap PLO leader Yasir Arafat and more than 14,000 Syrian and Palestinian troops among west Beirut's 500,-000 civilian population.

Lebanese Response. To save west Beirut from further destruction, Lebanon's President Elias Sarkis set in motion a political and diplomatic dialogue intended to resolve the crisis peacefully. Employing the good offices of U.S. Special Envoy Philip Habib to negotiate with the Israelis and six-time former Lebanese Prime Minister Saeb Salam to negotiate with the PLO, Sarkis also announced the formation of a six-member National Salvation Council on June 14. The Council, composed of representatives of Lebanon's major religious factions, embodied an attempt to end Israel's occupation and to solve Lebanon's internal problems. However, the bitter rivalries that were the cause and the legacy of the 1975–1976 civil war doomed the enterprise.

Phalange leader Gemayel, representing Maronite Christians, saw the Israeli invasion as an opportunity to drive out the PLO and to restore the Christian-led government's authority over the Muslim militias that had ruled west Beirut for eight years. Druze leader Walid Jumblatt, whose defiant boycott delayed the Council's first meeting until June 20, viewed Gemayel as an Israeli tool. Prime Minister Chafiq al-Wazan, representing Sunni Muslims, supported a PLO pullout under honorable conditions rather than the unconditional surrender demanded by Sarkis, Gemayel, and Foreign Minister Fuad Butros, who represented the Greek Orthodox.

Meanwhile, Israel continued to apply military pressure. On June 22 the Council's second meeting, during which the first of several PLO proposals to end the siege was discussed, had to be suspended after two hours because of Israeli shelling. The PLO proposal, which Arafat had presented to Salam and Wazan the previous night, was rejected by Israel on June 23.

Although June 25 ended in a cease-fire, the day's nearly continuous shelling caused the breakup of the short-lived Council. Wazan accused Habib of collusion with the Israelis and submitted his resignation as prime minister, though Sarkis refused to accept it and convinced him to stay on. Jumblatt also quit the Council and ordered two Druze cabinet members to resign. Henceforward, the Lebanese government was little more than an observer, as negotiations were carried out primarily by Habib and Salam.

Negotiations. Arafat agreed in principle on June 27 to disarm his troops and leave Beirut. Although Habib announced on June 30 that the negotiations were nearly completed, they dragged on for seven weeks, during which west Beirut was reduced to rubble.

The negotiations centered on the logistical complexities of the PLO evacuation, its timing, possible destinations for the PLO troops, and the future of 500,000 Palestinian civilians living in Lebanon. However, the talks foundered repeatedly over PLO delaying tactics, its efforts to use the crisis to develop a dialogue with the United States, and its demands for an Israeli pullback prior to the actual evacuation and maintenance of a symbolic Palestinian military presence.

While the negotiations lurched toward a final agreement, the civilian population of west Beirut had to endure a tremendous hardship and frightening ordeal. To force the PLO out of the city, the Israelis twice applied complete blockades—from July 3 to July 8 and from July 26 until August 8—cutting off water and electricity and denying the entry of food or medical supplies. The Israeli air force repeatedly dropped leaflets urging civilians to flee the city, but the toll of artillery fire and air bombardments was still devastating.

The arms-length PLO-Israeli negotiations were suspended for six days beginning July 22, when Habib left Lebanon to confer with Syrian, Egyptian, Saudi, and Jordanian leaders in an attempt to obtain commitments on the destinations to which the PLO could be evacuated. Exerting pressure for some settlement, Israel during the first two weeks of August stepped up its bombardments of west Beirut to the highest level of the war. The final obstacles to the PLO departure were apparently removed when Arafat dropped his last two demands on August 5 and Syria agreed to accept PLO evacuees on August 7. With major details still to be worked out and no formal agreement yet established, however, Israel bombed and shelled west Beirut for four straight days, culminating in a 10-hour attack on August 12.

By August 19, the final agreement was reached. On August 20 the first 350 troops of a French, Italian, and U.S. multinational peacekeeping force were deployed at Beirut's port facilities. The following day the first contingents of PLO troops left Beirut by sea, and by September 1 the last of some 14,400 PLO and Syrian men had been evacuated.

Throughout the war, there was great controversy over casualty and refugee reports. Based on police and hospital records, the respected Beirut daily an-Nahar reported—conservatively—that the 75-day war had left 17,200 dead, 30,000 wounded, and at least 150,000 homeless. It was estimated that $12,000,000,000 would be required to rebuild the country. Lebanon's tragedy, however, was not yet complete.

Presidential Election. Lebanon's confessional political system requires that the president be a Maronite Christian. Gemayel, the Phalangist militia leader, had no serious Christian rivals, but his candidacy was bitterly opposed by most Muslim factions because of his role during the civil war and his unofficial alliance with Israel.

Despite charges of Phalangist intimidation, Bashir Gemayel was elected president on August 23. To his credit, the president-elect made a genuine attempt to reunite opposing factions prior to his scheduled September 23 inauguration. He demanded an Israeli withdrawal despite their threat to occupy southern Lebanon unless he concluded a formal peace treaty with them, and he successfully persuaded Muslim militiamen to allow the deployment of government forces in west Beirut. Unfortunately, fears that he would use his presidency to settle old scores proved too powerful.

Assassination and Massacre. On September 14, at Phalangist party headquarters in east Beirut,

---

LEBANON · Information Highlights

Official Name: Republic of Lebanon.
Location: Southwest Asia.
Area: 4,000 sq mi (10 360 km²).
Population (1982 est.): 2,700,000.
Government: *Head of state,* Amin Gemayel, president (took office Sept. 1982). *Head of government,* Chafiq al-Wazan, prime minister (took office Oct. 1980). *Legislature* (unicameral)—National Assembly.
Monetary Unit: Lebanese pound (3.9565 pounds equal U.S.$1, Dec. 15, 1982).
Gross Domestic Product (1981 U.S.$): $4,190,000,-000.

Amin Gemayel dons the sash of office at the Presidential Palace in east Beirut after being sworn in September 23.

Bashir Gemayel was killed by an assassin's bomb. Israel invaded and occupied west Beirut the next day, justifying the action as a move to prevent anarchy and Christian retribution for the slaying of their leader.

Israel announced that its forces were "in control of all key points in Beirut" but claimed that the PLO had left behind some 2,000 guerrillas in the Sabra and Shatila refugee camps in southwest Beirut. Christian Phalangists were "entrusted" with a clearing out mission. On the evening of September 16, Phalangist troops entered the camps and proceeded to massacre hundreds of Palestinian men, women, and children before being ordered out at midday, September 18. Israel denied accountability for the act, saying that its forces were neither in the camps nor aware until September 18 that any massacre was taking place. Allegations of Israeli responsibility notwithstanding, the bloody event added another shameful chapter to Lebanon's history of sectarian violence.

A New President. On the same day the massacre began, Amin Gemayel, Bashir's older brother and a respected deputy of parliament, was nominated for the presidency. He was duly elected on September 21 and two days later was sworn in as Lebanon's seventh president since independence.

Amin Gemayel did not have the enemies his brother had, but his greatest domestic challenges continued to be consolidating government power and controlling the various militias. At the same time, Israel still occupied the southern half of the country, the PLO had upwards of 10,000 men in the north, and 30,000 Syrian troops were firmly entrenched in the Bekaa Valley. To complicate the issue, Israel on October 10 announced its intention to remain in Lebanon until all PLO forces were gone and then to withdraw only if the Syrians agreed to leave simultaneously.

With the occupying forces stalemated but the situation stable, Gemayel traveled to the United States, France, and Italy, meeting with U.S. President Ronald Reagan on October 19. On each stop Gemayel requested that the multinational force that had been redeployed after the September massacre be increased to 60,000 troops to assist his government in restoring order. The day following his October 22 return, President Gemayel opened the bargaining for an Israeli withdrawal by requesting a good-faith partial pullback by November 22, Lebanon's Independence Day.

U.S. Envoy Habib was again pressed into service since Gemayel, necessarily wary of the views of other Arab leaders, refused to enter direct negotiations with the Israelis. These talks were delayed until December 28 because Israel insisted that some of the negotiations must take place in Jerusalem. Gemayel could not agree to this, since meeting there would imply recognition of Israel's annexation of the holy city, and Israel withdrew its demand.

President Gemayel had better success on domestic issues. On October 24 the commander-in-chief of the Christian militias agreed to cooperate fully with Gemayel's efforts to remove all foreign forces. Earlier, the president had been successful in persuading Chafiq al-Wazan to stay on as prime minister. On November 9 the parliament gave a vote of confidence, 58–1, to Wazan and his cabinet. Coupled with the vote of confidence was a compromise measure giving President Gemayel and the 10-member cabinet power to rule by decree for six months on such matters as defense, security, taxation, justice, education, and reconstruction. Parliament retained its prerogative to exercise control over electoral law, citizenship requirements, and provincial boundaries.

F. NICHOLAS WILLARD

LIBRARIES

The U.S. federal government's financial commitment to library services was threatened in 1982 by the "let the states and localities do it" philosophy of President Reagan's New Federalism. At the same time, state and local support for libraries wavered menacingly.

U.S. Developments. The Reagan administration's budget proposal for the 1983 fiscal year contained no money for public and academic libraries or for the National Commission on Libraries and Information Science, and sharply reduced funding for the Education Consolidation and Improvement Act, a block grant arrangement within which elementary and secondary school libraries must compete for support with other educational services. By summer, however, it appeared that libraries would receive some funding—at about 1982 levels.

Earlier in 1982, the administration impounded funds appropriated by Congress via continuing resolution for the Library Services and Construction Act (LSCA). State library agencies in California, Florida, Kentucky, Maryland, Ohio, and Oklahoma joined New York in a legal action that would compel the Office of Management and Budget (OMB) to release the impounded LSCA funds. The General Accounting Office held that the administration could not legally withhold funds for public libraries under the Impoundment Control Act. The administration decided that it could not undermine the will of Congress, and released $19.7 million in LSCA funds.

In late 1981, President Reagan removed Joan Gross, Clara Jones, and Francis Naftalin from the 15-member National Commission on Libraries and Information Science although their terms did not expire until July 19, 1982. Since no other president had attempted to remove a commissioner before the expiration of a term, the administration's action was widely viewed as seeking to politicize a heretofore nonpartisan body. On April 27, the Postsecondary Education Subcommittee of the House of Representatives decided to pursue the matter with the Department of Justice. Meanwhile, the president named new members to the commission, with Elinor M. Hashim of Norwalk, CT, designated chair.

In other troubling developments for librarians, the Office of Personnel Management proposed on Dec. 8, 1981, a downgrading of the qualifications and classifications of federal librarians that would reduce the value of the Master of Library Science degree for those seeking federal employment. The library community was concerned that only library managers would be deemed professional. Reversing a trend that has made information about the federal government more widely available to the public, President Reagan signed on April 2, 1982, an executive order that expands the possible reasons for classifying information on national security grounds.

The Council on Library Resources provided $394,886 for an electronic link that will enable the Library of Congress, the Research Libraries Group, and the Washington Library Network to gain access to each other's bibliographic records. U.S. public libraries gave greater consideration to the charging of fees to nonresident users. In the spring, the St. Louis Public Library followed Denver and imposed an annual fee ($25) on nonresident borrowers. The Library of Congress continued to relocate to the new $160 million James Madison Memorial Building.

ALA. Struggling with a $875,000 cost overrun on its Chicago Huron Plaza building project, a shortfall in its operating revenues, the need to redefine its relationship with its membership divisions, and pressure to eliminate its national conference every fourth year, the ALA met in Philadelphia, July 10–15. President Elizabeth Stone presided. Carol A. Nemeyer, associate librarian for national programs, Library of Congress, and ALA's newly inaugurated president, called for a "new library declaration of interdependence." The American Association of School Librarians held its second national conference in Houston, October 21–24.

ALA again sponsored National Library Week, April 18–24, 1982, using as its theme, "A word to the wise—library," and marked Banned Books Week, September 5–11, to spotlight books being censored locally.

International. The 48th General Conference of the International Federation of Library Associations and Institutions (IFLA) convened in Montreal, Aug. 23–28, 1982. IFLA continued to be concerned with the development of librarianship in the Third World. The annual conference of the Canadian Library Association was held in Saskatoon, Saskatchewan, June 9–15, 1982. The Library Association in England called for an audit of that organization's finances at a general meeting on Jan. 6, 1982.

DAN BERGEN, *University of Rhode Island*

LIBRARY AWARDS OF 1982

Beta Phi Mu Award for distinguished service to education for librarianship: David K. Berninghausen, professor and former director, Library School, University of Minnesota

Randolph J. Caldecott Medal for the most distinguished picture book for children: Chris Van Allsburg, *Jumanji*

Melvil Dewey Award for creative professional achievement of a high order: Sarah K. Vann, professor, Graduate School of Library Studies, University of Hawaii

Grolier Foundation Award for unusual contribution to the stimulation and guidance of reading by children and young people: Spencer G. Shaw, professor, School of Librarianship, University of Washington, Seattle

Joseph W. Lippincott Award for distinguished service to the profession of librarianship: Keith Doms, director, Free Library of Philadelphia

John Newbery Medal for the most distinguished contribution to literature for children: Nancy Willard, *A Visit to William Blake's Inn: Poems for Innocent and Experienced Travelers*

Ralph R. Shaw Award for outstanding contribution to library literature: Sheila A. Egoff, *Thursday's Child: Trends and Patterns in Contemporary Children's Literature*

LIBYA

The rhetoric and actions of Libya's outspoken leader, Col. Muammar el-Qaddafi, combined with the resolve of the American government to punish Libya for what it deemed unacceptable international behavior, resulted in extremely poor political relations between the two countries in 1982, and a rupture of economic ties as well.

Foreign Relations. The Reagan administration, from its first days in office, had categorized Libya as an instigator of unrest in the Third World and a country that gave both economic and logistic assistance to a number of political organizations which the United States considered terrorist groups. After the confrontation between American and Libyan aircraft over the Gulf of Sidra in August 1981, the United States stepped up its efforts to undermine and discredit Qaddafi.

Early in 1982, Libya stridently criticized Arab states that cooperated with the United States, singling out Egypt and Saudi Arabia. Warning that leaders who came to terms with Israel would meet the same fate as the assassinated President Sadat of Egypt, Qaddafi accused the United States of supporting peace efforts designed to strengthen Israel at the expense of the Arabs. He further alleged that the Saudis were deliberately overproducing crude oil to keep world prices artificially low, thus helping the Western industrialized nations but damaging Libya and other OPEC militants.

Oil. In March, President Reagan placed an embargo on the importation of Libyan oil and the export of American technology to Libya. Despite the deteriorating relations between the two nations, Libya had spent more than $2 million for American material in 1981, while the United States was buying 150,000 barrels of Libyan oil per day at an annual cost of $2,000,000,-000, a quarter of Libya's total oil income. Since Libya provided only 2% of America's imported oil, and since the United States was enjoying an oil glut, the embargo imposed economic strictures on Libya but hardly affected the United States.

Libya found it difficult to maintain production, which had already dropped to a low level of a million barrels per day, and was forced to dip further into its dwindling reserves. Some international economic agencies estimated that, by midyear, Libyan revenues had fallen some 30% from 1981 levels.

Soon after the embargo, the American firm of Mobil Oil announced the termination of its operations in Libya. Mobil cited the world oil glut and the high price of Libyan crude as reasons its venture in Libya had become unprofitable. There was widespread speculation, however, that Mobil was responding to pressure from both the United States and Saudi Arabia. Mobil received no compensation for the assets lost in its withdrawal, many of which came into the hands of the Libyan National Oil Company.

The United States had encouraged American oil firms to leave Libya after the Gulf of Sidra incident. At that time Exxon did abandon property and equipment valued at $120 million, and early in 1982 Libya compensated Exxon to the extent of $95 million. This arrangement, plus the losses sustained by Mobil, prompted other American oil companies in Libya to reach agreements with the Libyan government and to continue their operations, although some replaced American personnel with Canadians.

African Relations. Colonel Qaddafi suffered another setback in August when the annual meeting of the Organization of African Unity (OAU), scheduled to be held in Tripoli with the Libyan leader assuming the chairmanship for 1982–1983, could not be convened because of the lack of a quorum of member nations. Most states that boycotted the meeting did so in protest against the granting of OAU membership to Polisario (the Western Saharan liberation movement that was carrying on a guerrilla war against Morocco)—a move strongly favored by Libya. Some OAU members, however, stayed away to express their displeasure with the policies of Qaddafi and to prevent his accession to the chairmanship.

Libyan diplomacy was not, however, without some triumphs during the year. Relations with neighboring Tunisia improved after both countries agreed to settle an offshore oil claims dispute in the Gulf of Gabès by accepting boundaries drawn by the Italian and French colonial authorities early in the 20th century. Libya and Malta referred a similar dispute to the International Court of Justice and then restored bilateral commissions on industrial, commercial, agricultural, and tourism projects that had been suspended during the controversy.

Again there were signs of internal opposition to Qaddafi. There were reports of an assassination attempt late in 1981, and the government acknowledged that the Soviet Union had helped it foil an attempted coup in January.

KENNETH J. PERKINS
University of South Carolina

LIBYA · Information Highlights

Official Name: Socialist People's Libyan Arab Jamahiriya ("state of the masses").
Location: North Africa.
Area: 679,360 sq mi (1 759 542 km²).
Population (1982 est.): 3,200,000.
Chief Cities (1973 census): Tripoli, the capital, 481,-295; Benghazi, 219,317; Misurata, 42,815.
Government: *Head of state,* Muammar el-Qaddafi, secretary-general of the General People's Congress (took office 1969). *Legislature*—General People's Congress (met initially Nov. 1976).
Monetary Unit: Dinar (0.29605 dinar equals U.S.$1, July 1981).
Gross National Product (1980 U.S.$): $39,100,000,-000.
Foreign Trade (1979 U.S.$): *Imports,* $5,311,000,-000; *exports,* $16,085,000,000.

LITERATURE

UPI

Gabriel García Márquez was awarded the Nobel Prize for "One Hundred Years of Solitude" and other works.

Gabriel García Márquez, a 54-year-old Colombian novelist, short-story writer, and journalist whom many regard as the leader of a renaissance in Latin American letters, was named by the Swedish Academy as the winner of the 1982 Nobel Prize for Literature. In its official statement October 10, the academy cited García Márquez "for his novels and short stories, in which the fantastic and the realistic are combined in a richly composed world of imagination, reflecting a continent's life and conflicts."

An active and outspoken leftist who lives in Mexico City, García Márquez was further recognized by the academy as "strongly committed politically on the side of the poor against domestic oppression and foreign economic exploitation." His masterpiece, the epic *Cien años de Soledad* (1967, translated as *One Hundred Years of Solitude,* 1970), recounts the rise and fall of an imaginary town called Macondo. Since the success of *One Hundred Years,* according to the Swedish Academy, "each new work of his is received by expectant critics and readers as an event of world importance." Among his other

works, in English translation, are: *No One Writes to the Colonel and Other Stories* (1968); *Leaf Storm and Other Stories* (1972); *The Autumn of the Patriarch* (1976), a novel; *Innocent Erendria and Other Stories* (1978); *Evil Hour* (1980), a novel; and *Chronicle of a Death Foretold,* a novella scheduled for publication in 1983.

American Literature

The deepening recession caused problems for U.S. publishers and writers in 1982. New authors found it harder to have first books accepted, and established writers made less money. Book sales were down, and prices for paperback rights fell drastically. A number of houses that benefited from an infusion of capital when bought by multimedia corporations proved unprofitable and were sold. All was not gloom, however. Simultaneous publication in hardback and paperback was promising for sales, and university presses, looking for broader markets, were interested in quality fiction by young writers.

Novels. John Cheever's posthumous short novel *Oh What a Paradise It Seems* was a fine grace note to his long, successful career. Cheever's eye is as sharp and his voice as sure as ever in this story of an elderly man who is not too old to get involved in life or to find out some new and curious things. (*See also* OBITUARIES.)

John Gardner's accidental death at age 49 cut short a promising career. His last novel, *Mickelsson's Ghosts,* concerns a professor of philosophy who seeks refuge from his problems in a farmhouse in the Adirondacks. Old woes follow him, new burdens arise, and even the land is mysteriously haunted.

Saul Bellow's *The Dean's December* comments gloomily on contemporary society. Eastern European culture, represented by events that befall the protagonist in bureaucratic Rumania, and Western culture, represented by a series of misfortunes in the United States, each seem soul-destroying in a different way: one creates a machinery which destroys the spirit of its people, and the other tolerates a level of violence which destroys human community.

Bernard Malamud's *God's Grace* is even more pessimistic. A fable in the future, the story begins with the only human survivor of a nuclear war, Calvin Cohn, arguing with a God who tells him that, "The cosmos is so conceived that I myself don't know what goes on everywhere." Cohn manages to create a new Eden, but sexual jealousy and unreason turn it to darkness and death. The parable suggests that no matter how often civilization starts afresh, it will bring upon itself its own destruction.

John Barth's *Sabbatical* was met with respect but little excitement. The story of a sailing trip by a married couple, it again shows Barth's intellect, verbal facility, and narrative inventiveness, but its self-conscious ingenuity seems to undercut the reality of the characters.

John Updike's *Bech is Back,* really a series of linked stories, continues the adventures the writer began in *Bech: A Book* (1970). With sympathy and irony, Updike depicts Bech's discovery of the indignities of marriage and success.

Anne Tyler's maturity as a novelist is demonstrated in her inquiry into family relationships, *Dinner at the Homesick Restaurant.* Pearl Tull does not understand why her husband left her with three small children, or what damage she has done to them by her denial of reality. The older children suffer from jealousy and repression. The youngest cannot understand why they do not get along better, or why his attempts to orchestrate a perfect family dinner consistently fail.

The brutalization is physical rather than psychological in Alice Walker's epistolary novel, *The Color Purple.* In letters to God, Celie tells about being raped by her stepfather and forced to marry a man who beats her regularly. The story of her growing strength and friendship with another woman is magnificently rendered in Celie's own language, a dialect of great natural beauty and power.

William Wharton, the pseudonymous author of *Birdy* (1979) and *Dad* (1981), continued in 1982 with *A Midnight Clear,* the story of World War II soldiers who attempt to maintain personal integrity amid psychological degradation and wanton destruction. John Del Vecchio's *The 13th Valley* is a minutely detailed account of life in Vietnam in 1970. Don DeLillo's *The Names* deals imaginatively with terrorism and international business.

Laurel Goldman's first novel, *Sounding the Territory,* tells of a mentally disturbed young man who leaves the institution for a transcontinental bus trip. The world of madness is depicted with depth and sensitivity. The protagonist is neither sentimentalized nor romanticized, but seen as a person reaching for a self.

Short Stories. It was clear in 1982 that no single school dominates American short fiction. On the one hand there was the nostalgic humor of Garrison Keillor's *Happy to Be Here,* and on the other there were the deeply felt situations of Maxine Kumin's *Why Can't We Live Together Like Civilized Human Beings?* There was even a revived interest in very brief stories, as reflected in Irving Howe and Ilana Wiener Howe's collection, *Short Shorts.*

A number of young writers found inspiration in the rootlessness of American life and the lack of commitment to family, culture, and religion. In Alice Adams' *To See You Again,* human relationships shift easily without guilt or remorse. Ann Beattie's *The Burning House* depicts characters who have no depth, not because they are shallow but because there is no depth to have. In Joy Williams' *Taking Care,* one feels this even more strongly; in the best stories, characters meet, part, and die almost weightlessly. In Bette Pesetsky's appropriately titled *Stories Up To A Point,* the form of the story itself changes to express the disappearance of meaningfulness.

Writers who have not moved in this direction tend to be those whose characters live within a rich cultural fabric. Cynthia Ozick's finely crafted *Levitations* often concern people whose traditions are in conflict with their circumstances. *The Collected Stories of Isaac Bashevis Singer* are based on the lively, complex traditions of Jewish life in Polish villages, in Warsaw, and even in Manhattan. Centuries of Biblical commentary, superstitions, and social customs accumulate in a world that is well populated with imps and demons, God and the Devil.

Poetry. As American fiction might be celebrated for its range, complaints are heard that there is a philosophical and formal sameness in contemporary poetry. In fact, for those who will but listen, there is a rich variety in preoccupation and voice. Galway Kinnell's *Selected Poems* alone demonstrates how many possibilities are available. As Kinnell moved through an evolution of styles—from alien landscapes to internal dramas to immediate experiences—his language became more powerful and penetrating. George Starbuck's *The Argot Merchant Disaster* dives from the abstract into the colloquial as he plays with the discrepancies between simple language and cosmic mysteries. John Haines' *News from the Glacier* is a fresh, clear voice from Alaska. Marge Piercy's *Circles on the Water* is warm, intimate, and emotionally direct rather than elegant. Stephen Dobyns' *The Balthus Poems* have

Three essays on the perils of nuclear war, "The Fate of the Earth" was one of the year's most talked-about books.

Alfred A. Knopf, Publisher, New York

THE FATE OF THE EARTH
JONATHAN SCHELL

AMERICAN LITERATURE: MAJOR WORKS | 1982

NOVELS

Barth, John, *Sabbatical*
Bellow, Saul, *The Dean's December*
Betts, Doris, *Heading West*
Cheever, John, *Oh What A Paradise It Seems*
Davis-Gardner, Angela, *Felice*
DeLillo, Don, *The Names*
Del Vecchio, John M., *The 13th Valley*
Dunne, William Gregory, *Dutch Shea, Jr.*
Elkin, Stanley, *George Mills*
Gardner, John, *Mickelsson's Ghosts*
Godwin, Gail, *A Mother And Two Daughters*
Goldman, Laurel, *Sounding the Territory*
Hawkes, John, *Virginie: Her Two Lives*
Howard, Maureen, *Grace Abounding*
Kluger, Richard, *Un-American Activities*
Kosinski, Jerzy, *Pinball*
Malamud, Bernard, *God's Grace*
McGuane, Thomas, *Nobody's Angel*
Merkin, Robert, *The South Florida Book of the Dead*
Michener, James, *Space*
Nova, Craig, *The Good Son*
Oates, Joyce Carol, *A Bloodsmoor Romance*
Piercy, Marge, *Braided Lives*
Plante, David, *The Woods*
Reed, Ishmael, *The Terrible Twos*
Rice, Anne, *Cry to Heaven*
Sarton, May, *Anger*
Settle, Mary Lee, *The Killing Ground*
Steiner, George, *The Portage to San Cristobal of A.H.*
Tyler, Anne, *Dinner at the Homesick Restaurant*
Updike, John, *Bech is Back*
Vonnegut, Kurt, *Deadeye Dick*
Walker, Alice, *The Color Purple*
Wharton, William, *A Midnight Clear*
White, Edmund, *A Boy's Own Story*
Williams, John A., *!Click Song*

SHORT STORIES

Adams, Alice, *To See You Again*
Beattie, Ann, *The Burning House*
Benedict, Dianne, *Shiny Objects*
Bosworth, David, *The Death of Descartes*
Keillor, Garrison, *Happy to be Here*
Kelley, William M., *Dancers on the Shore*
Kumin, Maxine, *Why Can't We Live Together Like Civilized Human Beings?*
Loeser, Katinka, *A Thousand Pardons*
Matthews, Jack, *Dubious Persuasions*
Pesetsky, Bette, *Stories Up To A Point*
Singer, Isaac Bashevis, *The Collected Stories*
Williams, Joy, *Taking Care*

POETRY

Ammons, A. R., *Worldly Hopes*
Barnes, Djuna, *Creatures in an Alphabet*
Bishop, Elizabeth, *The Complete Poems 1927–1979*
Chappell, Fred, *Midquest*
Creeley, Robert, *The Collected Poems of Robert Creeley 1945–1975*
Dobyns, Stephen, *The Balthus Poems*
Finkel, Donald, *What Manner of Beast*
Gilbert, Jack, *Monolithos*
Ginsberg, Allen, *Plutonian Ode and other Poems 1977–1980*
Goldbarth, Albert, *Faith*
Grossman, Allen, *Of The Great House*
Haines, John, *News From the Glacier: Selected Poems 1960–1980*
Kinnell, Galway, *Selected Poems*
Kumin, Maxine, *Our Ground Time Here Will Be Brief*
Levertov, Denise, *Candles in Babylon*
Levine, Philip, *One for the Rose*
Matthews, William, *Flood*
Morgan, Frederick, *Northbook*
Piercy, Marge, *Circles on the Water*
Pollitt, Katha, *Antarctic Traveller*

Price, Reynolds, *Vital Provisions*
Stafford, William, *A Glass Face in the Rain*
Starbuck, George, *The Argot Merchant Disaster*
Wakoski, Diane, *The Magician's Feastletters*
Weiss, Theodore, *Recoveries*
Wright, James, *This Journey*

HISTORY AND BIOGRAPHY

Anderson, Jervis, *This Was Harlem: A Cultural Portrait 1900–50*
Baker, Russell, *Growing Up*
Barrett, William, *The Truants: Adventures Among the Intellectuals*
Brinkley, Alan, *Voices of Protest: Huey Long, Father Coughlin, and the Great Depression*
Burns, James MacGregor, *The Vineyard of Liberty*
Carter, Jimmy, *Keeping Faith: Memoirs of a President*
Friedrich, Otto, *The End of the World: A History*
Givner, Joan, *Katherine Anne Porter*
Haffenden, John, *The Life of John Berryman*
Hamilton, Ian, *Robert Lowell*
Hayman, Ronald, *Kafka*
Kissinger, Henry, *Years of Upheaval*
McNeill, William H., *Pursuit of Power: Technology, Armed Force and Society since A.D. 1000*
Middlekauf, Robert, *The Glorious Cause: The American Revolution, 1763–1789*
Miller, William D., *Dorothy Day*
Murphy, Bruce Allen, *The Brandeis/Frankfurter Connection*
Oakes, James, *The Ruling Race: A History of American Slaveholders*
Robinson, Janice S., *H. D.*
Rose, Willie Lee, *Slavery and Freedom*
Rutland, Robert A., *James Madison and the Search for Nationhood*
Seebohm, Caroline, *The Man Who Was Vogue: The Life and Times of Conde Nast*
Sheed, Wilfred, *Clare Booth Luce*
Shivers, Alfred S., *The Life of Maxwell Anderson*
Simpson, Eileen, *Poets in Their Youth*
Stein, Jean, ed., with George Plimpton, *Edie: An American Biography*
White, G. Edward, *Earl Warren: A Public Life*
White, Theodore H., *America in Search of Itself: The Making of the President 1956–1980*
Young-Bruehl, Elisabeth, *Hannah Arendt: For Love of the World*

CRITICISM AND AMERICAN CULTURE

Angell, Roger, *Late Innings: A Baseball Companion*
Fiedler, Leslie, *What Was Literature? Class Culture and Mass Society*
Johnson, Diane, *Terrorists and Novelists*
Mailer, Norman, *Pieces and Pontifications*
Reeves, Richard, *American Journey: Traveling with Tocqueville in Search of "Democracy in America"*
Rooney, Andrew A., *And More by Andy Rooney*
Smith, Red, *The Red Smith Reader*, ed. Dave Anderson
Sontag, Susan, *A Susan Sontag Reader*
Styron, William, *This Quiet Dust*
Vidal, Gore, *The Second American Revolution and Other Essays (1976–82)*
Wolfe, Tom, *The Purple Decades: A Reader*

PAPERS

Clemens, Samuel L., *The Selected Letters of Mark Twain*, ed. Charles Neider
Dreiser, Theodore, *Theodore Dreiser American Diaries 1902–1926*, eds. Thomas P. Riggio, James L. W. West 3d and Neda M. Westlake
Emerson, Ralph Waldo, *Emerson In His Journals*, ed. Joel Porte
Le Sueur, Meridel, *Ripening: Selected Work 1927–1980*
Loy, Mina, *The Last Lunar Baedeker*, ed. Roger L. Conover
Nin, Anaïs, *The Early Diary of Anaïs Nin, Volume II, 1920–1923*
Plath, Sylvia, *The Journals of Sylvia Plath*, ed. Ted Hughes and Frances McCullough

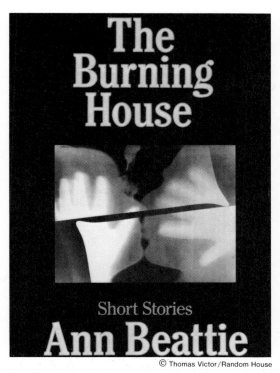

© Thomas Victor/Random House

The Dial Press

Beattie's stories depict the rootlessness of modern America; Plath's journals give insight into personal anguish.

the same balance of coolness and eroticism, detachment and obsessions, as the painter who inspired them.

Philip Levine's mastery of language in *One for the Rose* makes it clear that he must be regarded as an important poet. Maxine Kumin's *Our Ground Time Here Will Be Brief* focuses on the intimate bonds which humans develop, not only with each other, but also with animals. Another direction is seen in Reynolds Price's *Vital Provisions,* in which narrative is returned to poetry. William Stafford's *A Glass Face in the Rain* revives a more ancient form by having the poems speak as directives to the reader.

The Collected Poems of Robert Creeley 1945–1975 gathers the work of a writer who has been both praised and blamed for his strong influence on the development of free verse in America. Elizabeth Bishop's *The Complete Poems 1927–1979* demonstrates a considerable achievement that is not often fully appreciated.

Biography. Jean Stein's *Edie,* edited with George Plimpton, is based on interviews with dozens of people who knew Edith Sedgwick, a wealthy but vulnerable woman who had a moment of fame as part of Andy Warhol's circle in the 1960s before dying at the age of 28. The remarks of friends, relatives, and onlookers are cut up and arranged to give the reader several versions of the same story. The result is a brilliant collage which recreates an important and problematic time in American culture.

A generation of poets haunted by alcoholism and mental instability had their stories told in sympathetic but candid biographies. Ian Hamilton's *Robert Lowell* recounts the manic-depressive cycles that tortured him. John Haffenden's *The Life of John Berryman* tells of the poet's relentless drift toward suicide. In *Poets in Their Youth,* Eileen Simpson perceptively reflects on her marriage to Berryman and other poets she knew who died too young.

Editions. *Theodore Dreiser American Diaries, 1902–1926* preserves mundane details of the novelist's day-to-day life rather than ideas or reflections on art, but it is with the same zeal for minute documentation that gives his naturalistic novels their cumulative power. *The Journals of Sylvia Plath,* by contrast, provides insights into her tempestuous emotional life and her poetry.

In 1982 the Library of America produced the first four volumes of a long-needed uniform edition of classic American writers—Justin Kaplan's *Mark Twain,* G. Thomas Tanselle's *Herman Melville,* Kathryn Kish Sklar's *Harriet Beecher Stowe,* and Roy Harvey Pearce's *Nathaniel Hawthorne.* Additional volumes are planned.

Another cultural milestone was reached with the publication of an authoritative volume signaling the richness of the American literary heritage, Eugene Ehrlich and Gorton Carruth's *The Oxford Literary Guide to the United States.*

JEROME H. STERN, *Florida State University*

Children's Literature

The number of children's books produced in the United States during 1982 was several hundred more than the 2,000 published the previous year. With the drop in library purchases continuing, such a step up seemed contradictory. The increase, however, was in less expensive items that would produce high-volume sales. There were many new titles added to series of paperback teenage romances, dozens of new pop-up books, and numerous volumes with a movie or TV tie-in. More than a hundred newly illustrated editions of the classics—from *Aladdin* and *Alice in Wonderland* to *The Wizard of Oz* and *Wynken, Blynken, and Nod*—also appeared.

A somewhat controversial book was Japanese author-artist Toshi Maruki's *Hiroshima No Pika*, depicting the horrors of the first atomic bomb explosion in 1945. One of the most enthusiastically received books (for readers age 10 to 14) was Jean Fritz's autobiographical *Homesick*, an account of her growing up as the daughter of missionaries in China in the late 1920s and her journey to America.

The American Library Association's (ALA's) John Newbery Medal for the most distinguished contribution to American children's literature went to Nancy Willard for *A Visit to William Blake's Inn*, a book of poetry about life in an imaginary inn run by the English poet-artist. It was the first time in the 60-year history of the Newbery Medal that a book of poetry was honored. The ALA's Randolph Caldecott Medal for the most distinguished picture book was awarded to Chris Van Allsburg for his illustrations in *Jumanji*, in which two children play an imaginative and bizarre board game. The American Book Awards in various categories of children's literature were as follows: in hardcover picture books to Maurice Sendak for *Outside Over There*, a symbolic tale in which a little girl saves her baby sister from goblins; in paperback picture books to Peter Spier for his illustrations in *Noah's Ark;* in hardcover fiction to Lloyd Alexander for *Westmark*, a tale of high adventure in an imaginary kingdom; in paperback fiction to Ouida Sebestyen for *Words by Heart*, a poignant and tragic story of a black family in a southwestern town; and in paperback nonfiction to Susan Bonners for her illustrations and text in *A Penguin Year*. Athena Lord won the Child Study Children's Book Committee Award for *A Spirit to Ride the Whirlwind*, about a young girl's fight for justice in a New England mill town of the 1830s.

For the picture-book audience (ages 3 to 6), the most noteworthy books were Byron Barton's *Airport*, a young traveler's colorful tour of a plane and terminal; Chris Van Allsburg's somewhat surreal *Ben's Dream*, a tour of the world's great landmarks; William Steig's *Doctor De Soto*, in which a dentist mouse outfoxes a fox patient; Margot Zemach's *Jake and Honeybunch Go to Heaven*, the misadventures of a black man and his mule in Paradise; Peter Spier's *Rain*, a colorful pictorial presentation of two children in a downpour; *We Can't Sleep*, by James Stevenson, in which an old man tells his grandchildren a tall tale about when he was a boy; and Barbara Cooney's *Miss Rumphius*, an enjoyable story about a little girl who grew up to make the world more beautiful by sowing the Maine coastline with lupine seeds.

For children between 7 and 10, the best books were Karla Kuskin's *The Philharmonic Gets Dressed*, illustrated by Marc Simont, a text-and-picture description of musicians getting ready for an evening performance; *Marco Polo*, by Gian Paolo Ceserani and illustrated by Piero Ventura, a graceful account of the 13th-century Venetian merchant's travels in Asia; and the third of Mitsumasa Anno's "travel" books, *Anno's Britain*, which traces a pilgrim's journey through towns and villages as he encounters literary and historical surprises.

In the 9-to-12 category, the most outstanding books were Robbie Branscum's *The Murder of Hound Dog Bates*, a rural tale in which a 13-year-old boy tries to find out which of his three guardian aunts poisoned his pet hound dog; Isaac Bashevis Singer's compassionate retelling of a legend concerning the Jews of the old city of Prague in *The Golem;* Eleanor Cameron's *That Julia Redfern*, a sensitive story about a young girl's antics and yearnings to be a writer; Betsy Byars' *The Two-Thousand-Pound Goldfish*, about an 8-year-old boy with a vivid imagination and a mother on the run from the FBI; Lloyd Alexander's *The Kestrel*, in which intrigue and adventure abound in a sequel to the award-winning *Westmark;* and Roald Dahl's *The BFG*, about one Big Friendly Giant and nine other mean ones.

Among the year's best novels for teenagers were Virginia Hamilton's *Sweet Whispers, Brother Rush*, a compelling, richly characterized story of a young black girl discovering her family's past; Natalie Babbitt's *Herbert Rowbarge*, a fine and subtle tale about several sets of identical twins; Zibby Oneal's *A Formal Feeling*, a polished account of a 16-year-old girl reconciling herself to her mother's death and father's remarriage; Joyce Carol Thomas' *Marked by Fire*, a lyrical first novel about the joys and sorrows of a black girl's first 20 years in a small Oklahoma community; and Meredith Anne Pierce's *The Darkangel*, a romantic fantasy pitting a servant girl against a handsome but evil vampire.

Perhaps the most impressive work of children's nonfiction was Judith St. George's *The Brooklyn Bridge: They Said It Couldn't Be Built*, which covers the history, from dream to reality, of the New York suspension bridge which celebrates its centennial in 1983.

GEORGE A. WOODS
Children's Book Editor
"The New York Times"

Canadian Literature: English

In Canadian nonfiction, many English-language writers focused on present-day politics, economics, and the environment. In fiction, short story collections were unusually numerous.

Nonfiction. Publication of two volumes of the *Benjamin Disraeli Letters* marked the first results of an enormous scholarly task; Queen's University professors John Matthews and Donald Schurman have undertaken to edit Disraeli's letters in a projected 25-volume collection. Northrop Frye's *The Great Code: The Bible and Literature* demonstrates that book's great influence on literature; he plans further volumes on the Bible. *The Spice Box: An Anthology of Jewish Canadian Writing,* edited by Geri Sinclair and Morris Wolfe, is the first collection of its kind in Canada. *Beyond Sambation* collects essays and editorials by the poet A. M. Klein from 1928 to 1955. Klein, who died in 1972, is the subject of *Like One that Dreamed,* by Usher Caplan. In *A Genius at Work,* Dorothy Harley Eber quotes the letters and diaries of Alexander Graham Bell and tells of Bell's summers on Cape Breton Island.

Writings by Conservative politician Dalton Camp are collected in his *An Eclectic Eel.* Albert W. Truman's *A Second View of Things: A Memoir* is the reflections of a leading Canadian academic. In *The Establishment Man,* his fourth book about Canada's capitalists, Peter C. Newman concentrates on just one of them, Conrad Black. Anthony Sampson's *The Money Lenders* criticizes international bankers and pleads for development of the Third World.

Lorraine Monk's *Canada With Love/Canada Avec Amour,* written in honor of Canada's 115th birthday and the patriation of its constitution from Great Britain, collects items by leading Canadian authors, together with 50 spectacular photographs from across the land. Gerald Clark's *Montreal: The New Cité* is a careful study of the great metropolis. *British Columbia—This Favoured Land,* by Liz Bryan, is well researched and well illustrated. Ulli Steltzer's *Inuit—The North in Transition* is a first-hand description of Canada's Arctic people, with photographs by the author.

Why We Act Like Canadians, by the celebrated author Pierre Breton, is written as a letter to an American friend telling him how Canadians differ from Americans. In *Life With Uncle,* John W. Holmes discusses Canadian-U.S. relations more formally. And in *Essays on Canada,* Mordecai Richler, the well-known author of *Duddy Kravitz* and other novels, shoots some sacred cows.

In *Wildcatters,* Earle Gray gives the history of the Pacific Petroleum and Westcoast Transmission companies. David Carne's *Canada's Oil and Gas Industry* stresses the fact that a great deal of the country's petroleum industry is foreign-owned.

The Discovery of Insulin, by Michael Bliss, tells of the medical milestone reached by a research team in Toronto in 1923. Alwyn James' *Discovering Your Scottish Roots* gives practical advice to Canadians of Scottish descent who want to trace their ancestors.

On the Bridge of Time is the second volume of memoirs by the diplomat Hugh L. Keenlyside, and *Memoirs of an Art Dealer, 2* is the second volume of G. Blair Lang's intriguing tales about art and artists. In *Artists, Builders and Dreamers,* David Leighton gives the 50-year history of the Banff Centre, an international institution for the arts.

Ervin MacDonald's *The Rainbow Chasers* describes how his pioneer family battled the Canadian wilderness and survived. James K. Smith's *Wilderness of Fortune* is a lively history of Canada. *History in Their Blood* reproduces 64 paintings of Indians by Nicholas de Grandmaison, with text by Hugh A. Dempsey. And David Ricardo Williams' *Trapline Outlaw* tells about the famed Canadian outlaw Gunanoot.

Poetry. *Evening Dance of the Grey Flies* is a selection of poems by P. K. Page since 1969, and *The Phases of Love* is the work of another leading Canadian poetess, Dorothy Livesay.

bill bissett (who rejects capital letters) combines poems and short stories in *northern birds in color.* Susan Musgrave presents some old and new poems in *Tarts and Muggers.* And *Conflicts of Spring* is the 17th volume by Ralph Gustafson. A highly praised new volume was *A Sad Device* by Toronto poetess Roo Borson. George Amabile looks at life's problems in *The Presence of Fire.* And Irving Layton, now age 70, shows youthful zest in the selection of his works titled *A Wild Peculiar Joy, 1945–82.*

Fiction. Leon Rooke's *Death Suite* is a collection of funny and frightening short stories. George McWhirter, an Irishman living in Canada, deals with both Irishmen and Canadians in his third volume of short stories, *Coming to Grips with Lucy.* The *Black Queen Stories,* by poet Barry Callaghan, are all set in Toronto. Another Toronto poet, Don Coles, titled his third short story collection *The Prinzhorn Collection.* And Guy Vanderhaeghe's *Man Descending* presents 12 stories with Canadian settings.

David Helwig's novel *It is Always Summer* is about a love triangle. *Icarus,* the second novel by Prince Edward Island writer Christopher Hyde, is a thriller. And Ken Follett's latest, *The Man From St. Petersburg,* has to do with the events in England before World War I. Morley Torgov's *The Outside Chance of Maximilian Glick* is about a Jewish family in northern Ontario. David Adams Richards' *Lives of Short Duration* deals with a backwoods family in New Brunswick. Aviva Layton's *Nobody's Daughter* is about a poet's wife in Montreal. And Jack MacLeod's *Going Grand* takes an amusing look at Toronto's academic life.

DAVID SAVAGE, *Simon Fraser University*

Canadian Literature: Quebec

Quebec French publishing houses were extremely active in 1982. In general, novelists were more prolific than playwrights and short-story writers; essays and reference works abounded; and younger writers dominated the poetry scene.

Novels. Two important novels were published in December 1981. Jacque Godbout's *Têtes à Papineau* features a two-headed protagonist who symbolizes a Quebec that cannot choose between federalism and political independence. *Cent Ans dans le bois,* Antonine Maillet's sequel to the Goncourt Prize-winning *Pélagie-la-Charrette,* describes the life and traditions of Acadians in the 1860s.

In spring 1982, three well-known female novelists and a younger, promising male were published in Paris: Antonine Maillet (*La Gribouille*), Anne Hébert (*Les Fous de Bassan*), Marie-Claire Blais (*Visions d'Anna*), and Robert Lalonde (*Le Dernier Eté des Indiens*).

The third volume of Michel Tremblay's fictional chronicle of Mount Royal, *La Duchesse et la roturier,* was published in Montreal. Claude Jasmin's *L'Armoire de Pantagruel,* Jean-Marie Poupart's *Rétroviseurs,* and Jean-Paul Filion's *A Mes Ordres* also were published there.

Female writers from Montreal were equally productive. Yolande Villemaire's *Ange Amazone* and Monique La Rue's *Les Faux Fuyants* illustrate a concern about the ultimate meaning of words. France Théoret's *Nous parlerons comme on écrit* abandons traditional forms and divisions of genre to explore the gap separating the spoken or real world from the written or cultural world.

Poetry. The small presses continued to encourage promising young writers, including Yolande Villemaire (*Du côté hiéroglyphique ce qu'on appelle le réel*) and Claude Beausoleil (*Dans la matière rêvant comme d'une émeute*). Retrospectives of the poetry of the Québécoise Madeleine Gagnon and the Acadian Michel Gay vied for attention with Marie Uguay's third volume, *Autoportraits,* published posthumously.

Essays and Criticism. One of the most important essays of 1982 was feminist in orientation: Michèle Jean's *Histoire des femmes.*

Two former Quebec politicians tried their hand at writing. Lise Payette, a television interviewer and recently resigned Cabinet member of the Parti Québécois government, offers pointed observations on the Quebec political milieu in *Le Pouvoir? Connais pas!* In *Ecrits polémiques 1960–1981,* Pierre Bourgault, a dedicated though controversial separatist, comments with piquancy on the turbulent years during and after the Quiet Revolution.

Nonfiction. Brian Young's biography of former Prime Minister George-Etienne Cartier was published in 1982, as was Jacques Monet's life of Jules Léger, a former governor general.

Notable scholarly volumes published during the year include three French-language reference works: the *Dictionnaire biographique du Canada,* vol. XI; the *Encyclopédie de la musique canadienne;* and the third volume of Maurice Lemire's *Dictionnaire des oeuvres littéraires du Québec 1940–1959.*

The critic Jean Royer's *Ecrivains contemporains: Entretiens I* contains some 30 interviews with Quebec writers conducted from 1976 to 1979. Of a pictorial nature are Pierre Choinière's *Le Richelieu: une vallée du regard* and Linda Moser's *Québec á l'éte 1950,* with text by Roch Carrier.

Forthcoming Works. More titles by prominent Quebec writers were promised for the Christmas season: essays by the poets Nicole Brossard, Paul Chamberland, and Pierre Perrault; *Lectures* by Gérard Bessette; a study by the literary critic Gérard Tougas; and Louis Caron's second volume of fiction in the series *Les Fils de la liberté.*

Obituaries. The francophone literary world lost two prominent members during the summer: Jean Filiatrault, dramatist and novelist, and Monsignor Felix-Antoine Savard, the venerable 85-year-old cleric and classical scholar who created the patriarchal lumberjack Menand.

RAMON HATHORN, *University of Guelph*

English Literature

Four major events of the British year—the birth of Prince William, the papal visit, the Falklands War, and the raising of the *Mary Rose* (Henry VIII's warship that sank in the Solent in 1545)—were reflected in publishers' lists. Less immediate events were considered in scholarly books, memoirs, fiction, and poetry.

Nonfiction. Perhaps the best of recent books on the royal family was Penny Junor's *Diana, Princess of Wales.* In time for the papal visit, Lord Longford produced *Pope John Paul II.* Issues in the Falklands War were debated in *Authors Take Sides on the Falklands,* edited by Cecil Woolf and Jean Moorcroft Wilson. The archaeological significance of Henry VIII's vessel was discussed in Margaret Rule's *The Mary Rose.*

Several famous men were remembered in books by family members and friends. Philip Snow wrote of his brother in *Stranger and Brother: A Portrait of C.P. Snow* and T.R. Fyvel of a friend in *George Orwell: A Personal Memoir.* In *One of These Fine Days,* Myfanwy Thomas wrote of her father, Edward Thomas. In *A Half of Two Lives,* Alison Waley recalled her relationship with her late husband, Arthur Waley. William Buchan wrote of his father in *John Buchan.* And Nicholas Mosley recalled his parents in *Rules of the Game: Sir Oswald and Lady Cynthia Mosley.*

Notable biographies were Kenneth Harris' *Attlee* and Nigel Fisher's *Harold Macmillan;* Paul Ferris' *Richard Burton* and Garry O'Connor's *Ralph Richardson;* Michael Millgate's

Thomas Hardy, Peter Alexander's *Roy Campbell,* Martin Seymour-Smith's *Robert Graves,* George Jefferson's *Edward Garnett,* and Frances Donaldson's *P.G. Wodehouse.*

The first volumes of a major diary and of two major collections of letters were *The Diary of Beatrice Webb,* edited by Norman and Jeanne MacKenzie; *The Letters of Alfred, Lord Tennyson,* edited by Cecil Y. Lang and Edgar F. Shannon; and *The Letters of D.H. Lawrence,* edited by James T. Boulton and George J. Zytaruk. Smaller collections were *The Love Letters of William and Mary Wordsworth,* edited by Beth Darlington, and *The Noel Coward Diaries,* edited by Graham Payn and Sheridan Morley. Autobiographies of interest were Laurence Olivier's *Confessions of an Actor* and John Mortimer's *Clinging to the Wreckage.* William Golding's *A Moving Target* is a collection of literary essays and reviews.

Fiction. Well-known writers from several generations published novels in 1982. Graham Greene's *Monsignor Quixote* pays tribute to Cervantes in its account of the adventures of a Spanish priest and his "Sancho Panza," the Communist mayor of his village. John Fowles' *Mantissa* is mainly a dialogue about love and fiction between a writer and Erato, the muse of erotic poetry. John Wain's *Young Shoulders* describes the maturation of an adolescent after the accidental death of his sister. Allan Sillitoe's *Her Victory* chronicles the escape of a middle-aged woman from an unhappy marriage and her hard-won happiness thereafter. David Storey's realistic *A Prodigal Child* is about a young sculptor who has been lifted from his humble home by a benefactress.

Constance, set in Egypt and the south of France during World War II, is the third of Lawrence Durrell's "quincunx" group of novels. *Temporary Hearths* is the third novel in Stuart Evans' "Windmill Hill" sequence, which chronicles the aging of the generation that was young during World War II. *The Making of the Representative for Planet 8,* about a planet whose inhabitants are trapped by an ice age, is the fourth novel in Doris Lessing's "Canopus in Argos: Archives." *Funeral Games* completes Mary Renault's series on Alexander the Great.

Other notable novels were Thomas Keneally's *Schindler's Ark,* John Arden's *Silence Among the Weapons,* Kazuo Ishiguro's *A Pale View of Hills,* Stanley Middleton's *Blind Understanding,* Stephen Benatar's *Wish Her Safe at Home,* Alice Thomas Ellis' *The 27th Kingdom,* Elaine Feinstein's *The Survivors,* William Boyd's *An Ice Cream War,* A.N. Wilson's *A Wise Virgin,* and P.D. James' *The Skull Beneath the Skin.*

Collections of short stories included Edna O'Brien's *Returning,* Penelope Gilliatt's *Quotations from Other Lives,* Graham Swift's *Learning to Swim,* Dermot Healy's *Banished Misfortune,* Bernard Mac Laverty's *A Time to Dance,* and H.R.F. Keating's *The Lucky Alphonse.*

Photograph by Karsh

The latest work by prolific British author Graham Greene is a novel that takes place in modern-day Spain and pays tribute to Cervantes' picaresque classic, "Don Quixote."

Simon and Schuster

Poetry. The diversity of British verse published in 1982 was illustrated by Gavin Ewart's *The New Ewart,* R.S. Thomas' *Between Here and Now,* and D.M. Thomas' *Dreaming in Bronze.* Ewart's verse is energetic, topical, irreverent, bawdy, and funny. R.S. Thomas' poems are carefully controlled meditations on his own experiences and man's situation in the universe. D.M. Thomas' main subjects are sexuality and atrocities in war and peace, which he examines in cool, conversational verse or reveals in frenzied voices.

Collections by Vernon Scannell, Elizabeth Jennings, and John Heath-Stubbs show the individual coping with aging and other troubling circumstances, frequently finding pleasure in the process. In *Winterlude,* Scannell uses strategies of boxing, poetry, and lovemaking to survive. In *Celebrations and Elegies,* Jennings writes of bereavement and duress but also of the joys of living. And in *Naming the Beasts,* Heath-Stubbs turns from abrasive aspects of urban life to the pleasures of the countryside.

Other collections were Tom Paulin's *The Book of Juniper,* Wes Magee's *A Dark Age,* James Fenton's *Dead Soldiers,* E.J. Scovell's *The Space Between,* George Szirtes' *November and May,* and Peter Reading's *Tom O'Bedlam's Beauties.*

J. K. Johnstone
University of Saskatchewan

World Literature*

By the fall publishing season it had already become clear that 1982 was a sterling year in world letters. Major works of fiction from Latin America and Central Europe, excellent poetry and mixed-genre writing from France and the Orient, retrospectives by prominent literary figures, and several surprises from hitherto little-known or little-heeded names and areas were just some of the pleasures.

Spanish. To judge from worldwide commentary and number of translations, the year's single most spectacular success was Peruvian novelist Mario Vargas Llosa's best-selling epic *War of the End of the World.* Actually prereleased for the 1981 Christmas season, the work compares favorably with Tolstoyan and Stendhalian undertakings in its 600-page narrative of an enigmatic preacher whose defiance of authority in turn-of-the-century Brazil leads to armed rebellion.

Elsewhere in Latin America, Manuel Puig, the admired but sometimes outrageous Argentine author, also used a Brazilian setting in his new novel, *Blood of Requited Love,* a touching story about the pain of adolescent romance but also a marvelous elegy on the disguises and transformations of memory. Mexican poet-novelist Homero Aridjis' *Spectacle of the Year 2000* presents a myth-tinged, theatrical account of grotesquerie and ritual, welcoming the new millennium and reaffirming both spiritual and erotic love amid the final apocalypse. Nicaraguan poet-priest and Minister of Culture Ernesto Cardenal added to Latin America's distinguished tradition of the long poem with *The Dubious Predicament,* a lyrico-political meditation on the conquest of the Americas and the mixing of races and cultures. Mexican novelist Carlos Fuentes continued his recent efforts in shorter fiction with the fantasy-filled novella *Orchids by Moonlight.* The late Cuban José Lezama Lima's remaining unpublished verse and prose were brought together in *Kingdom of the Image.*

Writers from Spain again seemed to lag behind their creative American kinsmen. Only poet-critic Dámaso Alonso's *Joys of Sight,* a new longer poem with some selected early works; poet-novelist Gabriel Celaya's *Penultimate Poems;* and the late Ramón J. Sender's posthumous novel *Album of Secret Radiographs* stood out.

Italian. Italy, however, was blessed with first-rate new works by four of its classics and one highly promising newcomer. Leading novelists Leonardo Sciascia and Alberto Moravia continued their respective preoccupations with the intellectual-historical detective story and the exploration of Fascist-era mentality in *The Theatre of Memory* and *1934.* Nobel laureate Eugenio Montale's death in late 1981 did not prevent his seeing the first finished copies of his final poetry collection, *Other Verses,* but did deny him the joy

* Titles translated.

of hearing the chorus of praise for this compendium. And Ignazio Silone's brief novelette *Severina,* recounting the story of an activist nun, appeared four years after the author's death having been completed and annotated by his widow Darina. The imaginative newcomer was Annalisa Moncada, whose *Year by the Sea* narrates the symbolic "pilgrimage" to Jerusalem undertaken by a miraculously cured Sicilian prince entirely within the walls of his own palace.

French. The year brought new works by several French authors of established and lasting merit. Eighty-year-old novelist Nathalie Sarraute's *For the Slightest of Reasons* uses dialogue to explore typically Sarrautean "tropisms," the small and scarcely perceptible preverbal sensations underlying ordinary conversation and, in this case, producing distrust, alienation, and enmity between two good friends. Young prose writer J.M.G. Le Clézio turned to the short story in *The Rondo and Other Diverse Facts,* treating with gentle dignity and clear-eyed sympathy an array of banal incidents involving unimportant people and their uniformly sad fates. Mixed-genre *scripteur* Michel Butor's *Explorations* presents 15 short lyrical-prose texts and poems on such themes as the dawn of creation and the birth of narrative through magical threads and music on a mythical island. And aging poet Henri Michaux offered in *Roads Sought, Roads Lost* a lyrical but penetrating look back on the 1930s and other periods of his life and work. Memoirs, journals, and collected editions from Julien Green, Jean Cayrol, Zoé Oldenbourg, Bernard Delvaille, and Belgian author Marcel

Essays by the new president of France, written 1971–78 about a wide range of topics, came out in English.

Courtesy, Seaver Books

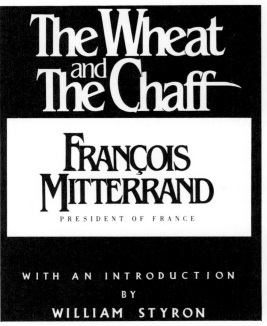

Thiry added to the delights of French readers.

German. As in several previous years, the best German-language writing of 1982 came not from West Germany but from the periphery—Switzerland and East Germany. Swiss playwright and novelist Max Frisch offered in the short prose work *Bluebeard* a disturbing but thoroughly engrossing examination of guilt and truth through the story of the enigmatic physician Felix Schaad, accused but soon acquitted of murdering the sixth of his seven wives.

Expatriated East German novelist and critic Joachim Seyppel's *I'm a Washout* gives a remarkably detailed look behind the scenes of the Democratic Republic's literary "industry," sparing neither former colleagues nor cultural hacks and political functionaries. One of the year's most startling and important documents, the book exposes the "great deceit of falsified voting results" that led to the expulsion of nine prominent authors from the Writers Union in the late 1970s. Hermann Kant, still a resident of the DDR, produced in the story collection *The Third Nail* a genuine rarity: an "acceptable" work of both realistic perceptiveness and genuine wit.

Austria's prolific Thomas Bernhard brought out *Cement,* a brooding parable of a young scholar stifled in his writing by solipsism and obsessive memories. West Germany welcomed the appearance of new books by such established writers as Gabriele Wohmann, Martin Walser, Herbert Achternbusch, Jurek Becker, Peter Härtling, Max von der Grün, and Christoph Meckel, as well as by East German exiles Günter Kunert and Reiner Kunze. But only newcomer Peter Schneider's *The Wall Jumper* rivaled the works of Frisch and Kant in both critical acclaim and popularity.

Scandinavian. The same situation—many good works but few that stood far above the others—applied to the other Germanic languages, with new publications by such leading literary lights as Sweden's Artur Lundkvist and Lars Gustafsson and by the late Johan Fabricius of the Netherlands, plus first-time English translations of the prolific Danish writer Klaus Rifbjerg and the recently deceased Johan Borgen of Norway. Also appearing in 1982 was a fine anthology, *Modern Scandinavian Poetry, 1900–1975,* introducing more than 270 poets to the English-speaking world.

Slavic. In Russian and Soviet literature, the year brought Konstantin Simonov's new trilogy *The So-Called Private Life,* Andrei Voznesensky's verse collection *Under Review,* exiled poet Joseph Brodsky's slim volume of a dozen poems *Roman Elegies,* and émigré author Fazil Iskander's satiric *Rabbits and Pythons,* as well as the second of five volumes in the definitive collected works of poet Marina Tsvetaeva.

Of perhaps wider interest, however, were outstanding new publications by several leading East European authors. Two novellas by Belorussian writer Vasil Bykov were issued together in English translation as *His Battalion/Live Until Dawn,* offering compelling and realistically detailed stories of the Soviet military during World War II. Czech author Jiří Gruša's 1974 underground novel *The Questionnaire,* which led to his arrest for "initiating disorder" and to his forced emigration in 1978, was issued in English. And Albanian novelist Ismaïl Kadaré continued to confound Western perceptions of that closed, ideological nation through a steady stream of engaging novels translated into French for European distribution; his latest book to be translated, *Twilight of the Gods of the Steppe,* draws on his years at Moscow's prestigious Gorky Institute to paint a wickedly satirical portrait of the Soviet intelligentsia.

Oriental. French and English continued to serve as important mediums of expression and dissemination of world literatures to Western audiences. Three particularly noteworthy volumes stood out among the year's many translations from the Chinese: *The Complete Stories of Lu Xun* is technically a misnomer but nonetheless is fully indicative of this classic modern author's satiric genius in attacking the hypocrisy and inhumanity of early 20th-century Chinese society; *Born of the Same Roots* offers six decades of writing by a wide range of authors on exclusively female protagonists, something of an oddity in male-dominated Chinese letters; and *Wandering in the Garden, Waking from a Dream* gathers stories which center on mainlanders who fled to Taiwan after the Nationalists' defeat, thus presenting through its characters a unique "history of the republic."

Junichirō Tanizaki, often called the finest modern Japanese novelist, was reintroduced to Western audiences in 1982 with two jointly-published short novels: the scandalous burlesque of Confucian chronicles *The Secret History of the Lord of Musashi,* and the meditative and poetic "essay novel" *Arrowroot.* Two notable collections of verse, both in the original and in translation, were Makoto Ōoka's *A String Around Autumn* and the late Kinoshita Yūji's *Treelike;* the former is an exquisite volume of controlled, consciously intellectual poetry by one of the leading figures in Tokyo's literary and art world, while the latter contains simple, colloquial lyrics by a provincial pharmacist.

African. The year in Africa brought admirable new works in Western languages, such as the South African writer André Brink's novel *A Chain of Voices* (Afrikaans), the Moroccan author Tahar Ben Jelloun's two long prose pieces *Solitary Confinement* and *Prayer of the Absent* (French), his countryman Abdellatif Laâbi's collection of prison verse *Under the Gag the Poem* (French), three new novels by José Luandino Vieira of Angola (Portuguese), and Kenyan novelist and playwright Ngugi wa Thiong'o's *Devil on the Cross,* his own English version of a novel originally written in Gikuyu. Of equal if not greater importance for African identity and heritage were two releases cast more in indigenous tradition: Ngugi's acclaimed but now banned folk-musical play *I Will Marry When I Want,* written in Gikuyu with Ngugi wa Miirie; and *Feti's Hatchet* by Henrique Abranches of Angola, the first part of a simulated oral epic gathered from Angolan history, ethnography, mythology, animal fables, and Ovambo legends.

Near Eastern. Two of the Near East's long-dominant literary figures, Turkish poet Nazim Hikmet and Egyptian dramatist Tawfiq al-Hakim, were represented in 1982 with important new translations: the verse collection *Human Landscapes* and the anthology *Theatre of the Mind* respectively. Israel's two principal poets, Yehuda Amichai and T. Carmi, brought out new collections, *Love Poems* and *At the Stone of Losses.* Benjamin Tammuz, one of Israel's most talented novelists, published the English version of his powerful *Requiem for Na'aman. Bread, Hashish, and Moon* is an all-too-brief anthology of four important Arabic poets. And last but certainly not least in light of the year's tragic events in the Mideast, *The Palestinian Wedding* introduces Westerners to 12 writers of Palestinian resistance poetry; far from rabid sloganeering, the verse is for the most part elegiac, expansive, and possessed of great historical awareness.

WILLIAM RIGGAN, *"World Literature Today"*

LONDON

London saw Irish Republican Army terrorist bombings again in 1982. In midsummer, eight soldiers were killed and 51 civilians injured after two bombs exploded during the changing of the guard ceremony at Whitehall and during a military band concert in Regents Park. Earlier in the year, the meeting of Queen Elizabeth II and Pope John Paul II, the first pope ever to visit Britain, brought a hope of greater religious peace and unity.

Londoners were offered two gifts during 1982. The Barbican Centre for Arts and Conferences near St. Paul's, which had been built amid controversy about costs escalating over the last twenty years, was opened in March. It provides in the City, London's financial area, an oasis of concert hall, theater, art galleries, exhibition and conference halls, and restaurants. Though fears had been expressed that the center might prove a white elephant, tens of thousands of Londoners ambled through its terraces and admired the fountains, while concerts and theatrical performances were packed. Financed from the taxes of the City, one of Britain's wealthiest local authorities, the center's cost was some £153 million.

The Greater London Council's gift to Londoners was later withdrawn somewhat acrimoniously after the House of Lords declared it unlawful. In October 1981, the GLC instituted a bold scheme to lower bus and subway fares by 32%, using massive subsidies from London's taxpayers, mostly householders. When one local authority contested this policy and queried its legality, the GLC was forced in March to admit defeat and remove subsidies, doubling London's fares overnight. A GLC decision to help fund London's "Safe Women's Transport" campaign was welcomed without controversy upon publication of surveys showing that in some boroughs 85% of women are afraid to go out at night.

MAUREEN GREEN

LOS ANGELES

Principal developments in Los Angeles during 1982 involved education, the fine arts, crime, the police, and the coroner. Also receiving attention were the prospects for building the Century Freeway, delayed for about a quarter century, and completion of the Artesia Freeway. Mayor Tom Bradley was unsuccessful in his November bid for the state governorship.

Education. After years of controversy, forced busing in the public schools came to an end on June 30, when the U.S. Supreme Court upheld Proposition 1, which prohibited judges from requiring busing to achieve school integration unless proof exists of intentional segregation. The school district faced the problems of a rapidly increasing number of non-English-speaking children and a growing number of both overcrowded and underused schools.

Fine Arts. The J. Paul Getty Museum in Malibu became the world's richest private museum with the transfer of $1,100,000,000 from the Getty estate on March 1.

Crime. On January 6, William G. Bonin, a truck driver, was convicted of killing ten young men and boys in the "Freeway Murders." A week later, Harold Rossfields Smith, a former boxing promoter, was convicted of embezzling $21.3 million from the Wells Fargo Bank, one of the largest such crimes in history. Arson continued to be a major problem. In the worst case, 24 people were killed in an apartment building fire on September 4.

Government. In a lean year, budgets were cut for the city, county, and school district.

On April 27, publicity-minded coroner Thomas T. Noguchi, who liked to be called "coroner to the stars," was removed from office by the County Board of Supervisors for poor administration, improper procedures, and a huge backlog of work. Noguchi appealed the decision.

Police. A burglary and sex scandal rocked the Hollywood division of the police department. By year's end, criminal charges had been brought against six officers, while others faced administrative hearings. Police Chief Daryl F. Gates ran into difficulties after he contrasted blacks with "normal people" and was accused of placing noncriminal groups under surveillance.

CHARLES R. ADRIAN
University of California, Riverside

LOUISIANA

The nationwide recession and the oil glut combined to put Louisiana's state government in serious economic difficulty in 1982. Thousands of Louisianans were driven from their homes by year-end floods.

Economic Problems. A sizable part of state revenues is derived from severance taxes on oil and gas production. For every drop of $1 in the price per barrel of oil, Louisiana's government loses approximately $35 million. The state was expected to run a deficit of some $120 million in the 1982 fiscal year. In November, Gov. David C. Treen ordered spending cuts totaling $78 million, which still left the budget $42 million short of the necessary revenues.

The outlook for the future was even bleaker. The state legislative fiscal office reported that unless Louisiana sharply reduces services it will face huge deficits over the next few years, including a shortage of up to $275 million in fiscal 1983–84 and $590 million by 1986–87. To cover its expenses in the coming years, oil prices would have to increase by $9 to $10 a barrel per year.

Legislature. The legislature defeated a bill known as the Coastal Wetlands Environmental Levy, which would have raised $450 million from taxes on minerals, primarily oil and gas, moving through the state's coastal wetland areas. It also rejected bills that would have reformed the workers' compensation system and allowed the use of inmate labor on new prisons. But it approved a tougher drunk-driving law, requiring first offenders to spend time in jail or perform public service, and it passed a bill requiring political candidates to reveal their finances.

Twice the legislature failed in a mail ballot to approve a $100,000 appropriation needed by the state attorney general's office for the defense of Louisiana's one-year-old "scientific creation" law, requiring the creation theory to be given equal time with the theory of evolution in public schools. The law was not enforced, pending the outcome of a suit against it.

UPI

Safety workers inspect the wreckage of a Pan Am plane that crashed near New Orleans in July, killing 154 persons.

Accidents. The second worst air disaster in U.S. history occurred on July 9 when a Pan American World Airways flight, leaving New Orleans for Las Vegas, crashed into the suburban city of Kenner. The death toll was 146 persons on the plane and eight on the ground, and nine homes were destroyed. The official cause of the crash was not immediately determined, but the plane attempted to take off during a heavy rainstorm when wind shears—sudden and violent changes in wind direction—had been reported at the airport.

Almost the entire population of the small town of Livingston, about 40 mi (65 km) east of Baton Rouge, was evacuated for two weeks after September 25, when a train hauling hazardous chemicals left the track and burned. About 20 houses were destroyed or seriously damaged. Nearly 3,000 persons lived in shelters or with relatives while the chemicals burned themselves out. Testimony at a federal hearing later indicated that the engineer and a brakeman had been drinking heavily, and that a woman railroad clerk was driving the locomotive at the time of the derailment.

Crime. Sen. Michael O'Keefe of New Orleans, president of the state Senate, was convicted of mail fraud and obstruction of justice by using the mails to cheat a business partner of $900,000. The trial judge overturned the conviction, ruling that the federal prosecutor had used inflammatory language in his summation. O'Keefe was reindicted later in the year.

JOSEPH W. DARBY III
"The Times-Picayune," New Orleans

LOUISIANA • Information Highlights

Area: 47,752 sq mi (123 678 km²).
Population (1980 census): 4,206,312.
Chief Cities (1980 census): Baton Rouge, the capital, 219,486; New Orleans, 557,927; Shreveport, 205,815; Lafayette, 81,961; Lake Charles, 75,051.
Government (1982): *Chief Officers*—governor, David C. Treen (R); lt. gov., Robert L. Freeman (D). *Legislature*—Senate, 39 members; House of Representatives, 105 members.
State Finances (fiscal year 1981): *Revenues*, $5,895,000,000; *expenditures*, $5,825,000,000.
Personal Income (1981): $41,001,000,000; per capita, $9,518.
Labor Force (Aug. 1982): Nonagricultural wage and salary earners, 1,608,600; unemployed, 207,100 (10.9% of total force).
Education: *Enrollment* (fall 1981)—public elementary schools, 543,275; public secondary, 238,778; colleges and universities (1981–82), 174,656. *Public school expenditures* (1980–81), $1,518,397,000 ($1,972 per pupil).

LUXEMBOURG

Weakness in the European economy posed problems for the duchy in 1982. Most serious was the 8.5% devaluation of the Belgian franc on Feb. 21, 1982. Although the Luxembourg franc was on a more sound basis than the Belgian, it was also devalued because the two currencies are linked. Duchy officials were angered, for Belgian consultation with Luxembourg had been late and limited. The concerns of the duchy, which imports 85% of its goods and would experience a sharp increase in prices, were scarcely addressed.

Duchy officials accepted the change because there seemed no other choice. Separation of the currencies would be difficult, and how would the Luxembourg franc fare on its own? But Luxembourg demanded and received assurances of better consultation in the future. Unresolved demands that the gold reserves of the two countries be kept separate reflect the extent of the strain placed on the monetary union.

To combat inflation, the ruling coalition of the Christian Social and Democratic parties adopted an austerity budget. Links between wages and the cost of living were broken, and salary increases were limited to 5% for 1982. Socialists and trade unions opposed these steps and on April 5 staged a rare general strike.

More cheerful news was the marriage of Princess Marie-Astrid to Christian of Hapsburg-Lorraine on Feb. 6, 1982.

During 1981 the national product fell by 1.2%; industrial production decreased by 6.8%, and that of steel by 17.9%. Imports increased by 4.6% and inflation by 8.1%. Unemployment was at 1%, kept low by the assignment of more than 3,000 workers to the anti-crisis odd-jobs division of ARBED. That steel conglomerate's declining fortunes, however, suggest that it cannot long maintain this division. Revenues produced by the banking community allowed a favorable balance of payments despite a trade deficit. Luxembourg's 114 banks make the duchy the third-largest banking center in Europe.

J. E. HELMREICH, *Allegheny College*

LUXEMBOURG • Information Highlights

Official Name: Grand Duchy of Luxembourg.
Location: Western Europe.
Area: 999 sq mi (2 587 km²).
Population (1982 est.): 400,000.
Chief Cities (1979 est.): Luxembourg, the capital, 79,-600; Esch-sur-Alzette, 25,500; Differdange, 16,-900.
Government: *Head of state,* Jean, grand duke (acceded 1964). *Head of government,* Pierre Werner, prime minister (took office July 1979). *Legislature* (unicameral)—Chamber of Deputies.
Monetary Unit: Franc (45.56 francs equal U.S.$1, March 1982).
Gross Domestic Product (1981 U.S.$): $3,770,000,-000.
Economic Indexes (1981): *Consumer Prices* (1970= 100), *all items,* 205.5; *food,* 195.9. *Industrial production* (1975=100), 92.
Foreign Trade (with Belgium) (1981 U.S.$): *Imports,* $62,133,000,000; *exports,* $55,646,000,000.

MAINE

For Maine's Democrats, 1982 was a notable year. And while many Maine citizens and much of the state's business community might not choose "notable" as their word to describe 1982, both are likely to say that the year in Maine was not as bad as it might have been, and in many cases better than elsewhere.

The Election. Maine Democrats were enthusiastic for a significant reason: for the first time since 1911, their party gained complete charge of state government. Democratic Gov. Joseph E. Brennan was reelected to a second, four-year term by a margin of nearly 2–1 over his Republican opponent, Charles L. Cragin. Another 93 Democrats were chosen for the 151-member Maine House, providing for a comfortable margin in that legislative body. Twenty-three Democratic senators were elected, leaving just 10 Senate Republicans, less than the one-third margin needed to sustain various parliamentary maneuvers.

George J. Mitchell, a Democrat who was named to the Senate when Edmund Muskie resigned to become U.S. secretary of state, won a full Senate term. He captured 61% of the vote to defeat his opponent, U.S. Rep. David F. Emery. In the face of that loss, Maine Republicans were pleased with the reelection of Olympia J. Snowe and the election of John R. McKernan, Jr., to the U.S. House of Representatives. Voters also rejected a motion to phase out Maine's only nuclear power plant by 1988.

According to some analysts, the state-level Democratic sweep was caused by a lack of strength at the "top of the ticket"—both Cragin and Emery proved to be mediocre campaigners. But other observers suggested that Governor Brennan would have been a difficult incumbent for any challenger because, in relative and historic terms, Maine has done well while he has been in the governor's mansion.

Population Growth and the Economy. For a state that recorded negative growth earlier in the 20th century, the news that Maine's population

---

MAINE • Information Highlights

Area: 33,265 sq mi (86 156 km²).
Population (1980 census): 1,125,027.
Chief Cities (1980 census): Augusta, the capital, 21,-819; Portland, 61,572; Lewiston, 40,481; Bangor, 31,643.
Government (1982): *Chief Officer*—governor, Joseph E. Brennan (D). *Legislature*—Senate, 33 members; House of Representatives, 151 members.
State Finances (fiscal year 1981): *Revenues,* $1,504,-000,000; *expenditures,* $1,420,000,000.
Personal Income (1981): $9,669,000,000; per capita, $8,535.
Labor Force (Aug. 1982): *Nonagricultural wage and salary earners,* 422,100; *unemployed,* 41,100 (7.6% of total force).
Education: *Enrollment*—public elementary schools (fall 1981), 148,769; public secondary, 67,524; colleges and universities (1981–82), 44,012. *Public school expenditures* (1980–81), $473,493,000 ($2,055 per pupil).

Former U.S. Secretary of State Edmund Muskie and John Mitchell join in celebrating the election victory of George J. Mitchell (center). The Maine Democrat won a six-year term to the U.S. Senate.

UPI

had increased 13% in the 1970s was a positive economic indicator. The population is now witnessing a current annual net in-migration of some 75,000, most of them young people under 35, according to the State Planning Office. These new arrivals, plus a strong and diversified economy, create a gross state product of nearly $10,-000,000,000, according to the index compiled by the Federal Reserve Bank of Boston. That activity, in turn, has kept Maine unemployment percentages below the national average.

It is the diverse and often small manufacturing and business enterprises that have contributed to Maine's economic growth. Only the pulp and paper industry, which owns more than half the state's 20 million acres (8.1 million ha), and supplies big business and heavy industry around the nation, is not sharing Maine's stability. Hurt by a drop in orders from such customers as General Motors and Ford, the state's paper companies cancelled expansion plans while they awaited a national economic recovery.

Meanwhile, Bath Iron Works, Maine's largest manufacturing employer, continues to grow and planned to construct a dry-dock facility in Portland.

JOHN N. COLE, *"Maine Times"*

MALAYSIA

Slumping international markets cut Malaysia's growth in 1982. Politically, the National Front government retained control of the federal and state parliaments in April elections.

Politics. Prime Minister Mahathir Mohamad's nine-month-old government won a new five-year mandate. The cabinet was little altered after the victory, but the National Front's parliamentary delegation, 132 of 154 seats, changed as 40% of the incumbents were retired before the contest in favor of younger candidates. The United Malays National Organization (UMNO), which dominates the Front coalition, gave youthful victors greater responsibilities.

Most dramatic was the rise of Anwar Ibrahim who, as leader of the Islamic youth move-

ment, had been the most vocal independent government critic. After defeating a strong Islamic Party opponent, Anwar was made a deputy minister under Mahathir and later edged the incumbent president to become head of the UMNO youth.

The Malaysian Chinese Association (MCA) of the National Front reversed its decline with important victories in peninsular Malaysia against the opposition Democratic Action Party (DAP), including the defeat of the DAP president by the MCA president. The MCA wins were partially offset by DAP victories in Sarawak and Sabah.

The murder of a state party leader before the election was a display of violence rare in Malaysian politics. Later, the minister of culture, youth, and sport was one of five persons charged with the murder. The trial was set for late 1982. On Independence Day, August 31, the nation was informed that Datuk Harun Idris, elected a vice-president of UMNO in 1981 after serving three and a half years in jail for corruption and forgery, had been pardoned.

The Economy. The petroleum glut and price decline, with low prices for other commodities such as palm oil and rubber, interrupted the country's prosperity. Growth in GNP was expected to slow to 3.5–4.5% in 1982. An antici-

---

MALAYSIA • Information Highlights

Official Name: Malaysia.
Location: Southeast Asia.
Area: 127,315 sq mi (329 746 km^2).
Population (1982 est.): 14,700,000.
Chief Cities (1975 est.): Kuala Lumpur, the capital, 500,000; George Town, 280,000; Ipoh, 255,000.
Government: *Head of state,* Sultan Ahmad Shah (took office April 1979). *Head of government,* Mahathir Mohamad, prime minister (took office July 1981). *Legislature*—Parliament: Dewan Negara (Senate) and Dewan Ra'ayat (House of Representatives).
Monetary Unit: Ringgit (Malaysian dollar) (2.3373 ringgits equal U.S.$1, March 1982).
Gross National Product (1981 U.S.$): $24,810,000,-000.
Economic Indexes (1981): *Consumer Prices* (1970= 100), *all items,* 194.4; *food,* 209. *Industrial production* (1975=100), 162.
Foreign Trade (1980 U.S.$): *Imports,* $12,139,000,-000; *exports,* $14,345,000,000.

---

pated trade deficit three times greater than in 1981 and a 50% increase in the current accounts deficit forced severe reductions in planned development spending. Countering the slump, the government arranged a $1,100,000,000 loan from foreign and local banks, which almost doubled the debt service ratio.

Despite the plunge in growth, government agencies and local companies virtually completed the Malaysianization of the plantation sector, buying out the major British trading companies. In the fall, Harrisons and Crosfield, a large British plantation, timber, and trading company, returned control of major resource and agricultural companies to Malaysian hands.

Mahathir ordered government buyers to avoid purchasing British goods in response to soaring educational fees levied by the British government on overseas students and to a law aimed at preventing Malaysia from major company takeovers on the British stock exchange.

Foreign Affairs. The candor of Deputy Prime Minister Musa Hitam upset officials of neighboring Thailand as he informed them that their campaigns against the Malaysian Communist Party were ineffective.

K. MULLINER, *Ohio University*

MANITOBA

Despite a serious national recession, Manitoba fared better than many other provinces in 1982. Unemployment was two to three percentage points below the national average, capital spending plans were slightly ahead of 1981, and by late September inflation in the province had fallen to 7.8%.

Economy and Politics. Thanks to a diversified manufacturing base and a record grain crop, Manitoba performed well in several economic areas. Manitoba housing prices showed a small increase, in sharp contrast to other provinces, where price drops of 20–25% were reported. Three projects touted by the previous Conservative administration—a potash mine, an aluminum smelter, and a hydroelectric grid—were shelved because of poor market conditions.

The New Democratic government of Premier Howard Pawley emphasized job-creation projects and refused to endorse a federal plan to limit public-service salary increases to 6%. The government maintained a freeze on Hydro rates and imposed freezes on gasoline taxes and tuition fees. It also imposed a 1.5% payroll tax on business to fund increased spending on education, health, and social services. A $50-million public housing project was announced to stimulate jobs, and the capital construction budget for health-care institutions was doubled. University funding was increased 15.65%, while student aid was raised 35%. Universities were warned not to ask for more than 9.5% in 1983 salary increases. Provincial doctors were granted a 10.3% fee increase, while civil servants were given 13%. Landlords were ordered to hold rent increases to 9% in 1982 and 8% in 1983.

The provincial business bankruptcy rate was almost double that of 1981. A projected government deficit of $334.5 million was being revised substantially upward as the year ended.

In September, Conservative Opposition Leader Sterling Lyon announced he would not lead the party in another election but agreed to stay on for a year until a successor was found.

Arts. The Manitoba Theatre Centre celebrated its 25th season with record season-ticket sales. The Royal Winnipeg Ballet performed in Greece and Cyprus in the summer and in October visited Great Britain, Northern Ireland, West Germany, and Egypt. Artistic Director Arnold Spohr celebrated his 25th season as director and was given a prestigious *Dance Magazine* award.

The Winnipeg Symphony, which was almost $1 million in debt two years earlier, announced that its deficit was down to $265,000 thanks to government and private sponsors. It also announced the appointment of Japanese conductor Kazuhiro Koizumi to replace Maestro Piero Gamba, who resigned in 1980.

General. In July, Princess Anne of Great Britain visited the province and stayed in Winnipeg as a guest of Lt.-Gov. Pearl McGonigal. Mother Teresa of Calcutta also visited the city in the summer to receive the International Award of the St. Boniface Hospital Research Foundation.

Winnipeg became headquarters of Canada's largest investment firm following the August merger of Richardson Securities of Canada Limited and Greenshields Inc.

In October, Winnipeg added $500,000 to its emergency welfare budget. Winnipeg M.P. Lloyd Axworthy vowed to resign if rumors of a major cutback in jobs at Canadian National Railways regional head office came true.

In an attempt to stimulate the economy, the provincial government held an economic summit of business, labor, and political leaders in Portage la Prairie in early November.

PETER CARLYLE-GORDGE
Manitoba Correspondent, "Maclean's" Magazine

MANITOBA • Information Highlights

Area: 251,000 sq mi (650 090 km²).
Population (1981 census): 1,026,241.
Chief Cities (1981 census): Winnipeg, the capital, 564,473; Brandon, 36,242; Thompson, 14,288.
Government (1982): *Chief Officers*—lt. gov. Pearl McGonigal; premier, Howard Pawley (New Democratic Party); atty. gen., Roland Penner. *Legislature*—Legislative Assembly, 57 members.
Education (1982–83): *Enrollment*—elementary and secondary schools, 213,000; postsecondary, 20,-320 students.
Public Finance (1982 fiscal year, est.): *Revenues,* $2,-423,000,000; *expenditures,* $2,674,500,000.
Personal Income (average weekly salary, June 1982): $345.94.
Unemployment Rate (August 1982, seasonally adjusted): 9.3%.
(All monetary figures are in Canadian dollars.)

MARYLAND

Elections dominated Maryland events in 1982.

Politics. Democrat Harry Hughes soundly defeated his Republican challenger, Anne Arundel County Executive Robert Pascal, to win a second term as Maryland's governor. Registered Democrats outnumber Republicans in the state 3-1.

Before the campaign, Hughes parted company with his first-term lieutenant governor, Samuel Bogley. The two had clashed over Bogley's desire for a larger role in the administration and over Hughes' more liberal position on abortion. Bogley accepted the lieutenant-governor candidacy on an opposition Democratic ticket and, when that was defeated in the primary, endorsed Republican Pascal.

Paul S. Sarbanes, another Democrat, retained his seat in the U.S. Senate by defeating Republican challenger Lawrence J. Hogan. The race had a third principal—The National Conservative Political Action Committee, which began campaigning against Sarbanes long before the primary and spent about $645,000 on advertising designed to convince voters that he was "too liberal for Maryland."

In the closest race for the U.S. House of Representatives, Democrat Clarence D. Long narrowly defeated Republican Helen Delich Bentley, a former U.S. maritime commissioner. It was her second attempt to unseat the ten-term congressman. The other seven members of the House of Representatives from Maryland, six Democrats and one Republican, were reelected by substantial margins.

After more than 11 years as president of the Baltimore city council, Walter S. Orlinsky resigned and entered into a plea bargain with federal prosecutors, who accused him of using his office to channel a sludge-hauling contract to a firm that allegedly would have shared its profits with him in subsequent years. He was disbarred and sentenced to six months at the Allenwood federal prison farm.

MARYLAND · Information Highlights

Area: 10,460 sq mi (27 091 km^2).
Population (1980 census): 4,216,975.
Chief Cities (1980 census): Annapolis, the capital, 31,-740; Baltimore, 786,775; Rockville, 43,811.
Government (1982): *Chief Officers*—governor, Harry R. Hughes (D); lt. gov., Samuel W. Bogley III (D). *General Assembly*—Senate, 47 members; House of Delegates, 141 members.
State Finances (fiscal year 1981): *Revenues,* $5,891,-000,000; *expenditures,* $5,788,000,000.
Personal Income (1981): $48,929,000,000; per capita, $11,477.
Labor Force (Aug. 1982): *Nonagricultural wage and salary earners,* 1,662,300; *unemployed,* 190,800 (8.7% of total force).
Education: *Enrollment* (fall 1981)—public elementary schools, 472,288; public secondary, 249,553; colleges and universities (1981–82), 229,936 students. *Public school expenditures* (1980–81), $1,818,494,000 ($2,541 per pupil).

Economy and Business. Despite the weak economy, the city of Baltimore enjoyed continued growth in its redeveloped Inner Harbor area, total renovation of its opera house, and major expansion of its 200-year-old Lexington Market. New buildings for eye research and neuroscience studies at the Johns Hopkins Hospital, a major concert hall, and a museum wing were opened during the year.

Bethlehem Steel Corporation, which recorded its lowest steel production in 40 years and a $209 million loss in the third quarter of 1982, laid off 7,000 of its 17,000 Baltimore-area steel mill employees. A $250 million contract to convert two container ships to Navy transports promised to provide work at Bethlehem's shipbuilding yard. But the company was asking $22 million for its unprofitable ship repair yard, where only 500 of the nearly 1,400 employees were still at work in November. Steelworkers' unions gave free groceries to members who had exhausted their unemployment benefits, using donations from members who were still working.

Westinghouse Corporation, which employs 14,500 persons in Maryland, most of them in defense work, announced plans to hire another 1,500 high-technology workers over the next four years.

General Motors resumed major renovation and expansion work—delayed by poor sales—and moved two new lines of cars to the Baltimore mid-size auto plant. But the additional production brought about the recall of relatively few workers.

Associated Dry Goods Inc. announced it would close its five prestigious Stewart's department stores in the Baltimore area early in 1983 and replace them with an upscale discount chain.

PEGGY CUNNINGHAM
"The News American," Baltimore

MASSACHUSETTS

Electoral contests dominated public events in Massachusetts in 1982.

Elections. The races for governor and U.S. senator attracted strong interest. The crucial events in the gubernatorial contest took place in the September primary. On the Democratic side, former Gov. Michael S. Dukakis defeated incumbent Edward J. King. The Dukakis strategy was to portray Governor King, a conservative Democrat, as a supporter of the economic policies of the Reagan administration, a tactic used successfully by other Democratic candidates. In the Republican primary, John W. Sears won over John Lakian, a political newcomer whose campaign was hurt by stories in the Boston *Globe* that statements and campaign literature gave false information about his background. Dukakis easily defeated Sears in November, winning 60% of the vote.

Peter Main/The Christian Science Monitor

Bay State voters elected a governor, reelected their senior senator, and decided several referendum questions.

U.S. Sen. Edward M. Kennedy (D), facing a surprisingly strong challenge from Raymond Shamie, a wealthy businessman, won 61% of the vote to secure his fourth six-year term. His continued ability to win by a wide margin prompted speculation that he would try again for the presidency in 1984, but Kennedy announced on December 1 that he would not run.

The other notable electoral confrontation took place in the fourth congressional district. New district boundaries were drawn early in the year because population losses forced a reduction of the Massachusetts delegation to the U.S. House from 12 to 11 seats. The new district combined parts of the old 4th, held by Republican incumbent Margaret Heckler and the old 10th district, held by first-term Democrat Barney Frank. Frank, a liberal, began a combative campaign after complaining earlier in the year that the redrawn district boundaries favored Heckler. Heckler, in Congress since January 1967, found herself on the defensive and trailing as Frank pressed her on her support of Reagan administration policies. A series of sharp debates heightened the tension of the contest. Frank emerged the winner with 60% of the vote. In the 10 other U.S. House races, incumbents won. Surprisingly, all incumbents but one in the state legislature won reelection.

One immediate consequence of the election was a further diminishing of Republican Party strength in the state. No Republican has won statewide office since 1972. In the legislature, Republicans lost one Senate and one House seat. In the state Senate, only seven Republicans will face 33 Democrats in 1983. As the year ended, Republican activists had begun what promised to be an extensive reexamination of strategy.

Referendums. The 1982 ballot included an unusually large number of referendum questions, which sparked considerable interest. A proposed amendment to the state constitution to allow state aid to private and parochial schools was resoundingly defeated by a margin of 3 to 2. A proposed constitutional amendment that would allow restoration of the death penalty was approved by a 2-1 margin. Also approved was a proposed statute that would place stringent local reviews and controls on new nuclear power plants or radioactive waste disposal sites. In the continuation of an ongoing battle, voters were asked if they wished to retain a law requiring refundable deposits on beverage bottles. They did, by a margin of almost 70%. Finally, voters strongly supported a nonbinding resolution advocating a mutual nuclear weapons freeze between the United States and the USSR.

Tax Limitation. Attempts to deal with the so-called Proposition 2½, a tax limitation law that went into full effect in 1982, preoccupied local officials during the year.

HARVEY BOULAY, *Boston University*

MASSACHUSETTS · Information Highlights

Area: 8,284 sq mi (21 456 km²).

Population (1980 census): 5,737,037.

Chief Cities (1980 census): Boston, the capital, 562,994; Worcester, 161,799; Springfield, 152,319.

Government (1982): *Chief Officers*—governor, Edward J. King (D); lt. gov., Thomas P. O'Neill III (D). *General Court*—Senate, 40 members, House of Representatives, 160 members.

State Finances (fiscal year 1981): *Revenues,* $7,676,000,000; *expenditures,* $7,986,000,000.

Personal Income (1981): $64,248,000,000; per capita, $11,128.

Labor Force (Aug. 1982): *Nonagricultural wage and salary earners,* 2,603,200; *Unemployed,* 238,400 (7.6% of total force).

Education: *Enrollment* (fall 1981)—public elementary schools, 645,218; public secondary, 351,337; colleges and universities (1981–82), 417,830. *Public school expenditures* (1980–81), $3,038,610,000 ($3,174 per pupil).

MEDICINE AND HEALTH

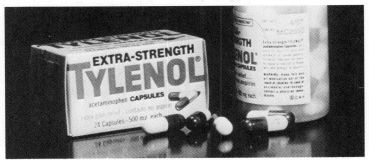

One of the scariest and most bizarre medical stories in many years began in late September 1982, when the first of seven persons in the Chicago area died from cyanide-laced Tylenol capsules. Within a few days of the first reports of the deaths, virtually everyone in the United States had heard the news, as well as urgings by authorities to discontinue use of the capsules. Johnson & Johnson, manufacturers of Tylenol, withdrew 11 million bottles of Tylenol capsules from the market. Meanwhile, dozens of investigators searched for the person who had loaded the capsules with the cyanide.

Other medical warnings were also issued during the year—against certain dietary aids, against giving aspirin to children with chicken pox, and against smoking during pregnancy. There were positive stories, too, in new drugs and technologies that promised better treatment of certain illnesses. But the story that probably affected the greatest number of people was a depressingly familiar one: the increasing cost of medical care.

Medical Costs. In July 1982, the U.S. Department of Health and Human Services reported that Americans spent $287,000,000,000 for health care in 1981. This was an increase of 15.1% from 1980 and represented a record 9.8% of the gross national product. The cost of physicians' services rose 11.7%, prescription drugs rose 12.6%, and hospital rooms rose 17%.

Secretary of Health and Human Services Richard S. Schweiker pointed out that users of health care are isolated from the true costs of the care because two thirds of such costs are financed by such "third parties" as government agencies, private health insurers, philanthropic groups, and industry. As a result, said Schweiker, patients do not have a strong incentive to economize.

Increased medical costs are due to a variety of factors, including governmental policies, the health insurance system, an aging population, labor costs, and the use of expensive technology. Experts agree that overhauling the nation's health care system is essential, but there is little agreement on what steps to take. In October, Schweiker proposed legislation that would establish set fees for each of 467 categories of treatment, and the government would reimburse

hospitals at these rates. Schweiker said that this would force hospitals to work within financial limits. Those that succeed could keep what they don't spend.

A report by the Congressional Office of Technology Assessment indicated that excessive or inappropriate use of medical technologies contributes significantly to the rising costs of medical care. It said that the nation's current policies and processes for evaluating medical technologies are inadequate, and concluded that a more integrated system of assessing medical technologies and spreading information about their safety, effectiveness, costs, and social effects is needed.

In a 4–3 decision, the U.S. Supreme Court ruled that agreements among competing doctors on maximum fees constituted illegal price fixing, even when the agreements were part of an insurance plan that might result in lower costs to patients. The decision meant that prepaid insurance plans known as "foundations for medical care" and sponsored by local medical organizations would have to change their fee-setting procedures.

Heart Implant. On December 2 surgeons at the University of Utah Medical Center in Salt Lake City performed the first implant of a permanent artificial heart in a human patient. The seven-and-a-half-hour procedure, performed by Wil-

U.S. HEALTH EXPENDITURES, 1965-81			
	Total Public & Private Spending*	Spending Per Person	Spending as % of GNP
1965	$ 41.7	$ 211	6.0%
1966	46.1	230	6.1
1967	51.3	254	6.4
1968	58.2	285	6.7
1969	65.6	318	7.0
1970	74.7	358	7.5
1971	83.3	394	7.7
1972	93.5	438	7.9
1973	103.2	478	7.8
1974	116.4	535	8.1
1975	132.7	604	8.6
1976	149.7	674	8.7
1977	169.2	755	8.8
1978	189.3	836	8.8
1979	215.0	938	8.9
1980	249.0	1,075	9.5
1981	286.6	1,225	9.8

* in U.S. billions

Source: U.S. Department of Health and Human Services

liam C. DeVries, chief of cardiovascular surgery, was declared a success. The patient, 61-year-old retired dentist Barney B. Clark from the Seattle area, regained consciousness a few hours later, and his vital signs gradually approached normal levels.

The artificial heart, made largely of polyurethane, was designed by Robert K. Jarvik, a bioengineer at the University of Utah. Jarvik-7, as the device is called, consists of two lower chambers (ventricles), as opposed to the four in a natural heart, and is driven by an air compressor attached to the body by hoses.

The first major complication in Clark's recovery was leakage from air-filled blisters in the lungs, corrected in a second operation only two days after the implant. The artificial heart continued to function well until another 10 days later, when a cracked valve caused the left ventricle to fail. The same team of surgeons went in a third time to replace the whole left side of the Jarvik-7. A medical spokesman said Clark would face "some awfully tough slugging," but the patient survived surgery again, made slow but steady progress, and by mid-January 1983 began looking forward to his release from the hospital.

Medical Technology. The U.S. National Eye Institute reported that an argon laser procedure has proven to be extremely effective in treating senile macular degeneration (SMD), a leading cause of blindness among the elderly. According to Carl Kupfer, director of the institute, the procedure "may save as many as 13,000 older Americans from going blind in the next year." SMD is characterized by the growth of new blood vessels into the macula, the yellowish center of the retina. The macula is needed for central (as opposed to peripheral) vision. As the blood vessels grow into the macula, they leak fluid, which kills the light-sensitive nerve cells. The nonsurgical laser treatment seals off the blood vessels, thereby preventing further leaking. To be effective, the treatment must be applied within the first few weeks after the onset of symptoms.

Fluosol-DA, an artificial blood designed to substitute for red blood cells in supplying the body with oxygen, has shown promising results in early clinical trials. Fluosol-DA, made by the Green Cross Corporation of Japan, is an emulsion of two perfluorocarbons (PFCs). These synthetic organic chemicals are noted for their ability to dissolve large quantities of oxygen. A number of companies are working to develop PFC-based artificial blood. In addition to being able to carry large amounts of oxygen, the ideal product must remain in the body a significant length of time before being exhaled through the lungs. It also must withstand the body's attempts to metabolize the chemicals.

Leland C. Clark, Jr., of the Children's Hospital Research Foundation in Cincinnati, views artificial blood as a way of modifying normal blood for specific purposes. He and others have found that PFC particles can reach parts of the body that are cut off from red blood cells by circulatory blockage. For this reason, partial replacement of normal blood with artificial blood can reduce the area of heart muscle deprived of oxygen by a heart attack, or similarly reduce the area of the brain that is deprived of oxygen by a stroke.

Pediatrics. In June the American Academy of Pediatricians and the U.S. government advised parents and physicians not to give aspirin to children suffering from chicken pox or influenza. The recommendation was based on evidence linking aspirin to Reye's Syndrome, a rare but sometimes fatal children's disease. According to several studies, children given aspirin for certain viral illnesses have an increased risk of developing the syndrome.

A Boston research team headed by John C. Leonidas reported an excessive use of skull X rays among children and infants who sustain falls or other mild blows to the head. A study of 354 such cases X-rayed in a hospital emergency room showed only a 4.2% incidence of skull fracture and no serious complications. Parental pressure, fear of litigation, and physicians' suspicions of injury all affect decisions to use X rays. The report suggested the adoption of clearer criteria for X-ray use, saying this would cut the number of X-rayed pediatric patients by more than half.

Orthopedic researchers reported the successful use of electrical impulses to treat young victims of scoliosis, a disease that causes disfiguring curvature of the spine. The painless impulses are applied to muscles on one side of the spine. They cause contractions that prevent the spine from curving further. With very young children, this treatment may actually reduce the existing curvature.

A study conducted by the U.S. government confirmed that levels of lead in the blood "were consistently higher" among black children than among white children. What was unexpected was that "this difference was found in children and adults, in rural residents and urban dwellers, and in families with low, moderate, and high incomes." The report said: "No clear-cut reason for the consistently higher mean blood lead concentrations . . . can be concluded from the results of this study."

Chicken pox, a usually mild infection, can be deadly in children who have leukemia and are being treated with anticancer drugs. Such drugs suppress the body's normal defenses against infection. A study organized by scientists at Stanford University indicates that interferon, a natural antiviral substance, reduces the severity of chicken pox infections in such children.

Arthritis. In April a new anti-arthritic drug, benoxaprofen, was approved for marketing in the United States by the Food and Drug Administration (FDA). Sold under the brand name

Oraflex, the medication was intended to reduce pain and inflammation caused by the two most common types of the disease, osteoarthritis and rheumatoid arthritis. But in August, the FDA announced that the manufacturer, Eli Lilly & Company, had suspended sales and distribution of Oraflex. The move was prompted by thousands of reports of adverse effects on the gastrointestinal tract, liver, skin, kidneys, eyes, and nails. In addition, some 61 deaths in Great Britain and 11 in the United States were tentatively linked to use of Oraflex.

Heart Disease. A study conducted by a research team from Massachusetts General Hospital in Boston indicated that the popular heart drug digitalis is often ineffective in patients with congestive heart failure, a condition in which blood and fluid back up into the lungs. An estimated two thirds of such patients have normal heart rhythms and no disease of the heart valves. The study found that 40% of this group were not helped by digitalis. Unlike other members of the group, they did not have a symptom called a third heart sound—an extra "dub" after the normal "lub dub" made by the pumping heart. This distinction can be used to determine which patients should receive digitalis.

In May the FDA approved the use of streptokinase in treating heart attacks. Streptokinase is a clot-dissolving enzyme which, when injected into the coronary arteries, liquifies blood clots. Clots in coronary arteries stop the flow of blood to heart muscle cells, resulting in destruction of the cells and, frequently, death of the individual. Streptokinase, administered while a heart attack is actually in progress, can dissolve clots in less than one hour, thereby stopping the heart attack and salvaging heart muscle that would otherwise be destroyed.

AIDS. There has been a marked rise in cases of Acquired Immune Deficiency Syndrome (AIDS), an illness that suppresses the body's immune system. More than one third of the people diagnosed with the disease have died; an average of two new cases are being reported daily. Victims of AIDS are very susceptible to deadly "opportunistic diseases" that strike when the body's defenses are down. Among these is Kaposi's Sarcoma, a rare form of skin cancer. Another is pneumocystis, a parasitic lung infection. Even if patients recover from these diseases, they remain prone to catching other life-threatening diseases.

The cause of AIDS is unknown, though doctors suspect it is an infectious agent. Most AIDS victims have been homosexual men, but the disease also afflicts heterosexual men and women, particularly hemophiliacs who use blood products to combat their illness, intravenous drug abusers, and recent Haitian immigrants to the United States.

Cancer. Researchers at Stanford University reported the first successful use of monoclonal antibodies to treat cancer. The antibodies, which must be custom-made for each cancer patient,

UPI

Dr. Thomas Glonek of the Chicago Osteopathic Hospital looks over a machine which, by use of a powerful magnet, detects chemical changes that cause eye disease.

were given to a man with an advanced case of B-cell lymphoma. The treatment resulted in long-lasting remission of the disease. The researchers stressed the experimental aspects of the treatment; practical use would depend on more testing.

New reports strengthened the evidence that certain human cancers may be caused by retroviruses. These viruses are known to cause leukemia in various animals. A retrovirus called human T-cell leukemia/lymphoma virus (HTLV) has been found in a number of cancer patients around the world. It is not known for certain how the virus is transmitted from person to person.

A study by radiologists at the University of Rochester indicates that X-ray studies can be used to detect extremely small tumors in the colon and rectum that, if allowed to grow, can spread and kill the patient. If caught early and surgically removed, however, the patient's prognosis for survival improves considerably.

A "flying intensive care unit" for transporting patients between hospitals began service in northeastern Ohio.

Smoking. In February, U.S. Surgeon General C. Everett Koop broadened the list of cancers associated with cigarette use. In addition to being "a major cause" of cancers of the lung, esophagus, and larynx, smoking is "a contributory factor" in bladder, kidney, and pancreatic cancers. Koop said that 30% of all cancer deaths and 85% of lung cancer deaths are attributable to smoking. He said that nonsmokers should avoid inhaling cigarette smoke, even though the possible danger of "sidestream smoke" is still a matter of debate.

Richard L. Naeye, a pathologist at Pennsylvania State University, reported that cigarette smoking during pregnancy increases the risk of Sudden Infant Death Syndrome (SIDS) by 50%. SIDS, also known as crib death, occurs when a baby mysteriously stops breathing. Smoking, says Naeye, reduces the flow of oxygen from the mother to the fetus, which in turn damages important structures in the brain stem.

According to Stephen K. Hall of Southern Illinois University, asbestos workers who quit smoking to improve their health may do more harm than good to their lungs. The surprising results of Hall's study may be explained by smokers' physical behavior when they light up. "They take a puff and inhale deeply," said Hall. "They exercise their lungs." When a worker gives up smoking, he no longer exercises. Hall believes the lung reacts like an unused muscle—it quickly turns to fat. Hall recommends that former smokers substitute another form of exercise to strengthen lungs, such as running or swimming.

Diet and Nutrition. Evidence of links between diet and health continues to mount. Ananda S. Prasad of Wayne State University found weight loss and low sperm counts in men marginally deficient in zinc, a nutrient commonly found in meat. The symptoms were produced experimentally by a low-zinc diet and disappeared after the men switched to a high-zinc diet.

David A. McCarron of the Oregon Health Services University reported that people with high blood pressure have reduced blood levels of calcium and a low intake of such calcium-rich dairy foods as cheese, butter, and ice cream.

Several researchers who have conducted studies with laboratory mammals believe that reducing food intake as a person gets older is the key to a longer life span and to less illness in one's later years. They have shown that "undernutrition without malnutrition" can result in a 10 to 20% increase in the life span of mice and rats. Roy Walford, a pathologist at the University of California at Los Angeles, said: "Long-term undernutrition is thus far the only method we know of that retards aging and extends the maximum life span of warm-blooded animals. The finding is undoubtedly applicable to humans because it works in every animal species thus far studied." Immunologist Robert A. Good of the Oklahoma Medical Research Foundation, says that there is "abundant evidence that even genetically determined diseases may be modified or even entirely prevented by limiting the protein, calories, or fat content of the diet."

The hottest diet craze of 1982 was starch-blockers, a protein concentrate derived from kidney beans. The pills purportedly reduce calorie consumption by blocking the digestion of starch, thereby allowing people to eat pasta, potatoes, pizza, and other starchy foods without gaining weight. However, many consumers reported such side effects as cramps, diarrhea, and nausea. In July, the FDA ordered manufacturers to discontinue sales. Two manufacturers filed a suit charging the FDA with exceeding its authority since, they said, starch-blockers are food supplements, not drugs. In October, a federal judge ruling on the suit banned the manufacture and sale of starch-blockers and ordered the destruction of existing stock.

JENNY TESAR
Science and Medical Writer

The Herpes Epidemic

Among the most common and notorious causes of human disease are a family of viruses called herpes. The five types of herpes that infect humans probably cause more illnesses than any other group of viruses. Chicken pox, shingles, mononucleosis, and certain types of cancer all are caused by these infectious organisms. Of particular concern at the present time is the spread of genital herpes, which has reached epidemic proportions. An estimated 20 million Americans have genital herpes, making it the nation's most common venereal disease. Between 300,000 and 500,000 new cases are being reported each year.

The Disease. Genital herpes is usually caused by the virus called herpes simplex type 2 (HSV-2), but it can also be caused by the closely related herpes simplex type 1 (HSV-1), which is better known as the cause of cold sores and fever blisters.

Genital herpes is usually transmitted sexually. The virus passes from a sore on the infected person's body to the noninfected skin and mucous membranes of the second person. Once it has entered the body, the virus multiplies rapidly. The first indication of infection is an itching or tingling sensation. Within 2 to 15 days, blisters appear on the genitals, buttocks, or thighs. Some people also experience fever, nausea, and headaches. A person becomes infected as soon as symptoms appear and remains capable of transmitting the virus until the lesions have healed, which takes about three weeks. Unfortunately, the end of the infection is not the end of the disease. Unlike other viruses, once herpes have invaded a person's body, they remain there for life.

When the body's immunological system brings a herpes attack under control, the virus retreats. In the case of genital herpes, the viruses travel through nerve fibers to the sacral ganglia, clusters of nerve cells near the lower end of the spinal cord, where they enter a latent stage. In some people the latent stage lasts forever. More commonly, the viruses eventually reawaken, travel back down the nerve fibers, and reinfect the genitals. Frequency of recurrence varies from person to person. The average person with herpes has four to six infections a year, but some have episodes as often as twice a month while others go for years without an episode.

Subsequent outbreaks are generally less severe than the initial episode. Symptoms are milder, and lesions are fewer and heal more rapidly. It is unclear what causes the viruses to reactivate, but there are indications that stress, negative emotions, sunlight, menstruation, illness, irritating foods, and immunosuppressive drugs all may trigger recurrences.

To complicate matters further, some herpes sufferers are asymptomatic or barely manifest disease symptoms. These people are unaware of outbreaks and the periods during which they are contagious. Another complication is that scientists know of more than 100,000 different strains of HSV-2, and there are at least as many different strains of HSV-1. A person who already has one strain of the disease may be infected with a different one.

In addition to the physical and psychological pain caused by the disease, genital herpes may have other adverse effects. Under laboratory conditions, the herpes simplex virus can turn normal human cells into cancer cells. Evidence that these viruses actually cause cancer in humans is inconclusive, but several researchers believe that the disease strongly increases the risk of developing cancers of the cervix and vulva.

Pregnant women with an active herpes infection risk passing the disease to their babies during delivery. Neonatal herpes is fatal to about 60% of infected newborns, and in babies who survive there is a very high risk of brain damage or blindness.

Treatment. At present there are no drugs that can cure or prevent genital herpes. Treatment of the disease is limited. In March 1982, the U.S. Food and Drug Administration announced its approval of an ointment form of acyclovir. This is the first drug on the U.S. market to "help manage" genital herpes. If applied during the initial episode, acyclovir alleviates symptoms and speeds healing. It is less effective in treating subsequent outbreaks, however, and it does not reduce the frequency of recurrences.

Herpes researchers are attacking the problems caused by these viruses on a number of fronts. In addition to trying to gather more basic information about the viruses, they are developing and testing vaccines that might be able to prevent the spread of disease. Researchers are also testing drugs that might be able to prevent the viruses from becoming dormant, as well as drugs that would prevent dormant viruses from reactivating.

Herpes sufferers can obtain information and receive emotional support from the Herpes Resource Center in Palo Alto, CA. This organization has some 50 chapters, known as HELP groups, throughout the United States.

JENNY TESAR

Dentistry

Americans will continue to enjoy better dental health during the 1980s, as the incidence of tooth decay will continue to decline among children. Periodontal or gum disease, the leading cause of tooth loss among adults, will also be curtailed as prevention, diagnosis, and treatment methods are constantly being improved. These and other predictions were the findings of a special committee of the American Dental Association (ADA) to study the future of dentistry. The report also predicted that despite the steady growth of alternate dental care delivery modes, such as dental centers in department stores and shopping malls, the traditional private practice system will continue to serve the majority of patients.

During 1982 the ADA also embarked on a national contact effort to enlist the support of organizations that share dentistry's interest in achieving the objectives of the previously adopted Access Program. The goal is to make dental care more accessible to currently underserved population groups, such as senior citizens and the handicapped. Representatives of the ADA and American Society of Geriatric Dentistry kicked off the effort at the National Council of Senior Citizens meeting in Detroit with a presentation on oral health measures for the elderly.

Sealants Cut Cavities. Long-term studies have confirmed that children's back teeth coated with a plastic sealant escape cavities at a rate of up to 90% and in one investigation remained totally decay-free for seven years, Dr. Leon M. Silverstone of the University of Iowa School of Dentistry told the annual meeting of the American Society for the Advancement of Science in Washington, DC. "Dental decay occurs mainly in two surfaces—the smooth and the biting," said Dr. Silverstone. "The biting surface accounts for about half the total amount of decay that occurs over a lifetime. So while fluoride is very effective in reducing decay, it works mainly on the smooth surface. Sealants are designed especially for the biting surfaces to 'wall off' the tooth from decay-causing bacteria," he explained. The technique can save money, too. The cost of sealant application averages $10.23, as opposed to the $21.15 that a control group spent for fillings in a single year, according to one study.

Anorexic Dental Patients. The life-threatening nature of anorexia nervosa often overshadows the dental problems associated with this disorder. Although dental manifestations of self-starvation and nutritional abuse are not fatal and may not become evident until late in the patient's illness, they are the only complications that cannot be reversed, says Dr. Patricia Stege of the Eastman Dental Center in Rochester, NY. A major drawback to providing dental care to the anorexic patient, usually a young woman, lies in her lack of regard for health and appearance until the final or reversal stages of the disorder. By the time she reaches the dental office, permanent damage has usually been done. Anorexic patients often present a variety of serious dental problems, including decay, enamel erosion, gum disease, increased dental sensitivity and pain, diminished chewing ability, and disfiguration of the teeth, explained Dr. Stege. In anorexic patients who depend on vomiting to maintain reduced body weight, extensive erosion and decalcification of enamel is frequently found. "In order to successfully treat these patients," Dr. Stege recommends, "the dentist must understand the ramifications of the illness. Restorative treatment and extensive patient education are necessary to prevent further damage to the mouth."

New Orthodontic Appliances. New orthodontic devices, which fit on the tongue side of the teeth, are being studied at different research centers. A principal advantage of this metalwork is that it may ease the trauma of conventional braces. On the other hand, the new appliances may prolong treatment and, since they may require more of the orthodontist's time, possibly will increase the cost of treatment. Because study results are still premature, the American Association of Orthodontists has not commented on the technique.

TMJ. Temporomandibular joint disorder (TMJ) is an often overlooked condition which affects the hinge connecting the jaw to the skull. Clinical studies have linked TMJ to an array of nagging physical problems, including pain in the jaw, head, neck, ears, and shoulders, as well as blurred vision, dizziness, and sinus trouble. As many as 60 million Americans, or 26% of the population, may have some form of TMJ. "While TMJ itself may not be a new disease, study of the syndrome is a relatively new area of research," 1982 ADA President Robert Griffiths told a special TMJ conference in Chicago.

Arthritis, psychological stress, excessive muscle tension, malocclusion (bad bite), and clenching or grinding of the teeth are considered possible causes of TMJ. Treatments range from drug therapy, mainly relaxants and tranquillizers, to surgery. The latter is a "last resort" and is effective only with certain forms of the disorder. TMJ studies have been intensified to learn more about causes and treatment.

Chocolate Research. Recent studies indicate that chocolate may be less apt to promote cavities than many people think. Dr. Paul F. DePaola of the Forsyth Dental Center told the 60th general session of the International Association for Dental Research in New Orleans that chocolate may actually offset the acid-producing effects of sugar in milk chocolate, the form in which most chocolate is consumed in the United States.

LOU JOSEPH
Senior Science Writer
Hill and Knowlton

Mental Health

In June 1982, a federal district court jury in Washington, DC, found John W. Hinckley, Jr., "not guilty by reason of insanity" in the 1981 shooting of President Reagan and three other persons. The eight-week trial, which revolved around the testimony of expert psychiatric witnesses called by both the defense and the prosecution, sparked persistent and complex questions about the insanity defense and the role of psychiatric testimony in criminal jurisprudence. (*See* special report, page 307.)

Neuroscience. The chemical and structural properties of the brain remained one of the hottest areas of biomedical research in 1982. At the National Institute of Mental Health (NIMH), scientists Candace Pert and Miles Herkenham developed a new method for mapping brain cell receptor sites—spots where neurotransmitters (the brain's chemical messengers) and drugs that mimic them attach to cells to inhibit or enhance neuronal communication. Understanding where and how receptors work will complement other advances in brain chemistry and lead to the development of safer and more precisely acting medications for mental disorders.

In Sweden, clinical researchers attempted the first human brain tissue transplant to reduce the crippling effects of Parkinson's disease, which stems from a deficiency of the neurotransmitter dopamine. The surgery—though its outcome is yet inconclusive—follows basic research in which implantation of dopamine-manufacturing tissue into animal brains successfully diminished artificially induced Parkinson-like symptoms.

Clinical Research. Recent studies of the neurotransmitter serotonin suggest that diminished levels of a serotonin metabolite or decreased serotonin receptor functioning may predispose some people to suicide. Low serotonin levels have also been found in persons suffering from alcoholism and schizophrenia, as well as in some highly aggressive and impulsive individuals. Though suicide is often associated with depression, the new finding suggests that "suicidal behavior is not necessarily linked to a particular mental disorder, but may be linked to other factors, such as low serotonergic functioning," according to NIMH psychiatrist Gerald Brown. The finding indicates a possible method for identifying suicide-prone persons and suggests the possibility of a biological approach to suicide prevention. Research is already underway to study the effectiveness of a combined drug and diet treatment in maintaining increased brain serotonin levels.

In "photobiological" studies of depression, scientists have found that either natural or high-intensity, full-spectrum fluorescent light may have therapeutic potential in treating affective disorders with distinct seasonal cycles. Drs. Thomas Wehr and Norman Rosenthal of NIMH based their research on earlier findings that, in contrast to the majority of manic-depressive patients whose depressive episodes peak in the spring, there exists a subgroup of patients who suffer "winter depression." This finding, in addition to the fact that the light-sensitive, pineal gland hormone melatonin—the basis of various seasonally occurring biological cycles—can be suppressed by light, prompted the research by Wehr and Rosenthal.

Television and Behavior. A comprehensive review of research conducted over the past decade supports and strengthens the 1972 finding of the U.S. surgeon general that violence on television leads to aggressive behavior by some children and teenagers who watch the programs. *Television and Behavior: Ten Years of Scientific Progress and Implications,* made public by the NIMH in May 1982, also notes the potential of TV as a positive social agent: "the evidence is persuasive—children can learn to be altruistic, friendly, and self-controlled by looking at television programs depicting such behavior patterns," the report states. The studies reviewed in the report were conducted in the United States and other countries by a variety of public and privately funded research organizations.

HERBERT PARDES
Director
National Institute of Mental Health

David Pearl headed a review by the NIMH of research on TV violence and aggressive behavior in children.

Courtesy, Dept. of Health and Human Services

METEOROLOGY

With the aid of new technology and innovative procedures, meteorologists continued to gain new understandings of atmospheric conditions and weather systems.

Observation Systems. Moored ocean buoys, which collect valuable data useful in tracking oceanic storms, beam their data to a geostationary satellite for relay to a central weather station. A new method of data transmission, using underwater sound signals, has now been successfully tested. Also recently developed is a new airborne Doppler radar system; a color radar screen in the plane's cockpit enables the pilot to keep better track of oncoming weather. Finally, a demonstration test of the controversial Automation of Field Operations and Services (AFOS) system successfully delivered weather guidance and warnings to local offices of the U.S. National Weather Service.

Satellite Meteorology. NASA's Solar Maximum satellite made it possible for scientists to follow daily changes in solar energy flux; the changes were generally very small, approximately one part in two thousand. Satellite infrared photography showed that cloud systems rarely persist more than two days; huge thunderstorm clusters seem to be a predominant feature in the tropics. TIROS-N satellite measurements demonstrated that the size of snow grains, and their water equivalents, can be determined from space.

Ozone Layer. Improved models of stratospheric chemistry resulted in a notable reduction in estimates of ozone destruction by man-made agents. No appreciable loss is anticipated during the current century, and with current chlorine emission rates, ozone depletion of no more than 5 to 9% is expected by the end of the 21st century. A NASA satellite launched in late 1981 now continuously observes processes leading to the formation and destruction of ozone.

Severe Storms. Doppler radar provided a detailed look inside an Oklahoma tornado. With winds of 195 mph (314 km/h), the 2,600-ft- (800-m-) wide funnel picked up cattle, farm machinery, and trucks and hurled them at 43 mph (70 km/h). Experimenters at the Denver airport are investigating intense downward bursts in thunderstorms, often called "wind shear," that have caused several aviation accidents.

Weather Patterns and Prediction. Weather anomalies, it is generally recognized, show global coherence. Their first manifestation is often a sea surface temperature anomaly over large areas of the equatorial Pacific. These gradually migrate, changing wind and sea current distributions as they move. Tropical rain systems shift, causing more rain in the eastern and central Pacific, less rain in Indonesia, and a weakening of the Asiatic winter monsoon. Studies of these patterns should yield improved forecasting of aberrant weather. Satellite measurements of rainfall rate reveal features of hurricane energetics, leading to improved predictions. Worldwide weather data collected during the first global atmospheric research program enabled the European Center for Medium Range Weather Forecasts to produce useful forecasts for periods of up to 10 days.

Cloud Physics. Precipitation enhancement studies still yield contradictory results. A recent repetition of earlier, successful experiments with cumulus seeding in Florida failed to produce statistically significant results. Israeli scientists, however, repeated randomized cloud seeding trials in the Lake Kinneret watershed and succeeded in increasing precipitation by 13 to 18%. The alcohol metaldehyde proved to be an effective cloud seeding agent, and an as yet unidentified bacterium was discovered to be an effective freezing nucleus.

Research on acid precipitation made slow progress. Oxides of sulfur and nitrogen from combustion processes are causing most of the acidity, but acid rain is also caused by volcanic exhalations and sea spray. Methane is a precursor of tropospheric ozone and carbon dioxide and of stratospheric water vapor. Scientists recently discovered that wood-eating termites produce about half the methane in the earth's atmosphere.

Turbidity. Atmospheric haze was much in the news in 1982. A widespread volcanic dust veil in the stratosphere circled the earth at an altitude of 11 to 14 mi (18 to 23 km). It was partly attributable to an eruption of El Chichon volcano in Mexico and perhaps partly due to an eruption of Mount Nyamaragira in Zaire. Research indicates that extensive dust veils many interrupt enough solar energy to cool the earth by a fraction of a degree in the years following an eruption. In August, the worst mass of wind-blown Sahara dust in a decade reached Florida, where it settled quickly. The haze that gave the Blue Ridge Mountains their name was found to be 75% man-made and 25% natural.

Turbulence. Turbulence remains one of the main hazards to aircraft. Ground-based radar has been used to detect gravity-wave phenomena related to wind shear layers containing clear air turbulence (CAT). Infrared sensors in aircraft can now warn pilots several minutes before impending encounters with CAT.

Lightning. Scientists also continue to study the menace of lightning. In the Midwest, 44% of all lightning strokes are from cloud to ground. In thunderstorms they average about one every five seconds and occur mostly where cloud updrafts, which create the electrical potential, are most intense. Particles of ice in the updrafts can be detected from the ground, giving ample warning. Measurement of global lightning frequency by new satellite sensors revealed a flash rate of 40 to 120 per second.

H. E. LANDSBERG and O. E. THOMPSON
University of Maryland

METEOROLOGY/SPECIAL REPORT

The Weather Year

December 1981–February 1982. The winter of 1982 was cold, snowy, and windy in the United States. More than 100 minimum temperature records were broken, and many new snowfall records were set. Average temperatures were 4 to 6°F (2 to 3°C) below expected values over much of the eastern half of the nation. Warmer than average temperature departures occurred in the central and southern intermountain region and in southern Florida. Precipitation was abundant in the Southeast and the northern Rockies, while dryness persisted in the central and southern Great Plains states.

In early December the Pacific Northwest was battered by rainstorms which triggered flooding and mudslides. Monthly precipitation was from 200 to 500% above average in parts of Oregon and northern California. A succession of rainstorms pounded the West Coast during the first week of January. Marin County, CA, recorded 12 inches (30 cm) of rain in a 24-hour period. Homes, roadways, and bridges were swept away in mudslides that took more than 30 lives and caused $300 million in damage. By mid-month severe blizzard conditions and record cold had affected the Upper Mississippi Valley and Great Lake states. Chicago shattered a 109-year record when it registered a low temperature of −26°F (−32°C) on December 10. A severe ice and snowstorm hit the Southeast, and a hard freeze in Florida damaged more than three quarters of the state's citrus crop. Atlanta recorded a temperature of −5°F (−2°C), the lowest in the century. At one point in January, every state except Hawaii reported snow cover.

Above-average rainfall continued in February along the northern Pacific Coast, causing flooding in parts of Washington and Oregon. Another major snowstorm pummeled the Midwest early in the month, with St. Louis receiving 22 inches (56 cm) in a two-day period. A warming trend began at mid-month, and the melting snow and ice, coupled with rainfall, caused local flooding in many areas. An intense Atlantic storm February 13–14 produced high seas and wind gusts of 110 mph (177 km/h) in the maritime provinces of Canada.

Winter was fierce in northern Europe and Great Britain, with many stations recording their coldest-ever December. Exceptional snowfalls occurred in England and France in December and January; drifts up to 15 ft (4.6 m) were common. Severe drought conditions continued throughout the winter in Sri Lanka, where crop prospects were poor. Typhoon Lee struck the Philippines on Christmas Day, leaving 137 dead and 500,000 homeless; it was the islands' 23rd typhoon of the season.

March–May. Warm temperatures combined with heavy rainfall in early spring caused quick thawing of the snowpack, which in turn caused flooding in the Ohio Valley, Great Lakes region, and parts of eastern Canada. Fort Wayne, IN, was hardest hit, with flooding of the St. Joseph, St. Mary, and Maumee rivers requiring the evacuation of 9,000 people during the week of March 14–22. In late March a freeze in the Southeast caused extensive damage to the peach and apple crops in the Carolinas and Georgia. Snows of up to 20 inches (51 cm) in the Sierra Nevada triggered avalanches which killed seven persons.

UPI

Tokyo residents wade in waist-high waters as the nearby Kanda River overflowed its banks after Typhoon Judy struck central Japan in September.

Wide World

Hurricane Iwa left Hawaii in shambles in late November.

A spring blizzard battered the Great Lakes and Northeast in early April. Satellite-estimated snow cover for April 5–11 was a record 6.3 million sq mi (16.4 million km²).

May was a stormy month in the Midwest, with a record 365 tornadoes reported, well beyond the previous high of 275, set in May 1965. Severe weather destroyed $300 million worth of property and claimed 19 lives.

China suffered a wet spring; heavy rains from mid-April to mid-May in Guangdong and Guangxi provinces left 385 dead, 36,000 buildings destroyed, and more than 800,000 people homeless. On March 2 the Tonga Islands in the southwest Pacific were devastated by Typhoon Isaac; half the total population of 100,000 was left homeless, and fatalities were high. A tropical disturbance stalled over Honduras and Nicaragua during the last week of May, dropping 12.8 inches (32.5 cm) of rain; severe flooding resulted, with 226 killed, 80,000 homeless, and extensive damage to crops and livestock. Continued drought in the southern African nations of Mozambique, Namibia, South Africa, and Zimbabwe resulted in reduced crop yields.

June–August. Favorable summer weather in the United States helped bring bumper crops of wheat, corn, and soybeans. Seasonal temperatures were below average in the northeastern and north central states and slightly above average in the Rocky Mountain region.

Rains of 7 to 10 inches (18 to 25 cm) in the first week of June caused severe flooding in parts of Connecticut, Massachusetts, and Rhode Island. During the last three weeks of June, severe thunderstorms accompanied by hail destroyed 2 million acres (800 000 ha) of Texas cotton, representing about 10% of the nation's yield. In the last week of August, cold Canadian air settled over the north central United States, producing numerous record low temperatures.

Alberto, an early season hurricane, dumped more than 12 inches (30 cm) of rain on western Cuba on June 3, causing 24 deaths. In Indonesia flooding and mudslides caused by heavy rains left 225 dead and more than 3,000 homeless. On June 25 a fierce winter storm in Brazil caused 40 deaths and 500 injuries; winds of up to 90 mph (145 km/h) were reported, causing damage to the coffee crop. From mid-July to mid-August, Japan and parts of China were battered by torrential rains from slowly moving storms propagating along a stationary polar front. More than 300 persons were killed and 50,000 left homeless in Japan, where flooding was reported to be the worst in more than a quarter century. In contrast, Australia suffered its worst drought in 25 years, and unseasonably dry and warm weather damaged grains in the eastern USSR.

September–November. Autumn precipitation was above average along the California coast and parts of the Pacific Northwest and below average in the Mid-Atlantic states. Temperatures were generally near seasonal averages.

In late September, rains from a tropical storm caused extensive damage to the raisin, grape, and tomato crops in California. In late October, high winds associated with a strong Atlantic coastal storm caused beach erosion from North Carolina to New Jersey. Record warmth blanketed the eastern half of the nation in late October and early November. An early winter storm swept into southern California during the first week of November, bringing torrential rains, marble-sized hail, and a rare phenomenon for California—three small tornadoes. Mudslides damaged homes and highways. The storm left several feet of snow in the Sierras. After re-forming over the Colorado Plateau, the storm swept into the Upper Midwest, bringing up to 15 inches (38 cm) of snow to parts of the Dakotas, Minnesota, and Wisconsin.

England, France, and parts of Spain recorded above-average rainfall at mid-season. Flooding in nothern Spain, October 20–22, took 113 lives. Dry weather prevailed in East Germany and Poland. Heavy rains from a developing tropical storm caused death and destruction in El Salvador and Guatemala in late September. Australia continued to suffer a severe drought, which nearly devastated the country's wheat crop. India also faced crop shortfalls, as the Southwest Monsoon retreated several weeks early. Continued dry weather affected much of the Sahel and East Africa, with 1983 crop prospects especially poor in parts of Chad and Egypt.

IDA HAKKARINEN

MEXICO

UPI

Miguel de la Madrid, Mexico's new president, is joined by his family for an official photo.

Mexico elected a new president in 1982, and he inherited one of the most serious crises in the nation's history. The peso was devalued three times during the year, and currency controls were established for the first time. In a dramatic move, outgoing President José López Portillo nationalized the domestic, private banks, an act prompted by the massive flight of capital from the country and the dangerous condition of the Mexican economy.

Elections. Elections held on July 4, 1982, produced few surprises. Miguel de la Madrid Hurtado, candidate of the government-backed Institutional Revolutionary Party, won the presidency with 71% of the votes cast, while Pablo Emilio Madero of the National Action Party ran second with 16.5%. The first female presidential candidate in Mexican history, Rosario Ibarra de Piedra of the Revolutionary Workers' Party, ran fourth but received only 2% of the vote. Countering recent trends, 71% of the registered voters went to the polls.

President de la Madrid, inaugurated on December 1, promised revolutionary nationalism, economic equality, full democracy, administrative decentralization, and moral renovation of the nation. (*See also* BIOGRAPHY.)

In congressional elections, also held on July 4, the government party took all 64 senatorial seats and all but one of the 300 federal deputy seats elected by district. The National Action Party, with 18% of the vote, was the big winner among the opposition parties, taking the remaining single-district federal deputy seat, the majority of the at-large federal deputy seats, and

some local offices in the state of Sonora. The Unified Socialist Party, which includes the former Communist Party, ran third but got only 4.4% of the vote. The new Revolutionary Workers' Party won permanent registration, but the Social Democratic and the Authentic Mexican Revolutionary parties lost their registrations by failing to obtain at least 1.5% of the vote. The remainder of the eight opposition parties split the other 6.6% of the vote.

Corruption. Government corruption dominated political conversation during much of the year as many persons saw corruption as a possible cause of the nation's economic difficulties. There were accusations that politicians had taken billions from the public purse and put the money to private use in Mexico, the United States, and Europe. Even President López Portillo was implicated. He was alleged to have participated, building a multimillion-dollar private housing complex in Mexico City and an extravagant home in California.

Economic Problems. The economic recession in the United States caught up with Mexico, which previously had countered international trends by increasing its gross domestic product an average of 7% per year. As interest rates rose, money supplies contracted, inventories grew, and unemployment increased in the United States, that country purchased less from Mexico and charged more for its exports. As the third-largest trading partner of the United States, Mexico suffered. For more than a year, income from petroleum, silver, copper, coffee, cotton, and other Mexican exports declined. In 1982, Mexico projected $27,000,000,000 in oil revenues but received only $14,000,000,000. Tourism income fell by $900 million. The staggering budget deficit programmed by Washington and the tight money policies of the Federal Reserve System drove interest rates up and increased Mexico's debt burden by some $2,500,000,000 in a single year.

The Mexican government, for its part, chose an economic development strategy that increased its exposure to the ills of the U.S. economy. It borrowed extensively from U.S. sources to finance investments in industry and agriculture, social services, and debt payments. The projected national budget for 1982 called for 34% of government revenues to come from borrowing. Mexico hoped that its income from tourism and exports, particularly petroleum, would enable it to service its debt, and that Mexico's importance as an oil power would force lenders to roll over the debt. The nation's foreign debt, 80% of which is owed by the government, grew by $11,000,000,000 during the first nine months of 1982, eventually totaling approximately $81,-000,000,000.

Mexico's strategy did not quite work. The U.S. government raised the cost of dollars to slow down its own inflation rate and inflated the Mexican economy in the process. Interest charges, which had been $2,600,000,000 in 1978, skyrocketed in 1981 to $8,200,000,000 and continued to climb in 1982. In January, economists were predicting a 60% inflation rate; by year's end, the rate was at least 100%.

Faced with an uncertain economy, private citizens switched from pesos to dollars and transferred some of their money to the United States. By July, $12,000,000,000 was held in dollar accounts in Mexican banks, some $14,000,000,000 had been deposited in U.S. bank accounts, and another $25,000,000,000 had been invested in Mexican real estate.

To counter this capital flight and to promote exports, the government three times devalued the peso. On February 17, the Banco de Mexico allowed the peso to float on the international money exchange, and the peso dropped 43% in value. On August 5, the peso was again devalued, bringing the year's total devaluation to 67%. Trading in foreign exchange was temporarily halted. A two-tier official exchange rate was created. For the payment of international debts and essential imports, the new rate was 49 to the dollar, and for nonessential imports the rate was 70. On December 20 the peso was floated again, resulting in a further 53% devaluation.

The government took several other steps to deal with the crisis. Spending was cut by 8%, and the expensive nuclear energy program was suspended. Prices were frozen on an additional 50 consumer items in February, and 10–30% wage increases were given. In August, income taxes were lowered, interest on savings accounts was increased, and prices on basic foods, subsidized by the government, were raised. Mexico obtained a $1,000,000,000 advance payment on oil sales to the United States, and a nearly $1,-000,000,000 credit from the Commodity Credit Corporation. In September the government suspended repayment on its short- and medium-term debts to 115 international banks until 1983. Finally, in November, the government agreed with the International Monetary Fund to impose an austerity program in exchange for a loan of $3,840,000,000 over three years.

Bank Nationalization. President López Portillo reorganized the Mexican financial system on September 1. He nationalized all private Mexican banks, converted the Banco de Mexico into a decentralized government agency, imposed strict currency controls, and made the peso the only legal tender in the country. He justified these dramatic steps by accusing speculators and banks of having looted the country and brought the nation close to financial collapse. Critics questioned the constitutionality of the nationalization move, but the government-dominated communications media and labor unions lauded the measure. The government now held more than 80% of the country's economic resources.

Foreign Relations. President López Portillo angered Washington in February by criticizing U.S. policy in Central America and offering Mexican aid in bringing about a negotiated settlement to the civil war in El Salvador and to resolve the differences between Nicaragua and the United States. He called for promises that the United States would not use force against Nicaragua. Successful elections in El Salvador subsequently reduced Mexico's concern for that nation's stability.

In spite of policy disagreements, the United States rushed to Mexico's aid in August because it was dependent on a healthy Mexico. The nine largest banks in the United States had loaned the equivalent of 40% of their capital and reserves to Mexico, and Washington could not afford to have Mexico default on its debt payments.

DONALD J. MABRY
Mississippi State University

MEXICO · Information Highlights

Official Name: The United Mexican States.
Location: Southern North America.
Area: 761,602 sq mi (1 972 549 km²).
Population (1980 census): 67,405,700.
Chief Cities (1980 census): Mexico City, the capital, 9,377,300; (1979 est.): Guadalajara, 1,906,145; Monterrey, 1,064,629.
Government: *Head of state and government,* Miguel de la Madrid Hurtado, president (took office Dec. 1982). *Legislature*—Congress: Senate and Chamber of Deputies.
Monetary Unit: Peso (95 pesos equal U.S.$, Dec. 26, 1982).
Gross National Product (1981 U.S.$): $229,040,000,-000.
Economic Indexes (1981): *Consumer Prices* (1970= 100), *all items,* 535.2; *food,* 533.6. *Industrial production* (Nov. 1981, 1975=100), 148.
Foreign Trade (1980 U.S.$): *Imports,* $19,517,000,-000; *exports,* $15,308,000,000.

MICHIGAN

Michigan voters, faced with the worst economic recession in 50 years, turned decisively to Democrats in the November elections. State services were slashed drastically. The auto industry struggled back to profitability, but on a relatively small scale.

Elections. U.S. Rep. James J. Blanchard, campaigning on a platform of "jobs, jobs, and jobs," was elected governor, the first Democrat in the office in 20 years. Voters gave him a majority of Democrats in both the state House and Senate. It was the first time since 1938 that Democrats controlled both houses as well as the governor's office. U.S. Sen. Donald W. Riegle, Jr., was elected to another six-year term, and the state's congressional delegation remained heavily Democratic.

The election underscored the collapse of the GOP in Michigan. Gov. William G. Milliken, who did not seek reelection after holding office for 14 years, backed Lt. Gov. James Brickley as his successor. But the moderate Brickley was beaten in the primary by Farmington Hills insurance executive Richard Headlee, whose subsequent defeat ended hopes for a more conservative party in the state.

Voters adopted two ballot proposals designed to curb automatic increases in utility rates. They rejected a proposal to replace with an elected body the Public Service Commission, currently appointed by the governor to regulate utilities. Voters in Wayne County (which includes Detroit) elected Sheriff William Lucas to the newly created office of county executive. The county executive replaced a governmental apparatus in which administrative power was exercised by a three-member board of auditors. The new form of government was approved by voters in 1981 as a way to make county government more responsive to residents.

Economy. The state's poor economy and declining tax revenues prompted Governor Milli-

Michigan's Employment Security Commission issued a brochure to benefit the state's 637,000 unemployed.

ken and the legislature to cut state services repeatedly. Measures to maintain a balanced budget included a six-month increase in the state income tax from 4.6% to 5.6%. Despite these efforts, Moody's Investors Service dropped Michigan's credit rating to the lowest of any state, citing "persistent and severe recession conditions."

The auto industry regained a measure of profitability. Combined results from the first nine months of the year showed an overall profit of $457.5 million, compared with a loss of $89.4 million for the 1981 period. But auto sales remained sluggish, and Volkswagen of America canceled plans to open a plant in the Detroit suburb of Sterling Heights.

General Motors and Ford Motor Company negotiated two-and-a-half-year cost-cutting contracts with the United Automobile Workers. The agreements included wage concessions in return for profit sharing. Chrysler Corporation employees rejected a proposed contract but voted not to strike until after Jan. 1, 1983.

Unemployment in Michigan remained high. The U.S. Labor Department reported 637,000 people out of work in October—14.9% of the state's labor force. Adjusted for seasonal employment trends, the jobless rate stood at a postwar high of 16.1%.

The J. L. Hudson Company, Detroit's largest department store, announced it would close its downtown store after the Christmas holidays. The firm, founded in 1881, had pioneered in the development of shopping malls in Detroit suburbs.

CHARLES THEISEN, *"The Detroit News"*

MICHIGAN · Information Highlights

Area: 58,527 sq mi (151 585 km²).

Population (1980 census): 9,262,078.

Chief Cities (1980 census): Lansing, the capital, 130,-414; Detroit, 1,203,339; Grand Rapids, 181,843; Warren, 161,134; Flint, 159,611; Sterling Heights, 108,999.

Government (1982): *Chief Officers*—governor, William G. Milliken (R); lt. gov., James H. Brickley (R). *Legislature*—Senate, 38 members; House of Representatives, 110 members.

State Finances (fiscal year 1981): *Revenues,* $15,-035,000,000; *expenditures,* $13,295,000,000.

Personal Income (1981): $99,314,000,000; per capita, $10,790.

Labor Force (Aug. 1982): *Nonagricultural wage and salary earners,* 3,190,600; *unemployed* (Oct. 1982), 637,000 (14.9% of total force).

Education: *Enrollment* (fall 1981)—public elementary schools, 1,178,255; public secondary, 591,305; colleges and universities (1981–82), 513,033 students. *Public school expenditures* (1980–81), $4,730,954,000 ($2,461 per pupil).

MICROBIOLOGY

The year 1982 was an eventful one for microbiologists. Successful medical use was made of recombinant-DNA products and of a bacterial toxin to correct an eye defect. The rise of antibiotic-resistant strains of disease-producing bacteria was disturbing, but the development of a microbial high-protein feed for animals held great promise. Also of interest was the discovery of higher-organism genes in some bacterial species and the widespread presence of hormones in microorganisms.

Recombinant-DNA Products. Through recombinant-DNA formation, also known as gene splicing, it has been possible to transfer human genes into bacteria and yeasts and to have these organisms produce the human chemical compounds specified by the transferred genes. In one such procedure, the human growth-hormone gene was transferred to the bacterium *Escherichia coli.* A deficiency of this hormone results in stunted growth, to a maximum of about 4 ft (1.21 m). Previously, hormone for the treatment of children with a deficiency was available only from the pituitaries of cadavers. Tests begun in 1982 demonstrated that the bacterially produced hormone is as effective in promoting growth as that obtained from pituitary glands. It offers great promise for the 15,000 children in the United States who suffer from this deficiency.

Another type of gene splicing involves the transfer of a number of genes, each responsible for the formation of a different type of interferon, into bacteria and yeasts. The interferon obtained from these organisms has been tested as an anticancer treatment and has been found to be effective in reducing the size of a tumor in about 12% of the cases.

Medical Use of a Bacterial Toxin. The anaerobe *Clostridium botulinum* produces a toxin that is responsible for a very lethal (50–100%) form of food poisoning. The toxin acts at the neuromuscular junction, preventing nerve stimuli from reaching the muscles. This results in a prolonged relaxation of body muscles, leading in most cases to death. Alan Scott of the Smith-Kettlewell Institute of Visual Sciences in San Francisco has developed a procedure to correct strabismus (crossed eyes) by using minute amounts of the toxin. It is injected into the muscle that makes the eye crossed, causing the muscle to relax. The muscle on the other side of the eye automatically pulls the eye into its proper position. Time will tell whether such cure is temporary or permanent and whether it will replace the 60,000 operations for strabismus performed each year in the United States.

Antibiotic Resistance. Bacterial infections are the fifth leading cause of death in the United States today. Pharmaceutical companies are constantly developing new antibiotics against disease-causing organisms, but resistant bacterial strains are continually making their appearance.

One example is a new strain of gonorrhea-causing bacteria that is resistant to penicillin. In this case, a newly developed antibiotic, called spectinomycin, appears to be effective against the penicillin-resistant organisms. A less promising situation involves the bacterium *Pseudomonas aeruginosa,* the causative agent of respiratory failure that kills nine out of ten patients afflicted with cystic fibrosis. These organisms avoid being killed by pumping the antibiotics out of themselves.

Gene Acquisition. It is well known that bacteria can acquire genes from one another. It has also been found that some bacteria have genes that could only have been acquired from higher organisms. One example of the latter is the gene for the enzyme *superoxide dismutase,* which protects cells against some of the effects of radiation and high levels of oxygen. In organisms whose cells contain nuclei (eukaryotes), the enzyme contains copper and zinc. In those whose cells do not have nuclei (prokaryotes), such as bacteria and blue-green algae, the enzyme contains iron. However, the bacterial species *Photobacter leiognathi,* a symbiont of the ponyfish, was found to have copper and zinc in its superoxide dismutase. It is assumed that the eukaryotic form of the gene was transferred to the bacterial species from the ponyfish sometime early in their association. Howard Steinman of the Albert Einstein College of Medicine in New York recently discovered that a free-living bacterium, *Caulobacter crescentus,* also has copper and zinc in this enzyme. Whether the eukaryotic form of the gene was obtained during some ancient symbiotic relationship or through some other mechanism remains to be determined.

Hormones in Bacteria. Hormones are usually thought of as the products of highly specialized endocrine glands of multicellular organisms. Certain hormones, however, such as insulin, ACTH, somatostatin, and calcitonin are found in protozoa, fungi and bacteria. What are hormones doing in unicellular organisms? Jesse Roth of the National Institutes of Health speculates that all hormones were originally substances that variously stimulated cell growth, cell migration and fusion, and biochemical reactions between cells. These are still their functions, he suggests, in unicellular organisms.

Microbial High-Protein Feed. A bacterial species, *Methylophilus methylotrophus,* that can be used as feed for pigs, poultry, and cattle has been discovered. The bacteria are grown in huge fermenters, separated out, dried, and sold. The product is called *pruteen* and contains more than 70% protein. One pruteen plant is expected to be able to produce about 50,000 T (45 360 t) of animal feed per year, freeing for human consumption the corn production of about 20,000 acres (8 000 ha) of cultivated land.

LOUIS LEVINE
Department of Biology
City College of New York

MIDDLE EAST

Rancinan/Sygma

French troops, part of a multinational force, arrive in war-torn Lebanon on August 21.

In the Middle East there were two areas of conflict that all but monopolized attention in 1982. These were Lebanon and the Iraqi-Iranian theater of war. In the latter case, a conflict that had begun in September 1980 continued into its third year. In Lebanon, a complicated and deteriorating situation passed into an entirely new phase at the beginning of June with the Israeli incursion and subsequent occupation of about one third of the country.

Conflict in Lebanon. The course of the year in Lebanon afforded a kaleidoscope of rapidly changing and significant events. It also produced a high degree of international involvement aimed at stabilizing the country and eliminating or reducing violence.

The purpose of the Israeli incursion on June 6 quickly proved to be more than the establishment of a security zone in the south, but rather a determined attempt—which ultimately proved successful—to root the PLO out of the entire country. There was a long period (June 18 to September 15) during which the Israelis occupied east Beirut but did not actually enter west Beirut. Negotiations on the PLO pullout took up almost all of July and August. The evacuation, which began by sea on August 21 and was completed by September 1, resulted in the PLO leadership going to Tunisia and their followers being dispersed to a variety of other Arab destinations. Some PLO members in arms, however, managed to remain in northern Lebanon under Syrian protection.

The crowded month of September saw the assassination of president-elect Bashir Gemayel and the Israeli move into west Beirut the next day; the appalling massacre of several hundred Palestinians in the Sabra and Shatila refugee camps by Phalangist militiamen; and the election to the presidency of Amin Gemayel, brother of the slain president-elect. Also, a strong international interest in the stability of Lebanon was manifested by the return, September 27–29, of French, Italian, and U.S. peacekeeping forces who had left the country only a few weeks before. Their original mission had been the short-lived one of monitoring the PLO departure. Their renewed stay was likely to prove considerably longer. It continued to the end of the year, and no termination was yet in prospect. Their presence in the Beirut area had a paradoxical aspect, for it appeared that the first step toward the highly desired end of removing foreign troops from Lebanese soil was to bring more foreign troops in.

Talks between Israel and Lebanon aimed at removing foreign troops from the latter were finally launched under U.S. sponsorship on December 28—after long delays, in part caused by the initial Israeli insistence, later abandoned, that some part of the discussions be held in Jerusalem. Envoys of Israel, Lebanon, and the United States began meeting alternately in Khalde (Lebanon) and Kiryat Shemona (Israel). The series of meetings seemed likely to be lengthy, since a vast distance separated Israeli and Lebanese objectives, and at first even an agreed agenda was hard to come by. The Lebanese aim was to secure the withdrawal of some 30,000 Israelis, 40,000 Syrians, and several thousand remaining PLO fighters. The Israeli objective (failing the *beau idéal* of a peace treaty, as with Egypt) was normalization of relations that would permit the borders to be opened for trade and tourism, eliminate any military threat from the north, and give Israel a stable and nonhostile

Israel's Defense Minister Ariel Sharon (center foreground) testifies before Israel's three-member commission, headed by the chief justice, investigating the murder of Palestinian civilians at two Beirut refugee camps in September.

neighbor. The minimum Israeli demand would no doubt be for a deep security zone in south Lebanon that would prevent that area from ever again being a threat. For Lebanon the inhibiting factor was what the reactions of other Arab states would be. For Israel the success or failure of the negotiations would answer the question of whether the entire operation was worth the costs—financial, military, diplomatic, and moral—that it entailed.

The international ramifications of Israel's incursion into Lebanon and the question—still unanswered in any conclusive manner at the end of the year—of the extent to which Israel was responsible for the September 17 massacre were considerable, yet perhaps less than might have been expected. Denunciations of course abounded—from the Arabs, the Soviet Union, the UN, the United States, and even many Israelis—but retaliatory measures were few. No Arab state except Syria took any military action at all to oppose Israel, and encounters between Israeli and Syrian forces were quite marginal. The Egyptian ambassador to Israel was recalled on September 20, and relations were certainly cool; but Egypt continued to sell oil to Israel and to observe the other conditions of the peace treaty between them. Egyptian President Hosni Mubarak publicly advised the PLO that it would be wise to recognize Israel formally. From some points of view, indeed, the most significant event of the year was the transfer by Israel to Egypt on April 25 of the last third of the Sinai region in accordance with their 1979 treaty. While both Israel and Egypt did abide by the treaty, their common-sense and realistic policy found few or no Arab imitators.

The Iraqi-Iranian War. Despite the preponderant attention paid to Lebanon, it may not have even constituted the most important series of events occurring in the Middle East in 1982.

That distinction belonged to the continuing conflict between Iraq and Iran. Not only was the level of casualties enormously higher, but the issues at stake were greater and the possible consequences graver. Iraq and Iran are two of the world's major oil producers. A clear Iranian victory could have consequences so unsettling for the world's industrialized nations as to be almost unforeseeable.

Because complete and reliable information about the conflict is controlled by both governments, it is only over a considerable period of time that it is possible to gain a clear outline of what has been happening. The broad, valid generalization is that the war, which began with Iraq's invasion of Iran, in 1982 saw Iraqi forces driven back to the border and to some extent even beyond it. The three major actions of the year were all initiated by Iran. In the first, which began on May 22, the Iranian city of Khorramshahr at the southern end of the front—the only major city which fell to the Iraqis in the early days of the war—was recaptured. This gave the war an entirely new aspect, as evidenced by the conciliatory statements in June by Iraq's President Saddam Hussein, offering a truce and total withdrawal from Iranian soil—offers which were spurned. The second major action, an attack on the great port city of Basra in southeastern Iraq, was launched on July 14. Six major attacks were made in a period of five weeks before it became clear that the offensive had stalled. The third major Iranian offensive of the year began on September 30 farther north, at the point where the border is nearest to Baghdad. If it had been successful, the capture of the Iraqi capital might have followed. But this attack, too, dwindled after a time.

During the course of these engagements, a clear pattern began to emerge. The standard Iranian tactic was that of massed, often suicidal infantry attacks by enthusiastic young volunteer troops. At the same time, Iraqi defenses were solid, making up for their manpower disadvantage with a solid professionalism. They also seem to have better armored support and, above all, superior air power.

On the diplomatic front, there was a good deal of evasion and ambiguity in the attitude of neighboring countries. King Hussein of Jordan was the one ruler to take an unequivocal pro-Iraqi stance. He paid numerous visits to Baghdad and continued to send Jordanian volunteers to fight at the front. For the countries of the Persian Gulf—rich, weak, and vulnerable—the theory of Arab unity took second place to considerations of expediency. They are sensitive to the glaring threat posed to their regimes and their very existence by the militant Islamic fundamentalism. If Iran succeeds in deposing Saddam Hussein and the Baathist regime in Baghdad—which Khomeini stated more than once to be the Iranian war aim—time would clearly be running out for the United Arab Emirates (UAE), Qatar, Bahrain, Kuwait, Oman, and even Saudi Arabia. It was such considerations that led Saudi Arabia in February 1981 to establish the Gulf Cooperation Council, with these six states as members. The countries of the Gulf group have contributed very heavy financial support to the Iraqi war effort, but their public stance has been more cautious, in keeping with their vulnerability and their fear of exasperating Iran into some action that would destroy or impair their oil industries. Kuwait, the sole port of entry now available to Iraq, was in fact attacked twice by Iran from the air. And the UAE therefore tries to hedge by maintaining diplomatic relations, as well as trade links, with Iran. No Arab state except Jordan has any of its nationals fighting in support of the Iraqi army. In a joint defensive move to strengthen their military posture, foreign ministers of the six states agreed in principle on January 26 to coordinate a regional defense plan, including a joint military-strike force. To this end they agreed to allocate more than $30,000,-000,000 in 1982.

The Iraqi-Iranian war is indeed a ruinous aberration which is estimated to have cost $200,000,000,000 and some 60,000 to 100,000 casualties, and has set back the economic development of the two states by many years. Efforts to settle it by diplomacy have been numerous. About 20 have been counted so far, including 9 separate initiatives by the Islamic Conference Organization, the last of 1982 in mid-October. Algeria, bolstered by its success in arranging both the 1975 Iraqi-Iranian accord and the release of the U.S. hostages, has been the most active state involved in attempting to arrange an armistice. By the end of 1982, all such attempts had failed and appeared likely to continue to fail while Khomeini still rules in Tehran and Hussein in Baghdad. In the Middle East, wars and other conflicts are easier to start than to stop.

Major Proposals for Arab-Israeli Peace. Peace plans, when they succeed, have an important place in history; when they fail, they have little but an antiquarian interest. At the end of 1982, no one knew which would be the fate of two general outlines for an Arab-Israeli settlement that were being promoted vigorously in the last third of the year. These were the U.S. peace initiative launched by President Ronald Reagan in a televised speech September 1 and the formula for Middle East peace adumbrated by Arab leaders meeting on September 9 at Fez, Morocco. Whatever their ultimate fate, these plans did have a hopeful aspect and demonstrated an advance, even on the part of the Arabs, toward a realization that some "fresh start," in President Reagan's words, was called for to achieve a general peace in a crucial area of the world. It would be an exaggeration, however, to claim either that the plans resembled each other very much or that they were very welcome to the parties most involved.

The Reagan plan was a coherent and positive approach, more so probably than any previous

UPI

U.S. Special Envoy Philip Habib (left) met with Egypt's President Hosni Mubarak and other Arab leaders during the summer. His mission was a solution to the Lebanon crisis.

U.S. formula for Mideast peace. It envisaged self-government for the Palestinians of the West Bank and Gaza, in association with Jordan. It also called for an immediate freeze on new Israeli settlements on the West Bank. Unhappily, the plan was rejected almost immediately by both Israel and the PLO, and on September 5 Israel announced that it was proceeding with its plans to promote Jewish settlements on the West Bank.

The Arab plan announced in Fez differed sharply from the Reagan plan on basic points. It envisaged a Palestinian state that would be independent, i.e. sovereign, not merely autonomous in some kind of link with Jordan. It also called for a rollback of Israeli settlements, not merely a freeze on new ones. The Fez plan also appeared to give implicit recognition to Israel's existence, but explicit recognition is the only kind likely to interest Israel.

King Hussein of Jordan played a key role in relation to both plans. He immediately embarked on a trip to all five permanent members of the UN Security Council to acquaint them with the Fez plan (which called for a Security Council guarantee of peace for "all states of the region"). Hussein's assent and cooperation was, of course, essential to the implementation of the Reagan plan, and U.S. diplomacy bent all its efforts to achieve that end. The king's attitude, however, even at the end of his December visit to Washington, was well short of full acceptance, though courteous and (up to a point) cooperative.

Year-end Reflections. The course of events in the Middle East during 1982 showed some elements of genuine novelty and provokes some reflections. First, many things that were anticipated, even in the course of the year, did not happen. The Iraqi-Iranian war did not reach any definite conclusion, catastrophic or otherwise. It ground on, with minority groups in neither of the two states supporting the national enemy; on the other hand, the war did not spread. Secondly, the general Arab-Israeli conflict was no longer central to developments in the Middle East. Individual Arab states intently pursued their respective national interests. For this very reason, some solution of Arab-Israeli relations appeared more achievable than before.

It was not a good year for organizations that professed to represent the common interests and policies of Mideast countries. Two attempts to hold meetings of the Organization of African Unity in Tripoli broke down. A meeting of the conference of nonaligned states scheduled for September in Baghdad was postponed until 1983 in India. The crucial December meeting of OPEC could not agree on oil quotas, prices, or general policy. Arab diplomacy once more demonstrated a certain self-defeating rigidity, as evidenced by their peace proposal at Fez and a hearing of the Reagan initiative that might have been more attentive.

Finally, it was noteworthy that the great fear that overlay the Middle East in recent years— that of increasing Soviet involvement—was replaced by another, that of rampant Islamic fundamentalism. Soviet diplomacy in the Middle East was relatively quiescent, and its arms were shown to be inferior to those provided by the United States, at least as wielded by the Israelis. The minimal role played by the Soviet Union in the Middle East is likely to be a temporary phenomenon, however, and Saudi Arabia, in a precautionary move of some significance, sent its foreign minister to Moscow in December. The two countries have not had formal diplomatic relations since 1938, but they agreed in the late-year meeting to establish regular channels of communication.

ARTHUR CAMPBELL TURNER
Department of Political Science
University of California, Riverside

Following a four-day closed-door conference in Fez, Morocco, Arab leaders announced their peace plan on September 9.

Thierry Campion/Gamma-Liaison

MILITARY AFFAIRS

Both rhetorically and substantively the arms competition between the world's two superpowers—the United States and the Soviet Union—increased in tempo during 1982. This trend was observed also in the military relationships between many of the smaller states.

The Arms Race. President Reagan continued to stress the theme that the United States had fallen behind the Soviet Union in important aspects of national defense, and that before arms control could become a serious possibility, weapons inequities between the two nations would have to be remedied.

Shortly before he died in early November, Soviet President Leonid Brezhnev delivered a tough speech in which he accused the Reagan administration of attempting to gain military superiority over the USSR. Speaking before the top command structure of the Soviet armed forces, Brezhnev said that the United States had "... raised the intensity of their military preparations to an unprecedented level," and was following "an aggressive policy which is threatening to push the world into the flames of a nuclear war." Brezhnev exhorted Soviet engineers and scientists to greater efforts in developing better military equipment. In a reference to American research and development, he stated: "A lag in this competition is inadmissible. We expect that our scientists, designers, engineers, and technicians will do everything possible to resolve successfully all tasks connected with this matter." Despite the generally harsh tone of Brezhnev's speech, however, the Soviet leader also called for détente and "reducing the danger of nuclear war."

U.S. Secretary of Defense Caspar Weinberger responded sharply to the Brezhnev speech, accusing him of pledging "... the Soviet Union to continue the path of an even more intensified quest for military superiority" and "a new technology race." Weinberger concluded: "This requires us to step up our efforts here in the United States, in Europe, and in Japan to counter this campaign."

The basic theme of the Reagan administration was well stated by Secretary Weinberger in October when he noted that 15 years of Soviet buildup had to be countered by the "rearming of America." Weinberger singled out expanded nuclear weapons deployment and the development of binary chemical (two chemicals that are inert when kept apart but which form a poisonous nerve gas when combined) warfare capability as areas needing particular attention. According to the defense secretary: "If we value our freedom, we must be prepared to fight at any level of conflict." To fight effectively, Weinberger argued, means that "... we have to have sufficient strength and strong friends and allies."

Major Weapons Developments. Throughout 1982 controversy swirled about the newly devel-

© 1982 by Marty Katz

In November, President Reagan announced his support of the deployment of 100 MX's in the "dense-pack" mode. Above, workers assemble the missile's re-entry vehicle.

oped American intercontinental ballistic missile (ICBM) called the "MX." Argument concerning the missile is not new. Since President Jimmy Carter approved development of the MX in 1979, technical and/or political objections have prevented a decision being made on exactly how the missile should be based.

Originally, under the Carter administration's proposal, several hundred MX's were to have been based in desolate areas of Utah and Nevada. In order to prevent a Soviet first strike from knocking out most of the missiles, they were to have been dispersed among a large number of shelters. The theory supporting this method of deployment was that the USSR would not know which shelters housed missiles and which were empty. As long as the United States built more shelters (some of which might be empty) than the Soviets had warheads to shoot at them, an attack would seem fruitless.

Strong opposition developed in Utah and Nevada against basing the MX's in those states. Local inhabitants feared the disruptions of their life-styles by construction of the missile complexes. Environmentalists worried about damage to the arid—and thus fragile—Western environment. Those living downwind from the proposed sites worried about nuclear fallout resulting from a Soviet attack on the missile shelters. Military strategists worried about some of the technical details of the proposed deployment. Economists worried about the cost.

The Reagan administration rejected the Utah and Nevada basing mode and the search began for a more suitable deployment plan. By midsummer 1982, several other basing proposals had been rejected for one reason or another. These included carrying the MX's on giant cargo planes from which they could be launched, placing them aboard submarines or surface ships, or adopting what was called the "deep-basing" plan. The latter was a proposal to construct very deep tunnels into the south-facing slopes of mountains in the western United States, in which the missiles could be kept before launch. South-facing slopes were desired for this deployment because Soviet warheads fired over the North Pole would have a more difficult time destroying the tunnels than if they were in north-facing slopes. While the discarded basing modes could yet be adopted, it appeared by late fall that President Reagan and his national security advisers preferred a basing plan known as "dense pack."

According to the dense-pack proposal, alternatively called the "closely spaced" basing mode, up to 100 MX's would be installed in heavily reinforced steel and concrete silos underground in an area 1 mi (1.6 km) wide and 14 mi (22.5 km) long. Proponents of the dense-pack scheme claim that placing the MX's close to each other will provide protection for most of the missiles because of a hypothetical principle known as "fratracide." According to this theory, an incoming Soviet nuclear warhead detonated over the MX missile complex would create radiation, intense heat, blast waves, and debris which would either deflect or detonate warheads that followed. An assumption of persons arguing the likelihood of fratracide is that one of the cluster of incoming warheads would explode a microsecond before its "brothers," thus destroying them. Before the area had cleared sufficiently for additional Soviet warheads to be targeted on the MX's, the U.S. missiles could be launched up through the mushroom clouds above their complex.

Some nuclear weapons specialists, such as William Van Cleave, former Reagan adviser, and William Perry, former under secretary for defense and engineering in the Carter administration, have voiced doubts about the validity of the fratracide concept, particularly regarding the probability that one or several Soviet warheads would in fact detonate early.

In midsummer a new argument was advanced in opposition to dense-pack deployment. Proponents of the "pindown" theory argued that the USSR might be able to prevent MX's from being fired for the first several hours of a nuclear exchange by utilizing a new tactic. According to this theory the Soviet Union would detonate a series of megaton nuclear explosions 75 to 100 mi (120–160 km) above the MX complexes. The consequences of such an attack could be a minienvironment characterized by radiation, intense heat, and electromagnetic pulse, such that U.S. missiles could not be fired upward and would in fact be "pinned down."

In an effort to resolve the technical controversy regarding the effectiveness of the dense-pack plan, Secretary Weinberger appointed a panel of experts to review the MX-basing matter. The group was headed by Dr. Charles Townes, professor of physics at the University of California. Prominent members of the panel were Dr. Edward Teller, long associated with U.S. nuclear weapons programs, and Herman Kahn of the Hudson Institute. The panel's decision supported the MX deployment.

On November 22, President Reagan announced his decision to ask the Congress for approximately $26,000,000,000 to fund the deployment of 100 MX's in the dense-pack mode near Cheyenne, WY. The president dubbed the new missile the "peacekeeper" by way of emphasizing his belief that peace is the consequence of military strength. A tough Congressional battle over the proposal was predicted.

The NATO Alliance. Despite opposition by various European peace organizations, the Reagan administration continued to support the previously announced plan to deploy nuclear-tipped Pershing II and ground-based cruise missiles to the NATO allies in 1983. This deployment would be made to counter the superiority that the Soviet Union is said to have gained with its previous deployment of SS-20 nuclear missiles in the Warsaw Pact region of Eastern Europe.

The debate among the European members of NATO, and in the United States, concerning the need for additional nuclear weapons for use in a potential battle in Europe was complicated in 1982 when a possible new strategy emerged. The new perspective, which reflects recent advances in nonnuclear weapons, is termed the "attack on the follow-on forces" concept. According to this view, NATO forces should be reinforced with new conventional equipment featuring precision-guided munitions (PGM's) and other "smart" weapons that can be guided with great accuracy to their targets. The new weapons and their implementing plan are designed to cut off Soviet troops in the front lines from reinforcement and fresh manpower held in reserve far behind the combat zone. Some NATO governments were not enthusiastic about the American plan because of higher costs associated with the

UPI

Benjamin Sasway, 21, was convicted and sentenced for failing to register for the draft. A federal judge in California later ruled that the registration law had not been legally promulgated and dismissed a similar case.

procurement of the new conventional weapons.

A potential problem for the NATO alliance was the victory in October of the Socialist Workers Party in the Spanish parliamentary elections. Before the elections the Socialist leader, Felipe González, had called for a referendum on Spain's continued membership in NATO and the renegotiation of the bilateral agreement with the United States concerning U.S. bases on Spanish soil. Fears over what the new Socialist governmen' might do were softened by recollection that a year earlier the newly elected Socialist government of Andreas Papandreou in Greece had also taken an anti-NATO stance, but the new government kept Greece in the NATO alliance throughout 1982.

Consequences of Small Wars. In 1982, defense analysts were busy attempting to determine the effects of weapons and tactics used in two small wars on any future war between the superpowers. In the Falkland Islands conflict between England and Argentina, the successful use by the latter of a French-built guided missile, the Exocet, to sink a British warship raised questions about the vulnerability of surface ships to surface- or air-launched missiles. In the Lebanese conflict between Israeli forces on the one hand and PLO and Syrian forces on the other, the technological superiority of U.S. planes and missiles over Soviet equipment was graphically demonstrated.

U.S. Domestic Problems: Women in the Army and Draft Registration. In the fall of 1982, the U.S. Army announced that it would discontinue training female recruits together with men. The reason given was that while women could learn the skills taught in basic training, they did so more slowly than men due to physical differences between men and women. Some analysts expressed the belief that the Army announcement was triggered by the defeat earlier in the year of the Equal Rights Amendment.

The year 1982 marked the first time since draft registration was reintroduced in 1980 that young men refusing to register for the draft were tried and convicted for disobeying the law. Two college students—Benjamin Sasway in California and Enten Eller in Virginia—argued unsuccessfully against compulsory registration in separate trials. Both were convicted in August. In November a federal judge in Los Angeles dismissed another case against David Wayte, partly on the grounds that the draft registration law had never been legally promulgated.

In the fall, President Reagan signed the defense authorization bill, which carried a provision requiring all eligible male students to be registered for the draft before they could receive financial assistance in college. The law, which was to become effective on July 1, 1983, was criticized by educators, students, and others on the ground that it is wrong for the government to require universities to participate in making draft registration a criterion for receiving assistance to stay in college, and that for universities to do so would destroy the academic freedom of students.

The Defense Budget. President Reagan's plans to continue increased spending for defense in 1983 appeared partially crippled by the changed composition of the House of Representatives. As a result of the November elections, 26 new Democrats were successful in replacing Republicans in the House. Typically the new members take a more critical view of Pentagon expenditures than did those whom they replaced.

Analysts thought it unlikely that such large procurements as additional Trident nuclear submarines and the B-1 intercontinental jet bomber would be scrapped. However, they were joined by both Republicans and Democrats in predicting some reductions in the president's defense budget.

See also ARMS CONTROL.

ROBERT M. LAWRENCE
Colorado State University

MINING

The year 1982 essentially was an extension of the previous year for the world's mineral industry. Continuing inflation and recessionary trends affected not only nonfuel mineral industry activities in market economy nations, but apparently also contributed to dampening growth trends in nations with centrally planned economies. Demand levels for most major mineral commodities were off as a result of continuing downtrends in demand for consumer goods. Other factors contributing to the generally poor year for the mineral industries included continued warfare in the Near East (Iran against Iraq and the Israeli-Syrian-PLO fighting in Lebanon); worker discontent in Poland; the Falkland Islands dispute; internal strife in several Central American republics; and an increasing array of political, economic, and social problems in other countries.

Value of World Output. The total value of world crude mineral production (including fuel minerals) in 1982 was tentatively estimated at about $530,000,000,000 (1978 constant dollars), about 4% below the record high of $566,000,000,-000 in 1979 and about 2% below the 1978 level of $540,000,000,000. Complete country-by-country results were not available for 1981, but the leading countries, in order of value of output, undoubtedly remained the USSR, United States, Saudi Arabia, China, and Canada. From the viewpoint of commodities, petroleum accounted for more than two fifths of the total, coal for about one sixth, and natural gas for one tenth. All nonfuel minerals together provided only about one third.

Law of the Sea. On April 30, the UN Law of the Sea Conference passed a comprehensive treaty governing the use and exploitation of the world's seas. (*See* LAW—International.) The United States voted against the pact on the grounds that it would "deter the development of the deep seabed resource." In fact, the effect of the treaty on mineral industry activity seemed academic, at least for the time being. Cutbacks in onshore output of the most prominent seabed minerals were so substantial that existing onshore industries were operating substantially below capacity. Thus, the prospect of commencing seabed mining, with the base investment that would be required, seemed remote.

Ferrous Ores and Metals. Optimistic predictions of higher world iron ore output in 1981 were dashed when the final results were all in. Partial data for 1982 suggested a further decline in production, from 946 million tons, or T (860 million metric tons, or t) in 1981 to 913-924 million T (830-840 million t). A similar decline in steel production, from 774 million T (704 million t) in 1981 to 748-759 million T (680-690 million t) in 1982, was expected.

The continued curtailment of steel industry activity led to further reductions in output of the principal steel alloying minerals—manganese, chromium, nickel, molybdenum, and tungsten—even though alloy steels again apparently accounted for a slightly increased share of total steel output.

Nonferrous Ores and Metals. Final returns for 1981 showed that copper and zinc were the only major nonferrous metals to register production gains over 1980. Expectations that aluminum output would rise were ill-founded, and lead, nickel, and tin all moved downward, as expected. Declines were expected for all of these commodities in 1982. Among nonferrous metals, mercury, which edged up slightly from 1980 to 1981, and antimony, magnesium, and titanium, all of which recorded slight downturns in that period, were expected to show declines in 1982.

Uranium. Indications were that world output of uranium in 1982 was about on par with 1981, with probable gains in the Soviet Union and China offset by declines among market economy nations.

Precious Metals. Marginal gains in output of gold and silver and approximate equality in platinum were expected for 1982, despite the fact that precious metal prices fell below 1981 levels and fell far short of the record highs set in 1980. The anticipated 1982 growth in gold output seemed somewhat more sure than did that for silver, because substantial amounts of silver are derived as a byproduct of copper, lead, and zinc, mining of which declined.

Asbestos. Continued publicity regarding the health hazards of asbestos, coupled with the general worldwide economic downturn, led to further declines in output of this key insulation material. In the United States, lawsuits against asbestos-producing companies led to two major firms filing for bankruptcy in 1982.

Diamond. A small decline in the total worldwide output of natural diamond was anticipated for 1982, with gains in the USSR and elsewhere more than offset by shortfalls in the former leading producer, Zaire. At least a portion of this drop was compensated by increased production of man-made industrial diamonds.

Fertilizer Materials. The critical need for maintaining world agricultural output contributed to a slight continued growth in output of all three major mineral fertilizer commodities (nitrogen, phosphate, and potash).

Salt. A slight decline in world salt production was expected in 1982, based chiefly on an anticipated decline in use in the manufacture of chemical products. In contrast, use of salt as a key foodstuff, both for animals and humans, was expected to fall little, if any.

Sulfur. World production of this key industrial nonmetal apparently edged lower in 1982, but its importance to the chemical industry in general and to fertilizer material producers specifically, tended to moderate the effect of the general industrial downturn.

CHARLES L. KIMBELL
U.S. Bureau of Mines

MINNESOTA

UPI

Record snows, high winds, and low temperatures swept through Minnesota in January.

The return to political dominance of the Democratic-Farmer-Labor Party (DFL), a bogged down economy, and a running battle over state finances highlighted the year in Minnesota.

Politics and Government. For the first time in the state's history, a former governor was returned to office. Rudy Perpich, who had lost to Al Quie in a Republican rout in 1978, led a strong DFL comeback, defeating Minneapolis businessman Wheelock Whitney. Quie was not seeking reelection.

In the nation's most costly U.S. Senate race, Republican Dave Durenburger, 48, was returned to office, defeating 35-year-old Mark Dayton, an heir to the Dayton-Hudson chain. Dayton spent $7.1 million, almost all of it his own, on the campaign; Durenberger spent $3.1 million.

The state's U.S. congressional delegation shifted from a 5–3 Republican advantage to 5–3 for the DFL. Rep. Tom Hagerdon (R) lost to State Rep. Tim Penney, and Rep. Arlen Erdahl (R) lost to Gerry Sikorski. Other incumbents were reelected. The shift was attributed to the effects of court-ordered redistricting and disaffection with Reagan policies.

In state legislative elections, the DFL retained control of both houses, promising an end to the gubernatorial-legislative stalemate that had dominated state government.

Voters in November approved constitutional amendments to 1) establish a state appeals court, 2) allow parimutuel betting on horse racing, 3) remove interest and borrowing limits on highway funding, and 4) provide state assistance for railroad rehabilitation.

State Sen. Hubert H. Humphrey III, son of the late vice-president, was elected the state's attorney general.

Economy and Finance. The state's economy was in its deepest slump since the 1974–75 recession. Although there was a fractional drop to 7.2% in September, the rate of unemployment remained critical, especially on the Iron Range, where four of every five iron ore miners were idle. Housing permits were at their lowest level in 12 years.

Revenue deficiencies forced sharp cuts in the 1981–83 biennial budget, unprecedented short-term borrowing, and enactment of a temporary 7% income tax surcharge as well as an extra one-cent sales tax.

Legislative actions suggested that the state was retreating from the nationally hailed "Minnesota Miracle," which in the early 1970s had greatly increased state support for public education and substantially reduced local reliance on the property tax by a statewide shift to sales and income taxes.

Newspaper Merger. In April the evening *Minneapolis Star* and morning *Minneapolis Tribune,* the city's only daily newspapers, were merged. About 110 employees reportedly lost their jobs and another 125 offered early retirement. Editor Charles Bailey resigned, and publisher Don Dwight was fired. John Cowles, Jr., chief executive officer of the parent Cowles Media Co., assumed personal control of the paper.

ARTHUR NAFTALIN, *University of Minnesota*

MINNESOTA • Information Highlights

Area: 84,402 sq mi (218 601 km²).
Population (1980 census): 4,075,970.
Chief Cities (1980 census): St. Paul, the capital, 270,-230; Minneapolis, 370,951; Duluth, 92,811.
Government (1982): *Chief Officers*—governor, Albert Quie (I-R); lt. gov. Lou Wangberg (I-R). *Legislature*—Senate, 67 members; House of Representatives, 134 members.
State Finances (fiscal year 1981): *Revenues,* $6,729,-000,000; *expenditures,* $6,050,000,000.
Personal Income (1981): $44,087,000,000; per capita, $10,768.
Labor Force (Aug. 1982): *Nonagricultural wage and salary earners,* 1,709,300; unemployed 159,900 (7.3% of total force).
Education: *Enrollment* (Fall 1981)—public elementary schools, 480,008; public secondary, 253,733; colleges and universities (1981–82), 210,713. *Public school expenditures* (1980–81), $2,030,251,000 ($2,484 per pupil).

MISSISSIPPI

UPI

Robert G. Clark, the grandson of a former slave, made an impressive run for a U.S. House seat, but narrowly lost.

Congressional elections attracted considerable attention in Mississippi in 1982, but it was fiscal and economic issues that dominated the public consciousness during the year. The legislature struggled to fund existing programs, and the economy remained severely troubled. The statewide unemployment rate climbed to more than 12%, its highest level since the Great Depression, and in several counties the jobless rate topped 20%.

The Legislature. Despite the tight-money situation facing the state government, the annual session that began January 5 saw legislators hold firm in their resolve to avoid a tax increase. No money was provided for new programs or for raises for state employees and schoolteachers, but the $1,200,000,000 general fund budget approved by the legislature did include for the first time a cash reserve fund with which to begin the new fiscal year.

Among the lawmakers' more significant actions was the approval of a legislative reseating plan that increased the number of House and Senate districts that have black voting age majorities. At year's end the plan had not gained the federal approval required under the Voting Rights Act.

Called into special session on December 6, lawmakers 14 days later approved the most significant education reform bill since 1953. Its provisions include a reading aid program beginning in 1983, mandated kindergartens starting in 1986, compulsory attendance, and teacher pay raises. To finance the program, the income tax was increased for the first time since 1968 and the general sales tax was raised by 0.5%.

Congressional Elections. In March the U.S. Justice Department disapproved Mississippi's 1981 Congressional redistricting map, forcing a postponement of House primaries scheduled for June 1. On June 8 a three-judge federal panel set August 17 as the new primary date and imposed a temporary plan containing a black-majority district for the first time since 1966. Incumbent David Bowen (D) chose not to seek reelection in the redrawn "Delta District," and Robert G. Clark, a black state representative, scored an impressive victory over several white opponents to gain the Democratic nomination. His bid to become the first black Mississippi congressman in the 20th century was rejected in the November 2 general election when Webb Franklin, a former circuit court judge from Greenwood, won a close victory for the Republicans (51%). Mississippi's four other House seats were won by incumbents, three Democrats and one Republican.

Democratic Sen. John C. Stennis easily defeated Republican Haley Barbour to win reelection (64%) to an unprecedented seventh term. His victory at age 81 made him the oldest person ever elected to the Senate.

Other Highlights. On July 1 the U.S. Supreme Court ruled that Mississippi University for Women must admit males to its nursing program, but the status of sex barriers to enrollment in the general undergraduate program was not made clear.

In the November general election, voters approved controversial constitutional amendments establishing a nine-member lay board of education and legalizing property classification for tax assessment purposes.

A fire in the Harrison county jail in Biloxi claimed the lives of 27 inmates on November 8. An additional 61 persons—including firefighters, police officers, and jailers—were injured.

DANA B. BRAMMER
The University of Mississippi

MISSISSIPPI • Information Highlights

Area: 47,689 sq mi (123 515 km²).
Population (1980 census): 2,520,638.
Chief Cities (1980 census): Jackson, the capital, 202,-895; Biloxi, 49,311; Meridian, 46,577.
Government (1982): *Chief Officers*—governor, William F. Winter (D); lt. gov., Brad Dye (D). *Legislature*—Senate, 52 members; House of Representatives, 122 members.
State Finances (fiscal year 1981): *Revenues,* $3,053,-000,000; *expenditures,* $2,985,000,000.
Personal Income (1981): $18,749,000,000; per capita, $7,408.
Labor Force (Aug. 1982): *Nonagricultural wage and salary earners,* 782,700; *unemployed,* 131,900 (12.5% of total force).
Education: *Enrollment* (fall 1981)—public elementary schools, 328,016; public secondary, 143,599; colleges and universities (1981–82), 105,974 students. *Public school expenditures* (1980–81), $761,790,000 ($1,536 per pupil).

354

MISSOURI

Missouri's overriding concern in 1982 was the sagging economy. The economic issues were paramount in voters' minds as they went to the polls for the November 2 elections.

The Economy. Unemployment continued high at an 8.8% level in 1982, while business remained largely stagnant and farm income fell. These factors translated into declining state revenues from sales and income taxes, requiring Gov. Christopher S. Bond (R) to withhold moneys appropriated to state agencies. The governor also moved to accelerate previous attempts to promote foreign markets for Missouri products, to attract new businesses to the state, and to propose a bond issue.

Late in its 1982 session, the General Assembly approved issuance of $600 million in bonds. The voters accepted the proposal by a narrow margin in a special referendum on June 8. The money is to be used for state building projects, and thus, it was hoped, would stimulate the economy and put a number of unemployed persons to work. It would be well into 1983, however, before any effects of this shot of economic adrenalin could be felt.

The Elections. Missouri voters on November 2 chose a U.S. senator, nine representatives in Congress, the state auditor, members of the lower house of the state legislature, and one third of the state senators.

The U.S. Senate race pitted incumbent Republican John C. Danforth against Democratic challenger Harriet Woods, state senator from University City. Woods had won the nomination in a divisive primary battle against 10 fellow Democrats, one of whom, Burleigh Arnold of Central Missouri Trust in Jefferson City, had the backing of party regulars. Danforth, although initially viewed as an easy victor, found himself increasingly on the defensive about his support of the Reagan administration's economic policies and his vote to deregulate natural gas. Woods sensed the distress current in the state

UPI

Gov. Christopher Bond personally inspects severe damage caused by floods in the Kansas City area in mid-August.

and became a symbol for labor, women, the elderly, and consumer groups. In the end she lost by a narrow margin, garnering 49% of the vote to Danforth's 51%, but, as she offered congratulations, she reminded him that her campaign had revealed the "very special concerns of the people of Missouri."

Missouri voters also favored incumbents in the races for seats in the House of Representatives. Five Democrats won reelection, and the seat of veteran Richard Bolling (who was not a candidate) remained in the Democratic column. Three Republicans also were returned to Washington, but a fourth, Wendell Bailey, lost his bid to Ike Skelton, a Democratic incumbent, when reapportionment (in which Missouri lost one congressional seat) threw the Bailey and Skelton districts together. The election of Alan D. Wheat to replace Bolling gave Missouri the distinction of having two black congressmen as William Clay, third in seniority in the Black Caucus, retained his seat.

State Auditor James T. Antonio, a Republican, was reelected, and the Democrats kept firm control of both houses of the General Assembly. Of 13 constitutional amendments and initiative or referendum propositions, most went down to defeat, but an additional 1 cent sales tax, earmarked for the public schools, was approved.

In a special election in April, voters repealed a law permitting larger trucks to operate on the state's highways. A major advertising campaign for and against the law had been waged by railroads and trucking firms.

RUTH W. TOWNE
Northeast Missouri State University

MISSOURI • Information Highlights

Area: 69,697 sq mi (180 515 km²).

Population (1980 census): 4,916,759.

Chief Cities (1980 census): Jefferson City, the capital, 33,619; St. Louis, 453,085; Kansas City, 448,159; Springfield, 133,116; Independence, 111,806.

Government (1982): *Chief Officers*—governor, Christopher S. Bond (R); lt. gov., Kenneth J. Rothman (D). *General Assembly*—Senate, 34 members; House of Representatives, 163 members.

State Finances (fiscal year 1981): *Revenues,* $4,435,-000,000; *expenditures,* $4,422,000,000.

Personal Income (1981): $47,682,000,000; per capita, $9,651.

Labor Force (Aug. 1982): *Nonagricultural wage and salary earners,* 1,955,900; *unemployed,* 210,600 (9.0% of total force).

Education: *Enrollment* (fall 1981)—public elementary schools, 553,012; public secondary, 265,693; colleges and universities (1981–82), 243,672. *Public school expenditures* (1980–81), $1,759,104,000 ($2,079 per pupil).

Paul Carter/Missoulian

Montana state troopers stand guard at Deer Lodge prison, where riots broke out in March.

MONTANA

The year was highlighted by general elections, prison problems, and mixed economic developments.

Elections. Republican Congressman Ron Marlenee won reelection to his eastern district seat. Otherwise it was a Democratic year, as Sen. John Melcher easily defeated Larry Williams, and western district Congressman Pat Williams crushed his opponent. In state legislative races a 12-seat gain in the House gave control to the Democrats, who also cut the Republican Senate margin to two votes. Voters faced a ballot that included three constitutional amendments, one referendum, and four initiatives. Voters defeated amendments liberalizing investment of state trust funds and mandating annual sessions of the legislature but approved a broadening of the legislature's power to overrule vetoes. The electorate overwhelmingly reaffirmed its opposition to storage of radioactive waste, solidly opposed MX missiles, refused to liberalize gambling laws and beer and wine licenses, and approved the investment of coal tax monies in in-state businesses.

Prison Riot. Officials blamed overcrowding at the state's Deer Lodge prison for a March 24 riot and subsequent disturbances. A special session of the legislature rejected Gov. Ted Schwinden's request for more than $12 million for new construction to expand the six-year-old prison. However, it set up two new pre-release centers, laid plans for an expanded work program, increased security forces, and established a committee to study prison problems and report to the 1983 legislature.

Economy. The year's economic developments were mixed. Oil and gas exploration slowed markedly. Western Montana experienced the lowest timber harvest in 21 years due to a stagnant wood-products industry. In Butte the Anaconda Minerals Company closed the Berkeley Pit and the Kelley Mine, laying off approximately 475 employees. Some 800 workers continued to operate the East Pit, expected to run for another 20 years. Although Anaconda's Columbia Falls aluminum plant was operating at only 60% capacity, officials predicted additional layoffs.

Anaconda's recent shutdowns in Great Falls and in Anaconda resulted in a temporary surplus of electricity and led Montana Power officials to postpone for a year construction of a coal-fired power plant east of Great Falls. Power-company officials also announced that construction of a new hydroelectric dam near Fort Benton would begin in 1994. The state's Public Service Commission temporarily stymied Montana Power's attempts to secure corporate reorganization. Under the plan, Montana Power Company and its 12 subsidiaries would become 13 subsidiaries of a new holding company, Montana Energy Company.

The Anaconda Company destroyed its 506-ft (154-m) Great Falls refinery smokestack despite the efforts of citizens to save the landmark as a historic monument.

Livingston's new windmill power system was interrupted when an improperly constructed tower blew down. Interest in development of wind power in the area continued to grow. Pan Aero Corporation of Denver, following public hearings, obtained a lease from the Bureau of Land Management and planned to begin the installation of 100 windmills in 1983.

Plentiful rainfall resulted in good ranges for cattle and an excellent grain harvest. The year's bounty was marred by careless use of pesticides, and public officials warned hunters of serious contamination of game animals.

RICHARD B. ROEDER, *Montana State University*

MONTANA · Information Highlights

Area: 147,046 sq mi (380 849 km²).

Population (1980 census): 786,690.

Chief Cities (1980 census): Helena, the capital, 23,938; Billings, 66,842; Great Falls, 56,725.

Government (1982): *Chief Officers*—governor, Ted Schwinden (D); lt. gov., George Turman (D). *Legislature*—Senate, 50 members; House of Representatives, 100 members.

State Finances (fiscal year 1981): *Revenues,* $1,269,000,000; *expenditures,* $1,096,000,000.

Personal Income (1981): $7,458,000,000; per capita, $9,410.

Labor Force (Aug. 1982): *Nonagricultural wage and salary earners,* 278,300; *unemployed,* 30,100 (7.7% of total force).

Education: *Enrollment* (fall 1981)—public elementary schools, 106,235; public secondary 47,200; colleges and universities (1981–82), 35,959. *Public school expenditures* (1980–81), $465,500,000 ($2,948 per pupil).

MOROCCO

Diplomatic efforts to find a negotiated solution to the war for control of the Western Sahara were superseded by the admission of the Polisario Front's self-proclaimed government, the Saharan Arab Democratic Republic (SADR), to the Organization of African Unity (OAU) as a member state. The SADR was granted membership at a February council of ministers meeting in Addis Ababa, Ethiopia.

The admission of the SADR as the OAU's 51st member state was a major factor behind the postponement of the annual OAU summit, scheduled for Tripoli, Libya, in August because of failure to reach a quorum. Morocco had lobbied intensely for a boycott of the Tripoli summit over the SADR's entry, and gained the support of enough African countries to jettison the summit. By late 1982, the problem remained.

Meanwhile, political and military ties between the United States and Morocco were strengthened in 1982 as the Reagan administration dropped a prior condition that arms sales to the kingdom be tied to progress on a negotiated settlement of the war. Weapons sales for Morocco's "legitimate defense needs" were increased. Former U.S. Secretary of State Alexander Haig and a host of other government officials visited Morocco for discussions with King Hassan II on ways to assist Rabat in the war. Haig concluded an agreement with Hassan in March forming a joint military commission.

Hassan paid an official visit to Washington in May, following which an agreement was signed granting transit rights to American military planes at Moroccan air bases during unspecified emergencies. Polisario warned that it might seek weapons from the Soviet Union if Washington continued to step up military assistance to Rabat, and intensified attacks against Moroccan positions in the Sahara as the Tripoli summit approached.

Morocco reopened the Bou Craa phosphate mines in the Sahara in July, after having completed a 400-mi (644-km) defense wall around them to protect against the Polisario attacks which had forced their closure in 1975.

Economy and Politics. In 1982, the Moroccan economy felt the effects of a two-year drought, low world demand for its major currency earner, phosphates, and the continuing cost of financing the Sahara war. Some hopeful signs of recovery were shown, however, with 1981–82 winter's rains and expected increased Arab aid and soft loans in the aftermath of hosting the Arab conference in Fez in September.

Food imports increased by 75% during the drought, and the trade deficit increased from $610 million in 1981 to $706 million, as export receipts for phosphate rock declined by 6% for the first quarter of 1982. Exports of fruit, vegetables, leather, and textile goods were hurt both by the drought and by the protectionist policies of

Michael Evans/The White House

The U.S. president and visiting King Hassan take time out from their May talks for a ride in the countryside.

the European Community. The International Monetary Fund approved two loans totalling $579 million in April.

Hassan granted clemency in February to Abderrahim Bouabid, head of the Socialist Union of Popular Forces (USFP), and to two other USFP members who had been jailed for criticizing Hassan's earlier agreement to OAU proposals for a referendum for the Sahara. And in April, the Democratic Labor Confederation (CDT) and the USFP were permitted to reopen their offices 10 months after they were closed following the Casablanca riots and demonstrations.

MARGARET A. NOVICKI, *"Africa Report"*

MOROCCO · Information Highlights

Official Name: Kingdom of Morocco.
Location: Northwest Africa.
Area: 180,602 sq mi (467 759 km²).
Population (1982 est.): 22,300,000.
Chief Cities (1973 est.): Rabat, the capital, 385,000; Casablanca, 2,000,000; Marrakesh, 330,000; Fez, 322,000.
Government: *Head of state,* Hassan II, king (acceded 1961). *Head of government,* Maati Bouabid, prime minister (took office March 1979).
Monetary Unit: Dirham (5.9 dirhams equal U.S.$1, March 1982).
Gross National Product (1980 U.S.$): $18,100,000,-000.
Economic Indexes (1981): *Consumer Prices* (1974= 100), *all items,* 192.8; *food,* 193.1. *Industrial production* (1980, 1975=100), 135.
Foreign Trade (1980 U.S.$): *Imports,* $4,185,000,-000; *exports,* $2,403,000,000.

MOTION PICTURES

Universal Pictures

The parting of E.T. and Elliott (Henry Thomas) will go down as one of the most memorable scenes in movie history.

There is nothing that Hollywood respects more than box office success. Steven Spielberg, once a fledgling director at Universal studios, was already considered one of the new movie moguls on the basis of the millions earned by *Jaws, Close Encounters of the Third Kind,* and *Raiders of the Lost Ark,* the latter coproduced with another new-generation titan, George Lucas. To have presented *Poltergeist* and *E.T. the Extra-Terrestrial* almost simultaneously was so stunning a feat that Spielberg promptly was recognized as the single most important force Hollywood had seen in years. (*See also* BIOGRAPHY, page 139.)

E.T. became a legend in the first weeks of its run. Business mounted so quickly that it was certain to become the highest grossing movie of all time. Children and adults alike stood in long lines, often more than once, and the film's evocation of childhood innocence and tug on the emotions made it difficult to imagine a country in which audiences would not react favorably to it. Although only 35 years old, Spielberg had attained economic power that would guarantee his ability to continue making the films of his choice and to take whatever risks he thought prudent.

As with Lucas' *Star Wars,* the merchandising aspects of *E.T.* were also phenomenal. E.T. dolls were everywhere, as were T-shirts and other mementos, and sales were helped by the popularity of catchwords, such as variations of "E.T., please call home."

Meanwhile, Hollywood also was heartened by the substantial box office business reported. Jack Valenti, president of the Motion Picture Association of America, projected close to a 9.1% rise in revenue over 1981's record of $2,900,000,-000. This was helped in part by a bonanza of summer business. However, the figures were deceptive with respect to the overall well-being of the industry. A few blockbusters accounted for a heavy proportion of the box office receipts. The public went to see their favorite films, not necessarily a broad variety of films, and unemployment was still high in an industry that turned out fewer pictures than in better times.

Technology. Rapid changes in entertainment possibilities and viewing habits of the American public pointed toward a time when motion pictures shown in theaters might be only a minor aspect of a company's overall market. International Resource Development, an organization which does market research, estimated that by 1984 the public would be spending $3,000,000,-000 on video games—about as much as Valenti said was spent by moviegoers in 1982. About $1,-700,000,000 in revenues was already projected for video games by year's end, and there was clear evidence that movie companies were tuned into the market potential. The possibility of planning films that would readily produce video-game spinoffs was attractive. For example, the Disney Studio produced *Tron*, a film about a video programmer who is pulled into one of the games and must fight for survival. Naturally, there was a Tron game as an offshoot. Such ploys are apart from the potential benefits to movie companies, namely, video games as a profitable subsidiary.

Anything that increases the use of television at home could also be a stimulus to watching more movies on the family set. The stakes in terms of revenues are still not defined, but film cassettes continued to be a burgeoning market, and the financing of films, as well as Broadway shows, increasingly was tied to cable or pay television enterprises.

Technology assumed heightened importance in the production of movies. While the film *Tron* itself was not the box office success that had been hoped for, it was significant in that computer technology was used extensively to provide settings and props. With such know-how, stars could enact their scenes, then be placed in complex environments through a process more sophisticated than old methods of rear projection.

Besides *Tron*, other 1982 films with various special effects included *E.T., Poltergeist, Star Trek II: The Wrath of Khan, Blade Runner, Firefox,* and *The Thing. The Dark Crystal,* released late in the year, was peopled entirely by mechanical beings.

In Focus. Numerous actors and actresses, some of whom had been in films previously, some who can be called "new faces," earned special recognition. Glenn Close, primarily a stage actress, won admiration for her striking portrayal of Jenny Fields in the screen version of John Irving's book *The World According to Garp.* In the same film, television's *Mork and*

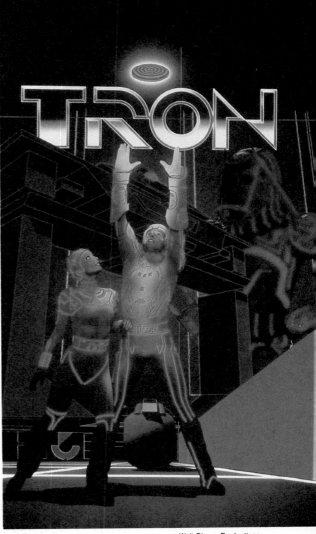

"Tron," a next-generation Walt Disney production, used elaborate computer graphics to create a video-game effect. "The World According to Garp" was an adroit adaptation of John Irving's best-selling novel; Robin Williams (left) and Glenn Close starred.

Robert Preston (seated), Julie Andrews, and James Garner play unconventional roles in "Victor/Victoria."

Mindy star Robin Williams also made an impressive showing in the title role, and John Lithgow was extraordinary as Roberta Muldoon, the transsexual.

An Officer and a Gentleman, an extremely popular and somewhat old-fashioned film that lauded the Navy Air Corps and involved audiences in the relationships of its characters, spotlighted the strengths of several performers. The film confirmed Richard Gere's magnetism; revealed that veteran actor Louis Gossett, Jr., was capable of dynamic work, evident by his tough drill sergeant role; was an excellent vehicle for rising star David Keith; and again showcased the much-lauded newcomer, Debra Winger, who had made a strong impression in *Urban Cowboy.*

Kevin Kline, who became a Broadway star in *The Pirates of Penzance,* made his movie debut

in *Sophie's Choice* as the charismatic but violent Nathan Landau. Peter MacNicol, applauded for his droll portrayal of the Mississippi lawyer in the Broadway production *Crimes of the Heart,* appeared in *Sophie's Choice* in the coveted role of Stingo, the alter ego of author William Styron. Mark Linn-Baker, an excellent stage actor, was introduced to movie audiences as the frantic young writer of a 1950s live television comedy show in the often funny *My Favorite Year.* Much excitement was generated by the performance of Matt Dillon, the young star of *Tex,* the teenage-oriented film presented by the Disney Studio as part of its new effort to make more mature movies.

Opera star Luciano Pavarotti, making his movie debut, was cast appropriately as a world-renowned opera star in the comedy, *Yes, Giorgio.* The film was feeble, but at least Pavarotti got to sing and the force of his voice and personality made him a promising addition to the screen.

History. Epics that attempt to recapture important periods of history have challenged filmmakers since the early days of the movies. Although the story of India's political and religious leader Mohandas K. Gandhi (1869–1948) has the sweep of history and the appeal of a deeply human and committed leading character, it took 20 years for British producer-director Sir Richard Attenborough to raise the money and bring *Gandhi* to the screen as a three and one-half hour film. With the help of India's late Prime Minister Jawaharlal Nehru and then of Nehru's daughter, Prime Minister Indira Gandhi, Attenborough was able to clear the obstacles for filming on location in India. Sir Richard was also fortunate to find a remarkable actor to portray Gandhi. Ben Kingsley both resembled the assassinated believer in nonviolent passive resistance and projected Gandhi's deep commitments. *Gandhi* was not only one of the year's most beautifully filmed and most graceful pictures, it also had the potential of informing a new generation of the significant role Gandhi played in his time.

Branching Out. Celebrated author Norman Mailer, who directed three films but had never written a screenplay that was produced, scripted the film version of his Pulitzer-Prize novel *The Executioner's Song.* The film was produced and directed by Lawrence Schiller.

Mailer's screenplay yielded a television movie, which was broadcast by NBC in a two-part installment, and also a theatrical version, which was sold for distribution outside the United States and which Mailer and Schiller hoped would ultimately reach American audiences in theaters. Despite shortcomings, Mailer's script revealed a sharp talent for screen dialogue and raised the possibility that if he attempted original screenplays instead of limiting his work to adaptations, this important American author also could contribute significantly to the cinema.

Going the Limit. There was a time in which films like those made today could not have been shown at all, or would have required considerable cutting before getting a seal of approval under the old Motion Picture Production Code. Many films released in 1982 were cases in point. *Victor/Victoria* dealt comically and candidly with the categorizing of the sexes. The film starred Julie Andrews as a woman nightclub singer who pretends to be a female impersonator, which results in complications when a macho Chicago gangster, charmingly played by James Garner, isn't sure which sex she is even though he has fallen in love. Robert Preston warmly played, without apology, Andrews' homosexual friend. In *The World According to Garp*, reference is made to an emasculating accident, although the incident is not so vividly depicted as in the book.

Broad, comically warped situations appeared in Paul Bartel's *Eating Raoul*, a selection at the 20th annual New York Film Festival. The story centers on a couple who decide to lure and kill sex deviants, then rob them to accumulate enough money to open a country gourmet restaurant. The picture sharply satirizes various aspects of Los Angeles life in particular and American life in general. Its message—murder can be less offensive to some people than sex. Bette Midler starred in *Jinxed*, a raunchy send-up of pictures along the lines of *The Postman Always Rings Twice*, and a film which contains language and situations that once was taboo.

Although filmmakers used to take particular pains to avoid anything explicit in films dealing with high school life, *Fast Times at Ridgemont High* was bold in its approach. A first film by Amy Heckerling and one admired by many critics upon its release by Universal Pictures, it certainly was not exploitative, but rather gently and openly recognized sexual experience as a fact of life and dealt intelligently with it.

What continued to worry many persons concerned with the welfare of youth was the violence still pervading the cinema—not surprising in view of the preoccupation with violence in most of the video games that have become the craze. *Blade Runner*, a futuristic version of the detective genre, had horrifying death scenes featuring exotic methods of killing. *The Road Warrior*, set in the bleak future when the world has been decimated by an atomic holocaust and only a few survivors exist, is almost nonstop violence. Parents were upset when youngsters found the film immensely exciting, as individuals fought each other for scarce gasoline in battered, but fortified cars.

Deaths. Moviegoers were saddened by the deaths of fabled personalities. Henry Fonda died at the age of 77 of chronic heart disease, Ingrid Bergman at 67 after a lengthy battle against cancer. Grace Kelly, who ended an illustrious career to fulfill her royal duties as Princess of Monaco, died at 52 following an auto accident. International cinema suffered a loss with the death at 36 of German director Rainer Werner Fassbinder. (*See also* OBITUARIES.)

Academy Awards. *Chariots of Fire* surprised the movie world when it achieved wide popularity and won the Oscar for best picture. Other Oscar winners were Warren Beatty, given the best directing award for *Reds;* and Henry Fonda and Katharine Hepburn, given best actor and actress awards for their work in *On Golden Pond.* (*See also* PRIZES AND AWARDS.)

WILLIAM WOLF, *"New York Magazine"*

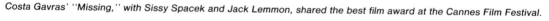

Costa Gavras' "Missing," with Sissy Spacek and Jack Lemmon, shared the best film award at the Cannes Film Festival.

Universal Pictures

Columbia Pictures

*German-made "Das Boot" (The Boat), with Jürgen Proch-
now as a U-boat captain, was a powerful World War II epic.*

ANNIE. Director, John Huston; screenplay by Carol
Sobleski, based on the Broadway play by Thomas
Meehan, which was based on "Little Orphan
Annie." With Albert Finney, Aileen Quinn.

AN OFFICER AND A GENTLEMAN. Director, Taylor
Hackford; screenplay by Douglas Day Stewart.
With Richard Gere, Louis Gossett, Jr.

AUTHOR! AUTHOR! Director, Arthur Hiller; screenplay
by Israel Horovitz. With Al Pacino.

BARBAROSA. Director, Fred Schepisi; screenplay by
William D. Wittliff. With Willie Nelson.

THE BEST LITTLE WHOREHOUSE IN TEXAS. Director, Colin Higgins; screenplay by Mr. Higgins,
Larry L. King, Peter Masterson. With Burt Reynolds, Dolly Parton.

BLADE RUNNER. Director, Ridley Scott; screenplay by
Hampton Fancher, David Peoples. With Harrison
Ford, Rutger Hauer.

THE BORDER. Director, Tony Richardson; screenplay
by Deric Washburn, Walon Green, David Freeman. With Jack Nicholson, Harvey Keitel.

BRIMSTONE & TREACLE. Director, Richard Loncraine; screenplay by Dennis Potter. With Sting,
Denholm Elliott, Joan Plowright.

CANNERY ROW. Written and directed by David S.
Ward, based on novels by John Steinbeck. With
Nick Nolte, Debra Winger.

CAT PEOPLE. Director, Paul Schrader; screenplay by
Alan Ormsby, based on a story by DeWitt Bodeen.
With Malcolm McDowell, John Heard, Nastassia
Kinski.

THE CHOSEN. Director, Jeremy Paul Kagan; screen-
play by Edwin Gordon, based on the novel by
Chaim Potok. With Maximilian Schell, Rod
Steiger, Robby Benson.

CHRISTIANE F. Director, Ulrich Edel; screenplay by
Herman Weigel. With Natja Brunkhorst.

CIRCLE OF DECEIT. Director, Volker Schlöndorff;
screenplay by Mr. Schlöndorff, Jean-Claude Car-
riere, Margarethe von Trotta, Kai Hermann, from a
novel by Nicolas Born. With Bruno Ganz.

**COME BACK TO THE 5 & DIME JIMMY DEAN, JIMMY
DEAN.** Director, Robert Altman; screenplay by Ed
Graczyk. With Sandy Dennis, Cher, Karen Black.

CONAN THE BARBARIAN. Director, John Milius;
screenplay by Mr. Milius and Oliver Stone, based
on the character created by Robert E. Howard.
With Arnold Schwarzenegger, James Earl Jones.

THE DARK CRYSTAL. Directors, Jim Henson and
Frank Oz; screenplay by David Odell; special dialogue by Alan Garner.

DAS BOOT. Written and directed by Wolfgang Petersen. With Jürgen Prochnow.

DEAD MEN DON'T WEAR PLAID. Director, Carl
Reiner; screenplay by Mr. Reiner, George Gipe,
Steve Martin. With Steve Martin, Rachel Ward.

DEATHTRAP. Director, Sidney Lumet; screenplay by
Jay Presson Allen, based on a play by Ira Levin.
With Michael Caine, Christopher Reeve.

DINER. Written and directed by Barry Levinson. With
Steve Guttenberg, Daniel Stern, Mickey Rourke,
Kevin Bacon.

EATING RAOUL. Director, Paul Bartel; screenplay by
Mr. Bartel, Richard Blackburn. With Mary
Waronov, Robert Beltran, Paul Bartel.

E.T. THE EXTRA-TERRESTRIAL. Director, Steven
Spielberg; screenplay by Melissa Mathison. With
Drew Barrymore, Robert Macnaughton, Henry
Thomas.

EVIL UNDER THE SUN. Director, Guy Hamilton;
screenplay by Anthony Shaffer. With Peter Ustinov, Maggie Smith, James Mason.

FIREFOX. Director, Clint Eastwood; screenplay by
Alex Lasker, Wendell Wellman. With Clint Eastwood.

FIRST BLOOD. Director, Ted Kotcheff; screenplay by
Michael Kozoll, William Sackheim, Sylvester Stallone.

FITZCARRALDO. Director, Werner Herzog; screenplay
by Mr. Herzog. With Klaus Kinski.

FRANCES. Director, Graeme Clifford; screenplay by
Eric Bergren, Christopher DeVore, Nicholas
Kazan. With Jessica Lange.

GANDHI. Director, Richard Attenborough; screenplay
by John Briley. With Ben Kingsley, John Gielgud,
Martin Sheen, Candice Bergen.

GREGORY'S GIRL. Written and directed by Bill Forsyth. With Dee Hepburn, Gordon John Sinclair.

HEALTH. Director, Robert Altman; screenplay by Mr.
Altman, Frank Barhydt, Paul Dooley. With Glenda
Jackson, Carol Burnett, James Garner, Lauren
Bacall.

I'M DANCING AS FAST AS I CAN. Director, Jack Hof-
siss; screenplay by David Rabe. With Jill Clay-
burgh.

I OUGHT TO BE IN PICTURES. Director, Herbert Ross;
screenplay by Neil Simon. With Walter Matthau,
Ann-Margret, Dinah Manoff.

JINXED. Director, Don Siegel; screenplay by Bert
Blessing, David Newman. With Bette Midler, Rip
Torn, Ken Wahl.

LE BEAU MARIAGE. Written and directed by Eric
Rohmer. With Béatrice Romand.

LOLA. Director, Rainer Werner Fassbinder; screenplay by Fassbinder, Peter Marthesheimer, Pea Frohlich. With Barbara Sukowa.

THE LONG GOOD FRIDAY. Director, John Mackenzie; screenplay by Barry Keeffe. With Bob Hoskins, Eddie Constantine.

MAKING LOVE. Director, Arthur Hiller; screenplay by Barry Sandler. With Michael Ontkean, Kate Jackson, Harry Hamlin, Wendy Hiller, Arthur Hill.

A MIDSUMMER NIGHT'S SEX COMEDY. Written and directed by Woody Allen. With Woody Allen, Mia Farrow, José Ferrer, Tony Roberts, Mary Steenburgen.

MISSING. Director, Costa-Gavras; screenplay by Mr. Costa-Gavras, Donald Stewart. With Jack Lemmon, Sissy Spacek, Melanie Mayron, John Shea.

THE MISSIONARY. Director, Richard Loncraine; screenplay by Michael Palin. With Michael Palin, Maggie Smith, Trevor Howard.

MY FAVORITE YEAR. Director, Richard Benjamin; screenplay by Norman Steinberg, Dennis Palumbo. With Peter O'Toole, Mark Linn-Baker.

NIGHT CROSSING. Director, Delbert Mann; screenplay by John McGreevey. With John Hurt, Beau Bridges, Jane Alexander.

ONE FROM THE HEART. Director, Francis Coppola; screenplay by Mr. Coppola, Armyan Bernstein. With Frederic Forrest, Teri Garr.

PARTNERS. Director, James Burrows; screenplay by Francis Veber. With Ryan O'Neal, John Hurt.

PERSONAL BEST. Written and directed by Robert Towne. With Mariel Hemingway, Patrice Donnelly.

POLTERGEIST. Director, Tobe Hooper; screenplay by Steven Spielberg, Michael Grais, Mark Victor. With Jobeth Williams, Heather O'Rourke.

PORKY'S. Written and directed by Bob Clark.

QUEST FOR FIRE. Director, Jean-Jacques Annaud; screenplay by Gerard Brach, based on a novel by J. H. Rosny, Sr. With Rae Dawn Chong.

RICHARD PRYOR LIVE ON THE SUNSET STRIP. Director, Joe Layton; screenplay by Richard Pryor. With Richard Pryor.

ROCKY III. Written and directed by Sylvester Stallone. With Sylvester Stallone, Talia Shire.

THE SECRET OF N.I.M.H. Director, Don Bluth; based on *Mrs. Frisby and the Rats of N.I.M.H.* by Robert

C. O'Brien, story adaptation by Mr. Bluth, John Pomeroy, and Gary Goldman. (animated)

SHOOT THE MOON. Director, Alan Parker; screenplay by Bo Goldman. With Albert Finney, Diane Keaton.

SIX WEEKS. Director, Tony Bill; screenplay by David Seltzer. With Dudley Moore, Mary Tyler Moore.

SOPHIE'S CHOICE. Director, Alan J. Pakula; screenplay by Mr. Pakula. With Meryl Streep, Kevin Kline, Peter MacNicol.

STAR TREK II: THE WRATH OF KHAN. Director Nicholas Meyer; screenplay by Jack B. Sowards. With William Shatner, Leonard Nimoy, Ricardo Montalban.

STILL OF THE NIGHT. Written and directed by Robert Benton. With Meryl Streep, Roy Scheider.

TEMPEST. Director, Paul Mazursky; screenplay by Mr. Mazursky, Leon Capetanos. With John Cassavetes, Raul Julia.

TEX. Director, Tim Hunter; screenplay by Mr. Hunter, Charlie Haas. With Matt Dillon.

TIME STANDS STILL. Director, Peter Gothar; screenplay by Mr. Gothar, Geza Beremenyi.

TOOTSIE. Director, Sydney Pollack; screenplay by Larry Gelbart and Murray Schisgal. With Dustin Hoffman, Jessica Lange.

TRAGEDY OF A RIDICULOUS MAN. Written and directed by Bernardo Bertolucci. With Ugo Tognazzi, Anouk Aimee.

TRON. Written and directed by Steven Lisberger. With Jeff Bridges.

THE VERDICT. Director, Sidney Lumet; screenplay by David Mamet, based on a novel by Barry Reed. With Paul Newman, James Mason, Jack Warden.

VERONIKA VOSS. Director, Rainer Werner Fassbinder; screenplay by Peter Marthescheimer, Pea Frohlich. With Rosel Zech, Hilmar Thate.

VICTOR/VICTORIA. Written and directed by Blake Edwards, based on *Victor und Victoria*. With Julie Andrews, James Garner, Robert Preston, Lesley Ann Warren.

THE WORLD ACCORDING TO GARP. Director, George Roy Hill; screenplay by Steve Tesich. With Robin Williams, Glenn Close.

YES, GIORGIO. Director, Franklin J. Schaffner; screenplay by Norman Steinberg. With Luciano Pavarotti.

Albert Finney played Daddy Warbucks and Aileen Quinn the title role in the colorful screen version of "Annie."

Wide World

MUSIC

Several new concert halls, including Toronto's Thomson Hall (above) and Peoria's Civic Center, opened in the fall.

Classical

If the creation of new facilities were the principal criterion for classical music, 1982 would have been a banner year. Five concert halls were opened in North America within two weeks in September, a sixth in October. Earlier, on March 3, the most extensive arts facility in Western Europe, London's almost $300 million Barbican Centre, was inaugurated. Initiated as much as 10 to 20 years ago when economic times and prospects were very different, these centers may yet have a positive, stimulating effect on the musical scene.

The Halls. Toronto's Roy Thomson Hall (September 13) and Baltimore's Joseph Meyerhoff Hall (September 16) are designed for concert use, mainly by the cities' symphonies. Thomson Hall, designed by Arthur Erickson at a cost of $39 million and seating 2,812, is architecturally striking, an inverted "cupcake" sheathed in glass and aluminum. The oval interior brings the audience near to the orchestra. The acoustics were generally praised.

Utilizing the same acousticians, the firm of Bolt, Beranek and Newman, Baltimore's $22 million Meyerhoff Hall, seating 2,467, features a similar system of sound-reflecting discs overhead. The hall was well received at its opening concert in which the pianist Leon Fleischer, 54, whose right hand mysteriously had been crippled for 17 years, made a successful return playing César Franck's *Symphonic Variations* with the Baltimore Symphony.

On September 10 the New Orleans Philharmonic inaugurated its new home in the Orpheum Theater, a 1921 Beaux-Arts style vaudeville and movie house, seating 1,950, and renovated at a cost of $2 million. The Peoria (IL) Civic Center (September 11) includes a 2,200-seat theater costing $22 million and a 10,000-seat arena and large Exhibition Hall. Designed by Philip Johnson and John Burgee, its total cost was $64.2 million. The theater's opera stage is adapted for concert use by a stage shell and an electronic acoustical-enhancement system designed by Christopher Jaffe. A similar system by Jaffe for the 2,500-seat Concert Hall in the Hult Center for the Performing Arts of Eugene, OR (September 24), proved effective in assisting the resonance and equalizing acoustics for what is really a multipurpose theater. Designed by Norman Pfeiffer in a colorful mix of styles, and including a 500-seat theater, the $22.4 million Hult arts building is part of a $55.5 million arts and convention center. Uniquely, it was financed by the city with no federal or state assistance, and despite the hard-hit condition of the region's lumber-based economy.

For the multipurpose El Pomar Great Hall of the Pikes Peak Center, Colorado Springs, CO (October 15), the acoustics and function of the approximately $14 million, 2,100-seat facility are adjustable by changing physical elements. The acoustician, Russell Johnson, provided retractable cloth banners and an adjustable canopy and movable stage towers to create a performing chamber for the musicians.

In the six months after its March 3 opening, London's Barbican Centre drew one million visitors. (*See also* LONDON.)

Opera. Of several new operas premiered under major auspices in the United States, all in conservative, tonal idioms, none seemed likely to be repeated, much less taken into the repertory. Robert Ward had two premieres. His *Abelard and Heloise,* presented by the Charlotte (NC) Opera in February was mildly received. On June 4 his *Minutes Till Midnight* was performed by the Greater Miami Opera to open Miami's first New World Festival of the Arts. Ward's romantic, Broadway-musical style of writing to a prosaic libretto on the moral dilemma of a nuclear physicist trivialized the subject.

Stephen Paulus' *The Postman Always Rings Twice,* presented by the Opera Theater of St. Louis, did not carry operatically the colloquial language drawn from James M. Cain's 1934 best-seller. The late Bernard Hermann's *Wuthering Heights,* given its premiere by the Portland Opera in November, harked back to a romantic film-score idiom of a much earlier day.

The Santa Fe Opera's premiere of George Rochberg's *The Confidence Man* (July 31) attracted much interest because of the composer's eminence and famous return to tonality in recent years. The libretto, based on a chapter in an obscure Herman Melville novel, was an awkward allegory. The music was a mix of easy, derivative writing; the opera was dramatically weak.

Opera repertory policies could not have reached a more conservative point, but the companies basically remained sound. However, experiencing real trouble at the box office and a $3 million deficit, the New York City Opera canceled its spring season for 1983 to create one continuous season from July to December. Bold new creations continued to be a European affair,

The occasion marking the debut of Baltimore's new $22 million Joseph Meyerhoff Symphony Hall also saw the triumphant return of pianist Leon Fleischer to dual-handed playing after a 17-year hiatus due to a mysterious illness which had crippled his right hand. Prior to corrective surgery, Mr. Fleisher had been able to play only music written for the left hand.

The New York City Opera company's premiere of Leonard Bernstein's "Candide" (above) was a smash hit of the fall, while Placido Domingo's performance in the title role of the Metropolitan Opera's "Les Contes d'Hoffmann" was well received during the spring season.

as exemplified by Luciano Berio's *La Vera Stória,* a far-flung work striving to become a mirror of the times, ambiguous and searching, given its premiere at La Scala in Milan on March 9.

Operatic adventure in America was found mostly in revivals of neglected works, including Haydn's *Orlando Paladino* (March 12), by the Pennsylvania Opera Theater, celebrating the 250th anniversary of Haydn's birth; Rameau's *Abaris ou les Boreades* by Opera Redeviva in New York (March 21); and Arrigo Boito's *Nerone* by Eve Queler's Opera Orchestra of New York (April 12).

Symphony Orchestras. In celebration of its centenary, the Berlin Philharmonic under Herbert von Karajan visited the United States in October, giving a six-program series in New York City and in Pasadena, CA. Christoph von Dohnányi, music director of the Hamburg State Opera, was named the Cleveland Orchestra's music director beginning in the summer of 1984. He succeeds Lorin Maazel, who became director of the Vienna State Opera in the fall of 1982.

On the eve of its 50th season, the Kansas City Philharmonic was disbanded and succeeded by a smaller, part-time orchestra, the Kansas City Symphony. The Philharmonic had suffered a steady decline in every aspect of orchestral operation. Plagued by financial and labor problems, the Florida Philharmonic was dissolved effective September 30.

Festivals. In April, the Filene Center at Wolf Trap Farm Park was destroyed by a fire of unknown origin. The only national park in the United States devoted to the performing arts, it had seen 11 years of classical and popular music performances. A special structure of fabric and aluminum arches was flown to the United States

from Saudi Arabia, where it had been in use, and the season was saved. In October, the U.S. Congress authorized a grant and loan to rebuild the Filene Center.

The centennial of Igor Stravinsky's birth (June 17, 1882) was celebrated nationwide. The events included a National Symphony concert on June 17 at the Washington, DC, cathedral, conducted by Leonard Bernstein and Michael Tilson Thomas, and telecast to Europe. Nationally, there were a five-concert series by the Pittsburgh Symphony, a three-hour marathon concert by the San Francisco Symphony, and other concerts by the Milwaukee, Omaha, Los Angeles, New Orleans, and Cleveland orchestras. Stravinsky was the subject of a month-long festival at Carleton College in Minnesota in February, of the June 4 weekend at the 36th Ojai Festival (CA), of an International Stravinsky Symposium (September 10–14) at the University of California, San Diego, with such illustrious participants as Robert Craft, Ernst Krenek, Virgil Thomson, and Charles Wuorinen.

The 13th Inter-American Music Festival in Washington, DC, presented five concerts (May 6–16) in which the *Piano Concerto* by Germán Cáceres (El Salvador) and Symphony No. 1 (*Age of Victory*) by Thomas Ludwig (United States) were considered outstanding. A project entitled "Scandinavia Today" was celebrated nationwide with the PBS telecast in September of the first of six programs of music by Nordic composers played by the Minnesota Orchestra. Other participating orchestras were the Seattle Symphony and the National Symphony, with five commissioned premieres of works by Arne Nordheim (Norway), Erik Abrahamsen (Denmark), Aulis Sallinen (Finland), and Ingmar Lidholm (Sweden).

Miami invested $4.8 million in a three-week marathon of more than 160 performances in hot, humid June, hoping (vainly, as it turned out) to lure tourists to its New World Festival of the Arts. The guest groups included the Israel Philharmonic, Zubin Mehta conducting, and the Chamber Music Society of Lincoln Center, which included in its 12 programs two noteworthy works commissioned for the festival—Morton Gould's suite for piano and cello and Lukas Foss' *Solo Observed* for piano with vibraphone, electric organ, and cello.

New Music. Proponents of music in avowedly tonal, so-called minimalist and experimental performance styles mounted a distinct and aggressive campaign against classical, so-called mainstream modern music. Although the works of Steve Reich (with his new *Tehillim*), Philip Glass, Frederic Rzewski, and performance-art musicians such as Meredith Monk and Joan La Barbara were being widely performed and received more media attention than "classicists" such as Milton Babbitt, Charles Wuorinen, Roger Sessions, and Elliott Carter, the younger generation pushed for polarization. The contrast between the traditionalist and the new populist views was reflected in the Fromm Festival of Contemporary Music at the Tanglewood Festival and the New Music America Festival in Chicago.

The Fromm Festival in August featured fully written out chamber works by Vivian Fine, Earl Kim, Shulamit Ran, Fred Lerdahl, and orchestral works by Jacob Druckman, György Ligeti, and Theodore Antoniou.

Chicago's new city-wide festival encompassed a broad span of experimental and exploratory music and music-theater pieces ranging from wind-activated sculptures, the Natural Sound Ensemble's singing with the animals at the zoo, and events on the water, including Alvin Curran's *Maritime Rites,* for singers in rowboats. The Chicago Symphony participated by playing Alvin Lucier's *Crossings,* for oscillators and amplified orchestra.

This confrontation did not occur at the Santa Fe Chamber Music Festival (July 11–August 16), where the mainstream was represented by composers-in-residence William Schuman, Ned Rorem, Richard Wernick, Yehudi Wyner, and John Harbison. Harbison's *Variations* for clarinet, violin and piano was singled out.

Awards. Named as fellows by the John and Catherine MacArthur Foundation were: Ralph Shapey, composer on the University of Chicago faculty, and Conlon Nancarrow, a composer of highly complex, original music for player piano and an expatriate American resident of Mexico.

In June, Michael Gurt, 23, Ypsilanti, MI, won the Sixth Gina Bachauer International Piano Competition in Salt Lake City, UT. Gurt's prize included a gold medal, Steinway grand piano, and recital engagements. In the first quadrennial International Violin Competition of Indianapolis, IN, in September, Mihaela Martin, 23, of Bucharest, Rumania, was awarded the first prize of $10,000, numerous appearances in America and Europe, and two recordings engagements.

ROBERT COMMANDAY
Music Critic, "San Francisco Chronicle"

In honor of the 80th birthday of Marian Anderson (center), opera stars Shirley Verrett (left) and Grace Bumbry sang.

UPI

Jazz

On the jazz scene of 1982, history repeated itself. In the midst of a harsh recession, new jazz clubs (like the Blue Note and Lush Life in New York) opened throughout the United States. Many more clubs changed from a pop/rock to a jazz format. Not since the 1940s has live jazz experienced so great an amount of exposure and artistic and commercial success. The popularity of jazz during the 1930s Great Depression, the mid-1950s recession, and today's hard times speaks well for the continued relevance of jazz.

In contrast to the surge in live performance popularity, jazz recording and publishing sales were drastically down. The reasons for this decline seemed to be threefold. First, the recording market has been saturated with new releases and re-releases, as well as new jazz charts, texts, and method books. Second, there have been severe cuts in the budgets of most public schools and universities. Third, the misuse of the tape, cassette, and xerox machines threatened the recording and publishing industries. To offset this downward trend, many record companies presented their jazz artists on pop-chart, commercially oriented releases, but with mediocre results. To survive the economic crunch, many important publishing firms sold out to large conglomerates. An important recent acquisition was that of Jim Houston's studio P/R Publishing Company by Columbia Pictures.

Festivals. The popularity of live jazz was evident again in the successful presentation of jazz festivals, such as the Kool Jazz Festivals in New York, Chicago, and San Diego; the New Orleans and Atlantic City Jazz Fests; and the Mayport and All That Jazz Festival in Mayport, FL. New York's Kool Festival produced the reunion of four very important groups—the Modern Jazz Quartet, the Benny Goodman Quartet, the original Herman "Four Brothers," and the Jazztet led by Benny Golson. This festival also included tributes to Sidney Bechet, Stan Kenton, Lester Young, Alec Wilder, and the women of jazz.

International jazz events included the North Sea Jazz Festival at The Hague, the Montreux Jazz Festival in Switzerland, and the Pori Jazz Festival in Finland.

Personalities. Trumpeter Wynton Marsalis and saxophonist Branford Marsalis, sons of the gifted New Orleans-based pianist Ellis Marsalis, were making names for themselves on the New York jazz circuit. Although still in his 20s, Wynton Marsalis is an exceptionally talented and spectacular jazz virtuoso. After a 10-year absence, 56-year-old Miles Davis made a triumphant return to Europe, playing two concerts in France —in Paris and Bordeaux. The Weather Report band made an impressive San Diego debut.

Awards. The winners in the 30th Annual International Jazz Critics Poll included: *Down Beat* Hall of Fame—Fats Navarro, big band—Toshiko Akiyoshi/Lew Tabackin, jazz group—Art Ensemble of Chicago, trumpet—Lester Bowie, trombone—Jimmy Knepper, alto sax—Phil Woods, tenor sax—Archie Shepp, baritone sax—Pepper Adams, clarinet—Anthony Braxton, violin—Stephane Grappelli, guitar—Jim Hall, acoustic bass—Charlie Haden, electric bass—Steve Swallow, drums—Max Roach, male singer—Joe Williams, female singer—Sarah Vaughan.

DOMINIC SPERA, *Indiana University*

Popular

In 1982 the depressed economy was a major factor in reshaping the pop music world. The two camps of art and commerce were clearly divided. Commercial popular music became increasingly bland as record companies with decreasing sales and radio stations with shrinking audiences aimed for the largest possible market.

Although technology provided many new sources of entertainment, a National Association of Broadcasters (NAB) study found that 35% of Americans 18 and older (the majority of the U.S. population) still listened to radio, once the primary disseminator of pop music. However, radio had become conservative, playing only established sellers and cutting off a potent means of exposure for new and peripheral artists. An untried performer first had to prove himself elsewhere. Innovative and artistically significant offerings appeared on major labels and on the airwaves after proving their audience appeal on a small label, generally aided by club exposure.

Radio returned to a programming philosophy reminiscent of the pre-rock 1940s, and cable TV took up the slack. The aforementioned NAB study found that 51% of Americans over age 18 listed television as their primary leisure activity. MTV, the cable music channel, grew ever more influential. When a new artist's video clip appeared on MTV, his record sales increased 15–20%. In this way, many British New Wave groups with odd names like Haircut 100, A Flock of Seagulls, and Soft Cell came to dominate American charts. Their sound was an intriguing blend of synthesizers, saxophones, minor keys, and 1960s American rhythm and blues (R&B).

As the urban cowboy craze repeated disco's fade-out, dance clubs offered more diversified music. They became entertainment centers as well as artists' springboards, purveying live and recorded music, video, and electronic games. The Go-Go's, the first all-female rock band ever to have a number one album, gained their first public notice in dance clubs.

Concert tours continued to be expensive, undertaken only by superstars like Elton John, Genesis, and Olivia Newton-John and newer stars Rick Springfield, Asia, and Joan Jett. The most significant rock concert event of 1982 was the Us Festival in California. It was the Woodstock of the 1980s, but better organized and with

More than 200,000 rock fans showed up at the Us Festival, a three-day concert in California in September.

an eye to technology. Its major acts ranged from mainstream rockers like Fleetwood Mac, Pat Benatar, and Tom Petty to New Wave's The Police and Talking Heads. The show had the best outdoor sound system ever constructed and special video games and computer technology.

Rock's maturity was driven home by the demise of many long-established acts and by the renewed careers of once-popular performers of the 1950s and 1960s. The Who's final concert tour was a massive success, heightened by the inclusion of The Clash, one of New Wave's foremost bands. The Doobie Brothers and The Eagles split; The Bee Gees broke up with plans to re-form in 1984. Back on the charts were old-timers Joe Cocker, Gary U.S. Bonds, Chicago, and Crosby, Stills & Nash.

Interest in the music of the past was evidenced by the inception of "Yesterhits," a feature charting the hits of 10 and 20 years ago in *Billboard,* the major music trade magazine. This hunger for the past, perhaps triggered by the bleak economy, applied to all categories of music. Larry Elgart, a big band leader of the 1940s, had the largest selling swing album of all time in *Hooked on Swing,* a medley of past hits. Both Smokey Robinson, one of Motown's earliest stars, and crooner Johnny Mathis celebrated their 25th anniversaries in the recording industry. A doo-wop revival was accelerated by the birth of a modern label. In country, Patsy Cline, Hank Williams, and Gene Autry resurfaced.

Country music on the air had gone the route of rock. The vocals of Ronnie Milsap, Alabama, and Eddie Rabbitt were almost MOR (Middle-of-the-Road) pop. What was considered country was so far from the traditional sound that the line between it and other categories blurred. Performers who exemplified this crossover ability were Juice Newton, Kenny Rogers, and Anne Murray. Willie Nelson, Merle Haggard, and Loretta Lynn continued to be successful.

Music identified with black audiences was neglected by commercial music interests. Black artists who survived on major labels were those with the broadest appeal to both black and white audiences. Thus, Stevie Wonder, Diana Ross, Kool & the Gang, and even Paul McCartney (because of his collaboration with Wonder) dominated black charts and airwaves. Once again, small labels and dance clubs were responsible for discovering many new black artists like The Dazz Band. A truly innovative sound emerged in black pop as synthesizers were coupled with RB vocals. Black groups like Time, The Bus Boys, and Kid Creole & the Coconuts experimented with new sounds and sophisticated lyrics that departed from black stereotypes.

Although the concert market was soft, the Budweiser Superfest package of black artists— Aretha Franklin, Ashford & Simpson, and Stephanie Mills among them—drew crowds. Jennifer Holliday of *Dreamgirls* joined the handful of black artists whose careers were launched on Broadway. Reggae continued as an important influence on 1980s pop.

Broadway fare was eclectic, from the country sound of *Pump Boys & Dinettes* to *Rock'n Roll: The First 5,000 Years. Cats* and *Nine* were the two most acclaimed musicals.

Vangelis's film score for *Chariots of Fire* was film's first number one sound track since 1978.

Artists who did not fit readily into a category abounded. They experimented with new combinations of styles and with modern electronics. Prominent among them were Steve Reich, the Swollen Monkeys, Brian Eno, Robert Fripp, and Keith Jarrett.

See also Rock 'n' Roll, page 61.

PAULETTE WEISS, *"Stereo Review"*

NEBRASKA

UPI

For Eric Salem, 15, election-night returns are good news. He was elected to the Lancaster County (NE) Weed Board.

Agriculture, legislative activities, and a controversial election campaign gained Nebraskans' attention in 1982.

Agriculture. A cool, wet growing season delayed both planting and maturing of fall grain crops. It also slowed the wheat harvest and decreased yields and quality in eastern Nebraska. Estimated grain crop production in millions of bushels was corn, 786.6; grain sorghum, 134.3; wheat, 103.25; and soybeans, 85.1. Production costs remained high and grain prices declined. Both soil erosion and nitrate pollution of groundwater were major concerns of Nebraska farmers.

The Legislature and State Government. The annual legislative session boosted the state sales tax from 3% to 3.5% and raised cigarette, gasoline, and corporate income taxes. Gov. Charles Thone vetoed pay raises for state constitutional officers and, by veto, delayed raises to other state employees until Jan. 1, 1983. The legislature passed a law regulating groundwater irrigation pumping and banned capital punishment for minors. It adopted an act guaranteeing equal opportunity in education, a vigorous drunken-driving law, and a controversial measure for distributing state funds to local governments. Efforts to resolve a private school controversy failed.

After the legislature adjourned, the state board of equalization raised the state income tax from 15% to 17% of federal liability. However, declining state revenues caused the governor to call a special legislative session in November to consider budget cuts.

Elections. The May 11 primary election nominated candidates to run for office in November. A proposed constitutional amendment to raise the pay for state legislators from $4,800 to $13,333 per year was soundly defeated. The November 2 general election had the second largest turnout of voters in Nebraska history. At the state level, the gubernatorial race and Initiative 300, aimed at regulating acquisition of Nebraska farmland by nonfarm corporations, were most controversial. Bob Kerrey (D) narrowly defeated incumbent Charles Thone (R) for governor. Initiative 300 was added as a constitutional amendment in spite of heavy contributions to the opposition by out-of-state insurance corporations interested in Nebraska land.

Edward Zorinsky (D) was easily elected to a second term in the U.S. Senate over Jim Keck (R), a retired Air Force lieutenant general. The three incumbent congressmen, Douglas Bereuter (R), Hal Daub (R), and Virginia Smith (R), were reelected. Proposed state constitutional amendments to remove final reading of bills in the legislature, to reduce the period of time for redemption of property to be sold for nonpayment of taxes, and to reimburse legislators for expenses were defeated. Constitutional amendments were approved authorizing issuance by local government of revenue bonds to acquire and develop real estate and issuance of revenue bonds for water development.

Miscellaneous. An illegal Christian school received continuous media coverage in Nebraska and nationwide. The Baptist church that housed the school was twice padlocked by court order and its pastor jailed. The issue remained unresolved.

The University of Nebraska football team, a special interest of Nebraskans and a longtime power in intercollegiate sports, had another winning year in 1982.

ORVILLE H. ZABEL
Midland Lutheran College

NEBRASKA · Information Highlights

Area: 77,355 sq mi (200 349 km²).
Population (1980 census): 1,569,825.
Chief Cities (1980 census): Lincoln, the capital, 171,932; Omaha, 313,911; Grand Island, 33,180.
Government (1982): *Chief Officers*—governor, Charles Thone (R); lt. gov., Roland A. Luedtke (R). *Legislature* (unicameral)—49 members (nonpartisan).
State Finances (fiscal year 1981): *Revenues,* $1,583,000,000; *expenditures,* $1,558,000,000.
Personal Income (1981): $16,346,000,000; per capita, $10,366.
Labor Force (Aug. 1982): *Nonagricultural wage and salary earners,* 604,400; *unemployed* 43,300 (5.5% of total force).
Education: *Enrollment* (fall 1981)—public elementary schools, 186,755; public secondary, 86,585; colleges and universities (1981–82), 93,507 students. *Public school expenditures* (1980–81), $583,426,000 ($2,105 per pupil).

NETHERLANDS

Although 1982 was highlighted by a year-long celebration of two centuries of friendship between the Netherlands and the United States, Dutch political life continued to be disturbed by the problems of a deepening economic recession and by uncertainties in international relations, especially with the United States.

The Bicentennial Year. The Netherlands marked 200 years of peaceful, friendly relations with America. Dutch recognition of John Adams as the first minister of the United States on April 19, 1782, was commemorated with a series of cultural, economic, scholarly, and political festivities. Queen Beatrix paid two visits to the United States on the occasion of the bicentennial and addressed a joint session of Congress. In the midst of the celebrations, however, the Netherlands found itself involved in a painful reappraisal of relations with the United States. U.S.-supported plans to base 48 NATO cruise missiles in the Netherlands aroused strong antinuclear sentiments among the Dutch people.

Politics. In September elections, Dutch voters shifted their support from a center-left to a center-right orientation in the Second (lower) Chamber of the States General (parliament). The parliamentary election was made necessary by the breakup in May of the coalition government headed by Premier Andreas van Agt, a Christian Democrat, and Vice-Premier Joop den Uyl, leader of the Labor party. Disagreement over ways to confront the economic recession and over foreign policy had grown too deep to permit continuation of the coalition. An interim coalition of the Christian Democrats and Democrats '66, a progressive, non-socialist party that also had been in the Van Agt-Den Uyl cabinet, had too narrow a base to continue long in office. The parliamentary election weakened the center forces, while the Labor party emerged with the largest representation, and the Liberals sharply increased their numbers. A surprising trend during the year was the growing amount of support among young people for the conservative Liberal party.

Although it was evident from the beginning that the new government would be composed of Christian Democrats and Liberals, the negotiations for its formation lasted almost two months. Van Agt, who had enjoyed considerable personal popularity, stunned the public in October by withdrawing from consideration as the new government's leader, citing health reasons. His place was taken by Rudolph (Ruud) F. M. Lubbers; at 43 years of age, Lubbers was only one of several younger men who took over the leadership of major political parties during the year. A new ministry was sworn in early in November, with the Christian Democrats holding the most important posts. It advocated reduction in government expenditures, especially in salaries and welfare payments.

These policies, as well as continued support of the Western alliance and of NATO defense measures, despite disagreements with the United States, increased the likelihood of clashes with the leftist parties and with the antinuclear movement. The strong outpouring of antinuclear forces and opposition to NATO policies, which verged on a revival of traditional Dutch neutralism, came not only from the customary left and environmental forces, but also from strong pacifist movements in the Catholic and Protestant churches. A march by several hundred thousand persons in Amsterdam was the high point of the antinuclear campaign.

Economic Developments. The recession deepened during the year. Foreign trade, on which the Dutch economy is largely based, was more sluggish than ever. Dutch manufacturing had difficulty maintaining its position in international competition, and the number of bankruptcies, including those of several very large firms, continued to rise. Unemployment rose implacably above the 12% figure, and strikes, which had become rare, broke out again, notably in the key port of Rotterdam. Government policy after the withdrawal of the Labor party from the cabinet was designed to mitigate the effects of the recession for business by reducing the levels of wages and taxes. It hoped thereby to reinvigorate economic activity and restore employment, but social conflict, generally quite limited since World War II, threatened to resume.

In a November policy statement to parliament, the new government announced plans for extensive spending cuts and a freeze on the wages of workers in the public sector. Unions representing the affected workers responded with threats of massive strikes.

It was not such direct labor-capital confrontation that brought new disorders to Dutch cities during the year. In Amsterdam renewed conflicts erupted over clearance of squatters from empty buildings and over construction of a new city hall and opera house.

HERBERT H. ROWEN, *Rutgers University*

NETHERLANDS · Information Highlights

Official Name: Kingdom of the Netherlands.
Location: Northwestern Europe.
Area: 13,104 sq mi (33 940 km²).
Population (1982): 14,310,526.
Chief Cities (Jan. 1981 est.): Amsterdam, the capital, 712,294; Rotterdam, 576,330; The Hague, the seat of government, 456,726.
Government: *Head of state,* Beatrix, queen (acceded April 30, 1980). *Head of government,* Rudolph F. M. Lubbers, prime minister (took office Nov. 1982). *Legislature*—States General: First Chamber and Second Chamber.
Monetary Unit: Guilder (2.721 guilders equal U.S.$1, Nov. 30, 1982).
Gross Domestic Product (1981 U.S.$): $139,076,-000,000.
Economic Indexes (1981): *Consumer Prices, all items* (1970=100), 216.5; *food* (1979=100), 131.1. *Industrial production* (1975=100), 109.
Foreign Trade (1981 U.S.$): *Imports,* $66,107,000,-000; *exports,* $68,756,000,000.

NEVADA

A faltering economy and November elections highlighted events in Nevada in 1982.

Elections. For the first time in 56 years, the Nevada electorate failed to return an incumbent governor for a second elected term. Democratic Attorney General Richard Bryan rode a landslide margin in his home county of Clark (including Las Vegas) to a 12% margin of victory over Republican Gov. Robert List, who was hurt by the economic recession and a large shortfall in state revenue projections.

In the U.S. Senate race, Democrat Howard Cannon, seeking a fifth term, was one of only two incumbent senators in the country to suffer defeat. Cannon had survived a hard-fought primary challenge from four-term Congressman James Santini in which the National Conservative Political Action Committee (NCPAC) used extensive negative advertising against the incumbent. The NCPAC ads seemed to backfire in the primary, so the group stayed out of the general election until the closing days. Little-known former state Sen. Jacob "Chic" Hecht won a narrow victory in November, overcoming a large Cannon lead in the final three weeks with negative television advertisements, a visit by President Ronald Reagan to Las Vegas, and the endorsement of popular Sen. Paul Laxalt. Nevada will have two elected Republicans in the U.S. Senate for the first time in 90 years.

Nevadans elected two members of the lower house of Congress for the first time in history, with Democrat Harry Reid, a former lieutenant governor, winning the Clark County district seat and Republican Barbara Vucanovich, longtime aide to Senator Laxalt, winning the seat representing the rest of the state. The Democrats increased their edge in the state senate to 17–4, but their margin in the expanded assembly was reduced to 23–19.

The voters turned down a proposed constitutional amendment, via the initiative process, that would have removed the sales tax from restaurant food. The same proposal had been ap-

UPI

Chic and Gail Hecht greet supporters after he unseated U.S. Sen. Howard Cannon, a four-term Democrat.

proved overwhelmingly in 1980. An amendment that would have allowed the state to pick up a percentage of the federal estate tax also was defeated, leaving Nevada the only state not to take advantage of the rebate.

Economy. Although the state had been considered recession-proof after the tourist-based economy continued to thrive during the national downturn in 1974, Nevada shared the nation's economic woes in 1982. Gaming officials pointed to the competition from casino gambling in Atlantic City as a factor in the decline of tourism. Sales tax revenue for the state's general fund increased by less than 2% for the 1981–82 fiscal year and fell below the previous year's total for the first quarter of the 1983 fiscal year. Gambling revenues, after allowing for the increase in taxes voted at the 1981 legislative session, increased by only 6% for the fiscal year. The unemployment rate rose to 11.7% in October, exceeding the national rate.

The problem of falling state revenues was compounded by the fact that the state appropriations for the 1981–83 biennium were based on an anticipated 10% annual increase in general fund revenue. Governor List responded to the shortfall by sharply cutting the budgets of state departments and agencies and by asking the University of Nevada system and the public schools to contribute their share of the cuts.

Don W. Driggs, *University of Nevada, Reno*

NEVADA • Information Highlights

Area: 110,561 sq mi (286 353 km²).
Population (1980 census): 800,493.
Chief Cities (1980 census): Carson City, the capital, 32,022; Las Vegas, 164, 674; Reno, 100,756.
Government (1982): *Chief Officers*—governor, Robert List (R); lt. gov., Myron E. Leavitt (D). *Legislature*—Senate, 20 members; Assembly, 40 members.
State Finances (fiscal year 1981): *Revenues,* $1,324,-000,000; *expenditures,* $1,230,000,000.
Personal Income (1981): $9,782,000,000; per capita, $11,576.
Labor Force (Aug. 1982): *Nonagricultural wage and salary earners,* 417,200; *unemployed,* 50,100 (10.2% of total force).
Education: *Enrollment* (fall 1981)—public elementary schools, 102,635; public secondary, 48,704; (1981–82): colleges and universities, 39,936 students. *Public school expenditures* (1980–81), $396,220,000 ($2,179 per pupil).

NEW BRUNSWICK

The Conservatives extended and strengthened their hold on political power in 1982. Power of a different kind began flowing when the province's first nuclear generating station went into operation.

Politics. The Conservative government of Premier Richard Hatfield scored its greatest triumph on October 12, winning 39 of the 58 legislature seats against 18 for the Liberals in a provincial general election. The left-wing New Democratic Party took the other seat. The victory gave the 51-year-old bachelor premier an unprecedented fourth term in office. The Tories' share of the popular vote climbed to 47% from the 42% they managed in the 1978 election, when they won 30 seats.

Nuclear Power. The Point Lepreau nuclear power station near Saint John began producing electricity in September. Part of the output from the 600-megawatt plant was to be exported to the United States. Now there is talk of a second, possibly larger unit at Point Lepreau, with power output also designated for the U.S. market.

Acadian Dissatisfaction. A report made public in May warned that New Brunswick risks serious social and political unrest unless it gives French-speaking Acadians a greater voice in provincial affairs. The report, based on a two-year, government-commissioned study, found that the province's 250,000 Acadians remain underrepresented in the civil service and are denied equal access to government, health, and legal institutions. "Overall it is clear that the Acadians feel trapped and that a growing number are demanding . . . an Acadian society more or less independent and self-determining within the New Brunswick territory."

Base Closing. The Miramichi region suffered a heavy blow with the announcement from Ottawa that the air force base at Chatham is to be closed in 1984. The base, home of 416 Fighter Squadron, employs 1,000 military personnel and gives work to hundreds of civilians.

JOHN BEST
"Canada World News"

NEWFOUNDLAND

The general downturn in the Canadian economy hit the province of Newfoundland especially hard in 1982. The year began with the closing of copper and asbestos mines in Baie Verte. In St. John's, delay in the offshore oil boom, high interest rates, and other factors forced numerous closings and bankruptcy for a firm whose name, Crosbie, was synonymous with commercial success. In the fishery, the second largest processing firm in the province sought massive infusions of money from both levels of government to save the jobs of 9,400 plant workers and to assure 11,000 fishermen that their catches would be processed. A federal task force was appointed to examine the floundering Atlantic fishery.

In February, 84 men were killed when the oil rig "Ocean Ranger" sank in a violent storm off the Grand Banks. The incident brought home the question of the safety and feasibility of oil exploration and production in this most difficult environment. A joint federal-provincial commission was appointed to investigate the accident. The disaster pointed up the need for resolution of ownership, jurisdictional, development, and revenue-sharing questions being disputed by the federal and provincial governments. After 10 months of unsuccessful negotiation, the matter was put before two courts.

An unexpected provincial election was held on April 6, specifically to obtain what Premier Brian Peckford called a "mandate to negotiate" offshore oil jurisdiction. The opposition parties immediately charged that this was a less important issue than the broad decline, even crisis, in the economy. Caught in a wave of provincial nationalism, the Liberal opposition was reduced to 8 seats, compared with 44 for the PC.

When the provincial budget was tabled in May, it was clear to voters that there was indeed an economic crisis. Nearly all provincially levied taxes were raised in an effort to close the gap on falling retail sales tax receipts and a 5.5% decline in federal transfer payments.

SUSAN MCCORQUODALE, *Memorial University*

NEW BRUNSWICK · Information Highlights

Area: 28,354 sq mi (73 437 km²).
Population (1981 census): 696,403.
Chief Cities (1981 census): Fredericton, the capital, 43,723; Saint John, 80,521; Moncton, 54,743.
Government (1982): *Chief Officers*—lt. gov., Hedard Robichaud; premier, Richard B. Hatfield (Progressive Conservative); min. of jus., Rodman E. Logan. *Legislative Assembly*, 58 members.
Education (1982–83): *Enrollment*—elementary and secondary, 148,800 pupils; postsecondary, 13,-590 students.
Public Finances (1982 fiscal year, est.): *Revenues,* $1,826,400,000; *expenditures,* $1,909,400,000.
Personal Income (average weekly salary, April 1982): $341.30.
Unemployment Rate (July 1982, seasonally adjusted): 14.2%.

(All monetary figures are in Canadian dollars.)

NEWFOUNDLAND · Information Highlights

Area: 156,185 sq mi (404 520 km²).
Population (1981 census): 567,681.
Chief Cities (1981 census): St. John's, the capital, 83,-770; Corner Brook, 24,339.
Government (1982): *Chief Officers*—lt. gov., Anthony J. Paddon; premier, A. Brian Peckford (Progressive Conservative); min. of jus., Gerald R. Ottenheimer. *Legislature*—Legislative Assembly, 52 members.
Education (1982–83): *Enrollment*—elementary and secondary schools, 142,800; postsecondary, 9,-790.
Public Finance (1982 fiscal year, est.): *Revenues,* $1,699,000,000; *expenditures,* $1,721,100,000.
Personal Income (average weekly salary, April 1982): $362.35.
Unemployment Rate (July 1982, seasonally adjusted): 16.6%.

(All monetary figures are in Canadian dollars.)

NEW HAMPSHIRE

Throughout 1982 politics and economic issues dominated state news.

The Elections. The gubernatorial contest between moderate incumbent Hugh Gallen (D) and conservative John Sununu (R) gave voters a clear choice. Gallen refused to take "the pledge" to veto any general sales or income tax, while Sununu said he would. The state biennial budget, passed in July 1981, had been running a large deficit forcing state employees to forgo an agreed upon pay raise in July 1982. The issue of a broad based tax surely hurt Gallen, but he also had to accept some responsibility for the financial problems incurred over the two prior years. Sununu used these issues effectively against Gallen in his 147,774–132,387 vote victory.

As incumbency hurt Republicans around the nation, so in New Hampshire it hurt the Democrats. The Republicans now totally dominate state and Congressional offices. Only veteran Congressman Norman D'Amours (D) bucked this Republican trend by turning back an aggressive challenger, Robert C. Smith, thereby remaining the state's only Democrat holding high office.

Governor Gallen was hospitalized following the elections. He died of kidney and liver failure on December 29.

The Economy. Despite the national economic climate, New Hampshire has escaped many of the most serious features of the recession. Unemployment reached 8.4% in April (the highest in seven years), but dropped to 6.3% in September when the national rate climbed to above 10%. New Hampshire's increased reliance on high-tech industries cushioned the impact as did a fine tourist season. Machine-tool companies and those dependent on the domestic auto industry, however, suffered and laid off workers.

Seabrook. The Seabrook nuclear power plant remained a major newsmaker because of the continued escalation of construction costs and the financial problems the project has caused Public Service Co., its builder. The Public Utilities Commission ordered a halt to construction on the second reactor until the first is finished. The controversial order was before the New Hampshire Supreme Court late in 1982. Most agree that Seabrook will cost far more than originally projected and many question whether it will actually keep electric rates down. A related dispute developed over the adequacy of the area evacuation plan in the event of a nuclear accident.

Other News. The U.S. Interstate Commerce Commission approved plans for Timothy Mellon to acquire the Boston & Maine Railroad. Mellon moved ahead with plans to put together a 4,000-mi (6437-km) rail network that would include the Boston & Maine, the Maine Central, and the Delaware & Hudson.

New Hampshire received national attention in the spring when four Catholic nuns claimed the church hierarchy dismissed them from their teaching positions in Hampton without proper cause. The nuns took their case to court where a lower court decision against them was overturned by the state Supreme Court at year-end.

WILLIAM L. TAYLOR, *Plymouth State College*

NEW JERSEY

Gov. Thomas H. Kean's first year in office, renewed evidence of political corruption, partisan wrangling over reapportionment of congressional districts, and election campaigns headed events in New Jersey in 1982.

The New Governor. As a gubernatorial candidate and upon taking office, Kean pledged to reduce taxes on corporations and to cut government spending. He proposed a $6,370,000,000 budget, which contained sales taxes on gasoline and cigarettes as a means of cutting the $730 million deficit. It also included the promised tax measures and reduced state aid to municipalities. The budget aroused considerable opposition in the Democratic-controlled legislature, which passed a $6,200,000,000 budget in June that eliminated the sales taxes and at the same time provided for $136 million in overall spending reductions. At the opposite end of the political spectrum, conservative Republicans attacked Kean for seemingly going back on his campaign promises to decrease spending. As 1982 ended, the legislature passed and the governor signed a package of tax measures that eliminated the need for budget cuts.

Kean emphasized law and order, signing bills that authorized the death penalty and that permitted stricter treatment of juvenile offenders. He successfully gained funds to double the state's prison system by 1988.

Political Corruption. In March, Sen. Harrison Williams resigned his seat in the U.S. Senate in order to forestall expulsion after having been convicted of bribery in the Abscam scandal the year before. Governor Kean appointed businessman Nicholas Brady to serve out Williams' unfinished term.

State Senator William V. Musto, also mayor of Union City, was convicted of extorting $440,000 from the Orlando Construction Company and sentenced to seven years in federal prison.

In the autumn, Hudson County Prosecutor Harold Ruvoldt, Jr., was indicted by a federal grand jury on charges of bribery and extortion allegedly committed during his tenure as a legal representative for shopping center projects.

Three New Jersey political figures were cleared of charges against them. A Justice Department prosecutor found insufficient evidence to indict U.S. Secretary of Labor Raymond Donovan for conducting improper dealings with union officials while he was president of Schiavone Construction Corporation in Secaucus. Newark Mayor Kenneth Gibson and City Council President Earl Harris were acquitted of charges of conspiring to offer Councilman Michael Bontempo a "no show" job as water commissioner.

Congressional Reapportionment. As a result of the 1980 census, a new apportionment plan was drawn up, but the original version did not pass the assembly. On January 19 outgoing Gov. Brendan Byrne signed a different plan into law. It reduced the number of congressional districts from 15 to 14 and was heavily gerrymandered to favor incumbent Democrats. Seven Republican congressmen appealed the case to a three-judge federal panel in Newark, which ruled in their favor on the grounds that the plan denied the principle of one man, one vote. The legislature was ordered to produce a new redistricting plan by March 22. Following an appeal, U.S. Supreme Court Justice William J. Brennan agreed to delay the invalidation order. The delay meant that a full Supreme Court review of the New Jersey reapportionment plan would not take place until 1983. Therefore, the 1982 elections were carried out under the disputed plan.

The Election. The major office at stake was the U.S. Senate seat vacated by Harrison Williams.

UPI

With a costly campaign and media blitz, Frank Lautenberg (D-NJ) won a come-from-behind U.S. Senate race.

On the Republican side, Congresswoman Millicent Fenwick, a moderate, and Jeffrey Bell, a conservative, were the contenders, with Fenwick winning the primary. The Democratic nomination went to Frank Lautenberg, a millionaire businessman with no previous political experience. In the early phases of the campaign, Millicent Fenwick, one of the most popular political figures in the state, was the heavy favorite. But the combination of increasing unemployment and Lautenberg's well-funded drive contributed to a substantial win for Lautenberg.

In the House of Representatives the Democrats picked up one seat, giving them a 9 to 5 margin. Harold Hollenbeck (R), from the new ninth district, was the only incumbent who lost.

Five public questions were on the ballot. One, involving a mutually verifiable freeze on nuclear arms production, received wide support.

HERMANN K. PLATT, *St. Peter's College*

NEW JERSEY · Information Highlights

Area: 7,787 sq mi (20 168 km²).
Population (1980 census): 7,364,823.
Chief Cities (1980 census): Trenton, the capital, 92,124; Newark, 329,248; Jersey City, 223,532; Paterson, 137,970; Elizabeth, 106,201; Camden, 84,910.
Government (1982): *Chief Officer*—governor, Thomas H. Kean (R). *Legislature*—Senate, 40 members; General Assembly, 80 members.
State Finances (fiscal year 1981): *Revenues,* $10,269,000,000; *expenditures,* $10,280,000,000.
Personal Income (1981): $89,788,000,000; per capita, $12,127.
Labor Force (Aug. 1982): *Nonagricultural wage and salary earners,* 3,098,400; *unemployed,* 320,200 (8.7% of total force).
Education: *Enrollment* (fall 1981)—public elementary schools, 787,700; public secondary, 411,300; colleges and universities (1981–82), 322,797 students. *Public school expenditures* (1980–81), $3,655,487,000 ($2,791 per pupil).

NEW MEXICO

Politics and the state of the economy engaged the attention of New Mexicans in 1982.

Politics. In January, Gov. Bruce King (D) called a special session of the New Mexico legislature to reapportion the state's legislative and congressional districts, in accordance with the 1980 census. Population growth allowed New Mexico a third seat in Congress.

The reapportionment bill passed by the legislature, however, later was ruled unconstitutional by a panel of three federal judges in Albuquerque. They declared that the redrawn districts discriminated against minority groups such as Indians and Hispanics. Indian leaders claimed the measure diluted their voting strength. On June 14 the governor called another special legislative session to revise the electoral districts. The plan adopted provided for 70 new House districts and 42 new Senate districts.

In the November 2 general election, former state Attorney General Toney Anaya (D) defeated John Irick (R) for governor. Incumbent Sen. Jack Schmitt (R) was defeated by Democrat Jeff Bingaman. Representatives Manuel Lujan, Jr. (R) and Joe Skeen (R) won reelection. In the newly created third congressional district, Bill Richardson (D) easily won election.

The Economy. While New Mexico's larger cities enjoyed modest prosperity and an unemployment rate below the national average, smaller towns, dependent upon the energy industry, experienced major economic hardships. Uranium mining in Grants and copper mining in Silver City all but collapsed. By summer, Amoco Production Company had shut down most of its 206 carbon dioxide wells drilled near Clayton during the previous two years. Drilling of oil and gas wells in the San Juan Basin slowed markedly.

Space Shuttle. Attention was focused on New Mexico on March 30, when *Columbia,* after an eight-day test flight, landed at Northrup Strip on the White Sands Missile Range.

NEW MEXICO · Information Highlights

Area: 121,592 sq mi (314 923 km²).
Population (1980 census): 1,302,981.
Chief Cities (1980 census): Santa Fe, the capital, 48,-899; Albuquerque, 331,767; Las Cruces, 45,086.
Government (1982): *Chief Officers*—governor, Bruce King (D); lt. gov., Roberto A. Mondragon (D). *Legislature*—Senate, 42 members; House of Representatives, 70 members.
State Finances (fiscal year 1981): *Revenues,* $2,687,-000,000; *expenditures,* $2,039,000,000.
Personal Income (1981): $11,324,000,000; *per capita,* $8,529.
Labor Force (Aug. 1982): *Nonagricultural wage and salary earners,* 474,800; *unemployed,* 60,600 (10.1% of total force).
Education: *Enrollment*—public elementary schools (fall 1981), 187,192; public secondary, 80,899; colleges and universities (1981–82), 60,413 students. *Public school expenditures* (1980–81), $704,814,000 ($2,219 per pupil).

Indian Affairs. Early in September, representatives of the state's tribes met in Albuquerque for an Indian political caucus. Called to endorse candidates for office and take stands on such issues as education, water resources, taxation, reapportionment, and mineral development, the gathering typified the growing political activism of Indian groups.

On January 25, in a precedent-setting decision, the U.S. Supreme Court upheld the right of the Jicarilla Apache tribe in northern New Mexico to impose a severance tax on non-Indian companies for resources they produce on the reservation.

Pueblo Indians and the Navajo Tribe protested vigorously when U.S. Interior Secretary James Watt announced plans to close the Southwestern Indian Polytechnic Institute (SIPI) as an economy measure. By July a compromise had been reached by which the Albuquerque Technical-Vocational Institute would manage SIPI until its future status could be determined.

Education. In late October, Britain's Prince Charles visited Las Vegas, NM, to dedicate the United World College of the American West. The school, with 103 students, opened in the fall.

MARC SIMMONS
Author of "Albuquerque: A Narrative History"

NEW YORK

After a stunning upset over New York City Mayor Edward I. Koch in the Democratic gubernatorial primary, Lt. Gov. Mario M. Cuomo gained an extremely close victory over Lewis E. Lehrman, the Republican-Conservative candidate, to become the next governor of New York State. He succeeds Gov. Hugh L. Carey (D), who had decided not to seek a third term. The governor's race, pitting a classic conservative who advocated supply-side economic theory against the liberal Cuomo, was widely viewed as a referendum on the economic policies of President Reagan. Lehrman's unsuccessful bid cost nearly $13 million.

Sen. Daniel Patrick Moynihan (D) won a second term in office by a record margin, defeating his Republican opponent, Florence M. Sullivan, by 65–35%. Attorney General Robert Abrams easily beat his GOP challenger, Fran Sclafani. Only one Republican was elected to statewide office—incumbent controller Edward Regan, who swamped his Democratic rival, Raymond Gallagher, by 56–40%.

Laws and Legislators. Earlier in the year, Governor Carey opened the 205th session of the New York State Legislature with a call for dramatic changes in the financing of health care for the poor, of education, and of the crumbling system of roads and bridges. The governor blamed New York's budget deficit, estimated at $579 million, on federal economic policies and the recession, which reduced the collection of many state taxes.

Yvonne Hemsey/Gamma-Liaison

A series of debates set the stage for the Lehrman-Cuomo gubernatorial race. Cuomo (D), right, won a squeaker.

Among the major actions of the legislature in 1982 were: passage of a bill that would provide $430 million to hospitals that face bankruptcy because they treat the working poor; the creation of a hazardous waste "superfund" to finance the cleanup of environmental disasters; and passage of a bill, signed into law by Governor Carey, requiring a 5-cent deposit on soda and beer containers. The bottle bill had been hotly contested for nearly a decade, and its passage was hailed by environmental groups across the state.

After a lengthy dispute, the U.S. Justice Department approved plans in July for the redistricting of congressional, state senate, and assembly district seats in Manhattan, Brooklyn, and the Bronx. The department had ruled earlier that the newly drawn lines discriminated against minorities, making it impossible for them to gain proper representation in legislative bodies.

Because of a reduction of almost 750,000 in the state's population since the 1970 U.S. Census, New York's congressional delegation was cut back from 39 to 34 members.

On August 26, Frederick Richmond (D) resigned his position as representative from Brooklyn's 14th U.S. Congressional District after pleading guilty to three federal charges, thus ending an eight-month federal investigation.

And on Long Island, Joseph M. Margiotta, the powerful Republican Party chairman of Nassau County, lost an appeal to overturn his conviction for fraud and extortion involving insurance kickbacks for political associates. He was sentenced to two years in prison.

Other Developments. In August the town of Glen Cove, Long Island, caused an international incident by halting swimming, golfing, and tennis privileges for Soviet diplomats living there, saying that they were using their tax-free Glen Cove residence to spy on Long Island's defense and technology industries. Shortly afterward, the Soviet Union retaliated by prohibiting American diplomats in Moscow from using a popular beach on the Moskva River.

A dispute over nuclear safety prompted the resignation of the chairman of a three-judge panel that has been conducting hearings on the safety of the Indian Point nuclear power plants. The chairman, Louis J. Carter, charged that the Nuclear Regulatory Commission, in issuing new rules, was not giving opponents of the Hudson Valley plants a fair chance to present their views.

In July the Federal Public Health Service declared the Love Canal "habitable" despite the nearby dumping of tens of thousands of tons of toxic waste in the 1940s and 1950s. The agency made the finding after the release of a study by the Environmental Protection Agency.

The State of New York sued the Hooker Chemical Company for $200 million, charging that the company "mishandled" toxic chemicals at its Buffalo Avenue plant in Niagara Falls, leading to the contamination of the Niagara River.

A fire in January ravaged the Roosevelt estate at Hyde Park, destroying much of the oldest part of the 35-room mansion. The house, birthplace of President Franklin D. Roosevelt, is a national monument maintained by the National Park Service, which began restorations.

MICHAEL SPECTER
"The New York Times"

NEW YORK • Information Highlights

Area: 49,108 sq mi (127 190 km²).
Population (1980 census): 17,558,072.
Chief Cities (1980 census): Albany, the capital, 101,-727; New York, 7,071,030; Buffalo, 357,870; Rochester, 241,741; Yonkers, 195,351; Syracuse, 170,105.
Government (1982): *Chief Officers*—governor, Hugh L. Carey (D); lt. gov., Mario M. Cuomo (D). *Legislature*—Senate, 60 members; Assembly, 150 members.
State Finances (fiscal year 1981): *Revenues,* $30,-003,000,000; *expenditures,* $27,780,000,000.
Personal Income (1981): $201,823,000,000; per capita, $11,466.
Labor Force (Aug. 1982): *Nonagricultural wage and salary earners,* 7,264,400; *unemployed,* 684,700 (8.4% of total force).
Education: *Enrollment*—public elementary schools (fall 1981), 1,778,207; public secondary, 982,567; colleges and universities (1981–82), 1,014,863. *Public school expenditures* (1980–81), $9,251,-000,000 ($3,358 per pupil).

NEW YORK CITY

© Bill Paciello/Duomo

More than 14,000 runners took part in the New City Marathon. Millions of spectators lined the streets.

The population of New York City shifted as dramatically during the 1970s as at any time in its history, according to final tabulations of the 1980 U.S. Census. On the whole the population declined, but there were more elderly people and young adults, with many fewer children and teenagers. Traditional minority groups—blacks, Hispanics, and Asians—combined to become a new majority in the city. In addition, by 1980 one in every four New Yorkers was foreign-born, an increase of more than 5% from 1970. Median income fell by thousands of dollars, as the city lost nearly seven times as many blue-collar as white-collar workers. Job losses were heaviest in the manufacturing, construction, wholesale, and retail industries.

Development. In July, Federal Judge Thomas P. Griesa blocked all federal funds for construction of Westway, the long-disputed 4.2-mi (6.8-km) stretch of highway on Manhattan's West Side, on the grounds that government agencies deliberately misrepresented the effects that the project would have on Hudson River fish.

The Lincoln West Housing Project, however, was approved by the city Board of Estimate, 10-1, after a steamy debate. The project will house some 10,000 people and be erected on the West Side between 59th and 72nd streets on the largest tract of undeveloped land in Manhattan.

Sweeping new zoning policies for midtown Manhattan were approved unanimously by New York City's Planning Commission. The regulations are designed to curb development on the congested East Side and to encourage it below 40th Street on the West Side.

Taxes. Several tax increases were granted for financially troubled New York City in 1982. Among them were a surcharge on the income tax paid by city residents for the following two years, and an increase in mortgage-recording and property-transfer taxes. The state legislature repealed a 10% tax on profits from the sale of buildings in the city worth $1 million or more.

Against the wishes of the Koch administration, the state legislature killed a bill that would have permitted New York City to continue lucrative tax benefits for real estate developers under its J-51 program. Critics argued that the program had been abused by landlords over the years.

Other Developments. Mayor Edward I. Koch suffered a surprise defeat at the hands of Lt. Gov. Mario Cuomo in the Democratic primary for governor of New York. Cuomo went on to win the governorship, defeating conservative Republican Lew Lehrman in November, and Koch returned to the municipal helm.

Hundreds of thousands of peaceful demonstrators overwhelmed Central Park and midtown on June 12, protesting the buildup of nuclear arms. It was the largest gathering of its kind in the nation's history.

In the most exciting finish in the history of the New York Marathon, Alberto Salazar outran Rudolfo Gomez by a mere four seconds; it was the third straight victory for Salazar, himself a New Yorker. Grete Waitz of Norway scored her fourth women's victory, as millions of New Yorkers poured into city streets to cheer the runners on.

In October, The Metropolitan Museum of Art announced a drive to raise $150 million over the next five years to halt rising deficits, reinforce the museum's endowment, and restore programs that have been eliminated for lack of funds. It is the first public fund-raising campaign in the 112-year history of the world-renowned museum.

MICHAEL SPECTER
"The New York Times"

NEW ZEALAND

The sluggish state of the economy and corrective measures taken by the government continued to dominate the national agenda. Successive public opinion polls showed that about 70% of the population regarded the interrelated issues of inflation, the economy, and unemployment as of the most serious concern.

The Economy. While unemployment remained modest by comparison with other developed nations, it did climb slowly, in midyear reaching 3.5% of the work force. The external balance of payments deficit rose alarmingly in the year to July 31, 1982, amounting to N.Z. $6,600,000,000, or in excess of 25% of the value of annual exports. This trend, coupled with a 1981 inflation rate of 15.7%, induced the government in June to impose a wage and price freeze for one year. Only 17% of those surveyed in a July poll believed that the freeze was then effective in curbing inflation. Similarly, the controversial "think-big" growth strategy, which had led in June to the resignation of Derek Quigley, minister of works and development, received the endorsement of only 27% in the same poll.

The 13th budget presented by Prime Minister Robert Muldoon, in his capacity as finance minister, featured massive tax cuts to complement the freeze. Taxes in 1982 took 29.5% out of the average wage packet and accounted for 31% of gross domestic product. Smokers, drinkers, motorists, lump-sum superannuation schemes, and tax-avoiders were all penalized. In seeking an anti-inflationary monetary policy, the Muldoon government restrained the budget deficit to an estimated N.Z. $1,879,000,000.

Foreign Affairs. In April, New Zealand severed diplomatic relations with Argentina for having invaded the Falkland Islands. In June the 14 partners in the Antarctic Treaty conferred in Wellington and reached an agreement in principle by which oil and other minerals could be exploited while safeguarding the polar environment. At the South Pacific Forum meeting at Rotorua in August, the heads of government and ministers concentrated discussions on decolonization of French territories.

Prime Minister Muldoon chaired the Organization for Economic Cooperation and Development's ministerial council meeting in Paris. In August he caused a stir at the Commonwealth finance ministers meeting in London by advocating urgent action to avert a possible collapse of the international monetary system.

Internal Affairs. Public opinion polls revealed a remarkable stability in support for the three major parties, with National and Labour each recording around 40%. The Social Credit Political League, trailing with 20%, changed its name to the Social Credit party. The National party made history by electing a woman, Sue Wood, a 33-year-old public relations consultant, to the post of party president.

A decision by the Privy Council in London that anyone born in Samoa between 1921 and 1949 was a British subject under New Zealand law threw immigration policy into disarray. A citizenship agreement hastily signed by the two governments effectively restored the *status quo ante*. In September the government failed to win approval through due planning processes for a vital project in its growth strategy, a hydroelectricity dam on the Clutha River. It thereupon passed legislation overriding legal decisions and authorizing construction. In August, Prince Edward arrived for a year as a junior house master at Wanganui Collegiate.

GRAHAM BUSH, *University of Auckland*

NEW ZEALAND · Information Highlights

Official Name: New Zealand.
Location: Southwest Pacific Ocean.
Area: 103,736 sq mi (268 676 km²).
Population (1982 est.): 3,100,000.
Chief Cities (1981 census): Wellington, the capital, 342,504; Auckland, 825,707; Christchurch, 321,-373.
Government: *Head of state,* Elizabeth II, queen, represented by David Beattie, governor general (took office Nov. 1980). *Head of government,* Robert Muldoon, prime minister (took office Dec. 1975). *Legislature* (unicameral)—House of Representatives.
Monetary Unit: New Zealand dollar (1.4079 N.Z. dollars equal U.S.$1, Nov. 23, 1982).
Gross National Product (1981 U.S.$): $21,190,000,-000.
Economic Indexes (1981): *Consumer Prices* (1970= 100), *all items,* 374.7; *food,* 397.8.
Foreign Trade (1981 U.S.$): *Imports,* $5,691,000,-000; *exports,* $5,568,000,000.

NIGERIA

Nigeria, the most populous state in Africa, began the long, expensive, and complex process of preparing for the 1983 general election of the legislators, governors, and president. Despite mounting economic problems, the government of President Alhaji Shehu Shagari was not seriously threatened. Some 300 persons were reported killed in religious rioting some 50 mi (80 km) northeast of Lagos in October.

Political Developments. A new election bill approved by the federal legislature was signed into law in August by President Shagari. New registration papers were designed, citizens over 18 years of age screened, polling places selected, and political parties and candidates certified. Most of the early details of registration went smoothly, although the Federal Election Commission (FEDECO), charged with conducting the election, discovered some cases of fraud. The most flagrant was in Lagos state where the courts in August canceled the first registration. Five state governors condemned the actions of FEDECO and its chairman and also demanded that the time for registration be extended.

An ill-conceived coup organized by a businessman was discovered in February. The coup implicated some elements of the army but never

UPI

Pope John Paul II was welcomed in Lagos by President Al-haji Shehu Shagari, February 12. Nigeria was the first stop on the pontiff's tour of Western Africa.

that lowered production by 20% until the break was repaired. Far more serious was the worldwide reduction of Nigeria's petroleum sales, particularly to its best customer, the United States. The OPEC meetings in March and again in July showed deep divisions within that group of states. Nigeria at first refused to adhere to the proposed cutback in production and lowering of the price of its benchmark oil from $34 a barrel. In July, although prices had been lowered and production cut, Nigeria, Libya, and Iran were accused by other OPEC members of ignoring the guidelines. After two years of protest by the oil companies, the government approved in August a new scale that allowed them a 100% increase in profits per barrel.

The shortfall of oil sales and continuing high level of imports created a minor crisis. Projected government revenue was revised downward from $17,300,000,000 to $13,300,000,000. Foreign currency reserves had fallen by February to less than $3,000,000,000, one third of the previous year's level. A temporary halt was made in March to issuing letters of credit, and the Central Bank was ordered not to process applications for foreign exchange to pay for imports. In April, President Shagari asked Parliament to agree to further stringent import restrictions.

Foreign Affairs. Nigeria became the focus of world attention in February when Pope John Paul II spent four days visiting its more populous cities.

President Shagari maintained Nigeria's moderate foreign policy by opposing South Africa as well as doctrinaire leftist regimes. Nigeria's attitude toward Libya had much to do with the failure of the Organization of African Unity summit meeting in Tripoli in August. Shagari's absence, his opposition to admission of the Polisario as a member of the OAU, and his continuing friendly relations with the Western powers clearly indicated Nigeria's position. Wherever possible, Nigeria sought to control the violence endemic in Africa. Nigerian armed forces were a part of the OAU peace-keeping force in Chad until they were withdrawn in the spring.

HARRY A. GAILEY, *San Jose State University*

developed beyond the planning stage. More of a threat to stability were the political divisions within some states. Fears of escalation of such quarrels led to the banning of all political activities in Niger state. There were also disagreements within a number of the many political parties, centering on quarrels between some of the political leaders and the elected governors. The most serious of these was in Kano state where the People's Redemption Party expelled Gov. Abubakr Remi.

Shagari's government took a major step toward internal reconciliation by dropping all outstanding charges against former head of state Gen. Yakubu Gowon. Even more difficult was the decision to pardon Col. Odumegwu Ojukwu, the leader of the Biafra secession (1967–1970).

Economic Developments. In January a leak in one of the main petroleum pipelines to the refinery at Forcados caused a shutdown of the facility

---

NIGERIA · Information Highlights

Official Name: Federal Republic of Nigeria.
Location: West Africa.
Area: 356,669 sq mi (923 773 km²).
Population (1982 est.): 82,300,000.
Chief Cities (1976 est.): Lagos, the capital, 1,100,000; Ibadan, 850,000; Ogbomosho, 435,000.
Government: *Head of state and government,* Alhaji Shehu Shagari, president (took office Oct. 1979). *Legislature*—Senate and House of Representatives.
Monetary Unit: Naira (0.65725 naira equals U.S.$1, Feb. 1982).
Gross National Product Per Capita (1980 U.S.$): $1,010.
Economic Index (1981): *Consumer Prices* (1972= 100), *all items,* 235.8; *food,* 235.
Foreign Trade (1980 U.S. $): *Imports,* $14,644,000,-000; *exports,* $21,345,000,000.

NORTH CAROLINA

The economy occupied the attention of North Carolinians in 1982.

Economy. The recession reached the state, and in October unemployment stood at 9.3%. Falling revenues led to a tightening of legislative appropriations (except for the usual pork-barrel allocations), and a freeze was placed on salaries of teachers and other state employees. By year's end 6% of appropriations was being withheld in an attempt to maintain the constitutionally mandated balanced budget.

North Carolina lost more than $241 million in federal funds after Oct. 1, 1981. Many of the cutbacks occurred in the state's education and employment programs and in services for children, the poor, and the handicapped.

Politics. Money appeared to be a minor problem for politicians as millions of dollars poured into the state from both liberal and conservative forces attempting to sway the voters in the election. The Democrats recaptured two Congressional seats—James McClure Clarke ousting William M. Hendon and Robin Britt defeating Eugene Johnston—and retained the fourth district seat occupied by Ike Andrews, whose repeated traffic violations became a campaign issue. In the second district, a write-in campaign for Henry M. Michaux, Jr., a black defeated in the Democratic primary, failed to prevent the election of Democrat Itimous T. Valentine, Jr., for the seat of the retiring L. H. Fountain (D). The Democrats maintained a commanding majority in the General Assembly, to which 11 blacks were elected. Blacks also made gains in local races—one clerk of court, four sheriffs, and representation on many boards of county commissioners and boards of education.

Each party lost one legislator to felony conviction: G. Ronald Taylor, Democratic representative from Bladen County, for conspiracy to burn buildings owned by a fellow legislator; and Harold A. Baker, a Republican senator from

Wide World

The Rev. Ben Chavia, a member of the "Wilmington 10," leads a protest against PCB dumping in Warren County.

Wilkes County, for possession of a stolen vehicle.

As in every previous session since its introduction, the Equal Rights Amendment failed to be ratified by the state legislature.

Thad Eure, who was first elected secretary of state in 1936, earned the record for having served longer in the office than any other person in American history.

Controversies. Opposition developed over the selection of sites for hazardous wastes repositories. Environmental and civil rights activists attempted unsuccessfully to block the deposit of PCB-contaminated soil in a Warren County dump, some associating the site selection with the high proportion of black residents in the county. Objections also arose to a planned privately built waste treatment plant in Anson County.

Gov. Jim Hunt announced his support for raising the legal drinking age and for stiffening penalties against persons convicted of driving while intoxicated. The governor continued his promotion of a microelectronics center in the Research Triangle Park in the face of questions raised by some environmentalists concerning the health of workers in such industries.

Crime. In a bizarre case, Mario E. V. Navas, a native of Colombia, held three persons hostage on an Amtrak train in Raleigh, leading to the deaths of a woman and a child. Subsequently,

---

NORTH CAROLINA • Information Highlights

Area: 52,669 sq mi (136 413 km²).

Population (1980 census): 5,881,813.

Chief Cities (1980 census): Raleigh, the capital, 149,-771; Charlotte, 314,447; Greensboro, 155,642; Winston-Salem, 131,885; Durham, 100,538.

Government (1982): *Chief Officers*—governor, James B. Hunt, Jr. (D); lt. gov., James C. Green (D). *General Assembly*—Senate, 50 members; House of Representatives, 120 members.

State Finances (fiscal year 1981): *Revenues,* $6,721,-000,000; *expenditures,* $6,571,000,000.

Personal Income (1981): $51,494,000,000; per capita, $8,649.

Labor Force (Aug. 1982): *Nonagricultural wage and salary earners,* 2,296,800; *unemployed,* 266,700 (9.0% of total force).

Education: *Enrollment* (fall 1981)—public elementary schools, 772,876; public secondary, 336,084; colleges and universities (1981–82), 295,771. *Public school expenditures* (1980–81), $2,219,000,000 ($1,992 per pupil).

Navas was indicted on charges of kidnapping and murder.

Education and Culture. The North Carolina School of Science and Mathematics graduated its first class, and the School of Veterinary Medicine admitted its first class. Faced with functional illiteracy among many high school graduates, sentiment grew for a writing competency test in the public schools.

The keel was laid for the *Elizabeth II,* a reproduction of a 16th-century English vessel, to be launched in 1984 at the beginning of a three-year observance of the quadricentennial of the English colonies on Roanoke Island. A bipartisan statewide campaign sought funds for the protection of the Cape Hatteras Lighthouse, threatened by the Atlantic Ocean. The first part of the new state art museum was opened, and the North Carolina Symphony observed its 50th anniversary as the first state-supported U.S. symphony. The University of North Carolina basketball team, coached by Dean Smith, won the NCAA championship.

H. G. JONES
University of North Carolina at Chapel Hill

NORTH DAKOTA

Financial problems overshadowed a bumper harvest, politics, two major court decisions, and continued expansion of energy development in North Dakota during 1982.

Government. Facing a revenue shortfall in excess of $140 million, Gov. Allen I. Olson cut state spending, refused an increase in salary, and denied state employees under his jurisdiction pay raises authorized by the legislature. State finances were strained by recession and by 1981 tax reforms that shifted part of the tax burden from real property to oil production. The Bank of North Dakota stopped buying FHA and VA home mortgage loans and suspended all direct loans.

Agriculture. The state's 38,000 farms—1,000 fewer than in 1981—produced another record crop with higher-than-average yields. With commodity prices 22% below 1980 levels, farmers put most of the huge harvest in storage. Stored wheat alone totaled 521 million bushels, up 30% from the 1981 record, and other grains added another 227 million bushels to the surplus. A bean cooperative failed, farm auctions and foreclosures increased, and retail sales of farm implements and supplies declined sharply. Two farm equipment manufacturers interrupted production due to labor strife, high interest rates, and surplus inventories.

The agricultural situation was not entirely bleak. Operations began at two huge sunflower processing plants, and a ten-year climb in farmland values continued. Governor Olson led a ten-day farm-products promotion trip to the People's Republic of China.

Politics. Voters defeated an initiated constitutional amendment to limit casino gambling for charity to bingo and raffles. Charitable and fraternal organizations operated 387 gambling sites and netted more than $11 million in 1982, mostly on $2-limit blackjack.

Voters returned two incumbent Democrats, Sen. Quentin Burdick and Rep. Byron Dorgan, to Congress; gave Democratic legislators a majority in the House for only the second time; and reelected a Democrat and a Republican to two contested statewide offices. A nuclear-freeze resolution and five of nine other constitutional measures were passed.

Court Actions. A federal judge ruled that North Dakota must reduce the resident population of two institutions for the retarded, upgrade both institutions to federal standards by mid-1985, and provide programs of services and living conditions for the deinstitutionalized. The suit was brought against the state by the Association for Retarded Citizens.

In another major decision, a federal appeals court overturned an order halting work on the Garrison Diversion water project and dismissed legal action against the project instituted in 1977 by the National Audubon Society.

Energy. Canadian natural gas flowed through the 279-mi (449-km), $436 million North Dakota segment of a pipeline linking Alberta to a five-state area. The total 823 mi (1 324 km) of pipeline was one of the largest projects in the United States. Other energy developments included construction of the country's first coal-gasification plant and congressional funding for work on the massive Garrison project. Although gas and oil production remained stable, the oil glut and falling prices slowed leasing, exploration, and drilling.

Weather. A record 69.2 inches (175.7 cm) of snow fell from January through April, and cold temperature marks were set in both January and June.

STAN CANN
"The Forum," Fargo

NORTH DAKOTA · Information Highlights

Area: 70,702 sq mi (183 118 km²).

Population (1980 census): 652,717.

Chief Cities (1980 census): Bismarck, the capital, 44,-485; Fargo, 61,308; Grand Forks, 43,765; Minot, 32,843.

Government (1982): *Chief Officers*—governor, Allen I. Olson (R); lt. gov., Ernest Sands (R). *Legislative Assembly*—Senate, 53 members; House of Representatives, 106 members.

State Finances (fiscal year 1981): *Revenues,* $1,204,-000,000; *expenditures,* $1,013,000,000.

Personal Income (1981): $6,725,000,000; per capita, $10,213.

Labor Force (Aug. 1982): *Nonagricultural wage and salary earners,* 251,400; *unemployed,* 15,700 (4.7% of total force).

Education *Enrollment* (fall 1981)—public elementary schools, 79,579; public secondary, 38,129; colleges and universities (1981–82), 35,446. *Public school expenditures* (1980–81), $249,612,000 ($2,062 per pupil).

NORTHWEST TERRITORIES

The question of whether the Northwest Territories (NWT) should be divided into two jurisdictions was a major concern of residents in 1982.

Division. A plebiscite on division of the NWT, long-favored by the Inuit population, was held throughout the Territories on April 14. By 56%, residents favored dividing the NWT into separate eastern and western jurisdictions. Support for the move was especially strong in the east, with more than 80% of the people favoring division. The Legislative Assembly supported the expressed will of the people and made sure that the federal government was also aware of that desire.

On November 26, federal Minister of Indian Affairs and Northern Development John Munro announced the long-awaited cabinet decision on the matter. Ottawa basically accepted the principle of division and supported greater responsibility and financial independence for the NWT government. The federal government would act on dividing the Territories as long as native land claims were settled and NWT residents reached a consensus on a boundary, new administrative centers, and distribution of powers among different levels of government. In preparation for the division, constitutional forums were set up in the eastern and western parts of the Territories to lay the foundations for new jurisdictions.

Economy. The general recession in Canada and other parts of the world was reflected in the NWT in the mining and mineral exploration sectors. Low mineral prices finally resulted in an announcement by Cominco Ltd. that its lead-zinc mine at Pine Point would shut down completely in January 1983. The shutdown would be reviewed monthly, as economic conditions were evaluated. Pine Point Mines is the largest in the NWT, employing about 450 people directly and affecting many support businesses indirectly.

On the positive side, work progressed at Norman Wells on Imperial Oil's oil field and on construction of a pipeline to transport crude oil south. Oil and gas exploration activity also continued in the Beaufort Sea.

ROSS M. HARVEY
Assistant Director of Information
Government of the Northwest Territories

**NORTHWEST TERRITORIES ·
Information Highlights**

Area: 1,304,903 sq mi (3 379 700 km²).
Population (1981 census): 45,741.
Chief City (1981 census): Yellowknife, the capital, 9,483.
Government (1981): *Chief Officers*—commissioner, John H. Parker. *Legislature*—Legislative Assembly, 22 elected members.
Education (1982–83): *Enrollment*—public and secondary schools, 13,100 pupils. *Public school expenditures* (1980–81), C$52,211,000.
Public Finance (1982 fiscal year, est.): *Revenues,* C$411,800,000; *expenditures,* C$385,800,000.

NORWAY

The main events in Norway in 1982 related to its economy, weakened by the continuing world recession, and the way in which the recently elected Conservative government dealt with it.

Economy. Unemployment, although still well below the levels prevailing in other countries, crept slowly upward during the first half of the year and in August hit a post-World War II record of 2.7% of the labor force. This compared with only 1.7% in 1981 and 1.3% in 1980.

The industries hardest hit by the slump were those selling raw materials or semifinished goods. Manufacturers of finished products also faced growing foreign competition and loss of market shares, both at home and abroad. The main reasons for this were the high cost of Norwegian products compared with those of competitors, declining productivity, adverse terms of trade, and slowness in adapting the industrial product to changing patterns in demand.

Budget. The minority Conservative government, led by Prime Minister Kare Willoch, had come to power in October 1981 on promises of substantial tax cuts and a budget in better balance. But it was not until the Conservatives unveiled their first draft budget on Oct. 6, 1982, that their new economic stategy was made explicit. It envisaged significant cuts in direct taxes, to be partly offset by substantially higher indirect taxes, and charges for public services. Public spending in most sectors was to be held at or below 1982 levels, in real terms, but there was to be a real increase in allocations for defense, law and order, hydro-power development, and telecommunications.

The budget got a hostile reception from the opposition on both Left and Right. The unions and the Labor Party said the real reductions in public spending would reduce employment, particularly in the country's less developed areas. The rightist Progress Party complained that the tax concessions were inadequate and that the Conservatives were simply continuing the social democratic policies of their predecessors. The Federation of Industry complained that there had been no reduction in the tax on investments or in the employers' share of social security contributions.

Currency Devaluations. The same day that the budget was proposed, a 4% devaluation by neighboring Finland set off a realignment of Scandinavian currencies that upset all plans. Sweden reacted to Finland's move by a 16% devaluation of the Swedish krone. This was almost immediately followed by a further 6% devaluation of the Finnish mark. Because Sweden is Norway's largest trading partner as well as one of its main competitors in certain exports, such as forest products, the Swedish devaluation gave Sweden a competitive price advantage in exports and thus posed a serious threat to employment in several of Norway's key industries.

NORWAY · Information Highlights

Official Name: Kingdom of Norway.
Location: Northern Europe.
Area: 125,056 sq mi (323 895 km²).
Population (1982 est.): 4,100,000.
Chief Cities (Jan. 1981): Oslo, the capital, 452,023; Bergen, 207,799; Trondheim, 134,976.
Government: *Head of state,* Olav V, king (acceded Sept. 1957). *Head of government,* Kare Willoch, prime minister (took office October 1981). *Legislature*—Storting; Lagting and Odelsting.
Monetary Unit: Krone (7.04 kroner equal U.S.$1, Dec. 21, 1982).
Gross Domestic Product (1981 U.S.$): $49,370,000,-000.
Economic Indexes (1981): *Consumer Prices* (1970= 100), all items, 254.0; food, 252.8. Industrial production (1975=100), 132.
Foreign Trade (1981 U.S.$): *Imports,* $15,646,000,-000; exports, $17,992,000,000.

The Norwegian government, however, decided not to devalue the krone again, since it had already dropped 9% in value in 1982, indirectly by 6% and directly by a 3% devaluation in September. Instead, to protect retailers from losing business to shops across the border, it more than halved the "tourist" quota of goods that Norwegians could import from Sweden free of duty.

Oil and Gas. The summer was marked by successful exploration drilling in the Tromsø Patch area, off northern Norway. Statoil, the state oil company, confirmed the existence of a large offshore gas field, containing an estimated 100,000,-000,000 to 150,000,000,000 m³ of recoverable reserves. It was named "Askeladd," after the "Ash Lad," hero of a well-known Norwegian folk tale. Norsk Hydro, the petroleum and industrial concern in which the government has a controlling interest, also found gas in the area. But its discovery, dubbed "Albatross," was only about half the size of Askeladd and only one fifth as large as Hydro had hoped, on the basis of advance seismic information. It was generally agreed, moreover, that more gas would have to be found to justify investing in production installations in these deep and stormy waters.

THØR GJESTER
"Økonomisk Revy," Oslo

NOVA SCOTIA

The year 1982 brought Nova Scotia high unemployment, higher interest rates, cuts in government spending, double-digit inflation, and only a moderate gain in real income. The discovery of gas off Sable Island was perhaps the year's only bright spot.

Government and Legislature. During the year, the Nova Scotia government, in its fight against inflation, froze annual wage increases in the public sector at 6% and launched an austerity drive with a $32.8 million cut in government spending on education, health, transportation, and government services. In March the government brought Nova Scotia a step closer to devel-oping offshore resources by signing an agreement with the federal government on the management of the province's oil and gas reserves.

Of the 133 bills introduced by the government in the provincial legislature, 108 became law, including acts protecting private property and creating the university of Cape Breton.

Economy. The year 1982 registered a moderate growth in real domestic product, due mainly to expansion in the mining and services sectors of the Nova Scotian economy. The former absorbed nearly 29% of the $2,570,000,000 of planned capital expenditure for the year. Relief from rising unemployment was not yet in sight. The goods-producing sector was hit hard by high interest rates and the general recession both in Canada and abroad. Consequently, a sharp decline occurred in the values of fish landings, pulpwood and lumber production, car sales, and manufacturing shipments. The economic slowdown caused record high unemployment, and the number of unemployment insurance recipients increased dramatically. The employed also experienced economic hardship. A negligible improvement in their economic well-being was recorded, as inflation absorbed a substantial fraction of their increased earnings.

Energy. However, Nova Scotian self-confidence gained momentum with the realization that offshore resources could transform Nova Scotia into a "have" province. A major breakthrough came on June 24, 1982, when Mobil Oil announced the discovery of the Venture natural gas field, located near the eastern tip of Sable Island. The government also announced a $551 million contract with a consortium led by Shell Canada to drill nine exploratory wells on the Scotian shelf. The gas finds have not reduced the importance of tidal power and coal mining in Nova Scotia. The first turbine to be installed at the Fundy Tidal Power project site arrived in 1982. The Cape Breton Development Corporation embarked on a 10-year, $2,000,000,000 expansion program involving three new mines. In the meantime, the provincial electric power utility continued to use coal instead of expensive oil to generate electricity.

R. P. SETH
Mount Saint Vincent University

NOVA SCOTIA · Information Highlights

Area: 21,425 sq mi (55 490 km²).
Population (1981 census): 847,442.
Chief Cities (1981 census): Halifax, the capital, 114,-594; Dartmouth, 62,277; Sydney, 29,444.
Government (1982): *Chief Officers*—lt. gov., John E. Shaffner; premier, John Buchanan (Progressive Conservative); atty. gen., Henry W. How. *Legislature*—Legislative Assembly, 52 members.
Education (1982–83): *Enrollment*—elementary and secondary schools, 180,200 pupils; postsecondary, 21,850.
Public Finance (1983 fiscal year, est.): *Revenues,* $2,087,228,800; expenditures, $2,216,514,600.
Unemployment Rate (Aug. 1982, seasonally adjusted): 13.1%.
(All monetary figures are in Canadian dollars.)

OBITUARIES[1]

SMITH, Walter Wellesley ("Red")

American sports columnist; b. Green Bay, WI, Sept. 25, 1905; d. Stamford, CT, Jan. 15, 1982.

Red Smith's newspaper writing career spanned 55 years. His gracefully written pieces, filled with insight, humor, understanding, and criticism, became the most widely syndicated sports columns in America. In 1976, when he won the Pulitzer Prize for distinguished commentary, the Pulitzer committee cited his work for being "unique in the erudition, the literary quality, the vitality, and freshness of viewpoint."

Background. Walter Wellesley Smith was the second son of three children of Walter Philip and Ida Richardson Smith. His father owned and operated a wholesale produce and retail grocery business. Growing up in Wisconsin, the youngster with bright red hair was not very athletic, but he learned to fish and enjoy the outdoors—avocations he pursued throughout his life. Red Smith went to the University of Notre Dame set on preparing himself for a career as a newspaperman. After he was graduated in 1927, he landed his first job at *The Milwaukee Sentinel* for $25 a week. A year later, at *The St. Louis Star,* he got a chance to write his first sports story, covering a night football game. His piece described a glowworm, and how it wished it could give off the same brightness as the stadium floodlights. It delighted his editors. Eight years later he moved to Philadelphia, and in 1945 he became full-time columnist for *The New York Herald Tribune.* He brought a wry wit and light touch to his columns, putting into perspective the nation's inclination to be entertained by games and athletic heroes. In 1971, four years after *The Tribune* ceased publication, he joined *The New York Times.*

Red Smith regarded sports writing as a significant endeavor. "Sports is not really a play world," he once said, "I think it's the real world. The people we're writing about ... they're suffering and living and dying and loving and trying to make their way through life just as the bricklayers and politicians are." He was in the vanguard when it came to criticizing those who would inflict injustice or commit foul play. He was the first columnist to propose a United States boycott of the 1980 Olympics in Moscow because of the Soviet invasion of Afghanistan. He was meticulous in his usage of words.

The Red Smith Reader, edited by Dave Anderson, and *To Absent Friends from Red Smith* were published shortly after his death.

He married Catherine Cody in 1933. They had a son and daughter. His wife died in 1967. In 1968 he married Phyllis Warner Weiss.

GEORGE DE GREGORIO

MacLEISH, Archibald

American poet, playwright, essayist, and public official: b. Glencoe, IL, May 7, 1892; d. Boston, MA, April 20, 1982.

Without official recognition, Archibald MacLeish seemed to be America's poet laureate. A contemporary of Frost, Stevens, Pound, and Eliot, he alone survived to speak for the generation of modernists who transformed poetry in the 20th century. His achievement as a writer was recognized by three Pulitzer Prizes and the Presidential Medal of Freedom. He was admired as a man of letters, public servant, and eloquent voice for freedom and democracy.

Background. MacLeish was graduated from Yale University in 1915, and his first collection of poems, *Tower of Ivory,* was published two years later. He took a degree at Harvard Law School in 1919 and, after serving in World War I, practiced law in Boston for three years.

MacLeish's most enduring poetry was written relatively early in his career. "Ars Poetica," the classic statement of poetry's right to be valued on its own terms as art rather than for its sincerity or philosophy, appeared in his striking 1926 collection *Streets in the Moon.*

After spending five years in France, he returned to the United States. Having early recognized the dangers of fascism, MacLeish came to believe that the artist has political as well as aesthetic responsibility. In an attempt to reach a wide audience, he wrote radio plays attacking defeatism, demagoguery, and materialism. In the 1930s, his poems admonished against perversions of the American ideal and spoke eloquently for the will of the common people.

In 1939 President Roosevelt appointed MacLeish librarian of Congress. An industrious public servant, he was responsible for a major reorganization of the library; served as assistant director of war information (1924-1943) and assistant secretary of state for cultural affairs (1944-45); contributed to Roosevelt's speeches; and helped set up UNESCO.

MacLeish continued to be an engaged artist, speaking out against McCarthyism, defending Ezra Pound, and supporting the publication of an unexpurgated version of *Lady Chatterley's Lover.* But in many ways he was isolated. His distaste for French existentialists and those they influenced led him to dismiss much that we find vital today. In 1958, his verse drama *J.B.* returned him to national prominence. A humanistic reinterpretation of the Book of Job, *J.B.* reflects a recurrent theme in MacLeish's work: although misery and failure pervade the world, there is redemptive power in love.

JEROME STERN

[1] Arranged chronologically by death date

PAIGE, Leroy Robert (Satchel)

Baseball player: b. Mobile, AL, July 7, 1906 (?); d. Kansas City, Mo. June 8, 1982.

One of the greatest pitchers of his time, Satchel Paige did not have a chance to compete in the major leagues until the age of 42. In the era before blacks were admitted to the big leagues, Paige had barnstormed with Negro teams for 22 years. Pitching as many as 2,500 games, the 6'3" (190 cm), 180 lb (82 kg) right-hander overwhelmed batters with his fastball and befuddled them with his breaking pitches. Major league stars who faced him in exhibition games were no less dazzled. Joe DiMaggio called him "the best I've ever faced, and the fastest." On July 7, 1948, the year after Jackie Robinson broke baseball's color line, Paige was signed to a contract by the Cleveland Indians. That October he made a brief appearance in the World Series, the first ever by a black.

Celebrated as much for his wit and home-spun philosophy as for his success on the mound, Paige became something of a folk hero. He had a lively sense of humor and an amused expression that belied the injustices he had faced. The mystery of his exact age was part of Paige's legend, though his appearance for the Kansas City A's in 1965 certainly made him the oldest player ever to take part in a major league game. His maxims for long living are part of baseball lore. "Don't look back," goes the most famous, "something might be gaining on you."

Background. Leroy Robert Paige is said to have been born on July 7, 1906, in Mobile, AL. He claimed, however, that the family's goat ate the Bible in which his birth certificate had been kept and that his exact age was unknown. The nickname "Satchel" was given to him as a boy, when he worked as a railroad porter.

Paige took up baseball at the Alabama Reform School, and in 1924 he won a job pitching for a semiprofessional black team called the Mobile Tigers. He began his full-time career with the Birmingham Black Barons and played for a variety of Negro teams over the next two decades. Billed as the "World's Greatest Pitcher," Paige was the major attraction in tours of the United States and Central America.

Paige had a 6-1 record in three months with the Indians in 1948. From 1951 to 1953 he was the most effective relief pitcher on the St. Louis Browns, being chosen for the All-Star Game in 1952. He was released after the 1953 season, but 12 years later—at the age of at least 59—he made a brief return.

Long past his prime, Paige compiled a major league record of 28-31, with an earned-run average of 3.29. In the Negro leagues he won at least 2,000 games, including some 250 shutouts and 45 no-hitters. He was elected to the Baseball Hall of Fame in 1971.

JEFF HACKER

CHEEVER, John

American writer: b. Quincy, MA, May 27, 1912; d. Ossining, NY, June 18, 1982.

John Cheever was one of the master story-tellers of his time and one of the few short-story writers to make the best-seller lists.

In brilliant prose that could be evasive, coy, or ironic, he evoked the failure of contemporary manners and morals. His novels and short stories shone a penetrating light into the deeper mysteries of modern American life. "The constants that I look for," he once wrote, "are a love of light and a determination to trace some moral chain of being." At a memorial service for Cheever, his friend Saul Bellow pointed out that "there are writers whose last novels are like the first. John Cheever was a writer of a different sort altogether. It is extraordinarily moving to come upon the inmost track of a man's life." Bellow also noted that Cheever put "human essences in the first place," leaving class, social origin, and the like behind.

Background. Precocious and apparently difficult as a child, John Cheever ended his formal education when, at 17, he was expelled from preparatory school. A talented writer even as a teenager, his stories found quick acceptance by a number of magazines, of which *The New Yorker* was his most important showcase over the years. After marrying Mary Winternitz in 1941 and serving in the army during World War II, he wrote television scripts and more short stories. He sought to earn "enough money to feed the family and buy a new suit every other year."

His first collection, *The Way Some People Live* (1943), won several awards and brought Cheever wide acclaim. His novels also received high praise. *The Wapshot Chronicle* (1957) won the National Book Award, and its sequel, *The Wapshot Scandal* (1964), won him the coveted Howells Medal for fiction. But there were critics who found the novelist too episodic and superficial. They scored Cheever, also, for dealing exclusively with bourgeois malaise from the point of view of orthodox morality. Cheever confounded his detractors, however, with *Falconer* (1977), a brutal portrait of life in prison.

In 1979, *The Stories of John Cheever* received both the Pulitzer Prize and the National Book Critics Circle Award. Three of the tales were adapted and televised by public TV. His last book, the novella *Oh What A Paradise It Seems*, was published in March 1982. The following month, he was awarded the National Medal for Literature for his "distinguished and continuous contribution to American letters."

In addition to his wife, he is survived by their three children. He spent his later writing years in Ossining, NY, where he enjoyed horseback riding, chopping wood, and raising Labador retrievers.

JEROME H. STERN

FONDA, Henry

American actor: b. Grand Island, NE, May 16, 1905; d. Los Angeles, CA, Aug. 12, 1982.

In a sense the American public had previewed Henry Fonda's death while being deeply moved by the film *On Golden Pond.* As the aging Norman Thayer, Fonda came to terms with approaching death by affirming life in a performance that epitomized the naturalness, sincerity, and humanity that were hallmarks of his career. Fonda had long held an exalted place as one of America's greatest screen and stage actors. When he died at 77 of chronic heart disease, it was as if the United States had lost not just one friend, but the many friends embodied in the characters he had made so real during nearly 50 years of acting in more than 100 films and plays.

Fonda was consistently able to project a basic decency that made audiences feel they were seeing something of themselves. Critics sometimes said his performances were "seemingly effortless." But infused in each portrayal was meticulous craftsmanship. Absent was even a hint of pretentiousness. "I don't think anybody has ever caught him in the act of acting," Jack Lemmon once said.

Fonda's triumph in *On Golden Pond* was fitting in several respects. Few actors faced with a deteriorating physical condition (Fonda had been having heart problems since 1974) get the opportunity to cap their careers with so demanding and effective a part. It was also the only time he appeared on screen with his daughter, Jane, who said she produced the film (through her company, IPC) as a "gift" to him. *On Golden Pond* also provided Fonda with his only Oscar for best actor. He had been given an honorary Oscar in 1981 but had never won one for a performance. In the year of his memorable depiction of Tom Joad in the John Steinbeck classic *Grapes of Wrath,* he lost out to his close friend James Stewart, honored for *The Philadelphia Story.*

Background. The celebrated actor was born Henry Jaynes Fonda. His father owned a small printing company in Omaha. After graduating from high school in 1923, Fonda studied journalism at the University of Minnesota, but left school to work and subsequently joined the Omaha Community Playhouse at the urging of a family friend, Dorothy Brando, the mother of Marlon Brando. After two years at the playhouse, he joined the procession of actors aspiring to success in New York. Fonda's big break came in 1934 with *New Faces,* in which he appeared in comedy sketches. He soon accepted a $1,000-a-week contract in Hollywood.

He was a success from the beginning. He could be dryly amusing at comedy, but was particularly apt at playing roles involving the quest for social justice. Tom Joad was the pinnacle, but Henry Fonda will be long remembered as

Culver Pictures, Inc.

the cowboy trying to stop a lynching in *The Ox-Bow Incident,* society's victim in *You Only Live Once,* and the juror committed to justice in *Twelve Angry Men.* His rich film legacy also includes a memorable performance as the future president in *Young Mr. Lincoln.*

Undoubtedly his greatest stage role was as the idealistic naval officer in *Mister Roberts,* a part he played on Broadway for three and a half years. (He also did the screen version.) Fonda openly professed a preference for theater. He was inspired by the challenge of doing a role all the way through, instead of in short takes, and by the perceptible reaction of a live audience.

Fonda's private life was often turbulent. "I've been married five times and I'm goddamned ashamed of it," he told Howard Teichmann, the collaborator on his autobiography *Fonda: My Life,* published in 1981. His wives included Margaret Sullavan; Frances Seymour Brokaw (the mother of Jane and Peter), who committed suicide; Susan Blanchard, with whom he adopted a daughter, Amy; Contessa Afdera Franchetti; and Shirlee Adams, to whom he was married at his death. His relations with Jane and Peter were sometimes strained, but he supported Jane in her crusade against the Vietnam war. The Fondas appeared close-knit in recent years, taking on a special aura as Hollywood's foremost acting family.

Fonda donated his eyes to an eye bank, and according to his instructions, he was cremated. His epitaph might well be a comment by Teichmann in the introduction to the autobiography: "He never thinks of himself as a star, only as an actor and a human being."

WILLIAM WOLF

Culver Pictures, Inc.

BERGMAN, Ingrid

Swedish actress: b. Stockholm, Aug. 29, 1915; d. London, Aug. 29, 1982.

An earthy peasant girl in *For Whom the Bell Tolls* (1943), a reluctant spy in Alfred Hitchcock's *Notorious* (1946), and a self-sacrificing lover in *Casablanca* (1942), Ingrid Bergman was one of Hollywood's most versatile and most adored leading ladies. Possessed of a wholesome beauty that sometimes overshadowed her considerable talents as an actress, she brought a unique combination of vulnerability, compassion, and moral strength to a broad diversity of roles. Her performances in *Gaslight* (1944) and *Anastasia* (1956) earned her Academy Awards for best actress, and a third Oscar was awarded for her supporting role in *Murder on the Orient Express* (1974). Bergman also won acclaim for her work on stage and television. In 1947 she was

Sovfoto

GOMULKA, Wladyslaw

Former Polish Communist party leader: b. Krosno, Poland, Feb. 6, 1905; d. Warsaw, Sept. 1, 1982.

From October 1956 to December 1970, Wladyslaw Gomulka was first secretary of the Polish United Workers' (Communist) Party and de facto ruler of Poland. No leader in modern Polish history has matched Gomulka's term of office. His outstanding accomplishment was the successful insistence on an autonomous, distinctively Polish brand of communism. In 1949 this stance brought him Stalin's wrath, expulsion from the party, and eventual imprisonment. In 1956, in the wake of destalinization and massive popular unrest, it brought him national leadership. As party leader, Gomulka secured greater independence from the Soviets, relaxed police controls, and pursued more conciliatory policies

Culver Pictures, Inc.

PRINCESS GRACE

Her Serene Highness Princess of Monaco; former American actress: b. Philadelphia, PA, Nov. 12, 1929; d. Monte Carlo, Monaco, Sept. 14, 1982.

For a little more than five years in the 1950s, Grace Kelly was one of Hollywood's most beautiful, popular, and successful actresses. Then for 26 years as the wife of His Serene Highness Prince Rainier III of Monaco she was a Grimaldi, a member of Europe's oldest royal family and the first lady of a 370-acre (150-ha) principality whose gambling casinos have made it a tourist mecca.

Although many considered the princess' life a "fairy tale," she detested the term. In an interview early in 1982, she said: "I think of myself as a modern, contemporary woman who has had to deal with all kinds of problems that many presented an Antoinette Perry (Tony) award for her portrayal of Joan of Arc in the Broadway production of *Joan of Lorraine*. In 1960 she won a television Emmy for her performance in *The Turn of the Screw*. And less than a month after her death from cancer on Aug. 29, 1982—her 67th birthday—Bergman was awarded another Emmy for her final role, that of Golda Meir in the TV movie *A Woman Called Golda*.

Background. Ingrid Bergman was born in Stockholm in 1915. Her mother, who was from Germany, and her father, a painter and photographer, both died when she was young. At age 17 she auditioned successfully for the Royal Dramatic Theater School in Stockholm, and studied there for two years. Still a teenager, she got the first movie role she tried out for and within five years had made 11 films, all in Swedish.

In 1939, American Producer David O. Selznick took her to Hollywood to star in a remake of her Swedish hit *Intermezzo*. After the filming, Ingrid returned to Sweden to be with her husband, Peter Lindstrom, and daughter, Pia, but U.S. audiences were enthralled by her performance and Selznick persuaded her to come back. Several more movies made her one of Hollywood's best-loved stars. Then came a fall from grace. In 1949 she fell in love with Italian director Roberto Rossellini and bore his child before getting a divorce from her husband. The American public was scandalized, and she did not appear in another Hollywood movie until her award-winning 1956 performance as an aging princess in *Anastasia*.

Though she regained favor, she spent most of the rest of her life in Europe. Her later career was marked by her portrayal of a middle-aged pianist in Ingmar Bergman's *Autumn Sonata* (1977).

JEFF HACKER

toward the Church and peasantry. By the late 1950s he was probably the only genuinely popular Communist leader Poland ever had. In the long run, however, he proved unable to reform Poland's communist system sufficiently to retain his wide popularity. When Polish workers rioted in response to food price increases during December 1970, Gomulka yielded power to Edward Gierek and went into obscure retirement.

Background. The son of an oil worker, Gomulka was born in the small southeastern town of Krosno in 1905. Having worked as a blacksmith and mechanic in his early years, he became active in Communist trade unions in the late 1920s. During the 1930s he was imprisoned several times for his radical labor involvements. It was during World War II, after the Kremlin created the Polish Workers' Party, that Gomulka became a prominent political leader. He was elevated to membership in the Central Committee and was active in the organization of Communist underground forces. In 1943 he became the party's secretary general and in 1945 a vice-premier in the Soviet-backed provisional government. After the break between Stalin and Tito in 1948, Gomulka, accused of "national deviationism," was eased out of power and imprisoned without a trial in 1951. Released in April 1954, he was readmitted to the party in 1956 and elected first secretary that October. When he took over, Poland was simultaneously threatened with a popular revolution against Communist rule and Soviet military intervention to quell it. Gomulka successfully negotiated with Soviet leader Nikita Khrushchev for more Polish autonomy and restored domestic tranquillity. His policies ultimately proved disappointing to most Poles, who had hoped for greater liberalization.

ALEXANDER GROTH

women have to deal with." In fact, Princess Grace spent considerable time working for charitable organizations, as well as serving as goodwill ambassador for Monaco. The princess was, however, first and foremost a wife and mother, rearing her children—Princess Caroline (b. 1957), Prince Albert (b. 1958), and Princess Stéphanie (b. 1965)—in a strict environment.

Princess Grace died following an auto accident in France above Monaco. Doctors later announced that the princess had suffered a stroke prior to the accident, in which Princess Stéphanie also was injured.

Background. Grace Patricia Kelly was the daughter of John Brendan and Margaret Majer Kelly. Her father, an Irish bricklayer, became a wealthy Philadelphia contractor and a force in the city's Democratic Party. Educated at private schools, Grace studied acting in New York's American Academy of Dramatic Arts. The future princess then practiced modeling and appeared in television commercials and TV dramatic productions. In 1949 she opened on Broadway in *The Father*. She then went to Hollywood.

Her movie credits include *High Noon* with Gary Cooper; *Mogambo* with Clark Gable; Alfred Hitchcock's *Dial M for Murder* with Ray Milland; Hitchcock's *Rear Window* with James Stewart; *The Country Girl* with Bing Crosby, for which she won an Oscar; *Bridge at Toko-Ri* with William Holden; Hitchcock's *To Catch a Thief* with Cary Grant; *High Society* with Crosby and Frank Sinatra; and *The Swan*. "True Love," the theme song of *High Society*, earned her and Crosby a gold record. In April 1956 she gave up acting to marry Prince Rainier, whom she had met at a Cannes Film Festival.

JAMES E. CHURCHILL, JR.

BREZHNEV, Leonid Ilyich

President of the USSR and secretary-general of the Soviet Communist Party: b. Kamenskoye, Russia, Dec. 19, 1906; d. Moscow, USSR, Nov. 10, 1982.

As both head of the Soviet Communist Party since 1964 and chairman of the Presidium of the Supreme Soviet from 1977, Leonid Brezhnev ruled the USSR longer than any previous leader except Stalin. Less cruel than his predecessors, Brezhnev exiled or imprisoned thousands of dissident intellectuals but never conducted a mass purge of the bureaucracy. While discriminating against Soviet Jewry, he allowed a quarter of a million to emigrate abroad. His regime improved the standard of living by raising urban salaries about 75%, doubling rural wages, building millions of one-family apartments, and manufacturing large quantities of home appliances.

Under Brezhnev's tutelage, Soviet industrial output increased by 75%, and the USSR became the world's largest producer of oil and steel. As he pursued the goal of military parity with the United States, however, industrial development concentrated largely on armaments. The armed forces were increased by one million men, the navy was equipped with twice as many warships as the U.S. fleet, and the arms industry outproduced the United States in number of intercontinental, intermediate, and submarine missiles.

The USSR having achieved approximate parity with the United States in strategic weapons, Brezhnev in the 1970s concluded with the U.S. government the world's first treaties limiting the means of delivering nuclear weapons. Although he carefully avoided atomic war, he callously sent Soviet troops into Czechoslovakia in 1968 to crush Czech liberalization, and into Afghanistan in 1979 to fight guerrillas rebelling against Kabul's Communist government. In foreign economic relations, he increased Soviet trade ninefold and doubled the number of developing countries receiving Soviet technical aid. The USSR became the world's largest exporter of arms to nations of the Third World.

Despite early successes, the Brezhnev regime ended in partial failure. Four consecutive years of poor harvests made the USSR the world's largest importer of grain. Annual industrial growth sank to its lowest level in 36 years. The Afghan war bogged down in stalemate, and U.S. anger over Soviet brutality there marked the beginning of a new cold war. Meanwhile, Soviet attempts to improve relations with Communist China were unsuccessful. Brezhnev, in short, left many problems for his successors.

Background. Born of Russian worker parentage in the Ukrainian factory town of Kamenskoye (now Dneprodzerzhinsk), Brezhnev was educated in an agricultural high school. In 1927 he became a land surveyor in the Ural mountains, rising by 1930 to the position of assistant

Camera Press

chief of the Ural agricultural administration. A year later he joined the Communist party and returned to his home town, where he enrolled in a college of metallurgical engineering, graduating in 1935. After working for two years as a steel engineer, he became deputy mayor of his city in 1937, and an official in the Communist party headquarters for his native Dnepropetrovsk region in 1938. In 1939 he was appointed party secretary in charge of the regional defense industry.

During the Nazi-Soviet war of 1941–45, Brezhnev was a political commissar for the army, serving in the Ukraine, Caucasus, and East Europe, rising to the rank of major-general. In the immediate postwar years he was, successively, first party secretary of two Ukrainian regions and the Moldavian Soviet republic. In 1952 he was transferred to Moscow as a national party secretary and alternate member of the Politburo. After Stalin's death in 1953, however, he was removed from the Politburo and made chief commissar of the Soviet navy. In 1954 he was sent to the Kazakh republic in Central Asia as party supervisor of a new lands program. He achieved a largely unexpected success and, for his loyalty to Nikita Khrushchev, was returned to Moscow in 1956 as a Politburo alternate and the national party secretary overseeing defense industry and rocket research. A full Politburo member in 1957, he was made president three years later. In 1964 he stepped down from the presidency, helped oust Khrushchev from power, and replaced him as first party secretary. Consolidating his power, Brezhnev named himself party secretary-general in 1966, army marshal in 1976, and president in 1977. Five years later, heart failure ended his life.

ELLSWORTH RAYMOND

RUBINSTEIN, Artur

Polish-American pianist: b. Łódź, Poland, Jan. 28, 1887 (?); d. Geneva, Switzerland, Dec. 20, 1982.

Performing in public for 85 years, Artur Rubinstein brought to the keyboard a unique combination of technical expertise, poetic sensitivity, and sheer exuberance that made him one of the most loved and respected piano virtuosos of the 20th century. Regarded as a peerless interpreter of Chopin, he professed a special liking for Mozart and won renown for his renditions of Debussy, Brahms, Beethoven, Liszt, and the Spanish composers. Stylistically, Rubinstein was often classified as a Romantic, but he resisted the exaggerated emotionalism of that period and interpreted its works with a distinctively free-flowing and unforced artistry. The tone he produced was described by one critic as "a firm, clear, colorful sonority that is one of the miracles of 20th-century pianism." Perhaps above all, the Rubinstein style was stamped with his own love of music and youthful joie de vivre. "Music is not a hobby, not even a passion with me; music *is* me," he once said. Always a fancier of wine, women, and song, he was asked at age 75 to explain his boyish spirit and enthusiasm for life. "What good are vitamins?" he scoffed. "Eat a lobster, eat a pound of caviar—live! Live!"

Background. Artur Rubinstein was the seventh child of a Jewish textile maker in Łódź, Poland. He took his first piano lesson at age 3 and was performing in public by age 4. After studying at the Warsaw Conservatory of Music he was sent to Berlin to perform for Joseph Joachim, a friend of Brahms and Schumann. Joachim took the boy under his wing and set up his Berlin debut at age 11. Recitals in Dresden, Hamburg, and Warsaw followed shortly.

In 1906 Rubinstein went on a 75-concert tour of the United States, but it was not a critical success. He returned to Paris, where he lived a somewhat bohemian life, practicing and making friends with artists and writers. He gradually es-

Photoreporters

tablished himself as one of Europe's top pianists and in 1916 made an especially successful tour of Spain and South America. Still, he was unenthusiastically received in New York in 1919. For the next decade, Rubinstein performed extensively but spent much of his time cavorting on the French Riviera. A turning point came in the early 1930s, when he married Aniela Mlynarski, the daughter of a Polish conductor, began recording, and set himself to practicing eight hours every day. In 1937 he made a historic reappearance at New York's Carnegie Hall and was acclaimed as "a giant." He settled in the United States during World War II and became a citizen in 1946.

In addition to hundreds of concerts and recordings over the years, Rubinstein played in several motion pictures and wrote compositions for piano and chamber ensemble. His many high honors included the U.S. Medal of Freedom (1976).

JEFF HACKER

The following is a selected list of prominent persons who died during 1982. Articles on major figures appear in the preceding pages.

Abdullah, Sheik Mohammad (76), political leader of the Indian state of Kashmir, known for many years as the Lion of Kashmir. He founded the Kashmir Muslim Conference in 1931 and fought first for independence from Britain and later for Kashmir's independence from India. He served as chief minister of Kashmir from 1948 until 1953; in 1975 he again became chief minister: d. Sept. 8.

Adams, Harriet Stratemeyer (89), author; under four pseudonyms she wrote nearly 200 children's books, including many of the Nancy Drew, Hardy Boys, Bobbsey Twins, and Tom Swift, Jr., series. Her father, Edward Stratemeyer, had created most of the series and their characters: d. Pottersville, NJ, March 27.

Aragon, Louis (85), French writer and prominent member of the French Communist party; he wrote novels, poetry, and essays, and at various times in his life embraced Dadaism, Surrealism, and Marxism. Among his critically acclaimed

novels were *The Bells of Basel, Residential Quarters, The Century Was Young, Aurelian,* and *Holy Week.* A visit to the Soviet Union in 1930 supplied the impetus for his turn toward Communism. He won the Lenin Peace Prize for his poem, *Ode to Stalin.* He had a falling-out with the Soviet Union over its handling of the unrest in Czechoslovakia in 1968, but later was brought back into the fold: d. Paris, Dec. 24.

Ashbrook, John M. (53), U.S. congressman (R-OH, 1961–82): d. Newark, OH, April 24.

Bader, Sir Douglas (72), British fighter pilot. After a Royal Air Force fighter plane crash in 1931 he lost both his legs, but was determined to fly again. He had artificial legs fitted and in 1939 persuaded the RAF to take him back as a pilot. He subsequently was credited with downing 24 Nazi planes in 1940–41 before being captured. He was knighted in 1976: d. London, England, Sept. 5.

UPI   UPI

John Belushi   *Lord Butler*

Bakr, Ahmed Hassan (68), president of Iraq (1968–79): d. Baghdad, Oct. 4.

Balmain, Pierre (68), French couturier; opened his couture house in 1945 and, along with Balenciaga, Fath, and Dior, perpetuated the postwar "New Look" which featured soft, rounded shoulders, small waistlines and bouffant skirts: d. Neuilly, France, June 29.

Barbour, Walworth (74), U.S. diplomat; was U.S. ambassador to Israel during three administrations (1961–73): d. Gloucester, MA, July 21.

Barnes, Djuna (90), American poet and novelist. A member of the Paris literary circle of the 1920s and 1930s. She is probably best known for her novel *Nightwood* (1937): d. New York City, June 18.

Barr, Stringfellow (84), author and educator; while president of St. Johns College (1937–46) in Annapolis, MD, he instituted a new curriculum consisting entirely of the study of 100 great books of man's past: d. Alexandria, VA, Feb. 2.

Bauer, Riccardo (86), Italian socialist; was a leader of the underground opposition to Mussolini during the 1930s and 1940s: d. Milan, Italy, Oct. 15.

Beaumont, Hugh (72), actor; best known for his role as the father Ward Cleaver in the television series *Leave It To Beaver:* d. Munich, West Germany, May 14.

Begin, Aliza (62), wife of Israeli prime minister Menahem Begin; she met Mr. Begin as a teenager in her native Poland when both were active in the Zionist Revisionist Party: d. Jerusalem, Nov. 14.

Belushi, John (33), comedian; rose to fame during the 1970s as a member of the troupe of the television series *Saturday Night Live.* He later appeared in such movies as *Animal House, 1941,* and *The Blues Brothers:* d. Hollywood, CA, March 5.

Benelli, Giovanni Cardinal (61), Roman Catholic archbishop of Florence, was considered in 1978 as a likely candidate to be elected pope: d. Italy, Oct. 26.

Benjamin, Adam (47), U.S. congressman (D-IN, 1977–82): d. Washington, DC, found Sept. 7.

Bettis, Valerie (62), choreographer and modern dancer. In 1947 she created *Virginia Sampler* for the Ballet Russe de Monte Carlo, becoming the first modern dancer to choreograph for a classical ballet company: d. New York City, Sept. 26.

Bhave, Vinoba (né Vinayak N.) (87), Indian social reformer and disciple of Mohandas K. Gandhi, considered by many as Gandhi's spiritual heir: d. Maharashtra (state), India, Nov. 15.

Biemiller, Andrew J. (75), lobbyist for the AFL-CIO (1956–78). He played an important role in attaching an equal employment provision to the Civil Rights Act of 1964. He was a U.S. congressman (D-WI, 1945–46; 1949–50): d. Bethesda, MD, April 3.

Bloch, Ray (79), musical conductor; composed and conducted for Ed Sullivan's and Jackie Gleason's television variety shows: d. Miami, March 29.

Bloomingdale, Alfred (66), businessman, was for many years head of the Diners' Club and a key figure in the growth of the credit-card business. Between 1939 and 1949 he was also a Broadway and Hollywood producer: d. Santa Monica, CA, Aug. 20.

Boyer, Ken (51), all-star third baseman for the St. Louis Cardinals for 11 years: d. St. Louis, Sept. 7.

Broderick, James (55), actor; probably best known for his roles in the television series *Brenner* and *Family:* d. New Haven, CT, Nov. 1.

Bruce, Virginia (née Briggs) (72), motion-picture actress; known for her portrayal of a Ziegfeld showgirl in *The Great Ziegfeld* (1936): d. Hollywood, CA, Feb. 24.

Bruehl, Anton (82), photographer; especially important during the 1920s and 1930s, he was one of the first to work in color: d. San Francisco, Aug. 10.

Buono, Victor (43), actor; appeared often in character roles in films and television and in 1962 received an Oscar nomination for his work in *Whatever Happened to Baby Jane?:* d. Apple Valley, CA, found dead Jan. 1.

Burnett, W. R. (82), author; his first book was *Little Caesar* (1927). He penned several screenplays, and wrote 39 novels in all: d. Santa Monica, CA, April 25.

Bushmiller, Ernie (76), cartoonist; creator of the comic strip "Nancy": d. Stamford, CT, Aug. 15.

Butler, Lord (Richard Austen Butler) (79), British political leader; one of the important figures of the modern Conservative Party. He was twice passed over for prime minister. In his more than 35 years of public service, he served in numerous governmental posts. As Britain's first minister of education, he pushed through the Education Act of 1944. In 1965 he retired from the House of Commons and became a master of Trinity College at Cambridge University: d. Great Yeldham, Essex, England, March 8.

Canham, Erwin D. (77), editor-in-chief of *The Christian Science Monitor* (1964–74): d. Agana, Guam, Jan. 3.

Carritt, David (55), English art critic, historian, and dealer; since the 1940s responsible for numerous discoveries of Old Master paintings: d. London, Aug. 3.

Case, Clifford P. (77), U.S. politician; served as a U.S. congressman (R-NJ, 1945–55) and U.S senator (1955–79): d. Washington, DC, March 6.

Chatfield-Taylor, Brenda (Frazier) (60), socialite; she was a famous debutante, and her 1938 coming-out party was the social event of the season: d. Boston, May 3.

Churchill, Sarah (67), British actress and the daughter of Sir Winston Churchill: d. London, Sept. 24.

Cody, John Cardinal (74), churchman; archbishop of Chicago (1965–82): d. Chicago, April 25.

Conried, Hans (66), actor and comedian; appeared in about 100 motion pictures and on television and the stage: d. Burbank, CA, Jan. 5.

Coote, Robert (73), British actor; his most famous stage role was that of Col. Pickering in *My Fair Lady:* d. New York City, Nov. 25.

Coppola, Frank (83), Mafia leader: d. Aprilia, Italy, April 26.

Cox, Allyn (86), American painter; did murals in the rotunda and corridors of the U.S. Capitol in Washington. He later did work in the Great Experiment Hall: d. Washington, DC, Sept. 26.

Curzon, Sir Clifford (75), British pianist. Sir Clifford entered the Royal Academy of Music in London at age 12 and early won acclaim. He made his first public appearance in London when he was 16 and thereafter began teaching at the Royal Academy. He was made a full professor at age 19. Until 1970 he performed in the United States frequently. He was knighted in 1977: d. London, Sept. 1.

Dannay, Frederic (76), coauthor of the Ellery Queen detective stories. He collaborated on more than 35 novels with his cousin Manfred B. Lee, who died in 1971: d. White Plains, NY, Sept. 3.

de Creeft, Jose (97), sculptor; an advocate of the direct method of sculpture—that is, working in the medium intended for the piece and not in clay first: d. New York City, Sept. 11.

Demara, Ferdinand Waldo, Jr. (60), impostor; was the inspiration for the film *The Great Impostor* (1960) and the book upon which it was based. During his life he lived as a Trappist monk, dean at a small college, law student, and surgeon: d. Anaheim, CA, June 7.

Deutsch, Helene (97), Austrian-born psychoanalyst; was the first woman analyst to be analyzed by Sigmund Freud. She is probably best known for describing the "as-if" personality, a concept which focuses on those whose lives seem to them to be lacking in genuineness. In the 1920s she started the Vienna Psychoanalytic Institute, staying there until she came to the United States in 1935: d. Cambridge, MA, March 29.

del Monaco, Mario (67), Italian operatic tenor. Having made his American debut in San Francisco in *Aïda* in 1950, he was associated with the Metropolitan Opera in New York (1951–59): d. near Venice, Italy, Oct. 16.

Dillard, Hardy Cross (79), jurist; dean of the University of Virginia law school (1963–68) and a judge of the International Court of Justice (1970–79): d. Charlottesville, VA, May 12.

Dubinsky, David (90), labor leader; president of the International Ladies Garment Workers Union (1932–66). Mr. Dubinsky held the belief that mass-production industries could not be effectively organized along craft-union lines and so joined with John L. Lewis in 1935 to set up the Committee for Industrial Organization which became the Congress of Industrial Organizations. At that time he was vice-president of the American Federation of Labor and when the AFL voted to suspend the CIO unions in 1936, he resigned. In 1940 he rejoined the AFL and in 1945 was again one of its vice-presidents. Long a crusader against racketeers, he established a code of ethics in dealing with them that was adopted by the labor movement. He helped eliminate sweatshops and worked within the union for health insurance, retirement and other benefits. He became active in New York politics, helping in 1936 to form the American Labor Party and in 1944 the Liberal Party: d. New York City, Sept. 17.

Dubos, Rene (81), bacteriologist and writer. His scientific career was spent primarily as a scientist and professor at the Rockefeller Institute and Rockefeller University, although from 1942 to 1944 he was at the Harvard Medical School. In recent years Dr. Dubos devoted full time to writing and lecturing in support of a healthy human environment. He wrote 20 books, including the Pulitzer prize-winning *So Human an Animal* and along with Barbara Ward, *Only One Earth*: d. New York City, Feb. 20.

Eldjarn, Kristjan (65), president of Iceland (1968–80), an archaeologist by profession, he was curator of the National Museum of Iceland (1947–1968): d. Cleveland, OH, Sept. 13.

Farber, Edward Rolke (67), photographer and electronic lighting engineer; credited with inventing the portable strobe flash for still cameras: d. Delafield, WI, Jan. 22.

Fassbinder, Rainer Werner (36), German motion-picture director; considered the man most responsible for the resurgence of the German cinema in the 1970s. He often made social and political satires concerned with what he considered a self-satisfied, post-World-War-II German society. One of his most famous films, *The Marriage of Maria Braun*, particularly exemplified this concern: d. Munich, West Germany, found dead June 10.

Feingold, Benjamin F. (81), pediatric allergist; believed that many hyperactive children could be helped by eliminating various foods from their diet: d. San Francisco, CA, March 23.

Feldman, Marty (48), British comedian; known for such films as *Young Frankenstein, The Adventure of Sherlock Holmes' Smarter Brother*, and *Silent Movie*: d. Mexico City, Dec. 2.

Felici, Pericle Cardinal (70), Roman Catholic Cardinal; an expert on church law and a noted Latin scholar. A member of the Curia, he recently presided over a special commission to revise canon law: d. Foggia, Italy, March 21.

Ferguson, Homer (94), U.S. senator (R-MI, 1943–55); was U.S. ambassador to the Philippines (1955–56) and a judge on the U.S. Court of Military Appeals (1956–76): d. Grosse Pointe, MI, Dec. 17.

Fitzgerald, Edward (89), radio broadcaster; he began working for WOR-AM radio in the 1930s. Along with his wife, Pegeen, he broadcast *The Fitzgeralds*. Together they are credited with originating husband-and-wife radio talk programs: d. New York City, March 22.

Fortas, Abe (71), American jurist; associate justice of the U.S. Supreme Court (1965–69). First in his class at the Yale Law School, Mr. Fortas became a protégé of William O. Douglas. Fortas later became a confidant of Lyndon Johnson and was a founding partner of one of Washington's most successful law firms. Prior to going into private practice, he had held various posts in the Roosevelt administration. It was Johnson who appointed him to the Supreme Court, and even after becoming an associate justice, Fortas continued to advise the president. In 1968 when Chief Justice Warren indicated that he wanted to retire, Johnson nominated Fortas for the post. A Senate filibuster ensued, and Fortas asked Johnson to withdraw his name. In 1969, Fortas resigned from the Supreme Court after an uproar on the discovery that he had accepted a $20,000

fee from a foundation controlled by Louis E. Wolfson, who at the time of the payment was under federal investigation. Mr. Fortas returned to private practice: d. Washington, DC, April 5.

Foster, Harold R. (89), cartoonist; creator of the "Prince Valiant" comic strip: d. Spring Hill, FL, July 25.

Frei, Montalva Eduardo (71), president of Chile (1964–70): d. Santiago, Chile, Jan. 22.

Freud, Anna (86), psychoanalyst; she was an authority on the teachings of her father, Sigmund Freud. Beginning a career as an elementary teacher, she switched to psychoanalysis and particularly child analysis early on. She published a number of books and established the Hampstead and Child Therapy Clinic, where she was director: d. London, Oct. 9.

Gale, Sir Richard (86), British Army general; played a major role in planning the Allied parachute invasion of Normandy during World War II: d. Kingston-on-Thames, England, July 29.

Gallen, Hugh (58), governor of New Hampshire (1978–82). A Democrat, he had gained national prominence in 1978 when he defeated the Republican incumbent. He was re-elected in 1980, but lost the election of 1982, attributing his defeat largely to his refusal to pledge to veto a state sales or income tax: d. Boston, MA, Dec. 29. (*See also* New Hampshire.)

Gardner, John (49), novelist, poet, and teacher; he wrote several novels, including *Grendel, The Sunlight Dialogues, October Light*, and *Mickelsson's Ghosts*, and a book of criticism, *On Moral Fiction*. He headed the creative writing program at the State University of New York in Binghamton and had taught at several other colleges and universities: d. near Susquehanna, PA, Sept. 14.

Garroway, Dave (69), television personality; served as the first host of the *Today* show (1952–61): d. Swarthmore, PA, July 21.

Gemayel, Bashir (34), president-elect of Lebanon: d. Beirut, Lebanon, Sept. 14.

George, Bill (51), football linebacker for the Chicago Bears (1952–65); became a member of the Pro Football Hall of Fame in 1974: d. Rockford, IL, Sept. 30.

Giauque, William F. (86), chemist; taught at the University of California at Berkeley. He won the Nobel Prize in Chemistry in 1949 for his contributions in the study of properties and substances at extremely low temperatures: d. Oakland, CA, March 28.

Gibbons, Edward F. (63), business executive, was chairman and chief executive officer of Woolworth Company (1978–82). He recently had announced decisions to close the 20-year-old Woolco discount chain and to sell the company's British subsidiary: d. Valhalla, NY, Oct. 26.

Gierow, Karl (78), Swedish theater director; led the Royal Dramatic Theater of Stockholm from 1951–63. He was an authority and intimate of Eugene O'Neill. Dr. Gierow was elected to the Swedish Academy in 1961 and became its permanent secretary: d. Stockholm, Oct. 31.

Goldmann, Nahum (87), Zionist leader; influential in the attainment of reparation payments from West Germany to Israel and the Jewish people for crimes against the Jews in World War II. He was president of the World Jewish Congress (1951–78) and for a time of the World Zionist Organization. Dr. Goldmann often found himself at odds with the state of Israel for his rather "dovish" views. He believed that there could be no future for a Jewish state unless agreement was reached with the Arabs: d. Bad Reichenhall, West Germany, Aug. 29.

Gosden, Freeman F. (83), radio performer; he created the role of Amos in the *Amos 'n Andy* radio series that began on NBC in 1929: d. Los Angeles, Dec. 10.

David Dubinsky
UPI

Abe Fortas
UPI

John Gardner
© Joel Gardner

Dave Garroway
UPI

Gould, Glenn H. (50), Canadian pianist; he had an important concert career but in 1964 retired from concert playing to become a recording artist. An eccentric, he chose a life of "isolation over society, recordings over live concerts, and musical reinterpretations over respect for musical 'authenticity.'" He made nearly 80 CBS recordings, many of which are considered outstanding. He was particularly well known for his Bach interpretations: d. Toronto, Oct. 4.

Gouzenko, Igor (65), Soviet turncoat; in 1945 he defected from the Soviet Embassy in Ottawa and provided Canadian police with documents uncovering Soviet espionage activities in Canada which revealed Soviet efforts to obtain American and British atomic bomb secrets: d. Canada (reported June 29 in Ottawa).

Grade, Chaim (72), Yiddish poet and novelist; in the late 1970s his two-volume *The Yeshiva* was published in English: d. New York City, June 26.

Grant, George (85), U.S. congressman (D–AL, 1938–65): d. Nov. 4 (aboard an ocean liner).

Greer, William Alexander (Sonny) (78), drummer for Duke Ellington's Orchestra: d. New York City, March 23.

Grosvenor, Melville B. (80), president of National Geographic Society and editor of the *National Geographic* magazine (1957–67); he became editor in chief and board chairman in 1967: d. Miami, April 22.

Grumman, Leroy (87), aeronautical engineer; founder of the Grumman Aerospace Corporation (1929). Mr. Grumman designed a revolutionary wing-retraction system that allowed double the number of planes to be stationed on an aircraft carrier: d. Manhasset, NY, Oct. 4.

Guest, Winston F.C. (76), polo champion; was the international champion of the 1930s. He maintained the Templeton racing stables: d. Mineola, NY, Oct. 25.

Guzmán, Antonio (71), president of the Dominican Republic (1978–81): d. Santo Domingo, July 4.

Haig, Al (58), jazz musician, was an early be-bop pianist and a member of the Charlie Parker Quintet: d. New York City, Nov. 16.

Hall, Joyce Clyde (91), founder of Hallmark Cards, Inc.: d. Leawood, KS, Oct. 29.

Hallstein, Walter (80), West German politician and diplomat; one of the founders of the European Economic Community (Common Market): d. Stuttgart, West Germany, March 29.

Hampton, Hope (84), entertainer; starred in silent films and in the 1930s sang with the Philadelphia Grand Opera: d. New York, Jan. 23.

Harkness, Rebekah West (67), American philanthropist; gave millions to the dance and medicine. In 1964 she founded the Harkness Ballet which disbanded in 1970 and then reformed that year and performed for five more years. In medicine Mrs. Harkness contributed to the building of the William Hale Harkness Medical Research Building at New York Hospital and supported Dr. Irvin S. Cooper's research on Parkinson's disease: d. New York City, June 17.

Harman, Fred (79), artist; creator of the "Red Ryder" cowboy comic series: d. Phoenix, AZ, Jan. 2.

Harnwell, Gaylord P. (78), atomic physicist and educator; was president of the University of Pennsylvania (1953–70). He was responsible for the development of sonar ranging: d. Haverford, PA, April 18.

Hemingway, Leicester (67), writer; younger brother of Ernest. He wrote the 1962 biography *My Brother, Ernest Hemingway* and five novels: d. Miami Beach, FL, Sept. 13.

Hicks, Granville (80), writer; leader of the proletarian literature movement of the 1930s. He joined the Communist Party in 1934, resigning in 1939 following the signing of a non-aggression pact between the Soviet Union and Nazi Germany. Although some critics took issue with his Marxist point of view, he was established as an important literary critic following the publication in 1938 of *The Great Tradition: An Interpretation of American Literature Since the Civil War*. His dismissal as an assistant professor of English at the Rensselaer Polytechnic Institute in 1935 brought on a furor regarding academic freedom. Mr. Hicks later taught at several major schools. In addition to criticism he wrote novels and biographies: d. Franklin Park, NJ, June 18.

Hillenkoetter, Roscoe (85), admiral, U.S. Navy; was the first director of the Central Intelligence Agency (1947–50): d. New York City, June 18.

Hofheinz, Roy Mark (70), public official and entrepreneur; was a Texas legislator at the age of 22, a Harris County judge at age 24, and a two-term mayor of Houston, TX, elected in 1952. In 1960 he proposed the world's first indoor stadium and persuaded Harris County residents to vote bonds to finance what was to become the Astrodome. Mr. Hofheinz also helped innovate artificial turf, now featured in many stadiums: d. Houston, TX, Nov. 21.

Holloway, Stanley (91), British actor; famed for the role of Alfred Doolittle in *My Fair Lady:* d. Littlehampton, Sussex, England, Jan. 30.

CBS Records   UPI

Glen H. Gould   *Leon Jaworski*

Hopkins, Sam (Lightnin') (69), musician; considered one of the great country blues singers and an influential guitarist: d. Houston, TX, Jan. 30.

Hosmer, Craig (67), U.S. congressman (R-CA, 1953–75): d. aboard a Mexico-bound cruise ship, Oct. 11.

Hughes, Emmet J. (61), writer, political adviser; was a speechwriter for President Dwight Eisenhower and a speechwriter and adviser to Nelson Rockefeller. His books include *The Ordeal of Power* and *The Living Presidency:* d. Kingston, NJ, Sept. 19.

Hunter, Frank (87), Major General, U.S. Army Air Force. He was a World War I flying ace and flew with Edward Rickenbacker. During World War II the Major General was the first U.S. air commander to put the P-47 Thunderbolt into combat: d. Savannah, GA, June 25.

Irish, Edward S. (Ned) (76), founder and former-president of the New York Knickerbockers basketball team: d. Venice, FL, Jan. 21.

Jakobson, Roman (85), Russian-born linguist; considered the father of modern structural linguistics. His work affected the disciplines of anthropology, art criticism, and brain research. In 1949 he joined the faculty of Harvard, becoming professor emeritus in 1967. He continued lecturing at other major universities. His papers totaled more than 600: d. Boston, MA, July 18.

Janson, Horst Waldemar (68), professor of art history at New York University (1949–82). He was probably best known for his top selling *History of Art*, first published in 1962. He died aboard a train between Milan, Italy, and Zurich, Switzerland: d. Sept. 30.

Jarman, John (66), U.S. congressman (OK, 1950–77). He was a Democrat until 1975 when he became a Republican: d. Oklahoma City, Jan. 15.

Jaworski, Leon (77), lawyer, was special prosecutor in the Watergate case that eventually brought about the resignation of Richard Nixon as president. Another important case in which Jaworski had a hand was the Nuremberg war criminal trials. His book on Watergate, *The Right and the Power*, was published in 1976: d. near Wimberley, TX, Dec. 9.

Jensen, Jackie (55), baseball player. In his 11-year major league career he played for the New York Yankees, the Washington Senators, and the Boston Red Sox and had a career batting average of .279. He was the American League's most valuable player in 1958: d. Charlottesville, VA, July 14.

Jeritza, Maria (née Mitzi Jedlicka) (94), opera soprano; internationally renowned, called the golden girl of opera's "golden age"; was an important artist from 1910–30, best known for the title role in *Tosca:* d. Orange, NJ, July 10.

Jessup, Richard (57), author; wrote more than 60 books, most of them paperback originals about crime. His best known work was *The Cincinnati Kid* (1964), which was later made into a movie: d. Nokomis, FL, Oct. 22.

Johnson, Dame Celia (73), English actress, probably best known for her role in the movie *Brief Encounter:* d. Nettlebed, Oxfordshire, England, April 26.

Jurgens, Curt (66), West German motion-picture actor: d. Vienna, June 18.

Kaufman, Murray (Murray the K) (60), disk jockey for several rock radio stations: d. Los Angeles, Feb. 21.

Khalid ibn Abdel Aziz Al Saud (69), king of Saudi Arabia (March 1975–1982): d. Taif, Saudi Arabia, June 13.

Khan, Fazlur R. (52), structural engineer and skyscraper design innovator: d. Saudi Arabia, March 27.

Kilgallen, James L. (94), newspaper reporter; joined the International News Service in 1920 after experience as a reporter on various U.S. newspapers and with The Associated Press and United Press. He was with the International News Service for 38 years. Important stories he covered were the Lindbergh baby kidnapping and the World War II German surrender at Rheims, France: d. New York City, Dec. 21.

King, Henry (91?), motion-picture director; directed more than 100 films, including *The Song of Bernadette, Twelve O'Clock High, Love Is a Many Splendored Thing,* and *The Sun Also Rises:* d. San Fernando Valley, CA, June 29.

Kistiakowsky, George (82), chemist; was professor of chemistry at Harvard University (1938–71). He worked on the development of the first atomic bomb and witnessed the first nuclear explosion at Alamagordo, NM, in July 1945. He later became a leading advocate of banning nuclear weapons: d. Cambridge, MA, Dec. 7.

Kogan, Leonid (58), Soviet violinist; known as a classicist who had achieved mastery but who played (in the view of some critics) without passion, he won various music prizes over the years. He was a professor at the Moscow State Conservatory and had played throughout the world; he made his U.S. debut in 1958 at Carnegie Hall. A Jew, he denied that the Soviet Union discriminated against Jewish people: d. Dec. 17 (place not disclosed).

Kollsman, Paul (82), aeronautical engineer, revolutionized aviation in the 1920s when he invented the altimeter, a device that measured the plane's altitude in flight: d. Los Angeles, CA, Sept. 26.

Kripalani, Jiwatram Bhagwandas (93), Indian nationalist, a close disciple of Mohandas Gandhi since 1919. He was president of the Congress Party at the time of India's independence from Great Britain in 1947. He later broke with the party over differences with Nehru and eventually helped to form the Janata Party: d. New Delhi, March 19.

Lamas, Fernando (67), actor; the Argentine-born Mr. Lamas appeared in numerous Latin-lover type roles: d. Los Angeles, Oct. 8.

Lawler, Richard (86), surgeon; successfully performed the first kidney transplant in 1950: d. Chicago, July 24.

Lay, Herman W. (73), entrepreneur; developer of Lay potato chips; his company merged with the Frito Company of Dallas in 1961. In 1965 Mr. Lay negotiated a merger with the Pepsi-Cola Company: d. Dallas, TX, Dec. 6.

Lee, Will (74), actor; portrayed Mr. Hooper on TV's *Sesame Street:* d. New York City, Dec. 7.

Lockridge, Richard (83), writer; with his wife Frances, he created the mystery-story characters of Mr. and Mrs. North: d. Tryon, NC, June 19.

Loughran, Tommy (79), boxer; won the light heavyweight championship in 1927: d. Hollidaysburg, PA, July 7.

Lynd, Helen Merrell (85), author and educator; taught social philosophy at Sarah Lawrence (1928–64) and was instrumental in devising the college's flexible, interdisciplinary curriculum and grading system. Along with her late husband Robert S. Lynd, she wrote *Middletown: A Study in American Contemporary Culture* (1929), the first sociological study of an American community: d. Warren, OH, Jan. 30.

Lynde, Paul (55), actor; appeared on Broadway in *Bye Bye Birdie* (1960) and in the film version of 1963. He was a regular panelist on television's *The Hollywood Squares:* d. Los Angeles, Jan. 9.

Lyons, Louis (84), journalist and curator of Harvard University's Nieman Foundation for Journalism; he was a long-time reporter for the *Boston Globe:* d. Cambridge, MA, April 11.

Macdonald, Dwight (76), writer, editor, and critic; books that he wrote include *Henry Wallace: The Man and the Myth, The Ford Foundation: The Man and the Millions, The Memoirs of a Revolutionist: Essays in Political Criticism, Parodies,* and *Essays and Afterthoughts: 1938–74.* A political leftist, he began as a Stalinist, then turned to Trotskyism, anarchism, and pacifism: d. New York City, Dec. 19.

McGivern, William P. (60), mystery writer; wrote 23 mystery novels, 14 of which were later adapted into motion pictures. His more popular novels were *The Big Heat, Odds Against Tomorrow, Night of the Juggler,* and *Soldiers of '44:* d. Palm Desert, CA, Nov. 18.

Magee, Patrick (58), Irish actor; won a 1965 Tony for his role in *Marat/Sade:* d. London, Aug. 14.

Malraux, Clara (85), French author and critic; she was a leading figure in the anti-Nazi resistance in France, organizing a network of shelters for German Jews fleeing the Nazis before and after the outbreak of World War II. A Jew herself, she was the first wife of author André Malraux, and despite their breakup in 1939 she kept his name. She wrote six volumes of memoirs: d. Paris, Dec. 15.

Markey, Lucille Parker (85), Calumet (horse) Farm owner: d. Lexington, KY, July 25.

Marsh, Dame Ngaio (82), New Zealand mystery writer; wrote 31 novels, most of which were best sellers, and an autobiography: d. Christchurch, New Zealand, Feb. 18.

Mendès-France, Pierre (75), prime minister of France (June 1954–February 1955); he was a leftist intellectual, lawyer, economist, and World War II pilot. He was admitted to the bar at the age of 21, the youngest lawyer in France, and became active in politics in the 1930s. After World War II, Mendès-France served a ministry and leadership role in the early government of Charles de Gaulle: d. Paris, Oct. 18.

Merrill, Henry Tindall (Dick) (88), aviator; in 1936 he made the first trans-Atlantic round-trip flight and made the first commercial trans-Atlantic flight in 1937: d. Lake Elsinore, CA, Oct. 31.

Merchant, Vivien (née Ada Thompson) (53), British actress; she starred in many stage plays written by her former husband Harold Pinter. Her films include *Alfie* (1966), *Accident* (1967), and *Frenzy* (1972): d. London, Oct. 3.

Mills, Harry (68), singer; a member of the Mills Brothers: d. Los Angeles, June 28.

Mitscherlich, Alexander (73), German psychoanalyst; credited with pioneering the study of aggression in large groups. He was the founder of the Hospital for Psychosomatic Disorders in Heidelberg in 1949 and the Sigmund Freud Institute in Frankfurt in 1959: d. Frankfurt, West Germany, June 26.

Monk, Thelonious (64), jazz pianist and composer, beginning in the 1930s and 1940s. During the 1960s he won widespread recognition: d. Englewood, NJ, Feb. 17.

Moore, Stanford (68), biochemist; was a professor at The Rockefeller University (1939–82). In 1972 he shared a Nobel Prize in Chemistry with Dr. William H. Stein for research into the chemical structure of pancreatic nuclease, a human enzyme: d. New York City, Aug. 23.

More, Kenneth (67), English actor; in a career spanning 40 years he was successful on stage, screen, and in television: d. London, July 12.

Morgan, Henry S. (81), investment banker; member of the famous banking family: d. New York City, Feb. 7.

Morrow, Vic (51), actor; probably best known for his role in the television series *Combat* (1962–66): d. Indian Dunes Park, CA, July 23.

Morton, Thruston B. (74), U.S. senator (R-KY, 1957–69); U.S. congressman (1947–53): d. Louisville, KY, Aug. 14.

Mueller, Reuben (85), Bishop of the United Methodist Church and president of the National Council of Churches (1963–66). He was a leading United Methodist ecumenist: d. Franklin, IN, July 6.

Mumford, Lawrence Q. (78), librarian of Congress (1954–74) and a past president of the American Library Association: d. Aug. 15.

Namgyal, Palden Thondup (58), former King of Sikkim; his rule was broken in 1973 by a coup; he was deposed in 1975. He had married American debutante Hope Cooke in 1963; together they attempted to modernize the state: d. New York City, Jan. 29.

Nesbitt, Cathleen (93), British character actress; famous for her role as Henry Higgins' mother in the Broadway musical *My Fair Lady* (1956): d. London, Aug. 2.

Nicholson, Ben (87), British artist; known for his abstract works: d. London, Feb. 6.

Lord Noel-Baker (né Philip Baker) (92), British statesman, Nobel Peace Prize recipient of 1959, and Olympic athlete in the 1920s. He was elected to Parliament for the Labor Party in 1929 and was reelected until 1970, when he retired. He was instrumental in founding the League of Nations after World War I and was a member of the British delegation to the UN in 1945 and from 1946 to 1947. He was made a life peer in 1977: d. London, Oct. 8.

Oates, Warren (52), motion-picture and television actor; known for character roles in such films as *Easy Rider, In the Heat of the Night, Dillinger,* and recently *The Border.* He occasionally appeared on television: d. Los Angeles, CA, April 3.

O'Brien, Leo W. (81), U.S. congressman (D-NY, 1952–66): d. Albany, NY, May 4.

O'Gorman, Juan (76), Mexican painter and architect: d. Mexico City, Jan. 18.

Okada, Kenzo (79), painter; his abstractionist works reflect both his Japanese origins and Western influences from his years in the United States: d. Tokyo, July 25.

Orff, Carl (86), German composer and music educator; best known for his *Carmina Burana:* d. Munich, West Germany, March 29.

Ovando Candia, Alfredo (65), former president of Bolivia. General Ovando was part of a military coup that ousted President Víctor Paz Estenssoro in 1964. He served as co-president, 1965–66. In 1969 he helped overthrow the government of Luis Adolfo Siles Salinas and became president. He resigned in 1970: d. La Paz, Bolivia, Jan. 24.

Pei, Wenzhong (79), Chinese archaeologist; in 1929 discovered the skull of Peking Man: d. Peking, Sept. 18.

Pelletier, Wilfrid (85), Canadian musical conductor: d. New York City, April 9.

Pemberton, Murdock (94), critic, was the first art critic for *The New Yorker* magazine, working there from 1925 until 1932 and then again in the 1950s. He believed that he had inadvertently started the literary luncheon at the Algonquin Hotel in the 1920s: d. Valatie, NY, Aug. 18.

Pepper, Art (56), musician; star saxophonist with Stan Kenton's orchestra during the 1940s; in recent years he rebuilt his career: d. Los Angeles, June 15.

Petri, Elio (53), Italian motion picture director; well known for his *Investigation of a Citizen Above Suspicion*, which in 1970 won an Academy Award as the best foreign film: d. Rome, Nov. 10.

Pilyugin, Nikolai (74), Soviet designer of space rockets, was a key figure in the development of the Soviet space program: d. Moscow, Aug. 2.

Pollard, H. Marvin (75), cancer specialist, was professor of internal medicine at the University of Michigan from 1933 to 1971. He was an authority on gastrointestinal diseases and headed the research team that invented the fiberoptic gastroscope in 1956: d. Ann Arbor, MI, July 15.

Powell, Eleanor (69), film and stage actress; known for her tap dancing skills: d. Beverly Hills, Feb. 11.

Prezzolini, Giuseppe (100), Italian-born author, teacher; in 1929 he joined the faculty of Columbia University, where he remained for more than 20 years. In all he wrote 57 books, a number of which were published in the United States, including *Fascism, Machiavelli,* and *The Legacy of Italy:* d. Lugano, Switzerland, July 14.

Primrose, William (77), musician; considered the greatest violist of his time. During his 50-year career, he was a soloist, chamber music player, orchestra musician, and teacher: d. Provo, UT, May 1.

Probst, Leonard (60), drama critic and radio news producer: d. Brooklyn Heights, NY, March 19.

Rambert, Dame Marie (née Cyvia Rambam) (94), British ballet leader; was director of the Ballet Rambert, established in 1931: d. London, June 12.

Rand, Ayn (77), writer and philosopher of "objectivism"; she advocated "rational selfishness" and capitalism, the economic system which she thought offered the best climate for the pursuit and practice of her ideas. Her novels include *The Fountainhead* (1943) and *Atlas Shrugged* (1957): d. New York City, March 6.

Rexroth, Kenneth (76), American author; was a poet, critic, translator of Chinese, Japanese, and classic Greek poetry, and painter, as well as a kind of father figure to the Beat Generation of the San Francisco literati in the 1950s. A correspondent for *The Nation* for 15 years, he also wrote a column for *The San Francisco Examiner* (1960–68) and lectured at the University of California: d. Montecito, CA, June 6.

Ritola, Willie (86), Finnish runner; won five Olympic gold medals—four in 1924 and in 1928: d. Helsinki, Finland, April 24.

Roa Garcia, Raúl (75), foreign minister of Cuba (1959–76); after 1976 he served as vice-president of the National Assembly and a member of the Council of State: d. Havana, July 6.

Robarts, John (65), Canadian politician; was premier of the province of Ontario (1961–71): d. Toronto, Oct. 18.

Robbins, Marty (57), country singer; twice a Grammy-award winner, he was a regular on the Grand Ole Opry: d. Nashville, TN, Dec. 8.

Robinson, Maurice (86), publisher; the founder and chairman of Scholastic Magazines Inc.: d. Pelham, NY, Feb. 7.

Roosevelt, Nicholas (88), diplomat and writer; he saw diplomatic service in Paris, Spain, Vienna, and Hungary and was a writer for *The Herald Tribune* and *The New York Times.* A cousin of President Theodore Roosevelt and a life-long Republican, his books include *The Philippines: A Treasure and a Problem* (1926) and *The Restless Pacific* (1928): d. Monterey, CA, Feb. 16.

Rothschild, Baron Alain de (72), member of the Rothschild banking family and a French Jewish leader. He was a strong supporter of the state of Israel and spoke out against anti-Semitism and terrorism: d. New York City, Oct. 17.

Sackler, Howard (52), playwright; best known for his Pulitzer-Prize-winning drama *The Great White Hope:* d. Ibiza, Spain, Oct. 14.

Sánchez, Salvador (23), boxer, was the World Boxing Council's featherweight champion, a title he won in February 1980: d. Mexico, Aug. 12.

Schilt, Jan (87), astronomer; considered a pioneer in stellar statistics, he invented the Schilt photometer which measures the brightness of stars and helps determine their distance from earth: d. New Jersey, Jan. 9.

Schneebeli, Herman T. (74), U.S. congressman (R-PA, 1961–71): d. Philadelphia, May 6.

Schneider, Romy (née Rose-Marie) (43), Austrian-born actress. In 1961 international acclaim came with her role in Luchino Visconti's segment of *Boccaccio '70:* d. Paris, May 29.

Sebelius, Keith (65), U.S. congressman (R-KS, 1969–81): d. Norton, KS, Sept. 5.

Seely-Brown, Horace, Jr. (73), U.S. congressman (R-CT, 1947–49; 1951–59; 1961–63): d. Boca Raton, FL, April 9.

Selye, Hans (75), endocrinologist; director of the International Institute of Stress at the University of Montreal and a pioneer in the studies on the effects of stress: d. Montreal, Oct. 16.

Shaginyan, Marietta S. (93), Soviet novelist; she was a minor poet of the Symbolist school and after the Russian Revolution began writing prose fiction. She helped develop the Soviet detective story, combining a mystery plot with revolutionary ideology. Later, she turned to industrial construction themes: d. Moscow, reported March 23.

Simmons, Calvin (32), music director of the Oakland (CA) Symphony (1979–82); considered one of the most promising young conductors in the United States: d. near Lake Placid, NY, Aug. 21.

Smith, Ray Winfield (85), Egyptologist: d. Houston, TX, April 17.

King Sobhuza II (83), king of Swaziland; was the world's longest-reigning sovereign, having reigned for 82 years. He ruled on his own starting in 1921. He was an absolute ruler who, following Swaziland's independence from Britain in 1969, allowed a British-style parliamentary system to exist for only four years. King Sobhuza actively supported foreign investment and management, much of it by a minority of whites. He had numerous wives, by some counts more than 100, and was thought to have had 600 children: d. near Mbabane, Swaziland, Aug. 21.

Spivak, Charlie (77), orchestra leader during the Big Band era of the 1940s: d. Greenville, SC, March 1.

Stanford, Sally (78), madam and mayor of Sausalito, CA, (1976–78): d. Greenbrai, CA, Feb. 1.

Stern, Max (83), industrialist and philanthropist; was the founder of the Hartz Mountain Products Corporation, the world's largest manufacturer of pet foods and related products. Stern was honorary chairman of the board of trustees of Yeshiva University and had donated more than $10 million to the university: d. New York City, May 20.

Stitt, Edward "Sonny" (58), jazz musician; was originally an alto saxophonist whom Charlie Parker regarded as the inheritor of his style and stature in jazz; later switched to tenor saxophone: d. Washington, DC, July 22.

Strasberg, Lee (né Israel Strassberg) (80), acting teacher and film performer; best known as the father of "method" acting in America. In 1931, along with Harold Clurman and Cheryl Crawford, he founded the Group Theater. In 1948 Strasberg joined the Actors Studio, which had been founded the year before: d. New York City, Feb. 17.

Stravinsky, Vera (93), actress, painter, and widow of composer Igor Stravinsky: d. New York City, Sept. 17.

Sunay, Cevdet (82), president of Turkey (1966–73): d. Istanbul, May 22.

Suslov, Mikhail (79), Soviet theorist; a powerful member of the Politburo and the national secretariat. Suslov was considered an ideological conservative and was influential in decisions to crush the Hungarian revolt in 1956, to end liberalism in Czechoslovakia in 1968, and to press for order in Poland in 1981. His main area of concentration was on interparty relations, and in the 1960s and 1970s he traveled abroad frequently to the congresses of other Communist parties: d. USSR, Jan. 25.

Eleanor Powell   *Ayn Rand*

UPI   UPI

TS IN **VIS**

UPI   UPI   UPI   Courtesy, RCA

Bess Truman   *Jack Webb*   *John Jay Whitney*   *Vladimir K. Zworykin*

Swart, Charles R. (87), the first South African State President (1961–67); he previously had served as minister of justice (1948–59): d. Bloemfontein, South Africa, July 16.

Swigert, John L., Jr. (51), astronaut and Republican congressman-elect from Colorado; he was a member of the crew of Apollo 13. The 1970 spacecraft launch was to be man's third landing on the moon, but an oxygen tank explosion altered that plan and all efforts were focused on getting the crew back to earth safely: d. Washington, DC, Dec. 27.

Swinnerton, Frank (98), British novelist; in all he wrote about 60 novels and was a literary critic, essayist, editor, and journalist, as well: d. Surrey, England, Nov. 6.

Szmuness, Wolf (63), Polish-born epidemiologist; he was in charge of the hepatitis-B vaccine field trials that began in 1978, and his studies are considered classics in the field: d. Flushing, NY, June 6.

Tanner, N. Eldon (84), Mormon church leader: d. Salt Lake City, UT, Nov. 27.

Tati, Jacques (né Tatischeff) (75), French actor, writer, and director; created the memorable Hulot character in *Mr. Hulot's Holiday, Mon Oncle, Playtime,* and *Traffic:* d. Paris, Nov. 5.

Theorell, Axel Hugo Teodor (79), Swedish biochemist; internationally known for his studies of enzymes involved in cell respiration. Dr. Theorell was the first to crystallize myoglobin (1932). In the mid-1930s he isolated and analyzed the structure of an oxidative enzyme then called the "yellow enzyme." He won a Nobel Prize in Medicine in 1955: d. Sweden, Aug. 15.

Trepper, Leopold (77), Polish-born spy; was one of the best known spymasters of World War II, the leader of the "Red Orchestra" network in Nazi Europe, important to the defeat of the Nazis at Stalingrad: d. Jerusalem, Jan. 19.

Truman, Bess (née Elizabeth Virginia) (97), widow of President Harry S. Truman, she was America's first lady from 1945 to 1953. President Truman indicated that she was his chief adviser always—politically and otherwise: d. Kansas City, MO, Oct. 18.

Turnbull, Agnes Sligh (93), novelist and short-story writer; her work often described the rural life of western Pennsylvania, where she was reared: d. Livingston, NJ, Jan. 31.

Tuve, Merle (80), physicist; his experiments with short-pulse radio waves aided in the development of radar: d. Bethesda, MD, May 20.

Twining, Nathan (84), U.S. general of the Air Force; was the Air Force Chief of Staff from 1953 to 1957 and Chairman of the Joint Chiefs until his retirement in 1960: d. San Antonio, TX, March 29.

Uris, Harold (76), builder and philanthropist; along with his brother Percy, he was instrumental in putting up many skyscrapers in New York City: d. Palm Beach, FL, March 28.

Valera, Fernando (83), president of the Spanish government in French exile opposed to Franco. He served from 1971 until 1977 when democratic elections were held in Spain, and was a founding member of the Spanish Radical Socialist Party: d. Paris, Feb. 13.

Vidor, King (88), motion-picture director; made his first feature film in 1919 and was known for two silent classics—*The Big Parade* (1925) and *The Crowd* (1928). He was nominated five times for an Academy Award. In 1979 he received a special Oscar for achievements over four decades. In his later years he taught film at several colleges: d. Paso Robles, CA, Nov. 1.

Wakely, Jimmy (68), country and western singer; he also starred in movie westerns. He was well known for such songs as *Tennessee Waltz* and *Beautiful Brown Eyes:* d. Los Angeles, Sept. 23.

Walker, Fred (Dixie) (71), baseball player; popular Brooklyn Dodger outfielder (1939–48), nicknamed "The People's Cherce." He compiled a lifetime .306 average in his 18 seasons in the major leagues and won the National League batting title in 1944 with a .357 average: d. Birmingham, AL, May 17.

Wallenberg, Marcus (82), Swedish banker-industrialist; Wallenberg headed an empire that encompassed a third of Swedish industry and dominated business life there: d. Stockholm, Sweden, Sept. 13.

Waner, Lloyd (76), baseball outfielder; joined the Pittsburgh Pirates in 1927, playing through the 1940 season. He played briefly for several clubs before ending his career with the Pirates in 1945. He was elected to the Baseball Hall of Fame in 1967 with 2,459 career hits: d. Oklahoma City, OK, July 22.

Warburg, Sir Siegmund (80), international banker, founded London's S.G. Warburg and Company merchant bank in 1946 through which he helped modernize London's financial district by providing standard money dealings and advisory services to individual clients. He was knighted in 1964: d. London, Oct. 18.

Webb, Jack (62), actor; best known for the role of Sgt. Joe Friday in the highly successful radio and television series *Dragnet.* He also had acting roles in several films, including *The Men, Sunset Boulevard,* and *The Halls of Montezuma* and later produced various television series: d. Los Angeles, Dec. 23.

Weiss, Peter (65), playwright; wrote *The Persecution and Assassination of Marat as Performed by the Inmates of the Asylum of Charenton Under the Direction of the Marquis de Sade* (usually referred to as *Marat/Sade*). The play, considered shocking in its time, opened on Broadway in December 1965: d. Stockholm, May 10.

Whitney, John Hay (77), capitalist; was a publisher, investor, and sportsman whose greatest disappointment was his inability to save *The New York Herald Tribune,* which he took over in 1961. At various times Whitney had an interest in 25 small newspapers, five television stations, six radio stations, and the International Herald Tribune Company, among others. Whitney was an early investor in the corporation that later evolved into Pan American World Airways. In 1946 he founded a venture capital company, the John Hay Whitney Foundation. A bridge and golfing partner of President Dwight Eisenhower, he served as ambassador to Great Britain (1957–61): d. Manhasset, NY, Feb. 8.

Wilson, Don (81), radio and TV announcer; was the foil for Jack Benny on his radio and TV shows for more than 40 years: d. Cathedral City, CA, April 25.

Wolff, Irving (88), vice-president for research of the RCA Laboratories, he was one of the developers of radar: d. Princeton, NJ, Dec. 5.

Woods, George D. (81), investment banker; was president of the World Bank (1963–1968): d. near Lisbon, Portugal, Aug. 20.

Ydigoras Fuentes, Miguel (88), president of Guatemala from 1958 to 1963 when he was overthrown in a coup: d. Guatemala City, Oct. 6.

Zaturenska, Marya (80), poet; received the Pulitzer Prize in 1938 for her volume *Cold Morning Sky:* d. Shelburne Falls, MA, Jan. 19.

Ziolkowski, Korczak (74), sculptor, he spent 35 years carving a monument (still incomplete) to the Sioux Indian Chief Crazy Horse out of a mountain in the Black Hills: d. Sturgis, SD, Oct. 20.

Zworykin, Vladimir (92), Russian-born scientist; held more than 120 patents, two of which were instrumental to the development of television—the iconoscope camera tube and the kinescope picture tube: d. Princeton, NJ, July 29.

OCEANOGRAPHY

A new technique allows oceanographers to see the profile of a body of water—in minutes instead of weeks. The technique employs an acoustic tomograph, an oceangoing cousin to the CAT (Computer-Assisted Tomograph) scanner which gives clinicians detailed views of our tissues and organs that traditional X rays do not reveal. Instead of X rays, the oceanographers' tool uses low frequency sound waves. Sound signals are sent through the water to submerged receivers, and their arrival time is recorded. The speed of sound in sea water varies with both pressure and temperature in such a way that a minimum speed is reached at a depth of about 3,280 ft (1 000 m), where the sound waves oscillate over great distances. Any variations in arrival time help to reveal the presence of warm and cold water eddies that lie between the source of the sound and the listening array.

A 186-mi (300-km) square of the Atlantic southwest of Bermuda was used as a test area, with four transmitters and five receivers placed at a depth of 6,560 ft (2 000 m). This gave a total of 20 different horizontal paths for the acoustical signals to travel. The results of the swift acoustical ranging were in good agreement with slowly accumulated shipboard measurements of temperature, salinity, and density. In the first experiment eddy patterns were reproduced as if in a photograph.

For many years, more traditional methods have been used to investigate the large gyres, or "rings," of water, between 93 and 186 mi (150–300 km) in diameter, that are produced by the Gulf Stream. Gyres to the northwest of the Gulf Stream form eddies and circulate clockwise, carrying tropical fish from the Sargasso Sea to the waters off New England. Gyres to the southwest of the stream carry cold water and rotate counterclockwise. In 1982 both aircraft and polar-orbiting satellites joined several research vessels in the study of the gyres' physical, chemical, and biological processes.

Still another example of this emphasis on understanding the mesoscale phenomena of circulation is a cooperative project of the United States and Spain. They are extensively studying a clockwise gyre 62 mi (100 km) in diameter that is formed in the westernmost Mediterranean, near El Alboran islet, by the water current flowing through the Straits of Gibraltar from the Atlantic.

Geological Research. An international group of institutions known as the Joint Oceanographic Institutions for Deep Earth Sampling (JOIDES) financially supports and gives scientific guidance to the Deep Sea Drilling Project (DSDP). In 1982, DSDP drilled and cored in a thick lens-shaped sedimentary belt lying parallel to and south of the equator in the Pacific. A new hydraulic piston corer was used that gives a minimal disturbance to the relatively soft sediment layers. Almost 7,000 ft (2 135 m) of oceanic sediment was collected from 16 holes located at five sites in the equatorial Pacific. Some 2,000 samples have been distributed to participating scientists for analysis. They will seek a better understanding of the factors of marine productivity in this fertile band of ocean water by elucidating the dynamics of the system through time and the reaction of the organisms to geography and climate.

On another DSDP cruise, three holes were drilled on the Shatsky Rise in the northwestern Pacific. Each effort recovered continuous sedimentary sections spanning the Cretaceous/Tertiary boundary some 75 million years ago, which was a time of many extinctions. Study of the cores will seek to determine the factors related to the faunal replacements. Other sites were drilled along a roughly north-south transect to study the history of the Japan, or Kuroshio, Current system over the past 5 million years. This system, analogous to the Gulf Stream in the northwest Atlantic, is a major demarcation of the Pacific warm and cold water masses. The northernmost site of the transect was drilled all the way into basaltic basement rocks to determine the total sediment thickness there. A fifth site recovered a typical red clay section with which to study the history of the input of wind-blown sediment from Asia.

Deep Sea Vents. In May, some 40 scientists from 20 universities and research institutions in the United States, Mexico, and France participated in the five-week Oasis expedition to the sites of hydrothermal vents off Baja California, Mexico. Located nearly 150 mi (240 km) south of the Baja peninsula, 21 degrees north of the equator, these hot water vents are at depths of about (8,360 ft) (2 550 m) along the East Pacific Rise. The rise is a volcanic ridge along the top of a spreading center on the boundary of two of the earth's crustal plates. Vent water reaches temperatures in excess of 660° F (350° C), whereas nearby sea water is only 36° F (2° C). While life is sparse over most of the ocean floor, dense communities of unique organisms surround the vents, thriving without the aid of sunlight in waters rich in bacteria and other microorganisms. In 18 dives the submersible ALVIN retrieved material for study of the physiology and ecology of the vent populations, which are remarkably adapted to their strange world. Some of them use chemicals from the vents as an energy source for producing usable organic compounds. Studies of the metabolisms of the special fauna show that they function much like more normal organisms but with the aid of special adaptations for a habitat rich in hydrogen sulfide, which normally poisons enzyme systems. The hydrothermal vents are also considered important sites for chemical processes and the formation of ore deposits.

DAVID A. MCGILL
U.S. Coast Guard Academy

OHIO

A single economic indicator explains Ohio's switching to a Democratic governor in the election of Nov. 2, 1982. The industrial state's unemployment rate jumped to 12.5% in August and 14.2% in November (the highest in 42 years), sharply up from 10% in January 1981.

The Election. Richard F. Celeste of Lakewood, former Peace Corps director and lieutenant governor of Ohio, won the governorship by carrying 61 of 88 counties. The new governor's vote was 1,979,000 to 1,303,000 for Republican Congressman Clarence J. Brown of Urbana. Of the 61 counties, 50 had suffered job losses since 1980. Celeste, to be inaugurated on Jan. 10, 1983, had lost in 1978 to Gov. James A. Rhodes. Under Ohio law, a governor cannot hold more than two consecutive terms. Rhodes, 73, held the remarkable record of filling the gubernatorial office for 16 years (1963–71 and 1975–83). (One researcher reported that Rhodes' tenure was surpassed only by New York Gov. George Clinton's 21 years in two tenures between 1777 and 1804.) Celeste's campaign was aimed at "Reaganomics" and spotlighted promises of more jobs. He will have Democratic majorities in the Senate (17D–16R) and House (63D–36R).

Democrats swept other elective offices in the state: lieutenant governor, attorney general, auditor, treasurer, and secretary of state. A fellow party member, Howard M. Metzenbaum of Lyndhurst, former airport parking lot magnate known as a champion of liberal and anti-oil company causes, won a second term as U.S. senator, defeating state Sen. Paul E. Pfeifer of Bucyrus. Pfeifer had been pressed into campaign service after Congressman John M. Ashbrook of Newark died on April 24.

Ohioans rejected constitutional proposals that would have: (1) required election, rather than appointment, of members of the Ohio Public Utilities Commission; and (2) added 1% to the state's sales tax (raised to 5% in late 1981) for funding a high-speed network of passenger

UPI

Richard F. Celeste (D), Ohio's governor-elect, and his five-year-old son, Stephen, relax after a long campaign.

trains between principal cities at an estimated cost of $8,000,000,000 through the mid-1990s.

The issuance of state revenue bonds to seed lower-than-market-rate single-family home mortgages was approved.

Taxes. No financial crises arose in 1982, but Celeste before his election hedged on whether he would seek a tax hike. He said that would depend on what happened in the first 100 days of his administration. Thanks to 1980 legislation (that included the 1981 sales tax rise) annual revenues had been increased by more than $300 million.

Newspapers. The afternoon *Cleveland Press,* the first Scripps newspaper, founded in 1878, closed on June 17 when businessman Joseph E. Cole, who bought control in 1980, said economic conditions prevented continuance. Some 900 employees were dismissed. Dayton Newspapers, Inc., reported in April that it would combine the editorial staffs of its *Journal-Herald* (morning) and *Daily News* (afternoon).

Schools. U.S. District Judge Frank Battisti on October 26 ordered the state of Ohio to pay $26.2 million to the Cleveland Board of Education as its 1978–1981 share of the schools' desegregation costs, including buses. Until a few months before, the state and school board could not agree on the costs. The state also claimed that its ordinary subsidies were all that it owed.

Corporations. Shareholders of Marathon Oil Co. in Findlay agreed to a merger into the U.S. Steel Corp. after Marathon's officials fought off an unwanted suitor. Standard Oil Co. (Ohio)

OHIO · Information Highlights

Area: 41,330 sq mi (107 045 km²).

Population (1980 census): 10,797,624.

Chief Cities (1980 census): Columbus, the capital, 565,032; Cleveland, 573,822; Cincinnati, 385,457; Toledo, 354,635; Akron, 237,177; Dayton, 193,444.

Government (1982): *Chief Officer*—governor, James A. Rhodes (R). *General Assembly*—Senate, 33 members; House of Representatives, 99 members.

State Finances (fiscal year 1981): *Revenues,* $14,241,000,000; *expenditures,* $13,269,000,000.

Personal Income (1981): $111,179,000,000; per capita, $10,313.

Labor Force (Aug. 1982): *Nonagricultural wage and salary earners,* 4,181,400; *unemployed,* 656,900 (12.5% of total force).

Education: *Enrollment* (fall 1981)—public elementary schools, 1,292,831; public secondary, 615,723; colleges and universities (1981–82), 521,396 students. *Public school expenditures* (1980–81), $4,095,800,000 ($2,143 per pupil).

completed purchase of enough land fronting on Euclid and Superior avenues and the edge of Public Square in Cleveland to ensure proceeding with a $200 million, 45-story headquarters building due for occupancy in mid-1985.

Crime. The U.S. Justice Department filed charges in Cleveland in October against six persons in an alleged organized-crime drug ring operating in northeastern Ohio. Two were indicted for having some connection with three murders, and bodies of other possible victims were being sought. The six pleaded not guilty; the seventh agreed to testify against them.

JOHN F. HUTH, JR.
Former Reporter, "The Plain Dealer," Cleveland

OKLAHOMA

Oklahoma celebrated the 75th anniversary of its statehood in November 1982.

Elections. Democrat George Nigh was reelected governor in a landslide victory over Republican Auditor and Inspector Tom Daxon. Nigh was the first Oklahoma governor to be reelected for a second term since the removal of the one-term limit in 1970. Nigh received 62% of the votes cast to defeat Daxon, who had campaigned on a Reaganomics platform of tax and spending reductions.

Incumbent congressmen received massive voter endorsement: all six were returned to office. The race in the first district was the closest, with Democrat James Jones winning by a 54% margin.

Voters defeated three state questions in the general election, including a congressional redistricting proposal that would have returned districts to the pre-1980 boundaries, and a water trust proposal. An initiative petition to legalize parimutuel betting on horse races passed at the runoff primary. County option will permit racetracks to exist subject to regulations established by the legislature and under supervision of commissioners appointed by the governor.

Legislative Session. Major initiatives adopted included a $37.2 million reduction in income taxes, increased corporate taxes, further reductions in inheritance taxes, and county government reforms. Increased support continued for common schools, higher education, mental health, corrections, and highways. A juvenile justice reform bill and a compulsory auto driver's liability insurance bill were passed. A university center was established at Tulsa, to be operated by existing state universities and colleges. The Senate refused to ratify the Equal Rights Amendment.

County Commissioners Scandal. Federal investigators continued to probe corruption charges against county commissioners who allegedly received kickbacks on supplies and road-building materials. Reform bills enacted to correct deficiencies in county government increased authority for the attorney general to prosecute violations, abolished the office of county surveyor, established an increased fine and prison term for those conspiring to defraud the state and its subdivisions, and required reapportionment of county commissioners' districts after each federal census.

Human Services. Lloyd Rader, the director of the state's department of human services for 31 years, resigned amid charges that children in state institutions were being physically and sexually abused. The charges led to U.S. Senate investigations and proposals to the state legislature to reorganize the department or transfer some functions to other agencies. Former U.S. Sen. Henry Bellmon was made interim director.

Business. Penn Square National Bank, the fourth-largest bank in Oklahoma, failed in July. The failure involved other major national lending institutions, such as Chase Manhattan Bank, Continental Illinois Corporation, the Seattle National Bank, and Northern Trust Company. These banks had purchased more than $2,000,000,000 worth of undercollateralized energy loans from Penn Square. The Federal Deposit Insurance Corporation (FDIC) estimated that some $250 million of uninsured deposits were defaulted. Many were held by credit unions, including the Congressional Credit Union, and savings and loan associations. The FBI and House Banking Committee launched investigations into possible criminal conduct by Penn Square officials.

The oil boom that peaked in 1981 appeared to be over as widespread layoffs of workers in oil and related industries occurred, and new drillings decreased.

Railroads. In a move to reestablish rail freight service in 11 western counties, the transportation department agreed to pay $15 million for 354 mi (570 km) of track abandoned by the Rock Island Railroad.

JOHN W. WOOD
University of Oklahoma

OKLAHOMA • Information Highlights

Area: 69,956 sq mi (181 186 km²).

Population (1980 census): 3,025,290.

Chief Cities (1980 census): Oklahoma City, the capital, 403,136; Tulsa, 360,919; Lawton, 80,054.

Government (1982): *Chief Officers*—governor, George Nigh (D); lt. gov., Spencer Bernard (D). *Legislature*—Senate, 48 members; House of Representatives, 101 members.

State Finances (fiscal year 1981): *Revenues,* $4,094,000,000; *expenditures,* $3,791,000,000.

Personal Income (1981): $31,771,000,000; per capita, $10,247.

Labor Force (Aug. 1982): *Nonagricultural wage and salary earners,* 1,201,000; *unemployed,* 82,800 (5.6% of total force).

Education: *Enrollment* (fall 1981)—public elementary schools, 408,579; public secondary, 173,993; colleges and universities (1981–82), 162,825 students. *Public school expenditures* (1980–81), $1,259,290,000 ($2,007 per pupil).

ONTARIO

As Canada's most industrialized province, Ontario felt the recession acutely during 1982. The automobile industry, centered in the south, and the mining industry, in the north, were especially hard hit. Sudbury, suffering from massive layoffs by Inco and Falcolnbridge Nickel, had one of the highest unemployment rates in the country.

Facing a rising deficit—up by 38% to $2,200,000,000—and falling revenue, Treasurer Frank Miller had little option but to raise taxes in his May 13 budget to finance his projected expenditures of $27,800,000,000. The 7% sales tax was extended to many new items, including plants, pets, magazines, labor charges, fast food, and personal hygiene products. Taxes were raised by 17.4% on beer, liquor, cigarettes, and health insurance premiums. Job creation was allotted $171 million, and $250 million went for tax relief for small businesses. Miller blamed the tax increases on the federal government, which he accused of reducing transfer payments for health programs, postsecondary education, and social services.

Spending on both hospitals and postsecondary education was held down tightly. Although Health Minister Larry Grossman announced an 11% increase in hospital funding, it was made clear that hospitals would no longer be permitted to run deficits and would be liable to provincial administration if they did. Layoffs of hospital staff occurred. Ontario physicians staged a series of walkouts after rejecting a government offer to raise fees by 34% over three years.

Although initially cool to the federal government's wage restraint program introduced during the summer, Ontario produced its own program in the fall. Bill 179 would hold wage increases of all public employees (including civil servants, hospital workers, university staff, and teachers) to 5% in 1983. All contracts were automatically extended and no increases above 5% were to take effect, even if previously negotiated.

The Canadian Press

Employees of Dominion Foundries and Steel read of layoffs at the Hamilton plant. Unemployment in Ontario soared.

In return there were to be no layoffs, although it was unclear how that would be guaranteed. Strikes were effectively banned. As a symbol of restraint, the premier's jet was to be sold and the proceeds to be spent on aircraft for fighting forest fires.

The new Liberal leader, David Peterson, bitterly attacked the Conservative government's economic programs as inadequate. He was especially critical of the 1981 purchase of $650 million worth of Suncor stock, arguing that the money should have been spent on job creation. Equally loud in demanding job-creation programs was Bob Rae, the new leader of the New Democratic Party (NDP). Rae resigned as federal NDP parliamentary finance critic to enter provincial politics. Hampered by the lack of a seat in the legislature, he also was embarrassed by the reluctance of any sitting NDP members to make way for him. He finally was elected in a by-election in November.

Despite the promulgation of the new Canadian constitution and pressure from both Franco-Ontarians and the federal government, Premier Davis reiterated that he would not see to make the province officially bilingual.

In October, the province was shocked by the suicide of former Premier John Robarts.

PETER J. KING
Carleton University

OREGON

During 1982, Oregon's timber-based economy continued to suffer the accumulated effects of several years' high mortgage rates and resulting record low housing starts.

Economy. Sawmill closures accelerated during the year, and by September the seasonally adjusted unemployment figure for Oregon stood at 11.2%.

A constitutional mandate for a balanced budget, plus the state's plummeting income, forced Gov. Victor Atiyeh to call three emer-

---

ONTARIO · Information Highlights

Area: 412,582 sq mi (1 068 587 km²).
Population (1981 census): 8,625,107.
Chief Cities (1981 census): Toronto, the provincial capital, 599,217; Ottawa, the federal capital, 295,163; North York, 559,521; Mississauga, 315,056; Hamilton, 306,434; London, 254,280.
Government (1982): *Chief Officers*—lt. gov., John Black Aird; premier, William G. Davis (Progressive Conservative); atty. gen., Roy McMurtry. *Legislature*—Legislative Assembly, 125 members.
Education (1982–83): *Enrollment*—elementary and secondary schools, 1,847,400 pupils; postsecondary, 246,200 students.
Public Finance (1982 fiscal year, est.): *Revenues,* $19,525,500,000; *expenditures,* $20,142,100,000.
Personal Income (average weekly salary, June 1982): $381.97.
Unemployment Rate (August 1982, seasonally adjusted): 10.8%.
(All monetary figures are in Canadian dollars.)

gency sessions of the Legislative Assembly. The first, from January to March, accomplished little. The second, lasting one day in June, cut state agency budgets severely. And the third, lasting one day in September, partially offset deficits by appropriating funds from the surplus accumulated by the State Accident Insurance Fund. Several legislators called for enactment of a sales tax—a distinct possibility in view of the increase in the state deficit to some $30 million.

Oregon became the only state in 1982 to cut funding for higher education below the levels of the previous biennium. While the average increase in higher education expenditures among the states was 15% in 1982, Oregon's outlay for higher education amounted to a 4% decline. Oregon now ranks 34th among the states in per capita appropriations for higher education.

Elections. Gov. Victor Atiyeh (R) won reelection by overwhelming Democrat Ted Kulongoski. Democratic incumbents Les AuCoin, Jim Weaver, and Ron Wyden were returned to Congress from the 1st, 4th, and 3d districts, respectively. Republican Denny Smith was elected to represent the new 5th district in the mid-Willamette Valley, and another Republican, Bob Smith, was elected from the 2d district vacated by Denny Smith.

Ballot propositions limiting property taxes, permitting self-service gasoline sales, and abolishing the state's model land-use planning law were defeated by narrow margins. A measure recommending a nuclear-weapons freeze was approved by the voters.

Education. A number of school levies were defeated during 1982, but school districts generally received more assistance than during previous years. The resignations of three regional state college presidents were attributed to faltering state funding of their institutions.

Other Events. Midsummer estimates of Coho salmon populations in coastal waters were alarmingly low, prompting early closure of both commercial and sports-fishing seasons. By September, however, counts of fish ascending the Columbia River and its tributaries were so high

that special seasons were opened on the Columbia. Moreover, allowable Indian takes were increased, and Indian fishing regions were enlarged.

The Washington Public Power Supply System (WPPSS) funding debacle (*see* WASHINGTON) affected a number of Oregon Public Power districts that had entered into contracts with WPPSS to share the costs of constructing five nuclear power plants in Washington. Several plants have been mothballed in midconstruction, and rate payers' lawsuits have resulted in a finding that Oregon utilities are not responsible for WPPSS debts without a precontract vote of approval by rate payers. The court's decision survived a first appeal.

In February, Betty Roberts, a judge in the State Court of Appeals, became a justice of the Oregon Supreme Court, the first woman to occupy a seat in the state's highest court.

L. CARL BRANDHORST
Western Oregon State College, Monmouth

OTTAWA

Despite the recession, Ottawa showed all the signs of a thriving city in 1982, buoyed by its federal civil service payroll and high-technology industries. The latter received a boost with the creation of a $20 million microelectronics center sponsored by the provincial government. The city enjoyed a minor building boom, fed by the construction of the $250 million Rideau Centre. The complex, covering several city blocks, altered the appearance of the downtown area and required radically new traffic patterns east of Confederation Square. "Transitways," part of Ottawa's experiment in urban mass transit, were under construction. The special highways, reserved for buses, were expected to speed commuting to the city center.

The city felt the impact of the recession despite its apparent prosperity. Welfare payments were expected to increase by 14%, higher than the national average.

City politics were fairly quiet during the year. The most contentious issue was the fate of the old Teachers College on the edge of Cartier Square. As a heritage building, it would survive the redevelopment of the area. Mayor Marion Dewar supported its use as a center for the performing arts. Alderman Darrel Kent, her major challenger for the mayoralty, was opposed, arguing that the city could not afford the annual maintenance cost of such a project.

In the November municipal elections, Mayor Dewar was reelected without difficulty to her second term. Operation Dismantle was successful in placing a general disarmament referendum on the ballot. (However, regional municipalities questioned its legality and refused to include it.) The referendum was carried easily.

PETER J. KING, *Carleton University*

OREGON • Information Highlights

Area: 97,073 sq mi (251 419 km²).
Population (1980 census): 2,633,149.
Chief Cities (1980 census): Salem, the capital, 89,233; Portland, 366,383; Eugene, 105,624.
Government (1982): *Chief Officers*—governor, Victor Atiyeh (R). *Legislative Assembly*—Senate, 30 members; House of Representatives, 60 members.
State Finances (fiscal year 1981): *Revenues,* $4,423,000,000; *expenditures,* $3,817,000,000.
Personal Income (1981): $26,526,000,000; per capita, $10,008.
Labor Force (Aug. 1982): *Nonagricultural wage and salary earners,* 964,600; *unemployed,* 131,900 (10.1% of total force).
Education: *Enrollment* (fall 1981)—public elementary schools, 315,388; public secondary, 141,777; colleges and universities (1981–82), 149,924. *Public school expenditures* (1980–81), $1,473,037,000 ($3,049 per pupil).

PAKISTAN

Pakistan continued in 1982 under the military rule of Gen. Mohammed Zia ul-Haq, assisted by an advisory council created in 1981.

Political Affairs. The new Majlis-i-Shura (Federal Advisory Council) held its first session in January 1982. General Zia, who has ruled Pakistan as military dictator since July 5, 1977, charged the new body with the tasks of advising the government, helping in the process of Islamization, and creating conditions and plans "conducive to the establishment of Islamic democracy." In creating the council in December 1981, General Zia had said that elections were "not possible despite our . . . best efforts."

Although the 287 members of the new Majlis were selected by the military, they quickly revealed a willingness to criticize governmental policies and officials. Majlis Chairman Khwaja Mohammad Safdar publicly urged the government to hold elections and return the country to civilian rule. General Zia frequently hinted that these actions might be taken. But whether political parties—which have officially been banned since 1979—would be allowed to participate, and what kind of governmental structure might result from such an exercise, remained problematical questions.

In January, Amnesty International issued a report which "noted a steady deterioration in respect for human rights in Pakistan, particularly since the beginning of 1981." Perhaps aided by public interest in the Majlis-i-Shura and by the general disarray of opposition forces in the country, the government seemed somewhat less repressive during 1982. Press censorship was reduced. However, terrorist acts against members of the Majlis and other regime supporters revealed a persistent undercurrent of discontent that is likely to remain as long as military rule continues.

The Economy. Pakistan's economy continued to show healthy growth during 1982. The gross

UPI

Pakistan's General Zia and his host, Indonesia's President Suharto, view the honor guard at Jakarta's airport.

domestic product grew by 5.7% despite shortfalls in wheat production due to adverse weather conditions. The country's economic policies, under the leadership of Finance Minister Ghulam Ishaq Khan, shifted still further in the direction of private sector development, looser import restrictions, and encouragement of foreign investment.

In January, Pakistan "delinked" its currency from the U.S. dollar and allowed the rupee to float in relationship to a basket of currencies. This action, which had the practical effect of gradual devaluation, provided economic benefits in the form of increased exports and higher exchange benefits from overseas workers' remittances. Worker migration to the Middle East continued to be a major positive factor in Pakistan's economy. A World Bank study in 1982 indicated that approximately 5% of Pakistan's labor supply was working in the Middle East. Remittances remained the largest single source of foreign exchange.

Foreign Affairs. Normalization of relations with India dominated Pakistan's foreign policy concerns in 1982. Talks between Indian and Pakistani officials over a possible no-war pact began in January but broke down in February when India objected to Pakistani public state-

---

PAKISTAN · Information Highlights

Official Name: Islamic Republic of Pakistan.
Location: South Asia.
Area: 310,403 sq mi (803 944 km²).
Population (1982 est.): 93,000,000.
Chief Cities (1974): Islamabad, the capital, 250,000; Karachi, 3,500,000; Lahore, 2,100,000.
Government: *Head of state and government,* Mohammed Zia ul-Haq, president (took power July 5, 1977). *Legislature*—Parliament: Senate and National Assembly (dissolved July 1977); Majlis-i-Shura (Federal Advisory Council, formed Dec. 1981).
Monetary Unit: Rupee (12.6 rupees equal U.S.$1, Nov. 4, 1982).
Gross National Product (1981 U.S.$): $27,300,000,-000.
Economic Indexes (1981): *Consumer Prices* (1971= 100), *all items,* 347.1; *food,* 353.7. *Manufacturing production* (1980, 1975=100), 138.
Foreign Trade (1980 U.S.$): *Imports,* $5,350,000,-000; *exports,* $2,588,000,000.

ments on Kashmir. Persistent Pakistani prodding led to a resumption of the dialogue in June, and on November 1, President Zia and Indian Prime Minister Indira Gandhi agreed to set up a commission that would settle future problems between the two countries.

The war in neighboring Afghanistan continued to burden Pakistan with refugees, officially estimated to number approximately 3 million. Pakistani and Afghan representatives met in Geneva in June under United Nations auspices, with Iranians also present as nonparticipants. Soviet troop withdrawal, restoration of political order, and return of refugees were the major issues under negotiation.

Despite disagreements over Afghanistan, Pakistan continued to seek friendly ties with the Soviet Union. Popular regard for the United States, revived since 1981 and reinforced by the influx of U.S. military aid, was somewhat eroded by developments in the Middle East, but President Zia visited the United States in December.

Pakistani Foreign Minister Agha Shahi retired in February and was replaced by veteran diplomat Sahibzada Yaqub Khan.

WILLIAM L. RICHTER

PARAGUAY

In August the Paraguayan government scheduled national elections for Feb. 6, 1983. The official Colorado, Liberal, Radical Liberal, and Febrerist Revolutionary parties would be allowed to participate. In September, President Alfredo Stroessner, 70, was nominated for a seventh consecutive term by the ruling Colorado Party. Also to be filled in the 1983 electoral contest were 30 senate and 60 lower house seats.

Six exiled members of opposition parties were prevented from deplaning in Asunción on September 11 and were forced to return to Buenos Aires. Among the partisans was Luis Alfonso Resck, president of the Christian Democratic Party, who had been banished in June 1981. On September 5, while attempting to gain a court order allowing the exiled politicians to return to Paraguay, Hermes Rafael Saquier had been seized. The detention of Saquier, a spokesman for an opposition coalition, prompted protests from political forces in Argentina, Brazil, the United States, and Venezuela.

The Stroessner government expelled Paraguayan novelist Augusto Roa Bastos in May, calling him an "active communist militant." Hernando Sevilla, an Argentine journalist who had been in a Paraguayan jail since February 1981 for alleged ties to the 1980 assassination in Asunción of Nicaraguan former President Anastasio Somoza, was released in October after UN intercession.

Milestone legislation was passed late in 1981 providing legal status to Indian communities. The new law guaranteed to indigenous groups the legal right to own and control the land on which they worked and lived. When the traditional homelands of the Ava Chiripa Indians in eastern Paraguay were flooded by waters rising behind the massive Itaipú hydroelectric enterprise, its administration reached a settlement with the displaced Indians, permitting them to obtain 10,000 acres (4 050 ha) of new land.

Foreign Relations. A third meeting between President Stroessner and Brazilian President João Figueiredo took place November 6. The meeting was set to coincide with the filling of Lake Itaipú, a reservoir 100 mi (161 km) long and four mi (6.4 km) wide created by Itaipú, the world's largest hydroelectric project. The U.S. $15,000,000,000 project was expected to become operational in April 1983.

Costly delays have plagued construction of the joint Paraguayan-Argentine Yacyretá hydroelectric project, downstream from the Itaipú installation. Argentine participation in the $8,000,000,000 project was hindered by that government's lack of finances for public investment projects. Although contracts for turbines and generators were awarded, work at Yacyretá could be delayed by as much as five years because of Argentina's South Atlantic crisis.

Economy. The once-booming Paraguayan economy slipped into a recession late in 1981, caused by the winding down of a construction boom at Itaipú and delays in the Yacyretá hydroelectric project. Also, currency devaluations in both Brazil and Argentina made Paraguayan products more expensive than imports from neighboring countries. Prices declined on Paraguay's principal exports.

The recession in industrialized nations also affected Paraguay. Bankruptcies increased in number and the stability of banking institutions was questioned. The Central Bank implemented new monetary policies dealing with speculation, free exchange, and export-import controls. The currency experienced a de facto devaluation of 20%. Inflation was expected to fall below 5%, and real GNP growth was forecast at about 5%.

LARRY L. PIPPIN, *Elbert Covell College*

PARAGUAY · Information Highlights

Official Name: Republic of Paraguay.
Location: Central South America.
Area: 157,047 sq mi (406 752 km²).
Population (1982 est.): 3,300,000.
Chief Cities (June 1979 est.): Asunción, the capital, 481,706; Caaguazú, 74,337; Coronel Oviedo, 67,-956.
Government: *Head of state and government,* Gen. Alfredo Stroessner, president (took office Aug. 1954). *Legislature*—Congress: Senate and Chamber of Deputies.
Monetary Unit: Guarani (126 guaranies equal U.S.$1, March 1982).
Gross National Product (1981 U.S.$): $5,330,000,-000.
Economic Index (1980): *Consumer Prices* (1970= 100), *all items,* 342.7; *food,* 386.5.
Foreign Trade (1980 U.S.$): *Imports,* $517,000,000; *exports,* $313,000,000.

PENNSYLVANIA

Citing the ailing economy, Pennsylvania Democrats in the 1982 election gained control of the congressional delegation and the state House of Representatives but failed to topple the state Republican (GOP) standard-bearers, Gov. Dick Thornburgh and U.S. Sen. John Heinz.

Election. Thornburgh, by virtue of a narrow victory over Democratic Congressman Allen Ertel, became the commonwealth's first Republican governor in more than a century to win a second term. Ertel, at the start of the campaign virtually unknown in all but his home district, linked Thornburgh with the Reagan administration and high unemployment. Heinz disassociated himself from "Reaganomics" and won handily over fellow Pittsburgher Cyril Wecht.

Although congressional reapportionment, drafted earlier in the year by the Republican-controlled legislature, was designed to favor the GOP, the Democrats eked out a 13-10 seat advantage in the lower house of Congress. The Republicans lost the slight majority they held in the state House of Representatives but maintained their tenuous control of the state Senate. The balloting was a replay—with role reversal—of the 1978 election, when the state GOP rode dissatisfaction with rising unemployment and slumping business to victory over a Democratic administration.

The Economy. As 1982 proceeded, unemployment topped 11% statewide and soared to more than 17% in some counties and communities. A number of steel plants closed, and workers in many other industries were furloughed. Agriculture, currently the state's No. 1 industry, experienced a good crop year, but depressed prices moderated the farmers' return.

Teacher Strikes. Although the economy generally acted as a damper on labor disputes, Pennsylvania continued to lead the nation in teacher strikes. As of Oct. 1, 1982, strikes were under way in 20 school districts, affecting more than 3,000 teachers and 60,000 pupils. Some walkouts continued into November. The disputes centered on salaries and attempts by many districts to cut faculties to comply with falling enrollments and budget limitations.

Nuclear Power. Clean-up work at the Three Mile Island Unit 2 reactor, badly damaged in March 1979 in the nation's worst nuclear power accident, made headway despite reluctance in Congress to commit the federal government to a major role in funding the project. Camera inspections showed the reactor core had been reduced to a "pile of rubble," but there was no evidence of meltdown. The plant operator, GPU Nuclear Corporation, appealed to the U.S. Supreme Court a lower court decision that ordered the Nuclear Regulatory Commission, in licensing and other such matters, to consider psychological stress of residents near nuclear power plants such as Three Mile Island.

A $20 million fund was created to pay expenses incurred by individuals and businesses as a result of the Three Mile Island accident, and there were 14,047 responses to the 550,000 notices sent out in an area within a 25-mile (40-km) radius of the plant, situated near Harrisburg.

Plans to restart the undamaged Unit 1 reactor were stalled by opposition from antinuclear groups and by technical problems connected with brittle conditions within the reactor wall.

Meanwhile, state courts weighed the legality of an order by the state Public Utility Commission halting construction of Unit 2 at the Limerick nuclear power plant near Philadelphia. The project has been troubled by escalating costs and antinuclear protests.

The state's newest nuclear installation, the Pennsylvania Power and Light Company plant at Berwick, began limited power production, and the nation's first commercial nuclear facility, Shippingport Atomic Power Station, near Pittsburgh, was retired after 25 years of service.

Legislation. Governor Thornburgh signed a bill restricting abortions less than six months after vetoing a similar measure because of reservations about some of its provisions. The legislature passed the governor's welfare reform bill and made the state's twice-a-year auto safety inspections an annual affair.

The state continued to fight a federal vehicle-emission-testing program drafted for the commonwealth. The opposition continued even after a contempt-of-court order froze more than $90 million in federal highway funds, and the U.S. Supreme Court refused to hear an appeal.

A new anticrime law, effective June 6, made a five-year minimum prison sentence mandatory for conviction of such violent crimes as murder, rape, burglary, and robbery with the use of a gun. The new law also applied to violent crimes committed at a transit stop or on public transportation, and to repeat felony offenders.

RICHARD ELGIN
"The Patriot-News," Harrisburg

PENNSYLVANIA · Information Highlights

Area: 45,308 sq mi (117 348 km²).
Population (1980 census): 11,863,895.
Chief Cities (1980 census): Harrisburg, the capital, 53,264; Philadelphia, 1,688,210; Pittsburgh, 423,959; Erie, 119,123; Allentown, 103,758; Scranton, 88,117.
Government (1982): *Chief Officers*—governor, Dick Thornburgh (R); lt. gov., William W. Scranton III (R). *General Assembly*—Senate, 50 members; House of Representatives, 203 members.
State Finances (fiscal year 1981): *Revenues,* $15,348,000,000; *expenditures,* $14,094,000,000.
Personal Income (1981): $123,096,000,000; per capita, $10,370.
Labor Force (Aug. 1982): *Nonagricultural wage and salary earners,* 4,482,400; *unemployed,* 574,900 (10.3% of total force).
Education: *Enrollment*—public elementary schools (fall 1981), 1,195,600; public secondary, 649,600; colleges and universities (1981–82), 517,879. *Public school expenditures* (1980–81), $5,492,707,000 ($2,798 per pupil).

PERU

A September 24 offer by Interior Minister José Gagliardi to negotiate personally with leftist guerrilla leaders and the declaration of an emergency in the mining sector highlighted 1982 events in Peru.

Terrorism Continues. Gagliardi's offer to meet with leaders of the Maoist-oriented *Sendero Luminoso* (Shining Path)—which has mounted more than 3,000 raids on public offices, foreign embassies, businesses, and institutions since 1980—was rejected by Prime Minister Manuel Ulloa Elias, who said that the government would punish "acts of brutality such as the murder of policemen and government officials." President Fernando Belaúnde Terry, trying to reconcile the differences between Gagliardi and the prime minister, refused to accept Gagliardi's subsequent letter of resignation and said that the government was "always ready to talk" with opposition members who were "disposed toward calming things down in the hope of saving lives."

Electric power was cut off to 9 million people in Lima and central and northern Peru when five high-tension towers were destroyed July 27. On August 11, police said they had broken up the principal cell of the Shining Path group, estimated to number about 500, with the arrest of mathematics professor Edgardo Liendo and 11 others. However, four more high-tension towers were destroyed August 19, blacking out the capital city and its environs. The foreign ministry, the Agrarian Bank, and several downtown stores were bombed under cover of darkness. The following day the government declared a state of emergency in Lima and in the nearby port of Callao.

In June, Javier Diaz Canseco, vice-president of the Peruvian Congress' Human Rights Commission, said there were "no less than 500 persons in Lima jails" accused of violating the 1981 anti-terrorist law or disturbing public order. In July, the Congress began consideration of legislation to restore the death penalty—abolished in 1980 by the new constitution—for those convicted of committing terrorist attacks.

Economy. In late July a decline in world metal prices prompted the government to declare a six-month state of economic emergency in the mining sector. The slump had brought many mining companies to the edge of bankruptcy. Under the government decree, all collective bargaining in mining was suspended. All but the largest mining companies were exempted from taxes and were forbidden to fire workers. After an earlier, one-month suspension of silver sales by MINPECO, the state-owned seller of mining products, silver prices crept up to $8.40 an ounce—helped in part by a six-month suspension of U.S. government stockpiles of silver.

President Belaúnde reported some "modest positive economic growth" in the first half of 1982 compared with 1981, owing to a recovery in exports of manufactured goods, tuna, and fishmeal. However, the foreign debt reached $6,890,000,000 on July 31, compared with $6,420,000,000 in July 1981. Inflation was reduced to about 60% in 1982, compared with 81% in 1981 and 50% in 1980, but the Peruvian sol fell in value from 467 to the U.S. dollar in November 1981 to 831 in late October 1982.

In July the International Monetary Fund approved a three-year loan of $975 million to Peru. The loan agreement, designed to reduce Peru's foreign debt, set strict limits on foreign borrowing by the public sector.

SIDERPERU, the state-owned steel company, closed its Chimbote plant for two months in September because of excess stocks. One bright note was the discovery of a new oil well in the Pavayacu area that was producing 3,500 barrels per day in April 1982.

Foreign Relations. Three weeks of efforts by Peruvian President Belaúnde Terry to mediate the Falkland (Malvinas) Islands War between Argentina and Great Britain started after the sinking of the Argentine cruiser *Belgrano* on May 2 and collapsed with the landing of British raiding parties on the main islands May 21.

In response to a call by Panama and Venezuela for a restructuring of the Organization of American States (OAS) without the United States, Peruvian Foreign Minister Javier Arias Stella stated July 19 that neither Cuba nor the United States should be excluded from the OAS. He admitted that the organization needed to be more efficient in both the political and economic fields.

Two Ecuadoran fishing boats were seized and fined for violating Peruvian waters on August 23. However, the two nations avoided a continuation of the border disputes that marred their relations in early 1981.

Peru was one of seven members of the International Whaling Commission to oppose a worldwide ban on commercial whaling. The commission approved the ban, which was to begin in 1985, at a July 23 meeting in England.

NEALE J. PEARSON, *Texas Tech University*

PERU · Information Highlights

Official Name: Republic of Peru.
Location: West Coast of South America.
Area: 496,223 sq mi (1 285 218 km²).
Population (1982 est.): 18,600,000.
Chief Cities (1972 census): Lima, the capital, 3,158,417 (met. area); Arequipa, 304,653; Callao, 296,220.
Government: *Head of state,* Fernando Belaúnde Terry, president (took office July 1980). *Head of government,* Manuel Ulloa Elías, prime minister (took office July 1980). *Legislature*—Congress: Senate and Chamber of Deputies.
Monetary Unit: Sol (831.73 soles equal U.S.$1, Oct. 26, 1982).
Gross National Product (1981 U.S.$): $19,500,000,000.
Economic Index (1980): *Consumer Prices (1970= 100),* all items, 159.2; food, 158.8.
Foreign Trade (1980 U.S.$): *Imports,* $2,541,000,000; *exports,* $3,364,000,000.

PHILADELPHIA

On an autumn day in 1682, the good ship "Welcome" sailed up the Delaware River, carrying with it William Penn. The English Quaker had crossed the Atlantic Ocean to survey the lands awarded to him by King Charles II of England—the Commonwealth of Pennsylvania. Penn dreamed of, and founded, an ordered city built on Quaker principles of religious tolerance and personal freedom. Within 50 years, Philadelphia had become a city second only to London in size and importance. In fact, the U.S. Constitution was adopted at Independence Hall in Philadelphia on Sept. 17, 1787, and the city served as the national capital from 1790 to 1800.

Three hundred years after its founding, in 1982, Philadelphia, Penn's "City of Brotherly Love," remembered in special celebrations the principles and traditions fostered by its founder. Philadelphia's 300th birthday celebration was called "Century IV"—the first year of Philadelphia's fourth century—symbolizing the necessity to use the past and the present to chart Philadelphia's future direction.

Hundreds of activities, exhibits, programs, and festivals were held throughout the year. They included: "A Philadelphia Portrait: 1682–1982," a combined exhibition by the Historical Society of Pennsylvania, the Library Company of Philadelphia, and the American Philosophical Society; "Of Color, Humanitas, and Statehood: The Black Experience in Pennsylvania over 300 Years," presented by the Afro-American Historical and Cultural Museum; "Changing Images of the Garden—300 Years of Horticulture in the Delaware Valley," the central exhibit of the Philadelphia Flower Show; "Destination Philadelphia: A Look at Philadelphia Immigration Over the Past Century" at the Balch Institute for Ethnic Studies; and "Children of '82—Youth Arts Festival," a weekend of performances by and for children. "Philadelphia Moving Past" was a traveling historical show produced by the Century IV Celebration in conjunction with the Philadelphia Area Cultural Consortium and the Center for Philadelphia Studies of the University of Pennsylvania. It brought unusual exhibits, storytelling, and historical games on Philadelphia's lifestyles and social changes of the past 100 years directly to the city's neighborhoods.

Beginning in April, the celebration staged six major "cornerstone" events as public happenings, designed for enjoyment as well as to focus attention on the city's strengths. The arrival on April 25 of the Cunard Line's *Queen Elizabeth II*, on her maiden voyage to Philadelphia, demonstrated the region's importance as an international port of call and the Delaware River port's continued vitality as the world's largest fresh water port. May's "Feasting Festival" culminated in the "Restaurant Festival on the Parkway," an open-air bounty of food from nearly

UPI

The Chilean tall ship Esmeralda *sails up the Delaware River as the City of Brotherly Love is 300 years old.*

100 of Philadelphia's nationally recognized restaurants.

More than 3.5 million people lined the banks of the Delaware River and flocked to Penn's Landing to see 35 Tall Ships of the World in full sail in June. The future of Philadelphia's downtown waterfront was reflected in the spirit of this visit. In July, the "American Music Festival" showcased American music styles—musical comedy, folk, jazz, pop, gospel, country and western, classical, rock, and rhythm and blues.

Philadelphia is a city of neighborhoods, nearly 130, and during August, the "Only in Philadelphia Neighborhoods Festival" highlighted 30 of them. The culmination of Century IV's activities occurred in October, with "William Penn Heritage Week." The city's 300th birthday party was marked on October 24, Penn's 338th birthday. Throughout "Heritage Week," Philadelphia joined with other communities in Pennsylvania, New Jersey, and Delaware to recreate Penn's voyage in 1682. This "Up River Festival" featured "Penn" taking part in historical commemorations at New Castle, DE; Camden, NJ; Chester, PA; Pennsbury Manor, Penn's country home in Bucks County, PA; as well as at Philadelphia's Penn's Landing and Penn Treaty Park. Descendants of families who arrived with Penn on the "Welcome" and of settlers already in the area and representatives of the Indian tribes who lived along the Eastern seaboard in the 17th century participated.

WILLIAM J. GREEN, *Mayor of Philadelphia*

PHILIPPINES

UPI

President and Mrs. Marcos call on UN Sec.-Gen. Pérez de Cuellar (center) in September.

President Ferdinand E. Marcos showed evidence in 1982 of heightened concern over succession to his nondemocratic rule. His trip in September to the United States was partly designed to promote the appearance of American approval of his personal political leadership and the governmental legacy that might be willed his countrymen.

Politics. President Marcos was hospitalized in August for mild pneumonia. In September, seemingly in response to this illness, the Philippine National Assembly sought to clarify the legal framework for a 15-member executive committee that would provide for a temporary successor to Marcos. The president's 53-year-old wife Imelda, already mayor of Manila, was named to the committee. Speculation was widespread within the country and abroad that this was a prelude to the first lady's possible future political succession to the presidency.

In August, on the eve of his departure for the United States, President Marcos charged that radical labor unionists were scheming to overthrow his government while he was out of the country, and more than 80 alleged plotters were arrested. The Marcos government also appointed 1,000 "secret marshals" to protect Manila's omnipresent "jeepneys" against a rising wave of passenger robberies.

Both moves, whatever their motivations, had the consequence of heading off demonstrations against President Marcos on the eve of his American trip. Former Senator José Diokno, an outspoken critic of the regime, charged that Marcos' actions were "partly designed to create the impression that the Philippine government is not getting enough military and economic support from the United States."

Opposition to Marcos expressed itself in diverse ways. Criticism of the president's authoritarian rule from the Catholic church continued, Manila's Jaime Cardinal Sim declaring that it

was time for Marcos to step down as the country's political leader.

Economy. The worldwide recession in 1982 had a particularly devastating effect on the Philippine economy. Overall foreign export earnings for the year were down 27%, and the country was forced to carry a $539 million balance of payments deficit. The external debt rose to $18,000,-000,000, and American banks—which carried much of this obligation—were unwilling to advance additional large "bail-out" loans. Inflation was at an annual rate of 13%, and the unemployment rate was 20%.

The increasing cost of imported oil weighed especially heavily on the Philippines, while prices for such Filipino exports as coconut products and copper dropped sharply. Other Philippine goods, including sugar, clothing, and wood products, fared almost as badly.

Because of heavy Filipino economic dependence on the United States, the Marcos government looked to increased sales of Filipino products to the United States as a partial solution to

---

PHILIPPINES · Information Highlights

Official Name: Republic of the Philippines.
Area: 115,830 sq mi (300 000 km^2).
Population (1982 est.): 51,600,000.
Chief Cities (1980 preliminary census): Manila, the capital, 1,626,249; Quezon City, 1,165,900; Davao, 611,311; Cebu, 489,208; Caloocan, 471,-289.
Government: *Head of state,* Ferdinand E. Marcos, president (took office Dec. 30, 1965). *Head of government,* Cesar Virata, premier (appointed April 8, 1981). *Legislature* (unicameral)—National Assembly.
Monetary Unit: Peso (8.7870 pesos equal U.S.$1, Nov. 1, 1982).
Gross National Product (1981 U.S.$): $39,500,000,-000.
Economic Indexes (1981): *Consumer Prices,* (1972=100), *all items,* 331.1; *food,* 308.2. *Industrial production* (1980, 1975=100), 129.
Foreign Trade (1980 U.S.$): *Imports,* $8,295,000,-000; *exports,* $5,788,000,000.

408

its economic problems. More than one fourth of Philippine trade is with the United States. The combined export-import value of trade with the United States in 1982 was estimated at approximately $3,500,000,000. Private American investment in the country—half of the total foreign investment—was estimated at $1,300,000,000.

Insurgencies. Two major insurrections continued to plague the country in 1982. The Communist New People's Army (NPA), numbering between 6,000 and 8,000 men, fought government forces or staged serious incidents in half of the provinces. In Bicol province alone, where incidents increased notably, 6,000 government troops had to be brought in. Soviet arms and ammunition, shipped through Yemen and brought ashore at changing points along the coast, provided weapons for the insurgency.

A second insurgency, that of the Moro (Muslim) National Liberation Front (MNLF), persisted on the major southern island of Mindanao. Elections were held in June for assemblies in two semiautonomous regions in very much delayed implementation of the Tripoli agreement of 1976 whereby the Islamic Conference of 42 Muslim nations sought to influence the resolution of this festering Philippine minority problem. Pro-government victories in the voting did not seem to ease the situation, and there were no talks between Manila and the MNLF.

Foreign Relations. President Marcos' 13-day state visit to the United States—his first official trip to the United States since 1966—resulted in agreement between the two governments to review the Philippine-American bases agreement beginning in April 1983. Two bases—Clark Airfield (the second largest American military facility in the world) and Subic Bay Naval Base—are key elements in U.S. western Pacific defense strategy.

The United States transfers to the Philippines more than $500 million a year in base rental payments, economic aid, and social security and veterans' benefits to Filipino nationals. U.S. and Filipino workers on these bases receive an additional $200 million a year. President Marcos reportedly sought greater Filipino control over the bases, more military equipment for fighting insurgents, and preferential access to American markets. Details of the agreement on these matters were not announced. However, President Reagan got President Marcos to agree to limited use of the bases to resupply U.S. forces in the Middle East if this were necessary for "the safety and security of the Philippines and Southeast Asia."

President Marcos also visited Saudi Arabia in March. The Saudis agreed to continue supplying the Philippines with 40,000 barrels of oil per day and to extend a $500 million loan. In exchange, Marcos agreed to improve the incomplete "autonomy" status of the 4 million Muslims in the southern part of the country.

The Philippines, together with its allies in the Association of Southeast Asian Nations (ASEAN)—Thailand, Singapore, Malaysia, and Indonesia—played a major role in bringing into being a new anti-Vietnamese coalition in Cambodia. (See also ASIA.)

RICHARD BUTWELL
The University of South Dakota

Early in 1983, President Marcos refused to accept the resignation of Foreign Minister Carlos P. Romulos, 84.

UPI

A Philippine customs inspector confiscates toy guns, which were banned "in the interest of public safety."

UPI

PHOTOGRAPHY

In 1982, economic hard times took the bloom off the art of photography as business. The boom of the 1970s in the collecting market was decisively at an end, and independent galleries that exhibit photographs or paintings exclusively showed signs of transforming their arenas into an amalgamation of the arts in order to survive. "Auto" continued to be the operative word as cameras and lenses became increasingly self-regulating in both focusing and programmed exposure, and Polaroid announced an "auto-processing" slide film for 35mm cameras not long before Edward H. Land, the founder and developer of Polaroid, stepped down as the corporation's chairman and director.

As the photography world stood on the brink of an influx of still video cameras with magnetic tape, expected later in the 1980s, Kodak took what may be its last stand in conventional silver-based photography with the introduction of its revolutionary Disc camera and film system. Despite the multifactorial impact of worldwide recession, all aspects of photography showed renewed vitality.

The Year of the Disk. A new space-age box camera, the size of a cigarette pack, uses a film disk instead of roll film and is Kodak's most important new product since the introduction of the Instamatic in 1963. Measuring 3 x 5 x 1 inches (7.6 x 12.7 x 2.5 cm) and weighing 6.5 ounces (.2 kg), it has an impressive high-speed f/2.8 four-element, 12.5mm wide-angle *glass* lens and a built-in electronic flash that recharges

Eastman Kodak officials demonstrate the new, slim Disc, an automatic exposure camera which features a disk, instead of film, that rotates behind the lens.

UPI

in 1 second. There are three camera models—the Disc 4000, the 6000, and the 8000, which list at $67.95, $89.95, and $142.95, respectively. The Kodacolor HR Disc film, priced at $3.19, is a disk-shaped cartridge 2.5 inches (6.3 cm) in diameter, containing 15 tiny 8 x 10mm color negatives rated at a film speed of ASA 200, that produces 3.5 x 4.25 inch (8.9 x 11 cm) sharp prints with rich tonal values. The Disc format is expected to be combined with processing equipment enabling image display on a television screen.

In single-lens reflex (SLR) 35mm cameras, Nikon's FM2 includes an entirely new feature—a titanium shutter capable of a top speed of 1/4,-000 second with electronic flash synchronization at 1/200 second. And in multi-mode exposure systems, in which the programmed mode is the latest achievement, Minolta introduced its first fully programmed camera, the X-700. When the X-700 is set on "P," it automatically picks the proper lens opening and shutter speed. While the first auto-focusing 35mm SLR was still awaited, Nikon introduced a prototype version, the F3/AF, and a pair of telephoto lenses. It was the first time that a major camera manufacturer applied auto-focus technology to an interchangeable lens, professional quality SLR, and to its flagship model, at that. Although electronic focusing aids were included in Pentax's ME-F and Canon's AL-1, actual working-model auto-focus cameras were limited to non-SLR versions, which proliferated in 1982.

In 110-format pocket cameras, Canon presented the Snappy 20 and 50, priced at $115 and $145, respectively. And in instant-picture technology, Kodak brought out an improved line of four cameras and more-than-twice-as-fast film (ASA 320) to replace its Colorburst line that fared badly in competition with Polaroid's Sun cameras, introduced in 1981.

In lenses, close-focusing compact zooms, especially telephotos, were favored by independent manufacturers, who showed considerable interest in stretching focal lengths, such as Tokina's end-all zoom, the 35-200mm. At 4.8 inches (12 cm) long, the Tokina is extremely compact, with a close-focusing capability down to 4.7 inches (11.9 cm).

In film, Polaroid demonstrated its new Auto-process color slide emulsion (ASA 40) for use in any 35mm camera—the first time Polaroid entered a market where its product can be used in competing cameras—plus a lightweight processor and slide mounter. The film is not developed instantly but is processed after the roll is shot. However, no darkroom, washing, or precise temperature control is required. And one year after Kodak sprang its revolutionary one-step color print-making process, it expanded that diffusion transfer system with a color slide film for making prints, called Ektaflex PCT Reversal Film. In a heated marketing battle with Kodak, Fuji Photo Film competed aggressively for a slice of the color film market. At the same time, Konishiroku was planning to introduce its own brand, Konica Color, in the United States.

In photo processing wares, another Japanese competitor, Sony, which during 1981 introduced the world's first video SLR, the Mavica, and a magnetic disk in place of film, added a printer to produce hard copies, Mavigraphs, from any still-frame color video image produced on a television screen or from original color negatives or slides. And Cibachrome announced an improved color print material, the A-II, which simplified the print-making process to six steps and allowed greater exposure/filtration latitude.

Exhibitions. Although some photographic galleries, including New York's Photograph, folded, others made the necessary adjustments to stay alive. But throughout the art and photography worlds, the most influential names continued to draw financially.

In New York City, Irving Penn exhibited 41 platinum-print still lifes concerned with the death of the spirit, made by combining long-established symbols of mortality with 20th-century debris, and artist Robert Rauschenberg showed straightforward, unmanipulated black-and-white photographs taken in the city and its environs. At the Museum of Modern Art (MoMA), "The Art of Old Paris" was 19th-century documentarian Eugène Atget's second annual exhibit in a series of four, comprising *The Work of Atget.* In northern California, the 80th birthday of nature photographer Ansel Adams was celebrated with three exhibits.

The Cubist-style work of the late Paul Outerbridge, a commercial photographer who pioneered in the development of color in the 1930s, was revived in a traveling show, "A Singular Aesthetic," which originated in California's Laguna Beach Museum of Art. Polaroids, including still lifes by Sandi Fellman and David Hockney's assemblages of 12 to 120 SX-70 images arrayed in a grid, mosaic-style, graced New York City gallery walls.

Among the important group shows were "China from Within: Contemporary Landscapes by Chinese Photographers," which opened at the National Academy of Sciences in Washington, DC; "Color as Form: A History of Color Photography" with more than 250 works from 1850 to 1981 at the Corcoran Gallery in Washington and later at the George Eastman House in Rochester, NY; a multi-exhibit tribute to German photography from 1840 to 1940 at the International Center of Photography in New York, as well as "Through Indian Eyes," Judith Mara Gutman's editing of 17,500 images she had unearthed in India of 19th- and early 20th-century work, including hand-painted portraits.

The Museum of Modern Art expanded its photographic facilities, as did the Chicago Art Institute, the first art museum with a major commitment to install a cold-storage facility to prevent color fading.

Smithsonian Institution Traveling Exhibition Service

"Mountain Village, Mist and Rain" was at the "China from Within" show at the National Academy of Sciences.

Publications. Two books, *Double Take* by art historian Richard Whelan and based on a show by the same name at New York's Metropolitan Museum of Art and *Counterparts* by curator Weston Naef, received extensive attention. The two authors explored the nature of photography by pairing pictures, an approach that again raised a question of the misapplication of the historical methods of art to photography. From André Kertész came the 88-year-old's first color, SX-70 Polaroids taken at home and published in *From My Window,* and his earliest black-and-white work, in *Hungarian Memories.* Selections from George Tice's major essays appeared in *Urban Romantic,* marketed both in cloth, at $50, and in a limited edition with an original print, at $300.

In magazines, *Camera 35* folded after 26 years, while *Camera Arts,* in its 2nd year, went from bimonthly to monthly publication. The latter won a 1982 National Magazine Award in the circulation under 100,000 category.

BARBARA LOBRON
Copy Editor, *Camera Arts*

PHYSICS

In 1982, the first magnetic monopole may have been observed, neutrino properties were debated, and the search for vector bosons was on.

Magnetic Monopole. Whereas isolated electric charges are common, magnets have regions of polarity—their north and south poles. Cutting a magnet in half does not separate the two magnetic charges, but creates two smaller magnets, each with its north and south poles.

In 1931 Paul A. M. Dirac proposed the existence of magnets with only one pole. Recent efforts to develop a theory that would explain all the forces of nature suggests that such a magnetic monopole would be extremely heavy—perhaps a million billion times the mass of a proton. The "Big Bang" that many scientists speculate was the way the universe was created can accommodate the magnetic monopole, but this particle should be heavy, slow-moving, and rare. No ordinary accelerator could possibly produce one, but that fact has not discouraged the searchers. On the contrary, their efforts have intensified and their studies have ranged from moon rocks to high altitude cosmic rays.

On Valentine's Day, 1982, a magnetic monopole may have been observed at Stanford University in California, when physicist Blas Cabrera, working with a superconducting ring, measured an event that was consistent with one unit of magnetic charge. In his experiment, a coil of superconducting niobium wire is connected to a superconducting quantum interference device (SQUID), to form an extremely sensitive magnetometer. A passing magnetic monopole would change the current in such a SQUID circuit.

One event consistent with the properties predicted for a monopole was observed. More will be required before the monopole can with confidence be said to have been observed. Cabrera is at work on a device that is 50 times more efficient than his initial system, and many other scientists have joined the search for the elusive monopole.

Neutrinos. The fundamental properties of neutrinos continue to be questioned. Three varieties of neutrinos are known—electron, muon, and tau neutrinos. All the neutrinos, which interact extremely weakly with matter, have been assumed to have zero mass and to travel at the speed of light. In 1980 Frederick Reines, the co-discoverer of neutrinos, reported that his experiments indicated that neutrinos can change identities, or oscillate. Such oscillation implies finite mass, and the existence of neutrino mass would have major implications for cosmology.

In 1982, the experiments reported by Felix Bohm of the California Institute of Technology cast doubt on the oscillation claim. The results of Bohm's measurements were consistent with zero oscillation and zero mass. A new, more stringent experiment must test for oscillation and mass.

Meanwhile, the measurements of neutrino mass are inferred by precisely measuring the energy of the other particles involved in the radioactive decay that creates neutrinos. The upper limit of the energy is now tens of electron volts (eV) of equivalent mass.

Elementary Particle Physics. In recent years physicists have taken major steps toward the goal of a unifying theory to explain all the forces of nature. The four forces are electromagnetism, gravity, and the strong and weak nuclear forces. Quantum chromodynamics (QCD) has made significant contributions toward a unified theory, including a merging of the electromagnetic and weak forces. The grand unified theory attempts to combine these forces with the strong force.

All interactions have particles that transfer a force. For electromagnetism the particle is the photon—the quantum of light. The particles for the strong force are the gluons, which have not been directly observed, but which are inferred from data obtained at the Deutsches Elektronen-Synchrotron Laboratory (DESY) in Hamburg, West Germany. Major attention focuses on the particles that carry the weak interaction, and specific predictions are made about three vector bosons—the W^+, W^-, and Z mesons. The existence of W and Z mesons is crucial to present theory.

The Super Proton Synchrotron at CERN in Geneva, Switzerland, has been converted into a proton-antiproton collider, to aid in the meson research. When a quark from the proton and an antiquark from the antiproton collide with a total energy of 80 to 90 GeV, they will be annihilated. Then a W or Z meson may be created. Their existence will have to be inferred from decay products, since the mesons are very unstable.

U.S. Science Policy, Manpower, and Education. Federal budget policy reflected the economic conditions of the United States in 1982. The future of the Isabelle high energy accelerator at Brookhaven National Laboratory, New York, remained very much in doubt. This huge colliding beam machine was to have been an integral part of the nation's elementary particle research. But the construction of the superconducting magnets to power it has been beset by difficulties, as the administrators of the laboratory have been by financial concerns. The several hundred million dollars needed to complete the accelerator can be obtained only at the expense of other key particle physics programs.

Science manpower continues to dwindle. In 1981 the percentage of foreign first year graduate students in physics rose to 37%. At the secondary and high school level, science and mathematics enrollments are down, and qualified science teachers are in short supply. Federal funding of science education has been drastically reduced; the Reagan administration considers it the concern of the individual states.

GARY MITCHELL
North Carolina State University

Nuclear Fusion

Controlled thermonuclear fusion is an appealing long-term solution to the energy problem; the same process that fuels the stars would provide an inexhaustible energy source on earth. In 1980 the U.S. Congress passed and President Jimmy Carter signed the Magnetic Fusion Energy Engineering Act, which mandated increased funding for fusion development and the construction by the year 2000 of a commercial demonstration power plant utilizing nuclear fusion. Yet the obstacles between the present state of controlled fusion development and the fabrication of power plants are quite formidable: exceptionally difficult technological problems, and money.

Nuclear fusion takes place when two light nuclei fuse to form a heavier nucleus. For example, two heavy hydrogen (deuterium) nuclei combine to form helium, while releasing a neutron plus extra energy. Since deuterium can be easily extracted from ocean water, the fuel supply is limitless. The problem is to overcome electric repulsion between the charged nuclei and force the two nuclei together. The kinetic energy required to accomplish that corresponds to a temperature of millions of degrees. In nature, such temperatures are found only in the centers of stars, where thermonuclear fusion reactions provide energy for the multibillion-year lifetime of a typical star, such as the sun.

The ultra-high temperature required for fusion leads to most of the technical problems. At such temperatures matter is neither a solid, liquid, nor ordinary gas, but instead it is highly ionized gas—a plasma, which must somehow be contained. The question is, how? Since solid walls vaporize, various indirect methods are utilized: magnetic confinement or inertial confinement.

Energy Sources. The properties of fusion make its advantages over alternative energy sources clear. Solar energy is limited by its low energy density, and its reliability is limited by weather and darkness. A highly dispersed energy source needs a large collecting structure; the economics of the solar collection process are poor.

In contrast to the fusion process that depends upon light nuclei, the fission process requires heavy nuclei, such as those of uranium, which release energy when they fission into smaller parts. The supply of uranium is limited, but more fissionable material could be created in a new type of fission rector—the breeder reactor. It would create more fuel than it consumes, thus extending the available fuel indefinitely. But the breeder reactor has not only all of the nontechnical problems presently encountered by the fission reactors now providing electricity, but also the problems of reprocessing and disposing of increased amounts of fuel and radioactive wastes.

History. Since controlled thermonuclear fusion would provide large quantities of highly localized power, with relatively few negative side effects, the appeal of the fusion approach is evident. A generation of large-scale research has brought controlled fusion to the brink of realization, as the passage of the 1980 fusion act attested. Even so, prototype plants are still some 20 years away.

The present status and division of fusion activity arise in part from military applications. Following the first thermonuclear weapons explosions, utilization of controlled fusion for peaceful purposes was an early goal in all nations with advanced technology. However, the

At Princeton University's Plasma Physics Laboratory, work continues on the Tokamak Fusion Test Reactor, designed to demonstrate energy breakeven.

Courtesy, Princeton University

enthusiasm of the early 1950s was much too optimistic. The problem of confining a hot plasma in a magnetic field proved exceptionally difficult. Magnetic fusion has come close to producing as much energy as it consumes in fuel, and magnetic confinement is fairly well understood. Magnetic fusion appears the most promising avenue to practical fusion reactors.

An alternative proposal to magnetic confinement is inertial confinement, wherein the fusion material is imploded either with particle or laser beams. However, the primary goal of research in fusion by inertial confinement is for military applications, with the generation of electric power secondary. This research is large-scale, and the development, much of which has possible military applications, is supported heavily by the U.S. government and is undertaken primarily at large national laboratories.

Magnetic Fusion. Since charged particles leak from a hot plasma, the shape of the confining magnetic field is crucial. From an open device, the particles leak out the ends. One way to prevent such leaks is to place magnetic mirrors at the ends. This approach was taken in the late 1970s in designing the large Mirror Fusion Test Facility (MFTF) at Lawrence Livermore Laboratory in Livermore, CA. The MFTF-B, an enlarged version, was meant to be capable of testing all open-confinement schemes.

In spite of some recent successes with open confinement, however, the preferred solution is to eliminate ends by closing the device on itself. The toroidal (doughnut) shape that results eliminates the problem of end leakage, but particles drift away from the center of the curved system. The simplest way to prevent drift is to apply electric current in helical field lines that trap the particles. With such a device, called a "tokamak," the Soviets in the late 1960s obtained the first significant results.

The tokamak approach has set the standard for magnetic fusion research. To produce net energy, the required temperature *and* a minimum value of the product of density and time are needed. The early test systems had been far below the required value for the breakeven point, and many attempts to scale up led to new instabilities and failures. Then the Princeton Large Torus (PLT) at Princeton University achieved conditions close to those required for a practical fusion reactor. The PLT worked according to plan. The next step, a very large tokamak facility, was the Tokamak Fusion Test Reactor (TFTR), also at Princeton. The TFTR, scheduled for completion in 1982, should demonstrate energy breakeven. Based on the information obtained by numerous studies in the United States and elsewhere, the tokamak approach is the preferred choice for the next step.

The U.S. Department of Energy (DOE) is planning a test facility to develop the technology for the final stage, an engineering prototype reactor. Although the test facility could be based on any fusion scheme, magnetic confinement of the tokamak type seemed favored.

One crucial question is whether to commit the United States to a definite system now or to wait for a final decision based on a more thorough scientific and engineering foundation. Most scientists prefer the latter approach, but there are pressures to get a development program launched. Well aware of the pressures, the DOE in 1982 had a set of timetables.

Inertial Confinement. In inertial confinement fusion (ICF), radially converging beams of energy must cause the target nuclei to implode and reach high temperature. Major technical problems include those of generating sufficient energy in the beams, coupling the energy to the target, and repeating the process often enough. The beams may consist of light ions, as in the Particle Beam Fusion Accelerator at Sandia National Laboratories in Albuquerque, NM. In this machine a power of tens of terawatts (1 TW = 1 million million watts) is concentrated in a very small volume. Some researchers feel that heavy ion beams would be even better suited for fusion.

However, most of the research and development efforts for ICF involve lasers. Livermore Laboratory plans a giant 100 TW glass laser facility called Nova. The first two-beam stage of this project (Novette) is near completion. At Los Alamos, NM, the Antares High Energy Gas Laser, a major carbon dioxide (CO_2) laser project, also nears completion. Laser fusion is hindered by poor coupling of the energy in the beam to the target material. This is especially true for the longer wavelength CO_2 laser. The glass laser at Livermore (with frequency multiplication) has a shorter wavelength and is more efficiently absorbed by the target pellets.

Repetition rate is another concern. If a device is to succeed as a power source, the implosion cycle must be repeated quite often. In this regard the glass laser is at a disadvantage; heat builds up in the glass and the system cannot be frequently cycled. The CO_2 laser can be rapidly pulsed, but the long wavelength disadvantages seem very difficult to overcome. Thus, no present laser fusion system seems a likely candidate for energy generation. The requirements for military applications (weapons research and effects simulation) are much less demanding. A few implosion cycles per day are sufficient, as in the glass laser system at Livermore or the Particle Beam Fusion Accelerator at Sandia. But for ICF to become a practical candidate for the production of electric power, a significant breakthrough is awaited.

GARY MITCHELL

POLAND

Conflict between the military government of Gen. Wojciech Jaruzelski (*see* BIOGRAPHY) and the dissident forces of Solidarity dominated developments in 1982. Lech Walesa and hundreds of other Solidarity activists spent most of the year in prison and internment camps, but still other leaders and hundreds of thousands of citizens kept up the struggle against the military regime. On November 13 Walesa was released from jail, and on December 30 the government announced a largely symbolic suspension of martial law, imposed in December 1981.

Strikes and Demonstrations. Early in January the government announced jail sentences for five workers accused of staging an illegal strike in a Katowice steel mill. Simultaneously, Solidarity leaders who had managed to escape arrest continued to conduct a mass struggle. Clandestine publications appealed to the people for continued resistance to military rule.

Government attempts to persuade the imprisoned Lech Walesa to give up Solidarity as an independent union and to support the martial law regime proved unavailing. Throughout most of the year, Walesa was allowed visits by his wife and children, although the family was subjected to occasional harassment. By the time Walesa was set free and returned home to Gdansk, Solidarity had been declared illegal, and Walesa's role was uncertain at best.

In public statements throughout the year, General Jaruzelski defended martial law as necessary to avoid civil war. He alluded to Polish independence, suggesting that the martial law regime had prevented direct Soviet military intervention. The government also accused the United States, as well as other Western nations, of gross interference in Polish domestic affairs. Voice of America, Radio Free Europe, and the BBC were all accused of inciting violence and disorder in Poland.

In mid-January some 100 Polish intellectuals addressed an open letter to the parliament, Catholic Primate Archbishop Josef Glemp, and the UN Human Rights Commission, demanding the lifting of martial law. On March 19 the government charged that an organization called Armed Forces of Underground Poland was active throughout the country. In late March, 50 Polish journalists circulated a letter protesting the suspension of their professional association. And in mid-April students and faculty at Warsaw University halted classes and circulated petitions protesting the ouster of outspoken university rector Henryk Samsonowicz. Meanwhile, Radio Solidarity reported strikes in various parts of the country.

On April 29 the government reported the outright release of 800 imprisoned activists and the "conditional" release of 200 others. On May 1, some 30,000 people demonstrated in Warsaw, calling for freedom and the release of Lech Walesa. There were also large demonstrations in the Baltic port of Szczecin. The government responded with shortened curfew hours, cuts in telephone and other communications, and the use of more troops. In turn, Radio Solidarity broadcast called for a 15-minute symbolic strike

In Warsaw and other cities, Poles took to the streets to protest martial law. The regime responded with force.

Achtner/Sygma

on May 9. Four days after that, 3,000 farmers demonstrated in Warsaw on behalf of Rural Solidarity; this was followed by brief work stoppages throughout Poland.

Official media disputed the success of these strikes and demonstrations, but Western diplomatic and news sources reported that they had caused widespread disruption. In mid-May, 16 interned Solidarity leaders, including Jan Rulewski, went on a hunger strike against martial law. On June 12 government sources reported that Gdansk Solidarity leader Jan Waszkiewicz was sent to a mental hospital for having organized an illegal strike. Thousands took part in illegal demonstrations in Wroclaw and Poznan in late June.

Relaxation and Crisis. Coinciding with the 38th anniversary of the founding of the Communist regime in Lublin on July 22, 1944, General Jaruzelski announced that 913 Solidarity internees would be released and 314 given "temporary leave." Anywhere from 4,000 to 6,000 remained in prison. Jaruzelski also declared that Pope John Paul II would not be allowed to visit Poland until sometime in 1983, after tensions had been lowered. The pontiff's 1979 visit was apparently remembered as a notable stimulant to Polish opposition. Jaruzelski credited the USSR with helping revive the Polish economy and said that future Polish trade unions would need to be independent of the administration but not political and "anti-Socialist" like Solidarity.

Jaruzelski promised to issue passports to Poles who have family abroad and relaxed postal and telephone controls. He also indicated that martial law might be lifted by year's end "if conditions warranted it." But, as the anniversary of the founding of Solidarity in August 1980 approached, the underground leadership called for peaceful mass demonstrations. The regime responded with an enormous buildup of police and military forces.

Despite martial law restrictions and government repression, construction of floral crosses to commemorate Solidarity and the victims of past repression was fairly commonplace, especially in Warsaw. On August 21 the regime employed troops and water cannons to disperse crowds in Warsaw's Old Town area. City authorities constructed a wall around Victory Square to prevent people from laying out flowered crosses on the spot where the coffin of Cardinal Wyszynski rested during his May 1981 funeral. Police also periodically dispersed crowds at the Gdansk Monument to workers killed in the 1970 riots. Mid-August demonstrations in several cities, including Gdansk, Warsaw, Cracow, and Wroclaw, led to scuffles with police.

On August 27 the regime began a trial of eight men on charges of joining an underground group which allegedly killed a Warsaw policeman and plotted to free jailed Solidarity activists. Solidarity leaders called for a two-week campaign of leaflet distribution and mass demonstrations to persuade the regime to release those it had jailed, lift martial law, and allow the union to operate freely once again. In a tough televised speech two days later, Interior Minister Kiszczak warned against demonstrations and blamed foreign sources, especially the United States, for promoting the disturbances. He threatened severe measures if necessary and accused Solidarity activists of stockpiling weapons for ostensibly peaceful demonstrations. In late August, Politburo member Kazimierz Barcikowski publicly accused Solidarity of plotting to "overthrow the socialist system in Poland," and massive Polish-Soviet maneuvers near Warsaw were reported in the official media. Police carried out raids on clandestine Solidarity printing shops in Lodz, Poznan, Jelenia Gora, Szczecin, Warsaw, and Wroclaw. General Jaruzelski declared that "martial law can be liked or disliked but it must be respected."

By the end of the month, widespread demonstrations were occurring throughout Poland. According to Western sources, between 65,000 and 70,000 people participated. Especially large were demonstrations in Wroclaw, Gdansk, Cracow, Nowa Huta, Lubin, and Warsaw. The regime used police and army units equipped with water cannons, armored vehicles, and tear gas launchers to disperse the demonstrators. It also extended curfew hours in various locations and banned the sale of alcohol. The government claimed to have uncovered evidence of clandestine terrorist activities aimed at the murder of officials and the overthrow of the state.

In September riots, four protestors were killed, and more than 100 civilian and police personnel were injured. Some 4,000 persons were arrested in more than 50 cities and towns; at least 1,000 were sentenced to prison terms of one to three months. Early in the month, the government announced that several political activists of the KOR (Committee of Worker Defense), including Jacek Kuron, Adam Michnik, Jan Litynski, and Henry Wujec, who had been imprisoned since the martial law decree, would face trial for "offenses against the state." On September 16 authorities arrested Jan Jozef Lipski,

---

POLAND · Information Highlights

Official Name: Polish People's Republic.
Location: Eastern Europe.
Area: 120,727 sq mi (312 683 km^2).
Population (1982 est.): 36,300,000.
Chief Cities (Dec. 1980): Warsaw, the capital, 1,596,-100; Lodz, 835,700; Cracow, 715,700.
Government: *Head of state,* Henryk Jablonski, president of the Council of State (took office 1972). *Head of government,* Gen. Wojciech Jaruzelski, chairman of the Council of Ministers (Feb. 1981) and first secretary of the Polish United Workers' Party (Oct. 1981). *Legislature* (unicameral)—Sejm.
Monetary Unit: Zloty (80.00 zlotys equal U.S.$1, March 1982).
Gross National Product (1981 U.S.$): $88,100,000,-000–$133,800,000,000.
Foreign Trade (1980 U.S.$): *Imports,* $19,089,000,-000; *exports,* $16,997,000,000.

a top Solidarity leader who had just returned from London.

Wladyslaw Gomulka, Communist Party leader from 1956 to 1970, died September 1. (*See* OBITUARIES.) The regime exploited his anti-Soviet reputation with a lavish funeral.

Solidarity Outlawed. As expected for some time, General Jaruzelski drafted legislation dissolving Solidarity, and on October 8 the parliament voted overwhelmingly to ban the independent union. The vote, by show of hands, was televised nationally. Simultaneously with the ban, Jaruzelski promised to release some of the still-jailed Solidarity activists but said that counterrevolutionary activity made the continuance of martial law a necessity. He promised that new unions would be formed, but the parliament passed legislation subjecting any future unions to party control. They would be created at the factory level and hence local rather than national in character; the right to strike would be severely curtailed; and no labor federation or coordinating bodies would be allowed until 1984.

A letter of protest by nine imprisoned union leaders was immediately signed and smuggled out of Warsaw's Bialoleka prison. Archbishop Glemp declared that he viewed the regime's decree with "pain" and "bitterness." Pope John Paul II declared that the action "violated the fundamental rights of man and society." The underground leadership of Solidarity called for a nationwide general strike on November 10; the proclamation was signed by four leaders of the Solidarity National Coordination Commission, in hiding somewhere in Poland. In what seemed to be a combination of regime repression and the popular mood of hopelessness, the strike failed to attract widespread backing.

Walesa Release and Martial Law Suspension. On November 13 Walesa was released from prison. Almost simultaneously he was subjected to official harassment. Allegations of sexual and financial misconduct and even pro-Nazi sympathies were circulated against him. On December 18 he was held by police for several hours in an apparent effort to prevent him from addressing Solidarity supporters in Gdansk.

On General Jaruzelski's initiative, parliament on December 18 passed an act authorizing the suspension of martial law by year's end. Nevertheless, the act incorporated some of the most severe features of martial law into ordinary law—allowing press censorship, telephone taps, the stationing of troops in work places, and compelling workers to stay on their jobs. Political prisoners who had been held without charges were released, but those charged with specific offenses remained in prisons.

Church and State. Throughout the year the Polish Catholic Church sought to promote conciliation and dialogue and to avoid bloodshed, but it also continued its support of Solidarity. Archbishop Glemp repeatedly called for the release of Lech Walesa and other unionists and condemned the military rule of force. In a mid-October sermon he condemned the decision to dissolve Solidarity, but he opposed Solidarity's call for a November general strike and deplored U.S. sanctions against Poland. Polish bishops joined together in condemning the harsh terms of the December 18 act.

Government and party press in Poland and the Soviet Union attacked the Roman Catholic Church and the Vatican for their alleged support of unrest and disorder in Poland. A bishop in Przemysl was attacked by the Communist press for a sermon in which he accused the regime of using brutal violence. In March a priest in Koszalin was sentenced to 3½ years in prison for "slandering the state" in a sermon.

Floral crosses were set up to mark Solidarity's second anniversary and commemorate victims of repression.

© J. Guichard/Sygma

In a largely tributary visit in March, Gen. Jaruzelski (third from left) was promised continued support by Soviet leaders. Close ties were expected to be maintained after the death of President Brezhnev later in the year.

Economic Developments. Early in the year the government announced serious shortages of bread and flour. It called on farmers to sell more grain to the state at fixed, low prices. The zloty was also substantially devalued.

In late July the government announced that the nation's cost of living had doubled in the first half of 1982. Production was officially estimated at 7.8% below 1981, with wages 45.4% higher and the cost of living 3.9% higher than in 1981. Estimates of the drop in production between 1980 and 1982 approached 25%. U.S. and other "capitalist" (Western) economic restrictions were blamed for the economic crisis. Heavy winter floods in central Poland augmented food shortages and transportation difficulties. Among the more important economic, as well as political, measures adopted by Poland in 1982 was the law of October 25 making unemployed persons or those living on undisclosed or "unsocialist" incomes liable to substantial forced labor or prison terms.

Government and Party Changes. At midyear, Stefan Olszowski, seen as a possible rival to General Jaruzelski, was dropped from the Politburo of the Polish United Workers' Party (PZPR) and replaced Jozef Czyrek as foreign minister. Three new Politburo members, believed to be Jaruzelski supporters, were Marian Wozniak, Stanislaw Kalkus, and Stanislaw Bejge. A purge of ineffectual and corrupt party members was in progress throughout the year. More than 100,000 party members were ousted, and special courts were set up to try former officials for corruption. Among those slated for trial were Maciej Szczepanski, former head of Polish television, and three of his associates.

Foreign Relations. At a January conference, member countries of NATO condemned Poland's martial law regime, blaming it on Soviet influence. Poland, in turn, accused NATO of interfering in its internal affairs. Denunciations and protests of this sort continued throughout the year.

In early January, Poland and the Soviet Union concluded an $11,800,000,000 trade agreement. Poland was to obtain fuel, raw materials, and $3,800,000,000 worth of Soviet credits. Reaffirming Poland's place in the Warsaw Pact bloc, General Jaruzelski made official visits to East Germany, Czechoslovakia, Hungary, Rumania, and the USSR. He conferred twice with Soviet President Leonid Brezhnev and traveled to Moscow in November for his funeral. The passing of Brezhnev and apparent ascendancy of Yuri Andropov was expected to bring little immediate change in the Polish situation.

According to UN sources, some 150,000 Poles sought refuge abroad in 1982. Several Polish planes were hijacked by persons seeking asylum in the West.

On September 6 the Polish embassy in Bern, Switzerland, was seized by a group of terrorists who held several diplomats hostage, demanding an end to martial law, the release of political prisoners in Poland, and large sums of money. Swiss police captured the terrorists and freed the hostages three days later.

U.S. President Ronald Reagan condemned the dissolution of Solidarity on October 9 and lifted Poland's most-favored-nation trading status with the United States; the measure only affected manufactured goods. Meanwhile, Polish exports to the United States declined from $427 million in 1979 to just $100 million in the first six months of 1982.

In February the United States decided not to declare Poland in default on loans from American banks. This action was in agreement with the policies of West European nations. By late March, Poland had completed interest payments on Western loans due in 1981.

ALEXANDER J. GROTH
University of California, Davis

POLAR RESEARCH

Antarctic. The National Science Foundation sponsored 81 Antarctic research projects in the earth sciences, ocean sciences, atmospheric sciences, marine and terrestrial biology, and glaciology during 1981–82. Approximately 280 U.S. scientists conducted these projects at four all-year stations, from two remote camps, and aboard the foundation's research ship and two Coast Guard icebreakers.

In February 1982, paleontologists from five universities discovered the first Antarctic fossil mammal on Seymour Island near the Antarctic Peninsula. These fossils of a small rodent-like marsupial (*Polydolopus*) suggest that Antarctica, South America, Australia, India, and Africa once were joined, forming the supercontinent Gondwanaland. The expedition also found the first Antarctic fossils of Tertiary reptiles (70 million years old) and Cretaceous bony fish (160 million years old), the first Antarctic Tertiary coal seam, and two Cretaceous marine reptiles, one 25 ft (7.6 m) long and the other 50 ft (15 m) long.

Thirteen U.S. and 13 Soviet ocean scientists aboard the Soviet research ship *Mikhail Somov* collected a comprehensive data set in the Weddell Sea pack ice during October and November 1981. The *Somov* was the first ship since 1912 to enter the Weddell Sea during the maximum extent of the pack ice. During the 550-mi (885-km), two-week expedition, the scientists studied physical oceanography, chemistry, biology, sea ice, and meteorology. One objective was to find and investigate a polynya, an ice-free "lake" which appears and disappears within the frozen pack ice. Because much of the ocean's deep bottom water (below 3,280 ft, or 1 000 m) comes from the southern ocean, polynyas may affect worldwide oceanic nutrient distribution. Although no polynyas appeared in 1981, 12-mi (19-km) eddies of relatively warm water rising to within 426 ft (130 m) of the surface were discovered. This upward movement brings large amounts of heat in contact with the atmosphere and may help form polynyas.

Between November 1981 and January 1982, 63 researchers from the United States, Australia, New Zealand, and West Germany participated in 22 geological and geophysical projects in Northern Victoria Land, some 370 mi (600 km) north of McMurdo Station. Their research included studies of present and past glaciation, gravity and airborne-radiometric surveys, a meteorite search, and a biological investigation of lichens living beneath the rock surfaces.

Biological research at McMurdo and Palmer stations provided new data on adaptive strategies of microorganisms living beneath Antarctic sea ice, the ecology and population dynamics of sea birds, behavioral and reproductive habits of Weddell seals, and survival mechanisms of Antarctic insects. Solar astronomy, atmospheric monitoring, meteorology, and upper atmospheric observations were continued at South Pole Station.

Arctic. During the last decade, Fram Strait, which lies between Greenland and Spitsbergen and is about 8,200 ft (2 500 m) deep and 217 mi (350 km) wide, has been the focus of heat-exchange investigations and long-term current measurements. During the summer of 1982, U.S. and Norwegian oceanographers aboard the M/V *Lance* conducted an integrated series of physical measurements in the strait. Pressure gauges, which measure the total flow of water, were deployed. Long-term measurements from the gauges will complement current measurements made during the cruise.

In Sondre Stromfjord, Greenland, U.S. upper atmosphere physicists constructed and installed an incoherent scatter radar, previously in operation near Fairbanks, AK. The radar, which began operation in the winter of 1982 and will continue until 1991, was relocated to a higher latitude to enable scientists to better observe upper atmosphere and magnetosphere phenomena.

WINIFRED REUNING
National Science Foundation

PORTUGAL

Following December municipal elections in which Portugal's governing coalition parties suffered setbacks at the hands of the Socialists, and with the economy weakening, Premier Francisco Pinto Balsemão resigned. The year ended with the government "adrift" and with new elections "almost inevitable." Earlier a constitutional reform had enhanced the premier's power and diminished the role of the armed forces.

Constitutional Reform. On August 12, Premier Balsemão mobilized the moderate-to-conservative Democratic Alliance (AD)—the governing coalition of Social Democrats, Center Democrats, and the tiny monarchist party—to win a stunning legislative victory. Specifically, the parliament amended the 1976 "radical" constitution to eliminate the Council of the Revolution (CR). The president and military officers who constituted the council had repeatedly employed sweeping veto power to block bills designed to enlarge the role of the private sector, which had been sharply restricted following the 1974 revolution that ended 48 years of dictatorship.

The required two-thirds majority for a constitutional change was assured when the Socialists threw their support behind the AD. The Communists used strikes, demonstrations, and pressure on Socialist deputies in an effort to stifle the measure, which they denounced as a "constitutional coup d'etat." However, the revision passed on August 12 by a vote of 197 to 40. This victory strengthened the hand of Balsemão in his struggle with Portugal's leftist president, António Ramalho Eanes, who had threatened to resign

Pope John Paul spent four days in Portugal in May. The trip was marred, however, by an assassination attempt.

and form his own political party if the parliament tried to reduce him to figurehead status.

The reform invested the parliament with the right to appoint judges to a constitutional court, which will assume the CR's authority to determine the constitutionality of legislation. A Council of State and a Superior Council of National Defense would take over the functions formerly discharged by the CR.

Economy. These political changes occurred amid difficult economic conditions. In June the Portuguese government devalued the escudo by 9.5% against the dollar as part of a general realignment of Western European currencies. Balsemão took this step reluctantly because of its inflationary impact on his country, which depends heavily on imported oil, grains, and other foreign goods.

While ordering a 7% boost in fuel charges, the government froze transport prices and those of essential food and clothing items until the end of the year. This action sprang from a desire to restrain the nation's 20% inflation rate. A wage freeze, decreed to run until the end of July, sparked protests by the Communist-run CGPT union and other labor organizations.

These demonstrations followed by five months a largely unsuccessful general strike on February 12, which the interior minister hinted had been called to trigger a Communist-inspired uprising. Such rhetoric appeared alarmist because a revolution can succeed only with the army's backing and, unlike many of their Spanish counterparts, most Portuguese officers seemed to have acquiesced in their country's nascent experiment in democracy.

Foreign Affairs. Balsemão flew to the United States on September 28 to address the UN General Assembly and meet with representatives of the Reagan administration. He urged officials in Washington to increase rent payments on the strategically important U.S. air base at Lajes in the Azores, the lease of which expires in February 1983. Portugal sought a financial package larger than the $60 million in military aid and $80 million in economic assistance stipulated under the old agreement. Negotiations continued in mid-October when Frank Carlucci, U.S. deputy defense secretary and former ambassador to Portugal, visited Lisbon, where his hosts reminded him both of their country's pressing economic needs and its unswerving loyalty to NATO and the United States.

While he was in the United States, Balsemão also held discussions with a number of executives of American banks, to which Portugal owes much of its $11,000,000,000 external debt.

GEORGE W. GRAYSON
College of William and Mary

PORTUGAL • Information Highlights

Official Name: Republic of Portugal.
Location: Southwestern Europe.
Area: 35,549 sq mi (92 072 km²).
Population (1982 est.): 9,900,000.
Chief Cities (1979 est.): Lisbon, the capital, 1,100,-000; Oporto, 350,000.
Government: *Head of state,* António Ramalho Eanes, president (took office July 1976). *Head of government,* Francisco Pinto Balsemão, prime minister (took office Jan. 1981, resigned Dec. 1982). *Legislature* (unicameral)—Assembly of the Republic.
Monetary Unit: Escudo (91.2 escudos equal U.S.$1, Nov. 1, 1982).
Gross Domestic Product (1981 U.S.$): $22,063,000,-000.
Economic Indexes (1980): *Consumer Prices* (1976=100), *all items,* 225.0; *food,* 228.3. *Industrial production* (1975=100), 142.
Foreign Trade (1980 U.S.$): *Imports,* $9,299,000,-000; *exports,* $4,632,000,000.

POSTAL SERVICE

During the fiscal year (FY) 1982, ending September 30, the revenues of the U.S. Postal Service (USPS) exceeded expenditures for the second time in four years. The surplus for 1982 was expected to total a little more than $600 million, as compared with $469 million in FY 1979. The last previous year the service showed a surplus was 1945.

That there should be two years of surplus close together is one important consequence of the Postal Reform Act of 1970. This act turned the old patronage-ridden cabinet department into a semi-independent government corporation with considerable power over its own rate structure and a mandate to make ends meet. The result has not always been a balanced set of books, but the deficits since 1970 (when it totaled $2,000,000,000) have been decreasing significantly in proportion to total funds involved. This has been especially true of the period since 1976, the last year to show a deficit of more than $1,000,000,000.

Postal Rates and Service. The 1982 surplus followed a general rise in postal rates in November 1981. Postmaster General William F. Bolger anticipated that the USPS would break even for FY 1983, but that it would be necessary to propose another rate increase for 1984. Much will depend on such uncertain factors as inflation, interest rates, and energy costs, as well as congressional attitudes toward reimbursing the USPS for such required but uneconomic functions as servicing distant rural post offices and for revenue foregone in the case of low rates for charitable organizations and the like. These reimbursements, termed subsidies, approached $700 million in FY 1982. However, they represent a rapidly decreasing proportion of USPS income, declining from about 25% of revenues a decade ago to about 4% in 1982.

An evaluative report by a panel of the National Academy of Public Administration in July 1982 gave the USPS good marks for its performance under the Postal Reform Act. However, this and several other recent studies have raised questions about the future of the service in light of competitive activities in electronic communications. Such activities are expected to make a considerable proportion of traditional communications techniques obsolete.

Meanwhile, contrary to some expectations, the traditional postal volume has continued to rise and is estimated to have reached an all-time high of about 113,000,000,000 pieces during FY 1982.

Electronic Mail. A decision by the District of Columbia Court of Appeals in the spring of 1982 dismissed a Department of Justice suit to prevent the USPS from proceeding with its electronic mail activities on the grounds they had not been properly authorized. The USPS had commenced its new E-COM (Electronic Computer-Originated Mail) service on Jan. 4, 1982. This allows volume mailers to send electronic messages to any of 25 postal centers, where they are automatically printed, put into envelopes, sorted, and entered into the regular first-class mail at a cost of 26 cents for one sheet and 31 cents for two.

However, by the late fall of 1982, E-COM was a financial disappointment. Instead of a predicted 400,000 messages a week the first year, the actual number by mid-1982 was closer to 10,000–15,000. By fall the weekly totals had risen to about 100,000, but volume must rise much higher for the system to justify its investment in equipment and personnel.

ZIP Code. The USPS received welcome support from a coalition of major mailers for its proposed nine-digit ZIP code. In 1981, Congress delayed inauguration of the new code until Oct. 1, 1983, but authorized purchase of the necessary automation equipment. "ZIP + 4" will pinpoint sorting and delivery down to individual apartment house or block units.

Labor. The labor contract of the Mail Handler Union, the one postal union to hold out during the July 1981 negotiations with the USPS, was settled by arbitration in January 1982 on terms close to those agreed to earlier by the other unions. The next collective bargaining talks with the postal unions will be in 1984.

In October 1982 the service settled a 1978 lawsuit over application of some 1974 amendments which applied the Fair Labor Standards Act to the USPS for the first time. About $400 million will be distributed to personnel employed between 1974 and 1978, mainly in settlement of overtime pay claims. As the money comes from contingency funds, there is no impact on current finances. Also in October, the Occupational Health and Safety Administration praised the USPS for safety improvements.

The principal immediate cloud on the horizon of the USPS consists of periodic attacks, in the name of free enterprise, on the Private Express Statutes, the laws guaranteeing the service a monopoly of most letter mail.

Canada. Large increases in postal rates early in 1982 (for example, 17 to 30 cents Canadian for domestic first-class mail) helped reduce the perennially large Canadian postal deficit. The $660 million deficit for the fiscal year ending March 1982 could fall to possibly half that amount in FY 1983. The newly formed (1981) Canada Post Corporation (CPC) proposed a second round of general rate increases for early 1983, which would increase domestic first-class mail by another 2 cents and raise the rate for mail to the United States to 37 cents and that to other countries to 64 cents.

Although the CPC's electronic mail, known as INTELPOST, has expanded, mail volume (about 6,500,000,000 pieces a year) was slightly below that of 1981.

PAUL P. VAN RIPER, *Texas A&M University*

PRINCE EDWARD ISLAND

© The Canadian Press

James Lee's Conservative Party won about 53% of the vote in Prince Edward Island's September election.

In 1982, a provincial general election and energy developments dominated events in Prince Edward Island (P.E.I.).

Politics. The Conservatives retained their hold on political power, winning 22 of the 32 legislature seats in the September 27 election. The Liberals won 10 seats in a straight two-party fight.

The Conservatives, led by Premier James Lee, campaigned on a good-government platform that eschewed explicit promises and emphasized fiscal restraint. In their campaign the Liberals, on the other hand, offered the voters millions of dollars worth of benefits.

Energy. Within a few years, energy-short P.E.I. may be using hydroelectric power from Quebec. Barry Clark, the island's energy minister, disclosed in August that he had a commitment from the Quebec government for the sale of about 50 megawatts of firm power from Hydro-Quebec to P.E.I. He also made an agreement with New Brunswick to transmit the power across that province, using New Brunswick transmission lines at a rental rate to be negotiated.

Prince Edward Island has enough generating capacity to meet its own needs until 1986, helped by oil-generated electricity from New Brunswick. Quebec power would supplant New Brunswick power under the proposed arrangement.

A few weeks after Clark's disclosure, a commission of inquiry into electric power in P.E.I. advocated a more definitive government policy. The report of inquiry commissioner Melvin McQuaid, nine months in preparation, called for a regional approach to power problems. The government should also keep open an option to purchase power eventually from the newly opened Point Lepreau nuclear station in New Brunswick.

Storm. For more than 10 days in March, the northwestern part of P.E.I.—a province accustomed to super snowstorms—was isolated by one of its worst storms in decades. Despite round-the-clock work by highway crews, some roads remained buried under 23 ft (7 m) of snow a week after the storm struck. Food, fuel, and medicine were delivered by volunteer snowmobilers to residents stranded in their homes.

College. After more than a decade of wrangling, Nova Scotia agreed in June that the proposed $14 million Atlantic provinces veterinary college should be situated in Charlottetown. Previously, Nova Scotia had held out for a Truro, N.S., location.

New questions arose when Premier Lee said the federal government had informed him it could not provide its promised half share of the cost. Yet in the election campaign, Lee referred to the college as virtually a fait accompli, saying it would provide 250 permanent jobs.

See also CANADA.

JOHN BEST
"Canada World News"

PRISONS

The decade-long trend of an increasing prison population continued in the United States in 1982. The official number of persons in federal and state prisons—in excess of 380,000, an increase of more than 15% over the previous year—was only the tip of the iceberg. While one in every 600 Americans was actually imprisoned, the millions serving short sentences, awaiting trial, or on probation left one citizen in every 100 under some form of penal supervision. In spite of expensive building programs in many areas, prison officials were unable to keep up with the spiraling prison population. There was some growth in public awareness that severe overcrowding was creating problems for which there were no easy solutions. Prisons in 30 states were under court order to end conditions that were judged unconstitutional. Although prison regulations and practices vary widely from state to state, almost all facilities across the United States faced the potentially serious consequences of overcrowding.

Expenses. Prisons are extremely expensive to construct and maintain. Costs vary greatly, but nowhere are they cheap. Texas, where inmates are building their own prisons and growing 70% of their food, nevertheless had to allocate $96.5 million for new construction. In most states it costs $15,000 per year to guard and feed each inmate, and construction costs for a single maximum security cell can exceed $75,000. Although the public seems to be calling for longer sentences, there is a growing reluctance to provide the staggering sums that such policies entail. Several states, including Michigan, Iowa, and Minnesota, have introduced laws that automatically release inmates when overcrowding rises beyond stipulated levels. Prison budgets in such states as Florida and Alabama have quadrupled in five years. Nationwide, nearly $5,000,000,000 is being spent on prisons, and conditions in many of them remain substandard. It has been estimated that $6,000,000,000 to $10,000,000,000 would be needed to bring them up to reasonable and humane standards.

Loss of Control. As prisons are strained beyond capacity, life behind bars becomes more difficult to control. Violence, often with racial overtones, is becoming more widespread. Two black inmates at Tennessee's Brushy Mountain Penitentiary were killed in February. Racial tension had been growing at the overcrowded maximum-security facility for some time. Four guards were taken hostage by white prisoners who had obtained a gun and shot four black inmates. After the attack the seven white prisoners released the guards and surrendered.

Twenty-five California inmates, alleged members of "Nuestra Familia," an organized crime ring, were indicted in January for a series of crimes including murder, armed robbery, extortion, and heroin traffic. Officials claimed that the group had been responsible for 136 murders in the previous five years.

In January, 200 state troopers raided the Massachusetts correctional institution at Framingham to break up a drug and gambling network operated by inmates with the active cooperation of a number of prison employees. In March three black inmates charging racial discrimination at a North Carolina prison took eight persons hostage for three days and demanded transfer to a federal prison. Officials agreed to the transfer and transported them to a federal facility in Virginia. Upon their arrival, however, it was immediately announced that they would be returned. Those who helped negotiate the settlement felt betrayed and complained of "bad faith" by authorities in a potentially volatile situation.

In April a fire of unknown origin broke out in a New Jersey cellblock and killed seven inmates. The facility was built to house 280 prisoners but actually contained more than 500. In early November, 27 prisoners died and dozens of others were injured when a fire broke out in the crowded county jail at Biloxi, MI. The fire, the worst in a U.S. jail since 1977, was started in the foam padding of a cell. The prisoner, being held for "lunacy," was charged with 27 counts of capital murder.

The death of college football star Ron Settles in a Los Angeles jail was the subject of a $12-million civil suit. His parents contended that he was beaten and strangled by police after being stopped for speeding. Police claimed that Settles had hanged himself in his cell.

Death Row. More than 1,000 convicted criminals await execution in the nation's prisons. Two out of three are in Deep South states—181 in Florida alone and 118 in Georgia. Almost half are black, and almost all are poor. U.S. Supreme Court rulings have required public defenders to act on behalf of the accused, but public defenders often drop out at some level of the appeal process and the defense is taken over by a small number of volunteer lawyers. The case of James C. McCray, on death row for eight years after conviction for rape and murder, is not atypical. The judge in his original trial joked publicly that lynching should be reinstated and sentenced McCray to execution, overruling the jury's recommendation of life imprisonment. The state-appointed clemency lawyer admitted that he had not read the trial transcripts and later was suspended from practice for embezzlement. A volunteer lawyer finally took up the case and won a new trial.

Unresolved Philosophies. The dangers of conflicting, unclear, or even absent philosophies regarding criminal punishment were illustrated in a case that played itself out over an almost two-year period. In a melodramatic scene in 1981, Baltimore police, with guns drawn and television crews on hand, raided two small buses of convicts returning to prison from work-release programs. Police spread-eagled the convicts against the buses and made 27 arrests; the charges ranged from murder to prison escape. In the uproar that followed, the state secretary of public safety and corrections was forced to resign, and his policy of reducing prison populations was reversed. As things turned out, however, the whole affair apparently was a ruse designed to further the careers of various political figures. Most of the charges were dropped.

See also CRIME.

DONALD GOODMAN
John Jay College of Criminal Justice
City College of New York

PRIZES AND AWARDS

NOBEL PRIZES

Chemistry ($157,000): Aaron Klug, South African-born research scientist, Medical Research Council's Laboratory of Molecular Biology, Cambridge, England, cited "for his development of crystallographic electron microscopy and his elucidation of biologically important nucleic acid-protein complexes."

Economics ($175,000): George J. Stigler, University of Chicago, cited for "seminal studies of industrial structures, functioning of markets and the causes and effects of public regulation."

Literature ($157,000): Gabriel García Márquez, Colombian-born writer, cited "for his novels and short stories, in which the fantastic and the realistic are combined in a richly composed world of imagination, reflecting a continent's life and conflicts."

Peace Prize ($157,000 shared): Alva Myrdal, Swedish writer and lecturer; Alfonso García Robles, Mexico's representative to the United Nations Disarmament Commission in Geneva; the citation read as follows: "There is the patient and meticulous work undertaken in international negotiations on mutual disarmament, and there is also the work of the numerous peace movements with their greater emphasis on influencing the climate of public opinion and appeal to the emotions . . . this year's prizewinners are worthy representatives of both."

Physics ($157,000): Kenneth G. Wilson, Cornell University, "honored for solving 'in a definite and profound way the critical phenomena' inherent in such changes as that of metal to liquid and water to steam."

Physiology or Medicine ($157,000 shared): Sune Bergstrom, Nobel Foundation, cited for the purification of prostaglandins, for determining their chemical structure, and showing that they were formed from unsaturated fatty acids; Bengt Ingemar Samuelsson, Karolinska Institute, cited for presenting a detailed picture of arachidonic acid from which all the various types of prostaglandins are created; John Robert Vane, Wellcome Research Laboratories, cited for discovering the subtype prostaglandin X, now called prostacyclin.

ART

American Academy and Institute of Arts and Letters Awards
Academy-Institute Awards ($5,000 ea.): art—Nizette Brennan, Michael David, George McNeil, Alan Motch, Manuel Neri; music—Douglas Allanbrook, James Tenney, George Walker, Ramon Zupko
Arnold W. Brunner Memorial Prize in Architecture ($1,000): Helmut John
The Award of Merit Medal for Painting: Myron Stout
Charles Ives Grant: The Charles Ives Society
Charles Ives Scholarship ($4,000 ea.): Michael Gandolfi, Peter Golub, Jeffrey Hall, Charles E. Porter, Preston Stahly, Jr., Karen P. Thomas
Distinguished Service to the Arts: Alfred A. Knopf
Goddard Lieberson Fellowship ($10,000 ea.): Stephen Dembski, Paul Dresher
Gold Medal in Music: William Schuman
Richard and Hinda Rosenthal Foundation Award ($3,000): Terry Winters (in painting)

American Institute of Architects Gold Medal Award: Romaldo Giurgola

Avery Fisher Prize ($10,000): Horacio Gutiérrez

Brandeis University Creative Arts Awards: medals—C. Vann Woodward, Stephen Sondheim, Trisha Brown, Jennifer Tipton, Peter Voulkos; notable achievement award—James Johnson Sweeney

Capezio Dance Award ($5,000): Alwin Nikolais

Dance Magazine Awards: Fernando Bujones, Laura Dean, Arnold Spohr, Lee Theodore

Edward MacDowell Medal: Isamu Noguchi

International American Music Competition ($10,000 cash award): Henry Herford (vocalist)

John F. Kennedy Center for the Performing Arts Awards for career achievement in the performing arts: George Abbott, Lillian Gish, Benny Goodman, Gene Kelly, and Eugene Ormandy

National Academy of Recording Arts and Sciences Grammy Awards for excellence in phonograph records
Album of the year: *Double Fantasy*, John Lennon, Yoko Ono
Classical album: *Mahler: Symphony No. 2 in C Minor;* Sir Georg Solti, conductor; Chicago Symphony Orchestra and chorus
Country music song: *9 to 5*, Dolly Parton, songwriter
Jazz vocal performance, female: Ella Fitzgerald, *Digital III at Montreux*
Jazz vocal performance, male: Al Jarreau, *Blue Rondo a la Turk*
New artist: Sheena Easton
Record of the year: *Bette Davis Eyes*, Kim Carnes
Song of the year: *Bette Davis Eyes*, Donna Weiss, Jackie DeShannon, songwriters

Naumberg International Viola Competition ($6,000): Thomas Reibl

Pritzker Prize in Architecture ($100,000): Kevin Roche

Pulitzer Prize for Music: Roger Sessions, *Concerto for Orchestra;* special citation for music—Milton Babbitt

Samuel H. Scripps-American Dance Festival Award ($25,000): Merce Cunningham

Tchaikovsky Competition: in cello—Antonio Meneses; vocal—(woman) Lidiya Zabilyasta, (man) Paata Burchchuladze; in violin—(shared) Viktoriya Mullova, Sergei Stadler

JOURNALISM

George Polk Memorial Awards
Book: Edwin R. Bayley, *Joe McCarthy and the Press*
Consumer reporting: Phil Norman, *The Louisville Courier-Journal*, "Sacred Cows: Power, Politics and Prices in the Milk Industry"
Foreign reporting: John Darnton, *The New York Times*
Local reporting: *The Orlando* (FL) *Sentinel-Star*, "The Federal Impact"
Magazine reporting: William Greider, *The Atlantic*, "The Education of David Stockman"
National reporting: Seymour M. Hersh, Jeff Gerth, Philip Taubman, *The New York Times*
Radio reporting: John Merrow, Institute for Educational Leadership and National Public Radio, *Juvenile Crime and Juvenile Justice*
Regional reporting: Stephanie Saul, W. Stevens Ricks, *The Jackson* (MS) *Clarion-Ledger*, "Mississippi Gulf Coast: Wide Open and Wicked"
Science reporting: *Science*, "News and Comment"
Television documentary: Pierre Salinger, ABC News, *America Held Hostage: The Secret Negotiations*
Television reporting: Ted Koppel, ABC News, *Nightline*

Maria Moors Cabot Prizes ($1,000 ea.): William Long, Daniel Samper; special citations to Frances R. Grant, United Press International

National Magazine Awards
Design: *Nautical Quarterly*
Essays and criticism: *The Atlantic*
Fiction: *The New Yorker*
General excellence awards: *Newsweek, Science 81, Rocky Mountain, Camera Arts*
Public service: *The Atlantic*
Reporting excellence: *The Washingtonian*
Single-topic issue: *Newsweek*

Overseas Press Club Awards
Book on foreign affairs: Pierre Salinger, *America Held Hostage: The Secret Negotiations*
Business news reporting from abroad: J.A. Livingston, *Philadelphia Inquirer*
Cartoon on foreign affairs: Don Wright, *Miami News*
Daily newspaper or wire service interpretation of foreign affairs: David K. Willis, *The Christian Science Monitor*

Daily newspaper or wire service reporting from abroad: David B. Ottaway, *The Washington Post*

Editorial or editorial series which "most effectively discloses abuse of human rights abroad and thereby lends support of the principle of human rights": Betty De Ramus, *Detroit Free Press*

Magazine interpretation of foreign affairs: Walter Isaacson, Bruce van Voorst, Johanna McGeary, *Time*

Magazine reporting from abroad: Lawrence Weschler, *The New Yorker*

Photographic reporting from abroad: (magazines and books)—Nakram Gadel Karim, *Time, The New York Times,* and Gamma; (newspapers and wire services)—Kent Kobersteen, *Minneapolis Tribune*

Radio interpretation of foreign affairs: ABC Radio

Radio spot news from abroad: ABC Radio

Television interpretation or documentary on foreign affairs: CBS for the *CBS Reports* "The Defense of the United States, 'The Russians' "

Television spot news reporting from abroad: ABC News special events coverage of the Sadat assassination

Robert Capa Gold Medal: Ruth Frey, *Time*

Madeline Dane Ross Award: Kent Kobersteen, Alan McConagha, *Minneapolis Tribune*

Pulitzer Prizes

Commentary: Art Buchwald, *Los Angeles Times* Syndicate

Criticism: Martin Bernheimer, *Los Angeles Times*

Editorial cartooning: Ben Sargent, *The Austin* (TX) *American-Statesman*

Editorial writing: Jack Rosenthal, *The New York Times*

Feature photography: John H. White, *The Chicago Sun-Times*

Feature writing: Saul Pett, The Associated Press

General local reporting: *The Kansas City Star/The Kansas City Times*

International reporting: John Darnton, *The New York Times*

National reporting: Rick Atkinson, *The Kansas City Times*

Public service: *The Detroit News*

Special local reporting: Paul Henderson, *The Seattle Times*

Spot news photography: Ron Edmonds, The Associated Press

LITERATURE

American Academy and Institute of Arts and Letters Awards

Academy-Institute Awards ($5,000 ea.): David H. Bradley, Jr., Frederick Buechner, Mac Donald Harris, Daryl Hine, Josephine Jacobsen, Donald Keene, Berton Rouché, Robert Stone

E.M. Forster Award ($5,000): F.T. Prince

Gold Medal in Biography: Francis Steegmuller

Harold D. Vursell Memorial Award ($5,000): Eleanor Perényi

Marjorie Peabody Waite Award ($1,500): Edouard Roditi

Morton Dauwen Zabel Award ($2,500): Harold Bloom

Richard and Hinda Rosenthal Foundation Award ($3,000): Marilynne Robinson

Sue Kaufman Prize for First Fiction ($1,000): Ted Mooney

Witter Bynner Prize for Poetry ($1,500): William Heyen

American Book Awards ($1,000 ea)

Hardcover—

Autobiography/Biography: David McCullough, *Mornings on Horseback*

Children's fiction: Lloyd Alexander, *Westmark*

Children's nonfiction: Susan Bonners, *A Penguin Year*

Fiction: John Updike, *Rabbit Is Rich*

First novel: Robb Forman Dew, *Dale Loves Sophie to Death*

© Christopher Casler/Camera Five

In the sentimental highlight of the March Oscar presentations, Jane Fonda accepts the best actor award for her ailing father, Henry Fonda. Mr. Fonda died in August.

General nonfiction: Tracy Kidder, *The Soul of a New Machine*

History: The Rev. Peter John Powell, *People of the Sacred Mountain*

Picture-book award: Maurice Sendak, *Outside Over There*

Science: Donald Johanson and Maitland Edey, *Lucy*

Translation: (shared) Robert Lyons Danly, *In the Shade of Spring Leaves;* Ian Hideo Levy, *The Ten Thousand Leaves*

Paperback—

Autobiography/Biography: Ronald Steel, *Walter Lippman and the American Century*

Children's fiction: Quida Sebestyen, *Words by Heart*

Children's picture books: Peter Spier, *Noah's Ark*

Fiction: William Maxwell, *So Long, See You Tomorrow*

History: Robert Wohl, *The Generation of 1914*

Nonfiction: Victor S. Navasky, *Naming Names*

Science: Fred Alan Wolf, *Taking the Quantum Leap*

Graphic—

Cover design—mass-market: Milton Charles, *The Best of John Sladek*

Cover design—trade: Fred Marcellino, *African Stories*

Design—pictorial: Susan Mitchell, *Nicaragua*

Design—typographical: Betty Anderson, *Edith Sitwell*

Illustration—collected art: Bill Katz, *The World of Donald Evans*

Illustration—original art: Chris Van Allsburg, *Jumanji*

Illustration—photographs: Deborah Turbeville, *Unseen Versailles*

Jacket design: Janet Odgis, *Remembrance of Things Past*

Bancroft Prizes ($4,000 ea.): Edward Countryman, *A People in Revolution: The American Revolution and Political Society in New York 1760–90;* Mary P. Ryan, *Cradle of the Middle Class: The Family in Oneida County, New York, 1780–1865*

Canada's Governor-General's Literary Awards
English drama: Sharon Pollock
French drama: Marie Laberge
English fiction: Mavis Gallant
French fiction: Denys Chabot
English nonfiction: George Calef
French nonfiction: Madeleine Oullette-Michalska
English poetry: F. R. Scott
French poetry: Michel Beaulieu

Cervantes Prize: Octavio Paz

Houghton Mifflin Literary Fellowship: W.P. Kinsella

Medal of Honor for Literature: Barbara Tuchman

National Medal for Literature ($15,000): John Cheever

Neustadt International Prize for Literature ($25,000): Octavio Paz

PEN/Faulkner Award ($5,000): David Bradley, *The Chaneysville Incident*

Pulitzer Prizes
Biography: William S. McFeely, *Grant: A Biography*
Fiction: John Updike, *Rabbit Is Rich*
General nonfiction: Tracy Kidder, *The Soul of a New Machine*
History: C. Vann Woodward, editor, *Mary Chesnut's Civil War*
Poetry: Sylvia Plath, *The Collected Poems*

MOTION PICTURES

Academy of Motion Picture Arts and Sciences ("Oscar") Awards
Actor: Henry Fonda, *On Golden Pond*
Actress: Katharine Hepburn, *On Golden Pond*
Cinematography: Vittorio Storaro, *Reds*
Costume design: Milena Canonero, *Chariots of Fire*
Director: Warren Beatty, *Reds*
Film: *Chariots of Fire*
Foreign language film: *Mephisto* (Hungary)
Music—original score: *Chariots of Fire*, Vangelis
Music—original song: *Arthur's Theme* (*Best That You Can Do*), Burt Bacharach, Carole Bayer Sager, Christopher Cross, Peter Allen
Original screenplay: Colin Welland, *Chariots of Fire*
Screenplay based on material from another medium: Ernest Thompson, *On Golden Pond*
Supporting actor: John Gielgud, *Arthur*
Supporting actress: Maureen Stapleton, *Reds*
Gordon E. Sawyer Award: Joseph B. Walker
Irving Thalberg Award: Albert R. (Cubby) Broccoli
Jean Hersholt Award: Danny Kaye
Honorary Award: Barbara Stanwyck
Special Achievement Award (sound effects): *Raiders of the Lost Ark*
Special Award: Fuji Photo Film Company

American Film Institute's Life Achievement Award: Frank Capra

Cannes Film Festival Awards
Actor: Jack Lemmon, *Missing*
Actress: Jadwiga Jankowska-Cieslak, *Another Look*
Director: Werner Herzog, *Fitzcarraldo*
Film: (shared) *Missing* (United States); *Yol* (Path) (Turkey)

National Society of Film Critics Awards
Actor: Burt Lancaster, *Atlantic City*
Actress: Marilia Pera, *Pixote*
Cinematographer: Gordon Willis, *Pennies from Heaven*
Director: Louis Malle, *Atlantic City*
Film: *Atlantic City*
Screenwriter: John Guare, *Atlantic City*
Supporting actor: Robert Preston, *S.O.B.*
Supporting actress: Maureen Stapleton, *Reds*

PUBLIC SERVICE

Albert Einstein Peace Prize: McGeorge Bundy, Robert S. McNamara, Gerard C. Smith

Alexander Onassis Foundation ($100,000 ea.): Manolis Andronikos, Bernard Kouchner

American Institute for Public Service Jefferson Awards
$1,000 awards: Dallas Doyle, Richard M. Garrett, Helena Kyle, Caroline Putman, Ruth Heinz, Lorraine Schreck
$5,000 awards: Howard H. Baker, Jr., Bob Hope, Claude Pepper, Henry Cisneros

Templeton Prize for progress in religion ($200,000): Billy Graham

U.S. Presidential Medal of Freedom: Philip C. Habib, Kate Smith

SCIENCE

Albert Lasker Awards
Basic research ($15,000 shared): J. Michael Bishop and Harold E. Varmus, University of California/San Francisco; Hidesaburo Hanafusa, Rockefeller University; Raymond L. Erikson, Harvard University; Robert C. Gallo, National Cancer Institute
Clinical research ($15,000 shared): Roscoe O. Brady, National Institute of Neurological and Communicative Diseases and Stroke; Elizabeth F. Neufeld, National Institute of Arthritis, Diabetes, Digestive, and Kidney Diseases

Bristol-Myers Award ($50,000 shared): Denis Parsons Burkitt, Michael Anthony Epstein

Crafoord Prize in mathematics ($30,000 ea.): Louis Nirenberg, Vladimir I. Arnold

General Motors Cancer Research Foundations Awards ($100,000 ea.): Denis Parsons Burkitt, Howard Earle Skipper, Stanley Cohen

Louisa Gross Horwitz Prize for research in biology or biochemistry ($22,000 shared): Barbara McClintock, Cold Spring Harbor Laboratory; Susumu Tonegawa, Massachusetts Institute of Technology

National Science Foundation's Vannevar Bush Award: Lee A. Dubridge

TELEVISION AND RADIO

Academy of Television Arts and Sciences ("Emmy") Awards
Actor—comedy series: Alan Alda, *M*A*S*H* (CBS)
Actor—drama series: Daniel J. Travanti, *Hill Street Blues* (NBC)
Actor—limited series: Mickey Rooney, *Bill* (CBS)
Actress—comedy series: Carol Kane, *Taxi* (ABC)
Actress—drama series: Michael Learned, *Nurse* (CBS)
Actress—limited series: Ingrid Bergman, *A Woman Called Golda* (SYN)
Children's program: *The Wave* (ABC)
Classical program in the performing arts: "La Bohème," *Live from the Met* (PBS)
Comedy series: *Barney Miller* (ABC)
Drama series: *Hill Street Blues* (NBC)
Individual achievement—special class: (performers)—Nell Carter, Andre De Shields, *Ain't Misbehavin'* (NBC); (costume supervisor)—Marilyn Matthews, *Fame,* "The Strike" (NBC)
Informational series: *Creativity with Bill Moyers* (PBS)
Informational special: *Making of "Raiders of the Lost Ark"* (PBS)
Limited series: *Marco Polo* (NBC)
Special drama: *A Woman Called Golda* (SYN)
Supporting actor—comedy series: Christopher Lloyd, *Taxi* (ABC)
Supporting actor—drama series: Michael Conrad, *Hill Street Blues* (NBC)
Supporting actress—comedy series: Loretta Swit, *M*A*S*H* (CBS)
Supporting actress—drama series: Nancy Marchand, *Lou Grant* (CBS)
Variety, music, or comedy program: *Night of 100 Stars* (ABC)
Governors Award: Hallmark Hall of Fame

© P. Cunningham/Jacksirja and Freedman

"Nine," an adaptation of Federico Fellini's "8½," won several Tonys, including best musical, musical direction, score.

George Foster Peabody Awards

Radio: Canadian Broadcasting Corp., Vancouver, for "Carl Sandburg at Connemara," from the *Signature* series; National Radio Theatre, Chicago, for *The Odyssey of Homer;* Timothy and Susan Todd for *The Todds' Teddy Bears Picnic;* WJR Radio, Detroit, for *Newsfile: A Bankrupt Court;* WQDR-FM, Raleigh, NC, for *Our Forgotten Warriors: Vietnam Veterans Face the Challenges of the 80's*

Television: ABC News, for *Viewpoint, Nightline,* and *America Held Hostage: The Secret Negotiations,* with special mention of the efforts of Ted Koppel; ABC and T.A.T. Communications, for "The Wave," *ABC Theatre for Young Americans;* CBS-TV and Alan Landsburg Productions for "Bill," *General Electric Theatre;* The Eighth Decade Consortium, Seattle, for *Fed Up with Fear;* Home Box Office and *Ms. Magazine* for *She's Nobody's Baby: The History of American Women in the 20th Century;* KATU-TV, Portland, for a series of documentaries including *Ready on the Firing Line, Out of the Ashes,* and *To Begin Again;* KJRH-TV, Tulsa, for *Project: China;* KTEH, San Jose, for *The Day After Trinity: J. Robert Oppenheimer and the Atomic Bomb;* NBC and MTM Enterprises for *Hill Street Blues;* The Nebraska Educational Television Network for *The Private History of a Campaign That Failed;* Société Radio-Canada, Montreal, for *Klimbo: le Lion et la Souris;* WGBH, Boston, and Granada TV, London, for "The Red Army," *World;* WLS-TV, Chicago, for *Eyewitness News;* WNET-Thirteen, NY, and PBS for *Dance in America: Nureyev* and the *Joffrey Ballet—Tribute to Nijinsky;* WSMV, Nashville, for a series of television documentaries

Individual awards: John Goldsmith, WDVM-TV; Danny Kaye, Bill Leonard, CBS News

Humanitas Awards

Long-form category ($25,000): Linda Elstad, Donald Wrye, *Divorce Wars*

One-hour category ($15,000): Gene Reynolds, *Lou Grant,* "Hunger"

One-half-hour category ($10,000): David Pollock, Elias Davis, *M*A*S*H,* "Where There's a Will, There's a War"

THEATER

Antoinette Perry ("Tony") Awards

Actor—drama: Roger Rees, *The Life and Adventures of Nicholas Nickleby*

Actor—musical: Ben Harney, *Dreamgirls*

Actress—drama: Zoe Caldwell, *Medea*

Actress—musical: Jennifer Holliday, *Dreamgirls*

Choreography: Michael Bennett and Michael Peters, *Dreamgirls*

Costume design: William Ivey Long, *Nine*

Director—drama: Trevor Nunn, John Caird, *The Life and Adventures of Nicholas Nickleby*

Director—musical: Tommy Tune, *Nine*

Featured actor—drama: Zakes Mokae, *Master Harold . . . and the Boys*

Featured actor—musical: Cleavant Derricks, *Dreamgirls*

Featured actress—drama: Amanda Plummer, *Agnes of God*

Featured actress—musical: Liliane Montevecchi, *Nine*

Musical: *Nine*

Musical—book: Tom Eyen, *Dreamgirls*

Musical—score: Maury Yeston, *Nine*

Play: *The Life and Adventures of Nicholas Nickleby*

Special awards: Tyrone Guthrie Theater, Actors Fund of America

New York Drama Critics Circle Theater Awards

Best new play: *The Life and Adventures of Nicholas Nickleby,* adapted from Charles Dickens by David Edgar

Best new American play: *A Soldier's Play* by Charles Fuller

Pulitzer Prize for Drama: Charles Fuller, *A Soldier's Play*

Charles Fuller won a Pulitzer for "A Soldier's Play."

UPI

PUBLISHING

The U.S. economy forced publishers to eye rising costs, seek lower-priced production processes, add computerized equipment, and update printing operations. New magazines and a few newspapers were started, while books flooded the markets. Postal rates were more stable than in the recent past, and paper supplies were plentiful. Courts tilted more to favor the public, away from the media, while censorship remained an issue. With fewer discretionary dollars to spend, consumers were more cautious.

Books. The book industry remained fairly stable. The U.S. Commerce Department predicted 3.2% annual gains for the next five years, below recent averages. Tradebooks sales would be higher than textbooks. In 1981, overall sales were up 9% to $7,700,000,000, according to the Association of American Publishers. For the first quarter of 1982, sales neared $1,500,000,000, up 5.6%.

Unit sales were down. Per-copy prices rose, with hardcovers averaging $26.64; mass market paperbacks, $2.65; and trade paperbacks, $9.70. According to preliminary figures by R. R. Bowker Co., 41,538 titles were issued in 1981, slightly below the output of 1980.

Reader's Digest presented a 40% condensed edition of the Revised Standard Version of the Bible in the fall.

Courtesy, Reader's Digest Association, Inc.

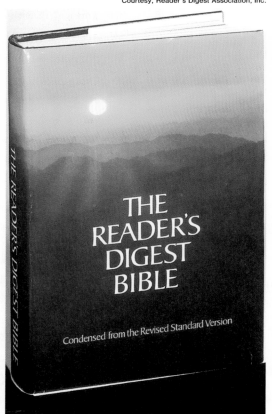

Some topics continued to lure readers. For the estimated 20 million readers of romantic novels, publishers issued 100 titles monthly, costing $200 million annually.

The Reader's Digest Corporation offered the first condensed version of the Bible, based on the Revised Standard Version. It was predicted that religious book sales would reach $300 million in 1983. Sunset Books, with total sales in excess of 100 million copies, celebrated its 50th anniversary. Golden Books passed 800 million copies in print, all within 40 years.

Increased sale of books discussing nuclear weapons and arms control reflected a national concern. Some 130 volumes were available, with 80% printed since 1980. For 1983 the public had its choice of 120 calendars. Rare volumes outperformed gold, diamonds, and stocks in investment returns.

The Rubik's Cube took the public's attention in 1981, and nearly 7 million copies of *The Simple Solution to Rubik's Cube* were sold. Video games took over as the fad of 1982, and publishers responded with *How to Master Video Games, Mastering Pac-Man,* and other books. Jim Davis and his Garfield accounts remained best-sellers, while the public paid nearly $20 a copy for James Clavell's *Noble House.*

The censorship trend was called "real, nationwide, and growing," and publishers and authors emphasized the public's right to read. Publishers remained unhappy with the Thor decision, a 1980 ruling by the U.S. Internal Revenue Service (IRS) that a producer (including a publisher) may not declare the value of inventory goods to decrease taxes on profits. As a result, some publishers cut back on initial press runs.

Best-seller lists were dominated by books on diet, exercise, money matters, and cooking. Colleen McCullough's *An Indecent Obsession,* Shel Silverstein's *A Light in the Attic,* James G. Nourse's *The Simple Solution to Rubik's Cube,* and Davis' *Garfield Bigger Than Life* were early 1982 leaders.

The popularity of television commentator Andy Rooney helped push his book, *A Few Minutes with Andy Rooney,* to the top. Other leaders included Jane Fonda's *Workout Book* and Richard Simmons' *Never-Say-Diet Cookbook.* John Jakes hit the charts with *North and South,* Martin Cruz Smith with *Gorky Park.*

Also on top were Robert Ludlum's *The Parsifal Mosaic* and *The Road to Gandolfo;* Robin Cook's *Fever;* Anton Myrer's *A Green Desire;* John Irving's *The Hotel New Hampshire;* Ken Follett's *The Man from St. Petersburg;* James Herriot's *The Lord God Made Them All;* Danielle Steel's *Once in a Lifetime;* and Theodore H. White's *America in Search of Itself: The Making of the President 1956–1980.*

William Kotzwinkle's *E.T.: The Extra-Terrestrial Storybook* capitalized on the movie's remarkable success. Other late 1982 leaders included Jeffrey Archer's *The Prodigal Daughter;* John D. MacDonald's *Cinnamon Skin;* Harold S. Kushner's *When Bad Things Happen to Good People;* Robert Lacey's *Princess;* Stephen King's *Different Seasons;* Rosemary Rogers' *Surrender to Love;* Durk Pearson and Sandy Shaw's *Life Extension;* James A. Michener's *Space;* Sidney Sheldon's *Master of the Game;* and Jean M. Auel's *The Valley of Horses.*

Magazines. "Nothing opens your eyes like magazines," proclaims the Magazine Publishers Association's (MPA) new slogan. Advertising revenues were up, and circulations were holding steady.

Reader's Digest recaptured first place among the circulation leaders, with a mid-1982 circulation of 18,171,628, edging out *TV Guide* (17,516,-896). *National Geographic's* 10,474,030 earned third. *Time,* with $253 million in 1981 ad revenues and $122 million for the first half of 1982, remained the top money producer. *TV Guide* was second with $239 million in 1981 and $117 million for the first half of 1982. Other circulation leaders were *Better Homes & Gardens,* 8,053,460; *Family Circle,* 7,010,192; *Modern Maturity,* 7,309,035; *Woman's Day,* 7,007,909; *McCall's,* 6,201,777; *Ladies' Home Journal,* 5,502,413; *Good Housekeeping,* 5,352,428. *Playboy, National Enquirer, Redbook, Time,* and *Penthouse* each topped 4 million circulation. The average magazine contained 48.5% ads and 51.5% editorial. The average cost of single magazine copies climbed to $1.63, annual subscriptions to $19.06.

George Allen, president of MPA, claimed, "Nine out of ten people read magazines." He noted the continued trend to new publications, more foreign publishers, printing process changes, record spinoff of books and electronic data banks, video text and teletext, and the like. Pretax operating profits in 1981 averaged 8.9%, up from 7.77% in 1980.

Robert Koen, vice-president of McCann Erickson, predicted that magazines would earn $3,800,000,000 in advertising in 1982. The business press experienced slower growth, according to Gallagher Reports. *Computerworld,* with revenues of $25 million in 1981, was number one and its $14.7 million led the first half of 1982. *Travel Agent* led in ad pages.

Time Inc. remained the world's leading publisher, with 1982 first half income of $1,710,000,-000. All of its publications were among the circulation/advertising leaders, including *Time, Sports Illustrated, People, Fortune, Money, Life,* and *Discover.* Its latest, *TV-Cable,* was announced for debut in early 1983.

Families, Saturday Review, and *Book Digest* were among the casualties. *Inside Sports, Ladies' Home Journal,* and *Redbook* were acquired by new owners. *Advertising Age* developed a magazine within a magazine, appropriately titled *Magazine. NRTA Journal* folded into *Modern Maturity.* Science magazines recorded circula-

NYT Pictures

Saturday Review, a magazine devoted since 1939 to society and culture, suspended publication in August.

tion gains. *Ms.* celebrated its tenth anniversary. Rodele passed $100 million in revenue with *Organic Farming and Gardening, Prevention, New Farm, Bicycling, New Shelter,* and *Spring.*

The growing competition from cable television forced magazine publishers "to make a greater effort to produce a product that really interests readers," according to George Green of *The New Yorker. Cosmopolitan's* editor-in-chief Helen Gurley Brown believes there is "a demand for more information in a more compact form."

Folio reported paper use up 2.1% in 1981, with a 5.3% hike predicted for 1982. *Folio's* Top 400 accounted for more than $8,000,000,000 of the $11,000,000,000 magazine industry's annual income. The magazine's study noted that there were nearly 11,000 active publications in its computerized database. *Magazine Age* issued its annual report on gross advertising by publications.

Newspapers. Wars, budget battles, elections, court cases, and economic developments made 1982 an exciting year for newspaper coverage. However, both the experts and the public began to ask such questions as: Will newspapers survive? Where will they fit as the computerized, electronic media world changes? The growth of cable, pay television, video cassettes, local radio and television stations, and other news sources drew from the newspaper audiences. Some predicted that there would be no letup for print journalism. William C. Marcil, president of the American Newspaper Publishers Association, predicted, in fact, that "the basic newspaper as we know it today is going to be around for a good long time."

Many papers, cautious about inflation and the future, expected a so-so 1982. The U.S. Department of Commerce predicted a 10.3% rise in 1982 revenues, slightly below 1981 gains. Some papers cut staffs and editions to survive. The International Typographical Union and the Newspaper Guild appeared closer to a merger.

"New technology is descending upon the industry with a vengeance," Canadian publishers were told. They also feared competition from video technology. Their readers thought television to be "most influential, most up-to-date, more fair and unbiased, more essential to Canada," yet newspapers were "more essential to the community" and presented the "widest range of opinion."

Newspapers did spend millions on expansion. *The Baltimore Sun* allocated $50 million for the first "fully automated plant in the world." The trend toward morning papers continued, with 347 morning editions accounting for nearly as much circulation as 1,330 afternoon papers. The United Press International, in its 75th year, was sold to Media News Corporation.

Allen H. Neuharth, president and chairman of Gannett, peruses USA Today, which made its debut in September.

© Roger P. Watts/USA Today

Noting resentment toward the U.S. media, Daniel Schoor observed: "We, the media, are not loved in this country anymore." Thirty-five newspapers now provide ombudsmen to act on public complaints.

Gannett, with nearly 90 dailies, launched *USA Today* during late 1982. In New York, the *Times* announced plans for a western edition printed in California. The *Daily News* gained concessions from unions and hoped to survive. The Cleveland *Press, The Tampa Times,* and the Buffalo (NY) *Courier-Express* faded away. In Philadelphia, the *Bulletin* ceased, but the *Inquirer* expanded coverage, gained circulation, and became the fifth-largest Sunday paper, trailing the New York *Daily News, The New York Times,* the *Los Angeles Times,* and the *Chicago Tribune.*

Evangelist Sun Myung Moon of the Unification Church established *The Washington Times* in mid-1982. *The Minneapolis Star* and the *Minneapolis Tribune* merged, as did the *Des Moines Tribune* and the larger *Des Moines Register.* The *Oregon Journal* and the *Portland Oregonian* joined to form the *Oregonian.* The editorial staffs of Atlanta's two daily newspapers, the *Constitution* and the *Journal,* were combined.

The Reagan administration acted to curb policy leaks. "What we have is a situation where every government employee and official must ask permission to talk to a reporter or suffer the consequence of an FBI probe," *Editor & Publisher* reported. Michael J. O'Neill, president of the American Society of Newspaper Editors, called for peace between the press and the Reagan administration. According to O'Neill, the press "should not be its (the administration's) enemy. No code of chivalry requires us to challenge every official action out of Pavlovian distrust of authority, upon the false premise that attack is the best way to flush out truth."

More laws and court decisions affected access to news. Specifically, the rights of reporters concerning the privacy of their news sources were curtailed. Larger awards in libel suits against newspapers alarmed media lawyers. A U.S. federal judge ruled that *The Washington Post* had published a libelous article about the president of Mobil Oil. The paper was assessed $2.05 million in damages.

The circulation of 1,715 dailies was up 67,475 to 62,041,176, while Sunday editions were up 836,940 to 54,993,965 for 722 newspapers. Weeklies gained 5 million, to reach 45 million circulation. Illinois with 700 weeklies and Texas with 513 were the leaders.

Circulation leaders in 1982 included *The Wall Street Journal,* 2,011,470; the New York *Daily News,* 1,540,218; the *Los Angeles Times,* 1,062,707; *The New York Times,* 947,681; the New York *Post,* 904,478; the *Chicago Tribune,* 770,798; and *The Washington Post,* 760,950.

WILLIAM H. TAFT
University of Missouri-Columbia

The Specialized Magazines

In the early days of U.S. publishing, general interest magazines achieved the mass circulation that made them economically viable by gauging what were perceived as the average tastes. Any magazines that failed to judge the average correctly soon vanished. But as the 20th century advanced general magazines lost hordes of readers to other diversions. Of the magazines flourishing today only a few are longtime or mass circulation publications.

Most current magazines seek their success in special-interest markets. One such market is that generated by the national women's movement. *Ladies' Home Journal, McCall's,* and *Good Housekeeping,* which had long catered to women's interests, suddenly had to compete against *MS.* (which marked its 10th year in 1982), *Playgirl, Working Woman, New Woman, Big Beautiful Woman,* and *Working Mother,* among others.

Growing numbers of retired people, active and able to devote time and resources to new pursuits, gave rise to magazines designed specifically to support their interests. *Modern Maturity,* introduced by the American Association of Retired Persons in 1958, now reaches more than 7 million readers bimonthly. *50 Plus* (1960), *Dynamic Years* (1965), and *Prime Time* (1980) are other magazines to serve those who are planning to retire or who have done so.

For the last 30 years, during which the civil rights movement gained strength, American blacks have had *Ebony* and *Jet* to focus their concerns. Since 1970, there are also *Black Enterprise,* which seeks to become the *Fortune* of the blacks, *Essence,* devoted to black women's interests, and *Black Collegian,* written for students.

Considerable growth in the field of computers, a renewed interest in space exploration caused by the recent space-shuttle flights, and a fascination with science generally have led to an expansion in the number of magazines devoted strictly to science and technology. By 1982 the pioneer *Scientific American* (1845) and *Science News* (1926) shared the market with *Science Digest* (1980), *Science 82* (first presented as *Science 80*), *Technology Illustrated* (1981), *High Technology* (1981), *Omni* (1978), and *Discover* (1980). The success of these new magazines is measured by their circulation. Both *Science 81* and *Discover,* for example, advanced by more than 50% in the second half of 1981 alone. As media analyst John S. Reidy noted, "there is clearly a demand for intelligently presented high-technology and science information—which is really an expansion of the trend of success among special-interest magazines."

Personal Computing (1977), *Popular Computing* (1973), *Creative Computing* (1974), *BYTE* (1975), *Computer Design* (1969), *Computer Decisions* (1969), and *Compute!* (1977) all were introduced to disseminate information about the computer explosion. Some of these magazines have a how-to-do-it approach; others cover sales and management.

There are an estimated 3,500 medical-health publications in the United States, and the medical-health periodicals clearly constitute the largest category of specialized magazine. *JAMA: The Journal of the American Medical Association, Medical Economics,* and the *New England Journal of Medicine* are examples of medical magazines with wide readership. *Prevention,* the layman's "magazine for better health," enjoys a circulation above 2 million.

Farmers who have long read the big three agricultural periodicals—*Successful Farming, Progressive Farmer,* and *Farm Journal*—can now benefit from more specialized editions of these publications, which are based on particular crop/animal interests. In addition, there are state-regional farm periodicals, and *Farm Chemicals* and *Farm Supplier* are examples of long-established magazines devoted to specific agricultural fields. In a related area, *Mother Earth News* debuted in 1972 to seek a "gentle revolution" to make Americans more ecology conscious.

The public has become increasingly aware of state and local issues and concerns. In fact, publishers in the field were led to form the City and Regional Magazine Association in 1978.

As the interests of the public shift, so does the U.S. magazine market. Magazines abound in the entertainment and recreation fields. For the sports fan, there are the general periodical (*Sports Illustrated, Inside Sports,* and *Sport*), the magazine on the fan's particular favorite sport, as well as the more specialized editions (for example, *Hot Rod* and *Fishing World*). *American Collector, Antique Monthly,* and *American Artist* have become leaders for those many Americans with the urge to collect anything old. Such publications as *Travelhost, Where, American Way,* and *Sky Delta* are devoted to the immediate concerns of the growing number of travelers. There are even magazines to guide the concerns of the animal lovers. It may be said that if there are two or more individuals interested in a given topic, another person will start a magazine to serve them.

WILLIAM HOWARD TAFT

PUERTO RICO

In its 30th year as a U.S. commonwealth, Puerto Rico faced difficult times. A bleak economic situation overshadowed all other events.

Economic Difficulties. The unemployment rate reached record levels in five of the first six months of 1982. Then in July the official rate of 24.6% was the highest since records have been kept; 248,000 people were out of work. There are, in fact, an estimated 2.5 million employable persons in Puerto Rico, and only 778,000 were actually working, giving an unofficial unemployment figure of more than 50% of the working-age population. This was about double the official figure, which represents only those actively seeking employment.

In the manufacturing sector the estimated number of employed was 139,000, the lowest level in eight years. With the absence of any formal housing program, the construction industry has been virtually eliminated, leaving only agriculture and the service sectors as sources of employment. By far the largest employer is the government. In late October, however, the government ordered a freeze on further employment in government agencies for the rest of the year. The decree came in response to an alarming drop in anticipated government revenues, which was expected to produce a $97-million deficit by the end of the fiscal year. The drop in revenues was in part brought about by an increasing number of bankruptcies. By the end of September, 1,409 bankruptcies had been registered, compared with 1,092 in all of 1981.

In previous years, under circumstances not so adverse as those of 1982, Puerto Ricans looked to the U.S. federal government to ease the island through hard times. In 1982, however, funds from Washington were cut back substantially. For example, under the defunct CETA program, Puerto Rico previously received $187 million yearly; under the new Job Training Partnership Act, which replaced CETA, the island could expect only $76 million in the first fiscal year. In the food stamp program, the local government was forced to accept a cutback of $300 million; under a new program there will be direct cash payment instead of stamps. Finally, more than $200 million in additional cutbacks were expected in federally funded health and education programs. Clearly the island was facing an even bleaker 1983.

Politics. In the face of such adversity, the local government found itself virtually paralyzed by party bickering. The executive branch was in the hands of the New Progressive Party, led by Gov. Carlos Romero Barceló. The legislative branch, however, was controlled in both houses by the opposition Popular Democratic Party. Cabinet members and agency heads nominated by the governor were frequently denied confirmation by the opposition-controlled Senate. For example, Romero was unable to secure approval for the post of secretary of agriculture.

A battle over the budget took most of the legislative session during the first part of 1982. Only on September 8, more than two months after the start of the fiscal year on July 1, was Romero able to sign into law a bill providing $1,500,000,-000 for government operations; this budget was $46.8 million higher than that of the previous fiscal year. The reason for the impasse was $16 million in pay increases for government employees. The governor had previously rejected two proposed budgets as inflationary.

THOMAS MATHEWS, *University of Puerto Rico*

QUEBEC

In Quebec, the harsh combined effects of inflation and recession were dominant concerns of government, business, and the general public.

Economy. Long-term reimbursement of its public debt and high rates of interest on current loans formed the bulk of the government's financial obligations. The government, which directly or indirectly employed more than 350,000 people, was forced to reduce the number of public jobs, to freeze salaries, and in some cases to impose a six-month 20% salary decrease in an effort to recover almost $700 million in the 1983 budget. Other financial measures were announced, including the closing of a number of programs and drastic cutting of others. Almost all targeted programs were in the domains of social welfare and education. A one-day symbolic illegal strike took place in early November.

Business was adversely affected by the drop in purchasing power and new savings habits of consumers, and by the steadily growing number of unemployed and socially assisted people. Most large private enterprises, such as Bell Canada, and large public businesses, such as Hydro-Quebec, decided to cut down their capital expenditures in the years to come. A number of firms, forced to slacken activities, faced impending bankruptcy. The asbestos mining companies at Asbestos, Thetford Mines, and East Broughton used less than half of the labor force they had to hire some years ago. Texaco and other large oil companies closed their Montreal-Est refineries.

In a major business achievement, Bombardier, located in Valcourt, was awarded a $1,000,-000,000 "contract of the century" to build 825 subway cars for the New York Metropolitan Transit Authority.

Political Scene. The stagnation of business seemed to affect political and administrative life. The provincial government, lacking the necessary tools, was unable to reactivate the economy, except by providing reasonable interest rates to boost the housing market and by helping local enterprises to remain in business.

Political personnel underwent several changes. Faced with growing criticism of his leadership abilities, Claude Ryan was compelled to abandon his leadership of the Parti Libéral du Québec. He was succeeded ad interim by Gerard D. Lévesque, deputy of Bonaventure and whip of his party. A national convention would not be held before the fall of 1983.

In the Parti Québécois (PQ), Claude Morin, who had been called the father of "étapisme" (gradualism) in the move toward independence and who for years had been in charge of major negotiations in provincial-federal issues, abandoned his ministry of intergovernmental affairs. The party was unable to retain his strategic constituency of Louis-Hébert, located in the western suburbs of Quebec City. Others who departed include Claude Charron, former whip of the party and a longtime representative of Montreal at the National Assembly, and Denis de Belleval, former minister of public service and deputy of Charlesbourg, who joined an office of international consultants headquartered in Algeria. Guy Bisaillon, complaining about his party's deviations, left the PQ to sit as an Independent. The PQ gained in none of the partial elections that took place during the year.

At the municipal level, Montreal Mayor Jean Drapeau, recently recovered from a severe illness, was reelected for the eighth time.

Quebec boycotted the April 17 constitution ceremonies in Ottawa. Instead, provincial Premier René Lévesque led a protest march in Montreal. In May the provincial government introduced a bill that used a clause in the new constitution to nullify other articles dealing with rights and freedoms. The move was an attempt to preserve Quebec's 1977 language legislation, known as Law 101, which calls for province-wide "frenchification." However, Quebec Chief Justice Jules Deschênes used the new Canadian bill of rights to overthrow a section of Law 101 that restricted English-language education.

Angry Anglophones. Encouraged by the decision of Chief Justice Deschênes, Alliance Quebec, a new umbrella organization for anglophones, undertook a campaign against frenchification. The group demanded full control of their school system, wide use of English on signs, smoothing of the linguistic tests enabling professionals to practice, free access of children to English-language schools, and proportionate representation of anglophones among the personnel of public and parapublic sectors. In November a major congress held in Quebec

Harold Rosenberg
As the new Canadian constitution was being proclaimed in Ottawa, more than 12,000 protestors rallied in Montreal.

City and devoted to the "Langue et Societé" theme concluded that English was still progressing among the francophones and that the frenchification of business, communication, and public life was far from being realized.

Culture. Quebec City's Festival d'Eté (Summer Festival), one of the outstanding arts events of the summer season, celebrated its 15th anniversary in July. Artists from Africa, the Caribbean, Latin America, and the United States joined with those of Quebec and the rest of Canada to entertain the public.

FERNAND GRENIER, *Interamerican Organization for Higher Education, Quebec*

QUEBEC · Information Highlights

Area: 594,860 sq mi (1 540 687 km²).

Population (1981 census): 6,438,403.

Chief Cities (1981 census): Quebec, the capital, 166,-474; Montreal, 980,354; Laval, 268,335; Longueil, 124,320.

Government (1981): *Chief Officers*—lt. gov., Jean-Pierre Coté; premier, René Lévesque (Parti Québécois). *Legislature*—Legislative Assembly, 122 members.

Education (1982–83): *Enrollment*—elementary and secondary schools, 1,160,640 pupils; postsecondary, 221,800 students.

Public Finance (1982 fiscal year, est.): *Revenues,* $20,800,500,000; *expenditures,* $21,547,900,-000.

Personal Income (average weekly salary, June 1982): $382.94.

Unemployment Rate (August 1982, seasonally adjusted): 15.9%.

(All monetary figures are in Canadian dollars.)

RECORDINGS

The sagging U.S. economy weighed heavily on the nation's recording industry in 1982. Although new technology opened exciting avenues of development, it also created new forms of entertainment that competed strongly for the consumer dollars once spent on audio recordings and equipment. As sales decreased sharply, such major commercial record labels as CBS and the WEA complex dismissed hundreds of employees, released fewer new products, and concentrated on material with proven mass appeal. Some smaller labels, including Inner City, went bankrupt, although tiny specialty labels—for example, Shanachie, Rounder, and Slash—prospered by catering to the smaller audiences ignored by the major companies.

The industry's ills most affected the popular sector, which continued to account for more than 90% of all commercial releases. The malaise was discussed hotly at meetings of major trade organizations such as the Recording Industry Association of America (RIAA). The problems most often cited were home taping, the encroachment of video games, the high prices and poor quality of the average audio recording, changing demographics, and the lackluster quality of the music.

Classical. Pop-flavored crossover albums, which sold well, helped companies which produce classical albums to maintain stable incomes despite the poor market. These records included *Hooked On Classics* (RCA) and, on the CBS label, Placido Domingo singing pop songs.

The sonic benefits of the digital-recording process helped sales of new recordings of standard classical works. Special audiophile pressings on various labels were a success.

To meet competition from European companies, CBS Masterworks improved the quality of their pressings and redesigned the packaging of their standard full-price line. At about $5 per disc, the CBS "Great Performances" series did well, and London Records introduced a successful mid-price line, Jubilee, listing for $6.98.

The improved quality of car-stereo systems and the popularity of tape players of the Sony Walkman type greatly stimulated the sales of prerecorded classical cassettes. Cassettes accounted for as much as 20–30% of sales of all Deutsche Grammophon recordings issued simultaneously in disc and cassette formats. DG introduced a mid-price line of "Doubletime Tapes," containing 90 minutes of music. CBS, RCA, and London all had budget cassette lines.

Popular. Pop-record companies attempted to adjust to the burgeoning popularity of the cassette and to combat home taping. An RIAA study found that the prerecorded cassette was the fastest growing music format. To take advantage of this trend, major labels created attractive cassette packages. Series like MCA's "Twin Pax" combined two pop albums on one tape for a reduced price. Island Records invented the "One Plus One," a cassette containing a full album on one side, with the other side geared for home taping. Columbia put an additional 15 minutes of material on the tape version of the original cast album of *Nine* to discourage home taping of the shorter disc. Some albums were released only as tape.

Home Taping. Despite these innovations, retail record shops found that renting records and selling blank tape often brought in bigger profits than selling a prerecorded product. National Public Radio in San Francisco implemented experimental taping from the airwaves for a fee with an encoded system by Codart. A controversial bill, introduced by Maryland's Sen. Charles Mathias, Jr., recommended a tax on blank tape and recorders to counteract the drain in profits caused by 39 million home tapers.

Disc Recordings. To stimulate sales of the disc format, record companies launched experiments like the one-sided single, priced under one dollar. Though album sales declined, the cheaper standard 45 rpm single and the 12-inch single sold steadily, and "mini" albums (EPs), containing about five selections, proliferated. Barry Manilow became the first pop superstar to market an EP. Budget lines, retailing for $5 to $6.98, became increasingly popular. Reissues and previously unreleased material appeared on disc, especially in jazz. They were highly profitable, involving no new recording costs. Thus the ABC/Impulse and Chess labels were rejuvenated, and Atlantic Deluxe was born.

The major companies shopped for superstars with guaranteed sales. RCA hooked Kenny Rogers with a reported $20 million contract, the largest in recording history. Underdeveloped markets were explored. Steady-selling children's records gained major-label interest as their share of the retail market expanded to 4%. For the first time, exercise records, including *Jane Fonda's Workout Record,* were high on the charts.

Despite price tags ranging from $15 to $50, audiophile pop pressings continued to sell briskly. The most expensive pop package ever, Mobile Fidelity's half-speed, re-mastered, complete catalog of the Beatles, sold well at $325.

Technological Advances. Sony, PolyGram, and Philips jointly initiated manufacture of the revolutionary compact disc in Germany. The CD, a small, laser-read encoded disc, was expected to become the world digital audio standard.

Although video clips of performers on cable television spurred sales of their audio recordings, commercial video discs and tapes of pop music did not yet encroach seriously on audio sales. Michael Nesmith's *Elephant Parts,* a musical created specifically for the home-video market, won the first video Grammy award. Audio-oriented companies of all kinds incorporated video facilities. New technology invaded the recording studio in other forms as Styx became the first performers to use solar power.

PAULETTE WEISS, *"Stereo Review"*

RECORDINGS | 1982

CLASSICAL

ALKAN: *Twelve Studies, Three Fantasies, and Other Works*, Ronald Smith, piano (Arabesque).

ARAIZA: *Opera Recital*, Francisco Araiza, Munich Radio Orchestra, Heinz Wallberg, conductor (Eurodisc).

BACH: *Goldberg Variations*, Glenn Gould, piano (CBS Masterworks).

BARTÓK: *String Quartets Nos. 1–6*, Lindsay String Quartet (Vanguard).

BERLIOZ: *Béatrice et Bénédict*, Yvonne Minton, Placido Domingo, Orchestre de Paris, Daniel Barenboim, conductor (Deutsche Grammophon).

BOYD: *Flute Music of "Les Six,"* Bonita Boyd, flute; Kimberly Schmidt, piano (Stolat).

BRAHMS: *Sonatas (2), Clarinet (or Viola) & Piano, Op. 120*, Richard Stoltzman, clarinet; Richard Goode, piano (RCA).

FRANÇAIX: *Paris à nous deux!*, Netherlands Saxophone Quartet (Nonesuch).

FRANCK: *Piano Quintet/WOLF: Italian Serenade*, Jorge Bolet, piano: Juilliard Quartet (CBS Masterworks).

GLASS: *Glassworks*, Instrumental Ensemble, Michael Riesman, conductor (CBS Masterworks).

HAYDN: *Complete Songs*, Elly Ameling, Jörg Demus (Philips).

MAHLER: *Symphony No. 7 in e*, Chicago Symphony Orchestra, James Levine, conductor (RCA).

PONCHIELLI: *La Gioconda*, Montserrat Caballé, Agnes Baltsa, Luciano Pavarotti, Sherrill Milnes, National Philharmonic Orchestra, Bruno Bartoletti, conductor (London).

PUCCINI: *Tosca*, Renata Scotto, Placido Domingo, Renato Bruson, Philharmonia Orchestra, James Levine, conductor (Angel).

RAVEL: *Daphnis et Chloé*, Montreal Symphony, Charles Dutoit, conductor (London).

STRAUSS: *Alpine Symphony*, Berlin Philharmonic, Herbert von Karajan, conductor (Deutsche Grammophon).

The Tango Project, William Schimmel, accordion; Michael Sahl, piano; Stan Kurtis, violin (Nonesuch).

WILD: *The Art of the Transcription*, Earl Wild, piano (Audiofon).

JAZZ

ART ENSEMBLE OF CHICAGO: *Urban Bushmen* (ECM/Warner Bros.).

CHET BAKER/LEE KONITZ: *In Concert* (India Navigation).

KENNY BARRON: *Golden Lotus* (MUSE).

ELLA FITZGERALD & COUNT BASIE: *A Classy Pair* (Pablo).

CHICO FREEMAN: *Traditions and Transitions* (Elektra/Musician).

DIZZY GILLESPIE: *The Source* (Jazz Man).

GRIFFITH PARK: *The Griffith Park Collection* (Elektra/Musician).

BILL HENDERSON: *A Tribute to Johnny Mercer* (Discovery).

AL JARREAU: *This Time* (Warner Bros.).

WYNTON MARSALIS: *Wynton Marsalis* (Columbia).

SUSANNAH McCORKLE: *Music of Harry Warren* (Inner City).

PAT METHENY GROUP: *Offramp* (ECM/Warner Bros.).

MUSICALS, MOVIES

ANNIE: sound track (Columbia).

CATS: original cast (Geffen).

DREAMGIRLS: original cast (Geffen).

NINE: original cast (Columbia).

AN OFFICER AND A GENTLEMAN: sound track (Island).

PUMP BOYS AND DINETTES: original cast (CBS).

POPULAR

ABC: *Lexicon of Love* (Mercury).

AIR SUPPLY: *Now & Forever* (Arista).

ALABAMA: *Mountain Music* (RCA).

ASIA: *Asia* (Geffen).

THE BEATLES: *Reel Music* (Capitol).

KIM CARNES: *Voyeur* (EMI America).

RAY CHARLES: *A Life in Music* (Atlantic/Deluxe).

CHICAGO: *Chicago 16* (Full Moon/Asylum).

THE CLASH: *Combat Rock* (Epic).

JOE COCKER: *Sheffield Steel* (Island).

ELVIS COSTELLO: *Imperial Bedroom* (Columbia).

JOHN COUGAR: *American Fool* (Riva).

MARSHALL CRENSHAW: *Marshall Crenshaw* (Warner Bros.).

CROSBY, STILLS & NASH: *Daylight Again* (Atlantic).

THE DAZZ BAND: *Keep It Live* (Motown).

NEAL DIAMOND. *Heartlight* (Columbia).

DIRE STRAITS: *Love Over Gold* (Warner Bros.).

PLACIDO DOMINGO with JOHN DENVER: *Perhaps Love* (CBS Masterworks).

DONALD FAGEN: *The Nightfly* (Warner Bros.).

FLEETWOOD MAC: *Mirage* (Warner Bros.).

ARETHA FRANKLIN: *Jump to It* (Arista).

PETER GABRIEL: *Security* (Geffen).

J. GEILS BAND: *Freeze-Frame* (EMI America).

GENESIS: *Three Sides Live* (Atlantic).

THE GO-GO'S: *Vacation* (I.R.S.).

MERLE HAGGARD/GEORGE JONES: *A Taste of Yesterday's Wine* (Epic).

HAIRCUT 100: *Pelican West* (Arista).

HALL & OATES: H_2O (RCA).

THE HUMAN LEAGUE: *Dare* (A&M).

JOE JACKSON: *Night & Day* (A&M).

RICK JAMES: *Throwin' Down* (Gordy/Motown).

JEFFERSON STARSHIP: *Winds of Change* (Grunt).

JOAN JETT: *I Love Rock 'n' Roll* (Boardwalk).

BILLY JOEL: *The Nylon Curtain* (Columbia).

ELTON JOHN: *Jump Up* (Geffen).

KID CREOLE & THE COCONUTS: *Wise Guy* (Sire/ZE).

EVELYN KING: *Get Loose* (RCA).

KENNY LOGGINS: *High Adventure* (Columbia).

LOVERBOY: *Get Lucky* (Columbia).

BARRY MANILOW: *Oh Julie* (Arista).

PAUL McCARTNEY: *Tug of War* (Columbia).

MICHAEL McDONALD: *If That's What It Takes* (Warner Bros.).

MEN AT WORK: *Business as Usual* (Columbia).

STEVE MILLER BAND: *Abracadabra* (Capitol).

RONNIE MILSAP: *Inside* (RCA).

ANNE MURRAY: *The Hottest Night of the Year* (Capitol).

WILLIE NELSON: *Always on My Mind* (Columbia).

JUICE NEWTON: *Quiet Lies* (Capitol).

RAY PARKER, JR.: *The Other Woman* (Arista).

ALAN PARSONS PROJECT: *Eye in the Sky* (Arista).

ROBERT PLANT: *Pictures at Eleven* (Swan Song).

THE POLICE: *Ghost in the Machine* (A&M).

QUEEN: *Hot Space* (Elektra).

EDDIE RABBITT: *Radio Romance* (Elektra).

LIONEL RICHIE: *Lionel Richie* (Motown).

KENNY ROGERS: *Love Will Turn You Around* (Liberty).

ROLLING STONES: *Still Life* (Rolling Stones).

LINDA RONSTADT: *Get Closer* (Asylum).

DIANA ROSS: *Silk Electric* (RCA).

RUSH: *Signals* (Mercury).

SANTANA: *Shango* (Columbia).

SKYY: *Skyyline* (Salsoul).

RICK SPRINGFIELD: *Success Hasn't Spoiled Me Yet* (RCA).

BRUCE SPRINGSTEEN: *Nebraska* (Columbia).

SQUEEZE: *Sweets from a Stranger* (A&M).

STEEL BREEZE: *Steel Breeze* (RCA).

DONNA SUMMER: *Donna Summer* (Geffen).

SUPERTRAMP: *Famous Last Words* (A&M).

SURVIVOR: *Eye of the Tiger* (Scotti Bros.).

RICHARD & LINDA THOMPSON: *Shoot Out the Lights* (Hannibal).

TOTO: *Toto 4* (Columbia).

VAN HALEN: *Diver Down* (Warner Bros.).

LUTHER VANDROSS: *Forever, for Always, for Love* (Epic).

SIPPIE WALLACE: *Sippie* (Atlantic).

DIONNE WARWICK: *Heartbreaker* (Arista).

THE WHO: *It's Hard* (Warner Bros.).

HANK WILLIAMS, JR.: *The Pressure Is On* (Elektra).

STEVE WINWOOD: *Talking Back to the Night* (Island).

STEVIE WONDER: *Original Musiquarium I* (Tamla).

WARREN ZEVON: *The Envoy* (Asylum).

REFUGEES AND IMMIGRATION

The United States appears to have reached a crossroad in its approach to immigration. Ongoing debate throughout much of 1982 centered on legislation introduced in April that would make the most sweeping change in U.S. immigration law since the Immigration and Nationality Act of 1952.

Companion bills sponsored in the Senate by Alan K. Simpson (R-WY) and in the House by Romano Mazzoli (D-KY) provided, for the first time, for sanctions—fines and jail—against employers who hire illegal aliens. Other portions of the legislation called on the president to devise, within three years, a fool-proof identification system to enhance enforcement of sanctions. In addition, the bills called for a ceiling of 425,000 legal immigrants per year not counting refugees; streamlining of asylum application determinations; and amnesty for most illegal aliens already in the United States. Those present before January 1977 would get immediate resident-alien status, and those present before January 1980 would become temporary residents for three years before receiving permanent status.

The legislation would also expand the nation's guest worker program, under which aliens receive temporary work permits for specific jobs. It also proposed an increase in immigration quotas for Canada and Mexico from 20,000 per year to 40,000 and provided that unused portions of the Canadian quota could be used by Mexico. Finally, the legislation sought elimination of the fifth quota preference in present law, which permits immigration by aliens who are brothers or sisters of U.S. citizens.

The Senate passed Simpson's bill (S 2222) on August 17 by a vote of 80 to 19. In the process it beat back amendments which would have eliminated employer sanctions and included refugees within the overall quota. A nonbinding "sense of the Congress" resolution, stating that English is the country's official language, was approved.

The House Judiciary Committee approved the Mazzoli version of the bill (HR 5872) in late September, but jurisdictional disputes forced the House leadership to refer it to three other committees for further consideration. The three committees were given a deadline of November 30 to finish work on the bill. The Congress recessed on October 2, setting a date of November 29 to reconvene. Since the lame duck session was largely intended to deal with appropriation bills, there was no time for floor action on immigration legislation, and supporters vowed to reintroduce similar legislation in the 98th Congress in January 1983.

Refugees and Illegals. Whatever changes are made in U.S. immigration law, the nation—and the world—will continue to grapple with the problems of refugees and illegal immigrants.

During 1982, international public opinion was horrified by the wholesale massacre of hundreds of Palestinians in refugee camps near Beirut in September. The victims of the carnage by right-wing Palestinian Phalangists were among the nearly two million Palestinians scattered around the world.

In 1982, according to the UN High Commissioner for Refugees and other sources, the number of stateless refugees worldwide continued at a level exceeding 10 million. In Africa, 2.5 million have been driven from their homes by wars, oppression, and persecution. An equal number of citizens of Afghanistan are in Pakistan, fleeing the savage war between the occupying Soviet army and Afghan guerrillas. Indochinese refugees still in camps or wandering about Southeast Asia number about 1.5 million.

A poignant example of the plight of refugees was the case of the Amerasians, children of U.S. servicemen and Indochinese mothers in Southeast Asia. Shunned by Indochinese society, the Amerasians are in effect refugees within their own countries. In September, the Vietnamese government permitted 11 Amerasians with proof of U.S. citizenship to emigrate to the United States, and Congress was debating legislation that would permit the entry of thousands more. A bill was passed just before recess, and President Reagan signed it into law on October 22.

In the Western Hemisphere, the principal sources of refugees in 1982 were Haiti and El Salvador, although strife in such other countries as Guatemala and Nicaragua contributed to the tide. Some 50,000 Haitians are reported to have entered the United States in recent years, the majority of them illegally. In July, a federal court ordered the release of 1,800 Haitians held in jail pending deportation hearings.

More than half a million Salvadorans have fled the civil war in their country. According to estimates by private refugee groups, between 180,000 and 300,000 are in other Latin American countries, and 300,000 to 500,000 are in the United States. Mexico reports it has some 140,000 Guatemalans and Salvadorans living along its southern border.

During 1981, the U.S. Immigration and Naturalization Service (INS) seized and deported more than 950,000 illegal aliens. It conducted a series of raids—dubbed "Operation Jobs"—on the workplaces of employers suspected of hiring illegal aliens, raising a storm of criticism from human rights groups. Still, the wave of persons seeking asylum rolled on in 1982. An estimated 98,500 refugees were admitted to the United States, and at midyear the INS said it had 105,000 requests pending.

A major problem lies in the definition of a refugee. Under present U.S. law, asylum may be granted to those fleeing persecution. "Economic refugees," however, are denied entry.

RICHARD C. SCHROEDER
Washington Bureau Chief, "Visión" Magazine

RELIGION

Survey

The pastoral travels of John Paul II took the pontiff to four countries of West Africa, Portugal, Britain, Argentina, Geneva (Switzerland), and Spain. The trip to Portugal was marred by another assassination attempt, this time by a deranged archconservative priest. The visits to Britain and Argentina were underscored by efforts toward peace in the Falklands (Malvinas) war. A highlight of the British tour was the ecumenical service held in Canterbury Cathedral, which emphasized the renewal of commitment to the reunion of the Church of England and the Church of Rome.

Religious leaders were in the forefront of opposition to the possibilities of nuclear destruction. In the United States, Roman Catholic bishops were increasingly vocal and forceful in their efforts to publicize the evil of nuclear war. Many theologians have concluded that nuclear weapons are unjustifiable. These theologians base their judgments on the "just war" theory, which requires that a licit conflict must produce more good than evil and must protect large populations from indiscriminate injury. There are those who feel that even possession of nuclear weapons as deterrents is unacceptable.

In May 1982, the Russian Orthodox Church sponsored a World Conference of Religious Workers for Saving the Sacred Gift of Life from Nuclear Catastrophe. The conference, which was approved by the Kremlin, was held in Moscow and was attended by more than 600 clergymen. Prominent among those in attendance was American evangelist Billy Graham, who drew considerable attention by his statements affirming religious freedom in the Soviet Union. The remarks were considered naive and irresponsible by many.

The Holocaust. The Holocaust is the name given to the destruction of approximately six million Jews in the Nazi death camps of World War II. The term itself is not of Jewish origin, and in recent years there has been some agitation among Jews to substitute a more appropriate name without diminishing the significance of the events. A "holocaust" is a burnt offering, one totally consumed by fire, made to the god or gods by representative priests. The massacre of Jews during World War II does not conform to such a definition. However improper the term may be, it is the name fixed in the mind of the public, which has become increasingly aware of the Holocaust. Symposia and conferences pursue the subject; films and television, and books and journals provide documentary expression.

During 1981–82 there were special commemorations. Survivors of Nazi brutality and representatives of nations that liberated concentration camps attended a special conference, sponsored by the U.S. Holocaust Memorial Council, at the

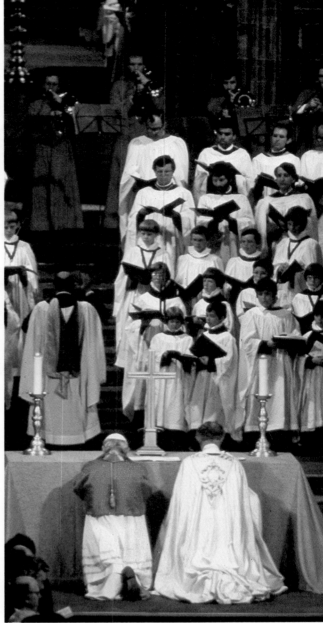

© Douglas Kirkland/Contact

Pope John Paul II (left) and the Archbishop of Canterbury, the Most Rev. Robert Runcie, kneel in prayer at the Canterbury Cathedral May 29. The churchmen later signed a pledge to move "in faith and hope" toward church unity.

State Department in October 1981. The Franklin Mint struck special medals for presentation to liberators. A collection of Jewish artifacts that survived Nazi destruction in Poland was exhibited at Harvard University, prior to a U.S. tour. Then the memorabilia were scheduled for display in Poland to commemorate in 1983 the 40th anniversary of the Warsaw ghetto uprising. The Judaica collection of Yale University's Sterling Memorial Library was named the repository for an acquisition of videotaped interviews with Holocaust survivors.

Elie Wiesel addresses a White House gathering April 20, 1982, a Day of Remembrance of the Holocaust.

In October 1981 the United States granted honorary citizenship to Raoul Wallenberg, a missing Swedish diplomat who saved thousands of Hungarian Jews from deportation and destruction during World War II. Wallenberg was seized by the USSR at the end of the war. A new book by Frederick E. Werbell and Thurston Clarke maintains that high Soviet officials gave evidence in 1965 to Swedish investigators that Wallenberg had died in a Soviet mental hospital. The fact that most reports regarding Wallenberg are inconclusive accounts for the U.S. action, which was aimed at pressing the Soviet Union to disclose the diplomat's fate and to free him if living.

The U.S. citizenship of several alleged Nazi executioners was revoked in 1981–1982. Renewed investigation of the massacre of Ukrainian Jews at Babi Yar called attention to the whereabouts of individuals involved in the extermination of Jews.

Increased public attention to the Holocaust accompanied a world-wide increase in reported incidents of anti-Jewish activities. The Anti-Defamation League of B'nai B'rith announced that such reports more than doubled for the three consecutive years 1979–1981. There also have been attempts to deny the historicity of Nazi extermination of Jews. The Institute of Historical Review, a right-wing organization, offered $50,-000 to anyone who could disprove its assertion that the Holocaust was a fabrication by Jews. A 1981 suit against the institute by Auschwitz survivor Mel Mermelstein led to "judicial notice" in Los Angeles Superior Court that "Jews were gassed to death at Auschwitz concentration camp in Poland during the summer of 1944." In France a Lyons University professor was convicted in July 1981 of inciting hatred and racial discrimination by calling the existence of Nazi gas chambers and the massacre of Jews "a historic lie."

Meanwhile, publication of new materials continued, including the paintings and words of Charlotte Saloman, who died in Auschwitz in 1943, and *The Auschwitz Album,* photographs taken at Birkenau by a Nazi officer and found by a camp survivor at the end of the war. Analysis of the Holocaust and its literature has entered a new phase. Such books as Lucy S. Dawidowicz's *The Holocaust and the Historians* serve notice that the issue of historical method has become crucial to understanding the Holocaust. Historians are constantly faced with the question of whether the general or the particular is to be emphasized. Like all academics, students of the Holocaust wish to classify, and may often obscure the issues by seeking that which is most general and fumbling over the unique. Many scholars who wish to comprehend the unique character of the Holocaust try to steer a course between Elie Wiesel's awe concerning its distinct sacredness and the penchant of the moralists for seeing it as a commentary on 20th century amorality.

RICHARD E. WENTZ
Department of Religious Studies
Arizona State University

Far Eastern

It is never safe to assume that Far Eastern religions are confined to the major traditions of China, India, and Japan. Japan is the site of many cults that illustrate this point. The Kakure Kirishitan inhabit the island of Ikitsuki. The sect is the result of a curious syncretism of Christian, Buddhist, and Shinto practices that emerged when a warlord suppressed the evangelistic efforts of Francis Xavier in the 16th century. The group's development was underground and insular. Today their doctrine diverges from orthodox Christianity. They do not use a Bible, and they practice an unusual form of house worship with elements of the three religious traditions.

India's President Sanjiva Reddy warned that without loyalty to moral values the political system itself would be undermined. In Punjab in April the severed heads of cows were found in front of Hindu temples. Violence broke out between Hindus and Sikhs, and the clashes spread to 20 villages. Two extremist Sikh groups, the Dal Khalsa and the National Council of Khalistan, were held responsible for the incidents and were banned by the government. They both advocate a separate Sikh state.

A call for the resignation of the Uttar Pradesh government of India was sounded as a result of continuing reports of massacres of harijans ("untouchables"). In the third such report since November 1981, upper caste Hindus were apparently responsible for the death in January 1982 of 13 members of a family from the state of Madhya Pradesh. It was believed that the killings occurred at the instigation of landlords who resent the legislative transfer of land to the harijans.

The 1982 gathering of pilgrims for the Fair of the Bowl at Allahabad was the largest in India's history. Approximately 10 million people bathed to cleanse their sins in the waters of the Ganges River at a point where it is joined by the Jamuna River. The festival has a major celebration every 12 years; 1982 was a midterm interval.

The first congress of Afghanistan's ruling People's Democratic Party ended in March with an appeal to Muslims to support the government. Delegates declared that party policy was based on respect for Islamic principles. Prior to the congress the government had ceded some of its authority back to traditional Muslim leaders as part of an attempt to promote solidarity.

RICHARD E. WENTZ

Islam

Although 1982 witnessed some examples of cooperation among Muslim nations, there were also examples of dissension within the Islamic community. This situation underscored the diversity of the Muslim world and illustrated that, while Islam is a universal creed, its followers diverge on points of interpretation and the means of applying their beliefs to daily life. Its practitioners are also influenced by the national interests of the states in which they live. The Iran-Iraq war and the controversies it has inspired within the predominantly Muslim Middle East reveal, on one hand, the extreme loyalty Islam is capable of fostering and, on the other, the religion's inability to override age-old national antagonisms. Above all, however, 1982 was marked by a continuation of the effort by Muslims to determine the role which their faith is to have in their societies, so many of which are rapidly moving away from their traditional roots.

A show of Muslim solidarity was triggered in the spring, when a Jewish gunman ran amok in Jerusalem's Dome of the Rock, the third most sacred mosque in the Islamic world, killing several worshipers. The Supreme Muslim Council, responsible for overseeing religious sites in Jerusalem, accused Israeli authorities of paying scant attention to security and called for a week-long general protest strike. The late King Khalid of Saudi Arabia joined in exhorting Muslims everywhere to protest the attack. The strike was heeded in at least 15 countries.

Another example of the Saudi regime's interest in the welfare of Muslims beyond its own borders was its effort, through the Organization of the Islamic Conference, to persuade Philippine President Ferdinand Marcos to implement a long-standing pledge of autonomy for his country's five million Muslims, some of whom had taken up arms against the Manila authorities. The Saudis used their position as the Philippine's major oil supplier to pressure Marcos to hold elections in Muslim regions. Amid charges of improprieties, pro-government candidates were elected, and disillusioned Muslim militants vowed to continue their campaign.

Pakistan, Nigeria, and Syria, all of which have largely Muslim populations, experienced domestic problems directly linked to Islamic issues during 1982. In Pakistan, President Zia ul-Haq announced his intention to instill what he called "Islamic democracy." While fundamentalists welcomed the move, other Pakistani Muslims were less enthusiastic. One group, the Ahmadiyya, experienced a wave of persecution as a result of its opposition to some of the proposals.

In Nigeria, another Islamic fundamentalist movement, known as Izala, accused the country's religious leaders of venality and corruption and demanded that these abuses be corrected, by revolution if necessary.

The call for reform and a return to the values of an earlier era are also slogans of the Muslim Brotherhood, or Ikhwan. Deftly combining political and religious concerns, the organization operates, openly or clandestinely, in many areas of the Mideast. Early in 1982 the Syrian government blamed it for a series of assaults on officials of the ruling Ba'ath Party. Shortly thereafter, government forces attacked the Brotherhood's strongest bastion in the northern city of Hama. Bitter fighting ensued, and thousands of lives were lost. Here, again, political and religious issues were closely interwoven. The Ba'ath is dominated by members of the Alawite sect—a politically powerful minority group whose views on Islam are often at variance with those of the Brotherhood. The government accused the Ikhwan of conspiring with external enemies, especially in Jordan, and used that charge to justify its crackdown on the group.

The clash between modern social and economic demands and traditional Muslim beliefs was also seen in Turkey. Although officially a secular state, Turkey's population is almost wholly Muslim. The demand of fundamentalist groups for a return to an Islamic-oriented government had grown increasingly strident in the late 1970s, and some extremist groups had turned to violence. The near anarchy which ensued led to a military coup in 1980. Since then, with parliament suspended, the secular military government has enacted various pieces of social legislation which the fundamentalist previously had blocked. In 1982, for example, laws allowing abortions and voluntary sterilization came into effect, but not without protest.

KENNETH J. PERKINS
University of South Carolina

Judaism

Repercussions of Israel's incursion into Lebanon had a global effect on Jewry during 1982. More than at any other time in recent history, Jews the world over were made answerable for the actions of the Israeli government and targets of violent abuse. Latent anti-Jewish animosities were brought into focus, and Jewish life everywhere was threatened.

Frequent comparisons in the world press between the Israeli action in Lebanon and the Holocaust, and between Israeli Prime Minister Menahem Begin and Adolph Hitler was a source of anguish for Jews. A French Catholic weekly called Israel "a terrorist state" and raised the medieval charge of deicide against Jews. The specter of 19th-century anti-Semitism was also revived; two articles circulated by a Guatemalan news service referred to Jews as the prime source of evil in the world and asserted that they have tried to introduce immorality among non-Jews. A group calling itself L'Action Directe was reminiscent of L'Action Française in its dedication to anti-Jewish violence.

France was a major scene of anti-Jewish violence throughout the year. In April, an Israeli diplomat was murdered outside his Paris apartment. In July, cafés owned by Jews were bombed; a young Israeli was killed and another wounded; a synagogue was damaged by fire; and commercial firms dealing with Israel were bombed. In August, random shooting into a kosher restaurant killed six persons and injured 22 others. In September an explosion in the car of an Israeli diplomat gravely injured its occupants and 47 others.

Attacks on Jews and Jewish property occurred on an unprecedented scale worldwide. In Copenhagen, youths hurled plastic bags containing pig's blood at the Israeli Embassy. In Brussels submachine gun fire wounded four worshipers in the main synagogue. In Vienna the home of the Austrian chief rabbi was bombed. In Rome a grenade and submachine gun attack at the main synagogue killed a two-year-old child and seriously injured several others. In Greece, Israeli basketball players were attacked, the premises of an Israeli firm were bombed, and a town magistrate refused to register the birth of a Jewish child. In Norway, anti-Israel demonstrations were held. And in the United States, a Hebrew school in Massachusetts was burned to the ground, and anti-Semitic slogans were sprayed on the synagogue.

Though there was considerable soul-searching over civilian losses, Jewry generally rallied in solidarity behind the Israeli campaign against the PLO in Lebanon. American rabbis reiterated the Israeli rabbinate's call for prayer. Thousands of Jews in New York and London publicly demonstrated their support. The World Jewish Congress adopted a resolution of "total solidarity" with Israel and "strong indignation at the widespread distortions of Israel's objectives and of the facts of the military operation." Hundreds of young Jewish volunteers traveled to Israel to fill in for workers drafted into war. Emigration from the United States to Israel, up 21%, escalated after the outbreak of war.

Jewish emigration from the Soviet Union was the lowest in 10 years. In addition to halting exit permits, Soviet authorities stepped up a campaign of harassment against Jewish dissidents and increased restrictions in Jewish entry into institutions of higher learning. Upon completion of her four-year sentence in Siberia, Ida Nudel, a well-known Moscow Jewish activist, was granted neither an exit permit to Israel nor a residence permit in any Soviet city. Petitions signed by millions of supporters in Europe and the United States were presented to the Parliament of Europe on her behalf and on behalf of Soviet Jewry in general.

In Israel, a cabinet decision to halt El Al flights on the sabbath and Jewish holidays created a confrontation between airline workers and Agudat Yisrael, the religious party responsible for the measure. The National Religious Party searched for a compromise to avoid the renewal of domestic religious controversy triggered earlier in the year by withdrawal from Yamit in southern Sinai and by archaeological excavations in Jerusalem.

See also ISRAEL; MIDDLE EAST.

LIVIA E. BITTON JACKSON
Herbert H. Lehman College, CUNY

Orthodox Eastern

The commission for the preparation of the Great and Holy Council of the Orthodox Church met in Switzerland in 1982 and affirmed traditional church positions on marriage and divorce, the priesthood, the date of Easter, and other issues until the council convenes. Representatives of the Orthodox met in Austria with Roman Catholics, continuing the official dialogue between the churches. At the same time, criticism of Vatican policies promoting the Uniate Eastern churches continued among the Orthodox.

Seminary enrollment in the Soviet Union in the last few years has increased, and reports have reached the West of some new church building. In addition, a published KGB statement declared that the Russian Orthodox Church is not a serious threat to Soviet society, indicating that there may be concessions regarding the church for political purposes. While visiting the USSR in May, the Protestant evangelist Billy Graham indicated that he sensed a degree of religious freedom in the USSR. His statements were criticized by the Orthodox outside the Soviet Union, especially in Western Europe and North America. Elsewhere in the Soviet bloc, Metropolitan Theodosius of the Orthodox Church in America visited Poland during the summer, expressing solidarity with the 500,000 Orthodox Poles and the Polish people in general.

In Greece, steps continued toward the formal separation of church and state. The move is strongly opposed by the hierarchy of the Greek Orthodox Church but is supported by a minority of churchmen, including several leading theology professors, who see it as an opportunity for greater freedom of Christian action and witness.

The monastic revival on Mount Athos and its influence throughout world Orthodoxy, including the United States and Canada, continues. The number of monks on the holy mountain has grown by about 1,000 during the last decade, and the number of Orthodox nuns is increasing at an even greater rate. This movement is attributed to improved education in Greece, coupled with disillusionment with the rapid secularization in Greece.

The bloodshed in the Middle East was of major concern to the Orthodox in the area, particularly in Lebanon, where the church generally attempts to maintain a neutral posture between Maronite Christians and Muslims. Metropolitan Elias of Beirut, together with other members of the Patriarchate of Antioch centered in Damascus, condemned Israeli military action.

In the United States, negotiations for greater cooperation and eventual union continued between the Orthodox Church in America and the American branch of the Patriarchate of Antioch, headed by Metropolitan Philip Saliba. The Greek Orthodox Archdiocese in America, under Constantinople, added several bishops to a growing church, in which a spiritual renewal movement, headed by Bishop Maximos of Pittsburgh, continues to thrive.

THE REV. THOMAS HOPKO
St. Vladimir's Orthodox Seminary

Protestantism

Church-state issues were at stake for Protestants during 1982.

Disputes over the teaching of Darwinian evolution theory in the public schools continued in several states. In Arkansas, a law calling for

Bishop David W. Preus presides as the American Lutheran Church agrees to merge with two other Lutheran bodies.

Courtesy, The American Lutheran Church

the balanced treatment of "creation science" along with Darwin-based biology was struck down as an unconstitutional attempt to introduce the biblical version of creation into public school curricula.

Debate over prayer in U.S. public schools became more heated. Many conservative Protestant groups, including the Southern Baptist Convention (SBC), backed President Ronald Reagan's proposal for an amendment authorizing voluntary prayer in the public schools. But the Baptist Joint Committee, an agency supported by nine denominations including the SBC, took the more traditional Baptist stance of strict church-state separation, and opposed such an amendment. (*See also* EDUCATION.) Legislation to curb legal abortion—another question seen by some as having implications for church-state relations—also failed to get through Congress.

The Supreme Court agreed to hear a case involving a Minnesota law that provides tax deductions to parents who send their children to sectarian schools. The president also proposed a plan for aiding families with children in private (parochial) schools. Many Protestant organizations contend that such a program is unconstitutional in that it aids religion.

Of the 11 young men who were the first indicted for failing to register for the draft, four were members of historic peace churches and cited religious reasons for their refusal to register. Three were Mennonites; the fourth was a member of the Church of the Brethren. A Mennonite official, pointing out that his church represents only a tiny minority of the population, suggested that the singling out of these individuals for indictment was discriminatory against religion.

The United Presbyterian Church, the Lutheran Church in America, the Episcopal Church, and others went on record in favor of a nuclear freeze. (*See also* pages 108–09.) Heads of four U.S. Protestant denominations—Avery Post, United Church of Christ; William P. Thompson, United Presbyterian Church; Arie Brouwer, Reformed Church in America; and David Preus, American Lutheran Church—participated in a conference in Moscow in May at which 580 persons from 90 countries, representing eight world religions, urged the governments of the world "to guard the sacred gift of life from nuclear catastrophe."

Ecumenism. There were major ecumenical developments in 1982. Three Lutheran bodies voted to unite by 1988; they set up a 70-member commission to work out structural matters. When the three denominations—the Lutheran Church in America (2.9 million), the American Lutheran Church (2.3 million), and the Association of Evangelical Lutheran Churches (180,-000)—come together, their new 5.5-million-member church will be the fourth largest U.S. Protestant body. Not included in the proposed merger is the Lutheran Church-Missouri Synod (2.6 million), which contends that serious doctrinal differences preclude its having closer relations with other Lutheran bodies.

Another significant step toward ecumenical rapprochement came when the three soon-to-unite Lutheran bodies entered into a relationship of "interim eucharistic fellowship" with the Episcopal Church (3 million)—the first time any of these churches has taken such a step with any church outside its own confessional family. Each church officially recognized the other as one in which "the gospel is preached and taught."

Two major Presbyterian bodies divided since the Civil War—the United Presbyterian Church (2.4 million) and the largely southern Presbyterian Church in the U.S. (840,000)—moved toward merger. General Assemblies of the two denominations approved a Plan of Union. The regional presbyteries of both churches were to vote on the plan in February 1983.

The National Council of Churches put off for a year a decision on whether a church made up largely of homosexuals is eligible for membership in the council. The applicant body, the Universal Fellowship of Metropolitan Community Churches, had been deemed to meet formal criteria in the judgment of a preliminary screening committee.

Five Reformed churches outside South Africa took strong action against a sister Dutch Reformed body in that country that supports the South African government's policies of racial separation. (*See also* SOUTH AFRICA.)

An ecumenical study sponsored by the National Council of Churches and others found growth of church membership in the U.S. falling behind population gains. The study, based on 1980 census figures, disclosed that the U.S. population grew three times faster than church membership in the 1970s.

The Reader's Digest organization issued a condensed version of the Bible, based on the Revised Standard Version. Bruce Metzger, New Testament professor at Presbyterian-related Princeton Theological Seminary, was general editor. The new version, considered a "reading Bible" and not for serious study or scholarship, reduces the Old Testament by 50% and the New Testament by 25%. (*See also* PUBLISHING.)

The General Convention of the Episcopal Church approved 600 hymn texts for *The Hymnal 1982,* the church's first new hymnal in 42 years. The book was expected to be off the press in late 1985.

A United Church of Christ congregation in Chicago, and a Presbyterian congregation in Tucson began providing public sanctuary for illegal Salvadoran refugees who were said to fear torture and death if they were forced to return to the strife-torn Central American nation.

JEAN CAFFEY LYLES
Associate Editor
"The Christian Century"

Roman Catholicism

An intensification of antinuclear sentiments, a deepening commitment to ecumenical dialogue, and the continuation of papal visits to world trouble spots highlighted the Catholic Church's growing concern over the world's socioeconomic and political ills.

The Pope. In messages throughout the year, Pope John Paul II punctuated his appeals for an end to the arms race, international terrorism, and civil strife by urging the world's superpowers to use the money spent on weapons to feed the hungry and spur development of Third and Fourth World nations. The pope, often preoccupied with the repressive situation in his native Poland, seemed bent on making up for time lost following the 1981 assassination attempt—an attempt which some 1982 media reports laid at the door of the Soviet Union.

The pope found time to make another visit to Africa, give personal attention to the reorganization of the Jesuits, meet with a wide variety of world leaders, and promulgate the church's new Code of Canon Law. Two of the most dramatic developments in the pope's year were the pastoral visits to Great Britain and Argentina at a time when the two countries were at war over the Falkland Islands.

The pope later addressed himself to the Mideast crisis which saw Israel invade Lebanon to oust the Palestine Liberation Army (PLO). After making a strong plea for a Palestinian homeland, he incurred the wrath of Israeli leaders by meeting PLO leader Yasir Arafat.

Pope John Paul kept up a low key but persistent criticism of Poland's communist regime, calling for an end to martial law and the restoration of the labor union, Solidarity. He condemned the terrorism and strife in Central America, promising to visit several of the predominantly Catholic nations there.

U.S. News. Catholic opposition to the arms buildup reached new heights when more than 130 bishops called for a "freeze" on nuclear arms. The debate widened with the issuance of a draft document by a bishops' committee condemning U.S. nuclear policies.

Peace became a preoccupation, as pressure from Catholic leaders and activists led to a change in the name of the Navy's attack submarine, *Corpus Christi,* which in Latin means "body of Christ." Archbishop Raymond Hunthausen of Seattle announced he would withhold a portion of his 1982 income tax as a protest against the U.S. participation in the arms buildup.

U.S. church leaders also provided strong support to federal legislation proposing tax credits for parents of students in private and parochial schools. The bishops continued to endorse attempts in Congress to ban abortions via a constitutional amendment and gave support "in principle" to a bill that would allow prayer in public schools.

James Kilcoyne

Archbishop Joseph Bernardin was installed as the head of the 2.4 million Catholics of the Chicago archdiocese.

The first married Episcopal priest was ordained to serve a Catholic diocese in South Carolina, and the debate over optional celibacy for Catholic priests heated up despite a strong statement by Pope John Paul affirming celibacy.

John Cardinal Cody, controversial head of the Chicago archdiocese, died in April. He was succeeded by Archbishop Joseph Bernardin of Cincinnati, former general secretary of the U.S. National Conference of Catholic Bishops. Earlier, the Rev. Daniel Hoye was named general secretary of the conference.

International News. Catholic scholars were among those participating in a global interfaith dialogue in Lima, Peru, that claimed a "breakthrough" on the general acceptance by Christian participants of baptism, Eucharist, and ministry. In addition, the Anglican-Catholic dialogue, after 12 years, issued its final report making a strong plea for unity.

Catholics worldwide celebrated the 800th anniversary of the birth of St. Francis of Assisi and the 400th anniversary of the death of St. Teresa of Ávila, two of the church's best-known saints and religious founders. Pope John Paul in October raised to sainthood one of his fellow countrymen, Blessed Maximilian Kolbe, a Conventual Franciscan who was killed in a Nazi death camp during World War II.

See also special report, page 551.

ROBERT L. JOHNSTON, *"The Catholic Review"*

RETAILING

The Great Factory Store/Reading, PA

Everyone loves a bargain! Reading, PA, above, has many factory stores and is the "outlet capital of the world."

For U.S. retailers, 1982 proved to be the most difficult year since the 1974–75 recession. High interest rates, the largest jobless rate in some 40 years, and inflation combined to curb sales and pressure profits. Both large and small companies engaged in heavy price promotion in a general effort to jar the consumer out of lethargy. But it was only partially successful because Americans' disposable income could not keep pace with living cost increases.

The inroads affected almost every retailer, including the finest specialty fashion chains which in 1981 had appeared impervious to the economic turndown. Attempting to explain the turnabout, the fashion merchants cited a drop in foreign tourism because of the strengthening dollar and added that many well-heeled Americans were spending cautiously because of high interest rates and an erratic stock market. But, as sales demonstrated, the hardest-hit consumers were the low- and middle-income families.

Chains and Stores. Reacting to reduced stock values and the burdens faced by struggling companies, the merger trend which began in 1981 intensified in 1982, throwing some venerable, family- or closely-controlled chains into the arms of the public giants. Thus, the Limited Stores Corporation of Columbus, OH, acquired Lane Bryant, the largest seller of extra-size apparel; the Batus Retail Division of Batus Inc., owned by BAT Industries of England, took control of Marshall Field and Company, Chicago; Federated Department Stores, Inc., bought The Children's Place; and Allied Stores Corporation succeeded in 1981, in spite of opposition, in buying Garfinkel, Brooks Brothers, and Miller and Rhoads, Inc. Allied had begun the recent merger cycle in 1979 by acquiring the Bonwit Teller fashion chain.

Two major takeovers, however, did not concern retailing although they involved Sears Roebuck & Co., the country's largest merchandiser. Eager under a new management to capitalize on its already huge public franchise, Sears acquired (effective Jan. 1, 1982) both Coldwell Banker & Co., the largest real estate brokerage, and Dean Witter Reynolds Inc., one of the biggest stock brokerages. And then, in a move to digest it all, Sears refined its structure into three appropriate divisions under a headquarters holding-company.

The tough economy produced some unusual results. Although the do-it-yourself (D-I-Y) trend generally withstood the recession, Wickes Cos., San Diego, one of the largest D-I-Y retailers, filed for voluntary bankruptcy status to stave off creditor suits. One primary reason was its 1980 purchase of Gamble-Skogmo, a diversified retailer battling difficult times. The cost of paying for that acquisition and the tendency of consumers to postpone buying big-ticket items, such as furniture and appliances, kept Wickes from remaining current on paying debts. Dayton Hudson Corporation decided to concentrate on its department, discount, and book stores and accordingly sold its jewelry chain. For the same reasons, J. C. Penney Company discontinued its Treasury discount stores. And Federated, which had three separate discount chains, closed the Gold Triangle home goods discount units which had not been earning their keep.

Some companies elected to follow the old maxim, "You can make more money out of real estate than retailing." Vornado Inc., the New Jersey operator of the Two Guys discount chain, shut all its 49 stores and became a real estate development business. Others reduced the size of their urban and suburban stores and subleased portions to bowling alleys, movie theaters, banks, and other retailers. Others leased portions of their frontage to opticians, dentists, and fast-food restaurants.

Discount Stores. Discounters mostly thrived and expanded as they met the public's demand for values. But F. W. Woolworth stunned the in-

444

The 120-store Ashley Stores, a division of Kellwood Company in St. Louis, is an example of a new trend in retailing, the factory outlet chain. Catalog showroom companies, which originated in the suburbs in the mid-1950s, enjoyed sales above the average during 1982.

dustry by announcing that it would close all of its 337 U.S. Woolco discount stores. A spotlight fell upon Wal-Mart Stores, an aggressive discounter based in Arkansas, which some analysts hailed as a possible giant growth company in the manner of the K Mart Corporation. That company, where skillful strategy and rapid expansion over the last decade had built sales of $16,500,000,000, second only to Sears' $26,000,-000,000, grappled with problems of digesting its expansion and rising local competition. It decided to offer more expensive ("trade up") fashion merchandising, as did J. C. Penney, and showed improved earnings.

Factory outlets, flea markets, and specialty stores offering brand apparel at off-prices multiplied, taking an increasing market share. Despite the general slowdown in shopping centers, centers composed entirely or mostly of discounters or the cut-price, brand stores opened for business. So successful is the factory outlet trend that entire chains are sprouting. One is the 120-store Ashley Stores division of the Kellwood Company in St. Louis.

Catalog sales did somewhat better than the over-the-counter business. Large retailers either invested in or researched more sophisticated catalog selling or closed circuit television home shopping, the latter, however, only beginning to make its entry. Catalog showroom companies, which distribute catalogs to consumers who then appear in the store to buy preselected items, also found their business crimped. But a major merger involved Best Products Company, Richmond, VA, the largest in the field, which acquired Modern Merchandising Inc., Minne-

tonka, MN, the third-largest showroom concern.

Food, the Auto, Other Trends. In the food field, retailers also found profits under stress. But the loss-ridden Great Atlantic and Pacific Tea Company (A & P) produced its first quarterly profit in several years by cutting its operations and overhead. Others, such as Safeway Stores, Oakland, CA, the largest of the food retailers, continued their policy of closing small, obsolete stores and increasing their number of more productive large or "super-stores." Automated checkouts involving optical scanners to speed traffic through the store's front-end came into wider use. And the number of combination food-drug stores also grew as consumers, still concerned by the cost of gasoline, continued to show more interest in one-stop shopping.

The severe erosion in the automobile business hurt the economy of the Midwest, as well as other areas where the auto makers have plants or subcontractors. This especially affected the year's business for those retailers with a big stake in the Midwest, including Sears, the Montgomery Ward division of Mobil Corporation, and K Mart. In addition, to the retailers' disappointment, the vaunted economy of the Sun Belt states faltered, owing to overexpansion and the washover from the auto industry slump. As a result, such retailers as Federated, Allied, and Marshall Field, with stores in either Florida or Texas or both, were hurt. This was also complicated by the devaluation of the Mexican peso, which adversely affected Texas retailers catering to nationals across the border.

A fallout of the auto industry's troubles was the decision by the J. L. Hudson division of Dayton Hudson to close its famous downtown Detroit store, a 2-million-sq-ft (185 800-m^2) facility that had lost business for 20 consecutive years. It was a trauma typical of many large, outmoded downtown stores but was especially aggravated in Detroit where suburban stores were better able to withstand the economic blows. As P. Gerald Mills, Hudson's board chairman, observed: "The size of the building and its age make it an expensive and inefficient arena to do business in. Consumers have changed their shopping patterns in recent decades. They prefer a multifaceted shopping environment with several major anchor stores, a variety of specialty shops, and nearby free parking."

The July 1 federal income tax cut and the higher Social Security pay increment affected retail sales at a slower pace than retailers would have preferred. And back-to-school shopping was less than expected. But retailers did not have to swallow only bad news. The consumers' more discriminating interests helped specialty stores of various kinds, except the highest-priced ones. So the hard year was not felt so severely at stores specializing in sporting goods, camping gear, health-and-beauty aids, and footwear. The proliferating home computer stores enjoyed a terrific boom. All age segments apparently enjoyed the products' novelty and potential utility. (*See also* COMPUTERS.)

As the year drew to a close, many retail executives consoled themselves with the thought that they had built well in a tough period for a coming turnaround. The theory that problems also create opportunities seemed to sink in. It was a comforting realization, particularly after they enjoyed the normally strong Christmas selling season.

ISADORE BARMASH
Business Writer
The New York Times

With personal computer sales expected to reach $2,700,000,000 in 1982, the number of stores specializing in such equipment skyrockets. According to one estimate, there were 1,500 such stores in the United States at midyear.

Radio Shack, A Division of Tandy Corp.

RHODE ISLAND

© Bruce Flynn/Picture Group

Labor problems, including a strike at toolmaker Brown & Sharpe, a major employer, compounded economic woes.

The state was preoccupied during 1982 with the impact of the national recession, politics, and a celebrated murder trial. In the latter, Claus von Bülow was accused of attempting to kill his wealthy Newport socialite wife by insulin injections. An avidly reported six-week trial culminated with a conviction in mid-March. (*See also* CRIME.)

The Economy. Rhode Island's unemployment was at 9.2% of the work force by May and had changed little by the year's end. Unlike similar past circumstances, the rate remained somewhat below the 10%-plus national level during the year. There was a rising number of bankruptcies; some employers closed their doors, while others cut their work forces.

It was a discouraging year for Rhode Island labor. The toolmaker Brown & Sharpe, one of the state's long-established major employers, continued in the throes of a strike which had begun in October 1981. There was violence on the picket line, and appeals were made to the public and to elected officials by the union. In the face of shrinking business, the company hired a small replacement force. At Quonset Point, the Electric Boat plant (maker of submarine components) went through its third bargaining election with another union defeat.

The Legislature. In the January session of the General Assembly, the Democratic majority enacted redistricting legislation amid accusations of gerrymandering and other constitutional violations. Opponents won a court challenge to the Senate plan, which the legislature thereupon revised. Complex maneuvering ensued to find a basis for holding the fall legislative elections. Opponents shifted to federal court, which stayed all senatorial electoral activity. Meanwhile a parallel challenge to the House district plan failed, and on November 2, the House elections were held. In January 1983 the newly chosen House and the holdover Senate were to convene, pending a resolution of the latter's status.

During the January session, the legislature also approved a complex and carefully negotiated overhaul of worker compensation legislation designed to improve the state's business climate. It raised the tax on cigarettes and gross oil-company sales, stiffened drunken driving penalties, and regulated the siting of hazardous waste facilities. A bottle-deposit bill again failed.

Elections. Former state Attorney General Julius Michaelson challenged Republican Sen. John Chafee, and state representative James Aukerman sought Republican Congresswoman Claudine Schneider's second-district seat. Both Democrats were unsuccessful. Among other candidates, victorious Democratic Gov. J. Joseph Garrahy had only token opposition, and first-district Congressman Fernand St. Germain easily defeated his Republican opponent. Democratic Attorney General Dennis J. Roberts II, won his nationally reported contest with Arlene Violet, a Catholic nun of the Sisters of Mercy. Republican Susan Farmer became the first woman to win statewide office when she was elected secretary of state.

In a surprising comeback from his 1980 defeat for governor, Providence's Republican mayor, Vincent A. Cianci, Jr., running as an Independent, defeated his 1978 opponent, Frank Darigan (D), and Frederick Lippitt (R).

ELMER E. CORNWELL, JR., *Brown University*

RHODE ISLAND • Information Highlights

Area: 1,212 sq mi (3 139 km^2).

Population (1980 census): 947,154.

Chief Cities (1980 census): Providence, the capital, 156,805; Warwick, 87,123; Cranston, 71,992.

Government (1982): *Chief Officers*—governor, J. Joseph Garrahy (D); lt. gov., Thomas R. DiLuglio (D). *Assembly*—Senate, 50 members; House of Representatives, 100 members.

State Finances (fiscal year 1981): *Revenues,* $1,535,000,000; *expenditures,* $1,461,000,000.

Personal Income (1981): $9,676,000,000; per capita, $10,153.

Labor Force (Aug. 1982): *Nonagricultural wage and salary earners,* 392,600; *unemployed,* 46,200 (9.5% of total force).

Education: *Enrollment* (fall 1981)—public elementary schools, 91,642; public secondary, 51,173; colleges and universities (1981–82), 68,339 students. *Public school expenditures* (1980–81), $362,750,000 ($2,559 per pupil).

RUMANIA

The paradox of Rumania's independent foreign policy and its repressive Stalinist internal rule continued in 1982.

Domestic Affairs. According to official publications, 1981 economic targets were not reached, particularly in agriculture, transportation, and industrial investments. Industrial production rose by 2.6% instead of the projected 7%, labor productivity grew by 2.4% instead of the planned 7%, and national real income increased by 2.2% instead of the expected 4.4%.

In January severe restrictions on consumption of electricity and fuel were announced that affected domestic life, factories, and transportation. A few months later, price increases were imposed on electricity, natural gas, coal, firewood, and liquid fuels. Rumania's per capita energy consumption became one of the lowest in Europe.

Food and cigarette prices were raised by 35% in February. Stiff customs regulations were instituted, aimed at limiting imports and enhancing exports, even of consumer goods. Fees were raised for passports as well as for entry and exit visas. Wages were increased by an average of 16.5%.

In the spring several high government officials, including Premier Ilie Verdet, Minister of Foreign Trade Cornel Burtica, and Education Minister Aneta Spornic, were dismissed or demoted for economic transgressions.

At the beginning of June, President Nicolae Ceauşescu addressed the plenum of the Central Committee of the Communist party. He blamed the state bureaucracy for failures, absolved the party and himself from any guilt, and called for further industrialization with emphasis on machines, chemicals, and petrochemicals.

In July the 17th anniversary of the "Ceauşescu Era" was celebrated, featuring glorification of the party, state, and supreme government leader.

Foreign Affairs and Trade. Rumania's foreign debts to more than 200 Western banks (mostly French, English, and German) surpassed $11,000,000,000. Some $500 million were in ar-

UPI

President Ceauşescu marked his 17th year in power.

rears for 1981, and $2,400,000,000 were due in 1982. Unable to pay, the government requested that 80% of 1981 arrears and all 1982 maturities be rescheduled over six and a half years.

In May the World Bank approved a 15-year loan for advanced oil technology. In June the International Monetary Fund (IMF) released $500 million of previously suspended credit to Rumania on the condition that Bucharest introduce various economic reforms. By November, however, the IMF stopped dispersing sums to Rumania out of a standby credit of almost $1,500,000,000.

Rumania's foreign trade became increasingly West-oriented. Exchanges with Eastern bloc countries fell to one third of its total trade.

Exports to the United States in 1981 amounted to nearly $1,100,000,000, an increase of some $800 million over 1980, resulting for the first time in a positive balance of trade. However, in consideration of Rumania's failure to pay its debts to American banks, U.S. President Ronald Reagan declined to approve new agricultural credits of $65 million. The most-favored-nation status of Rumania continued.

As in the past, Rumania was highly visible in the international arena. In the late fall of 1981, West German President Karl Carstens paid an official visit. Pakistan's President Mohammed Zia ul-Haq, then U.S. Secretary of State Alexander Haig, and Turkish Head of State Gen. Kenan Evren also visited Rumania. In June, Polish Prime Minister Wojciech Jaruzelski paid "an official visit of friendship." Soon after, UN Secretary-General Javier Pérez de Cuellar conferred with Ceauşescu in the Rumanian resort of Neptun.

In April, Ceauşescu visited the People's Republic of China and North Korea. A few weeks later he visited Syria and Greece. In July he went to Jordan, Iraq, and Lebanon to mediate in the Middle East conflict.

JAN KARSKI, *Georgetown University*

RUMANIA · Information Highlights

Official Name: Socialist Republic of Rumania.
Location: Southeastern Europe.
Area: 91,700 sq mi (237 503 km²).
Population (1982 est.): 22,600,000.
Chief Cities: (July 1980 est.): Bucharest, the capital, 2,090,408; Brasov, 304,670; Timisoara, 287,543.
Government: *Head of state,* Nicolae Ceauşescu, president (took office 1967) and secretary-general of the Communist Party (1965). *Head of government,* Dascalescu Constantin, premier (took office May 1982). *Legislature* (unicameral)—Grand National Assembly.
Monetary Unit: Leu (15 lei equal U.S.$1, Dec. 1981).
Gross National Product (1981 est. U.S.$): $77,100,-000,000 to $120,000,000,000.
Foreign Trade (1980 U.S.$): *Imports,* $13,201,000,-000; *exports,* $12,230,000,000.

SASKATCHEWAN

Government. Grant Devine, leader of the Progressive Conservative Party (PC), led his party to a resounding political victory on April 26, 1982, and brought to an end 11 years of New Democratic Party (NDP) rule in Saskatchewan. Devine appealed to the electorate with a call for less government involvement in the economic sector and the promise of a series of tax cuts. The Conservative platform rapidly gained in popularity in a time of voter dissatisfaction with high interest rates and slow economic growth.

Incumbent Premier Allan Blakeney (now leader of the opposition) was not able to maintain voter support with his election platform. He called on the electorate to give the government a mandate to fight the federal government's attempt to abolish the statutory Crow freight rate and to continue the NDP resource policy of mixed public and private enterprise. Traditional support for the NDP from organized labor was weakened during this campaign as a result of back-to-work legislation passed by the government prior to the election call. Liberal leader Ralph Goodale attempted to generate electoral support with a platform of financial initiatives. These included tax cuts, a freeze on university tuition, and an expanded health care program.

Two new parties entered the election race during the 1982 campaign: the Aboriginal Peoples party and the Western Canada Concept party.

Standings at the dissolution of the 61-seat legislature were NDP 44, PC 15, and Unionest 2. Redistribution of seats resulted in a new total of 64 seats, of which the PC won 55 seats and the NDP 9.

Economy. The Conservative platform included a change in fiscal policy from public investment through the Crown corporation sector to stimulative tax cuts. To this end, the new government abolished the 20% provincial gas tax, instituted a three-year-mortgage interest program guaranteeing home owners 13.25% interest rates on new mortgages, and eliminated the Sas-

CANAPRESS

A 37-year-old farmer who never held elective office, Grant Devine was elected premier of Saskatchewan.

katchewan Land Bank. A White Paper on the economy presented by Finance Minister Bob Andrew revealed the initiation of deficit financing as a result of poor development opportunities for the resource sector.

Resources. While the coal mining industry was stable during 1981, the world oil glut and the weakening of pricing power in OPEC brought oil prices down. This delayed plans for a heavy oil upgrading operation in the province. During the year there was a substantial increase over 1981 in the production of sodium sulphate.

Agriculture. High snowfall levels and adequate rainfall created excellent growing conditions across most of the province, although some areas in the southeast missed the higher-than-average moisture levels brought on by heavy July rains. Prospects were good for the harvest of grain crops, with forecasts projecting a yield of 44.7 million metric tons (49.2 million T) for the province, up 3 tons (3.3 T) from the previous year. In spite of good harvest expectations, it was likely that net farm incomes would be reduced as a result of lower grain prices and high interest costs. Livestock operators benefited in 1982 from a provincial beef stabilization program that came into effect on January 1. It covered cattle fed to slaughter weight and was under review to determine possible applications to other livestock.

JENNIFER JOHNSON
Regina Public Library

SASKATCHEWAN · Information Highlights

Area: 251,700 sq mi (651 900 km²).

Population (1981 census): 968,313.

Chief Cities (1981 census): Regina, the capital, 162,-613; Saskatoon, 154,210; Moose Jaw, 33,941.

Government (1982): *Chief Officers*—lt. gov., C. Irwin McIntosh; premier, Grant Devine (Progressive Conservative); atty. gen., R. J. Romanow. *Legislature*—Legislative Assembly, 64 members.

Education (1982–83): *Enrollment*—elementary and secondary schools, 208,600 pupils; postsecondary, 17,320 students.

Public Finance (1982 fiscal year, est.): *Revenues* $3,-322,100,000; *expenditures* $2,842,900,000.

Personal Income (average weekly salary, April 1982): $368.75.

Unemployment Rate (July 1982, seasonally adjusted): 6.5%.

(All monetary figures are in Canadian dollars.)

SAUDI ARABIA

© Sipa-Press/Black Star

Egypt's President Mubarak pays a condolence call on Saudi Arabia's new king, Fahd.

New political leadership, decreasing oil production, and some challenging foreign policy initiatives made for dramatic changes in Saudi Arabia in 1981–82.

Government and Military. King Khalid died of a heart attack in Taif on June 13, 1982, and was succeeded by Crown Prince Fahd, who became prime minister as well as king. (*See* BIOGRAPHY.) Khalid had reigned since 1975, but Fahd had managed the government as deputy prime minister, and there were few immediate changes in policy or personnel upon his accession. He did name Prince Abdullah, head of the National Guard, as crown prince and first deputy prime minister, and Prince Sultan, the minister of defense, as second deputy prime minister. The death of King Khalid delayed the expected announcement of a constitution and the establishment of a consultative council.

Internal security after the accession of Fahd was challenged only by small pro-Khomeini demonstrations by Iranian pilgrims in September. Twenty-one of them were sent back to Iran by Saudi authorities.

The Iran-Iraq war, Iranian intervention in the Persian Gulf region, and Israeli military superiority remained sources of concern both for the old and new Saudi kings. Saudi Arabia provided financial aid to Iraq; 13 Saudis were arrested in mid-December 1981 for complicity in an attempted pro-Iranian coup in Bahrain; and Israel admitted that it was making overflights of the new Saudi airbase at Tabuk.

U.S. support of the Saudi regime included the delivery of six F-15 fighter planes in January, a visit by Secretary of Defense Caspar Weinberger in February, and an offer of joint military maneuvers in July. Saudi Arabia publicly backed away from joint military exercises and the deployment of the U.S. rapid strike force in the Gulf region.

Oil and Finance. As world demand for oil declined, Saudi Arabia reduced its own production and tried, unsuccessfully, to secure a united policy of decreased production by all members of the Organization of Petroleum Exporting Countries (OPEC). In 1981, Saudi production averaged 9.8 million barrels per day, and total Saudi income from oil was more than $100,000,-000,000. In 1982, production was cut in stages, reaching a low in August of about 6 million barrels per day, which Oil Minister Ahmed Zaki Yamani estimated would still yield enough revenue to meet the nation's needs.

An emergency OPEC meeting in July was suspended without an agreement on pricing structures or how to curb overproduction. Venezuela and Iran successfully opposed Saudi Deputy Oil Minister Abdul Aziz al-Turki, even though Saudi Arabia provided more than 40% of all OPEC oil.

One result of changes in oil policy was that the 1982–83 Saudi budget called for only 9% more in expenditures than the 1981–82 budget. However, economic development sponsored by the government continued at a massive rate. The new industrial cities of Jubail and Yanbu neared completion, while major strides were taken in housing, transportation, and electricity.

Foreign Affairs. The failure of the Saudi plan to resolve the Arab-Israeli dispute at the Arab

---

SAUDI ARABIA · Information Highlights

Official Name: Kingdom of Saudi Arabia.
Location: Arabian peninsula in southwest Asia.
Area: 830,000 sq mi (2 149 690 km²).
Population (1982 est.): 11,100,000.
Chief Cities (1976 est.): Riyadh, the capital, 667,000; Jidda, 651,000; Mecca, 367,000.
Government: *Head of state and government,* Fahd ibn Abd al-Aziz, king and prime minister (acceded June 1982).
Monetary Unit: Riyal (3.44 riyals equal U.S.$1, Oct. 1982).
Gross National Product (1981 U.S.$): $118,990,000,-000.
Foreign Trade (1981 U.S.$): *Imports,* $35,244,000,-000; *exports,* $120,240,000,000.

summit of November 1981 in Fez, Morocco, left Saudi diplomacy in shambles. Iran's apparent role in the Bahrain coup attempt of December upset the Saudis even more and created new tensions.

By assuming its usual low diplomatic profile, Saudi Arabia in subsequent months began to gain back its prestige and influence. Relations with Libya were resumed despite a prior declaration by the Saudi Council of High Ulema that Libya's leader Col. Muammar el-Qaddafi was a heretic. On April 11, King Khalid, acting as head of the 42-nation Islamic Conference, called for a one-day strike by the world's Muslims to protest the shooting incident at the Aqsa Mosque in Israeli-controlled East Jerusalem.

In June and July, Saudi Arabia appealed urgently to the United States to put pressure on Israel to stop the bombing of Beirut and to withdraw from Lebanon. Bashir Gemayel, then the leader of the Lebanese Christian militia, met in Saudi Arabia with King Fahd and Arab League officials on July 1 in a futile attempt to reach a compromise that would end the fighting. A Syrian and Saudi plan for the evacuation of Palestinian Arab troops from Beirut to northern Lebanon was presented to U.S. President Ronald Reagan on July 20 but was rejected by Israel.

After the removal of Palestinians from Beirut and the full revelation of Arab diplomatic and military weaknesses during the Lebanon crisis, King Fahd once more tried to unite the Arab states and the Palestine Liberation Organization (PLO) on a common peace proposal. In September at Fez, Saudi Arabia and Morocco secured unanimous Arab agreement on a slightly modified version of the 1981 Saudi plan which was presented to Reagan in October.

WILLIAM OCHSENWALD
Virginia Polytechnic Institute

SINGAPORE

The presence of an opposition member in Parliament for the first time since independence did little to change government policies but did embarass other opposition parties.

Politics. In an October 1981 by-election to fill the seat vacated by C. V. Devan Nair when he was named president, opposition parties united behind J. B. Jeyaretnam, who broke the ruling People's Action Party's (PAP) complete dominance of Parliament. Shocked at its first defeat in 16 years, the government and the PAP moved to remove many of the community leadership responsibilities that usually fall to the district representative. By mid-1982, Jeyaretnam faced charges of conflict of interest and breach of privilege which forced him to apologize to Parliament and to accept a reprimand by that body.

His Workers' Party had suffered in January 1982 when the arrest of a number of Muslims for planning to distribute inflammatory literature

SINGAPORE • Information Highlights

Official Name: Republic of Singapore.
Location: Southeast Asia.
Area: 224 sq mi (580 km^2).
Population (1982 est.): 2,500,000.
Chief City (1974 est.): Singapore, the capital, 1,327,-500.
Government: *Head of state*, C. V. Devan Nair, president (took office October 1981). *Head of government*, Lee Kuan Yew, prime minister (took office 1959). *Legislature* (unicameral)—Parliament.
Monetary Unit: Singapore dollar (2.1875 S. dollars equal U.S.$1, Oct. 20, 1982).
Gross National Product (1981 U.S.$): $12,400,000,-000.
Economic Index (1981): *Consumer Prices* (1978= 100), *all items*, 122.1; *food*, 121.3.
Foreign Trade (1981 U.S.$): *Imports*, $27,571,000,-000; *exports*, $20,993,000,000.

and foment disorder netted some party members. To stem criticism of political intent, some of those arrested were formally charged and others were released, rather than simply detained for a number of months or years as had been the practice. In September, Lim Hock Siew, who had been jailed for 15 years and had spent another 4 years restricted to a small island, was permitted to return to the main city.

As the government moved to shape future generations through its promulgation of a standard Chinese language for the Chinese majority (rather than the present potpourri of regional dialects), moral education in the schools which will present Confucianist principles for the Chinese who are not members of a world religion, and standard English against colorful local variations, newspapers carried lively debates in their letters columns. Emerging as a vocal and influential opponent of many government social policies was Toh Chin Chye, a founder of the PAP and former deputy prime minister. The government also ordered the *Straits Times* newspaper group to give up its afternoon edition, *The New Nation*, which was taken over by a rival Chinese language newspaper group. The government also made certain that its candidate was named the new head of the *Straits Times*.

Economics. Prosperity continued, but government forecasts predicted that the 10% growth rate of 1981 would decline to 5.6% in 1982. A regulation was enacted that would force the withdrawal of foreign laborers by the end of 1984.

Foreign Affairs. The Association of Southeast Asian Nations (ASEAN), especially its efforts to form a coalition against the Vietnamese-backed government in Cambodia, continued as the main orientation of Singapore's foreign policy. A visit by Vietnam's Foreign Minister Nguyen Co Thach in July culminated in a confrontation with Singapore's Foreign Minister S. Dhanabalan. It was indicated that Vietnam might support opposition elements in ASEAN nations if ASEAN continued to support anti-Vietnamese forces in Cambodia. Prime Minister Lee Kuan Yew met with President Reagan in July.

K. MULLINER, *Ohio University*

SOCIAL WELFARE

Diana Walker/Liaison

Americans frequently went to the protest lines during 1982 to demand their share of social-welfare benefits.

The intensifying worldwide recession magnified welfare problems almost everywhere during the year. In the industrial nations the most obvious effect was rising unemployment; in many less developed nations it was the reduced capacity of governments and private agencies to alleviate the plight of refugees from political turmoil and the worsened shortages of food, water, and other necessities.

The World. During the year the jobless rolls in Western Europe climbed to well above 10 million, more than 2 million above the year before,

with jobless rates in such hard hit countries as Spain and Great Britain reaching 16%. While government fiscal deficits grew rapidly in virtually every advanced industrial nation, indebtedness to foreign banks and international agencies reached catastrophic levels in such newly developing nations as Poland, Mexico, Argentina, and Brazil, exerting great strains on welfare systems that had buffered the impact of declining or disappearing incomes on the unemployed and underemployed. The relative deterioration of support in richer countries for foreign aid programs led United Nations Secretary-General Javier Pérez de Cuellar to warn at the fall convention of the Society for International Development that by the end of the decade 200 million people globally would "join the ranks of those living in absolute poverty," a category currently holding about 800 million, roughly 20% of the world population. The second annual World Food Day, sponsored by the UN Food and Agriculture Organization (FAO), the U.S. Department of Agriculture, and 262 private voluntary organizations, on October 16 called attention to the global plight of an estimated 400 to 500 million on the brink of starvation, a disproportionate number of them children.

The UN Children's Fund reported that in 1981 more than 17 million children died from hunger or related diseases. According to a study for the Worldwatch Institute, the world's infant mortality rate averaged roughly 97 per thousand, but in the poorer nations ran as high as 200 per thousand and showed some increases in such widely different societies as the USSR, Brazil, and America's Washington, DC. In the USSR during the last decade, the rate increased from 26 to 36 per thousand, three times the rate in the United States. The Washington-based Children Defense Fund warned in August that reductions in welfare programs had increased the number of Americans officially classified as poor by about 2.2 million in 1981, the highest rate in 15 years, and that most of those entering poverty were children. One in five of the American children had been classified as poor, and the numbers were growing. In late October the Ford Foundation announced its support, with grants expected to total $6 million in the next two years, for a new program to improve the health and mental development of poor children in the United States and in Third World countries. The program, called "A Fair Start for Children," emphasizes grants targeted for prenatal care, contraception, and nutrition among specific immigrant and refugee groups, for depressed areas, and for such special projects as a collaboration between medical specialists at Columbia University and those in Cuba who had achieved dramatic reductions in infant mortality from gastroenteritis, a major threat to children in the Third World.

The worsening situation for developing economies forced the Reagan administration to soften its opposition to increasing the U.S. contribution to the International Monetary Fund (IMF). At the joint meeting in September of the IMF and World Bank, representatives from the Group of 10 (the leading industrialized nations) urged the creation of a special crisis fund to meet the problems of an increasingly fragile world economy. The United States agreed, though still pressing at year's end for a modest increase rather than the doubling of quotas which other group members urged. Earlier, a U.S. Treasury Department effort to reduce by 30–45% U.S. direct contributions to development funds for low income countries came under attack from Robert S. McNamara, chairman of the Overseas Development Council and former head of the World Bank, who pointed out that the United States had fallen to the bottom of the list of 17 donor nations in the ratio of aid contributions to gross national product.

Delegates from 123 nations met in Vienna July 26–August 6 for the first United Nations World Assembly on Aging. A Plan of Action, calling for improved employment, housing, and participation in the mainstream of life for the elderly in all societies, was developed and was to be submitted to the General Assembly for review and adoption.

In Europe political disputes, sometimes involving changes in governments, increasingly centered on the issues of maintaining or reducing welfare programs. Sporadic rioting in Britain's slum district, though on a much smaller scale than in 1981, punctuated a rash of strikes, including an especially bitter one by the one million workers in health services. In the fall, a debate raged over the mounting cost of the National Health Service, which had tripled in real terms since it was established in 1948, and of social security benefits. A government-sponsored study recommended replacing the British health service with a private insurance scheme and brought an outcry that prompted Prime Minister Margaret Thatcher to disavow the study and to promise voters that the welfare state "is safe with us." Similar pressures and unresolved problems appeared in Canada, where both inflation and unemployment levels stayed above 10%.

A change in government in Germany, putting more conservative leaders in charge, led to large protest marches in November against rising unemployment and reduced public services. In France, too, the cost of increased welfare provisions which the Socialist regime had enacted in 1981 required considerable fiscal juggling and some retreat. A budget dispute in the Netherlands dissolved a coalition government and brought a shift to the right in September. The change was marked by a surge of vandalism and rioting in Amsterdam by squatters in deserted buildings calling for the government to provide additional housing, an unrelieved problem in much of Europe. Meanwhile, a new study of the Soviet population revealed that a growth in European Russia of influenza, in pandemic alcoholism, and in limits on medical care had contributed to falling birth rates, rising death rates, and a drop in male life expectancy.

Much of Asia, too, saw deteriorating conditions for ordinary people. In Japan, unemployment reached 1.5 million by year-end, and the three quarters of the labor force working outside those firms with more than 500 employees saw a reduction in living standards, continuing a trend unbroken since the 1973 oil crisis. In the Philippines, the struggle between the Catholic Church and the state over contraception and abortion grew fiercer as unemployment spread and officials expressed fears that unless the population growth was reduced shortly, the nation would become "another India." India itself had a number of protest riots over welfare issues, but had made enough progress in development to be taken off the "critical list" by the World Bank, from which it had been the largest borrower. It was Bangladesh, rather, which still had Asia's largest proportion of citizens on the verge of starvation; both the government and private agencies from many nations were seeking ways to provide aid that was more than merely palliative. In Pakistan, progress in food output was counterbalanced by the weight of more than 2 million refugees from Afghanistan. In Sri Lanka, there was a reelection of a government for a six-year term that had been dismantling many welfare programs there. In sub-Sahara Africa and much of Latin America there was little general improvement. In many instances conditions were much worse. The major positive news for those regions was the announcement of a new drug, ivermectin, for treating effectively "river blindness," a parasitic disease endemic to tropical Africa and lowland parts of equatorial Latin America.

The United States. In the United States unemployment rose gradually during 1982, reaching 10.8% in December, the highest level in 42 years. Particularly hard hit was the industrial northeastern and midwestern states. More than one half of teenage black males found no chance to get on a payroll, and on many Indian reservations the jobless rate was hitting 70% by late autumn. The loss of jobs by about eight million Americans between 1980 and 1982 also led to losses of hospital- and medical-insurance coverage for about 16 million, with the consequent postponement of treatment when possible and rising claims on public facilities when not.

The "new federalism" program submitted by President Reagan was attacked in a study by the National Black Child Development Institute. The study, released in the summer, indicated that the plan would cut child-welfare programs 30%, deprive as many as three million children (one third of them black) of remedial-education services, and change the eligibility requirements for food stamps, medicaid, and Aid to Families with Dependent Children. There was a consider-

© John Hillery/Picture Group

The U.S. government offered surplus cheese and butter, bought to maintain dairy prices, to low-income Americans.

which each major party sought to exploit, with mixed success. The nagging short-term problem of a cash shortage in the Old Age and Survivors Insurance (OASI) funds was twice relieved during the year by Congress granting authority to borrow from the Medicaid and Disability funds, temporarily averting the suspension of payments for the last two months of the year. The National Commission on Social Security Reform was scheduled to submit its report by Dec. 31, 1982, but was given a 15-day extension. The new session of Congress was expected to be embroiled in choosing between various options. To increase revenues, hard hit by the recession as well as the shrinking number of contributors relative to retirees, there were proposals to extend coverage more universally. But the main thrust was toward reducing the outflow by changing the cost of living adjustment formula, raising the retirement age, and reducing benefits for those who choose to retire early. Meanwhile, resentment grew over the stricter rules for disability insurance claims on the system. Some 400,000 cases were reviewed between March 1981 and April 1982, with 190,948 recipients declared ineligible. Just as critical for many observers was the obsolescence of the record-keeping machinery of the Social Security Administration, whose antiquated computers were making it difficult to provide more than basic services for the 36 million recipients.

A study by Data Resources, Inc. for the National Association of Retired Persons claimed that proposed cost of living adjustments would push up to 1.2 million elderly people below the poverty line. Meanwhile, the relatively new federal insurance plan for private pensions was running into similar trouble, due to a growing number of under-funded pension plans, often abandoned as firms sell off their subsidiaries. One reduction in costs to the federal government came in the tax bill compromise of August, which trimmed the Medicare program for those over 65 by imposing strict new controls on payments to hospitals. Congress also authorized state governments to charge small fees for most services they provide under Medicaid.

The Villers Foundation began operating in 1982 to support research, programs, and lobbying activity on behalf of the aged poor. Yet a study, released in October by ICF, inc., for the American Council on Life Insurance, confirmed the rather rosy general picture of retirees in the United States contained in the final report of the 1981 White House Conference on Aging, which concluded that the nation had the "wealthiest, best-fed, best-housed, healthiest, most self-reliant older population in our history." The study nevertheless called for more geriatric day-care on the British model, for more emphasis on gerontology as a field of medicine, and for tax incentives for home-care programs.

able retreat from that set of proposals during the summer, but even more reversal over jobs, as one state after another exhausted their unemployment insurance funds and new jobless claims continued to rise. On September 3, President Reagan signed a bill extending unemployment insurance for the estimated 2.2 million who had exhausted their eligibility, in effect canceling scheduled cuts in benefits and eligibility levels. In October, he signed a bill to provide retraining for about 1 million workers, taking up some of the slack in such efforts created by the death of the Comprehensive Employment and Training Act (CETA) program.

Besides jobs, the other major social welfare issue in the election year was Social Security,

MORTON ROTHSTEIN
University of Wisconsin-Madison

SOUTH AFRICA

Fundamental political realignments took place in South Africa in 1982, resulting in the first major split in Afrikaner solidarity since the National party came to power in 1948. The division was caused by proposed constitutional reforms intended to partially incorporate the Coloured and Indian population into the political process.

In February, Prime Minister P. W. Botha confronted Dr. Andries P. Treurnicht, the minister for statistics and state administration, who for some time had challenged Botha's leadership of the ruling National party and his proposed racial reforms. Treurnicht, an advocate of the extreme right wing of the party, opposed the proposed shifts in policy, which he claimed would fundamentally alter race relations in South Africa. At a meeting of the Transvaal branch of the National Party, Treurnicht was removed from the party's executive committee and a vote of confidence in Botha's leadership was passed.

As a result of the split in the National party, the government for the first time had formal opposition to its right in Parliament. Sixteen members of the House of Assembly—including two cabinet ministers, Treurnicht, and Minister of Education Ferdinand Hartzenberg—resigned from the party. On March 20, Treurnicht founded a new political party, the Conservative party, which was opposed to racial integration.

Constitutional Reforms. On July 31, Prime Minister Botha received unanimous endorsement for proposed constitutional changes from a special federal congress of the National party, meeting in Bloemfontein. Botha called a national congress of the party, the first in 20 years and the third in the history of the party, to win support for these proposals, which he viewed as a significant program of reform. The congress also was summoned in an effort to rally support in areas known to be strongholds of Andrias Treurnicht.

The new proposals called for the establishment of three separate parliaments, one each for whites, Coloureds, and Indians or Asians. (South Africa contains some 4.5 million whites, 2.5 million Coloureds, and 800,000 Indians. The more than 16 million blacks, who comprise 70% of the population, would not be given a separate parliament under the plan.) Differences among the parliaments would be debated by multiracial committees, which would seek a consensus. If a consensus could not be reached, the existing multiracial President's Council would make a final decision, which would be binding on the president.

Considerable power would be concentrated in an executive president, who would have a fixed five-year term of office. Proponents argued that a strong presidency would enable a leader to move decisively in enacting racial reforms. Those opposed feared the danger of a dictatorship. The president would be elected by a multiracial electoral college consisting of members of the parliaments. Whites would be in the majority in the electoral college and in the President's Council.

The proposals were severely criticized by the Conservative party, the Progressives, and African leaders. Chief Gatsha Buthelezi, chief minister of KwaZulu, condemned the plan for excluding blacks. The government argued that Africans have representation through the "homelands."

Germiston By-Election. In August the National party narrowly avoided defeat in a by-election for a seat on the provincial council for Germiston, near Johannesburg. Two parties to the right of the National party did surprisingly well. Andries P. Treurnicht's newly formed Conservative Party polled 3,559 votes, while the Herstigte Nasionale party (HNP) received 1,638 votes. The National Party received 3,867 votes.

Ceding of Homelands. Early in June the South African government decided to cede the KaNgwane "homeland" and parts of KwaZulu to Swaziland. By doing this, South Africa hoped to draw Swaziland into its regional organization of homelands, the "Constellation of States." The inclusion in the organization of a sovereign, independent state with international recognition would give legitimacy to South Africa's homeland policy. In addition, the action would enhance Swaziland's strategic importance as a buffer between South Africa and the more radical regime in Mozambique. It also would decrease the black-white population ratio in South Africa, since 900,000 Africans would automatically lose their South African citizenship if the transfer took place. Landlocked Swaziland would gain a coastline and the possibility of developing a port of its own. Its population would be more than doubled by the change.

In September, South Africa's highest court, the Appeals Court, issued a ruling that at least temporarily blocked ceding the territory to Swaziland. The decision was in many ways a victory for Chief Gatsha Buthelezi of KwaZulu because

---

SOUTH AFRICA • Information Highlights

Official Name: Republic of South Africa.
Location: Southern tip of Africa.
Area: 471,445 sq mi (1 221 043 km^2).
Population (1980 census): 23,771,970.
Chief Cities (1980 census): Pretoria, the administrative capital, 528,407; Cape Town, the legislative capital, 213,830; Johannesburg, 1,536,457; Durban, 505,963.
Government: *Head of state,* Marais Viljoen, president (took office June 1979). *Head of government,* P. W. Botha, prime minister (took office Sept. 1978). *Legislature*—Parliament: President Council and House of Assembly.
Monetary Unit: Rand (1.1659 rands equal U.S.$1, Nov. 1, 1982).
Gross Domestic Product (1981 U.S.$): $81,100,000,-000.
Economic Index (1980): *Consumer Prices* (1970= 100), *all items,* 277.1; *food,* 314.5.

Damage is extensive following a confrontation between striking black miners and security forces in South Africa.

he had brought the government to court based on laws that originally established the homelands. The Appeals Court judges ruled that the creation of the "self-governing" homelands meant that the homeland leaders should be consulted on such fundamental questions.

Economy. In June 1982 the price of gold fell to less than $300 an ounce. It later recovered somewhat, but at no time approached its high boom price of $875 an ounce in January 1981. Gold accounts for nearly half of South Africa's export earnings as well as a significant proportion of South Africa's tax revenues. Other major exports, such as manganese and diamonds, also brought low returns. In addition, South Africa's maize crop suffered from a severe drought.

All of this placed pressure on South Africa's balance-of-payments situation (there was a $4,000,000,000 deficit in 1981) and made it necessary for South Africa to borrow in the international market. In early November the International Monetary Fund agreed to lend South Africa $1,100,000,000.

During the year the South African rand fell substantially in relation to the U.S. dollar; it was quoted at $0.85 in early November. The inflation rate was running between 15% and 16%.

Social Issues. In July black miners at the West Rand mining complex refused to go to work because of a dispute over a low pay increase. A confrontation lasting several days developed between the workers and the mines' internal security forces. Ten workers died and 300 were arrested. Eventually, thousands of workers were dismissed from their jobs. Similar crises developed at several other mines. The salaries of black workers average about $216 a month, while those of white workers average $1,080.

Guerrilla activities continued during the year. Government offices, fuel depots, and power lines were bombed in the days preceding the June 16 anniversary of the 1976 Soweto riots. The African National Congress (ANC) was assumed to be responsible.

On February 5, Dr. Neil Aggett, a 28-year-old white physician who became an organizer of a black trade union, died while in police custody. In a statement written before his death, Aggett described harsh police torture. Allegations of police abuse were admitted as evidence in a subsequent court investigation of his death.

In June the government decided not to implement plans to control the press through required licensing of journalists. Nonetheless, newspapers were required to monitor themselves by establishing a media council and submitting to its code of conduct.

Namibia. Over the course of the year, hopes for independence for Namibia waned. The Reagan administration linked the settlement to the withdrawal of 20,000 Cuban troops and advisers from Angola, a contingency that South Africa considered nonnegotiable.

See also AFRICA.

PATRICK O'MEARA
Africa Studies Program, Indiana University

SOUTH CAROLINA

Sen. Ernest F. Hollings (D) was a leading critic of Reagan budget policy and the "dense pack" MX missile proposal. In August he addressed the Sheet Metal Workers' Union convention in New York, which some called a preview of the 1984 presidential election because it featured seven potential candidates.

UPI

In South Carolina elections, Democratic Gov. Richard W. Riley was reelected over Republican William D. Workman, Jr., by a 69.8% majority. A 1981 constitutional amendment permits the governor to serve a second consecutive four-year term.

Government. Democrats made two significant gains in the elections, rewinning the sixth congressional district and defeating incumbent Republican Agriculture Commissioner G. Bryan Patrick, Jr. Blacks won five additional seats in the House of Representatives and the Republicans two. The state-adopted congressional reapportionment plan was adjusted by the federal court to provide a better racial and population distribution.

The recession caused state expenditures to be reduced twice during the year. Governor Riley vetoed numerous provisions increasing expenditures for 1982-83, including salary raises for state employees. Conflict arose between the Supreme Court and the legislature over rule-making and the establishment of an intermediate court of appeals.

The general assembly strengthened laws pertaining to alcohol and drug abuse, arson, and theft, and provided for a victim compensation act permitting awards of up to $10,000. It reaffirmed the application of reassessed property values to 1982 taxes, providing a reduction for industries. The electorate defeated a constitutional amendment that would have allowed municipalities to grant new industries a five-year tax exemption.

Economy. The recession hit South Carolina very hard, as evidenced by reduced tax collections, an unemployment rate higher than the national average, and the permanent closing of numerous textile plants. Even so, capital invested in new industry matched the 1981 amount. Foreign industrial investments equaled about 20% of the total. Substantially fewer jobs were created, however. Several mergers were effected among savings and loan institutions. Development of downtown complexes continued in Greenville, Charleston, and Columbia.

The agricultural year was unimpressive, producing only half the normal crop of peaches and average soybean yields. Tobacco prices increased and wheat acreage grew by one third.

The disposal of low-level nuclear waste in South Carolina was a major issue, and the state joined the Southeast Low-Level Nuclear Waste Compact. Regulations governing nuclear waste disposal and toxic chemical plants were more strictly enforced. Plans for two nuclear power plants were canceled, but authorization was given for a major new facility to begin operation.

Education. Reduced revenue was a source of concern for both higher and public educational institutions. Controversies developed over the

---

SOUTH CAROLINA • Information Highlights

Area: 31,113 sq mi (80 583 km²).
Population (1980 census): 3,121,833.
Chief Cities (1980 census): Columbia, the capital, 100,385; Charleston, 69,510; Greenville, 58,242.
Government (1982): *Chief Officers*—governor, Richard W. Riley (D); lt. gov., Nancy Stevenson (D). *General Assembly*—Senate, 46 members; House of Representatives, 124 members.
State Finances (fiscal year 1981): *Revenues,* $3,948,-000,000; *expenditures,* $3,952,000,000.
Personal Income (1981): $25,457,000,000; per capita, $8,039.
Labor Force (Aug. 1982): *Nonagricultural wage and salary earners,* 1,164,100; *unemployed,* 167,700 (11.3% of total force).
Education: *Enrollment* (fall 1981)—public elementary schools, 420,664; public secondary, 188,494; colleges and universities (1981–82), 132,394 students. *Public school expenditures* (1980–81), $1,-028,628,000 ($1,560 per pupil).

retrenchment of higher education programs, the appointment of blacks to college boards, and tuition charges. Former federal Energy Secretary James B. Edwards assumed the presidency of the Medical University of South Carolina.

Although SAT scores increased, South Carolina students continued to fall near the bottom of national rankings. The state continued to stress kindergarten programs and the measurement of achievement in selected grades. Overall, achievement scores improved, but reflected major deficiencies. Additional districts began to require minimum achievement scores before promoting students. Salary raises were granted to public school teachers.

Social and Cultural Issues. Medicaid rules for nursing homes were revised, saving the state money. Overcrowding in the state correctional system remained a major problem; a plan to increase the number of parolees was stymied by the courts. Keen competition surfaced for development of new authorized hospital facilities.

Tourism flourished, especially in the coastal areas, and state facilities were expanded significantly. However, the water quality of the major recreational lakes deteriorated.

ROBERT H. STOUDEMIRE
University of South Carolina

SOUTH DAKOTA

Republicans held an advantage in the November elections, with approximately 5% more registered Republican than Democratic voters. Gov. William Janklow was especially strong, and he was elected to a second term with a record 71% of the vote. His record of achievement in the attraction of clean industry, the revival of railroad transportation, the development of water resources, and restraint in spending earned him wide support. Lowell Hansen II was chosen lieutenant governor, Alice Kundert secretary of state, David Volk treasurer, and Mark Meierhenry attorney general. Republicans enlarged their majorities in the state legislature to 54 (R) to 16 (D) for the house and 26 (R) to 9 (D) for the senate. Among Democrats, only Congressman Tom Daschle led a Republican in the polls for high office. He defeated Clint Roberts for the state's single seat in the U.S. House of Representatives.

Legislation. Restraint on spending by majority Republicans drew criticism from minority Democrats. Democrats charged that road repairs, tax reforms, and other urgent needs were shortchanged. Yet all members took credit for voting a record $796 million for fiscal year 1982–83, making no substantial tax increases, and providing adequately for normal state operations, while maintaining a balanced budget.

Economy. The economy, on the whole, was stable. Unemployment declined from 4.4% as the year opened to 4.3% in August. The state's economy continued to depend on agriculture, tourism, small industry, and the professions. Personal income increased by 8.6%.

Many farmers suffered gravely, however, because of a decline in the prices of all farm products except hogs and cattle. Most farmers harvested bumper crops, despite late plantings because of spring rains and acreage losses caused by summer weather damage. Yet high production costs, high interest rates, and sagging prices caused by large yields brought a substantial percentage of farmers to the brink of bankruptcy. Various remedial plans were proposed and pursued. Democratic gubernatorial candidate Mike O'Connor proposed a regional cartel with other agrarian states to drive up farm prices by withholding agricultural products from the market. Farm organization leaders outlined programs of narrower scope to achieve the same end.

Urban workers enjoyed better conditions, yet there were strikes by the United Steelworkers Union against the Homestake Mining Company and by the United Food and Commercial Workers Union International against the John Morrell and Company packing plant.

Native Americans. Distress unparalleled since the 1920s came to most reservations, where reductions in federal housing and job training programs drove unemployment up to levels between 75% and 90%. Tensions mounted near Yellow Thunder Indian Camp, where American Indian Movement spokesmen continued their demand for the return of the Black Hills to the Sioux.

Missouri River Water Controversy. Environmentalists, Sioux leaders, and officials in states downstream all registered protests as Governor Janklow—having won federal approval for water sales—concluded a long-term agreement with private industry to supply as much as 16,-300,000,000 gallons (61,702,020,000 liters) of river water a year to operate a crushed coal slurry line from Wyoming to Oklahoma and Arkansas.

HERBERT T. HOOVER
University of South Dakota

SOUTH DAKOTA · Information Highlights

Area: 77,116 sq mi (199 730 km²).
Population (1980 census): 690,768.
Chief Cities (1980 census): Pierre, the capital, 11,973; Sioux Falls, 81,343; Rapid City, 46,492.
Government (1982): *Chief Officers*—governor, William J. Janklow (R); lt. gov., Lowell C. Hansen II (R). *Legislature*—Senate, 35 members; House of Representatives, 70 members.
State Finances (fiscal year 1981): *Revenues,* $805,-000,000; *expenditures,* $836,000,000.
Personal Income (1981): $6,056,000,000; per capita, $8,833.
Labor Force (Aug. 1982): *Nonagricultural wage and salary earners,* 231,700; *unemployed,* 14,400 (4.3% of total force).
Education: *Enrollment* (fall 1981)—public elementary schools, 85,887; public secondary, 39,770; colleges and universities (1981–82), 35,015 students. *Public school expenditures* (1980–81), $273,500,-000 ($1,995 per pupil).

SPACE EXPLORATION

Thomas K. Mattingly 2d, STS 4 crew commander, prepares a meal in the mid-deck area of Columbia.

The year 1982 marked the 25th anniversary of Sputnik, the first man-made earth satellite, which was launched on Oct. 4, 1957. During 1982 the USSR launched and manned an improved space station, Salyut 7, to a new manned endurance record of 211 days. The U.S. space shuttle *Columbia* completed its development phase and conducted its first operational mission designated as Space Transportation System 5 (STS 5) with four astronauts aboard. In interplanetary space exploration, the USSR landed two probes on Venus and the U.S. Voyager 2 continued on its course toward encounters with Uranus in 1986 and Neptune in 1989.

Manned Space Flight. The U.S. space shuttle *Columbia* conducted three missions in 1982 to complete the test series of flights and initiate the operational phase. The STS 3 mission was launched with the orbiter *Columbia* from Kennedy Space Center on March 22, commanded by Col. Jack R. Lousma and piloted by Col. C. Gordon Fullerton. *Columbia* landed successfully at White Sands Missile Range, NM, on March 30. STS 3 carried an Office of Space Science (OSS 1) payload, which supported investigations in space plasma physics, solar physics, astronomy, life sciences, and space technology.

The final test of shuttle operational readiness was successfully completed with the STS 4 mission. The shuttle orbiter *Columbia* was again employed for this mission, which was launched from Kennedy Space Center on June 27 and made the first landing on a hard-surface runway at Edwards Air Force Base on July 4.

The STS 4 crew commander, Thomas K. Mattingly 2d, and pilot, Henry W. Hartsfield, Jr., were greeted by President Reagan on their return. The president summarized the significance of the STS 4 mission on the 206th anniversary of America's independence when he said: "The fourth landing of the *Columbia* is the historic equivalent to the driving of the golden spike which completed the first transcontinental railroad. It marks our entrance into a new era. The test flights are over. The groundwork has been laid. And now we will move forward to capitalize on the tremendous potential offered by the ultimate frontier of space.... We must look aggressively to the future by demonstrating the potential of the shuttle and establishing a more permanent presence in space."

Two anomalies occurred during the mission: the failure of the solid rocket booster deceleration system during the launch, and the inability to operate one of the payloads during the flight. An unmanned tethered robotic underwater ocean vehicle was used by NASA to assist in the recovery of the parachute mechanisms and flight data recorded from the sunken boosters in order to conduct a failure analysis.

The principal cargo aboard STS 4 consisted of a Department of Defense payload, a cryogenic infrared telescope. Unfortunately the payload could not be operated properly because the protective cover would not open. Other experiments included a NASA-industry-sponsored continuous-flow electrophoresis system to separate biological materials in a fluid in zero gravity according to their surface electrical charge. NASA's first "get-away special," a 5-cubic-foot (0.14-m^3) payload canister, was also flown in support of nine experiments constructed by Utah State University students.

STS 5 was launched on November 11 as the first operational shuttle mission with four astronauts aboard the *Columbia* orbiter: Vance D. Brand, commander; Robert F. Overmyer, copilot; William B. Lenoir, electrical engineer; and Joseph P. Allen, physicist. STS 5 carried two spin-stabilized communication satellites, Satellite Business Systems' SBS 3 and Telesat Canada's Anik C, valued at approximately $30 million each. These satellites, weighing approximately 7,200 lbs (1,452 kg) each, were spun up to 50 revolutions per minute and ejected from the payload bay. Solid rocket propellant Payload Assist Modules (PAM) were used to boost the satellites from 185 mi (300 km) to a geosynchronous altitude of 22,300 mi (36,000 km). These spacecraft contained individual apogee kick motors to place them in circular orbit. The launch of these satellites marked a first-time use of the space shuttle for launching and deploying free-flying satellites.

In August, Svetlana Savitskaya, a 34-year-old Soviet test pilot, became the second woman to orbit the earth.

Tass from Sovfoto

Astronauts Allen and Lenoir were scheduled to conduct extravehicular activity (EVA) on STS 5. However, malfunctions in the new pressurized suits that contained integral life-support systems caused the space walks to be canceled. The solid rocket boosters were successfully recovered after launch and STS 5 completed its first operational mission on November 16.

The Soviet Union's highly successful Salyut 6 space station ended almost five years of operation on July 29 with a destructive reentry over the Pacific Ocean. The Salyut 6 had 23 dockings of Soyuz vehicles from five basic expeditions and 11 visiting missions, and 12 dockings of Progress supply craft during its operational life, which began in September 1977. Salyut 6 was manned for 676 days by 27 cosmonauts, with 185 of those days occupied continuously by Leonid Popov and Valeri Ryumin for a manned space record. Cosmos 1267, a prototype space station module, was docked with Salyut 6 for more than a year, during which time it was successfully tested for use with Salyut 7.

The new modular space station, Salyut 7, was launched on April 19, 1982, to an altitude of 186 mi (300 km). The new space station was manned by cosmonauts Lt. Col. Anatoly Berezovoy, commander, and Valentin Lebedev, flight engineer, who were launched in a Soyuz T-5 spacecraft on May 13 and docked with Salyut 7 on May 14. The cosmonauts were resupplied by an unmanned Progress 13 supply craft, which was launched on May 23 and docked on May 25. Progress 13 carried more than 4,400 lbs (2,000 kg) of supplies to Salyut 7 in preparation for another cosmonaut team: Jean-Loup Chrétien of France, copilot, and Soviet members Vladimir Dzhanibekov, pilot, and Aleksandr Ivanchenkov, flight engineer. This international team utilized a Soyuz T-6 spacecraft for their one-week visit that began with launch on June 24, docking on June 25, and successful return on July 2. Their visit coincided with the fourth launch of the U.S. space shuttle *Columbia,* although no contact was made between the orbiting astronauts and cosmonauts. The team carried a number of experiments aboard Alyut 7, among them various French metal alloy samples for the Soviet magma furnace aboard the space station.

A Progress 14 supply craft was launched on July 12, docking with Salyut 7 on July 13, to prepare for the next group of visiting cosmonauts. This team consisted of the second woman to orbit the earth, Svetlana Savitskaya, accompanied by Commander Leonid Popov and Flight Engineer Aleksandr Serebrov. They were launched aboard Soyuz T-7 on August 19, docked with Salyut 7 on August 20, and returned in the Soyuz T-5 spacecraft on August 27. The switch in returning spacecraft allowed cosmonauts Berezovoy and Lebedev to use the newer Soyuz T-7 for their return. One hundred days in orbit is considered maximum for a qualified reentry vehicle.

Cosmonauts Berezovoy and Lebedev returned to earth in the Soyuz T-7 spacecraft on December 10 after a continuous stay of 211 days aboard the Salyut 7 space station.

Planetary Probes. U.S. spacecraft Voyager 1 and 2, Pioneer Venus Orbiter, Pioneer probes 6–11, and Viking Lander 2 all continued successful operation in extended mission modes.

Voyager 2 continued toward an encounter with Uranus in 1986 and Neptune in 1989. Analysis of Saturn 1981 flyby data revealed the presence of four—and possibly six—new satellites of that planet. These discoveries bring the number of known Saturnian satellites to between 21 and 23. Analysis has also identified an extremely hot plasma zone near Saturn. Temperatures in a region from 170,000 mi (274,000 km) to 450,000 mi (724,000 km) altitude above Saturn were found to be 300 million to 500 million degrees centigrade (540 million to 900 million degrees Fahrenheit), or about 300 times hotter than the solar corona.

Voyager 2 passed safely through this corona because of its extremely low density of 30 particles per cubic foot (1,000 particles per cubic meter). This region was previously identified by Pioneer 11 and Voyager 1 as a relatively "cold" plasma with temperatures of a few million degrees and densities a thousand times those identified by Voyager 2. There is presently no obvious explanation for the heating mechanism of this gas.

The USSR continued a more detailed investigation of Venus, utilizing two probes, Venera 13 and 14, which were launched Oct. 30 and Nov. 4, 1981, and parachute-landed on March 1 and 5, 1982. The previous spacecrafts to study Venus were the USSR's Venera 11 and 12, which landed on the planet in December 1978, and the U.S. Pioneer Venus 1 and 2, which orbited the planet and deployed probes also in December 1978. A camera and moisture meter aboard the Venera 13 lander took color pictures for 127 minutes and reported a very low water vapor content of less than 0.1% in the atmosphere of Venus. This contrasted with U.S. findings, which indicated a higher water vapor content. Inert gases of neon, krypton, and possibly xenon also were discovered in an atmosphere that is composed principally of carbon dioxide. This confirmed previous U.S. Pioneer Venus findings. Venera 14 operated for about an hour on the planet and found surface temperatures of 465° C (870° F) with a pressure of 94 atmospheres. Approximately 40 spectra were obtained from Venusian soil samples.

On Mars, the Thomas Mutch Memorial Station (Viking Lander 1) continued to operate satisfactorily in automatic mode, collecting and storing data on seven-day cycles. Analysis of Viking photos and data from Mars has indicated evidence of surface water in the form of ground ice, indications that north polar cap layers influence climate as on earth, and recognition of sea-

Conestoga I, *a rocket built privately for commercial use, underwent a successful suborbital test flight in Texas.*

sonal variations such as cloud forms and motion, frost accumulation, and temperature and pressure variations.

Scientific Satellites. The existence of a polar wind has been proved by measurements from the U.S. Dynamics Explorer (DE) satellites launched in 1981. The polar wind is a flow of particles from the ionosphere into space.

The DE satellites used three retarding-ion mass spectrometers, which enabled the satellite to make measurements in all directions, including the earth-facing or polar wind side. The spectrometer recorded hydrogen and helium ions flowing upward at the predicted speed of 22,000 mph (10 km/sec). Surprisingly, ions were also seen above the polar cap flowing at 112,000 mph (50 km/sec). The origin and cause of this unexpected phenomenon are not yet understood.

The International Sun Earth Explorer (ISEE 3) is being maneuvered to intercept the Comet Giacobini-Zinner at a distance of 44 million mi (71 million km) from the earth in 1985.

The International Ultraviolet Explorer (IUE)

satellite, which is orbiting the earth between 15,500 and 28,000 mi (25,000 and 45,000 km) altitude, was used to acquire imagery in the ultraviolet spectrum of Comet Austin, which entered our solar system in 1982, passing closest to the earth on August 10 and closest to the sun on August 24. This was expected to reveal details of the comet's composition. IUE images will be complemented by ground-based telescope observations.

These data will be compared with Comet Halley observations, which will be acquired by an international group of scientists with ground-based telescopes and satellite platforms in 1985–1986. It is hoped that ISEE 3 and Pioneer satellites may be used to assist in this measurement program.

The Solar Maximum Mission (SMM) spacecraft, launched in 1980, has detected an 18-month decrease in the sun's energy output. The Active Cavity Radiometer Irradiance Monitor experiment was used to detect a reduction of 0.1% in the total amount of solar energy reaching the earth. This reduction was detected from February 1980 to August 1981 and presents a possible explanation of the recent harsh winter and the relationship between the sun's energy output and changes in the earth's weather and climate. The earth's climate is very sensitive to changes in the solar output and resultant earth surface temperature. The SMM has been operating in a degraded mode after only 10 months of normal operation because of an attitude-control system malfunction. The SMM was designed to be serviced by the space shuttle, and a repair mission has been under consideration.

Earth Observation Satellites. The highlight of 1982 was the successful launch of Landsat 4, the fourth in a series of experimental earth-resources remote-sensing satellites. Landsat 4 was launched from the Western Test Range by a Delta launch vehicle on July 16. The spacecraft is the most complex and advanced land-observing satellite launched by NASA. Its orbit enables it to view the entire cloud-free land surface of the earth every 16 days from its 438-mi (705-km) polar sun synchronous orbit. Landsat 4 complements Landsat 3, launched in 1978 and operating in a degraded mode in 1982.

The Thematic Mapper (TM) aboard Landsat 4 represents the first significant advancement in sensing capability since 1972, when Landsat 1 was launched with the Multispectral Scanner (MSS). The MSS operated in four visible near-infrared wavelengths, from 0.5 to 1.1 micrometers with 80-m (263-ft) spatial resolution. The TM is operating in seven wavelengths through the visible near-infrared, shortwave-infrared, and thermal-infrared bands from 0.45 to 12.5 micrometers at 30-m (98-ft) spatial resolution. This increased capability should significantly improve our ability to classify and monitor the earth's surface cover. It represents a significant improvement over the MSS capability and should pro-

vide insights heretofore unavailable because of the broader spectral coverage.

Landsat data have been used for scientific investigations in botany, hydrology, geology, and geography. These investigations have supported many applications in agricultural crop forecasting and condition monitoring, forest inventory and condition assessment, range-forage assessment, land-cover classification, urban-area delineation, wetlands and irrigated lands mapping, and geologic mapping.

Landsat 4 carries both the MSS and TM sensors. This will afford an opportunity for researchers and resource managers to make an orderly transition to the new TM data, which will contain almost ten times the amount of data per scene as was obtained by the MSS. The Landsat 4 spacecraft uses the same bus as the SMM.

Approximately six months after launch, the operation of the satellite and the MSS was turned over to the National Oceanographic and Atmospheric Administration (NOAA). NASA will continue to operate the experimental TM and will develop techniques to extract information from the data. The TM operation is scheduled to be turned over to NOAA in 1985. A second satellite, Landsat D, is being held in ground storage to back up Landsat 4 in the event of a failure or to continue data acquisition after the end of Landsat 4's useful life.

Communications Satellites. During 1982 the United States launched nine communications satellites; the USSR, eight; and India, one. Two communication satellites were launched by Delta vehicles for the Radio Corporation of America—RCA-C on January 15 and RCA-E on November 18. Westar IV and V were launched by Delta vehicles on February 25 and June 8 for the Western Union Company. Two Intelsat communication satellites were launched by Atlas Centaur vehicles for the International Telecommunications Satellite Organization: Intelsat V-D on March 4 and Intelsat V-E on September 23. Telesat satellites were launched for Canada on August 26 by a Delta vehicle and on November 12 by the space shuttle STS 5. A Satellite Business Systems (SBS 3) communication satellite also was launched by STS 5 on November 11.

A Delta vehicle was used also to launch an Indian National Satellite System (INSAT 1A) on April 10. This multipurpose telecommunications-meteorology spacecraft was designed to provide for nationwide direct broadcasting to community TV receivers in rural areas. Unfortunately the satellite failed 150 days after launch.

Civilian communications satellites launched by the USSR in 1982 included three Molniya 1 satellites on February 26, March 24, and May 29; two EKRAN (STRATSIONAR-T) on February 5 and September 16; Gorizont on March 15 and October 21; and a radio ham communication satellite, ISKRA 2, on May 17.

MICHAEL A. CALABRESE

SPAIN

A sweeping victory by the Socialist Workers Party in the parliamentary elections of October 1982 has changed the political course of Spain's young experiment in democracy, which began after the death of Generalissimo Francisco Franco in 1975. The decisive shift to the left excited fears that diehard civilian backers of the deceased dictator and their military supporters might attempt a coup d'etat to reverse the outcome of the elections.

Politics and Government. Headed by Felipe González Márquez, a boyishly handsome 40-year-old lawyer, the Socialists captured more than 45% of the vote on October 28 to win 201 seats in the 350-member national parliament (Cortés), as well as 134 of the 208 seats in the largely ceremonial Senate. (*See* BIOGRAPHY—González Márquez, Felipe.)

The triumph for the Socialists, who for 40 years in exile had opposed Franco's repressively authoritarian regime, came largely at the expense of the Communists, who lost 18 of their 22 seats, and the centrist Union of the Democratic Center (UDC), whose legislative representation plunged from 167 to 12 seats. The badly fragmented UDC was all but eliminated as a political force as voters ousted Prime Minister Leopoldo Calvo Sotelo, 11 other ministers, and the party's secretary general. Communist Party leader Santiago Carrillo Solares resigned after the election defeat and was replaced by Gerardo Iglesias.

The right-wing Popular Alliance, led by ex-Francoist minister Manuel Fraga Iribarne, staged an impressive comeback, electing 106 deputies and converting Spain into a virtual two-party system. The 59-year-old Fraga attracted support from rural areas, business organizations, and army officers.

The magnetic personality of González, who took office in December as his country's first Socialist prime minister since before the civil war of the 1930s, helped trigger his party's landslide. Also important was a moderate platform that avoided pledges to nationalize banks or industry, with the sole exception of the national power grid. The Socialists promised to create 800,000 jobs in four years—a modest target in view of the widespread unemployment afflicting the country. Greater controversy surrounded the goal of reforming the armed forces, with advancement based on merit and performance, rather than on seniority.

The prospect of a Socialist victory nourished rumors that the army would seize power. Indeed, just before campaigning began, three colonels were arrested for plotting a putsch. Although the balloting took place peaceably, the postelection assassination of the nation's top field general, Gen. Victor Lago Román—allegedly carried out by Basque terrorists—appeared designed to destabilize a fragile democracy that King Juan Carlos, as head of the armed forces, has worked tirelessly to preserve.

During his historic visit to Spain from October 31 to November 9, Pope John Paul II condemned violence and emphasized the importance of strengthening democratic principles.

Economy. A severe recession enhanced González's electoral appeal. The increase in gross national product rose from 0.4% in 1981 to approximately 2.5% in 1982, while the rate of inflation dipped from 15% to 13%.

Still, one in six workers remained unemployed—Western Europe's highest rate in 1982. This situation inspired a three-part program, announced in April, to spur development and create jobs. The effort involved providing $1,100,000,000 in credits to promote exports; establishing a new agency to reduce impediments to exports; and launching a major government investment program to build highways, railroads, agricultural facilities, and other projects.

Dependence on oil imports has exacerbated Spain's economic problems. A national energy plan, revised at the end of 1981, called for the country to produce 50% of all energy requirements domestically by 1985, with emphasis on coal, nuclear, and hydro power.

Foreign Relations. González has expressed misgivings about Spain's affiliation with NATO, which occurred in May. He has advocated a referendum on whether Spain should assume a relationship with the alliance similar to that of France—namely, membership without participation in allied military planning or exercises.

Officials in Washington predict "long, hard bargaining" with the Socialist regime to retain air bases at Torrejón and Zaragoza and a naval base at Rota. González has stressed his desire to renegotiate the five-year leases under which the United States operates these facilities. The Socialists seem less enthusiastic than the outgoing UDC government in promoting Spain's membership in the European Community.

GEORGE W. GRAYSON
College of William and Mary

SPAIN · Information Highlights

Official Name: Spanish State.
Location: Iberian Peninsula in southwestern Europe.
Area: 194,897 sq mi (504 783 km^2).
Population (1982 est.): 37,900,000.
Chief Cities (1982 est.): Madrid, the capital, 3,271,-834; Barcelona, 1,720,998; Valencia 770,277.
Government: *Head of state,* Juan Carlos 1, king (took office Nov. 1975). *Head of government,* Felipe González Márquez, prime minister (took office Dec. 1982). *Legislature*—Cortés: Senate and Chamber of Deputies.
Monetary Unit: Peseta (120.5 pesetas equal U.S.$1, Nov. 15, 1982).
Gross Domestic Product (1981 U.S.$): $191,700,-000,000.
Economic Indexes (1981): *Consumer Prices* (1970= 100), *all items,* 474.8; *food,* 423.6. *Industrial production* (Nov. 1981, 1975=100), 124.
Foreign Trade (1981 U.S.$): *Imports,* $32,159,000,-000; *exports,* $20,338,000,000.

SPORTS

© Duomo

At the World Cup soccer tournament in Spain, Italy defeated West Germany, 3-1, for the championship. Italy's Paolo Rossi (20), who netted the first goal of the match and led the tournament in scoring, became a national hero.

The Year in Review

Both for better and for worse, the 1982 sports year was one of repeats. In actual competition, past champions gave refreshing encore performances. But in the latest installment of the *Wide World of Money,* there was no thrill of victory, only the agony of another strike.

Lest any fan had doubts about what the national pastime really is—football, baseball, or labor negotiation—NFL players followed close on the heels of their baseball brethren by calling a strike after the second week of the season. Much like the diamond walkout of 1981, the football strike involved union demands which few fans understood—or cared about. "It's a matter of dignity," said Gene Upshaw, president of the NFL Players Association.

On the fields and courts, dignity of a different kind did show itself time and again. Teams and individuals who had won in the past put on inspired performances to retain their titles, make comebacks, or even exceed previous successes.

In *real* football—soccer—1982 was a World Cup year. Italy, which had won the tournament in 1934 and 1938 but was considered an underdog in 1982, captured its third championship, tying the record. In the North American Soccer

League, the New York Cosmos returned to the top with its fourth Soccer Bowl triumph in six years. Other scripts might have been written by the same hand. Coach Dean Smith of North Carolina had taken his basketball teams to the NCAA Final Four on six previous occasions, and he did so again in 1982. Not only that, the team won for the first time in 25 years. In the pro ranks, the Los Angeles Lakers put on championship rings for the second time in three seasons. And in the National Hockey League, the New York Islanders won a third consecutive Stanley Cup.

Individual stars were no less resurgent. At age 30, Jimmy Connors retooled his tennis game and was his old invincible self at Wimbledon and the U.S. Open. Tom Watson reaffirmed his status as golf's best by taking the British and U.S. opens, while Jack Nicklaus came back to win his first tournament in two years. And Larry Holmes, undefeated heavyweight boxing champion since 1979, finally got some respect by knocking out challenger Gerry Cooney.

In an exciting baseball season, St. Louis beat the expansion Milwaukee Brewers in the World Series. All in all, it was a bad year for upstarts—and football fans.

JEFF HACKER

© Richard Mackson/Sport Illustrated

© Tony Duffy/Duomo

© Jerry Wachter/Focus on Sports

The way the ball bounced: *In the U.S. Open golf championship at Pebble Beach, Tom Watson, top left, faced a nearly impossible chip shot at the 17th hole of the final round. The ball went in, and Watson edged Jack Nicklaus for the title. Jimmy Connors, above, who last won at Wimbledon in 1974, reached the finals against defending champion John McEnroe. In the longest men's singles final in Wimbledon history, Connors used a serve-and-volley attack to dethrone McEnroe. Julius "Dr. J." Erving of the Philadelphia '76ers pulled out all the stops to win an NBA championship, but even his acrobatics could not keep the Los Angeles Lakers from taking their second title in three years.*

© Paul J. Sutton/Duomo

Mary Decker Tabb, right, came into her own in 1982. The versatile American runner set a total of seven world records, four indoors and three outdoors. In the fight of the year, heavyweight Larry Holmes (below, left) scored an impressive 13th-round TKO over touted challenger Jerry Cooney.

© Dan Helms/Duomo

Auto Racing

An incredibly close finish in the Indianapolis 500-mile race was about the only bright spot in an otherwise grim year for all of motor racing.

Gordon Johncock nicked Rick Mears by the flick of an eyelash, 0.16 seconds, the closest finish in Indianapolis history. It was Johncock's second Indianapolis victory; he also won in 1973.

Mears, however, nearly was unbeatable through most of the season and captured his second straight Championship Auto Racing Teams (CART) title.

Gordon Smiley was killed while practicing at Indianapolis, and Jim Hickman died at Milwaukee. The grim casualty total continued in Europe. Gilles Villeneuve, a Canadian national hero, died in Belgium; Riccardi Paletti of Italy was fatally injured during the Canadian Grand Prix. Dean Chenoweth, one of powerboat racing's all-time greats, was killed, as was stock-car driver Gene Richards.

Finland's Keke Rosberg used one victory and consistent finishes to capture the 1982 world title after point leader Didier Pironi was seriously injured during the French Grand Prix.

Veteran Bobby Allison won the Daytona "500," the top event on the National Association for Stock Car Racing (NASCAR) circuit.

And another Unser made headlines. Al, Jr., son of three-time Indianapolis champion Al, won the Can-Am title and announced that he would campaign Indy cars in 1983. His uncle, Bobby, another three-time Indy winner, said he was retiring from Indy car competition. For the first time in 35 years of racing, the 48-year-old driver said that he had agreed to let his family decide his future.

BOB COLLINS
"The Indianapolis Star"

AUTO RACING

Major Race Winners
Indianapolis 500: Gordon Johncock, U.S.
Pocono 500: Rick Mears, U.S.
Michigan 500: Gordon Johncock
Daytona 500: Bobby Allison, U.S.

1982 Champions
World Championship: Keke Rosberg, Finland
CART: Rick Mears, U.S.
Can-Am: Al Unser, Jr., U.S.
NASCAR: Darrell Waltrip

Grand Prix for Formula One Cars, 1982
South Africa: Alain Prost, France
Brazil: Nelson Piquet
Long Beach: Niki Lauda, Austria
San Marino: Didier Pironi, France
Belgium: John Watson, Great Britain
Monaco: Riccardo Patrese, Italy
Detroit: John Watson
Canada: Nelson Piquet
Netherlands: Didier Pironi
Britain: Niki Lauda
France: Rene Arnoux, France
Germany: Patrick Tambay, France
Austria: Elio de Angelis, Italy
Switzerland: Keke Rosberg
Italy: Rene Arnoux, France
Las Vegas: Michele Alboreto, Italy

Baseball

Major league baseball made a remarkable recovery from the 1981 strike that sliced seven weeks off the schedule.

With labor peace restored, a record 44,580,822 fans watched the 26 teams play uninterrupted 162-game schedules. When the season ended on October 3, four new divisional champions advanced to post-season play.

Play-offs and World Series. Though the Milwaukee Brewers won 95 regular-season games, the most in baseball, they had to defeat the Baltimore Orioles on the final day to finish first in the American League (AL) East. Baltimore had beaten Milwaukee in three previous games to force the showdown.

The Brewers again faced elimination when the veteran-packed California Angels, winners of the AL West, took 8–3 and 4–2 decisions in the first two games of the league championship series. But the Brewers rebounded to win all three games at their own County Stadium, 5–3, 9–5, and 4–3, and became the first team to overcome a 2–0 play-off deficit.

Milwaukee drew St. Louis as a World Series opponent when the Cardinals swept the Atlanta Braves by scores of 7–0, 4–3, and 6–2, in the National League (NL) play-offs. The Braves had narrowly escaped a one-game divisional play-off when the San Francisco Giants defeated the Los Angeles Dodgers on the last day of the season, ending a three-team scramble for the NL West flag. After a record 13-game winning streak to open the season, Atlanta had fallen four games behind Los Angeles before regrouping in September to finish one game ahead of the Dodgers and two ahead of the Giants.

In the World Series opener on October 12, the powerful Brewers showed why the absence of a solid left-handed pitcher had hurt Atlanta, which was loaded with righties, in the play-offs. Milwaukee southpaw Mike Caldwell blanked St. Louis, 10–0, and teammate Paul Molitor became the first player to get five hits in a World Series game.

St. Louis won Game 2, 5–4, when Brewers' reliever Bob McClure—subbing for injured bullpen ace Rollie Fingers—walked in the winning run in the eighth inning. The Cards then showed unexpected power—a pair of home runs from rookie Willie McGee—to post a 6–2 win in Game 3. But the Brewers erupted for a six-run seventh to win Game 4, 7–5, and got a 6–4 win from Caldwell in Game 5.

Rookie right-hander John Stuper stunned veteran Don Sutton, a late-season acquisition by Milwaukee, to give St. Louis a 13–1 win in Game 6; the contest was held up for several hours by rain. The Cards then overcame a 3–1 Milwaukee lead to win the seventh game, 6–3, with airtight relief from crack fireman Bruce Sutter, who led the majors with 36 saves during the regular season.

Milwaukee's Robin Yount led both teams with a .414 average—thanks to a pair of four-hit games (a World Series record)—but St. Louis catcher Darrell Porter, who hit .286, was named World Series most valuable player (MVP). Porter had also been MVP in the NL play-offs. Cardinal manager Whitey Herzog was named UPI manager of the year, though Atlanta's Joe Torre, who had been fired one year earlier by the New York Mets, was the choice of an AP panel for the same honor.

Milwaukee manager Harvey Kuenn, who had succeeded Buck Rodgers on June 2, became only the 18th rookie pilot to participate in a World Series, but his AL play-off opponent, veteran Gene Mauch, failed to reach the Fall Classic after 23 years of managing—a record for fu-

St. Louis catcher Darrell Porter was the MVP in both the National League play-offs and the World Series.

© John McDonough/Duomo

BASEBALL

Professional—Major Leagues

Final Standings, 1982

AMERICAN LEAGUE

Eastern Division	W.	L.	Pct.	Western Division	W.	L.	Pct.
Milwaukee	95	67	.586	California	93	69	.574
Baltimore	94	68	.580	Kansas City	90	72	.556
Boston	89	73	.549	Chicago	87	75	.537
Detroit	83	79	.512	Seattle	76	86	.469
New York	79	83	.488	Oakland	68	94	.420
Cleveland	78	84	.481	Texas	64	98	.395
Toronto	78	84	.481	Minnesota	60	102	.370

NATIONAL LEAGUE

Eastern Division	W.	L.	Pct.	Western Division	W.	L.	Pct.
St. Louis	92	70	.568	Atlanta	89	73	.549
Philadelphia	89	73	.549	Los Angeles	88	74	.543
Montreal	86	76	.531	San Francisco	87	75	.537
Pittsburgh	84	78	.519	San Diego	81	81	.500
Chicago	73	89	.451	Houston	77	85	.475
New York	65	97	.401	Cincinnati	61	101	.377

Play-offs—American League: Milwaukee defeated California, 3 games to 2; National League: St. Louis defeated Atlanta, 3 games to 0.

World Series—St. Louis defeated Milwaukee, 4 games to 3. First Game (Busch Stadium, St. Louis, Oct. 12, attendance 53,-723): Milwaukee 10, St. Louis 0; Second Game (Busch Stadium, Oct. 13, attendance 53,723): St. Louis 5, Milwaukee 4; Third Game (County Stadium, Milwaukee, Oct. 15, attendance 56,566): St. Louis 6, Milwaukee 2; Fourth Game (County Stadium, Oct. 16, attendance 56,560): Milwaukee 7, St. Louis 5; Fifth Game (County Stadium, Oct. 17, attendance 56,562): Milwaukee 6, St. Louis 4; Sixth Game (Busch Stadium, Oct. 19, attendance 53,723): St. Louis 13, Milwaukee 1; Seventh Game (Busch Stadium, Oct. 20, attendance 53,723): St. Louis 6, Milwaukee 3.

All-Star Game (Olympic Stadium, Montreal, July 13, attendance 59,057): National League 4, American League 1.

Most Valuable Players—American League: Robin Yount, Milwaukee; National League: Dale Murphy, Atlanta.

Cy Young Memorial Awards (outstanding pitchers)—American League: Pete Vuckovich, Milwaukee; National League: Steve Carlton, Philadelphia.

Managers of the Year—American League: Harvey Kuenn, Milwaukee (AP and UPI); National League: Joe Torre, Atlanta (AP) and Whitey Herzog, St. Louis (UPI).

Rookies of the Year—American League: Cal Ripken, Jr., Baltimore; National League: Steve Sax, Los Angeles.

Leading Hitters—(Percentage) American League: Willie Wilson, Kansas City, .332; National League: Al Oliver, Montreal, .331. (Runs Batted In) American League: Hal McRae, 133; National League: Dale Murphy, Atlanta, and Oliver (tied), 109. (Home Runs) American League: Reggie Jackson, California, and Gorman Thomas, Milwaukee (tied), 39; National League: Dave Kingman, New York, 37. (Hits) American League: Yount, 210; National League, Oliver, 204. (Runs) American League: Paul Molitor, Milwaukee, 136; National League: Lonnie Smith, St. Louis, 120.

Leading Pitchers—(Earned Run Average) American League: Rick Sutcliffe, Cleveland, 2.96; National League: Steve Rogers, Montreal, 2.40; (Victories) American League: Lamarr Hoyt, Chicago, 19; National League: Carlton, 23; (Strikeouts) American League: Floyd Bannister, Seattle, 209; National League: Carlton, 286; (Shutouts) American League: Dave Stieb, Toronto, 5; National League: Carlton, 6; (Saves) American League: Dan Quisenberry, Kansas City, 35; National League: Bruce Sutter, St. Louis, 36. No-Hit Games—None.

Stolen Bases—American League: Rickey Henderson, Oakland, 130; National League: Tim Raines, Montreal, 78.

Professional—Minor Leagues, Class AAA

American Association (play-offs): Indianapolis
International League (Governor's Cup): Tidewater
Pacific Coast League (play-offs): Albuquerque

Amateur

NCAA Division I: Miami; Division II: California—Riverside; Division III: Eastern Connecticut State
NAIA: Grand Canyon (Arizona)

Little League World Series: Kirkland

tility. Criticized for his handling of the California pitching staff, Mauch announced his resignation in late October.

Regular Season. The 1982 campaign got a late start because of an April 6 blizzard that erased numerous games. When the New York Yankees postponed their opener four times, they joined the 1933 New York Giants and 1939 St. Louis Browns as the only teams to cancel their first four regular-season games.

Once the season started, fans had much to cheer about. Seattle's Gaylord Perry won his 300th game on May 6. Ferguson Jenkins of the Chicago Cubs notched his 3,000th strikeout on May 25. Jerry Reuss of Los Angeles threw two one-hitters early in the year. (By the end of the season, however, no one had pitched a no-hitter.) Steve Carlton of the Philadelphia Phillies became the oldest man to lead the National League in strikeouts (286) en route to a record fourth Cy Young Award. Carlton, 37, fanned 16 Cubs, the major-league high, on June 9 and finished the season with 23 victories, four more than AL leader Lamarr Hoyt of the Chicago White Sox. Baltimore's ace right-hander, Jim Palmer, won 11 in a row, but two eight-game winning streaks allowed Pete Vuckovich of Milwaukee to post an 18–6 mark that earned him his first Cy Young Award.

Robin Yount, also of the Brewers, became the first AL shortstop to lead the league in both slugging percentage and total bases, and he also led in hits, tied for first in doubles, and was runner-up in batting and runs scored. Willie Wilson of Kansas City (.332) and Al Oliver of Montreal (.331) were the batting champions, and Oliver tied Atlanta's Dale Murphy for the National League leadership with 109 runs batted in. Six AL hitters bettered that figure, with Kansas City's Hal McRae the leader at 133—a record for a designated hitter (DH). Cleveland's Andre Thornton hit 32 homers, 31 as a DH, tying a record. Milwaukee slugger Gorman Thomas and Reggie Jackson, now of California, led the majors with 39 homers each, two more than the National League leader Dave Kingman of the New York Mets.

Steve Rogers of Montreal led both leagues with a 2.40 earned run average; AL leader Rick Sutcliffe of Cleveland was at 2.96. California's Rod Carew, a seven-time batting champion, posted the year's longest hitting streak (25 games), but a base-stealer, Rickey Henderson of the Oakland Athletics, captured more headlines. On August 27, he stole his 119th base, exceeding the 1974 record of Lou Brock. Henderson finished the year with 130 steals. (*See also* BIOGRAPHY.)

Pete Rose was also a record-breaker. On June 22, the Philadelphia first baseman recorded his 3,772d career hit, moving him past Hank Aaron and into second place on the career-hit list. Also in June, Rose became the fifth player to appear in 3,000 games.

Rose's teammate Manny Trillo played in a record 89 consecutive errorless games (same season), while San Francisco reliever Greg Minton extended to 269.1 his mark for innings pitched without yielding a home run. Lonnie Smith of St. Louis tied an NL mark when he swiped five bases in a game on September 4. The Baltimore Orioles set an American League record by slamming 11 pinch-hit homers, three of them with the bases loaded.

Baltimore manager Earl Weaver was fined $2,000 and suspended for a week after hitting umpire Terry Cooney during a July argument, but he rebounded to coax a strong comeback from his club down the stretch. Weaver retired in October after more than 14 years as boss of the Orioles. During that time, he recorded a .596

After a slow start, Philadelphia lefty Steve Carlton won 23 games and a record fourth Cy Young Award.

Focus on Sports

Rickey Henderson of the Oakland A's was a basepath terror, notching a phenomenal 130 steals by season's end.

winning percentage, third on the all-time list behind Joe McCarthy (.614) and Frank Selee (.598). The colorful ex-skipper made his debut as a network television commentator during post-season play.

Baseball also said goodbye to Pittsburgh slugger Willie Stargell, who hung up his spikes at age 41. In his final season, Stargell hit three home runs—all as a pinch hitter—to tie Stan Musial for 14th place on the career list with 475.

Two other veteran players remained productive at advanced ages. Atlanta knuckleballer Phil Niekro, 43, pitched shutouts in his last two starts to finish with a 17–4 record and .810 winning percentage, best in the majors. On September 1, Carl Yastrzemski, the 43-year-old star of the Boston Red Sox, collected his 100th hit, giving him that many safeties in 21 different seasons—a feat accomplished only once previously.

Jim Kaat, who turned 44 in November 1982, worked in his 24th season, a record for a pitcher, while Gaylord Perry incurred a 10-day suspension and $250 fine for allegedly throwing a spitball on August 23. It was his first ejection for ball-tampering in his 21-year career.

The National League won its 11th straight All-Star Game, 4–1, at Montreal's Olympic Stadium on July 13. Cincinnati shortstop Dave Concepcion, who hit the only home run, was the game's MVP. It was the first All-Star Game to be played outside the United States. Prime Minister Trudeau threw out the first pitch.

Former All-Star outfielders Hank Aaron and Frank Robinson joined former commissioner A. B. (Happy) Chandler and one-time New York Giants' shortstop Travis Jackson as new members of the Baseball Hall of Fame. Aaron, the all-time home run king with 755, received 97.8% of the vote, second to Ty Cobb in the history of Hall of Fame voting, but was left off four ballots. Robinson is the only player ever to be named MVP in both leagues (Cincinnati, 1961 and Baltimore, 1966).

After the World Series ended, team owners voted not to renew the contract of Commissioner Bowie Kuhn, who became the game's chief executive in 1969. Kuhn planned to remain in office until the expiration of his seven-year contract in August 1983. The search for a successor was threatened by widespread dissatisfaction over procedures and by misgivings over the very function of the commissioner's office.

DAN SCHLOSSBERG
Baseball Writer

Basketball

For the 13th year in succession, a reigning National Basketball Association (NBA) champion failed to retain its crown, as the 1980–81 titlist Celtics ventured no farther than the Eastern Conference play-off finals, and the Los Angeles Lakers carried off the league's tallest trophy. In college competition, the North Carolina Tar Heels rolled to their second NCAA men's championship exactly 25 years after their first. Louisiana Tech took the first-ever NCAA women's championship.

The Professional Season

Invincible was one word used to describe the Boston team during the regular season. Awesome was another. After winning 26 of their last 30 games to post a 63–19 record—the best in the league—and winning their third consecutive Atlantic Division championship, the Celtics were proclaimed the team to beat in postseason play. Again the club was led by gifted forward Larry Bird—the 1982 All-Star Game most valuable player (MVP)—as well as 7'1" (2.16 m) center Robert Parish and slick playmaker Nate "Tiny" Archibald. The rival Philadelphia '76ers, who finished five games back after playing half the regular season with center Darryl Dawkins on the injured list, and the banged-up Milwaukee Bucks, winners of the Central Division, were given slim chances to beat out the Celtics.

In the Eastern finals, however, the '76ers, behind star forward Julius Erving, put the Celtic tradition on the shelf at least for another year. When Boston's Archibald went down with an injured shoulder early in the series, the Celtics' chances seemed to go with him. Though the Celts managed to come back from a three-games-to-one deficit and forced Game Seven in Boston, they couldn't complete the miracle finish that would have given them a chance for a second straight, and 15th all-time, championship. Instead, the '76ers were bound for the championship series for the third time in six years, hoping to win it all after having been turned back twice.

Philadelphia's opponent would be the L.A. Lakers, who survived a rocky start to finish the regular season five games ahead of Seattle in the Pacific Division and with the best record (57–25) in the Western Conference. The events of the previous months, though, made it difficult to expect so lofty a finish.

First there was disenchantment among the players, which led to the firing of coach Paul Westhead and his replacement by former assistant Pat Riley. Then there was the early, season-ending injury to newcomer Mitch Kupchak, the power forward believed to have been the club's missing link. Still, the Lakers endured, featuring perennial all-star center Kareem Abdul-Jabbar and guard Earvin "Magic" Johnson, who was a central figure in the move to fire Westhead.

The L.A. juggernaut rolled over Phoenix and San Antonio by four games to none in the Western Conference play-offs. It faltered only briefly in the championship series against Philadelphia. Having been knocked out of the 1981 play-offs in the very first round, the revenge-minded Lakers sealed the championship with a 114–104 victory in Game Six at the L.A. Forum. It was the Lakers' second NBA crown in three years and, as in 1980, Magic Johnson was the key. In the title series he averaged 16.2 points, 10.8 rebounds, and 8.0 assists per game, and he was voted MVP of the play-offs (see BIOGRAPHY).

Houston's Moses Malone—the league's top rebounder (14.7 per game) and second-leading scorer (31.1 points per game)—was voted the

PROFESSIONAL BASKETBALL

National Basketball Association
(Final Standings, 1981–82)

Eastern Conference

Atlantic Division	W	L	Pct.
*Boston Celtics	63	19	.768
*Philadelphia '76ers	58	24	.707
*New Jersey Nets	44	38	.537
*Washington Bullets	43	39	.524
New York Knicks	33	49	.402
Central Division			
*Milwaukee Bucks	55	27	.671
*Atlanta Hawks	42	40	.512
Detroit Pistons	39	43	.476
Indiana Pacers	35	47	.427
Chicago Bulls	34	48	.415
Cleveland Cavaliers	15	67	.183

Western Conference

Midwest Division	W	L	Pct.
*San Antonio Spurs	48	34	.585
*Denver Nuggets	46	36	.561
*Houston Rockets	46	36	.561
Kansas City Kings	30	52	.366
Dallas Mavericks	28	54	.341
Utah Jazz	25	57	.305
Pacific Division			
*Los Angeles Lakers	57	25	.695
*Seattle SuperSonics	52	30	.634
*Phoenix Suns	46	36	.561
Golden State Warriors	45	37	.549
Portland Trail Blazers	42	40	.512
San Diego Clippers	17	65	.207

*Made play-offs

Play-Offs
Eastern Conference

First Round	Philadelphia	2 games	Atlanta	0
	Washington	2 games	New Jersey	0
Semifinals	Philadelphia	4 games	Milwaukee	2
	Boston	4 games	Washington	1
Finals	Philadelphia	4 games	Boston	3

Western Conference

First Round	Seattle	2 games	Houston	1
	Phoenix	2 games	Denver	1
Semifinals	Los Angeles	4 games	Phoenix	0
	San Antonio	4 games	Seattle	1
Finals	Los Angeles	4 games	San Antonio	0
Championship:	Los Angeles	4 games	Philadelphia	2
All-Star Game:	East 120, West 118			

Individual Honors

Most Valuable Player: Moses Malone, Houston
Most Valuable Player (play-offs): Earvin Johnson, Los Angeles
Most Valuable Player (all-star game): Larry Bird, Boston
Rookie of the Year: Buck Williams, New Jersey
Coach of the Year: Gene Shue, Washington
Leading Scorer: George Gervin, San Antonio; 2,551 points, 32.3 per game
Leading Rebounder: Moses Malone, Houston; 14.7 per game

regular season MVP. Rookie of the year honors went to New Jersey forward Buck Williams, the only first-year man since 1972 to collect 1,000 rebounds. At 32.3 points per game, George Gervin won his fourth scoring title in five years, while San Antonio teammate Johnnie Moore won the assists crown with 9.6 per game.

The College Season

When it was all over, the University of North Carolina Tar Hells, runners-up in the 1981 NCAA tournament, stood at the top of the college basketball world. Before the largest crowd ever to see a basketball game—more than 61,000 at the Louisiana Superdome—the Tar Heels defeated the Georgetown University Hoyas, 63–62, in the closest NCAA final since 1963. For North Carolina coach Dean Smith it was the first championship after six previous trips to the Final Four (*see* BIOGRAPHY).

Led by tourney MVP James Worthy, the 6′9″ (2.06 m) junior All-American forward, Carolina stormed past James Madison, Alabama, and Villanova to win the NCAA East Regional and a berth in the national semifinals against Houston. The Tar Heels won that contest, 68–63, and all that stood in their way was Georgetown, which featured 7′0″ (2.13 m) freshman Patrick Ewing. The dominating center was at his shotblocking best and scored 23 points, but UNC prevailed, thanks to Worthy's 28-point performance and a last-minute basket by freshman guard Michael Jordan.

Sam Perkins tries for two, as North Carolina wins the NCAA crown. Ewing (63) and Floyd (21) led the Hoyas.

Focus on Sports

COLLEGE BASKETBALL

Conference Champions*
Atlantic Coast: North Carolina
Big East: Georgetown
Big Eight: Missouri
Big Sky: Idaho
Big Ten: Minnesota
East Coast: St. Joseph's
Eastern Athletic: Pittsburgh
Ivy League: Pennsylvania
Metro: Memphis State
Mid-American: Northern Illinois
Missouri Valley: Tulsa
Ohio Valley: Middle Tennessee State
Pacific Coast Athletic: Fresno State
Pacific-10: Oregon State
Southeastern: Alabama
Southern: Tennessee-Chattanooga
Southland: Southwestern Louisiana
Southwest: Arkansas
Southwestern: Alcorn State
Sun Belt: Alabama-Birmingham
West Coast Athletic: Pepperdine
Western Athletic: Wyoming
　　*Based on post-season conference tournaments, where applicable.

Tournaments
NCAA: North Carolina
NIT: Bradley
NCAA Div. II: District of Columbia
NCAA Div. III: Wabash
NAIA: South Carolina-Spartanburg
NCAA (women's): Louisiana Tech
AIAW: Rutgers

During the regular season, Carolina did have a turn as the top team in the weekly polls, but other major contenders were: UCLA, which began the season with optimism but ended it on NCAA probation; Louisville, which lost its hold on the Metro Conference championship but rallied to reach the NCAA semifinals before losing to Georgetown, 50-46; Missouri, which won its first 19 games and the Big Eight championship; Virginia, which was led by 7′4″ (2.24 m) Player of the Year Ralph Sampson and tied North Carolina for first place in the Atlantic Coast Conference's regular season race; and DePaul, which replaced one All-American (Mark Aguirre) with another (Terry Cummings) but still couldn't solve its first-round NCAA Tournament jinx.

Statistically, Kevin Magee of the University of California at Irvine stood out. His 25.2 points per game, 12.2 rebounds, and .642 field goal accuracy ranked him among the top ten nationally in all three categories. Texas Southern's Harry Kelly was the scoring champ at 29.7, Texas' La-Salle Thompson the rebound leader at 13.5, and California's Mark McNamara the most accurate field goal shooter at .702. UCLA's Rod Foster set an NCAA record for free-throw accuracy with 95%.

In other men's postseason play, Bradley stopped Purdue, 67–58, for the National Invitation Tournament (NIT) crown.

Louisiana Tech wrapped up the first NCAA women's title by blasting Cheyney State, 76–62. Rutgers went to the top of the watered-down AIAW by edging Texas, 83–77.

MARK ENGEL
Managing Editor, "Basketball Weekly"

Boxing

Few heavyweight-title fights, even those involving Muhammad Ali, stirred the public imagination as much as the Larry Holmes-Gerry Cooney bout did in 1982. Boxing also lost two of its brightest stars, Salvador Sanchez, who was killed in an auto accident, and Sugar Ray Leonard, who announced his retirement November 9 after undergoing eye surgery in May.

The Holmes-Cooney match was the richest in boxing history, grossing more than $40 million. It drew a crowd of 32,000 and a record live gate of $8.4 million to a stadium erected in a parking lot at Caesars Palace in Las Vegas to watch two undefeated fighters battle in what was billed as "the fight of the 1980s." Postponed from its original March 15 date because of a shoulder injury to the 25-year-old Cooney, the fight had a long publicity buildup that created a highly partisan atmosphere, with racial overtones among the fans and in the press. Each fighter received $8.5 million.

The 32-year-old Holmes, who weighed 212½ lbs. (96.4 kg), won on a knockout in the 13th round, but not before Cooney had displayed a powerful and dangerous left hook and had gained the respect, not only of Holmes, but of boxing experts as a tough and courageous fighter. For 12 rounds in sweltering heat, Holmes skillfully outboxed the Huntington, NY, challenger, who was penalized twice for low blows. Then in the 13th, with Cooney's strength sapped, Holmes battered Cooney into submission at 2:52 of the round. Cooney's nose and left eye were bloodied, and his trainer rushed into the ring to plead with the referee to halt the fight.

For the champion from Easton, PA, the victory was the 40th overall, his 30th by a knockout, in a 10-year pro career. It was his 11th by knockout in a record 12 defenses of the World Boxing Council title, and many experts regarded it as his finest triumph.

In a stunning upset, Michael Dokes took the World Boxing Association (WBA) heavyweight title from Mike Weaver in 63 seconds of the first round in Las Vegas.

Sanchez, the WBC featherweight champion who was widely regarded as one of the world's finest boxers, had won the title in February 1980 from Danny Lopez. In May 1982 he won a unanimous decision from Jorge (Rocky) Garcia at Dallas, and late in July he scored a 15-round knockout of Azumah Nelson at New York's Madison Square Garden. Two weeks after the Nelson bout, the 23-year-old Mexican champion was killed in a three-car crash near Queretaro, Mexico. His career record of 43 victories, one defeat, and one draw included 31 knockouts. In September, fighting for the title vacated by Sanchez's death, Juan LaPorte won the crown in New York, beating Mario Miranda.

Leonard, the undisputed welterweight champion, had one defense in 1982, scoring a third-round knockout of Bruce Finch at Reno, NV, before he discovered his eye problem in May.

Ray (Boom Boom) Mancini, a lightweight from Youngstown, OH, won the World Boxing Association title from Arturo Frias with a sixth-round knockout on May 8 at Las Vegas. Mancini insisted that his first defense be held before the fans in his hometown area. On July 24 he knocked out Ernesto España in the sixth round in Warren, OH. The fight was held in a high-school football stadium and drew more than 15,000 fans. It was a county-fair setting, with fireworks and high-school cheerleaders rooting for the popular 21-year-old Mancini. His next defense, at Las Vegas, ended in tragedy for his opponent, Duk Koo Kim of South Korea. Mancini knocked Kim unconscious in the 14th round. Kim underwent surgery for a blood clot in the brain, went into a coma, and died November 17.

Alexis Arguello, the WBC lightweight champion and one of only six fighters ever to hold titles in three different divisions, made two successful title defenses with knockouts of Bubba Busceme and Andy Ganigan. On November 12 he lost on a knockout in the 14th round to the unbeaten WBA junior welterweight titleholder, Aaron Pryor.

Wilfred Benitez, the WBC junior middleweight titleholder, and like Arguello the holder of three divisions titles during his career, lost his crown to Thomas Hearns on a majority decision December 3 in New Orleans. Hearns, known as a strong puncher, simply outboxed Benitez.

Michael Spinks, the WBA light-heavyweight champion, was the busiest fighter of the year, taking on virtually all comers. He made four defenses of his title, all in Atlantic City, and won each time on a knockout.

GEORGE DE GREGORIO, *"The New York Times"*

BOXING

World Champions

Junior Flyweight—Katsuo Tokashiki, Japan (1981), World Boxing Association (WBA); Hilario Zapata, Panama (1980), World Boxing Council (WBC).
Flyweight—Santos Laciar, Mexico (1982), WBA; Eleoncio Mercedes, Dominican Republic (1982), WBC.
Junior Bantamweight—Jiro Watanabe, Japan (1982), WBA; Rafael Orono, Venezuela (1982), WBC.
Bantamweight—Jeff Chandler, Philadelphia (1980), WBA; Lupe Pintor, Mexico (1979), WBC.
Junior Featherweight—Leo Cruz, Dominican Republic (1982), WBA; Wilfredo Gomez, Puerto Rico (1977), WBC.
Featherweight—Eusebio Pedroza, Panama (1978), WBA; Juan LaPorte, Brooklyn, NY (1982), WBC.
Junior Lightweight—Sammy Serrano, Puerto Rico (1981), WBA; Bobby Chacon, Oroville, CA (1982), WBC.
Lightweight—Ray Mancini, Youngstown, OH (1982), WBA; Alexis Arguello, Nicaragua (1981), WBC.
Junior Welterweight—Aaron Pryor, Cincinnati (1980), WBA; Leroy Haley, Las Vegas, NV (1982), WBC.
Welterweight—vacant
Junior Middleweight—Davey Moore, New York City (1981), WBA; Thomas Hearns, Detroit (1982), WBC.
Middleweight—Marvelous Marvin Hagler, Brockton, MA (1980), WBA and WBC.
Light-Heavyweight—Michael Spinks, St. Louis (1981), WBA; Dwight Muhammed Qawi (Dwight Braxton), Camden, NJ (1981), WBC.
Cruiserweight—Ossie Ocasio, Puerto Rico (1982), WBA; S. T. Gordon, Las Vegas, NV (1982), WBC.
Heavyweight—Michael Dokes, Akron, OH (1982), WBA; Larry Holmes, Easton, PA (1978), WBC.

* Year of achieving title in parentheses

Football

Fittingly, Penn State became the No. 1 college football team in the nation by containing the No. 1 player, Herschel Walker. The Nittany Lions were declared national champions for the first time after devising a special defense for Walker and defeating Georgia, 27–23, in the Sugar Bowl. A strike by the National Football League Players Association (NFLPA) forced armchair quarterbacks to settle for a shortened season. They were treated, however, to some additional play-off action, as the championship series was rearranged because of the strike into the Super Bowl XVII Tournament. For the fifth consecutive year, the Edmonton Eskimos captured Canada's Grey Cup.

The College Season

Coach Joe Paterno, in his 17th year at Penn State, finally achieved his long-standing ambition. He had had three undefeated and untied teams (1968, 1969, and 1973), none of which was awarded the top ranking. In Penn State's best previous chance, the unbeaten and No. 1–rated Lions of 1978 were upset by Alabama, 14–7, in the Sugar Bowl.

This time Penn State arrived in New Orleans as No. 2 to Georgia's No. 1, in a rare bowl matchup of the two top-ranked elevens. The Lions had faced the more difficult schedule, counting Nebraska, Pitt, Notre Dame, and Maryland among their 10 victims, but a midseason loss to Alabama had hurt. The Bulldogs were accorded the top spot as the only major college eleven with an undefeated and untied mark, thanks mostly to the incomparable Walker, their Heisman Trophy winner.

Penn State used a shifting defensive line to confuse Georgia's blockers and limited Walker to 107 yards on 28 carries. (His longest gain was 12 yards). That was the lowest rushing total for the Bulldogs' star since his freshman year except for the opener against Clemson, when he was injured.

Going into the game, the Lions boasted the most diversified attack in the country, with 2,369 yards and 22 touchdowns passing and 2,283 yards and 21 touchdowns rushing. Quarterback Todd Blackledge and tailback Curt Warner sparked the two-pronged offense. In the Sugar Bowl the duo again were the Penn State leaders. Blackledge, who was voted the game's most valuable player, threw for 228 yards, including 47 yards to Gregg Garrity for the deciding touchdown early in the final period. Plagued by leg cramps, Warner still managed to run for 117 yards and two touchdowns on only 18 carries.

Southern Methodist, unbeaten but once-tied, entertained hopes of receiving the No. 1 ranking after the Mustangs' stout defense prevailed over Pittsburgh, 7–3, in rain and sleet in the Cotton Bowl. But SMU, which had a comparatively weak schedule, was placed second in both national wire-service polls.

Two major upsets made it possible for UCLA to go to the Rose Bowl. First, Washington State denied Washington a third consecutive trip to Pasadena with a 24–20 stunner, and then Arizona threw a 28–18 roadblock in Arizona State's path. Michigan had its share of luck and became

Georgia's junior running back Herschel Walker powered his way to 1,752 yards and the Heisman Trophy.

Perry McIntyre, Jr./University of Georgia

the Big Ten representative only by virtue of having played one more conference game than Ohio State, which defeated the Wolverines, 24–14. Earlier in the season UCLA had beaten Michigan, but contrary to the trend of the loser winning the rematch, the Bruins were 24–14 Rose Bowl victors.

Without a doubt the season's most bizarre and spectacular play—and a game winner at that—was California's five-lateral kickoff return as time ran out for the touchdown that upset Stanford, 25–20. Mark Harmon's 35-yard field goal with 4 seconds remaining had given Stanford a 20–19 lead and apparently a lock on a trip to the Hall of Fame Bowl. But then the fun began. Kevin Moen caught the ensuing kickoff, which was made from the Stanford 25 because of a penalty, on the California 45. Moen was about

COLLEGE FOOTBALL

Conference Champions	Atlantic Coast—Clemson Big Eight—Nebraska Big Ten—Michigan Pacific Coast—Fresno State Pacific Ten—UCLA Southeastern—Georgia Southwest—Southern Methodist (SMU) Western Athletic—Brigham Young
Individual Honors	Heisman Trophy—Herschel Walker, Georgia Lombardi Trophy—David Rimington, Nebraska Outland Trophy—David Rimington
NCAA Champions	Division I—AA—E. Kentucky Division II—Southwest Texas State Division III—West Georgia
NAIA Champions	Division I—Central State Oklahoma Division II—Linfield

Major Bowl Games

Independence Bowl (Shreveport, LA, Dec. 11)—Wisconsin 14, Kansas State 3
Holiday Bowl (San Diego, CA, Dec. 17)—Ohio State 47, Brigham Young 17
California Bowl (Fresno, CA, Dec. 18)—Fresno State 29, Bowling Green 28
Tangerine Bowl (Orlando, FL, Dec. 18)—Auburn 33, Boston College 26
Sun Bowl (El Paso, TX, Dec. 25)—North Carolina 26, Texas 10
Aloha Bowl (Honolulu, HI, Dec. 25)—Washington 21, Maryland 20
Liberty Bowl (Memphis, TN, Dec. 29)—Alabama 21, Illinois 15
Gator Bowl (Jacksonville, FL, Dec. 30)—Florida State 31, West Virginia 12
Hall of Fame Bowl (Birmingham, AL, Dec. 31)—Air Force 36, Vanderbilt 28
Peach Bowl (Atlanta, GA, Dec. 31)—Iowa 28, Tennessee 22
Bluebonnet Bowl (Houston, TX, Dec. 31)—Arkansas 28, Florida 24
Cotton Bowl (Dallas, TX, Jan. 1)—Southern Methodist University 7, Pittsburgh 3
Fiesta Bowl (Tempe, AZ, Jan. 1)—Arizona State 32, Oklahoma 21
Orange Bowl (Miami, FL, Jan. 1)—Nebraska 21, LSU 20
Rose Bowl (Pasadena, CA, Jan. 1)—UCLA 24, Michigan 14
Sugar Bowl (New Orleans, LA, Jan. 1)—Penn State 27, Georgia 23

Final College Rankings

	AP Writers	UPI Coaches
1	Penn State	Penn State
2	SMU	SMU
3	Nebraska	Nebraska
4	Georgia	Georgia
5	UCLA	UCLA
6	Arizona State	Arizona State
7	Washington	Washington
8	Clemson	Arkansas
9	Arkansas	Pitt
10	Pitt	Florida State

to be tackled when he lateraled to Richard Rodgers, who ran 10 yards and flipped the ball to Dwight Garner. By now time had expired and fans were closing in on the sidelines. After running about 20 yards, Garner tossed the ball back to Rodgers, who lateraled to Marriet Ford. Ford then made the fifth lateral to Moen, who had started it all. Not only were spectators moving onto the field, but members of the Stanford band were lined up preparing to strike up a victory march they never got to play. Moen darted through the crowd and into the end zone, bowling over a trombone player.

One of the coaching greats, Paul (Bear) Bryant, holder of the record for the most major college victories, abruptly retired as Alabama's head coach. The sudden announcement came after the Crimson Tide lost the last three games of the regular season, the first time during his 25-year reign that one of his Alabama teams had lost three in a row. Appropriately, the 69-year-old Bryant went out a winner as Alabama beat Illinois, 21–15, in the Liberty Bowl for his 323rd career triumph. His overall record showed only 85 losses and 17 ties in 38 seasons as a head coach. He eclipsed the previous mark for most victories in 1981, when he surpassed Amos Alonzo Stagg's standard of 314. So as not to lose time in recruiting high school prospects, Alabama quickly named as his successor Ray Perkins, the New York Giants' head coach, who had played for Bryant in the mid-1960s.

For his regular-season performance, Herschel Walker was a runaway victor in the balloting to become the 48th recipient of the Heisman Trophy. Georgia's junior tailback garnered 1,926 votes. John Elway, Stanford's strong-armed quarterback, was second with 1,231 votes, and Eric Dickerson, Southern Methodist's fine running back, was third with 465. The 6-1, 222-lb Walker had finished third as a freshman and second as a sophomore in the Heisman voting. In 1982 he rushed for 1,752 yards despite being hampered early in the season by a thumb injury. He ended the season with a three-year total of 5,259 yards, the most ever gained by a player through his junior year.

From high times to hard times was the fate of Clemson. The Cinderella team of 1981, capturing the national title after being unranked at the start of the season, in 1982 won nine games in a row after an opening loss to Georgia and a tie with Boston College. But the win streak was small comfort, as the Tigers were hit by the most severe penalty in NCAA history—two years probation, which prohibits appearances in bowl and televised games, and the loss of 20 scholarships—for recruiting violations.

The victory drought ended at Northwestern. The Wildcats, who stretched their record losing streak to 34 by dropping their first three games in 1982, defeated Northern Illinois, 31–6. To show it could be done again, they beat Minnesota and Michigan State later in the season.

The Professional Season

For the National Football League, 1982 was a year of travail: revelations of drug abuse, a team moving without league permission, a 57-day strike (*see* page 477), and a new rival on the horizon, the U.S. Football League.

The interrupted season was called tainted by critics because of the abbreviated schedule. After the players' walkout ended, only one of the eight games missed was made up, creating a nine-game slate instead of the regular 16 games. To compensate, the NFL decided on a 16-team play-off format. The eight teams in each conference with the best won-lost records (divisional groupings were ignored) qualified for post-season play. The new setup was sneered at because

PROFESSIONAL FOOTBALL

National Football League
Final Standings

AMERICAN CONFERENCE

	W	L	T	Pct.	Points For	Points Against
*L.A. Raiders	8	1	0	.889	260	200
*Miami	7	2	0	.778	198	131
*Cincinnati	7	2	0	.778	232	177
*Pittsburgh	6	3	0	.667	204	146
*San Diego	6	3	0	.667	288	221
*N.Y. Jets	6	3	0	.667	245	166
*New England	5	4	0	.556	143	157
*Cleveland	4	5	0	.444	140	182
Buffalo	4	5	0	.444	150	154
Seattle	4	5	0	.444	127	147
Kansas City	3	6	0	.333	175	184
Denver	2	7	0	.222	148	226
Houston	1	8	0	.111	136	245
Baltimore	0	8	1	.056	113	236

Super Bowl XVII Tournament

Los Angeles Raiders 27, Cleveland 10
Miami 28, New England 13
New York Jets 44, Cincinnati 17
San Diego 31, Pittsburgh 28

New York Jets 17, Oakland Raiders 14
Miami 34, San Diego 13

Miami 14, New York Jets 0

NATIONAL CONFERENCE

	W	L	T	Pct.	Points For	Points Against
*Washington	8	1	0	.889	190	128
*Dallas	6	3	0	.667	226	145
*Green Bay	5	3	1	.611	226	169
*Minnesota	5	4	0	.556	187	198
*Atlanta	5	4	0	.556	183	199
*Tampa Bay	5	4	0	.556	158	178
*St. Louis	5	4	0	.556	135	170
*Detroit	4	5	0	.444	181	176
N.Y. Giants	4	5	0	.444	164	160
New Orleans	4	5	0	.444	129	160
San Francisco	3	6	0	.333	209	206
Philadelphia	3	6	0	.333	191	195
Chicago	3	6	0	.333	141	174
L.A. Rams	2	7	0	.222	200	250

* Clinched play-off spot

Super Bowl XVII Tournament

Washington 31, Detroit 7
Green Bay 41, St. Louis 16
Dallas 30, Tampa 17
Minnesota 30, Atlanta 24

Washington 21, Minnesota 7
Dallas 37, Green Bay 26

Washington 31, Dallas 17

Super Bowl XVII

Washington 27, Miami 17

of the probability that clubs with losing records would get into the play-offs (two did—the Cleveland Browns and the Detroit Lions, each with a 4–5 mark).

Some of the first-round results were lopsided, but overall the new format justified itself competitively. In fact, Super Bowl XVII had the same cast as Super Bowl VII, which the Miami Dolphins won from the Washington Redskins, 14–7, completing an all-winning season.

In Super Bowl XVII, however, the Redskins defeated the Dolphins, 27–17. Washington's John Riggins was MVP.

In the 1983 National Conference championship, the Redskins beat the Cowboys, 31–17, finally gaining the respect that had eluded them during the season. The reason: five of their eight season victories were due to Mark Moseley's field goals. In the championship, the Hogs, the nickname Washington's linemen gave themselves, paved the way for John Riggins who rushed for 140 yards on 36 carries and two touchdowns.

The Dolphins reached the Super Bowl by defeating the Jets, 14–0, for the third time this season. Freeman McNeil, the Jets' star back noted for his cutback abilities, and the New York receivers were hampered by a muddy Orange Bowl field, which had not been covered before the game. New York's Richard Todd suffered five interceptions, three by A. J. Duhe.

Earlier, Al Davis scored a victory over the NFL after two years of legal battling when a court decision allowed the owner to move the Raiders from Oakland to Los Angeles. However, in effect, the Raiders became a road club. With training facilities inadequate at the Los Angeles Coliseum, they practiced in Oakland and flew to L.A. for their home games. The arrangement did not harm the Raiders' on-field performance as they lost only once on their way to an eight-one finish. Jim Plunkett was again in the quarterback form he showed in winning the 1981 Super Bowl. He was helped greatly by Marcus Allen, the former USC all-American back.

One of the few records to emerge from the reduced season was Moseley's field goal streak. Moseley booted 23 in a row, breaking Garo Yepremian's old mark of 20.

The San Francisco 49ers, the defending Super Bowl champions, were a major disappointment. The 49ers stumbled to six losses as they suffered from injuries, defensive woes, and overconfidence. The Philadelphia Eagles' losing season so upset Coach Dick Vermeil that he abruptly resigned, describing himself as "emotionally burned out."

Fans showed their displeasure at the labor dispute by posting a record number of no-shows (those who have bought tickets, but do not attend). TV ratings were also down for the second portion of the season, reflecting the public's disenchantment.

LUD DUROSKA, *"The New York Times"*

The Pro Football Strike

From the start of contract negotiations in February at Miami, it was apparent that the National Football League Players Association (NFLPA) and the team owners were on a collision course. After months of off-and-on talks, the result was the longest strike (57 days) in U.S. sports history and the first regular-season walkout in the 63-year existence of the National Football League (NFL).

The players, all too mindful that they had the lowest average salary in any major sport, were in a militant mood. They were further nettled by the news that the league had completed a record television deal: $2,100,000,000 over a five-year span. With the slogan "We Are the Game," the players' union made as its paramount demand that 55% of the league's gross revenues be placed in a central fund and paid to the players under a salary-bonus system. "There is a good possibility of a strike as long as they don't take us seriously," warned Ed Garvey, the union's executive director.

The owners were shocked by the proposal, considering it the equivalent of giving away half their franchises. Jack Donlan, chief negotiator for the Management Council, declared that no settlement tied to a percentage of revenues was possible.

The July 15 expiration date of the old five-year contract came and went without any progress. It seemed as if the owners were testing player unity. Only when the season was a mere four days away in September did the council put its first meaningful offer on the table: a five-year, $1,600,000,000 package. The figures were disputed by Garvey. The NFLPA, finding that its 55% concept was unpopular with the public, substituted a proposal for a fund of $1,600,000,000 over four years, to be financed mostly by TV revenues.

But the movement on both sides came too late. As Dan Rooney, president of the Pittsburgh Steelers, acknowledged afterward, "We waited much too long. By September we should have been deep in negotiations."

Matters were at a standstill as the season opened, and after two weeks of play, on September 20, NFLPA President Gene Upshaw called the strike. The Raiders' veteran guard estimated that 94% of the players concurred in the union's decision.

Federal mediator Sam Kagel was brought in, but his efforts proved unavailing. The owners walked out of the talks on November 8, and it looked as if the entire season would be cancelled. Then Paul Martha came to the rescue. General counsel for the San Francisco

Huddle, 1982

Langley in The Christian Science Monitor © 1982

49ers and a former Steeler defensive back, Martha acted as an intermediary in the talks and was instrumental in hammering out an agreement by November 16. Eight weeks of the season had been washed out.

For the players, the wage scale was increased, though a far cry from what the union had sought; the range was from $30,000 for rookies to $200,000 for 18-year veterans. A new bonus plan guaranteed $10,000 for rookies to a maximum of $60,000 for players in their fourth year; in some cases the bonus more than made up for the loss of eight weeks salary. A severance plan—starting at $5,000 for two years of experience, increasing to $140,000 for 12 or more years—was set up for the first time. Other beneficial items were increased postseason pay, the right of the union to disqualify player agents and, with the player's approval, negotiate for the player itself. Also, in the event of a rule change that involves player safety, the union has the right to take the case to arbitration.

For the owners, there were at least two important victories: the system of paying player salaries—or at least the bulk of them—through individual contract negotiations was preserved; and none of the money allocated for player costs over the term of the contract was fixed to any percentage.

Lud Duroska

Golf

Craig Stadler led the money-winners, Tom Kite won the Vardon Trophy, and Calvin Peete showed the most improvement, but in 1982 Tom Watson, after a year's absence, regained his place, atop the world of men's professional golf. On the LPGA Tour, JoAnne Carner dominated as few have before and was named LPGA Player of the Year.

The 33-year-old Watson won two early tournaments on the PGA Tour. Then, in June at Pebble Beach, he holed a nearly impossible pitch from the rough on the 71st hole and went on to beat Jack Nicklaus by two strokes for his first U.S. Open Championship. A month later, at Royal Troon in Scotland, he won his fourth British Open, boosting his major championship total to seven and earning him the Professional Golfers Association Player of the Year award for the fifth time in six years.

Stadler won the Masters and three other tournaments. The last of these was the World Series of Golf, a $100,000 payoff that boosted his year's money total to $446,462.

Peete, a winner only once in his first six years on tour, also triumphed four times and was named *Golf Digest*'s Most Improved Male Professional. But Stadler won the magazine's Byron Nelson Award for most tour victories on the strength of two second-place finishes.

Kite repeated as the Vardon Trophy winner with a 70.21 stroke average and also as *Golf Digest*'s Jack Nicklaus Performance Average winner, finishing third on the money list with $341,081. The No. 2 money winner was Raymond Floyd, who won the PGA Championship and two other events and banked $386,809. Peete was fourth in money winnings with $318,419 and Watson was fifth with $316,483.

Carner, the likable "Big Momma" of the LPGA Tour, had her finest year ever at the age of 43. She won five tournaments and qualified for the LPGA Hall of Fame with a total of 37 career victories. She earned her fifth money title with a record $310,399, repeated as the Vare Trophy winner with a 71.49 scoring average, and won *Golf Digest*'s Kathy Whitworth Performance Average Trophy and the Mickey Wright Award for most victories.

In the majors, Jan Stephenson won the LPGA Championship; veteran Sandra Haynie continued her comeback by winning the Peter Jackson Classic; and Janet Alex made the U.S. Open her first tournament victory.

Patty Sheehan, a second-year professional, won three tournaments and $225,022 and was named *Golf Digest*'s Most Improved Female Professional. Hal Sutton and Patti Rizzo were named Rookies of the Year on their respective tours by *Golf Digest*. Miller Barber won the U.S. Senior Open and was the leading money-winner on the burgeoning men's Senior Tour.

LARRY DENNIS, *"Golf Digest"*

GOLF

PGA Tour 1982 Tournament Winners

Joe Garagiola-Tucson Open: Craig Stadler (266)
Bob Hope Desert Classic: Ed Fiori (335)
Phoenix Open: Lanny Wadkins (263)
Wickes-Andy Williams-San Diego Open: Johnny Miller (270)
Bing Crosby National Pro-Am: Jim Simons (274)
Hawaiian Open: Wayne Levi (277)
Glen Campbell-Los Angeles Open: Tom Watson (271)
Bay Hill Classic: Tom Kite (278)
Honda Inverrary Classic: Hale Irwin (269)
Tournament Players Championship: Jerry Pate (280)
Sea Pines Heritage Classic: Tom Watson (280)
Greater Greensboro Open: Danny Edwards (285)
Masters Tournament: Craig Stadler (284)
Magnolia Classic: Payne Stewart (270)
Mony-Tournament of Champions: Lanny Wadkins (280)
Tallahassee Open: Bob Shearer (272)
New Orleans Open: Scott Hoch (206)
Byron Nelson Classic: Bob Gilder (266)
Michelob-Houston Open: Ed Sneed (275)
Colonial National Invitational: Jack Nicklaus (273)
Georgia Pacific-Atlanta Classic: Keith Fergus (273)
Memorial Tournament: Raymond Floyd (281)
Kemper Open: Craig Stadler (275)
Danny Thomas Memphis Classic: Raymond Floyd (271)
United States Open: Tom Watson (282)
Manufacturers Hanover Westchester Classic: Bob Gilder (261)
Western Open: Tom Weiskopf (276)
Greater Milwaukee Open: Calvin Peete (274)
Quad Cities Open: Payne Stewart (268)
Anheuser-Busch Golf Classic: Calvin Peete (203)
Canadian Open: Bruce Lietzke (277)
PGA Championship: Raymond Floyd (272)
Sammy Davis Jr.-Greater Hartford Open: Tim Norris (259)
Buick Open: Lanny Wadkins (280)
World Series of Golf: Craig Stadler (278)
B. C. Open: Calvin Peete (265)
Bank of Boston Classic: Bob Gilder (271)
Hall of Fame Tournament: Jay Haas (276)
Southern Open: Bobby Clampett (266)
Texas Open: Jay Haas (262)
LaJet Classic: Wayne Levi (271)
Pensacola Open: Calvin Peete (268)
Walt Disney World Golf Classic: Hal Sutton (269)

LPGA 1982 Tournament Winners

Whirlpool Championship of Deerfield Beach: Hollis Stacy (282)
Elizabeth Arden Classic: JoAnne Carner (283)
S & H Golf Classic: Hollis Stacy (204)
Bent Tree Ladies Classic: Beth Daniel (276)
Arizona Copper Classic: Ayako Okamoto (281)
American Express Sun City Classic: Beth Daniel (278)
Olympia Gold Classic: Sally Little (288)
J & B Scotch Pro-Am: Nancy Lopez (279)
Women's Kemper Open: Amy Alcott (286)
Nabisco Dinah Shore Invitational: Sally Little (278)
CPC International: Kathy Whitworth (281)
Orlando Lady Classic: Patty Sheehan (209)
Birmingham Classic: Beth Daniel (203)
UVB Golf Classic: Sally Little (208)
Lady Michelob: Kathy Whitworth (207)
Chrysler Plymouth Charity Classic: Cathy Morse (216)
Corning Classic: Sandra Spuzich (280)
McDonald's Kids Classic: JoAnne Carner (276)
LPGA Championship: Jan Stephenson (279)
Rochester International: Sandra Haynie (276)
Lady Keystone Open: Jan Stephenson (211)
Peter Jackson Classic: Sandra Haynie (280)
West Virginia Classic: Hollis Stacy (209)
Mayflower Classic: Sally Little (275)
U.S. Women's Open: Janet Alex (283)
Columbia Savings Classic: Beth Daniel (276)
Boston Five Classic: Sandra Palmer (281)
WUI Classic: Beth Daniel (276)
Chevrolet World Championship of Women's Golf: JoAnne Carner (284)
Henredon Classic: JoAnne Carner (282)
Rail Charity Golf Classic: JoAnne Carner (202)
Mary Kay Classic: Sandra Spuzich (206)
Portland Ping Team Championship: Sandra Haynie/Kathy McMullen (196)
Safeco Classic: Patty Sheehan (276)
Inamori Classic: Patty Sheehan (277)
Mazda Japan Classic: Nancy Lopez (207)

Other Tournaments

British Open: Tom Watson (284)
U.S. Men's Amateur: Jay Sigel
U.S. Women's Amateur: Julie Inkster
U.S. Men's Public Links: Billy Tuten
U.S. Women's Public Links: Nancy Taylor
U.S. Senior Open: Miller Barber
U.S. Senior Men's Amateur: Alton Duhon
U.S. Senior Women's Amateur: Edean Ihlanfeldt
U.S. Men's Mid-Amateur: William Hoffer

Horse Racing

Thoroughbred racing lost two genuine stars in the fall of 1982 with the tragic deaths of Timely Writer and Landaluce.

Timely Writer was destroyed after he shattered a bone in his left foreleg during the Jockey Club Gold Cup in October at New York's Belmont Park. Earlier in the season the three-year-old colt had won the Flamingo and Florida Derby. He had been the Kentucky Derby favorite until he was sidelined from the race with abdominal surgery.

Landaluce, a two-year-old filly from the first crop of 1977 Triple Crown winner Seattle Slew, died from a bacterial infection. The unbeaten filly won five starts by a total of 46½ lengths, including a 21-length triumph in the Hollywood Lassie Stakes. Landaluce, trained by D. Wayne Lukas, had earnings of $372,365.

For the first time since 1934, no horse ran in all three Triple Crown races. Gato del Sol, a 21-1 shot owned by Arthur B. Hancock III and Leone Peters, rallied from last place under Eddie Delahoussaye's handling to win the Kentucky Derby. Aloma's Ruler, with 16-year-old Jack Kaenel in the saddle, captured the Preakness by a half-length over Linkage, the overrated favorite. Conquistador Cielo, ridden by Laffit Pincay, Jr., triumphed by 14½ lengths in the Belmont Stakes. The Belmont victory was the first in the Triple Crown series for Pincay, who had failed in 16 previous rides in the series.

Just five days before the Belmont, Conquistador Cielo won the Metropolitan Handicap by 7¼ lengths in a time of 1:33 for the mile, a Belmont Park track record. The Florida-bred colt, a son of Mr. Prospector, captured seven races—all in a row—in nine 1982 starts and was honored as Horse of the Year. Conquistador Cielo, trained by W. C. "Woody" Stephens, was retired and syndicated for a record $36.4 million.

Lemhi Gold won stakes races on both coasts, the San Marino and San Juan Capistrano in California and the Sword Dancer, Marlboro, and Jockey Club Gold Cup in New York. Perrault, winner of the Budweiser Million, led the money winners with earnings of $1,197,400.

Jockey Angel Cordero's mounts earned $9.7 million, a record for a single season.

Harness Racing. Cam Fella, a three-year-old colt pacer, won 28 of 33 starts in 1982 and was selected as the Harness Horse of the Year. Trenton set a new world record for the mile pace with a time of 1:51.6.

Quarter Horse Racing. Mr Master Bug, with Jackie Martin up, won the $2.5-million All American Futurity at Ruidoso Downs in New Mexico.

Horse Sales. A colt sired by Nijinsky II sold for a world-record $4.25 million at Keeneland's July Selected Yearling Sale.

JIM BOLUS
"The Louisville Times"

Dan Helms/Duomo

Gato del Sol, with Eddie Delahoussaye up, won the 108th running of the Kentucky Derby at Churchill Downs.

HORSE RACING

Major U.S. Thoroughbred Races

Belmont Stakes: Conquistador Cielo, $266,200 (value of race)
Beldame: Weber City Miss, $223,500
Budweiser Million: Perrault, $1,000,000
Californian: Erins Isle, $335,200
Champagne: Copelan, $240,000
Florida Derby: Timely Writer, $250,000
Hollywood Futurity: Roving Boy, $811,400
Hollywood Gold Cup Handicap: Perrault, $500,000
Hollywood Invitational Handicap: Exploded, $300,000
Hollywood Lassie: Landaluce, $77,500
Jockey Club Gold Cup: Lemhi Gold, $563,000
Kentucky Derby: Gato del Sol, $542,600
Man o' War Stakes: Naskra's Breeze, $173,100
Marlboro Cup Handicap: Lemhi Gold, $400,000
Meadowlands Cup Handicap: Mehmet, $400,000
Metropolitan Handicap: Conquistador Cielo, $153,000
Oak Tree Invitational: John Henry, $300,000
Preakness: Aloma's Ruler, $279,900
Ruffian Handicap: Christmas Past, $166,800
Santa Anita Handicap: John Henry, $543,800
Suburban Handicap: Silver Buck, $167,700
Turf Classic: April Run, $476,800
Washington D.C. International: April Run, $250,000
Woodward: Island Whirl, $227,500

Major U.S. Harness Races

Cane Pace: Cam Fella, $513,300
Hambletonian: Speed Bowl, $875,000
Kentucky Futurity: Jazz Cosmos, $116,200
Kentucky Pacing Derby: Trim the Tree, $312,200
Little Brown Jug: Merger, $259,577
Meadowlands Pace: Hilarion, $1,000,000
Messenger: Cam Fella, $259,577
Peter Haughton Memorial: Dancer's Crown, $653,250
Woodrow Wilson: Fortune Teller, $1,957,500
Yonkers Trot: Mystic Park, $415,160

Ice Hockey

The 1981–82 National Hockey League (NHL) season may be remembered as much for its losers as for its winners. While the New York Islanders became only the third franchise in the league's history to win a third straight Stanley Cup—and the first U.S.-based team ever to do so—it was the absence of such powerhouses as Montreal, Minnesota, and Edmonton from the Stanley Cup finals that was truly stunning. In one of the oddest turnabouts the league had seen in years all three of these teams won their respective divisions but were eliminated in the first play-off round. By the time the semifinals began, the only teams with winning records were the Islanders, who had finished with the best regular season mark and had also set an NHL record with 15 consecutive victories, and Quebec. For the players individually, the year was just as topsy-turvy. The biggest headlines were shared by superstar Wayne Gretzky, who launched an assault on the record book, and by journeyman Paul Mulvey, who refused to assault anyone. (*See* special report, page 481).

Gretzky, the 21-year-old "wunderkind" of the Edmonton Oilers, established himself as one of the greatest centers in the game's history by shattering two scoring marks once thought to be unapproachable. His 92 goals easily bested the previous record of 76 by Boston's Phil Esposito in 1971. Gretzky's 212 points surpassed his own

Wayne Gretzky signed a longtime contract with Edmonton, set scoring records, and again won the MVP award.

UPI

record of 164 set the previous season. His 65-point lead over runner-up Mike Bossy of the Islanders represented the largest margin ever. In addition, Gretzky's averages of 1.5 assists and 2.65 points per game both were records, as were his ten three-goal games. He also scored the fastest 50 goals in NHL history, taking just 39 games. Those achievements earned Gretzky the Hart Trophy as the league's most valuable player (MVP) for the third straight season, equaling the record set by the great Bobby Orr from 1970 to 1972.

Gretzky was one of ten 50-goal scorers and one of 13 players who had more than 100 points, both records. He was one of three 60-goal scorers, along with Bossy and Washington's Dennis Maruk, yet another mark. Gretzky's Oilers had 417 goals, the most ever. Even the lowly Pittsburgh Penguins, who finished fourth in the five-team Patrick Division, set a scoring record with 99 power-play goals. But high scoring wasn't the only news. The Mulvey incident grabbed many headlines, and the biggest surprise was the upside-down play-off field produced by the league's new system for postseason play.

The first-place team in each of the four divisions played the fourth-place team, and the second-place team met the third-place team. The winners met for the division title, and the four division champions went on to play for the two conference titles. Finally, the two conference winners met for the Stanley Cup.

In a season that was remarkably short of predictable winners, even the powerful Islanders were almost eliminated early. They met Pittsburgh in the best-of-five first-round series and were trailing, 3–1, in the decisive fifth game. Averting a major upset, the defending champions rallied for two goals in the final six minutes and won the game with an overtime score by John Tonelli. Then the Isles took the Patrick Division title by defeating the rival New York Rangers in six games.

Other first-place finishers were not so fortunate. Montreal suffered a first-round upset to Quebec, which was fourth in the Adams Division. Minnesota, the finalist against the Islanders the season before, finished first in the Norris Division but was ousted in the initial play-off round by Chicago. Edmonton, leader of the Smythe Division, was upset in the first round by Los Angeles, which had the worst record of any play-off team. The Vancouver Canucks, runners-up in the Smythe, beat Calgary, Los Angeles, and Chicago for the championship of the Campbell Conference and the right to play the Islanders, who had swept Quebec in four games for the Prince of Wales Conference title. The Canucks were bidding to become the first team since 1949 to win the Stanley Cup after completing the regular season with a losing record.

Vancouver put on a surprisingly solid performance in the first game of the finals at the Nassau Coliseum on Long Island. The teams

Violence in Hockey

Fighting is an old issue in the National Hockey League (NHL), but bloody assaults by players against players and by players against referees stirred major new controversies during the 1981–82 season. On one notable occasion, the issue was brought to the fore not by players who fought but by one who didn't. Paul Mulvey, a journeyman forward for the Los Angeles Kings, attracted wide publicity when he refused a command by coach Don Perry to join in a fight against the Vancouver Canucks.

Upswing. Perry's order to Mulvey seemed to reflect an upswing in violence around the NHL. Paul Baxter of the Pittsburgh Penguins set a league record with an astonishing 407 minutes in penalties. Jimmy Mann of the Winnipeg Jets was banned for ten games and fined $500 by a provincial court for attacking Pittsburgh's Paul Gardner and fracturing his jaw. Perhaps most disturbing was the increase in attacks against referees. Terry O'Reilly of the Boston Bruins was suspended for ten games and fined $500 for slapping referee Andy Van Hellemond in a play-off game. Paul Holmgren of the Philadelphia Flyers was suspended for five games and fined $2,000 for striking Van Hellemond. And Denis Savard of the Chicago Black Hawks was fined $500 for spitting at a referee. The most severe fine, however, was not handed down by the NHL.

Tim Coulis, a player for Dallas in the Central Hockey League, was suspended for an entire season after jumping out of the penalty box and attacking a referee in a play-off game at Salt Lake City. It was among the harshest penalties ever assessed a hockey player, and the NHL was criticized for not being as tough.

So concerned were NHL referees that they threatened job and legal actions if players were not disciplined more quickly and harshly. After the Holmgren-Van Hellemond incident, Jim Beatty, counsel for the referees, recommended that the officials go on strike or refuse to break up fights.

Backlash. If Perry's order to Mulvey was characteristic of NHL thinking, Mulvey's refusal to fight seemed to be part of a growing resistance to violence in the sport. It was an especially brave act by Mulvey, whose 6′4″ (1.93 m), 220 lb (100 kg) frame and menacing stares had earned him a place in the league. A more unlikely peacemaker there couldn't have been. After playing for three different teams in two years, however, Mulvey believed his career was in peril, and he desperately wanted to display his hockey skills at left wing. Privately he vowed to fight for a job——or rather, not to fight for one.

When Perry ordered him on to the ice, he waited until several other Kings had leaped from the bench and then did not throw a punch.

The decision cost both Perry and Mulvey dearly. Mulvey was placed on waivers by the Kings and eventually demoted to the minor leagues. After an investigation by NHL president John Ziegler, Perry was suspended for 15 days, and the Kings were fined $5,000. More importantly, serious questions were asked about the conduct of coaches and players.

While Perry was the object of much criticism, Mulvey gained sympathy from around the league. Mike Bossy, a right wing for the Stanley Cup champion New York Islanders and the leading voice against fighting, declared flatly, ''I'll never drop my gloves to fight. I don't consider it a part of the game.'' Even several NHL roughnecks became dismayed by the continued fighting in the league.

Perhaps the best examples of how unnecessary fighting is were the remarkable seasons of Edmonton's Wayne Gretzky and New York's Bossy. Gretzky set an NHL record with 212 points while receiving a mere 26 minutes in penalties. Bossy finished second in scoring with only 22 penalty minutes.

Reform Efforts. For years the NHL has had trouble coping with on-ice fighting and rising fan participation. Rules committees have attempted to reduce fighting by ordering all players not involved in a fight to move to a neutral area. However, many of the new rules simply have not worked. Although certain old-time league officials defend fighting as an acceptable ''outlet of frustration,'' those newer to the league have campaigned hard for stricter rules and more diligent enforcement. Finally on September 8, the NHL Board of Governors voted in favor of an automatic 20-game suspension for physical abuse of officials and made other rule changes to reduce fighting.

Another frequent recommendation is that league discipline should be more consistent. While many fines for fighting total only a few hundred dollars and a handful of games, Vancouver coach Roger Neilson cost his team $10,-000 by waving a white towel at a ref.

That was hardly the season's biggest irony. Mulvey finished the year in the American Hockey League, toiling in dark, cramped minor-league rinks. (After the season he was traded to Edmonton of the NHL.) But Mulvey resisted any suggestions of heroism. He didn't intend to start a crusade, he said. He only wanted to play the game.

PAT CALABRIA

ICE HOCKEY

National Hockey League
(Final Standings, 1981–82)

Wales Conference

Patrick Division	W	L	T	Pts	Goals For	Goals Against
*N.Y. Islanders	54	16	10	118	385	250
*N.Y. Rangers	39	27	14	92	316	306
*Philadelphia	38	31	11	87	325	313
*Pittsburgh	31	36	13	75	310	337
Washington	26	41	13	65	319	338
Adams Division						
*Montreal	46	17	17	109	360	223
*Boston	43	27	10	96	323	285
*Buffalo	39	26	15	93	307	273
*Quebec	33	31	16	82	356	347
Hartford	21	41	18	60	264	351

Campbell Conference

Norris Division	W	L	T	Pts	For	Against
*Minnesota	37	23	20	94	346	288
*Winnipeg	33	33	14	80	319	332
*St. Louis	32	40	8	72	315	349
*Chicago	30	38	12	72	332	363
Toronto	20	44	16	56	298	380
Detroit	21	47	12	54	271	350
Smythe Division						
*Edmonton	48	17	15	111	417	295
*Vancouver	30	33	17	77	290	286
*Calgary	29	34	17	75	334	345
*Los Angeles	24	41	15	63	314	369
Colorado	18	49	13	49	241	362

*Made play-offs

Stanley Cup: New York Islanders

INDIVIDUAL HONORS

Hart Trophy (most valuable player): Wayne Gretzky, Edmonton Oilers
Ross Trophy (leading scorer): Wayne Gretzky
Vezina Trophy (top goaltender): Bill Smith, N.Y. Islanders
Norris Trophy (best defenseman): Doug Wilson, Chicago Black Hawks
Selke Award (best defense forward): Steve Kasper, Boston Bruins
Calder Trophy (rookie of the year): Dale Hawerchuk, Winnipeg Jets
Lady Byng Trophy (sportsmanship): Rick Middleton, Boston
Conn Smythe Trophy (most valuable in play-offs): Mike Bossy, N.Y. Islanders
Coach of the Year: Tom Watt, Winnipeg Jets

Intercollegiate Champions

NCAA: University of North Dakota

were tied, 5–5, after regulation play and appeared headed for a second overtime until, with two seconds left in the first sudden-death period, Bossy intercepted a pass and fired a shot past the Vancouver goalie for a 6–5 victory. In Game Two, the Isles rallied for four goals in the third period to win, 6–4. New York had not registered a shutout all season, but in Game Three at the Pacific Coliseum in Vancouver they blanked the Canucks, 3–0, behind goalie Bill Smith. The Islanders finished off the series with a 3–1 victory, making them the first team in 12 years to sweep both the semifinal and final play-off rounds. Smith won a record 15 play-off games, and Bossy, who tied a record with seven goals in the final series, won the Conn Smythe Trophy as play-off MVP. The Isles became only the third franchise, along with Toronto and Montreal, to win at least three straight championships and kept alive their hopes of matching Montreal's record five straight cups.

There was history in the making off the ice, as well. The financially-troubled Colorado Rockies were sold to millionaire John McMullen and transferred from Denver to the Meadowlands Arena in East Rutherford, NJ.

Canada Cup. The Soviet Union defeated Canada, 8–1, in the championship game to win the six-team Canada Cup international tournament in Montreal. The Soviets had gained the final with a 4–1 semifinal victory over Czechoslovakia, which finished third.

PAT CALABRIA, *"Newsday"*

Ice Skating

Scott Hamilton of Denver became the first U.S. figure skater since Tom Wood to win the senior men's world championship two years in a row. Wood had turned the trick in 1969 and 1970. And Elaine Zayak, a 16-year-old from Paramus, NJ, gave the United States a sweep of the world individual titles by winning the senior women's event at Copenhagen, Denmark, in March.

Hamilton, a 5'3" (1.6 m), 110-pounder (50 kg), also retained his United States crown at Indianapolis in January. The 23-year-old Hamilton took the world title with relative ease. Zayak, who had been the runner-up in the 1981 world championships, rallied from seventh place with a brilliant display of free skating to beat Katarina Witt of East Germany, who was second. Claudia Kristofics-Binder of Austria finished third. In the free skating program, which counted 50% in the overall scoring, Miss Zayak made seven triple

Scott Hamilton, 23-year-old figure skater from Denver, retained the senior men's world and U.S. titles.

Ralph Martin/Duomo

jumps without faltering, to lead the field of 33 competitors.

Zayak especially enjoyed her triumph at Copenhagen since it ended a series of poor performances, including the loss of her United States title in the January championships at Indianapolis. She became the sixth American to win the world title since World War II and the first since Linda Fratianne won it in 1979.

At Copenhagen, the dance crown went to the British team of Jayne Torvill and Christopher Dean for the second straight year, and in the pairs Sabine Baess and Tassilo Thierbach of East Germany became the new champions. Miss Torvill and Dean received five perfect scores of 6.0 and two 5.9s for artistry.

Rosalynn Sumners of Edmonds, WA, dethroned Zayak for the U.S. title. Sumners rallied from fourth place entering the freestyle program. Zayak missed three of six triple jumps, a maneuver in which she usually excels, and finished third. Vikki de Vries, 17, of Colorado Springs, was second.

Hamilton was at his best in the nationals, scoring several 5.9s in beating Mark Wagenhoffer of Fontana, CA, the runner-up, and David Santee of Park Ridge, IL, who was third.

Peter and Caitlin Carruthers of Wilmington, DE, retained the pairs title and, for the second year in a row, Judy Blumberg of Colorado Springs and Michael Seibert of Carmel, IN, won the dance. The junior dance title went to Amanda Newman of Short Hills, NJ, and Jerry Santoferrara of Syracuse, NY.

Speed Skating. Hilbert van der Duim of the Netherlands won the men's world speed skating title. Karin Busch of East Germany was the overall women's champion.

GEORGE DE GREGORIO

Skiing

Phil Mahre of Yakima, WA, who became the first American to win the overall World Cup skiing championship in 1981, retained the title in 1982, clinching it as early as January 24, barely halfway through the season. Mahre's victory total was 309 points, and he took the slalom (120 points), giant slalom (105), and combined (75) crowns, as well. The women's overall championship went to Erika Hess of Switzerland, with 297 points. Christin Cooper of Sun Valley, ID, was third with 198, trailing Irene Epple of West Germany (282).

Mahre led American World Cup skiers to their best showing ever, as his twin brother, Steve, placed third behind Ingemar Stenmark of Sweden in both the overall category and in the slalom and was seventh in the giant slalom. Among American women, Cindy Nelson of Reno, NV, was fifth and Tamara McKinney of Olympic Valley, CA, was ninth in the World Cup overall category.

UPI

Steve Mahre is the first American to win a gold medal in a regular men's event at the World Alpine Championships.

The men's downhill champion was Steve Podborski of Canada, who narrowly won the title from Peter Mueller of Switzerland by having placed among the top three finishers in races more times than Mueller. Each had finished the campaign with 115 points. Harti Weirather of Austria, the 1981 champion, was third.

Marie Cecile Gros-Gaudenier of France won the women's downhill, with 84 points, beating Doris de Agostini of Switzerland and Holly Flanders of Deerfield, NH, who were second and third.

Hess won the slalom, with 125 points, but Cooper turned in a strong American effort for third place, with 88 points. Irene Epple beat out her sister, Maria, for the giant slalom laurels, with 120 points. She was followed by Hess, McKinney (fourth), Cooper (fifth), and Nelson (seventh). The combined went to Irene Epple, with Hess runner-up.

At the World Alpine Championships in Schladming, Austria, Steve Mahre became the first U.S. skier to win a gold medal in a regular men's event, taking the giant slalom. Stenmark, Weirather, and France's Michel Vion captured the slalom, the downhill, and the combined, respectively. Hess dominated the women's competition at Schladming, winning the slalom, giant slalom, and the combined. Canada's Gerry Sorensen was victorious in the women's downhill.

Bill Koch of Putney, VT, was the overall cross-country Nordic World Cup winner, with 121 points, and Armin Kogler of Austria captured the jumping title, with 189 points.

Austria won the Alpine Nations Cup with 1,492 points. The United States was third, with 1,196. Colorado earned the NCAA skiing crown.

GEORGE DE GREGORIO

Soccer

Both around the world and in the United States, 1982 was the year of the Italians in professional soccer.

World Cup. On the international level, the Italians stunned the soccer world by winning the 12th World Cup championship, held in Spain during June and July. At the outset of the quadrennial tournament, Italy was no better than a 25–1 shot to capture the coveted Havelange Cup. After the first round of games, the odds seemed entirely justified. Although it did advance to the second round, Italy had survived only as the Group I runner-up (to Poland), playing three tedious tie matches. To add to its problems, its runner-up status found them paired with powerful Brazil and Argentina in the second round. A quiet exit seemed probable.

But the Italians shocked the world by beating the tournament favorite, Brazil, 3–2, on three goals by Paolo Rossi and then by earning a berth in the semifinals with a 3–1 defeat of the defending champion, Argentina.

Italy disposed of Poland in the semifinals and then completed its miraculous performance by beating West Germany, 3–1, in the finals. Rossi, who had returned for the tournament after a two-year suspension because of alleged involvement in a game-fixing scandal, was the tournament's leading scorer with six goals.

Giorgio Chinaglia (right) of the Cosmos, the NASL's top scorer, challenges for the ball in the play-offs.

UPI

NASL. In the United States, a transplanted Italian—Giorgio Chinaglia of the New York Cosmos—scored the biggest goal of the year in the troubled North American Soccer League (NASL). His tally at 30:17 of the first half in Soccer Bowl-82, played at San Diego's Jack Murphy Stadium on September 18, gave the Cosmos a 1–0 victory over the Seattle Sounders. It also gave New York its fourth NASL title in six years and climaxed another brilliant season for Chinaglia, who had played for the Italian national team before becoming a U.S. citizen. Chinaglia again won the league scoring title, was named most valuable player (MVP) of Soccer Bowl, and continued to reign as the NASL's all-time leading scorer.

Despite Chinaglia's accomplishments, the league MVP award went to Seattle's English forward, Peter Ward, who was playing in the NASL for the first time. Ward's teammate at Seattle, Mark Peterson, was named North American player of the year, while Pedro De-Brito of the Tampa Bay Rowdies was named rookie of the year, and John Giles of the Vancouver Whitecaps was honored by his peers as coach of the year.

DeBrito's play was one of the few bright spots for the normally potent Rowdies, who fell to a record of 12–20 and failed to make the play-offs for the first time in their eight-year history. The defending Soccer Bowl champion Chicago Sting also failed to qualify, as the balance of power in the NASL shifted slightly. In a new league alignment, Seattle won the Western Division title, Fort Lauderdale the Southern Division championship, and New York the Eastern Division title. Joining these teams in the play-offs were Montreal, Toronto, Tulsa, Vancouver, and San Diego.

It was a tumultuous year in the NASL, which had lost seven franchises since the previous season and then experienced a league-wide drop in attendance. Howard Samuels was appointed the NASL's chief executive officer, replacing Phil Woosnam as the top policymaker, and immediately took steps to merge with the Major Indoor Soccer League (MISL). San Diego, Chicago, and San Jose of the NASL indoor league were admitted to the MISL for the 1982–83 season and will play in both leagues, setting the stage for an eventual merger. Two NASL outdoor teams, Edmonton and Portland, folded after the season, and Jacksonville appeared to be not far behind. The Tea Men were attempting to move to Detroit, but the deal was in question.

MISL. It was business as usual in the MISL, as the New York Arrows won the league title for the fourth straight year. No other team has ever won the championship.

Two MISL franchises—Denver and Philadelphia—asked for and received a year's "sabbatical" because of financial problems, and the Arrows merged with the New Jersey Rockets. On the other hand, there were successful fran-

SOCCER

NORTH AMERICAN SOCCER LEAGUE
(Final Standings, 1982)

Eastern Division

	W	L	G.F.	G.A.	Pts.
*New York	23	9	73	52	203
*Montreal	19	13	60	43	159
*Toronto	17	15	64	47	151
Chicago	13	19	56	67	129

Southern Division

	W	L	G.F.	G.A.	Pts.
*Ft. Lau'dale	18	14	64	74	163
*Tulsa	16	16	69	57	151
Tampa Bay	12	20	47	77	112
Jacksonville	11	21	41	71	105

Western Division

	W	L	G.F.	G.A.	Pts.
*Seattle	18	14	72	48	166
*San Diego	19	13	71	54	162
*Vancouver	20	12	58	48	160
Portland	14	18	49	44	122
San Jose	13	19	47	62	114
Edmonton	11	21	38	65	93

*Made play-offs

NASL Champion: New York Cosmos
NASL MVP: Peter Ward, Seattle Sounders
NASL Indoor Champion: San Diego Sockers

ASL Champion: Detroit Express
MISL Champion: New York Arrows
European Cup: Aston Villa, England
NCAA Champion: Indiana University

World Cup: Italy

chises in St. Louis and Baltimore, and the league expanded to Los Angeles for 1982–83.

ASL. The American Soccer League appeared to be in serious trouble. Some teams had to forfeit regular season games, and the Pennsylvania team dropped out of the play-offs.

U.S. Amateur. Karl-Heinz Heddergott, a former assistant trainer for the West German national team, was named the first director of coaching for the United States Soccer Federation (USSF). Still to be named, however, were the national and Olympic team coaches; both spots were held previously by Walt Chyzowych. Meanwhile, interim coaches Angus McAlpine and Manny Schellscheidt piloted the U.S. junior national team to a runner-up spot in CONCAF youth World Cup qualifying play. The United States was to play Israel and the champion of the Oceania area for the right to go to Mexico for the 1983 Junior World Cup.

Soccer in the United States continued to grow at the grass roots level. Participation at the youth and amateur levels were at all-time highs for both men and women—about nine million.

JIM HENDERSON, *"Tampa Tribune"*

Swimming

Numerous world records fell during 1982, seven in the World Aquatic Championships at Guayaquil, Ecuador, in August. East Germany excelled with 12 gold medals, and Americans swept the diving competition. Overall the U.S. team was a disappointment. American men set two relay world marks, but the team failed to produce an individual world standard and won only eight events. An 18-year-old Canadian, Victor Davis, broke David Wilkie's six-year-old world record in the 200-meter backstroke by .34 of a second, with a time of 2:14.77. Ricardo Prado of Brazil shattered the four-year-old record held by American Jesse Vassallo in the 400 individual medley; Prado's 4:19.78 bettered Vassallo's mark by .27 of a second. U.S. men set world marks in the 400 freestyle and 400 medley relays, with Rowdy Gaines, who lowered his world record in the 200 freestyle to 1:48.93 in July, anchoring both teams. The freestylers' 3:19.26 bettered the 3:19.74 set in 1978 by a U.S. team that also included Gaines. The medley mark of 3:40.84 erased the 3:42.22 standard of the 1976 U.S. Olympic team.

Steve Lundquist was the only other American to set a world mark in 1982; he did it twice. His 1:02.62 for the 100 breaststroke at the U.S. trials for the world championships lowered the mark held by West Germany's Gerald Mörken. A month later, Lundquist did it in 1:02.53 at the U.S. Long Course Nationals in Indianapolis. Alex Baumann of Canada lowered his record to 2:02.25 in the 200 individual medley at the Commonwealth Games in Australia, October 4.

The American sweep of the diving laurels at Guayaquil was unprecedented. Greg Louganis won the men's springboard and platform titles, Wendy Wyland took the women's platform event, and Megan Neyer took the women's springboard.

Vladimir Salnikov of the Soviet Union broke three world freestyle records early in the year, and Tracy Caulkins became the U.S. swimmer with the most wins by surpassing former Olympic great Johnny Weissmuller's record of 36 national titles. Caulkins, a freshman at the University of Florida, won her 37th in the 400 individual medley at the U.S. Short Course Championships in Gainesville, FL, April 8. Salnikov, who broke the 15-minute barrier for the 1,500 freestyle at the 1980 Olympics, lowered his record to 14:56.35 on March 13 in Moscow. The day before he broke the 400 freestyle mark of 3:50.49 set by Peter Schmidt of Canada at the 1980 Olympics, with 3:49.57. In February, Salnikov reduced the 800 freestyle record to 7:52.82, breaking the 7:56.48 he had set in 1979. In July at Kiev, he equaled his 3:49.57 for the 400.

Cornelia Sirch of East Germany replaced countrywoman Rica Reinisch as world record holder in the 200 backstroke; Sirch's 2:09.91 erased Reinisch's 2:11.77. Petra Schneider, also of East Germany, lowered her world mark in the 400 medley by .19 to 4:36.10. The East German medley relay team clipped .79 from the 4:06.67 set by their counterparts at the 1980 Olympics.

UCLA won the men's NCAA championship, and Caulkins, winning all five of her races, led Florida to the first NCAA women's title.

GEORGE DE GREGORIO

Tennis

Professional tennis is anything but predictable. Just when pundits were certain that John McEnroe and Martina Navratilova would consolidate their position as the world's best, two veteran champions, Chris Evert-Lloyd and Jimmy Connors, reasserted themselves.

Mrs. Lloyd had a frustrating early season, competing only randomly on the Avon Circuit and then losing in both the French and Wimbledon championships. However, two months later, with pride and resolution more her allies than altered tactics or strokes, she won the 1982 U.S. Open for a record sixth time and later the Australian Open for the first time.

Until September, Martina Navratilova's performance was so impressive that she was regarded as a sure bet to win a Grand Slam (revised by ITF, the International Tennis Federation, officials as any of the four major titles—French, Wimbledon, U.S. and Australian opens—won consecutively rather than in the same year). Since Navratilova had won the Australian at the end of 1981 and added the French and Wimbledon in 1982, she only had to win the U.S. championship to become the third woman in history (Maureen Connolly and Margaret Smith Court were the others) to achieve a Grand Slam. Historians and the international press corps scorned the fiddling with tradition and, without wishing ill on Navratilova, were not unhappy that fate deprived her of a short cut into the record books. At the Open she was upset by her doubles partner Pam Shriver in the quarterfinals. Previously in 1982 she had lost only in the Avon finals.

McEnroe fared far worse than Navratilova. The American Davis Cup star lost his world's number one ranking as he failed to capture a single Grand Slam title. A series of nagging leg injuries reduced McEnroe's service power, and without a terrorizing delivery to keep foes off balance, he was particularly vulnerable to rivals Ivan Lendl and Jimmy Connors.

Lendl "owned" McEnroe by beating him in the Volvo Masters semifinals and then stopping him in a $250,000 eight-man Invitation in Canada, the WCT (World Championship Tennis) finals in Dallas, as well as the U.S. Open semifinals. Lendl also won the WCT Tournament of Champions at Forest Hills and the ATP (Association of Tennis Professionals) championships in Mason, OH, where McEnroe was entered but did not reach the finals. Along the way the Czech star was compiling incredible statistics dating back to the fall of 1981, winning 91 of 95 matches before losing to teenage Swedish sensation Mats Wilander at the French Open. Wilander at 17 became the youngest man ever to triumph in a Grand Slam event—eclipsing by several months countryman Björn Borg's record at the same championships in 1975. After unheralded South African Johan Kriek's surprise victory at the Australian Open in January 1982, scribes forecast the end of the superstar era with the year's first two "slams" being won by unknown youngsters.

Connors, 30, squashed this "rookie revolution" by recapturing Wimbledon over McEnroe in a five-set final, a title he had not earned since 1974. Connors' success was popular because over the years he has shed his shroud as the game's "bad boy" and now was comfortably wearing the mantle of a family man while maintaining his trademark as a fighter to the final punch. But even his fans thought Connors' Wimbledon conquest was the final stroke on his plaque of accomplishments. Connors, however, has made a career of not conforming to people's expectations. He won the U.S. Open, defeating Guillermo Vilas in the semis and Lendl in the finals with remarkable ease.

John McEnroe, certainly no conformist either, saved his best for Davis Cup where for the fourth time in five years he led the United States to victory. The United States also won the women's Federation and Wightman cups for a perfect record in the world's team competitions.

Politically, professional tennis was as chaotic as ever. First Avon, the overall sponsor of the women's tour, decided that its cosmetic products were not compatible with the image of ladies' tennis. Virginia Slims, the women's circuit first benefactor in 1971, signed on again for 1983 promising a more cohesive organized season than ever.

The men's tour remained fragmented and disoriented. First the ATP (players' union) quit the Pro Council which administers the worldwide Grand Prix (only to rejoin later) in order to be neutral in the council's conflict with Lamar Hunt's competing circuit. Ultimately, the players were the only beneficiaries of the squabbles by virtue of inflated prize money for an overload of tournaments. As a result, such journeyman players as Tomas Smid were able to win more than $500,000 on court alone. Lendl, the most opportunistic of all, earned $1,628,850 excluding exhibitions and endorsements.

By far the weirdest political happening, however, was the Pro Council's refusal to let Björn Borg play the French Open or Wimbledon without qualifying despite his record 11 Grand Slam titles (1974–82). Borg had refused to enter the required 10 tournaments because he wanted to rest the first three months of the year.

EUGENE L. SCOTT, *"Tennis Week"*

Track and Field

Mary Decker Tabb, who feared several years ago that a calf injury would end her career, turned in track's most dazzling performances in 1982. She set three world records (her mile mark fell later to Maricica Puica of Rumania), four American records, and four world-best indoor

TENNIS

Major Team Competitions

Davis Cup: United States
Federation Cup: United States
Wightman Cup: United States

Major Tournaments

U.S. Open—men's singles: Jimmy Connors; women's singles: Chris Evert Lloyd; men's doubles: Kevin Curren (South Africa) and Steve Denton; women's doubles: Rosie Casals and Wendy Turnbull; mixed doubles: Ann Smith and Curren; men's 35 singles: Jaime Fillol (Chile); women's 35 singles: Billie Jean King; junior boys: Patrick Cash (Australia); junior girls: Beth Herr.

U.S. Clay Courts—men's singles: José Higueras (Spain); women's singles: Virginia Ruzici (Rumania); men's doubles: Sherwood Stewart and Ferdi Taygan; women's doubles: Ivanna Madruga-Osses (Argentina) and Catherine Tanvier (France).

U.S. National Indoor—men's singles: Johan Kriek (South Africa); men's doubles: Kevin Curren and Steve Denton.

National Men's 35 Clay Court Championships—Jaime Fillol.

U.S.T.A. Women's Clay Court Championships—35 singles: Judy Alvarez; 35 doubles: Alvarez and Katherine Willette; 45 singles: Nancy Reed; 45 doubles: Jane Crofford and Olga Palafox; 55 singles: Betty Pratt; 55 doubles: Jeanie Dattan and June Gay.

National Boy's 18 Championships—singles: John Letts; doubles: Rick Leach and Tim Pawsat.

National Girl's 18 Championships—singles: Leigh Anne Eldredge; doubles: Cathy Holton and Amy Holton.

Volvo Grand Prix Masters—singles: Ivan Lendl (Czechoslovakia); doubles: John McEnroe and Peter Fleming.

Other U.S. Championships

NCAA (Division 1)—singles: Mike Leach; doubles: Peter Doohan and Pat Serrete; team: UCLA.

NAIA—men's singles: Chuck Nunn; doubles: Jeff Bramlett and Russell Angell; team: Southwest Texas State; women's singles: Tarja Koho; doubles: Karen Regman and Pat Smith; team: Westmont College.

AIAW—singles: Heather Crowe; doubles: Tracie Blumentritt and Susan Rudd; team: Indiana.

Professional Championships

U.S. Pro Indoor Championships—singles: John McEnroe; doubles: McEnroe and Peter Fleming.

World Championship Tennis Tour—singles: Ivan Lendl.

Avon Championship Tennis Tour—singles: Sylvia Hanika (West Germany); doubles: Martina Navratilova and Pam Shriver.

Toyota Championship Tennis Tour—singles: Martina Navratilova; doubles: Navratilova and Pam Shriver.

Other Countries

Wimbledon—men's singles: Jimmy Connors; women's singles: Martina Navratilova; men's doubles: Peter McNamara and Paul McNamee (Australia); women's doubles: Navratilova and Pam Shriver.

Australian Open—men's singles: Johan Kriek; women's singles: Chris Evert Lloyd.

French Open—men's singles: Mats Wilander (Sweden); men's doubles: Sherwood Stewart and Ferdi Taygan; women's singles: Martina Navratilova; women's doubles: Navratilova and Pam Shriver; mixed doubles: Wendy Turnbull and John Lloyd.

Italian Open—men's singles: Andres Gomez (Ecuador); women's singles: Chris Evert Lloyd; men's doubles: Heinz Gunthardt (Switzerland) and Balazs Taroczy (Hungary); women's doubles: Kathy Horvath and Yvonne Vermaak (South Africa).

Canadian Open—men's singles: Vitas Gerulaitis; women's singles: Martina Navratilova; men's doubles: Steve Denton and Mark Edmondson; women's doubles: Navratilova and Candy Reynolds.

N.B. All players are from the United States, unless otherwise noted.

Leading Money Winners
As of Dec. 31, 1982

Ivan Lendl	$1,628,850	M. Navratilova	$1,475,055
José-Luis Clerc	590,400	Chris Evert Lloyd	689,458
Tomas Smid	552,200	Andrea Jaeger	423,315
Jimmy Connors	543,850	Wendy Turnbull	371,196
Wojtek Fibak	533,626	Pam Shriver	354,168
John McEnroe	525,725	Barbara Potter	270,015
Guillermo Vilas	502,150	Bettina Bunge	248,598
Johan Kriek	364,098	Hana Mandlikova	231,283
Vitas Gerulaitis	340,875	Sylvia Hanika	215,151
Kevin Curren	293,427	Anne Smith	212,754

UPI

The top money winners—Ivan Lendl and Martina Navratilova—frequently raised their arms in victory in 1982. Lendl failed, however, to win a Grand Slam event.

UPI

Carl Lewis continued to make track headlines. His prime goal is Bob Beamon's long jump record of 29'2½".

records in aiming her sights at the 1984 Olympics in Los Angeles, where she grew up.

Although indoor times are not recognized as world records by the international track federation, the extensive indoor season serves as a gauge for an athlete's potential proficiency during the outdoor campaign. Mrs. Tabb's indoor ledger began on January 22 at Los Angeles, with a 4:24.6 mile, a time she reduced to 4:21.47, then 4:20.5, on successive weekends in New York and San Diego in February. Her 8:47.3 for 3,000 meters indoors set a world-best and an American mark on February 5 at Inglewood, CA.

She began her outdoor assault in June, setting world and American records of 15:08.26 for 5,000 meters at Eugene, OR. At Oslo on July 7, she set an American standard of 8:29.71 for 3,000. Two days later, she broke the world and American marks for the mile at Paris, with 4:18.08. Her fourth American record came in the 10,000 at Eugene—31:35.3. Miss Puica, who also won the world cross-country title in March (14:38.9), lowered the mile to 4:17.44 on September 16 at Rieti, Italy. The women's 3,000-meter world record was broken by Svetlana Ulmasova of the Soviet Union with 8:26.78 at Kiev in July.

The much-awaited and publicized match-up in the mile between Sebastian Coe, England's world-record holder in the mile and 800, and Steve Ovett, his countryman and world-record holder in the 1,500, did not materialize. Both runners pulled out of races in which they were to compete because of injuries or personal reasons. The best time for the mile for the year was posted by an American, Steve Scott, whose 3:47.69 at Oslo became the second-best mile ever, just behind Coe's 1981 record 3:47.33 and ahead of Ovett's 3:48.40.

Coe, however, managed to break into the world-record listings. He anchored England's national team, which ran a record 7:03.89 in the 3,200-meter relay, at London on August 30. The other members were Peter Elliott, Garry Cook, and Steve Cram. Their time bettered the 1978 Soviet national team's mark by 4.21 seconds.

A 1981 record held by Henry Rono, the Kenyan who is the world-record holder in the 3,000 and 10,000 and the 3,000 steeplechase, fell to 29-year-old Englishman David Moorcroft, who has been competing in the shadow of Coe and Ovett. His time of 13:00.42 at Oslo on July 7 knocked 5.78 seconds off Rono's record in the 5,000 and was the greatest reduction of the record for that event since 1966.

At the European championships at Athens, Greece, three world records fell on September 8. Daley Thompson of England scored 8,743 points in the decathlon to reclaim the mark from Jurgen Hingsen, who had set the record with 8,723 points three weeks earlier. Marita Koch of East Germany, world-record holder in the 200 dash, lowered her 1979 mark in the 400 by .45 of a second to 0:48.15, and Ulrike Meyfarth of West Germany bettered the 1979 high jump of 6'7¼" by the Italian Sara Simeoni with a leap of 6'7½". Three days later, the East German national 1,600-meter relay team, anchored by Miss Koch, broke the six-year-old record of another East German team, with 3:19.05.

In field events, Soviet hammer-thrower Sergei Litvinov set a record of 275'6" in July. Among the women, Sofia Sakorafa of Greece threw the javelin 243'5" on September 26 to erase the 237'6" mark set by Tiina Lillak of Finland in July, and Vali Ionescu of Rumania set a long jump record of 23'7½" at Bucharest. Ralph Kowalsky of East Germany set marks in walking, 17 miles 1,092 yards for 2 hours, and 2:06.54 for 30,000 meters.

Alberto Salazar, who set American records in the 5,000 and 10,000, won the 86th Boston Marathon in 2:08.51, a record for the event and only .38 of a second off his world record for the marathon. Charlotte Teske of West Germany (2:29.33) was first among the women. Later in the year, Salazar (2:09.29) and Norway's Grete Waitz (2:27.14) captured the New York City Marathon. Mohammad Kedir of Ethiopia won the men's world cross-country title (33:40.5). In a dual meet at Indianapolis, the USSR beat the United States for the 14th time in 17 years.

In October the International Olympic Committee agreed to return the two gold medals Jim Thorpe won at the 1912 Olympic Games in Stockholm. The American-Indian athlete, who died in 1953, had been deprived of the medals for accepting about $60 per month playing professional baseball.

GEORGE DE GREGORIO

SPORTS SUMMARIES[1]

ARCHERY—U.S. Champions: men: Rich McKinney, Glendale, AZ; women: Luann Ryon, Parker Dam, CA.
BADMINTON—World Champions: men's singles: Rudy Hartono, Indonesia; women's singles: Wiharjo Verawaty, Indonesia. **U.S. Champions:** men's singles: Gary Higgins, Alhambra, CA; women's singles: Cheryl Carton, San Diego.
BIATHLON—World Champions: men's 20 km: Frank Ullrich, E. Germany; 10 km: Erik Kvalfoss, Norway; world cup: F. Ullrich.
BILLIARDS—World Champions: men's pocket: Steve Mizerak, Fords, NJ; women's pocket: Jean Balukas, Brooklyn.
BOBSLEDDING—World Champions: two-man: Erich Schaerer, Switzerland; four-man: Silvio Giobellina, Switzerland.
BOWLING—Professional Bowling Association: leading money winner: Earl Anthony, Dublin, CA; national champion: Earl Anthony; men's world cup: Arnie Stroem, Norway; women's world cup: Jeannette Baker, Australia. **American Bowling Congress:** singles: Bruce Bohm, Chicago (748); doubles: Rich Wonders, Racine, WI, and Darold Meisel, Milwaukee (1,364); all-events: Rich Wonders (2,076); masters: Joe Berardi, Brooklyn, NY; team: Carl's Bowlers Paddock, Cincinnati (3,268). **Women's International Bowling Congress:** open division: singles: Gracie Freeman, Alexandria, VA (652); doubles: (tie) P. Costello, Fremont, CA, and D. Adamek, Duarte, CA; S. Hintz, Merrit Island, FL, and L. Wrathgeber, Palmetto, FL (1,264).
CANOEING—U.S. Champions (flatwater): men's kayak: 500 m: Greg Barton, Homer, MI; 1,000 m: Greg Barton; 10,000 m: Greg Barton; women's kayak: 500 m: Cathy Marino-Gregory, Huntington Beach, CA; men's canoe: 500 m: Rob Plakenhorn, Roselle, IL; 1,000 m: Blaise Stanek, New York City; 10,000 m: Rob Plakenhorn.
CRICKET—World Champion: West Indies.
CROSS-COUNTRY—World Champions: men: Mohammed Kedir, Ethiopia; women: Maricica Puica, Rumania. **NCAA:** men: Mark Scrutton, Colorado; women: Lesley Welch, Virginia.
CURLING—World Champions: men: Canada; women: Denmark. **U.S. Champions:** men: Madison, WI; women: Illinois.
CYCLING—Tour de France: Bernard Hinault, France. **World Pro Champions:** sprint: Connie Paraskevin, Detroit; pursuit: Rebecca Twig, Seattle; road: Giuseppe Saronni, Italy; women's road: Mandy Jones, Britain. **U.S. Road Racing Champions:** men: G. Demgen, Lacrosse, WI; women: Sue Novara-Reber, Flint, MI.
DOG SHOWS—Westminster (New York): best: Ch. St. Aubrey Dragonara of Elsdon, Pekingese owned by Anne Snelling, Ottawa. **International** (Chicago): best: Ch. Beaucrest Ruffian, Bouvier des Flandres owned by Pat and Roy Schiller, Ijamsville, MD.
FENCING—World Champions: men: foil: Aleksandr Romankov, USSR; épée: Jeno Pap, Hungary; saber: Viktor Krovopouskov, USSR; Women: foil: Naila Giliazova, USSR. **North American Cup:** men: foil: Greg Massialas, U.S.; épée: Lee Shelley, U.S.; saber: Pete Westwood, U.S.; women: foil: Jana Angelakis, U.S.
FIELD HOCKEY—World Cup (men): Pakistan. **International Cup** (women): Netherlands.
GYMNASTICS—U.S. Gymnastics Federation Champions: men's all-around: Peter Vidmar, Los Angeles; women's all-around: Tracee Talavera, Walnut Creek, CA. **NCAA:** men: all-around: Peter Vidmar, UCLA; team: Nebraska. Women: all-around: Sue Stednitz, Utah; team: Utah.
HANDBALL—U.S. Handball Association Champions (4-wall): men: singles: Naty Alvarado, Hesperia, CA; doubles: Naty Alvarado and Vern Roberts, Chicago; women: singles: Rosemary Bellini, New York City; doubles: Allison Roberts, Ohio, and Glorian Motal, Houston.
HORSE SHOWS—World Cup: Melanie Smith, United States, on Calypso. **U.S. Equestrian Team Champions:** three-day eventing: Grant Schneidman on Flying Dutchman; show jumping: Conrad Homfeld on Balbucl; dressage: Kay Meredith on Domino.
ICE SKATING, SPEED—U.S. Outdoor Champions: men: Greg Oly, Minneapolis; women: Lisa Merrifield, Butte, MT. **U.S. Indoor Champions:** men: (tie) Jack Mortell, Evanston, IL, and Paul Jacobs, Park Ridge, IL; women: Lydia Stephans, Northbrook, IL.
JUDO—U.S. Champions: men: 132-lb class: Rod Condurages, Wantagh, NY; 143: James Martin, San Gabriel, CA; 156: Mike Swain, Bridgewater, NJ; 172: Brett Barron, San Mateo, CA; 189: Robert Berland, Wilmette, IL; under 209: Leo White, U.S. Army; over 209: Douglas Nelson, Englewood, NJ; open: Mitch Santa Maria, Rochelle Park, NJ. Women: 106: Darlene Anaya, Albuquerque, NM; 114: Mary Lewis, Albany, NY; 123: Geri Bindell, New Milford, NJ; 134: Cindy Sovljanski, Sterling Heights, MI; 145: Chris Penick, San Jose, CA; 158: Eileen O'Connell, Bayside, NY; over 158: Margaret Castro, New York City; open: Heidi Baversachs, New York City.
KARATE—U.S. Champions (AAU): 60 kg and under: George Gino, Cleveland; 70 kg: Michael Sledge, New York City; 75 kg: John DiPasquale, Chicago; 80 kg: Terrance Tokey Hill, Chillicothe, OH; open heavyweight class: Bob Allen, New Orleans.

[1] *Sports not covered separately in pages 467–488.*

LACROSSE—NCAA: men's Division I: North Carolina; Division III: Hobart; women: Massachusetts.
LUGE—U.S. Champions: men: singles: Frank Masley, Newark, DE; doubles: Terry Morgan, Saranac Lake, NY, and Bo Jamieson, Hudson, OH; Women: singles: Erica Terwillegar, Lake Placid, NY.
PLATFORM TENNIS—U.S. Champions: open singles: Doug Russell, New York City; men's doubles: Steve Baird, Harrison, NY, and Rich Maier, Allendale, NJ; women's doubles: Evonne Hackenberg, Kalamazoo, MI, and Hilary Hilton, Glen Ellyn, IL; mixed doubles: Doug Russell and Hillary Marold, New York City.
POLO—Gold Cup: Boehm, Palm Beach, FL; **World Cup:** Boehm; **America Cup:** Aiken (SC) Polo Club; **U.S. Open:** Retama, San Antonio, TX.
RACQUETBALL—U.S. Champions: men's amateur open: Jack Newman, Morton Grove, IL; women's open: Diane Bullard, Gainesville, FL; men's pro: Marty Hogan, San Diego, CA; women's pro: Heather McKay, Toronto.
RODEO—Professional Rodeo Cowboy Association: all-around: Chris Lybbert, Coyote, CA.
ROWING—World Champions: men: four with coxswain: E. Germany; double sculls: Norway; pair without coxswain: Norway; single sculls: E. Germany; pair with coxswain: Italy; four without coxswain: Switzerland; four without coxswain (small): United States; quad: E. Germany; eight: New Zealand. **U.S. Collegiate Champions:** men: pair with coxswain: Northeastern; pair without coxswain: Wisconsin; four with coxswain: Wisconsin; four without coxswain: University of Pennsylvania; eight: Cornell. Women's nationals: single: Dartmouth; quad: Boston, Dartmouth, California Irvine, Zlac (CA); pair without coxswain: Lake Washington; four with coxswain: College Boat Club, PA; double: Dartmouth; eight: College Boat Club.
RUGBY—U.S. Champions: club: Old Blues, Berkeley, CA; collegiate: University of California, Berkeley. **Test Matches:** United States 3, Canada 3; England 59, United States 0.
SOFTBALL—U.S. Amateur Softball Association Champions: men: major fast pitch: Peterbilt Western, Seattle; class-A fast pitch: Tee House, Stockton, CA; major slow pitch: Triangle, Minneapolis; class-A slow pitch: Lawson Auto Parts, Altamonte Springs, FL. Women: major fast pitch: Raybestos Brakettes, Stratford, CT; class-A fast pitch: San Diego Astros; major slow pitch: Stompers, Richmond, VA; class-A slow pitch: Circle K Roadrunners, Phoenix.
SQUASH RACQUETS—World Champion: pro: Michael Desaulniers, New York City. **U.S. Squash Racquets Association Champions:** men: singles: John Nimick, Narbeth, PA; doubles: Lawrence Heath, Cos Cob, CT, and John Reese, Cold Spring Harbor, NY; North American Open: Michael Desaulniers: college team: Harvard. Women: singles: Alicia McConnell, Brooklyn, NY; doubles: Joyce Davenport, King of Prussia, PA, and Carol Thesieres, Broomall, PA.
TABLE TENNIS—U.S. Open Champions: men: singles: Zoran Kosanovic, Canada; doubles: Danny and Ricky Seemiller, Pittsburgh; team: Japan. Women: singles: Kayoko Kawahigashi, Japan; doubles: Shin Deuk Hwa and Jung Kyung, South Korea; team: South Korea.
VOLLEYBALL—U.S. Champions: USVBA Open: men: Chuck's Steak House, Los Angeles; women: Monarch, Honolulu. **NCAA:** men: UCLA; women: Southern California. **AIAW:** Texas-Austin.
WATER POLO—U.S. Champions: outdoor: men: Industry Hills, CA; women: Slippery Rock, PA. **NCAA:** University of California, Irvine.
WEIGHTLIFTING—U.S. Weightlifting Federation Champions: 114-lb class: Brian Okada, Wailuku, HI; 123: Albert Hood, Chicago; 132: Philip Sanderson, Billings, MT; 148: Don Abrahamson, San Jose, CA; 165: Cal Schake, Butler, PA; 181: Curt White, Colorado Springs; 198: Kevin Winter, San Jose, CA; 220: Ken Clark, Pacifica, CA; 242: Jeff Nickels, Chicago; over 242: Mario Martinez, San Francisco.
WRESTLING—World Cup Champions (freestyle): 105.5-lb class: Adam Cuestas, United States; 114.5: Joe Gonzalez, United States; 125.5: Sergei Beloglazov, USSR; 136.5: Viktor Alexeev, USSR; 149.5: Mikhail Kharachura, USSR; 163: Lee Kemp, United States; 180.5: Mark Schultz, United States; 198: Clark Davis, Canada; 220: Magomed Magomedov, USSR; heavyweight: Salman Chasimikov, USSR; team: United States. **AAU Freestyle:** 105.5: Bill Rosado, Sunkist Kids; 114.5: Bob Weaver NYAC; 125.5: Gene Mills, NYAC; 136.5: Lee Roy Smith, Cowboy Wrestling Club; 149.5: Andy Rein, Wisconsin Wrestling Club; 163: Lee Kemp, Wisconsin Wrestling Club; 180.5: Bruce Kinseth, Hawkeye Wrestling Club; 198: Bill Scherr, Nebraska Olympic Club; 220: Greg Gibson, U.S. Marines; heavyweight: Bruce Baumgartner, NYAC; team: NYAC. **AAU Greco-Roman:** 105.5: T. J. Jones, U.S. Navy; 114.5: Mark Fuller, Little C Athletic Club; 125.5: Dan Mello, U.S. Marines; 136.5: Frank Famiano, Adirondack 3-Style Club; 149.5: Doug Yates, Canada; 163: John Matthews, Michigan Wrestling Club; 180.5: Tom Press, Minnesota Wrestling Club; 198: Steve Fraser, Michigan Wrestling Club; 220: Greg Gibson, U.S. Marines; heavyweight: Pete Lee, Grand Rapids, MI; team: U.S. Marines.
YACHTING—U.S. Yacht Racing Union: champion of champions: John Kostecki, Novato, CA; world women's champion: Marit Soderstrom, Sweden; Mallory Cup (men): M.J.B. Golison, Long Beach, CA; Adams Trophy (women): Heidi Backus, Vermilion, OH.

SRI LANKA

The United National government, headed by President Junius R. Jayewardene, commemorated the fifth anniversary of its accession to power on July 22, 1982. Its political position remained strong, as was demonstrated by Jayewardene's victory in the October elections. While the level of communal violence declined, Sri Lanka's internal situation remained unstable.

Political Events. Opposition groups leveled charges of corruption against the United National Party in 1982, and in reply the party launched an anticorruption campaign. Both the Sri Lanka Freedom Party and the Lanka Sama Samaj Party remained weak and divided. President Jayewardene was able to win the support of the largest labor union and the mainstream group (the Tamil United Liberation Front) among the Tamils, the largest minority.

On January 16 the prolonged national emergency, in effect since August 1981, was lifted. But because of internal conflict, mainly between Sinhalese and Muslims, the emergency was reimposed on July 30.

Although presidential elections were not due until 1984, President Jayewardene decided to hold them in October. In the elections of October 20, Jayewardene received about 52% of the vote, while his main opponent, Hector Kobbekaduwa, received about 37%. This was the first election under the presidential system established in the 1978 constitution. Tensions had been high during the campaign, and after the polls had closed the government proclaimed a limited state of emergency as a precautionary measure.

The Economy. The economic situation was adversely affected by severe droughts early in the year. They were a major factor in the slump in tea and coconut production, both major export items. High levels of public spending, relatively low levels of economic growth, and a large deficit in the balance of payments also affected the country's economic situation.

At a meeting in Tokyo in July, members of the Sri Lanka aid consortium pledged $682 million in economic assistance for the next fiscal year, while at the same time urging greater efforts to meet long-term problems. The new budget for fiscal 1983 called for more rigorous financial management, but it still envisioned a large deficit in the balance of payments. Significant achievements included the lowering of the rate of inflation and the successful promotion of foreign investment.

Foreign Affairs. A highlight of the year was the six-day visit in February of N. Sanjiva Reddy, president of India. A new Sino-Sri Lankan trade pact was signed in January. In March, Sri Lanka extended diplomatic recognition to the Palestine Liberation Organization. In June, Sri Lanka's application for membership in the Association of Southeast Asian Nations was turned down on geographic grounds.

NORMAN D. PALMER, *University of Pennsylvania*

SRI LANKA • Information Highlights

Official Name: Democratic Socialist Republic of Sri Lanka.
Location: Island off the southeastern coast of India.
Area: 25,332 sq mi (65 610 km^2).
Population (1982 est.): 15,200,000.
Chief City (1978 est.): Colombo, the capital, 624,000.
Government: *Head of state,* Junius R. Jayewardene, president (took office Feb. 1978). *Head of government,* Ranasinghe Premadasa, prime minister (took office Feb. 1978). *Legislature* (unicameral)—National State Assembly.
Monetary Unit: Rupee (20.7 rupees equal U.S.$1, March 1982).
Gross National Product (1980 U.S.$): $4,070,000,-000.
Economic Index: *Consumer Prices* (Feb. 1982, 1970= 100), *all items,* 294.8; *food,* 322.7.
Foreign Trade (1981 U.S.$): *Imports,* $1,803,000,-000; *exports,* $1,036,000,000.

STAMPS AND STAMP COLLECTING

In 1982, philately saw the overdue end of a boom that had plagued it for about a decade. When profits on highly touted stamps did not materialize, withdrawal of speculators from the market drove prices to more realistic levels. Many of the firms that promoted and catered to the investment trade since the 1970s were forced out of business by the slump. The two largest were sold by conglomerates who had acquired them as potential moneymakers at the market's peak a few years before.

A number of Third World nations with ties to the British Commonwealth marked the 21st birthday of the princess of Wales and the birth of the royal baby with commemorative stamps. Catering to a widespread interest in Prince Charles and Lady Diana, the "omnibus" sets were not popular follow-ups to the 1981 royal wedding commemoratives.

Other events marked by commemoratives included the 75th anniversary of scouting and the 125th birth anniversary of its founder, Lord Robert Baden-Powell; the centenary of Dr. Robert Koch's discovery of the TB bacillus; the 800th birth anniversary of St. Francis of Assisi; the death centenary of Charles Darwin; and the 250th birth anniversary of George Washington. The Argentine invasion of the Falkland Islands sparked a temporary boom in Falklands stamps, but interest dwindled when Britain recaptured the islands.

To increase sales to collectors, the U.S. Postal Service not only turned out more stamps than official guidelines stipulate, but it contracted with dealers in Europe and Japan to sell them abroad on a commission basis.

Records were set at a New York auction in April, when two U.S. stamps with "inverted center" misprints sold for $198,000 apiece ($180,000 plus a 10% buyer's premium). One stamp,

SELECTED U.S. COMMEMORATIVE STAMPS, 1982

Subject	Denomination	Date
Ralph Bunche	20¢	Jan. 12
Crazy Horse	13¢	Jan. 15
Robert Millikan	37¢	Jan. 26
F. D. Roosevelt	20¢	Jan. 30
LOVE	20¢	Feb. 1
George Washington	20¢	Feb. 22
Francis Marion	13¢ postal card	April 3
LaSalle Expedition	13¢ postal card	April 7
Birds and Flowers	50x20¢	April 14
Netherlands Friendship	20¢	April 20
Library of Congress	20¢	April 21
Consumer Education	20¢	April 27
World's Fair	4x20¢	April 29
Aging Together	20¢	May 21
Barrymores	20¢	June 8
Mary Walker	20¢	June 10
Academy of Music	13¢ postal card	June 18
Peace Gardens	20¢	June 30
American Libraries	20¢	July 13
Jackie Robinson	20¢	Aug. 2
Purple Heart	20¢ envelope	Aug. 6
Touro Synagogue	20¢	Aug. 22
Wolf Trap	20¢	Sept. 1
World Trade	30¢ aerogramme	Sept. 16
Architecture	4x20¢	Sept. 30
St. Francis of Assisi	20¢	Oct. 7
Ponce de Leon	20¢	Oct. 12
Christmas	5x20¢	Oct. 28
Christmas	13¢	Nov. 3

printed in 1869, portrays Columbus' landing in the New World—upside down. The other, a 1918 airmail stamp known as an "upside-down Jenny," depicts a Curtiss biplane.

Because of organizational mismanagement and lack of publicity, the international exhibitions in Tokyo and Paris proved disappointing. Only the exhibition in Vaduz, for the 70th anniversary of the first Liechtenstein stamps, proved to be an outstanding success.

Responding to the desire of many beginning collectors to learn more about the avocation's appeals, more than a dozen colleges began to offer courses as part of adult education programs. The Philatelic Foundation, the American Philatelic Society, and other institutions conducted seminars and found them so popular that they planned to expand them in the future. Programs also were inaugurated to encourage more youngsters to collect stamps.

ERNEST A. KEHR, *Director, Stamp News Bureau*

STOCKS AND BONDS

The stock and bond markets of Wall Street staged a historic rally in 1982, raising hopes for a recovery from the worst recession in the U.S. economy since the 1930s. (See also feature article, page 38.)

In a whirlwind advance from mid-August to early November, the Dow Jones average of 30 industrial stocks, which represents "the market" to millions of investors, soared almost 40% from a two-year low to a record high. Bond prices also ran up dramatic gains as interest rates dropped sharply and evidence mounted that the virulent inflation of the past several years was abating.

Trading volume records toppled at the New York Stock Exchange as the rally progressed. Before Aug. 18, 1982, the exchange had never had a trading day in which more than 100 million shares changed hands. In the few months that followed, that milestone was passed more than 20 times.

At the close on December 31, the Dow Jones industrials stood at 1,046.54, up 171.54 points, or 19.6%, from a year earlier. NYSE volume, at 16,460,000,000 shares, far surpassed the record of 11,850,000,000 set in 1981.

One of the rally's most exuberant days came on November 3, when the "Dow" climbed a record 43.41 points to 1,065.49. With that upsurge, the average surpassed a peak that had stood as a financial Everest for almost a decade—a 1,051.70 close reached on Jan. 11, 1973. That record was broken, however, on December 27 when the Dow jumped 25.48 points to close at a new high of 1,070.55.

But if a new bull market was dawning on Wall Street, many businessmen, workers, and consumers were in no mood to join in the celebration. The unemployment rate, as reported by the U.S. Labor Department, rose above 10% for the first time in more than four decades. Other economic statistics showed American factories operating at less than 70% of capacity, and business failures at their highest level since the 1930s.

Yet many followers of the securities markets argued that the rise of stock prices and the decline of interest rates were harbingers of better times ahead for Main Street as well as Wall Street. Stock prices are traditionally considered a good, if not perfect, advance indicator of business and economic trends. Donald T. Regan, secretary of the Treasury and former chairman of Merrill Lynch & Co., the nation's largest investment firm, borrowed from his old employer's advertising slogan to declare, "the stock market is bullish on America."

The enthusiasm that swept Wall Street had some echoes in European investment markets. Stock prices in Great Britain, where inflation also slowed, showed a 25.45% gain for the first 10 months of the year, according to statistics compiled by the U.S. investment management firm of T. Rowe Prices Associates. The Dutch market was up 19.41%; France 14.57%; West Germany 8.52%; and Switzerland 5.63%.

But the story was far different in the Pacific Basin, with the volatile Hong Kong market down 39.02%. Australia was off 8.94% and Japan was down 4.95%. The Canadian markets recorded a 4.42% drop during the same period.

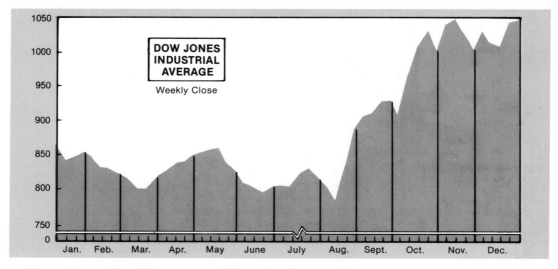

The early months of the year gave little evidence of the fireworks to come on Wall Street. The Dow Jones industrials, which had fallen 88.99 points in 1981, dropped almost 100 points further to 776.92 by August 12. The markets were jolted by a series of unpleasant surprises in the spring and early summer, including the collapse of a government-securities trading firm, Drysdale Government Securities, and the failure of the Penn Square Bank of Oklahoma City, OK. Professional stock traders who had speculated on the plans of Gulf Oil Corp. to acquire Cities Service Co. got a bad scare when Gulf backed out of the deal. But a third energy concern, Occidental Petroleum Corp., emerged soon afterward as a buyer for Cities Service.

Merger specialists in the financial community also drew some criticism for their role in perhaps the most bizarre takeover struggle in U.S. business history, involving Bendix Corp., Martin Marietta Corp., United Technologies Corp., and Allied Corp. Bendix began the month-long battle with a bid to buy Martin Marietta; Martin Marietta, backed by United Technologies, retaliated with an offer for Bendix, setting the two parties on a collision course. The brawl reached its apparent denouement when Allied stepped in to buy Bendix and a minority interest in Martin Marietta, which otherwise remained independent.

While events like those were dominating the financial headlines, another important development was quietly taking shape. Slowly at first, more rapidly later on, the high interest rates that had been depressing economic activity for two years were coming down. Rates on three-month Treasury bills, as high as 17% in 1981, stood at about 8% by the fall of 1982. Tax-exempt municipal bonds that carried rates as high as 13.4% in January 1982 were yielding 9.25% nine months later. Because prices of existing bonds rise when interest rates decline, bond holders were able to reap big profits from that decline. A long-term

Treasury bond worth about $940 in June was selling for about $1,300 in early November.

Lending impetus to the decline of rates, and to the stock market's boom, was an apparent shift in strategy by the Federal Reserve in its job of overseeing the supply of money and credit in the economy. "The Fed," as it is commonly referred to, lowered its discount rate—the charge it sets on loans to private financial institutions—from 12% at midsummer to 8.5% by year-end. Paul Volcker, the Fed's chairman, repeated his aim of controlling inflation by restricting the growth of the money supply. But many observers outside the Fed concluded that the central bank was successful enough in that mission, and worried enough about the depressed state of business, to shift its sights toward stimulating the economy.

In contrast to the double-digit inflation rates that had prevailed at the start of the decade, the Consumer Price Index rose at an annual rate of 4.8% in the first nine months of 1982. Some private economists predicted lower figures for 1983.

Despite the markets' strong performance, many economists remained doubtful that anything more than a slight improvement in business activity was in prospect for early 1983. Politicians and financial experts alike voiced concern over huge and growing deficits in the accounts of the U.S. government.

There was great uneasiness, as well, about financial woes afflicting other countries as diverse as Argentina, Mexico, and Poland, and the possibility that they could lead to an international credit crisis. Indeed, analysts pointed out, some of the fuel for the U.S. markets' gains came from international investors engaging in a "flight to safety" into U.S. government securities and blue-chip stocks. To the extent that that was true, there were elements of fear as well as hope in the Great Wall Street Rally of 1982.

CHET CURRIER
The Associated Press

SUDAN

In January, rioting in Khartoum, Omdurman, and other cities over the elimination of subsidies on sugar and gasoline, and a 12% devaluation in the currency—required in return for a $250 million loan from the International Monetary Fund (IMF)—resulted in a political shakeup. Khartoum's universities and secondary schools were closed in the wake of the violence.

In late January, President Jaafar al-Nemery fired his first vice-president and defense minister, Abdel Majed Hamid Khalil, assuming the positions himself, and dissolved the central committee and politburo of the ruling Sudanese Socialist Union (SSU). A 41-member "popular committee" was named to replace the SSU structures and to reorganize the party leadership.

Tensions between the central government and the semiautonomous, predominantly Christian South flared a decade after the signing of the Addis Ababa Agreement which ended the North-South civil war. In January, more than 20 leading southern politicians were detained after forming the Council for the Unity of Southern Sudan to resist government measures to divide the South into three smaller regions.

In late June, Nemery removed second vice-president Abel Alier from his post and replaced him with Joseph Lagu. Alier, a veteran southern politician, had opposed the redivision plans. Elections for a new regional assembly for the South were held in late June. Nemery had dissolved the legislature in October 1981, and had appointed a transitional administration. Joseph Tembura, formerly minister of public works, transport, and communications, was elected president of the South's High Executive Council.

In March, the Paris Club of 13 Western creditor countries agreed to reschedule $500 million of Sudan's official debt, the final phase of a $1,000,000,000 rescheduling program. The move followed the IMF's approval of a $250 million one-year credit for Sudan in October 1981, contingent upon the adoption of the austerity measures that provoked the January riots.

SUDAN • Information Highlights

Official Name: Democratic Republic of Sudan.
Location: Northeast Africa.
Area: 967,500 sq mi (2 505 825 km²).
Population (1982 est.): 19,900,000.
Chief Cities (April 1973): Khartoum, the capital, 333,-906; Omdurman, 299,399; Khartoum North, 150,-989.
Government: *Head of state,* Gen. Jaafar Mohammed al-Nemery, president (took office following election, Oct. 1971). *Legislature* (unicameral)—National People's Assembly.
Monetary Unit: Pound (0.90090 pound equals U.S.$1, March 1982).
Gross Domestic Product (1981 U.S.$): $12,160,000,-000.
Economic Index (1979): *Consumer Prices* (1970= 100), *all items,* 385.9; *food,* 398.3.
Foreign Trade (1980 U.S.$): *Imports,* $1,616,000,-000; *exports,* $543,000,000.

Sudan's total external debt was estimated at $6,000,000,000, and in September it was feared that the country would have to reschedule its $600 million commercial debt for a second time because of delays in the payment of the latest IMF tranche. Sudan failed to make a $22 million interest payment to commercial banks in June and told bankers it did not have funds available for the payment due in September.

Sudan's hopes to become an oil exporter received a boost with the news in September that Standard Oil of California would build a 900-mi (1 448-km) pipeline from its oil fields in south-central Sudan to a terminal on the Red Sea, thus speeding up the schedule for projected oil deliveries from 1986 to 1985.

Foreign Relations. In October, Sudan and Egypt signed a "charter of integration," aimed at pooling their resources. The pact provides for the establishment of a Higher Council headed by the two presidents, a joint Nile Valley parliament, and a joint fund to finance ventures with international monetary support.

Under a 1976 mutual defense treaty, the Khartoum government held discussions in May about deploying Egyptian troops on the 1,200-mi (1 931-km) Sudan-Ethiopia border to intercept alleged Libyan-trained saboteurs. Sudan's relations with Ethiopia were rocky in 1982, despite a June agreement to end activities within each country by dissidents.

MARGARET A. NOVICKI, *"Africa Report"*

SWEDEN

The year in Sweden was climaxed by the return to power of the Social Democratic party and of Olof Palme as prime minister.

Elections. The campaign preceding the September 19 general elections was dominated by the issues of the economy and employment. A very rapidly growing deficit in the national budget and a low level of industrial investment demanded a change in economic policy. The opposition also attacked government cutbacks in social programs. The single most controversial proposal was that of the Social Democrats for the establishment of wage-earner funds. Financed by payroll and excess-profit taxes, the fund would buy shares in private companies on behalf of workers. The government and industrial sector said the program would mean "socialization of the Swedish economy" and argued that the existing system of subsidized share investment savings was adequate.

All 349 seats in the one-chamber Riksdag (parliament) were up for election, as well as every seat in the nation's 23 county councils and 279 municipal councils. As predicted in the pre-election public opinion polls, the Social Democrats won a substantial victory. Garnering 46% of the vote, the party increased its representation in parliament by 12 seats, to 166. The three nonsocialist parties together won 163 seats—Conservatives 86, Center Party 56, and Liberals 21. The Communist Party took 5.6% of the vote to retain its 20 mandates.

Outgoing Prime Minister Thorbjörn Fälldin resigned September 20 and was asked by the speaker of parliament to continue as caretaker until a Social Democratic government, under party leader Olof Palme, could be formed. On October 7, six years after leaving office, the 55-year-old Palme was sworn in as premier. His cabinet was installed the next day. For the stated purpose of strengthening exports and thereby creating jobs, the government immediately announced a 16% devaluation of the krona. A general price freeze was also put into effect.

Economy. The October devaluation followed a 10% currency cut in September 1981, which did allow export-oriented industries to meet the expected increase in demand with added competitive clout. But exports were the only reasonably strong sector in the Swedish economy, and some analysts even questioned the improvement in that area. A burdensome foreign debt, heavy balance of payment deficit, inflation rate of about 9%, and uncharacteristically high unemployment prompted Palme's initiatives. Unemployment was regarded as the key matter. Sweden in 1982 was witnessing its highest unemployment figures since World War II. In June there were 131,000 workers out of a job, 52% more than at the same time in 1981. In subsequent months, the jobless rate moved toward 5%, alarmingly high by Swedish standards.

As a result of both currency devaluations, Swedish export volume, which had been losing ground for several years, was expected to outstrip the rate of increase for overall exports worldwide. Similarly, the reduction in cost-level was expected to make Swedish industry more competitive against the world's 14 most important industrialized nations than at any time during the 1970s or 1980s. New orders from abroad, even before the October devaluation, confirmed that an improvement was taking place.

Submarine Incident. As in 1981, the public was alarmed and the government angered when, on October 1, a foreign submarine—assumed to be Soviet—was detected in coastal waters near a top-secret naval base south of Stockholm. Unlike the previous incident, however, no submarine actually surfaced. For more than three weeks, Swedish surface vessels maintained a net, trying to force the sub to come up. By the end of the month it appeared that the sub had slipped away, and the waiting game was abandoned.

MAC LINDAHL
Free-lance writer and translator

SWEDEN · Information Highlights

Official Name: Kingdom of Sweden.
Location: Northern Europe.
Area: 173,229 sq mi (448 663 km²).
Population (1982 est.): 8,300,000.
Chief Cities (1980 est.): Stockholm, the capital, 647,214; Göteborg, 431,273; Malmö, 233,803.
Government: *Head of state,* Carl XVI Gustaf, King (acceded Sept. 1973). *Head of government,* Olof Palme, prime minister (took office Oct. 7, 1982). *Legislature* (unicameral)—Riksdag.
Monetary Unit: Krona (7.43 kronor equal U.S.$1, Oct. 26, 1982).
Gross National Product (1981 U.S.$): $110,900,000,000.
Economic Indexes (1981): *Consumer Prices* (1970= 100), *all items,* 270.8; *food,* 286.2. *Industrial production* (1975=100), 94.
Foreign Trade (1981 U.S.$): *Imports,* $28,855,000,000; *exports,* $28,597,000,000.

Olof Palme, prime minister from 1969 to 1976, led his Socialist party back to power in October general elections.

Milsson/Sygma

SWITZERLAND

New policies and old issues predominated in Switzerland during 1982.

United Nations Membership. Departing from its longstanding policy of noninvolvement in international organizations, the government on March 22 asked parliament to authorize it to seek Swiss membership in the United Nations. On August 18 the government announced it had also approved in principle plans to join the International Monetary Fund and the World Bank. Government officials were quick to point out that the decision-making processes would take time, with a national referendum on U.N. membership unlikely before 1984.

In anticipation of hostilities in the Falkland Islands, Switzerland on April 6 banned the sale of arms to both Britain and Argentina. Subsequently the Swiss embassy in Buenos Aires served as a link between Britain and Argentina as they sought to end hostilities in the Falklands. In a unique arrangement engineered by the International Red Cross, Switzerland also agreed to serve as the interning site and supervising authority for Soviet soldiers captured by resistance fighters in the Afghanistan conflict.

Conservative Political Reaction. For the second straight year, voters rejected, on June 6, government proposals that would have liberalized restrictive provisions regarding residence, work, and civil rights for foreign seasonal workers. In a similarly conservative vein, male voters of Appenzell-Innerrhoden canton on April 25 denied the franchise to women in town and cantonal elections.

Terrorism and Violence. Reacting to several years of political terrorist acts and youth demonstrations, voters on June 6 overwhelmingly approved an increase in penalties for violent crimes, in particular acts of terrorism, kidnapping, and taking of hostages. The government was also empowered to bring criminal charges against demonstrators who caused physical injury or property damage to others, even if the victims did not choose to lodge a complaint. When, in September, four gunmen seized hostages and held the Polish embassy in Bern for three days, the Swiss government refused Polish extradition requests, electing instead to try them under the new law.

Swiss Bank Accounts. On September 1 the Swiss and U.S. governments announced an agreement allowing the U.S. Securities and Exchange Commission to obtain information regarding U.S. citizens suspected of using Swiss bank accounts to bypass U.S. regulations that forbade purchase or sale of stock based on privileged "insider" information. This agreement constituted a major relaxation in Switzerland's famous confidentiality provisions regarding private bank accounts.

International Trade. Exports for the first six months of 1982 rose 4.6% to $13,707,000,000, while imports declined 1.6% to $14,919,000,000. The projected trade deficit for 1982 was in the vicinity of $2,400,000,000, substantially less than the $6,700,000,000 deficit experienced in 1980.

PAUL C. HELMREICH
Wheaton College

SWITZERLAND · Information Highlights

Official Name: Swiss Confederation.
Location: Central Europe.
Area: 15,943.4 sq mi (41 293.4 km²).
Population (1980 census): 6,365,960.
Chief Cities (1980): Bern, the capital, 145,254; Zurich, 369,522; Basel, 182,143.
Government: *Head of state,* Fritz Honegger, president, (took office Jan. 1982). *Legislature*—Federal Assembly: Council of States and National Council.
Monetary Unit: Franc (2.225 francs equal U.S.$1, Nov. 4, 1982).
Gross Domestic Product (1981 U.S.$): $100,030,-000,000.
Economic Indexes (1981): *Consumer Prices* (1970= 100), *all items,* 173.1; food, 179.8. *Industrial production* (1975=100), 115.
Foreign Trade (1981 U.S.$): *Imports,* $30,689,000,-000; *exports,* $27,051,000,000.

SYRIA

In 1982, Syria's President Hafez al-Assad was confronted with violent domestic insurrections and a series of political and military failures that typified Syria's inability to affect significantly the outcome of Israel's invasion of Lebanon, where Syria's 22,000-member Arab Deterrent Force was stationed. In the wake of the Lebanese debacle, Assad lost much of his power to influence the leadership of the Palestine Liberation Organization (PLO) and was compelled, by year's end, to switch his support from Iran to Iraq in the bitter Gulf War and to maneuver to recoup his loss of influence in Arab politics.

Internal Unrest. In the bloodiest incident since Assad gained power in 1970, Syrian security forces battled fundamentalist Muslim Brotherhood dissidents in the city of Hama for three weeks before finally quelling the insurrection on February 23. Hama was sealed off for nearly a month, most of its central sections was destroyed, and more than 3,000 civilians were killed.

Assad also faced military opposition. On January 30–31, some 150 officers implicated in a planned coup were arrested and executed.

Disaster in Lebanon. By the last week of June, Syria's armed forces had ceased to be a factor in Israel's military campaign to crush the PLO in Lebanon. Beginning with a devastating air attack on June 9, Israel's technologically superior forces dealt Syria a string of embarrassing defeats that reduced Assad's options to facesaving diplomacy.

By June 11, Syria had lost its entire anti-aircraft missile defense system in Lebanon and 80 combat aircraft without inflicting a single loss on the Israeli air force. Syria's 2,200-troop 85th

Syrian positions in Lebanon came under Israeli air attack. President Assad's forces were dealt serious blows.

Brigade was completely trapped in Beirut by June 17 and, by the fourth cease-fire of the war on June 25, Syria had lost control of the strategic Beirut-Damascus highway, and the bulk of its troops were sealed off in Lebanon's Bekaa Valley.

Negotiations. With Beirut besieged, the Lebanese government sought to avert the capital's destruction by means of U.S.-mediated negotiations to remove PLO troops from Lebanon. Knowing that finding a destination for the PLO fighters encircled in Beirut was the key element in the talks, Assad successfully carried out a strategy designed to demonstrate that there would be no peaceful settlement without full consultations with his government.

After conferring with Saudi Arabia's King Fahd on July 4–5, Assad accordingly announced on July 9 that PLO combatants could not be evacuated to Syria. Assad's plan also included embarrassing Yasir Arafat, the PLO leader, who openly scorned Syria's military performance. On July 16 Assad went a step further in not only demanding a formal PLO request to be evacuated to Syria but also in stipulating that the request would only be acceptable if it were part of a substantive plan for the withdrawal of all foreign troops, including Syria's, from Lebanon.

Despite the July 27 termination of the Arab League mandate by which Syria had legal sanction to be in Lebanon, Assad insisted he would not withdraw his troops until Israel withdrew. It was not until August 10 that Assad announced he had received the necessary PLO request and that PLO troops could be evacuated to Syria. With a full agreement on Beirut reached on August 19, the evacuation was completed by August 30 and serious discussions of a joint Syrian-Israeli withdrawal could begin.

Arab Summit. However, the September 1 unveiling of a new U.S. peace proposal—which Syria rejected—delayed substantive negotiations in Lebanon until Arab leaders completed their September 5–9 summit conference in Fez, Morocco. Assad, who was personally responsible for the failure of the previous summit, surprisingly cooperated fully with his counterparts. He concurred in the Arabs' eight-point peace plan and joined a consensus declaration of support for Iraq. Separately, Assad announced he would meet with Iraqi rival Saddam Hussein to resolve their longstanding feud. In addition, Syria's foreign minister joined the Arab delegation that presented the peace proposal to U.S. President Ronald Reagan on October 22.

Assad's apparent fence mending did not extend to Jordan's King Hussein. While Hussein, with whom Assad has had poor relations for years, attempted to effect a rapprochement with Arafat so that Jordan could participate in the U.S. peace plan, the Syrian president spent the duration of the year trying to bring about a split within the PLO, to be engineered by those Palestinian factions loyal to Damascus. Such a split would ultimately diminish Hussein's role in shaping the way the Arab world would react to the American initiative.

F. Nicholas Willard

SYRIA • Information Highlights

Official Name: Syrian Arab Republic.
Location: Southwest Asia.
Area: 71,500 sq mi (185 185 km^2).
Population (1982 est.): 9,700,000.
Chief Cities (1975 est.): Damascus, the capital, 1,042,245; Aleppo, 778,523; Homs, 267,132.
Government: *Head of state,* Lt. Gen. Hafez al-Assad, president (took office officially March 1971). *Head of government,* Abdel Raouf al-Kasm, prime minister (took office Jan. 1980). *Legislature* (unicameral)—People's Council.
Monetary Unit: Pound (3.925 pounds equal U.S.$1, March 1982).
Gross National Product (1981 U.S.$): $11,980,000,-000.
Economic Index (1980): *Consumer Prices* (1970= 100), *all items,* 285; *food,* 310.
Foreign Trade (1980 U.S.$): *Imports,* $4,119,000,-000; *exports,* $2,108,000,000.

TAIWAN (Republic of China)

Undaunted by what it perceived as Peking's menace, Taiwan in 1982 made extensive efforts to advance the capability of its armed forces through securing sophisticated weapons and developing the defense industries. The Nationalists deplored the U.S. decision gradually to reduce arms sales to Taiwan, but they were determined not to negotiate with Peking unless it renounced Communism. On the economic front, growth slowed down but prices were stable.

Reunification. As Peking continued its campaign of "peaceful reunification" with Taiwan, the Nationalists stiffened their resolution not to deal with the Communists unless the mainland abandoned Communism. In a lengthy speech on June 10, Premier Sun Yun-suan set forth his government's position. There was no "Taiwan issue," he said, but only the "China issue" of whether the people should forever live under Communist rule. Taiwan called for Chinese reunification under Sun Yat-sen's Three Principles of the People, but the Chinese Communists wanted to "communize free China" through "deceptive formulas." The premier then concluded: "If the political, economic, social, and cultural gaps between the Chinese mainland and free China continue to narrow, the conditions for peaceful reunification can gradually mature. The obstacles to reunification will be reduced naturally with the passage of time."

These concluding remarks gave rise to the speculation that Sun saw a chance of accord with Peking. Actually the premier had no intention of dealing with Peking. In this statement and elsewhere, Sun consistently maintained that China could be reunified only when Peking discarded Communism.

The Economy. Worldwide economic recession in 1982 affected Taiwan severely because its economy was just moving from labor-intensive to capital-intensive levels. The rise of wages diminished the competitiveness of its products, thereby depressing exports and discouraging investments. To strengthen the economy, Taiwan reduced interest rates on bank loans and took

UPI

Once a family craft, umbrella-making in Taiwan is now a light industry. The growing manufacturing sector relies heavily on export of nonessential consumer goods.

vigorous measures to curb inflation. Aided by price stability in imported goods, consumer prices during the first five months of 1982 rose only 5.6% over the same period of the previous year.

To foster the development of high-technology industries, the government established a science and technology agency entrusted with the task of granting loans at very easy terms to private companies involved in these enterprises. An association for science and technology was also formed in Taipei, with the participation of ten U.S.-based consulting firms, to provide advice and assistance on the transfer of technology from the United States. In agriculture, attention was given to the enlargement of farmland units and to extending the use of farm machinery.

Taiwan continued to develop trade relations with friendly countries, including those with which it had no diplomatic relations. The government encouraged small companies to merge so that they would be in a stronger position to compete in the world market. Various measures were taken to simplify customs procedures and to facilitate the transportation of goods and passengers.

Taiwan's foreign trade declined in the first eight months of 1982: 2% for exports and 12.4% for imports. It showed a favorable balance of $1,780,000,000. Trade with the United States for the first seven months had a surplus of $2,260,000,000, but large deficits with Japan ($3,450,000,000 in 1981) called for correction. In July 1982, Tokyo agreed to remove tariff barriers on imports from Taiwan, especially agricultural products. In return, Taiwan lifted its ban on imports of 1,533 items from Japan, mostly consumer goods.

TAIWAN (Republic of China) · Information Highlights

Official Name: Republic of China.
Location: Island off the southeastern coast of mainland China.
Area: 13,885 sq mi (35 962 km²).
Population (Sept. 1982): 18,357,467.
Chief Cities: (Dec. 1979): Taipei, the capital, 2,196,237; Kaohsiung, 1,172,977; Taichung, 585,205.
Government: *Head of state,* Chiang Ching-kuo, president (installed May 1978). *Head of government,* Sun Yunsuan, premier (took office May 1978). *Legislature* (unicameral)—Legislative Yüan.
Monetary Unit: New Taiwan dollar (35 NT dollars equal U.S.$1, Oct. 1982).
Gross National Product (1980 U.S.$): $38,000,000,000.
Foreign Trade (1981 U.S.$): *Imports,* $21,199,000,000; *Exports,* $22,611,000,000.

Foreign Affairs. On August 17 Washington and Peking issued a joint communiqué in which the United States agreed gradually to reduce arms sales to Taiwan, while Peking would strive for a peaceful reunification with the island. Taipei expressed "profound regret" over the communiqué, charging that it was "in contradiction of the letter and spirit" of the Taiwan Relations Act, which provided for continued armed sales to Taiwan. Although President Reagan declared that the communiqué did not undercut Taiwan's security and needs, the Nationalists were not convinced. They felt they could no longer rely on the United States for security.

Uncertain of Washington's future policy, Taiwan began to seek arms supplies from European countries. A large share of its military budget was earmarked for the purchase of advanced military equipment so as to ensure a qualitative edge over the Chinese Communists. Said Premier Sun Yun-suan: "If there are countries willing to sell their sophisticated weapons, we would buy them even if it means we have to borrow money for the purchase."

Taiwan expanded its economic and cultural relations with Western European countries, which had ten liaison offices and nine banks on the island. In June, Taipei disclosed plans to seek French nuclear technology to reprocess nuclear waste materials. The move was seen as an effort to reduce reliance on the United States.

Premier Sun's visit to Indonesia in December 1981 paved the way for industrial and agricultural cooperation with that Southeast Asian country. Taiwan's relations with Saudi Arabia remained close and mutually beneficial.

See also CHINA, PEOPLE'S REPUBLIC OF.

CHESTER C. TAN, *New York University*

TANZANIA

A continued slide into economic disaster and the first open, violent opposition to the Nyerere regime highlighted the year in Tanzania.

The Economy. Despite the drastic economic decline in 1982, President Julius K. Nyerere stuck to Tanzania's course of Socialist self-reliance. The entire economy was under the control of government-run "parastatal" organizations. Even Nyerere admitted that the more than 300 parastatals were choking the economy, being inefficient at best and totally corrupt at worst, and that the regular government bureaucracy was "corrupt," "greedy," and virtually engaged in economic war with the average Tanzanian. However, he refused to return to the free-enterprise system that had existed before 1969. As a result, Tanzania faced severe hunger in its cities because it could not import enough food, and hunger in the countryside because the faltering transportation system prevented aid from being distributed outside of Dar es Salaam.

The near shutdown of internal transportation was due to a severe shortage of foreign exchange. Spare parts could not be bought for lack of funds, and foreign airlines began refusing to fly to Dar if they were to be paid only in Tanzanian currency. Even the International Monetary Fund, which had arranged for massive aid in years past, ceased sending money to Tanzania, citing the total inability of the country to make effective use of the funds. With inflation at 60% for the year, the shilling devalued by 10% (and of little value on the world market), oil imports climbing, and the economy working at 30% of capacity, Tanzania appeared headed for collapse. Outright starvation was prevented only by the gift late in 1981 of 260,000 t (286,000 T) of food—which Tanzania at first had scorned out of pride—and by the fact that most people lived in a subsistence economy, providing much of their own needs. The image of the government in the crisis was further tarnished when Vice-President Aboud Jumbe spent more than $5 million of scarce foreign exchange on fancy cars and accommodations during a trip to Europe.

Hijacking. A sign of growing popular anger and frustration was the hijacking on February 27 of a Tanzanian passenger jet by the leftist "Revolutionary Youth Movement of Tanzania," which demanded the resignation of Nyerere and the ending of corruption. The hijackers finally surrendered in London, but the affair greatly damaged Nyerere's reputation in the West. Moreover, leadership of the hijacking by a former army officer suggested dangerous unrest in the Tanzanian armed forces and thus a potential threat to the government's authority.

Foreign Affairs. Tanzania kept a generally low international profile in 1982. But it did send 1,000 troops to the Seychelles to prop up a leftist regime in the Indian Ocean archipelago after an attempted invasion by white mercenaries from South Africa in November 1981. Nyerere announced that the Tanzanian forces would stay in the Seychelles "as long as needed."

ROBERT GARFIELD, *DePaul University*

TANZANIA · Information Highlights

Official Name: United Republic of Tanzania.
Location: East Coast of Africa.
Area: 364,900 sq mi (945 091 km^2).
Population (1982 est.): 19,900,000.
Chief Cities (1978 est.): Dar es-Salaam, the capital, 870,020; Mwanza, 170,823; Tanga, 143,878.
Government: *Head of state,* Julius K. Nyerere, president (took office Jan. 1964). *Head of government,* Cleopa Msuya, prime minister (took office Nov. 1980). Aboud Jumbe, vice-president and president of Zanzibar (elected Nov. 1980). *Legislature* (unicameral)—National Assembly, 230 members.
Monetary Unit: Tanzanian shilling (8.359 shillings equal U.S.$1, Feb. 1982).
Gross National Product Per Capita (1980 U.S.$): $260.
Economic Index (1980): *Consumer Prices* (1970= 100), *all items,* 369.5; *food,* 425.3.
Foreign Trade (1980 U.S.$): *Imports,* $1,226,000,- 000; *exports,* $508,000,000.

TAXATION

Worsening economic conditions and rising government deficits were a major source of concern in industrial nations throughout the world. Accordingly, tax-policy changes reflected a mixture of measures cautiously designed to provide a mild stimulus to economic recovery and to narrow threatening budget deficits.

The United States

Congressional Action. Congress approved the Tax Equity and Fiscal Responsibility Bill of 1982, which was signed by President Ronald Reagan on Sept. 3, 1982. The law scaled back substantial amounts of business-tax reductions approved in 1981 and included other provisions to raise new revenues. Over the three years 1983 through 1985 the law is expected to raise taxes by $98,321,000,000. The increase will be $17,959,-000,000 in fiscal year 1983, rising to $42,698,000,000 by fiscal year 1985. Most major taxes, including those levied on individual incomes, business profits, employer payrolls, and certain commodities and services, will be affected. In addition, the law provided for stricter compliance and enforcement of tax laws.

Among changes directly affecting individuals are those requiring withholding on interest and dividends, restricting medical deductions and casualty losses, imposing a new and higher minimum tax, and raising excise taxes on several items. Beginning July 1, 1983, the law imposes withholding on dividends and interest earned by individuals at a flat 10% rate, similar to the graduated withholding that applies to wages. Exemptions from withholding were granted for those who paid no more than $600 in federal income tax for the previous year ($1,000 on joint returns) and for persons 65 and older who paid less than $1,500 in taxes in the previous year ($2,500 on joint returns). There will also be 10% withholding on current payments for pensions and annuities, unless recipients elect not to have the amounts withheld. The law limits medical deductions to costs in excess of 5% of adjusted gross income (previously 3%), beginning after Dec. 31, 1982. In addition, taxpayers will no longer be allowed the separate deduction of up to $150 for health-insurance premiums. Starting in 1984, the deduction for drugs in excess of 1% of income is repealed, and costs for prescription drugs only (including insulin) will be grouped with other expenses in computing the medical deduction. Also starting in 1983, taxpayers can deduct personal casualty and theft losses only to the extent that they exceed 10% of adjusted gross income. The law also imposed higher taxes on wealthier persons subject to the minimum tax, which applies to tax on certain income not subject to regular taxation. Moreover, the threshold for taxation of unemployment-compensation benefits was lowered from $20,000 to $12,000 (from $25,000 to $18,000 on joint returns), effective Jan. 1, 1982.

For three years beginning Jan. 1, 1983, the 1982 law raised the federal excise tax on cigarettes from 8 cents to 16 cents a pack and the tax on telephone service from 1% to 3%. Increases in airport and airway levies included a rise in the air-passenger ticket tax from 5% to 8% and a $3-per-passenger tax on all international air transportation that starts in the United States.

Higher business taxes will account for more than one third of the revenue increase under the new law. The law repealed a provision of the 1981 legislation that would increase depreciation allowances on property placed in service after 1984, as well as a controversial provision in the 1981 law, known as safe-harbor leasing, that allows companies to sell unused tax benefits to other firms. Such leasing is repealed after 1983 and curtailed significantly before then; beginning in 1984 the tax treatment of traditional leasing will be liberalized. In addition, the 1982 law reduced depreciation-tax allowances available through the investment-tax credit and limited the percentage of tax liability the credit may offset to 85% (formerly 90%). Corporate quarterly income-tax payments were accelerated to 90% (formerly 80%) of tax liability for the year. In addition, certain corporate-tax preferences will be scaled back by 15%, including percentage depletion in coal and iron, bad debt reserves for financial institutions, and interest on debt used to carry tax-exempt securities acquired after 1982. A wide range of other business provisions included limiting the tax advantages of companies operating in Puerto Rico, imposing higher windfall oil profit taxes on Alaskan oil companies, and tightening the taxation of income from oil and gas extracted in foreign countries.

The 1982 law also affected employment taxes. The federal unemployment tax, paid by employers, will rise from a maximum of $204 per employee in 1982 to $245 in 1983 and $434 in 1984, as a result of increases in both the base and rate of the tax. The law also subjects federal employees to the hospital-insurance portion of the social-security tax and makes them eligible for Medicare. As a compliance measure, restaurants employing 11 or more persons must report estimated employee income from tips.

In other action, during its lame-duck session, Congress approved legislation that would raise the federal excise tax on gasoline and diesel fuel from 4 cents to 9 cents a gallon, starting April 1, 1983. The measure, which President Reagan signed into law in early January 1983, also imposed higher taxes on heavy trucks. The annual proceeds of about $5,500,000,000 would finance highway and related projects. The new legislation was seen as a means to help repair the nation's deteriorating roads, bridges, and transit systems, while creating some 320,000 new jobs a year.

GIVE US FIVE CENTS WORTH

ROAD REPAIR INC.

Prolonged debate over a bill to increase the federal excise tax on gasoline to finance highway and related projects delayed Congressional adjournment until just before Christmas. A bill was enacted.

Englehart © 1982, The Hartford Courant

Reprinted with permission The Los Angeles Times Syndicate

Supreme Court. The two major tax cases that came before the Supreme Court in 1982 dealt with the right of states to tax certain investment income of corporations doing some business in the states but with headquarters elsewhere. Both cases focused on the concept of the unitary business method of taxation, which has been a source of controversy between corporate taxpayers and state taxing authorities. After the states' highest courts ruled against them, the companies appealed their cases to the Supreme Court. It ruled in favor of the companies.

In *ASARCO Inc. v. Idaho State Tax Commission,* the case involved $325,515 in corporate-income taxes that Idaho had sought to levy on the parent company for the years 1968, 1969, and 1970. ASARCO carries on mining and related activities in various states. Its primary Idaho business is the operation of a silver mine. The company is incorporated in New Jersey and maintains its headquarters in New York. The taxes at issue were assessed on dividends, interest, and capital gains—so-called intangible income—that the parent company earned from holdings in three foreign and two domestic corporations. In considering the case, the court fell back on its previous decisions in *Mobile Oil Corp. v. Commissioner of Taxes of Vermont* and *Exxon Corp. v. Wisconsin Dept. of Revenue,* in which it held that "the linchpin of apportionality in the field of state-income taxation is the unitary business principle" and that a state may not tax value earned outside its borders. Although the court had decided in 1980 that a unitary relationship existed in the Mobil and Exxon cases, it held that ASARCO had succeeded in proving that such a relationship did not exist between the company and its subsidiaries. Idaho's law was

thus declared in violation of the due process clause of the Constitution. The state had argued that intangible income should be considered part of a unitary business if the income-producing property is "acquired, managed, or disposed of for purposes relating to or contributing to the taxpayers' income," but the court said that such a definition "would destroy the concept of unitary business," because almost any investment could logically fall within that concept. Although the court noted that in some cases ASARCO's stake in the subsidiaries was large enough to permit it to control them, it said that the potential to control did not make the subsidiaries part of a unitary business. While the dividend-paying subsidiaries "add to the riches" of the appellant, the court said that, "in any business or economic sense, they have nothing to do with the activities" of the company in Idaho.

In *F.W. Woolworth Co. v. Taxation and Revenue Department of New Mexico,* the case also involved whether the due process clause allowed a state to tax a portion of dividends and gains from foreign subsidiaries of a parent company domiciled outside the state. Woolworth's principal place of business and commercial domicile is in New York, but it engages in chain-store retailing throughout the United States. New Mexico's tax laws distinguish between "business" income, which it apportions between it and other states, and "nonbusiness" income, which it generally allocates to a single state on the basis of commercial domicile. Woolworth reported its dividend income from four of its foreign subsidiaries—in Germany, Canada, Mexico, and England—as nonbusiness income. Similarly, the company did not report as New Mexico business income "gross-up" amounts that it did not actually receive from its foreign subsidiaries but that the federal government (for purposes of calculating the company's foreign-tax credit) deemed it to have received. Again the issue hinged on the unitary business principle. The court held that principle did not hold in the case and that New Mexico's tax on the income in question therefore failed to meet established due process standards. The fact that Woolworth had the potential to operate the subsidiaries as integrated divisions of a single unitary business was irrelevant, the court said, since each of the subsidiaries operated as a discrete business enterprise. The court also held that New Mexico's efforts to tax the "fictitious" gross-up income contravened the due process clause, because the foreign-tax credit, requiring use of the gross-up, arose from the taxation by foreign nations of Woolworth's foreign subsidiaries that had no unitary business relationship with New Mexico.

In another case involving state taxing powers, *United States v. New Mexico et al.,* the court held that private contractors managing federal atomic facilities in New Mexico under Department of Energy agreements are subject to the state's gross receipts and use taxes. The federal government had challenged the tax, holding that certain of its contractors are instruments of the United States and immune from state taxes. But the justices held that immunity cannot be conferred simply because the tax is paid from government funds and that tax immunity is appropriate only "when the levy falls on the United States itself, or on an agency or instrumentality so closely connected to the government that the two cannot realistically be viewed as separate entities, at least insofar as the activity being taxed is concerned." As a result of the court's decision, federal officials indicated that the government may owe the state of New Mexico more than $100 million in back taxes and $20 million a year in the future.

State and Local Taxes. Tax collections of state and local governments in fiscal year 1982 totaled $265,722,000,000, an increase of $23,741,000,000 or 9.8% over fiscal year 1981. The percentage rise was similar to the 9.4% gain of a year earlier.

For the second consecutive year, state legislatures in 1982 enacted a near-record volume of tax-raising measures, with 21 states approving net statutory increases totaling $2,930,000,000 annually. These were minimally offset by net reductions in eight other states amounting to $50 million, for an overall net rise of $2,880,000,000. Higher sales taxes, enacted in six states, will bring in more than $1,317,000,000 of the new revenues. Increases in personal income taxes in four states were expected to yield $990.8 million in new annual revenues.

International

Canada. In a budget message in June, the second in eight months, Finance Minister Allan J. MacEachen proposed various measures to al-
leviate Canada's economic problems, including modest tax changes. A revenue increase of about C $1.3 million would be attained by holding the indexation factor for personal income taxes below the rate of inflation. The adjustment would be limited to 6% for 1983 and 5% for 1984.

The government also presented new tax proposals for investment income, which were to be examined by a committee of specialists. Included were indexing bank deposits and loans to eliminate taxes on the inflation component of interest income, and setting up a new shareholder investment plan through which capital gains on common stock in Canadian corporations would be taxable only to the extent they exceed the rate of inflation.

Europe. Britain's Chancellor of the Exchequer, Sir Geoffrey Howe, presented a budget calling for slight reductions in the overall tax burden. Taxpayers' personal exemptions were raised to 14%, which was about the current 12% rate of inflation; and the employers' payroll tax, or social security surcharge, was reduced from 3.5% to 2.5%. Other provisions of the Finance Act of 1982, approved in July, increased capital-gains tax deductions and introduced an inflation adjustment in computing taxable income from capital gains. On the other hand, the law raised the petroleum revenue tax from 70% to 75% (while abolishing a supplementary petroleum duty) and increased excise taxes on beer, liquor, gasoline, and automobile registrations.

The West German Parliament approved a temporary 10% investment premium for additional plant and equipment ordered during 1982 and delivered by the end of 1983. In October, Chancellor Helmut Kohl's cabinet approved the government's 1983 budget, which included a rise in the value-added tax from 13% to 14%.

In May the French Ministers' Council agreed on a bill to increase the standard value-added tax rate from 17.6% to 18.6%, to introduce a "super reduced" rate of 5.5% for certain necessities (the normal reduced rate is 7%), to cut the business tax substantially, and to provide new tax incentives for farming enterprises. The 1983 Finance Bill called for reductions in rates of individual income tax to reflect inflation, introduction of a new 65% rate bracket on higher incomes, and a 7% surcharge on income-tax assessments in excess of 28,000 French francs (about $3,800).

In Italy, a decree-law, published in July, raised the corporate-income tax rate from 25% to 30%, increased the value-added tax on gasoline, and hiked excise duties on oil products, beer, gas, and bananas. On July 31 a measure increasing value-added tax rates was announced.

Japan. It was reported that the Japanese government was seeking to reduce the budget deficit by being less generous with respect to allowable tax deductions for entertainment expenses, reserves for pension schemes, and reserves for bad debts.

ELSIE M. WATTERS, *Tax Foundation, Inc.*

TELEVISION AND RADIO

Television in the United States reached a watershed in 1982. The rhetoric of boosterism and bonanza that had accompanied the growth of cable TV for the previous decade was suddenly hushed, as a litany of bad news came over the wire.

"CBS-C," the Tiffany of cable networks featuring first-rate cultural programming, collapsed after less than one year and losses of $30 to $50 million; analysts claimed the network had spent extravagantly without establishing a firm advertising base. ABC's equally ambitious cultural cable network, "ARTS," lost $6 million in its first year, while a number of other specialized cable services, such as the arts-oriented "Bravo," and "Daytime" for women, cut their staffs and lowered their profit projections.

Even as it celebrated its 10th year in operation, "Home Box Office" (HBO), the biggest of the cable networks, began to sense its limits. HBO reached an all-time high rating of 13.3% of all subscribers in June, then declined steadily for the rest of the year despite the growing number of subscribers signed on. (Some 35% of the nation's households were wired for cable by 1982.) To analysts, this suggested that viewers were trying out new channels during the "summer reruns," returning loyally to the networks with the new fall season.

But the broadcast networks could take little comfort in cable's mixed fortunes, for their own viewership eroded apace. The American Broadcasting Companies (ABC), the National Broadcasting Company (NBC), and the Columbia Broadcasting System (CBS) lost roughly 1.3 million regular viewers during the 1981–82 season, and the networks' combined share of prime-time viewers had declined from 91% in 1977 to 83% in 1982. Add to this a government study that concluded—far more conclusively than ever before—that television violence caused violence in children, a 25% cut in federal aid to the Corporation for Public Broadcasting through 1984, and a National Football League strike that eliminated eight weekends of lucrative fall programming, and it's easy to see why 1982 appeared to most television executives to be a season of discontent.

Network Programming. *Dynasty* was a popular show on ABC, but it was a more apt description of CBS' programming, which won the ratings race for the third consecutive season. *Dallas* was the top-rated show for the second year in a row, with such other established CBS hits as *60 Minutes* and *M*A*S*H* among the top 10. For the 26-week season ending April 26, CBS had a 19.0 rating (percentage of households with televisions), ABC an 18.1, and NBC a 15.2.

Not surprisingly, the critics found the most to admire on the least popular network. NBC's intelligent police drama, *Hill Street Blues,* swept

© Granada Television of England

Jeremy Irons (left) and Anthony Andrews starred in the serial dramatization of "Brideshead Revisited," on PBS.

most of the Emmy awards, and reviews were excellent for two NBC late-night programs geared for a young market—*The David Letterman Show,* featuring the gap-toothed Letterman as its irreverent host, and *SCTV,* featuring sharp satire and ingenious send-ups.

Notices were mixed on the new 1982–83 season. Certainly there weren't many surprises—*St. Elsewhere,* an NBC hospital drama, and *Square Pegs,* an offbeat CBS comedy about contemporary high-school students, were among the few attempts at social realism. Instead, action-adventure seemed to be the theme. ABC's *Tales of the Gold Monkey* and CBS' *Bring 'Em Back Alive* were serial cliff-hangers set in the 1930s, clearly imitations of the smash movie, *Raiders of the Lost Ark.* Bob Newhart and Sally Struthers returned to CBS with new comedy vehicles, and a stable of young "beefcake" actors were introduced in such series as ABC's *Matt Houston* and NBC's *The Powers of Matthew Starr.*

Pay-TV/Home Video. Despite the more subdued outlook in new television technologies, pay-TV executives moved boldly into Broadway and legitimate theater as a fresh source of programming product. Unlike previous theater productions which consisted of fixed cameras filming a stage performance, *Camelot* on HBO and *Sweeney Todd* on "The Entertainment Channel" were produced especially for pay-TV, combining the freshness of continuous stage performance with the close-ups of a taped studio production. The shows were true blockbusters, featuring Richard Harris and Angela Lansbury, respectively, from the original Broadway casts.

On the other hand, one of the season's most closely watched theatrical experiments was a commercial failure. On November 5, Oak Media Inc. telecast the first live performance of a Broadway musical, *Sophisticated Ladies,* for distribution on several over-the-air, pay-TV channels at a fee of $15. But less than 10% of the potential audience purchased the telecast, leaving boxing as the sole attraction that had proven itself a profitable pay-per-view item.

Recent-release movies continued to be the staple of pay-TV, and to challenge the dominance of HBO, three major film studios—Paramount, MCA Inc., and Warner Bros.—planned to set up their own pay-TV outlet, "The Movie Channel." ABC also moved to exploit this market by planning a "Home View Network" in which movies would be telecast on a scrambled signal in the early morning hours, to be recorded on subscribers' video cassettes and played back later.

Television News. The networks stepped up competition for ratings on the news programs, using some of the same eye-catching graphics that had proved so successful in other programming, and leading many industry critics to question whether journalistic content was actually being enhanced.

In a move that precisely mirrored one made previously at ABC, CBS moved its chief of sports programming, Van Gordon Sauter, into the director's chair at the news division. Like Roone Arledge, who continued to run both the news and sports operations at ABC, Sauter had a reputation for using dazzling visual effects. Shortly after he assumed his new post, CBS News began to regain some of the ratings ground it had lost to ABC in 1981 after the beloved Walter Cronkite was replaced by Dan Rather as weeknight anchorman.

However slick the presentation of news may have become, there was undoubtedly much more of it on the air in 1982. All three networks introduced news programs—*Overnight* on NBC, *The Last Word* on ABC, and *Nightwatch* on CBS—to air after 1 A.M. EST, in time slots that had always been given over to local stations. Industry analysts attributed these sweeping changes in part to "Cable News Network" (CNN), which in two years had reached into more than 14 million households, demonstrating the appeal of 24-hour news and keeping the networks alert with impressive scoops.

Although Ted Turner's CNN was reportedly losing $1 million per month, the Atlanta entrepreneur in January launched a second channel, CNN II, a "headline service" to provide capsules of the news. In an effort to tap the same "fast news" market on cable, ABC and Westinghouse Electric Corp. launched a joint venture called "Satellite News," based in Stamford, CT.

Television and the Law. The networks' increasing tendency to package news in an entertaining "magazine" format and historical fact in a "docudrama" format was seen by some as an abuse of the broadcasters' power. Several public figures who felt they had been injured by such presentations decided to fight back.

CBS with "Nightwatch," as well as ABC and NBC, added wee-hour news shows. News in general got more air time.

CBS News

TELEVISION | 1982

Some Sample Programs

ABC News Special—The centennial of Franklin D. Roosevelt was commemorated. ABC, Jan. 29.

Ain't Misbehavin'—The original cast of the Broadway musical recreated their roles in this television adaptation. NBC, June 21.

American Playhouse—A 25-week series featuring an eclectic collection of drama, comedy, musicals, and biography—some written originally for television and others, adaptations. PBS, Jan. 12.

Baryshnikov in Hollywood—A variety special starring Mikhail Baryshnikov; with Dom DeLuise, Shirley MacLaine, Bernadette Peters. CBS, April 21.

Bataan, The Forgotten Hell—An *NBC Reports* telecast of the World War II battle and its aftermath. NBC, Dec. 5.

Bennett and Basie Together—Tony Bennett and Count Basie teamed up in Boston. PBS, Mar. 7.

Bernstein/Beethoven—Eleven-part series in which Leonard Bernstein conducted the Vienna Philharmonic Orchestra in their playing of Beethoven's nine symphonies and certain other music. PBS, Jan. 25.

The Blue and the Gray—A three-part miniseries on the American Civil War; with Gregory Peck, Stacy Keach, John Hammond. CBS, Nov. 14.

Brideshead Revisited—Eleven-part dramatic adaptation of Evelyn Waugh's novel; with Jeremy Irons, Anthony Andrews. PBS, Jan. 18.

Caruso Remembered—Tenor Placido Domingo and conductor Zubin Mehta presented a concert in tribute to Enrico Caruso. NBC, Jan. 16.

Central America in Revolt—A CBS News Special; with Dan Rather, Bill Moyers, Mike Wallace, and Ed Rabel. CBS, Mar. 20.

Creativity with Bill Moyers—A 17-week series exploring creativity through the lives and ideas of some gifted and inventive people. PBS, Jan. 8.

Eleanor, First Lady of the World—A dramatization of Eleanor Roosevelt's life after President Roosevelt's death; with Jean Stapleton. CBS, May 12.

The Elephant Man—TV-movie adapted from the Broadway play; with Philip Anglim. ABC, Jan. 4.

The Executioner's Song—Two-part dramatization of Norman Mailer's novel, for which Mr. Mailer wrote the screenplay; with Tommy Lee Jones, Eli Wallach, Rosanna Arquette. NBC, Nov. 28.

The Hitchhikers Guide to the Galaxy—A seven-part science-fiction production, based on a novel by Douglas Adams; with Simon Jones, David Dixon. PBS, Nov. 4.

Horowitz in London: A Royal Concert—Pianist Vladimir Horowitz performed a benefit concert, his first European concert in 31 years. PBS, May 22.

The Hunchback of Notre Dame—Adaptation of the Victor Hugo novel; with Anthony Hopkins, Leslie-Anne Down. CBS, Feb. 4.

I Heard It Through the Grapevine—Author James Baldwin's assessment of the 1960s civil-rights struggle. PBS, June 30.

Illusions—A Shirley MacLaine special; with Gregory Hines. CBS, June 24.

In Concert at the Met—Mezzo-soprano Tatiana Troyanos and tenor Placido Domingo in a recital; with James Levine conducting. PBS, Mar. 3.

Inside the Third Reich—A 1982 TV-movie, based on the memoirs of the Nazi architect Albert Speer; with Rutger Hauer, Derek Jacobi. ABC, May 9.

Ireland—A 13-part history series on Ireland. PBS, April 17.

I Remember Nelson—A *Masterpiece Theatre* four-part production of the life of British admiral Horatio Nelson; with Kenneth Colley. PBS, Feb. 21.

Itzhak Perlman in Concert—Perlman and the New York Philharmonic performed works by Vivaldi, Mendelssohn, and Brahms. PBS, Feb. 10.

Ivanhoe—A 1982 TV-movie of Sir Walter Scott's novel; with Anthony Andrews, James Mason, Olivia Hussey, Lysette Anthony. CBS, Feb. 23.

J. Edgar Hoover—An *ABC News Closeup* telecast on former FBI director J. Edgar Hoover. ABC, June 3.

Johnny Belinda—The story of a young deaf woman who finds hope and love; with Rosanna Arquette, Richard Thomas. CBS, Oct. 19.

Kennedy Center Tonight—A tribute to jazz great Lionel Hampton was presented. PBS, Jan. 27.

La Bohème—Puccini's opera was given a production from the Academy of Music in Philadelphia; with Luciano Pavarotti. PBS, Aug. 28.

The Letter—A television adaptation of W. Somerset Maugham's play; with Lee Remick. ABC, May 3.

Life on Earth—Thirteen-part natural history documentary. PBS, Jan. 12.

A Lincoln Center Special: Balanchine and Stravinsky—Genius Has a Birthday!—In honor of Stravinsky's centennial, the New York City Ballet performed *Apollo* and *Orpheus*. PBS, Oct. 4.

Little Gloria . . . Happy at Last—A 1982 TV-movie dramatizing the custody battle waged over Gloria Vanderbilt; with Lucy Gutteridge, Jennifer Dundas, Angela Lansbury, Bette Davis. NBC, Oct. 24.

Lucia di Lammermoor—A *Live from Lincoln Center* telecast of the Donizetti opera; performed by the New York City Opera. PBS, April 10.

Madama Butterfly—Puccini's tragic opera was performed from Lincoln Center by the New York City Opera; with Judith Haddon. PBS, Oct. 20.

Marcel Marceau—The French mime was interviewed in this two-part profile. PBS, Aug. 11.

Marco Polo—Ten-hour miniseries dramatizing the adventures of Marco Polo; with Ken Marshall, John Gielgud, Anne Bancroft. NBC, May 16.

The Member of the Wedding—A live broadcast of the Carson McCuller's play; with Pearl Bailey, Dana Hill, Howard Rollins. NBC, Dec. 20.

Mexico—Times of Crisis—An *ABC News Closeup* telecast on Mexican social and economic problems, with correspondent Bill Redeker. ABC, July 25.

Middletown—Inspired by the study on Muncie, IN, made by sociologists Robert and Helen Lynd in the 1920s, producer Peter Davis returned to Muncie to film *cinema-verite* documentaries on contemporary American life. PBS, Mar. 24.

Murder Is Easy—TV-movie adapted from an Agatha Christie novel; with Helen Hayes. CBS, Jan. 2.

Night of 100 Stars—Gala with some 200 celebrities participating in a benefit for the Actors' Fund. ABC, Mar. 8.

Oliver Twist—A TV-movie of the Charles Dickens' novel; with George C. Scott. CBS, Mar. 23.

Pleasure Drugs: The Great American High—An *NBC White Paper* documentary on cocaine and methaqualone (Quaaludes). NBC, April 20.

Rehearsal for Murder—Drama about a playwright attempting to solve a murder via a new play written for his suspects (most of them actors) to perform; with Robert Preston. CBS, May 26.

A Report on the United Nations—An *ABC News Closeup* documentary. ABC, Aug. 13.

Saudi Arabia—Three-part documentary series on Saudi Arabia. PBS, April 27.

Shakespeare Plays—In the six-year season, 1982's presentations included *A Midsummer Night's Dream, Troilus and Cressida, King Lear,* and *Cymbeline.* PBS, April 19, May 17, Oct. 18, Dec. 20.

The Sharks—A *National Geographic* special. PBS, Jan. 13.

Smiley's People—A six-part miniseries depicting the encounter of the British master spy George Smiley with his Soviet counterpart, Karla; with Alec Guinness, Curt Jurgens. Independent, Oct. 25.

Summer and Smoke—The 1971 opera based on the Tennessee Williams' play was presented by the Chicago Opera Theater. PBS, June 23.

The Wall—A 1982 TV-movie dramatizing the Warsaw ghetto uprising of 1943. CBS, Feb. 16.

Witness for the Prosecution—A 1982 TV-movie re-make of the Agatha Christie whodunit; with Ralph Richardson, Diana Rigg, Deborah Kerr, Wendy Hiller, Beau Bridges. CBS, Dec. 4.

A Woman Called Golda—Two-part film biography of former Israeli Prime Minister Golda Meir; with Ingrid Bergman. Independent, April 26.

Norman Lear (left), producer of "All in the Family" and other television hits, discusses his work for a segment of "Creativity with Bill Moyers." In the 17-part, Emmy-winning series, Moyers explored the creative process with people in the arts, science, industry, and education.

Courtesy, The Corporation for Entertainment and Learning, Inc.

Gen. William Westmoreland, former commander of U.S. forces in Vietnam, sued CBS for $120 million for a January 23 *60 Minutes* segment accusing him of "conspiracy" to falsify information about the strength of enemy forces in Vietnam. At first CBS News stood by its report, then admitted several errors and offered Westmoreland 15 minutes of unedited air time for a rebuttal. But Westmoreland refused, filing suit in a South Carolina federal court September 13. Also, ABC News apologized publicly to Mobil Oil Corporation—known for its combative, anti-media vice president, Herbert Schmertz—for inaccuracies in the June 20 documentary, *The Oil Game*. The two incidents suggested that perhaps the network news departments had begun to retreat from their traditional position that the reporter is always right.

Docudramas, hybrids of documentary and fiction, became more prevalent and more controversial in 1982, examining—and annoying—such celebrities as Gloria Vanderbilt and Jacqueline Kennedy Onassis. Elizabeth Taylor, the subject of a docudrama being produced by ABC, decided to test the legality of these often-sensational presentations, and sued to block the production. "This docudrama technique has gotten out of hand," said the 51-year-old actress, "It is simply a fancy new name for old-fashion invasion of privacy."

People in Television. Ed Asner, who played the gruff city editor Lou Grant on the CBS series of the same name, seemed to be at the center of controversy wherever he went. He was criticized by many of his colleagues for using his credibility as a "journalist" and his platform as president of the Screen Actors' Guild to raise money for the leftist rebels in El Salvador. Because of Asner's outspokenness, the pharmaceutical firm Kimberly-Clark withdrew its advertising from *Lou Grant* on May 4, and the next day the series was cancelled by CBS. Asner's supporters claimed it was politics, not poor ratings, that had killed the show.

Perhaps the most important television milestone of the year was the retirement of William S. Paley, 81, who had founded CBS and over 54 years had built it into one of the largest communications empires in the world. Paley announced that as of April 20, 1983, Thomas H. Wyman, president and chief executive officer, would take over his post as chairman.

Two men symbolizing different eras in television history died under tragic circumstances during 1982. Dave Garroway, the affable host of NBC's *Today* program from 1952 to 1961, committed suicide at his Swarthmore, PA, home. He was 69. John Belushi, the stocky, manic comedian who starred in the ground-breaking series *Saturday Night Live* from 1975 to 1979, died March 5 in Hollywood of a drug overdose. He was 33.

Radio. Seemingly neglected by the proliferation of new television technologies, radio in fact was moving to exploit some of the cable channels that television programmers were unable to fill. National Public Radio began planning a network called "Cable Audio," to begin transmission on cable lines in 1983, specifically designed for the needs of the visually impaired. Programming will emphasize readings from newspapers and technical journals.

The splintering of the rock-music market into crossover formats combining adult/contemporary, country and western, and progressive rock threatened some of the longtime powers in Top 40 rock. WABC in New York, which had watched its national preeminence in Top 40 eroded over the years, switched to all-talk.

Other stations and networks juggled schedules in an attempt to adjust to new listening and advertising patterns. NBC Radio eliminated all of its short-format public affairs programs, featuring such personalities as Gene Shalit, Willard Scott, and Dr. Joyce Brothers, to make room for what a network official called "more hard news, because it sells."

DAN HULBERT, *"The Dallas Times Herald"*

Soap Operas: Bigger Than Ever

A media event to rival the shooting of *Dallas'* J.R. Ewing occurred in late 1981, when superstar and *General Hospital* fan Elizabeth Taylor appeared in a few episodes of that series, becoming a party to the wedding of the young lovers, Luke and Laura. The wedding episode, watched by about 16 million fans, was indicative of the great attraction that television serials, commonly called soap operas, currently have for people of all ages and socioeconomic backgrounds. The term is a throwback to the time of radio serials when many of the shows' advertisers were soap companies, but it has taken on a meaning suggestive of the programs' nearly maniacal concern with human relationships.

With millions of viewers (estimates range from 30 to 70 million) and the ability to generate tremendous profits for the networks, soaps are no longer the stepchildren of the broadcasting world. In early 1982, CBS unveiled its afternoon soap opera *Capitol* with a prime-time premier episode and the fanfare usually reserved for shows permanently slotted in prime time.

Serialization as a means of telling a tale is not unique to the broadcasting industry, but radio, and later television, with their ability to enter into any home, provide an intimacy particularly well suited to the method. Radio serials, which began in the 1930s and were 15 minutes in length and broadcast five days weekly, were frequently tales of domestic tragedy, medical ailments, and unrequited love. The major char-

acters were of two sorts—either constantly balanced on the brink of disaster and about to be done in, or of a saintly nature, ever ready to offer a helping hand. Often they were both. Radio soaps made money, sometimes producing about 60% of the advertising revenues of the broadcasting networks. Many were the brainstorms of Frank and Anne Hummert, associates of a Chicago advertising firm, who became the virtual rulers of daytime radio. One of their earliest shows was *Just Plain Bill*. Another was the popular *Ma Perkins,* which aired from 1933–60. The programs did not attempt to be realistic. In *The Romance of Helen Trent,* Helen remained 35 years old for 27 years.

With the advent of television, the genre continued. Some radio soaps—*One Man's Family* and *The Guiding Light*—made the transition to the new medium. In fact, in 1982, the Emmy award-winning *Guiding Light* celebrated its 45th broadcast year—30 years on TV and 15 on radio. Other soaps, including the longest-running, *Search for Tomorrow* (1951), were created for TV. The television soaps, like the radio ones, took over the afternoon broadcasting slots, where most remain.

In recent years soap operas have changed. Most of the serials broadcast in 1982 were one hour in length, making possible complex plot twists, multiple subplots, and huge casts. Production costs, while low in comparison to those of prime time shows, have risen; sets and cos-

Search for Tomorrow, the longest-running television soap opera, is the story of Joanne, her family, and their neighbors in the town of Henderson. Mary Stuart (left) has portrayed Joanne since the show's beginning in 1951.

CBS

Wide World   © 1981 American Broadcasting Companies, Inc.

Left: Larry Hagman as J.R. (center), Linda Gray as Sue Ellen, and Steven Kanaly as Ray star in the evening hit, Dallas. *Right: Liz Taylor guest stars on the daytime favorite,* General Hospital; *Anthony Geary plays Luke Spencer.*

tumes have been upgraded; and on-location filming is now routine. With the aim of drawing an audience from the 18-to-34 age group so highly valued by advertisers, the programs are currently populated with younger stars who struggle with contemporary problems. Drug and alcohol abuse, divorce, child abuse, rape, murder, suicide, and sex (usually outside of marriage) are all subjects of extensive treatment.

General Hospital, a top-rated afternoon soap opera in 1982, had a regular following of as many as 14 million viewers and earned its network about $1 million weekly in profits. By comparison, even a big evening hit can generate only about half that amount. In 1980, daytime television shows (of which 80% were soap operas) accounted for $1,000,000,000 of the total $5,100,000,000 in network advertising revenues.

In addition, the soaps have affected other aspects of the communications and entertainment industries. The twice-monthly *Soap Opera Digest,* which gives a synopsis of the shows, began publishing in 1975. "Dial-Soap-Fone," a service which audiences may telephone for a plot synopsis, is available in Philadelphia, and there are plans to expand it. Likewise, a number of radio stations give listeners capsule updates of the soaps. Within the entertainment industry, the shows have provided a training ground for many performers who have gone on

to greater stardom, and in a turnabout, several celebrities have made guest appearances.

Undoubtedly the biggest change in recent years was the expansion of the genre from its traditional afternoon time period to evening prime time. The innovator in the new time arena was *Dallas,* which began broadcasting in 1978 and rose to the top of television's Nielsen ratings. In 1980, with the shooting of the sinister J.R. Ewing, the series produced a cliffhanger and drew the biggest audience of the season for a series episode. Following in *Dallas'* footsteps, and with a similar format, came other prime-time soaps, including *Knots Landing, Dynasty, Flamingo Road,* and *Falcon Crest.*

Why do soaps have the enduring capacity to draw and hold an audience? One theory suggests that they create a bond of loyalty with viewers that no other programming type has duplicated. The soaps' characters are so vividly drawn that many in the audience personally relate to them, particularly when the same actor is in the role for years. Many fans find soaps stars approachable and caring.

Whatever the reasons behind the attachment, soap operas continue to stir interest in all regions and in many professional groups. Long considered the fare of housewives, they are now the subject of college classes, doctoral theses, and television research grants.

SAUNDRA FRANCE

TENNESSEE

Politics and the World's Fair dominated Tennessee news in 1982.

The Election. After campaigns which generated little excitement, Gov. Lamar Alexander and U.S. Sen. James Sasser were reelected by comfortable majorities. Alexander, a Republican aided by disenchanted Democrats, handily defeated Knoxville Mayor Randall Tyree and became the first governor to be elected to two successive four-year terms and the only Republican ever to be chosen for eight years. Sasser was challenged by veteran sixth-district Republican Congressman Robin Beard. In the U.S. congressional races, only the fourth and seventh districts generated much interest. In the fourth, Democrat Jim Cooper, 28-year-old son of a former governor, surprisingly defeated Cissy Baker, 26-year-old daughter of Republican senator and majority leader Howard Baker, by a two-to-one margin. In the seventh district, Memphis Republican leader and businessman Don Sundquist narrowly defeated Democrat Bob Clement, son of former governor Frank Goad Clement. Five members of the state Supreme Court—one Republican and four Democrats—were reelected.

Legislation. Legislation passed in 1982 included a state law requiring one minute of prayer daily in the public schools. The statute subsequently was ruled unconstitutional by a federal district court in Nashville. Other enacted legislation provided stiffer penalties for drunken driving; that judges rather than juries sentence persons convicted of non-capital crimes; and a 7% pay increase to state employees.

The Fair. The World's Fair opened on May 1 in Knoxville for a six-month stand. By mid-October its success was such that all debts had been paid and 11 million people had viewed the exhibits of the $173 million extravaganza. While an exhibit from the Soviet Union notably was absent, those from two dozen other nations were brilliantly displayed. Tourist trade within a 200-mi (322-km) radius of Knoxville increased considerably.

The Economy. The unemployment rate of 11.2% in October exceeded the national rate. Rural Van Buren and Stewart counties each suffered a 40% jobless rate, while urban counties averaged less than 10%. Even so, new manufacturing investments had exceeded $300 million at midyear—an increase of nearly $140 million over that of 1981.

Agriculture. Soybeans continued to be the chief crop, with wheat, corn, cotton, sorghum, and tobacco following in that order. Farmland values, while experiencing double-digit increases during most of the preceding decade, fell by 1%—the first decline since 1954.

Education. Tennessee State University, the state's only predominantly black university, experienced its first enrollment increase since the 1979 merger with the University of Tennessee-Nashville. Inadequate state funding continued to be a major problem for higher education, and authorities shifted more of the burden of college costs to students. After a search of more than a year, trustees at Vanderbilt University chose Harvard's Joe B. Wyatt as the school's sixth chancellor.

Crime. Crime continued to increase, especially in the cities, with little in the way of exemplary conduct from some state officials. House majority leader Thomas Burnett was sentenced in federal court to a prison term for failure to file timely tax returns; Memphis state senator Edgar Gillock was convicted on 11 counts of conspiracy, fraud, extortion, and tax evasion. Former representative Emmitt Ford, serving a term for insurance fraud, was denied parole when he became eligible in October. The sentence of former legislator and governor Ray Blanton, convicted of accepting payoffs, remained on appeal.

ROBERT E. CORLEW
Middle Tennessee State University

TENNESSEE · Information Highlights

Area: 42,144 sq mi (109 153 km²).
Population (1980 census): 4,591,120.
Chief Cities (1980 census): Nashville, the capital, 455,651; Memphis, 646,174; Knoxville, 175,045; Chattanooga, 169,588; Clarksville, 54,777.
Government (1982): *Chief Officers*—governor, Lamar Alexander (R); lt. gov., John S. Wilder (D). *General Assembly*—Senate, 33 members; House of Representatives, 99 members.
State Finances (fiscal year 1981): *Revenues,* $4,271,-000,000; *expenditures,* $4,231,000,000.
Personal Income (1981): $38,957,000,000; per capita, $8,447.
Labor Force (Aug. 1982): *Nonagricultural wage and salary earners,* 1,703,600; *unemployed,* 234,600 (11.1% of total force).
Education: *Enrollment* (fall 1981)—public elementary schools, 593,556; public secondary, 244,741; colleges and universities (1981–82), 200,183. *Public school expenditures* (1980–81), $1,337,037,000 ($1,458 per pupil).

TEXAS

Economic growth and expansion continued to describe the state of Texas in 1982. The unemployment rate was among the lowest in the nation, and the population increased as many job seekers arrived from the depressed Northeast and Midwest.

Politics. Two strenuously contested races dominated the political year. U.S. Rep. Jim Collins, a Republican from the 3rd District in Dallas, challenged Democratic incumbent Lloyd Bentsen for a U.S. Senate seat. Although Bentsen had never been thought of as a liberal and often voted in support of President Reagan's economic policies, Collins presented himself as the conservative candidate. Collins emphasized the crime and law and order issues, yet Bentsen proved a relatively easy winner. In the race for governor, State Attorney General Mark White mounted a strong challenge against Republican

Texas gubernatorial candidate Mark White (D) and wife Linda Gale wave to supporters while awaiting election results in Austin. White was the surprise winner over the Republican incumbent, William Clements.

incumbent William Clements. White hit hard at Clements' refusal to endorse a salary increase for public school teachers and at utility rate increases that had consumers up in arms. To the surprise of many political pundits, White was a strong winner.

Economy. While jobs were relatively plentiful, the economy was hurt somewhat by hard times in the oil and gas industry. As worldwide oil prices declined, many small Texas oil companies were forced into bankruptcy. A drive was also under way to lobby in Washington for accelerated deregulation of natural gas prices. Complete decontrol and a resulting free market is not scheduled until 1985, but leaders of the Texas oil and gas industry were already pushing hard for immediate decontrol as a solution for falling prices. On the other hand, the health of the economy was evidenced by new construction. More building permits were issued in Houston during 1982 than in any other city in the nation.

Constitutional Issues. In a landmark decision, Federal Judge William Justice ordered immediate improvement in the Texas prison system. Responding to charges of overcrowding and brutality, the legislature met in special session and granted a one-time appropriation of $56 million to the state prison system. Because of lack of space, some convicts were forced to live in tents at the Huntsville prison.

Another area of federal reform addressed by Judge Justice was the matter of educating Mexican children whose parents had entered the United States illegally. Although attorneys for the state pointed to the extreme financial hardship that would be visited on already overburdened school districts, the court held that the state must bear the expense of educating all children, whatever the status of their parents. The order was somewhat modified on appeal, but the principle remained generally intact.

Education. For the first time in recent years, there was no shortage of teachers in elementary and secondary schools. The void was filled by teachers from other states who came to Texas seeking jobs. No strikes were recorded in the public schools, and the drive for unionization of faculty appeared to be lagging. Attempts in some cities to implement examinations proving a level of 8th-grade competency were resisted.

In higher education, most state universities experienced an increase in enrollment. With the state universities already hard-pressed for finances, the increase will only intensify the struggle for appropriations in the state legislature. Rice University, the prestigious private institution in Houston, ranked among the nation's leaders in the number of Merit Scholars it attracts. Southern Methodist University (SMU) in Dallas and Baylor University in Waco also enjoyed national reputations.

Sports. Avid football fans, Texans generally deplored the National Football League strike, though the absence of professional competition did serve to heighten interest in the fortunes of such ranking college teams as SMU and the University of Texas. Finally, the legalization of horse racing in Oklahoma encouraged Texas enthusiasts who hope to bring the question before the legislature once again.

STANLEY E. SIEGEL, *University of Houston*

TEXAS • Information Highlights

Area: 226,807 sq mi (691 030 km²).
Population (1980 census): 14,229,288.
Chief Cities (1980 census): Austin, the capital, 345,-496; Houston, 1,594,086; Dallas, 904,078; San Antonio, 786,023; El Paso, 425,259; Fort Worth, 385,141.
Government (1982): *Chief Officers*—governor, William P. Clements, Jr. (R); lt. gov., William P. Hobby (D). *Legislature*—Senate, 31 members; House of Representatives, 150 members.
State Finances (fiscal year 1981): *Revenues,* $15,-252,000,000; *expenditures,* $12,910,000,000.
Personal Income (1981): $158,431,000,000; per capita, $10,729.
Labor Force (Aug. 1982): *Nonagricultural wage and salary earners,* 6,223,100; *unemployed,* 518,600 (7.0% of total force).
Education: *Enrollment* (fall 1981)—public elementary schools, 2,098,126; public secondary, 837,421; colleges and universities (1981–82), 716,297. *Public school expenditures* (1980–81), $6,140,-941,000 ($1,955 per pupil).

THAILAND

In the bicentennial year of the royal dynasty, the Prem government survived and the general who saved the government in 1981 was named army commander-in-chief.

Political Events. Two unsolved grenade attacks on Prime Minister Prem Tinsulanonda in July and August, one on his home and one against a motorcade in which he was traveling, led many persons to suspect dissatisfied army officers who might be attempting to thwart the rise of Prem protégé and assistant commander-in-chief of the army Lt. Gen. Arthit Kamlang-ek. But Arthit, who rushed forces to protect Prem's house after the second attack, and who had suppressed the coup attempt by "Young Turk" army officers in April 1981, was named the new army commander in September.

In December 1981, Prem broadened his cabinet in a reorganization that brought the Social Action Party (SAP) back into the government coalition, minus former economic czar Boonchu Rojanasathien, who resigned as deputy SAP leader. With former Prime Minister Kriangsak Chamanan seeking to regain influence through his new National Democratic Party, political jousting continued as a prelude to elections scheduled for 1983.

The reported death of the Communist Party head in January and the defection of a high Politburo member left that party's leadership in disarray. Defections and internal struggles reduced its armed threat.

In January the army attacked the base of opium warlord Khun Sa in northern Thailand. The raid and subsequent military operations disrupted his activities on the Thai side of the Burmese border but failed to capture him. During the year the government repelled a number of attacks by Khun Sa's Shan United Army to regain an operational base in Thailand.

The year 1982 marked the bicentennial of the Chakri Dynasty, and led to large celebrations, centered on the April birthday of the dynasty, and also of the royal identification of the city of Bangkok as the capital. The present king, now in the 37th year of his reign, ninth in the ruling line, is identified as Rama IX but is better known as King Bhumibol Adulyadej. In July he was stricken with a severe case of pneumonia. A relapse in August raised fears for his survival. A generally popular constitutional ruler, his recovery in late August was welcomed.

The Economy. Thailand's economy remained relatively strong, and its growth rate for the year was expected to exceed that of Singapore. Loans from the World Bank and the United States, plus substantial natural gas reserves, were important economic stimuli. To strengthen international trade, the government joined the new tin producers association, as well as the International Tin Agreement, in June and ratified a rubber trade pact aimed at stabilizing prices in April.

Foreign Affairs. The government continued to back the Association of Southeast Asian Nations (ASEAN) in its opposition to the Vietnamese presence in Cambodia, even to the extent of hosting former arch foe Prince Norodom Sihanouk, the rallying point of the Kampuchean anti-Vietnamese coalition.

A prisoner-exchange treaty, expected to permit the transfer of 42 American prisoners to the United States for completion of their sentences, was signed by Thai and American officials in Bangkok in October.

See also ASIA.

K. MULLINER
Ohio University

In July, Prince Norodom Sihanouk was greeted warmly by refugees at a camp near the Thailand-Cambodia border.

UPI

THAILAND · Information Highlights

Official Name: Kingdom of Thailand.
Location: Southeast Asia.
Area: 198,000 sq mi (512 820 km^2).
Population (1982 est.): 49,800,000.
Chief Cities (1980 est.): Bangkok, the capital, 4,870,-509; Chiang Mai, 105,230.
Government: *Head of state,* Bhumibol Adulyadej, king (acceded June 1946). *Head of government,* Gen. Prem Tinsulanonda, prime minister (took office March 1980).
Monetary Unit: Baht (23.00 baht equal U.S.$1, March 1982).
Gross National Product (1980 U.S.$):$31,100,000,-000.
Economic Index (1981): *Consumer Prices* (1970=100), *all items,* 282.2; *food,* 299.6.
Foreign Trade (1981 U.S.$): *Imports,* $9,931,000,-000; *exports,* $6,999,000,000.

THEATER

In 1982 theatrical activity in New York was in decline. At year's end the famous perennial shortage of Broadway theaters was no longer a problem. Although two fine Broadway theaters had, in the face of the dogged opposition of show-business leaders, been razed to make room for a hotel, the remaining playhouses went begging for plays.

Big Hits. The three great commercial hits of the year were, as might be expected, musicals—*Dreamgirls* (which opened in the last days of 1981), *Nine,* and *Cats.* Taking show business as its subject (like its comparably successful predecessors *A Chorus Line* and *42nd Street*), *Dreamgirls* used its music to tell its story, about a group of black girl singers, rather like the Supremes, who drop their gifted but unbecomingly stout lead singer and adapt their style to suit white preferences. Michael Bennett created a dazzling production, Jennifer Holliday shone as the discarded singer, Henry Krieger's score sounded authentic, and Tom Eyen's book bore a general resemblance to the recent history of popular music. *Nine* (based on the film *8½,* by Federico Fellini, who wished not to be mentioned in publicity for the play) showed us a filmmaker bedeviled by his women and seeking a new project for a film. Tommy Tune's inventive direction and a few entertaining character songs (notably Liliane Montevecchi's witty evocation of the Folies Bergère) won their audiences without pretending that anyone involved had the slightest real concern with the hero's problems. *Cats,* an English importation consisting mainly of poems out of T.S. Eliot's *Old Possum's Book of Practical Cats,* set to music by Andrew Lloyd Webber, commanded attention first of all by its virtues as a spectacle. The inside of a Broadway theater was torn apart and reassembled to form a suitably intimate setting for feline disguises and gyrations, heaps of junk for cats to play with, fireworks, and other amusing sights.

Broadway Musicals. The year's other durable musicals were two transfers from Off Broadway—*Joseph and the Amazing Technicolor Dreamcoat* (also with a score by Webber), a delightful biblical trifle first seen in New York a few years ago and now enlivened by the presence, amid its normally all-male voices, of an engaging girl, Laurie Beechman, singing the narration, and *Pump Boys and Dinettes,* a diverting low-keyed concert of country-rock music, set in a roadside filling station and diner. *Little Me,* the pleasantly loony 1962 saga of a resilient woman (with a book written by Neil Simon), was revived with James Coco giving a lively rendition of five bizarre roles but did not enjoy the success it deserved. The more pretentious *A Doll's Life,* an unimaginative and entirely unnecessary sequel to Ibsen's *A Doll's House,* conceived and directed by Harold Prince, fared no better. *Seven Brides for Seven Brothers,* based on

the Hollywood film about primitive courtship in the Wild West, failed to win New Yorkers with its forced heartiness and quickly failed.

Broadway Plays. Among straight plays on Broadway, Harvey Fierstein's *Torch Song Trilogy,* another transfer from Off Broadway, surely ranks first; it is a sensitive but frequently hilarious portrait of a homosexual drag queen, brilliantly played by the dramatist, and his struggle to bring some regularity to his life. By being frank, witty, defensive, and self-critical, Fierstein added a bold, innovative chapter to the theater's interpretation of homosexuality. The leader among Broadway's foreign plays was Athol Fugard's *Master Harold . . . and the Boys,* a South African work which came from the Yale Repertory Theatre, where it had had its world premiere. There can be no question of the great dramatic effect of this play's moment of explosive confrontation between two blacks and the unsteady adolescent son of their employer. The long exposition is the price we necessarily pay for this moment, but Zakes Mokae's extraordinarily vigorous performance as the older of the blacks made the waiting tolerable.

There is remarkably little to say for the rest of the American plays that reached Broadway. Many Hollywood actors came East to appear in them, and several may have come to wonder why they bothered. Those who possibly had least cause to wonder had a long run in John Pielmeier's *Agnes of God,* in which a former Catholic psychoanalyst (Elizabeth Ashley) interrogates a mother superior (Geraldine Page) and a young nun to investigate the nun's murder of her newly born child. Their conversation has more the effect of exploring the terrain and of entertaining us than of making real discoveries. Amanda Plummer, making her Broadway debut as the nun, earned a Tony award. By appearing in William Alfred's *The Curse of an Aching Heart,* Faye Dunaway paid a debt to the author of the play in which she had had her first New York success, but, otherwise, she did no more than create an oddly limited picture of a Brooklyn woman 50 years ago. Hollywood arrived in force in Ed Graczyk's *Come Back to the 5 & Dime Jimmy Dean, Jimmy Dean.* Taking leave from films, Robert Altman directed Cher, Sandy Dennis, and Karen Black in this sluggish drama of Texas girls tenderly recalling the making of James Dean's last film, *Giant.* Suzanne Pleshette returned to give one performance (as it turned out) in Bernard Slade's excessively lightweight romantic comedy *Special Occasions.* Jane Alexander was not seen much longer in William Gibson's *Monday after the Miracle,* a sequel to *The Miracle Worker,* his famous play about Helen Keller.

Two married couples acted together on Broadway late in the year and gave better reports of their personal qualities than of their plays. Jessica Tandy and Hume Cronyn were seen in *Foxfire,* adapted by Mr. Cronyn and

Susan Cooper from the popular *Foxfire* compilations of American folk customs. In an earlier manifestation, when it played Stratford, Ontario, in 1980, it was packed full of fascinating folklore, most of which was pruned away for Broadway, leaving mainly the less interesting story of an ancient rustic couple and their wayward son. Even so, Miss Tandy is, in the bigger role, exceptionally impressive. Like Miss Dunaway, Anne Jackson and Eli Wallach returned gratefully to the dramatist of their former triumphs, who, in this case, happened to be Murray Schisgal. His two one-act plays, *Twice around the Park,* provided a mild exercise in ironic urban humor.

The younger dramatists had trouble, too. Beth Henley, who had won a Pulitzer Prize with her first Broadway play, *Crimes of the Heart,* combined some of the same comic materials less happily in *The Wake of Jamey Foster,* a farcical treatment of a widow's fortunate bereavement. While his earlier play, *Sister Mary Ignatius Explains It All for You,* continued to run prosperously Off Broadway, Christopher Durang's

Beyond Therapy satirized both sex and psychoanalysis with a bold excess of exuberant abandon and failed to find an audience.

English plays, possibly still benefiting from the enormous success of the Royal Shakespeare's *Nicholas Nickleby* the year before, carried a special cachet. Understandably, the Royal Shakespeare chose to remind Americans of its *Nickleby* when it announced Cecil P. Taylor's *Good,* a conscientious but oddly stiff chronicle of a decent German's gradual transformation into a Nazi, featuring a cool but accurate performance by Alan Howard. David Hare's *Plenty,* which opened Off Broadway at Joseph Papp's Public Theater before moving to Broadway for an official opening in early 1983, had more to say in its cynical assault on British politics of the last few decades, and it gave the astonishing Kate Nelligan a chance to repeat her London triumph. *84 Charing Cross Road* might well be judged to be an American work because it is based on the correspondence of an American, Helene Hanff, with a London book dealer, but James Roose-Evans, who is English, first adapted and di-

© Ken Howard

Amanda Plummer (left) won a Tony for her supporting role in "Agnes of God," which also starred Geraldine Page.

BROADWAY OPENINGS | 1982

MUSICALS

Cats, music by Andrew Lloyd Webber, based on *Old Possum's Book of Practical Cats,* by T. S. Eliot; directed by Trevor Nunn; choreographed by Gillian Lynne; Oct. 7–

Do Black Patent Leather Shoes Really Reflect Up?, book by John R. Powers, music and lyrics by James Quinn and Alaric Jans; directed by Mike Nussbaum; with Russ Thacker; May 27–30.

A Doll's Life, book and lyrics by Betty Comden and Adolph Green, music by Larry Grossman; directed by Harold Prince; with Betsy Joslyn, George Hearn; Sept. 23–26.

Is There Life After High School?, book by Jeffrey Kindley, music and lyrics by Craig Carnelia, suggested by the book by Ralph Keyes; directed by Robert Nigro; May 7–16.

Joseph and the Amazing Technicolor Dreamcoat, music by Andrew Lloyd Webber, lyrics by Tim Rice; directed by Tony Tanner; with Laurie Beechman; Jan. 18–

Little Johnny Jones, book, music, and lyrics by George M. Cohan; directed by Gerald Gutierrez; with Donny Osmond; March 21.

Little Me, book by Neil Simon, music by Cy Coleman, lyrics by Carolyn Leigh; directed by Robert Drivas; with James Coco, Victor Garber, Jessica James; Jan. 21–Feb. 21.

Nine, book by Arthur Kopit; music and lyrics by Maury Yeston; directed by Tommy Tune; with Raul Julia, Karen Akers, Anita Morris, Shelly Burch, Taina Elg, Liliane Montevecchi; May 9–

Play Me a Country Song, book by Jay Broad, music and lyrics by John R. Briggs and Harry Manfredini; directed by Jerry Adler; June 27–29.

Seven Brides for Seven Brothers, book by Lawrence Kasha and David Landay, music by Gene de Paul, lyrics by Johnny Mercer; new songs by Al Kasha and Joel Hirschorn; directed by Lawrence Kasha; with Debby Boone; July 8–11.

Your Arms Too Short to Box with God, conceived from the Book of St. Matthew by Vinnette Carroll, music and lyrics by Alex Bradford and Micki Grant; directed by Miss Carroll; with Patti LaBelle, Al Green; Sept. 9–Nov. 7.

rected it for the London stage before presenting a slightly broader version in New York so that Anglo-American cultural contrasts might be made even plainer. Set in a public bath for women, Nell Dunn's *Steaming* mildly engages us with feminist issues and throws in some naked bodies for good measure.

Broadway's only French entry of 1982 was *A Little Family Business,* by Barillet and Grédy, the authors of *Cactus Flower* and *Forty Carats.* Pursuing as always the favorite thesis of Parisian boulevard comedy, the notion that middle-aged ladies are always right, demonstrated here in a contest with a bigoted philandering husband, the dramatists at least managed to provide Angela Lansbury with a fat part.

Broadway had more than its usual ration of classic plays in 1982. An *Othello* which had begun its life in 1981 in Stratford, CT, offered James Earl Jones, mustering all of his dignity in the title role, and Christopher Plummer, stealing attention with the sparks he set off as Iago. Zoe Caldwell gave a vigorous performance in the title role of Robinson Jeffers' adaptation of Euripides' *Medea,* supported by Judith Anderson, who had played Medea in 1947. Liv Ullmann made a better impression than the production that surrounded her in her short run as Mrs. Alving in Ibsen's *Ghosts.* The Circle in the Square made its annual contribution to Broadway's complement of classics—a quirky *Macbeth* directed by the unpredictable Nicol Williamson with himself in the lead, Ugo Betti's *The Queen and the Rebels* with the commanding Colleen Dewhurst, and Noel Coward's *Present Laughter* with George C. Scott as the self-loving actor (and so good at it that this comedy extended its run), accompanied by one new play, Percy Granger's *Eminent Domain,* a study of academic and literary life.

Off Broadway. The most considerable hit of the Off-Broadway year was *Little Shop of Horrors,* a wild musical farce about a man-eating plant; freely adapted by Howard Ashman from a modest horror film, it has a score by Alan Menken. The other long-running Off-Broadway offerings of the year were both products of Playwrights Horizons—*The Dining Room,* by

PLAYS

Agnes of God, by John Pielmeier; directed by Michael Lindsay-Hogg; with Elizabeth Ashley, Geraldine Page, Amanda Plummer; March 30–

Alice in Wonderland, adapted by Eva Le Gallienne and Florida Friebus from Lewis Carroll's stories; directed by Eva Le Gallienne and John Strasberg; with Eva Le Gallienne, Kate Burton; Dec. 23–

Almost an Eagle, by Michael Kimberley; directed by Jacques Levy; with James Whitmore; Dec. 16–19.

Beyond Therapy, by Christopher Durang; directed by John Madden; with John Lithgow, Dianne Wiest; May 26–June 13.

Come Back to the 5 & Dime Jimmy Dean, Jimmy Dean, by Ed Graczyk; directed by Robert Altman; with Cher, Sandy Dennis, Karen Black; Feb. 18–April 4.

The Curse of an Aching Heart, by William Alfred; directed by Gerald Gutierrez; with Faye Dunaway; Jan. 25–Feb. 21.

84 Charing Cross Road, adapted and directed by James Roose-Evans from Helene Hanff's book; with Ellen Burstyn, Joseph Maher; Dec. 7–

Eminent Domain, by Percy Granger; directed by Paul Austin; with Philip Bosco, Betty Miller; March 28–May 23.

Foxfire, by Susan Cooper and Hume Cronyn; directed by David Trainer; with Jessica Tandy, Hume Cronyn, Keith Carradine, Nov. 11–

Ghosts, by Henrik Ibsen; directed by John Neville; with Liv Ullmann, John Neville; Aug. 30–Oct. 2.

Good, by C. P. Taylor, directed by Howard Davies; with Alan Howard; Oct. 13–

A Little Family Business, by Jay Presson Allen, adapted from a French play by Pierre Barillet and Jean-Pierre Grédy; directed by Martin Charnin; with Angela Lansbury; Dec. 15–28.

Macbeth, by William Shakespeare; directed by Nicol Williamson; with Nicol Williamson; Jan. 28–Feb. 14.

Master Harold . . . and the Boys, written and directed by Athol Fugard; with Zakes Mokae, Danny Glover, Lonny Price; May 4–

Medea, adapted from Euripides' play by Robinson Jeffers; directed by Robert Whitehead; with Zoe Caldwell, Judith Anderson; May 22–June 27.

Monday after the Miracle, by William Gibson; directed by Arthur Penn; with Jane Alexander, Karen Allen; Dec. 14–Dec. 18.

Othello, by William Shakespeare; directed by Peter Coe; with James Earl Jones, Christopher Plummer, Dianne Wiest; Feb. 3–May 23.

Present Laughter, by Noel Coward; directed by George C. Scott; with George C. Scott, Christine Lahti; July 15–

The Queen and the Rebels, by Ugo Betti; directed by Waris Hussein; with Colleen Dewhurst; Sept. 30–Nov. 7.

Solomon's Child, by Tom Dulack; directed by John Tillinger; with John McMartin; April 8–11.

Special Occasions, by Bernard Slade; directed by Gene Saks; with Suzanne Pleshette; Feb. 7.

Steaming, by Nell Dunn; directed by Roger Smith; with Judith Ivey; Dec. 12–

Torch Song Trilogy, by Harvey Fierstein; directed by Peter Pope; with Harvey Fierstein; June 10–

Twice around the Park, by Murray Schisgal; directed by Arthur Storch; with Eli Wallach, Anne Jackson; Nov. 4–

The Wake of Jamey Foster, by Beth Henley; directed by Ulu Grosbard; Oct. 14–23.

Waltz of the Stork, written, directed, and featuring Melvin Van Peebles; Jan. 5–May 25.

Whodunnit, by Anthony Shaffer; directed by Michael Kahn; with George Hearn, Hermione Baddely, Barbara Baxley, Gordon Chater, Fred Gwynne; Dec. 30–

The World of Sholom Aleichem, by Arnold Perl; directed by Milton Moss; with Jack Gilford; Feb. 11–28.

OTHER ENTERTAINMENT

Blues in the Night, conceived and directed by Sheldon Epps; with Leslie Uggams; June 2–July 4.

Dance Theatre of Harlem; Jan. 20–Feb. 14.

Herman Van Veen: All of Him; Dec. 8–12.

Merce Cunningham Dance Company; March 16–28.

Pump Boys and Dinettes, revue featuring bluegrass, rockabilly, ballads, and blues music, conceived and written by John Foley, Mark Hardwick, Debra Monk, Cass Morgan, John Schimmel, Jim Wann; Feb. 4–

Rock 'n Roll! The First 5,000 Years, conceived by Bob Gill and Robert Rabinowitz; directed and choreographed by Joe Layton; musical continuity and supervision by John Simon; Oct. 24–Nov. 2.

Yves Montand; Sept. 7–12.

© Martha Swope

In October, "Cats," a musical based on T.S. Eliot poems, began playing to standing-room-only Broadway audiences.

A. R. Gurney, Jr., a witty collage of disconnected scenes in the history of a middle-class American dining room, and Jonathan Reynolds' *Geniuses,* a farcical report on filmmaking in an exotic locale, apparently suggested by Reynolds' employment by Francis Ford Coppola on *Apocalypse Now.* Playwrights Horizons, it should be added, won favorable notice also for a musical play, *Herringbone,* which permitted David Rounds to distinguish himself in ten roles.

Off Broadway's other major producing organizations had more or less uneven records in 1982. Papp's New York Shakespeare Festival sent *Plenty* on its way to Broadway, and it concluded the year by bringing over a Royal Court production from London, Caryl Churchill's feminist fantasy *Top Girls,* but it also presented an extremely elaborate production of a musical play that seemed not to justify all that elaboration, Des McAnuff's *The Death of von Richtofen as Witnessed from Earth;* David Rabe's *Goose and Tomtom,* a gangster play which the author dis-

avowed; *Hamlet,* in which the lead was, for no discernible reason, played by an actress who shows promise but not as yet much notable fulfillment; and Sophocles' *Antigone,* directed with heavy overemphasis by Joseph Chaikin. During the summer in Central Park the festival offered two classics—Molière's *Don Juan,* curiously interpreted by the *avant-garde* director Richard Foreman in a version previously seen at the Guthrie Theater of Minneapolis, and an uneven but generally entertaining staging of *A Midsummer Night's Dream* which made good use of its natural outdoor setting. The high spot of the Circle Repertory's season was Lanford Wilson's *Angels Fall,* about some personal encounters that come about at an isolated mission in New Mexico, but the year's roster also included Jules Feiffer's trivial play about an unhappy housewife, *A Think Piece,* and, with the film actor John Hurt in the lead, a *Richard II,* moved, it is said, to the dawn of England's history, which the critics were finally asked not to attend. The Manhattan Theater Club produced some plays of interest but nothing that called for a longer run—a Louisville production of *Talking with,* by Jane Martin (a pseudonym), a program of monologues by women; Sybille Pearson's *Sally and Marsha,* about the friendship between two very different women; John Olive's *On My Knees,* a portrait of a schizophrenic woman; and *Gardenia,* a new representative of John Guare's series of plays about 19th-century American life. A companion play by Guare also had its Off-Broadway debut in the course of the year, *Lydie Breeze.* The Roundabout Theater continued to offer us the plays of yesterday—Enid Bagnold's *The Chalk Garden* (with Irene Worth and Constance Cummings), Terence Rattigan's *The Browning Version,* and, no doubt representing the day before yesterday, Molière's *The Learned Ladies.* Elsewhere Off Broadway, Sam Shepard's *True West* at last found a production to the dramatist's liking, and David Mamet's *Edmond,* visiting from Chicago, was a record of one man's catastrophes ending on a rather startling note of hope. Harold Pinter's *The Hothouse,* a belatedly discovered early comedy which brutally but hilariously assails mental hospitals, arrived in a regional production from Providence but never won much attention.

Among the regional theaters, the Guthrie of Minneapolis reinterpreted classics by Beaumarchais and Goldoni, while New Haven's Long Wharf premiered Arthur Miller's awkward double bill *2 by A. M.,* and Chicago's Goodman proffered Edward Albee's *The Man Who Had Three Arms.* The failure of *Hamlet* and *Henry IV, Part One* at Stratford, CT, raised doubts as to the continued life of this Shakespeare theater. Responding to the vogue of *Nicholas Nickleby,* a Cleveland theater staged *Nickleby,* and a St. Louis playhouse dramatized *A Tale of Two Cities.*

HENRY POPKIN
State University of New York at Buffalo

THIRD WORLD

Much of the Third World was on the verge of financial bankruptcy in 1982 because of difficulty in paying back the enormous debts that had been accrued in recent years. The problem had potentially serious consequences for the United States and other industrially developed countries. A massive debt default by Third World states could set off an international depression from which no country would be immune.

The debt of the Third World countries exceeded $500,000,000,000 and was constantly growing because of interest charges. In addition, new loans were needed to complete industrial, agricultural, and other development projects that had been started with earlier loans. A number of countries could neither pay the interest nor make principal payments on their debts.

Causes. The causes of this near bankruptcy were numerous. The recession hit Third World countries particularly hard, as it brought a decline in prices and demand for raw materials, the major exports of underdeveloped countries. Protectionism on the part of both the rich and poor countries further restricted trade. Corruption, bureaucratic inefficiency, and political demagoguery continued to slow progress.

Ironically, falling oil prices did not help the situation very much. In fact, they sometimes hurt. Mexico, Nigeria, Venezuela, and Indonesia, all major oil producers, found that they did not have the revenues from oil exports which they had counted on to pay for ambitious development projects.

Shock. The inability of Mexico to service its more than $80,000,000,000 debt sent shock waves through the international financial system. It was soon clear that other countries—including Brazil, Argentina, Turkey, and Egypt—were in a similar predicament.

U.S. Policy Reversal. The Reagan administration began its term in Washington with a Third World policy stressing self-help and capitalistic initiative rather than foreign aid. But circumstances during the course of 1982 forced the administration to reverse its position. American political and economic interests were too closely linked with the fate of many Third World countries for Washington to maintain a laissez-faire, hands-off attitude.

A major worry for the United States was that economic chaos in the Third World could lead to political upheaval, particularly in Latin America, already a target for Soviet and Cuban subversion.

Another important factor was that one half the Third World debt was owed to private banks in the West, among them several major U.S. institutions. A permanent default by a country like Mexico or Brazil could cause some of those banks to go under. Finally, Washington realized that U.S. trade with the Third World could come to a virtual halt if new financing were not arranged.

Aid. The United States was quick to extend special financial aid to Mexico and Brazil, and late in the year was putting together a large Western aid package for Yugoslavia. Other countries were also counting on emergency assistance from Washington.

At the September meetings in Toronto of the International Monetary Fund (IMF) and World Bank, the United States agreed reluctantly to increase the financial resources of both agencies so that they could help debt-ridden countries.

Outlook. While resource-rich countries like Mexico and Brazil might be able to pay off their debts in the long run, the situation remained extremely bleak for countries not blessed with great natural resources. In the final analysis, Western efforts to prevent default in the Third World meant pouring in more good money after bad. For the United States and other rich countries, however, there seemed to be no choice.

Forums. During the year the Third World states and the developed countries often found themselves at odds in international forums such as the UN General Assembly and the International Atomic Energy Agency. The United States had to threaten to withdraw from the UN and its agencies in order to stop a drive by Third World states to have Israel expelled.

At the Paris conference in December of UNESCO (UN Educational, Scientific and Cultural Organization), the West and the Third World states agreed to disagree on the question of the free flow of information. The Third World had demanded a "new world information order," which the United States and other Western countries regarded as an attempt to use international bodies like UNESCO to throttle freedom of the press.

Nonaligned Movement. Adding to the economic crisis facing much of the Third World in 1982 was a political fiasco—the failure to successfully mediate an end to the Iran-Iraq war. The Nonaligned Movement, the political organization of the Third World, had been scheduled to hold its summit meeting in the Iraqi capital of Baghdad in September. But the ongoing conflict between the two Third World countries made this impossible, and the summit had to be ignominiously canceled and rescheduled for New Delhi in 1983.

Positive. If anything positive could be found in the Third World picture in 1982, it was simply that the economic crisis had underscored the interdependence and mutual interests of the rich and poor states. If this lesson is fully learned, the way may be open for greater cooperation and understanding between the Third World and the West.

See also articles on individual countries; NATIONS OF THE WORLD (page 572).

AARON R. EINFRANK
Free-lance International Correspondent

TRANSPORTATION

The performance of the U.S. transportation industries in 1982 was dominated by a continuing worldwide economic recession. All modes of transportation found traffic either stagnant or declining. The construction, steel, and automotive industries remained deeply depressed. But the scope of recession widened to include all sections of the United States. Early in the third quarter, a sudden collapse in domestic oil drilling traceable to lagging demand and prices dealt a serious blow to a wide range of supply industries. Only aerospace and other defense-related industries experienced increasing activity.

By the end of the third quarter, estimated cumulative rail ton miles were down 11.4% from 1981. All major commodity groups were down. A lag in export coal and grain movements added to the impact of domestic traffic declines. Only trailer on flatcar and container on flatcar movements were up, but some of the growth represented diversion from conventional rail carload service. Truck freight appeared to decline for the third year in a row. Traffic on the Great Lakes and on the inland rivers was down, reflecting the sharp decline in iron ore tonnage and the deferral of grain movement into export position. Domestic air cargo was off, although international cargo showed a modest increase. Passenger miles by air staged a minor recovery, but the intercity bus industry was seriously depressed.

The earnings of carriers of all modes were, of course, adversely affected even though a number of rate increases were put into effect. In the motor carrier industry, the general level of freight rates increased more than 14% during the year, but discounting continued on consolidated, multiple package, and volume shipments. In the first quarter, 64 of the 100 largest motor carriers reported losses. Upward of 140 large truckers had gone out of business or sought refuge under Chapter 11 of the Bankruptcy Act since mid-1980. Rail earnings for the six months ending June 30, 1982, produced a return on investment of 3%, well below the 5.4% reported for calendar year 1981. Many U.S. airlines experienced mounting losses, and the overall industry result appeared likely to be no better than in 1981 when U.S. airlines contributed most of worldwide airline losses of more than $600 million. Traffic declines generated surplus capacity in all modes of transportation. By July 31, more than 500 locomotives and 250,000 freight cars, 15% of ownership, were surplus. Orders for new rail equipment were virtually nonexistent and the heavy truck business was severely down.

Regulation. The year was not an active one in terms of new federal legislation. However, the Bus Regulatory Reform Act, signed by President

A strike by the Brotherhood of Locomotive Engineers left many U.S. railroads idle for four days in September. Fearing the damage to an already depressed economy, Congress passed legislation ending the walkout.

© Tom Ebenhoh/Black Star

Reagan on September 20, eased restraint on entry into the intercity bus industry, route abandonment and adjustment, and fare changes. A bill to reform maritime regulation was passed by the House of Representatives and awaited action in the Senate. Some progress was made on a bill designed to grant eminent domain to slurry pipelines, a number of which are planned for the long-haul transport of coal. For the most part, however, 1982 was marked by rule making and litigation designed to resolve uncertainties and conflicts with respect to the application of the major rail and motor carrier legislative changes made in 1980. Conrail was realizing advantages from application of the Northeast Rail Service Act of 1981 in the way of accelerated abandonment or disposal of unprofitable lines and progress toward relief from the operation of commuter services.

The statute that reforms bus regulation also contains a provision for a two-year moratorium on the grant of trucking rights within the United States to Canadian and Mexican motor carriers. The greater ease of entry into trucking provided by the Motor Carrier Act of 1980 had resulted in many grants of operating rights to carriers domiciled in the two adjacent countries. The Mexican constitution, however, prohibits the granting of operating rights to foreign carriers within Mexico. While the Canadian federal government does not regulate motor carriers, many of the provinces do. Ontario and Quebec, in particular, have regulations similar to those that prevailed in the United States prior to 1980. U.S. motor carriers successfully charged unfairness in light of the absence of reciprocity and convinced Congress to incorporate the moratorium. Some Canadian provincial officials threatened retaliation.

Perhaps the most important of many disputed regulatory issues is that of acceptable levels for coal rates under the terms of the Staggers Rail Act of 1980. Utilities and railroads are in continuing contention and the Interstate Commerce Commission (ICC) has yet to promulgate an acceptable set of regulations. Effective October 1, the statutory threshold for market dominance became 170% of rail variable cost. Below that level the commission lacks jurisdiction in the matter of rate reasonableness. The basis for calculating variable cost had not been finally settled by late 1982. Nor does it follow that a rate above 170% is necessarily unreasonable. Major investment has been made by railroads in the improvement of lines subject to heavy and growing coal traffic. Some new mileage has been built. The question of what compensation railroads are entitled to is still an open issue.

Air Transportation. Braniff, after strenuous efforts to preserve solvency, including the sale of routes and aircraft, filed under Section II of the Bankruptcy Act and ceased all operations. Eastern assumed operations in many of Braniff's Latin American markets, and other carriers moved to expand service in its domestic markets. Braniff later defaulted on its pension plans, raising the possibility that the government's Pension Benefits Guaranty Corporation might face the largest claim in its history. The carrier was the victim of extensive and unwise expansion of its route network immediately following deregulation as well as competitive fare-cutting on some of its key routes. In late October, however, Braniff and Pacific Southwest Airlines (P.S.A.) announced a tentative agreement in which P.S.A. would use some Braniff equipment and employ some of its work force. Other airlines in precarious financial condition in 1982 included Pan American, Continental, World Airlines, and Western. In September, Pan Am abandoned its effort to recoup by expansion of its routes and service and announced drastic curtailments. Florida Air, recently one of the fastest growing airlines, announced that it would cut its operations by approximately one third.

The service curtailments occasioned by the 1981 firing of striking air traffic controllers gradually eased. As additional takeoff slots became available, the Federal Aviation Administration (FAA) resorted to a lottery system in allocating such slots. Meanwhile, the Civil Aeronautics Board (CAB) sought to reduce airline subsidies from $113 million to $94 million in 1982 and by $48 million in the following year. Carriers may apply to "bump" commuter airlines from serving a community after two years by an offer of improved service and lower subsidy requirement. Even prior to this policy, some 100 small communities lost all commercial air service.

In the international sphere, tentative and temporary accord was reached between the United States and Japan after some 10 years of fruitless negotiations over air service between the two nations. Whereas some nations have accepted the U.S. view, which favors increased competition on international routes, Japan has strongly resisted such policies. The agreement, which satisfied neither government, did not settle all issues in dispute. The CAB approved numerous increases in international passenger fares between the United States and member countries of the European Common Market. The increases were responsive to an agreement between the United States and the European Civil Aviation Conference. Similar increases were denied to and from Scandinavian countries which are not members of the conference.

Motor Carrier Developments. The growth of nonunion trucking and the severe economic pressures to which unionized carriers are subjected led to an unusually restrained National Master Freight Agreement with the International Brotherhood of Teamsters. Some 120,000 of the 300,000 members subject to the agreement had been laid off. Under the agreement, cost-of-living (COL) increases would be limited to one per year, and a portion of each increase would be diverted to health, welfare, and pension plans.

In the fall, Boeing introduced the 767, said to be 35% more fuel efficient than the aircraft it would displace.

Work rule changes were also granted in some of the 31 supplemental area agreements reached at the same time. Two of a number of carriers which decided to negotiate separately, Time-D.C. and Hemingway, were subsequently struck and found it necessary to discontinue their less-than-truckload operations. Faced with a drop of 49% in revenues in the first six months, the Greyhound Corporation sought to reopen its contract with the Amalgamated Transit Union.

In its continuing effort to improve efficiency, the trucking industry again sought the liberalization of vehicle size and weight limits and the repeal of limitations more restrictive than the national pattern in the few remaining states that have such limitations. The industry was prepared to accept a 50% increase in user taxes both as a quid pro quo and to assist in funding rehabilitation and improvement of the rapidly deteriorating federal highway system. Highway excise taxes have remained essentially unchanged since 1956, while the escalation in highway construction costs has outrun general inflation. Hence, for many years, funding has been inadequate to maintain the system. Some 40% of the Interstate Highway System needs resurfacing, along with much of the remaining mileage. The condition of the highways is a source of increased operating and vehicle maintenance costs for all highway users.

Despite numerous failures in trucking, many of the larger carriers of general commodities showed good earnings and continued to grow by the opening of new terminals. It appeared that the less-than-truckload business will eventually be dominated by a small number of carriers operating nationwide networks. Some smaller carriers expanded their territorial reach by utilizing railroad piggyback service to connect their existing service territory to new areas in which they opened terminals. Shippers adjusting to changed circumstances were consolidating shipments to take advantage of volume discounts and were generally reducing the number of carriers with which they do business.

Railroads. The merger movement continued as a dominant trend among U.S. railroads. The consummation of the merger of Norfolk & Western Railway Co. and the Southern Railway created a strong competitor for CSX (which had been formed by the merger of Chessie System and the Seaboard Coast Line Industries) in the Southeast and the Midwest. The ICC approved the merger of Union Pacific Railroad with the Missouri Pacific and Western Pacific railroads, subject to specified grants of trackage rights to the St. Louis-Southwestern, Denver and Rio Grande, and Missouri/Kansas Texas. The decision was immediately challenged in the courts by the Southern Pacific and the Rio Grande. If consummated, the union would produce a major change in the railroad structure in the West and threaten other carriers with loss of traffic. Merger negotiations among some of those other railroads were rumored. Meanwhile the Grand Trunk, a subsidiary of Canadian National, sought control of the bankrupt Milwaukee Road, which had been reduced from a transcontinental system to a compact core operation in the Midwest. The Rock Island was still in the process of liquidation and various portions of its trackage were sold to other railroads for incorporation in their systems. Guilford Transportation Industries, which already controls Maine Central, was given authority to control Boston and Maine and Delaware & Hudson thus promising a 3,830-mi (6 164-km) New England system.

Despite a greater decline of traffic than was experienced in other parts of the country, Conrail, the government corporation controlling rail operations in the Northeast, continued to show modest earning ability. Careful cost control, shop closings, disposition of unprofitable lines, and aggressive use of the rate freedom accorded by the Staggers Act all contributed to this result. Since its main routes have been thoroughly rehabilitated as a result of heavy government funding, the railroad is in a position to render good service and to compete effectively for available business. Ultimate sale of the corporation to private parties now seems a reasonable expectation.

Progress was made with several kinds of innovative technology and control arrangements. Congestion at coal ports and long delay to ships awaiting loading were virtually eliminated by a booking plan for ship arrivals developed by the railroads serving Hampton Roads ports. Better car utilization was obtained as communications and car reporting using satellites reached a high degree of perfection. Improvements in track maintenance equipment continued to be made. Road Railers, a highway trailer with retractable steel wheels to permit movement on railroads without loading onto flat cars, continued to be tested on the Illinois Central Gulf between Chicago and Memphis. Service for perishables was also instituted between Florida points and the Hunts Point produce market in New York City. Because of restricted tunnel clearance north of Washington, conventional piggyback service has been impossible over this route. The service operates through the Hudson River and East River tunnels hitherto utilized only by passenger trains.

Despite growing unemployment, railroad workers did not feel the same economic pressure experienced by airline and motor carrier employees. Railroad earnings in 1981 were excellent in comparison with past performance for the industry, and the carriers could hardly argue a profit squeeze. Agreements, comparatively liberal by 1982 standards, were reached with the 11 nonoperating unions. Negotiations with the Brotherhood of Locomotive Engineers and the United Transportation Union along similar lines were not successfully concluded. To stay a strike, emergency boards were appointed by President Reagan under the Railway Labor Act. The engineers refused to accept the emergency board report and struck the carriers on September 19. The principal unsettled issue was maintenance of the traditional 15% wage differential for engineers. The president called for legislation to terminate the strike and to impose the agreement recommended by the emergency board. Such legislation became law on September 23, and the union ordered the engineers to return to their jobs. Conrail, which had previously worked out separate contracts, was not struck. Hence, commuter and Amtrak service in much of the Northeast was not affected. Few rules concessions were obtained by the carriers as the emergency board recommended a tripartite commission to study rule proposals.

Ocean Transportation. The deep sea trades have been characterized by depressed volumes of bulk cargo since 1979. Worldwide recession, increased conservation, and the growing availability of crude petroleum from closer sources, such as Mexico and the North Sea, have reduced long-haul petroleum movement from the Persian Gulf. Hence, some 15% of the world's tankship tonnage was either in lay-up or used for storage. Charter rates were deeply depressed. Under the circumstances larger crude carriers were being scrapped, sometimes after only 10 years of service. New buildings were at the lowest level since the 1930s. The dry cargo market was better than that for tankers, but the drop in iron ore and coking coal shipments produced by the low operating rates in the steel industry worldwide had an adverse effect on ship demand and charter rates.

Liner cargoes were not so deeply affected. Heavy carryings continued to and from the Pacific Basin, but the eastbound North America-Europe trade route suffered a loss of cargo due primarily to the strength of the U.S. dollar, which inhibited exports.

Mass Transit. Federal mass transit policy remained unchanged, and transit operators were scrambling for funds to replace the prospective loss of federal subsidies for operating expenses. Transit systems still under construction as well as those long in operation were adversely affected. In some cases increased state funding ameliorated the pressure, but transit operators were contemplating more stringent labor negotiations, negotiated contracts, and other efforts to tighten up on costs. New construction, especially of stations, was expected to be more austere. Construction continued on incomplete planned systems but at a reduced rate. The light rail system in Buffalo, NY, reached the equipment purchase state.

Controversy arose when the New York City Transit Authority awarded a large contract for news cars to Bombardier of Canada. The cars would be assembled in a new plant in Vermont but employ a large content of Canadian components. The Budd Company, the only remaining U.S. builder of transit cars, unsuccessfully contested the award since it was supported by a low-interest loan granted by the Canadian government. Most U.S. requirements for transit cars are now filled by foreign manufacturers.

For many years the Department of Transportation (DOT) has held that the mass transit needs of American cities not presently served by rail are best met by an expansion of bus operations. A report, issued by the Regional Plan Association of New York, New Jersey, and Connecticut under contract to DOT, contests that point of view. It found that Los Angeles, Seattle, Honolulu, and Houston have traffic which justifies investment in rapid transit while 10 other cities merit light-rail systems. Further, the report found that many cities which are presently served by rapid transit or light rail could justify extension of their systems.

Ernest W. Williams, Jr., *Columbia University*

TRAVEL

Gamma/Liaison

San Francisco's cable cars closed for 20 months of repairs, costing the city tourist revenue.

In 1982, world economic conditions affected travel much as they did other details of modern living but, as in other areas, directional signs were confusing, even in some ways downright contradictory.

U.S. Dollar. As the U.S. economy gave feeble signs of recovery, the dollar started an upward climb in value against other currencies, reaching a record 7-plus French francs, 2.5 deutsche marks, or 260 yen to the dollar by September. As early as June, U.S. passport offices were swamped by an 11% increase in applications. This reflected travel expectations, and the trend continued into fall. Yet as year's end approached, actual departures from the United States showed only a modest rise, while tourism to the United States, which has been increasing since 1979, fell from 3 to 17%, according to country of origin. Only the number of Japanese visitors increased, by 5%.

Some of this decline was attributable to the crisis in the Mexican economy and subsequent currency controls. Mexican tourism to the United States fell by 15% from 1981, reflecting limits on the amount of money that could be taken out of the country. Visitors from Great Britain accounted for the sharpest slide. Domestic travel within the United States also decreased by an estimated 7 to 10%, as noted by all elements of the travel industry over the usually crowded Labor Day weekend.

Airlines. Continuing a trend that began conspicuously with government deregulation in 1978, U.S. airlines engaged in a competitive struggle, alternately lowering fares or offering discounts, then raising them higher than before. In the resultant daily confusion, most travel agencies that had not done so invested in computers to enable them to find for their clients the most advantageous rates to desired destinations at given times. Particularly on intrastate routes, the rate battles continued through the autumn. But after an emergency meeting in Geneva of the world's major air carriers, the International Air Transport Association (IATA) announced fare raises of 5 to 7% on most international routes, effective October 1.

Even with the calculations of their own computers, airlines scarcely benefited from the scramble. In May, Braniff International declared bankruptcy, and in September asked the government for an additional 60 days to reorganize to put its fleet back in service. A similar jolt was the bankruptcy of Britain's Laker Airways, which started cut-rate transatlantic service in 1977. By late 1982, bouncy Sir Freddie Laker was appearing on television in commercials for Bell Telephone, publicizing overseas phone calls.

Such manifestations of airline vulnerability were not all. Other carriers continued to post losses, including Pan American, TWA, World, and United. Texas International swallowed Continental and assumed the victim's name. Pan Am said that it would reduce its staff 15%. Although United put some new Boeing 767s, considered to be the U.S. answer to Europe's Airbus, into service, it postponed taking delivery on 20 of 39 of the new planes it had bespoken.

Also in August, a year after the Professional Air Traffic Controllers Organization (PATCO) went on strike in defiance of the government, the union went into bankruptcy. Although air traffic was but 86% of 1981 volume, according to federal officials, it was flowing smoothly and with fewer delays despite reduced service. And the government announced that by January 1983, nearly half the control towers at 80 small airports that had been closed because of the strike would have reopened. While these control towers handle only private planes and some small commuter air lines, it was expected that reactivating them would relieve the burden at nearby major airports.

Other. However, not all indicators regarding the travel industry were discouraging. Some companies specializing in charter tours experienced a 35% increase in business, compared with 1981, and extended their "season" into late October. Special-interest travel to unusual destinations held up, showing a slight increase over 1981. Cruise travel demonstrated a still growing market, but so marginally that companies offered more incentives, such as free air fares to ports of departure, since competition on the seas also is increasing. Pearl Cruises, a new entry from Scandinavia with headquarters in San Francisco, joined the fleets with fly/cruises to China and other oriental ports, as well as the Pacific islands.

In Japan, rail travel continued to be popular on Bullet trains. France put its new high speed TGV express into regular service between Paris and Lyons. On that run, and on those to come, not only are rates less expensive than air fares, but travelers alighting in the center of town also save time by not having to go to and from airports.

Sales of France Vacances passes, which offer bargains in addition to rail tickets, were about the same as in 1981, but sales of Eurailpasses, providing for similar privileges to overseas visitors on Europe's entire rail system, were down by a puzzling 40%. U.S. train travel declined by about 5% per passenger, though passenger miles were up, indicating that people were taking longer rail trips. A late-in-the-year blow to Amtrak was a rail strike in mid-September but, after government intervention, it lasted only four days.

See also TRANSPORTATION.

CAROLYN STULL
Free-lance Travel Writer

TRINIDAD AND TOBAGO

On Aug. 31, 1982, Trinidad and Tobago celebrated its 20th anniversary as an independent nation. The festive mood was tempered by a general awareness that the era of prosperity brought about by petrodollars was coming to an abrupt end.

Declining oil production coupled with a softening of oil prices markedly reduced the income of the government. Texaco, which at one point had reached a production high of 300,000 barrels per day at the island's largest refinery, cut back to a mere 50,000 barrels per day. On top of that, Texaco announced its willingness to sell the refinery and pull out of Trinidad altogether. Earlier in the year, the government was given the opportunity to purchase the remaining 49.9% of shares of the jointly held Trinidad-Tesoro oil drilling company.

During the first six months of fiscal 1982, the government registered an alarming deficit of $1,400,000,000 (T&T), about $1,200,000,000 more than in the corresponding period of the previous year. Since more than 90% of the government's export earnings come from petroleum, it was obvious that the oil boom was over. Recognizing that fact, the government sought to cut expenditures and reverse the carefree spending habits of its citizens. The importation of certain consumer articles was restricted, and an extravagant horse racing complex being built by a U.S. corporation was canceled.

Other expenditures were harder to control. The government agreed to a costly settlement with some 52,000 federal employees who had gone on strike in late 1981. In August 1982 the parliament passed a bill providing $500 million to pay part of the increased wages. Workers in the government electric power corporation demanded a 170% wage increase. Power outages occurred with alarming frequency, forcing some industries to suspend operations for extended periods.

Charges of inefficiency and corruption in government clearly marked the end of the euphoria with which Prime Minister George Chambers and his People's National Movement had begun the 20th year of independence.

THOMAS MATHEWS
Institute of Caribbean Studies
University of Puerto Rico

TRINIDAD AND TOBAGO · Information Highlights

Official Name: Republic of Trinidad and Tobago.

Location: Caribbean Islands.

Area: 1,980 sq mi (5 128 km²).

Population (1982 est.): 1,100,000.

Chief Cities (1977 est.): Port of Spain, 120,000; San Fernando, 60,000; Arima, 20,000.

Government: Head of state, Ellis Clarke, president (took office Dec. 1976). Head of government, George Chambers, prime minister (took office Nov. 1981). Legislature—Parliament: Senate and House of Representatives.

Monetary Unit: Trinidad and Tobago dollar (2.4 TT dollars equal U.S.$1, March 1982).

Gross National Product Per Capita (1980 U.S.$): $4,370.

Economic Index (1981): *Consumer Prices* (1970=100), *all items,* 388.5; food, 417.5.

Foreign Trade (1980 U.S.$): *Imports,* $3,178,000,-000; *exports,* $4,077,000,000.

TUNISIA

Some 1,100 Palestinians were guarded by members of Tunisia's Army upon their arrival in Bizerte from Lebanon.

In 1982, the Tunisian government was successful in maintaining mutually beneficial relations with the powerful trade confederation, the General Union of Tunisian Workers (UGTT), despite an increase in the unemployment rate and strikes in several sectors of the economy. Relations with the United States were strengthened with increased sales of military equipment.

Politics and Labor Relations. Following his pardon by President Habib Bourguiba in late November 1981, Habib Achour was reelected leader of the UGTT, a position he had lost after the January 1978 labor unrest. Achour had been imprisoned and then under house arrest since the disturbances. The pardon of the labor leader was seen as part of an ongoing government effort to achieve an accommodation with the UGTT, with which the ruling Socialist Destour Party (PSD) had formed an electoral alliance and

swept the country's first multiparty legislative elections in November 1981.

Opposition parties protested the outcome of the elections, accusing the government of having falsified the results. And on the 26th anniversary of Tunisia's independence in March, the main opposition groups—the Movement of Democratic Socialists, the Communist party, the Movement for Popular Unity, and the Islamic Movement—issued a joint declaration calling for "an improvement in the political climate."

Prime Minister Mohamed Mzali implemented a general salary increase for workers in February after conducting complex negotiations with labor groups representing industry, agriculture, and the public sector.

Foreign Relations and the Economy. Mzali's April visit to Washington, DC, culminated in the signing of an agreement for the purchase of F-5E jet fighters, M-60 tanks, and antiaircraft weaponry. The deal represented part of the Reagan administration's policy to bolster Tunisia and Morocco militarily in a "strategic consensus." Tunisia had been seeking increased military cooperation with the United States after the 1980 commando raid on the mining town of Gafsa, allegedly carried out with Libyan assistance. However, Mzali said in Washington that relations with Libya had improved since the attack, following two visits to Tunis in 1982 by Libyan leader Muammar el-Qaddafi.

While the United States was shifting its policy emphasis from economic to military assistance, Tunisia continued to suffer from high levels of unemployment, estimated as high as 25%. The $14,000,000,000 five-year development plan now in effect had envisioned the creation of 60,000 new jobs per year, but Mzali conceded that it would fall short by at least 10,000.

Tunisia turned increasingly to Libya and Arab Gulf states in 1982 for financial assistance and markets for its excess manpower, while facing obstacles to trade with the European Community (EC). The French prime minister, Pierre Mauroy, visited Tunis in February to promote economic cooperation between the two coun-

---

TUNISIA • Information Highlights

Official Name: Republic of Tunisia.
Location: North Africa.
Area: 63,170 sq mi (163 610 km²).
Population (1982 est.): 6,700,000.
Chief City (1975 census): Tunis, the capital, 550,404.
Government: *Head of state,* Habib Bourguiba, president-for-life (took office 1957). *Chief minister,* Mohamed Mzali, prime minister (took office April 1980). *Legislature* (unicameral)—National Assembly.
Monetary Unit: Dinar (.5666 dinar equals U.S.$1, March 1982).
Gross Domestic Product (1980 U.S.$): $8,600,000,000.
Economic Indexes (1981): *Consumer Prices* (1970= 100), *all items,* 136.1; *food,* 143.7. *Industrial production* (1980, 1975=100), 149.
Foreign Trade (1981 U.S.$): *Imports,* $3,479,000,000; *exports,* $2,189,000,000.

tries. France agreed to participate in the Tunisia-Qatar-France Investment Bank and will provide 30% of the $100 million in capital required. An outstanding issue between the two countries—French property and assets blocked and retained in Tunisia—was not addressed during the French prime minister's trip, but further negotiations were planned. France also will cooperate in developing the industrial and agricultural sectors in Tunisia.

MARGARET A. NOVICKI, *"Africa Report"*

TURKEY

In 1982, there was some improvement in the economy, and attempts were made to control militant elements in the population. Gen. Kenan Evren assured the people that parliamentary democratic government would be restored under a new constitution, replacing the 1961 document.

Economy. Economic development was placed within the framework of the stabilization plan of Jan. 24, 1980. The plan was reaffirmed when Adnan Basar Kafaoglu took office as finance minister in July 1982. Turkish exports in the first five months of 1982 amounted to $2,100,000,000, a 29% increase over the same period in 1981; imports were down by 6%. The foreign trade deficit fell to $1,370,000,000 in January–May 1982, as against $2,840,000,000 in the same period of 1981. It was hoped that the inflation rate, cut to 35% in 1981, would be half that figure in 1982. Remittances from Turks working abroad, mainly in Germany, remained the same. Because of the high external debt, basic recovery could not take place without assistance from allies in NATO and the OECD; the major contributor was the United States, with $40 million per year. In June 1982 the World Bank approved a $304.5-million loan to support recovery.

Foreign Affairs. In addition to Turkey's basically homogeneous population of Muslims, there are Kurdish and Armenian communities whose most ardently nationalistic members again claimed credit for violent actions throughout 1982. In October some 574 suspects were brought to trial. Terrorist acts beyond the borders of Turkey resulted in the deaths of Kemal Arikan, the Turkish consul general in Los Angeles, and of Orhan Gunduz, the Turkish honorary consul general in Boston. In Ottawa the Turkish commercial attaché was wounded.

Turkey sought to improve its position among its Arab neighbors to the south and Balkan neighbors to the north. It was unable, however, to solve the problem of Cyprus and the Aegean Islands, and relations with Greece therefore did not show much improvement.

New Constitution. General Evren proceeded to the task of giving Turkey a new constitution. A Consultative Assembly to draft the charter first met in October 1981, at which time Evren said that he stood by his pledge "to pave the way

---

TURKEY · Information Highlights

Official Name: Republic of Turkey.
Location: Southeastern Europe and southwestern Asia.
Area: 300,947 sq mi (779 452 km^2).
Population (1980 census): 44,736,957.
Chief Cities (1980 census): Ankara, the capital, 2,585,293; Istanbul, 3,904,588; Izmir, 1,673,966.
Government: *Head of state,* Gen. Kenan Evren, president (took office Nov. 10, 1982). *Head of government,* Bülent Ulusu, prime minister (took office Sept. 1980). *Legislature*—Grand National Assembly
Monetary Unit: Lira (176.15 liras equal U.S.$1, Oct. 26, 1982).
Gross Domestic Product (1980 U.S.$): $51,320,000,000.
Economic Index (1980): *Consumer prices* (1970= 100), *all items,* 1,638.7; *food,* 1,638.4
Foreign Trade (1981 U.S.$): *Imports,* $8,973,000,000; *imports,* $4,697,000,000.

---

for a smooth functioning democracy." He also said there had not been, nor would there be, "any attempt by persons or authority to make suggestions or exert any pressure on the Consultative Assembly."

A preliminary draft of the new document, which retained most of the provisions of the 1961 constitution, was published July 17, 1982. It provided that the president of the republic would be elected for a seven-year term by a two-thirds majority of the legislature. The Grand National Assembly, as the legislative body would be called, would comprise 400 members, each elected to five-year terms.

The final version of the new constitution was approved by Turkey's military leaders on October 19. The most controversial provision was the automatic election of General Evren as president for seven years if the document were approved in a popular referendum on November 7. Another provision arousing criticism was one banning former political leaders from politics for ten years and former members of parliament for five years. This would bar activity by former prime ministers Bülent Ecevit and Suleiman Demirel; Ecevit had served time in jail for violating the ban on political activity promulgated in 1981. Finally, parliamentary elections were tentatively scheduled for late 1983.

General Evren immediately began his campaign in favor of the constitution in the November referendum. The military imposed a ban on criticism of key provisions, saying there had been sufficient discussion. The constitution was overwhelmingly approved in the referendum, and Evren became the nation's seventh president.

HARRY N. HOWARD, *Middle East Institute*

UGANDA

A revival of the Ugandan economy after the chaos of the Idi Amin years appeared to be under way at last in 1982, but it was jeopardized by the personal and political violence that continued to plague the country.

The Economy. The government of President Milton Obote adopted strong measures to bring the economy back to life. Devaluation of the Uganda shilling by 1,000% and raising the price guaranteed to coffee growers ended a four-year lapse in coffee exports, which earn 97% of the nation's foreign exchange. Tea cultivation also resumed on a commercial scale, and the strong possibility of mineral exports, especially copper, further brightened the economic outlook. Meanwhile the International Monetary Fund arranged $197 million in loans to Uganda and agreed to provide up to $225 million more. The money was to be used for general rebuilding.

Unrest. Despite Obote's endorsement of a non-Socialist, multiparty political system for Uganda, armed opposition groups continued to battle his regime for control of the country. The accurate charges of corruption attending his election and his personal unpopularity among the large and powerful Ganda tribe made the legitimizing of Obote's government almost impossible. At least four well-organized guerrilla groups were determined to overthrow Obote.

A daring raid on the Kampala army headquarters in February led to a violent reaction in which thousands of people were arrested and more than 1,000 executed, many after torture. The new Ugandan armed forces were still largely undisciplined and little better than the guerrillas and common criminals they were fighting. The murder by unknown gunmen of leaders of the opposition Democratic Party and the enticing of some of its members of Parliament into Obote's Uganda People's Congress further embittered national politics. Personal violence and danger, though not as bad as in years past, remained a serious problem.

Foreign Affairs. Uganda took little part in foreign affairs in 1982. However, there was a brief border war with the Sudan, whose troops crossed a disputed section of the frontier into northern Uganda and decimated animal life in Kidepo National Park. Both governments seemed unable or unwilling to end the slaughter. Since the loss of animal herds could mean the end of Ugandan hopes to revive the tourism attracted by the country's once magnificent wildlife parks, the incident had economic implications.

ROBERT GARFIELD, *DePaul University*

UGANDA • Information Highlights

Official Name: Republic of Uganda.
Location: Interior of East Africa.
Area: 91,134 sq mi (236 037 km²).
Population (1982 est.): 13,700,000.
Chief City (1980 census): Kampala, the capital, 458,-423.
Government: *Head of state,* Milton Obote, president (elected Dec. 1980). *Head of government,* Otema Alimadi, prime minister (appointed Dec. 1980). *Legislature* (unicameral)—Parliament, 126 members.
Monetary Unit: Uganda shilling (85.75 shillings equal U.S.$1, March 1982).
Gross National Product Per Capita (1980 U.S.$): $280.

USSR

An era of Soviet history ended with the death of President Leonid I. Brezhnev at age 75 on Nov. 10, 1982. Two days later a new era appeared to begin as Yuri V. Andropov, 68, former head of the KGB, was named the new secretary-general of the Soviet Communist Party. The presidency itself, a largely ceremonial post, was also expected to go to Andropov, but as the year came to an end no replacement for Brezhnev had yet been named.

Throughout 1982, meanwhile, new economic difficulties at home and a number of setbacks abroad were the fate of the Soviet state. For the fourth consecutive year, industrial output stagnated, and bad weather resulted in a grain crop insufficient for national needs. Despite these factory and farm troubles, the regime stepped up munitions production to compete with the growing armaments of the United States. In Afghanistan, for the third year, a 100,000-man Soviet army was unable to defeat poorly armed guerrillas harassing Kabul's Communist government. Elsewhere, Soviet friends suffered military defeat: Syria and the PLO at the hands of Israel in Lebanon, and Argentina at the hands of Great Britain in the Falklands. Finally, Soviet attempts to improve relations with China failed to resolve basic disagreements.

Domestic Affairs

Politics. In poor health for half a decade, President Brezhnev finally died from heart failure after 18 years as the top leader of the Soviet Union. (*See* OBITUARIES.) As appropriate for a high-ranking veteran of World War II, Brezhnev was given an elaborate military funeral on November 15. In attendance were officials representing more than 100 foreign countries and constituting the largest assemblage of foreign dignitaries to come to Moscow in the history of the USSR.

The realignment of power came swiftly after Brezhnev's passing. Politburo-member Yuri Andropov, who in May had relinquished his long-time chairmanship of the Committee for State Security (KGB) to become a national party secretary, on November 12 was chosen by the party's Central Committee to succeed Brezhnev in the top post of secretary-general. (*See* BIOGRAPHY.) On November 22 the Central Committee promoted Geidar A. Aliyev, 59, from alternate to full member of the party Politburo. Meeting November 23–24, the governmental Supreme Soviet made Andropov a member of its Presidium and appointed Aliyev a first deputy premier in the cabinet. Apparently because of behind-the-scenes disputes, Brezhnev's additional post of chairman of the Presidium of the Supreme Soviet (president) was not immediately filled.

The rise of Andropov had actually begun earlier in the year. Mikhail A. Suslov, the influential chief party ideologist and a member of the Politburo since 1955, died in Moscow on January 25 at age 79. Andropov is said to have made a bid for Suslov's role in the Secretariat over the following months; his return to that powerful 10-member body in May (he had been a party secretary earlier in his career) signaled success. Further maneuvering put him in line as Brezhnev's eventual successor.

In other changes during the year, Andrei P. Kirilenko, 76, the party secretary for heavy industry, tendered his resignation from the Politburo in the fall. Vladimir Dolgikh, a 57-year-old technocrat regarded as an up-and-coming force, was made an alternate member of the Politburo in May. And Andropov's successor as KGB chief was Vitaly V. Fedorchuk, the former head of that organization in the Ukraine.

Armed Forces. Military buildup remained a top priority of the old leadership as well as the new. In 1982 the total Soviet armed forces comprised about 4.2 million men. The USSR ranked first in the world in number of tanks, intercontinental ballistic missiles, intermediate and submarine-based missiles, medium-range bombers, submarines, and surface naval vessels. But the Soviet arsenal lagged behind that of the United States in number of aircraft carriers, long-range bombers, tactical atomic weapons, and total nuclear warheads. In July the USSR government stated that, in the Lebanese war, Soviet military equipment in Arab hands was not proving inferior to Western equipment used by Israel. Later, however, President Brezhnev did say that the overall quality of Soviet armaments must be improved.

In 1982 President Brezhnev made two major statements on military policy. In June he informed the United Nations Disarmament Conference that the USSR renounced the first use of nuclear weapons in future war. Then, in an October speech to Soviet military officers, he said that the USSR would increase munitions output to compete with U.S. armament expansion. Both statements were immediately qualified by other leading Soviet spokesmen. It was explained that if NATO or the United States were about to launch an atomic attack upon the USSR, Soviet nuclear weapons would be fired first. And, while increasing its armaments, the USSR would continue arms-limitation talks with the United States.

In March, East German, Polish and Soviet troops conducted joint Warsaw Pact maneuvers in northwest Poland to intimidate Poles resisting the martial law regime. In June the USSR made test flights of seven long-range and short-range missiles within Soviet territory. And in late summer, several intercontinental missiles were test-fired into the Pacific Ocean.

Only days after taking office, Secretary-General Andropov reaffirmed the nation's commit-

Tass from Sovfoto

Despite a cold rain, Red Square was packed for annual May Day ceremonies. A frail Leonid Brezhnev observed the parade from atop the Lenin Mausoleum (center, front).

ment to military buildup, saying "we will multiply our forces in our struggle for security."

Dissidents. Many Soviet dissidents were imprisoned during 1982 for demanding freedom of religion, other civil liberties, equality for minorities, release of political prisoners, or permission to emigrate abroad. Emigration was officially authorized for some 3,000 Soviet Jews, compared with 9,400 in 1981 and 21,500 in 1980.

During the year, some 48 million citizens attended officially organized meetings and marches opposing nuclear war throughout the USSR. In July a large group of Scandinavian pacifists was permitted to make a train tour of European USSR, holding peace rallies in several cities.

In June, however, when West European amateur sailors distributed leaflets in Leningrad urging the USSR to stop nuclear testing, their yacht was towed out of Leningrad harbor by Soviet tugs. Meanwhile KGB police repeatedly harassed a group of Moscow intellectuals who

In a speech to the Young Communist League, May 18, President Brezhnev proposed a U.S.-Soviet nuclear freeze.

tried to form a private organization to promote disarmament.

Population. In mid-1982 the total population of the USSR stood at approximately 270 million. The largest public organizations were the Soviet Communist Party, with more than 17.5 million members; the Young Communist League, with 41 million; the trade unions, with 130 million; and the sports societies, with 80 million.

Because of a longtime low birthrate, the economy in 1982 suffered from an acute shortage of labor. Though there were 50 million Soviet people on pension, extra income induced only 7.4 million retirees to return to work. As a result, the Soviet labor force in 1982 increased by only 1.1%, and there were more than 2 million vacant jobs.

Space. A major series of spaceflights began on April 19, 1982, when the Salyut 7 space research station was launched to replace the obsolete Salyut 6, which was allowed to burn up in the atmosphere. After being launched in Kazakhstan with Lt. Col. Anatoly Berezovoy and Valentin Lebedev on board, the Soyuz T-5 manned rocket on May 13 docked with Salyut 7, where the two men stayed to receive six visitors. The first three guests were Col. Vladimir Dzhanibekov, Aleksandr Ivanchenkov, and Frenchman Jean-Loup Chrétien, who were launched in Soyuz T-6 on June 24 and returned to earth July 2. They were followed by Lt. Col. Leonid Popov, Aleksandr Serebrov, and a woman, Svetlana Savitskaya, who were lofted in Soyuz T-7 on August 19, and returned to earth August 27. Chrétien was the first Frenchman and Savitskaya the second woman ever to fly in space. The two hosts on Salyut 7, Berezovoy and Lebedev, finally returned on December 10 after setting a new space longevity record of 211 days.

On March 1 and 5, two Soviet unmanned rockets landed on the planet Venus and trans-

mitted back to earth the first color photographs of the planetary surface.

Economy

Industry. The labor shortage and military buildup caused the 1979–1981 industrial recession to continue during 1982. As the year drew to a close, the growth of industrial production was only 2.8%, the lowest annual increase since 1946. Some 22 major Soviet industries in 1982 were producing less or no more than in 1981, while 17 could not exceed the 1978 level. Among the inefficient industries were coal mining and steel smelting, resulting in a nationwide shortage of metal and fuel. Petroleum production increased very little because of mining difficulties and a labor shortage in Western Siberian wooded swamps.

These and other difficulties occurred in an industrial establishment which, according to government statistics, was only 54% of the size of the U.S. industrial sector.

Agriculture. Because of bad spring and summer weather, the 1982 grain harvest of approximately 170 million metric tons (187 million T) was even smaller than the poor 1981 crop of 175 million tons (193 million T) and far below the 1982 goal of 237 million tons (261 million T). Meat production in 1982 was below the level of any of the previous four years.

As a result of the poor grain harvest, the USSR in 1982 had to purchase about 40 million metric tons (44 million T) of foreign grain, with Argentina and the United States being the chief suppliers. Meat was also imported from West Europe.

Food Program. To cope with all these agricultural difficulties, the Central Committee on May 24 unveiled a special food program for the years 1982–1990. The program has two main goals: to make the USSR self-sufficient in grain, and to end the longtime store shortages of vegetables, livestock products, and fruit. Instead of concentrating on farm output alone, the program will strive to improve everything connected with food supply, including the farm machinery and fertilizer industries, rural roads, railway crop transportation, food storage and processing facilities, and even grocery stores.

As a start, state agro-industrial commissions to enforce the program were established at the district, regional, republic, and national levels. Collective farm debts to the government totaling 9,700,000,000 rubles were canceled, and repayment of another 11,000,000,000 rubles was deferred. State farm salaries were raised by 30%. As of Jan. 1, 1983, the prices paid by the state for collective farm produce were increased for grain, sugar beets, vegetables, meat, and milk.

For the first time in Soviet history, collective and state farms were allowed to fulfill only 90% of their compulsory sales to government agencies of fruit and vegetables. The remaining 10% was sold directly to the public in city markets. The Soviet press explained that there were too few urban refrigerated warehouses and that the 10% would otherwise be lost to spoilage.

In the cities, the program ordered restaurants not to waste food in preparing meals. Every factory and mine was encouraged to organize its own large farm so that industrial workers would be well fed despite store shortages.

Standard of Living. Because of the industrial recession and poor harvest, the Soviet standard of living remained mediocre in 1982. There were admitted store shortages of butter, cheese, eggs, fish, fruit, margarine, meat, milk, potatoes, vegetables, vegetable oil, clothing, furs, home appliances, leather goods, and shoes. Housing was overcrowded, and there were not enough nurseries and kindergartens for pre-school children. Salaries continued to be low, the average urban annual wage being 2,124 rubles ($2,992).

Transportation. Contributing to the 1982 industrial recession was the poor performance of the Soviet transportation network, the railways and inland waterways being the worst offenders. Except for pipeline transport of natural gas, total haulage of internal freight was little higher than in 1981.

Aeroflot, the Soviet state aviation company, claimed in 1982 to be the world's largest airline, transporting more than 100 million passengers and flying to 3,600 Soviet cities and 91 foreign countries.

The Soviet merchant marine in 1982 operated 1,750 ships and in tonnage was sixth largest in the world. On February 16, the Soviet cargo ship *Mekhanik Tarasov* sank in a violent storm east of Newfoundland, drowning most of its crew.

Trade. Total Soviet foreign trade increased by about 11% over 1981. The USSR continued to be the world's largest exporter of raw materials and one of the biggest importers of food. Because of heavy borrowing to pay for imports, the USSR in 1982 owed $20,000,000,000 to Western and Japanese banks and governments.

All in all, the new Soviet leadership inherited a difficult economic situation from the Brezhnev era.

Foreign Affairs

Though the USSR was experiencing grave economic difficulties at home, its technical aid to developing nations was still extensive. In 1982,

Sluggish industry and a poor harvest left trading centers in short supply of clothing, appliances, and fresh foods.

Tass from Sovfoto

the Soviet Union was building hundreds of installations in 76 Asian, African, and Latin American countries. Relations with the other superpowers remained adverse at best.

United States. Throughout 1982 the United States and USSR waged a war of words, each accusing the other of inciting violence in Asia, Africa, and Latin America. Blaming the USSR for the imposition of martial law in Poland in December 1981, the U.S. government took several measures in retaliation: Aeroflot, the official Soviet airline, was ordered in January to discontinue its Moscow-Washington service; from May to July, the State Department refused to renew previous treaties for cooperation in space, energy, and technology research; and on June 18, President Reagan expanded his December 1981 ban on the sale of oil and gas equipment to the USSR, now applying it to foreign subsidiaries and licensees of U.S. companies. The Soviet government claimed that it was not responsible for Polish martial law.

U.S.-Soviet relations were further aggravated by the Middle East conflict in June–September. Moscow accused the United States of encouraging the Israeli invasion of Lebanon, asked the U.S. government to stop the Israeli bombardment of PLO positions in west Beirut, and protested the stationing of U.S. peacekeeping troops in the Lebanese capital.

Minor incidents also clouded relations. In February the chief military attaché of the Soviet Embassy in Washington was expelled from the United States for attempted espionage. In August an American correspondent was expelled from the USSR for allegedly masquerading as a Soviet citizen, and the United States ousted a Soviet journalist in retaliation. Also in August, the Kremlin forbade U.S. diplomats to use a beach near Moscow, after the Long Island (NY) town of Glen Cove had barred resident Soviet diplomats from its recreational facilities.

No issue was the subject of more rhetoric and posturing than the arms buildup. In May the Soviets proposed an immediate freeze of U.S. and Soviet strategic weapons, stopping further production and deployment. In rejecting the offer, Washington explained that a freeze would leave the USSR superior to the United States in number of nuclear missiles. Warnings and accusations continued even as the strategic arms reduction talks (START) went on in Geneva.

Despite all the friction, President Reagan in August offered a one year extension of the grain sales agreement, which the Soviets accepted, and in October offered to sell 23 million metric tons (25 million T) of American grain. Total 1982 trade between the two superpowers exceeded the level of the year before.

On November 11, the day after Brezhnev's death, President Reagan sent a message to the Kremlin expressing condolences and the U.S. desire to improve relations. On November 13 the United States lifted its embargo on the sale of equipment for the natural-gas pipeline. Vice-President George Bush headed the U.S. delegation to Brezhnev's funeral and while in Moscow met privately with Secretary-General Andropov.

Europe. Soviet relations with Western Europe were poor politically but good in terms of trade. All major West European governments and even the Italian Communist Party disapproved of the Polish military dictatorship and held the Kremlin largely responsible. Blaming the Soviet Union, the British government in February restricted travel by Soviet diplomats in the United Kingdom and reduced Soviet-British cooperation in scientific research.

Britain, France, Italy, and West Germany all supplied equipment for the giant pipeline, however, which was to transport natural gas from Siberia to Western Europe. A January 23 treaty obligated France to purchase 280,000,000,000 cubic feet of gas annually for 25 years, beginning in 1984, when the pipeline was expected to be completed. On February 10 a consortium of French banks lent $140 million to the USSR to buy French pipeline machinery.

The USSR made several peaceful gestures toward Western Europe during 1982. On March 16, President Brezhnev announced that it would freeze the number and type of its intermediate nuclear missiles in European USSR until a Soviet-U.S. pact was concluded limiting such weapons in Europe, or until the United States started to deploy medium-range missiles in West European countries. In May the USSR paid $170,000 to Sweden for refloating a Soviet submarine which ran ashore in late 1981 near a Swedish naval base on the Baltic Sea.

The Soviet Union continually denied rumors that the attempted assassination of Pope John Paul II in 1981 was engineered by the Bulgarian intelligence service operating under Soviet directives.

Near East. In 1982, as before, the 100,000-man Soviet army in Afghanistan was unable to suppress the nationwide Islamic rebellion against Kabul's Communist government. Soviet troops controlled only cities and major high-

---

USSR · Information Highlights

Official Name: Union of Soviet Socialist Republics.
Location: Eastern Europe and northern Asia.
Area: 8,649,540 sq mi (22 402 308 km²).
Population (1982 est.): 270,000,000.
Chief Cities (1979 census): Moscow, the capital, 8,011,000; Leningrad, 4,588,000; Kiev, 2,144,000.
Government: *Head of state,* president (vacant). *Head of government,* Nikolai A. Tikhonov, premier (took office Oct. 1980). *Secretary-general of the Communist party,* Yuri V. Andropov (took office Nov. 1982). *Legislature*—Supreme Soviet: Soviet of the Union, Soviet of Nationalities.
Monetary Unit: Ruble (0.71 ruble equals U.S.$1, March 1982—noncommercial rate).
Economic Indexes: *Consumer Prices* (1978; 1970= 100), *all items,* 100.7; *food,* 101.9. *Industrial production* (1980; 1975=100), 124.
Foreign Trade (1980 U.S.$): *Imports,* $68,522,000,000; *exports,* $76,449,000,000.

ways, while the countryside was ruled by Afghan nationalist guerrillas. To aid Soviet troop supply, a railway-highway bridge was completed in May from the Soviet city of Termez across the Amu Darya river border into Afghanistan. In early 1982, the Soviet press claimed that the Afghan rebels were using toxic weapons manufactured in the United States. In response, the U.S. State Department said that Soviet troops in Afghanistan were using poison gas and other chemical weapons against Afghan guerrillas.

In 1982, nine Near Eastern countries were receiving technical aid from the USSR, which was building 49 economic enterprises in Iran alone. In January, the Soviet Union and Turkey signed a treaty that would increase mutual trade over the 1981 level.

Far East. High-level negotiations between the USSR and Communist China in the fall failed to achieve any major mutual concessions. The USSR continued to send economic aid worth $3 million per day to China's enemy, Vietnam, and about 11,000 Vietnam laborers were receiving work-training in the USSR. In July the Soviet Union concluded a technical aid treaty with Vietnamese-occupied Cambodia.

Africa. In 1982 the USSR rendered technical aid to 39 African countries, about half of which were receiving Soviet weapons. In addition, Soviet arms were supplied to two guerrilla armies: the South West Africa People's Organization (SWAPO) fighting South Africa, and the Polisario Front rebelling against Morocco. In January, a Soviet-Angolan technical aid treaty was concluded for 1982–1985.

Latin America. The Soviet attitude toward the Falklands war was strongly anti-British. In April, soon after Argentina seized the islands, the USSR contracted to supply uranium fuel to Argentina, and two Soviet-Argentine companies were formed for joint fishing in the South Atlantic. In May, Moscow proclaimed that the British naval blockade of the Falkland Islands was illegal, though Soviet ships did avoid the blockaded waters.

In its continuing effort to weaken U.S. influence, the USSR rendered technical aid to 13 Latin American nations, with Cuba receiving the largest amount. During the year, the USSR concluded treaties of cultural exchange, trade, and technical aid with Grenada. Another Soviet technical aid pact granted a credit of $166.8 million to Nicaragua, whose 1981 Soviet assistance amounted to only $9 million.

Directions. In his first major foreign policy statement as secretary-general November 22, Yuri Andropov expressed confidence in détente with the West but said the Soviet Union would reject any demands for "preliminary concessions." He promised to continue efforts at better relations with China and emphasized the importance of the nonaligned nations.

ELLSWORTH RAYMOND
Professor Emeritus, New York University

In an address to the Communist Party Central Committee before his election as secretary-general November 12, Yuri V. Andropov spoke of his predecessor: "Leonid Ilyich said that not a single day in his life could be separated from the affairs of the Communist Party of the Soviet Union and the entire Soviet country." "It is our prime duty," Andropov went on, "to translate consistently into life the domestic and foreign policy course of our party and the Soviet state, a course which was worked out under the leadership of Leonid Ilyich Brezhnev."

Maggie Steber

The 37th regular session of the General Assembly opens at UN headquarters in New York, September 21.

The advent of a new secretary-general and a frustrating series of failures in the organization's prime function—keeping the peace—turned 1982 into a year of introspection and self-criticism for the United Nations. Javier Pérez de Cuellar of Peru took office on Jan. 1, 1982, proclaiming that "first we must get our own house in order" before tackling the problems of the world. (*See* BIOGRAPHY.) Early in the year the world body faced criticism from Ed Koch, the mayor of the UN's host city, who said, "If the UN would leave New York, nobody would hear of it again." And a group of prominent Americans, including three former secretaries of state, complained in a report that the UN had failed to act on threats to peace and had adopted "grossly biased resolutions." They urged the United States to reassess its policy toward the UN.

The organization's image was further tarnished by its inability to resolve conflicts in the Falkland Islands, Lebanon, and the Persian Gulf. Pérez de Cuellar enhanced his personal reputation with his mediation effort between Great Britain and Argentina, though it failed in the end. The future of the UN's peacekeeping role was cast into doubt by the Israeli invasion, which saw the UN peace force in southern Lebanon overrun. Its functions were later taken over by the multinational force composed of U.S., French, and Italian troops.

Pérez de Cuellar startled the diplomatic community by admitting the UN's shortcomings in his first annual report in September and proposing reforms designed to restore the institution's ability to serve as a vital negotiating forum. As the year drew to a close, the UN remained under attack. The staff was threatening to strike. The major donors were demanding a lid on the growing UN budget. And U.S. Ambassador Jeane J. Kirkpatrick, who earlier in the year had complained that the United States was "ignored, despised, and reviled" at the UN, now charged that the "arrogant" bureaucrats running the organization were engaged in a Marxist "class war" against the United States and U.S. corporations, trying to achieve "global socialism."

General Assembly. In addition to its regular fall conclave, which began September 21, the General Assembly held three special sessions during 1982—on Israel's annexation of the Golan Heights, on disarmament, and on Palestinian rights.

On February 5, by a vote of 86 to 21, with 34 abstentions, the Assembly declared that Israel's annexation of the Syrian territory showed it was "not a peace-loving state" and had not carried out its obligations as a UN member.

The special session on disarmament—the second of its kind—attracted a number of world leaders between June 7 and July 10, including U.S. President Ronald Reagan. Despite the high-level participation, it failed to reach agreement on a broad disarmament program. Its only achievement was the launching of a global drive to promote public backing for arms control.

The special session on Palestinian rights, first held in 1980, reconvened four times in 1982—in April, June, August, and September. Among the measures adopted were calls for a cease-fire in Lebanon (in June), a condemnation of Israel for failure to do so (August), and a call for a UN investigation of the Beirut massacre of several hundred Palestinian civilians (September).

The regular Assembly session, three months long, dealt with 142 agenda items, the first of which was the election of Hungarian diplomat Imre Hollai as its president. One item not debated was the status of Puerto Rico. A Cuban attempt to treat it as a "colonial" issue was soundly defeated (30 to 70, with 43 abstentions), in a major triumph for the United States.

The Soviet bloc suffered three other big setbacks. The Assembly seated the Cambodian regime represented by Prince Sihanouk, rather than the government backed by Vietnam, and called for the withdrawal of Vietnamese troops from that country. The Assembly also called for Soviet troop withdrawal from Afghanistan (114 to 21, with 13 abstentions). And a team of UN experts investigating U.S. charges that the USSR used outlawed chemical weapons in Afghanistan and Indochina concluded that there is "circumstantial evidence" indicating toxins were used. U.S. officials, disappointed by the vagueness of the report, pursued the issue through a French resolution (adopted on December 13, 86–19, with 33 abstentions) calling on the UN to investigate any new reports of chemical weapon use. U.S. officials promptly revealed reports that nerve gas had been used in Ethiopia, another Soviet ally.

An intense U.S. lobbying campaign helped block a drive to oust Israel from the General Assembly and various UN agencies. After Israeli delegates were expelled from a meeting of the UN atomic energy agency, Secretary of State George Shultz declared a freeze on U.S. funding and warned that a total cutoff of American funds—one quarter of the UN budget—would follow any similar move. Most Arab nations, anxious to stay on good terms with the West, opposed any confrontation on the issue, but on October 25 Iran demanded a vote on the credentials of Israel's Assembly delegates. The next day the Iranian motion was pigeonholed by a vote of 74–9, with 32 abstentions, ending the crisis—for 1982 at least.

The United States split with its European allies—but moved to rebuild ties to Latin America—by voting in November for an Argentine resolution calling on Great Britain to resume talks on the Falklands dispute. Britain rejected the proposal.

Washington also voted with Latin America (and split with NATO nations) by opposing a winning resolution that called for the suspension of military aid to El Salvador and demanded that its government respect human rights.

Other U.S. setbacks included resolutions backing a ban on the neutron bomb, an end to all nuclear tests, and a freeze on production and deployment of atomic weapons. The United States was on the losing side when the General Assembly elected Nicaragua rather than the Dominican Republic to a two-year term on the Security Council.

The United States and USSR did find themselves allied on budget issues. Both insisted that future UN budgets show no growth, not even for inflation. Britain joined them in asking the secretary-general to ensure that the cost of new UN activities be covered in the current UN budget ($722 million in 1982) by cuts in existing but "marginal" programs. Together, the three nations pay 40% of UN costs, but without a budget lid the Third World majority controls spending, while paying minimal dues—one or two hundredths of one percent each.

Security Council. Though preoccupied by events in the Middle East throughout the year, the Security Council was unable to exert much influence. It adopted two unanimous resolutions calling for a cease-fire between Iran and Iraq (in July and October), but Iran rejected both.

The United States vetoed six major anti-Israel resolutions during the year. The first three dealt with the Golan Heights, the treatment of West Bank residents, and the April 11 attack on a Jerusalem mosque by an American-born Israeli resident. The three others condemned Israel for its military campaign in Lebanon that began on June 6. However, the Council did adopt a string of resolutions during the Lebanon crisis. The first, on June 7, called for a cease-fire and an immediate and unconditional Israeli withdrawal. Others called for the safety of Lebanese civilians (June 19), demanded an end to the siege of Beirut (July 4 and July 29), censured Israel for its failure to end the blockade (August 4), ordered the stationing of UN observers in Beirut (August 1 and August 12), and condemned the massacre of Palestinians at the Sabra and Shatila ref-

ORGANIZATION OF THE UNITED NATIONS

THE SECRETARIAT

Secretary-General: Javier Pérez de Cuellar (until Dec. 31, 1986)

THE GENERAL ASSEMBLY (1982)

President: Imre Hollai (Hungary).
The 157 member nations were as follows:

Afghanistan	Central African	German Demo-	Laos	Papua New	Sweden
Albania	Republic	cratic Republic	Lebanon	Guinea	Syria
Algeria	Chad	Germany, Federal	Lesotho	Paraguay	Tanzania
Angola	Chile	Republic of	Liberia	Peru	Thailand
Antigua and	China, People's	Ghana	Libya	Philippines	Togo
Barbuda	Republic of	Greece	Luxembourg	Poland	Trinidad and Tobago
Argentina	Colombia	Grenada	Madagascar	Portugal	Tunisia
Australia	Comoros	Guatemala	Malawi	Qatar	Turkey
Austria	Congo	Guinea	Malaysia	Rumania	Uganda
Bahamas	Costa Rica	Guinea-Bissau	Maldives	Rwanda	Ukrainian SSR
Bahrain	Cuba	Guyana	Mali	Saint Lucia	USSR
Bangladesh	Cyprus	Haiti	Malta	Saint Vincent and	United Arab Emirates
Barbados	Czechoslovakia	Honduras	Mauritania	the Grenadines	United Kingdom
Belgium	Denmark	Hungary	Mauritius	São Tomé and	United States
Belize	Djibouti	Iceland	Mexico	Principe	Upper Volta
Belorussian SSR	Dominica	India	Mongolia	Saudi Arabia	Uruguay
Benin	Dominican	Indonesia	Morocco	Senegal	Vanuatu
Bhutan	Republic	Iran	Mozambique	Seychelles	Venezuela
Bolivia	Ecuador	Iraq	Nepal	Sierra Leone	Vietnam
Botswana	Egypt	Ireland	Netherlands	Singapore	Western Samoa
Brazil	El Salvador	Israel	New Zealand	Solomon Islands	Yemen
Bulgaria	Equatorial Guinea	Italy	Nicaragua	Somalia	Yemen, Democratic
Burma	Ethiopia	Ivory Coast	Niger	South Africa	Yugoslavia
Burundi	Fiji	Jamaica	Nigeria	Spain	Zaire
Cambodia	Finland	Japan	Norway	Sri Lanka	Zambia
Cameroon	France	Jordan	Oman	Sudan	Zimbabwe
Canada	Gabon	Kenya	Pakistan	Surinam	
Cape Verde	Gambia	Kuwait	Panama	Swaziland	

COMMITTEES

General. Composed of 29 members as follows: The General Assembly president; the 21 General Assembly vice presidents (heads of delegations or their deputies of Austria, China, Congo, Cyprus, Democratic Yemen, France, Haiti, Jamaica, Kuwait, Libya, Mali, Nicaragua, Philippines, Qatar, Turkey, Uganda, USSR, United Kingdom, United States, Upper Volta, and Zambia); and the chairmen of the following main committees, which are composed of all 157 member countries.

First (Political and Security): James Victor Gbeho (Ghana)
Special Political: Abduldayem Mubarez (Yemen)
Second (Economic and Financial): O.O. Fafowora (Nigeria)
Third (Social, Humanitarian and Cultural): Carlos Calero Rodrigues (Brazil)
Fourth (Decolonization): Raul Roa-Kouri (Cuba)
Fifth (Administrative and Budgetary): Andrzej Abraszewski (Poland)
Sixth (Legal): Philippe Kirsch (Canada)

THE SECURITY COUNCIL

Membership ends on December 31 of the year noted; asterisks indicate permanent membership.

China*	Netherlands (1984)	USSR*
France*	Nicaragua (1984)	United Kingdom*
Guyana (1983)	Pakistan (1984)	United States*
Jordan (1983)	Poland (1983)	Zaire (1983)
Malta (1984)	Togo (1983)	Zimbabwe (1984)

Military Staff Committee: Representatives of chief of staffs of permanent members.

Disarmament Commission: Representatives of all UN members.

THE ECONOMIC AND SOCIAL COUNCIL

President: Miljan Komatina (Yugoslavia).
Membership ends on December 31 of the year noted.

Algeria (1985)	France (1984)	Peru (1983)
Argentina (1983)	German Democratic	Poland (1983)
Austria (1984)	Republic (1985)	Portugal (1984)
Bangladesh (1983)	Germany, Federal	Qatar (1984)
Belorussian SSR	Republic of (1984)	Rumania (1984)
(1983)	Greece (1984)	St. Lucia (1984)
Benin (1984)	India (1983)	Saudi Arabia (1985)
Botswana (1985)	Japan (1984)	Sierra Leone (1985)
Brazil (1984)	Kenya (1983)	Sudan (1983)
Bulgaria (1985)	Lebanon (1985)	Surinam (1985)
Burundi (1983)	Liberia (1984)	Swaziland (1984)
Cameroon (1983)	Luxembourg (1985)	Thailand (1985)
Canada (1983)	Malaysia (1985)	Tunisia (1984)
China (1983)	Mali (1984)	USSR (1983)
Colombia (1984)	Mexico (1985)	United Kingdom
Congo (1983)	Netherlands (1985)	(1983)
Denmark (1983)	New Zealand (1985)	United States (1985)
Djibouti (1985)	Nicaragua (1983)	Venezuela (1984)
Ecuador (1985)	Norway (1983)	
Fiji (1983)	Pakistan (1984)	

THE TRUSTEESHIP COUNCIL

President: Paul Poudade (France)

China[2]   France[2]   USSR[2]   United Kingdom[2]   United States[1]

[1] Administers Trust Territory. [2] Permanent member of Security Council not administering Trust Territory.

THE INTERNATIONAL COURT OF JUSTICE

Membership ends on February 5 of the year noted.

President: Taslim O. Elias (Nigeria, 1985)
Vice President: José Sette Camara (Brazil, 1988)

Roberto Ago (Italy, 1988)	Kéba Mbaye (Senegal, 1991)
Mohammed Bedjaoui (Algeria, 1988)	Platon D. Morozov (USSR, 1988)
Guy Ladreit De Lacharrière (France, 1991)	Hermann Mosler (Fed. Rep. of Germany, 1985)
Abdallah Fikri El-Khani (Syria, 1985)	Shigeru Oda (Japan, 1985)
Robert Y. Jennings (United Kingdom, 1991)	José María Ruda (Argentina, 1991)
Manfred Lachs (Poland, 1985)	Stephen Schwebel (United States, 1988)
	Nagendra Singh (India, 1991)

INTERGOVERNMENTAL AGENCIES

Food and Agricultural Organization (FAO); General Agreement on Tariffs and Trade (GATT); International Atomic Energy Agency (IAEA); International Bank for Reconstruction and Development (World Bank); International Civil Aviation Organization (ICAO); International Fund for Agricultural Development (IFAD); International Labor Organization (ILO); International Maritime Organization (IMO); International Monetary Fund (IMF); International Telecommunication Union (ITU); United Nations Educational, Scientific and Cultural Organization (UNESCO); Universal Postal Union (UPU); World Health Organization (WHO); World Intellectual Property Organization (WIPO); World Meteorological Organization (WMO).

ugee camps (September 18). But Israel ignored or rejected all the UN appeals, and the cease-fire was finally negotiated by the United States without the use of UN machinery. An attempt to launch an investigation of the Beirut massacre was stymied by differences between Lebanon and the PLO over the scope of the inquiry.

During 1982 the Council also dealt with a Nicaraguan complaint against U.S. subversion (a resolution was vetoed by the Americans in April) and with the Falklands crisis. The day after Argentina's takeover of the islands on April 2, the Council called for its withdrawal. Later it backed the secretary-general's negotiating effort. Finally, as British commandos were retaking the islands by force, Great Britain vetoed a June 4 resolution calling for a cease-fire on the ground that the text did not specify the withdrawal of Argentine troops. The United States also vetoed the Argentine draft but later announced that its vote should have been an abstention.

Secretariat. As part of his proposal for the strengthening of the UN as a forum for negotiation, the secretary-general promised to take a more active personal role in defusing differences before they reach the crisis point. When he took office, Pérez de Cuellar inherited the task of mediating disputes in Cyprus, Afghanistan, Indochina, and the Persian Gulf. In his first year he worked out an arbitration pact between Malta and Libya, and offered his services to resolve differences between Nicaragua and Honduras and between Guyana and Venezuela.

Pérez de Cuellar's reputation within the diplomatic community soared as a result of his intense effort to avert the Falklands fighting. He met daily with each side from April 30 to May 20, narrowing differences and bringing agreement within reach. Both sides credited Pérez de Cuellar for dependability and deft timing, though in the end the gap over sovereignty in the Falklands could not be bridged.

Despite his stated goal of making the UN staff more efficient, Pérez de Cuellar experienced the same difficulties with personnel policy as had all his predecessors. He started out on good terms with the staff, but by fall three brief job actions had been staged over issues ranging from pay scales to the continued imprisonment of more than a score of UN employees around the world.

There was also controversy over the secretary-general's executive appointments, including a protest by Western diplomats at the naming of Indian diplomat Brajesh Mishra as commissioner for Namibia, and African objections to the reappointment of Denmark's former prime minister, Poul Hartlins, as the UN high commissioner for refugees.

On November 30 the UN paid the United States the last $1 million on a $65 million interest-free loan that went for the building of UN Headquarters in 1948.

Trusteeship and Decolonization. In December the United States asked for a special meeting of the Trusteeship Council to arrange UN observation of 1983 plebiscites in the last remaining trust territory, Micronesia. The U.S. hope was that voting in the three segments of the far-flung Pacific territory—the Marshall Islands, Palau, and the Federated States of Micronesia—would result in "free association" with the United States (akin to Commonwealth status). The islanders were being offered the alternatives of independence or closer association with the United States; in any event, the object was to end trust territory status.

Negotiations on independence for Namibia, the last major colonial territory under UN auspices, continued on the periphery of UN affairs throughout the year. Talks in New York in July and August were inconclusive, but the first direct negotiations between South Africa and Angola on the issue were held in December.

Economic and Social Council. Miljan Komantina of Yugoslavia was elected ECOSOC president in February. The Council sponsored a World Assembly on Aging in Vienna in July and August.

One of the UN's major economic agencies, the UN Development Program (UNDP), reported that because of the recession, voluntary contributions had plummeted to the level of 10 years earlier and that recipients would have to cut their expectations by 45% for 1983. The recession, said UNDP administrator Bradford Morse, had become a depression.

The Human Rights Commission, an ECOSOC subsidiary, took action on rights violations in Poland for the first time since martial law was declared. It also named investigators to look into the status of human rights in El Salvador, Chile, Guatemala, and Bolivia. Theo van Boven, head of the UN's Human Rights Division, was fired by Pérez de Cuellar in February for speaking out rather than operating as a "civil servant."

Legal Activities. The Third UN Conference on the Law of the Sea ended December 10 after eight years of negotiation, when 118 countries signed the resultant treaty at a ceremony in Jamaica. The U.S. opposed the treaty provisions on deep-sea mining and urged others not to sign. Britain and West Germany were among the other holdouts. The massive text (320 treaty articles and nine annexes) was approved April 30 by a vote of 130 to 4, with 17 abstentions. Its provisions are comprehensive, defining coastal state jurisdiction and setting out rules for fishing, shipping, economic exploitation of the ocean floor, scientific exploration, pollution control, and naval rights. The treaty will go into force one year after the 60th nation ratifies it. (*See also* LAW—International.)

On December 30 President Reagan announced that the United States would not pay a UN assessment, up to $1 million per year, for a commission set up under the sea treaty.

MICHAEL J. BERLIN
"New York Post"

Cherry blossom time, 1982, Jefferson Memorial, Washington, DC.

Domestic Affairs

"The economy will face difficult moments in the months ahead," President Ronald Reagan declared in his State of the Union Address to a joint session of Congress on Jan. 26, 1982. "But the program for economic recovery that is in place will pull the economy out of its slump and put us on the road to prosperity and stable growth by the latter half of this year."

As it turned out, though, the difficulties persisted longer than the president predicted. The severe recession cast a pall over the Reagan administration and over the lives of many Americans in 1982, and as the year ended there was little evidence to show that the anticipated recovery had begun.

The Economy. The grimmest evidence of the slump was provided by unemployment statistics. The year started out on a slightly hopeful note, when the jobless rate in January fell to 8.5% from 8.8% in December 1981. But that improvement was short-lived. Unemployment rose to 8.8% in February, beginning a steady climb that carried it to 9.8% in July and then through the double digit mark to 10.1% in September. By October unemployment had soared to 10.4%, or more than 11,551,000 persons, the highest rate since 1940, when the annual rate was 14.6%.

As unemployment rose through the year administration spokesmen pointed out that the jobless rate was a lagging indicator, which traditionally remained high even after the rest of the economy had begun to recover. But there were few signs of such an improvement.

The gross national product (GNP), which had decreased by 5.1% in real terms in the first quarter of the year, climbed slightly (2.1%) in the second quarter. But figures released late in the year showed that the GNP had grown by 0.7% in the third quarter of the year and government officials estimated that it was declining in the fourth quarter.

One of the economy's big problems, particularly during the first half of the year, was high interest rates. In February, the prime rate, charged by banks to their best credit risks, reached 16.5%, and other interest rates were at correspondingly high levels. The rate levels reflected the tight money policy of the Federal Reserve, which sought to restrict growth of the money supply and to curb inflation. In midsummer, as the recession continued, the Federal Reserve began easing its restrictions and interest rates began falling. By October the prime rate had dropped to 12%. One result of the interest rate decline was a spurt in buying on the stock market. The Dow Jones average, which had been below the 800 level, pushed past 1,000 in a series of record trading sessions as many investors concluded that the interest rate drop portended prosperity ahead.

There was also encouraging news on the inflation front. As a result of the worldwide oil glut, bumper farm crops, and the recession, inflation as measured by the Consumer Price Index averaged only about 5% during the year, compared with 8.9% in 1981.

The easing of inflation, along with concern over unemployment, helped bring about relatively moderate wage settlements in a number of industries. And administration officials cited these contract agreements as evidence of a sound foundation for the eventual recovery. Nevertheless, economic analysts found reason for concern in the size of the federal deficit, swollen by the massive federal tax cuts enacted in 1981 and by the decline in federal revenues as a result of the economic slump. In November, *The Washington Post* reported that David Stockman, director of the Office of Management and Budget, had informed the president that without further spending cuts or tax increases, the deficit for the fiscal year beginning Oct. 1, 1983, would grow to between $185,000,000,000 and $195,000,000,000.

The Administration. In his State of the Union Address, President Reagan unveiled his "new federalism" plan, which he sought to make the centerpiece of his 1982 legislative program. The purpose of new federalism, Reagan said, was "to make government again accountable to the people," by reducing waste and confusion caused by "the overpowering growth of federal grants-in-aid programs." (*See* special report, page 539.)

Because of budgetary and other economic concerns, the president had little time to develop other major legislative initiatives. Meanwhile, controversies led to the replacement of two of his top-level foreign policy advisers. On January 4, Richard V. Allen resigned as national security adviser to be succeeded by William P. Clark, a longtime Reagan associate, who had been serving as deputy secretary of state. Allen's reputation had been damaged by the disclosure that he had accepted gifts from Japanese journalists and had maintained contact with clients of his former consulting business.

On June 25 the president announced the resignation of Secretary of State Alexander M. Haig, Jr. Haig had disagreed with the president on a number of foreign policy issues, including policy toward Israel and the ban on American-designed equipment for the Soviet Union's natural gas pipeline to Western Europe. To succeed Haig the president selected George P. Shultz, 61, who headed Bechtel Group, Inc., a construction firm with large interests in Saudi Arabia. Before that he had served in the Nixon administration.

On November 5 the president nominated Donald P. Hodel, undersecretary of the interior, as energy secretary, replacing James B. Edwards, who resigned to return to private life. As the year ended, Drew Lewis announced his resignation as secretary of transportation.

The Congress. The 97th Congress, which had been largely dominated by Reagan during its first session in 1981, became increasingly resistant to his will under the pressures of the recession and budget deficit. The rebellion began in February when the president submitted his fiscal 1983 budget, which called for an 18% increase in defense spending as well as freezes or cuts in most domestic spending. A $250,000,000,-000 deficit over the next three years was contemplated. Critics complained about the hike in defense spending, questioned the economic assumptions on which the budget projections were based, and denounced the size of the deficit. Opposition developed not only in the Democrat-controlled House but also in the Republican Senate, where the budget committee rejected the president's proposal by a vote of 16 to 1.

At first the president refused to heed his critics' demands for a tax increase to reduce the deficit. In April, however, he did allow White House advisers to enter into negotiations with Congressional leaders, climaxing with a face-to-face meeting between the president and Rep. Thomas

On the campaign trail and in Washington, President Reagan promoted the importance of his economic program.

John Ficara/Newsweek

Some 11 million unemployed Americans tried to send their message to Washington: "We want jobs."

P. O'Neill, Jr. (D-MA), speaker of the House, on April 28. The preident said he would agree to a tax increase if the Democrats would support spending cutbacks, including a delay in cost-of-living increases for Social Security recipients. But the talks failed and the Senate Budget Committee, chaired by Sen. Pete Domenici (R-NM), took the initiative in drafting a compromise budget. Ultimately the budget developed by the Senate Committee, calling for $769,820,000,000 in expenditures, won approval in both Houses.

The focus of the legislative battle then shifted to a three-year $98,300,000,000 tax-increase proposal, backed by the president, despite his original pledge not to raise taxes. The measure was opposed in the House by a group of conservative Republicans, led by Rep. Jack Kemp (R-NY), a longtime Reagan ally who charged that the president had made "a U-turn" on economic policy. But with the strong support of Speaker O'Neill, the measure passed the House August 19 by a 226–207 vote, with more Democrats (123) supporting it than Republicans (103). The bill passed the Senate by 52 to 47, with the support of nine liberal Democrats.

The president then sought to reassure his conservative supporters by vetoing a $14,100,-000,000 supplemental appropriations bill that he charged would "bust the budget by nearly $1,000,000,000." But the Democrats pointed out that the vetoed bill actually called for $1,300,-000,000 less in spending than the president's own original requests. And the House on September 9 and the Senate on September 10 voted to over-ride the veto by substantial margins, the most significant setback the president had suffered in Congress.

The president was rebuffed again on October 1, when the House failed to provide the two-thirds majority required to approve an administration-backed constitutional amendment requiring a balanced federal budget. The measure got 236 votes, 46 fewer than was needed. The proposal had passed the Senate by 69 to 31. Critics charged that it was hypocritical for the president to advocate the amendment when his own budgets carried record deficits, but he maintained the amendment was needed to ensure fiscal restraint.

The president did pretty much get his way on defense spending. In August, Congress approved a $178,000,000,000 authorization bill, which was only $5,400,000,000 less than Reagan had requested, and which funded most of the weapon systems he had sought.

The president also won in another area related to national security, when the House on August 5 rejected by a 204–202 vote a resolution calling for a U.S.-Soviet nuclear freeze. Reagan had opposed the resolution.

One piece of legislation that did pass, for which both president and Democratic leaders claimed credit, was a $3,800,000,000 job training program, aimed mainly at helping disadvantaged youths. The law stipulates that 70 cents of each dollar spent be used directly for training activities. The new program replaces the Comprehensive Employment and Training Act (CETA), which expired on Sept. 30, 1982, after 10 years of providing public-service employment for the disadvantaged.

In other legislation prompted by the troubled economy, Congress adopted a measure to aid the savings and loan industry, which had been badly squeezed by high interest rates. The law allows savings and loans institutions and commercial banks to establish a new type of insured account to help them compete against money-market funds, which have been drawing funds away from conventional passbook-savings accounts.

In its rush to adjourn early in October so that its members could campaign for reelection, Congress passed a number of stopgap appropriations measures. Complaining that this practice "amounts to both bad economics and bad management," President Reagan requested a special session, which convened November 29.

The house remained in session until December 21, but filibusters by conservative Republicans over a bill to increase the federal excise tax on gasoline to pay for highway and related projects kept the Senate in session until two days later. Although the gasoline bill passed, the Senate went through some of the longest "all nighters" in more than 20 years. In addition to the gasoline bill, the lame-duck session saw enactment of various appropriation bills, stop-gap money bills for six departments and agencies that had not received such funding previously, a bill providing salary increases for members of the House and some top government officials and judges, a bill strengthening protection of migrant farm workers, and a bill establishing a long-term system for burial of radioactive nuclear waste. President Reagan said that "after taking all factors into account," the session was a "worthwhile" effort. Most members of Congress had little good to say of the session.

Among significant issues that the 97th Congress failed to deal with was the financially troubled Social Security system. The National Commission on Social Security Reform, appointed by President Reagan, reported in November that the system needed an infusion of $150,000,000,000 to $200,000,000,000 during the next seven years. But at a three-day meeting that followed months of study, the commission could not agree on a solution. Generally, the commission's Democratic members favored some method of in-

Diana Walker/Gamma-Liaison

Majority Leader Tip O'Neill speaks for House Democrats.

creasing revenues, one possibility being an acceleration of scheduled increases in the payroll taxes. Republicans by and large wanted to slow the growth of benefits, mainly by restricting future cost-of-living increases, which now are tied to inflation.

Social Issues and Civil Rights. Advocates of civil rights and civil liberties, who appeared to be in danger of losing ground to New Right conservatives in the wake of the 1980 elections, rallied in 1982 and scored some notable successes. Their major accomplishment was an extension and strengthening of the Voting Rights Act, originally passed in 1965. The measure, which had been approved by the House in 1981, passed the Senate June 18 by an 85–8 vote. A key issue was an attempt by conservatives to make it necessary to prove "intent" as evidence of discrimination. This move was defeated, and the new law instead allows federal courts to consider "a totality of circumstances" surrounding a case, including election results, in judging whether discrimination has taken place. A portion of the act requiring jurisdictions that had discriminated in the past to clear any changes in voting laws with the Justice Department was extended for 25 years, although such jurisdictions can "bail out" of this requirement by demonstrating they had not discriminated for 10 years.

Legislative initiatives by Sen. Jesse Helms (R-NC) and other New Right conservatives in the controversial areas of abortion and school prayer were beaten back. On September 15, after weeks of filibuster by liberal opponents, the Senate voted 47 to 46 to table a Helms proposal, endorsed by President Reagan, which contended that the Supreme Court had erred in its 1973 decision guaranteeing abortion rights. And on September 23, the Senate tabled a Helms amendment that would prohibit courts from rul-

---

UNITED STATES • Information Highlights

Official Name: United States of America.
Location: Central North America.
Area: 3,615,123 sq mi (9 363 169 km²).
Population (1980 census): 226,547,346.
Chief Cities (1980 census): Washington, DC, the capital, 638,432; New York, 7,071,639; Chicago, 3,005,072; Los Angeles, 2,966,850; Philadelphia, 1,688,210.
Government: *Head of state and government,* Ronald Reagan, president (took office Jan. 20, 1981). *Legislature*—Congress: Senate and House of Representatives.
Monetary Unit: Dollar.

© Shelly Katz/Black Star

Braniff, the nation's eighth largest airline, filed for bankruptcy. Many other companies, large and small, did likewise.

ing on cases of voluntary prayer in public schools.

There was disappointment for civil rights advocates when the proposed Equal Rights Amendment to the Constitution failed to win ratification by the necessary 38 state legislatures by the June 30 deadline. The women's rights proposal had been approved by 35 states. It was reintroduced in Congress, but ERA strategists said they would concentrate on trying to elect supporters in state legislatures before launching another drive to change the constitution.

On another front, civil rights forces won a court victory in Los Angeles in November when U.S. District Judge Terry J. Hatter, Jr., invalidated former President Carter's 1980 reestablishment of draft registration. The judge ruled that Carter had waited only 21 days from the time of publication of the registration regulation until it was put into effect, instead of the required 32 days. The ruling came in the case of David Alan Wayte, 21, a Yale philosophy student, who was defended by the American Civil Liberties Union. The judge also criticized the government for selective prosecution because only young men who had publicly announced their resistance to registration had been indicted.

Crime and the Law. Crime was a cause of concern for Americans in 1982.

On June 21, John Hinckley, Jr., who had been charged with the attempted assassination of President Reagan in March of 1981, was found not guilty by reason of insanity by a federal court jury in Washington. The 27-year-old Hinckley subsequently was committed to a mental hospital for an indefinite period by U.S. District Judge Barrington D. Parker, who held that Hinckley was mentally ill and dangerous.

The Hinckley verdict stirred indignation from the public and criticism by legal experts of the so-called insanity defense used by Hinckley's lawyers. On September 13 President Reagan sent Congress an anticrime legislative package, including a proposal for restricting the use of the insanity defense by focusing attention on whether the accused knew what he or she was doing, rather than on whether he or she was mentally disturbed. The White House said the proposal was not prompted by the Hinckley verdict. Reagan also proposed narrowing the scope of the exclusionary rule, under which illegally obtained evidence cannot be introduced in criminal trials. And the president sought to limit the right of persons convicted in state courts to appeal to the federal courts. But John Shattuck of the American Civil Liberties Union said that Reagan's recommendations would do little to curb crime and accused the president of trying to divert attention from the economy.

On October 14 the president moved to cut down on illegal drug traffic by announcing plans for the establishment of 12 regional antidrug task forces. These would be based in large cities and would be staffed by agents of the Federal Bureau of Investigation, the Drug Enforcement Agency, and the U.S. Customs Office. Attorney General William French Smith said that illegal drug sales totaled more than $79,000,000,000 in 1980. The lame-duck session of Congress passed a compendium of anticrime measures, including a provision establishing a Cabinet-level director of federal efforts to combat narcotics traffic. The president, saying that the measure was "enacted hastily," refused to sign it. Since the Congress that passed it had adjourned, it died.

ROBERT SHOGAN, *"Los Angeles Times"*

The New Federalism Plan

Early in 1982 President Ronald Reagan unveiled his "new federalism" plan calling for a massive shift of federal government programs and taxes to the states. Although economic worries prevented Congress from seriously considering the proposal in 1982, it was viewed as a major step to sort out the duties and finances of federal, state, and local governments.

The Proposal. Under the plan, as outlined in Reagan's State of the Union speech, the federal government would turn over dozens of existing education, welfare, health, and transportation programs to the states. In return, the states would turn over to the federal government the spiraling costs of the Medicaid health program for the poor. While states would get interim federal funding for their new programs, eventually they would have to pay for the programs out of their own funds.

"In a single stroke, we will be accomplishing a realignment that will end cumbersome administration and spiraling costs at the federal level, while we ensure these programs will be more responsive to both the people they are meant to help and the people who pay for them," Reagan said in introducing his plan.

The new federalism has two parts. In a welfare swap, the federal government would assume Medicaid costs. Under existing law, states share Medicaid spending with the federal government, at an estimated cost to states of $19,000,000,000 in fiscal year 1984. While taking over Medicaid, the federal government would abolish its other two main welfare programs, Aid to Families with Dependent Children (AFDC) and food stamps. States could then establish their own welfare programs.

Under the half of the plan, known as the "turnback," the federal government would establish a trust fund with money from tobacco, alcohol, and other excise taxes. These funds (estimated at $28,000,000,000 in 1984) would be distributed to states, to pay for some 40 programs that would have cost the federal government about $30,000,000,000. States would use their trust fund money to operate such programs as energy aid to the poor, foster care, highways, sewer construction, and vocational rehabilitation. The trust fund money would be reduced gradually. By 1991, the federal excise taxes and trust fund would be eliminated, leaving states to fund the programs independently.

Reaction. The new federalism plan received a mixed reaction. State governors, who had advocated a similar revamping of federal-state relations, viewed the plan as a positive step. Big-city mayors were less favorable. Knowing that support from such groups as the National Governors Association was essential for the plan to pass Congress, the administration undertook negotiations for a compromise. A key point in the administration argument for the plan was that there would be "no winners or losers"—that some states and regions would not benefit at the expense of others because of the shift.

But the swap of food stamps and AFDC for Medicaid seemed likely to hurt southern states. Many states in the South rely much more heavily on federally-financed food stamps than on AFDC and Medicaid to help their poor. So they would lose much more in paying for food stamps than they would save by giving up their restrictive Medicaid programs. Northern industrial states could realize large savings by giving up Medicaid. States determine the levels of Medicaid health benefits and the northern industrial states generally have generous, expensive programs. But the disparities in Medicaid standards raised a difficult problem for a national program. If national standards for eligibility and benefits were set at the level of the northern states, the costs would be enormous. But if standards were set at the lower levels of the South, then many poor people in such states as New York and California would lose medical benefits.

Another regional issue was created by the proposal to make states raise their own taxes to pay for the turnback program. States have widely different abilities to levy their own taxes. Such oil-producing states as Louisiana are more able to raise energy taxes than the oil-importing states of New England. "Sin taxes" on liquor and gambling are a much greater source of revenue in Nevada than in Utah. Many state officials argue that, in the long run, the federal government would have to help poor states.

After months of negotiations, state and Reagan administration officials were moving toward agreement on a number of points. In late June, Richard S. Williamson, assistant to the president for intergovernmental affairs, announced a modification of the federalism proposal. Under the revision, states would continue to take over the AFDC program but would be given more authority over the financing-plan for Medicaid. Specifically, states could establish rules for Medicaid in accord with their needs. The administration also said that it was discontinuing its plan to have the states oversee the food stamp program. In spite of these revisions and other proposals, the future of new federalism awaited 1983 developments.

HARRISON DONNELLY

The Economy

The year 1982 was the year of the big test for supply-side economics—the concept that economic growth can be restored by directing revenues primarily into production rather than consumption, as had been the case for at least two decades. Conclusive results were not evident as the year ended, but the report card was speckled with poor marks, and opponents of President Ronald Reagan's administration were ready to give it a flunking grade. These opponents pointed to the highest jobless rate since the Great Depression of the 1930s; the biggest budget deficit ever; thousands of home mortgage foreclosures each week; and an industrial sector operating at less than 70% of capacity, with steels, autos, and construction the worst hit.

The president, however, held his ground stating repeatedly that he would "stay the course." At one point, however, his own treasury secretary, Donald Regan, said that the economy was a ship dead in the water, and George Stigler, being honored at the White House after being named winner of the 1982 Nobel Prize in economics, said the president's program was something between a gimmick and a slogan.

Throughout it all, the president retained his smile and, in fact, seldom if ever permitted any doubts to show in his many public appearances. Eventually, he kept promising, results would show. But just as regularly, the results were pushed back. As the year ended the economy was still mired in recession. Consumers and producers alike were digging in their heals, watching their pennies, and postponing big purchases.

There were some successes. Inflation diminished month after month, and in late summer and early fall interest rates began an almost steady decline for the rest of the year. The stage was being set for an economic rebound, said the president, but his opponents claimed the only reason either was falling was because the economy was in such bad shape.

Budget Deficit and the President. Was it that way because of the budget deficit? Many people thought so. For fiscal 1982, which ended September 30, the deficit amounted to $110,660,000,-000, nearly twice the $57,930,000,000 deficit of fiscal 1981, and $44,250,000,000 more than the previous record budget of $66,410,000,000 in fiscal 1976. A study by the House Budget Committee showed that more than half the expansion in deficits from 1981 to 1982 stemmed from increased defense spending and the lower business and individual tax rates that Reagan had helped push through Congress.

The budget problem presented the administration with two major dilemmas; each seemed to contradict the president's stated intentions. First, if he failed to contain defense spending, how could he balance the budget, as he had promised? And second, if he could not balance the budget, how could he transfer economic power from the public to the private sector? The president's response was clearer on the first than on the other. Asked about deficits and defense spending at a news conference on December 10, he replied: "Well, as I said all during the campaign and continue to say, the first responsibility of the federal government is the security and freedom of the people of this country. And if it comes down to a choice in a deficit period of this kind, of deficit or national defense, national security, I have to come down on the side of national security."

The president had fewer troubles in explaining the delay in rebuilding the private sector. If business was not very good, then it will be very good, he said. In their public statements, many business leaders supported the administration's policies, but in a practical sense they did not back them. Capital spending plans fell all year long as the private sector decided to play cautiously. Since consumers also were cutting back, that left government as the big spender.

Interest Rates and the Federal Reserve. For much of the year interest rates remained high, and some investment community economists said they would move even higher. But after reaching a peak of 16.5% in the second quarter, with the Federal Reserve holding a tight hand over the money supply, a decline set in during late summer. Some attributed it to relief over passage of the administration's $98,300,000,000 tax increase, which they felt would help reduce the budget deficit, but the Fed also was easing up on its tight money actions, and in early October it shifted decidedly to a more accommodative policy. Paul Volcker, its chairman, indicated he was now more concerned about the pallid economy than he was about interest rates.

Wall Street went on a wild rally, with the Dow Jones industrial average soaring to a record high 1,065.49 points on November 3 and, according to economists at Morgan Guaranty Trust, adding more than $300,000,000,000 to consumer net worth. By year-end, the Dow record was topped at 1,070.55, the prime rate was down to 11.5% and the discount rate had been lowered to 8.5%.

Volcker's concern about the economy was well placed, although his angry critics thought it should have begun much earlier. The economy seemed to be closing down, despite the hopes expressed by the Morgan Bank people. With the exception of investment markets and housing, which quickly rose from their badly depressed bases, the economy barely responded to the lower borrowing rates.

Unemployment, Foreclosures, Profits. The economic situation was worst in the industrial heartland, from the mills of Pennsylvania through most of the "smokestack" towns that line the rivers and lakes in the Midwest, and on up through northern Minnesota's iron ore pits and ports, where jobless rates ranged in excess of 19%. Unemployment nationwide reached 10.8%

in December, and even the Reagan administration conceded that 11% or more was possible in 1983. But the popular statistics failed to relate the true devastation. There were, for example, more than 20 million workers directly affected at one time in December. Nearly 12 million were listed officially as without jobs. More than 6.5 million were underemployed, meaning they were involuntarily working part-time rather than full-time. And 1.6 million were listed as discouraged workers because they had given up looking. Of those officially listed as jobless, 2.3 million were out of work six months or more. And, according to *Business Week* magazine, 40% of the jobless had no hope of being recalled because their jobs had been abolished.

It was more than a recession in the old industrial belt, now sometimes referred to as the "Rust Bowl," an uncomfortable reminder of the farmland dust bowls which accompanied the Depression of the 1930s. Industry was changing. The nation was becoming more a producer of services, and many of those services were associated with the new electronic technology. According to the American Productivity Center in Houston, white-collar workers accounted for nearly 53% of the work force and 70% of industry's annual payroll. By 1985, the Bureau of Labor Statistics said, the white-collar work force would grow to 65%, and by the turn of the century to 90%. The handwriting was scribbled on the walls of old mills and factories. While unemployment in Michigan rose to 17.2% in November, it fell to 7.2% in Massachusetts, largely because of a boom in electronic computers.

Farmers were hurting too. Profits plunged and bankruptcies grew, mainly because of a drop in farm prices but also because of high interest rates. Farmers banded together to forestall property foreclosures, sometimes by demonstrating at auction sales. From January 1 to September 30, the Farmers Home Administration handled 844 foreclosures, 2,753 liquidations for financial reasons, and 1,245 bankruptcies.

Businesses, especially small ones, were hurt badly, although huge corporations also went under. International Harvester, one of the grand old names of industry, teetered on the edge of collapse and remained alive only because, as it was popularly said, it was into the banks for too much money. Statistics compiled by Merrill Lynch, the investment house, told the story of corporate after-tax profits: down 28.8% in the first quarter, compared with a year earlier; down 20.5% in the second, 22.1% in the third, and an estimated 17.2% in the fourth.

The Populace. In spite of such grim statistics, Americans seemed to remain optimistic. President Reagan retained a great deal of personal popularity, and his almost weekly assurances that better times were ahead retained their credibility.

And, in spite of it all, there were some things to reassure. Inflation was down to an average of just more than 6% for the year, and the decline in interest rates was spreading to consumer loans. The savings rate was rising slowly, to more than 6.5%, and so was industrial productivity. Although many families were in deep trouble, the statistical averages still showed the consumer debt load was being repaid and that the total of debt, after rising for 10 straight months, was beginning to shrink.

JOHN CUNNIFF, *The Associated Press*

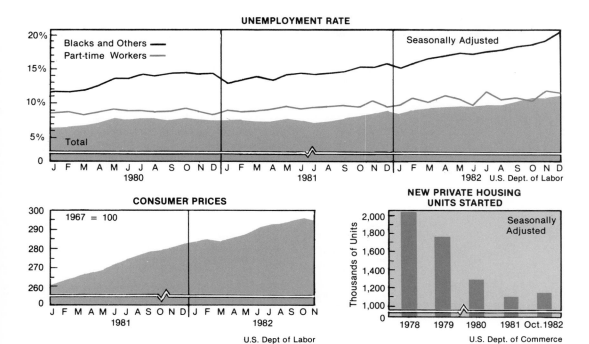

UNEMPLOYMENT RATE

CONSUMER PRICES

NEW PRIVATE HOUSING UNITS STARTED

U.S. Dept of Labor

U.S. Dept. of Commerce

The National Debt

In spring or early summer, about as regularly as the flowers bloom anew, after a spate of hearings and the sounding of some pieties about the dangers of deficit financing, Congress votes to boost the national debt ceiling. In 1982, the vote was for a $210 billion increase in the government's borrowing authority. The "temporary" debt lid was put at $1.143 trillion (U.S.) through Sept. 30, 1982, and $1.290 trillion until Sept. 30, 1983. Written out, that last figure is $1,290,000,000,000. To count out one dollar bill each second would take almost 32,000 years to reach just $1 trillion, or, as it is sometimes called, $1,000 billion.

Some conservatives moan, as they have for decades, that the debt is economically sinful, dumping a terrible financial burden on future generations. The lid is "temporary" because it is due to drop on Sept. 30, 1983, to the "permanent" level of $400 billion. But Congress has boosted the debt ceiling some 47 times since it was first set in 1946, and it will undoubtedly raise the level again. Administration officials claim the ceiling complicates their task of funding the debt.

The Problem. Economists do not regard the national debt as a desirable condition for the good reason that annual interest payments nowadays exceed $100 billion, a sizable chunk of the total budget. However, economists generally are not alarmed by the immense size of

© Voltman '79/Rothco

'I DON'T KNOW OF ANY CEILING THAT HAS KEPT HIM FROM BREAKING THROUGH'

the debt. National debt, they note, merely involves the transfer of resources from one broad group of citizens—taxpayers—to a somewhat smaller but still large group—the owners of Treasury bills, bonds, and other federal securities. A growing portion of the debt is owned by foreigners, but most of the money is going from one set of American pockets to another.

What does concern economists to a greater degree is the annual increase in the national debt as a result of budget deficits. Some portion of any deficit is financed by the creation of new money. In that process, the Federal Reserve System buys more federal securities than it sells. In payment, the Fed gives paper IOUs—checks. These checks are deposited in banks, and the money is spent. New money is thus created. The Treasury then pays interest to the Fed on the debt the central bank has acquired. Almost all of that interest returns to the Treasury in the form of the Fed's annual surplus after expenses. Thus, the federal government has practically free use of the money represented in the Fed's portfolio of securities. It never has to repay the money or even, in reality, pay interest on it.

Most of the remainder of the annual federal debt is financed by sales to the public and is bought by banks, pension funds, insurance companies, and numerous other institutions, as well as by individuals. The money comes from the capital markets. In 1982, for instance, Salomon Brothers Inc., a Wall Street brokerage firm, reckoned that of a total national demand for credit of $468.4 billion, the government's demand would be $135.4 billion. In other words, Washington would need more than 28% of every single dollar saved. That, many economists noted, was one reason why interest rates remained so high despite the recession. By paying whatever interest was needed to sell that new debt and refinance the old debt, Federal debt issues were "crowding out" private borrowers from the capital market.

How Bad Is It Really? Despite increasingly huge figures, the debt and deficit may not be so bad as many people think. The gross debt certainly has grown—from $16.9 billion in 1929 to the trillion dollar level in the fall of 1981. In the quarter century from the end of 1956 to the end of 1981, gross federal debt increased at an average annual rate of 5.9%. Debt held by the public (defined to include the Fed) climbed at an average annual rate of 5.2%. If the Fed is excluded, the average annual increase was 4.9%. During that period the Fed was creating a lot of money. But since World War II, the national debt held by the public has declined in relation to total credit market debt owed by nonfinancial sectors of the market. During the Great Depression of the 1930s and during World War II, Federal debt held by the public (including the Fed) rose from 13% at the end of 1929 to 70% at the end of 1945. The ratio declined steadily until 1975, when a severe recession prompted a large deficit. The percentage has remained at about 18 ever since.

Federal debt has also declined relative to gross national product (GNP). Debt held by the public equaled 61.6% of GNP at the end of 1954 but declined steadily to 25.1% by the end of 1974. It climbed somewhat after that, probably running about 29–30% in 1982.

More importantly, however, interest rates grew faster than GNP in the period 1954–81. In the late 1950s interest was equal to 1.4% of GNP. By 1971 it was 1.6%, and by 1981 a record high of 2.8%. The ratio was undoubtedly even higher in 1982, despite some decline in interest rates. Nonetheless, two economists at the Federal Reserve Bank of Philadelphia have done some calculations which show that the "crowding out" of private debtors from the credit markets may be exaggerated and, indeed, far less serious than at the conclusion of the last serious recession in 1975.

The calculation by the two economists, Brian Horrigan and Aris Protopapadakis, corrects for several factors not usually taken into account in measuring the "crowding out" effect. Added to the overall deficit are federal borrowing that does not appear in the budget, as well as state and local borrowing, all of which have an impact on private credit markets. Subtracted from that figure are the federal debt bought by the Fed as it creates new money and the debt bought by federal agencies and by state and local governments for investment purposes. The remainder is the privately held total government debt, or "gross borrowing." Because that figure does not take account of inflation, it exaggerates the effect of government sector borrowing on the credit market. In the calculation, therefore, the inflation rate for the year in question is multiplied by the total federal debt held by the public, and that amount is subtracted from gross borrowing to get "federal net borrowing." The same subtraction is done to determine net borrowing for all levels of government.

The numbers derived from this calculation seem surprisingly small to most people. For instance, "federal net borrowing" was only $23.2 billion in calendar 1981. Figuring in state and local government finances, "total government net borrowing" was just $19 billion, far lower than the $52.8 billion in the 1975 recession year. The $19 billion figure for 1981 was only 14% of the net private investment of $130.2 billion. Thus, there wasn't as much

THE NATIONAL DEBT

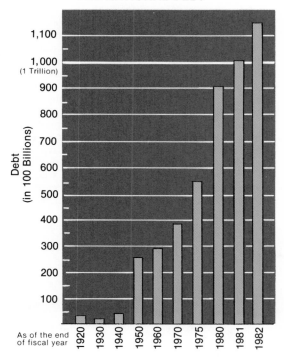

Debt (in 100 Billions)

1,100
1,000 (1 Trillion)
900
800
700
600
500
400
300
200
100

As of the end of fiscal year

1920 1930 1940 1950 1960 1970 1975 1980 1981 1982

Source of information: U.S. *Statistical Abstract;* Office of Management and Budget

"crowding out" as the raw deficit numbers might indicate. That, the two Philadelphia bank economists maintain, has been the case for the past decade. Only during the 1975 recession year was government borrowing large relative to private investment.

Uncertain Future. Even if the current U.S. national debt is not so bad as many people think, the situation could worsen. If the federal government does not restrain the size of its deficit, total net government borrowing could swell to a size more uncomfortable for the capital markets. Projections have shown deficits growing to more than $200 billion by 1985 if Congress were to do nothing. But for fiscal 1983, at least, the legislators have already passed a budget resolution which restrains the deficit.

Whatever other measures are taken, the national debt and deficit will remain a hot issue in the United States for years to come. Most people can't spend beyond their own incomes for too long or they get into financial trouble. Consequently, they feel that the nation should not do so either. There are differences between nations and individuals: only governments can create money, and the U.S. government maintains a top credit rating—even if it is not always deserved. Still, politicians are under public pressure to reduce fiscal deficits.

DAVID R. FRANCIS

Elections

Long before voters went to the polls on November 2, the 1982 midterm national elections had assumed more than usual significance.

One reason was Ronald Reagan's landslide victory in 1980. Some Republican leaders likened that triumph to the Democratic sweep in 1932 which elected Franklin Roosevelt as president, and foresaw a broad political realignment with the Republican Party (GOP) emerging as the nation's new majority party. They predicted that in 1982 the GOP would gain control of the Democratic-held House of Representatives and extend its dominance of the Senate.

Meanwhile, though, the Democrats, who had been demoralized by the 1980 results, became increasingly assertive as national economic condi-

Steve Liss/Gamma-Liaison

tions worsened. The Democrats blamed high unemployment on President Reagan's economic policy and sought to make the 1982 election a referendum on "Reaganomics." Reagan accepted the opposition's challenge. He called upon the voters to show their support for his programs and to "stay the course."

The partisan disagreements on economic policy were blurred somewhat, however, by the tendency of some Republican officeholders in areas hard hit by the recession to put some distance between themselves and the president's policies. Out of deference to their wishes, Reagan avoided campaigning in some parts of the country.

The Democrats found themselves at a disadvantage in pressing their attack because the Republican National Committee and the Republican House and Senate campaign committees were able to raise and spend more than six times as much money as their Democratic counterparts. The financial handicap was particularly severe for Democrats challenging incumbent Republican House members and Senators. Another problem for the Democrats was their inability to agree on clear alternatives to the president's program. Then, too, public opinion polls showed that many voters blamed the Democrats as much or more than the president for the ailing economy.

The Results. Nevertheless, the election showed that the president's failure to deliver on his campaign promises of prosperity weighed heavily on the electorate. Republican hopes of a party re-

Sen. Ted Kennedy campaigned hard for his own reelection and for other Democrats. In California's closely watched Senate race, Pete Wilson, below, defeated Jerry Brown.

Cindy Charles/Gamma-Liaison

alignment were dashed, and the returns indicated that the president would be forced to compromise on his legislative goals.

In the House of Representatives the Democrats, who held a majority of 243 (counting two vacancies originally held by Democrats) to 192 in the 97th Congress, won 269 seats to 166 for the Republicans in the 98th Congress, a net gain of 26. This was about twice the average in recent midterm elections for the party not in control of the White House.

As a result of reapportionment and retirements, as well as election defeats, the House of Representatives in the 98th Congress would have 81 new faces, the biggest changeover since the big Democratic gain in 1974, following the Watergate scandal. And analyses suggested that the 98th would not only be more Democratic, but also more inclined to resist the president. A *Los Angeles Times* computer study of voting records rated 55% of the departing members of the 97th Congress as pro-Reagan on key economic votes, while their returning colleagues were only 42% pro-Reagan. And a *New York Times*-CBS News survey of the new members showed that overall the 98th Congress will be more likely than the 97th to try to curb proposed increases in defense spending, to oppose cuts in social programs, and generally to differ with the president.

In the Senate, where the Democrats held 46 seats (including that of retiring Independent Harry Byrd of Virginia) to 54 for the Republicans, the Democrats managed to hold their own, though they had more seats at risk. Of the 19 incumbent Democratic senators standing for reelection, only Howard Cannon of Nevada was defeated, by Republican Jacob ("Chic") Hecht. The Democrats offset that loss in New Mexico where their candidate, Jeff Bingaman, defeated Republican Sen. Harrison Schmitt, the only one of 11 incumbent GOP senators to be defeated. In the three contests where incumbents did not seek reelection, Republicans won in California, where Pete Wilson took the seat formerly held by S. I. Hayakawa (R), and in Virginia, where Paul S. Trible, Jr., would replace Harry Byrd, while in New Jersey, Democrat Frank R. Lautenberg won the seat held by Republican-appointee Nicholas Brady. The net result was the same (54R-46D).

The most dramatic Democratic successes came in the gubernatorial races, in which Democrats scored a net gain of seven in the 36 contests, to give them control of 34 states to only 16 for the Republicans. The Democrats won 9 of 16 Republican-held governorships that were at stake. They elected Richard F. Celeste in Ohio, James J. Blanchard in Michigan, Rudy Perpich in Minnesota, Anthony S. Earl in Wisconsin, and William (Bill) Sheffield in Alaska. In those five states Republican governors had retired. In four other states Republican incumbents were defeated, by Mark White in Texas, Richard H. Bryan in Nevada, Bill Clinton in Arkansas, and Bob Kerrey in Nebraska.

"WHAT'S IT DONE TO THE CONTENTS OF THIS BOX?"

© 1982 by Herblock in The Washington Post

In New Hampshire, Republican John H. Sununu defeated Democratic incumbent Hugh Gallen, and in California, Republican George Deukmejian defeated Democrat Tom Bradley, who was trying to become the first elected black governor. In New York, Democrat Mario Cuomo defeated Republican Lewis Lehrman to maintain Democratic control of the nation's second largest state, while in Alabama, former Gov. George Wallace, disavowing the segregationist doctrines he had once proclaimed, rode a tide of support from black voters back to the governor's chair.

Referenda and Turnout. The election results also heartened advocates of a U.S.-Soviet freeze on nuclear weapons. Ballot proposals advocating the freeze were endorsed in eight states, as well as in more than a score of cities and counties. The total vote on the various pro-freeze proposals was 10.8 million in favor and 7.2 million opposed. (*See also* special report, page 108.)

Proponents of gun control suffered a setback when a stringent handgun registration proposal was defeated in California by a margin of two to one. And in New Hampshire and Nevada, state constitutional amendments reaffirming the right of citizens to bear arms were approved.

Concern over the economy and interest in the freeze and other ballot proposals produced a turnout of about 40% of eligible voters, up from 37.9% in the 1978 election and reversing a steady decline in voter turnout since 1960.

ROBERT SHOGAN

Foreign Affairs

During 1982 crises continued to rage in Afghanistan, Central America, the Middle East, Poland, and elsewhere. The Iraqi-Iranian War—which the United States, though not directly involved, regarded as crucial to American interests in the Mideast—escalated, and new conflicts broke out in the Falkland Islands and Lebanon. The Reagan administration further refined its foreign policies, enunciating changes piecemeal, and emphasizing realism, American national interests, and the linkage principle.

Major decisions related to arms reduction, the Caribbean Basin, the Falklands war, the Palestinian issue, the Law of the Sea Treaty, and double standards in the United Nations. Because of Cuba's and the Soviet Union's foreign adventurism, the United States applied sanctions against those two nations and against Poland in response to its martial rule, but moderated its policy on banning grain sales to Moscow and, late in the year, on European export to the USSR of U.S. high technology products for building the trans-European gas line.

The Conduct of Foreign Affairs. In January, William P. Clark (*see* BIOGRAPHY) succeeded Richard V. Allen as the president's national security adviser, and in June, George P. Shultz (*see* BIOGRAPHY) was named secretary of state to replace Alexander Haig. Some 30 summit visitors came to the United States during the year, and President Reagan made several foreign trips—to Barbados for a Caribbean meeting in April, and to Europe in June to attend a meeting of the Western industrial powers at Versailles, a NATO session in Bonn, and a five-day goodwill trip to

Brazil, Colombia, Costa Rica, and Honduras late in the year. He declined, however, to meet with President Leonid Brezhnev or to attend the Soviet leader's funeral.

To tighten controls over information and intelligence matters, the Central Intelligence Agency (CIA) adopted a revised code of conduct for its agents, and President Reagan announced new guidelines to prevent unauthorized disclosure of classified information and signed an intelligence protection act providing stiff penalties for divulging the identity of covert U.S. agents.

During the year the Department of State maintained 145 diplomatic and 98 consular missions throughout the world. The United States participated in approximately 750 international conferences and sessions of international agencies—including UN conferences on aging, the law of the sea, and outer space; a UNESCO conference on cultural policies; and a special General Assembly session on disarmament. On Jan. 1, 1982 the United States was a party to 7,354 treaties and agreements, and signed some 125 during the year—including arrangements for U.S. peacekeeping forces in the Mideast, taxation, and claims and debt settlements. After the Law of the Sea Conference, convened in its tenth session in New York, approved its draft treaty on April 30 without the modifications respecting deep-sea mining that were sought by the United States, President Reagan announced on July 9 that the United States would not sign the treaty.

Arms and Defense. The United States negotiated arrangements with several countries for the use of air facilities by American military planes, agreed with China to reduce U.S. arms sales to Taiwan, and urged Japan to rearm suffi-

Secretary of State Shultz (right) and Soviet Foreign Minister Gromyko discuss East-West relations September 29.

UPI

ciently during the 1980s to provide its own defense. Although the Reagan administration increased its military budget to strengthen its armaments negotiating posture and U.S. security,
it established new policy for arms negotiations
with the Soviet Union, shifting its objective from
limitation to the *reduction* of nuclear arms. It opposed both unilateral relinquishment of the
"first-strike option" in Europe and a blanket
East-West nuclear freeze, which were demanded
by popular action groups in the United States.

Negotiations on theater nuclear weapons in
Europe commenced in Geneva in November
1981, and President Reagan suggested a phased,
eventually complete elimination of such weapons. In March 1982 the NATO allies rejected a
Soviet plan for a European nuclear freeze, and
the president countered with an offer to negotiate "dramatic" reductions of medium-range nuclear forces based on East-West parity.

To produce negotiated strategic nuclear
equality and to reduce American ICBM vulnerability, President Reagan in May proposed a
phased plan for substantial reduction of strategic
nuclear weapons by at least one third, producing
a ceiling parity, with agreed verification procedures. The same month the Defense Department
revealed a five-year plan, accepting the premise
of protracted nuclear conflict. The U.S.-Soviet
strategic arms reduction talks (START)—super-
seding earlier strategic arms limitation talks
(SALT)—were convened in Geneva late in June.
In a TV speech on November 22, the president
called for the deployment of 100 MX missiles in
the dense-pack basing system. The president said
that he intended to "search for peace along two
parallel paths—deterrence and arms reductions." He said that modernizing the U.S. military "keeps others from threatening."

Terrorism. Terrorist outbreaks occurred in
Central America, the Mideast, Africa, the Philippines, the Seychelles, and elsewhere. On January
18 an American military attaché at the U.S. embassy in Paris was assassinated in that city. In
December 1981, Red Brigade terrorists kidnapped Brig. Gen. James L. Dozier, a U.S.
NATO official in Verona, and threatened to exe-
cute him, but he was rescued by Italian antiterrorist forces in Padua on January 28. Also late in
1981 it was reported that a Libyan-supported assassination squad was dispatched to kill President Reagan and other American officials. Security was intensified, and the United States
prohibited travel to Libya, urged Americans in
that country to return to the United States, and
banned the importation of Libyan oil and the
exportation of high technology products to that
country.

Western Hemisphere. With revolutionary
flames crackling over the Caribbean Basin, President Reagan in February announced a six-point
"mini-Marshall plan" for the area. He proposed
increasing U.S. financial and military assistance,
a twelve-year period of free trade, and greater

private investment incentives, credits, and business to promote regional development. He also
warned that the United States would do whatever is necessary to counter Soviet and Cuban
moves in order to ensure peace and security in
the area. In April he met in Barbados with the
leaders of five Caribbean microstates to discuss
his plans.

When Argentina seized the British-controlled
Falkland Islands in April, the United States
wrestled with the dilemma of supporting Argentina, its ally under the inter-American Rio
Treaty, or the United Kingdom, its ally under
the North Atlantic Treaty. Initially the United
States sought to mediate the dispute and cooperate with the Organization of American States
(OAS) to achieve a negotiated settlement. When
this failed, the president called Argentina guilty
of armed aggression, ordered sanctions against
it, and offered matériel support to Britain. In late
April the OAS voted its support of Argentina's
claim, and in early June the United States joined
Britain in vetoing a UN Security Council resolution calling for a cease-fire. (The United States
later announced that it really intended to abstain
in the UN vote.) Argentinian forces surrendered
in mid-June, and the United States lifted its
sanctions, but the strain on the inter-American
system remained.

Central America's political malaise sim-
mered. Conflict intensified in Guatemala; newly
independent Belize was on the verge of being
drawn into the struggle; previously tranquil
Honduras became the haven of neighboring dissidents; guerrilla activities surfaced in Costa
Rica; and Nicaragua drifted more toward the
Left and initiated a war of words with the United
States. The vortex of the conflict was El Salvador, tormented by civil strife. The White House
accepted the outcome of El Salvador's national
election in March, and indicated that it would
support the government and provide financial
assistance, but would not send U.S. combat
troops. To help stabilize the situation in Central
America, the United States proposed an eight-
point plan to mend relations with Nicaragua and
suggested the curbing of weapons transfers, and
the establishment of a "common ceiling" for military advisers in the area. Mexico intervened to
try for a cease-fire and political settlement, and
to scale down tensions between Nicaragua and
its neighbors. But internal struggles for national
political control and conflicts between neighbors
persisted throughout 1982, threatening the stability of the region and the vital interests of the
United States.

Mideast. On April 25 Israel withdrew from
occupied Sinai in accordance with 1978 commitments and returned jurisdiction to Egypt, and
the United States joined an 11-nation Sinai
peacekeeping force. Late in 1981 the Saudi government had proposed a peace plan for the area,
as an alternative to the Camp David accords,
which the Palestine Liberation Organization

Then Secretary of State Alexander M. Haig, Jr., and U.S. Ambassador to the UN Jeane Kirkpatrick listen intently to President Reagan's UN talk on disarmament. Mrs. Kirkpatrick was reported to have welcomed Mr. Haig's departure from the cabinet.

UPI

(PLO), Israel, and several Arab countries rejected. Despite U.S. mediatory efforts in the spring of 1982, Egyptian-Israeli negotiations on Palestinian autonomy were deadlocked.

The area erupted in early June when Israel launched a full-scale military invasion of Lebanon—to destroy PLO forces and their bases. Originally limited in scope, eventually it became a bloody siege of Beirut. The United States approved Israeli objectives, but not its tactics. By means of the shuttle diplomacy of Philip Habib (*see* BIOGRAPHY), the United States was instrumental in producing a settlement. Despite several violated cease-fires, general condemnation of Israel, and U.S. pressure on the Israeli government of Menahem Begin, it was not until late August that arrangements were negotiated for 15,000 PLO and Syrian forces to withdraw, unarmed—under the supervision of a multilateral contingent consisting of American, French, and Italian troops—and they were given sanctuary in a number of Arab countries. Throughout, the United States pressed for a binding cease-fire, minimizing civilian casualties and destruction, withdrawing all foreign forces from Lebanon, and restoring the Lebanese government and its military control over its domain.

On September 1, just hours after the last PLO troops left Beirut, President Reagan promulgated a comprehensive peace plan for the Mideast—a freeze on Israeli settlements in occupied territory, return of Israel to its pre-1967 borders by withdrawing from the West Bank and Gaza Strip and linking them with Jordan, Palestinian autonomy in the West Bank, negotiated settlement of the status of Jerusalem, recognition of Israel by the Arab countries, and continued U.S. commitment to Israeli security.

Within the next weeks the international forces were withdrawn from Lebanon, its presi-

dent-elect was assassinated, and hundreds of unarmed Palestinians were massacred by Christian militiamen who were permitted into Beirut refugee camps by Israel. American, French, and Italian troops returned for constabulary duty, pending stabilization under the Lebanese government and the rapid withdrawal of Israeli and other foreign forces.

United Nations System. Major developments occurred reflecting mounting U.S. dissatisfaction with the UN system. Concerned with the growing inability of nations to pay off their international indebtedness, the United States, resisting calls for substantial increases in government contributions to the international lending pool, insisted that borrowing countries do more to improve their own financial systems, curb extravagance, and rely more on private resources and lending institutions. Yet, in August the United States joined other states in taking action to alleviate the critical financial plight of Mexico, and in December the Reagan administration acted to assist Brazil in resolving its international economic difficulties.

When in October the UN considered branding Israel a "non-peace-loving state"—as a prelude to expelling it—the United States responded that if this were done, and if the double standards permeating the UN were carried to such an extreme, it would withdraw from the General Assembly and halt its contributions. The United States also threatened to walk out of the International Telecommunication Plenipotentiary Conference and stop its payments, as it had done with the International Atomic Energy Agency following a vote to reject Israeli representational credentials. The United States made it clear that it would do the same if similar actions were taken in other UN agencies.

ELMER PLISCHKE

548

URUGUAY

Tortuously slow progress back toward democratic government, and continuing economic crises characterized Uruguay in 1982.

Political Affairs. The president, Gen. Gregorio Alvarez, had approved a decree law on reorganization of political parties drawn up by the Political Commission of the Armed Forces in the last days of 1981. However, it was the first week of June 1982 before that law was finally approved by the military regime's Council of State.

According to the new law, three parties would legally be allowed to reorganize: the traditional National (Blanco) Party, the Colorado Party, and the conservative Catholic Civic Union Party. These would have internal elections to choose party officials and nominees for president of the republic and other offices on November 28. More than 1.2 million voters went to the polls, and the result was a defeat for the military regime. Opposition candidates outpolled government candidates heavily.

On August 1, another decree provided that these parties would be permitted to hold indoor meetings without prior government authorization. They also could hold outdoor meetings during the 60 days prior to the November 28 election and were promised that candidates would have radio and television time.

Within the National Party, the Pro-Patria faction of exiled Wilson Ferreira (headed within Uruguay by his wife, Susana Sionra de Ferreira) emerged as the largest group. In the Colorado Party, there was division between the followers of former-President Jorge Pacheco, who resigned in March as the military regime's ambassador to Washington, and his opponents. The latter were divided into several factions.

All three parties tended to be opposed to the military regime. However, in September, retired Col. Nestor Bolentini, a member of the Council of State and former minister of the interior and labor, announced formation of a fourth, progovernment party. The new Patriotic Union for the Salvation of Democracy would uphold the principles of the "civilian-military process."

Meanwhile, military men continued to indicate that only a severely circumscribed democratic regime could be expected to result from "liberalization." In May a group of civilian politicians were warned by the Political Commission of the Armed Forces that there would be no return to the "democratic system, the political pluralism and liberalism that existed before 1973." On October 5, Gen. Julio Cesar Bonelli, commander of the army's Second Division, warned that a return to democracy would depend on the politicians' willingness to allow the military to continue to have a role in government. He urged amending the constitution to give such a role to the National Security Council.

The government continued to hold political prisoners. In May, it was announced that there were still 858 in jail, although 3,238 had been released. A number of opposition leaders also remained in exile.

Economy. The economic situation was serious. Inflation continued at a high level, and the balance of payments picture was critical. In October the military government announced the use of some of the country's gold reserves held abroad to help correct the situation.

In pursuance of its "Chicago school" economic policies, the military regime in March announced plans for denationalizing substantial parts of the economy. These include sale of 49% of the shares of the government airline PLUNA; disposal of part of ANCAP, the government's petroleum and alcohol monopoly; reduction of the role of the government gas company; and ending of the monopoly of seal fishing by the National Fishing Institute.

In the face of a wave of bankruptcies and the threat of many more, the government announced in September that the Central Bank would help in refinancing one third of the debts of business firms, totaling about $600 million. These debts would be extended over a five-year period with a two-year period of grace. At the same time, the country's agricultural interests were demanding refinancing of all of their debts.

In spite of foreign exchange problems, Uruguay received some foreign aid and investment during the year. In August a group of Inter-American Development Bank officials were in Montevideo arranging details of loans totaling $200 million for construction of rural roads and other projects.

Foreign Relations. Uruguay became tangentially involved in the Anglo-Argentine crisis over the Falkland Islands. Montevideo was the entrepôt for exchange of prisoners between the two sides. Also as a consequence of the Falkland Islands conflict, a consortium of three British banks and one Portuguese bank withdrew from financing the joint Uruguay-and-Argentine Salto Grande hydroelectric project on the Uruguay River.

ROBERT J. ALEXANDER, *Rutgers University*

URUGUAY • Information Highlights

Official Name: Eastern Republic of Uruguay.
Location: Southeastern coast of South America.
Area: 68,536 sq mi (177 508 km²).
Population (1982 est.): 3,000,000.
Chief City (1975 census): Montevideo, the capital, 1,229,748.
Government: *Head of state,* Gregorio Alvarez, president (took office Sept. 1981). *Head of government,* Lt. Gen. Luis Vicente Quevedo, head of the military junta. *Legislature*—Council of state.
Monetary Unit: Peso (13.17 pesos equal U.S.$1, Oct. 1982).
Gross National Product (1980 U.S.$): $9,770,000,-000.
Economic Index (1980): *Consumer Prices* (1970= 100), *all items,* 13,007; *food,* 13,620.
Foreign Trade (1980 U.S.$): *Imports,* $1,727,000,-000; *exports,* $1,059,000,000.

UTAH

Elections, unemployment, and a rash of child kidnappings marked the scene in Utah in 1982. In early December a team of surgeons at the University of Utah Medical Center made medical history by implanting a permanent artificial heart in a dying patient.

Elections. In the November 1982 elections, Utah Republicans gained a landslide victory over Democratic, Libertarian, and American Party candidates. In a key race for the U.S. Senate, which drew nationwide attention and two personal visits by President Ronald Reagan, incumbent Orrin Hatch (R) won a second term decisively over challenger Ted L. Wilson, mayor of Salt Lake City. The large margin of victory was directly attributable to the TV message to Utahns by President Reagan that "I need Orrin Hatch in the Senate."

In the closest congressional race, Democratic State Sen. Frances Farley lost to the incumbent, Republican Dan Marriott, who was elected for a fourth term in Utah's second district. In the new third district, Republican Howard C. Nielson, a Brigham Young University professor, easily won by a 3–1 margin. Rep. James V. Hanson (R) defeated his opponent, A. Stephen Dirks (D), mayor of Ogden, in the first district by a nearly 2–1 margin.

The GOP further demonstrated its firm grip on the Utah electorate in statewide races. Republicans now outnumber Democrats in the Utah Senate 24 to 5. In the House, the imbalance is not quite so decisive; there are 58 Republicans and 17 Democrats. The GOP dominance was also pervasive in major county elections. This overwhelming victory of the GOP reflected the popularity of President Reagan in the state and a fundamental conservative political philosophy that characterizes the Utah electorate.

Unemployment. By October, Utah's economic condition had grown considerably weaker as reflected in a 9% unemployment figure. Although this was below the national average, it reflects a disturbing trend. For example, the state's unemployment rate jumped from 6.8% in March to 7.6% in April, reaching 9% in October. Many Utah areas had unemployment above the October figure. The central portion of the state, comprising Juab, Millard, Piute, Sanpete, Sevier, and Wayne counties, had a combined 12.5% rate, with Juab County having the highest rate, at 20.1%. The seasonally adjusted figures, released by the Utah Department of Job Security, show 58,900 people out of work, up 42% from January. The basic goods-producing industries in Utah continue to be hit the hardest by the recession. Mining jobs decreased 15.2%, construction work was off 8%, and manufacturing jobs decreased 5.1%.

Kidnappings. The abduction and brutal murder of a three-year-old girl from Sunset, following the kidnapping of a 10-year-old Kaysville girl, created fear and concern throughout the state in 1982. Parents began holding neighborhood meetings to deal with prevention; several local PTA's and other community groups started safety programs; and law-enforcement agencies began programs in elementary schools to warn children against involvement with strangers.

LORENZO K. KIMBALL, *University of Utah*

At the University of Utah Medical Center in Salt Lake City, Dr. William DeVries led a team of surgeons who implanted a permanent artificial heart for the first time.

UPI

UTAH · Information Highlights

Area: 84,899 sq mi (219 888 km^2).
Population (1980 census): 1,461,037.
Chief Cities (1980 census): Salt Lake City, the capital, 163,697; Provo, 73,907; Ogden, 64,407.
Government (1982): *Chief Officers*—governor, Scott M. Matheson (D); lt. gov., David S. Monson (R). *Legislature*—Senate, 29 members; House of Representatives, 75 members.
State Finances (fiscal year 1981): *Revenues*, $2,053,-000,000; *expenditures*, $1,896,000,000.
Personal Income (1981): $12,619,000,000; per capita, $8,313.
Labor Force (Aug. 1982): *Nonagricultural wage and salary earners,* 558,800; *unemployed,* 50,400 (7.5% of total force).
Education: *Enrollment* (fall 1981)—public elementary schools, 261,722; public secondary, 93,832; colleges and universities (1981–82), 97,048. *Public school expenditures* (1980–81), $781,806,000 ($1,742 per pupil).

The Vatican Bank Case

A months-long series of probes into the Vatican bank's involvement in the dubious dealings and dramatic collapse of Italy's largest private banking institution, Banco Ambrosiano, cost the Vatican in prestige and credibility and left the European banking community reeling. The case combined all the elements of a mystery thriller, including the mysterious death of Ambrosiano's president, Roberto Calvi; the apparent loss of more than $1,000,000,000; the possible involvement of sinister international criminal elements; and more.

Most of the notoriety of the case centered on the relationship between the Vatican bank and Calvi's worldwide financial escapades. On a larger scale it involved the Vatican's status as a sovereign state, the Vatican bank's peculiar mission and position in the banking community, and the reasons for the failure of Banco Ambrosiano despite "letters of patronage" from the Vatican bank. The Vatican bank—officially L'Istituto per le Opere di Religione (IOR), the Institute for Works of Religion—became the focus of investigations by banking authorities in Italy and other nations, and the subject of a special probe by a select Vatican commission. Founded in 1942, IOR is the Vatican's principal financial institution.

The Case Itself. The controversy came to a head June 18 when Calvi's body was found hanging from the Blackfriar's Bridge in London. The death was ruled a suicide by British authorities, but claims surfaced that Calvi was murdered by underworld elements involved in his financial dealings. Shortly after Calvi's death, Italian banking authorities declared Banco Ambrosiano bankrupt. A major factor was the $1,200,000,000 in unpaid loans which Calvi arranged from Ambrosiano subsidiaries on behalf of highly questionable Panamanian finance companies in which Calvi himself is said to have had major investment holdings.

The previous year IOR issued letters of patronage allegedly approving the lending of at least some of the Ambrosiano money to the Panamanian groups. The letters were signed after Calvi had been convicted by an Italian court of illegal money transfers. To some, the letters of patronage gave the impression that IOR exercised some measure of control over the Panamanian operations and afforded the loans some credibility. Reportedly, the Vatican bank received from Calvi a special letter absolving it from any financial responsibility for the loans.

Calvi's death eventually set off a highly publicized investigation by the Italian banking authority into Banco Ambrosiano's links to the IOR. It, too, focused on the $1,200,000,000 in unpaid loans which Calvi arranged. Similar probes were launched in at least a dozen other countries to which Banco Ambrosiano had financial ties.

The Italian government began pressing the Vatican—in particular, Archbishop Paul Marcinkus, 60-year-old IOR president—for a fuller disclosure of the bank's role in Ambrosiano affairs. Under direct investigation were Archbishop Marcinkus, a native of Cicero, IL, and a veteran of 30 years of Vatican service, and his two closest aides, both laymen, IOR managing director Luigi Mennini, 71, and chief accountant Pellegrino de Strobel, 70. Soon after the probe began, Archbishop Marcinkus moved into the Vatican, a separate state under Italian law, to avoid being served a judicial notice that he was under investigation. Such notices usually contain accusations. In addition to the Italian government's probe, a special commission was established by Pope John Paul II. A team of international bankers not connected to IOR and appointed by Agostino Cardinal Casaroli, papal secretary of state, began conducting a separate study of the IOR connection to Banco Ambrosiano.

In mid-October, reports in the Vatican newspaper, L'Osservatore Romano, indicated that both the commission and the IOR's own officials had concluded separately that the IOR was clear of responsibility to Banco Ambrosiano's creditors. They also claimed that the foreign (Panamanian) finance companies in debt to Banco Ambrosiano were never under the direction or control of the Vatican Bank, that all loans made by Banco Ambrosiano to the finance companies were approved before the Vatican bank's letters were issued, and that these letters did not influence any of the loans. The October 16 issue of L'Osservatore Romano claimed that conclusions reached by IOR officials and those of the papal commission could be proven after a full investigation.

Shortly afterward, Archbishop Marcinkus, who had been under fire for failing to respond to Italian government queries into the Ambrosiano affair, broke silence. He said that the Vatican bank was not responsible for the failure of Banco Ambrosiano and instead suggested that the Italian government take some of the blame because Ambrosiano investors, including the Vatican, relied on Italian financial authorities to closely monitor the defunct bank's operations.

Earlier, Italian Treasury Minister Beniamino Andreatta suggested in a speech to Italy's Par-

François Lochon/Gamma-Liaison

Archbishop Marcinkus, American-born banking chief of the Holy See, came under fire in the Banco Ambrosiano affair.

liament that the Vatican bears some moral responsibility for Banco Ambrosiano's default on the $1,200,000,000 in loans because of the letters of patronage. He said some Italian banking sources claimed the letters in effect vouched for the credit-worthiness of the Panamanian groups. Andreatta asked Pope John Paul point blank to order the Vatican bank to help pay the $1,200,000,000 in Banco Ambrosiano debts caused by the bad loans to companies with possible Mafia connections. The Italian official pointed out that the Vatican could not be forced to make good the bad debts because the Italian government regards the Vatican as a sovereign state not subject to Italian banking regulations.

Archbishop Marcinkus claimed the letters of patronage "never had the value of a guarantee." He noted that the IOR "is and was extraneous to all operations carried out at the time by any of the companies controlled by the Ambrosiano group." The prelate also said that the IOR carried on normal banking relations with Calvi and his bank. But he said he knew nothing of the bank's plans or strategies, observing that the Banco Ambrosiano "seemed to operate with great success and with apparent approval of the Italian financial authority. This, without a doubt, encouraged people to invest."

Claiming that the IOR also suffered financial damage, Archbishop Marcinkus continued to argue for independence of the Vatican bank from Italian control or regulation. The IOR

funds religious and social projects in many countries, and its supporters say that independence from Italian regulation makes the flow of funds to these countries easier.

In late November the pope himself spoke out on the case for the first time. At a meeting of the College of Cardinals, the pontiff promised the full cooperation of the Vatican in discovering "the whole truth" of the IOR involvement with Ambrosiano. An overhaul of the Vatican's system for conducting its financial affairs also was proposed.

Findings and Effects. Since its inception, the IOR has existed to do what its name implies—to help religious orders and institutions carry out apostolic projects by overseeing the use of their financial resources. The bank also helps dioceses which are experiencing economic difficulties and funds projects which might not otherwise get off the ground.

Vatican sources claim that there is no question that the Catholic Church's image and credibility has been harmed by the investigations into IOR's operations and allegations regarding its connection with Banco Ambrosiano's questionable activities. By year's end the IOR, currently supervised by five cardinals making up a Commission of Vigilance, had no public accusations leveled against it by Italian officialdom. Few Italian banking experts believe that the IOR benefited from the Banco Ambrosiano collapse; few bankers hold that the IOR acted illegally in its dealings. Critics of the IOR's questionable involvement with Calvi and his cohorts indicated the belief that the letters of patronage may have spurred what was already foreseen as the imminent collapse of the Banco Ambrosiano. Calvi, at the time of his death, was out on bail during an appeal of his four-year prison sentence for illegally exporting some $26.4 million out of Italy.

In late December, the Vatican and the Italian government announced the formation of a joint commission of six lay banking and legal experts to study the links between the bankrupt Banco Ambrosiano and the IOR. Government sources said that the new commission was expected to conclude its work within two months. The Vatican said four international banking experts appointed earlier to probe the situation were asked to assist the Holy See's appointees to the joint commission.

As the year ended, there were concerns in the Vatican that the good name of the Church was used to assist in a financial operation that was quite irregular and possibly dishonest. Until the conclusions of the joint commission are published (sometime in early 1983), the extent of the Vatican's bank's involvement and responsibility in the matter of Banco Ambrosiano's dealings remains decidedly unclear.

ROBERT L. JOHNSTON

VENEZUELA

A sagging economy marked by declining oil revenues and increased imports was a major concern of Venezuela in 1982, along with efforts by President Luis Herrera Campíns to restructure Venezuela's relationships with the United States and Cuba in the wake of the Falkland Islands War between Argentina and Britain.

Economic Measures. Early in October, President Herrera ordered all state-owned firms to turn over control of their overseas revenues to the Central Bank in a move to increase monetary reserves, which fell from $8,600,000,000 in December 1981 to $6,300,000,000 in July 1982. An increasingly unfavorable balance of payments was due to increased imports of food, automobiles, and other consumer goods that totaled $12,000,000,000 in 1981, along with a decline in oil export revenue from $19,600,000,000 in 1981 to $14,000,000,000 in 1982. It appeared likely that Venezuela might not be able to meet $1,800,000,000 in short-term debts due in late 1982 and early 1983.

While inflation was down from 23% in 1980 and 15% in 1981 to 10% in September 1982, unemployment in August 1982 was expected to increase beyond 8% as private investment stagnated. Earlier in the year, President Herrera ordered a 10% cut in public spending and a 15% cut in the total of 1.1 million persons in government employment; levied a $70 departure tax on overseas travel; outlawed the importing of 8-cylinder cars; and doubled gasoline prices.

Oil Production. In both June and September 1982, Venezuela rejected efforts by the Organization of Petroleum Exporting Countries (OPEC) to reduce its daily production by 400,000 barrels to an assigned OPEC quota of 1.9 million barrels per day. President Herrera and Energy Minister Humberto Calderón Berti said that Venezuela needed the income to meet foreign debt demands and the cost of imports. It also needed to supply oil on preferential terms to Central American and Caribbean nations that had meager or no oil supplies of their own.

PDVSA, the state-owned oil company, in January and February reduced the price of a barrel of residual fuel oil with 1.5% sulfur content by $1.70 to $26.42 in an effort to increase exports to the United States and other countries importing the oil for heating purposes. On September 11, PDVSA increased the export price of fuel oil by 50 cents a barrel in response to increased demand in world markets.

Political Parties Name 1983 Candidates. The continued economic stagnation increased the probability that Jaime Lusinchi, a 58-year-old pediatrician from Anzoátegui, nominated by the Democratic Action Party in June, might win the December 1983 presidential election. Lusinchi said he would put a high priority on reviving agriculture, which has been in the doldrums since the oil boom began in the 1920s. He would also pay special attention to the needs of young people under 21, and support a transition government in El Salvador that included the left-wing guerrilla opposition.

In August, President Herrera's COPEI (Christian Democratic) Party selected 66-year-old former President Rafael Caldera (1969–1974), who wanted to be the first Venezuelan to be elected to the presidency twice.

Leftist extremists abandoned their efforts in August to present a joint candidate when the People's Electoral Movement (MEP) and Nueva Alternativa (the New Alternative) named José Vicente Rangel as their candidate, and the Movement of the Revolutionary Left (MIR) and the Movement to Socialism (MAS) named Teodore Petkoff as their candidate.

Foreign Policy Shifts. President Herrera signaled a policy shift on March 23 when he criticized U.S. policy in Central America, saying that the Reagan administration "should make an effort to comprehend" Latin America in order to "act in a realistic way." The Venezuelan president said his government would reevaluate its Central American policies regardless of which party won the Salvadoran elections.

The Venezuelan president was the only Latin American chief of state to attend July 19 ceremonies marking the third anniversary of the overthrow of Anastasio Somoza in Nicaragua. In early July, President Herrera announced that his government was "seriously considering" joining the 94-nation Nonaligned Movement, which generally takes an anti-U.S. stance in its foreign policy statements. In September a spokesman said that Venezuela would upgrade its status in the movement from observer to full member.

For many years, an area of 53,000 square miles (137 270 sq km) in Guyana, called the "Guyana Essequibo," has been in dispute between Venezuela and Guyana. A 12-year agreement to delay settlement of the dispute, signed by the two countries in 1970, expired in 1982. On September 20, Venezuela announced that it was asking UN Secretary General Javier Perez de Cuellar to help resolve the Essequibo problem.

NEALE J. PEARSON, *Texas Tech University*

VENEZUELA • Information Highlights

Official Name: Republic of Venezuela.
Location: Northern coast of South America.
Area: 352,143 sq mi (912 050 km²).
Population (1982 est.): 18,400,000.
Chief Cities (1976 est.): Caracas, the capital, 2,576,-000; Maracaibo, 792,000; Valencia, 439,000.
Government: *Head of state and government,* Luis Herrera Campins, president (took office March 1979). *Legislature*—Congress: Senate and Chamber of Deputies.
Monetary Unit: Bolivar (4.2942 bolivares equal U.S.$1, Oct. 26, 1982).
Gross National Product (1980 U.S.$): $60,430,000,-000.
Economic Index (1981): *Consumer Prices* (1970=100), *all items,* 260; *food,* 371.2
Foreign Trade (1979 U.S.$): *Imports,* $9,618,000,-000; *exports,* $14,159,000,000.

VERMONT

Incumbent Republican Gov. Richard Snelling celebrates his Election Day victory with a dance with wife Barbara.

As the state withstood the 1981–82 recession with an unemployment rate about half the national average, Vermonters' attention was drawn to environmental matters and escalating health costs—in particular, acid rain, retention of open lands, health insurance, and nuclear power. One hundred seventy-seven towns voted to instruct their representatives in Congress to work for a U.S.-Soviet freeze on nuclear weapons, and both houses of the state legislature endorsed their appeal.

The 1982 session of the Republican-dominated legislature was distinguished by action on educational funding, criminal justice, and highway taxes. After years of wrangling, a revision of the formula for state aid to education was adopted, taking into account the average income of municipalities as well as real estate wealth; simultaneously, a one-third increase in total aid was funded by an increase in the sales tax and the state income tax. A juvenile detention center was voted after bitter debate over its location. Vermont's anomalous position as the only state without a diesel motor fuel tax was corrected as part of an omnibus revenue measure to bring the ailing highway fund into balance. A bill raising the minimum drinking age from 18 to 19 was successfully vetoed by Gov. Richard Snel-

ling. In the area of social legislation, the General Assembly created an Independence Fund to support noninstitutional forms of care for the elderly. Workmen's compensation was revised to eliminate a five-year limit on support of the permanently disabled. Governor Snelling, as chairman of the National Governor's Conference, defended the "new federalism" while campaigning against the transfer of responsibilities to states without the funds to meet them.

Elections. The decision by Republican U.S. Sen. Robert Stafford to seek reelection was the pivotal event of the 1982 campaign season. Governor Snelling and U.S. Rep. James Jeffords, considered aspirants for Stafford's seat, at first declined to mount a primary challenge. In response to a draft spearheaded by the Burlington *Free Press,* however, Snelling reversed plans to retire and sought an unprecedented fourth two-year term as governor. Jeffords, who had eyed the governorship, then announced his reelection bid as the state's lone representative in the U.S. House.

Democratic hopes were buoyed by a bitter primary challenge in the opposing camp. Two-term Democratic Lt. Gov. Madeleine Kunin and former Secretary of State James Guest conducted vigorous and well-financed campaigns for governor and U.S. senator respectively. Nevertheless the entire Republican slate prevailed in November, Governor Snelling by 55% of the vote and Senator Stafford by 51%. Representative Jeffords easily won reelection.

Democrats made slight gains in the Republican-controlled state House of Representatives, while Republicans widened their Senate margin to 17–13. Third-party politics enlivened the state's largest city, Burlington, with the Citizens' Party allied with Socialist Mayor Bernard Sanders adding two aldermanic seats in the March election. However, the numerous splinter parties on the November ballot failed to make a significant showing.

ROBERT V. DANIELS and SAMUEL B. HAND
University of Vermont

VERMONT • Information Highlights

Area: 9,614 sq mi (24 900 km²).

Population (1980 census): 511,456.

Chief Cities (1980 census): Montpelier, the capital, 8,241; Burlington, 37,712; Rutland, 18,436.

Government (1982): *Chief Officers*—governor, Richard A. Snelling (R); lt. gov., Madeleine M. Kunin (D). *General Assembly*—Senate, 30 members; House of Representatives, 150 members.

State Finances (fiscal year 1981): *Revenues,* $795,-000,000; *expenditures,* $724,000,000.

Personal Income (1981): $4,497,000,000; per capita, $8,723.

Labor Force (Aug. 1982): *Nonagricultural wage and salary earners,* 201,800; *unemployed,* 17,200 (6.3% of total force).

Education: *Enrollment* (fall 1981)—public elementary schools, 64,988; public secondary, 28,195; colleges and universities (1981–82), 30,573. *Public school expenditures* (1980–81), $195,402,000 ($2,017 per pupil).

VIETNAM

During 1982, Vietnam's Communist leaders struggled to make the best of a very unfavorable situation. After decades of war and mismanagement, the country's economic performance was among the poorest in the world. This could not be changed overnight, and there seemed to be no immediate alternative to accepting Soviet aid—at a rate of several million dollars per day. Meanwhile, because of the occupation of Cambodia by Vietnamese troops, very few countries were willing to trade with Vietnam or to provide badly needed aid.

Politics. The Fifth Congress of the Vietnamese Communist party was held in 1982. It produced no major policy or leadership changes. Vietnam's close ties with Moscow were confirmed, despite somewhat lower aid levels and Soviet complaints that Vietnam had misused its aid.

Professional military officers, as opposed to political commissars, were given a leading role in running the war against small resistance units in Cambodia. Many top party leaders were relieved of their government assignments so they could concentrate on supervising lower party cadres, whose poor morale and discipline have become a major problem. The party congress also approved some economic policies that were already in use on a trial basis—mainly to provide more wage and profit incentives to the people to raise their low levels of production.

While morale appeared to be low throughout the country, it was probably worse in the south and among the tribal minority groups that inhabit the central mountain areas. Unemployment was very high in the south, and travelers reported that malnutrition was widespread, especially among children. There is a strong sense of regional identity among Vietnamese of the north, central, and southern regions; until quite recently, people from different regions did not intermarry. Among southerners, there is widespread resentment of Communist cadres from the North who have been running the South since 1975. Southerners believe that their needs and preferences are generally ignored by the Hanoi government and by the cadres whom it sends south. All too often, these cadres are corrupt and incompetent as well.

The ethnic minority groups who live in the central mountain region have a long tradition of resisting political or economic domination by governments in Hanoi or Ho Chi Minh City (formerly Saigon). These tribal groups have reportedly received arms from China to resist Hanoi's control. The Chinese, who resent Vietnam's close ties with Moscow, also maintain a large army on Vietnam's northern border, and they reportedly seek to subvert the loyalty of minority groups in Vietnam's northern provinces.

Economics. Eighty-seven percent of the Vietnamese people are literate, and they are highly productive workers when given the right incentives. But Vietnam's state-controlled economy is one of the few in the world that has achieved virtually no progress in the last 40 years, according to World Bank reports. The Hanoi government has had to abandon its elaborate schemes for development and concentrate on food production and the distribution of basic necessities.

To achieve even minor improvement in these areas, Hanoi has had to condone an increasing amount of open market activity—both legal and black market. Farmers have been allowed to keep a larger share of their crops and to sell some of their products on the open market. This has helped to raise food production, and Vietnam might be able to achieve self-sufficiency in food in the near future, particularly if it can slow its rate of population growth. Factory workers are now sometimes rewarded on the basis of a system of piecework.

Some of the ethnic Chinese who have not fled Vietnam to escape persecution have been encouraged by the government to set up export firms to earn badly needed foreign exchange. Even so, Vietnam's foreign exchange reserves are almost nil, and most foreign banks are unwilling to finance Vietnamese imports.

Foreign Relations. Foreign Minister Nguyen Co Thach visited a number of European countries in the spring and several Southeast Asian countries in the summer to try to prove to the world that Vietnam is no longer politically and economically isolated. The results of his travels were not spectacular. France was the only Western European country Thach visited that agreed to provide a small amount of aid. Belgium and West Germany refused to help Vietnam until it withdraws its troops from Cambodia. Most countries not allied with Moscow took a similar position. Sweden is one of a small group of neutral countries that continued to provide assistance.

In Southeast Asia, Thach tried to gain acceptance of Vietnamese control of Cambodia. But the non-Communist countries of the region support a coalition of Cambodian resistance groups, as do a majority of UN members.

See also ASIA.

PETER A. POOLE

VIETNAM · Information Highlights

Official Name: Socialist Republic of Vietnam.
Location: Southeast Asia.
Area: 127,246 sq mi (329 567 km^2).
Population (1982 est.): 56,600,000.
Chief Cities (1979 census): Hanoi, the capital, 2,570,-905; Ho Chi Minh City, 3,419,067; Haiphong, 1,279,067.
Government (1982): Communist party secretary, Le Duan; State Council chairman, Truong Chinh; Council of Ministers, chairman, Pham Van Dong.
Monetary Unit: Dong (2.18 dongs equal U.S.$1, 1982).
Gross National Product (1980–81 U.S.$): est. $9,-500,000,000 to $16,000,000,000.
Foreign Trade (1979 U.S.$): *Imports,* $1,225,000,-000; *exports,* $535,000,000.

Wide World

Opponents of capital punishment protest the state's first execution in 20 years, August 10.

In 1982 elections, Republican Paul S. Trible, Jr., edged Democratic Lt. Gov. Richard J. Davis for the Senate seat left open when Harry F. Byrd, Jr., an Independent, decided to retire. Trible, a lawyer who had been the first-district congressman, captured 51% of the vote. His term would be the first time in 50 years that a Byrd did not represent Virginia in the Senate.

Trible and Davis disagreed most strongly on President Ronald Reagan's economic program, with Davis calling for a "midcourse correction" and Trible urging voters to "stay the course." Davis painted his opponent as an overly ambitious young man and a "do-nothing" congressman. Trible described Davis as a tool of organized labor who knew little about foreign policy.

Democrats captured three more of Virginia's 10 congressional seats than they had in 1980, bringing their total to four. In addition to re-electing fifth-district Democratic Rep. Dan Daniel, who was unopposed, voters chose Democratic candidates in the fourth, sixth, and ninth districts, ousting two veteran legislators—fourth-district Rep. Robert W. Daniel, Jr., and ninth-district Rep. William C. Wampler. But Wampler would not concede his apparent loss by fewer than 1,150 votes to state Sen. Frederick Boucher. A recount showed that he lost.

Democrats retained their solid hold on the 100-member House of Delegates, with a total of 65 seats in official returns. The elections were for one-year terms because of problems with the state's redistricting plan. The plan was not ready by November 1981, and federal courts said Virginia had to have a special election in 1982. General Assembly members wrangled over numerous proposals, and the U.S. Justice Department finally approved a single-member district plan after rejecting earlier plans as racially biased or violating the one-man, one-vote principle. The House traditionally had several multi-member districts. Elections would return to the regular schedule in 1983.

Legislative and Other Matters. The General Assembly passed a $13,700,000,000 budget for 1982–1984. Among the measures approved to pay for it were a 3% wholesale gasoline tax and higher liquor taxes. The assembly also approved tougher sentencing laws for drunk drivers. It killed several attempts to allow the interbasin transfer of water; a bill to create a state holiday in honor of the Rev. Martin Luther King, Jr.; and proposals to reduce sales taxes on food and nonprescription drugs.

Virginia attracted nationwide attention when convicted murderer Frank J. Coppola died in the electric chair on August 10—one hour after the U.S. Supreme Court overruled a stay of execution granted by a lower court. It was the first execution in Virginia since 1962.

In November, Virginia Electric and Power Company (Vepco) announced plans to cancel construction of the third nuclear unit at the North Anna Power Station, signaling the end of the utility's nuclear reactor construction program, at least for the decade. Vepco, which was left with four operating nuclear units, originally had planned to build eight. Two were canceled in 1977 and one in 1980. The North Anna 3 cancellation—blamed on the cost of new regulations—resulted in a $540 million writeoff.

VIRGINIA MUNSCH, *"Richmond Times-Dispatch"*

VIRGINIA • Information Highlights

Area: 40,767 sq mi (105 587 km²).

Population (1980 census): 5,346,818.

Chief Cities (1980 census): Richmond, the capital, 219,214; Norfolk, 266,979; Virginia Beach, 262,-199; Newport News, 144,903; Hampton, 122,617.

Government (1982): *Chief Officers*—governor, Charles S. Robb (D); lt. gov., Richard J. Davis (D). *General Assembly*—Senate, 40 members; House of Delegates, 100 members.

State Finances (fiscal year 1981): *Revenues,* $6,484,-000,000; *expenditures,* $6,092,000,000.

Personal Income (1981): $56,191,000,000; per capita, $10,349.

Labor Force (Aug. 1982): *Nonagricultural wage and salary earners,* 2,164,000; *unemployed,* 191,900 (7.3% of total force).

Education: *Enrollment* (fall 1981)—public elementary schools, 690,736; public secondary, 298,812; colleges and universities (1981–82), 286,015. *Public school expenditures* (1980–81), $2,367,736,000 ($2,223 per pupil).

VIRGIN ISLANDS

In the Virgin Islands, 1982 was an election year. Voters on St. Thomas, St. John, and St. Croix went to the polls to elect the governor, the resident commissioner, and the 15 members of the unicameral legislature.

Five candidates vied for the post of governor, including incumbent Gov. Juan Luis, an independent from the island of St. Croix. The other candidates were Sen. Ruby Rouss, president of the Senate; Lt. Gov. Henry Millin; St. Croix attorney Derek Hodge, and Hector Cintron, former senator from St. Croix. Governor Luis won easily over all contenders, despite an ongoing U.S. Justice Department investigation of charges that his administration misused some $19 million in public funds. He received 56% of the total valid votes cast for the post, thus avoiding the need for a run-off election between the two top contenders. The only question that clouded the results was whether or not blank or damaged ballots should be counted as part of the total votes cast. The attorney general ruled that these ballots should not be taken into consideration in determining the majority.

Incumbent Resident Commissioner Ron de Lugo (D) won reelection for his fifth term even more decisively, winning 77% of the vote against two challengers whose combined total was less than 4,000 votes.

In the race for the legislature, most of the incumbents who sought reelection were returned to their seats. The election was characterized more by personalities than by party labels.

The reelection of Juan Luis confirmed his popularity, although his relations with the local press were strained and he continually found himself in dispute with members of the legislature. During his first term, the St. Thomas hospital underwent a multimillion dollar reconstruction; the runway for the Harry S. Truman airport in St. Thomas was extended; the fisherman's pier of Fredericksted in St. Croix was rebuilt after having been damaged by two hurricanes; modern library facilities were inaugurated at Grove Place; and a large criminal justice complex was built in the capital city, Charlotte Amalie.

Despite the new construction, the unemployment rate in the islands hit an all-time high of about 9% in 1982. Labor disputes were frequent. Schoolteachers went on strike for two weeks in October before the government agreed to negotiate a new contract with substantial wage increases. At the end of October a group of public employees threatened to strike but accepted a $600 bonus hastily offered by an anxious government facing an election.

Tourism in the islands remained strong, with winter tour-ship visits to St. Croix expected to quadruple over the previous year.

THOMAS MATHEWS
University of Puerto Rico

WASHINGTON

In its 90-day regular session in 1982, the legislature continued its struggle of recent years to reduce state expenditures to meet anticipated revenues—revenues that continued to fall short of periodic projections.

Economic Measures. No new taxes were levied during the legislature's regular session, but a 4.4% surcharge was added to all except property taxes, and the sales tax again was applied to food after having been removed in 1977. By midyear it was obvious that revenues in a declining economy would continue to fall short of expenditure requirements, and Gov. John Spellman called a 10-day special session to deal with the crisis as an alternative to ordering all state agencies to accept an 8.2% budget cut for the remaining year of the biennium. No new consumer taxes were passed in the special session, but a number of "business loopholes" were closed, including taxing electric energy produced in the state but exported. These remedies were seen as temporary at best.

Pipeline. On April 8 Governor Spellman rejected the application of Northern Tier Pipeline Company, a consortium of oil producers and distributors, to build a pipeline from Port Angeles on the Straits of Juan de Fuca across the bottom of Puget Sound and east across Washington to the Midwest. The most serious concerns of the governor were the engineering feasibility of traversing the Puget Sound bottom with strong assurances of safety, and the possibility of oil spills at Port Angeles.

Nuclear Energy. After a protracted series of emergency efforts to prevent the termination of construction (or at least to postpone further construction) of two of five nuclear energy plants being constructed by the Washington Public Power Supply System (WPPSS) for 88 utility districts and power companies, WPPSS was forced to terminate construction on one plant 23% finished at Hanford near Richland, and one 14% finished at Satsop.

Success of a plan to mothball the two unfin-

WASHINGTON · Information Highlights

Area: 68,139 sq mi (176 480 km²).
Population (1980 census): 4,132,180.
Chief Cities (1980 census): Olympia, the capital, 27,-447; Seattle, 493,846; Spokane, 171,300; Tacoma, 158,501; Bellevue, 73,903; Everett, 54,413.
Government (1982): *Chief Officers*—governor, John Spellman (R); lt. gov., John A. Cherberg (D). *Legislature*—Senate, 49 members; House of Representatives, 98 members.
State Finances (fiscal year 1981): *Revenues*, $6,916,-000,000; *expenditures*, $6,911,000,000.
Personal Income (1981): $47,557,000,000; per capita, $11,277.
Labor Force (Aug. 1982): *Nonagricultural wage and salary earners*, 1,546,900; *unemployed*, 240,100 (12.0% of total force).
Education: *Enrollment* (fall 1981)—public elementary schools, 513,018; public secondary, 237,170; colleges and universities (1981–82), 278,680. *Public school expenditures* (1980–81), $2,519,378,000 ($2,653 per pupil).

ished nuclear energy plants depended on the sponsoring utilities' funding the additional money needed to suspend but not terminate construction. More than one third of the utility owners refused to contribute to the mothballing plan, thus dooming it. Already the most expensive civil-works project in history, the costs of the three remaining plants plus the cost of terminating two plants will mean substantially higher electric rates for the customers of the sponsoring utilities.

Election. In the general election of November 2, Washington voters gave Democrats slim majorities in the legislature while soundly defeating two initiatives generally supported by Democrats—one that would have replaced the unpopular sales tax on food with a corporate income tax, and one that would have imposed an interest-rate ceiling on retail-sales transactions. All incumbent congressmen—five Democrats and two Republicans—were reelected, and Rodney Chandler (R) won election to the new 8th congressional district. Sen. Henry M. Jackson (D) was reelected for his sixth term.

National Monument. On August 17, Congress completed approval of a bill creating the Mount St. Helens National Volcanic Monument, covering approximately 110,000 acres (44 515 ha) of the area devastated in the volcano's eruption of May 18, 1980. The monument will be administered by the U.S. Forest Service.

WARREN W. ETCHESON
University of Washington

December 8: An antinuclear activist parks a truck said to be filled with dynamite at the Washington Monument.

UPI

WASHINGTON, DC

Several noteworthy issues in the U.S. capital came to a head in the November elections.

Statehood. The city moved one step closer to statehood when the proposed constitution obtained voter approval. The 18,000-word constitution, which would call the state "New Columbia," establishes a governorship and lieutenant governorship, a 40-member unicameral legislature, a two-tiered court system, full budget and taxing authority, and the power to create semiautonomous neighborhoods. The document contained several controversial sections, however, prompting many supporters to seek revisions and another submission to voters before formally submitting it to Congress. Public debate centered on six of the document's 18 articles. Criticized most often were provisions requiring the new state to provide jobs or adequate incomes to all residents and giving firefighters and police officers the right to strike.

Initiatives. An initiative committing the city to support a bilateral nuclear-weapons freeze won strong approval. It requires the mayor to appoint an unpaid advisory board to urge the federal government to begin negotiation of a U.S.-Soviet nuclear-weapons freeze and to redirect federal resources to human needs.

Another successful initiative provided for mandatory minimum sentencing for persons convicted of using a firearm in the commission of a violent crime and for selling or distributing illegal drugs or controlled substances.

Offices. Mayor Marion Barry (D) won reelection to a second term with nearly 80% of the vote. David A. Clark, former ward councilmember, was elected City Council chairperson. Betty Ann Kane and Hilda Mason were reelected to at-large seats; and Frank Smith, Polly Shackleton, William R. Spaulding, and Nadine Winters won ward positions. The Democrats retained their majority on the City Council, holding 11 of 13 seats. Walter E. Fauntroy (D) retained his seat as delegate to Congress.

Monuments. The Vietnam Veterans Memorial was dedicated in mid-November, during a five-day salute that brought more than 200,000 veterans and their families to Washington. The memorial is a set of polished black granite walls shaped as a chevron, on which the names of war dead and missing are carved. (*See* page 75.)

On December 8, at the nearby Washington Monument, a 66-year-old antinuclear activist took control of the structure and threatened to blow it up. His daylong siege ended when police gunned him down inside a van that he said was packed with dynamite. The truck turned out to be empty.

Lottery. An instant lottery game was begun August 25. Tickets sell for $1, and prizes range from $2 to $1 million. About one third of the revenue goes into the city treasury.

MORRIS J. LEVITT, *Howard University*

WEST VIRGINIA

UPI

A retaining wall collapses on Interstate-64, causing Charleston traffic problems.

Sagging under one of the country's highest unemployment rates in key industries, West Virginia's voters turned out in near-record numbers for the 1982 election, chose an all-Democratic Congressional delegation, and all but eliminated Republicans from the state senate.

Election. U.S. Senate minority leader Robert Byrd (D) led the ticket with a crushing win over Procter & Gamble heir Cleve Benedict, the Republican challenger, who had given up his one-term House of Representatives seat to seek the Senate post. That seat went to Democrat Harley O. Staggers, Jr., son of the 32-year House veteran who retired in 1980. Another second-generation Congressman was chosen when Alan B. Mollohan won in the first district, replacing his father, Robert, an 18-year legislator. The state's only other Republican Congressman, first-termer Mick Staton, was beaten by Democratic newcomer Robert Wise. Nick Joe Rahall easily won reelection to Congress.

The Democrats, long in control of the state senate, won all but one seat in that body, retaining a firm grip on the lower house as well.

Referendums. For much of the year, voters debated court decisions that had originally addressed equity in school-financing formulas and that threatened drastic and immediate increases in property taxes. A brief special legislative session proposed an amendment that would equalize and control levy procedures among the counties (and delay any substantial increases for at least two years). Voters overwhelmingly approved the measure on November 2. A related amendment, which would allow excess and special levies to pass with only majority approval, also was adopted. A third, which would have removed all limits on terms a sheriff might serve consecutively, was defeated.

The Economy. Unemployment statewide climbed from 9% in August of 1981 to 13.6% one year later, a level close to the nation's highest. In the southern coal fields unemployment soared to almost 25%, as the bituminous industry hit a decade low. Employed miners numbered only 48,-000 in the fall, down 12,700 from the same period in 1981. By mid-November, company, union, and government representatives were discussing ways of pumping new life into the state's major producer. They were also reexamining federal and state mining regulations, as well as contracts with East Coast ports and railways.

West Virginia's number-one individual employer, National Steel's plant in Weirton, was marked for closing by the parent company. Employees explored various ways to purchase and operate the huge installation, including government-backed bond issues as a method of raising the money for the acquisition.

Legislative Session. The state legislature smarted under charges that it had conducted a "do nothing" session. Both parties blamed the lack of constructive legislation on the same thing—"no money." The same reason had been used by Gov. John D. (Jay) Rockefeller IV in January when he announced a 10% cutback in expenditures by state agencies (as he had done in 1981) and the discharge of 1,500 workers. Another 5% cut was mandated in November.

Ignoring the governor's recommendations, the lawmakers turned down pay raises for state employees and teachers. They further expanded their own powers—at the executive branch's expense—over regulations issued by state agencies and over the distribution of federal revenue-sharing funds. They finally approved (after two decades of debate) a limited branch-banking law.

DONOVAN H. BOND, *West Virginia University*

WEST VIRGINIA • Information Highlights

Area: 24,231 sq mi (62 758 km^2).
Population (1980 census): 1,950,279.
Chief Cities (1980 census): Charleston, the capital, 63,968; Huntington, 63,684; Wheeling, 43,070.
Government (1982): *Chief Officers*—governor, John D. Rockefeller IV (D); secy. of state, A. James Manchin (D). *Legislature*—Senate, 34 members; House of Delegates, 100 members.
State Finances (fiscal year 1981): *Revenues,* $2,931,-000,000; *expenditures,* $2,863,000,000.
Personal Income (1981): $16,352,000,000; per capita, $8,377.
Labor Force (Aug. 1982): *Nonagricultural wage and salary earners,* 603,400; *unemployed,* 107,600 (13.6% of total force).
Education *Enrollment:* (fall 1981)—public elementary schools, 266,944; public secondary, 110,828; colleges and universities (1981–82), 82,375. *Public school expenditures* (1980–81), $739,829,000 ($1,816 per pupil).

WISCONSIN

Courtesy, The Grand Avenue

The restored Plankinton Arcade (ca. 1916) is part of The Grand Avenue shopping center that opened in Milwaukee.

A budget crisis, legislative squabbles over redistricting, and the election of a new governor highlighted the year in Wisconsin.

State Finances. Wisconsin's economy had been doing better than much of the nation, but the effects of the recession became increasingly evident in 1982. Faced with a projected deficit of $149 million by mid-1983, Gov. Lee S. Dreyfus, a Republican, went to the people in February and asked them to support an increase in the sales tax from 4% to 5%, along with corporate and cigarette tax increases.

In an election year, the Democratic legislature was at first cool to the idea, but reluctantly accepted it. The solution was only temporary, however, for there were forecasts later in the year that the state would have a deficit of some $100 million in mid-1983.

Just as the legislature was approving his budget repair bill, Dreyfus announced on April 23 that he would not seek a second term. The 55-year-old governor, always an independent, later accepted an executive position with an insurance company.

Elections. Governor Dreyfus' announcement surprised both Democrats and Republicans, for it was widely believed that he would seek, and win, a second term. The Democrats already were organized for the campaign, but the Republicans had to scramble for a likely candidate.

In the September 14 primary, Democrat Anthony S. Earl, a former head of the Depart-

ment of Natural Resources, defeated two opponents, one of them former Acting Governor Martin Schreiber. The GOP winner was Terry Kohler, a businessman whose father and grandfather were Wisconsin governors.

The state economy became the main issue in the campaign, with Kohler declaring that the state needed business experience to deal with its problems. But Earl, who had argued that a tax increase might be necessary, achieved a 57% to 42% victory, one of the biggest margins in modern times.

Other elections resulted in few major changes. The congressional delegation remained at five Democrats and four Republicans, with Democrat Jim Moody of Milwaukee replacing retiring Henry Reuss (D). Both houses of the legislature remained in Democratic control, but the election was a painful one for many incumbents because of redistricting. Legislators had squabbled for months trying to preserve their districts but finally left the effort to a federal court in Milwaukee. The court announced its plan three weeks before the deadline for filing for office.

Downtown Milwaukee. For years, downtown Milwaukee had been injured by the flight of businesses to outlying shopping centers and by a widespread reputation for being both dull and dangerous. That changed in late August with the opening of The Grand Avenue, a $70 million shopping center stretching the length of four blocks and containing 143 stores. The center, developed by the Rouse Company of Columbia, MD, preserved many of the historic buildings.

Economy. The unadjusted unemployment rate for the year was more than 10%, the highest since World War II. In a state where the capital goods industry is significant, the weak demand for new machinery was worrisome, and recovery was expected to lag in that area for one or two quarters. Farm income was expected to be down significantly from 1981 because of unchanged dairy support prices, sluggish export grain demand, and higher production expenses.

PAUL SALSINI, *"The Milwaukee Journal"*

WISCONSIN • Information Highlights

Area: 56,153 sq mi (145 436 km^2).
Population (1980 census): 4,705,521.
Chief Cities (1980 census): Madison, the capital, 170,616; Milwaukee, 636,236; Green Bay, 87,899.
Government (1982): *Chief Officers*—governor, Lee S. Dreyfus (R); lt. gov., Russell A. Olson (R). *Legislature*—Senate, 33 members; Assembly, 99 members.
State Finances (fiscal year 1981): *Revenues,* $7,201,000,000; *expenditures,* $6,838,000,000.
Personal Income (1981): $47,579,000,000; per capita, $10,035.
Labor Force (Aug. 1982): *Nonagricultural wage and salary earners,* 1,872,400; *unemployment,* 256,900 (10.4% of total force).
Education: *Enrollment* (fall 1981)—public elementary schools, 512,831; public secondary, 291,431; colleges and universities (1981–82), 275,325. *Public school expenditures* (1980–81), $2,167,011,000 ($2,769 per pupil).

WOMEN

The decade-long struggle to add the Equal Rights Amendment (ERA) to the U.S. Constitution ended in defeat on June 30, 1982. When the midnight deadline passed, the amendment was still three states short of the 38 needed for ratification.

ERA. Although ERA supporters never gave up hope, the amendment had been in trouble for years. The last state to ratify it was Indiana, which did so in January 1977. Meanwhile, five states—Idaho, Kentucky, Nebraska, South Dakota, and Tennessee—voted to rescind or nullify earlier ratifications. Fifteen states, most of them in the South, never ratified it.

The amendment's supporters won an important victory in 1978 when they convinced Congress to extend the ratification deadline from March 22, 1979, to June of 1982. But the extension failed to revive the stalled equal rights drive.

ERA was defeated despite widespread support. Public opinion surveys consistently indicated that a majority of Americans favored the amendment. A Gallup Poll released the day the ratification drive expired reported that 56% of those who knew about the ERA supported it, while 34% opposed it. A CBS poll released the same day found 52% in favor and 35% opposed.

Given this level of public support, why did the amendment fail? ERA supporters say the chief obstacle was the large sums of money poured into the anti-ERA campaign by conservative political groups and fundamentalist churches. According to Eleanor Smeal, the retiring president of the National Organization for Women (NOW), another hindrance was "the special corporate interests that profit from sex discrimination." ERA proponents also admit that they underestimated both the difficulty of their task and the effectiveness of the opposition. Convinced of the righteousness of their cause, they at first neglected the grassroots lobbying needed to get the amendment approved by enough state legislatures.

According to Phyllis Schlafly, leader of the anti-ERA forces, the amendment was defeated because its supporters "never could show any benefit, any advantage to women in ERA." While most feminists dismiss that argument as ridiculous, they do concede that Schlafly's attempts to link ERA with abortion, homosexual rights, and other controversial issues put them on the defensive. (*See* BIOGRAPHY—.)

On July 14, ERA was reintroduced in both houses of Congress, but women's rights advocates indicated that their top priority for the next few years was to elect more women to Congress and the state legislatures.

Election News. Even before the ERA ratification drive ended, political analysts were talking about the importance of the "gender gap"—indications in public opinion polls of a political parting-of-the-ways between men and women. As the results of the 1982 elections made clear, the gender gap was no statistical fluke. In statewide races across the United States, women showed a marked preference for Democratic

Women office-seekers had mixed results. Millicent Fenwick (right) ran strong but lost her New Jersey Senate bid.

UPI

Judy Goldsmith, above, 43-year-old former professor of English, was elected president of NOW. Bertha Wilson, 58-year-old member of Ontario's Court of Appeals, is the first woman to serve on Canada's Supreme Court.

candidates, while men favored Republicans. According to NOW, female voters provided the margin of victory in the gubernatorial races in Michigan, Texas, and New York. Women also were an important source of support for nuclear-freeze proposals, which won in eight of the nine states where they were on the ballot.

The gender gap did not always translate into victories for women candidates. Of the 55 women running for the U.S. House of Representatives, only 21 were elected, including 16 incumbents. The five newcomers were Democrats Barbara Boxer of California, Marcy Kaptur of Ohio, and Katie Hall of Indiana and Republicans Nancy Johnson of Connecticut and Barbara Vucanovich of Nevada.

Not returning to the House were Republicans Margaret Heckler of Massachusetts, who lost to Barney Frank, and Millicent Fenwick of New Jersey, who lost her Senate bid against Frank R. Lautenberg. Also not returning was Democrat Shirley Chisholm of New York, who retired.

Women made no gains in the U.S. Senate and only modest gains at the state level, where they increased their presence in state legislatures from 12 to 14%. Both women candidates for governor—Vermont Lt. Gov. Madeleine M. Kunin and Roxanne Conlin of Iowa—were defeated.

The NOW Election. One of the hardest fought campaigns of 1982 was for the presidency of the National Organization for Women. At their October convention in Indianapolis, NOW members chose Judith B. Goldsmith to succeed Eleanor Smeal. Goldsmith's chief opponent was Sonia Johnson, who gained national attention when she was excommunicated from the Morman Church in 1979 for her activities on behalf of ERA. Johnson was one of seven women who participated in a 37-day fast earlier in the year in an unsuccessful attempt to get ERA passed by the Illinois legislature.

International News. Nearly two decades after they sent the first woman in space (Valentina Tereshkova in 1963), the Soviet Union launched a second female cosmonaut, Svetlana Savitskaya. She and two crewmates, launched on August 19 aboard a Soyuz spacecraft, spent eight days in space. (*See* SPACE EXPLORATION.)

On March 4, Bertha Wilson became the first woman appointed to the Canadian Supreme Court. Wilson had been a member of the Ontario Court of Appeals since 1975. The Yugoslav Parliament on May 16 elected Milka Planinc premier. She is the first woman to head that government. Voters in the Bahamas on June 10 elected their first woman representative to parliament, Janet J. Bostwick.

The Venezuelan congress voted in July to modify a 40-year-old civil code that included such provisions as "A woman must follow her husband wherever he decides to live" and "A husband shall make all decisions related to married life."

SANDRA STENCEL, *"Editorial Research Reports"*

Trends in Childbearing

Babies were news in 1982. Although the birthrate rose only slightly, the public's interest was caught by the growing number of women who choose to postpone childbearing until they are in their 30s. At the other end of the age spectrum, the number of teenage pregnancies continued to be of concern.

Perhaps the public's current fascination with birth trends derives from the large number of women of childbearing age. In 1980, there were 29.3 million women between ages 20 and 34, the traditional childbearing years. These women are part of the first full generation to sample birth-control techniques, such as pills and intrauterine devices (IUDs), and abortion, all of which no doubt have encouraged pregnancy delay.

Many social, psychological, and economic benefits add to the allure of postponed childbearing as well. Most women now use the time before giving birth to a first child to establish a career. "Postponers" have the opportunity to gain job-related skills at the same time in life as male competitors. Because women who delay pregnancy have had a chance for self development, they are thought to be better prepared psychologically for motherhood. Women who postpone childbearing, particularly for a career, often have accrued financial resources that translate into good medical care and, later, educational opportunities for the child.

However, some women who delay childbearing may discover an inability to become pregnant. A French study published in 1982 found that a woman's fertility drops more sharply after age 30 than previously thought. The fertility experts in France found that, over a year's time, 73% of women under 25 and 74% of women ages 26–30 were able to conceive. After 30, the conception rate dropped dramatically to 61% for women ages 31–35 and 54% for women over 35. In the light of these findings some social scientists and demographers speculated that women should delay career pursuits and make childbearing a priority during their 20s. This interpretation was challenged by fertility experts in the United States.

Despite the increased risk of infertility, many women do wait until the "biological clock" strikes 30 to begin childbearing, and most are able to conceive. In 1972 only 58,000 women waited until past age 30 to start a family. More than 100,000 such women gave birth in 1982.

Conception is not the most severe challenge to childbearing for women over 35. The chances that a woman over 35 will bear a child with a birth defect are much greater than those faced by women in their 20s. The most common age-related defect is Down's syndrome, or mongolism. Women of ages 25–29 have a one-in-1,200 chance of bearing a child with Down's syndrome. By the time a woman is in the 35–39 age group, the chance of the defect appearing is one in 290, accelerating to one in 46 for women of 45–49. Many other chromosomal and some biological defects are associated with advanced maternal age.

Because of the increased risk of birth defects, pregnant women over 35 now routinely undergo amniocentesis. This is a method of analyzing the amniotic fluid in which the fetus floats. The analysis can uncover major chromosomal defects, including Down's syndrome, and some biochemical defects (also detectable by a newly developed maternal blood test). While scientists can pinpoint subtle chromosomal defects, they cannot always predict whether a slight aberration will result in any measurable retardation. Screening techniques still in the experimental stage include inserting a periscope into the uterus to view the fetus and sampling fetal blood from the placenta or from the fetus itself.

Pregnant teenagers face almost as many physical problems as pregnant women over age 35, but for different reasons. Teenagers are less likely to seek medical help early in pregnancy and to take steps to ensure maternal and fetal health. They are also more likely to use drugs that will endanger themselves and their unborn children. This carelessness results in high rates of toxemia and anemia. And the costs of teenage pregnancy are not only physical. Teenage mothers often are forced to forgo much needed schooling, and many enter into hasty and generally unsuccessful marriages.

Although the number of births to teenagers has declined in recent years, it still remains astronomically high: 560,000 in 1979, the last year for which age-specific birthrates are available. Teenagers account for one in every five births in the United States, and one in two in many cities. The number of terminated pregnancies almost doubles the number of pregnant teenagers. It is estimated that 449,000 teenagers had abortions in 1979. Experts predict that if current trends prevail, four out of every 10 girls now age 14 will have at least one pregnancy before age 20.

Many concerned adults blame the number of teenage pregnancies on a breakdown in family values.

JULIA McCUE

WYOMING

A downturn in the state's economic activity, the legislative session, the November general elections, and the MX missile made news in Wyoming in 1982.

The Economy. The nationwide recession had a marked impact on Wyoming's energy-related mineral industries. Reduced demand for electric power softened the market for the state's coal and uranium. During 1982 about 107 million tons of coal came from Wyoming mines, a 5% increase over 1981 but some five million tons less than earlier projections. A continuing weak market for uranium brought the state's production of this mineral to about half that of 1981. Oil and gas drilling activity reached a four-year low in the summer of 1982; the active rig count was 112, while a year earlier the figure was 201. Refineries in Casper and Cody closed with lay-offs of some 300 workers. Long-term prospects for Wyoming's coal, oil, and gas remained favorable, however. The Hampshire Energy Synfuels Plant, a $2,000,000,000 project located near Gillette and scheduled for completion in 1987, received necessary water permits from the state and continued in the planning stage.

Wyoming's unemployment rate was slightly over 5% in 1982, marginally higher than in 1981 but well below the national average. The state's labor force grew at an annual rate of 4%, twice the national figure yet well below the 9% rate experienced by Wyoming in the late 1970s.

Legislation. The 20-day budget session of Wyoming's 46th legislature convened in February with Republican majorities in both the House and Senate. Beyond the mandatory money appropriations, the lawmakers adopted Gov. Ed Herschler's comprehensive water development package and allocated $114 million for its implementation.

Politics. The November elections reflected the traditional edge held by Republicans over Democrats in Wyoming and the propensity of state voters to cross party lines freely. Republicans are favored over Democrats in voter registration by a ratio of 51 to 37, and 12% are registered as independents. Governor Herschler (D) demonstrated his continued popularity with voters in both parties as he won an unprecedented third term. He carried 63% of the vote in defeating Warren Morton, a Casper businessman and former Republican speaker of the state House. Sen. Malcolm Wallop (R) and Rep. Dick Cheney (R) won reelection to the U.S. Congress by wide margins. (The state has but one representative in the U.S. House.)

In other statewide races, Secretary of State Thyra Thompson (R) won reelection over Leslie Petersen (D); State Auditor Jim Griffith (R) defeated Sid Kornegay (D); Superintendent of Public Instruction Lynn Simons (D) won over Gary Elliott (R); and Republicans retained the state treasurer's office with Stan Smith's victory over C. R. Engstrom (D). In the legislature, Democrats picked up four seats in the newly reapportioned House, though Republicans retained control with a 38–25 edge. In the Senate a 19–11 margin for the Republicans remained unchanged.

MX Missile. President Reagan's plan for basing the controversial MX system in a 20 sq mi (52 km^2) "dense pack" near Cheyenne got a mixed reaction from state residents. Opponents questioned its feasibility and environmental impact.

H. R. DIETERICH, *University of Wyoming*

A Casper refinery closed its doors after 59 years with a message to employees. Recession hurt Wyoming.

Bob Kennedy/Star Tribune

TEXACO

THANK YOU
FOR A JOB
WELL DONE

WYOMING • Information Highlights

Area: 97,809 sq mi (253 325 km^2).
Population (1980 census): 469,557.
Chief Cities (1980 census): Cheyenne, the capital, 47,-283: Casper, 51,016; Laramie, 24,410.
Government (1982): *Chief Officers*—governor, Ed Herschler (D). *Legislature*—Senate, 30 members; House of Representatives, 62 members.
State Finances (fiscal year 1981): *Revenues*, $1,158,-000,000; *expenditures*, $968,000,000.
Personal Income (1981): $5,738,000,000; per capita, $11,665.
Labor Force (Aug. 1982): *Nonagricultural wage and salary earners*, 213,900; *unemployed*, 14,900 (5.8% of total force).
Education: *Enrollment* (fall 1981)—public elementary schools, 71,842; public secondary, 27,699; colleges and universities (1981–82), 21,235. *Public school expenditures* (1980–81), $335,249,000 ($2,596 per pupil).

YUGOSLAVIA

Christian Vioujard/Gamma-Liaison

Milka Planinc, Yugoslavia's first woman head of government, led a 28-member cabinet.

In a resounding speech on September 13, Mitja Ribičič, temporary head of the League of Communists of Yugoslavia (LCY), forewarned of a generalized "crisis of confidence in our system." The London *Economist* wrote of Yugoslavia's "worst economic crisis since 1945." And to many observers, internal LCY conflicts were the most severe since the 1971 purge. Still, Tito's collective heirs at both the state and LCY levels maintained formal cohesion through 1982.

Domestic Affairs. On May 16 the Yugoslav parliament elected Milka Planinc, 57, as president of the Federal Executive Council (prime minister). A Croatian and protegée of Tito, Planinc formed a 28-member government evenly divided between those without portfolios and those with. Most prominent among the latter were Stane Dolanc (internal affairs), Lazar Mojsov (foreign affairs), and Adm. Branko Mamula (national defense).

From the outset the Planinc cabinet faced problems caused by localist and autarkic tendencies in the federal republics and autonomous provinces, the malfunctioning of the parliamentary system of indirectly elected delegates, and the failure of the workers' self-management system to live up to original expectations.

The 12th Congress of the LCY was held in Belgrade, June 26–29. It formally pledged to follow Tito's policies and approved the government's long-term program of economic stabilization. However, sharp discussions and unprecedented proposals to change the very nature of the LCY, while rejected, pointed up the post-Tito party crisis.

The problem of ethnic exclusivism among Albanians in the autonomous province of Kosovo, which exploded in the spring of 1981, became more intractable in 1982. Initial demands for the status of a separate republic or incorporation into a "Greater Albania" escalated into aspirations for a "pure" Albanian Kosovo, cleansed of all Slavs. Physical violence and economic pressure were applied, particularly against the Serbian minority. More than 20,000 Serbs fled Kosovo during 1982, and media coverage of the forced exile caused a strong emotional reaction, especially in Belgrade. State and LCY leaders, particularly non-Serbs, disagreed on the causes of the Kosovo insurgency and ways to deal with it. Units of the Yugoslav army and militia maintained a highly visible presence in Kosovo, while state security organs arrested ringleaders whom the courts sentenced to harsh jail terms. Political purges also took place, but many local, state, and LCY officials were hesitant to repress their radical compatriots. Disagreements and vacillation at the top of civil, state, and LCY authorities caused irritation among Army generals within the LCY.

Factionalism in the LCY was conducive to acerbic polemics in the press on practically every aspect of Yugoslav society. The year 1982 was one of publicly aired discontent—"an explosion in radical thinking"—but genuine democratization did not ensue. Repression continued under different forms. LCY leaders assailed the non-conformist press and denounced any opposition. Student demonstrators in favor of Polish Solidarity were dispersed and some arrested. Noted professors were also arrested and briefly detained. Heavy sentencing was reserved for those committing "hostile" acts against the state.

YUGOSLAVIA · Information Highlights

Official Name: Socialist Federal Republic of Yugoslavia.

Location: Southwestern Europe.

Area: 98,766 sq mi (255 804 km²).

Population (1981 census): 22,352,000.

Chief Cities (1981 census): Belgrade, the capital, 1,209,360 (1971); Zagreb, 763,426; Skopje, 503,449.

Government: *Head of state,* collective state presidency, Petar Stambolić, president (took office May 1982). *Head of government,* Milka Planinc, prime minister (took office May 1982). *Legislature*—Federal Assembly: Federal Chamber and Chamber of Republics and Provinces.

Monetary Unit: Dinar (63.41 dinars equal U.S.$1, October 1982).

Gross National Product (1980 U.S.$): $69,867,000,-000.

Economic Indexes (1981): *Consumer Prices* (1970=100), *all items,* 789.4; *food,* 853.3. *Industrial production* (1975=100), 144.

Foreign Trade (1981 U.S.$): *Imports,* $15,757,000,-000; *exports,* $10,929,000,000.

Perhaps the most significant domestic development was the accelerated process of Tito's eclipse, leading to the muted but clearly perceptible phenomenon of de-Titoization.

Economy. The dire state of the Yugoslav economy was reflected in the basic indicators, which forced the government to revise downward its entire 1981–85 plan. Inflation was more than 30%; the foreign hard-currency debt reached $20,000,000,000; some 850,000 (nearly 15%) were unemployed and about 30% of industrial workers were underemployed; industrial production rose by only 0.7% (the goal was 3.5%); strikes were numerous; and the foreign trade balance remained negative. Shortages of consumer goods were extensive and led to a widespread black market.

To counter negative trends, the government on October 17 introduced a series of stern, and unpopular, austerity measures. Drastic gasoline rationing was ordered; foreign travel was sharply curbed; and use of fuel, electricity, and other energy sources was cut back. On October 22 the dinar was devalued by 18%.

Throughout the year Yugoslav authorities sought new loans from the West and certain Arab countries. In December the U.S. government, in cooperation with West European governments and banks, was preparing a rescue package for Yugoslavia involving $1,000,000,000.

Foreign Relations. Economic and political difficulties at home reduced Yugoslavia's role in international affairs. Inability to compete in Western markets forced Yugoslavia to enter even greater cooperation with the Soviet Union; trade volume between the two countries reached $7,-000,000,000 in 1982. An official visit by Soviet Foreign Minister Andrei Gromyko in early April testified to the Soviet aim of intensifying relations across-the-board.

Anxious to counter Yugoslav-Soviet rapprochement, the U.S. State Department hailed Yugoslavia's "independence and nonalignment" and stressed the United States' "excellent and constructive relations with Yugoslavia."

Extolling the virtues of nonalignment, Yugoslav officials visited all Arab and some African and Mediterranean countries during the year.

Yugoslavia's relations with its neighbors were predictable: maximally unfriendly with Albania because of Kosovo; frosty with Bulgaria because of the perennial Macedonian question; friendly with Rumania and Hungary; and warm with the new Socialist regime in Greece. Tense Greek-Turkish relations notwithstanding, the Turkish head of state, Gen. Kenan Evren, was warmly received September 20–23.

As for Poland, Belgrade was pleased with the banning of Solidarity and hopeful that General Jaruzelski would be able to recreate an effective Communist party while remaining independent from the USSR.

MILORAD M. DRACHKOVITCH
The Hoover Institution, Stanford University

YUKON

In a territorial election in June, the Yukon Progressive Conservative Party was returned to power with a reduced majority, winning nine seats in the 16-member legislative assembly. The Yukon Liberal Party lost the two seats it previously held, while the New Democratic Party formed the official opposition with six seats. One independent member was elected.

Economy. Due to a slumping economy, the government faced a revenue shortfall of $13 million, or 10% of the projected budget. To reduce government expenditures, capital project funds were cut by 46%. The territory's 1,100 civil servants received a 10% increase in salaries, negated in August by a corresponding 10% decrease in working hours.

The territory's unemployment rate stood at 15.5% in September and was expected to continue to rise through the spring of 1983.

The tourist industry continued at record levels with an estimated 350,000 visitors during the year, generating $51 million in revenues.

However, the territory suffered a virtual collapse of the mining industry. For the first time since the Klondike gold rush of 1898, not one mine was operating in Yukon by year's end. Cyprus Anvil, Yukon's largest operating mine, closed in June due to low world metal prices for its lead-zinc ore. The United Keno Hill silver mine followed suit soon after. The Whitehorse Copper Mine announced during the summer that its ore reserves had been depleted, resulting in the closure of the mine in December, some nine months earlier than expected.

Business bankruptcies more than doubled over 1981 and included the territory's largest gold placer mine, Territorial Gold Placers Ltd., which went into receivership during the summer.

Oil and gas explorations in the Beaufort Sea provided hope for economic revitalization. Stokes Point on Yukon's north coast was being considered as the site of a deep-sea port to service Beaufort exploration activities. The Stokes Point port, if approved, would result in a $100 million capital investment in port facility construction. Native land claims and environmental concerns remained obstacles to development.

ANDREW HUME
Free-lance Writer, Yukon

YUKON · Information Highlights

Area: 207,076 sq mi (536 327 km²).
Population (1981 census): 23,153.
Chief City (1981 census): Whitehorse, the capital, 14,814.
Government (1982): *Chief Officers*—commissioner, Douglas Bell; government leader, Christopher Pearson. *Legislature*—16-member legislative assembly.
Education (1982–83): *Enrollment*—elementary and secondary schools, 4,800 pupils.
Public Finance (1982 fiscal year, est.): *Revenues*, $143,200,000; *expenditures*, $135,700,000.

ZAIRE

Zaire faced a major financial crisis as it was unable to meet the performance criteria of the International Monetary Fund (IMF) program. Opposition groups challenged the government. Parliamentary elections took place.

Domestic Affairs. The University of Kinshasa was closed as students staged protests, demanding higher grants and improved living conditions. Thirteen parliamentarians were sentenced to 15 years in prison for plotting to form a party to oppose the sole political party, the Popular Movement of the Revolution (MPR). The MPR announced in October that it would hold its third ordinary congress in December 1982.

Opposition also came from the Front de Liberation National du Congo (FLNC). It was partly responsible for the 1977 and 1978 invasions of Shaba province. Another armed group operated in the northeasterly mountainous areas. The most prominent exile critic to attack President Mobutu Sese Seko was former Prime Minister Nguza Karl-I-Bond. Only 62 people's commissioners were reelected to the new 310-seat parliament.

Economy and Mining. Zaire faced a crisis in its inability to comply with a three-year IMF program agreed to in June 1981. This agreement assumed high export receipts. The slide in world prices for cobalt and industrial diamonds, of which Zaire is the world's largest producer, as well as poor copper sales generated lower receipts. The IMF granted a loan for export losses.

Zaire's industry, already functioning below 50% of capacity, remained strapped for equipment and spare parts. To boost output, the cabinet announced the return of 38 public enterprises to private owners. Offshore oil output went up, but cash crop production in coffee, sugar, and cotton lagged.

Foreign Affairs. Zaire's poor economy necessitated the recalling of 141 members of its diplomatic corps. However, Zaire resumed diplomatic relations with Israel, becoming the first of the 22 African states that severed diplomatic relations during the 1973 Middle East war to so act. Zaire later bought Israeli military equipment.

ZAIRE • Information Highlights

Official Name: Republic of Zaire.
Location: Central equatorial Africa.
Area: 905,365 sq mi (2 344 895 km²).
Population (1982 est.): 30,300,000.
Chief City (1980 est.): Kinshasa, the capital, 3,000,-000.
Government: *Head of state and government,* Mobutu Sese Seko, president (took office 1965). *Legislature* (unicameral)—National Legislative Council.
Monetary Unit: Zaire (5.62 zaires equal U.S.$1, October 1982).
Gross National Product (1980 U.S.$): $5,710,000,-000.
Economic Index (1980): *Consumer Prices* (1970= 100), *all items,* 1,339.0; *food,* 1,313.3.
Foreign Trade (1980 U.S.$): *Imports,* $725,000,000; *exports,* $1,639,000,000.

Although the U.S. House Foreign Affairs and the Senate Foreign Relations committees voted to cut military sales credits in an attempt to move Mobutu toward reforms, relations with the United States stayed on good terms. In France the Mitterrand government unexpectedly announced an increase in military sales. Border tensions with Zambia temporarily flared up.

THOMAS H. HENRIKSEN, *Hoover Institution*

ZIMBABWE

Events in Zimbabwe in 1982 threatened to upset the delicate balance that exists between the Shona people, who comprise 80% of the population, and the minority Ndebele people. The coalition government of Prime Minister Robert Mugabe's Shona-supported Zimbabwe African National Union (ZANU) and Joshua Nkomo's Ndebele-backed Zimbabwe African People's Union (ZAPU) was shattered in February. The coalition was formed after the 1980 election as a positive move toward reconciling the major cultural, historical, and linguistic differences between the two groups.

Internal Discord. In February government troops found several large caches of arms on farms and other properties owned by Joshua Nkomo and ZAPU. Mugabe accused Nkomo of planning a coup d'etat and immediately dismissed him from the cabinet. At that point, between 1,000 and 2,000 former Zimbabwe People's Revolutionary Army (ZIPRA) guerrillas deserted the national army and went into hiding in Matabeleland, in the west of the country. Nkomo denied that he had planned a coup and maintained that he had been dismissed for political reasons.

Armed violence in the countryside increased as some of the army deserters who had gone underground in Matabeleland engaged in lootings and robberies. Nkomo denied that he had any connection with these forces.

Another sign of the increasing unrest was an armed attack in June on Mugabe's residence, Zimbabwe House. The attack was made by eight men in army combat dress, who were thought to be former ZAPU guerrillas. The attackers were repulsed by armed guards, and Mugabe was not harmed. In late July six Western tourists were kidnapped and held hostage in western Zimbabwe. Their captors, presumably former ZAPU guerrillas, threatened to kill the hostages unless the government released 200 political prisoners.

In August, Mugabe blamed Nkomo supporters for bombing 13 of Zimbabwe's warplanes at the Thornhill Air Base in Gweru. The attack resulted in the destruction of eight new Hawk fighters and one Cessna spotter plane—25% of Zimbabwe's combat force. The Zimbabwean air force was decimated by these acts of sabotage. Various rumors associated Nkomo or South Africa with the destruction.

Zimbabwe Prime Minister Robert Mugabe seeks popular support following his rift with cabinet minister Joshua Nkomo.

In the wake of the violence, the prime minister dispatched thousands of troops to Matabeleland. The large, predominantly Shona military presence caused further discontent among the Ndebele. The security forces were allowed to arrest without charges and also engaged in harsh interrogation procedures.

In July the government extended the state of emergency originally imposed by the white Rhodesian government 17 years before. The action enabled the government to detain suspected criminals indefinitely without a trial. Another definite indication of a government crackdown was the return of capital punishment; in October, the country's first executions since independence took place.

One-Party State. After independence there had been much discussion in Zimbabwe about the creation of a one-party state. In August, Mugabe confirmed that he planned to begin the process of transforming Zimbabwe's multiparty rule into a one-party state. Specifically, ZANU would campaign in the 1985 election on a one-party platform.

Cabinet Changes. In April, Prime Minister Mugabe reshuffled the cabinet in an effort to "accommodate . . . friends and allies." The appointments included three new ZAPU supporters, Dr. Callistus Ndlovu as minister of construction, John Nkomo as minister of state in the prime minister's office with special responsibility to the deputy prime minister, and Cephas Msipa as minister of water resources and development. Of the three, Ndlovu was the most controversial

and independent. In May the Central Committee of ZAPU refused to recognize these three new appointments as well as that of Jane Ngwenya to the position of deputy minister. Chris Anderson, a white Zimbabwean, was appointed minister of state in the prime minister's office with special responsibility for the public service. John Landau was appointed a deputy minister of trade and commerce.

Military. The major military crises in 1982 were the discovery of arms caches that led to Nkomo's dismissal from the cabinet and the detention of the deputy commander of the Zimbabwean army, Gen. Lookout Masuru. Masuru was formerly Nkomo's top military aide. Despite the desertion of some of Nkomo's supporters from the military, the army appeared to be holding together. One third of the army, which was left with 54,000 men, was still composed of loyal former ZAPU guerrillas. Maj.-Gen. Jevan Maseko became the senior former ZIPRA officer-guerrilla and Lt.-Gen. Rex Nhongo, formerly of ZANLA, was the army commander.

Plans were made to further reduce the size of the nation's army to 35,000, although this would depend in part on land resettlement. The 128 North Korean military advisers who were brought in to train the Fifth Brigade in 1981 left.

Economy. Several important trends were apparent in the budget speech delivered in July by Dr. B. T. Chidzero, minister of finance, economic planning, and development. Inflation for 1982 was estimated at 16%. (In 1981 it had been 14% and in 1980, 7%.) The balance-of-payments situation was under severe strain, with a deficit of $496 million. Employment opportunities would be lower than the 1981 figure of 30,000 new jobs. The budget deficit for 1982–83 would probably be $771.6 million, giving little chance for relief in the availability of credit or in foreign exchange to the private sector. The deficit was to be met by increased foreign and local borrowing by the government. Chidzero also indicated that strong efforts would be made to obtain the $615 million still pledged but unpaid from Zimbabwe Conference on Reconstruction and Development (ZIMCORD) donors.

A sum of $14 million was set aside for state participation in private enterprise. Of the total budget, 22% was allocated to education and 15.8% to defense.

Since independence, Zimbabwe has suffered from food and diesel shortages and from transportation difficulties. Some of these problems were alleviated in 1982. It remained to be seen whether radical social reform packages could coexist with outside foreign investment in Zimbabwe's mixed economy.

The severe drought in 1982 was expected to reduce the nation's agricultural output by 20%. Depressed prices for chrome, nickel, and copper were also expected because of prevailing world economic conditions. It was projected that Zimbabwe's growth rate would drop from 8% in 1981 to 3% in 1982.

Zimbabwe's exporters were less competitive because of currency depreciations in South Africa, Botswana, and Malawi. Some exporters lost their export market because of the depreciation of the South African rand.

The government refused to devalue the Zimbabwean dollar, said to be at least 30% overvalued in relation to the currencies of neighboring nations.

A $20 million deal negotiated by a U.S. food-processing firm, H. J. Heinz & Co., could stimulate foreign investment. After protracted negotiations, Heinz will own 51% and the Zimbabwe government 49% of Olivine Industries.

On March 1, Zimbabwe became the 61st member of the European Community's Lomé Trade and Aid Convention and was offered aid under this program.

The oil pipeline from Beira, Mozambique, owned by the LONRHO corporation, was again operative in 1982. This was expected to improve Zimbabwe's oil position, enabling it to avoid South African ports and tariffs.

Social Issues. In 1982 the government continued to be responsive to the needs of the black population, taking steps to improve wages for labor and social services in addition to subsidizing food. There was an overall improvement in the lives of black Zimbabweans. The minimum wage was increased by 66% on Jan. 1, 1982.

In 1982 there were 186,000 landless African families (one out of every eight) and 75,000 squatters. The land resettlement program announced in November 1981 proceeded. Under the plan, Zimbabwe would resettle 163,000 families onto formerly white-owned land (for which compensation would be paid) over a three-year period. While this move is politically expedient and socially necessary, it could cost as much as $65 million in foreign exchange farm exports.

Whites. Close to 20,000 whites left the country in 1981, leaving a white population of approximately 180,000, 2.1% of the total population of 7.5 million. Whites in their 20s and 30s have emigrated at five times the rate of those in their 50s. However, in the first quarter of 1982, the number leaving the country fell to 4,619. The government continued to be concerned about the departure of skilled white workers.

A split occurred in the Republican Front (RF) party of Ian Smith. Jonas Christian Andersen and eight other members of Parliament (MPs) left the Republican Front and became independents, thus reducing the strength of the RF from 20 to 11. One white MP, Wally Stuttaford, was detained for 10 months. He was accused of plotting against the government. In December, Ian Smith, who criticized the government during a U.S. visit, had his passport confiscated.

South Africa. In an effort to keep Zimbabwe from being used as a base of operations by black opponents to the South African regime, and also as a general policy to limit the development and strength of Zimbabwe, South Africa took actions that hurt Zimbabwe's economy. In August three white soldiers, former Rhodesians who joined South African forces, were killed in a clash with Zimbabwean forces 18 mi (29 km) inside the Zimbabwean border. Mugabe saw this as "... part of a South African plan to destabilize Zimbabwe." Through propaganda and diplomatic channels, Zimbabwe also pursued a policy of symbolic hostility against South Africa. Nonetheless, in 1982 a preferential trade agreement that had existed for 17 years between the two countries was renewed. South Africa continued to be Zimbabwe's main trading partner.

PATRICK O'MEARA, *Indiana University*

ZIMBABWE · Information Highlights

Official Name: Zimbabwe.
Location: Southern Africa.
Area: 150,673 sq mi (390 243 km²).
Population (1982 est.): 7,500,000.
Chief cities (1979 est.): Harare (formerly Salisbury), the capital, 650,000; Bulawayo, 350,000.
Government: *Head of state,* Canaan Banana, president (took office April 1980). *Head of government,* Robert Mugabe, prime minister (took office March 1980). *Legislature*—Parliament: Senate and House of Assembly.
Monetary Unit: Zimbabwe dollar (0.723 Z. dollar equals U.S.$1, July 1981).
Gross Domestic Product (1980 U.S.$): $5,080,000,000.
Economic Indexes (1981): *Consumer Prices* (1970= 100), *all items,* 233.5; *food,* 221.4. *Industrial production* (1975=100), 113.
Foreign Trade (1980 U.S.$): *Imports,* $1,322,000,000; *exports,* $1,423,000,000.

ZOOLOGY

Photos UPI

Newborns: Snow Cap, top left, the Bronx Zoo's newest polar bear, made his debut in April. A Malayan tapir, top right, was born at the St. Louis Zoo. And Baby Geraldine, a gerenuk, was born in Tampa's Busch Gardens.

Items about zoology in the popular press during 1982 most often concerned endangered species and the breeding of various rare species. In the technical books and journals, a wide variety of noteworthy reports were published. The year was recognized as the Charles Darwin centennial, since it marked the 100th anniversary of his death; many books and review articles concerning Darwin's influence on modern concepts of evolution were produced. As a result of recent findings, new emphases have been made in zoological studies. For example, the study of behavior in animals has changed markedly with the recognition that animals systematically attempt to lie to each other.

Evolution. The finches of the Galapagos Islands were singled out by Charles Darwin as demonstrating evolution by natural selection. Though "Darwin's finches" have been studied many times and provide a textbook example of the results of evolution, few studies anywhere have demonstrated the actual process. In 1982, Peter T. Boag and Peter R. Grant of McGill University in Montreal documented the process. On Daphne Major Island in the Galapagos, a major drought resulted in limited growth of plants that provided food for the Medium Ground Finch. Survivorship through the drought period was not random. Males and females with large beaks managed to survive by feeding on large, hard-shelled plant seeds not usually eaten by this species. Smaller birds with lighter bills could not crack the shells, and few survived.

R. M. Robertson of the University of Alberta and associates presented evidence from the structure of the nervous system that insect wings probably evolved from modified movable, articulated appendages and not from rigid structures as proposed by others. One set of theories holds that the rigid ancestral lateral structures were used in temperature regulation, parachuting, and even sexual displays. The jointed appendage theories variously propose that the ancestral flaps which evolved into wings were used as spiracle covers, gill covers, or fins.

Behavior. Relatively few zoologists have ever engaged in the study of spiders. A new book, edited by Peter N. Witt and Jerome S. Rovner, reviews the results of various studies on how spiders communicate. Although more than 30,000 different kinds of spiders have been recognized, the few in which communication has been studied demonstrate specialization in the means of communicating. Some use vibratory signals that are transmitted through webs; others use sounds, produced in different ways; several species use various chemical communications; and many others, especially the jumping spiders, use visual communication.

Swarming of social bees and wasps as a means of population dispersal and establishment of new colonies is well known. Recently, however, Yeal D. Lubin and Michael H. Robinson reported from the Smithsonian Tropical Research Institute in Panama that some kinds of tropical spiders also exhibit swarming behavior. In studies conducted in Papua New Guinea, adult spiders built communal webs for the capture of insects. Colonies of different sizes were examined, with swarming occurring only in those with more than 100 spiders. Dispersing individuals were mostly fertilized females which moved along a communal web "highway" and laid eggs one to two weeks after swarming.

Physiology. Professor Robert M. Silverstein of the State University of New York at Syracuse assessed the case against pesticide insect control and reviewed the scattered reports of the isolation of insect pheromones (biochemicals, produced by the insects themselves, which modify such behaviors as sexual attraction, aggregation, and trail following). Silverstein concluded that chemical pesticides will continue to be used in the future but that the application of pheromones in controlling insect populations is still in the experimental stage.

Old age and senility are physiological states that are rarely found in wild animals but well known in captive animals. The occurrence of mental degeneration was observed in a 47-year-old male monkey (*Cebus capucinus*), believed to be the oldest documented monkey alive. Though long-term memory had deteriorated, the monkey could remember recent events, a condition often prominent in old humans.

Paleontology. As evidenced by fragmentary skull remains, ancestors of modern artiodactyls (cows, deer, and relatives), lived during the Eocene (some 50 million years ago). Zoologists have commonly assumed that these animals were short-limbed. However, Kenneth D. Rose of Johns Hopkins University reported the discovery in Wyoming of an almost complete skeleton which shows many specializations that had been presumed to be modern. This extinct mammal was about the size of a rabbit and highly specialized for feeding on plant materials, as evidenced by the relatively long leg structure.

Ulrich Lehmann wrote an insightful new book on the subject of fossil ammonites. These extinct mollusks, related to the chambered nautilus, disappeared some 100 million years ago.

Natural Rabbit Repellants. John P. Bryant of the University of Alaska found that during population explosions in snowshoe rabbits (about every 10 years), various trees and shrubs suffer from overbrowsing. At such times, such food plants as the Alaska paper birch and quaking aspens produce special growths that contain heavy concentrations of terpene and phenolic resins that actually repel the rabbits.

Endangered Species. The number of bald eagles in the United States appeared to be increasing in 1982. In May, Daniel Jones of the Department of the Interior reported that the number had increased greatly since 1960, when the species was classified as almost extinct. Now there are about 5,000 living in the country. During the winter, when many move southward from Canada, the population reaches almost 14,000.

The marine green turtle, however, is in danger of extinction. Stephen J. Morreale of the State University of New York at Buffalo and associates reported that some of the efforts to increase populations by incubating eggs in artificial hatcheries are probably not working. They found that the temperature of the eggs during development determines the sex of the hatchlings; low temperatures produce almost no females, while warm nests produce almost 95% females. If the hatchery produces mainly individuals of one sex, restocking efforts are seriously hindered.

See also ENVIRONMENT.

E. LENDELL COCKRUM
University of Arizona

Statistical and Tabular Data

Table of Contents

NATIONS OF THE WORLD*

A Profile and Synopsis of Major 1982 Developments

Nation, Region	Population in millions[1]	Capital	Area Sq mi (km[2])	Head of State/Government[2]
Antigua and Barbuda, Caribbean	0.1	St. John's	170 (440)	Sir Wilfred E. Jacobs, *governor general* Vere C. Bird, *prime minister*

Gross National Product (GNP) Per Capita (1980 U.S.$): $1,270. Foreign Trade (1980): Imports, $76 million; exports, $21 million.

Bahamas, Caribbean	0.2	Nassau	5,382 (13 939)	Sir Gerald C. Cash, *governor general* Lynden O. Pindling, *prime minister*

Incumbent Prime Minister Lynden Pindling was reelected to another five-year term in June. Charges against Pindling of bribery and influence peddling had been dropped in April. GNP Per Capita (1980 U.S.$): $3,300. Foreign Trade (1980): Imports, $5,481,000,000; exports, $4,834,000,000.

Bahrain, W. Asia	0.4	Manama	258 (668)	Isa ibn Salman, *emir* Khalifa ibn Salman, *prime minister*

The worldwide oil glut forced Bahrain to postpone several development projects scheduled for 1982. In May, 73 Shiite Muslims were convicted of sabotage in connection with an Iranian-backed coup attempt in December 1981. Bahrain took part in two meetings of six Persian Gulf states (Bahrain, Kuwait, Oman, Qatar, Saudi Arabia, and the United Arab Emirates) in 1982. One resulted in a mutual defense agreement and the other established a joint investment corporation. GNP (1980 U.S.$): $2,210,000,000. Foreign Trade (1980): Imports, $3,484,000,000; exports, $3,602,000,000.

Barbados, Caribbean	0.3	Bridgetown	166 (430)	Sir Deighton Ward, *governor general* John M. G. Adams, *prime minister*

In Barbados in April, U.S. President Ronald Reagan met with the leaders of Antigua and Barbuda, Barbados, Dominica, Saint Kitts-Nevis, and Saint Vincent and the Grenadines. GNP Per Capita (1980 U.S.$): $3,040. Foreign Trade (1981): Imports, $571 million; exports $194 million.

Benin, W. Africa	3.7	Porto Novo	43,484 (112 624)	Mathieu Kérékou, *president*

A reshuffling of the cabinet in April resulted in the first civilian majority government since the coup d'etat of 1972. The ministers of foreign affairs and rural development were replaced as being too pro-Soviet, and the provincial administrations were reorganized. Benin was given a $14 million, 50-year grant by the International Development Association for improvement of its educational system, including construction of three teacher-training colleges. On February 17, Pope John Paul II visited Benin briefly and heard President Kérékou speak against "foreign domination in Africa." GNP (1980 U.S.$): $1,140,000,000. Foreign Trade (1980): Imports, $410 million; exports, $170 million.

Nation, Region	Population in millions[1]	Capital	Area Sq mi (km^2)	Head of State/Government[2]
Bhutan, S. Asia	1.4	Thimphu	18,000 (46 620)	Jigme Singye Wangchuk, *king*

GNP *(fiscal year 1981 U.S.$): $116 million. Foreign Trade (fiscal year 1981): Imports, $19 million; exports, $12 million.*

Botswana, S. Africa	0.9	Gaborone	224,711 (582 000)	Quett Masire, *president*

A depressed diamond market, together with reduced copper and nickel production, caused an increasing deficit in the balance of payments. A third diamond mine, owned jointly by Botswana and the De Beers company, was opened at Jwaneng. In April, the currency was devalued by 10.3% against the U.S. dollar, interest rates were increased, government spending was curtailed, and wages were frozen. The worst drought in years caused Botswana to appeal for food aid from abroad. In foreign affairs, Botswana officials charged South Africa with violating its air space and kidnapping some of Botswana's people. In turn, the South African press accused Botswana of becoming increasingly pro-Soviet and permitting African National Congress insurgents (the South African black liberation movement) to launch attacks on South Africa from Botswana. GNP Per Capita (1980 U.S.$): $910. Foreign Trade (1980): Imports, $643.9 million; exports, $478.4 million.

Burundi, E. Africa	4.4	Bujumbura	10,747 (27 835)	Jean-Baptiste Bagaza, *president*

In April, as a result of Zambian President Kaunda's visit to Burundi, a Burundi-Zambia cooperation commission was established; trade, air service, and cultural cooperation agreements were signed; and it was agreed that new transportation facilities on Lake Tanganyika and at the port of Mpulungu in Zambia would be built. On October 22, legislative elections for the 65-member National Assembly were held under the new constitution approved by referendum in November 1981. GNP (1980 U.S.$): $889 million. Foreign Trade (1980): Imports, $168 million; exports, $65 million.

Cameroon, Cen. Africa	8.9	Yaoundé	183,569 (475 444)	Paul Biya, *president*

President Ahidjo made three notable state visits in 1982: to Nigeria in January, to seek agreements on economic and administrative cooperation; to Britain in April, to promote trade and British investment in Cameroon; and to the United States in July, to seek increased U.S. aid and investment. During the year, refugees from the civil war in Chad found sanctuary in Cameroon, including President Goukhouni, who was driven from Chad by the forces of rebel leader Hissene Habré. On November 6, Ahidjo retired from the presidency and was succeeded by the prime minister, Paul Biya. GNP (1980 U.S. $): $5,500,000,000. Foreign Trade (1980): Imports, $1,602,000,000; exports, $1,384,000,000.

Cape Verde, W. Africa	0.3	Praia	1,557 (4 033)	Aristides Maria Pereira, *president* Pedro Pires, *prime minister*

In March, 18 persons accused of plotting to sabotage the government's land-reform program for 1982–85 were sentenced to prison terms. The presidents of Cape Verde and Guinea-Bissau, meeting in Mozambique in June, agreed to restore diplomatic relations between their countries, broken after the coup d'etat of November 1980 in Guinea-Bissau. A meeting of their ministers in July set up machinery for economic cooperation and improvement of communications. In September the heads of the five former Portuguese colonies in Africa, meeting in Cape Verde, announced plans to bolster the defenses of Mozambique and Angola, accused South Africa of "waging war" against the two countries, and declared their support of the United Nations proposal for independence for Namibia. GNP Per Capita (1980 U.S.$): $300.

Central African Republic Cen. Africa	2.4	Bangui	240,535 (622 986)	André Kolingba, *president of the military committee*

On January 3, 12 officials of the Movement for the Liberation of the Central African People (MLPC) were arrested on command of the head of state, Gen. André Kolingba. Late in March, following an attempted coup led by opposition leader Ange Patasse of the MLPC, General Kolingba purged his government of MLPC members. Gen. François Bozize, a principal in the attempted coup, was forced to flee the country. Patasse was arrested and offered exile, and in April he sought refuge in Lomé, Togo. On May 15, five men were sentenced to death for plotting to blow up the French military base in Bouar in July 1981. On September 1, General Kolingba announced a gradual return to civilian rule within three years. GNP (1980 U.S.$): $550 million.

Comoros, E. Africa	0.4	Moroni	838 (2 170)	Ahmed Abdallah, *president* Ali Mroudjae, *prime minister*

President Abdallah, visiting Libya, signed an agreement on January 13 for economic, cultural, and scientific cooperation between Libya and the Comoros. On January 25 he dissolved the government and the National Assembly, indicating his intention to give the next government a "new direction." In February, Foreign Minister Ali Mroudjae was named prime minister. Parliamentary elections followed in March, with 37 out of 38 seats won by candidates favoring President Abdallah. GNP (1980 U.S.$): $78.8 million. Foreign Trade (1980): Imports, $33 million; exports, $11 million.

Congo, Cen. Africa	1.6	Brazzaville	132,047 (342 000)	Denis Sassou-Nguesso, *president* Louis-Sylvain Goma, *prime minister*

President Sassou-Nguesso visited Brazil, Cuba, and Spain in July. French President Mitterrand visited the Congo on October 10–11 in the hopes of establishing better relations with the Marxist government. GNP (1980 U.S.$): $1,000,000,000. Foreign Trade (1980): Imports, $545 million; exports, $910.6 million.

Djibouti, E. Africa	0.5	Djibouti	8,494 (22 000)	Hassan Gouled Aptidon, *president* Barkat Gourad Hamadou, *prime minister*

Legislative elections were held on May 21, confirming the election of 65 nominated candidates of the People's Group for Progress, the only legal party. Prime Minister Barkat Gourad Hamadou formed a new cabinet. GNP (1980 U.S.$): $350 million.

Dominica, Caribbean	0.1	Roseau	289 (749)	Aurelius Marie, *president* Mary Eugenia Charles, *prime minister*

In September, Alexander McQuirter, who in 1981 had plotted to overthrow the government of Dominica, was sentenced in Canada to two years' imprisonment. GNP Per Capita (1980 U.S.$): $620. Foreign Trade (1980): Imports, $49 million; exports, $8.9 million.

Dominican Republic, Caribbean	5.7	Santo Domingo	18,818 (48 739)	Salvador Jorge Blanco, *president*

See Caribbean. GNP (1981 U.S.$): $7,100,000,000. Foreign Trade (1981): Imports, $1,450,000,000; exports, $1,199,000,000.

Nation, Region	Population in millions[1]	Capital	Area Sq mi (km²)	Head of State/Government[2]
Equatorial Guinea, Cen. Africa	0.3	Malabo	10,831 (28 052)	Teodoro Obiang Mbasogo, *president*

A new constitution was approved in a referendum on August 15. It provided that the head of state, Lt. Col. Teodoro Obiang Mbasogo, would remain in office for another seven years. Pope John Paul II visited the country on February 18. GNP (1980 U.S.$): $100 million. Foreign Trade (1980): Imports, $37.1 million; exports, $13.3 million.

Fiji, Oceania	0.7	Suva	7,055 (18 272)	Ratu Sir George Cakobau, *governor general* Ratu Sir Kamisese Mara, *prime minister*

In July general elections, Prime Minister Ratu Sir Kamisese Mara's ruling Alliance Party defeated the opposition National Federation Party by a slim margin. GNP (1981 U.S.$): $1,529,000,000. Foreign Trade (1981): Imports, $632 million; exports, $311 million.

Gabon, Cen. Africa	0.7	Libreville	103,346 (267 666)	Omar Bongo, *president* Léon Mébiame, *prime minister*

Following demonstrations late in 1981, President Bongo closed the University of Libreville for a month. Pope John Paul II visited Gabon briefly on February 17. In March and April several persons opposed to President Bongo were arrested. Late in May, a consortium representing six Western European countries agreed to help finance construction of the final 211 mi (340 km) of the Trans-Gabon Railway, to be completed by 1987 at a cost of $560 million. GNP (1981 U.S.$): $3,700,000,000.

Gambia, W. Africa	0.6	Banjul	4,361 (11 295)	Sir Dawda K. Jawara, *president*

The Confederation of Senegambia, agreed upon in 1981 by the presidents of Senegal and Gambia, came into effect on Feb. 1, 1982. The first protocol of the pact was approved by the Gambian parliament in late August, providing that the president and vice-president of the new confederation would be the presidents of Senegal and Gambia, respectively. President Sir Dawda Jawara was reelected in May, and 27 of the 35 contested seats in parliament were won by the president's People's Progressive Party. Meanwhile, on February 4, six Gambians were sentenced to death for complicity in their attempted coup against President Jawara in July 1981. Five more were sentenced to death in June, but Sheriff Dibba, opposition leader of the National Convention Party, who had been in jail since the coup attempt, was acquitted of high treason and released. GNP (1980 U.S.$): $200 million. Foreign Trade (1980): Imports, $163 million; exports, $31 million.

Grenada, Caribbean	0.1	St. George's	133 (344)	Sir Paul Scoon, *governor general* Maurice Bishop, *prime minister*

A bilateral economic agreement between Grenada and the Soviet Union was announced in the spring. Prime Minister Maurice Bishop announced in August that the Soviet Union would establish a diplomatic mission in Grenada. Bishop visited Paris in September. GNP Per Capita (1980 U.S.$): $690. Foreign Trade (1980): Imports, $55 million; exports, $16 million.

Guinea, W. Africa	5.3	Conakry	94,926 (245 858)	Ahmed Sékou Touré, *president* Louis Lansana Beavogni, *prime minister*

Guinea suspended its participation in the Organization of African Unity (OAU) in March because of OAU's recognition of the Polisario Front in the Western Sahara. President Touré went to Iran and Iraq in an unsuccessful effort to mediate the war between those countries. President Touré was reelected for another seven-year term on May 9. He visited the United States in late June and France in September. Meanwhile, in August the UN Human Rights Commission listed Guinea as one of 22 countries in which political opponents were being abducted and often murdered. GNP (1980 U.S.$): $1,500,000,000. Foreign Trade (1980): Imports, $380 million; exports, $410 million.

Guinea-Bissau, W. Africa	0.8	Bissau	13,948 (36 125)	João Bernardo Vieira, *president of the Council of the Revolution* Victor Saude Maria, *prime minister*

President Vieira visited Cuba in March and reached agreements with the Castro government on economic, political, and cultural cooperation. On his return to Guinea-Bissau, several army officers were arrested for allegedly attempting a coup d'etat in Vieira's absence. In a purge of cabinet leftists in May, the president took over the defense and interior ministries and appointed former Foreign Minister Victor Saude Maria as prime minister. GNP (1980 U.S.$): $200 million. Foreign Trade (1980): Imports, $48.3 million; exports, $9.6 million.

Haiti, Caribbean	6.1	Port-au-Prince	10,714 (27 750)	Jean-Claude Duvalier, *president*

In January government troops repulsed a Haitian exile force that had invaded Tortuga Island in an attempt to overthrow the Haitian government. President Jean-Claude Duvalier shuffled his Cabinet in July, removing Finance Minister Marc Bazin, who had launched an anticorruption drive and introduced economic reforms. In August the International Monetary Fund (IMF) made the first payment of a $37 million loan to Haiti, on the condition that Bazin's reforms would be carried out. GNP (1980 U.S.$): $1,550,000,000.

Ivory Coast, W. Africa	8.8	Abidjan	124,503 (322 463)	Félix Houphouët-Boigny, *president*

The Ivory Coast's national oil company, Petroci, was granted a World Bank loan of $102 million in July to help develop the new Espoir oil field, and in September it was announced that oil production had begun in the field. GNP Per Capita (1980 U.S.$): $1,150. Foreign Trade (1980): Imports, $2,600,000,000; exports, $3,000,000,000.

Kiribati, Oceania	0.06	Tarawa	331 (857)	Ieremia Tabai, *president*
Kuwait, W. Asia	1.5	Kuwait	6,880 (17 819)	Jabir al-Ahmad al-Sabah, *emir* Saad al-Abdullah al-Sabah, *prime minister*

In response to its declining oil income, Kuwait reduced its expenditures for fiscal 1982 by 40% to $11,200,000,-000. The country had its first budget deficit despite the cuts. The drop in oil revenue, caused by a worldwide glut, resulted in a loss of capital and the subsequent collapse of Kuwait's unofficial stock market in August. GNP (1981 U.S.$): $30,700,000,000. Foreign Trade (1980): Imports, $6,560,000,000; exports, $19,767,000,000.

Lesotho, S. Africa	1.4	Maseru	11,720 (30 355)	Moshoeshoe II, *king* Leabua Jonathan, *prime minister*

In February and March, a series of explosions in the capital were blamed on the Lesotho Liberation Army (LLA), a division of the Basotho Congress Party (BCP), which was opposed to King Moshoeshoe II. Another wave of violence occurred in August as the LLA attempted to overthrow the government of Prime Minister Jonathan. The Lesotho government frequently accused South Africa of harboring the BCP rebels. After the assassination of the minister of public works in August, Prime Minister Jonathan reshuffled his Cabinet. Lesotho was one of 22 countries named by the UN Commission on Human Rights in August as having abducted political opponents and occasionally murdering them. On December 9, South African forces invaded the capital city of Maseru, killing 42 persons, including 30 members of the underground African National Congress which is banned in South Africa.

Nation, Region	Population in millions[1]	Capital	Area Sq mi (km²)	Head of State/Government[2]
Liberia, W. Africa	2.0	Monrovia	43,000 (111 370)	Samuel K. Doe, chairman, People's Redemption Council

Numerous cabinet and other official changes occurred during the year. The head of state visited several nations, seeking financial aid for his country. He announced in June that a new capital would be built in a rural area, not yet named, to replace Monrovia. GNP Per Capita (1980 U.S.$): $520. Foreign Trade (1981): Imports, $449 million; exports, $538 million.

Liechtenstein, Cen. Europe	0.3	Vaduz	62 (161)	Franz Joseph II, prince Hans Brunhart, prime minister

The ruling Fatherland Union Party, led by Prime Minister Hans Brunhart, won nearly 54% of the vote in general elections held early in the year. In April Liechtenstein's highest court found no conflict between the law limiting the vote to men and the constitutional guarantee to all citizens of equality before the law.

Madagascar, E. Africa	9.2	Antananarivo	226,657 (587 039)	Didier Ratsiraka, president

The early part of the year saw several persons arrested for allegedly plotting against the government, as well as student riots in northern Madagascar. The currency was devalued by 15% in May, as economic aid was obtained. Late in the year, prospecting for oil was under way off the west coast. On November 7, Ratsiraka was reelected president. GNP Per Capita (1980 U.S.$): $350. Foreign Trade (1980): Imports, $600 million; exports, $402 million.

Malawi, E. Africa	6.6	Lilongwe	45,747 (118 485)	Hastings Kamuzu Banda, president

On Dec. 24, 1981, Orton Chirwa, former minister of justice and a founder of the Malawi Congress Party, who had been exiled to Tanzania in 1964 and who had become leader of the opposition Malawi Freedom Movement, was arrested after allegedly being tricked into returning to Malawi. Brought to trial in July, he pleaded not guilty to charges of treason. Early in January, Zambia protested Malawi's holding 10 Zambians who had strayed across the border, but relations between the two countries improved in February when Zambian President Kaunda made his first state visit to Malawi. In mid-April the currency was devalued by 15%. GNP (1980 U.S.$): $982 million. Foreign Trade (1981): Imports, $362 million; exports, $284 million.

Maldives, S. Asia	0.2	Malé	115 (298)	Maumoon Abdul Gayoom, president and prime minister

GNP Per Capita (1980 U.S.$): $260. Foreign Trade (1980): Imports, $26.9 million; exports, $10.7 million.

Mali, W. Africa	7.1	Bamako	478,776 (1 204 021)	Moussa Traoré, president

In late February, the Democratic Union of Malian People (UDPM), Mali's only legal political party, held its second congress and replaced 8 of the 19 members of its central executive bureau. In the June 13 elections for 82 National Assembly members, UDPM candidates won 99.82% of the votes cast. It was reported in 1982 that Soviet specialists were assisting in mining newly found deposits of gold in the Kalan region. GNP (1980 U.S.$): $1,100,000,000. Foreign Trade (1980): Imports, $309.9 million; exports, $175.4 million.

Malta, S. Europe	0.4	Valletta	122 (316)	Agatha Barbara, president Dominic Mintoff, prime minister

Agatha Barbara, a former education minister, was elected president in February, the first woman to hold the mainly ceremonial office. The election was boycotted by the opposition Nationalist Party. Libyan leader Muammar el-Qaddafi visited Malta in March. The two countries agreed to refer their dispute over Mediterranean oil-drilling rights to the International Court of Justice at The Hague. GNP (1981 U.S.$): $1,200,000,000. Foreign Trade (1981): Imports, $855 million; exports, $448 million.

Mauritania, W. Africa	1.7	Nouakchott	397,950 (1 030 691)	Mohammed Khouna Ould Haidala, president Maaouya Ould Sidi Taya, prime minister

On March 5, several former government officials, including a prime minister and an interior minister, and Col. Mustapha Ould Mohamed Salek, who had engineered the overthrow of President Ould Daddah in 1978, were given prison sentences for an attempted coup on February 6–7. The president ordered a major Cabinet reshuffle in mid-July. GNP Per Capita (1980 U.S.$): $320. Foreign Trade (1980): Imports, $264 million; exports, $194 million.

Mauritius, E. Africa	1.0	Port Louis	790 (2 046)	Sir Dayendranath Burrenchobay, governor general Aneerood Jugnauth, prime minister

The parliamentary elections of June 11 resulted in a landslide victory for the socialist Militant Mauritian Movement led by Paul Bérenger, and the defeat of the pro-Western Labor Party government of Prime Minister Sir Seewoosagur Ramgoolam. A new leftist coalition government, headed by Aneerood Jugnauth as prime minister, was installed on June 16. GNP (1980 U.S.$): $890 million. Foreign Trade (1981): Imports, $553 million; exports, $326 million.

Monaco, S. Europe	0.025	Monaco-Ville	0.7 (1.81)	Rainier III, prince

In September, Monaco was shaken by the death of Princess Grace. (See Obituaries.)

Mongolia, E. Asia	1.8	Ulan Bator	604,251 (1 565 000)	Yumjaagiyn Tsedenbal, president Jambyn Batmönh, prime minister

Mongolia held six weeks of border talks with China, February 13–April 3, the first since the 1964 agreement that provided for such meetings. The presence of Soviet forces in Mongolia along the Chinese border continued to be a stumbling block to improved Sino-Soviet relations.

Mozambique, E. Africa	12.7	Maputo	302,330 (783 035)	Samora Machel, president

Increasing sabotage of rail, road, and pipeline facilities by the South African-supported Mozambique Resistance Movement (MRM), based in South Africa and Malawi, caused President Machel to appoint military commanders for the provinces, to begin arming residents in the affected areas, and to take measures to stop MRM infiltration into the country. There were some indications that the Marxist Machel government might be trying to establish some contacts with the West—for example, a food-aid agreement with West Germany, small-arms and military-training agreements with Portugal, and a meeting between the foreign minister and U.S. Secretary of State Shultz in New York. Portugal's Prime Minister Balsemão visited Mozambique in June and signed a number of cooperation and aid agreements. GNP (1980 U.S.$): $2,800,000,000.

Nauru, Oceania	0.008	Nauru	8 (21)	Hammer DeRoburt, president

Nation, Region	Population in millions[1]	Capital	Area Sq mi (km²)	Head of State/Government[2]
Nepal, S. Asia	14.5	Katmandu	55,304 (143 237)	Birendra Bir Bikram, *king* Surya Bahadur Thapa, *prime minister*

A United Nations study published in March reported that Nepal was one of nine Asian nations that could not produce enough food to meet the caloric requirements of its people. In November, Nepal was linked with the outside world via a communication satellite earth station partially funded by Great Britain. GNP Per Capita (1980 U.S.$): $140. Foreign Trade (1981 fiscal year): Imports, $373 million; exports, $116 million.

Niger, W. Africa	5.8	Niamey	489,191 (1 267 005)	Seny Kountché, *president*

In March the government restored diplomatic relations with Libya, suspended in January 1981 because of Libya's involvement in Chad. Also in March, President Kountché visited Saudi Arabia to discuss aid and other matters, including the forthcoming Islamic Conference of foreign ministers in Niamey. The conference ended on August 26 with condemnations of U.S. and USSR policies. In April, President Kountché announced transformation of the National Development Council into a constituent assembly. GNP Per Capita (1980 U.S.$): $330. Foreign Trade (1980): Imports, $801 million; exports, $557.9 million.

Oman, W. Asia	0.9	Muscat	89,029 (230 585)	Qabus ibn Said, *sultan*

In May, Sultan Said traveled to Cairo, becoming the first Arab head of state to visit Egypt since its 1979 peace treaty with Israel. Said met with Egyptian President Hosni Mubarak and urged other Arab leaders to restore normal relations with Egypt. GNP (1981 U.S.$): $3,910,000,000. Foreign Trade (1980): Imports, $17,320,000,000; exports, $32,020,000,000.

Papua New Guinea, Oceania	3.3	Port Moresby	178,704 (462 843)	Sir Tore Lokoloko, *governor general* Michael Somare, *prime minister*

Former Prime Minister Michael Somare, who had presided over Papua New Guinea's transition to independence in 1975, won the office again as the result of June elections. GNP (1981 U.S.$): $2,682,000,000. Foreign Trade (1980): Imports, $1,023,000,000; exports, $1,031,000,000.

Qatar, W. Asia	0.3	Doha	4,402 (11 400)	Khalifa ibn Hamad al-Thani, *emir*

GNP (1981 U.S.$): $6,580,000,000. Foreign Trade (1980): Imports, $1,429,000,000; exports, $5,698,000,000.

Rwanda, E. Africa	5.4	Kigali	10,169 (26 338)	Juvénal Habyarimana, *president*

Formation of Rwanda's first National Assembly since 1973 was followed in February by a reshuffling of the Cabinet. GNP Per Capita (1980 U.S.$): $200. Foreign Trade (1981): Imports, $188 million; exports, $115 million.

Saint Lucia, Caribbean	0.1	Castries	238 (616)	John Compton, *prime minister*

Widespread strikes in January compelled Prime Minister Winston Cenac to step down and schedule new elections. The United Workers Party, led by former Prime Minister John Compton, won the May elections, taking 14 of the 17 seats in the assembly. GNP Per Capita (1980 U.S.$): $850. Foreign Trade (1980): Imports, $115 million; exports, $26 million.

Saint Vincent and the Grenadines, Caribbean	0.1	Kingstown	150 (389)	Sir Sydney Gun-Munro, *governor general* Robert Milton Cato, *prime minister*

GNP Per Capita (1980 U.S.$): $520. Foreign Trade (1980): Imports, $57 million; exports, $17 million.

San Marino, S. Europe	0.021	San Marino	24 (62)	Co-regents appointed semiannually

São Tomé and Príncipe, W. Africa	0.1	São Tomé	372 (964)	Manuel Pinto da Costa, *president*

GNP Per Capita (1980 U.S.$): $490.

Senegal, W. Africa	5.9	Dakar	75,955 (196 723)	Abdou Diouf, *president* Habib Thíam, *prime minister*

The National Assembly in the spring approved new laws governing elections to the National Assembly and banning opposition coalitions. In September the government requested European Community aid in developing the Falémé iron mines, and the cornerstone was laid for a 60,000-seat Friendship Stadium and sports complex in a suburb of Dakar, to be built with Chinese aid. GNP Per Capita (1980 U.S.$): $450. Foreign Trade (1980): Imports, $1,022,-200,000; exports, $570.3 million. (See GAMBIA.)

Seychelles, E. Africa	0.1	Victoria	119 (308)	F. Albert René, *president*

In November 1981 a group of mercenaries based in South Africa was caught in the Seychelles while attempting to overthrow the government of President René. In July a South African supreme court judge sentenced four of the mercenaries to death for treason and 43 others to prison terms for air piracy of an Air Indian plane. In mid-August a mutiny among soldiers in Victoria, the capital, demanding removal of senior army officers, was crushed by government forces aided by Tanzanian troops. GNP Per Capita (1980 U.S.$): $1,770. Foreign Trade (1980): Imports, $74 million; exports, $5.2 million.

Sierra Leone, W. Africa	3.7	Freetown	27,699 (71 740)	Siaka Stevens, *president*

Violence and widespread irregularities occurred during the parliamentary elections on May 1. President Stevens, who had said earlier that he would retire after the elections, decided to remain in office. He appointed a Cabinet of 25 ministers and retained the defense post for himself. Sierra Leone faced a serious economic and financial crisis. GNP Per Capita (1980 U.S.$): $270.

Solomon Islands, Oceania	0.2	Honiara	10,983 (28 446)	Baddeley Devesi, *governor general* Solomon Mamaloni, *prime minister*

GNP Per Capita (1980 U.S.$): $460. Foreign Trade (1980): Imports, $74 million; exports, $73 million.

Somalia, E. Africa	4.6	Mogadishu	246,201 (637 661)	Mohammed Siad Barre, *president*

Fighting between Somali forces and Ethiopian troops and Ethiopian-aided guerrillas on the Somali-Ethiopian border near the Ogaden area escalated in mid-1982. In mid-June, seven high-ranking government and army officials were reported to have been arrested for conspiring with an unnamed "enemy country." On March 1, President Siad Barre announced a reorganization of both the government and the ruling Somali Revolutionary Socialist Party. The president visited Washington in March, seeking U.S. economic and military aid; and on July 24, the United States announced that it was sending arms to Somalia. Foreign Trade (1981): Imports, $199 million; exports, $200 million.

Nation, Region	Population in millions[1]	Capital	Area Sq mi (km²)	Head of State/Government[2]
Surinam, S. America	0.4	Paramaribo	63,037 (163 266)	Col. Daysi Bouterse, *head of National Military Council*

The civilian government of President Henk R. Chin A Sen resigned in February and was replaced by a four-man National Military Council, led by Col. Daysi Bouterse. In March, after thwarting a coup attempt by right-wing forces, the military installed a civilian Cabinet. In December the government, claiming to have uncovered a second coup attempt, detained and shot some 35 leading opposition figures—including labor leaders, journalists, and academics. The United States suspended its $1.5 million aid program. GNP Per Capita (1980 U.S.$): $2,840. Foreign Trade (1980): Imports, $504 million; exports, $514 million.

Swaziland, S. Africa	0.6	Mbabane	6,704 (17 363)	Prince Mabandla Dlamini, *prime minister*

On June 30, South Africa's plan to transfer 3,000 sq mi (7 770 sq km) of Zulu tribal homeland in Natal Province to Swaziland was overruled by the province's supreme court. King Sobhuza II died in Mbabane. GNP Per Capita (1980 U.S.$): $680.

Togo, W. Africa	2.8	Lomé	21,622 (56 000)	Gnassingbe Eyadéma, *president*

GNP (1980 U.S.$): $1,200,000,000. Foreign Trade (1980): Imports, $550 million; exports, $335 million.

Tonga, Oceania	0.1	Nuku'alofa	289 (749)	Taufa'ahau Tupou IV, *king* Prince Fatafehi Tu'ipelehake, *prime minister*

In March, Cyclone Isaac left thousands homeless and damaged 80% of the buildings in the capital city.

Tuvalu, Oceania	0.01	Funafuti	10 (26)	Fiatau Penitala Teo, *governor general* Tomasi Puapua, *prime minister*

United Arab Emirates, W. Asia	1.2	Abu Dhabi	32,278 (83 600)	Zaid ibn Sultan al-Nuhayan, *president* Rashid ibn Said al-Maktum, *vice-president, premier*

The country anticipated a budget deficit of about $620 million—its first since independence—despite actions to cut spending. GNP Per Capita (1980 U.S.$): $30,070. Foreign Trade (1980): Imports, $8,752,000,000; exports, $20,-742,000,000.

Upper Volta, W. Africa	6.7	Ouagadougou	105,870 (274 203)	Jean-Baptiste Ouedraogo, *head of state*

Following the banning of strikes and suspension of the Voltaic Trade Union Confederation (CSV) late in 1981, Col. Saye Zerbo lifted most of the restrictions on strikes in late February. Labor unrest continued, however, and demands grew for the release of persons arrested at the time of Zerbo's November 1980 coup. In September, CSV leader Soumana Toure, sought by the Voltaic government since November 1981, was captured near the Ghana border. On November 7, the Zerbo government was overthrown by a group calling itself the Provisional People's Salvation Council. GNP (1980 U.S.$): $1,000,000,000. Foreign Trade (1981): Imports, $338 million; exports, $75 million.

Vanuatu, Oceania	0.1	Vila	5,700 (14 763)	Ati George Sokomanu, *president* Walter Lini, *prime minister*

GNP Per Capita (1980 U.S.$): $530.

Vatican City, S. Europe	0.001	Vatican City	0.17 (0.44)	John Paul II, *pope*

The Vatican announced in March that it anticipated a budget deficit of more than $27.6 million. The deficit was attributed to the high rate of inflation in Italy and to increased salaries of Vatican officials. (See also special report, p. 551.)

Western Samoa, Oceania	0.2	Apia	1,095 (2 836)	Malietoa Tanumafili II, *head of state* Va'ai Kolone, *prime minister*

In February elections Va'ai Kolone, leader of the Human Rights Protection Party, was elected prime minister. In September the Western Samoan supreme court nullified the election, citing fraud. However, the party could remain in power until one year after the election, and Kolone would be entitled to nominate a successor.

Yemen, North, S. Asia	5.5	San'a	75,000 (194 250)	Al Abdullah Saleh, *president* Abdel Karim al-Iryani, *prime minister*

In March, North Yemen joined Jordan's King Hussein in pledging to send volunteers to fight with Iraq against Iran. North Yemen received a number of PLO guerrillas evacuated from Beirut, although the country's offer of asylum originally had been rejected by the PLO for geographic reasons. A severe earthquake in mid-December left more than 2,800 persons dead. GNP Per Capita (1980 U.S.$): $460. Foreign Trade (1980): Imports, $1,685,000,000; exports, $12.7 million.

Yemen, South, S. Asia	2.0	Aden	112,000 (290 080)	Ali Nasser Mohammed al-Hasani, *chairman, Council of Ministers*

The U.S. government in March eased controls on the sale of civilian aircraft to South Yemen, provided that the aircraft were not used for military purposes. The discovery of light crude oil in Hadraumaut Province in April was expected to boost the South Yemen economy. In September, South Yemen was reported to have received about 700 PLO guerrillas evacuated from Beirut. GNP (1980 U.S.$): $996.5 million.

Zambia, E. Africa	6.0	Lusaka	290,585 (752 615)	Kenneth D. Kaunda, *president* Nalumino Mundia, *prime minister*

Despite President Kaunda's meeting with President Mobutu of Zaire in August, frequent skirmishes occurred along the Zambia-Zaire border. GNP (1980 U.S.$): $2,800,000,000. Foreign Trade (1980): Imports, $1,383,000,000; exports, $1,378,000,000.

---

* Independent nations not covered separately, or under Central America, in alphabetical section (pages 76–571).
[1] Mid-1982 estimates.
[2] As of Dec. 31, 1982.

AGRICULTURAL PRODUCTION: SELECTED COUNTRIES (1981)
(in thousand metric tons)

	Barley	Corn	Eggs (million pieces)	Milk	Potatoes	Rice[1]	Soybeans	Sugar[2]	Wheat
AFGHANISTAN	365	770	——	——	——	380	——	20	2 200
ALBANIA	10	260	——	——	——		——	20	400
ALGERIA	600	1	——	——	611	1	——	15	1 400
ANGOLA	——	250	——	——		31	——	40	10
ARGENTINA	200	9 700	3 250	5 300	2 247	323	3 500	1 715	7 800
AUSTRALIA	3 430	176	3 600	5 333	896	793	73	3 389	16 350
AUSTRIA	1 220	1 374	1 730	3 400	1 310	——	——	480	1 025
BANGLADESH	15	——			999	20 218	——	155	900
BELGIUM[3]	824	38	3 200	3 895	1 498	——	——	873	926
BOLIVIA	65	310	——	——	720	106	40	242	54
BRAZIL	142	23 300	10 200	10 500	1 908	9 300	15 200	8 508	2 207
BULGARIA	1 401	2 477	2 350	——	407	68	107	215	4 429
BURMA	——	95	——	——	54	13 650	17	135	70
CAMEROON	——	410	——	——		45	——	57	
CANADA	13 384	6 214	5 975	7 986	2 555	——	713	92	24 519
CHILE	91	490	——	1 220	1 007	100	1	267	686
CHINA	7 400	59 000	——	——	28	143 204	7 880	3 052	58 500
COLOMBIA	66	815	——	——	1 900	1 788	89	1 225	67
COSTA RICA	——	47	——	——		168	——	189	——
CUBA	——	20	——	——	235	462	——	6 400	——
CZECHOSLOVAKIA	3 392	706	4 900	5 980	3 500	——	5	847	4 325
DENMARK	6 257	——	1 351	5 037	1 060	——	——	464	846
DOM. REP.		50	——	——	25	369	——	1 107	——
ECUADOR	31	246	——	——	323	391	31	368	22
EGYPT	103	3 232	2 013	——	1 210	2 236	92	658	1 938
EL SALVADOR	——	487	——	——		52	——	180	——
ETHIOPIA	700	980	——	——		——	——	165	400
FINLAND	1 080	——	1 370	3 232	478	——	——	114	235
FRANCE	10 231	9 200	15 250	28 150	6 256	21	14	4 195	22 857
GERMANY, E.	3 476	4	5 662	8 325	11 500	——	——	797	2 942
GERMANY, W.	8 687	832	13 310	24 800	7 585	——	——	2 988	8 314
GHANA	——	420	——	——		79	——	20	——
GREECE	768	1 304	2 420	714	978	75	——	182	2 780
GUATEMALA	——	997	——	——		52	——	442	50
GUYANA	——	5	——	——		289	——	280	——
HAITI	——	250	——	——		105	——	47	——
HUNGARY	900	6 800	4 500	2 653	1 128	37	39	486	4 600
INDIA	2 242	6 500	——	16 500	9 590	81 081	450	6 534	36 460
INDONESIA	——	4 648	——	——		32 776	687	1 350	——
IRAN	1 100	60	——	——	718	1 212	50	250	5 300
IRAQ	800	100	——	——		188	——	25	1 500
IRELAND	1 425	——	510	4 770	950	——	——	160	250
ISRAEL	15	2	1 550	——	208	——	——	10	230
ITALY	983	7 197	11 300	10 660	2 864	837	——	1 935	8 828
IVORY COAST	——	300	——	——		475	——	135	——
JAPAN	383	3	33 150	6 620	3 095	12 824	174	822	587
KENYA	100	2 200	——	——		41	——	426	175
KOREA, N.	——	1 900	——	——		4 300	330	——	350
KOREA, S.	897	145	——	——	554	7 032	216	——	57
LEBANON	10	2	785	——		——	——	10	25
MADAGASCAR	——	130	——	——		1 998	——	115	——
MALAYSIA	——	9	——	——		2 109	——	59	——
MEXICO	430	12 500	12 150	6 980	892	562	280	2 518	3 050
MOROCCO	1 039	90	——	——	217	18	——	330	892
MOZAMBIQUE	——	350	——	——		45	——	170	3
NEPAL	25	770	——	——	305	2 477	——	17	350
NETHERLANDS	249	——	9 400	12 160	6 196	——	——	936	882
NEW ZEALAND	399	198	——	6 690	215	——	——	——	302
NICARAGUA	——	243	——	——		103	——	193	——
NIGERIA	——	1 750	——	——		1 200	5	42	20
NORWAY	650	——	758	1 960	544	——	——	——	61
PAKISTAN	120	960	——	——	449	4 955	——	911	11 470
PANAMA	——	68	——	——		135	——	215	——
PARAGUAY	——	450	——	——	9	69	600	78	40
PERU	160	590	940	630	1 650	706	8	493	120
PHILIPPINES	——	3 350	——	——	30	8 131	10	2 373	——
POLAND	3 575	79	8 800	15 527	42 600	——	——	1 134	4 229
PORTUGAL	38	367	1 117	665	900	112	——	4	310
RUMANIA	2 580	11 870	6 500	——	4 700	60	448	553	5 320
SAUDI ARABIA	28	30	——	——		3	——	——	275
SOUTH AFRICA	99	8 535	3 270	2 260	650	——	26	1 709	2 230
SPAIN	4 709	2 151	11 670	6 000	5 571	441	14	983	3 356
SRI LANKA	——	——	——	——	38	2 212	——	45	——
SWEDEN	2 452	——	1 800	3 493	1 279	——	——	312	1 066
SWITZERLAND	220	128	720	3 640	1 150	——	——	103	389
SYRIA	1 400	66	——	——	238	——	——	32	1 800
TAIWAN	——	100	——	——	30	3 127	26	770	3
TANZANIA	——	800	——	——		185	——	125	60
THAILAND	——	4 000	——	——		19 250	105	1 671	——
TUNISIA	270	——	——	——	140	——	——	6	963
TURKEY	5 500	1 300	4 800	——	2 900	323	3	930	13 200
USSR	41 900	8 400	70 900	88 500	70 000	2 400	525	6 900	88 000
UN. KINGDOM	10 145	——	13 500	15 940	6 280	——	——	1 202	8 585
USA	10 414	208 314	69 604	60 162	15 136	8 408	48 772	5 345	76 025
URUGUAY	100	121	——	——	130	351	45	76	400
VENEZUELA	——	415	2 656	1 385	171	730	——	253	1
VIETNAM	——	475	——	——		10 500	——	45	——
YEMEN	60	90	——	——	116	——	——		50
YUGOSLAVIA	720	9 766	4 550	4 402	2 500	42	34	709	4 270
ZAIRE	——	520	——	——		246	——	54	4
ZIMBABWE	——	1 614	——	——			65	358	201

Source: U.S. Department of Agriculture.   [1] Rough rice   [2] Centrifugal sugar   [3] Includes Luxembourg

ENERGY
(quadrillion [10^{15}] Btu)

	Primary Energy Production[2]	Crude Oil Production	Natural Gas Plant Liquids Production	Natural Gas Production (Dry)	Coal Production	Hydroelectric Power Production	Nuclear Electric Power Production
PRODUCTION BY REGION (1981)[1]							
N. America	81.67	25.95	3.20	23.46	20.05	5.65	3.41[4]
Central and S. America	12.17	7.88	.17	1.60	.39	2.10	
Western Europe	29.54	5.77	.22	6.40	9.38	4.70	3.07
E. Europe and USSR	69.10	24.36	.61	17.53	23.27	2.14	1.19
Middle East	36.13	33.56	1.01	1.47	—	.08	
Africa	15.45	9.56	.42	1.44	3.37	.65	
Far East and Oceania	40.45	10.15	.30	2.75	23.21[3]	3.04	1.02
World Total[5]	284.51	117.23	5.92	54.65	79.66	18.35	8.69
PRODUCTION BY SELECTED COUNTRIES (1981)[1]							
Algeria	3.20	1.64	.34	1.22	—	—	
Argentina	1.62	1.09	.02	.32	—	.15	.03
Australia	4.94	.84	.10	.41	3.41	.19	
Belgium	—	—	—	—	.16	—	.13
Bolivia	—	—	.01	.07	—	—	
Brazil	2.05	.45	.01	—	.20	1.35	
Brunei	—	.35	.04	.34	—	—	
Bulgaria	—	—	—	—	.41	.04	.06
Canada	9.85	2.73	.52	2.47	.92	2.74	.48
Chile	—	—	.02	.14	—	.08	
China	20.20	4.32	—	.48	14.79	.62	—
Colombia	—	.27	.01	.13	.15	.14	
Czechoslovakia	1.96	—	—	—	1.82	.04	.06
Egypt	1.41	1.25	.03	—	—	.10	
Finland	—	—	—	—	—	.11	.14
France	2.80	—	.04	.26	.57	.75	1.10
Germany, E.	2.45	—	—	.12	2.18	—	.14
Germany, W.	5.37	—	—	.64	3.81	.20	.54
Hungary	—	—	.03	.24	.30	—	—
India	3.72	.61	—	—	2.49	.51	.03
Indonesia	4.22	3.36	.15	.66	—	—	
Iran	3.10	2.97	.01	.06	—	.04	
Iraq	2.18	2.09	.01	.07	—	—	
Italy	1.11	—	—	.51	—	.47	.03
Japan	2.37	—	—	.09	.44	.97	.85
Korea, N.	1.51	—	—	—	1.26	.25	—
Kuwait	2.87	2.43	.15	.29	—	—	
Libya	2.58	2.37	.06	.16	—	—	
Mexico	6.84	5.07	.38	1.06	.14	.18	
Netherlands	2.48	—	.01	2.38	—	—	.04
Nigeria	3.07	3.03	—	—	—	—	
Norway	3.15	1.06	.08	1.05	—	.95	
Pakistan	—	—	—	.41	—	.11	
Peru	—	.41	—	—	—	.08	
Poland	5.10	—	—	.22	4.83	—	
Qatar	—	.84	.04	—	—	—	
Rumania	2.76	.50	.02	1.62	.49	.12	
Saudi Arabia	22.08	20.94	.69	.46	—	—	
South Africa	3.27	—	—	—	3.24	—	
Spain	1.12	—	—	—	.65	.31	.10
Sweden	—	—	—	—	—	.60	.36
Trinidad and Tobago	—	.42	—	.20	—	—	
USSR	55.50	23.64	.55	15.30	13.22	1.86	.92
United Arab Emirates	3.45	3.11	.10	.24	—	—	
United Kingdom	9.00	3.89	.08	1.42	3.08	.06	.48
United States	64.99	18.15	2.30	19.93	18.98	2.73	2.90
Venezuela	5.57	4.66	.09	.66	—	.15	
Zimbabwe	—	—	—	—	.08	.04	

[1] preliminary; [2] includes crude oil, lease condensate natural gas plant liquids, dry natural gas, coal, net hydroelectric power, and net nuclear power; [3] includes Middle East; [4] includes Central and South America; [5] sum of components may not equal total due to rounding.

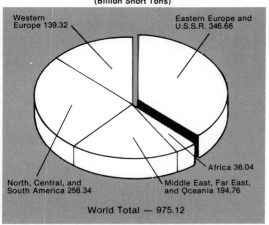

WORLD CRUDE OIL RESERVES
(Billion Barrels)

Central and South America 28.1
Western Europe 24.8
Eastern Europe and U.S.S.R. 66.0
North America 93.7
Far East and Oceania 39.0
Africa 56.6
Middle East 362.6

World Total — 670.3

WORLD ESTIMATED RECOVERABLE RESERVES OF COAL
(Billion Short Tons)

Western Europe 139.32
Eastern Europe and U.S.S.R. 346.66
North, Central, and South America 258.34
Africa 36.04
Middle East, Far East, and Oceania 194.76

World Total — 975.12

1981 International Energy Annual, U.S. Department of Energy

UNITED STATES: Major Legislation Enacted During Second Session of the 97th Congress

SUBJECT	PURPOSE
Federal Courts	Establishes a new U.S. Court of Appeals for the Federal Circuit and a U.S. Claims Court. Signed April 2. Public Law 97-164.
Idaho-Wyoming	Authorizes the exchange of certain lands in Idaho and Wyoming. Signed April 6. Public Law 97-168.
Government Employees	Permits an officer or employee of the U.S. government injured during an assassination attempt to receive contributions from charitable organizations. Signed April 13. Public Law 97-171.
Housing	Extends the authority of the secretary of housing and urban development to enter into contracts to provide mortgage assistance payments for lower income families. Signed May 24. Public Law 97-185.
Dance	Designates the square dance as the U.S. national folk dance. Signed June 1. Public Law 97-188.
Commerce Department	Establishes the position of undersecretary of commerce for economic affairs. Signed June 15. Public Law 97-195.
Voting Rights	Extends for 25 years the enforcement provisions of the Voting Rights Act of 1965. Signed June 29. Public Law 97-205.
Lebanon	Authorizes emergency humanitarian assistance to victims of the hostilities in Lebanon. Signed June 30. Public Law 97-208.
Environment	Designates certain new national wildlife refuge lands. Signed June 30. Public Law 97-211.
Postal Service	Repeals outdated size and weight limitations imposed on the U.S. Postal Service. Signed August 24. Public Law 97-242.
Tax Increase	*See* page 499. Signed September 3. Public Law 97-248.
World's Fair	Provides for U.S. participation in the 1984 Louisiana World Exposition in New Orleans. Signed September 8. Public Law 97-254.
Bus Deregulation	Gives intercity bus operators greater freedom to establish routes and prices. Signed September 20. Public Law 97-261.
The Bible	Authorizes and requests the president to proclaim 1983 as the "Year of the Bible." Signed October 4. Public Law 97-280.
Crime	Makes it a federal crime to kill, kidnap, or assault Supreme Court justices and senior executive officials. Signed October 6. Public Law 97-285.
Export Trade	Promotes exports by allowing financing from banking holding companies and by providing protection from antitrust laws. Signed October 8. Public Law 97-290.
Crime	Makes the federal courts more sensitive to crime victims and witnesses. Signed October 12. Public Law 97-291.
Missing Children	Expands the National Crime Information Center to facilitate the search for missing children. Signed October 12. Public Law 97-292.
Arson	Makes it a federal crime to use fire to destroy or damage property in or affecting interstate commerce. Signed October 12. Public Law 97-298.
Job Training	Establishes a program to provide job training for economically disadvantaged youths. Signed October 13. Public Law 97-300.
Endangered Species	Tightens procedures for removing plants or animals from the endangered-species list. Signed October 13. Public Law 97-304.
Banking	*See* page 125. Signed October 15. Public Law 97-320.
Coastal Barriers	Tightens federal protection of coastal barriers, beaches, and islands by blocking federal subsidies for development projects. Signed October 18. Public Law 97-348.
Crime	Makes it a federal crime to obtain nuclear materials and use them to threaten or harm individuals. Signed October 18. Public Law 97-351.
Amerasians	Grants preferential immigration status to Amerasian children who could prove U.S. parentage. Signed October 22. Public Law 97-359.
Productivity	Establishes a White House Conference on Productivity. Signed October 25. Public Law 97-367.
Drugs	Encourages drug companies to develop drugs for the treatment of rare diseases. Signed Jan. 4, 1983. Public Law 97-414.
Gasoline Tax	*See* page 499. Signed Jan. 6, 1983. Public Law 97-424.
Nuclear Waste	Establishes a national plan for the disposal of highly radioactive nuclear waste. Signed Jan. 7, 1983. Public Law 97-425.
Trade	Reduces customs duties on more than 200 imported items and extends the international sugar and coffee agreements until Jan. 1, 1985, and Oct. 1, 1983, respectively. Signed Jan. 12, 1983. Public Law 97-446.
Migrant Workers	Establishes new federal protections for migrant and seasonal farm workers. Signed Jan. 14, 1983. Public Law 97-470.

THE UNITED STATES GOVERNMENT

(selected listing, as of Jan. 15, 1983)

President: Ronald Reagan

Vice-President: George Bush

Executive Office of the President
The White House

Counsellor to the President: Edwin Meese III
Chief of Staff and Assistant to the President: James A. Baker III
Deputy Chief of Staff and Assistant to the President: Michael K. Deaver
Assistant to the President for National Security Affairs: William P. Clark
Assistant to the President for Policy Development: Edwin L. Harper
Assistant to the President and Press Secretary: James S. Brady
Assistant to the President for Public Liaison: Faith Ryan Whittlesey
Counsel to the President: Fred R. Fielding
Assistant to the President for Legislative Affairs: Kenneth M. Duberstein
Assistant to the President for Communications: David R. Gergen
Deputy Counsellor to the President: James Jenkins

Assistant to the President for Presidential Personnel: E. Pendleton James
Assistant to the President for Political Affairs: Edward J. Rollins, Jr.
Assistant to the President for Intergovernmental Affairs: Richard S. Williamson
Deputy Press Secretary: Larry Speakes
Office of Management and Budget, Director: David A. Stockman
Council of Economic Advisers, Chairman: Martin S. Feldstein
Office of United States Trade Representative, U.S. Trade Representative: William E. Brock
Council on Environmental Quality, Chairman: A. Alan Hill
Office of Science and Technology Policy, Director: George A. Keyworth II
Office of Administration, Director: John F. W. Rogers II

The Cabinet

Secretary of Agriculture: John R. Block
Secretary of Commerce: Malcolm Baldrige
Secretary of Defense: Caspar W. Weinberger
    Joint Chief of Staff, Chairman: Gen. John W. Vessey, USA
    Secretary of the Air Force: Verne Orr
    Secretary of the Army: John O. Marsh, Jr.
    Secretary of the Navy: John F. Lehman, Jr.
Secretary of Education: Terrel H. Bell
Secretary of Energy: Donald P. Hodel
Secretary of Health and Human Services: Margaret M. Heckler[1]
    National Institutes of Health, Director: James B. Wyngaarden
    Surgeon General: C. Everett Koop
    Commissioner of Food and Drugs: Arthur Hull Hayes, Jr.

    Commissioner of Social Security: John A. Svahn
Secretary of Housing and Urban Development: Samuel R. Pierce, Jr.
Secretary of the Interior: James G. Watt
Department of Justice, Attorney General: William French Smith
    Federal Bureau of Investigation, Director: William H. Webster
Secretary of Labor: Raymond J. Donovan
    Women's Bureau, Director: Lenora Cole-Alexander
    Commissioner of Labor Statistics: Janet L. Norwood
Secretary of State: George P. Shultz
Secretary of Transportation: Elizabeth H. Dole[1]
Secretary of the Treasury: Donald T. Regan
    Internal Revenue Service, Commissioner: Roscoe L. Egger

Independent Agencies

ACTION, Director: Thomas W. Pauken
    Peace Corps, Director: Loret M. Ruppe
Central Intelligence Agency, Director: William J. Casey
Civil Aeronautics Board, Chairman: Clinton D. McKinnon
Commission on Civil Rights, Chairman: Clarence M. Pendleton, Jr.
Commission of Fine Arts, Chairman: J. Carter Brown
Consumer Product Safety Commission, Chairman: Nancy H. Steorts
Environmental Protection Agency, Administrator: Anne McGill Gorsuch
Equal Employment Opportunity Commissioner: Clarence Thomas
Export-Import Bank, President and Chairman: William H. Draper III
Federal Communications Commission, Chairman: Mark S. Fowler
Federal Deposit Insurance Corporation, Chairman: William M. Isaac
Federal Election Commission, Chairman: Frank P. Reiche
Federal Emergency Management Agency, Director: Louis O. Giuffrida
Federal Farm Credit Board, Chairman: Owen Cooper
Federal Home Loan Bank Board, Chairman: Richard T. Pratt
Federal Labor Relations Authority, Chairman: Ronald W. Haughton
Federal Maritime Commission, Chairman: Alan Green, Jr.
Federal Reserve System, Chairman: Paul A. Volcker
Federal Trade Commission, Chairman: James C. Miller III

General Services Administrator: Gerald P. Carmen
International Communication Agency, Director: Charles Z. Wick
Interstate Commerce Commission, Chairman: Reese H. Taylor, Jr.
National Aeronautics and Space Administration, Administrator: James M. Beggs
National Foundation on the Arts and Humanities
    National Endowment for the Arts, Chairman: Francis S. M. Hodsoll; National Endowment for the Humanities, Chairman: William J. Bennett
National Labor Relations Board, Chairman: John R. Van de Water
National Science Foundation, Director: John B. Slaughter
National Transportation Safety Board, Chairman: James E. Burnett, Jr.
Nuclear Regulatory Commission, Chairman: Nunzio J. Palladino
Postal Rate Commission, Chairman: Janet D. Steiger
Securities and Exchange Commission, Chairman: John S. R. Shad
Selective Service System, Director: Maj. Gen. Thomas K. Turnage
Small Business Administrator: James C. Sanders
Tennessee Valley Authority, Chairman: Charles H. Dean, Jr.
U.S. Arms Control and Disarmament Agency, Director: Kenneth L. Adelman[1]
U.S. International Trade Commission, Chairman: Alfred Eckes
U.S. Postmaster General: William F. Bolger
Veterans Administrator: Harry N. Walters

The Supreme Court
Chief Justice, Warren E. Burger

William J. Brennan, Jr.	Byron R. White	Thurgood Marshall	Harry A. Blackmun
Lewis F. Powell, Jr.	William H. Rehnquist	John Paul Stevens	Sandra Day O'Connor

[1] Nominated but not confirmed

UNITED STATES: 98th CONGRESS
First Session

SENATE MEMBERSHIP

(As of January 1983: 54 Republicans, 46 Democrats) Letters after senators' names refer to party affiliation—D for Democrat, R for Republican. Single asterisk (*) denotes term expiring in January 1985; double asterisk (**), term expiring in January 1987; triple asterisk (***), term expiring in January 1989.

ALABAMA
*H. Heflin, D
**J. Denton, R
ALASKA
*T. Stevens, R
**F. H. Murkowski, R
ARIZONA
**B. Goldwater, R
***D. DeConcini, D
ARKANSAS
**D. Bumpers, D
*D. Pryor, D
CALIFORNIA
**A. Cranston, D
***P. Wilson, R
COLORADO
**G. Hart, D
*W. Armstrong, R
CONNECTICUT
***L. P. Weicker, Jr., R
**C. J. Dodd, D
DELAWARE
***W. V. Roth, Jr., R
*J. R. Biden, Jr., D
FLORIDA
***L. M. Chiles, Jr., D
*P. Hawkins, R
GEORGIA
*S. Nunn, D
**M. Mattingly, R
HAWAII
*D. K. Inouye, D
***S. M. Matsunaga, D
IDAHO
*J. A. McClure, R
**S. D. Symms, R
ILLINOIS
*C. H. Percy, R
**A. J. Dixon, D

INDIANA
***R. G. Lugar, R
**D. Quayle, R
IOWA
*R. Jepsen, R
**C. E. Grassley, R
KANSAS
*R. J. Dole, R
*N. Kassebaum, R
KENTUCKY
*W. Huddleston, D
**W. H. Ford, D
LOUISIANA
**R. B. Long, D
*J. B. Johnston, D
MAINE
*W. Cohen, R
***G. Mitchell, D
MARYLAND
**C. M. Mathias, Jr., R
***P. S. Sarbanes, D
MASSACHUSETTS
***E. M. Kennedy, D
*P. Tsongas, D
MICHIGAN
***D. W. Riegle, Jr., D
*C. Levin, D
MINNESOTA
***D. Durenberger, R
*R. Boschwitz, R
MISSISSIPPI
***J. C. Stennis, D
*T. Cochran, R
MISSOURI
**T. F. Eagleton, D
***J. C. Danforth, R
MONTANA
***J. Melcher, D
*M. Baucus, D

NEBRASKA
***E. Zorinsky, D
*J. Exon, D
NEVADA
**P. Laxalt, R
***C. Hecht, R
NEW HAMPSHIRE
*G. Humphrey, R
**W. Rudman, R
NEW JERSEY
*B. Bradley, D
***Frank R. Lautenberg, D
NEW MEXICO
*P. V. Domenici, R
***J. Bingaman, D
NEW YORK
***D. P. Moynihan, D
**A. D'Amato, R
NORTH CAROLINA
*J. Helms, R
**J. P. East, R
NORTH DAKOTA
***Q. N. Burdick, D
**M. Andrews, R
OHIO
*J. H. Glenn, Jr., D
***H. M. Metzenbaum, D
OKLAHOMA
*D. Boren, D
**D. Nickles, R
OREGON
*M. O. Hatfield, R
**B. Packwood, R
PENNSYLVANIA
***J. Heinz, R
**A. Specter, R
RHODE ISLAND
*C. Pell, D
***J. H. Chafee, R

SOUTH CAROLINA
*S. Thurmond, R
**E. F. Hollings, D
SOUTH DAKOTA
*L. Pressler, R
**J. Abdnor, R
TENNESSEE
*H. H. Baker, Jr., R
***J. Sasser, D
TEXAS
*J. G. Tower, R
***L. M. Bentsen, D
UTAH
**J. Garn, R
***O. Hatch, R
VERMONT
***R. T. Stafford, R
**P. J. Leahy, D
VIRGINIA
*J. Warner, R
***P. S. Trible, Jr., R
WASHINGTON
***H. M. Jackson, D
**S. Gorton, R
WEST VIRGINIA
*J. Randolph, D
***R. C. Byrd, D
WISCONSIN
***W. Proxmire, D
**R. W. Kasten, Jr., R
WYOMING
***M. Wallop, R
*A. Simpson, R

HOUSE MEMBERSHIP

(As of Jan. 15, 1983, 267 Democrats, 165 Republicans, 3 vacancies). "At-L." in place of Congressional district number means "representative at large." * Indicates first elected Nov. 2, 1982; all others served in a previous Congress.

ALABAMA
1. J. Edwards, R
2. W. L. Dickinson, R
3. W. Nichols, D
4. T. Bevill, D
5. R. Flippo, D
6. *B. Erdreich, D
7. R. Shelby, D

ALASKA
At-L. D. Young, R

ARIZONA
1. *J. McCain, R
2. M. K. Udall, D
3. B. Stump, D
4. E. Rudd, R
5. *J. McNulty, D

ARKANSAS
1. W. V. Alexander, Jr., D
2. E. Bethune, Jr., R
3. J. P. Hammerschmidt, R
4. B. Anthony, Jr., D

CALIFORNIA
1. *D. H. Bosco, D
2. G. Chappie, R
3. R. Matsui, D
4. V. Fazio, D
5. P. Burton, D
6. *B. Boxer, D
7. G. Miller, D
8. R. V. Dellums, D
9. F. H. Stark, Jr., D
10. D. Edwards, D
11. T. Lantos, D

12. *E. Zschau, R
13. N. Y. Mineta, D
14. N. Shumway, R
15. T. Coelho, D
16. L. E. Panetta, D
17. C. Pashayan, Jr., R
18. *R. Lehman, D
19. R. J. Lagomarsino, R
20. W. M. Thomas, R
21. B. Fiedler, R
22. C. J. Moorhead, R
23. A. C. Beilenson, D
24. H. A. Waxman, D
25. E. R. Roybal, D
26. *H. L. Berman, D
27. *M. Levine, D
28. J. Dixon, D
29. A. F. Hawkins, D
30. M. G. Martinez, D
31. M. Dymally, D
32. G. M. Anderson, D
33. D. Dreier, R
34. *E. Torres, D
35. J. Lewis, R
36. G. E. Brown, Jr., D
37. *A. McCandless, R
38. J. M. Patterson, D
39. W. Dannemeyer, R
40. R. E. Badham, R
41. B. Lowery, R
42. D. Lungren, R
43. *R. Packard, R
44. *J. Bates, D
45. D. L. Hunter, R

COLORADO
1. P. Schroeder, D
2. T. E. Wirth, D

3. R. Kogovsek, D
4. H. Brown, R
5. K. Kramer, R
6. Vacant

CONNECTICUT
1. B. Kennelly, D
2. S. Gejdenson, D
3. *B. Morrison, D
4. S. B. McKinney, R
5. W. Ratchford, D
6. *N. L. Johnson, R

DELAWARE
At-L. *T. R. Carper, D

FLORIDA
1. E. Hutto, D
2. D. Fuqua, D
3. C. E. Bennett, D
4. W. V. Chappell, Jr., D
5. B. McCollum, R
6. *B. MacKay, D
7. S. M. Gibbons, D
8. C. W. Young, R
9. *M. Bilirakis, R
10. A. Ireland, D
11. B. Nelson, D
12. *T. Lewis, R
13. *C. Mack, R
14. D. A. Mica, D
15. E. C. Shaw, Jr., R
16. *L. Smith, D
17. W. Lehman, D
18. C. Pepper, D
19. D. B. Fascell, D

GEORGIA
1. *L. Thomas, D
2. C. Hatcher, D
3. *R. Ray, D
4. E. H. Levitas, D
5. W. Fowler, D
6. N. Gingrich, R
7. L. P. McDonald, D
8. *J. R. Rowland, D
9. E. L. Jenkins, D
10. D. D. Barnard, Jr., D

HAWAII
1. C. Heftel, D
2. D. K. Akaka, D

IDAHO
1. L. Craig, R
2. G. V. Hansen, R

ILLINOIS
1. H. Washington, D
2. G. Savage, D
3. M. A. Russo, D
4. G. M. O'Brien, R
5. *W. O. Lipinski, D
6. H. J. Hyde, R
7. C. Collins, D
8. D. Rostenkowski, D
9. S. R. Yates, D
10. J. Porter, R
11. F. Annunzio, D
12. P. M. Crane, R
13. J. N. Erlenborn, R
14. T. Corcoran, R
15. E. R. Madigan, R
16. L. Martin, R
17. *L. Evans, D

18. R. H. Michel, R
19. D. B. Crane, R
20. *R. J. Durbin, D
21. M. Price, D
22. P. Simon, D

INDIANA
1. K. Hall, D
2. P. R. Sharp, D
3. J. Hiler, R
4. D. Coats, R
5. E. H. Hillis, R
6. *D. Burton, R
7. J. T. Myers, R
8. *F. X. McCloskey, D
9. L. H. Hamilton, D
10. A. Jacobs, Jr., D

IOWA
1. J. A. S. Leach, R
2. T. Tauke, R
3. C. Evans, R
4. N. Smith, D
5. T. R. Harkin, D
6. B. W. Bedell, D

KANSAS
1. P. Roberts, R
2. *J. Slattery, D
3. L. Winn, Jr., R
4. D. Glickman, D
5. R. Whittaker, R

KENTUCKY
1. C. Hubbard, Jr., D
2. W. H. Natcher, D
3. R. L. Mazzoli, D
4. G. Snyder, R
5. H. Rogers, R
6. L. Hopkins, R
7. C. D. Perkins, D

LOUISIANA
1. R. L. Livingston, Jr., R
2. L. Boggs, D
3. W. J. Tauzin, D
4. B. Roemer, D
5. J. Huckaby, D
6. W. H. Moore, R
7. J. B. Breaux, D
8. G. W. Long, D

MAINE
1. *J. R. McKernan, Jr., R
2. O. Snowe, R

MARYLAND
1. R. Dyson, D
2. C. D. Long, D
3. B. A. Mikulski, D
4. M. S. Holt, R
5. S. Hoyer, D
6. B. Byron, D
7. P. J. Mitchell, D
8. M. Barnes, D

MASSACHUSETTS
1. S. O. Conte, R
2. E. P. Boland, D
3. J. D. Early, D
4. B. Frank, D
5. J. Shannon, D
6. N. Mavroules, D
7. E. J. Markey, D
8. T. P. O'Neill, Jr., D
9. J. J. Moakley, D
10. G. E. Studds, D
11. B. Donnelly, D

MICHIGAN
1. J. Conyers, Jr., D
2. C. D. Pursell, R
3. H. Wolpe, D
4. M. Siljander, R
5. H. S. Sawyer, R
6. B. Carr, D
7. D. E. Kildee, D
8. B. Traxler, D
9. G. A. Vander Jagt, R
10. D. Albosta, D
11. R. Davis, R
12. D. E. Bonior, D
13. G. Crockett, Jr., D
14. D. Hertel, D
15. W. D. Ford, D
16. J. D. Dingell, D
17. *S. Levin, D
18. W. S. Broomfield, R

MINNESOTA
1. *T. J. Penny, D
2. V. Weber, R

3. B. Frenzel, R
4. B. F. Vento, D
5. M. Sabo, D
6. *G. Sikorski, D
7. A. Stangeland, R
8. J. L. Oberstar, D

MISSISSIPPI
1. J. L. Whitten, D
2. *W. Franklin, R
3. G. V. Montgomery, D
4. W. Dowdy, D
5. T. Lott, R

MISSOURI
1. W. L. Clay, D
2. R. A. Young, D
3. R. A. Gephardt, D
4. I. Skelton, D
5. *A. Wheat, D
6. E. T. Coleman, R
7. G. Taylor, R
8. B. Emerson, R
9. H. L. Volkmer, D

MONTANA
1. P. Williams, D
2. R. Marlenee, R

NEBRASKA
1. D. Bereuter, R
2. H. Daub, R
3. V. Smith, R

NEVADA
1. *H. Reid, D
2. *B. Vucanovich, R

NEW HAMPSHIRE
1. N. E. D'Amours, D
2. J. Gregg, R

NEW JERSEY
1. J. J. Florio, D
2. W. J. Hughes, D
3. J. J. Howard, D
4. C. Smith, R
5. M. Roukema, R
6. B. J. Dwyer, D
7. M. J. Rinaldo, R
8. R. A. Roe, D
9. *R. G. Torricelli, D
10. P. W. Rodino, Jr., D
11. J. G. Minish, D
12. J. Courter, R
13. E. B. Forsythe, R
14. F. Guarini, D

NEW MEXICO
1. M. Lujan, Jr., R
2. J. Skeen, R
3. *B. Richardson, D

NEW YORK
1. W. Carney, R
2. T. J. Downey, D
3. *R. J. Mrazek, D
4. N. F. Lent, R
5. R. McGrath, R
6. J. P. Addabbo, D
7. Vacant
8. H. J. Scheuer, D
9. G. Ferraro, D
10. C. E. Schumer, D
11. *E. Towns, D
12. *M. R. Owens, D
13. S. J. Solarz, D
14. G. V. Molinari, R
15. B. Green, R
16. C. B. Rangel, D
17. T. Weiss, D
18. R. Garcia, D
19. M. Biaggi, D
20. R. L. Ottinger, D
21. H. Fish, Jr., R
22. B. A. Gilman, R
23. S. S. Stratton, D
24. G. B. H. Solomon, R
25. *S. L. Boehlert, R
26. D. Martin, R
27. G. C. Wortley, R
28. M. F. McHugh, D
29. F. Horton, R
30. B. B. Conable, Jr., R
31. J. F. Kemp, R
32. J. J. LaFalce, D
33. H. J. Nowak, D
34. S. N. Lundine, D

NORTH CAROLINA
1. W. B. Jones, D
2. *I. T. Valentine, Jr., D

3. C. O. Whitley, Sr., D
4. I. F. Andrews, D
5. S. L. Neal, D
6. *R. Britt, D
7. C. Rose, D
8. W. G. Hefner, D
9. J. G. Martin, R
10. J. T. Broyhill, R
11. *J. M. Clarke, D

NORTH DAKOTA
At-L. B. Dorgan, D

OHIO
1. T. A. Luken, D
2. W. D. Gradison, Jr., R
3. T. Hall, D
4. M. Oxley, R
5. D. L. Latta, R
6. B. McEwen, R
7. *M. DeWine, R
8. T. N. Kindness, R
9. *M. Kaptur, D
10. C. E. Miller, R
11. D. E. Eckart, D
12. *J. R. Kasich, R
13. D. J. Pease, D
14. J. F. Seiberling, D
15. C. P. Wylie, R
16. R. Regula, R
17. L. Williams, R
18. D. Applegate, D
19. *E. F. Feighan, D
20. M. R. Oakar, D
21. L. Stokes, D

OKLAHOMA
1. J. R. Jones, D
2. M. Synar, D
3. W. W. Watkins, D
4. D. McCurdy, D
5. M. Edwards, R
6. G. English, D

OREGON
1. L. AuCoin, D
2. *R. F. Smith, R
3. R. Wyden, D
4. J. Weaver, D
5. D. Smith, R

PENNSYLVANIA
1. T. Foglietta, D
2. W. Gray, D
3. *R. A. Borski, Jr., D
4. *J. P. Kolter, D
5. R. T. Schulze, R
6. G. Yatron, D
7. R. W. Edgar, D
8. P. H. Kostmayer, D
9. B. Shuster, R
10. J. M. McDade, R
11. *F. Harrison, D
12. J. P. Murtha, D
13. L. Coughlin, R
14. W. Coyne, D
15. D. Ritter, R
16. R. S. Walker, R
17. *G. W. Gekas, R
18. D. Walgren, D
19. W. F. Goodling, R
20. J. M. Gaydos, D
21. *T. J. Ridge, R
22. A. J. Murphy, D
23. W. Clinger, Jr., R

RHODE ISLAND
1. F. J. St Germain, D
2. C. Schneider, R

SOUTH CAROLINA
1. T. Hartnett, R
2. F. D. Spence, R
3. B. C. Derrick, Jr., D
4. C. Campbell, Jr., R
5. *J. Spratt, D
6. *R. M. Tallon, Jr., D

SOUTH DAKOTA
At-L. T. Daschle, D

TENNESSEE
1. J. H. Quillen, R
2. J. J. Duncan, R
3. M. L. Bouquard, D
4. *J. Cooper, D
5. W. H. Boner, D
6. A. Gore, Jr., D
7. *D. Sundquist, R
8. E. Jones, D
9. H. E. Ford, D

TEXAS
1. S. B. Hall, Jr., D
2. C. Wilson, D
3. *S. Bartlett, R
4. R. Hall, D
5. *J. Bryant, D
6. Vacant
7. B. Archer, R
8. J. Fields, R
9. J. Brooks, D
10. J. J. Pickle, D
11. J. M. Leath, D
12. J. C. Wright, Jr., D
13. J. E. Hightower, D
14. W. Patman, D
15. E. de la Garza, D
16. *R. Coleman, D
17. C. Stenholm, D
18. M. Leland, D
19. K. Hance, D
20. H. B. Gonzalez, D
21. T. Loeffler, R
22. R. Paul, R
23. A. Kazen, Jr., D
24. M. Frost, D
25. *M. Andrews, D
26. *T. Vandergriff, D
27. *S. P. Ortiz, D

UTAH
1. J. Hansen, R
2. D. D. Marriott, R
3. *H. C. Nielson, R

VERMONT
At-L. J. M. Jeffords, R

VIRGINIA
1. *H. H. Bateman, R
2. G. W. Whitehurst, R
3. T. Bliley, Jr., R
4. *N. Sisisky, D
5. D. Daniel, D
6. *J. R. Olin, D
7. J. K. Robinson, R
8. S. Parris, R
9. *F. C. Boucher, D
10. F. Wolf, R

WASHINGTON
1. J. M. Pritchard, R
2. A. Swift, D
3. D. L. Bonker, D
4. S. Morrison, R
5. T. S. Foley, D
6. N. D. Dicks, D
7. M. Lowry, D
8. *R. Chandler, R

WEST VIRGINIA
1. *A. B. Mollohan, D
2. *H. O. Staggers, Jr., D
3. *B. Wise, D
4. N. J. Rahall, II, D

WISCONSIN
1. L. Aspin, D
2. R. W. Kastenmeier, D
3. S. Gunderson, R
4. C. J. Zablocki, D
5. *J. Moody, D
6. T. E. Petri, R
7. D. R. Obey, D
8. T. Roth, R
9. F. J. Sensenbrenner, Jr., R

WYOMING
At-L. R. Cheney, R

AMERICAN SAMOA
Delegate, Fofo Sunia

DISTRICT OF COLUMBIA
Delegate, W. E. Fauntroy, D

GUAM
Delegate, Antonio Borja Won Pat

PUERTO RICO
Resident Commissioner
B. Corrada

VIRGIN ISLANDS
Delegate, Ron de Lugo

CANADA'S CONSTITUTION

Before a crowd of 30,000 on Parliament Hill in Ottawa, Canada, on April 17, 1982, Queen Elizabeth II proclaimed the Constitution Act, 1982, bringing into effect Canada's new constitution. The constitutional reform resolution, which had been agreed to by the English-speaking provinces of Canada in late 1981 and approved by Britain's House of Lords in March 1982, granted Canada independence and the power to amend its laws without the approval of the British Parliament. It officially ended the British North America Act of 1867. Speaking in French, the Queen noted that the province of Quebec had boycotted the ceremony. ''Despite the regretted absence of the Premier of Quebec,'' the Queen said, ''it is only just to associate Quebecers with this celebration of renewal because without them Canada would not be what it is today.''

UPI

CONSTITUTION ACT, 1982

PART I
SCHEDULE B

CANADIAN CHARTER OF RIGHTS AND FREEDOMS

Whereas Canada is founded upon principles that recognize the supremacy of God and the rule of law:

Guarantee of Rights and Freedoms

1. The *Canadian Charter of Rights and Freedoms* guarantees the rights and freedoms set out in it subject only to such reasonable limits prescribed by law as can be demonstrably justified in a free and democratic society.

Fundamental Freedoms

2. Everyone has the following fundamental freedoms:
   (a) freedom of conscience and religion;
   (b) freedom of thought, belief, opinion and expression, including freedom of the press and other media of communication;
   (c) freedom of peaceful assembly; and
   (d) freedom of association.

Democratic Rights

3. Every citizen of Canada has the right to vote in an election of members of the House of Commons or of a legislative assembly and to be qualified for membership therein.
4. (1) No House of Commons and no legislative assembly shall continue for longer than five years from the date fixed for the return of the writs at a general election of its members.
   (2) In time of real or apprehended war, invasion or insurrection, a House of Commons may be continued by Parliament and a legislative assembly may be continued by the legislature beyond five years if such continuation is not opposed by the votes of more than one-third of the members of the House of Commons or the legislative assembly, as the case may be.

5. There shall be a sitting of Parliament and of each legislature at least once every twelve months.

Mobility Rights

6. (1) Every citizen of Canada has the right to enter, remain in and leave Canada.
   (2) Every citizen of Canada and every person who has the status of a permanent resident of Canada has the right
       (a) to move to and take up residence in any province; and
       (b) to pursue the gaining of a livelihood in any province.
   (3) The rights specified in subsection (2) are subject to
       (a) any laws or practices of general application in force in a province other than those that discriminate among persons primarily on the basis of province of present or previous residence; and
       (b) any laws providing for reasonable residency requirements as a qualification for the receipt of publicly provided social services.
   (4) Subsections (2) and (3) do not preclude any law, program or activity that has as its object the amelioration in a province of conditions of individuals in that province who are socially or economically disadvantaged if the rate of employment in that province is below the rate of employment in Canada.

Legal Rights

7. Everyone has the right to life, liberty and security of the person and the right not to be deprived thereof except in accordance with the principles of fundamental justice.

8. Everyone has the right to be secure against unreasonable search or seizure.

9. Everyone has the right not to be arbitrarily detained or imprisoned.

10. Everyone has the right on arrest or detention
   (a) to be informed promptly of the reasons therefor;
   (b) to retain and instruct counsel without delay and to be informed of that right; and
   (c) to have the validity of the detention determined by way of *habeas corpus* and to be released if the detention is not lawful.

11. Any person charged with an offence has the right
   (a) to be informed without unreasonable delay of the specific offence;
   (b) to be tried within a reasonable time;
   (c) not to be compelled to be a witness in proceedings against that person in respect of the offence;
   (d) to be presumed innocent until proven guilty according to law in a fair and public hearing by an independent and impartial tribunal;
   (e) not to be denied reasonable bail without just cause;
   (f) except in the case of an offence under military law tried before a military tribunal, to the benefit of trial by jury where the maximum punishment for the offence is imprisonment for five years or a more severe punishment;
   (g) not to be found guilty on account of any act or omission unless, at the time of the act or omission, it constituted an offence under Canadian or international law or was criminal according to the general principles of law recognized by the community of nations;
   (h) if finally aquitted of the offence, not to be tried for it again and, if finally found guilty and punished for the offence, not to be tried or punished for it again; and
   (i) if found guilty of the offence and if the punishment for the offence has been varied between the time of commission and the time of sentencing, to the benefit of the lesser punishment.

12. Everyone has the right not to be subjected to any cruel and unusual treatment or punishment.

13. A witness who testifies in any proceedings has the right not to have any incriminating evidence so given used to incriminate that witness in any other proceedings, except in a prosecution for perjury or for the giving of contradictory evidence.

14. A party or witness in any proceedings who does not understand or speak the language in which the proceedings are conducted or who is deaf has the right to the assistance of an interpreter.

Equality Rights

15. (1) Every individual is equal before and under the law and has the right to the equal protection and equal benefit of the law without discrimination and, in particular, without discrimination based on race, national or ethnic origin, colour, religion, sex, age or mental or physical disability.
   (2) Subsection (1) does not preclude any law, program or activity that has as its object the amelioration of conditions of disadvantaged individuals or groups including those that are disadvantaged because of race, national or ethnic origin, colour, religion, sex, age or mental or physical disability.

Official Languages of Canada

16. (1) English and French are the official languages of Canada and have equality of status and equal rights and privileges as to their use in all institutions of the Parliament and government of Canada.
   (2) English and French are the official languages of New Brunswick and have equality of status and equal rights and privileges as to their use in all institutions of the legislature and government of New Brunswick.

(3) Nothing in this Charter limits the authority of Parliament or a legislature to advance the equality of status or use of English and French.

17. (1) Everyone has the right to use English or French in any debates and other proceedings of Parliament.
   (2) Everyone has the right to use English or French in any debates and other proceedings of the legislature of New Brunswick.

18. (1) The statutes, records and journals of Parliament shall be printed and published in English and French and both language versions are equally authoritative.
   (2) The statutes, records and journals of the legislature of New Brunswick shall be printed and published in English and French and both language versions are equally authoritative.

19. (1) Either English or French may be used by any person in, or in any pleading in or process issuing from, any court established by Parliament.
   (2) Either English or French may be used by any person in, or in any pleading in or process issuing from, any court of New Brunswick.

20. (1) Any member of the public in Canada has the right to communicate with, and to receive available services from, any head or central office of an institution of the Parliament or government of Canada in English or French, and has the same right with respect to any other office of any such institution where
   (a) there is a significant demand for communications with and services from that office in such language; or
   (b) due to the nature of the office, it is reasonable that communications with and services from that office be available in both English and French.
   (2) Any member of the public in New Brunswick has the right to communicate with, and to receive available services from, any office of an institution of the legislature or government of New Brunswick in English or French.

21. Nothing in sections 16 to 20 abrogates or derogates from any right, privilege or obligation with respect to the English and French languages, or either of them, that exists or is continued by virtue of any other provision of the Constitution of Canada.

22. Nothing in sections 16 to 20 abrogates or derogates from any legal or customary right or privilege acquired or enjoyed either before or after the coming into force of this Charter with respect to any language that is not English or French.

Minority Language Educational Rights

23. (1) Citizens of Canada
   (a) whose first language learned and still understood is that of the English or French linguistic minority population of the province in which they reside, or
   (b) who have received their primary school instruction in Canada in English or French and reside in a province where the language in which they received that instruction is the language of the English or French linguistic minority population of the province,

   have the right to have their children receive primary and secondary school instruction in that language in that province.

   (2) Citizens of Canada of whom any child has received or is receiving primary or secondary school instruction in English or French in Canada, have the right to have all their children receive primary and secondary school instruction in the same language.

   (3) The right of citizens of Canada under subsections (1) and (2) to have their children receive primary and secondary school instruction in the language of the English or French linguistic minority population of a province

(a) applies wherever in the province the number of children of citizens who have such a right is sufficient to warrant the provision to them out of public funds of minority language instruction; and

(b) includes, where the number of those children so warrants, the right to have them receive that instruction in minority language educational facilities provided out of public funds.

Enforcement

24. (1) Anyone whose rights or freedoms, as guaranteed by this Charter, have been infringed or denied may apply to a court of competent jurisdiction to obtain such remedy as the court considers appropriate and just in the circumstances.

(2) Where, in proceedings under subsection (1), a court concludes that evidence was obtained in a manner that infringed or denied any rights or freedoms guaranteed by this Charter, the evidence shall be excluded if it is established that, having regard to all the circumstances, the admission of it in the proceedings would bring the administration of justice into disrepute.

General

25. The guarantee of this Charter of certain rights and freedoms shall not be construed so as to abrogate or derogate from any aboriginal, treaty or other rights or freedoms that pertain to the aboriginal peoples of Canada including

(a) any rights or freedoms that have been recognized by the Royal Proclamation of October 7, 1763; and

(b) any rights or freedoms that may be acquired by the aboriginal peoples of Canada by way of land claims settlement.

26. The guarantee in this Charter of certain rights and freedoms shall not be construed as denying the existence of any other rights or freedoms that exist in Canada.

27. This Charter shall be interpreted in a manner consistent with the preservation and enhancement of the multicultural heritage of Canadians.

28. Notwithstanding anything in this Charter, the rights and freedoms referred to in it are guaranteed equally to male and female persons.

29. Nothing in this Charter abrogates or derogates from any rights or privileges guaranteed by or under the Constitution of Canada in respect of denominational, separate or dissentient schools.

30. A reference in this Charter to a province or to the legislative assembly or legislature of a province shall be deemed to include a reference to the Yukon Territory and the Northwest Territories, or to the appropriate legislative authority thereof, as the case may be.

31. Nothing is this Charter extends the legislative powers of any body or authority.

Application of Charter

32. (1) This Charter applies

(a) to the Parliament and government of Canada in respect of all matters within the authority of Parliament including all matters relating to the Yukon Territory and Northwest Territories; and

(b) to the legislature and government of each province in respect of all matters within the authority of the legislature of each province.

(2) Notwithstanding subsection (1), section 15 shall not have effect until three years after this section comes into force.

33. (1) Parliament or the legislature of a province may expressly declare in an Act of Parliament or of the legislature, as the case may be, that the Act or a provision thereof shall operate notwithstanding a provision included in section 2 or sections 7 to 15 of this Charter.

(2) An Act or a provision of an Act in respect of which a declaration made under this section is in effect shall have such operation as it would have but for the provision of this Charter referred to in the declaration.

(3) A declaration made under subsection (1) shall cease to have effect five years after it comes into force or on such earlier date as may be specified in the declaration.

(4) Parliament or a legislature of a province may re-enact a declaration made under subsection (1).

(5) Subsection (3) applies in respect of a re-enactment made under subsection (4).

Citation

34. This part may be cited as the *Canadian Charter of Rights and Freedoms*.

PART II
RIGHTS OF THE ABORIGINAL PEOPLES OF CANADA

35. (1) The existing aboriginal and treaty rights of the aboriginal peoples of Canada are hereby recognized and affirmed.

(2) In this Act, "aboriginal peoples of Canada" includes the Indian, Inuit and Métis peoples of Canada.

PART III
EQUALIZATION AND REGIONAL DISPARITIES

36. (1) Without altering the legislative authority of Parliament or of the provincial legislatures, or the rights of any of them with respect to the exercise of their legislative authority, Parliament and the legislatures, together with the government of Canada and the provincial governments, are committed to

(a) promoting equal opportunities for the well-being of Canadians;

(b) furthering economic development to reduce disparity in opportunities; and

(c) providing essential public services of reasonable quality to all Canadians.

(2) Parliament and the government of Canada are committed to the principle of making equalization payments to ensure that provincial governments have sufficient revenues to provide reasonably comparable levels of public services at reasonably comparable levels of taxation.

PART IV
CONSTITUTIONAL CONFERENCE

37. (1) A constitutional conference composed of the Prime Minister of Canada and the first ministers of the provinces shall be convened by the Prime Minister of Canada within one year after this Part comes into force.

(2) The conference convened under subsection (1) shall have included in its agenda an item respecting constitutional matters that directly affect the aboriginal peoples of Canada, including the identification and definition of the rights of those peoples to be included in the Constitution of Canada, and the Prime Minister of Canada shall invite representatives of those peoples to participate in the discussions on that item.

(3) The Prime Minister of Canada shall invite elected representatives of the governments of the Yukon Territory and the Northwest Territories to participate in the discussions on any item on the agenda of the conference convened under subsection (1) that, in the opinion of the Prime Minister, directly affects the Yukon Territory and the Northwest Territories.

PART V
PROCEDURE FOR AMENDING CONSTITUTION OF CANADA

38. (1) An amendment to the Constitution of Canada may be made by proclamation issued by the Governor General under the Great Seal of Canada where so authorized by

  (a) resolutions of the Senate and House of Commons; and

  (b) resolutions of the legislative assemblies of at least two-thirds of the provinces that have, in the aggregate, according to the then latest general census, at least fifty per cent of the population of all the provinces.

  (2) An amendment made under subsection (1) that derogates from the legislative powers, the proprietary rights or any other rights or privileges of the legislature or government of a province shall require a resolution supported by a majority of the members of each of the Senate, the House of Commons and the legislative assemblies required under subsection (1).

  (3) An amendment referred to in subsection (2) shall not have effect in a province the legislative assembly of which has expressed its dissent thereto by resolution supported by a majority of its members prior to the issue of the proclamation to which the amendment relates unless that legislative assembly, subsequently, by resolution supported by a majority of its members, revokes its dissent and authorizes the amendment.

  (4) A resolution of dissent made for the purposes of subsection (3) may be revoked at any time before or after the issue of the proclamation to which it relates.

39. (1) A proclamation shall not be issued under subsection 38(1) before the expiration of one year from the adoption of the resolution initiating the amendment procedure thereunder, unless the legislative assembly of each province has previously adopted a resolution of assent or dissent.

  (2) A proclamation shall not be issued under subsection 38(1) after the expiration of three years from the adoption of the resolution initiating the amendment procedure thereunder.

40. Where an amendment is made under subsection 38(1) that transfers provincial legislative powers relating to education or other cultural matters from provincial legislatures to Parliament, Canada shall provide reasonable compensation to any province to which the amendment does not apply.

41. An amendment to the Constitution of Canada in relation to the following matters may be made by proclamation issued by the Governor General under the Great Seal of Canada only where authorized by resolutions of the Senate and House of Commons and of the legislative assembly of each province:

  (a) the office of the Queen, the Governor General and the Lieutenant Governor of a province;

  (b) the right of a province to a number of members in the House of Commons not less than the number of Senators by which the province is entitled to be represented at the time this Part comes into force;

  (c) subject to section 43, the use of the English or the French language;

  (d) the composition of the Supreme Court of Canada; and

  (e) an amendment to this Part.

42. (1) An amendment to the Constitution of Canada in relation to the following matters may be made only in accordance with subsection 38(1):

  (a) the principle of proportionate representation of the provinces in the House of Commons prescribed by the Constitution of Canada;

  (b) the powers of the Senate and the method of selecting Senators;

  (c) the number of members by which a province is entitled to be represented in the Senate and the residence qualifications of Senators;

  (d) subject to paragraph 41(d), the Supreme Court of Canada;

  (e) the extension of existing provinces into the territories; and

  (f) notwithstanding any other law or practice, the establishment of new provinces.

  (2) Subsections 38(2) to (4) do not apply in respect of amendments in relation to matters referred to in subsection (1).

43. An amendment to the Constitution of Canada in relation to any provision that applies to one or more, but not all, provinces, including

  (a) any alteration to boundaries between provinces, and

  (b) any amendment to any provision that relates to the use of the English or the French language within a province,

may be made by proclamation issued by the Governor General under the Great Seal of Canada only where so authorized by resolutions of the Senate and House of Commons and of the legislative assembly of each province to which the amendment applies.

44. Subject to sections 41 and 42, Parliament may exclusively make laws amending the Constitution of Canada in relation to the executive government of Canada or the Senate and House of Commons.

45. Subject to section 41, the legislature of each province may exclusively make laws amending the constitution of the province.

46. (1) The procedures for amendment under sections 38, 41, 42 and 43 may be initiated either by the Senate or the House of Commons or by the legislative assembly of a province.

  (2) A resolution of assent made for the purposes of this Part may be revoked at any time before the issue of a proclamation authorized by it.

47. (1) An amendment to the Constitution of Canada made by proclamation under section 38, 41, 42 or 43 may be made without a resolution of the Senate authorizing the issue of the proclamation if, within one hundred and eighty days after the adoption by the House of Commons of a resolution authorizing its issue, the Senate has not adopted such a resolution and if, at any time after the expiration of that period, the House of Commons again adopts the resolution.

  (2) Any period when Parliament is prorogued or dissolved shall not be counted in computing the one hundred and eighty day period referred to in subsection (1).

48. The Queen's Privy Council for Canada shall advise the Governor General to issue a proclamation under this Part forthwith on the adoption of the resolutions required for an amendment made by proclamation under this Part.

49. A constitutional conference composed of the Prime Minister of Canada and the first ministers of the provinces shall be convened by the Prime Minister of Canada within fifteen years after this Part comes into force to review the provisions of this Part.

PART VI
AMENDMENT TO THE CONSTITUTION ACT, 1867

50. The *Constitution Act, 1867* (formerly named the *British North America Act, 1867*) is amended by adding thereto, immediately after section 92 thereof the following heading and section:

"Non-renewable Natural Resources, Forestry Resources and Electrical Energy

92A. (1) In each province, the legislature may exclusively make laws in relation to

(a) exploration for non-renewable natural resources in the province;

(b) development, conservation and management of non-renewable natural resources and forestry resources in the province, including laws in relation to the rate of primary production therefrom; and

(c) development, conservation and management of sites and facilities in the province for the generation and production of electrical energy.

(2) In each province, the legislature may make laws in relation to the export from the province to another part of Canada of the primary production from non-renewable natural resources and forestry resources in the province and the production from facilities in the province for the generation of electrical energy, but such laws may not authorize or provide for discrimination in prices or in supplies exported to another part of Canada.

(3) Nothing in subsection (2) derogates from the authority of Parliament to enact laws in relation to the matters referred to in that subsection and, where such a law of Parliament and a law of a province conflict, the law of Parliament prevails to the extent of the conflict.

(4) In each province, the legislature may make laws in relation to the raising of money by any mode or system of taxation in respect of

(a) non-renewable natural resources and forestry resources in the province and the primary production therefrom, and

(b) sites and facilities in the province for the generation of electrical energy and the production therefrom,

whether or not such production is exported in whole or in part from the province, but such laws may not authorize or provide for taxation that differentiates between production exported to another part of Canada and production not exported from the province.

(5) The expression "primary production" has the meaning assigned by the Sixth Schedule.

(6) Nothing in subsections (1) to (5) derogates from any powers or rights that a legislature or government of a province had immediately before the coming into force of this section."

51. The said Act is further amended by adding thereto the following Schedule:

"THE SIXTH SCHEDULE

Primary Production from Non-renewable Natural Resources and Forestry Resources

1. For the purposes of section 92A of this Act,

(a) production from a non-renewable natural resource is primary production therefrom if

(i) it is in the form in which it exists upon its recovery or severence from its natural state, or

(ii) it is a product resulting from processing or refining the resource, and is not a manufactured product or a product resulting from refining crude oil, refining upgraded heavy crude oil, refining gases or liquids derived from coal or refining a synthetic equivalent of crude oil; and

(b) production from a forestry resource is primary production therefrom if it consists of sawlogs, poles, lumber, wood chips, sawdust or any other primary wood product, or wood pulp, and is not a product manufactured from wood."

PART VII
GENERAL

52. (1) The Constitution of Canada is the supreme law of Canada, and any law that is inconsistent with the provisions of the Constitution is, to the extent of the inconsistency, of no force or effect.

(2) The Constitution of Canada includes

(a) the *Canada Act*, including this Act;

(b) the Acts and orders referred to in Schedule I; and

(c) any amendment to any Act or order referred to in paragraph (a) or (b).

(3) Amendments to the Constitution of Canada shall be made only in accordance with the authority contained in the Constitution of Canada.

53. (1) The enactments referred to in Column I of Schedule I are hereby repealed or amended to the extent indicated in Column II thereof and, unless repealed, shall continue as law in Canada under the names set out in Column III thereof.

(2) Every enactment, except the *Canada Act*, that refers to an enactment referred to in Schedule I by the name in Column I thereof is hereby amended by substituting for that name the corresponding name in Column III thereof, and any British North America Act not referred to in Schedule I may be cited as the *Constitution Act* followed by the year and number, if any, of its enactment.

54. Part IV is repealed on the day that is one year after this Part comes into force and this section may be repealed and this Act renumbered, consequential upon the repeal of Part IV and this section, by proclamation issued by the Governor General under the Great Seal of Canada.

55. A French version of the portions of the Constitution of Canada referred to in Schedule I shall be prepared by the Minister of Justice of Canada as expeditiously as possible and, when any portion thereof sufficient to warrant action being taken has been so prepared, it shall be put forward for enactment by proclamation issued by the Governor General under the Great Seal of Canada pursuant to the procedure then applicable to an amendment of the same provisions of the Constitution of Canada.

56. Where any portion of the Constitution of Canada has been or is enacted in English and French or where a French version of any portion of the Constitution is enacted pursuant to section 55, the English and French versions of that portion of the Constitution are equally authoritative.

57. The English and French versions of this Act are equally authoritative.

58. Subject to section 59, this Act shall come into force on a day to be fixed by proclamation issued by the Queen or the Governor General under the Great Seal of Canada.

59. (1) Paragraph 23(1) (a) shall come into force in respect of Quebec on a day to be fixed by proclamation issued by the Queen or the Governor General under the Great Seal of Canada.

(2) A proclamation under subsection (1) shall be issued only where authorized by the legislative assembly or government of Quebec.

(3) This section may be repealed on the day paragraph 23(1) (a) comes into force in respect of Quebec and this Act amended and renumbered, consequential upon the repeal of this section, by proclamation issued by the Queen or the Governor General under the Great Seal of Canada.

60. This Act may be cited as the *Constitution Act, 1981*, and the Constitution Acts 1867 to 1975 (No. 2) and this Act may be cited together as the *Constitution Acts, 1867 to 1981*.

See also CANADA.

Contributors

ADRIAN, CHARLES R., Professor of Political Science, University of California, Riverside; Coauthor, *Governing Urban America:* CALIFORNIA; LOS ANGELES

ALEXANDER, ROBERT J., Professor of Economics and Political Science, Rutgers University: BOLIVIA; ECUADOR; GUYANA; URUGUAY

AMBRE, AGO, Economist, Bureau of Economic Analysis, U.S. Department of Commerce: INDUSTRIAL PRODUCTION

BARMASH, ISADORE, Business Writer, *The New York Times;* Author, *The Chief Executives:* RETAILING

BATRA, PREM P., Professor of Biochemistry, Wright State University: BIOCHEMISTRY

BECK, KAY, School of Urban Life, Georgia State University: ATLANTA; GEORGIA

BERGEN, DANIEL P., Professor, Graduate Library School, University of Rhode Island, Kingston, RI: LIBRARIES

BERLIN, MICHAEL J., Diplomatic Correspondent, *New York Post:* BIOGRAPHY—*Javier Pérez de Cuellar;* UNITED NATIONS

BERNHARDT, ARTHUR D., President, Program in Industrialization of the Housing Sector; Author, *Building Tomorrow: The Mobile/Manufactured Housing Industry:* HOUSING—*Manufactured Homes*

BEST, JOHN, Chief, *Canada World News,* Ottawa: NEW BRUNSWICK; PRINCE EDWARD ISLAND

BÖDVARSSON, HAUKUR, Coeditor, *News From Iceland:* ICELAND

BOLUS, JIM, Sports Department, *The Louisville Times;* Author, *Run for the Roses:* SPORTS—*Horse Racing*

BOND, DONOVAN H., Professor of Journalism, West Virginia University: WEST VIRGINIA

BOULAY, HARVEY, Assistant Professor of Political Science, Boston University; Author, *The Twilight Cities:* MASSACHUSETTS

BRADY, RAY, Business-Financial Commentator, CBS-TV; member, board of governors, New York Financial Writers Association: PERSONAL INVESTING IN THE 1980s

BRAMMER, DANA B., Associate Director, Bureau of Governmental Research, University of Mississippi: MISSISSIPPI

BRANDHORST, L. CARL, Associate Professor of Geography, Western Oregon State College, Monmouth, OR: OREGON

BURKS, ARDATH W., Professor Emeritus of Asian Studies, Rutgers University; Author, *Japan: Profile of a Postindustrial Power:* JAPAN

BUSH, GRAHAM W.A., Associate Professor of Political Studies, University of Auckland, New Zealand; Author, *Local Government & Politics in New Zealand:* NEW ZEALAND

BUTWELL, RICHARD, Vice President for Academic Affairs and Professor of Political Science, University of South Dakota, Vermillion, SD; Author, *Southeast Asia, a Political Introduction, Southeast Asia Today and Tomorrow, U Nu of Burma, Foreign Policy and the Developing State:* ASIA; BURMA; LAOS; PHILIPPINES

CALABRESE, MICHAEL A., Program Manager, National Aeronautics and Space Administration: SPACE EXPLORATION (article written independently of NASA)

CALABRIA, PAT, Sports Department, *Newsday,* Long Island, NY: SPORTS—*Ice Hockey, Violence in Hockey*

CANN, STANLEY, Consultant, *The Forum,* Fargo, ND: NORTH DAKOTA

CARLYLE-GORDGE, PETER, Manitoba Correspondent, *Maclean's* magazine; writer for *The Financial Post, Toronto Star, Montreal Gazette,* and *Winnipeg Sun:* MANITOBA

CHALMERS, JOHN W., Concordia College, Edmonton, Alberta; Editor, *Alberta Diamond Jubilee Anthology:* ALBERTA

CLARK, DICK, Host, *American Bandstand;* Author, *Dick Clark's First 25 Years of Rock 'n' Roll* (1981): Dick Clark Remembers . . . 25+ Years of Rock 'n' Roll

CLARKE, JAMES W., Professor of Political Science, University of Arizona: ARIZONA

CLIFT, ELEANOR, White House Correspondent, *Newsweek* magazine: BIOGRAPHY—*William P. Clark, George Shultz, Caspar Weinberger*

COCKRUM, E. LENDELL, Professor and Head, Department of Ecology and Evolutionary Biology, University of Arizona: ZOOLOGY

COHEN, SIDNEY, Clinical Professor of Psychiatry, UCLA School of Medicine; Author, *The Beyond Within: The LSD Story, The Substance Abuse Problems, The Drug Dilemma:* DRUG AND ALCOHOL ABUSE

COLE, GORDON H., Senior Staff Associate, George Meany Center for Labor Studies: LABOR

COLE, JOHN N., Contributing Editor, *Maine Times;* Author, *From the Ground Up, Countryside/Cityside:* MAINE

COLLINS, BOB, Sports Editor, *The Indianapolis Star:* SPORTS—*Auto Racing*

COMMANDAY, ROBERT, Music Critic, *San Francisco Chronicle:* BIOGRAPHY—*Placido Domingo;* MUSIC—*Classical*

CONNALLY, EUGENIA HORSTMAN, Editor, *National Parks* magazine; Editor, *National Parks in Crisis:* ENVIRONMENT—*The U.S. National Park System*

CORLEW, ROBERT E., Dean, School of Liberal Arts, Middle Tennessee State University: TENNESSEE

CORNWELL, ELMER E., JR., Professor of Political Science, Brown University: RHODE ISLAND

CUNNIFF, JOHN, Business News Analyst, The Associated Press; Author, *How to Stretch Your Dollar:* HOUSING; UNITED STATES—*The Economy*

CUNNINGHAM, PEGGY, Staff Reporter, *Baltimore News American:* MARYLAND

CURRIER, CHET, Financial Writer, The Associated Press: STOCKS AND BONDS

CURTIS, L. PERRY, JR., Professor of History, Brown University: IRELAND

DANIELS, ROBERT V., Professor of History, University of Vermont: VERMONT

DARBY, JOSEPH W., III, Reporter, *The Times-Picayune/States-Item:* LOUISIANA

DE GREGORIO, GEORGE, Sports Department, *The New York Times;* Author, *Joe DiMaggio, An Informal Biography:* OBITUARIES—*Red Smith;* SPORTS—*Boxing, Ice Skating, Skiing, Swimming, Track*

DELZELL, CHARLES F., Professor of History, Vanderbilt University; Author, *Italy in the Twentieth Century:* ITALY

DENNIS, LARRY, Senior Editor, *Golf Digest;* Coauthor, *How to Become a Complete Golfer:* SPORTS—*Golf*

DIETERICH, H. R., Professor, History/American Studies, University of Wyoming, Laramie: WYOMING

DONNELLY, HARRISON, Reporter, *Congressional Quarterly:* UNITED STATES—*The New Federalism Plan*

DORPALEN, ANDREAS, late Professor Emeritus of History, The Ohio State University: BIOGRAPHY—*Helmut Kohl;* GERMANY

DRACHKOVITCH, MILORAD M., Senior Fellow, The Hoover Institute on War, Revolution, and Peace, Stanford University; Author, *U.S. Aid to Yugoslavia and Poland:* YUGOSLAVIA

DRIGGS, DON V., Professor of Political Science, University of Nevada; Coauthor, *The Nevada Constitution: Its Origin and Growth:* NEVADA

DUFF, ERNEST A., Professor of Political Science, Randolph-Macon Woman's College; Author, *Agrarian Reform in Colombia:* COLOMBIA

DUFFY, HELEN, Art Critic and Curator to The Art Centre, Queen's University, Kingston, Ontario: CANADA—*The Arts*

DURNIAK, ANTHONY, Data Processing Editor, *Business Week:* COMPUTERS

DUROSKA, LUD, *The New York Times;* Author/editor, *Football Rules in Pictures, Great Pro Quarterbacks,* and *Great Pro Running Backs:* SPORTS—*Football, The Pro Football Strike*

DURRENCE, J. LARRY, Department of History and Political Science, Florida Southern College; mayor of Lakeland, FL: FLORIDA

EINFRANK, AARON R., Free-lance Foreign Correspondent, Specialist in the Middle East, Third World, and Soviet Affairs: IRAN; IRAQ; THIRD WORLD

ELGIN, RICHARD, Metro Desk, *The Patriot, The Evening News,* and *The Sunday Patriot-News,* Harrisburg, PA: PENNSYLVANIA

ELKINS, ANN M., Fashion Director, *Good Housekeeping Magazine:* FASHION

ENGEL, MARK, Managing Editor, *Basketball Weekly:* BIOGRAPHY—*Dean Smith;* SPORTS—*Basketball*

ENSTAD, ROBERT H., Writer, *Chicago Tribune:* CHICAGO; ILLINOIS

ETCHESON, WARREN W., Graduate School of Business Administration, University of Washington: WASHINGTON

EWEGEN, BOB, Editorial Writer, *The Denver Post:* COLORADO

FAGEN, M. D., Bell Telephone Laboratories (retired); Editor, *A History of Engineering and Science in the Bell System,* Vols. I and II: COMMUNICATION TECHNOLOGY

FINGARETTE, HERBERT, Professor of Philosophy, University of California, Santa Barbara; Author, *The Meaning of Criminal Insanity* and *Mental Disabilities and Criminal Responsibility:* LAW—*The Insanity Defense*

FLEMING, JAMES, Business Editor, Maclean's magazine: CANADA—*The Economy*

FRANCIS, DAVID R., Business Editor, *The Christian Science Monitor:* INTERNATIONAL TRADE AND FINANCE; UNITED STATES—*The National Debt*

FRIIS, ERIK J., Editor-Publisher, *The Scandinavian-American Bulletin;* Author, *The American-Scandinavian Foundation 1910–1960: A Brief History:* DENMARK; FINLAND

GAILEY, HARRY A., Professor of History and Coordinator of African Studies, San Jose State University, California: CHAD; GHANA; NIGERIA

GARFIELD, ROBERT, Associate Professor of History, Co-Director, Afro-American Studies Program, De Paul University, Chicago, IL; Editor, *Readings in World Civilizations:* KENYA; TANZANIA; UGANDA

GEIS, GILBERT, Professor, Program in Social Ecology, University of California, Irvine; Author, *Man, Crime and Society:* CRIME

GJESTER, THOR, Editor, *Økonomisk Revy,* Oslo: NORWAY

GOODMAN, DONALD, Associate Professor of Sociology, John Jay College of Criminal Justice, City University of New York: PRISONS

GORDON, MAYNARD M., Editor, *Motor News Analysis:* AUTOMOBILES

GRAYSON, GEORGE W., Professor of Government, College of William and Mary; Author, *Politics of Mexican Oil:* BIOGRAPHY—*Felipe González Márquez;* PORTUGAL; SPAIN

GREEN, MAUREEN, British Author and Journalist: GREAT BRITAIN—*The Arts;* LONDON

GRENIER, FERNAND, Interamerican Organization for Higher Education, Quebec: QUEBEC

GROTH, ALEXANDER J., Professor of Political Science, University of California, Davis; Author, *People's Poland: Government and Politics:* BIOGRAPHY—*Wojciech Jaruzelski;* OBITUARIES—*Wladyslaw Gomulka;* POLAND

GRUBERG, MARTIN, Professor of Political Science, University of Wisconsin, Oshkosh: LAW—*International*

HAKKARINEN, IDA, Research Meteorologist, Severe Storms Research Program, Support Group GSFC, General Software Corporation: METEOROLOGY—*The Weather Year*

HAND, SAMUEL B., Professor of History, University of Vermont: VERMONT

HARVEY, ROSS M., Assistant Director of Information, Government of the Northwest Territories: NORTHWEST TERRITORIES

HATHORN, RAMON, Associate Professor of French, University of Guelph, Guelph, Ontario: LITERATURE—*Canadian Literature: Quebec*

HAYES, KIRBY M., Professor of Food Science and Nutrition, University of Massachusetts: FOOD

HEADY, EARL O., Distinguished Professor of Agricultural Economics, Iowa State University; Author, *Economics of Agricultural Production and Resource* and *Agricultural Policies Under Economic Development:* AGRICULTURE

HECHINGER, FRED M., President, The New York Times Company Foundation, Inc.; Educational Columnist, *The New York Times;* Author, *The Big Red Schoolhouse;* Coauthor, *Teen-Age Tyranny* and *Growing Up in America:* EDUCATION—*The College Cost Factor*

HELMREICH, E. C., Thomas B. Reed Professor of History and Political Science, Bowdoin College, Bowdoin, ME; Author, *The German Churches Under Hitler: Background, Struggle, and Epilogue:* AUSTRIA

HELMREICH, JONATHAN E., Professor of History, Allegheny College, Meadville, PA; Author, *Belgium and Europe: A Study in Small Power Diplomacy:* LUXEMBOURG

HELMREICH, PAUL C., Professor of History, Wheaton College, Norton, MA: SWITZERLAND

HELMS, ANDREA R. C., Associate Professor of Political Science, University of Alaska: ALASKA

HENBERG, MARVIN, Department of Philosophy, University of Idaho: IDAHO

HENDERSON, JIM, Sportswriter, *The Tampa Tribune,* Tampa, FL; Former Publisher, *Annual Soccer Guide:* SPORTS—*Soccer*

HENRIKSEN, THOMAS H., Research Fellow, Hoover Institution on War, Revolution, and Peace, Stanford, CA; Author, *Mozambique: A History;* Coauthor, *The Struggle for Zimbabwe: Battle in the Bush:* ANGOLA; ZAIRE

HOGGART, SIMON, Special Correspondent, *The Observer,* London: BIOGRAPHY—*Roy Jenkins;* GREAT BRITAIN

HOOVER, HERBERT T., Professor of History, University of South Dakota: SOUTH DAKOTA

HOPKO, THE REV. THOMAS, Assistant Professor, St. Vladimir's Orthodox Theological Seminary, Crestwood, NY: RELIGION—*Orthodox Eastern*

HOTTELET, RICHARD C., United Nations Correspondent, CBS News: THE FALKLAND—*An Unlikely War*

HOWARD, HARRY N., Board of Governors Emeritus, Middle East Institute, Washington, DC; Author, *Turkey, The Straits and U.S. Policy:* TURKEY

HOYT, CHARLES K., Associate Editor, *Architectural Record,* Author, *Buildings for Commerce and Industry, Public, Municipal and Community Buildings, Interior Spaces Designed by Architects,* and *More Places for People:* ARCHITECTURE

HULBERT, DAN, *The Dallas Times-Herald:* TELEVISION AND RADIO

HULL, RICHARD W., Associate Professor of African History, New York University; Author, *Southern Africa: Civilization in Turmoil, Modern Africa: Change and Continuity,* and *African Cities and Towns Before the European Conquest:* AFRICA

HUME, ANDREW, Free-lance Writer/Photographer, Former Reporter, *The Whitehorse* (Yukon) *Star;* Author, *The Yukon:* YUKON

HUTH, JOHN F., JR., Free-lance Writer, Retired Reporter, *The Plain Dealer,* Cleveland: OHIO

JACKSON, LIVIA E. BITTON, Professor of Judaic and Hebraic Studies, Herbert H. Lehman College, City University of New York; Author, *Elli: Coming of Age in the Holocaust* and *Madonna or Courtesau? The Jewish Woman in Christian Literature:* ISRAEL; RELIGION—*Judaism*

JAFFE, HERMAN J., Department of Anthropology and Archaeology, Brooklyn College, City University of New York: ANTHROPOLOGY

JENNINGS, PETER, Chief Foreign Correspondent, ABC News; THE YEAR IN REVIEW

JEWELL, MALCOLM E., Professor of Political Science, University of Kentucky; Coauthor, *Kentucky Politics:* KENTUCKY

JOHNSON, JENNIFER, Librarian, Prairie History Room, Regina Public Library, Regina, Saskatchewan: SASKATCHEWAN

JOHNSON, WILLIAM OSCAR, Senior Writer, *Sports Illustrated:* SPORTS ON TELEVISION—*The Game Changes . . .*

JOHNSTON, ROBERT L., Editor, *The Catholic Review,* Baltimore, MD: RELIGION—*Roman Catholicism;* VATICAN CITY—*The Vatican Bank Case*

JOHNSTONE, J. K., Professor of English, University of Saskatchewan; Fellow of the Royal Society of Literature; Author, *The Bloomsbury Group:* LITERATURE—*English*

JONES, H. G., Curator, North Carolina Collection, University of North Carolina Library: NORTH CAROLINA

JOSEPH, LOU, Senior Science Writer, Hill and Knowlton: MEDICINE AND HEALTH—*Dentistry*

JOYAL, MARY JANE, Associate Editor, *The Numismatist,* Colorado Springs, CO: COINS AND COIN COLLECTING

KARNES, THOMAS L., Chairman, Department of History, Arizona State University; Author, *Latin American Policy of the United States* and *Failure of Union: Central America 1824–1960:* CENTRAL AMERICA

KARSKI, JAN, Professor of Government, Georgetown University; Author, *Story of a Secret State:* BULGARIA; HUNGARY; RUMANIA

KASH, DON E., George Lynn Cross Research Professor of Political Science, University of Oklahoma; Coauthor, *Our Energy Future* and *Energy Under the Oceans:* ENERGY

KEHR, ERNEST A., Stamp News Bureau; Author, *The Romance of Stamp Collecting:* STAMPS AND STAMP COLLECTING

KIMBALL, LORENZO K., Professor of Political Science, University of Utah: UTAH

KIMBELL, CHARLES L., Supervisory Physical Scientist, United States Bureau of Mines: MINING

KING, PETER J., Associate Professor of History; Carleton University, Ottawa: ONTARIO; OTTAWA

KISSELGOFF, ANNA, Chief Dance Critic, *The New York Times:* DANCE

LAI, CHUEN-YAN DAVID, Associate Professor of Geography, University of Victoria, B.C.: HONG KONG

LANDSBERG, H. E., Professor, University of Maryland; Author, *Physical Climatology, Weather and Health,* and *The Urban Climate:* METEOROLOGY

LAURENT, PIERRE-HENRI, Professor of History, Tufts University; Adjunct Professor of Diplomatic History, Fletcher School of Law and Diplomacy: BELGIUM

LAWRENCE, ROBERT M., Professor of Political Science, Colorado State University; Author, *Arms Control and Disarmament: Promise and Practice, Nuclear Proliferation: Phase II:* ARMS CONTROL; ARMS CONTROL—*The Nuclear Freeze Movement;* MILITARY AFFAIRS

LEVINE, LOUIS, Professor of Biology, City College of New York: GENETICS; MICROBIOLOGY

LEVITT, MORRIS J., Professor, Department of Political Science, Howard University; Coauthor, *Of, By and For the People: State and Local Government and Politics:* WASHINGTON, DC

LEWIS, JEROME R., Director for Public Administration, College of Urban Affairs and Public Policy, University of Delaware: DELAWARE

LIDDLE, R. WILLIAM, Professor of Political Science, The Ohio State University; Author, *Political Participation in Modern Indonesia:* INDONESIA

LINDAHL, MAC, Free-lance writer and translator: SWEDEN

LOBRON, BARBARA, Writer, Editor, Photographer; Copy Editor, *Camera Arts:* PHOTOGRAPHY

LYLES, JEAN CAFFEY, Associate Editor, *The Christian Century;* Author, *A Practical Vision of Christian Unity:* RELIGION—*Protestantism*

MABRY, DONALD J., Professor of History, Mississippi State University; Author, *Neighbors—Mexico and the United States:* BIOGRAPHY—*Miguel de la Madrid Hurtado;* MEXICO

McCORQUODALE, SUSAN, Associate Professor of Political Science, Memorial University of Newfoundland: NEWFOUNDLAND

McCUE, JULIA, Congressional Quarterly: WOMEN—*Trends in Childbearing*

McGILL, DAVID A., Professor of Marine Science, U.S. Coast Guard Academy, New London, CT: OCEANOGRAPHY

MADIER, MONIQUE, Free-lance Writer and Editor, Paris, France: FRANCE

MALONE, JULIA, Staff Correspondent, Washington Bureau, *The Christian Science Monitor:* BIOGRAPHY—*Phyllis Schlafly, Eleanor Smeal*

MARCOPOULOS, GEORGE J., Associate Professor of History, Tufts University, Medford, MA: CYPRUS; GREECE

MASOTTI, LOUIS H., Professor of Political Science, Urban Affairs and Policy Research, Northwestern University, Evanston, IL; Author, *The New Urban Politics* and *The City in Comparative Perspective:* CITIES AND URBAN AFFAIRS

MATHEWS, THOMAS G., Secretary General of the Association of Caribbean Universities, University of Puerto Rico; Author, *Politics and Economics in the Caribbean* and *Puerto Rican Politics and the New Deal:* CARIBBEAN; PUERTO RICO; TRINIDAD AND TOBAGO; VIRGIN ISLANDS

MEYER, EDWARD H., President and Chairman of the Board, Grey Advertising Inc.: ADVERTISING

MICHAELIS, PATRICIA A., Curator of Manuscripts, Kansas State Historical Society: KANSAS

MIRE, JOSEPH, Former Executive Director, National Institute for Labor Education: LABOR

MITCHELL, GARY, Professor of Physics, North Carolina State University, Raleigh: PHYSICS; PHYSICS—*Nuclear Fusion*

MORTON, DESMOND, Professor of History, University of Toronto; Author, *A Peculiar Kind of Politics, Canada and War,* and *Working People: An Illustrated History of Canadian Labour:* CANADA

MULLINER, K., Assistant to the Director of Libraries, Ohio University; Coeditor, *Southeast Asia, An Emerging Center of World Influence?* and *Malaysian Studies:* MALAYSIA; SINGAPORE; THAILAND

MUNSCH, VIRGINIA, Reporter and Assistant Editor, *The Richmond Times-Dispatch,* Richmond, VA: VIRGINIA

MURPHY, ROBERT F., *The Hartford Courant:* CONNECTICUT

NADLER, PAUL S., Professor of Finance, Rutgers University; Author, *Commercial Banking in the Economy* and *Paul Nadler Writes About Banking:* BANKING

NAFTALIN, ARTHUR, Professor of Public Affairs, Hubert H. Humphrey Institute of Public Affairs, University of Minnesota; MINNESOTA

NOLAN, WILLIAM C., Professor of Political Science, Southern Arkansas University: ARKANSAS

NOVICKI, MARGARET A., Assistant Editor, *Africa Report,* The African-American Institute: ALGERIA; MOROCCO; SUDAN; TUNISIA

OCHSENWALD, WILLIAM L., Associate Professor of History, Virginia Polytechnic Institute, Blacksburg, VA; Author, *The Hijaz Railroad;* Editor, *Nationalism in a Non-National State: The Dissolution of the Ottoman Empire:* BIOGRAPHY—*King Fahd;* SAUDI ARABIA

O'MEARA, PATRICK, Director, African Studies Program, Indiana University, Bloomington, IN; Coeditor, *Southern Africa: The Continuing Crisis* and *International Politics in Southern Africa:* SOUTH AFRICA; ZIMBABWE

O'ROURKE, E. N., Professor of Horticulture, Louisiana State University, Baton Rouge, LA: GARDENING AND HORTICULTURE

PALMER, NORMAN O., Professor Emeritus of Political Science and South Asian Studies, University of Pennsylvania: INDIA; SRI LANKA

PANO, NICHOLAS C., Professor of History, Western Illinois University; Author, *The People's Republic of Albania:* ALBANIA

PARDES, HERBERT, Director, National Institute of Mental Health: STRESS; MEDICINE AND HEALTH—*Mental Health*

PARKER, FRANKLIN, Benedum Professor of Education, West Virginia University; Author, *British Schools and Ours* and *U.S. Higher Education: A Guide to Education Sources;* coauthor, *Crucial Issues in Education:* EDUCATION

PEARSON, NEALE J., Associate Professor of Political Science, Texas Tech University, Lubbock, TX: CHILE; PERU; VENEZUELA

PERKINS, KENNETH J., Assistant Professor of History, University of South Carolina: LIBYA; RELIGION—*Islam*

PIPPIN, LARRY L., Professor of Political Science, Elbert Covell College, University of the Pacific; Author, *The Remon Era:* ARGENTINA; PARAGUAY

PLATT, HERMANN K., Professor of History, Saint Peter's College, Jersey City: NEW JERSEY

PLISCHKE, ELMER, Professor Emeritus, University of Maryland; Adjunct Professor, Gettysburg College; Adjunct Scholar, American Enterprise Institute; Author, *Foreign Relations Decisionmaking: Options Analysis, United States Diplomats and Their Missions, Microstates in World Affairs,* and *U.S. Foreign Relations: A Guide to Information Sources:* UNITED STATES—*Foreign Affairs*

POOLE, PETER A., Author, *ASEAN in the Pacific Community* and *The Vietnamese in Thailand:* CAMBODIA; VIETNAM

POPKIN, HENRY, Professor of English, State University of New York at Buffalo: THEATER

POULLADA, LEON B., Professor of Political Science, Northern Arizona University; Author, *Reform and Rebellion in Afghanistan:* AFGHANISTAN

PRITCHETT, C. HERMAN, Professor of Political Science, University of California, Santa Barbara; Author, *The Roosevelt Court and The American Constitution:* LAW—*U.S. Supreme Court*

QUIRK, WILLIAM H., Construction Consultant; Former North American Editor, *Construction Industry International* magazine: ENGINEERING, CIVIL

RAGUSA, ISA, Research Art Historian, Department of Art and Archaeology, Princeton University: ART

RAYMOND, ELLSWORTH L., Professor of Politics (retired), New York University; Author, *Soviet Economic Progress and The Soviet State:* BIOGRAPHY—*Yuri Andropov;* OBITUARIES—*Leonid Brezhnev;* USSR

REDITT, JACQUELINE, Free-lance Correspondent, Seoul, South Korea: KOREA

REUNING, WINIFRED, Writer, Polar Programs, National Science Foundation: POLAR RESEARCH

RICCIUTI, EDWARD R., Free-lance Writer; Author, *Audubon Society Book of Wild Animals* and *The Beachwalker's Guide:* ENVIRONMENT

RICHTER, WILLIAM L., Director, South Asia Center, Kansas State University: BANGLADESH; PAKISTAN

RIGGAN, WILLIAM, Associate Editor, *World Literature Today,* University of Oklahoma; Author, *Picaros, Madmen, Naifs, and Clowns: The Unreliable First-Person Narrator* and *Comparative Literature and Literary Theory:* LITERATURE—*World Literature*

ROBINSON, LEIF J., Editor, *Sky & Telescope:* ASTRONOMY

ROEDER, RICHARD B., Professor of History, Montana State University: MONTANA

ROSS, RUSSELL M., Professor of Political Science, University of Iowa; Author, *Iowa Government & Administration:* IOWA

ROTHSTEIN, MORTON, Professor of History, University of Wisconsin, Madison: SOCIAL WELFARE

ROWEN, HERBERT H., Professor, Rutgers University, New Brunswick, NJ; Editor, *The Low Countries in Early Modern Times: A Documentary History:* NETHERLANDS

ROWLETT, RALPH M., Professor of Anthropology, University of Missouri, Columbia: ARCHAEOLOGY

RUFF, NORMAN J., Assistant Professor, University of Victoria: BRITISH COLUMBIA

SALSINI, PAUL, State Editor, *The Milwaukee Journal:* WISCONSIN

SAMANSKY, ARTHUR W., Federal Reserve Bank of New York: CHINA—*Foreign Investment*

SAVAGE, DAVID, Course Supervisor, Continuing Studies Department, Simon Fraser University: LITERATURE—*Canadian Literature: English*

SCHERER, RON, Business and Financial Correspondent, *The Christian Science Monitor:* BUSINESS AND CORPORATE AFFAIRS; BUSINESS AND CORPORATE AFFAIRS—*Mergers and Antitrust*

SCHLOSSBERG, DAN, Baseball Writer; Author, *The Baseball Catalog, Barons of the Bullpen,* and *Hammerin' Hank: The Henry Aaron Story:* SPORTS—*Baseball*

SCHROEDER, RICHARD C., Washington Bureau Chief, Vision, Latin American News magazine, and syndicated writer for U.S. newspapers; Author, *The Politics of Drugs: An American Dilemma:* BRAZIL; LATIN AMERICA; REFUGEES AND IMMIGRATION

SCHWAB, PETER, Professor, Political Science, State University of New York at Purchase; Author, *Decision-Making in Ethiopia* and *Haile Selassie I:* ETHIOPIA

SCOTT, EUGENE L., Publisher and Founder, *Tennis Week;* Author, *Björn Borg: My Life & Game, Tennis: Game of Motion,* and *The Tennis Experience:* SPORTS—*Tennis*

SETH, R. P., Professor of Economics, Mount Saint Vincent University, Halifax: NOVA SCOTIA

SEYBOLD, PAUL G., Professor of Chemistry and Biological Chemistry, Wright State University, Dayton, OH: CHEMISTRY

SHOGAN, ROBERT, National Political Correspondent, Washington Bureau, *Los Angeles Times;* Author, *A Question of Judgement* and *Promises to Keep:* UNITED STATES—*Domestic Affairs, Elections*

SIEGEL, STANLEY E., Professor of History, University of Houston; Author, *A Political History of the Texas Republic, 1836-1845:* TEXAS

SIMMONS, MARC, Author, *New Mexico, A Bicentennial History:* NEW MEXICO

SPECTER, MICHAEL, *The New York Times:* NEW YORK; NEW YORK CITY

SPERA, DOMINIC, Associate Professor of Music, Indiana University; Author, *The Prestige Series—16 Original Compositions for Jazz Band:* MUSIC—*Jazz*

STENCEL, SANDRA, Managing Editor, *Editorial Research Reports:* WOMEN

STERN, JEROME H., Associate Professor of English, Florida State University: BIOGRAPHY—*John Updike;* LITERATURE—*American;* OBITUARIES—*John Cheever, Archibald MacLeish*

STEWART, WILLIAM H., JR., Associate Professor of Political Science, The University of Alabama; Author, *The Alabama Constitutional Commission* and *Alabama and the Energy Crisis:* ALABAMA

STOKES, WILLIAM LEE, Professor, Department of Geology and Geophysics, University of Utah; Author, *Essentials of Earth History* and *Introduction to Geology:* GEOLOGY

STOUDEMIRE, ROBERT H., Professor of Government, University of South Carolina: SOUTH CAROLINA

STULL, CAROLYN, Free-lance Travel Writer: TRAVEL

SYLVESTER, LORNA LUTES, Associate Editor, *Indiana Magazine of History,* Indiana University, Bloomington; Editor, *No Cheap Padding: Seventy-Five Years of the Indiana Magazine of History:* INDIANA

TABORSKY, EDWARD, Professor of Government, University of Texas, Austin; Author, *Communism in Czechoslovakia, 1948-1960* and *Communist Penetration of the Third World:* CZECHOSLOVAKIA

TAFT, WILLIAM HOWARD, Professor Emeritus of Journalism, University of Missouri; Author, *American Journalism History, American Magazines for the 1980s:* PUBLISHING; PUBLISHING—*The Specialized Magazines*

TAN, CHESTER C., Department of History, New York University; Author, *The Boxer Catastrophe* and *Chinese Political Thought in the 20th Century:* CHINA; TAIWAN

TAYLOR, WILLIAM L., Professor of History, Plymouth State College, Plymouth, NH: NEW HAMPSHIRE

TESAR, JENNY, Free-lance Science Writer: MEDICINE AND HEALTH; MEDICINE AND HEALTH—*The Herpes Epidemic*

THEISEN, CHARLES W., Assistant News Editor, *The Detroit News:* MICHIGAN

THOMPSON, O. E., Associate Professor, University of Maryland: METEOROLOGY

TOWNE, RUTH W., Professor of History, Northeast Missouri State University: MISSOURI

TURNER, ARTHUR CAMPBELL, Professor of Political Science, University of California, Riverside; Author, *Tension Areas in World Affairs;* Coauthor, *Control of Foreign Relations:* EGYPT; MIDDLE EAST

TURNER, CHARLES H., Staff Writer, *The Honolulu Advertiser:* HAWAII

VAN RIPER, PAUL P., Professor and Head (retired), Department of Political Science, Texas A&M University: POSTAL SERVICE

VOLSKY, GEORGE, Center for Advanced International Studies, University of Miami: CUBA

WATTERS, ELSIE M., Director of Research, Tax Foundation, Inc.: TAXATION

WEEKS, JEANNE G., Member, American Society of Interior Designers; Coauthor, *Fabrics for Interiors:* INTERIOR DESIGN

WEISS, PAULETTE, Popular Music Editor, *Stereo Review* magazine: MUSIC—*Popular;* RECORDINGS

WENTZ, RICHARD E., Professor of Religious Studies, Arizona State University; Author, *Saga of the American Soul:* RELIGION—*Survey, Far Eastern*

WILLARD, F. NICHOLAS, Professor, Washington, D.C.: JORDAN; LEBANON; SYRIA

WILLIAMS, DENNIS A., General Editor, *Newsweek:* BIOGRAPHY—*John E. Jacob;* ETHNIC GROUPS

WILLIAMS, ERNEST W., JR., Professor of Transportation, Graduate School of Business, Columbia University; Coauthor, *Transportation and Logistics* and *Shipping Conferences in the Container Age:* TRANSPORTATION

WILLIS, F. ROY, Professor of History, University of California, Davis; Author, *Italy Chooses Europe* and *France, Germany and the New Europe:* EUROPE

WOLF, WILLIAM, Contributing Editor, *New York* magazine; Author, *The Marx Brothers* and *The Landmark Films: The Cinema and Our Century:* MOTION PICTURES; OBITUARIES—*Henry Fonda*

WOOD, JOHN, Professor of Political Science, University of Oklahoma: OKLAHOMA

WOODS, GEORGE A., Children's Book Editor, *The New York Times;* Author, *Vibrations* and *Catch a Killer:* LITERATURE—*Children's*

YOUNGER, R. M., Author, *Australia and the Australians, Australia's Great River,* and *Australia! Australia! March to Nationhood:* AUSTRALIA

ZABEL, ORVILLE H., Midland Lutheran College, Fremont, NE. Professor of History (retired), Creighton University, Omaha: NEBRASKA

Index

Main article headings appear in this index as bold-faced capitals; subjects within articles appear as lower-case entries. Both the general references and the subentries should be consulted for maximum usefulness of this index. Illustrations are indexed herein. Cross references are to the entries in this index.

C

Put The World At Your Fingertips . . .
ORDER THIS EXQUISITELY DETAILED LENOX GLOBE!

The world's never looked better! Why? Because this Lenox Globe — the most popular raised-relief model made by Replogle — is as stunning to look at as the living planet it represents.

Handsomely crafted and easy-to-use, the Lenox is the latest word in the state of the mapmaker's art — an ingenious marriage of classic, antique styling with clean, modern readability.

The Lenox is a giant 12-inch globe, beautifully inscribed with eye-catching "cartouches" and colorful compass "roses" . . . solidly-mounted on an elegantly sturdy, 18-inch Fruitwood stand . . . and covered with three dimensional "mountain ranges" children love to touch!

Five pounds light, the Lenox comes complete with a 32-page **STORY OF THE GLOBE** — a richly-illustrated, full-color handbook you and your whole family will refer to over and over again.

TO ORDER, simply send us your name and address, along with a check or money order for $29.95* to:

Grolier Yearbook, Inc.
Lenox Globe
Sherman Turnpike
Danbury, Connecticut 06816

*Please note: New York and Connecticut residents must add state sales tax.

THE LENOX GLOBE . . . by Replogle. Make it yours *today.*